Children

TENTH EDITION

JOHN W. SANTROCK
University of Texas at Dallas

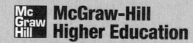
**McGraw-Hill
Higher Education**

Boston   Burr Ridge, IL   Dubuque, IA   New York   San Francisco   St. Louis
Bangkok   Bogotá   Caracas   Kuala Lumpur   Lisbon   London   Madrid   Mexico City
Milan   Montreal   New Delhi   Santiago   Seoul   Singapore   Sydney   Taipei   Toronto

**McGraw-Hill
Higher Education**

Published by McGraw-Hill, an imprint of The McGraw-Hill Companies, Inc., 1221 Avenue of the Americas, New York, NY 10020. Copyright © 2008, 2007, 2005, 2003, 2001, 1998. All rights reserved. No part of this publication may be reproduced or distributed in any form or by any means, or stored in a database or retrieval system, without the prior written consent of The McGraw-Hill Companies, Inc., including, but not limited to, in any network or other electronic storage or transmission, or broadcast for distance learning.

This book is printed on acid-free paper.

1 2 3 4 5 6 7 8 9 0 QPD/QPD 0 9 8 7
ISBN: 978-0-07-338260-9
MHID: 0-07-338260-4

Editor in Chief: *Mike Ryan*
Publisher: *Beth Ann Mejia*
Executive Editor: *Michael J. Sugarman*
Executive Marketing Manager: *James R. Headley*
Director of Development: *Dawn Groundwater*
Developmental Editor: *Maureen Spada*
Supplements Editor: *Emily Pecora*
Production Service: *Marilyn Rothenberger*
Production Editor: *Melissa Williams*
Manuscript Editor: *Beatrice Sussman*
Senior Designer: *Preston Thomas*
Interior Design: *Glenda King*
Cover Photo: © *Ariel Skelley/Corbis*
Photo Research: *LouAnn Wilson*
Supplements Producer: *Louis Swain*
Senior Production Supervisor: *Tandra Jorgensen*
Composition: *9.5/12 Meridien by Aptara, Inc.*
Printing: *Quebecor World*

Credits: The credits section for this book begins on page C-1 and is considered an extension of the copyright page.

Library of Congress Cataloging-in-Publication Data

Santrock, John W.
    Children / John W. Santrock.—10th ed.
      p. cm.
    Includes biographical references and indexes
    ISBN: 978-0-07-338260-9; ISBN: 0-07-338260-4 (alk. paper)
    1. Child development. 2. Adolescence. I. Title.
HQ767.9.S268 2007b
305.23—dc22

2007036677

The Internet addresses listed in the text were accurate at the time of publication. The inclusion of a Web site does not indicate an endorsement by the authors or McGraw-Hill, and McGraw-Hill does not guarantee the accuracy of the information presented at these sites.

www.mhhe.com

With Special appreciation to my grandchildren,
Jordan, Alex, and Luke

Jordan Bowles

Alex and Luke, the Bellucci Brothers.

ABOUT THE AUTHOR

JOHN W. SANTROCK

Received his Ph.D. from the University of Minnesota in 1973. He taught at the University of Charleston and the University of Georgia before joining the psychology department at the University of Texas at Dallas. He has been a member of the editorial boards of *Developmental Psychology and Child Development*. His research on father custody is widely cited and used in expert witness testimony to promote flexibility and alternative considerations in custody disputes. John has also authored these exceptional McGraw-Hill texts: Child Development, Eleventh Edition; Adolescence, Twelfth Edition; Life-Span Development, Eleventh Edition; Essentials of Life-Span Development, First Edition. A Topical Approach to Life-Span Development, Fourth Edition; Human Adjustment, First Edition; and Educational Psychology, Third Edition.

For many years, John was involved in tennis as a player, teaching professional, and coach of professional tennis players. He has been married for more than 35 years to his wife, Mary Jo, who is a realtor. He has two daughters— Tracy, who is studying to become a financial planner at Duke University, and Jennifer who is a medical sales specialist at Medtronic. He has one granddaughter, Jordan, age 16, and two grandsons, Alex age 3 and Luke, age 2. Tracy recently completed the New York Marathon, and Jennifer was in the top 100 ranked players on the Women's Professional Tennis Tour. In the last decade, John also has spent time painting expressionist art.

John Santrock, teaching an undergraduate class

BRIEF CONTENTS

CONTENTS

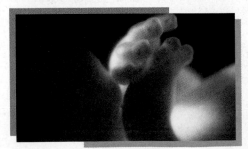

**Section Three
INFANCY 138**

Section Four
EARLY CHILDHOOD   246

Section Five
MIDDLE AND LATE CHILDHOOD   352

Section Six
ADOLESCENCE   462

Children's development has become an enormous, complex field, and no single author, or even several authors, can possibly keep up with the rapidly changing content in many areas of children's development. To solve this problem, author John Santrock sought the input of leading experts about content in all age periods of children's development. The experts provided detailed evaluations and recommendations for topics in their area(s) of expertise. The biographies and photographs of the experts, who literally represent a who's who in the field of children's development, follow.

NEL NODDINGS

Dr. Noddings is one of the world's leading experts on children's education. She is Lee L. Jacks Professor of Education, Emerita, at Stanford University. Dr. Noddings is a past president of the National Academy of Education, the Philosophy of Education Society, and the John Dewey Society. In addition to fifteen books—among them, *Caring: A Feminine Approach to Ethics and Moral Education, Women and Evil, The Challenge to Care in Schools, Educating for Intelligent Belief or Unbelief,* and *Philosophy of Education*—she is the author of more than 200 articles and chapters on various topics, ranging from the ethics of care to mathematical problem solving. Her latest books are *Starting at Home: Caring and Social Policy, Educating Moral People, Happiness and Education, Educating Citizens for Global Awareness,* and *Critical Lessons: What Our Schools Should Teach.* Dr. Noddings spent fifteen years as a teacher, administrator, and curriculum supervisor in public schools and served as mathematics department chairperson in New Jersey and as director of the Laboratory Schools at the University of Chicago. At Stanford, she received the Award for Teaching Excellence three times and served as Associate Dean and as Acting Dean at Stanford for four years. Dr. Noddings is a Laureate member of Kappa Delta Pi, and holds a number of awards, among them the Anne Rowe Award for contributions to the education of women (Harvard University); the Willystine Goodsell Award for contributions to the education of women (AREA); the Medal for Distinguished Service, Teachers College, Columbia University; the Lifetime Achievement Award from AREA (Division B); the Award for Distinguished Leadership in Education, Rutgers University; and honorary doctorates from Columbia College, Montclair State University, and Queen's University, Canada.

ROSS THOMPSON

Dr. Thompson is one of the world's leading experts on children's socioemotional development. He currently is a professor of psychology at the University of California, Davis. His research interests are in two fields. As a developmental psychologist, he studies early parent-child relationships, the development of emotional understanding and emotion regulation, conscience development, and the growth of self-understanding. As a psycholegal scholar, he works on the applications of developmental research to public policy concerns, including the effects of divorce and custody arrangements on children, child maltreatment prevention, school readiness, research ethics, and early brain development and early intervention. Dr. Thompson is a founding member of the National Scientific Council on the Developing Child and was a member of the Committee on Integrating the Science of Early Childhood Development of the National Academy of Sciences that produced the book, *From Neurons to Neighborhoods.* He is a member of the Board of Directors of Zero to Three: National Center for Infants, Toddlers, and Families, and is on the Editorial Advisory Board of *Wondertime* magazine. He has twice been associate editor of *Child Development* and is consulting editor for a series of topical texts in developmental psychology published by McGraw-Hill. His books include *Preventing Child Maltreatment Through Social Support, The Postdivorce Family* (co-edited with Paul Amato); and *Toward a Child-Centered, Neighborhood-Based Child Protection System* (co-edited with Gary Melton and Mark Small). Dr. Thompson is currently writing two books: (1) *Early Brain Development, the Media, and Public Policy* and (2) *Emotional Development.* He received his undergraduate degree from Occidental College and his master's and doctoral degrees from the University of Michigan. Dr. Thompson has been a Visiting Scientist at the Max Planck Institute for Human Development and Education in Berlin, a Senior NIMH Fellow in Law and Psychology at Stanford University, and a Harris Visiting Professor at the University of Chicago. He also received the Boyd McCandless Young Scientist Award for Early Distinguished Achievement from the American Psychological Association, the Scholarship in Teaching Award and the Outstanding Research and Creative Activity Award from the University of Nebraska, where he was also a lifetime member of the Academy of Distinguished Teachers.

ALGEA HARRISON

Dr. Harrison is a leading expert on diversity and children's development. She is a professor of psychology at Oakland University, Rochester, Michigan. Dr. Harrison obtained her doctoral degree from the University of Michigan and has been a visiting professor and scholar at the University of Zimbabwe, the Free University of Amsterdam, and Nanjing University, China. Her research interests have focused on the contextual and diversity aspects of working women's lives and how they influence adolescent development. She also has been collaborating with international colleagues on a series of cross-cultural studies of adolescent development. Dr. Harrison has been a pioneer in the creation and development of the Black Caucus of the Society for Research in Child Development and recently (2006) co-edited the *Monographs of the Society for Research in Child Development* issue titled "Our Children Too: A History of the First 25 Years of the Black Caucus of the Society for Research in Child Development."

MARYLOU HYSON

Dr. Hyson is one of the world's leading experts on young children's development. She currently is a senior consultant with the National Association for the Education of Young Children (NAEYC) in Washington, DC, and is an affiliate faculty member in Applied Developmental Psychology at George Mason University. A former preschool and kindergarten teacher and child-care director, over the past six years she has served as NAEYC's Associate Executive Director for Professional Development and as senior advisor for Research and Professional Practice. While at NAEYC, Marilou helped to revise standards for early childhood professional preparation and worked on accreditation and national recognition for two- and four-year higher education programs. She has also helped develop position statements on early learning standards, early childhood mathematics, and curriculum/assessment/program evaluation. Before joining NAEYC's staff, she was a professor and chair of the University of Delaware's Department of Individual and Family Studies. A former editor of *Early Childhood Research Quarterly*, Dr. Hyson is also a former SRCD Executive Branch Policy Fellow in the U.S. Department of Education's National Institute on Early Childhood Development and Education. She currently co-chairs the Committee on Policy and Communications of the Society for Research in Child Development. Her research and publications have focused on emotional development, parents' and teachers' beliefs and educational practices, and teacher preparation. She is lead author of the chapter "Early Childhood Development and Education," co-authored with Carol Copple and Jacqueline Jones, recently published (2006) in the sixth edition of the *Handbook of Child Psychology*. Marilou also consults on international early childhood projects and is currently writing a book on young children's positive approaches to learning, to be published by Teachers College Press.

CAMPBELL LEAPER

Dr. Leaper is a leading expert on gender development. He currently is a professor at the University of California, Santa Cruz. He obtained his undergraduate degree at Boston University and his doctoral degree at the University of California, Los Angeles. Following his graduate training, Dr. Leaper was a research fellow at Harvard Medical School. His research examines the socialization and the social construction of gender and sexism during childhood, adolescence, and early adulthood. Dr. Leaper has investigated gender-related variations in the these areas: language and communication, self-concepts and attitudes, play activities, academic and athletic achievement, parenting, and friendship. Currently, he is studying adolescent girls' and young women's experiences with sexism, focusing on how they cope with sexual harassment, as well as discrimination in math, science, or computers, and in sports.

LINDA PUGH

Dr. Pugh is a leading expert in the field of pediatric nursing. She obtained her undergraduate, master's, and doctoral degrees in nursing from the University of Maryland, Baltimore. Dr. Pugh currently is a professor at York College of Pennsylvania and formerly was a professor at Johns Hopkins University School of Nursing, where she also was director of Professional Education, director of the Center for Nursing Research at Milton Hersey Medical Center, and a professor in the School of Health Evaluation Research at Pennsylvania State University. She has received numerous awards in the field of nursing, including the Nursing Research Award from Pennsylvania's Nurse's Association, excellence in teaching award at Johns Hopkins University, and the award for significant contributions to nursing research (Sigma Theta Tau International). Dr. Pugh's research interests include breast feeding, nursing interventions with low-income women, discovering ways to prevent fatigue during childbearing, and using breathing exercises during labor.

JAMES MARCIA

Dr. Marcia has been a pioneer in the study of adolescent identity development. He currently is Professor Emeritus at Simon Fraser University in Burnaby, British Columbia, Canada. He obtained his doctoral degree from Ohio State University and formerly was a professor at State University of New York, Buffalo, where was director of the Psychological Clinic. From 1972 until 2002, he was Associate and Full Professor at Simon Fraser University and director of the Psychological Clinic there. Dr. Marcia has served on the editorial boards of *The Journal of Youth and Adolescence, Journal of Applied Developmental Psychology, The Narrative Study of Lives,* and *Identity: An International Journal of Theory and Research.* In addition to his numerous conceptual and research contributions to the study of identity development, he has practiced psychotherapy since 1964 and has served as consultant on a number of community mental health projects.

JANE COUPERUS

Dr. Couperus is a an expert on developmental neuroscience. She obtained her Ph.D. at the Institute of Child Development at the University of Minnesota. Dr. Couperus did her undergraduate work at Wesleyan University in psychology and music and also received a master's degree in applied developmental psychology at Claremont University. Her research focuses on the brain's role on the developmental aspects of learning, attention, and memory. Dr. Couperus' research uses both behavioral and physiological techniques, primarily event-related potentials to gain a better understanding of the brain's development.

PREFACE

Children have a very special place in every society because they are every society's future. The study of development gives those who care for children many tools for improving the lives of children throughout the world and, therefore, contributing to a better future for humankind. This is an ambitious goal, but not an impossible one. As research in child development has progressed and the information has been applied to family, education, health, child care, and a variety of other contexts, it has become clear that developmentalists can make a difference in children's lives.

In a broad sense, this text seeks to convey a clear understanding of what we know about child development, how we arrived at this level of understanding, and how research in child development can be applied in the various settings in which children develop. To achieve this goal, I have continued to emphasize and update *Children* in three main areas:

- Research and content
- Applications
- Accessibility and interest

First, I will generally describe the thrust of the changes in the tenth edition of *Children*. Then I will specify the key changes in each chapter.

EXTENSIVE INCREASE IN COVERAGE OF BRAIN DEVELOPMENT

The creation of brain-imaging techniques, such as fMRI, have led to remarkable increases in our knowledge about brain development in recent years. I have substantially expanded the coverage of children's brain development in this new edition and where appropriate incorporated images of brains scans. Here are some of the main changes related to brain development:

- Chapter 3, Prenatal Development: new major section on the early formation of the brain and key neurological processes (Nelson, Thomas, & de Haan, 2006)
- Chapter 5, Physical Development in Infancy: expanded coverage of the function of myelination, as well as new graphics that highlight specific functions of brain regions (Haynes & others, 2006)
- Chapter 6, Cognitive Development in Infancy: new description of the main brain region involved in attention; new discussion of the connections between development of the brain and memory, including new Figure 6.6; and new coverage of the numerous brain

regions that are likely activated in imitation
- Chapter 8, Physical Development in Early Childhood: much expanded section on the brain, including more specific aspects of brain changes in early childhood (Lenroot & Giedd, 2006)
- Chapter 11, Physical Development in Middle and Late Childhood: new section on changes in the brain during middle and late childhood that focuses on brain regions involved in cognitive control and changes in cortical thickening (Durston & others, 2007; Toga, Thompson, & Sowell, 2006); new discussion of brain pathways involved in learning disabilities (Shaywitz, Lyon, & Lyon, 2006)
- Chapter 14, Physical Development in Adolescence: expansion, revision, and updating of brain development in adolescence, including new Figure 14.6.

RESEARCH AND CONTENT

Four ways I have attempted to provide students with an understanding of research and content on children development focus on (1) research coverage, (2) *Research in Child Development interludes*, (3) expert consultants, and (4) diversity.

Research Coverage

Above all, a text on child development must include a solid research foundation. This edition of *Children* presents the latest, most contemporary research. *Children*, tenth edition, has more than 1,600 citations from 2000 through 2007. More than 1,000 of these are 2004 through 2007 citations, making *Children*, tenth edition, truly a twenty-first-century rendition of the field of child development.

Coverage has been updated and expanded throughout the book. Notably, I have incorporated information from the sixth edition of the *Handbook of Child Psychology* (Damon & Lerner, 2006).

Research in Children's Development Interludes

New to this edition are *Research in Children's Development* interludes that appear once in each chapter and provide a more in-depth look at research related to a topic in the chapter. I call them interludes rather than boxes because they follow directly in the text after they have been introduced. In most instances they consist of a description of a research study, including the identity of the participants, the methods used to obtain data, and the main results. In most cases, they are research studies that have been conducted in the twenty-first century. Because students often have more difficulty reading about research studies than other text material, I wrote these with an eye toward student understanding. The new *Research in Children's Development* interludes include Expectant Mothers' Cigarette Smoking and Cigarette Smoking by Their Adolescent Offspring (Porath & Fried, 2005) (Chapter 3); Physical Activity in Young Children Attending Preschools (Pate & others, 2004) (Chapter 8); Aggressive Victims, Passive Victims, and Bullies (Hanish & Guerera, 2004) (Chapter 13); and Evaluating a Service Learning Program Designed to Increase Civic Engagement (Metz & Youniss, 2005) (Chapter 15).

Expert Research Consultants

Also new to this edition are expert research consultants. Children's development has become an enormous, complex field, and no single author, or even several authors, can possibly be an expert in many different areas of children's development. To solve this problem, I sought the input of leading experts in many different research and applied areas of children's development. The experts provided me with detailed evaluations and recommendations for a chapter(s) in their area(s) of expertise. The expert research consultants for *Children*, tenth edition, were:

Expert	Topics
Nel Noddings *Stanford University*	Education throughout the book
Ross Thompson *University of California–Davis*	Socioemotional development throughout the book
Algea Harrison *Oakland University*	Diversity throughout the book
Marylou Hyson *National Association for the Education of Young Children*	Early childhood
Campbell Leaper *University of California–Santa Cruz*	Gender throughout the book
Linda Pugh *Johns Hopkins University*	Nursing/health, prenatal development, birth, and infancy
James Marcia *Concordia University*	Adolescence
Jane Couperus *Hampshire College*	Neuroscience throughout the book

The photographs and biographies of the expert consultants appear on page xi.

Diversity

In addition, this text has always emphasized diversity and culture, and this tradition continues in this edition. *Diversity in*

Children's Development interludes are new in this edition. They appear once in each chapter and focus on a topic related to the chapter's content. Among the topics of the *Diversity* interludes are Gender, Families, and Children's Development (Chapter 1); Language Environment, Poverty, and Language Development (Chapter 6); Early Childhood Education in Japan and Developing Countries (Chapter 9); Bilingual Education (Chapter 12); and Cross-Cultural Comparisons of Secondary Schools (Chapter 15).

REDUCTION OF NUMBER OF CHAPTERS

At the request of adopters and reviewers, I have reduced and combined the material in Chapters 1 and 2 of the tenth edition into a single opening chapter.

APPLICATIONS

It is important not only to present the scientific foundation of child development to students, but also to demonstrate that research has real-world applications, to include many applied examples of concepts, and to give students a sense that the field of child development has personal meaning for them. Here are some of the ways I incorporated applications in the text:

- Applications of research in child development to health, parenting, and education receive special attention throughout the text. Here are just a few of these many applications: a new main section in Chapter 1 titled "Why Is Caring for Children Important?"; new coverage of the Hip-Hop to Health Jr. program to reduce overweight and obesity in minority children attending Head Start programs (Fitzgibbon & others, 2005); recently developed school/family programs for preventing child obesity (Lindsay & others, 2006; Paxon & others, 2006; Story, Kaphingst, & French, 2006); and recent research on parenting styles and developmental outcomes (Steinberg, Blatt-Eisengart, & Cauffman, 2006);
- *Caring for Children* interludes in every chapter that outline important ways to improve the lives of children. These are new *Caring for Children* interludes for this edition: Exercise Guidelines for Expectant Mothers (Chapter 3); From Waterbirth to Music Therapy (Chapter 4); Tools of the Mind (Chapter 9); Strategies for Increasing Children's Creative Thinking (Chapter 12); Reducing Adolescent Pregnancy (Chapter 14); Strategies for Parenting Adolescents (Chapter 16).
- Every chapter also has at least one *Careers in Child Development* profile that describes an individual whose career relates to the chapter's content. Most of the *Careers* inserts include a photograph of the person at work. In addition, the Careers in Child Development Appendix that follows Chapter 1 describes a number of careers in the education/research, clinical/counseling, medical/nursing/physical, and family/relationship categories.

- At the end of each chapter, two features—*Making a Difference* and *Resources for Improving Children's Lives*—provide valuable information about ways to improve children's lives.
- On the book's Web site, students can hone their decision-making skills by completing exercises related to children's health and well-being, parenting, and education.

ACCESSIBILITY AND INTEREST

Many students today juggle numerous responsibilities in addition to their coursework. To help them make the most of their study time, I have made this book as accessible as possible without watering down the content. The writing, organization, and learning system of *Children* will engage students and provide a clear foundation in child development.

Writing and Organization

For *Children*, tenth edition, every sentence, every paragraph, and every section of every chapter was carefully considered and, if appropriate, moved, streamlined, expanded, or eliminated in order to integrate new research and to make the book more accessible.

The Learning System

I strongly believe that students not only should be challenged to study hard and think more deeply and productively about child development, but also should be provided with an effective way to learn the content. Instructors and students continue to provide extremely positive feedback about the book's learning system and student-friendly presentation.

Students often struggle to find the main ideas in their courses, especially in child development, which includes so much material. This book's learning system centers on learning goals that, together with the main text headings, keep the key ideas in front of the reader from the beginning to the end of the chapter. Each chapter has no more than six main headings and corresponding learning goals, which are presented side-by-side in the chapter-opening spread. At the end of each main section of a chapter, the learning goal is repeated in a feature called Review and Reflect, which prompts students to review the key topics in the section and poses a question to encourage them to think critically about what they have read. At the end of the chapter, under the heading, Reach Your Learning Goals, the learning goals guide students through the chapter review.

In addition to the learning tools just described, visual organizers, or maps, that link up with the learning goals are presented at the beginning of each major section in the chapter. The complete learning system, including many additional features not mentioned here, is illustrated in a section titled Visual Tour for Students, which follows this Preface on page xxviii.

CHAPTER-BY-CHAPTER CHANGES

I made a number of changes in all 16 chapters of *Children*, tenth edition. Highlights of these changes follow.

Chapter 1
INTRODUCTION

- Combined Chapters 1 and 2 from the ninth edition into a single opening chapter at the request of instructors
- New main first section: Why Is Caring for Children Important?
- Updated *Caring for Children* interlude: Improving Family Policy
- New *Diversity in Children's Development* interlude: Gender, Families, and Children's Development
- New discussion of research on poverty and children's development, including new research figure
- Moved coverage of Careers in Child Development to an Appendix that follows Chapter 1
- Expanded discussion of research on children from ethnic minority backgrounds (Parke & Buriel, 2006)
- New *Research in Children's Development* interlude: Research Journals

Chapter 2
BIOLOGICAL BEGINNINGS

- Extensive line-by-line rewriting of chapter and inclusion of a number of new introductions to topics and transitions between topics for improved clarity and understanding.
- Description of recent search documenting how stress hormones can damage DNA (Flint & others, 2007)
- New material on the specification of the number of genes humans possess (21,774) (Ensembl Human, 2007)
- Expanded coverage of phenylketonuria and how its link with nutrition reflects the principle of heredity-environment interaction
- New coverage of the increasing use of fetal MRI for detecting fetal malformations (Laifer-Narin & others, 2007; Muhler & others, 2007)
- Description of recent large-scale study that found no difference in pregnancy loss between chronic villus sampling and amniocentesis (Caughey, Hopkins, & Norton, 2006).
- New *Research in Children's Development* interlude: In Vitro Fertilization and Developmental Outcomes in Adolescence
- New *Diversity in Children's Development* interlude: The Increased Diversity of Adopted Children and Adoptive Parents
- New coverage of recent large-scale study on adoption and learning disabilities (Altarac & Saroha, 2007)

- New description of two recent meta-analyses: one that focused on behavioral problems and mental health referrals in adopted and nonadopted children (Juffer & van IJzendoorn, 2005) and one that examined the cognitive development on adopted and nonadopted children (van IJendoorn, Juffer, & Poelhuis, 2005)
- Coverage of recent study of the antisocial behavior of adopted and nonadopted young adults (Grotevant & others, 2006)
- Updated and expanded discussion of the epigenetic view, including criticisms of the heredity-environment correlation view (Gottlieb, 2007)

Chapter 3
PRENATAL DEVELOPMENT

- Extensive rewriting of chapter on a line-by-line basis and rearrangement of some sections
- Important new section on the development of the brain in the prenatal period, including a photo of the tubular appearance of the human nervous system six weeks after conception (Nelson, Thomas, & de Haan, 2006)
- New coverage of the rapidly increasing program, CenteringPregnancy, that brings pregnant women into relationship-oriented groups (Massey, Rising, & Ickovics, 2006)
- New discussion of neural tube defects and what characterizes anencephaly and spina bifida
- Coverage of recent study on prescription drug use during pregnancy (Riley & others, 2005)
- Description of recent research on caffeine, pregnancy, and fetal death (Matijasevich & others, 2006)
- Description of recent research on the continuing negative outcomes of fetal alcohol syndrome in early adulthood (Spohr, Willms, & Steinhausen, 2007)
- Discussion of recent research on maternal use of cocaine during pregnancy and attention deficits in preschool children (Noland & others, 2005)
- Description of recent survey on methamphetamine use by pregnant women (Arria & others, 2006)
- Coverage of recent study on prenatal marijuana exposure and depression in 10-year-old children (Gray & others, 2005) and revised conclusions about the effects of marijuana by pregnant women on offspring (de Moares & others, 2006; Williams & Ross, 2007)
- New description of maternal diabetes as a risk factor for pregnant outcomes, including recent research (Rosenberg & others, 2005)
- Inclusion of two recent research studies on maternal obesity, central nervous birth defects in offspring, and neonatal death (Anderson & others, 2005; Kristensen & others, 2005)
- Coverage of recent study on maternal age and stillbirth (Bateman & Simpson, 2006)

- Description of two longitudinal studies linking high maternal anxiety and high maternal levels of cortisol during pregnancy with higher levels of cortisol in offspring during preschool and middle and late childhood (Gutteling, de Weerth, & Buitelaar, 2005; O'Connor & others, 2005).
- Discussion of recent research on pregnancy outcomes in women of very advanced maternal age (Callaway, Lust, & McIntyre, 2005)
- Description of research linking heavy paternal smoking to increased risk of early pregnancy loss (Venners & others, 2004)
- New *Research in Children's Development* interlude: Expectant Mothers' Cigarette Smoking and Cigarette Smoking by their Adolescent Offspring (Porath & Fried, 2005)
- New Caring for Children interlude: Exercise Guidelines for Expectant Mothers
- New Diversity in Children's Development interlude: Cultural Beliefs About Pregnancy
- Expanded and updated *Resources for Improving Children's Lives*

Chapter 4
BIRTH

- Extensive rewriting of chapter on a line-by-line basis and rearrangement of some sections (placing material on assessing the newborn before low birth weight and preterm infants, for example) to improve clarity and understanding
- Updated figures on percentage of U.S. babies delivered in hospitals, delivered by physicians, and attended by a midwife (Martin & others, 2005)
- Coverage of recent study showing positive effects of doula support for low-income pregnant women and their newborns (Campbell & others, 2006)
- Description of recent study showing adverse outcomes on newborns when their mothers were given oxytocin during childbirth (Oscarsson & others, 2006)
- Expanded and updated coverage of why cesarean delivery has increased in the United States and recent data on trends in cesarean delivery (Hoyert & others, 2006)
- New *Caring for Children* interlude: From Waterbirth to Music Therapy (Field, 2007)
- Description of recent studies on the benefits of massage and acupuncture during labor (Beckmann & Garrett, 2006; Gaudernack, Forbord, & Hole, 2006)
- Discussion of trends in Apgar scale scores for U.S. newborns (Martin & others, 2005)
- Update on the percentage of African American infants born preterm (Ashton, 2006)
- Inclusion of recent research support for the use of progestin in the second trimester of pregnancy in reducing the risk of preterm birth (Coomarasamy & others, 2006; Mackenzie & others, 2006)

- New *Diversity in Children's Development* interlude: Incidence and Causes of Low Birth Weight Around the World
- New coverage of a recent survey on techniques used in the NICU (Field & others, 2006)
- Discussion of recent study documenting the positive effects of exercise in the postpartum period on maternal well-being (Blum, Beaudoin, & Caton-Lemos, 2005)
- Description of recent national study on the incidence of depressive symptoms in mothers and fathers in the postpartum period (Paulson, Dauber, & Leiferman, 2006)
- Coverage of recent large-scale Danish study on the increase in psychological disorders in mothers, but not fathers, in the postpartum period (Munk-Olsen & others, 2006)
- Updated and revised *Resources for Improving Children's Lives*

- Recent research on breast feeding and a lower percentage of developmental delays in gross motor development (Sacker & others, 2006)
- New *Research in Children's Development* interlude: Studying the Infant's Perception
- New *Diversity in Children's Development* interlude: Cultural Variations in Guiding Infants' Motor Development
- Revised and updated discussion of color vision in infancy (Kellman & Arterberry, 2006)
- New section on perception of faces infancy, including recent research (Kelly & others, 2007a, b; Slater, Field, & Hernandez-Reif, 2007)
- New section: Nature, Nurture, and the Development of Infants' Visual Perception (Kellman & Arterberry, 2006)
- New coverage of developmental changes in stereoacuity during infancy (Birch & others, 2005; Takai & others, 2005)
- Updated *Resources for Improving Children's Lives* to include *The Amazing Infant*

Chapter 5
PHYSICAL DEVELOPMENT IN INFANCY

- Extensive rewriting and editing of chapter for improved student understanding
- Expanded graphics on the brain to emphasize specific functions of regions, such as the visual association cortex and somatosensory cortex (Figure 5.4)
- Updated coverage of the development of the brain (Nelson, 2007; Coch, Fischer, & Dawson, 2007)
- Expanded description of the function of myelination (Haynes & others, 2006)
- Expanded and updated discussion of links between spurts in brain growth and cognitive functioning (Immordino-Yang & Fischer, 2007)
- Expanded discussion of REM sleep in infancy and question raised about whether we can know for sure whether infants dream
- Updated and expanded discussion of the shared sleeping and SIDS controversy (Bajanowoski & others, 2007; Mitchell, 2007)
- Expanded and updated research on SIDS, including recent information about the role of the neurotransmitter serotonin in the brain stem (Shani, Fifer, & Myers, 2007)
- New coverage of recent research showing that babies who use a pacifier when they go to sleep are less likely to experience SIDS (Li & others, 2006; Mitchell, Blair, & L'Hoir, 2006)
- New discussion of a recent research on the percentage of overweight babies in the United States, including new Figure 5.11 (Kim & others, 2006)
- Coverage of recent information about breast feeding and type II diabetes (Das, 2007)

Chapter 6
COGNITIVE DEVELOPMENT IN INFANCY

- Extensive editing and rewriting of Piagetian material for improved student understanding
- New discussion of Elizabeth Spelke's research on infants' expectations and research photo of a 4-month-old in a perception study in Elizabeth Spelke's laboratory to illustrate perception researchers' conclusions that infants have a better understanding of how the world works at earlier ages than Piaget envisioned
- New description of the main region of the brain involved in infant attention
- New coverage of joint attention and its role in infants' language development
- Coverage of recent research on the emergence of gaze following in infants, including new Figure 6.5, showing the research setting and sequence involved in the study (Brooks & Meltzoff, 2005)
- Description of recent research on deferred imitation as a predictor of communicative gestures (Heimann & others, 2006)
- New discussion of connections between development of the brain and development of memory in infancy, including new Figure 6.6 (Nelson, Thomas, & de Haan, 2006)
- New description of the numerous areas of the brain likely involved in infant imitation, including the role that mirror neurons might play in infant imitation (Jackson, Meltzoff, & Decety, 2006; Nash, 2006; Nelson, Thomas, & de Haan, 2006)
- Important new section on concept formation and categorization in infancy (Mandler, 2004, 2006)

- New Figure 6.8 showing stimuli in research on concept formation in infancy
- Updated coverage of predicting IQ later in childhood from information-processing tasks in infancy (Kavsek, 2004)
- New coverage of Michael Tomasello's (2006) interactionist view of language that stresses the role of intentions
- New *Diversity in Children's Development* interlude, including recent research indicating that the type of maternal speech, vocabulary, and gestures are more important than the sheer amount of verbal input in predicting children's vocabulary development in low-income families (Pan & others, 2005)
- Updated and improved coverage of language development based on input from leading expert Jean Berko Gleason
- Coverage of a study on the importance of social interaction in advancing the language of infants including new research Figure 6.15 (Goldstein, King West, & West, 2003)
- Updated *Resources for Improving Children's Lives* to include two additional books: *How Babies Talk* and *Blackwell Handbook of Language Development*

Chapter 7
SOCIOEMOTIONAL DEVELOPMENT IN INFANCY

- Extensive rewriting of chapter for improved student understanding, including addition of numerous concrete examples of concepts and more descriptions of infants' behaviors and emotions
- Expanded and updated coverage of the controversy regarding the onset of early emotions (Campos, Anderson, & Babu-Roth, 2008; Lewis, 2007)
- New discussion of why studying the self in infancy is difficult based on the view of leading expert Ross Thompson (2007)
- Important new major section, Social Orientation/ Understanding, that includes coverage of infants' developing social interest, locomotion, joint attention, and social referencing (Thompson, 2006)
- New discussion of recent research on becoming a social partner with a peer in 1- and 2-year-olds, including a photograph of the research setting and task (Figure 7.5) (Brownell, Ramani, & Zerwas, 2006)
- New description of Bowlby's internal working model of attachment based on expert consultant Ross Thompson's recommendation
- Expanded discussion of cultural variations in attachment (Saarni & others, 2006)
- Connection of turn-taking and games like peek-a-boo to the development of joint attention (Meltzoff & Brooks, 2006)

- Discussion of recent research on acculturation in Latino families and links to infant cognitive development (Cabrera & others, 2006)
- New *Research in Children's Development* interlude, A National Longitudinal Study of Child Care, including recent research discussed from the NICHD Child Care Research Network (2005, 2006) study
- New *Diversity in Children's Development* interlude: Child-Care Policies Around the World
- Description of recent research on quality of child care and children's vocabulary development (Belsky & others, 2007)
- Updated *Resources for Improving Children's Lives* to include *Touchpoints; Birth to 3*

Chapter 8
PHYSICAL DEVELOPMENT IN EARLY CHILDHOOD

- Significant expansion of material on short stature, growth hormone deficiency, and growth hormone treatment in children (Dunkel, 2006; Stanford University Medical Center, 2007)
- New Figure 8.3 that shows an electron microscope image of myelination
- Description of diffusion tensor imaging (DTI) and its improved ability to detect microstructural changes in the brains of infants and children (Mukherjee & McKinstry, 2006)
- Expanded and updated coverage of the brain and cognitive development, including more specific aspects of brain changes during early childhood (Craik, 2006; Lenroot & Giedd, 2006)
- New *Research in Children's Development* interlude: Physical Activity in Young Children Attending Preschools
- New description of the recent trend in reducing physical activity opportunities in preschool and kindergarten programs (American Academy of Pediatrics, 2006)
- New coverage of cultural variations in promoting right-handedness (Zverev, 2006)
- New description of recent recommendations by the World Health Organization that on average children 7 years and younger need to reduce their energy intake by about 20 percent for girls and 18 percent for boys (Butte, 2006)
- Added description of what body mass index is and how it is used to categorize a child as being overweight or at risk for being overweight (Centers for Disease Control and Prevention, 2007)
- Discussion of recent research linking being overweight at age 3 with being overweight at age 12 (Nader & others, 2006)
- New coverage of the Hip-Hop to Health Jr. program to reduce overweight and obesity in African American and Latino children attending Head Start programs (Fitzgibbon & others, 2005)

- Discussion of recent study on parents' misperceptions of their children's overweight (Eckstein & others, 2006)
- Coverage of recent study on parents' misperceptions of children's firearm access in the home (Baxley & Miller, 2006)
- Description of recent fMRI study linking extensive exposure to lead in infancy and early childhood to deficits in brain regions that are involved in language (Weihong & others, 2006)
- Recent research on iron deficiency anemia in children and their affective behavior (Lozoff & others, 2007)
- Expanded and updated coverage of young children's nutrition in low-income families (Darton-Hill & others, 2007; Sausenthaler & others, 2007)
- New *Diversity in Children's Development* interlude: The State of Illness and Health in the World's Children (2006, 2007)
- Updated resources for improving children's lives

Chapter 9
COGNITIVE DEVELOPMENT IN EARLY CHILDHOOD

- Extensively edited and rewritten for improved student understanding
- Updated and improved coverage of Vygotsky's concept of private speech (John-Steiner, 2007)
- New *Caring for Children* interlude: Tools of the Mind (Bodrova & Leong, 2001, 2007; Hyson, Copple, & Jones, 2006)
- Recent recommendations for three changes to improve interviewing techniques with children to reduce their suggestibility (Bruck, Ceci, & Principe, 2006)
- Expanded and updated description of the young child's theory of mind (Harris, 2006)
- Creation of new section: Theory of Mind and Autism
- Expanded and updated discussion of language development in early childhood, including increased emphasis on the regularities in which young children acquire their particular language (Berko Gleason, 2005)
- Description of recent data on the positive outcomes of the Perry Preschool program at age 40 (Schweinhart & others, 2005)
- Update on the number of states providing education for 3- and 4-year-old children and the percentage of 3- and 4-year-old children who attend center-based programs (NAEYC, 2005)
- New *Research in Children's Development* interlude: Suggesting False Events to Children
- Recent information about the surge of interest in Montessori schools in the United States (Whitescarver, 2006)
- Updated coverage of characteristics of developmentally appropriate and inappropriate early childhood education (Figure 9.13)

- New section on the controversy about whether universal preschool education should be implemented (Zigler, Gilliam, & Jones, 2006)
- New *Diversity in Children's Development* interlude: Early Childhood Education in Japan and Developing Countries (Rooparnine & Metingdogan, 2006)
- New discussion of the difficulty in making generalizations about the effectiveness of developmentally appropriate education and how developmentally appropriate education is an evolving concept; coverage of what recently been emphasized more in this approach (Hyson, Copple, & Jones, 2006)

Chapter 10
SOCIOEMOTIONAL DEVELOPMENT IN EARLY CHILDHOOD

- New chapter-opening *Images of Children's Development:* Craig Lesley's Complicated Early Emotional and Social Life (Lesley, 2005)
- New description of young children's use of psychological traits in their self-descriptions at about 4 to 5 years of age (Thompson, 2006)
- Expansion of section on Self-Understanding to Self-Understanding and Understanding Others, including new introduction on how young children are more psychologically sophisticated than used to be thought (Thompson, 2006)
- Coverage of research on how even 4-year-olds understand that people will sometimes make statements that aren't true to get what they want or to avoid trouble (Gee & Heyman, 2007; Lee & others, 2002)
- Reorganization of emotion regulation coverage with a new introduction paragraph on its importance in children's development
- Important new section, Parenting and Young Children's Moral Development, that focuses on the quality of parent-child relationships, parents' use of proactive strategies, and conversational dialogue about moral issues (Thompson, 2006; Thompson, Meyer, & McGinley, 2006)
- Discussion of recent research on links between parenting styles and psychosocial maturity and academic achievement (Steinberg, Blatt-Eisengart, & Cauffman, 2006)
- New description of recent research review of mothers' and fathers' socialization strategies (Bronstein, 2006)
- Discussion of recent research studies on the negative developmental outcomes of punishment (Aucoin, Frick, & Bodin, 2006; Bender & others, 2007)
- New description of low-income families having less resources than higher-income families (Conger & Dogan, 2007; Patterson & Hastings, 2007)

- Coverage of Ann Crouter's (2006) recent research on how parents' poor conditions at work can be brought home to negatively influence parenting behavior and child outcomes
- Description of Kathleen McCartney's (2006) recent research on family factors being more important predictors of children's behavior and competence than child-care factors
- New *Research in Children's Development* interlude: Marital Conflict, Individual Hostility, and the Use of Physical Punishment (Kanoy & others, 2003)
- New coverage of research that examined the positive/negative aspects of sibling relationships and children's adjustment (Pike, Coldwell, & Dunn, 2005)
- New material included from Laurie Kramer's research on how frequently siblings have conflicts, how parents react when siblings have conflicts, and teaching siblings skills to improve their sibling interaction
- New section, Emotional Regulation and Peer Relations (Saarni & others, 2006)
- Description of Paul Amato's (2006) longitudinal research on adult outcomes of individuals who experienced their parents' divorce in childhood and adolescence
- New *Resources for Improving Children's Lives* to include *The Emotional Development of Young Children* and *A World of Difference*

Chapter 11
PHYSICAL DEVELOPMENT IN MIDDLE AND LATE CHILDHOOD

- Important new section, The Brain, including recent research on changes in the prefrontal cortex and diffuse/focused activation in the brain, as well as the connection of these changes to cognitive functioning in areas such as cognitive control (Durston & Casey, 2006; Durston & others, 2007)
- Discussion of cortical thickening in children 5 to 11 years of age (Toga, Thompson, & Sowell, 2006)
- Description of recent research on factors linked with whether children will be physically active when they have free time (Heitzler & others, 2006)
- Discussion of recent research linking TV viewing in childhood with exercising less and eating fewer servings per day (Salmon, Campbell, & Crawford, 2006)
- In keeping with the Centers for Disease Control and Prevention's (2007) policy, change in the description of children from obese to overweight or risk for being overweight and statement of how those categories are defined in terms of body mass index (BMI)
- Description of recent research that links being overweight in middle and late childhood with being overweight in adolescence (Nader & others, 2006; Thompson & others, 2007)

- Recent commentary about overweight children more likely to come from low-income families (Longo-Mbenza & others, 2007)
- Description of recent study of parental monitoring of Latino children's eating habits (Arrendono & others, 2006)
- New coverage of recent school/family programs for preventing the likelihood that children will become overweight (Lindsay & others, 2006; Paxon & others, 2006; Story, Kaphingst, & French, 2006)
- New *Research in Children's Development* interlude: Heart Smart (Chen & others, 2007; Friedman & others, 2007)
- Coverage of recent study in four developing countries linking caregiver depression with child injuries (Howe, Hutley, & Abramsky, 2006)
- New discussion of the brain pathways that are involved in reading disabilities based on recent MRI brain scans (Shaywitz, Lyon, & Lyon, 2006)
- New figure of a 9-year-old boy with dyslexia going through an MRI scanner in a research study
- Recent national data on the percentage of U.S. children who have a learning disability or ADHD (National Health Survey, 2006)
- New description of the U.S. government's 2006 warning about the cardiovascular risks of ADHD stimulant medication
- New coverage of the possible role of exercise in reducing ADHD (Ferrando-Lucas, 2006; Rebollo & Montiel, 2006)
- New description of the effort to align IDEA with the government's No Child Left Behind legislation (Rosenberg, Westling, & McLeskey, 2008)
- New *Diversity in Children's Development* interlude: Disproportionate Representation of Minority Students in Special Education

Chapter 12
COGNITIVE DEVELOPMENT IN MIDDLE AND LATE CHILDHOOD

- New *Images of Children's Development* opening: Marva Collins, Challenging Children to Achieve
- Extensive rewriting, updating, and reorganization of sections for improved student understanding
- Revised definition of creativity based on Robert Sternberg's (2007a) view
- Revised and updated material on culture-fair tests, which an increasing number of experts such as Robert Sternberg (2007a) now prefer to label as *culture-reduced tests*
- Moved the major section on achievement after language to fit with the sequence in earlier chapters of having the discussion of language follow cognition
- New *Caring for Children* interlude: Strategies for Increasing Children's Creative Thinking
- Revised and updated conclusion about the best strategy for teaching beginning readers to now emphasize

direct instruction in phonics (Mayer, 2004; Rasinski & Padak, 2008)

- Coverage of recent study on gender differences in mastery and performance orientations (Kenney-Benson & others, 2006)
- New section in Achievement: Social Relationships and Contexts, including Nel Noddings' (2006) view on caring for students
- New *Research in Children's Development* interlude: Children's Math Achievement in the United States, China, Taiwan, and Japan
- New *Diversity in Children's Development* interlude: Bilingual Education
- New section, Mindset, that describes Carol Dweck's (2006) recent emphasis on the importance of children developing a growth rather than a fixed mindset

Chapter 13
SOCIOEMOTIONAL DEVELOPMENT IN MIDDLE AND LATE CHILDHOOD

- Expanded *Images of Children's Development* opening story that now includes vivid descriptions of elementary school children in the South Bronx
- Updated coverage of developmental changes in self-descriptions during middle and late childhood (Harter, 2006)
- New section, Understanding others, including information about perspective taking and recent research on children's increasing psychological sophistication in understanding others, especially showing more skepticism of others' self-reports of value-laden terms (Heyman, Fu, & Lee, 2007)
- New *Caring for Children* interlude: Increasing Children's Self-Esteem
- New section, Self-Regulation, that describes the increased capacity for self-regulation in middle and late childhood, including its link to advances in managing one's own behavior, emotions, and thoughts that lead to increased social competence and achievement (Laible & Thompson, 2007)
- Connection of increased self-regulation to the discussion of developmental advances in the brain's prefrontal cortex in Chapter 11, "Physical Development in Middle and Late Childhood" (Durston & others, 2007)
- New section on social conventional reasoning (Smetana, 2006; Turiel, 2006)
- New section on personality that emphasizes moral identity, moral character, and moral exemplars (Blasi, 2005; Lapsley & Narvaez, 2006)
- Description of recent research on an increase in gender stereotyping from preschool through the fifth grade (Martin & others, 2007)

- Updating of discussion of relational aggression (Young, Boye, & Nelson, 2006)
- Updated national assessment of the gender gap in reading (National Assessment of Educational Progress, 2005)
- New coverage of the importance of parenting in middle and late childhood as gatekeepers for children's behavior as children spend less time with parents (Huston & Ripke, 2006)
- New section, Parents as Managers, which describes the important roles that parents play as managers of children's opportunities, monitors of their behavior, and social initiators and arrangers (Eccles, 2007; Parke & Buriel, 2006)
- Discusssion of Hetherington's (2006) recent conclusions about which type of stepfamily arrangement is linked to better adjustment in children and adolescents
- Updated coverage of children with gay male or lesbian parents (Patterson & Hastings, 2007)
- New discussion of longitudinal study linking peer competence in middle and late childhood with competence at work and in close relationships in early adulthood (Collins & van Dulmen, 2006)
- Coverage of recent research on links between bullying and negative developmental outcomes (Brunstein & others, 2007; Srabstein & others, 2006)
- New *Research in Children's Development* interlude, Aggressive Victims, Passive Victims, and Bullies (Hanish & Guerera, 2004)
- New coverage of recent conclusions by experts in educational psychology that the most effective teachers often use both constructivist and direct instruction approaches (Bransford & others, 2006)
- Updated discussion of accountability and the No Child Left Behind legislation (McMillan, 2007)
- Coverage of Jonathan Kozol's (2005) recent book *The Shame of the Nation*, that portrays the continuing educational segregation and inequities of many minority students living in low-income circumstances

Chapter 14
PHYSICAL DEVELOPMENT IN ADOLESCENCE

- Extensive editing and restructuring for improved student understanding
- Important new section on developmental transitions from childhood to adolescence and from adolescence to adulthood, with a new description of what characterizes emerging adulthood (Arnett, 2006, 2007)
- Considerable updating and revision of material on hormones and adolescent behavior (DeRose & Brooks-Gunn, 2006; DeRose, Wright, & Brooks-Gunn, 2006)
- Coverage of seven recent research studies on body image and body dissatisfaction during adolescence that focus on ethnicity, appearance, developmental changes,

mental health problems, health, and the best and worst aspects of being a boy or a girl (Bearman & others, 2006; Dyl & others, 2006; Gillen & others, 2006; Grabe & Hyde, 2006; Neumark-Sztainer & others, 2006; Schooler & others, 2004; Zittleman, 2006)

- New section, Body Art, that describes the increase use of tattooing and body piercing by adolescents and college students (Armstrong, Caliendo, & Roberts, 2006; Armstrong & others, 2004)

- Extensive expansion, revision, and updating of brain development in adolescence with an emphasis on brain structure, cognition, and emotion

- New discussion of the implications of the recent research on brain development in adolescence for the legal system, including whether this research can be used to decide whether an adolescent should be given the death penalty (Ash, 2006)

- Description of recent research on patterns of TV viewing by high school students and links to their sexual stereotyping and sexual experience (Ward & Friedman, 2006)

- Updated data on developmental changes in adolescents' sexual activities (MMWR, 2006)

- New discussion of the dramatic increase in oral sex by U.S. adolescents (Bersamin & others, 2006)

- Description of longitudinal study from 10 to 12 years of age to 25 years of age involving early sexual intercourse and problems in emerging adulthood (Cornelius & others, 2007)

- Discussion of recent longitudinal study on adolescent contraceptive use (Anderson, Santelli, & Morrow, 2006)

- Updated statistics on the number of U.S. adolescents and emerging adults who have AIDS (Centers for Disease Control and Prevention, 2007)

- Inclusion of recent research on factors involved in inconsistent contraceptive use by African American female adolescents living in low-income circumstances (Davies & others, 2006)

- New *Caring for Children* interlude, Reducing Adolescent Pregnancy, that includes information from a recent review of research on whether schools should have an abstinence-only or contraceptive-knowledge approach to sex education (Bennett & Assefi, 2005)

- New *Diversity in Children's Development* interlude: Cross-Cultural Comparisons of Adolescent Pregnancy

- Updated description of the reduction in U.S. adolescent pregnancy rates (Child Trends, 2006)

- Recent research on the increasing recognition of the importance of family functioning in anorexia nervosa and its treatment (Benninghoven & others, 2007; Bulik & others, 2007)

- Inclusion of recent research on a link between adolescent girls who hang out together and weight problems (Hutchinson & others, 2007)

- Inclusion of recent data from the National Youth Risk Survey (2005) on high school students decreased intake of fruits and vegetables, including new Figure 14.9 (MMWR, 2006)

- Description of recent data on the increase in the percentage of adolescents who are overweight (Eaton & others, 2006)

- Discussion of recent data from the National Youth Risk Survey (2005) on adolescents' exercise patterns with a special focus on gender and ethnic variations (MMWR, 2006)

- Coverage of recent data on ethnic variations in U.S. adolescents' exercise patterns, including new Figure 14.10

- Description of results from the recent National Sleep Foundation (2006) survey on adolescent sleep patterns and new research photo of adolescent being assessed in Mary Carskadon's sleep laboratory

- Coverage of two recent research studies that linked sleep deprivation in adolescence to health-compromising behaviors (Chen, Wang, & Jeng, 2006; Fuligni & Hardway, 2006)

- New *Research in Children's Development* interlude: Evaluation of a Family Program Designed to Reduce Drinking and Smoking in Young Adolescents

- Discussion of recent research review of school-based obesity interventions in adolescence (Sharma, 2006)

- Description of recent information about including obesity prevention/intervention in after-school programs and healthier eating at school (Paxson & others, 2006; Story, Kaphingst, & French, 2006)

- Updated results from the Monitoring the Future Study regarding adolescent substance use and abuse (Johnston & others, 2007)

Chapter 15
COGNITIVE DEVELOPMENT IN ADOLESCENCE

- Updated statistics that reveal the continuing decline in school dropout rates across ethnic groups (National Center for Education Statistics, 2007)

- New material on two conditions that improve the likelihood that service learning will generate positive outcomes (Nucci, 2006)

- Updated and expanded coverage of service learning outcomes (Hart, Atkins, & Donnelly, 2006)

- New *Research in Children's Development* interlude: Evaluating a Service Learning Program Designed to Increase Civic Engagement

- Description of recent research on outcomes of character education programs and the most common strategies used in effective programs (Berkowitz & Bier, 2006; Berkowitz & others, 2006)

- New coverage of Darcia Narvaez' integrative moral education approach

- New *Diversity in Children's Development* interlude: Cross-Cultural Comparisons of Secondary Schools

- Expanded and updated coverage of the positive role of religion in adolescent development (Cotton & others, 2006)
- Description of a recent large-scale study connecting religiosity in adolescence to a lower level of problem behaviors (Sinha, Cnaan, & Gelles, 2007)
- Expanded description of the link between identity development and spirituality (Templeton & Eccles, 2006)
- Updated discussion of the importance of various aspects of values in first-year college students' lives and their participation in religious activities and discussion of religion (Pryor & others, 2005)
- New section, Extracurricular Activities, reflecting increased interest in this aspect of school experiences (Fredricks & Eccles, 2006)
- Updated description of school dropout rates (Figure 15.3)
- Updated of The *Caring for Children* interlude: "I Have a Dream" Program to prevent school dropout (2007)

Chapter 16
SOCIOEMOTIONAL DEVELOPMENT IN ADOLESCENCE

- New chapter-opening *Images of Children's Development*: Jewel Cash, Teen Dynamo
- New *Research in Children's Development* interlude: Adolescents' Self-Images
- Coverage of recent research studies on self-esteem in adolescence and emerging adulthood (Galambos, Barker, & Krahn, 2006; Trzesniewski & others, 2006)
- New discussion of James Cote's (2006) view on identity development in emerging adulthood
- New description of the importance of emotion regulation in adolescence and research linking emotional control to higher grades (Gumora & Arsanio, 2002)
- Inclusion of information about early-maturing adolescents experiencing more conflict with parents than those who mature on time or late (Collins & Steinberg, 2006)
- Discussion of recent longitudinal study on a number of dimensions of parenting linked with competent or deviant outcomes in adolescents (Goldstein & others, 2005)
- New *Caring for Children* interlude, Strategies for Parenting Adolescents
- Description of three recent studies linking affiliation with deviant, antisocial peers in adolescence to drug use, delinquency, and depression (Connell & Dishion, 2006; Laird & others, 2006; Nation & Heflinger, 2006)
- Commentary about developmental changes in reputation-based crowds in adolescence (Collins & Steinberg, 2006)
- New section on immigration in the discussion of ethnicity and culture (Parke & Buriel, 2006)
- New discussion of recent research on discrimination of ethnic minority adolescents, including new Figure 16.7 (DeGarmo & Martinez, 2006; Sellers & others, 2006)

- New description of early- and late-onset antisocial behavior and their links with outcome in emerging adulthood (Schulenberg & Zarrett, 2006)
- New coverage of gangs in adolescence, including recent research (Dishion, Nelson, & Yasui, 2005; Lauber, Marshall, & Meyers, 2005)
- Updated trends on the incidence of various aspects of school violence in a national study (Eaton & others, 2006)
- New discussion of the onset of depression in early versus late adolescence and links with developmental outcomes (Schulenberg & Zarrett, 2006)
- Coverage of recent study linking adolescent depression to parent-adolescent conflict and low parental support (Sheeber & others, 2007)
- Updated coverage of suicide rates in adolescence and emerging adulthood (Minino, Heron, & Smith, 2006; Park & others, 2006)
- Description of recent research on suicidal thoughts in adolescence and a link with physical or sexual abuse (Evans, Hawton, & Rodham, 2005)
- Coverage of recent research linking suicidal thoughts to eating disorders in adolescence (Whetstone, Morrissey, & Cummings, 2007)
- Updated coverage of Joy Dryfoos' view on at-risk youth and successful programs to prevent or intervene in adolescent problems (Dryfoos & Barkin, 2006)
- Updated description of recent research involving the Fast Track intervention program (Dodge & the Conduct Problems Prevention Research Group, 2007)

ACKNOWLEDGMENTS

I very much appreciate the support and guidance provided to me by many people at McGraw-Hill. Beth Ann Mejia, Publisher, has provided outstanding guidance and support for this text. Mike Sugarman, Executive Editor, has brought a wealth of publishing knowledge and vision to bear on improving my texts. Dawn Groundwater, Director of Development, and Maureen Spada, Developmental Editor, did a superb job of editing, organizing, and monitoring the many tasks necessary to move this book through the editorial and production process. Jillian Allison, Editorial Coordinator, skillfully coordinated the reviews and juggled many editorial duties related to the book's development. Glenda King provided a beautiful design. Beatrice Sussman did an excellent job as the book's copy editor. Marilyn Rothenberger was superb as Project Manager. James Headley, Executive Marketing Manager, has provided excellent marketing strategies for the text.

I also want to thank my wife, Mary Jo, our children, Tracy and Jennifer, and our grandchildren, Jordan, Alex, and Luke for their wonderful contributions to my life and for helping me to better understand the marvels and mysteries of children's development.

REVIEWERS

I owe a special gratitude to the reviewers who provided detailed feedback about the book.

Expert Consultants

I already listed the expert consultants earlier in the preface. Their photographs and biographies appear on pages xi–xiii. Feedback from the Expert Consultants has especially helped me to include very recent, cutting-edge research in this new edition.

General Text Reviewers

I also owe a great deal of thanks to the instructors who teach child development and who have provided feedback about the book. Many of the changes in *Children,* tenth edition, are based on their input. For their help and encouragement, I thank these individuals:

TENTH EDITION REVIEWERS

Helen Swanson, *U of Wisconsin*
Kate Byerwalter, *Grand Rapids Community*
Bonnie Wright, *Gardner-Webb University*
John Addleman, *Messiah College*
Jean W. Hunt, *University of Cumberlands*
Charles L. Reid, *Essex County College*
Janet Fuller, *Mansfield University*
Joe Price, *San Diego State*
Paul Vonnahme, *University of New Mexico, Las Cruces*
Caroline Olko, *Nassau Community College*
Karen Falcone, *San Joaquin Delta College*
Sabine Gerhardt, *Akron University*
Minhnoi Wroble Biglan, *Penn State Beaver*
Ramona Knight, *Yuba College*
Pamela A. Schulze, *University of Akron*
Susan Witt, *U of Akron*
Jody Miller, *Moorpark College*

REVIEWERS OF PREVIOUS EDITIONS

I also remain indebted to the individuals who reviewed previous editions and whose recommendations have been carried forward into the present edition.

Bonnie Wright, *Gardner Webb University*
Teion Wells, *Florida State University–Tallahassee*
Naomi Wagner, *San Jose State University*
Pamela Schuetze-Pizarro, *Buffalo State College*
Beverly Edmondson, *Buena Vista University*
Sara Lawrence, *California State University–Northridge*
Linda Anderson, *Northwestern Michigan College*
Lynne Rompelman, *Concordia University–Wisconsin*

Art Gonchar, *University of La Verne*
Anita Thomas, *Northeastern Illinois University*
John A. Addleman, *Messiah College*
Harry H. Avis, *Sierra College*
Diana Baumrind, *University of California–Berkeley*
Lori A. Beasley, *University of Central Oklahoma*
Patricia J. Bence, *Tompkins Cortland Community College*
Michael Bergmire, *Jefferson College*
Belinda Blevins-Knabe, *University of Arkansas–Little Rock*
Ruth Brinkman, *St. Louis Community College, Florissant Valley*
Eileen Donahue Brittain, *City College of Harry S Truman*
Urie Bronfenbrenner, *Cornell University*
Phyllis Bronstein, *University of Vermont*
Dan W. Brunworth, *Kishwaukee College*
Carole Burke-Braxton, *Austin Community College*
Alison S. Carson, *Hofstra University*
Rosalind Charlesworth, *Weber State University*
Nancy Coghill, *University of Southwest Louisiana*
Malinda Jo Colwell, *Texas Tech University*
Jennifer Cousins, *University of Houston*
Dixie R. Crase, *Memphis State University*
Kathleen Crowley-Long, *The College of Saint Rose*
Florence Denmark, *Pace University*
Sheridan DeWolf, *Grossmont Community College*
Swen H. Digranes, *Northeastern State University*
Ruth H. Doyle, N.C.C., L.P.C., *Casper College*
Laura Duvall, *Heartland Community College*
Celina V. Echols, *Southeastern Louisiana State University*
Beverly Edmonson, *Buena Vista University*
Timothy P. Eicher, *Dixie Community College*
Sarah Erikson, *University of New Mexico*
Jennifer Fager, *Western Michigan University*
JoAnn Farver, *Oklahoma State University*
Greta Fein, *University of Maryland*
Tiffany Field, *University of Miami (Florida)*
Johanna Filp, *Sonoma State University*
Cheryl Fortner-Wood, *Winthrop College*
Janet Fuller, *Mansfield University*
Thomas Gerry, *Columbia Greene Community College*
Sam Givhan, *Minnesota State University*
Sandra Graham, *UCLA*
Susan Hale, *Holyoke Community College*
Barbara Springer Hammons, *Palomar College*
Cory Anne Hansen, *Arizona State University*
Barbara H. Harkness, *San Bernardino Valley College*
Algea Harrison, *Oakland University*
Susan Heidrich, *University of Wisconsin*
Ashleigh Hillier, *Ohio University*
Alice S. Hoenig, *Syracuse University*
Sally Hoppstetter, *Palo Alto College*
Robert J. Ivy, *George Mason University*
Diane Carlson Jones, *Texas A&M University*
Ellen Junn, *Indiana University*
Marcia Karwas, *California State University–Monterey*
Melvyn B. King, *State College of New York at Cortland*
Kathleen Kleissler, *Kutztown University*

Dene G. Klinzing, *University of Delaware*
Claire B. Kopp, *UCLA*
Cally Beth Kostakis, *Rockland Community College*
Tara L. Kuther, *Western Connecticut State University*
Linda Lavine, *State University of New York–Cortland*
Sara Lawrence, *California State University at Northridge*
Gloria Lopez, *Sacramento City College*
James E. Marcia, *Simon Fraser University*
Deborah N. Margolis, *Boston College*
Julie Ann McIntyre, *Russell Sage College*
Mary Ann McLaughlin, *Clarion University*
Chloe Merrill, *Weber State College*
Karla Miley, *Black Hawk College*
Jody Miller, *Los Angeles Pierce College*
Carrie L. Mori, *Boise State University*
Joyce Munsch, *California State University at Northridge*
Barbara J. Myers, *Virginia Commonwealth University*
Jeffrey Nagelbush, *Ferris State University*
Sonia Nieves, *Broward Community College*
Caroline Olko, *Nassau Community College*
Sandy Osborne, *Montana State University*
William H. Overman, *University of North Carolina at Wilmington*
Michelle Paludi, *Michelle Paludi & Affiliates*
Susan Peet, *Bowling Green State University*
Pete Peterson, *Johnson County Community College*
Pamela Schuetze Pizarro, *Buffalo State College*
Joe Price, *San Diego State University*
Charles L. Reid, *Essex County College*
Barbara Reynolds, *College of the Sequoias*
Richard Riggle, *Coe College*
Lynne Rompelman, *Concordia University, Wisconsin*
James A. Rysberg, *California State University, Chico*
Marcia Rysztak, *Lansing Community College*
David Sadker, *The American University, Washington, D.C.*
Peter C. Scales, *Search Institute*
Pamela A. Schulze, *University of Akron*
Diane Scott-Jones, *University of Illinois*
Clyde Shepherd, *Keene State College*
Carol S. Soule, *Appalachian State University*
Dorothy D. Sweeney, *Bristol Community College*
Ross A. Thompson, *University of Nebraska, Lincoln*
Naomi Wagner, *San Jose State University*
Richard L. Wagner, *Mount Senario College*
Patricia J. Wall, *Northern Arizona University*
Dorothy A. Wedge, *Fairmont State College*
Carla Graham Wells, *Odessa College*
Becky G. West, *Coahoma Community College*
Alida Westman, *Eastern Michigan University*
Allan Wigfield, *University of Maryland, College Park*
Marilyn E. Willis, *Indiana University of Pennsylvania*
Mary E. Wilson, *Northern Essex Community College*
Susan D. Witt, *University of Akron*
Sarah Young, *Longwood College*
William H. Zachry, *University of Tennessee, Martin*

SUPPLEMENTS

For The Instructor

The instructor side of the Online Learning Center at http://www.mhhe.com/santrockc10e contains the Instructor's Manual, Test Bank files, PowerPoint slides, Image Gallery, and other valuable material to help you design and enhance your course. Ask your local McGraw-Hill representative for your password.

Instructor's Manual

by Andrea Rosati, Elmira College

Each chapter of the *Instructor's Manual* is introduced by a Total Teaching Package Outline. This fully integrated tool helps instructors more easily locate and choose among the many resources available for the course by linking each element of the Instructor's Manual to a particular teaching topic within the chapter. These elements include chapter outline, suggested lecture topics, classroom activities and demonstrations, suggested student research projects, essay questions, critical thinking questions, and implications for guidance.

Test Bank and Computerized Test Bank

by John Addleman, Messiah College

This comprehensive Test Bank includes more than 2,000 multiple-choice and approximately 75 essay questions. Organized by chapter, the questions are designed to test factual, applied, and conceptual understanding. All test questions are compatible with EZ Test, McGraw-Hill's Computerized Test Bank program.

Powerpoint Slides

by L. Ann Butzin, Owens Community College

These presentations cover the key points of each chapter and include charts and graphs from the text. They can be used as is, or you may modify them to meet your specific needs.

CPS Questions

by Alisha Janowsky, University of Central Florida

These questions, formatted for use with the interactive Classroom Performance System, are organized by chapter and designed to test factual, applied, and conceptual understanding. These test questions are also compatible with EZTest, McGraw-Hill's Computerized Test Bank program.

McGraw–Hill's Visual Asset Database for Lifespan Development ("VAD")

McGraw-Hill's Visual Assets Database for Lifespan Development (VAD 2.0) www.mhhe.com/vad is an on-line database of videos for use in the developmental psychology classroom, created specifically for instructors. You can customize classroom presentations by downloading the videos to your computer and showing the videos on their own or insert them into your course cartridge or PowerPoint presentations. All of the videos are available with or without captions. Ask your McGraw-Hill representative for access information.

Multimedia Courseware For Child Development

Charlotte J. Patterson, University of Virginia

This video-based set of two CD-ROMS covers classic and contemporary experiments in child development. Respected researcher Charlotte J. Patterson selected the content and wrote accompanying modules that can be assigned to students. These modules include suggestions for additional projects as well as a testing component. Multimedia Courseware can be packaged with the text at a discount.

Annual Editions: Child Growth and Development 08/09

This reader is a collection of articles on topics related to the latest research and thinking in human development. Annual Editions are updated regularly and include useful features such as a topic guide, an annotated table of contents, unit overviews, and a topical index.

Taking Sides: Clashing Views in Childhood and Society

Current controversial issues are presented in a debate-style format designed to stimulate student interest and develop critical thinking skills. Each issue is thoughtfully framed with an issue summary, an issue introduction, and a postscript.

Cases in Child and Adolescent Development for Teachers

Containing more than 40 cases, *Case Studies in Child and Adolescent Development for Teachers* brings developmental issues to life. The reality-based cases address a variety of developmental issues, giving students an opportunity to think critically about the way development influences children everyday.

FOR THE STUDENT:

Online Learning Center (OLC)

This companion website, at www.mhhe.com/santrockc10e offers a wide variety of student resources. Multiple Choice, True/False, and Matching Tests for each chapter reinforce key principles, terms, and ideas, and cover all the major concepts discussed throughout the text. Entirely different from the test items in the Test Bank, the questions have been written to quiz students but also to help them learn. Key terms from the text are reproduced in a Glossary of Key Terms where they can be accessed in alphabetical order for easy reference and review. Decision Making Scenarios present students with the opportunity to apply the information in the chapter to realistic situations, and see what effects their decisions have.

VISUAL TOUR FOR STUDENTS

This book provides you with important study tools to help you more effectively learn about child development. Especially important is the learning goals system that is integrated throughout each chapter. In the visual walk-through of features, pay special attention to how the learning goals system works.

THE LEARNING GOALS SYSTEM

Using the learning goals system will help you to learn the material more easily. Key aspects of the learning goals system are the learning goals, chapter maps, Review and Reflect, and Reach Your Learning Goals sections, which are all linked together. At the beginning of each chapter, you will see a page that includes both a chapter outline and three to six learning goals that preview the chapter's main themes and underscore the most important ideas in the chapter. Then, at the beginning of each major section of a chapter, you will see a mini–chapter map that provides you with a visual organization of the key topics you are about to read in the section. At the end of each section is Review and Reflect, in which the learning goal for the section is restated, a series of review questions related to the mini–chapter map are asked, and a question that encourages you to think critically about a topic related to the section appears. At the end of the chapter, you will come to a section titled Reach Your Learning Goals. This includes a restatement of the chapter's learning goals and a summary of the chapter's content that is directly linked to the chapter outline at the beginning of the chapter and the questions asked in the Review part of Review and Reflect within the chapter. The summary essentially answers the questions asked in the within-chapter Review sections.

THE LEARNING GOALS SYSTEM

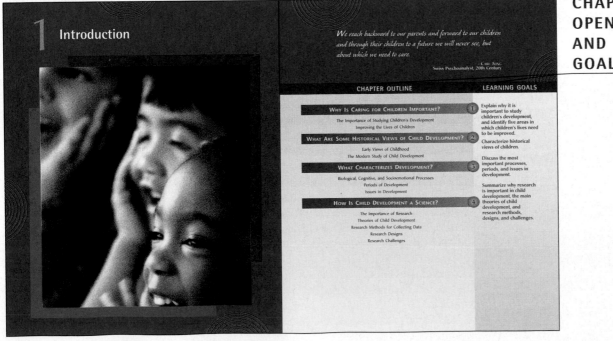

CHAPTER-OPENING OUTLINE AND LEARNING GOALS

MINI-CHAPTER MAP

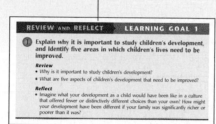

REVIEW AND REFLECT

REACH YOUR LEARNING GOALS

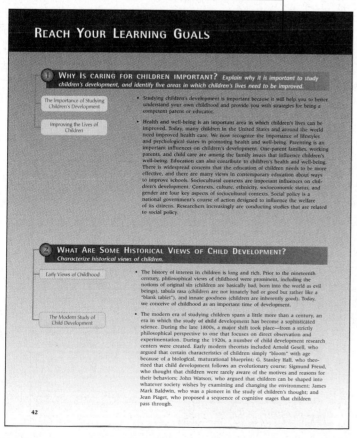

OTHER LEARNING SYSTEM FEATURES

RESEARCH IN CHILDREN'S DEVELOPMENT INTERLUDE

One *Research in Children's Development* interlude appears in every chapter. The *Research* interludes describe a research study or program and are designed to acquaint you with how research on child development is conducted.

Research in Children's Development

RESEARCH JOURNALS

Regardless of whether you pursue a career in child development, psychology, or some related scientific field, you can benefit by learning about the journal process. As a student you might be required to look up original research in journals. As a parent, teacher, or nurse you might want to consult journals to obtain information that will help you understand and work more effectively with people. And as an inquiring person, you might look up information in journals after you have heard or read something that piqued your curiosity.

A journal publishes scholarly and academic information, usually in a specific domain—like physics, math, sociology, or, our current interest, child development. Scholars in these fields publish most of their research in journals, which are the source of core information in virtually every academic discipline.

An increasing number of journals publish information about child development. Among the leading journals in child development are *Developmental Psychology, Child Development, Developmental Psychopathology, Pediatrics, Pediatric Nursing, Infant Behavior and Development, Journal of Research on Adolescence, Human Development,* and many others. Also, a number of journals that do not focus solely on development include articles on various aspects of human development. These journals include *Journal of Educational Psychology, Sex Roles, Journal of Cross-Cultural Research, Journal of Marriage and the Family, Exceptional Children,* and *Journal of Consulting and Clinical Psychology.*

Every journal has a board of experts who evaluate articles submitted for publication. Each submitted paper is accepted or rejected on the basis of such factors as its contribution to the field, methodological excellence, and clarity of writing. Some of the most prestigious journals reject as many as 80 to 90 percent of the articles submitted.

Journal articles are usually written for other professionals in the specialized field of the journal's focus; therefore, they often contain technical language and terms specific to the discipline that are difficult for nonprofessionals to understand. Their organization often takes this course: abstract, introduction, method, results, discussion, and references.

The *abstract* is a brief summary that appears at the beginning of the article. The abstract lets readers quickly determine whether the article is relevant to their interests. The *Introduction* introduces the problem or issue that is being studied. It includes a concise review of research relevant to the topic, theoretical ties, and one or more hypotheses to be tested. The *method* section consists of a clear description of the subjects evaluated in the study, the measures used, and the procedures that were followed. The method section should be sufficiently clear and detailed so that by reading it another researcher could repeat or replicate the study. The *results* section reports the analysis of the data collected. In most cases, the results section includes statistical analyses that are difficult for nonprofessionals to understand. The *discussion* section describes the author's conclusions, inferences, and interpretation of what was found. Statements are usually made about whether the hypotheses presented in the introduction were supported, limitations of the study, and suggestions for future research. The last part of the journal article, called *references,* includes bibliographic information for each source cited in the article. The references section is often a good source for finding other articles relevant to the topic that interests you.

Where do you find journals such as those we have described? Your college or university library likely has some of them, and some public libraries also carry journals. Online resources such as PsycINFO, which can facilitate the search for journal articles, are available to students on many campuses.

CARING FOR CHILDREN INTERLUDE

Every chapter has one *Caring for Children* interlude, which provides applied information about parenting, education, or health and well-being related to a topic in the chapter.

Caring for Children

IMPROVING FAMILY POLICY

In the United States, the national government, state governments, and city governments all play a role in influencing the well-being of children (Children's Defense Fund, 2007; Corbett, 2007). When families fail, governments often step in to help (Ross & Kirby, 2006). At the national and state levels, policy makers for decades have debated whether helping poor parents ends up helping their children as well. Researchers are providing some answers by examining the effects of specific policies (Adams & Snyder, 2006; Sandefur & Meier, 2007).

For example, the Minnesota Family Investment Program (MFIP) was designed in the 1990s primarily to affect the behavior of adults—specifically, to move adults off the welfare rolls and into paid employment. A key element of the program was that it guaranteed that adults who participated in the program would receive more money if they worked than if they did not. When the adults' income rose, how did that affect their children? A study of the effects of MFIP found that increases in the incomes of working poor parents were linked with benefits for their children (Gennetian & Miller, 2002). The children's achievement in school improved, and their behavior problems decreased.

Developmental psychologists and other researchers have examined the effects of many other government policies. They are seeking ways to help families living in poverty improve their well-being, and they have offered many suggestions for improving government policies (Coley, Li-Grining, & Chase-Lansdale, 2006; Gennetian, Crosby, & Houston, 2006).

DIVERSITY IN CHILDREN'S DEVELOPMENT INTERLUDE

Once each chapter, a *Diversity in Children's Development* interlude appears to provide information about diversity related to a chapter topic.

Diversity in Children's Development

GENDER, FAMILIES, AND CHILDREN'S DEVELOPMENT

Around the world, the experiences of male and female children and adolescents continue to be quite different (Brown & Larson, 2002; Kagitcibasi, 2007; UNICEF, 2007). Except in a few areas, such as Japan, the Philippines, and Western countries, males have far greater access to educational opportunities than females. In many countries, adolescent females have less freedom to pursue a variety of careers and engage in various leisure acts than males. Gender differences in sexual expression are widespread, especially in India, Southeast Asia, Latin America, and Arab countries—where there are far more restrictions on the sexual activity of adolescent females than males. In certain areas around the world, these gender differences do appear to be narrowing over time. In some countries, educational and career opportunities for women are expanding, and in some parts of the world control over adolescent girls' romantic and sexual relationships is weakening. However, in many countries females still experience considerable discrimination, and much work is needed to bridge the gap between the rights of males and females.

In certain parts of the world, children grow up in closely knit families with extensive extended kin networks "that provide a web of connections and reinforce a traditional way of life" (Brown & Larson, 2002, p. 6). For example, in Arab countries, adolescents are required to adopt strict codes of conduct and loyalty. However, in Western countries such as the United States, children and adolescents are growing up in much larger numbers in divorced families and stepfamilies. Parenting in Western countries is less authoritarian than in the past.

QUOTATIONS

These appear occasionally in the margins to stimulate further thought about a topic.

Ah! What would the world be to us
If the children were no more?
We should dread the desert behind us
Worse than the dark before.

—Henry Wadsworth Longfellow
American Poet, 19th Century

of examples to follow in studying children. In addition, philosophers of the time debated, on both intellectual and ethical grounds, whether the methods of science were appropriate for studying people.

The deadlock was broken when some daring thinkers began to try new methods of studying infants, children, and adolescents. For example, near the turn of the century, French psychologist Alfred Binet invented many tasks to study attention and memory. He used them to study his own daughters, other normal children, children with mental retardation, extremely gifted children, and adults. Eventually, he collaborated in the development of the first modern test of intelligence (the Binet test). At about the same time, G. Stanley Hall pioneered the use of questionnaires with large groups of children. In one investigation, Hall tested 400 children in the

CRITICAL-THINKING AND CONTENT QUESTIONS IN PHOTOGRAPH CAPTIONS

Most photographs have a caption that ends with a critical-thinking or knowledge question in italics to stimulate further thought about a topic.

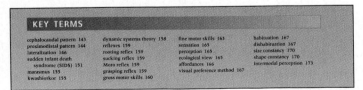

Albert Bandura has been one of the leading architects of social cognitive theory. *What is the nature of his theory?*

KEY TERMS AND GLOSSARY

Key terms appear in boldface. Their definitions appear in the margin near where they are introduced.

The **prenatal period** is the time from conception to birth, roughly a nine-month period. During this amazing time, a single cell grows into an organism, complete with a brain and behavioral capabilities.

Infancy is the developmental period that extends from birth to about 18 to 24 months of age. Infancy is a time of extreme dependence on adults. Many psychological activities are just beginning—the ability to speak, to coordinate sensations and physical actions, to think with symbols, and to imitate and learn from others.

Early childhood is the developmental period that extends from the end of infancy to about 5 to 6 years of age; sometimes this period is called the preschool years. During this time, young children learn to become more self-sufficient and to care for themselves, they develop school readiness skills (following instructions, identifying letters), and they spend many hours in play and with peers. First grade typically marks the end of this period.

Middle and late childhood is the developmental period that extends from about 6 to 11 years of age; sometimes this period is referred to as the elementary school years. Children master the fundamental skills of reading, writing, and arithmetic, and they are formally exposed to the larger world and its culture. Achievement becomes a more central theme of the child's world, and self-control increases.

Adolescence is the developmental period of transition from childhood to early adulthood, entered at approximately 10 to 12 years of age and ending at 18 to 22 years of age. Adolescence begins with rapid physical changes—dramatic gains in height and weight; changes in body contour; and the development of sexual

cognitive processes Changes in an individual's thought, intelligence, and language.

socioemotional processes Changes in an individual's relationships with other people, changes in emotions, and changes in personality.

prenatal period The time from conception to birth.

infancy The developmental period that extends from birth to 18 to 24 months of age.

early childhood The developmental period that extends from the end of infancy to about 5 to 6 years of age sometimes called the preschool years.

middle and late childhood The developmental period that extends from about 6 to 11 years of age, sometimes called the elementary school years.

adolescence The developmental period of transition from childhood to early adulthood, entered at approximately 10 to 12 years of age and ending at 18 to 22 years of age.

Key terms also are listed and page-referenced at the end of each chapter.

KEY TERMS

cephalocaudal pattern 143
proximodistal pattern 144
lateralization 146
sudden infant death syndrome (SIDS) 151
marasmus 155
kwashiorkor 155
dynamic systems theory 158
reflexes 159
rooting reflex 159
sucking reflex 159
Moro reflex 159
grasping reflex 159
gross motor skills 160
fine motor skills 163
sensation 165
perception 165
ecological view 165
affordances 166
visual preference method 167
habituation 167
dishabituation 167
size constancy 170
shape constancy 170
intermodal perception 173

Key terms are alphabetically listed, defined, and page-referenced in a Glossary at the end of the book.

GLOSSARY

A

accommodation Piagetian concept of adjusting schemes to fit new information and experiences. 183

acculturation Cultural changes that occur when one culture comes into contact with another. 339

active (niche-picking) genotype-environment correlations Correlations that exist when children seek out environment they find compatible and stimulating. 75

tion in an area of the body or to block consciousness. 117

anger cry A variation of the basic cry, with more excess air forced through the vocal cords. 219

animism The belief that inanimate objects have lifelike qualities and are capable of action. 279

anorexia nervosa An eating disorder that involves the relentless pursuit of thinness through starvation. 491

A-not-B error Also called AB error, this occurs when infants make the mistake of selecting the familiar hiding place (A) rather than the new

their directions and to respect work and effort. The authoritarian parent places firm limits and controls on the child and allows little verbal exchange. Authoritarian parenting is associated with children's social incompetence. 326

authoritative parenting A parenting style in which parents encourage their children to be independent but still place limits and controls on their actions. Extensive verbal give-and-take is allowed, and parents are warm and nurturant toward the child. Authoritative parenting is associated with children's social competence. 326

CAREERS IN CHILD DEVELOPMENT PROFILES

Throughout the book, *Careers in Child Development* profiles feature a person working in a child development field related to the chapter's content.

40 Chapter 1 Introduction

Careers in CHILD DEVELOPMENT

Pam Reid
Educational and Development Psychologist

When she was a child, Pam Reid liked to play with chemistry sets. She majored in chemistry during college and wanted to become doctor. However, when some of her friends signed up for a psychology class as an elective, she also decided to take the course. She was intrigued by learning about how people think, behave, and develop—so much so that she changed her major to psychology. Reid went on to obtain her Ph.D. in psychology (American Psychological Association, 2003, p. 16).

For a number of years, Reid was professor of education and psychology at the University of Michigan, where she also was a research scientist at the Institute for Research on Women and Gender. Her main focus has been on how children and adolescents develop social skills with a special interest in the development of African American girls (Reid & Zalk, 2001). In 2004, Reid became Provost and Executive Vice-President at Roosevelt University in Chicago.

Pam Reid (*center, back row*) with some of the graduate students she mentored at the University of Michigan.

must ensure that the deception will not harm the participants and that the participants will be told the complete nature of the study (debriefed) as soon as possible after the study is completed.

Minimizing Bias Studies of life-span development are most useful when they are conducted without bias or prejudice toward any particular group of people. Of special concern is bias based on gender and bias based on culture or ethnicity.

Gender Bias For most of its existence, our society has had a strong gender bias, a preconceived notion about the abilities of males and females that prevented individuals from pursuing their own interests and achieving their potential (Matlin, 2008; Worell & Goodheart, 2006). Gender bias also has had a less obvious effect within the field of child development. For example, it is not unusual for conclusions to be drawn about females' attitudes and behaviors from research conducted with males as the only participants.

Furthermore, when researchers find gender differences, their reports sometimes magnify those differences (Denmark & others, 1988). For example, a researcher might report that 74 percent of the boys in a study had high achievement expectations versus only 67 percent of the girls and go on to talk about the differences in some detail. In reality, this might be a rather small difference. It also might disappear if the study were repeated, or the study might have methodological problems that don't allow such strong interpretations.

Pam Reid is a leading researcher who studies gender and ethnic bias in development. To read about Pam's interests, see the *Careers in Child Development* profile.

Cultural and Ethnic Bias The realization that research on children's development needs to include more children from diverse ethnic groups has also been building (Graham, 1992, 2006). Historically, children from ethnic minority groups (African American, Latino, Asian American, and Native American) were excluded from most research in the United States and simply thought of as variations from the norm or average. If minority children were included in samples and their scores

KEY PEOPLE

The most important theorists and researchers in each chapter are listed and page-referenced at the end of each chapter.

KEY PEOPLE

Mark Rosenzweig •••	Karen Adolph •••	Robert Fantz •••
Ernesto Pollitt •••	Eleanor and James	William James •••
T. Berry Brazelton •••	J. Gibson •••	Richard Walk •••
Esther Thelen •••		

MAKING A DIFFERENCE

At the end of each chapter, this feature provides practical information that individuals can use to improve the lives of children.

MAKING A DIFFERENCE

Supporting the Infant's Physical Development

What are some good strategies for helping the infant develop in physically competent ways?

- *Be flexible about the infant's sleep patterns.* Don't try to put the infant on a rigid sleep schedule. By about 4 months of age, most infants have moved closer to adultlike sleep patterns.
- *Provide the infant with good nutrition.* Make sure the infant has adequate energy and nutrient intake. Provide this in a loving and supportive environment. Don't put an infant on a diet. Weaning should be gradual, not abrupt.
- *Breast feed the infant, if possible.* Breast feeding provides more ideal nutrition than bottle feeding. If because of work demands the mother cannot breast feed the infant, she should consider "pumping."
- *Toilet train the infant in a warm, relaxed, supportive manner.* Twenty months to 2 years of age is a recommended time to begin toilet training, so that it is accomplished before

the "terrible twos." Like good strategies for the infant's sleep and nutrition, toilet training should not be done in a harsh, rigid way.

- *Give the infant extensive opportunities to explore safe environments.* Infants don't need exercise classes. What they should be provided are many opportunities to actively explore safe environments. Infants should not be constricted to small, confined environments for any length of time.
- *Don't push the infant's physical development or get uptight about physical norms.* In American culture, we tend to want our child to grow faster than other children. Remember that there is wide individual variation in normal physical development. Just because an infant is not at the top of a physical chart doesn't mean parents should start pushing the infant's physical skills. Infants develop at different paces. Respect and nurture the infant's individuality.

RESOURCES FOR IMPROVING CHILDREN'S LIVES

At the end of each chapter, resources provide information about books, Web sites, and organizations relevant to the chapter's topics.

RESOURCES FOR IMPROVING CHILDREN'S LIVES

Child Art in Context
by Claire Golomb (2002)
Washington, DC: American Psychological Association

One of the world's leading experts on children's art reviews the latest research and presents her contextual theory of children's art. Includes many children's drawings to illustrate points related to the theory.

American Academy of Pediatrics
www.aap.org

This Web site provides extensive information about strategies for improving children's health.

How Children Learn to Be Healthy
by Barbara Tinsley (2003)
New York: Cambridge University Press

A leading expert explores the ways in which health behavior develops in children, especially focusing on the roles of parents, schools, and the media in influencing children's health.

E-LEARNING TOOLS

This feature appears at the end of each chapter and consists of three parts: *Taking It to the Net* Internet problem-solving exercises; *Video Clips,* which provide interesting visual material related to the chapter's content, and *Health and Well-Being, Parenting, and Education* exercises, which provide an opportunity to practice decision-making skills related to real-world applications. By going to the Online Learning Center for this book, you can complete these valuable and enjoyable exercises, and you will find many learning activities to improve your knowledge and understanding of the chapter.

E-LEARNING TOOLS

Connect to **www.mhhe.com/santrock10** to research the answers and complete these exercises. In addition, you'll find a number of other resources and valuable study tools for Chapter 4, "Birth," on this Web site.

Taking It to the Net

1. Jessica and Eric have just given birth to their first child. Eric has noticed that since the birth three months ago, Jessica has seemed a bit withdrawn and sad. He remembers from their Lamaze classes that there is a condition called postpartum depression. What can Eric do to help Jessica through this difficult time period?
2. The author of your text provides a summary of the most widely used birthing methods in the United States. What other birthing methods might a woman consider?

3. You have just given birth, and the nurse has informed you that tomorrow your baby will be assessed using the Brazelton Neonatal Behavioral Assessment Scale. What will your baby's experience be like during this assessment?

Health and Well-Being, Parenting, and Education

Build your decision-making skills by trying your hand at the health and well-being, parenting, and education exercises.

Video Clips

The Online Learning Center includes the following video for this chapter:

1. *Midwifery*—1524
   A certified midwife discusses midwives and how they differ from obstetricians.

If I had my child to raise over again

If I had my child to raise over again,

I'd finger paint more, and point the finger less.

I'd do less correcting, and more connecting.

I'd take my eyes off my watch, and watch more with my eyes.

I would care to know less, and know to care more.

I'd take more hikes and fly more kites.

I'd stop playing serious, and seriously play.

I would run through more fields, and gaze at more stars.

I'd do more hugging, and less tugging.

I would be firm less often, and affirm much more.

I'd build self-esteem first, and the house later.

I'd teach less about the love of power,

And more about the power of love.

—Diane Loomans

Section One

THE NATURE OF CHILDREN'S DEVELOPMENT

In every child who is born, under no matter what circumstances, and of no matter what parents, the potentiality of the human race is born again.

—JAMES AGEE
American Writer, 20th Century

Examining the shape of childhood allows us to understand it better. Every childhood is distinct, the first chapter of a new biography in the world. This book is about children's development, its universal features, its individual variations, its nature at the beginning of the twenty-first century. *Children* is about the rhythm and meaning of children's lives, about turning mystery into understanding, and about weaving together a portrait of who each of us was, is, and will be. In Section 1 you will read "Introduction" (Chapter 1).

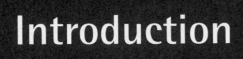

1 Introduction

We reach backward to our parents and forward to our children and through their children to a future we will never see, but about which we need to care.

—CARL JUNG
Swiss Psychoanalyst, 20th Century

CHAPTER OUTLINE

LEARNING GOALS

WHY IS CARING FOR CHILDREN IMPORTANT? ①

The Importance of Studying Children's Development
Improving the Lives of Children

WHAT ARE SOME HISTORICAL VIEWS OF CHILD DEVELOPMENT? ②

Early Views of Childhood
The Modern Study of Child Development

WHAT CHARACTERIZES DEVELOPMENT? ③

Biological, Cognitive, and Socioemotional Processes
Periods of Development
Issues in Development

HOW IS CHILD DEVELOPMENT A SCIENCE? ④

The Importance of Research
Theories of Child Development
Research Methods for Collecting Data
Research Designs
Research Challenges

1 Explain why it is important to study children's development, and identify five areas in which children's lives need to be improved.

2 Characterize historical views of children.

3 Discuss the most important processes, periods, and issues in development.

4 Summarize why research is important in child development, the main theories of child development, and research methods, designs, and challenges.

Images of Children's Development
The Stories of Ted Kaczynski and Alice Walker

Ted Kaczynski, the convicted Unabomber, traced his difficulties to growing up as a genius in a kid's body and not fitting in when he was a child.

Alice Walker
What might be some reasons that she overcame trauma in her childhood to develop in positive ways?

Ted Kaczynski sprinted through high school, not bothering with his junior year and making only passing efforts at social contact. Off to Harvard at age 16, Kaczynski was a loner during his college years. One of his roommates at Harvard said that he avoided people by quickly shuffling by them and slamming the door behind him. After obtaining his Ph.D. in mathematics at the University of Michigan, Kaczynski became a professor at the University of California at Berkeley. His colleagues there remember him as hiding from social circumstances—no friends, no allies, no networking.

After several years at Berkeley, Kaczynski resigned and moved to a rural area of Montana where he lived as a hermit in a crude shack for 25 years. Town residents described him as a bearded eccentric. Kaczynski traced his own difficulties to growing up as a genius in a kid's body and sticking out like a sore thumb in his surroundings as a child. In 1996, he was arrested and charged as the notorious Unabomber, America's most wanted killer. Over the course of 17 years, Kaczynski had sent 16 mail bombs in 17 years that left 23 people wounded or maimed, and 3 people dead. In 1998, he pleaded guilty to the offenses and was sentenced to life in prison.

A decade before Kaczynski mailed his first bomb, Alice Walker spent her days battling racism in Mississippi. She had recently won her first writing fellowship, but rather than use the money to follow her dream of moving to Senegal, Africa, she put herself into the heart and heat of the civil rights movement. Walker had grown up knowing the brutal effects of poverty and racism. Born in 1944, she was the eighth child of Georgia sharecroppers who earned $300 a year. When Walker was 8, her brother accidentally shot her in the left eye with a BB gun. Since her parents had no car, it took them a week to get her to a hospital. By the time she received medical care, she was blind in that eye, and it had developed a disfiguring layer of scar tissue. Despite the counts against her, Walker overcame pain and anger and went on to win a Pulitzer Prize for her book *The Color Purple*. She became not only a novelist but also an essayist, a poet, a short-story writer, and a social activist.

What leads one individual, so full of promise, to commit brutal acts of violence and another to turn poverty and trauma into a rich literary harvest? If you have ever wondered why people turn out the way they do, you have asked yourself the central question we explore in this book.

PREVIEW

Why study children? Perhaps you are or will be a parent or teacher, and responsibility for children will be a part of your everyday life. The more you learn about children, the better you can guide them. Perhaps you hope to gain an understanding of your own history—as an infant, as a child, and as an adolescent. Perhaps you accidentally came across the course description and found it intriguing. Whatever your reasons, you will discover that the study of child development is provocative, intriguing, and informative. In this first chapter, we explore why caring for children is so important, describe historical changes in the study of children's development, examine the nature of development, and outline how science helps us to understand it.

1 WHY IS CARING FOR CHILDREN IMPORTANT?

| The Importance of Studying Children's Development | Improving the Lives of Children |

Caring for children is an important theme of this text. To think about why caring for children is such an important theme, we explore why it is beneficial to study children's development and some areas in which children's lives need to be improved. Just what do we mean when we speak of an individual's development? **Development** is the pattern of change that begins at conception and continues through the life span. Most development involves growth, although it also includes decay.

The Importance of Studying Children's Development

How might you benefit from examining children's development? Perhaps you are, or will be, a parent or teacher and you want to learn about children so that you can become a better parent or educator. Perhaps you hope to gain some insight about your own history—as an infant, a child, and an adolescent. Or perhaps you think that the study of children's development might raise some provocative issues. Whatever your reasons for reading this book, you will discover that the study of children's development is intriguing and filled with information about who we are and how we came to be this way.

Most human development involves growth, but it also includes decline. For example, think about how your ability to speak and write your native language has grown since you were a young child. But your ability to learn to speak a new language has probably declined. In this book we examine children's development from the point of conception through adolescence. You will see yourself as an infant, as a child, and as an adolescent, and be stimulated to think about how those years influenced you.

Children are the legacy we leave for the time we will not live to see.

—ARISTOTLE
Greek Philosopher,
4th Century B.C.

Improving the Lives of Children

If you were to pick up a newspaper or magazine in any U.S. town or city, you might see headlines like these: "Political Leanings May Be Written in the Genes," "Mother Accused of Tossing Children into Bay," "Gender Gap Widens," and "FDA Warns About ADHD Drug." Researchers are examining these and many other topics of contemporary concern. The roles that health and well-being, parenting, education, and sociocultural contexts play in children's development, as well as how social policy is related to these issues, are a particular focus of this textbook.

Health and Well-Being Does a pregnant woman endanger her fetus if she has a few beers a week? How does a poor diet affect a child's ability to learn? Are children exercising less today than in the past? What roles do parents and peers play in whether adolescents abuse drugs? Throughout this text we discuss many questions like these regarding health and well-being. Investigating these questions, and their answers, are important goals for just about everyone.

Health professionals today recognize the power of lifestyles and psychological states in health and well-being (Hahn, Payne, & Lucas, 2007; Insel & Roth, 2008; Robbins, Powers, & Burgess, 2008). In every chapter of this book, issues of health and well-being are integrated into our discussion. They also are highlighted through the Internet connections that appear with World Wide Web icons throughout the book.

Clinical psychologists are among the health professionals who help people improve their well-being. In this chapter's *Careers in Child Development* profile, you

development The pattern of movement or change that begins at conception and continues through the human life span.

Careers
in CHILD DEVELOPMENT

Luis Vargas
Clinical Child Psychologist

Luis Vargas is Director of the Clinical Child Psychology Internship Program and a professor in child and adolescent psychiatry at the University of New Mexico School of Medicine. Vargas obtained an undergraduate degree in psychology from Trinity University in Texas and a Ph.D. in clinical psychology at the University of Nebraska–Lincoln.

Vargas' work includes assessing and treating children, adolescents, and their families, especially when a child or adolescent has a serious mental disorder. He also trains mental health professionals to provide culturally responsive and developmentally appropriate mental health services. In addition, he is interested in cultural and assessment issues with children, adolescents, and their families. He co-authored (with Joan Koss-Chiono, a medical anthropologist) (1999) *Working with Latino Youth: Culture, Context, and Development.*

Vargas' clinical work is heavily influenced by contextual and ecological theories of development (which we discuss later in this chapter). His first undergraduate course in human development, and subsequent courses in development, contributed to his decision to pursue a career in clinical child psychology.

Luis Vargas (*left*) conducting a child therapy session.

can read about clinical psychologist Luis Vargas, who helps adolescents with problems. A Careers Appendix that follows Chapter 1 describes the education and training required to become a clinical psychologist and other careers in child development.

Parenting   Can two gay men raise a healthy family? Are children harmed if both parents work outside the home? Do adopted children fare as well as children raised by their biological parents? How damaging is divorce to children's development? We hear many questions like these related to pressures on the contemporary family (Grusec & Davidov, 2007; Patterson & Hastings, 2007). We examine these questions and others that provide a context for understanding factors that influence parents' lives and how effectively they rear their children. How parents, as well as other adults, can make a positive difference in children's lives is a major theme of this book.

You might be a parent someday or might already be one. You should take seriously the importance of rearing your children, because they are the future of our society. Good parenting takes considerable time. If you plan to become a parent, commit yourself day after day, week after week, month after month, and year after year to providing your children with a warm, supportive, safe, and stimulating environment that will make them feel secure and allow them to reach their full potential as human beings. The poster on page 9 that states "Children learn to love when they are loved" reflects this theme.

Understanding the nature of children's development can help you become a better parent (Parke & Buriel, 2006; Pipe & others, 2007; Voydanoff, 2007). Many parents learn parenting practices from their parents. Unfortunately, when parenting practices and child-care strategies are passed from one generation to the next, both desirable and undesirable ones are usually perpetuated. This book and your instructor's lectures in this course can help you become more knowledgeable about children's development and sort through which practices in your own upbringing you should continue with your own children and which you should abandon.

Education   There is widespread agreement that something needs to be done to improve the education of our nation's children (Aldridge & Goldman, 2007; Jonassen & others, 2008; Sunal & Haas, 2008). A number of questions are involved in improving schools. For example, are U.S. schools teaching children to be immoral? Are they failing to teach them how to read and write and calculate adequately? Should there be more accountability in schools with accountability of student learning and teaching assessed by formal tests? Have schools become too soft and watered down? Should they make more demands on, and have higher expectations of, children? Should schooling involve less memorization and more attention to the development of children's ability to process information more efficiently? Should schools focus only on developing the child's knowledge and cognitive skills, or should they pay more attention to the whole child and consider the child's socioemotional and physical development as well? For example, should schools be dramatically changed so that they serve as a locus for a wide range of services, such as primary health care, child care, preschool education, parent education, recreation, and family counseling, as well as the traditional educational activities, such as learning in the classroom? In this text we examine such questions about the state of education in the United States and consider recent research on solutions to educational problems.

Sociocultural Contexts and Diversity   Health and well-being, parenting, and education—like development itself—are all shaped by their sociocultural context. The term **context** refers to the settings in which development occurs. These settings are influenced by historical, economic, social, and cultural factors. Four contexts that we pay special attention in this text are culture, ethnicity, socioeconomic status, and gender.

Culture encompasses the behavior patterns, beliefs, and all other products of a particular group of people that are passed on from generation to generation. Culture results from the interaction of people over many years (Matsumoto, 2008). A cultural group can be as large as the United States or as small as an isolated Appalachian town. Whatever its size, the group's culture influences the behavior of its members (Shiraev & Levy, 2007). **Cross-cultural studies** compare aspects of two or more cultures. The comparison provides information about the degree to which development is similar, or universal, across cultures, or is instead culture-specific (Kagitcibasi, 2007; Rothbaum & Trommsdorff, 2007).

Ethnicity (the word *ethnic* comes from the Greek word for "nation") is rooted in cultural heritage, nationality, race, religion, and language. African Americans, Latinos, Asian Americans, Native Americans, Polish Americans, and Italian Americans are a few examples of ethnic groups. Diversity exists within each ethnic group (Banks, 2008; Kottak & Kozaitis, 2008). Contrary to stereotypes, not all African Americans live in low-income circumstances; not all Latinos are Catholics; not all Asian Americans are high school math whizzes.

Race and ethnicity are sometimes misrepresented. *Race* is a controversial classification of people according to real or imagined biological characteristics such as skin color and blood group (Corsini, 1999). An individual's ethnicity can include his or her race but also many other characteristics. Thus, an individual might be White (a racial category) and a fifth-generation Texan who is a Catholic and speaks English and Spanish fluently.

Socioeconomic status (SES) refers to a person's position within society based on occupational, educational, and economic characteristics. Socioeconomic status implies certain inequalities. Generally, members of a society have (1) occupations that vary in prestige, and some individuals have more access than others to higher-status occupations; (2) different levels of educational attainment, and some individuals have more access than others to better education; (3) different economic resources; and (4) different levels of power to influence a community's institutions. These differences in the ability to control resources and to participate in society's rewards produce unequal opportunities (Borkowski & others, 2007; Conqer & Dogan, 2007).

Gender   Gender is another key dimension of children's development. Whereas sex refers to the biological dimension of being female or male, **gender** involves the psychological and sociocultural dimensions of being female or male. Few aspects of our development are more central to our identity and social relationships than gender

Children learn to love when they are loved

context The settings, influenced by historical, economic, social, and cultural factors, in which development occurs.

culture The behavior patterns, beliefs, and all other products of a group that are passed on from generation to generation.

cross-cultural studies Comparisons of one culture with one or more other cultures. These provide information about the degree to which children's development is similar, or universal, across cultures, and to the degree to which it is culture-specific.

ethnicity A characteristic based on cultural heritage, nationality, race, religion, and language.

socioeconomic status (SES) The grouping of people with similar occupational, educational, and economic characteristics.

gender The psychological and sociocultural dimensions of being female or male.

Shown here are two Korean-born children on the day they became U.S. citizens. Asian American children are the fastest-growing group of ethnic minority children in the United States.

(Hyde, 2007; Matlin, 2008; Ruble, Martin, & Berenbaum, 2006; Smith, 2007). How you view yourself, your relationships with other people, your life, and your goals are shaped to a great extent by whether you are male or female and how your culture defines the proper roles of males and females.

Each of these dimensions of the sociocultural context—culture, ethnicity, SES, and gender—helps mold how an individual develops through life, as discussions in later chapters demonstrate. We explore, for example, questions such as the following:

- Do infants around the world form attachments with their parents in the same way, or do these attachments differ from one culture to another?
- Does poverty influence the likelihood that young children will be aggressive?
- Is there a parenting style that is universally effective, or does the effectiveness of different types of parenting depend on the ethnic group or culture?
- If adolescents from minority groups identify with their ethnic culture, is that likely to help or hinder their social development?

In the United States, the sociocultural context has become increasingly diverse in recent years. Its population includes a greater variety of cultures and ethnic groups than ever before. This changing demographic tapestry promises not only the richness that diversity produces but also difficult challenges in extending the American dream to all individuals (Banks, 2008; Nieto & Bode, 2008). We discuss sociocultural contexts and diversity in each chapter. In addition, a *Diversity in Children's Development* interlude appears in every chapter. The first Diversity interlude, which focuses on gender, families, and children's development around the world, follows.

Diversity in Children's Development

GENDER, FAMILIES, AND CHILDREN'S DEVELOPMENT

Muslim school in Middle East with boys only

Around the world, the experiences of male and female children and adolescents continue to be quite different (Brown & Larson, 2002; Kagitcibasi, 2007; UNICEF, 2007). Except in a few areas, such as Japan, the Philippines, and Western countries, males have far greater access to educational opportunities than females. In many countries, adolescent females have less freedom to pursue a variety of careers and engage in various leisure acts than males. Gender differences in sexual expression are widespread, especially in India, Southeast Asia, Latin America, and Arab countries—where there are far more restrictions on the sexual activity of adolescent females than males. In certain areas around the world, these gender differences do appear to be narrowing over time. In some countries, educational and career opportunities for women are expanding, and in some parts of the world control over adolescent girls' romantic and sexual relationships is weakening. However, in many countries females still experience considerable discrimination, and much work is needed to bridge the gap between the rights of males and females.

In certain parts of the world, children grow up in closely knit families with extensive extended kin networks "that provide a web of connections and reinforce a traditional way of life" (Brown & Larson, 2002, p. 6). For example, in Arab countries, adolescents are required to adopt strict codes of conduct and loyalty. However, in Western countries such as the United States, children and adolescents are growing up in much larger numbers in divorced families and stepfamilies. Parenting in Western countries is less authoritarian than in the past.

Some of the trends that are occurring in many countries around the world "include greater family mobility, migration to urban areas, family members working in distant cities or countries, smaller families, fewer extended-family households, and increases in mothers' employment" (Brown & Larson, 2002, p. 7). Unfortunately, many of these changes may reduce the ability of families to provide time and resources for children and adolescents.

Resilience, Social Policy, and Children's Development   Some children develop confidence in their abilities despite negative stereotypes about their gender or their ethnic group. And some children triumph over poverty or other adversities. They show *resilience*. Think back to the chapter-opening story about Alice Walker. In spite of racism, poverty, her low socioeconomic status, and a disfiguring eye injury, she went on to become a successful author and champion for equality.

Are there certain characteristics that make children like Alice Walker resilient? Are there other characteristics that make children like Ted Kaczynski, who despite his intelligence and education, became a killer? After analyzing research on this topic, Ann Masten and her colleagues (2001, 2004, 2006; Masten, Burt, & Coatsworth, 2006; Masten & Obradovic, 2007) concluded that a number of individual factors, such as good intellectual functioning, influence resiliency. In addition, as Figure 1.1 shows, their families and extrafamilial contexts tend to show certain features. For example, resilient children are likely to have a close relationship to a caring parent figure and bonds to caring adults outside the family.

Thus factors outside the individual child may act as buffers to adversity, helping the child to show resilience. Norman Garmezy (1993) described a setting in a Harlem neighborhood of New York City that demonstrated the adult competence and concern for children that might bolster resilience. In the entranceway of a walkup apartment building, there is a large frame on a wall. It displays the photographs of children. With the photographs is a written request that if anyone sees any of the children endangered on the street, they bring them back to the apartment house.

Should governments also take action to improve the contexts of children's development and aid their resilience? **Social policy** is a government's course of

Asian Indian adolescents in a marriage ceremony

social policy The government's course of action designed to promote the welfare of its citizens.

If our American way of life fails the child, it fails us all.

—PEARL BUCK
American Author, 20th Century

Source	Characteristic
Individual	Good intellectual functioning
	Appealing, sociable, easygoing disposition
	Self-confidence, high self-esteem
	Talents
	Faith
Family	Close relationship to caring parent figure
	Authoritative parenting: warmth, structure, high expectations
	Socioeconomic advantages
	Connections to extended supportive family networks
Extrafamilial context	Bonds to caring adults outside the family
	Connections to positive organizations
	Attending effective schools

FIGURE 1.1 Characteristics of Resilient Children and Their Contexts

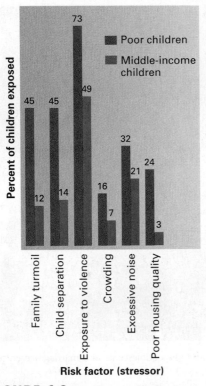

FIGURE 1.2 Exposure to Six Stressors Among Poor and Middle-Income Children One study analyzed the exposure to six stressors among poor children and middle-income children (Evans & English, 2002). Poor children were much more likely to face each of these stressors.

These children live in a slum area of a small Vermont town where the unemployment rate is very high because of a decline in industrial jobs. *What should be the government's role in improving the lives of these children?*

action designed to promote the welfare of its citizens. The shape and scope of social policy related to children are tied to the political system. The values held by citizens and elected officials, the nation's economic strengths and weaknesses, and partisan politics all influence the policy agenda.

When concern about broad social issues is widespread, comprehensive social policies often result. Child labor laws were established in the early twentieth century to protect not only children but also jobs for adults; federal child-care funding during World War II was justified by the need for women laborers in factories; and Head Start and other War on Poverty programs in the 1960s were implemented to decrease intergenerational poverty.

Out of concern that policy makers are doing too little to protect the well-being of children, researchers increasingly are undertaking studies that they hope will lead to wise and effective decision making about social policy (Brown, 2007; Eccles, Brown, & Templeton, 2007). Children who grow up in poverty represent a special concern (McLoyd, Aikens, & Burton, 2006). In 2005, 17.8 percent of U.S. children lived in poor families, and about 4.6 million children lived in families that do not have an employed parent (U.S. Census Bureau, 2006). As indicated in Figure 1.2, one study found that a higher percentage of children in poor families than in middle-income families were exposed to family turmoil, separation from a parent, violence, crowding, excessive noise, and poor housing (Evans & English, 2002). What can we do to lessen the effect of these stressors on the lives of children, and those who care for them? To read more about improving the lives of children through social policies, see the *Caring for Children* interlude that follows.

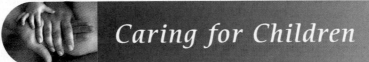

Caring for Children

IMPROVING FAMILY POLICY

In the United States, the national government, state governments, and city governments all play a role in influencing the well-being of children (Children's Defense Fund, 2007; Corbett, 2007). When families fail, or seriously endanger a child's well-being, governments often step in to help (Ross & Kirby, 2006). At the national and state levels, policy makers for decades have debated whether helping poor parents ends up helping their children as well. Researchers are providing some answers by examining the effects of specific policies (Adams & Snyder, 2006; Sandefur & Meier, 2007).

For example, the Minnesota Family Investment Program (MFIP) was designed in the 1990s primarily to affect the behavior of adults—specifically, to move adults off the welfare rolls and into paid employment. A key element of the program was that it guaranteed that adults who participated in the program would receive more money if they worked than if they did not. When the adults' income rose, how did that affect their children? A study of the effects of MFIP found that increases in the incomes of working poor parents were linked with benefits for their children (Gennetian & Miller, 2002). The children's achievement in school improved, and their behavior problems decreased.

Developmental psychologists and other researchers have examined the effects of many other government policies. They are seeking ways to help families living in poverty improve their well-being, and they have offered many suggestions for improving government policies (Coley, Li-Grining, & Chase-Lansdale, 2006; Gennetian, Crosby, & Houston, 2006).

REVIEW AND **REFLECT**   **LEARNING GOAL 1**

1 **Explain why it is important to study children's development, and identify five areas in which children's lives need to be improved.**

Review
- Why is it important to study children's development?
- What are five aspects of children's development that need to be improved?

Reflect
- Imagine what your development as a child would have been like in a culture that offered fewer or distinctively different choices than your own? How might your development have been different if your family was significantly richer or poorer than it was?

2 WHAT ARE SOME HISTORICAL VIEWS OF CHILD DEVELOPMENT?

Early Views of Childhood   The Modern Study of Child Development

Anywhere you turn today, the development of children captures public attention. Historically, though, interest in the development of children has been uneven.

Early Views of Childhood

Childhood has become such a distinct period that it is hard to imagine that it was not always thought of as markedly different from adulthood. However, in medieval Europe laws generally did not distinguish between child and adult offenses. After analyzing samples of art along with available publications, historian Philippe Ariès (1962) concluded that European societies prior to 1600 did not give any special status to children (see Figure 1.3).

Were children actually treated as miniature adults with no special status in medieval Europe? Ariès primarily sampled aristocratic, idealized subjects, which might have been misleading. Childhood probably was recognized as a distinct phase of life more than Ariès believed, but his analysis helped to highlight cultural differences in how children are viewed and treated.

Throughout history, philosophers have speculated at length about the nature of children and how they should be reared. The ancient Egyptians, Greeks, and Romans held rich conceptions of children's development. More recently in European history, three influential philosophical views portrayed children in terms of original sin, tabula rasa, and innate goodness:

- In the **original sin view,** especially advocated during the Middle Ages, children were perceived as being born into the world as evil beings. The goal of child rearing was to provide salvation, to remove sin from the child's life.
- Toward the end of the seventeenth century, the **tabula rasa view** was proposed by English philosopher John Locke. He argued that children are not innately bad but, instead, are like a "blank tablet." Locke believed that childhood experiences are important in determining adult characteristics. He advised parents to spend time with their children and to help them become contributing members of society.

FIGURE 1.3 Historical Perception of Children This artistic impression shows how some children were viewed as miniature adults earlier in history. Many artists' renditions of children as miniature adults may have been too stereotypical.

original sin view Advocated during the Middle Ages, the belief that children were born into the world as evil beings and were basically bad.

tabula rasa view The idea, proposed by John Locke, that children are not innately bad but are like a "blank tablet."

- In the eighteenth century, the **innate goodness view** was presented by Swiss-born French philosopher Jean-Jacques Rousseau. He stressed that children are inherently good. Because children are basically good, said Rousseau, they should be permitted to grow naturally, with little parental monitoring or constraint.

Today, the Western view of children holds that childhood is a highly eventful and unique period of life that lays an important foundation for the adult years and is markedly different from them. Most current approaches to childhood identify distinct periods in which children master specific skills and tasks that prepare them for adulthood. Childhood is no longer seen as an inconvenient waiting period during which adults must suffer the incompetencies of the young. Instead, we protect children from the stresses and responsibilities of adult work through strict child labor laws. We handle their crimes in a special system of juvenile justice. We also have provisions for helping children when families fail. In short, we now value childhood as a special time of growth and change, and we invest great resources in caring for and educating children.

The Modern Study of Child Development

The modern era of studying children began with some important developments in the late 1800s (Cairns & Cairns, 2006). Since then, the study of child development has evolved into a sophisticated science with major theories, as well as elegant techniques and methods of study that help organize our thinking about children's development (Damon & Lerner, 2006). This new era began during the last quarter of the nineteenth century when a major shift took place—from a strictly philosophical approach to human psychology to an approach that includes systematic observation and experimentation.

Methods for a New Science   Most of the influential early psychologists were trained either in the natural sciences such as biology or medicine or in philosophy. The natural scientists valued experiments and reliable observations; after all, experiments and systematic observation had advanced knowledge in physics, chemistry, and biology. But these scientists were not at all sure that people, much less children or infants, could be studied in this way. Their hesitation was due, in part, to a lack of examples to follow in studying children. In addition, philosophers of the time debated, on both intellectual and ethical grounds, whether the methods of science were appropriate for studying people.

The deadlock was broken when some daring thinkers began to try new methods of studying infants, children, and adolescents. For example, near the turn of the century, French psychologist Alfred Binet invented many tasks to study attention and memory. He used them to study his own daughters, other normal children, children with mental retardation, extremely gifted children, and adults. Eventually, he collaborated in the development of the first modern test of intelligence (the Binet test). At about the same time, G. Stanley Hall pioneered the use of questionnaires with large groups of children. In one investigation, Hall tested 400 children in the Boston schools to find out how much they "knew" about themselves and the world, asking them such questions as "Where are your ribs?"

Later, during the 1920s, many child development research centers were created and their professional staffs began to observe and chart a myriad of behaviors in infants and children. Research centers at the Universities of Minnesota, Iowa, California at Berkeley, Columbia, and Toronto became famous for their investigations of children's play, friendship patterns, fears, aggression and conflict, and sociability. This work became closely associated with the so-called child study movement, and a new organization, the Society for Research in Child Development, was formed at about the same time.

*Ah! What would the world be to us
If the children were no more?
We should dread the desert behind us
Worse than the dark before.*

—HENRY WADSWORTH LONGFELLOW
American Poet, 19th Century

innate goodness view The idea, presented by Swiss-born French philosopher Jean-Jacques Rousseau, that children are inherently good.

Another ardent observer of children was Arnold Gesell. With his photographic dome (shown in Figure 1.4), Gesell (1928) could systematically observe children's behavior without interrupting them. He strove for precision in charting what a child is like at specific ages.

The direct study of children, in which investigators directly observe children's behavior, conduct experiments, and obtain information about children by questioning their parents and teachers, had an auspicious start in the work of these child study experts. The flow of information about children, based on direct study, has not slowed since that time.

Theories for a New Science Gesell not only developed sophisticated strategies for studying children but also had provocative views on children's development. His views were strongly influenced by Charles Darwin's evolutionary theory (Darwin had made the scientific study of children respectable when he developed a baby journal for recording systematic observations of children). Gesell argued that certain characteristics of children simply "bloom" with age because of a biological, maturational blueprint.

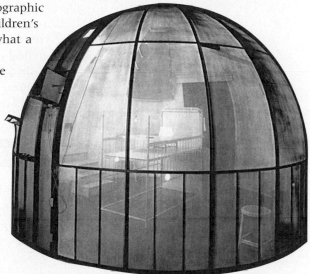

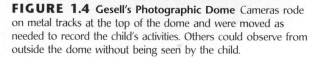

FIGURE 1.4 **Gesell's Photographic Dome** Cameras rode on metal tracks at the top of the dome and were moved as needed to record the child's activities. Others could observe from outside the dome without being seen by the child.

Evolutionary theory also influenced G. Stanley Hall. Hall (1904) argued that child development follows a natural evolutionary course that can be revealed by child study. He theorized that child development unfolds in stages, with distinct motives and capabilities at each stage.

Stages are also a feature of Sigmund Freud's portrait of child development. According to Freud's psychoanalytic theory, children are rarely aware of the motives and reasons for their behavior, and the bulk of their mental life is unconscious. Freud's ideas were compatible with Hall's, emphasizing conflict and biological influences on development, although Freud stressed that a child's experiences with parents in the first five years of life are important determinants of later personality development. Freud envisioned the child moving through a series of stages, filled with conflict between biological urges and societal demands. Since the early part of the twentieth century, Freud's theory has had a profound influence on the study of children's personality development and socialization.

A competing view that gained prominence during the 1920s and 1930s was John Watson's (1928) theory of behaviorism. Watson argued that children can be shaped into whatever society wishes by examining and changing the environment. He believed strongly in the systematic observation of children's behavior under controlled conditions. Watson had some provocative views about child rearing as well. He claimed that parents are too soft on children. "Quit cuddling and smiling at babies so much," he told parents.

Whereas John Watson was observing the environment's influence on children's behavior, and Sigmund Freud was probing the depths of the unconscious mind to discover clues about our early experiences with our parents, others were more concerned about the development of children's conscious thoughts—that is, the thoughts of which they are aware. James Mark Baldwin was a pioneer in the study of children's thought (Cairns & Cairns, 2006). He gave the term **genetic epistemology** to the study of how children's knowledge changes over the course of their development. (The term *genetic* at that time was a synonym for "developmental," and the term *epistemology* means "the nature or study of knowledge.")

Baldwin's ideas initially were proposed in the 1880s. Later, in the twentieth century, Swiss psychologist Jean Piaget adopted and elaborated on many of Baldwin's themes, keenly observing the development of his own children and devising clever experiments to investigate how children think. Piaget became a giant in developmental psychology. Some of you, perhaps, are already familiar with his view that children pass through a series of cognitive, or thought, stages from infancy through adolescence. According to Piaget, children think in a qualitatively different manner than adults do.

genetic epistemology The study of how children's knowledge changes over the course of their development.

This introduction to several theories of children's development has been brief, designed to give you a glimpse of some of the different ways children have been viewed as the study of child development unfolded. You will read more about theoretical perspectives later in this chapter and in later chapters. These theories helped push forward the scientific study of child development. New knowledge about children—based on direct observation and testing—is accumulating at a breathtaking place.

REVIEW AND REFLECT ▸ **LEARNING GOAL 2**

2 **Characterize historical views of children.**

Review
- What are three philosophical views of children?
- How can development of the modern study of children be described?

Reflect
- Which of the three philosophical views of children—original sin, tabula rasa, and innate goodness—appeals to you? Why?

---

3 WHAT CHARACTERIZES DEVELOPMENT?

| Biological, Cognitive, and Socioemotional Processes | Periods of Development | Issues in Development |

Each of us develops in certain ways like all other individuals, like some other individuals, and like no other individuals. Most of the time, our attention is directed to a person's uniqueness, but psychologists who study development are drawn to our shared characteristics as well as what makes us unique. As humans, we all have traveled some common paths. Each of us—Leonardo da Vinci, Joan of Arc, George Washington, Martin Luther King, Jr., and you—walked at about the age of 1, engaged in fantasy play as a young child, and became more independent as a youth. What shapes this common path of human development, and what are its milestones?

Biological, Cognitive, and Socioemotional Processes

The pattern of human development is created by the interplay of several processes—biological, cognitive, and socioemotional. **Biological processes** produce changes in an individual's body. Genes inherited from parents, the development of the brain,

biological processes Changes in an individual's body.

PEANUTS © United Feature Syndicate, Inc.

height and weight gains, motor skills, and the hormonal changes of puberty all reflect the role of biological processes in development.

Cognitive processes refer to changes in an individual's thought, intelligence, and language. The tasks of watching a mobile swinging above a crib, putting together a two-word sentence, memorizing a poem, solving a math problem, and imagining what it would be like to be a movie star all involve cognitive processes.

Socioemotional processes involve changes in an individual's relationships with other people, changes in emotions, and changes in personality. An infant's smile in response to her mother's touch, a child's attack on a playmate, another's development of assertiveness, and an adolescent's joy at the senior prom all reflect socioemotional development.

Biological, cognitive, and socioemotional processes are intricately intertwined. Consider a baby smiling in response to its mother's touch. Even this simple response depends on biological processes (the physical nature of the touch and responsiveness to it), cognitive processes (the ability to understand intentional acts), and socioemotional processes (smiling often reflects positive emotion, and smiling helps to connect infants with other human beings).

We typically study each type of process—biological, cognitive and socioemotional—in separate chapters of the book. For each period of development, we explore how the process influences children's development. However, keep in mind that you are studying the development of an integrated human child who has only one interdependent mind and body (see Figure 1.5).

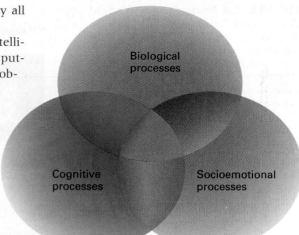

FIGURE 1.5 Biological, Cognitive, and Socioemotional Processes Changes in development are the result of biological, cognitive, and socioemotional processes. These processes interact as individuals develop.

Periods of Development

For the purposes of organization and understanding, a child's development is commonly described in terms of periods, which are given approximate age ranges. The most widely used classification of developmental periods describes a child's development in terms of the following sequence: the prenatal period, infancy, early childhood, middle and late childhood, and adolescence. We use these classifications as the titles of the main sections of this text.

The **prenatal period** is the time from conception to birth, roughly a nine-month period. During this amazing time, a single cell grows into an organism, complete with a brain and behavioral capabilities.

Infancy is the developmental period that extends from birth to about 18 to 24 months of age. Infancy is a time of extreme dependence on adults. Many psychological activities are just beginning—the ability to speak, to coordinate sensations and physical actions, to think with symbols, and to imitate and learn from others.

Early childhood is the developmental period that extends from the end of infancy to about 5 to 6 years of age; sometimes this period is called the preschool years. During this time, young children learn to become more self-sufficient and to care for themselves, they develop school readiness skills (following instructions, identifying letters), and they spend many hours in play and with peers. First grade typically marks the end of this period.

Middle and late childhood is the developmental period that extends from about 6 to 11 years of age; sometimes this period is referred to as the elementary school years. Children master the fundamental skills of reading, writing, and arithmetic, and they are formally exposed to the larger world and its culture. Achievement becomes a more central theme of the child's world, and self-control increases.

Adolescence is the developmental period of transition from childhood to early adulthood, entered at approximately 10 to 12 years of age and ending at 18 to 22 years of age. Adolescence begins with rapid physical changes—dramatic gains in height and weight; changes in body contour; and the development of sexual

cognitive processes Changes in an individual's thought, intelligence, and language.

socioemotional processes Changes in an individual's relationships with other people, changes in emotions, and changes in personality.

prenatal period The time from conception to birth.

infancy The developmental period that extends from birth to 18 to 24 months of age.

early childhood The developmental period that extends from the end of infancy to about 5 to 6 years of age sometimes called the preschool years.

middle and late childhood The developmental period that extends from about 6 to 11 years of age, sometimes called the elementary school years.

adolescence The developmental period of transition from childhood to early adulthood, entered at approximately 10 to 12 years of age and ending at 18 to 22 years of age.

FIGURE 1.6 Processes and Periods of Development Development moves through the prenatal, infancy, early childhood, middle and late childhood, and adolescence periods. These periods of development are the result of biological, cognitive, and socioemotional processes. Development is the creation of increasingly complex forms.

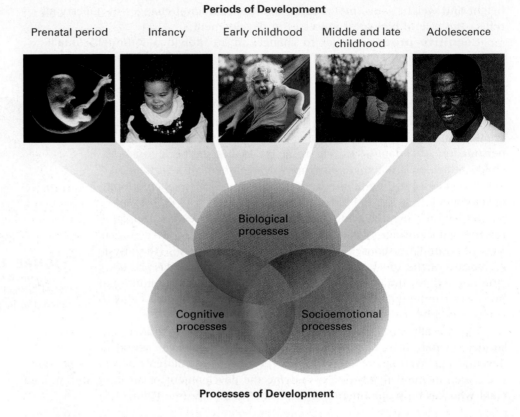

Periods of Development

Prenatal period   Infancy   Early childhood   Middle and late childhood   Adolescence

Biological processes

Cognitive processes   Socioemotional processes

Processes of Development

characteristics such as enlargement of the breasts, development of pubic and facial hair, and deepening of the voice. The pursuit of independence and an identity are prominent features of this period of development. More and more time is spent outside of the family. Thought becomes more abstract, idealistic, and logical.

Today, developmentalists do not believe that change ends with adolescence (Baltes, Lindenberger, & Staudinger, 2006; Birren, 2007; Schaie, 2007). They describe development as a life-long process. However, the purpose of this text is to describe the changes in development that take place from conception through adolescence. All of these periods of development are produced by the interplay of biological, cognitive, and socioemotional processes (see Figure 1.6).

Issues in Development

Many questions about children's development remain unanswered. For example, what exactly drives the biological, cognitive, and socioemotional processes of development, and how does what happens in infancy influence middle childhood or adolescence? Despite all of the knowledge that researchers have acquired, debate continues about the relative importance of factors that influence the developmental processes and about how the periods of development are related. The most important issues in the study of children's development include nature and nurture, continuity and discontinuity, and early and later experience.

Nature and Nurture The **nature-nurture issue** involves the debate about whether development is primarily influenced by nature or by nurture (Rutter, 2007). *Nature* refers to an organism's biological inheritance, *nurture* to its environmental experiences. Almost no one today argues that development can be explained by nature alone or by nurture alone. But some ("nature" proponents) claim that the most important influence on development is biological inheritance, and others ("nurture" proponents) claim that environmental experiences are the most important influence.

nature-nurture issue The issue regarding whether development is primarily influenced by nature or nurture. The "nature" proponents claim biological inheritance is the most important influence on development; the "nurture" proponents claim that environmental experiences are the most important.

According to the nature proponents, just as a sunflower grows in an orderly way—unless it is defeated by an unfriendly environment—so does a person. The range of environments can be vast, but evolutionary and genetic foundations produce commonalities in growth and development (Hartwell, 2008; Plomin, DeFries, & Fulker, 2007). We walk before we talk, speak one word before two words, grow rapidly in infancy and less so in early childhood, and experience a rush of sexual hormones in puberty. Extreme environments—those that are psychologically barren or hostile—can stunt development, but nature proponents emphasize the influence of tendencies that are genetically wired into humans.

By contrast, other psychologists emphasize the importance of nurture, or environmental experiences, to development (Grusec & Hastings, 2007; Maccoby, 2007). Experiences run the gamut from the individual's biological environment (nutrition, medical care, drugs, and physical accidents) to the social environment (family, peers, schools, community, media, and culture). For example, a child's diet can affect how tall the child grows and even how effectively the child can think and solve problems. Despite their genetic wiring, a child born and raised in a poor village in Bangladesh and a child in the suburbs of Denver are likely to have different skills, different ways of thinking about the world, and different ways of relating to people.

Continuity and Discontinuity Think about your own development for a moment. Did you become the person you are gradually, like the seedling that slowly, cumulatively grows into a giant oak? Or did you experience sudden, distinct changes, like the caterpillar that changes into a butterfly (see Figure 1.7)?

The **continuity-discontinuity issue** focuses on the extent to which development involves gradual, cumulative change (continuity) or distinct stages (discontinuity). For the most part, developmentalists who emphasize nurture usually describe development as a gradual, continuous process, like the seedling's growth into an oak. Those who emphasize nature often describe development as a series of distinct stages, like the change from caterpillar to butterfly.

Consider continuity first. As the oak grows from seedling to giant oak, it becomes more oak—its development is continuous. Similarly, a child's first word, though seemingly an abrupt, discontinuous event, is actually the result of weeks and months of growth and practice. Puberty, another seemingly abrupt, discontinuous occurrence, is actually a gradual process occurring over several years.

Viewed in terms of discontinuity, each person is described as passing through a sequence of stages in which change is qualitatively rather than quantitatively different. As the caterpillar changes to a butterfly, it is not more caterpillar, it is a different kind of organism—its development is discontinuous. Similarly, at some point a child moves from not being able to think abstractly about the world to being able to. This change is a qualitative, discontinuous change in development, not a quantitative, continuous change.

Early and Later Experience The **early-later experience** issue focuses on the degree to which early experiences (especially in infancy) or later experiences are the key determinants of the child's development. That is, if infants experience harmful circumstances, can those experiences be overcome by later, positive ones? Or are the early experiences so critical—possibly because they are the infant's first, prototypical experiences—that they cannot be overridden by a later, better environment? To those who emphasize early experiences, life is an unbroken trail on which a psychological quality can be traced back to its origin (Kagan, 1992, 2000). In contrast, to those who emphasize later experiences, development is like a river, continually ebbing and flowing.

The early-later experience issue has a long history and continues to be hotly debated among developmentalists (Egelund, 2007; Thompson, 2006). Plato was sure that infants who were rocked frequently become better athletes. Nineteenth-century New England ministers told parents in Sunday afternoon sermons that the

FIGURE 1.7 Continuity and Discontinuity in Development Is our development like that of a seedling gradually growing into a giant oak? Or is it more like that of a caterpillar suddenly becoming a butterfly?

continuity-discontinuity issue The issue regarding whether development involves gradual, cumulative change (continuity) or distinct stages (discontinuity).

early-later experience issue The issue of the degree to which early experiences (especially infancy) or later experiences are the key determinants of the child's development.

What characterizes the early and later experience issue?

way they handled their infants would determine their children's later character. Some developmentalists argue that, unless infants experience warm, nurturing care during the first year or so of life, their development will never quite be optimal (Sroufe, 2007).

In contrast, later-experience advocates argue that children are malleable throughout development and that later sensitive caregiving is just as important as earlier sensitive caregiving. A number of children's developmentalists stress that too little attention has been given to later experiences in development (Baltes, Lindenberger, & Staudinger, 2006; Birren, 2007; Schaie, 2007). They accept that early experiences are important contributors to development, but no more important than later experiences. Jerome Kagan (2000) points out that even children who show the qualities of an inhibited temperament, which is linked to heredity, have the capacity to change their behavior. In his research, almost one-third of a group of children who had an inhibited temperament at 2 years of age were not unusually shy or fearful when they were 4 years of age (Kagan & Snidman, 1991).

People in Western cultures, especially those influenced by Freudian theory, have tended to support the idea that early experiences are more important than later experiences (Chan, 1963; Lamb & Sternberg, 1992). The majority of people in the world do not share this belief. For example, people in many Asian countries believe that experiences occurring after about 6 to 7 years of age are more important to development than are earlier experiences. This stance stems from the long-standing belief in Eastern cultures that children's reasoning skills begin to develop in important ways during middle childhood.

Evaluating the Developmental Issues   Most developmentalists recognize that it is unwise to take an extreme position on the issues of nature and nurture, continuity and discontinuity, and early and later experiences. Development is not all nature or all nurture, not all continuity or all discontinuity, and not all early or later experiences (Gottlieb, 2007; Rutter, 2007). Nature and nurture, continuity and discontinuity, and early and later experiences all play a part in development through the human life span. Along with this consensus, there is still spirited debate about how strongly development is influenced by each of these factors (Laible & Thompson, 2007; Plomin, DeFries, & Fulker, 2007). Are girls less likely to do well in math mostly because of inherited characteristics or because of society's expectations and because of how girls are raised? Can enriched experiences during adolescence remove deficits resulting from poverty, neglect, and poor schooling during childhood? The answers also have a bearing on social policy decisions about children and adolescents, and consequently on each of our lives.

REVIEW AND REFLECT   LEARNING GOAL 3

3   Discuss the most important processes, periods, and issues in development.

Review
- What are biological, cognitive, and socioemotional processes ?
- What are the main periods of development?
- What are three important issues in development?

Reflect
- Can you identify an early experience that you believe contributed in important ways to your development? Can you identify a recent or current (later) experience that you think had (is having) a strong influence on your development?

4 HOW IS CHILD DEVELOPMENT A SCIENCE?

The Importance of Research

Research Methods for Collecting Data

Research Challenges

Theories of Child Development

Research Designs

This section introduces the theories and methods that are the foundation of the science of child development. We describe why research is important in understanding children's development and examine the main theories of children's development, as well as the main methods and research designs that researchers use. At the end of the section, we explore some of the ethical challenges and biases that researchers must guard against to protect the integrity of their results and respect the rights of the participants in their studies.

The Importance of Research

Some individuals have difficulty thinking of child development as a science like physics, chemistry, and biology. Can a discipline that studies how parents nurture children, how peers interact, the developmental changes in children's thinking, and whether watching TV hour after hour is linked with being overweight be equated with disciplines that study the molecular structure of a compound and how gravity works? Is child development really a science? The answer is yes. Science is defined not by *what* it investigates, but by *how* it investigates. Whether you're studying photosynthesis, butterflies, Saturn's moons, or children's development, it is the way you study that makes the approach scientific or not.

Scientific research is objective, systematic, and testable. It reduces the likelihood that information will be based on personal beliefs, opinions, and feelings (Graziano & Raulin, 2007; McMillan, 2007, 2008). Scientific research is based on the **scientific method,** an approach that can be used to discover accurate information. It includes these steps: conceptualize the problem, collect data, draw conclusions, and revise research conclusions and theory.

The first step, *conceptualizing a problem*, involves identifying the problem. At a general level, this may not seem like a difficult task. However, researchers must go beyond a general description of the problem by isolating, analyzing, narrowing, and focusing more specifically on what they want to study. For example, a team of researchers decide to study ways to improve the achievement of children from impoverished backgrounds. Perhaps they choose to examine whether mentoring that involves sustained support, guidance, and concrete assistance can improve the children's academic performance. At this point, even more narrowing and focusing takes place. For instance, what specific strategies should the mentors use? How often will they see the children? How long will the mentoring program last? What aspects of the children's achievement will be assessed?

As part of the first step in formulating a problem to study, researchers often draw on *theories* and *develop hypothesis*. A **theory** is an interrelated, coherent set of ideas that helps to explain and to make predictions. For example, a theory on mentoring might attempt to explain and predict why sustained support, guidance, and concrete experience make a difference in the lives of children from impoverished backgrounds. The theory might focus on children's opportunities to model the behavior and strategies of mentors, or it might focus on the effects of individual attention, which might be missing in the children's lives. A **hypothesis** is a specific testable assumption or prediction. A hypothesis is often written as an *if-then* statement. In our example, a

> *Science refines everyday thinking.*
>
> —ALBERT EINSTEIN
> *German-born American Physicist, 20th Century*

scientific method An approach that can be used to obtain accurate information. It includes these steps: (1) conceptualize the problem, (2) collect data, (3) draw conclusions, and (4) revise research conclusions and theory.

theory An interrelated, coherent set of ideas that helps to explain and make predictions.

hypothesis A specific assumption or prediction that can be tested to determine its accuracy.

sample hypothesis might be: If children from impoverished backgrounds are given individual attention by mentors, the children will spend more time studying and make higher grades. Testing a hypothesis can inform researchers whether or not a theory may be accurate.

The second step in the scientific method is to *collect information (data)*. In the study of mentoring, the researchers might decide to conduct the mentoring program for six months. Their data might consist of classroom observations, teachers' ratings, and achievement tests given to the mentored children before the mentoring began and at the end of six months of mentoring.

Once data have been collected, child development researchers use *statistical procedures* to understand the meaning of the data (Sprinthall, 2007). Then they try to *draw conclusions*. In this third step, statistics help to determine whether or not the researchers' observations are due to chance.

After data have been collected and analyzed, researchers compare their findings with those of other researchers on the same topic. The final step in the scientific method is *revising research conclusions and theory*.

Theories of Child Development

A wide range of theories makes understanding children's development a challenging undertaking (Newman & Newman, 2007). Just when you think one theory has the most helpful explanation of children's development, another theory crops up and makes you rethink your earlier conclusion. To keep from getting frustrated, remember that child development is a complex, multifaceted topic. No single theory has been able to account for all aspects of child development. Each theory contributes an important piece to the child development puzzle. Although the theories sometimes disagree, much of their information is complementary rather than contradictory. Together they let us see the total landscape of development in all its richness.

We briefly explore five major theoretical perspectives on development: psychoanalytic, cognitive, behavioral and social cognitive, ethological, and ecological. As you will see, these theoretical approaches examine in varying degrees the three major processes involved in children's development: biological, cognitive, and socioemotional.

Psychoanalytic Theories   **Psychoanalytic theories** describe development as primarily unconscious (beyond awareness) and heavily colored by emotion. Psychoanalytic theorists emphasize that behavior is merely a surface characteristic and that a true understanding of development requires analyzing the symbolic meanings of behavior and the deep inner workings of the mind. Psychoanalytic theorists also stress that early experiences with parents extensively shape development. These characteristics are highlighted in the psychoanalytic theory of Sigmund Freud.

Freud's Theory   Freud (1917) proposed that personality has three structures: the id, the ego, and the superego. The *id* is the Freudian structure of personality that consists of instincts, which are an individual's reservoir of psychic energy. In Freud's view, the id is totally unconscious; it has no contact with reality. As children experience the demands and constraints of reality, a new structure of personality emerges—the *ego*. It deals with the demands of reality and is called the "executive branch" of personality because it uses reasoning to make decisions. The id and the ego have no morality—they do not take into account whether something is right or wrong. The *superego* is the Freudian structure of personality that is the moral branch of personality, the part that considers whether something is right or wrong. Think of the superego as what we often refer to as our "conscience."

As Freud listened to, probed, and analyzed his patients, he became convinced that their problems were the result of experiences early in life. He thought that as children grow up, their focus of pleasure and sexual impulses shifts from the mouth to the anus and eventually to the genitals. As a result, we go through five stages of

Sigmund Freud, the pioneering architect of psychoanalytic theory. *How did Freud believe each individual's personality is organized?*

psychoanalytic theories Describe development as primarily unconscious and heavily colored by emotion. Behavior is merely a surface characteristic, and the symbolic workings of the mind have to be analyzed to understand behavior. Early experiences with parents are emphasized.

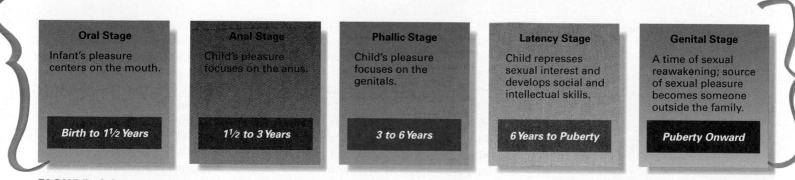

FIGURE 1.8 Freudian Stages

psychosexual development: oral, anal, phallic, latency, and genital (see Figure 1.8). Our adult personality, Freud claimed, is determined by the way we resolve conflicts between sources of pleasure at each stage and the demands of reality.

Freud's theory has been significantly revised by a number of psychoanalytic theorists. Many contemporary psychoanalytic theorists maintain that Freud overemphasized sexual instincts; they place more emphasis on cultural experiences as determinants of an individual's development. Unconscious thought remains a central theme, but most contemporary psychoanalysts stress that conscious thought plays a greater role than Freud envisioned. Next, we outline the ideas of an important revisionist of Freud's ideas—Erik Erikson.

Erikson's Psychosocial Theory   Erik Erikson (1902–1994) recognized Freud's contributions but argued that Freud misjudged some important dimensions of human development. For one thing, Erikson (1950, 1968) said we develop in *psychosocial* stages, rather than in *psychosexual* stages, as Freud maintained. According to Freud, the primary motivation for human behavior is sexual in nature; according to Erikson, it is social and reflects a desire to affiliate with other people. According to Freud, our basic personality is shaped in the first five years of life; according to Erikson, developmental change occurs throughout the life span. Thus, in terms of the early versus later experience issue described earlier in this chapter, Freud argued that early experience is far more important than later experiences, whereas Erikson emphasized the importance of both early and later experiences.

In **Erikson's theory,** eight stages of development unfold as we go through life (see Figure 1.9). At each stage, a unique developmental task confronts individuals with a crisis that must be resolved. According to Erikson, this crisis is not a catastrophe but a turning point marked by both increased vulnerability and enhanced potential. The more successfully an individual resolves the crises, the healthier development will be.

Trust versus mistrust is Erikson's first psychosocial stage, which is experienced in the first year of life. Trust in infancy sets the stage for a lifelong expectation that the world will be a good and pleasant place to live.

After gaining trust in their caregivers, infants begin to discover that their behavior is their own. They start to assert their sense of independence, or autonomy. If infants are restrained too much or punished too harshly, they are likely to develop a sense of shame and doubt. This is Erikson's second stage of development, *autonomy versus shame and doubt,* which occurs in late infancy and toddlerhood (1 to 3 years of age).

Initiative versus guilt, Erikson's third stage of development, occurs during the preschool years. As preschool children encounter a widening social world, they face new challenges that require active, purposeful behavior. Children are asked to assume responsibility for their bodies, their behavior, their toys, and their pets—and they take initiative. Feelings of guilt may arise, though, if the child is irresponsible and is made to feel too anxious.

Erikson's theory Includes eight stages of human development. Each stage consists of a unique developmental task that confronts individuals with a crisis that must be resolved.

Erikson's stages	Developmental period
Integrity versus despair	Late adulthood (60s onward)
Generativity versus stagnation	Middle adulthood (40s, 50s)
Intimacy versus isolation	Early adulthood (20s, 30s)
Identity versus identity confusion	Adolescence (10 to 20 years)
Industry versus inferiority	Middle and late childhood (elementary school years, 6 years to puberty)
Initiative versus guilt	Early childhood (preschool years, 3 to 5 years)
Autonomy versus shame and doubt	Infancy (1 to 3 years)
Trust versus mistrust	Infancy (first year)

FIGURE 1.9 Erikson's Eight Life-Span Stages

Industry versus inferiority is Erikson's fourth developmental stage, occurring approximately in the elementary school years. Children's initiative brings them in contact with a wealth of new experiences. As they move into middle and late childhood, they direct their energy toward mastering knowledge and intellectual skills. At no other time is the child more enthusiastic about learning than at the end of early childhood's period of expansive imagination. The danger is that the child can develop a sense of inferiority—feeling incompetent and unproductive.

During the adolescent years, individuals are faced with finding out who they are, what they are all about, and where they are going in life. This is Erikson's fifth developmental stage, *identity versus identity confusion*. Adolescents are confronted with many new roles and adult statuses—vocational and romantic, for example. If they explore roles in a healthy manner and arrive at a positive path to follow in life, then they achieve a positive identity. If parents push an identity on adolescents, and if adolescents do not adequately explore many roles and define a positive future path, then identity confusion reigns.

Intimacy versus isolation is Erikson's sixth developmental stage, which individuals experience during the early adulthood years. At this time, individuals face the developmental task of forming intimate relationships. Erikson describes *intimacy* as finding oneself yet losing oneself in another. If the young adult forms healthy friendships and an intimate relationship with another, intimacy will be achieved; if not, isolation will result.

Generativity versus stagnation, Erikson's seventh developmental stage, occurs during middle adulthood. By *generativity* Erikson means primarily a concern for helping the younger generation to develop and lead useful lives. The feeling of having done nothing to help the next generation is stagnation.

Integrity versus despair is Erikson's eighth and final stage of development, which individuals experience in late adulthood. During this stage, a person reflects on the past. Through many different routes, the person may have developed a positive outlook in most or all of the previous stages of development. If so, the person's review of his or her life will reveal a life well spent, and the person will feel a sense of satisfaction—integrity will be achieved. If the person had resolved many of the earlier stages negatively, the retrospective glances likely will yield doubt or gloom—the despair Erikson described.

Each of Erikson's stages has a "positive" pole, such as trust, and a "negative" pole, such as mistrust. In the healthy solution to the crisis of each stage, the positive pole dominates, but Erikson maintained that some exposure or commitment to the negative side is sometimes inevitable. For example, learning to trust is an important outcome of Erikson's first stage, but you cannot trust all people under all circumstances and survive. We discuss Erikson's theory again in the chapters on socioemotional development.

Erik Erikson with his wife, Joan, an artist. Erikson generated one of the most important developmental theories of the twentieth century. *Which stage of Erikson's theory are you in? Does Erikson's description of this stage characterize you?*

Evaluating the Psychoanalytic Theories The contributions of psychoanalytic theories include these ideas: (1) early experiences play an important part in development; (2) family relationships are a central aspect of development; (3) personality can be better understood if it is examined developmentally; (4) the mind is not all conscious—unconscious aspects of the mind need to be considered; and (5) in Erikson's theory, changes take place in adulthood as well as in childhood.

There are some criticisms of psychoanalytic theories. First, the main concepts of psychoanalytic theories have been difficult to test scientifically. Second, much of the data used to support psychoanalytic theories come from individuals' reconstruction of the past, often the distant past, and are of unknown accuracy. Third, the sexual underpinnings of development are given too much importance (especially in Freud's theory), and the unconscious mind is given too much credit for influencing development. In addition, psychoanalytic theories (especially in Freud's theory) present an image of humans that is too negative and are culture- and gender-biased, treating Western culture and males as the measure for evaluating everyone.

Cognitive Theories

Whereas psychoanalytic theories stress the importance of the unconscious, cognitive theories emphasize conscious thoughts. Three important cognitive theories are Piaget's cognitive developmental theory, Vygotsky's sociocultural cognitive theory, and information-processing theory.

Piaget's Cognitive Developmental Theory **Piaget's theory** states that children actively construct their understanding of the world and go through four stages of cognitive development. Two processes underlie the four stages of development in Piaget's theory: organization and adaptation. To make sense of our world, we organize our experiences. For example, we separate important ideas from less important ideas, and we connect one idea to another. In addition to organizing our observations and experiences, we *adapt,* adjusting to new environmental demands (Mooney, 2006).

Piaget (1954) also proposed that we go through four stages in understanding the world (see Figure 1.10). Each stage is age-related and consists of a distinct way of thinking, a *different* way of understanding the world. Thus, according to Piaget, the child's cognition is *qualitatively* different in one stage compared with another. What are Piaget's four stages of cognitive development like?

The *sensorimotor stage,* which lasts from birth to about 2 years of age, is the first Piagetian stage. In this stage, infants construct an understanding of the world by coordinating sensory experiences (such as seeing and hearing) with physical, motoric actions—hence the term *sensorimotor.*

Jean Piaget, the famous Swiss developmental psychologist, changed the way we think about the development of children's minds. *What are some key ideas in Piaget's theory?*

Piaget's theory States that children actively construct their understanding of the world and go through four stages of cognitive development.

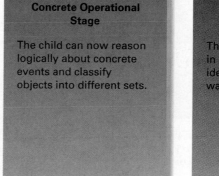

Sensorimotor Stage	Preoperational Stage	Concrete Operational Stage	Formal Operational Stage
The infant constructs an understanding of the world by coordinating sensory experiences with physical actions. An infant progresses from reflexive, instinctual action at birth to the beginning of symbolic thought toward the end of the stage.	The child begins to represent the world with words and images. These words and images reflect increased symbolic thinking and go beyond the connection of sensory information and physical action.	The child can now reason logically about concrete events and classify objects into different sets.	The adolescent reasons in more abstract, idealistic, and logical ways.
Birth to 2 Years of Age	*2 to 7 Years of Age*	*7 to 11 Years of Age*	*11 Years of Age Through Adulthood*

FIGURE 1.10 Piaget's Four Stages of Cognitive Development

The *preoperational stage,* which lasts from approximately 2 to 7 years of age, is Piaget's second stage. In this stage, children begin to go beyond simply connecting sensory information with physical action and represent the world with words, images, and drawings. However, according to Piaget, preschool children still lack the ability to perform what he calls *operations,* which are internalized mental actions that allow children to do mentally what they previously could only do physically. For example, if you imagine putting two sticks together to see whether they would be as long as another stick, without actually moving the sticks, you are performing a concrete operation.

The *concrete operational stage,* which lasts from approximately 7 to 11 years of age, is the third Piagetian stage. In this stage, children can perform operations that involve objects, and they can reason logically as long as reasoning can be applied to specific or concrete examples. For instance, concrete operational thinkers cannot imagine the steps necessary to complete an algebraic equation, which is too abstract for thinking at this stage of development.

The *formal operational stage,* which appears between the ages of 11 and 15 and continues through adulthood, is Piaget's fourth and final stage. In this stage, individuals move beyond concrete experiences and think in abstract and more logical terms. As part of thinking more abstractly, adolescents develop images of ideal circumstances. They might think about what an ideal parent is like and compare their parents to this ideal standard. They begin to entertain possibilities for the future and are fascinated with what they can be. In solving problems, they become more systematic, developing hypotheses about why something is happening the way it is and then testing these hypotheses. This is a brief introduction to Piaget's theory. It is provided here, along with other theories, to give you a broad understanding. Later in the text, when we study cognitive development in infancy, early childhood, middle and late childhood, and adolescence, we return to Piaget and examine his theory in more depth.

Vygotsky's Sociocultural Cognitive Theory   Like Piaget, the Russian developmentalist Lev Vygotsky (1896–1934) said that children actively construct their knowledge. However, Vygotsky (1962) gave social interaction and culture far more important roles in cognitive development than Piaget did. **Vygotsky's theory** is a sociocultural cognitive theory that emphasizes how culture and social interaction guide cognitive development.

Vygotsky portrayed the child's development as inseparable from social and cultural activities (Bodrova & Leong, 2007; Cole & Gajdamaschko, 2007). He argued that development of memory, attention, and reasoning involves learning to use the inventions of society, such as language, mathematical systems, and memory strategies. Thus in one culture, children might learn to count with the help of a computer; in another, they might learn by using beads. According to Vygotsky, children's social interaction with more-skilled adults and peers is indispensable to their cognitive development (Alvarez & de Rio, 2007). Through this interaction, they learn to use the tools that will help them adapt and be successful in their culture. For example, if you regularly help a child learn how to read, you not only advance a child's reading skills but also communicate to the child that reading is an important activity in their culture.

Vygotsky's theory has stimulated considerable interest in the view that knowledge is *situated* and *collaborative* (Bodrova & Leong, 2007). In this view, knowledge is not generated from within the individual but rather is constructed through interaction with other people and objects in the culture, such as books. This suggests that knowledge can best be advanced through interaction with others in cooperative activities.

Vygotsky's theory, like Piaget's, remained virtually unknown to American psychologists until the 1960s, but eventually both became influential among educators as well as psychologists. We examine ideas about learning and teaching that are based on Vygotsky's theory when we study cognitive development in early childhood.

There is considerable interest today in Lev Vygotsky's sociocultural cognitive theory of child development. *What were Vygotsky's basic ideas about children's development?*

Vygotsky's theory A sociocultural cognitive theory that emphasizes how culture and social interaction guide cognitive development.

The Information-Processing Theory   Early computers may be the best candidates for the title of "founding fathers" of information-processing theory. Although many factors stimulated the growth of this theory, none was more important than the computer. Psychologists began to wonder if the logical operations carried out by computers might tell us something about how the human mind works. They drew analogies between a computer's hardware and the brain and between computer software and cognition.

This line of thinking helped to generate **information-processing theory,** which emphasizes that individuals manipulate information, monitor it, and strategize about it. Unlike Piaget's theory, but like Vygotsky's theory, information-processing theory does not describe development as stage-like. Instead, according to this theory, individuals develop a gradually increasing capacity for processing information, which allows them to acquire increasingly complex knowledge and skills (Munakata, 2006; Reed, 2007).

Robert Siegler (2006; Siegler & Alibali, 2005), a leading expert on children's information processing, states that thinking is information processing. In other words, when individuals perceive, encode, represent, store, and retrieve information, they are thinking. Siegler emphasizes that an important aspect of development is learning good strategies for processing information. For example, becoming a better reader might involve learning to monitor the key themes of the material being read.

Evaluating the Cognitive Theories   The primary contributions of cognitive theories are that (1) they present a positive view of development, emphasizing conscious thinking; (2) they (especially Piaget's and Vygotsky's) emphasize the individual's active construction of understanding; (3) Piaget's and Vygotsky's theories underscore the importance of examining developmental changes in children's thinking; and (4) information-processing theory offers detailed descriptions of cognitive processes.

There are several criticisms of cognitive theories. First, Piaget's stages are not as uniform as he theorized. Piaget also underestimated the cognitive skills of infants and overestimated the cognitive skills of adolescents. Second, the cognitive theories do not give adequate attention to individual variations in cognitive development. Third, information-processing theory does not provide an adequate description of developmental changes in cognition. In addition, psychoanalytic theorists argue that the cognitive theories do not give enough credit to unconscious thought.

Behavioral and Social Cognitive Theories   At about the same time as Freud was interpreting patients' unconscious minds through their early childhood experiences, Ivan Pavlov and John B. Watson were conducting detailed observations of behavior in controlled laboratory settings. Their work provided the foundations of *behaviorism*, which essentially holds that we can study scientifically only what can be directly observed and measured. Out of the behavioral tradition grew the belief that development is observable behavior that can be learned through experience with the environment (Bugental & Grusec, 2006; Watson & Tharp, 2007). In terms of the continuity-discontinuity issue discussed earlier in this chapter, the behavioral and social cognitive theories emphasize continuity in development and argue that development does not occur in stage-like fashion. The three versions of the behavioral and social cognitive theories that we explore are Pavlov's classical conditioning, Skinner's operant conditioning, and Bandura's social cognitive theory.

Pavlov's Classical Conditioning   In the early 1900s, the Russian physiologist Ivan Pavlov (1927) knew that dogs innately salivate when they taste food. He became curious when he observed that dogs salivate to various sights and sounds before eating their food. For example, when an individual paired the ringing of a bell with the food, the bell ringing subsequently elicited salivation from the dogs when it was presented by itself.

information-processing theory Emphasizes that individuals manipulate information, monitor it, and strategize about it. Central to this theory are the processes of memory and thinking.

B. F. Skinner was a tinkerer who liked to make new gadgets. The younger of his two daughters, Deborah, was raised in Skinner's enclosed Air-Crib, which he invented because he wanted to control her environment completely. The Air-Crib was sound-proofed and temperature-controlled. Debbie, shown here as a child with her parents, is currently a successful artist, is married, and lives in London. *What do you think about Skinner's Air-Crib?*

Albert Bandura has been one of the leading architects of social cognitive theory. *What is the nature of his theory?*

social cognitive theory The view of psychologists who emphasize behavior, environment, and cognition as the key factors in development.

With this experiment, Pavlov discovered the principle of *classical conditioning*, in which a neutral stimulus (in our example, ringing a bell) acquires the ability to produce a response originally produced by another stimulus (in our example, food).

In the early twentieth century, John Watson demonstrated that classical conditioning occurs in human beings. He showed an infant named Albert a white rat to see if he was afraid of it. He was not. As Albert played with the rat, a loud noise was sounded behind his head. As you might imagine, the noise caused little Albert to cry. After several pairings of the loud noise and the white rat, Albert began to cry at the sight of the rat even when the noise was not sounded (Watson & Rayner, 1920). Albert had been classically conditioned to fear the rat. Similarly, many of our fears may result from classical conditioning: fear of the dentist may be learned from a painful experience, fear of driving from being in an automobile accident, fear of heights from falling off a high chair when we were infants, and fear of dogs from being bitten.

Skinner's Operant Conditioning   Classical conditioning may explain how we develop many involuntary responses such as fears, but B. F. Skinner argued that a second type of conditioning accounts for the development of other types of behavior. According to Skinner (1938), through *operant conditioning* the consequences of a behavior produce changes in the probability of the behavior's occurrence. A behavior followed by a rewarding stimulus is more likely to recur, whereas a behavior followed by a punishing stimulus is less likely to recur. For example, when a person smiles at a child after the child has done something, the child is more likely to engage in the activity than if the person gives the child a nasty look.

According to Skinner, such rewards and punishments shape development. For example, Skinner's approach argues that shy people learned to be shy as a result of experiences they had while growing up. It follows that modifications in an environment can help a shy person become more socially oriented. Also, for Skinner the key aspect of development is behavior, not thoughts and feelings. He emphasized that development consists of the pattern of behavioral changes that are brought about by rewards and punishments.

Bandura's Social Cognitive Theory   Some psychologists agree with the behaviorists' notion that development is learned and is influenced strongly by environmental interactions. However, unlike Skinner, they argue that cognition is also important in understanding development. **Social cognitive theory** holds that behavior, environment, and cognition are the key factors in development.

American psychologist Albert Bandura (1925–) is the leading architect of social cognitive theory. Bandura (2001, 2005, 2006; 2007a,b) emphasizes that cognitive processes have important links with the environment and behavior. His early research program focused heavily on *observational learning* (also called *imitation*, or *modeling*), which is learning that occurs through observing what others do. For example, a young boy might observe his father yelling in anger and treating other people with hostility; with his peers, the young boy later acts very aggressively, showing the same characteristics as his father's behavior. A girl might adopt the dominant and sarcastic style of her teacher, saying to her younger brother, "You are so slow. How can you do this work so slowly?" Social cognitive theorists stress that people acquire a wide range of behaviors, thoughts, and feelings through observing others' behavior and that these observations form an important part of children's development.

What is *cognitive* about observational learning in Bandura's view? He proposes that people cognitively represent the behavior of others and then sometimes adopt this behavior themselves.

Bandura's (2001, 2005, 2006; 2007a,b) most recent model of learning and development includes three elements: behavior, the person/cognition, and the environment. An individual's confidence that he or she can control his or her success is an example of a person factor; strategies are an example of a cognitive factor. As shown in Figure 1.11, behavior, person/cognitive, and environmental factors operate interactively. Behavior can influence person factors and vice versa. Cognitive activities can influence the environment, the environment can change the person's cognition, and so on.

Evaluating the Behavioral and Social Cognitive Theories   Contributions of the behavioral and social cognitive theories include (1) their emphasis on the importance of scientific research; (2) their focus on environmental determinants of behavior; (3) the identification and explanation of observational learning (by Bandura); and (4) the inclusion of person/cognitive factors (in social cognitive theory)

Criticisms of the behavioral and social cognitive theories include the objections that they give (1) too little emphasis on cognition (in Pavlov's and Skinner's theories); (2) too much emphasis on environmental determinants; (3) inadequate attention to developmental changes; and (4) inadequate consideration of human spontaneity and creativity.

Behavioral and social cognitive theories emphasize the importance of environmental experiences in human development. Next we turn our attention to a theory that underscores the importance of the biological foundations of development—ethological theory.

Ethological Theory
American developmental psychologists began to pay attention to the biological bases of development thanks to the work of European zoologists who pioneered the field of ethology. **Ethology** stresses that behavior is strongly influenced by biology, is tied to evolution, and is characterized by critical or sensitive periods. These are specific time frames during which, according to ethologists, the presence or absence of certain experiences has a long-lasting influence on individuals.

European zoologist Konrad Lorenz (1903–1989) helped bring ethology to prominence. In his best-known experiment, Lorenz (1965) studied the behavior of greylag geese, which will follow their mother as soon as they hatch.

In a remarkable set of experiments, Lorenz separated the eggs laid by one goose into two groups. One group he returned to the goose to be hatched by her. The other group was hatched in an incubator. The goslings in the first group performed as predicted. They followed their mother as soon as they hatched. However, those in the second group, which saw Lorenz when they first hatched, followed him everywhere, as though he were their mother. Lorenz marked the goslings and then placed both groups under a box. Mother goose and "mother" Lorenz stood aside as the box lifted. Each group of goslings went directly to its "mother." Lorenz called this process *imprinting*, the rapid, innate learning within a limited critical period of time that involves attachment to the first moving object seen.

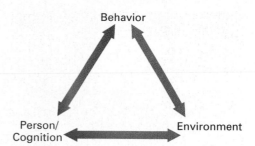

FIGURE 1.11 Bandura's Social Cognitive Model The arrows illustrate how relations between behavior, person/cognition, and environment are reciprocal rather than unidirectional.

ethology Stresses that behavior is strongly influenced by biology, is tied to evolution, and is characterized by critical or sensitive periods.

Konrad Lorenz, a pioneering student of animal behavior, is followed through the water by three imprinted greylag geese. Describe Lorenz's experiment with the geese. *Do you think his experiment would have the same results with human babies? Explain.*

Ethological research and theory at first had little or nothing to say about the nature of social relationships across the human life span, and the theory stimulated few studies with humans. Ethologists' view that normal development requires that certain behaviors emerge during a *critical period*, a fixed time period very early in development, seemed to be overdrawn.

However, John Bowlby (1969, 1989) illustrated an important application of ethological theory to human development. Bowlby argued that attachment to a caregiver over the first year of life has important consequences throughout the life span. In his view, if this attachment is positive and secure, the individual will likely develop positively in childhood and adulthood. If the attachment is negative and insecure, life-span development will likely not be optimal. Thus, in this view the first year of life is a *sensitive period* for the development of social relationships. In Chapter 7, "Socioemotional Development in Infancy," we explore the concept of infant attachment in much greater detail.

Contributions of ethological theory include (1) an increased focus on the biological and evolutionary basis of development; (2) use of careful observations in naturalistic settings; and (3) an emphasis on sensitive periods of development.

Criticisms of ethological theory include the following: (1) the concepts of critical and sensitive periods are perhaps too rigid; (2) there is too strong an emphasis on biological foundations; (3) inadequate attention is given to cognition; and (4) it is better at generating research with animals than with humans.

Another theory that emphasizes the biological aspects of human development—evolutionary psychology—is be presented in Chapter 2, "Biological Beginnings," along with views on the role of heredity in development.

Ecological Theory   Ethological theory stresses biological factors, whereas ecological theory emphasizes environmental factors. One ecological theory that has important implications for understanding children's development was created by Urie Bronfenbrenner (1917–2005).

Bronfenbrenner's ecological theory (1986, 2000, 2004; Bronfenbrenner & Morris, 1998, 2006) holds that development reflects the influence of several environmental systems. The theory identifies five environmental systems (see Figure 1.12):

- *Microsystem*—the setting in which the individual lives. These contexts include the person's family, peers, school, neighborhood, and work. It is in the microsystem that the most direct interactions with social agents take place—with parents, peers, and teachers, for example.
- *Mesosystem*—relations between microsystems or connections between contexts. Examples are the relation of family experiences to school experiences, school experiences to church experiences, and family experiences to peer experiences. For example, children whose parents have rejected them may have difficulty developing positive relations with teachers.
- *Exosystem*—links between a social setting in which the individual does not have an active role and the individual's immediate context. For example, a husband's or child's experience at home may be influenced by a mother's experiences at work. The mother might receive a promotion that requires more travel, which might increase conflict with the husband and change patterns of interaction with the child.
- *Macrosystem*—the culture in which individuals live. Remember from earlier in this chapter that culture refers to the behavior patterns, beliefs, and all other products of a group of people that are passed on from generation to generation. Remember also that cross-cultural studies—the comparison of one culture with one or more other cultures—provide information about the generality of development (Shiraev & Levy, 2007).
- *Chronosystem*—the patterning of environmental events and transitions over the life course, as well as sociohistorical circumstances (Schaie, 2007). For

Bronfenbrenner's ecological theory An environmental systems theory that focuses on five environmental systems: microsystem, mesosystem, exosystem, macrosystem, and chronosystem.

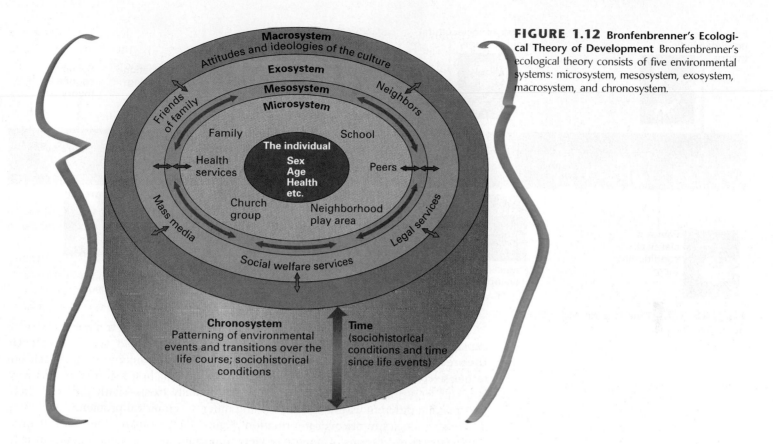

FIGURE 1.12 Bronfenbrenner's Ecological Theory of Development Bronfenbrenner's ecological theory consists of five environmental systems: microsystem, mesosystem, exosystem, macrosystem, and chronosystem.

example, divorce is one transition. Researchers have found that the negative effects of divorce on children often peak in the first year after the divorce (Hetherington, 1993, 2006). By two years after the divorce, family interaction is less chaotic and more stable. As an example of sociohistorical circumstances, consider how the opportunities for women to pursue a career have increased during the last thirty years.

Bronfenbrenner (2000, 2004; Bronfenbrenner & Morris, 1998, 2006) has added biological influences to his theory and now describes it as a *bioecological* theory. Nonetheless, ecological, environmental contexts still predominate in Bronfenbrenner's theory.

The contributions of ecological theory include (1) a systematic examination of macro and micro dimensions of environmental systems; (2) attention to connections between environmental settings (mesosystem); and (3) consideration of sociohistorical influences on development (chronosystem).

Some criticisms of ecological theory include (1) too little attention to biological foundations of development, even with the added discussion of biological influences; and (2) inadequate attention to cognitive processes.

An Eclectic Theoretical Orientation   The theories that we have discussed were developed at different points in the twentieth century, as Figure 1.13 shows. No single theory described in this chapter can explain entirely the rich complexity of children's development, but each has contributed to our understanding of development. Psychoanalytic theory best explains the unconscious mind. Erikson's theory best describes the changes that occur in adult development. Piaget's, Vygotsky's, and the information-processing views provide the most complete description of cognitive development. The behavioral and social cognitive and ecological theories have been the most adept at examining the environmental determinants of development. The ethological theories have highlighted biology's role and the importance of sensitive periods in development.

Urie Bronfenbrenner developed ecological theory, a perspective that is receiving increased attention. *What is the nature of ecological theory?*

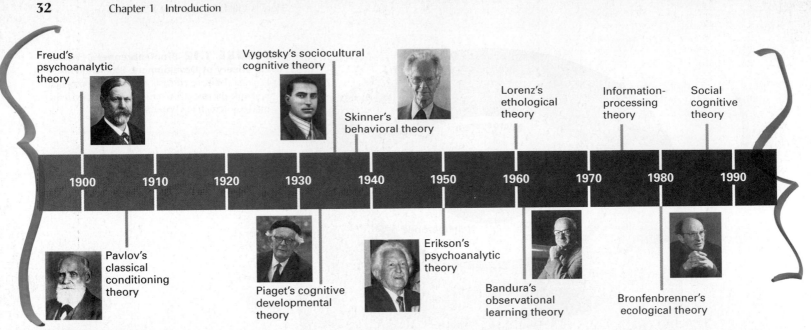

FIGURE 1.13 Time Line for Major Developmental Theories

In short, although theories are helpful guides, relying on a single theory to explain development is probably a mistake. This book instead takes an **eclectic theoretical orientation,** which does not follow any one theoretical approach but rather selects from each theory whatever is considered its best features. In this way, you can view the study of development as it actually exists—with different theorists making different assumptions, stressing different empirical problems, and using different strategies to discover information. Figure 1.14 compares the main theoretical perspectives in terms of how they view important developmental issues in children's development.

Research Methods for Collecting Data

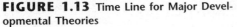
eclectic theoretical orientation An orientation that does not follow any one theoretical approach but rather selects from each theory whatever is considered the best in it.

If they follow an eclectic orientation, how do scholars and researchers determine that one feature of a theory is somehow better than another? The scientific method discussed at the beginning of this chapter provides the guide. Recall that the steps

THEORY	ISSUES	
	Continuity/discontinuity, early versus later experiences	**Biological and environmental factors**
Psychoanalytic	Discontinuity between stages—continuity between early experiences and later development; early experiences very important; later changes in development emphasized in Erikson's theory	Freud's biological determination interacting with early family experiences; Erikson's more balanced biological-cultural interaction perspective
Cognitive	Discontinuity between stages in Piaget's theory; continuity between early experiences and later development in Piaget's and Vygotsky's theories; no stages in Vygotsky's theory or information-processing theory	Piaget's emphasis on interaction and adaptation; environment provides the setting for cognitive structures to develop; information-processing view has not addressed this issue extensively but mainly emphasizes biological-environmental interaction
Behavioral and social cognitive	Continuity (no stages); experience at all points of development important	Environment viewed as the cause of behavior in both views
Ethological	Discontinuity but no stages; critical or sensitive periods emphasized; early experiences very important	Strong biological view
Ecological	Little attention to continuity/discontinuity; change emphasized more than stability	Strong environmental view

FIGURE 1.14 A Comparison of Theories and Issues in Children's Development

in the scientific method involve conceptualizing the problem, collecting data, drawing conclusions, and revising research conclusions and theories. Through scientific research, the features of theories can be tested and refined.

Whether we are interested in studying attachment in infants, the cognitive skills of children, or the peer relations of adolescents, we can choose from several ways of collecting data. Here we outline the measures most often used, including their advantages and disadvantages, beginning with observation.

Observation   Scientific observation requires an important set of skills (McBurney & White, 2007). Unless we are trained observers and practice our skills regularly, we might not know what to look for, we might not remember what we saw, we might not realize that what we are looking for is changing from one moment to the next, and we might not communicate our observations effectively.

For observations to be effective, they have to be systematic. We have to have some idea of what we are looking for. We have to know whom we are observing, when and where we will observe, how the observations will be made, and how they will be recorded.

Where should we make our observations? We have two choices: the laboratory and the everyday world.

When we observe scientifically, we often need to control certain factors that determine behavior but are not the focus of our inquiry (Rosnow & Rosenthal, 2008). For this reason, some research in life-span development is conducted in a **laboratory,** a controlled setting with many of the complex factors of the "real world" removed. For example, suppose you want to observe how children react when they see other people act aggressively. If you observe children in their homes or schools, you have no control over how much aggression the children observe, what kind of aggression they see, which people they see acting aggressively, or how other people treat the children. In contrast, if you observe the children in a laboratory, you can control these and other factors and therefore have more confidence about how to interpret your observations.

Laboratory research does have some drawbacks, however. First, it is almost impossible to conduct research without the participants' knowing they are being studied. Second, the laboratory setting is unnatural and therefore can cause the participants to behave unnaturally. Third, people who are willing to come to a university laboratory may not fairly represent groups from diverse backgrounds. Fourth, people who are unfamiliar with university settings, and with the idea of "helping science," may be intimidated by the laboratory setting. In addition, some aspects of life-span development are difficult, if not impossible, to examine in the laboratory. Last, Laboratory studies of certain types of stress may even be unethical.

Naturalistic observation provides insights that we sometimes cannot achieve in the laboratory (Billman, 2003). **Naturalistic observation** means observing behavior in real-world settings, making no effort to manipulate or control the situation. Life-span researchers conduct naturalistic observations at sporting events, child-care centers, work settings, malls, and other places people live in and frequent.

Naturalistic observation was used in one study that focused on conversations in a children's science museum (Crowley & others, 2001). Parents were over three times as likely to engage boys than girls in explanatory talk while visiting exhibits at the science museum, suggesting a gender bias that encourages boys more than girls to be interested in science (see Figure 1.15). In another study, Mexican American parents who had completed high school used more explanations with their children when visiting a science museum than Mexican American parents who had not completed high school (Tenenbaum & others, 2002).

Survey and Interview   Sometimes the best and quickest way to get information about people is to ask them for it. One technique is to *interview* them directly. A

What are some important strategies in conducting observational research with children?

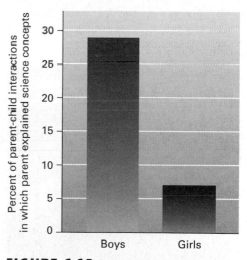

FIGURE 1.15 **Parents' Explanation of Science to Sons and Daughters at a Science Museum** In a naturalistic observation study at a children's science museum, parents were over three times more likely to explain science to boys than girls (Crowley & others, 2001). The gender difference occurred regardless of whether the father, the mother, or both parents were with the child, although the gender difference was greatest for fathers' science explanations to sons and daughters.

laboratory A controlled setting in which many of the complex factors of the "real world" are removed.

naturalistic observation Observing behavior in real-world settings.

related method is the *survey* (sometimes referred to as a questionnaire), which is especially useful when information from many people is needed (Nardi, 2006). A standard set of questions is used to obtain peoples' self-reported attitudes or beliefs about a particular topic. In a good survey, the questions are clear and unbiased, allowing respondents to answer unambiguously.

Surveys and interviews can be used to study a wide range of topics from religious beliefs to sexual habits to attitudes about gun control to beliefs about how to improve schools. Surveys and interviews today are conducted in person, over the telephone, and over the Internet.

One problem with surveys and interviews is the tendency of participants to answer questions in a way that they think is socially acceptable or desirable rather than telling what they truly think or feel (Creswell, 2008). For example, on a survey or in an interview some individuals might say that they do not take drugs even though they do.

Standardized Test   A **standardized test** has uniform procedures for administration and scoring. Many standardized tests allow a person's performance to be compared with the performance of other individuals—thus they provide information about individual differences among people (Gregory, 2007; Gronlund, 2006). One example is the Stanford-Binet intelligence test, which is described in Chapter 12, "Cognitive Development in Middle and Late Childhood." Your score on the Stanford-Binet test tells you how your performance compares with that of thousands of other people who have taken the test.

Standardized tests also have three key weaknesses. First, they do not always predict behavior in nontest situations. Second, standardized tests are based on the belief that a person's behavior is consistent and stable, yet personality and intelligence—two primary targets of standardized testing—can vary with the situation. For example, individuals may perform poorly on a standardized intelligence test in an office setting but score much higher at home, where they are less anxious. This criticism is especially relevant for members of minority groups, some of whom have been inaccurately classified as mentally retarded on the basis of their scores on intelligence tests. A third weakness of standardized tests is that many psychological tests developed in Western cultures might not be appropriate in other cultures (Shiraev & Levy, 2007). The experiences of people in differing cultures may lead them to interpret and respond to questions differently.

Case Study   A **case study** is an in-depth look at a single individual. Case studies are performed mainly by mental health professionals, when—for either practical or ethical reasons—the unique aspects of an individual's life cannot be duplicated and tested in other individuals (Dattilio, 2001). A case study provides information about one person's fears, hopes, fantasies, traumatic experiences, upbringing, family relationships, health, or anything that helps the psychologist understand the person's mind and behavior. In later chapters we discuss vivid case studies, such as studies of Michael Rehbein, who had much of the left side of his brain removed at 7 years of age to end severe epileptic seizures.

Case histories provide dramatic, in-depth portrayals of people's lives, but remember that we must be cautious when generalizing from this information. The subject of a case study is unique, with a genetic makeup and personal history that no one else shares. In addition, case studies involve judgments of unknown reliability. Psychologists who conduct case studies rarely check to see if other psychologists agree with their observations.

Physiological Measures   Researchers are increasingly using *physiological measures* when they study children's development. For example, as puberty unfolds, the blood levels of certain hormones increase. To determine the nature of these

Mahatma Gandhi was the spiritual leader of India in the middle of the twentieth century. Erik Erikson conducted an extensive case study of his life to determine what contributed to his identity development. *What are some limitations of the case study approach?*

standardized test A test with uniform procedures for administration and scoring. Many standardized tests allow a person's performance to be compared with the performance of other individuals.

case study An in-depth look at a single individual.

hormonal changes, researchers take blood samples from willing adolescents (Dorn & others, 2006).

Another physiological measure that is increasingly being used is neuroimaging, especially *functional magnetic resonance imaging (fMRI)*, in which electromagnetic waves are used to construct images of a person's brain tissue and biochemical activity (Nelson, Thomas, & de Haan, 2006). We have much more to say about neuroimaging and other physiological measures at various points in this book.

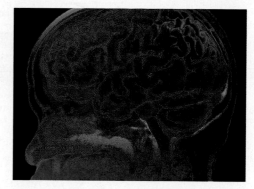

A functional magnetic resonance image of a child's brain.

Research Designs

Suppose you want to find out whether the children of permissive parents are more likely than other children to be rude and unruly. The data-collection method that researchers choose often depends on the goal of their research. The goal may be simply to describe a phenomenon, or it may be to describe relationships between phenomena, or to determine the causes or effects of a phenomenon.

Perhaps you decide that you need to observe both permissive and strict parents with their children and compare them. How would you do that? In addition to a method for collecting data, you would need a research design. There are three main types of research design: descriptive, correlational, and experimental.

Descriptive Research   All of the data-collection methods that we have discussed can be used in **descriptive research,** which aims to observe and record behavior. For example, a researcher might observe the extent to which people are altruistic or aggressive toward each other. By itself, descriptive research cannot prove what causes some phenomenon, but it can reveal important information about people's behavior.

Correlational Research   In contrast to descriptive research, correlational research goes beyond describing phenomena to provide information that will help us to predict how people will behave. In **correlational research,** the goal is to describe the strength of the relationship between two or more events or characteristics. The more strongly the two events are correlated (or related or associated), the more effectively we can predict one event from the other (McBurney & White, 2007).

For example, to study if children of permissive parents have less self-control than other children, you would need to carefully record observations of parents' permissiveness and their children's self-control. The data could then be analyzed statistically to yield a numerical measure, called a **correlation coefficient,** a number based on a statistical analysis that is used to describe the degree of association between two variables. The correlation coefficient ranges from +1.00 to −1.00. A negative number means an inverse relation. For example, researchers often find a negative correlation between permissive parenting and children's self-control. By contrast, they often find a positive correlation between parental monitoring of children and children's self-control.

The higher the correlation coefficient (whether positive or negative), the stronger the association between the two variables. A correlation of 0 means that there is no association between the variables. A correlation of −.40 is stronger than a correlation of +.20 because we disregard whether the correlation is positive or negative in determining the strength of the correlation.

A caution is in order, however. Correlation does not equal causation (Aron, Aron, & Coups, 2008). The correlational finding just mentioned does not mean that permissive parenting necessarily causes low self-control in children. It could mean that, but it also could mean that a child's lack of self-control caused the parents to simply throw up their arms in despair and give up trying to control the child. It also

descriptive research A research design that has the purpose of observing and recording behavior.

correlational research A research design whose goal is to describe the strength of the relationship between two or more events or characteristics.

correlation coefficient A number based on statistical analysis that is used to describe the degree of association between two variables.

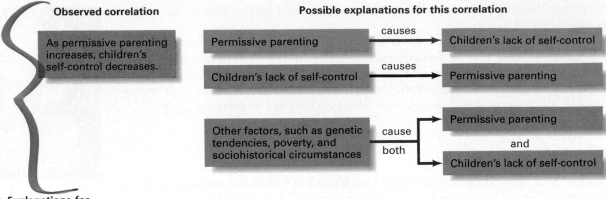

Observed correlation

As permissive parenting increases, children's self-control decreases.

Possible explanations for this correlation

Permissive parenting — causes → Children's lack of self-control

Children's lack of self-control — causes → Permissive parenting

Other factors, such as genetic tendencies, poverty, and sociohistorical circumstances — cause both → Permissive parenting and Children's lack of self-control

FIGURE 1.16 Possible Explanations for Correlational Data An observed correlation between two events cannot be used to conclude that one event caused the other. Some possibilities are that the second event caused the first event or that a third, unknown event caused the correlation between the first two events.

could mean that other factors, such as heredity or poverty, caused the correlation between permissive parenting and low self-control in children. Figure 1.16 illustrates these possible interpretations of correlational data.

Throughout this book, you will read about numerous correlational research studies. Keep in mind how easy it is to assume causality when two events or characteristics merely are correlated.

Experimental Research To study causality, researchers turn to *experimental research*. An **experiment** is a carefully regulated procedure in which one or more factors believed to influence the behavior being studied are manipulated, while all other factors are held constant. If the behavior under study changes when a factor is manipulated, we say that the manipulated factor has caused the behavior to change. In other words, the experiment has demonstrated cause and effect. The cause is the factor that was manipulated. The effect is the behavior that changed because of the manipulation. Nonexperimental research methods (descriptive and correlational research) cannot establish cause and effect because they do not involve manipulating factors in a controlled way (Jackson, 2008).

Independent and Dependent Variables Experiments include two types of changeable factors, or variables: independent and dependent. An independent variable is a manipulated, influential, experimental factor. It is a potential cause. The label independent is used because this variable can be manipulated independently of other factors to determine its effect. One experiment may include several independent variables.

A dependent variable is a factor that can change in an experiment, in response to changes in the independent variable. As researchers manipulate the independent variable, they measure the dependent variable for any resulting effect.

For example, suppose that you conducted a study to determine whether aerobic exercise by pregnant women changes the breathing and sleeping patterns of newborn babies. You might require one group of pregnant women to engage in a certain amount of exercise each week; the amount of exercise is thus the independent variable. When the infants are born, you would observe and measure their breathing and sleeping patterns. These patterns are the dependent variable, the factor that changes as the result of your manipulation.

Experimental and Control Groups Experiments can involve one or more experimental groups and one or more control groups. An experimental group is a group whose experience is manipulated. A control group is a comparison group that is as much like the experimental group as possible and that is treated in every way like the experimental group except for the manipulated factor (independent variable). The

experiment A carefully regulated procedure in which one or more of the factors believed to influence the behavior being studied are manipulated, while all other factors are held constant.

control group serves as a baseline against which the effects of the manipulated condition can be compared.

Random assignment is an important principle for deciding whether each participant will be placed in the experimental group or in the control group. Random assignment means that researchers assign participants to experimental and control groups by chance. It reduces the likelihood that the experiment's results will be due to any preexisting differences between groups (Martin, 2008). In the example of the effects of aerobic exercise by pregnant women on the breathing and sleeping patterns of their newborns, you would randomly assign half of the pregnant women to engage in aerobic exercise over a period of weeks (the experimental group) and the other half to not exercise over the same number of weeks (the control group). Figure 1.17 illustrates the nature of experimental research.

Time Span of Research

Researchers in child development have a special concern with studies that focus on the relation of age to some other variable. To do this, they can study different individuals of different ages and compare them, or they can study the same individuals as they age over time.

Cross-Sectional Approach

The **cross-sectional approach** is a research strategy in which individuals of different ages are compared at one time. A typical cross-sectional study might include a group of 5-year-olds, 8-year-olds, and 11-year-olds. The groups can be compared with respect to a variety of dependent variables: IQ, memory, peer relations, attachment to parents, hormonal changes, and so on. All of this can be accomplished in a short time. In some studies, data are collected in a single day. Even in large-scale cross-sectional studies with hundreds of participants, data collection does not usually take longer than several months to complete.

The main advantage of the cross-sectional study is that researchers don't have to wait for children to grow older. Despite its efficiency, the cross-sectional approach has its drawbacks. It gives no information about how individual children change or about the stability of their characteristics. It can obscure the increases and decreases of development—the hills and valleys of growth and development.

Longitudinal Approach

The **longitudinal approach** is a research strategy in which the same individuals are studied over a period of time, usually several years or more.. For example, if a study of self-esteem were conducted longitudinally, the same children might be assessed three times—at 5, 8, and 11 years of age, for example. Some longitudinal studies take place over shorter time frames, even just a year or so.

Longitudinal studies provide a wealth of information about such important issues as stability and change in development and the importance of early experience for later development, but they are not without their problems (Hofer & Sliwinski, 2006). They are expensive and time-consuming. Also, the longer the study lasts, the more participants drop out. For example, children's families may move, get sick, lose interest, and so forth. Those who remain in the study may be dissimilar to those who drop out, biasing the results. Those individuals who remain in a longitudinal study over a number of years may be more compulsive and conformity-oriented, for example, or they might have more stable lives.

So far we have discussed many aspects of scientific research in child development. In the *Research in Children's Development* interlude, you can read about the research journals in which this research is published.

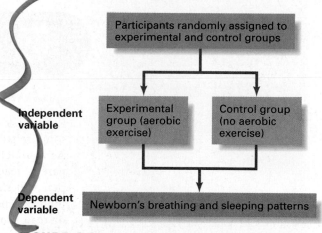

FIGURE 1.17 Principles of Experimental Research
Imagine that you decide to conduct an experimental study of the effects of aerobic exercise by pregnant women on their newborns' breathing and sleeping patterns. You would randomly assign pregnant women to experimental and control groups. The experimental-group women would engage in aerobic exercise over a specified number of sessions and weeks. The control group would not. Then, when the infants are born, you would assess their breathing and sleeping patterns. If the breathing and sleeping patterns of newborns whose mothers were in the experimental group are more positive than those of the control group, you would conclude that aerobic exercise caused the positive effects.

cross-sectional approach A research strategy in which individuals of different ages are compared to one time.

longitudinal approach A research strategy in which the same individuals are studied over a period of time, usually several years or more.

Research in Children's Development

RESEARCH JOURNALS

Regardless of whether you pursue a career in child development, psychology, or some related scientific field, you can benefit by learning about the journal process. As a student you might be required to look up original research in journals. As a parent, teacher, or nurse you might want to consult journals to obtain information that will help you understand and work more effectively with people. And as an inquiring person, you might look up information in journals after you have heard or read something that piqued your curiosity.

A journal publishes scholarly and academic information, usually in a specific domain—like physics, math, sociology, or, our current interest, child development. Scholars in these fields publish most of their research in journals, which are the source of core information in virtually every academic discipline.

An increasing number of journals publish information about child development. Among the leading journals in child development are *Developmental Psychology, Child Development, Developmental Psychopathology, Pediatrics, Pediatric Nursing, Infant Behavior and Development, Journal of Research on Adolescence, Human Development*, and many others. Also, a number of journals that do not focus solely on development include articles on various aspects of human development. These journals include *Journal of Educational Psychology, Sex Roles, Journal of Cross-Cultural Research, Journal of Marriage and the Family, Exceptional Children*, and *Journal of Consulting and Clinical Psychology*.

Every journal has a board of experts who evaluate articles submitted for publication. Each submitted paper is accepted or rejected on the basis of such factors as its contribution to the field, methodological excellence, and clarity of writing. Some of the most prestigious journals reject as many as 80 to 90 percent of the articles submitted.

Journal articles are usually written for other professionals in the specialized field of the journal's focus; therefore, they often contain technical language and terms specific to the discipline that are difficult for nonprofessionals to understand. Their organization often takes this course: abstract, introduction, method, results, discussion, and references.

The *abstract* is a brief summary that appears at the beginning of the article. The abstract lets readers quickly determine whether the article is relevant to their interests. The *introduction* introduces the problem or issue that is being studied. It includes a concise review of research relevant to the topic, theoretical ties, and one or more hypotheses to be tested. The *method* section consists of a clear description of the subjects evaluated in the study, the measures used, and the procedures that were followed. The method section should be sufficiently clear and detailed so that by reading it another researcher could repeat or replicate the study. The *results* section reports the analysis of the data collected. In most cases, the results section includes statistical analyses that are difficult for nonprofessionals to understand. The *discussion* section describes the author's conclusions, inferences, and interpretation of what was found. Statements are usually made about whether the hypotheses presented in the introduction were supported, limitations of the study, and suggestions for future research. The last part of the journal article, called *references*, includes bibliographic information for each source cited in the article. The references section is often a good source for finding other articles relevant to the topic that interests you.

Where do you find journals such as those we have described? Your college or university library likely has some of them, and some public libraries also carry journals. Online resources such as PsycINFO, which can facilitate the search for journal articles, are available to students on many campuses.

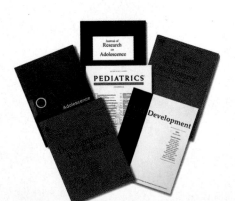

Research journals are the core of information in virtually every academic discipline. Those shown here are among the increasing number of research journals that publish information about child development. *What are the main parts of a research article that presents findings from original research?*

Research Challenges

The scientific foundation of research in child development helps to minimize the effect of research bias and maximize the objectivity of the results. Still, subtle challenges remain for each researcher to resolve. One is to ensure that research is conducted in an ethical way; another is to recognize, and try to overcome, deeply buried personal biases.

Conducting Ethical Research The explosion in technology has forced society to grapple with looming ethical questions that were unimaginable only a few decades ago. The same line of research that enables previously sterile couples to have children might someday let prospective parents "call up and order" the characteristics they prefer in their children or tip the balance of males and females in the world. For example, should embryos left over from procedures for increasing fertility be saved or discarded? Should people with inheritable fatal diseases (such as Huntington disease) be discouraged from having children?

Researchers also face ethical questions both new and old. They have a responsibility to anticipate the personal problems their research might cause and to at least inform the participants of the possible fallout. Safeguarding the rights of research participants is a challenge because the potential harm is not always obvious (Myers & Hansen, 2006).

Ethics in research may affect you personally if you ever serve as a participant in a study. In that event, you need to know your rights as a participant and the responsibilities of researchers to assure that these rights are safeguarded.

If you ever become a researcher in child development yourself, you will need an even deeper understanding of ethics. Even if you only carry out experimental projects in psychology courses, you must consider the rights of the participants in those projects.

Today, proposed research at colleges and universities must pass the scrutiny of a research ethics committee before the research can be initiated. In addition, the American Psychological Association (APA) has developed ethics guidelines for its members. The code of ethics instructs psychologists to protect their participants from mental and physical harm. The participants' best interests need to be kept foremost in the researcher's mind (Jackson, 2006). APA's guidelines address four important issues: informed consent, confidentiality, debriefing, and deception.

- *Informed consent*. All participants must know what their participation will involve and what risks might develop. For example, participants in a study on dating should be told beforehand that a questionnaire might stimulate thoughts about issues in their relationship that they have not considered. Participants also should be informed that in some instances a discussion of the issues might improve their relationship, but in others might worsen the relationship and even end it. Even after informed consent is given, participants must retain the right to withdraw from the study at any time and for any reason.
- *Confidentiality*. Researchers are responsible for keeping all of the data they gather on individuals completely confidential and, when possible, completely anonymous.
- *Debriefing*. After the study has been completed, participants should be informed of its purpose and the methods that were used. In most cases, the experimenter also can inform participants in a general manner beforehand about the purpose of the research without leading participants to behave in a way they think that the experimenter is expecting. When preliminary information about the study is likely to affect the results, participants can at least be debriefed after the study has been completed.
- *Deception*. This is an ethical issue that researchers debate extensively. In some circumstances, telling the participants beforehand what the research study is about substantially alters the participants' behavior and invalidates the researcher's data. In all cases of deception, however, the psychologist

Careers in CHILD DEVELOPMENT

Pam Reid
Educational and Development Psychologist

When she was a child, Pam Reid liked to play with chemistry sets. She majored in chemistry during college and wanted to become doctor. However, when some of her friends signed up for a psychology class as an elective, she also decided to take the course. She was intrigued by learning about how people think, behave, and develop—so much so that she changed her major to psychology. Reid went on to obtain her Ph.D. in psychology (American Psychological Association, 2003, p. 16).

For a number of years, Reid was professor of education and psychology at the University of Michigan, where she also was a research scientist at the Institute for Research on Women and Gender. Her main focus has been on how children and adolescents develop social skills with a special interest in the development of African American girls (Reid & Zalk, 2001). In 2004, Reid became Provost and Executive Vice-President at Roosevelt University in Chicago.

Pam Reid (*center, back row*) with some of the graduate students she mentored at the University of Michigan.

ethnic gloss Using an ethnic label such as African American or Latino in a superficial way that portrays an ethnic group as being more homogeneous than it really is.

must ensure that the deception will not harm the participants and that the participants will be told the complete nature of the study (debriefed) as soon as possible after the study is completed.

Minimizing Bias Studies of life-span development are most useful when they are conducted without bias or prejudice toward any particular group of people. Of special concern is bias based on gender and bias based on culture or ethnicity.

Gender Bias For most of its existence, our society has had a strong gender bias, a preconceived notion about the abilities of males and females that prevented individuals from pursuing their own interests and achieving their potential (Matlin, 2008; Worell & Goodheart, 2006). Gender bias also has had a less obvious effect within the field of child development. For example, it is not unusual for conclusions to be drawn about females' attitudes and behaviors from research conducted with males as the only participants.

Furthermore, when researchers find gender differences, their reports sometimes magnify those differences (Denmark & others, 1988). For example, a researcher might report that 74 percent of the boys in a study had high achievement expectations versus only 67 percent of the girls and go on to talk about the differences in some detail. In reality, this might be a rather small difference. It also might disappear if the study were repeated, or the study might have methodological problems that don't allow such strong interpretations.

Pam Reid is a leading researcher who studies gender and ethnic bias in development. To read about Pam's interests, see the *Careers in Child Development* profile.

Cultural and Ethnic Bias The realization that research on children's development needs to include more children from diverse ethnic groups has also been building (Graham, 1992, 2006). Historically, children from ethnic minority groups (African American, Latino, Asian American, and Native American) were excluded from most research in the United States and simply thought of as variations from the norm or average. If minority children were included in samples and their scores didn't fit the norm, they were viewed as confounds or "noise" in data and discounted. Given the fact that children from diverse ethnic groups were excluded from research on child development for so long, we might reasonably conclude that children's real lives are perhaps more varied than research data have indicated in the past.

Researchers also have tended to overgeneralize about ethnic groups (Banks, 2008; Kottak & Kozaitis, 2008). **Ethnic gloss** is using an ethnic label such as African American or Latino in a superficial way that portrays an ethnic group as being more homogeneous than it really is (Trimble, 1988). For example, a researcher might describe a research sample like this: "The participants were 60 Latinos." A more complete description of the Latino group might be something like this: "The 60 Latino participants were Mexican Americans from low-income neighborhoods in the southwestern

(a)   (b)

Look at these two photographs, (*a*) one of all non-Latino White boys, the other (*b*) of boys and girls from diverse ethnic backgrounds. Consider a topic in child development such as independence seeking, cultural values, parenting education, or health care. *If you were conducting research on this topic, might the results of the study be different depending on whether the participants in your study were the children in the photo on the left or the photo on the right?*

area of Los Angeles. Thirty-six were from homes in which Spanish is the dominant language spoken, 24 from homes in which English is the main language spoken. Thirty were born in the United States, 30 in Mexico. Twenty-eight described themselves as Mexican American, 14 as Mexican, 9 as American, 6 as Chicano, and 3 as Latino." Ethnic gloss can cause researchers to obtain samples of ethnic groups that are not representative of the group's diversity, which can lead to overgeneralization and stereotyping.

Research on ethnic minority children and their families has not been given adequate attention, especially in light of their significant rate of growth (Parke & Buriel, 2006). Until recently, ethnic minority families were combined in the category "minority," which masks important differences among ethnic groups as well as diversity within an ethnic group. At present and in the foreseeable future, the growth of minority families in the United States will be mainly due to the immigration of Latino and Asian families. Researchers need to take into account their acculturation level and generational status of parents and children, and how they influence family processes and child outcomes (Berry, 2007). More attention also needs to be given to biculturalism because the complexity of diversity means that some children of color identify with two or more ethnic groups (Phinney, 2006).

REVIEW AND REFLECT › LEARNING GOAL 4

4 **Summarize why research is important in child development, the main theories of child development, and research methods, designs, and challenges.**

Review

- Why is research on child development important?

- What are the main theories of child development?

- What are the main research methods for collecting data about children's development?

- What types of research designs do child development researchers use?

- What are some research challenges in studying children's development?

Reflect

- Imagine that you are conducting a research study on the sexual attitudes and behaviors of adolescents. What ethical safeguards should you use in conducting the study?

REACH YOUR LEARNING GOALS

1 **WHY IS CARING FOR CHILDREN IMPORTANT?** *Explain why it is important to study children's development, and identify five areas in which children's lives need to be improved.*

The Importance of Studying Children's Development

Improving the Lives of Children

- Studying children's development is important because it will help you to better understand your own childhood and provide you with strategies for being a competent parent or educator.

- Health and well-being is an important area in which children's lives can be improved. Today, many children in the United States and around the world need improved health care. We now recognize the importance of lifestyles and psychological states in promoting health and well-being. Parenting is an important influences on children's development. One-parent families, working parents, and child care are among the family issues that influence children's well-being. Education can also contribute to children's health and well-being. There is widespread concern that the education of children needs to be more effective, and there are many views in contemporary education about ways to improve schools. Sociocultural contexts are important influences on children's development. Contexts, culture, ethnicity, socioeconomic status, and gender are four key aspects of sociocultural contexts. Social policy is a national government's course of action designed to influence the welfare of its citizens. Researchers increasingly are conducting studies that are related to social policy.

2 **WHAT ARE SOME HISTORICAL VIEWS OF CHILD DEVELOPMENT?** *Characterize historical views of children.*

Early Views of Childhood

The Modern Study of Child Development

- The history of interest in children is long and rich. Prior to the nineteenth century, philosophical views of childhood were prominent, including the notions of original sin (children are basically bad, born into the world as evil beings), tabula rasa (children are not innately bad or good but rather like a "blank tablet"), and innate goodness (children are inherently good). Today, we conceive of childhood as an important time of development.

- The modern era of studying children spans a little more than a century, an era in which the study of child development has become a sophisticated science. During the late 1800s, a major shift took place—from a strictly philosophical perspective to one that focuses on direct observation and experimentation. During the 1920s, a number of child development research centers were created. Early modern theorists included Arnold Gesell, who argued that certain characteristics of children simply "bloom" with age because of a biological, maturational blueprint; G. Stanley Hall, who theorized that child development follows an evolutionary course; Sigmund Freud, who thought that children were rarely aware of the motives and reasons for their behaviors; John Watson, who argued that children can be shaped into whatever society wishes by examining and changing the environment; James Mark Baldwin, who was a pioneer in the study of children's thought; and Jean Piaget, who proposed a sequence of cognitive stages that children pass through.

3 WHAT CHARACTERIZES DEVELOPMENT? *Discuss the most important processes, periods, and issues in development.*

Biological, Cognitive, and Socioemotional Processes

- Three key processes of development are biological, cognitive, and socioemotional. Biological processes (such as genes inherited from parents) involve changes in an individual's physical nature. Cognitive processes (such as thinking) consist of changes in an individual's thought, intelligence, and language. Socioemotional processes (such as smiling) include changes in an individual's relationships with others, in emotions, and in personality.

Periods of Development

- Childhood's five main developmental periods are (1) prenatal—conception to birth, (2) infancy—birth to 18 to 24 months, (3) early childhood—end of infancy to about 5 to 6 years of age, (4) middle and late childhood—about 6 to 11 years of age, and (5) adolescence—begins at about 10 to 12 and ends at about 18 to 22 years of age.

Issues in Development

- The nature-nurture issue focuses on the extent to which development is mainly influenced by nature (biological inheritance) or nurture (environmental experience). Some developmentalists describe development as continuous (gradual, cumulative change), others describe it as discontinuous (a sequence of abrupt stages). The early-later experience issue focuses on whether early experiences (especially in infancy) are more important in development than later experiences. Most developmentalists recognize that extreme positions on the nature-nurture, continuity-discontinuity, and early-later experience issues are not supported by research. Despite this consensus, they continue to debate the degree to which each position influences children's development.

4 HOW IS CHILD DEVELOPMENT A SCIENCE? *Summarize why research is important in child development, the main theories of child development, and research methods, designs, and challenges.*

The Importance of Research

- When we base information on personal experience, we aren't always objective. Research provides a vehicle for evaluating the accuracy of information. Scientific research is objective, systematic, and testable. Scientific research is based on the scientific method, which includes these steps: conceptualize the problem, collect data, draw conclusions, and revise theory.

Theories of Child Development

- Psychoanalytic theories describe development as primarily unconscious and as heavily colored by emotion. The two main psychoanalytic theories in developmental psychology are Freud's and Erikson's. Freud also proposed that individuals go through five psychosexual stages—oral, anal, phallic, latency, and genital. Erikson's theory emphasizes eight psychosocial stages of development. The three main cognitive theories are Piaget's cognitive developmental theory, Vygotsky's sociocultural cognitive theory, and information-processing theory. Cognitive theories emphasize conscious thoughts. In Piaget's theory, children go through four cognitive stages: sensorimotor, preoperational, concrete operational, and formal operational. Vygotsky's sociocultural cognitive theory emphasizes how culture and social interaction guide cognitive development. The information-processing theory emphasizes that individuals manipulate information, monitor it, and strategize about it. Three versions of the behavioral and social cognitive approach are Pavlov's classical conditioning, Skinner's operant conditioning, and Bandura's social cognitive theory. Ethology stresses that behavior is strongly influenced by biology, is tied to evolution, and is characterized by critical or sensitive periods. Ecological theory is Bronfenbrenner's environmental systems view of development. It consists of five environmental systems: microsystem, mesosystem, exosystem, macrosystem, and chronosystem. An eclectic theoretical orientation does not follow any one theoretical approach but rather selects from each theory whatever is considered the best in it.

Research Methods for Collecting Data

- Research methods for collecting data about child development include observation (in a laboratory or a naturalistic setting), survey (questionnaire) or interview, standardized test, case study, and physiological measures.

Research Designs

- Descriptive research aims to observe and record behavior. In correlational research, the goal is to describe the strength of the relationship between two or more events or characteristics. Experimental research involves conducting an experiment, which can determine cause and effect. An independent variable is the manipulated, influential, experimental factor. A dependent variable is a factor that can change in an experiment, in response to changes in the independent variable. Experiments can involve one or more experimental groups and control groups. In random assignment, researchers assign participants to experimental and control groups by chance. When researchers decide about the time span of their research, they can conduct cross-sectional or longitudinal studies.

Research Challenges

- Researchers' ethical responsibilities include seeking participants' informed consent, ensuring their confidentiality, debriefing them about the purpose and potential personal consequences of participating, and avoiding unnecessary deception of participants. Researchers need to guard against gender, cultural, and ethnic bias in research. Every effort should be made to make research equitable for both females and males. Individuals from varied ethnic backgrounds need to be included as participants in child research, and overgeneralization about diverse members within a group must be avoided.

KEY TERMS

KEY PEOPLE

MAKING A DIFFERENCE

Lessons for Life

Marian Wright Edelman (1992, 2000, 2004) is one of America's foremost crusaders in the quest for improving the lives of children. Here are some of the main strategies she advocates for improving not only children's lives but our own as well (Edelman, 1992, pp. xxi, 42, 60):

- *"Don't feel as if you are entitled to anything that you don't sweat and struggle for."* Take the initiative to create opportunities. Don't wait around for people to give you favors. A door never has to stay closed. Push on it until it opens.
- *"Don't be afraid of taking risks or of being criticized."* We all make mistakes. It is only through making mistakes that we learn how to do things right. "It doesn't matter how many times you fall down. What matters is how many times we get up." We need "more courageous shepherds and fewer sheep."
- *"Don't ever stop learning and improving your mind or you're going to get left behind."* College is a great investment, but don't think you can park your mind there and everything you need to know will somehow be magically poured into it. Be an active learner. Be curious and ask questions. Explore new horizons.
- *Stand up for children.* According to Edelman, this is the most important mission in the world. Parenting and nurturing the next generation of children are our society's most important functions, and we need to take them more seriously than we have in the past.

CHILDREN RESOURCES

Children's Defense Fund

25 E Street
Washington, DC 20001
800–424–9602
www.childrensdefense.org

The Children's Defense Fund exists to provide a strong and effective voice for children and adolescents who cannot vote, lobby, or speak for themselves. The Children's Defense Fund is especially interested in the needs of poor, minority, and handicapped children and adolescents. The fund provides information, technical assistance, and support to a network of state and local child and youth advocates. The Children's Defense Fund publishes a number of excellent books and pamphlets related to children's needs.

Handbook of Child Psychology

edited by William Damon and Richard Lerner (6th ed., Vols. 1–4, 2006).
New York: John Wiley
The *Handbook of Child Psychology* is the standard reference work for overviews of theory and research in this field. It has in-depth discussions of many topics that we explore in this book.

E-LEARNING TOOLS

Connect to **www.mhhe.com/santrockc10** to research the answers and complete these exercises. In addition, you'll find a number of other resources and valuable study tools for Chapter 1, "Introduction," on this Web site.

Taking It to the Net

1. George is teaching fourth grade. He wants his students to learn about the difficulties and challenges of being a child

in colonial America. What was life like for children in the early history of our country?

2. Janice thinks that better and stricter gun control laws will help decrease violent crime among children. Her husband, Elliott, disagrees. Janice found a March 2000 Department of Justice study that provides support for her argument. What facts in the report can she point to in order to convince Elliott?

3. For his political science class, Darren has to track federal funding appropriations in the most recent Congress for any issue of his choice. He has chosen children's issues. How did children and families fare in terms of congressional appropriations in the current Congress?

Health and Well-Being, Parenting, and Education

Build your decision-making skills by trying your hand at the health and well-being, parenting, and education exercises.

Video Clips

The Online Learning Center includes the following videos for this chapter:

1. *Career in Child Development*–905
   Dr. Richard Lerner gives a humorous account of decision to major in psychology in college.

2. *Career in Developmental Psychology*–245
   Dr. Weinraub, one of the leading researchers on the NICHD Early Child care Study, describes how she became interested in developmental psychology.

3. *Ethical Issues in Studying Infants*—274
   Renowned infant researcher Albert Yonas discusses the ethical issues he faces when studying infants.

4. *Schools and Public Policy*—931
   Dr. Jacquelynne Eccles describes how her research on gender and school transitions has influenced public policy.

Careers in Child Development

Each of us wants to find a rewarding career and enjoy the work we do. The field of child development offers an amazing breadth of career options that can provide extremely satisfying work.

If you decide to pursue a career in child development, what career options are available to you? There are many. Colleges and university professors teach courses in areas of child development, education, family development, nursing, and medicine. Teachers impart knowledge, understanding, and skills to children and adolescents. Counselors, clinical psychologists, nurses, and physicians help parents and children of different ages to cope more effectively with their lives and well-being. Various professionals work with families to improve the quality and family functioning.

Although an advanced degree is not absolutely necessary in some areas of child development, you usually can expand your opportunities (and income) considerably by obtaining a graduate degree. Many careers in child development pay reasonably well. For example, psychologists earn well above the median salary in the United States. Also, by working in the field of child development you can guide people in improving their lives, understand yourself and others better, possibly advance the state of knowledge in the field, and have an enjoyable time while you are doing these things.

If you are considering a career in child development, would you prefer to work with infants? Children? Adolescents? Parents? As you go through this term, try to spend some time with children of different ages. Observe their behavior. Talk with them about their lives. Think about whether you would like to work with children of this age in your life's work.

Another important aspect of exploring careers is to talk with people who work in various jobs. For example, if you have some interest in becoming a school counselor, call a school, ask to speak with a counselor, and set up an appointment to discuss the counselor's career and work.

Something else that should benefit you is to work in one or more jobs related to your career interests while you are in college. Many colleges and universities have internships or work experiences for students who major in such fields as child development. In some instances, these jobs earn course credit or pay; in others, they are strictly on a volunteer basis. Take advantage of these opportunities. They can provide you with valuable experiences to help you decide if this is the right career for you—and they can help you get into graduate school, if you decide you want to go.

In the upcoming sections, we profile careers in four areas: education and research; clinical and counseling; medical, nursing, and physical development; and families and relationships. These are not the only career options in child development, but they should provide you with an idea of the range of opportunities available and information about some of the main career avenues you might pursue. In profiling these careers, we address the amount of education required, the nature of the training, and a description of the work.

EDUCATION AND RESEARCH

Numerous career opportunities in child development involve education or research. These range from a college professor to child-care director to school psychologist.

College/University Professor Courses in child development are taught in many programs and schools in college and universities, including psychology, education, nursing, child and family studies, social work, and medicine. The work that college professors do includes teaching courses either at the undergraduate or graduate level (or both), conducting research in a specific area, advising students and/or directing their research, and serving on college or university committees. Some college instructors do not conduct research as part of their job but instead focus mainly on teaching. Research is most likely to be part of the job description at universities with master's and Ph.D. programs. A Ph.D. or master's degree almost always is required to teach in some area of child development in a college or university. Obtaining a doctoral degree usually takes four to six years of graduate work. A master's degree requires approximately two years of graduate work. The training involves taking graduate courses, learning to conduct research, and attending and presenting papers at professional meetings. Many graduate students work as teaching or research assistants for professors in an apprenticeship relationship that helps them to become competent teachers and researchers.

If you are interested in becoming a college or university professor, you might want to make an appointment with your instructor in this class on child development to learn more about his or her profession and work. To read about the work of one college professor, see the *Careers in Child Development* Profile.

Researcher Some individuals in the field of child development work in research positions. In most instances, they have either a master's or Ph.D. in some area of child development. The researchers might work at a university, in some cases in a university professor's research program, in government at such agencies as the National Institute of Mental Health, or in private industry. Individuals who have full-time research positions in child development generate innovative research ideas, plan studies, carry out the research by collecting data, analyzing the data, and then interpreting it. Then, they will usually attempt to publish the research in a scientific journal. A researcher often work in a collaborative manner with other researchers on a project and may present the research at scientific meetings. One researcher might spend much of his or her time in laboratory; another researcher might work out in the field, such as in schools, hospitals, and so on.

Valerie Pang
Professor of Teacher Education

Valerie Pang is a professor of teacher education of San Diego State University and formerly was an elementary school teacher. Like Dr. Pang, many professors of teacher education have a doctorate and have experience in teaching at the elementary or secondary school level.

Pang earned a doctorate at the University of Washington. She has received a Multicultural Educator Award from the National Association of Multicultural Education for her work on culture and equity. She also was given the Distinguished Scholar Award from the American Educational Research Association's Committee on the Role and Status of Minorities in Education.

Pang (2005) believes that competent teachers need to:

• Recognize the power and complexity of cultural influences on students.

• Be sensitive to whether their expectations for students are culturally biased.
• Evaluate whether they are doing a good job of seeing life from the perspective of students who come from different cultures.

Valerie Pang is a professor in the School of Education of San Diego State University and formerly an elementary school teacher. Valerie believes it is important for teachers to create a caring classroom that affirms all students.

Elementary School Teacher The work of an elementary or secondary school teacher involves teaching in one or more subject areas, preparing the curriculum, giving tests, assigning grades, monitoring students' progress, conducing parent-teacher conferences, and attending in-service workshops. Becoming an elementary or secondary school teacher requires a minimum of an undergraduate degree. The training involves taking a wide range of courses with a major or concentration in education, as well as completing a supervised practice-teaching internship.

Exceptional Children (Special Education) Teacher A teacher of exceptional children spends concentrated time with individual children who have a disability or are gifted. Among the children a teacher of exceptional children might work with are children with learning disabilities, ADHD (attention deficit hyperactivity disorder), mental retardation, or a physical disability such as cerebral palsy. Some of this work will usually be done outside of the student's regular classroom, some of it will be carried out when the student is in the regular classroom. The exceptional children teacher works closely with the student's regular classroom teacher and parents to create the best educational program for the student. Becoming a teacher of exceptional children requires a minimum of an undergraduate degree. The training consists of taking a wide range of courses in education and a concentration of courses in educating children with disabilities or children who are gifted. Teachers of exceptional children often continue their education after obtaining their undergraduate degree and attain a master's degree.

Early Childhood Educator Early childhood educators work on college faculties and have a minimum of a master's degree in their field. In graduate school, they take courses in early childhood education and receive supervisory training in child-care or early childhood programs. Early childhood educators usually teach in community colleges that award an associate degree in early childhood education.

Preschool/Kindergarten Teacher Preschool teachers teach mainly 4-year-old children, and kindergarten teachers primarily teach 5-year-old children. They usually have an undergraduate degree in education, specializing in early childhood education. State certification to become a preschool or kindergarten teacher usually is required.

Family and Consumer Science Educator Family and consumer science educators may specialize in early childhood education or instruct middle and high school students about such matters as nutrition, interpersonal relationships, human sexuality, parenting, and human development. Hundreds of colleges and universities throughout the United States offer two- and four-year degree programs in family and consumer science. These programs usually include an internship requirement. Additional education courses may be needed to obtain a teaching certificate. Some family and consumer educators go on to graduate school for further training, which provides a background for possible jobs in college teaching or research.

Educational Psychologist An educational psychologist most often teaches in a college or university and conducts research in such areas of educational psychology as learning, motivation, classroom management, and assessment. Most educational psychologists have a doctorate in education, which takes four to six years of graduate work. They help to train students who will take various positions in education, including educational psychology, school psychology, and teaching.

School Psychologist School psychologists focus on improving the psychological and intellectual well-being of elementary and secondary school students. They may work in a centralized office in a school district or in one or more schools. They give psychological tests, interview students and their parents, consult with teachers, and may provide counseling to students and their families.

School psychologists usually have a master's or doctoral degree in school psychology. In graduate school, they take courses in counseling, assessment, learning, and other areas of education and psychology.

CLINICAL AND COUNSELING

There are a wide variety of clinical and counseling jobs that are linked with child development. These range from child clinical psychologist to adolescent drug counselor.

Clinical Psychologist Clinical psychologists seek to help people with psychological problems. They work in a variety of settings, including colleges and universities, clinics, medical schools, and private practice. Some clinical psychologists only conduct psychotherapy, others do psychological assessment and psychotherapy, and some also do research. Clinical psychologists may specialize in a particular age group, such as children (child clinical psychologist).

Clinical psychologists have either a Ph.D. (which involves clinical and research training) or a Psy. D. degree (which only involves clinical training). This graduate training usually takes five to seven years and includes courses in clinical psychology and a one-year supervised internship in an accredited setting toward the end of the training. In most cases, they must pass a test to become licensed in a state and to call themselves clinical psychologists.

Psychiatrist Like clinical psychologists, psychiatrists might specialize in working with children (child psychiatry) or adolescents (adolescent psychiatry). Psychiatrists might work in medical schools in teaching and research roles, in a medical clinic, or in private practice. In addition to administering drugs to help improve the lives of people with psychological problems, psychiatrists also may conduct psychotherapy. Psychiatrists obtain a medical degree and then do a residency in psychiatry. Medical school takes approximately four years, and the psychiatry residency another three to four years. Unlike psychologists (who do not go to medical school) in most states, psychiatrists can administer drugs to clients.

Counseling Psychologist Counseling psychologists work in the same settings as clinical psychologists and may do psychotherapy, teach, or conduct research. In many instances, however, counseling psychologists do not work with individuals who have a severe mental disorder. A counseling psychologist might specialize in working with children, adolescents, and/or families.

Counseling psychologists go through much of the same training as clinical psychologists, although in a graduate program in counseling rather than clinical psychology. Counseling psychologists have either a master's degree or a doctoral degree. They also must go through a licensing procedure. One type of master's degree in counseling leads to the designation of licensed professional counselor.

School Counselor School counselors help to identify students' abilities and interests, guide students in developing academic plans, and explore career options with students. They may help students cope with adjustment problems. They may work with students individually, in small groups, or even in a classroom. They often consult with parents, teachers, and school administrators when trying to help students with their problems.

High school counselors advise students on choosing a major, admissions requirements for college, taking entrance exams, applying for financial aid, and on appropriate vocational and technical training. Elementary school counselors are mainly involved in counseling students about social and personal problems. They may observe children in the classroom and at play as part of their work. School counselors usually have a master's degree in counseling.

Career Counselor Career counselors help individuals to identify their best career options and guide them in applying for jobs. They may work in private industry or at a college/university. They usually interview individuals and give them vocational or psychological tests to help them provide students with information about careers that fit their interests and abilities. Sometimes they help individuals to create résumés or conduct mock interviews to help them feel comfortable in a job interview. They may create and promote job fairs or other recruiting events to help individuals obtain jobs.

Social Worker Social workers often are involved in helping people with social or economic problems. They may investigate, evaluate, and attempt to rectify reported cases of abuse, neglect, endangerment, or domestic disputes. They can intervene in families if necessary and provide counseling and referral services to individuals and families.

Social workers have a minimum of an undergraduate degree from a school of social work that includes course work in various areas of sociology and psychology. Some social workers also have a master's or doctoral degree. They often work for publicly funded agencies at the city, state, or national level, although increasingly they work in the private sector in areas such as drug rehabilitation and family counseling.

In some cases, social workers specialize in a certain area, as in true of a medical social workers, who has a master's degree in social work (MSW). This involves graduate course work and supervised clinical experiences in medical settings. A medical social worker might coordinate a variety of support services to people with a severe or long-term disability. Family-care social workers often work with families who need support services.

Drug Counselor Drug counselors provide counseling to individuals with drug abuse problems. They may work on an individual basis with a substance abuser or conduct group therapy sessions. They may work in private practice, with a state or federal government agency, with a company, or in a hospital setting. Some drug counselors specialize in working with adolescents or families. Most states provide a certification procedure for obtaining a license to practice drug counseling.

At a minimum, drug counselors to through an associates or certificate program. Many have an undergraduate degree in substance-abuse counseling, and some have master's and doctoral degrees.

MEDICAL, NURSING, AND PHYSICAL DEVELOPMENT

This third main area of careers in child development includes a wide range of careers in the medical and nursing areas, as well as jobs pertaining to improving some aspect of the child's physical development.

Obstetrician/Gynecologist An obstetrician/gynecologist prescribes prenatal and postnatal care and performs deliveries in maternity cases. The individual also treats diseases and injuries of the female reproductive system. Obstetricians may work in private practice, in a medical clinic, in a hospital, or in a medical school. Becoming an obstetrician/ gynecologist requires a medical degree plus three to five years of residency in obstetrics/ gynecology.

Pediatrician A pediatrician monitors infants' and children's health, works to prevent disease or injury, helps children attain optimal health, and treats children with health problems. Pediatricians may work in private practice, in a medical clinic, in a hospital, or in a medical school. As medical doctors, they can administer drugs to children and may counsel parents and children on ways to improve the children's health. Many pediatricians on the faculty of medical schools also teach and conduct research on children's health and diseases. Pediatricians have attained a medical degree and completed a three- to five-year residency in pediatrics.

Neonatal Nurse A neonatal nurse is involved in the delivery of care of the newborn infant. The neonatal nurse may work to improve the health and well-being of infants born under normal circumstances or be involved in the delivery of care to premature and critically ill neonates.

A minimum of an undergraduate degree in nursing with a specialization in the newborn is required. This training involves course work in nursing and the biological sciences, as well as supervisory clinical experiences.

Nurse–Midwife A nurse-midwife formulates and provides comprehensive care to selected maternity patients, cares for the expectant mother as she prepares to give birth and guides her through the birth process, and cares for the postpartum patient. The nurse-midwife also may provide care to the newborn, counsel parents on the infant's development and parenting, and provide guidance about health practices. Becoming a nurse-midwife generally requires an undergraduate degree from a school of nursing. A nurse-midwife most often works in a hospital setting.

Pediatric Nurse Pediatric nurses have a degree in nursing that takes from two to five years to complete. Some also may obtain a master's or doctoral degree in pediatric nursing. Pediatric nurses take courses in biological sciences, nursing care, and pediatrics, usually in a school of nursing. They also undergo supervised clinical experiences in medical settings. They monitor infants' and children's health, work to prevent disease or injury, and help children attain optimal health. They may work in hospitals, schools of nursing, or with pediatricians in private practice or at a medical clinic. To read about the work of one pediatric nurse practitioner, see the *Careers in Child Development* profile.

Audiologist An audiologist has a minimum of an undergraduate degree in hearing science. This includes courses and supervisory training. Audiologists assess and identify the presence and severity of hearing loss, as well as problems in balance. Some audiologists also go on to obtain a master's and/or doctoral degree. They may work in a medical clinic, with a physician in private practice, in a hospital, or in a medical school.

Speech Therapist Speech therapists are health-care professionals who are trained to identify, assess, and treat speech and language problems. They may work with physicians, psychologists, social workers, and other health-care professionals as a team to help individuals with physical or psychological problems that include speech and language problems. Speech pathologists have a minimum of an undergraduate degree in the speech and hearing science or communications disorders area. They may work in private practice, in hospitals and medical schools, and in government agencies with individuals

of any age. Some specialize in working with children or with a particular type of speech disorder.

Genetic Counselor
Genetic counselors work as members of a health-care team, providing information and support to families who have members with birth defects or genetic disorders and to families who may be at risk for a variety of inherited conditions. They identify families at risk and provide supportive counseling. They serve as educators and resource people for other health-care professionals and the public. Almost half work in university medical centers, and another one-fourth work in private hospital settings.

Most genetic counselors enter the field after majoring in undergraduate school in such disciplines as biology, genetics, psychology, nursing, public health, and social work. They have specialized graduate degrees and experience in medical genetics and counseling.

FAMILIES AND RELATIONSHIPS

A number of careers are available for working with families and relationship problems. These range from being a child welfare workers to marriage and family therapist.

Child Welfare Worker
A child welfare worker is employed by the child protective services unit of each state. The child welfare worker protects the child's rights, evaluates any maltreatment the child might experience, and may have the child removed from the home if necessary. A child social worker has a minimum of an undergraduate degree in social work.

Child Life Specialist
Child life specialists work with children and their families when the child needs to be hospitalized. They monitor the child patient's activities, seek to reduce the child's stress, help the child cope effectively, and assist the child in enjoying the hospital experience as much as possible. Child life specialists may provide parent education and develop individualized treatment plans based on an assessment of the child's development, temperament, medical plan, and available social supports.

Child life specialists have an undergraduate degree. As undergraduates, they take courses in child development and education and usually taking additional courses in a child life program.

Marriage and Family Therapist
Marriage and family therapists work on the principle that many individuals who have psychological problems benefit when psychotherapy is provided in the context of a marital or family relationship. Marriage and family therapists may provide marital therapy, couple therapy to individuals in a relationship who are not married, and family therapy to two or more members of a family.

Marriage and family therapists have a master's or doctoral degree. They go through a training program in graduate school similar to that of a clinical psychologist but with the focus on martial and family relationships. To practice marital and family therapy in most states, it is necessary to go through a licensing procedure.

Section Two

BEGINNINGS

There are one hundred and ninety-three living species of monkeys and apes. One hundred and ninety-two of them are covered with hair. The exception is the naked ape, self-named Homo sapiens.

—DESMOND MORRIS
British Zoologist, 20th Century

The rhythm and meaning of life involve beginnings. Questions are raised about how, from so simple a beginning, endless forms develop, grow, and mature. What was this organism, what is the organism, and what will this organism be? In Section 2, you will read three chapters: "Biological Beginnings" (Chapter 2), "Prenatal Development" (Chapter 3), and "Birth" (Chapter 4).

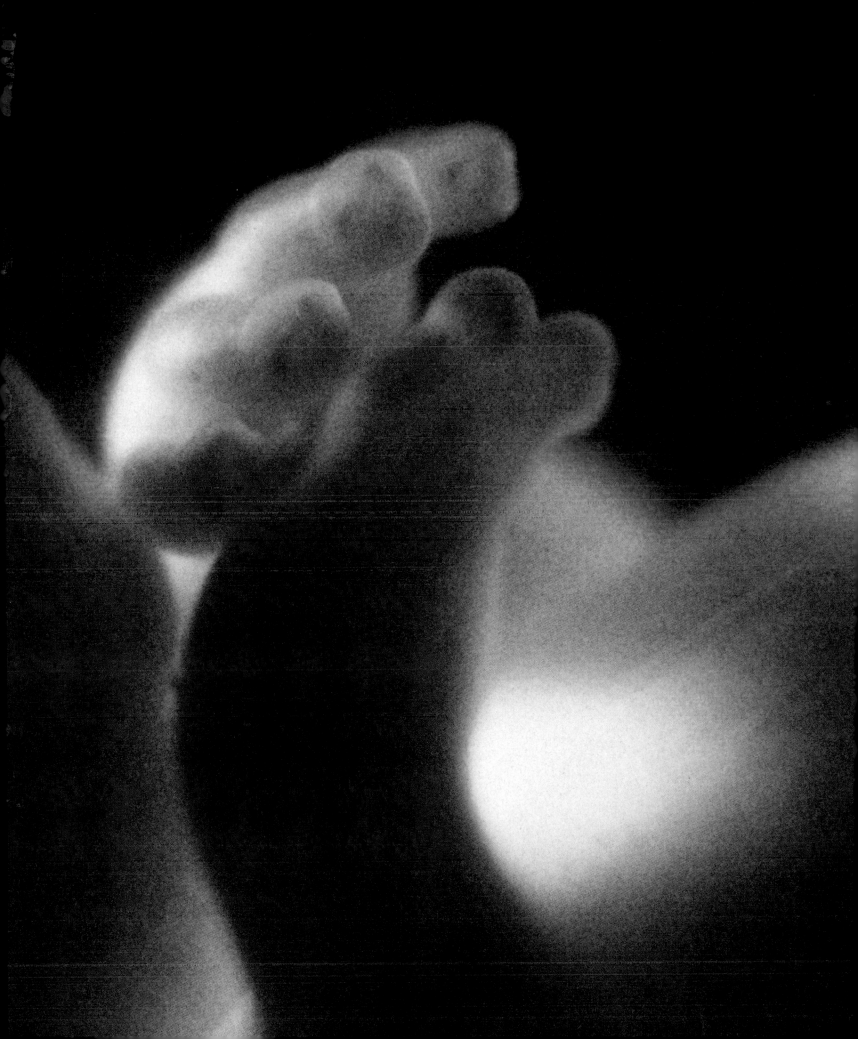

2 Biological Beginnings

What endless questions vex the thought, of whence and whither, when and how.

—Sir Richard Burton
British Explorer, 19th Century

CHAPTER OUTLINE

LEARNING GOALS

WHAT IS THE EVOLUTIONARY PERSPECTIVE?

Natural Selection and Adaptive Behavior

Evolutionary Psychology

1 Discuss the evolutionary perspective on development.

WHAT ARE THE GENETIC FOUNDATIONS OF DEVELOPMENT?

The Collaborative Gene

Genes and Chromosomes

Genetic Principles

Chromosomal and Gene-Linked Abnormalities

2 Describe what genes are and how they influence human development.

WHAT ARE SOME REPRODUCTIVE CHALLENGES AND CHOICES?

Prenatal Diagnostic Tests

Infertility and Reproductive Technology

Adoption

3 Identify some important reproductive challenges and choices.

HOW DO HEREDITY AND ENVIRONMENT INTERACT? THE NATURE-NURTURE DEBATE

Behavior Genetics

Heredity-Environment Correlations

Shared and Nonshared Environmental Experiences

The Epigenetic View

Conclusions About Heredity-Environment Interaction

4 Characterize some of the ways that heredity and environment interact to produce individual differences in development.

Images of Children's Development
The Story of the Jim and Jim Twins

Jim Lewis (*left*) and Jim Springer (*right*).

Jim Springer and Jim Lewis are identical twins. They were separated at 4 weeks of age and did not see each other again until they were 39 years old. Both worked as part-time deputy sheriffs, vacationed in Florida, drive Chevrolets, had dogs named Toy, and married and divorced women named Betty. One twin named his son James Allan, and the other named his son James Alan. Both liked math but not spelling, enjoyed carpentry and mechanical drawing, chewed their fingernails down to the nubs, had almost identical drinking and smoking habits, had hemorrhoids, put on 10 pounds at about the same point in development, first suffered headaches at the age of 18, and had similar sleep patterns.

Jim and Jim do have some differences. One wears his hair over his forehead; the other slicks it back and has sideburns. One expresses himself best orally; the other is more proficient in writing. But, for the most part, their profiles are remarkably similar.

Jim and Jim were part of the Minnesota Study of Twins Reared Apart, directed by Thomas Bouchard and his colleagues. The study brings identical twins (identical genetically because they come from the same fertilized egg) and fraternal twins (who come from different fertilized eggs) from all over the world to Minneapolis to investigate their lives. There the twins complete personality and intelligence tests, and they provide detailed medical histories, including information about diet and smoking, exercise habits, chest X-rays, heart stress tests, and EEGs. The twins are asked more than 15,000 questions about their family and childhood, personal interests, vocational orientation, values, and aesthetic judgments (Bouchard & others, 1990).

Another pair of identical twins in the Minnesota study, Daphne and Barbara, are called the "giggle sisters" because, after being reunited, they were always making each other laugh. A thorough search of their adoptive families' histories revealed no gigglers. The giggle sisters ignored stress, avoided conflict and controversy whenever possible, and showed no interest in politics.

Two other identical twin sisters were separated at 6 weeks of age and reunited in their fifties. Both described hauntingly similar nightmares in which they had doorknobs and fishhooks in their mouths as they were smothered to death. The nightmares began during early adolescence and stopped within the past 10 to 12 years. Both women were bed-wetters until about 12 or 13 years of age, and their educational and marital histories are remarkably similar.

When genetically identical twins who were separated as infants show such striking similarities in their tastes and habits and choices, can we conclude that their genes must have caused the development of those tastes and habits and choices? Other possible causes need to be considered. The twins shared not only the same genes but also some experiences. Some of the separated twins lived together for several months prior to their adoption; some of the twins had been reunited prior to testing (in some cases, many years earlier); adoption agencies often place twins in similar homes; and even strangers who spend several hours together and start comparing their lives are likely to come up with some coincidental similarities (Joseph, 2006). The Minnesota study of identical twins points to both the importance of the genetic basis of human development and the need for further research on genetic and environmental factors (Bouchard, 1995).

The examples of Jim and Jim, the giggle sisters, and the identical twins who had the same nightmares stimulate us to think about our genetic heritage and the biological foundations of our existence. Organisms are not like billiard balls, moved by simple, external forces to predictable positions on life's pool table.

Environmental experiences and biological foundations work together to make us who we are. Our coverage of life's biological beginnings focuses on evolution, genetic foundations, challenges and choices regarding reproduction, and the interaction of heredity and environment.

1 WHAT IS THE EVOLUTIONARY PERSPECTIVE?

Natural Selection and Adaptive Behavior

Evolutionary Psychology

As our earliest ancestors left the forest to feed in the savannahs, and then to form hunting societies on the open plains, their minds and behaviors changed, and they eventually established humans as the dominant species on earth. How did this evolution come about?

Natural Selection and Adaptive Behavior

Natural selection is the evolutionary process by which those individuals of a species that are best adapted are the ones that survive and reproduce. To understand what this means, let's return to the middle of the nineteenth century, when the British naturalist Charles Darwin was traveling around the world, observing many different species of animals in their natural surroundings. Darwin, who published his observations and thoughts in *On the Origin of Species* (1859), noted that most organisms reproduce at rates that would cause enormous increases in the population of most species and yet populations remain nearly constant. He reasoned that an intense, constant struggle for food, water, and resources must occur among the many young born each generation, because many of the young do not survive. Those that do survive, and reproduce, pass on their characteristics to the next generation. Darwin believed that these survivors are better *adapted* to their world than are the nonsurvivors (Johnson, 2008). The best-adapted individuals survive to leave the most offspring. Over the course of many generations, organisms with the characteristics needed for survival make up an increased percentage of the population. Over many, many generations, this could produce a gradual modification of the whole population. If environmental conditions change, however, other characteristics might become favored by natural selection, moving the species in a different direction (Enger, 2007).

All organisms must adapt to particular places, climates, food sources, and ways of life. An eagle's claws are a physical adaptation that facilitates predation. *Adaptive behavior* is behavior that promotes an organism's survival in the natural habitat (Freeman & Herron, 2007). For example, attachment between a caregiver and a baby ensures the infant's closeness to a caregiver for feeding, and protection from danger, thus increasing the infant's chances of survival. Or consider pregnancy sickness, which is a tendency for women to avoid certain foods and become nauseous during pregnancy (Schmitt & Pilcher, 2004). Women with pregnancy sickness tend

How does the attachment of this Vietnamese baby to its mother reflect the evolutionary process of adaptive behavior?

to avoid foods that are higher in toxins, such as coffee, that may harm the fetus. Thus, pregnancy sickness may be an evolution-based adaptation that enhances the offspring's ability to survive.

Evolutionary Psychology

Although Darwin introduced the theory of evolution by natural selection in 1859, his ideas only recently have become a popular framework for explaining behavior. Psychology's newest approach, **evolutionary psychology,** emphasizes the importance of adaptation, reproduction, and "survival of the fittest" in shaping behavior. "Fit" in this sense refers to the ability to bear offspring that survive long enough to bear offspring of their own. In this view, natural selection favors behaviors that increase reproductive success, the ability to pass your genes to the next generation (Bjorklund, 2006, 2007).

David Buss (1995, 2000, 2004, 2008) has been especially influential in stimulating new interest in how evolution can explain human behavior. He believes that just as evolution shapes our physical features, such as body shape and height, it also pervasively influences how we make decisions, how aggressive we are, our fears, and our mating patterns. For example, assume that our ancestors were hunters and gatherers on the plains and that men did most of the hunting and women stayed close to home, gathering seeds and plants for food. If you have to travel some distance from your home in an effort to find and slay a fleeing animal, you need not only certain physical traits but also the ability for certain types of spatial thinking. Men born with these traits would be more likely than men without them to survive, to bring home lots of food, and to be considered attractive mates—and thus to reproduce and pass on these characteristics to their children. In other words, these traits would provide a reproductive advantage for males and, over many generations, men with good spatial thinking skills might become more numerous in the population. Critics point out that this scenario might or might not have actually happened.

Evolutionary Developmental Psychology   Recently, interest has grown in using the concepts of evolutionary psychology to understand human development (Geary, 2006). Here are a few ideas proposed by evolutionary developmental psychologists (Bjorklund & Pellegrini, 2002, pp. 336–340):

- *An extended juvenile period evolved because humans require time to develop a large brain and learn the complexity of human social communities.* Humans take longer to become reproductively mature than any other mammal (see Figure 2.1). During this juvenile period they develop a large brain and the experiences required for mastering the complexities of human society.
- *Many dimensions of childhood functions serve as preparations for adulthood and were selected by evolution.* Play is one possible example. Beginning in the preschool years, boys in all cultures engage in more rough-and-tumble play than girls. Perhaps rough-and-tumble play prepares boys for fighting and hunting as adults. In contrast to boys, girls engage in play that involves more imitation of parents, such as caring for dolls, and less physical dominance. This, according to evolutionary psychologists, is an evolved tendency that prepares females for becoming the primary caregivers for their offspring.
- *Some characteristics of childhood were selected because they are adaptive at specific points in development, not because they prepare children for adulthood.* For example, some aspects of play may function not to

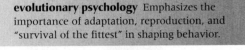
evolutionary psychology Emphasizes the importance of adaptation, reproduction, and "survival of the fittest" in shaping behavior.

FIGURE 2.1 The Brain Sizes of Various Primates and Humans in Relation to the Length of the Juvenile Period

prepare us for adulthood, but to help children adapt to their immediate circumstances, perhaps to learn about their current environment.

- *Many evolved psychological mechanisms are domain-specific.* That is, the mechanisms apply only to a specific aspect of a person's makeup (Finn, 2006). According to evolutionary psychology, information processing is one example. In this view, the mind is not a general-purpose device that can be applied equally to a vast array of problems. Instead, as our ancestors dealt with certain recurring problems, specialized modules evolved that process information related to those problems, such as a module for physical knowledge, a module for mathematical knowledge, and a module for language. Also in this view, infants come into the world ready to learn some information more easily than others, and this readiness provides a foundation for socioemotional and cognitive development. For example, much as goslings in Lorenz' experiment (described in Chapter 1) were "prepared" to follow their mother, human infants are biologically prepared to learn the sounds that are part of human language.

- *Evolved mechanisms are not always adaptive in contemporary society.* Some behaviors that were adaptive for our prehistoric ancestors may not serve us well today. For example, the food-scarce environment of our ancestors likely led to humans' propensity to gorge when food is available and to crave high-calorie foods, a trait that that might lead to an epidemic of obesity when food is plentiful.

Evaluating Evolutionary Psychology   Although evolutionary psychology is getting increased attention, it remains just one theoretical approach. Like the theories described in Chapter 1, it has limitations, weaknesses, and critics (Buller, 2005). Albert Bandura (1998), whose social cognitive theory was described in Chapter 1, acknowledges the important influence of evolution on human adaptation. However, he rejects what he calls "one-sided evolutionism," which sees social behavior as the product of evolved biology. An alternative is a *bidirectional view,* in which environmental and biological conditions influence each other. In this view, evolutionary pressures created changes in biological structures that allowed the use of tools, which enabled our ancestors to manipulate the environment, constructing new environmental conditions. In turn, environmental innovations produced new selection pressures that led to the evolution of specialized biological systems for consciousness, thought, and language.

In other words, evolution gave us bodily structures and biological potentialities; it does not dictate behavior. People have used their biological capacities to produce diverse cultures—aggressive and pacific, egalitarian and autocratic. As American scientist Steven Jay Gould (1981) concluded, in most domains of human functioning, biology allows a broad range of cultural possibilities

Children in all cultures are interested in the tools that adults in the cultures use. For example, this 11-month-old boy from the Efe culture in the Democratic Republic of the Congo in Africa is trying to cut a papaya with a sharp stick. *Might the infant's behavior be evolutionary-based or be due to both biological and environmental conditions?*

REVIEW AND REFLECT ◆ LEARNING GOAL 1

1 **Discuss the evolutionary perspective on development.**

Review
- How can natural selection and adaptive behavior be defined?
- What is evolutionary psychology? What are some basic ideas about human development proposed by evolutionary developmental psychologists? How can evolutionary psychology be evaluated?

Reflect
- Which is more persuasive to you: the views of evolutionary psychologists or their critics? Why?

2 WHAT ARE THE GENETIC FOUNDATIONS OF DEVELOPMENT?

The Collaborative Gene

Genetic Principles

Genes and Chromosomes

Chromosomal and Gene-Linked Abnormalities

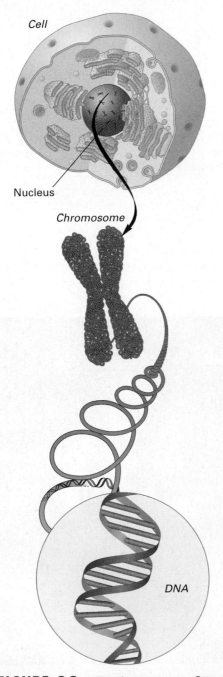

FIGURE 2.2 Cells, Chromosomes, Genes, and DNA (*Top*) The body contains trillions of cells. Each cell contains a central structure, the nucleus. (*Middle*) Chromosomes are threadlike structures, located in the nucleus of the cell. Chromosomes are composed of DNA. (*Bottom*) DNA has the structure of a spiraled double chain. A gene is a segment of DNA.

How are characteristics that suit a species for survival transmitted from one generation to the next? Darwin did not know because genes and the principles of genetics had not yet been discovered. Each of us carries a "genetic code" that we inherited from our parents. Because a fertilized egg carries this human code, a fertilized human egg cannot grow into an egret, eagle, or elephant.

The Collaborative Gene

Each of us began life as a single cell weighing about one twenty-millionth of an ounce! This tiny piece of matter housed our entire genetic code—instructions that orchestrated growth from that single cell to a person made of trillions of cells, each containing a replica of the original code. That code is carried by our genes. What are genes and what do they do? For the answer, we need to look into our cells.

The nucleus of each human cell contains **chromosomes,** which are threadlike structures made up of deoxyribonucleic acid, or DNA. **DNA** is a complex molecule has a double helix shape, like a spiral staircase, and contains genetic information. **Genes,** the units of hereditary information, are short segments of DNA, as you can see in Figure 2.2. They direct cells to reproduce themselves and to assemble proteins. Proteins, in turn, are the building blocks of cells as well as the regulators that direct the body's processes (Hartwell, 2008).

Each gene has its own location, its own designated place on a particular chromosome. Today, there is a great deal of enthusiasm about efforts to discover the specific locations of genes that are linked to certain functions (Lewis, 2007; Plomin & Schalkwyck, 2007; Weaver, 2008). An important step in this direction was accomplished when the Human Genome Project and the Celera Corporation completed a preliminary map of the human *genome*—the complete set of developmental instructions for creating proteins that initiate the making of a human organism.

One of the big surprises of the Human Genome Project was a report indicating that humans have only about 30,000 genes (U.S. Department of Energy, 2001). More recently, the number of human genes has been revised further downward to an exacting figure of 21,774 (Ensembl Human, 2007). Scientists had thought that humans had as many as 100,000 or more genes. They had also believed that each gene programmed just one protein. In fact, humans appear to have far more proteins than they have genes, so there cannot be a one-to-one correspondence between genes and proteins (Commoner, 2002; Moore, 2001). Each gene is not translated, in automaton-like fashion, into one and only one protein. A gene does not act independently, as developmental psychologist David Moore (2001) emphasized by titling his book *The Dependent Gene*.

Rather than being a group of independent genes, the human genome consists of many genes that collaborate both with each other and with nongenetic factors inside and outside the body. The collaboration operates at many points. For example, the cellular machinery mixes, matches, and links small pieces of DNA to reproduce the genes, and that machinery is influenced by what is going on around it.

Whether a gene is turned "on," working to assemble proteins, is also a matter of collaboration. The activity of genes (*genetic expression*) is affected by their environment (Gottlieb, 2007; Gottlieb, Wahlsten, & Lickliter, 2006). For example, hormones that circulate in the blood make their way into the cell where they can turn genes "on" and "off." And the flow of hormones can be affected by environmental conditions, such as light, day length, nutrition, and behavior. Numerous studies have shown that external events outside of the original cell and the person, as well as events inside the cell, can excite or inhibit gene expression (Gottlieb, 2007). For example, one recent study revealed that an increase in the concentration of stress hormones such as cortisol produced a fivefold increase in DNA damage (Flint & others, 2007).

In short, a single gene is rarely the source of a protein's genetic information, much less of an inherited trait (Gottlieb, Wahlsten, & Lickliter, 2006). Rather than being a group of independent genes, the human genome consists of many genes that collaborate both with each other and with nongenetic factors inside and outside the body.

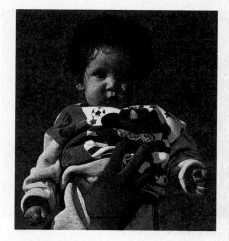

A positive result from the Human Genome Project. Shortly after Andrew Gobea was born, his cells were genetically altered to prevent his immune system from failing.

Genes and Chromosomes

Genes are not only collaborative, they are enduring. How do the genes manage to get passed from generation to generation and end up in all of the trillion cells in the body? Three processes explain the heart of the story: mitosis, meiosis, and fertilization.

Mitosis, Meiosis, and Fertilization

All cells in your body, except the sperm and egg, have 46 chromosomes arranged in 23 pairs. These cells reproduce by a process called **mitosis.** During mitosis, the cell's nucleus—including the chromosomes—duplicates itself and the cell divides. Two new cells are formed, each containing the same DNA as the original cell, arranged in the same 23 pairs of chromosomes.

However, a different type of cell division—**meiosis**—forms eggs and sperm (or *gametes*). During meiosis, a cell of the testes (in men) or ovaries (in women) duplicates its chromosomes but then divides *twice*, thus forming four cells, each of which has only half of the genetic material of the parent cell. By the end of meiosis, each egg or sperm has 23 *unpaired* chromosomes.

During **fertilization,** an egg and a sperm fuse to create a single cell, called a **zygote.** In the zygote, the 23 unpaired chromosomes from the egg and the 23 unpaired chromosomes from the sperm combine to form one set of 23 paired chromosomes—one chromosome of each pair from the mother's egg and the other from the father's sperm. In this manner, each parent contributes half of the offspring's genetic material.

chromosomes Threadlike structures made up of deoxyribonucleic acid, or DNA.

DNA A complex molecule with a double helix shape, contains genetic information.

genes Units of hereditary information composed of DNA. Genes direct cells to reproduce themselves and manufacture the proteins that maintain life.

mitosis Cellular reproduction in which the cell's nucleus duplicates itself with two new cells being formed, each containing the same DNA as the parent cell, arranged in the same 23 pairs of chromosomes.

meiosis A specialized form of cell division that occurs to form eggs and sperm (or gametes).

fertilization A stage in reproduction whereby an egg and a sperm fuse to create a single cell, called a zygote.

zygote A single cell formed through fertilization.

Calvin and Hobbes

by Bill Watterson

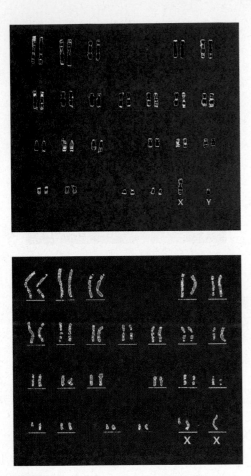

FIGURE 2.3 The Genetic Difference Between Males and Females Set (*a*) shows the chromosome structure of a male, and set (*b*) shows the chromosome structure of a female. The last pair of 23 pairs of chromosomes is in the bottom right box of each set. Notice that the Y chromosome of the male is smaller than the X chromosome of the female. To obtain this kind of chromosomal picture, a cell is removed from a person's body, usually from the inside of the mouth. The chromosomes are stained by chemical treatment, magnified extensively, and then photographed.

genotype A person's genetic heritage; the actual genetic material.

phenotype The way an individual's genotype is expressed in observed and measurable characteristics.

Figure 2.3 shows 23 paired chromosomes of a male and a female. The members of each pair of chromosomes are both similar and different: Each chromosome in the pair contains varying forms of the same genes, at the same location on the chromosome. A gene for hair color, for example, is located on both members of one pair of chromosomes, in the same location on each. However, one of those chromosomes might carry the gene for blond hair; the other chromosome in the pair might carry the gene for brown hair.

Do you notice any obvious differences between the chromosomes of the male and the chromosomes of the female in Figure 2.3? The difference lies in the 23rd pair. Ordinarily, in females this pair consists of two chromosomes called *X chromosomes*; in males the 23rd pair consists of an X and a *Y chromosome*. The presence of a Y chromosome is what makes an individual male.

Sources of Variability   Combining the genes of two parents in offspring increases genetic variability in the population, which is valuable for a species because it provides more characteristics for natural selection to operate on (Brooker & others, 2008; Mader, 2007). In fact, the human genetic process creates several important sources of variability.

First, the chromosomes in the zygote are not exact copies of those in mother's ovaries and the father's testes. During the formation of the sperm and egg in meiosis, the members of each pair of chromosomes are separated, but which chromosome in the pair goes to the gamete is a matter of chance. In addition, before the pairs separate, pieces of the two chromosomes in each pair are exchanged, creating a new combination of genes on each chromosome. Thus, when chromosomes from the mother's egg and the father's sperm are brought together in the zygote, the result is a truly unique combination of genes (Raven & others, 2008).

If each zygote is unique, how do identical twins like those discussed in the opening of the chapter exist? *Identical twins* (also called monozygotic twins) develop from a single zygote that splits into two genetically identical replicas, each of which becomes a person. *Fraternal twins* (called dizygotic twins) develop from separate eggs and separate sperm, making them genetically no more similar than ordinary siblings.

Another source of variability comes from DNA. Chance, a mistake by cellular machinery, or damage from an environmental agent such as radiation may produce a *mutated gene*, which is a permanently altered segment of DNA (Cummings, 2006).

Even when their genes are identical, however, people vary. The difference between genotypes and phenotypes helps us to understand this source of variability. All of a person's genetic material makes up his or her **genotype.** However, not all of the genetic material is apparent in our observed and measurable characteristics. A **phenotype** consists of observable characteristics. Phenotypes include physical characteristics (such as height, weight, and hair color) and psychological characteristics (such as personality and intelligence).

For each genotype, a range of phenotypes can be expressed, providing another source of variability (Gottlieb, Wahlsten, & Lickliter, 2006; Wong, Gottesman, & Petronis, 2005). An individual can inherit the genetic potential to grow very large, for example, but good nutrition, among other things, will be essential to achieving that potential. The giggle sisters introduced in the chapter opening might have inherited the same genetic potential to be very tall, but if Daphne had grown up malnourished, she might have ended up noticeably shorter than Barbara. This principle is so widely applicable it has a name: heredity-environment interaction (or gene-environment interaction) (Gottlieb, 2005).

Genetic Principles

What determines how a genotype is expressed to create a particular phenotype? Much is unknown about the answer to this question (Lewis, 2007; Talaro, 2008).

However, a number of genetic principles have been discovered, among them those of dominant-recessive genes, sex-linked genes, genetic imprinting, and polygenically determined characteristics.

Dominant–Recessive Genes Principle   In some cases, one gene of a pair always exerts its effects; it is *dominant*, overriding the potential influence of the other gene, called the *recessive* gene. This is the *dominant-recessive genes principle*. A recessive gene exerts its influence only if the two genes of a pair are both recessive. If you inherit a recessive gene for a trait from each of your parents, you will show the trait. If you inherit a recessive gene from only one parent, you may never know you carry the gene. Brown hair, farsightedness, and dimples rule over blond hair, nearsightedness, and freckles in the world of dominant-recessive genes. Can two brown-haired parents have a blond-haired child? Yes, they can. Suppose that each parent has a dominant gene for brown hair and a recessive gene for blond hair. Since dominant genes override recessive genes, the parents have brown hair, but both are carriers of blondness and pass on their recessive genes for blond hair. With no dominant gene to override them, the recessive genes can make the child's hair blond (see Figure 2.4).

Sex-Linked Genes   Most mutated genes are recessive. When a mutated gene is carried on the X chromosome, the result is called *X-linked inheritance*. It may have very different implications for males than females (Pan, Ober, & Abney, 2007; Zhang & others, 2007). Remember that males have only one X chromosome. Thus, if there is an altered, disease-creating gene on the X chromosome, males have no "backup" copy to counter the harmful gene and therefore may carry an X-linked disease. However, females have a second X chromosome, which is likely to be unchanged. As a result, they are not likely to have the X-linked disease. Thus, most individuals who have X-linked diseases are males. Females who have one changed copy of the X gene are known as "carriers," and they usually do not show any signs of the X-linked disease. Hemophilia and fragile X syndrome, which we discuss later in the chapter, are examples of X-linked inherited diseases (Pierce & others, 2007).

Genetic Imprinting   *Genetic imprinting* occurs when genes have differing effects depending on whether they are inherited from the mother or the father (Munshi & Duvvuri, 2007; Smith & others, 2007). A chemical process "silences" one member

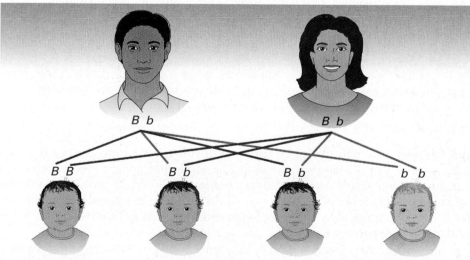

B = Gene for brown hair   *b* = Gene for blond hair

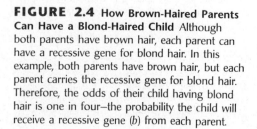

FIGURE 2.4 How Brown-Haired Parents Can Have a Blond-Haired Child Although both parents have brown hair, each parent can have a recessive gene for blond hair. In this example, both parents have brown hair, but each parent carries the recessive gene for blond hair. Therefore, the odds of their child having blond hair is one in four—the probability the child will receive a recessive gene (*b*) from each parent.

Name	Description	Treatment	Incidence
Down syndrome	An extra chromosome causes mild to severe retardation and physical abnormalities.	Surgery, early intervention, infant stimulation, and special learning programs	1 in 1,900 births at age 20 1 in 300 births at age 35 1 in 30 births at age 45
Klinefelter syndrome	An extra X chromosome causes physical abnormalities.	Hormone therapy can be effective	1 in 800 male births
Fragile X syndrome	An abnormality in the X chromosome can cause mental retardation, learning disabilities, or short attention span.	Special education, speech and language therapy	More common in males than in females
Turner syndrome	A missing X chromosome in females can cause mental retardation and sexual underdevelopment.	Hormone therapy in childhood and puberty	1 in 2,500 female births
XYY syndrome	An extra Y chromosome can cause above-average height.	No special treatment required	1 in 1,000 male births

FIGURE 2.5 Some Chromosomal Abnormalities *Note:* Treatment does not necessarily erase the problem but may improve the individual's adaptive behavior and quality of life.

of the gene pair. For example, as a result of imprinting, only the maternally derived copy of a gene might be active, while the paternally derived copy of the same gene is silenced—or vice versa. Only a small percentage of human genes appear to undergo imprinting, but it is a normal and important aspect of development. When imprinting goes awry, development is disturbed, as in the case of Beckwith-Wiedemann syndrome, a growth disorder, and Wilms tumor, a type of cancer (Gropman & Adams, 2007).

Polygenic Inheritance Genetic transmission is usually more complex than the simple examples we have examined thus far (Lewis, 2007; Nester & others, 2007). Few characteristics reflect the influence of only a single gene or pair of genes. Most are determined by the interaction of many different genes; they are said to be *polygenically determined*. Even simple characteristics such as height, for example, reflects the interaction of many genes, as well as the influence of the environment.

Chromosomal and Gene-Linked Abnormalities

Sometimes, abnormalities characterize the genetic process. Some of these abnormalities involve whole chromosomes that do not separate properly during meiosis. Other abnormalities are produced by harmful genes.

Chromosomal Abnormalities Sometimes, when a gamete is formed, the sperm and ovum do not have their normal set of 23 chromosomes. The most notable examples involve Down syndrome and abnormalities of the sex chromosomes (see Figure 2.5).

Down Syndrome An individual with **Down syndrome** has a round face, a flattened skull, an extra fold of skin over the eyelids, a protruding tongue, short limbs, and retardation of motor and mental abilities (Zitanova & others, 2006). The syndrome is caused by the presence of an extra copy of chromosome 21 (Visootsak & Sherman, 2007). It is not known why the extra chromosome is present, but the health of the male sperm or female ovum may be involved (Hodapp & Dykens, 2006).

Down syndrome appears approximately once in every 700 live births. Women between the ages of 16 and 34 are less likely to give birth to a child with Down

These athletes, many of whom have Down syndrome, are participating in a Special Olympics competition. Notice the distinctive facial features of the individuals with Down syndrome, such as a round face and a flattened skull. *What causes Down syndrome?*

Down syndrome A chromosomally transmitted form of mental retardation, caused by the presence of an extra copy of chromosome 21.

syndrome than are younger or older women. African American children are rarely born with Down syndrome.

Sex-Linked Chromosomal Abnormalities   Recall that a newborn normally has either an X and a Y chromosome, or two X chromosomes. Human embryos must possess at least one X chromosome to be viable. The most common sex-linked chromosomal abnormalities involve the presence of an extra chromosome (either an X or Y) or the absence of one X chromosome in females.

Klinefelter syndrome is a genetic disorder in which males have an extra X chromosome, making them XXY instead of XY (Itti & others, 2006). Males with this disorder have undeveloped testes, and they usually have enlarged breasts and become tall (Bojesen & Gravhott, 2007). Klinefelter syndrome occurs approximately once in every 800 live male births.

Fragile X syndrome is a genetic disorder that results from an abnormality in the X chromosome, which becomes constricted and often breaks (Penagarikano, Mulle, & Warren, 2007). Mental deficiency often is an outcome, but it may take the form of mental retardation, a learning disability, or a short attention span (Lewis, 2007). This disorder occurs more frequently in males than in females, possibly because the second X chromosome in females negates the effects of the other abnormal X chromosome (Kochi & others, 2007).

Turner syndrome is a chromosomal disorder in females in which either an X chromosome is missing, making the person XO instead of XX, or part of one X chromosome is deleted (Kanaka-Gantenbein, 2006). Females with Turner syndrome are short in stature and have a webbed neck (Carel, 2005). They might be infertile and have difficulty in mathematics, but their verbal ability often is quite good. Turner syndrome occurs in approximately 1 of every 2,500 live female births.

The **XYY syndrome** is a chromosomal disorder in which the male has an extra Y chromosome (Briken & others, 2006). Early interest in this syndrome focused on the belief that the extra Y chromosome found in some males contributed to aggression and violence. However, researchers subsequently found that XYY males are no more likely to commit crimes than are XY males (Witkin & others, 1976).

Gene-Linked Abnormalities

Abnormalities can be produced not only by an uneven number of chromosomes but also by harmful genes. More than 7,000 such genetic disorders have been identified, although most of them are rare.

Phenylketonuria (PKU) is a genetic disorder in which the individual cannot properly metabolize phenylalanine, an amino acid (Hvas, Nexos, & Nielsen, 2006). It results from a recessive gene and occurs about once in every 10,000 to 20,000 live births. Today, phenylketonuria is easily detected, and it is treated by a diet that prevents an excess accumulation of phenylalanine. If phenylketonuria is left untreated, however, excess phenylalanine builds up in the child, producing mental retardation and hyperactivity. Phenylketonuria accounts for approximately 1 percent of institutionalized individuals who are mentally retarded, and it occurs primarily in non-Latino Whites.

The story of phenylketonuria has important implications for the nature-nurture issue. Although phenylketonuria is a genetic disorder (nature), how or whether a gene's influence in phenylketonuria is played out depends on environmental influences since the disorder can be treated (nurture) (Brosco, Mattingly, & Sanders, 2006; Schindler & others, 2007). That is, the presence of a genetic defect *does not* inevitably lead to the development of the disorder *if* the individual develops in the right environment (one free of phenylalanine) (Cipriano, Rupar, & Zaric, 2007). This is one example of the important principle of heredity-environment interaction (Gottlieb, 2005). Under one environmental condition (phenylalanine in the diet), mental retardation results, but when other nutrients replace phenylalnine, intelligence develops in the normal range. The

Klinefelter syndrome A genetic disorder in which males have an extra X chromosome, making them XXY instead of XY.

fragile X syndrome A genetic disorder involving an abnormality in the X chromosome, which becomes constricted and often breaks.

Turner syndrome A chromosomal disorder in females in which either an X chromosome is missing, making the person XO instead of XX, or the second X chromosome is partially deleted.

XYY syndrome A chromosomal disorder in which males have an extra Y chromosome.

phenylketonuria (PKU) A genetic disorder in which an individual cannot properly metabolize phenylalanine, an amino acid. PKU is now easily detected—but if left untreated, results in mental retardation and hyperactivity.

During a physical examination for a college football tryout, Jerry Hubbard, 32, learned that he carried the gene for sickle-cell anemia. Daughter Sara is healthy but daughter Avery (in the print dress) has sickle-cell anemia. *If you were a genetic counselor, would you recommend that this family have more children? Explain.*

same genotype has different outcomes depending on the environment (in this case, the nutritional environment).

Sickle-cell anemia, which occurs most often in African Americans, is a genetic disorder that impairs the body's red blood cells. Red blood cells carry oxygen to the body's cells and are usually shaped like a disk. In sickle-cell anemia, a recessive gene causes the red blood cell to become a hook-shaped "sickle" that cannot carry oxygen properly and dies quickly. As a result, the body's cells do not receive adequate oxygen, causing anemia and early death (Smith & others, 2006). About 1 in 400 African American babies is affected by sickle-cell anemia. One in 10 African Americans is a carrier, as is 1 in 20 Latin Americans.

Other diseases that result from genetic abnormalities include cystic fibrosis, diabetes, hemophilia, spina bifida, and Tay-Sachs disease (Gregory & others, 2007; Oakley, 2007). Figure 2.6 provides further information about these diseases. Someday,

sickle-cell anemia A genetic disorder that affects the red blood cells and occurs most often in people of African descent.

Name	Description	Treatment	Incidence
Cystic fibrosis	Glandular dysfunction that interferes with mucus production; breathing and digestion are hampered, resulting in a shortened life span.	Physical and oxygen therapy, synthetic enzymes, and antibiotics; most individuals live to middle age.	1 in 2,000 births
Diabetes	Body does not produce enough insulin, which causes abnormal metabolism of sugar.	Early onset can be fatal unless treated with insulin.	1 in 2,500 births
Hemophilia	Delayed blood clotting causes internal and external bleeding.	Blood transfusions/injections can reduce or prevent damage due to internal bleeding.	1 in 10,000 males
Phenylketonuria (PKU)	Metabolic disorder that, left untreated, causes mental retardation.	Special diet can result in average intelligence and normal life span.	1 in 10,000 to 20,000 births
Sickle-cell anemia	Blood disorder that limits the body's oxygen supply; it can cause joint swelling, as well as heart and kidney failure.	Penicillin, medication for pain, antibiotics, and blood transfusions.	1 in 400 African American children (lower among other groups)
Spina bifida	Neural tube disorder that causes brain and spine abnormalities.	Corrective surgery at birth, orthopedic devices, and physical/medical therapy.	2 in 1,000 births
Tay-Sachs disease	Deceleration of mental and physical development caused by an accumulation of lipids in the nervous system.	Medication and special diet are used, but death is likely by 5 years of age.	One in 30 American Jews is a carrier.

FIGURE 2.6 Some Gene-Linked Abnormalities

scientists may identify why these and other genetic abnormalities occur and discover how to cure them.

Dealing with Genetic Abnormalities   Every individual carries DNA variations that might predispose the person to serious physical disease or mental disorder. But not all individuals who carry a genetic disorder display the disorder. Other genes or developmental events sometimes compensate for genetic abnormalities (Gottlieb, Wahlsten, & Lickliter, 2006). For example, recall the example of phenylketonuria from the previous section: Even though individuals might carry the genetic disorder of phenylketonuria, it is not expressed when phenylalanine is replaced by other nutrients in their diet.

Thus, genes are not destiny, but genes that are missing, nonfunctional, or mutated can be associated with disorders (Almeida & others, 2007; Spry & others, 2007). Identifying such genetic flaws could enable doctors to predict an individual's risks, recommend healthy practices, and prescribe the safest and most effective drugs (Holloway & Koppelmann, 2007). A decade or two from now, parents of a newborn baby may be able to leave the hospital with a full genome analysis of their offspring that reveals disease risks.

However, this knowledge might bring important costs as well as benefits. Who would have access to a person's genetic profile? An individual's ability to land and hold jobs or obtain insurance might be threatened if it is known that a person is considered at risk for some disease. For example, should an airline pilot or a neurosurgeon who is predisposed to develop a disorder that makes one's hands shake be required to leave that job early?

Genetic counselors, usually physicians or biologists who are well versed in the field of medical genetics, understand the kinds of problems just described, the odds of encountering them, and helpful strategies for offseting some of their effects (Forrester & Merz, 2007; Latimer, 2007). To read about the career and work of a genetic counselor, see the *Careers in Child Development* profile.

Careers in CHILD DEVELOPMENT

Holly Ishmael
Genetic Counselor

Holly Ishmael is a genetic counselor at Children's Mercy Hospital in Kansas City. She obtained an undergraduate degree in psychology and then a master's degree in genetic counseling from Sarah Lawrence College.

Genetic Counselors, like Holly, work as members of a health-care team, providing information and support to families with birth defects or genetic disorders. They identify families at risk by analyzing inheritance patterns and explore options with the family. Some genetic counselors, like Holly, become specialists in prenatal and pediatric genetics; others might specialize in cancer genetics or psychiatric genetic disorders.

Holly says, "Genetic counseling is a perfect combination for people who want to do something science-oriented, but need human contact and don't want to spend all of their time in a lab or have their nose in a book" (Rizzo, 1999, p. 3).

Genetic counselors have specialized graduate degrees in the areas of medical genetics and counseling. They enter graduate school with undergraduate backgrounds from a variety of disciplines, including biology, genetics, psychology, public health, and social work. There are approximately thirty graduate genetic counseling programs in the United States. If you are interested in this profession, you can obtain further information from the National Society of Genetic Counselors at www.nsgc.org.

Holly Ishmael (*left*) in a genetic counseling.

REVIEW AND REFLECT   LEARNING GOAL 2

2 **Describe what genes are and how they influence human development.**

Review
- What are genes?
- How are genes passed on?
- What basic principles describe how genes interact?
- What are some chromosomal and gene-linked abnormalities?

Reflect
- What are some possible ethical issues regarding genetics and development that might arise in the future?

3 WHAT ARE SOME REPRODUCTIVE CHALLENGES AND CHOICES?

| Prenatal Diagnostic Tests | Infertility and Reproductive Technology | Adoption |

The facts and principles we have discussed regarding meiosis, genetics, and genetic abnormalities are a small part of the recent explosion of knowledge about human biology. This knowledge not only helps us understand human development but also opens up many new choices to prospective parents, choices that can also raise ethical questions (Bromage, 2006; Gotz & Gotz, 2006).

Prenatal Diagnostic Tests

One choice open to prospective mothers is the extent to which they should undergo prenatal testing. A number of tests can indicate whether a fetus is developing normally, including ultrasound sonography, fetal MRI, chorionic villus sampling, amniocentesis, and maternal blood screening (Karpin & Bennett, 2006).

A 6-month-old infant poses with the ultrasound sonography record taken four months into the baby's prenatal development. *What is ultrasound sonography?*

An ultrasound test is often conducted seven weeks into a pregnancy and at various times later in pregnancy. *Ultrasound sonography* is a prenatal medical procedure in which high-frequency sound waves are directed into the pregnant woman's abdomen. The echo from the sounds is transformed into a visual representation of the fetus's inner structures. This technique can detect many structural abnormalities in the fetus, including microencephaly, a form of mental retardation involving an abnormally small brain; it can also determine the number of fetuses and give clues to the baby's sex (Oepkes & others, 2006; Sonek, 2007). There is virtually no risk to the woman or fetus in this test.

The development of brain-imaging techniques has led to increasing use of *fetal MRI* to diagnose fetal malformations (Huisman & Kellenberger, 2007; Lee & Simpson, 2007). MRI stands for magnetic resonance imaging and uses a powerful magnet and radio images to generate detailed images of the body's organs and structure. Currently, ultrasound is still the first choice in fetal screening, but fetal MRI can provide more detailed images than ultrasound. In many instances, ultrasound will indicate a possible abnormality, and then fetal MRI will be used to obtain a clearer, more detailed image (Muhler & others, 2007). Among the fetal malformations that fetal MRI may be able to detect better than ultrasound sonography are certain central nervous system, chest, gastrointestinal, genital/urinary, and placental abnormalities (Dietrich & Cohen, 2006; Fratelli & others, 2007; Laifer-Narin & others, 2007).

At some point between the 10th and 12th weeks of pregnancy, chorionic villus sampling may be used to detect genetic defects and chromosomal abnormalities, such as the ones discussed in the previous section. (Csaba, Bush, & Saphier, 2006). Diagnosis takes approximately 10 days. *Chorionic villus sampling (CVS)* is a prenatal medical procedure in which a small sample of the placenta (the vascular organ that links the fetus to the mother's uterus) is removed. There is a small risk of limb deformity when CVS is used.

Between the 15th and 18th weeks of pregnancy, amniocentesis may be performed. *Amniocentesis* is a prenatal medical procedure in which a sample of amniotic fluid is withdrawn by syringe and tested for chromosomal or metabolic disorders (Nagel & others, 2007). The amnionic fluid is found within the amnion, a thin sac in which the embryo is suspended. Ultrasound sonography is often used during amniocentesis so that the syringe can be placed precisely. The later amniocentesis is performed, the better its diagnostic potential. The earlier it is performed, the more useful it is in deciding how to handle a pregnancy (Pinette & others, 2004). It may take two weeks for enough cells to grow and amniocentesis test results to be obtained. Amniocentesis brings a small risk of miscarriage—about 1 woman in every 200 to 300 miscarries after amniocentesis.

Both amniocentesis and chorionic villus sampling provide valuable information about the presence of birth defects, but they also raise difficult issues for parents about whether an abortion should be obtained if birth defects are present (Bromage, 2006; Quadrelli, 2007). Chorionic villus sampling allows a decision to be made sooner, near the end of the first 12 weeks of pregnancy, when abortion is safer and less traumatic than later. Although earlier reports indicated that chorionic villus sampling brings a slightly higher risk of pregnancy loss than amniocentesis, a recent U.S. study of more than 40,000 pregnancies found that loss rates for CVS decreased from 1998–2003, and that there is no longer a difference in pregnancy loss risk between CVS and amniocentesis (Caughey, Hopkins, & Norton, 2006).

During the 16th to 18th weeks of pregnancy, maternal blood screening may be performed. *Maternal blood screening* identifies pregnancies that have an elevated risk for birth defects such as spina bifida (a defect in the spinal cord) and Down syndrome (Palomaki & others, 2006). The current blood test is called the *triple screen* because it measures three substances in the mother's blood. After an abnormal triple screen result, the next step is usually an ultrasound examination. If an ultrasound does not explain the abnormal triple screen results, amniocentesis is typically used.

Singer Celine Dion became pregnant through in vitro fertilization and gave birth to her son Rene-Charles in 2001.

Infertility and Reproductive Technology

Recent advances in biological knowledge have also opened up many choices for infertile people. Approximately 10 to 15 percent of couples in the United States experience infertility, which is defined as the inability to conceive a child after 12 months of regular intercourse without contraception. The cause of infertility can rest with the woman or the man (Kumar & others, 2006). The woman may not be ovulating (releasing eggs to be fertilized), she may be producing abnormal ova, her fallopian tubes by which ova normally reach the womb may be blocked, or she may have a disease that prevents implantation of the embryo into the uterus. The man may produce too few sperm, the sperm may lack motility (the ability to move adequately), or he may have a blocked passageway (Hesmet & Lo, 2006).

In the United States, more than 2 million couples seek help for infertility every year. In some cases of infertility, surgery may correct the cause; in others, hormone-based drugs may improve the probability of having a child. Of the 2 million couples who seek help for infertility every year, about 40,000 try high-tech assisted reproduction. The three most common techniques follow:

- *In vitro fertilization (IVF)*. Eggs and sperm are combined in a laboratory dish. If any eggs are successfully fertilized, one or more of the resulting fertilized eggs is transferred into the woman's uterus.
- *Gamete intrafallopian transfer (GIFT)*. A doctor inserts eggs and sperm directly into a woman's fallopian tube.
- *Zygote intrafallopian transfer (ZIFT)*. This is a two-step procedure. First, eggs are fertilized in the laboratory; then, any resulting fertilized eggs are transferred to a fallopian tube.

A national study in the United States in 2000 by the Centers for Disease Control and Prevention found that IVF is by far the most frequently used technique (98 percent of all cases in the study) and had the highest success rate (slightly more than 30 percent).

The creation of families by means of the new reproductive technologies raises important questions about the physical and psychological consequences for children (El-Toukhy, Khalaf, & Braude, 2006; Gurgan & Demirol, 2007). One result of fertility treatments is an increase in multiple births (Jones, 2007; Reddy & others, 2007). Twenty-five to 30 percent of pregnancies achieved by fertility treatments—including in vitro fertilization—now result in multiple births. Any multiple birth increases the likelihood that the babies will have life-threatening and costly problems, such as extremely low birth weight (Cheung, 2006).

Not nearly as many studies have examined the psychological outcomes of IVF as the physical outcomes. To read about a study that addresses these consequences, see the *Research in Children's Development* interlude that follows.

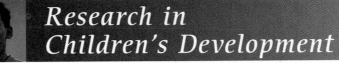

Research in Children's Development

IN VITRO FERTILIZATION AND DEVELOPMENTAL OUTCOMES IN ADOLESCENCE

A longitudinal study examined 34 in vitro fertilization families, 49 adoptive families, and 38 families with a naturally conceived child (Golombok, MacCallum, & Goodman, 2001). Each type of family included a similar portion of boys and girls. Also, the age of the young adolescents did not differ according to family type (mean age of 11 years, 11 months).

Children's socioemotional development was assessed by (1) interviewing the mother and obtaining detailed descriptions of any problems the child might have, (2) administering a Strengths and Difficulties questionnaire to the child's mother and teacher, and (3) administering the Social Adjustment Inventory for Children and Adolescents, which examines functioning in school, peer relationships, and self-esteem.

No significant differences between the children from the in vitro fertilization, adoptive, and naturally conceiving families were found. The results from the Social Adjustment Inventory for Children and Adolescents are shown in Figure 2.7. Another study also revealed no psychological differences between IVF babies and those not conceived by IVF, but more research is needed to reach firm conclusions in this area (Hahn & Dipietro, 2001).

FIGURE 2.7 Socioemotional Development at Adolescence of Children in Three Family Types: In Vitro Fertilization, Naturally Conceived, and Adopted In this study, there were no significant differences in socioemotional development at the beginning of adolescence in terms of school functioning, peer relations, and self-esteem (Golombok, MacCallum, & Goodman, 2001). The mean scores shown for the different measures are all in the normal range of functioning.

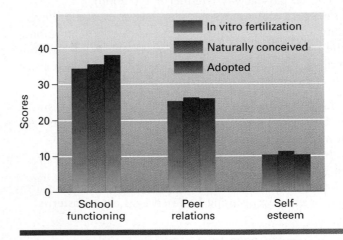

Adoption

Although surgery and fertility drugs can sometimes solve the infertility problem, another choice is to adopt a child (Fontehot, 2007; Grotevant & others, 2006). Adoption is the social and legal process by which a parent-child relationship is established between persons unrelated at birth. As we see next in the *Diversity in Children's Development* interlude, an increase in diversity has characterized the adoption of children in the United States in recent years.

Diversity in Children's Development

THE INCREASED DIVERSITY OF ADOPTED CHILDREN AND ADOPTIVE PARENTS

Several changes occurred during the last several decades of the twentieth century in the characteristics both of adopted children and of adoptive parents (Brodzinsky & Pinderhughes, 2002, pp. 280–282). Until the 1960s, most U.S. adopted children were healthy, European American infants, who were adopted within a few days or weeks after birth. However, in recent decades, an increasing number of unmarried U.S. mothers decided to keep their babies, and the number of unwanted births decreased as contraception became readily available and abortion was legalized. As a result, the number of healthy European American infants available for adoption dropped dramatically. Increasingly, U.S. couples adopted children who were not European Americans, children from other countries, and children in foster care whose characteristics—such as age, minority status, exposure to neglect or abuse, or physical or mental health problems—"were once thought to be barriers to adoption" (p. 281).

An increasing number of Hollywood celebrities are adopting children from developing countries. Actress Angelina Jolie recently adopted a baby girl, Zahara (*above*), in Ethiopia.

Changes also have characterized adoptive parents. Until the last several decades of the twentieth century, most adoptive parents had a middle or upper socioeconomic status and were "married, infertile, European American couples, usually in their 30s and 40s, and free of any disability. Adoption agencies *screened out* couples who did not have these characteristics" (p. 281). Today, however, many adoption agencies *screen in* as many applicants as possible and have no income requirements for adoptive parents. Many agencies now permit single adults, older adults, and gay and lesbian adults to adopt children (Matthews & Cramer, 2006; Ryan, Pearlmutter, & Groza, 2004).

Do these changes matter? They open opportunities for many children and many couples, but possible effects of changes in the characteristics of parents on the outcomes for children are still unknown. For example, in one study, adopted adolescents were more likely to have problems if the adopted parents had low levels of education (Miller & others, 2000). In another study, international adoptees showed fewer behavior problems and were less likely to be using mental health services than domestic adoptees (Juffer & van Ijzendoorn, 2005). More research is needed before definitive conclusions can be reached about the changing demographic characteristics of adoption.

The changes in adoption practice over the last several decades make it difficult to generalize about the average adopted child or average adoptive parent. As we see next, though, some researchers have provided useful comparisons between adopted children and nonadopted children and their families.

How do adopted children fare after they are adopted? Children who are adopted very early in their lives are more likely to have positive outcomes than children adopted later in life. In one study, the later adoption occurred, the more problems the adoptees had. Infant adoptees had the fewest adjustment difficulties; those adopted after they were 10 years of age had the most problems (Sharma, McGue, & Benson, 1996).

In general, adopted children and adolescents are more likely to experience psychological and school-related problems than nonadopted children (Brodzinksy, Lang, & Smith, 1995; Brodzinsky & Pinderhuges, 2002; Brodzinsky & others, 1984). For example, a recent meta-analysis (a statistical procedure that combines the results of a number of studies) revealed that adoptees were far more likely to be using mental health services than their nonadopted counterparts. (Juffer & van IJzendoorn, 2005). Adopted children also showed more behavior problems than nonadoptees, but this difference was small. A recent large-scale study revealed that adopted children are more likely to have a learning disability than nonadopted children (Attarac & Saroha, 2007).

Research that contrasts adopted and nonadopted adolescents has also found positive characteristics among the adopted adolescents. For example, in one study, although adopted adolescents were more likely than nonadopted adolescents to use illicit drugs and to engage in delinquent behavior, the adopted adolescents were also less likely to be withdrawn and engaged in more prosocial behavior, such as being altruistic, caring, and supportive of others (Sharma, McGue, & Benson, 1996).

Do adopted children show differences in cognitive development as well? A recent meta-analysis (a statistical technique that combines the results of a number of studies) of 62 studies involving almost 18,000 adopted children compared (1) the cognitive development of adopted children with children who remained in institutional care or in the birth family, and (2) the same group of adopted children to their current nonadopted siblings or peers in their current environment (van IJzendoorn, Juffer, & Poelhuis, 2005). In this meta-analysis, the adopted children scored higher on IQ tests, and performed better in school, than the children who stayed behind in institutions or with their birth families. The IQ of adopted children did not differ from that of nonadopted peers or siblings in their current environment, but their school performance and language abilities were at lower levels, and they were more likely to have learning difficulties. Overall, the meta-analysis documented the positive influence of adoption on children's cognitive development, and the normal intellectual ability of adopted children, but a lower level of performance in school.

In short, the vast majority of adopted children (including those adopted at older ages, transracially, and across national borders) adjust effectively, and their parents report considerable satisfaction with their decision to adopt (Brodzinsky & Pinderhughes, 2002). In one recent national study, there were no differences in the antisocial behavior of adopted and nonadopted young adults (Grotevant & others, 2006). Furthermore, adopted children fare much better than children in long-term foster care or in an institutional environment (Brodzinsky & Pinderhughes, 2002). To read more about adoption, see the *Caring for Children* interlude in which we discuss effective parenting strategies with adopted children.

Caring for Children

PARENTING ADOPTED CHILDREN

Many of the keys to effectively parenting adopted children are no different from those for effectively parenting biological children: Be supportive and caring, be involved and monitor the child's behavior and whereabouts, be a good communicator, and help the child to learn to develop self-control. However, parents of adopted children face some unique circumstances (Fontenot, 2007). These need to recognize the differences involved in adoptive family life, communicate about these differences, show respect for the birth family, and support the child's search for self and identity.

David Brodzinsky and Ellen Pinderhughes (2002, pp. 288–292) discussed how to handle some of the challenges that parents face when their adopted children are at different points in development:

- *Infancy.* Researchers have found few differences in the attachment that adopted and nonadopted infants form with their parents, but attachment can be compromised "when parents have difficulty in claiming the child as their own either because of unresolved fertility issues, lack of support from family and friends, and/or when their expectations about the child have not been met" (p. 288). Competent adoption agencies or counselors can help prospective adoptive parents develop realistic expectations.
- *Early childhood.* Because many children begin to ask where they came from when they are about 4 to 6 years old, this is a natural time to begin to talk

in simple ways to children about their adoption status (Warshak, 2004). Some parents (although not as many as in the past) decide not to tell their children about the adoption. This secrecy may create psychological risks for the child if he or she later finds out about the adoption.

- *Middle and late childhood.* During the elementary school years, children begin to express "much more curiosity about their origins: *Where did I come from? What did my birthmother and birthfather look like? Why didn't they keep me? Where are they now? Can I meet them?*" (p. 290). As they grow older, children may become more ambivalent about being adopted and question their adoptive parents' explanations. It is important for adoptive parents to recognize that this ambivalence is normal. Also, problems may come from the desire of adoptive parents to make life too perfect for the adopted child and to present a perfect image of themselves to the child. The result too often is that adopted children feel that they cannot release any angry feelings and openly discuss problems (Warshak, 2004).
- *Adolescence.* Adolescents are likely to develop more abstract and logical thinking, to focus their attention on their bodies, and to search for an identity. These characteristics provide the foundation for adopted adolescents to reflect on their adoption status in more complex ways, to become "preoccupied with the lack of physical resemblance between themselves and others in the family" (p. 291), and to explore how the fact that they were adopted fits into their identity.

Adoptive parents "need to be aware of these many complexities and provide teenagers with the support they need to cope with these adoption-related tasks" (p. 292).

What are some strategies for parenting adopted children at different points in their development?

REVIEW AND REFLECT   ▶ LEARNING GOAL 3

③ Identify some important reproductive challenges and choices.

Review
- What are some common prenatal diagnostic tests?
- What are some techniques that help infertile people to have children?
- How does adoption affect children's development?

Reflect
- We discussed a number of studies indicating that adoption is linked with negative outcomes for children. Does that mean that all adopted children have more negative outcomes than all nonadopted children? Explain.

---

④ HOW DO HEREDITY AND ENVIRONMENT INTERACT? THE NATURE-NURTURE DEBATE

| Behavior Genetics | Shared and Nonshared Environmental Experiences | Conclusions About Heredity-Environment Interaction |

| Heredity-Environment Correlations | The Epigenetic View |

In each section of this chapter so far, we have examined parts of the nature-nurture debate. We have seen how the environment exerts selective pressures on the characteristics of species over generations, examined how genes are passed from parents to children, and discussed how reproductive technologies and adoption influence the course of children's lives. But in all of these situations, heredity and environment interact to produce development. After all, Jim and Jim (and each of the other

Identical twins develop from a single fertilized egg that splits into two genetically identical organisms. Twin studies compare identical twins with fraternal twins. Fraternal twins develop from separate eggs, making them genetically no more similar than nontwin siblings. *What is the nature of the twin study method?*

pairs of identical twins discussed in the opening of the chapter) have the same genotype, but they are not the same person; each is unique. What made them different? Whether we are studying how genes produce proteins, their influence on how tall a person is, or how PKU might affect an individual, we end up discussing heredity-environment interactions.

Is it possible to untangle the influence of heredity from that of environment and discover the role of each in producing individual differences in development? When heredity and environment interact, how does heredity influence the environment, and vice versa?

Behavior Genetics

Behavior genetics is the field that seeks to discover the influence of heredity and environment on individual differences in human traits and development (Plomin, DeFries, & Fulker, 2007; Saudino, 2005). Note that behavior genetics does not determine the extent to which genetics or the environment affects an individual's traits. Instead, what behavior geneticists try to do is to figure out what is responsible for the differences among people—that is, to what extent do people differ because of differences in genes, environment, or a combination of these? To study the influence of heredity on behavior, behavior geneticists often use either twins or adoption situations.

In the most common **twin study,** the behavioral similarity of identical twins (who are genetically identical) is compared with the behavioral similarity of fraternal twins. Recall that although fraternal twins share the same womb, they are no more genetically alike than are brothers or sisters. Thus by comparing groups of identical and fraternal twins, behavior geneticists capitalize on the basic knowledge that identical twins are more similar genetically than are fraternal twins (Bishop & others, 2006; Whitfield & others, 2007). For example, one study revealed that conduct problems were more prevalent in identical twins than fraternal twins; the researchers concluded that the study demonstrated an important role for heredity in conduct problems (Scourfield & others, 2004).

However, several issues complicate interpretation of twin studies (Vogler, 2006). For example, perhaps the environments of identical twins are more similar than the environments of fraternal twins. Adults might stress the similarities of identical twins more than those of fraternal twins, and identical twins might perceive themselves as a "set" and play together more than fraternal twins do. If so, the influence of the environment on the observed similarities between identical and fraternal twins might be very significant.

In an **adoption study,** investigators seek to discover whether the behavior and psychological characteristics of adopted children are more like those of their adoptive parents, who have provided a home environment, or more like those of their biological parents, who have contributed their heredity (Haugaard & Hazen, 2004; Loehlin, Horn, & Ernst, 2007). Another form of the adoption study compares adopted and biological siblings.

Heredity–Environment Correlations

The difficulties that researchers encounter when they interpret the results of twin studies and adoption studies reflect the complexities of heredity-environment interaction. Some of these interactions are *heredity-environment correlations,* which means that individuals' genes may influence the types of environments to which they are exposed. In a sense, individuals "inherit" environments that may be related or linked to genetic "propensities" (Plomin & others, 2003). Behavior geneticist Sandra Scarr (1993) described three ways that heredity and environment are correlated (see Figure 2.8):

- **Passive genotype-environment correlations** occur because biological parents, who are genetically related to the child, provide a rearing environment for the child. For example, the parents might have a genetic predisposition to

Heredity-Environment Correlation	Description	Examples
Passive	Children inherit genetic tendencies from their parents and parents also provide an environment that matches their own genetic tendencies.	Musically inclined parents usually have musically inclined children and they are likely to provide an environment rich in music for their children.
Evocative	The child's genetic tendencies elicit stimulation from the environment that supports a particular trait. Thus genes evoke environmental support.	A happy, outgoing child elicits smiles and friendly responses from others.
Active (niche-picking)	Children actively seek out "niches" in their environment that reflect their own interests and talents and are thus in accord with their genotype.	Libraries, sports fields, and a store with musical instruments are examples of environmental niches children might seek out if they have intellectual interests in books, talent in sports, or musical talents, respectively.

FIGURE 2.8 Exploring Heredity-Environment Correlations

be intelligent and read skillfully. Because they read well and enjoy reading, they provide their children with books to read. The likely outcome is that their children, given their own inherited predispositions from their parents and their book-filled environment, will become skilled readers.

- **Evocative genotype-environment correlations** occur because a child's characteristics elicit certain types of environments. For example, active, smiling children receive more social stimulation than passive, quiet children do. Cooperative, attentive children evoke more pleasant and instructional responses from the adults around them than uncooperative, distractible children do.

- **Active (niche-picking) genotype-environment correlations** occur when children seek out environments that they find compatible and stimulating. *Niche-picking* refers to finding a setting that is suited to one's abilities. Children select from their surrounding environment some aspect that they respond to, learn about, or ignore. Their active selections of environments are related to their particular genotype. For example, outgoing children tend to seek out social contexts in which to interact with people, whereas shy children don't. Children who are musically inclined are likely to select musical environments in which they can successfully perform their skills. How these "tendencies" come about is discussed shortly under the topic of the epigenetic view.

Scarr argues that the relative importance of the three genotype-environment correlations changes as children develop from infancy through adolescence. In infancy, much of the environment that children experience is provided by adults. Thus, passive genotype-environment correlations are more common in the lives of infants and young children than they are for older children and adolescents who can extend their experiences beyond the family's influence and create their environments to a greater degree.

Notice that this analysis gives the preeminent role in development to heredity—the analysis describes how heredity may influence the types of environments that children experience. Critics argue that the concept of heredity-environment correlation gives heredity too much of a one-sided influence in determining development because it does not consider the role of prior environmental influences in shaping the correlation itself (Gottlieb, Wahlsten, & Lickliter, 2006). Before considering this criticism and a different view of the heredity-environment linkage, let's take a closer look at how behavior geneticists analyze the environments involved in heredity.

Shared and Nonshared Environmental Experiences

Behavior geneticists have argued that to understand the environment's role in differences between people, we should distinguish between shared and nonshared

evocative genotype-environment correlations Correlations that exist when the child's characteristics elicit certain types of physical and social environments.

active (niche-picking) genotype-environment correlations Correlations that exist when children seek out environment they find compatible and stimulating.

Tennis stars Venus and Serena Williams. *What might be some shared and nonshared environmental experiences they had while they were growing up that contributed to their tennis stardom?*

environments. That is, we should consider experiences that children share in common with other children living in the same home, and experiences that are not shared (Feinberg & Hetherington, 2001; Gelhorn & others 2006; Slomkowski & others, 2005).

Shared environmental experiences are siblings' common experiences, such as their parents' personalities or intellectual orientation, the family's socioeconomic status, and the neighborhood in which they live. By contrast, **nonshared environmental experiences** are a child's unique experiences, both within the family and outside the family, that are not shared with a sibling. Even experiences occurring within the family can be part of the "nonshared environment." For example, parents often interact differently with each sibling, and siblings interact differently with parents (Hetherington, Reiss, & Plomin, 1994). Siblings often have different peer groups, different friends, and different teachers at school.

Behavior geneticist Robert Plomin (2004) has found that shared environment accounts for little of the variation in children's personality or interests. In other words, even though two children live under the same roof with the same parents, their personalities are often very different. Further, Plomin and his colleagues (2003, 2007) argue that heredity influences the nonshared environments of siblings through the heredity-environment correlations we described earlier. For example, a child who has inherited a genetic tendency to be athletic is likely to spend more time in environments related to sports; a child who has inherited a tendency to be musically inclined is more likely to spend time in environments related to music.

What are the implications of Plomin's interpretation of the role of shared and nonshared environments in development? In the *Nurture Assumption*, Judith Harris (1998) argued that what parents do does not make a difference in their children's and adolescents' behavior. Yell at them. Hug them. Read to them. Ignore them. Harris says it won't influence how they turn out. She argues that genes and peers are far more important than parents in children's and adolescents' development.

Genes and peers do matter, but Harris' descriptions of peer influences do not take into account the complexity of peer contexts and developmental trajectories (Hartup, 1999). In addition, Harris is wrong in saying that parents don't matter. For example, in the early child years parents play an important role in selecting children's peers and indirectly influencing children's development. Volumes of parenting literature with many research studies document the importance of parents in children's development (Grusec & Davidov, 2007; Maccoby, 2007). We discuss parents' important roles throughout this book.

The Epigenetic View

Does the concept of heredity-environment correlation downplay the importance of environment in our development? The concept emphasizes how heredity directs the kind of environmental experiences individuals have. However, earlier in the chapter we discussed how genes are collaborative, not determining an individual's traits in an independent manner, but rather in an interactive manner with the environment. In line with the concept of a collaborative gene, Gilbert Gottlieb (2007; Gottlieb, Wahlsten, & Lickliter, 2006) emphasizes the **epigenetic view,** which states that development is the result of an ongoing, bidirectional interchange between heredity and the environment. Figure 2.9 compares the heredity-environment correlation and epigenetic views of development.

Let's look at an example that reflects the epigenetic view. A baby inherits genes from both parents at conception. During prenatal development, toxins, nutrition, and stress can influence some genes to stop functioning while others become stronger or weaker. During infancy, environmental experiences such as toxins, nutrition, stress, learning, and encouragement continue to modify genetic activity and

shared environment experiences Siblings' common experiences, such as their parents' personalities and intellectual orientation, the family's socioeconomic status, and the neighborhood in which they live.

nonshared environment experiences The child's own unique experiences, both within the family and outside the family, that are not shared by another sibling. Thus, experiences occurring within the family can be part of the "nonshared environment."

epigenetic view Emphasizes that development is the result of an ongoing, bidirectional interchange between heredity and environment.

the activity of the nervous system that directly underlies behavior (Gottlieb, 2005). Heredity and environment operate together—or collaborate—to produce a person's intelligence, temperament, height, weight, ability to pitch a baseball, ability to read, and so on (Gottlieb, 2007; Rutter, 2007).

Conclusions About Heredity–Environment Interaction

If an strong, fast, athletic girl wins a championship tennis match in her high school, is her success due to heredity or to environment? Of course, the answer is both.

The relative contributions of heredity and environment are not additive. That is, we can't say that such-and-such a percentage of nature and such-and-such a percentage of experience make us who we are. Nor is it accurate to say that full genetic expression happens once, around conception or birth, after which we carry our genetic legacy into the world to see how far it takes us. Genes produce proteins throughout the life span, in many different environments. Or they don't produce these proteins, depending in part on how harsh or nourishing those environments are.

The emerging view is that complex behaviors have some *genetic loading* that gives people a propensity for a particular developmental trajectory (Plomin, DeFries, & Fulker, 2007; Plomin & Schalkwyck, 2007; Walker, Petrill, & Plomin, 2005). However, the actual development requires more: an environment. And that environment is complex, just like the mixture of genes we inherit (Grusec & Hastings, 2007; Laible & Thompson, 2007). Environmental influences range from the things we lump together under "nurture" (such as parenting, family dynamics, schooling, and neighborhood quality) to biological encounters (such as viruses, birth complications, and even biological events in cells) (Greenough, 1997, 1999; Greenough & others, 2001).

Consider for a moment the cluster of genes associated with diabetes. The adolescent who carries this genetic mixture might experience a world of loving parents, nutritious meals, and regular medical intervention. Or the adolescent's world might include parental neglect, a diet high in sugar, and little help from competent physicians. In which of these environments are the adolescent's genes likely to result in diabetes?

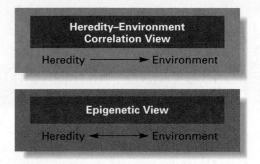

FIGURE 2.9 Comparison of the Heredity-Environment Correlation and Epigenetic Views

---

REVIEW AND **REFLECT**   **LEARNING GOAL 4**

4 **Characterize some of the ways that heredity and environment interact to produce individual differences in development.**

Review
- What is behavior genetics?
- What are three types of heredity-environment correlations?
- What is meant by the concepts of shared and nonshared environmental experiences?
- What is the epigenetic view of development?
- What conclusions can be reached about heredity-environment interaction?

Reflect
- Someone tells you that she has analyzed her genetic background and environmental experiences and reached the conclusion that environment definitely has had little influence on her intelligence. What would you say to this person about her ability to make this self-diagnosis?

REACH YOUR LEARNING GOALS

1 WHAT IS THE EVOLUTIONARY PERSPECTIVE? *Discuss the evolutionary perspective on development.*

Natural Selection and Adaptive Behavior

- Natural selection is the process by which those individuals of a species that are best adapted survive and reproduce. Darwin proposed that natural selection fuels evolution. In evolutionary theory, adaptive behavior is behavior that promotes the organism's survival in a natural habitat.

Evolutionary Psychology

- Evolutionary psychology holds that adaptation, reproduction, and "survival of the fittest" are important in shaping behavior. Ideas proposed by evolutionary developmental psychology include the view that an extended juvenile period is needed to develop a large brain and learn the complexity of human social communities. Many evolved psychological mechanisms are domain-specific. Like other theoretical approaches to development, evolutionary psychology has limitations. Bandura rejects "one-sided evolutionism" and argues for a bidirectional link between biology and environment. Biology allows for a broad range of cultural possibilities.

2 WHAT ARE THE GENETIC FOUNDATIONS OF DEVELOPMENT? *Describe what genes are and how they influence human development.*

The Collaborative Gene

- Except in the sperm and egg, the nucleus of each human cell contains 46 chromosomes, which are composed of DNA. Short segments of DNA constitute genes, the units of hereditary information that direct cells to reproduce and manufacture proteins. Genes act collaboratively, not independently.

Genes and Chromosomes

- Genes are passed on to new cells when chromosomes are duplicated during the processes of mitosis and meiosis, which are two ways in which new cells are formed. When an egg and a sperm unite in the fertilization process, the resulting zygote contains the genes from the chromosomes in the father's sperm and the mother's egg. Despite this transmission of genes from generation to generation, variability is created in several ways, including the exchange of chromosomal segments during meiosis, mutations, and the distinction between a genotype and a phenotype.

Genetic Principles

- Genetic principles include those involving dominant-recessive genes, sex-linked genes, genetic imprinting, and polygenic inheritance.

Chromosomal and Gene-Linked Abnormalities

- Chromosomal abnormalities produce Down syndrome, which is caused by the presence of an extra copy of chromosome 21, as well as sex-linked chromosomal abnormalities such as Klinefelter syndrome, fragile X syndrome, Turner syndrome, and XYY syndrome. Gene-linked abnormalities involve harmful genes. Gene-linked disorders include phenylketonuria (PKU) and sickle-cell anemia. Genetic counseling offers couples information about their risk of having a child with inherited abnormalities.

3 WHAT ARE SOME REPRODUCTIVE CHALLENGES AND CHOICES? *Identify some important reproductive challenges and choices.*

Prenatal Diagnostic Tests

- Amniocentesis, ultrasound sonography, fetal MRI, chorionic villus sampling, and maternal blood screening are used to determine whether a fetus is developing normally.

| Infertility and Reproductive Technology | • Approximately 10 to 15 percent of U.S. couples have infertility problems, some of which can be corrected through surgery or fertility drugs. Additional options include in vitro fertilization and other more recently developed techniques. |

| Adoption | • Although adopted children and adolescents have more problems than their nonadopted counterparts, the vast majority of adopted children adapt effectively. When adoption occurs very early in development, the outcomes for the child are improved. Because of the dramatic changes that occurred in adoption in recent decades, it is difficult to generalize about the average adopted child or average adoptive family. |

4 HOW DO HEREDITY AND ENVIRONMENT INTERACT? THE NATURE–NURTURE DEBATE *Characterize some of the ways that heredity and environment interact to produce individual differences in development.*

| Behavior Genetics | • Behavior genetics is the field concerned with the degree and nature of behavior's hereditary basis. Methods used by behavior geneticists include twin studies and adoption studies. |

| Heredity-Environment Correlations | • In Scarr's heredity-environment correlations view, heredity directs the types of environments that children experience. She describes three genotype-environment correlations: passive, evocative, and active (niche-picking). Scarr maintains that the relative importance of these three genotype-environment correlations changes as children develop. |

| Shared and Nonshared Environmental Experiences | • Shared environmental experiences refer to siblings' common experiences, such as their parents' personalities and intellectual orientation, the family's socioeconomic status, and the neighborhood in which they live. Nonshared environmental experiences involve the child's unique experiences, both within a family and outside a family, that are not shared with a sibling. Many behavior geneticists argue that differences in the development of siblings are due to nonshared environmental experiences (and heredity) rather than shared environmental experiences. |

| The Epigenetic View | • The epigenetic view emphasizes that development is the result of an ongoing, bidirectional interchange between heredity and environment. |

| Conclusions About Heredity-Environment Interaction | • Complex behaviors have some genetic loading that gives people a propensity for a particular developmental trajectory. However, actual development also requires an environment, and that environment is complex. The interaction of heredity and environment is extensive. Much remains to be discovered about the specific ways that heredity and environment interact to influence development. |

KEY TERMS

evolutionary psychology 58	genes 61	fertilization 61	phenotype 62
chromosomes 61	mitosis 61	zygote 61	Down syndrome 64
DNA 61	meiosis 61	genotype 62	Klinefelter syndrome 65

KEY PEOPLE

MAKING A DIFFERENCE

Some Prepregnancy Strategies

Even before a woman becomes pregnant, some strategies can be adopted that may make a difference in how healthy the pregnancy is and its developmental outcomes:

- *Become knowledgeable about prepregnancy planning and health-care providers.* The kinds of health-care providers who are qualified to provide care for pregnant women include an obstetrician/gynecologist, a family practitioner, a nurse practitioner, and a certified nurse-midwife.
- *Meet with a health professional before conception.* A good strategy is for both potential parents to meet with a health

professional prior to conception to assess their health and review personal and family histories. During this meeting, the health professional will discuss nutrition and other aspects of health that might affect the baby.

- *Find a health-care provider who is competent.* The health-care provider should (1) take time to do a thorough family history; (2) not be patronizing; (3) be knowledgeable and stay current on prenatal testing; (4) be honest about risks, benefits, and side effects of any tests or treatments; and (5) inspire trust.

CHILDREN RESOURCES

American Fertility Association

www.theafa.org

The American Fertility Association provides information about infertility and possible solutions to it.

How Healthy Is Your Family Tree?

by Carol Krause (1995)
New York: Simon & Schuster

In this book, you will learn how to create a family medical tree. Once you put together a family medical tree, a specialist or genetic counselor can help you understand it.

National Organization for Rare Disorders (NORD)

www.rarediseases.org

NORD supports awareness and education about rare birth defects and genetic disorders.

The Twins Foundation

www.twinsfoundation.com

For information about twins and multiple births, contact The Twins Foundation.

E-LEARNING TOOLS

Connect to **www.mhhe.com/santrockc10** to research the answers and complete these exercises. In addition, you'll find a number of other resources and valuable study tools for Chapter 2, "Biological Beginnings," on this Web site.

Taking It to the Net

1. Ahmahl, a biochemistry major, is writing a psychology paper on the potential dilemmas that society and scientists

may face as a result of decoding the human genome. What are some of the main issues or concerns that Ahmahl should address in his class paper?

2. Brandon and Katie are thrilled to learn that they are expecting their first child. They are curious about the genetic makeup of their unborn child and want to know (a) what disorders might be identified through prenatal genetic testing, and (b) which tests, if any, Katie should undergo to help determine this information?

3. Greg and Courtney have three boys. They would love to have a girl. Courtney read that there is a clinic in Virginia where you can pick the sex of your child. How successful are such efforts? Would you want to have this choice available to you?

Health and Well-Being, Parenting, and Education

Build your decision-making skills by trying your hand at the health and well-being, parenting, and education exercises.

Video Clips

The Online Learning Center includes the following videos for this chapter:

1. *Interview with Adoptive Parents*—3004
   An interview with a couple that adopted a second child.

3 Prenatal Development

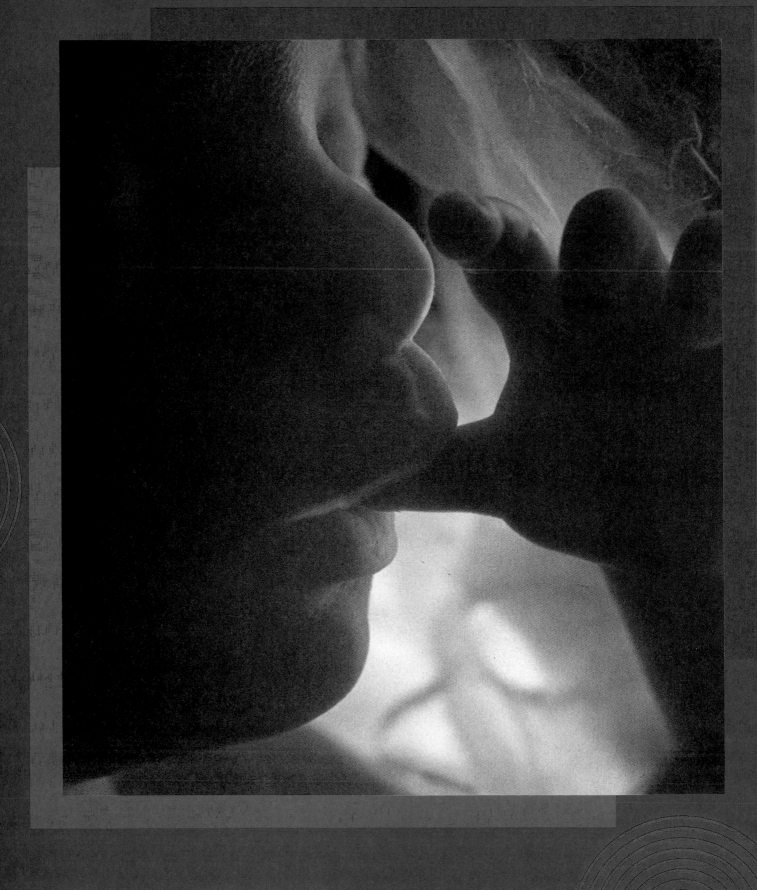

The history of man for nine months preceding his birth would probably be far more interesting and contain events of greater moment than all three score and ten years that follow it.

—SAMUEL TAYLOR COLERIDGE
English Poet Essayist, 19th Century

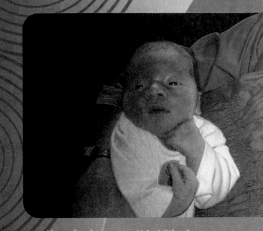

Alex, also known as "Mr. Littles."

Images of Children's Development
The Story of Mr. Littles

Diana and Roger married when he was 38 and she was 34. Both worked full-time and were excited when Diana became pregnant. Two months later, Diana began to have some unusual pains and bleeding. Just two months into her pregnancy she had lost the baby. Diana thought deeply about why she was unable to carry the baby to full term. It was about the time she became pregnant that the federal government began to warn that eating certain types of fish with a high mercury content during pregnancy on a regular basis can cause a miscarriage. Now she eliminated these fish from her diet.

Six months later, Diana became pregnant again. She and Roger read about pregnancy and signed up for birth preparation classes. Each Friday night for eight weeks they practiced simulated contractions. They talked about what kind of parents they wanted to be and discussed what changes in their lives the baby would make. When they found out that their offspring was going to be a boy, they gave him a name: Mr. Littles.

This time, Diana's pregnancy went well, and Alex, also known as Mr. Littles, was born. During the birth, however, Diana's heart rate dropped precipitously and she was given a stimulant to raise it. Apparently, the stimulant also increased Alex's heart rate and breathing to a dangerous point, and he had to be placed in a neonatal intensive care unit (NICU).

Several times a day, Diana and Roger visited Alex in the NICU. A number of babies in the NICU who had a very low birth weight had been in intensive care for weeks, and some of these babies were not doing well. Fortunately, Alex was in better health. After several days in the NICU, his parents were permitted to take home a very healthy Alex.

PREVIEW

This chapter chronicles the truly remarkable changes that take place from conception to birth. Imagine . . . at one time you were floating around in a sea of fluid in your mother's womb. In this chapter, we explore the course of prenatal development, expectant parents' experiences, and some potential hazards to prenatal development.

1 WHAT IS THE COURSE OF PRENATAL DEVELOPMENT?

| The Germinal Period | The Fetal Period | The Brain |

The Embryonic Period

Imagine how Alex ("Mr. Littles") came to be. Out of thousands of eggs and millions of sperm, one egg and one sperm united to produce him. Had the union of sperm and egg come a day or even an hour earlier or later, he might have been very different—maybe even of the opposite sex. Conception occurs when a single sperm cell from the male unites with an ovum (egg) in the female's fallopian tube in a

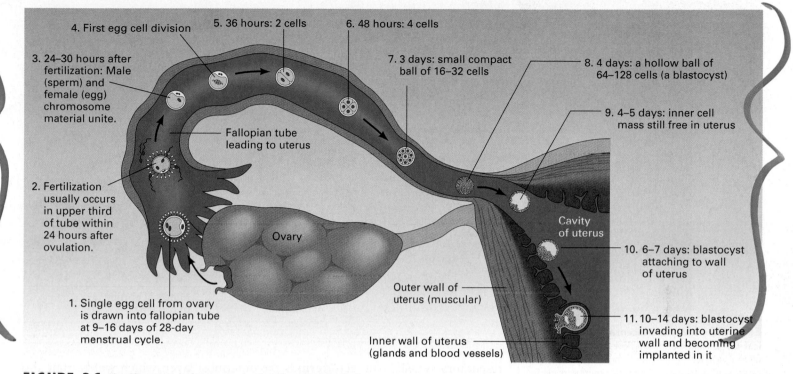

FIGURE 3.1 Significant Developments in the Germinal Period

process called fertilization. Over the next few months, the genetic code, discussed in Chapter 2, directs a series of changes in the fertilized egg, but many events and hazards will influence how that egg develops and becomes tiny Alex.

Prenatal development lasts approximately 266 days, beginning with fertilization and ending with birth. It can be divided into three periods: germinal, embryonic, and fetal.

The Germinal Period

The **germinal period** is the period of prenatal development that takes place in the first two weeks after conception. It includes the creation of the fertilized egg, called a zygote, cell division, and the attachment of the zygote to the uterine wall.

Rapid cell division by the zygote begins the germinal period (recall from Chapter 2 that this cell division occurs through a process called *mitosis*). By approximately one week after conception, the differentiation of these cells—their specialization for different tasks—has already begun. At this stage, the group of cells, now called the **blastocyst,** consists of an inner mass of cells that will eventually develop into the embryo and the **trophoblast,** an outer layer of cells that later provides nutrition and support for the embryo. *Implantation*, the attachment of the zygote to the uterine wall, takes place about 10 to 14 days after conception. Figure 3.1 illustrates some of the most significant developments during the germinal period.

The Embryonic Period

The **embryonic period** is the period of prenatal development that occurs from two to eight weeks after conception. During the embryonic period, the rate of cell differentiation intensifies, support systems for the cells form, and organs appear.

This period begins as the blastocyst attaches to the uterine wall. The mass of cells is now called an *embryo*, and three layers of cells form. The embryo's **endoderm** is the inner layer of cells, which will develop into the digestive and

germinal period The period of prenatal development that takes place in the first two weeks after conception. It includes the creation of the zygote, continued cell division, and the attachment of the zygote to the uterine wall.

blastocyst The inner layer of cells that develops during the germinal period. These cells later develop into the embryo.

trophoblast The outer layer of cells that develops in the germinal period. These cells provide nutrition and support for the embryo.

embryonic period The period of prenatal development that occurs two to eight weeks after conception. During the embryonic period, the rate of cell differentiation intensifies, support systems for the cells form, and organs appear.

endoderm The inner layer of cells, which develops into digestive and respiratory systems.

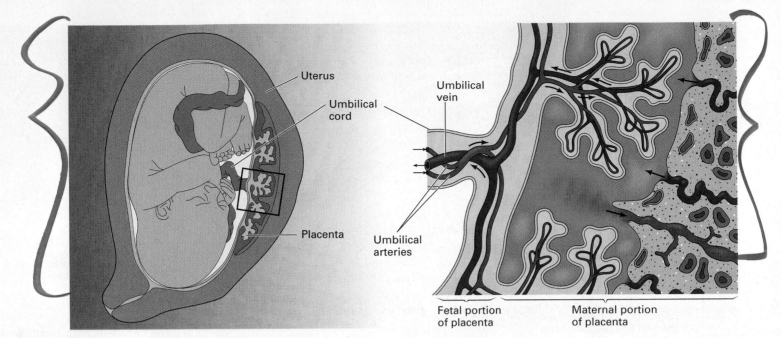

Uterus

Umbilical cord

Placenta

Umbilical vein

Umbilical arteries

Fetal portion of placenta

Maternal portion of placenta

FIGURE 3.2 The Placenta and the Umbilical Cord Maternal blood flows through the uterine arteries to the spaces housing the placenta, and it returns through the uterine veins to the maternal circulation. Fetal blood flows through the umbilical arteries, which transport oxygen-poor blood into the capillaries of the placenta, and returns oxygen-rich blood to the fetal circulation through the umbilical vein. This exchange of materials occurs across the layer separating the maternal and fetal blood supplies, so the maternal blood never comes into contact with the fetal blood. *Note:* The area bounded by the square is enlarged in the right half of the illustration. Arrows indicate the direction of blood flow.

ectoderm The outermost layer of cells, which becomes the nervous system and brain, sensory receptors (ears, nose, and eyes, for example), and skin parts (hair and nails, for example).

mesoderm The middle layer of cells, which becomes the circulatory system, bones, muscles, excretory system, and reproductive system.

amnion The life-support system that is a thin bag or envelope that contains a clear fluid in which the development embryo floats.

umbilical cord Contains two arteries and one vein, and connects the baby to the placenta.

placenta Consists of a disk-shaped group of tissues in which small blood vessels from the mother and the offspring intertwine but don't join.

organogenesis Process of organ formation that takes place during the first two months of prenatal development.

respiratory systems. The **ectoderm** is the outermost layer, which will become the nervous system and brain, sensory receptors (ears, nose, and eyes, for example), and skin parts (hair and nails, for example). The **mesoderm** is the middle layer, which will become the circulatory system, bones, muscles, excretory system, and reproductive system. Every body part eventually develops from these three layers. The endoderm primarily produces internal body parts, the mesoderm primarily produces parts that surround the internal areas, and the ectoderm primarily produces surface parts.

As the embryo's three layers form, life-support systems for the embryo develop rapidly. These life-support systems include the amnion, the umbilical cord (both of which develop from the fertilized egg, not the mother's body), and the placenta. The **amnion** is like a bag or an envelope and contains a clear fluid in which the developing embryo floats. The amniotic fluid provides an environment that is temperature and humidity controlled, as well as shockproof. The **umbilical cord** contains two arteries and one vein, and connects the baby to the placenta. The **placenta** consists of a disk-shaped group of tissues in which small blood vessels from the mother and the offspring intertwine but do not join.

Figure 3.2 illustrates the placenta, the umbilical cord, and the blood flow in the expectant mother and developing organism. Very small molecules—oxygen, water, salt, food from the mother's blood, as well as carbon dioxide and digestive wastes from the offspring's blood—pass back and forth between the mother and embryo or fetus. Large molecules cannot pass through the placental wall; these include red blood cells and harmful substances, such as most bacteria, maternal wastes, and hormones. The mechanisms that govern the transfer of substances across the placental barrier are complex and are still not entirely understood (Giequel & Le Boue, 2006; Xu & others, 2006).

By the time most women know they are pregnant, the major organs have begun to form. **Organogenesis** is the name given to the process of organ formation during the first two months of prenatal development. While they are being formed, the organs are especially vulnerable to environmental changes. In the third week after conception, the neural tube that eventually becomes the spinal cord forms. At about 21 days, eyes begin to appear, and at 24 days the cells for the heart begin to differentiate. During the fourth week, the urogenital system becomes apparent, and arm and leg buds emerge. Four chambers of the heart take shape, and blood vessels appear. From the fifth to the eighth week, arms and legs differentiate further; at this time, the face starts to form but still is not very recognizable. The intestinal tract develops and the facial structures fuse. At eight weeks, the developing organism weighs about 1/30 ounce and is just over 1 inch long.

The Fetal Period

The **fetal period** is the prenatal period of development that begins two months after conception and lasts for seven months, on the average. Growth and development continue their dramatic course during this time.

Three months after conception, the fetus is about 3 inches long and weighs about 3 ounces. It has become active, moving its arms and legs, opening and closing its mouth, and moving its head. The face, forehead, eyelids, nose, and chin are distinguishable, as are the upper arms, lower arms, hands, and lower limbs. The genitals can be identified as male or female. By the end of the fourth month, the fetus has grown to 6 inches in length and weighs 4 to 7 ounces. At this time, a growth spurt occurs in the body's lower parts. For the first time the mother can feel arm and leg movements.

By the end of the fifth month, the fetus is about 12 inches long and weighs close to a pound. Structures of the skin have formed—toenails and fingernails, for example. The fetus is more active, showing a preference for a particular position in the womb. By the end of the sixth month, the fetus is about 14 inches long and has gained another half pound to a pound. The eyes and eyelids are completely formed, and a fine layer of hair covers the head. A grasping reflex is present and irregular breathing movements occur.

At about seven months, the fetus for the first time has a chance of surviving outside of the womb—that is, it is *viable*. But even when infants are born in the seventh month, they usually need help breathing. By the end of the seventh month, the fetus is about 16 inches long and now weighs about 3 pounds.

During the last two months of prenatal development fatty tissues develop, and the functioning of various organ systems—heart and kidneys, for example—steps up. During the eighth and ninth months, the fetus grows longer and gains substantial weight—about another 4 pounds. At birth, the average American baby weighs 7½ pounds and is about 20 inches long.

Figure 3.3 gives an overview of the main events during prenatal development. Notice that instead of describing development in terms of germinal, embryonic, and fetal periods, Figure 3.3 divides prenatal development into equal periods of three months, called *trimesters*. Remember that the three trimesters are not the same as the three prenatal periods we have discussed. The germinal and embryonic periods occur in the first trimester. The fetal period begins toward the end of the first trimester and continues through the second and third trimesters. Viability (the chances of surviving outside the womb) occurs at the beginning of the third trimester.

The Brain

One of the most remarkable aspects of the prenatal period is the development of the brain. By the time babies are born, they have approximately 100 billion **neurons,** or nerve cells, which handle information processing at the cellular level. During prenatal development, neurons spend time moving to the right locations and are starting to become connected. The basic architecture of the human brain is assembled during the first two trimesters of prenatal development. The third trimester of prenatal development and the first two years of postnatal life are characterized by connectivity and functioning of neurons (Nelson, Thomas, & de Haan, 2006).

fetal period The prenatal period of development that begins two months after conception and lasts for seven months, on the average.

neurons The term for nerve cells, which handle information processing at the cellular level.

First trimester (first 3 months)

Prenatal growth	**Conception to 4 weeks**	**8 weeks**	**12 weeks**
	• Is less than ¹/₁₀ inch long • Beginning development of spinal cord, nervous system, gastrointestinal system, heart, and lungs • Amniotic sac envelopes the preliminary tissues of entire body • Is called a "zygote"	• Is just over 1 inch long • Face is forming with rudimentary eyes, ears, mouth, and tooth buds • Arms and legs are moving • Brain is forming • Fetal heartbeat is detectable with ultrasound • Is called an "embryo"	• Is about 3 inches long and weighs about 1 ounce • Can move arms, legs, fingers, and toes • Fingerprints are present • Can smile, frown, suck, and swallow • Sex is distinguishable • Can urinate • Is called a "fetus"

Second trimester (middle 3 months)

Prenatal growth	**16 weeks**	**20 weeks**	**24 weeks**
	• Is about 6 inches long and weighs about 4 to 7 ounces • Heartbeat is strong • Skin is thin, transparent • Downy hair (lanugo) covers body • Fingernails and toenails are forming • Has coordinated movements; is able to roll over in amniotic fluid	• Is 10 to 12 inches long and weighs ½ to 1 pound • Heartbeat is audible with ordinary stethoscope • Sucks thumb • Hiccups • Hair, eyelashes, eyebrows are present	• Is 11 to 14 inches long and weighs 1 to 1½ pounds • Skin is wrinkled and covered with protective coating (vernix caseosa) • Eyes are open • Waste matter is collected in bowel • Has strong grip

Third trimester (last 3 months)

Prenatal growth	**28 weeks**	**32 weeks**	**36 to 38 weeks**
	• Is 14 to 17 inches long and weighs 2½ to 3 pounds • Is adding body fat • Is very active • Rudimentary breathing movements are present	• Is 16½ to 18 inches long and weighs 4 to 5 pounds • Has periods of sleep and wakefulness • Responds to sounds • May assume the birth position • Bones of head are soft and flexible • Iron is being stored in liver	• Is 19 to 20 inches long and weighs 6 to 7½ pounds • Skin is less wrinkled • Vernix caseosa is thick • Lanugo is mostly gone • Is less active • Is gaining immunities from mother

FIGURE 3.3 The Three Trimesters of Prenatal Development Both the germinal and embryonic periods occur during the first trimester. The end of the first trimester as well as the second and third trimesters are part of the fetal period.

As the human embryo develops inside its mother's womb, the nervous system begins forming as a long, hollow tube located on the embryo's back. This pear-shaped *neural tube*, which forms at about 18 to 24 days after conception, develops out of the ectoderm. The tube closes at the top and bottom ends at about 24 days after conception. Figure 3.4 shows that the nervous system still has a tubular appearance six weeks after conception.

Two birth defects related to a failure of the neural tube to close are anencephaly and spina bifida. The highest regions of the brain fail to develop when fetuses have anencephaly, and they die in the womb, during childbirth, or shortly after birth (Koukoura & others, 2006). Spina bifida results in varying degrees of paralysis of the lower limbs (Ghi & others, 2006). Individuals with spina bifida usually need assistive devices such as crutches, braces, or wheelchairs. A strategy that can help to prevent neural tube defects is for women to take adequate amounts of the B vitamin folic acid, a topic we further discuss later in the chapter (Bell & Oakley, 2006; Pitkin, 2007).

In a normal pregnancy, once the neural tube has closed, a massive proliferation of new immature neurons begins to take place about the fifth prenatal week and continues throughout the remainder of the prenatal period. The generation of new neurons is called **neurogenesis.** At the peak of neurogenesis, it is estimated that as many as 200,000 neurons are being generated every minute (Brown, Keynes, & Lumsden, 2001).

At approximately 6 to 24 weeks after conception, *neuronal migration* occurs (Couperus & Nelson, 2006). This involves cells moving outward from their point of origin to their appropriate locations and creating the different levels, structures, and regions of the brain (Hepper, 2007). Once a cell has migrated to its target destination, it must mature and develop a more complex structure. In the 20th to 23rd prenatal weeks, connections between neurons begin to occur, a process that continues postnatally. We have much more to say about the more complex structure of neurons, their connectivity, and the development of the brain in infancy in Chapter 5.

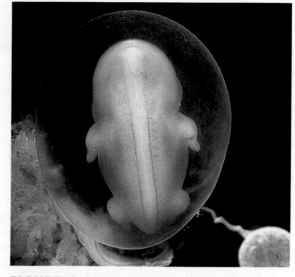

FIGURE 3.4 Early Formation of the Nervous System The photograph shows the primitive, tubular appearance of the nervous system at 6 weeks in the human embryo.

These individuals are members of the Spina Bifida Association of Greater New Orleans. The association is made up of parents, family members, children, and adults with spina bifida, and health professionals who provide care for individuals born with spina bifida and their families.

REVIEW AND REFLECT ◆ LEARNING GOAL 1

① Discuss the three periods of prenatal development.

Review
- How can the germinal period be characterized?
- What is the embryonic period like?
- How can the fetal period be described?
- How does the brain develop in the prenatal period?

Reflect
- What is the most important thing you learned in the section on exploring prenatal development that you did not previously know?

neurogenesis The formation of new neurons.

② WHAT ARE EXPECTANT PARENTS' EXPERIENCES LIKE DURING PRENATAL DEVELOPMENT?

Confirming the Pregnancy and Calculating the Due Date

The Expectant Mother's Nutrition, Weight Gain, and Exercise

Prenatal Care

The Three Trimesters and Preparation for Birth

Most pregnancies involve prenatal development that results in a healthy baby. In this section, we explore the experiences of expectant parents during prenatal development and examine ways to maximize the likelihood of having a healthy baby.

For many people, becoming parents is one of the greatest life changes they will experience. Parenthood is permanent, and the physical and emotional nurturing of a child is both a time-intensive responsibility and a wonderful opportunity. So far, most of our discussion has focused on the embryo and the fetus, but it is also important to examine the effects of pregnancy on the expectant parents. An important first consideration is to confirm the pregnancy and then to calculate the due date. Then, as the pregnancy proceeds, a number of family issues emerge in the first, second, and third trimesters of pregnancy.

Confirming the Pregnancy and Calculating the Due Date

Although pregnancy can be detected soon after conception, a woman might not suspect she is pregnant until she has missed a menstrual period. A pregnancy test checks the woman's urine or blood for human chorionic gonadotropin (HCG), a hormone produced during pregnancy. If a woman thinks she is pregnant, she should have her pregnancy confirmed early, so she can obtain prenatal care, avoid environmental hazards, and give special attention to nutritional needs. Figure 3.5 describes the early signs and symptoms of pregnancy.

Fetal life begins with the fertilization of the ovum, which occurs about two weeks after the woman's last menstrual period. However, the length of the pregnancy is calculated from the first day of the woman's last menstrual period and lasts an average of 280 days, or 40 weeks. When a doctor or midwife says that a woman is eight weeks pregnant, it means that the fetus is six weeks old. Birth is likely to occur anytime between two weeks before and after the so-called due date. Approximately two-thirds of all babies are born within 10 days of their due dates.

The Three Trimesters and Preparation for Birth

A common way of thinking about issues that arise during pregnancy is in terms of pregnancy's trimesters. Each of the three phases of prenatal development contains major milestones including the expectant mother's physical and emotional changes, feeling the baby's first movements, and adjustments in the parents' sexual activity.

The First Trimester Earlier in this chapter, we learned that the first three calendar months of pregnancy (the first trimester) is a time when prenatal organ systems are being formed and begin to function. For the pregnant woman, the first trimester is a time of physical and emotional adjustment to her pregnant state.

The expectant mother may feel extraordinarily tired and require more sleep because of the new demands on her energy and because of the subsequent shift in her metabolic rate, especially in the second and third months of pregnancy. She also may experience nausea and vomiting during the early months of pregnancy.

- Missed menstrual period

- Breast changes—a heavy and full feeling, tenderness, tingling in the nipple area, and a darkened areola

- Fullness or aching in the lower abdomen

- Fatigue and drowsiness, faintness

- Nausea, vomiting, or both

- Frequent urination

- Increased vaginal secretions

FIGURE 3.5 Early Signs and Symptoms of Pregnancy

Although this is usually referred to as pregnancy sickness or "morning sickness," it can occur at any time of day and may be caused by human chorionic gonadotropin, produced by the developing placenta.

Although the female's breasts develop in puberty, the glandular tissue that produces milk does not completely develop until the woman becomes pregnant. As the levels of estrogen and other hormones change during pregnancy, the expectant mother's breasts change. They enlarge, veins are often more prominent, and a tingling sensation is often felt in the nipples. The expectant mother may also need to urinate more frequently as the enlarging uterus puts increased pressure on the bladder. In addition, her vagina and cervix become bluish in color, the cervix becomes softer, and vaginal secretions increase.

Emotional changes accompany physical changes in the early months of pregnancy. It is not unusual for the expectant mother to experience emotional ups and downs. The thought of motherhood may at times be pleasing or disturbing. Mood swings, such as crying, may be difficult to understand, for both the expectant mother and her partner.

Finding out that she is pregnant may bring about a mixture of emotions not only in the expectant mother but also in her partner: pride in the ability to produce a child; fear of losing independence; apprehension about changes in the marital relationship; doubts about one's ability to parent; and happiness about becoming parents. Sharing thoughts and feelings with each other can help expectant couples develop a closer relationship during the transition to parenthood.

A couple's sexual relationship may change during the first trimester. The expectant mother may experience an increased interest in spontaneous sexual activity because she no longer has to worry about trying to become pregnant or about avoiding pregnancy, or an expectant mother's sexual interest may decrease because of fatigue, nausea, breast changes, or fear of miscarriage. The expectant couple should discuss their feelings about sexual intercourse and do what is mutually desired.

Expectant parents benefit from a parent education class on pregnancy and prenatal development in the first trimester of pregnancy. It is important for expectant parents to become knowledgeable about the nature of pregnancy and prenatal development.

The Second Trimester During the middle months of pregnancy, the expectant mother will probably feel better than she did earlier or than she will later. Nausea and fatigue usually lessen or disappear. As the baby's growth continues, the expectant mother's uterus expands into the abdominal cavity. By the end of the fifth month of pregnancy, the top of the uterus (called the fundus) reaches the navel. During monthly visits, the physician or caregiver measures the height of the fundus to ensure that the fetus is growing adequately and to estimate the length of the pregnancy. The expectant mother's breasts do not increase much in size during the second trimester, but colostrum (a yellowish fluid produced before breast milk) is usually present in the milk glands by the middle of pregnancy. This is the time for expectant mothers to begin preparing their breasts for breast feeding if they have decided to breast feed the baby.

Psychological changes accompany physical changes in the second trimester in response to advancing pregnancy and a changing body. Some expectant mothers enjoy how they look; others consider themselves unattractive, inconvenienced, and restricted.

During the second trimester, pregnancy becomes more of a reality for the expectant mother's partner. The baby's movement can be felt by a hand placed on the abdomen or when she is in close contact with her partner. This contact with the baby may increase her partner's feelings of closeness and interest in the pregnancy. A woman's partner may or may not like the changing appearance of the expectant mother. In a normal pregnancy, the expectant couple can continue to have sexual intercourse without harming the fetus, which is believed to be adequately protected from penetrations and the strong contractions that sometimes accompany orgasm.

In the third trimester of pregnancy, the expectant couple may feel protective of the developing baby. *What are some good communication strategies between the expectant mother and her partner about their needs?*

How much do you know about prenatal development and maintaining a healthy pregnancy? How much weight gain on average should occur during pregnancy?

The Third Trimester During the third trimester, the expectant mother's uterus expands to a level just below her breastbone. Crowding by the uterus, in addition to high levels of progesterone, may give the expectant mother heartburn and indigestion. She may also experience shortness of breath as her uterus presses upward on her diaphragm and ribs. Varicose veins in the legs, hemorrhoids, and swollen ankles sometimes appear because of the increased pressure within the abdomen, the decreased blood return from the lower limbs, and the effect of progesterone, which relaxes the walls of the blood vessels.

By the ninth month, the expectant mother often looks forward to the end of the pregnancy, relief from physical restrictions, and the long-awaited joy of having the baby. She may become more introspective and, at times, worry about labor, birth, and the baby. Through childbirth classes, the expectant couple can learn more about how to cope with the stress of the latter part of pregnancy. In Chapter 4, we discuss different types of childbirth and childbirth classes.

In the third trimester of pregnancy, the expectant couple may feel protective of the developing baby. Adjustments in sexual activity continue as the expectant mother's abdomen enlarges. Lines of communication should be open between the expectant mother and her partner about their needs, feelings, and desires.

Preparation for the Baby's Birth About two weeks before the baby's birth, the expectant mother's profile may change as the fetus descends into the pelvic cavity. The expectant mother may now feel less pressure on her diaphragm and thus find it easier to breathe and eat. However, because the head of the fetus can press on the expectant mother's bladder, she may need to urinate more frequently.

Toward the end of the pregnancy, noticeable contractions of the uterus (called Braxton Hicks contractions) increase in frequency. These contractions, which have occurred intermittently throughout pregnancy and which may or may not be felt by the expectant mother, help increase the efficiency of uterine circulation. Though usually not directly associated with labor, these contractions prepare the uterine muscles for labor. As the pregnancy comes to an end, and the baby's head presses against the expectant mother's pelvis, her cervix becomes softer and thinner. This thinning is a sign of readiness for labor and birth.

Awkwardness and fatigue may add to the expectant mother's desire for the pregnancy to end. She may feel as if she has been and will be pregnant forever. At the same time, the expectant mother may feel a "nesting urge" in the form of a spurt of energy that often results in preparations for the arrival of the new baby. She now visits her physician or midwife more often as these physical changes signal that her body is preparing for labor and birth.

The Expectant Mother's Nutrition, Weight Gain, and Exercise

The mother's nutrition can have a strong influence on the development of the fetus. Here we discuss the mother's nutritional needs and optimal nutrition during pregnancy, as well as the role of exercise in the expectant mother's health.

Nutrition and Weight Gain The best assurance of an adequate caloric intake during pregnancy is a satisfactory weight gain over time (Butte & King, 2005; London & others, 2007). The optimal weight gain depends on the expectant mother's height, bone structure, and prepregnant nutritional state. However, maternal weight gains that average from 25 to 35 pounds are associated with the best reproductive outcomes.

Approximately one-third of pregnant women gain more than this recommended amount (Cogswell & others, 2001). Maternal obesity adversely impacts pregnancy outcomes through increased rates of hypertension, diabetes, respiratory complications, and infections in the mother (Villamor & Cnattinguis, 2006). Also, pregnancies in obese women are characterized by a high incidence of neural tube defects, preterm deliveries, and late fetal deaths (Siega-Riz, Siega-Riz, & Laraia, 2006). We further discuss obesity as a potential hazard to prenatal development later in the chapter.

The pattern of weight gain is also important. The ideal pattern of weight gain during pregnancy is 2 to 4.4 pounds during the first trimester, followed by an average gain of 1 pound per week during the last two trimesters. In the second trimester, most of the weight gain is due to increased blood volume; the enlargement of breasts, uterus, and associated tissue and fluid; and the deposit of maternal fat. In the third trimester, weight gain mainly involves the fetus, placenta, and amniotic fluid. A 25-pound weight gain during pregnancy is generally distributed in this way: 11 pounds: fetus, placenta, and amniotic fluid; 5 pounds: maternal stores; 4 pounds: increased blood volume; 3 pounds: tissue fluid; and 2 pounds: uterus and breasts.

During the second and third trimesters, inadequate gains of less than 2.2 pounds per month or excessive gains of more than 6.6 pounds per month should be evaluated and the need for nutritional counseling considered. Inadequate weight gain has been associated with low birth weight infants. Sudden sharp increases in weight of 3 to 5 pounds in a week may result from fluid retention and may require evaluation.

The recommended daily allowance (RDA) for all nutrients increases during pregnancy. The expectant mother should eat three meals a day, with nutritious snacks of fruits, cheese, milk, or other foods between meals if desired. More frequent, smaller meals also are recommended. Water is an essential nutrient. Four to six 8-ounce glasses of water and a total of 8 to 10 cups (64 to 80 ounces) of total fluid should be consumed daily. The need for protein, iron, vitamin D, folacin, calcium, phosphorus, and magnesium increases by 50 percent or more. Recommended increases for other nutrients range from 15 to 40 percent (see Figure 3.6). Researchers have recently found that women who take a multivitamin prior to pregnancy may be at a reduced risk for delivering a preterm infant (Vahratian & others, 2004).

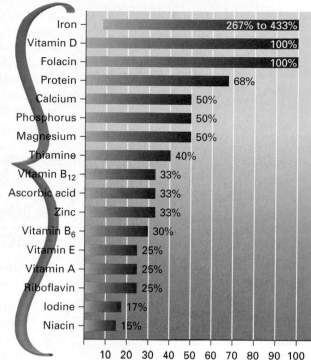

FIGURE 3.6 Recommended Nutrient Increases for Expectant Mothers

Exercise   How much and what type of exercise is best during pregnancy depends to some degree on the course of the pregnancy, the expectant mother's fitness, and her customary activity level (Kramer & McDonald, 2006; Schmidt & others, 2006). Normal participation in exercise can continue throughout an uncomplicated pregnancy. In general, the skilled sportswoman is no longer discouraged from participating in sports she participated in prior to her pregnancy. However, pregnancy is not the appropriate time to begin strenuous activity.

Because of the increased emphasis on physical fitness in our society, more women routinely jog as part of a physical fitness program prior to pregnancy. There are few concerns about continuing to jog during the early part of pregnancy, but in the latter part of pregnancy there is some concern about the jarring effect of jogging on the breasts and abdomen. As pregnancy progresses, low-impact activities, such as walking, swimming, and bicycling, are safer and provide fitness as well as greater comfort, eliminating the bouncing associated with jogging.

Exercise during pregnancy helps prevent constipation, conditions the body, and is associated with a more positive mental state (Paisley, Joy, & Price, 2003; Poudevigne & O'Conner, 2006). However, it is important to remember to not overdo it. Pregnant women should always consult their physician before starting any exercise program.

Might the mother's exercise during pregnancy be related to the development of the fetus and the birth of the child? Few studies have been conducted on this topic, but recently several studies indicated that moderate exercise three to four times a week was linked to healthy weight gain in the fetus and a normal birth weight, whereas the risk of low birth weight increased for women who exercised intensely most days of the week and for women who exercised less than twice a week or not at all (Campbell & Mottola, 2001).

Elizabeth Noble is a physical therapist and childbirth educator who has influenced many women to engage in prenatal and postnatal exercise. To read about her work, see the *Careers in Child Development* profile. We discuss some guidelines for exercise in the following *Caring for Children* interlude.

Caring for Children

EXERCISE GUIDELINES FOR EXPECTANT MOTHERS

These guidelines for exercise are recommended for expectant mothers (Olds, London, & Ladewig, 1988, pp. 387–388):

- *"Exercise for shorter intervals.* By exercising for 10 to 15 minutes, resting for a few minutes, and then exercising for an additional 10 to 15 minutes, the woman decreases potential problems associated with the shunting of blood to the musculoskeletal system and away from organs, such as the uterus."
- *"As pregnancy progresses, decrease the intensity of exercise.* This helps compensate for the decreased cardiac reserve, increased respiratory effort, and increased weight of the pregnant woman."
- *"Avoid prolonged overheating.* Strenuous exercise, especially in a humid environment, can raise the core body temperature" and increase the risk of fetal problems. Remember to avoid overheating in saunas and hot tubs.
- *"As pregnancy increases, avoid high-risk activities such as skydiving, mountain climbing, racquetball, and surfing."* An expectant mother's changed center of gravity and softened joints may decrease her coordination and increase the risk of falls and injuries in such sports.
- *"Warm up and stretch to help prepare the joints for activity, and cool down with a period of mild activity to help restore circulation. . . ."*
- *"After exercising, lie on the left side for ten minutes to rest.* This improves return of circulation from the extremities. . . ."
- *"Wear supportive shoes and a supportive bra."*
- *"Stop exercising and contact the caregiver if dizziness, shortness of breath, tingling, numbness, vaginal bleeding, or abdominal pain occur."*
- *"Reduce exercise significantly during the last four weeks of pregnancy.* Some evidence suggests that strenuous exercise near term increases the risk of low birth weight, stillbirth, and infant death. . . ."*

Prenatal Care

Although prenatal care varies enormously, it usually involves a defined schedule of visits for medical care, which typically include screening for manageable conditions and treatable diseases that can affect the baby or the mother (Kuppermann & others, 2006). In addition to medical care, prenatal programs often include comprehensive educational, social, and nutritional services (Massey, Rising, & Ickovics, 2006; Moos, 2006).

The education provided in prenatal care varies during the course of pregnancy. Those in the early stages of pregnancy, as well as couples who are anticipating a pregnancy, may participate in early prenatal classes (Davidson, London, & Ladewig,

2008). In addition to providing information on dangers to the fetus, early prenatal classes often discuss the development of the embryo and the fetus; sexuality during pregnancy; choices about the birth setting and care providers; nutrition, rest, and exercise; common discomforts of pregnancy and relief measures; psychological changes in the expectant mother and her partner; and factors that increase the risk of preterm labor and possible symptoms of preterm labor. Early classes also may include information about the advantages and disadvantages of breast feeding and bottle feeding (50 to 80 percent of expectant mothers decide how they will feed their infant prior to the sixth month of pregnancy). During the second or third trimester of pregnancy, prenatal classes focus on preparing for the birth, infant care and feeding, choices about birth, and postpartum self-care.

An innovative program that is rapidly expanding in the United States is CenteringPregnancy (Massey, Rising, & Ickovics, 2006; Moos, 2006). This program is relationship-centered and provides complete prenatal care in a group setting. CenteringPregnancy replaces traditional 15-minute physician visits with 90-minute peer group support settings and self-examination led by a physician or certified nurse-midwife. Groups of up to 10 women (and often their partners) meet regularly beginning at 12 to 16 weeks of pregnancy. The sessions emphasize empowering women to play an active role in experiencing a positive pregnancy.

Does prenatal care matter? Information about pregnancy, labor, delivery, and caring for the newborn can be especially valuable for first-time mothers (Chang & others, 2003). Prenatal care is also very important for women in poverty because it links them with other social services (Hogan & others, 2007). The legacy of prenatal care continues after the birth because women who experience this type of care are more likely to get preventive care for their infants (Bates & others, 1994).

Research contrasting the experiences of mothers who had prenatal care and those who did not supports the significance of prenatal care (Chen & others, 2007a, Daniels, Noe, & Mayberry, 2006). One study found that U.S. women who had no prenatal care were far more likely than their counterparts who received prenatal care to have infants who had low birth weight, increased mortality, and a number of other physical problems (Herbst & others, 2003). In other recent studies, low birth weight and preterm deliveries were common among U.S. mothers who received no prenatal care, and the absence of prenatal care increased the risk for preterm birth by almost threefold in both non-Latino White and African American women (Stringer & others, 2005).

Inadequate prenatal care may help explain a disturbing fact: rates of infant mortality and low birth weight indicate that many other nations have healthier babies than the United States (Thornton & others, 2006). In many countries that have a lower percentage of low birth weight infants than the United States, mothers

Careers
in CHILD DEVELOPMENT

Elizabeth Noble
Physical Therapist and Childbirth Educator

Elizabeth Noble grew up in Australia where she obtained undergraduate degrees in physiotherapy, philosophy, and anthropology. She moved to the United States in the 1970s and founded the Women's Health section of the American Physical Therapy Association.

Dr. Noble has authored numerous books such as *Essential Exercises for the Childbearing Years*. She also is a consultant, lecturer, and workshop leader. More than 2,000 instructors in prenatal and postpartum exercise have been trained by Dr. Noble. Currently, she is the director of Women's Health Resources in Harwich, Massachusetts.

Elizabeth Noble, demonstrating an effective postpartum exercise.

A CenteringPregnancy program. This rapidly increasing program alters routine prenatal care by bringing women out of exam rooms and into relationship-oriented groups.

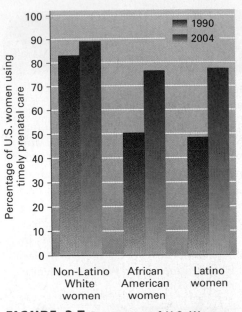

FIGURE 3.7 Percentage of U.S. Women Using Timely Prenatal Care: 1990 to 2004 From 1990 to 2004, the use of timely prenatal care increased by 7 percent (to 89.1) for non-Latino White women, by 25 percent (to 76.5) for African American women, and by 28 percent (to 77.4) for Latino women in the United States.

receive either free or very low cost prenatal and postnatal care, and can receive paid maternity leave from work that ranges from 9 to 40 weeks. In Norway and the Netherlands, prenatal care is coordinated with a general practitioner, an obstetrician, and a midwife.

Why do some U.S. women receive inadequate prenatal care? Sometimes the reasons are tied to the health-care system, to provider practices, and to their own individual and social characteristics (Conway & Kutinova, 2006). Women who do not want to be pregnant, who have negative attitudes about being pregnant, or who unintentionally become pregnant are more likely to delay prenatal care or to miss appointments. As we noted earlier, adolescent girls are less likely than adult women to obtain prenatal care. Within the United States, there are differences among ethnic groups both in the health of babies and in prenatal care (Madan & others, 2006; Wasserman, Bender, & Lee, 2007). In the 1980s, more than one-fifth of all non-Latino White mothers and one-third of all African American mothers did not receive prenatal care in the first trimester of their pregnancy, and 5 percent of White mothers and 10 percent of African American mothers received no prenatal care at all (Wegman, 1987).

The situation has been improving. From 1990 to 2004, the use of timely prenatal care increased for women from a variety of ethnic backgrounds in the United States, although non-Latino White women were still more likely to obtain prenatal care than African American and Latino women (Martin & others, 2005) (see Figure 3.7). The United States needs more comprehensive medical and educational services to improve the quality of prenatal care and to reduce the number of low birth weight and preterm infants (Daniels, Noe, & Mayberry, 2006; Thornton & others, 2006).

Cultures around the world have differing views of pregnancy than the United States. In the *Diversity in Children's Development* interlude that follows, we explore these beliefs.

Diversity in Children's Development

CULTURAL BELIEFS ABOUT PREGNANCY

All cultures have beliefs and practices that surround life's major events, and one such event is pregnancy. When a woman who immigrated to the United States becomes pregnant, the beliefs and practices of her native culture may be as important as, or more so than, those of the mainstream U.S. culture that now surrounds her. The conflict between cultural tradition and Western medicine may pose a risk for the pregnancy and a challenge for the health-care professional who wishes to give proper care while respecting the woman's values.

The American Public Health Association (2006) has identified a variety of cultural beliefs and practices that are observed among various immigrant groups, such as:

- *Food cravings.* Latin American, Asian, and some African cultures believe that it is important for a pregnant woman's food cravings to be satisfied because they are thought to be the cravings of the baby. If cravings are left unsatisfied, the baby might take on certain unpleasant personality and/or physical traits, perhaps characteristic of the food (Taylor, Ko, & Pan, 1999). As an example, in African cultures women often eat soil, chalk, or clay during pregnancy; this is believed to satisfy the baby's hunger as well as affirming soil as a symbol of female fertility (American Public Health Association, 2006).

- *"Hot-cold" theory of illness.* Many cultures in Latin America, Asia, and Africa characterize foods, medications, and illnesses as "hot" or "cold"; this has nothing to do with temperature or spiciness, but with traditional definitions and categories. Most of these cultures view pregnancy as a "hot" condition, although the Chinese view it as "cold" (Taylor, Ko, & Pan, 1999). As a result, a woman may resist taking a prescribed medication because of concern that it could create too much "heat" and cause a miscarriage; in Indian culture iron-rich foods are also considered unacceptably "hot" for pregnant women (DeSantis, 1998).

- *Extended family.* In many immigrant cultures, the extended family is a vital support system, and health-care decisions are made based on the needs of the family over those of the individual. Western health-care providers need to be sensitive to this dynamic, which runs counter to today's practices of protecting patient confidentiality and autonomy.

- *Stoicism.* In many Asian cultures, stoicism is valued, as suffering is seen as part of life (Uba, 1992). Physicians are also viewed with great respect. As a result, a pregnant Asian woman may behave submissively and avoid voicing complaints to her health-care provider, but may privately fail to follow the provider's advice (Assanand & others, 1990).

In India, a midwife checks on the size, position, and heartbeat of a fetus. Midwives deliver babies in many cultures around the world. *What are some cultural variations in prenatal care?*

Some cultures treat pregnancy simply as a natural occurrence; others see it as a medical condition (Walsh, 2006). How expectant mothers behave during pregnancy may depend in part on the prevalence of traditional home-care remedies and folk beliefs, the importance of indigenous healers, and the influence of health-care professionals in their culture. In various cultures, women may consult herbalists and/or faith healers during pregnancy (Mbonye, Neema, & Magnussen, 2006).

Health-care workers should assess whether a woman's beliefs or practices pose a threat to her or the fetus. If they do, health-care professionals should consider a culturally sensitive way to handle the problem (Jansen, 2006).

REVIEW AND REFLECT ▸ LEARNING GOAL 2

2 **Characterize expectant parents' experiences during prenatal development.**

Review
- How can the pregnancy be confirmed and the due date calculated?
- What are some positive strategies for expectant parents in the three trimesters of prenatal development and preparation for the birth?
- What are some recommendations for the expectant mother's nutrition, weight gain, and exercise?
- What are some important aspects of prenatal care?

Reflect
- What are some beliefs about pregnancy and prenatal development in your culture?

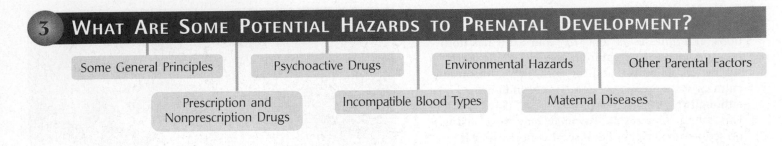

For Alex, the baby discussed at the opening of this chapter, the course of prenatal development went smoothly. His mother's womb protected him as he developed. Despite this protection, the environment can affect the embryo or fetus in many well-documented ways.

Some General Principles

A **teratogen** is any agent that can potentially cause a birth defect or negatively alter cognitive and behavioral outcomes. (The word comes from the Greek word *tera*, meaning "monster"). The field of study that investigates the causes of birth defects is called *teratology*. Teratogens include drugs, incompatible blood types, environmental pollutants, infectious diseases, nutritional deficiencies, maternal stress, advanced maternal and paternal age, and environmental pollutants. In fact, thousands of babies are born deformed or mentally retarded every year as a result of events that occurred in the mother's life as early as one or two months *before* conception. As we further discuss teratogens, you will see that factors related to the father also can influence prenatal development.

So many teratogens exist that practically every fetus is exposed to at least some teratogens. For this reason, it is difficult to determine which teratogen causes which problem. In addition, it may take a long time for the effects of a teratogen to show up. Only about half of all potential effects appear at birth.

The dose, genetic susceptibility, and the time of exposure to a particular teratogen influence both the severity of the damage to an embryo or fetus and the type of defect:

- *Dose.* The dose effect is rather obvious—the greater the dose of an agent, such as a drug, the greater the effect.
- *Genetic susceptibility.* The type or severity of abnormalities caused by a teratogen is linked to the genotype of the pregnant woman and the genotype of the embryo or fetus (Lidral & Murray, 2005). For example, how a mother metabolizes a particular drug can influence the degree to which the drug effects are transmitted to the embryo or fetus. Differences in placental membranes and placental transport also affect exposure. The extent to which an embryo or fetus is vulnerable to a teratogen may also depend on its genotype (Graham & Shaw, 2005).
- *Time of exposure.* Teratogens do more damage when they occur at some points in development than at others (Nava-Ocampo & Koren, 2007; Rifas-Shiman & others, 2006). Damage during the germinal period may even prevent implantation. In general, the embryonic period is more vulnerable than the fetal period.

Figure 3.8 summarizes additional information about the effects of time of exposure to a teratogen. The probability of a structural defect is greatest early in the embryonic period, when organs are being formed (Hill, 2007). Each body structure has its own critical period of formation. Recall from Chapter 1 that a *critical period* is a fixed time period very early in development during which certain experiences or events can have a long-lasting effect on development. The critical period for the nervous system (week 3) is earlier than for arms and legs (weeks 4 and 5).

After organogenesis is complete, teratogens are less likely to cause anatomical defects. Instead, exposure during the fetal period is more likely instead to stunt

teratogen From the Greek word *tera*, meaning "monster," any agent that can potentially cause a birth defect on negatively alter cognitive or behavioral outcomes. The field of study that investigates the causes of birth defects is called teratology.

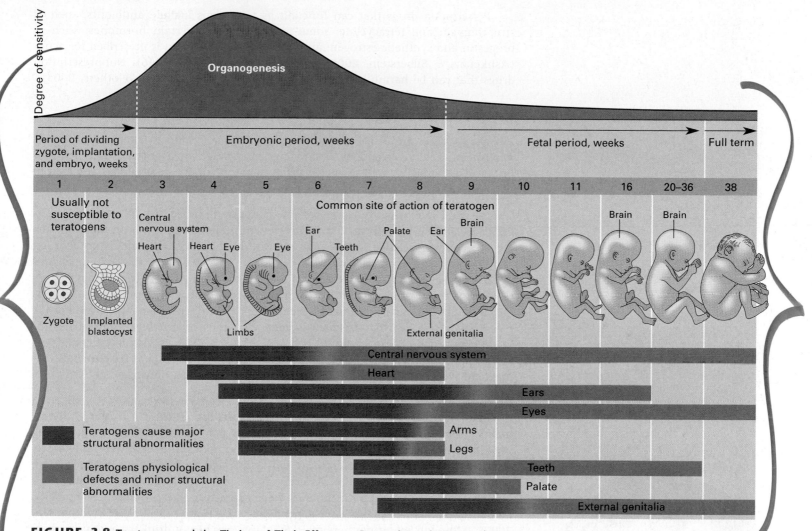

FIGURE 3.8 Teratogens and the Timing of Their Effects on Prenatal Development The danger of structural defects caused by teratogens is greatest early in embryonic development. The period of organogenesis (red color) lasts for about six weeks. Later assaults by teratogens (blue color) mainly occur in the fetal period and instead of causing structural damage are more likely to stunt growth or cause problems of organ function.

growth or to create problems in the way organs function. To examine some key teratogens and their effects, let's begin with drugs.

Prescription and Nonprescription Drugs

Many U.S. women are given prescriptions for drugs while they are pregnant—especially antibiotics, analgesics, and asthma medications (Riley & others, 2005). Prescription as well as nonprescription drugs, however, may have effects on the embryo or fetus that the women never imagined.

The damage that drugs can do was tragically highlighted in 1961, when many pregnant women took a popular tranquilizer, thalidomide, to alleviate their morning sickness. In adults, the effects of thalidomide are mild; in embryos, however, they are devastating. Not all infants were affected in the same way. If the mother took thalidomide on day 26 (probably before she knew she was pregnant), an arm might not grow. If she took the drug two days later, the arm might not grow past the elbow. The thalidomide tragedy shocked the medical community and parents and taught a valuable lesson: taking the wrong drug at the wrong time is enough to physically handicap the offspring for life (Knobloch, Shaughnessy, & Ruther, 2007).

Prescription drugs that can function as teratogens include antibiotics, such as streptomycin and tetracycline; some antidepressants; certain hormones, such as progestin and synthetic estrogen; and Accutane (which often is prescribed for acne) (Ashkenazi & Silberstein, 2006; Scheinfeld & Bangalore, 2006). Nonprescription drugs that can be harmful include diet pills and aspirin (Norgard & others, 2005).

Psychoactive Drugs

Psychoactive drugs are drugs that act on the nervous system to alter states of consciousness, modify perceptions, and change moods. Examples include caffeine, alcohol, and nicotine, as well as illegal drugs such as cocaine, marijuana, and heroin (Alvik & others, 2006)).

Caffeine   People often consume caffeine by drinking coffee, tea, or colas, or by eating chocolate (Bech & others, 2007). A review of studies on caffeine consumption during pregnancy concluded that a small increase in the risks for spontaneous abortion and low birth weight occurs for pregnant women consuming more than 150 milligrams of caffeine—approximately two cups of brewed coffee or two to three 12-ounce cans of cola—per day (Fernandez & others, 1998). (Low birth weight is linked to a variety of health and developmental problems, which we discuss later in the chapter.) A recent study revealed that pregnant women who consumed 300 or more milligrams of caffeine a day had an increased risk of fetal death (Matijasevich & others, 2006). Taking into account such results, the Food and Drug Administration recommends that pregnant women either not consume caffeine or consume it only sparingly.

Alcohol   Heavy drinking by pregnant women can be devastating to offspring (Shankaran & others, 2007). **Fetal alcohol syndrome (FAS)** is a cluster of abnormalities that appears in the offspring of mothers who drink alcohol heavily during pregnancy. The abnormalities include facial deformities and defective limbs, face, and heart. Most of these children are below average in intelligence, and some are mentally retarded (Abel, 2006). A recent study revealed that as young adults individuals diagnosed with FAS in infancy were characterized by intellectual disability, limited occupational options, and dependent living (Spohr, Willms, & Steinhausen, 2007). Although many mothers of FAS infants are heavy drinkers, many mothers who are heavy drinkers do not have children with FAS or have one child with FAS and other children who do not have it.

Drinking alcohol during pregnancy, however, can have serious effects on offspring even when they are not afflicted with FAS (Pollard, 2007; Sayal & others, 2007). One study found that prenatal exposure to binge drinking was linked to a greater likelihood of having IQ scores in the mentally retarded range and a higher incidence of acting-out behavior at seven years of age (Bailey & others, 2004). Serious malformations such as those produced by FAS are not found in infants born to mothers who are moderate drinkers, but even moderate drinking can have an effect on the offspring (Burden & others, 2005). In one study, children whose mothers drank moderately (one to two drinks a day) during pregnancy were less attentive and alert, even at 4 years of age (Streissguth & others, 1984). Also, one study found that pregnant women who had three or more drinks a day faced an increased risk of preterm birth (Parazzini & others, 2003). And in a longitudinal study, the more alcohol mothers drank in the first trimester of pregnancy, the more 14-year-olds fell behind on growth markers such as weight, height, and head size (Day & others, 2002).

What are some guidelines for alcohol use during pregnancy? Even drinking just one or two servings of beer or wine or one serving of hard liquor a few days a week can have negative effects on the fetus, although it is generally agreed that this level of alcohol use will not cause fetal alcohol syndrome. The U.S. Surgeon General recommends that *no* alcohol be consumed during pregnancy. And recent research suggests that it may not be wise to consume alcohol at the time of conception. One study revealed that "both male and female alcohol intakes during the week of conception increased the risk of early pregnancy loss" (Henriksen & others, 2004, p. 661).

A child with fetal alcohol syndrome. Notice the wide-set eyes, flat cheekbones, and thin upper lip.

fetal alcohol syndrome (FAS) A cluster of abnormalities that appears in the offspring of mothers who drink alcohol heavily during pregnancy.

Nicotine Cigarette smoking by pregnant women can also adversely influence prenatal development, birth, and postnatal development (Noakes & others, 2007; Slykerman & others, 2007). Preterm births and low birth weights, fetal and neonatal deaths, respiratory problems and sudden infant death syndrome (SIDS, also known as crib death) are all more common among the offspring of mothers who smoked during pregnancy (Adgent, 2006; Roza & others, 2007). Prenatal exposure to heavy smoking has been linked in one study to nicotine withdrawal symptoms in newborns (Godding & others, 2004). Prenatal exposure to cigarette smoking during pregnancy is also related to increased incidence of attention deficit hyperactivity disorder at 5 to 16 years of age (Thapar & others, 2003).

One analysis indicated a decline in smoking during pregnancy from 1990 to 2002, although smoking by pregnant adolescents still remained high (Centers for Disease Control and Prevention, 2004). Intervention programs designed to help pregnant women stop smoking can reduce some of smoking's negative effects, especially by raising birth weights (Barron & others, 2007; Klesges & others, 2001). To read further about the negative outcomes for smoking during pregnancy, see the *Research in Children's Development* interlude.

What are some links between Expectant mothers' cigarette smoking and outcomes for their offspring?

Research in Children's Development

EXPECTANT MOTHERS' CIGARETTE SMOKING AND CIGARETTE SMOKING BY THEIR ADOLESCENT OFFSPRING

Nicotine and other substances in cigarette smoke cross the placental barrier and pass from the expectant mother to the fetus, stimulating the fetal brain as early as the first trimester of pregnancy (Helmstrom-Lindahl & Nordberg, 2002). Researchers are exploring the possibility that this prenatal exposure of the brain to cigarette smoke may predispose individuals to be more vulnerable to addiction in adolescence.

A recent study examined whether expectant mothers' cigarette smoking and marijuana use were linked to an increased risk for substance use in adolescence by their offspring (Porath & Fried, 2005). One hundred fifty-two 16- to 21-year-olds were asked to complete a drug history questionnaire that included their past and current cigarette smoking. A urine sample was also obtained from the participants and analyzed for the presence of drugs. The adolescent participants' mothers had been asked about the extent of their cigarette smoking during their pregnancy several decades earlier as part of the Ottawa Prenatal Prospective Study.

The results indicated that adolescent offspring of mothers who reported that they smoked cigarettes during pregnancy were more than twice as likely to have initiated smoking during adolescence than their counterparts whose mothers reported not smoking during their pregnancy. These findings indicate that cigarette smoking by expectant mothers is a risk factor for later cigarette smoking by their adolescent offspring. Such results add to the strength of the evidence that supports drug use prevention and cessation among expectant mothers.

Cocaine Does cocaine use during pregnancy harm the developing embryo and fetus? The most consistent finding is that cocaine exposure during prenatal development is associated with reduced birth weight, length, and head circumference (Smith & others, 2001). Also, in other studies, prenatal cocaine exposure has been linked to impaired motor development at 2 years of age (Arendt & others, 1999); to lower arousal, less effective self-regulation, higher excitability, and lower quality of reflexes at 1 month of age (Lester & others, 2002); and to impaired language

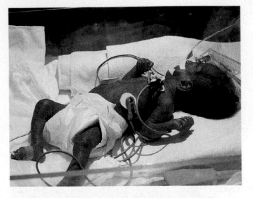

This baby was exposed to cocaine prenatally. *What are some of the possible effects on development of being exposed to cocaine prenatally?*

development and information processing (Beeghly & others, 2006), including attention deficits in preschool children (Noland & others, 2005).

These findings should be interpreted cautiously (Accornero & others, 2006). Why? Because other factors in the lives of pregnant women who use cocaine (such as poverty, malnutrition, and other substance abuse) often cannot be ruled out as possible contributors to the problems found in their children (Hurt & others, 2005). For example, cocaine users are more likely than nonusers to smoke cigarettes, use marijuana, drink alcohol, and take amphetamines.

Despite these cautions, the weight of research evidence indicates that children born to mothers who use cocaine are likely to have neurological and cognitive deficits (Field, 2007; Forrester & Mertz, 2007; Mayes, 2003; Shankaran & others, 2007). Cocaine use by pregnant women is not recommended.

Methamphetamine Methamphetamine, like cocaine, is a stimulant, speeding up an individual's nervous system. Babies born to mothers who use methamphetamine, or "meth," during pregnancy are at risk for a number of problems, including high infant mortality, low birth weight, and developmental and behavioral problems (Chang & others, 2004). Meth use during pregnancy is increasing, and some experts conclude that meth use during pregnancy has become a greater problem in the United States than cocaine use (Elliott, 2004). A recent survey revealed that 5 percent of U.S. women used methamphetamine during their pregnancy (Arria & others, 2006).

Marijuana An increasing number of studies find that marijuana use by pregnant women has negative outcomes for offspring (de Moraes Barros & others, 2006; Huizink & Mulder, 2006; Williams & Ross, 2007). A review of the research concluded that marijuana use by pregnant women is related to negative outcomes in memory and information processing in their offspring (Kalant, 2004). For example, in a longitudinal study, prenatal marijuana exposure was related to learning and memory difficulties at age 11 (Richardson & others, 2002). Another study revealed that prenatal marijuana exposure was linked with depressive symptoms at 10 years of age (Gray & others, 2005). Further, a recent study indicated that prenatal exposure to marijuana was linked to marijuana use at 14 years of age (Day, Goldschmidt, & Thomas, 2006). In sum, marijuana use is not recommended for pregnant women.

Heroin It is well documented that infants whose mothers are addicted to heroin show several behavioral difficulties (Yang & others, 2006). The difficulties include withdrawal symptoms, such as tremors, irritability, abnormal crying, disturbed sleep, and impaired motor control. Many still show behavioral problems at their first birthday, and attention deficits may appear later in development. The most common treatment for heroin addiction, methadone, is associated with very severe withdrawal symptoms in newborns.

Incompatible Blood Types

Incompatibility between the mother's and father's blood type poses another risk to prenatal development. Blood types are created by differences in the surface structure of red blood cells. One type of difference in the surface of red blood cells creates the familiar blood groups—A, B, O, and AB. A second difference creates what is called Rh-positive and Rh-negative blood. If a surface marker, called the *Rh factor,* is present in an individual's red blood cells, the person is said to be Rh positive; if the Rh marker is not present, the person is said to be Rh negative. If a pregnant woman is Rh negative and her partner is Rh positive, the fetus may be Rh positive. If the fetus' blood is Rh positive and the mother's is Rh negative, the mother's immune system may produce antibodies that will attack the fetus. This can result in any number of problems, including miscarriage or stillbirth, anemia, jaundice, heart defects, brain damage, or death soon after birth (Moise, 2005).

Generally, the first Rh-positive baby of an Rh-negative mother is not at risk, but with each subsequent pregnancy the risk increases. A vaccine (RhoGAM) may be given to the mother within three days of the first child's birth to prevent her body from making antibodies that will attack any future Rh-positive fetuses in subsequent pregnancies. Also, babies affected by Rh incompatibility can be given blood transfusions before or right after birth (Mannessier & others, 2000).

Environmental Hazards

Many aspects of our modern industrial world can endanger the embryo or fetus. Some specific hazards to the embryo or fetus that are worth a closer look include radiation, toxic wastes, and other chemical pollutants (Bellinger, 2005; Kaufman & Groters, 2006).

Radiation can cause a gene mutation (an abrupt, permanent change in DNA). Chromosomal abnormalities are elevated among the offspring of fathers exposed to high levels of radiation in their occupations (Schrag & Dixon, 1985). X-ray radiation also can affect the developing embryo or fetus, especially in the first several weeks after conception, when women do not yet know they are pregnant (Urbano & Tait, 2004). Possible effects include microencephaly (an abnormally small brain), mental retardation, and leukemia. Women and their physicians should weigh the risk of an X-ray when an actual or potential pregnancy is involved (Hurwitz & others, 2006; Menias & others, 2007). However, a routine diagnostic X-ray of a body area other than the abdomen, with the women's abdomen protected by a lead apron, is generally considered safe (Loughlin, 2007).

Environmental pollutants and toxic wastes are also sources of danger to unborn children. Among the dangerous pollutants are carbon monoxide, mercury, and lead, as well as certain fertilizers and pesticides. Exposure to lead can come from lead-based paint that flakes off the walls of a home or from leaded gasoline emitted by cars on a nearby busy highway. Early exposure to lead can affect children's mental development (Yang & others, 2003). For example, in one study, 2-year-olds who prenatally had high levels of lead in their umbilical-cord blood performed poorly on a test of mental development (Bellinger & others, 1987).

Maternal Diseases

Maternal diseases and infections can produce defects in offspring by crossing the placental barrier, or they can cause damage during birth (Avgil & Ornoy, 2006; Tappia & Gabriel, 2006). Rubella (German measles) is one disease that can cause prenatal defects. The greatest damage occurs if a mother contracts rubella in the third or fourth week of pregnancy, although infection during the second month is also damaging (Kobayashi & others, 2005). A rubella outbreak in 1964–1965 resulted in 30,000 prenatal and neonatal (newborn) deaths, and more than 20,000 affected infants were born with malformations, including mental retardation, blindness, deafness, and heart problems. Elaborate preventive efforts ensure that rubella will never again have such disastrous effects. A vaccine that prevents German measles is now routinely administered to children, and women who plan to have children should have a blood test before they become pregnant to determine if they are immune to the disease (Best, 2007).

Syphilis (a sexually transmitted infection) is more damaging later in prenatal development—four months or more after conception. Rather than affecting organogenesis, as rubella does, syphilis damages organs after they have formed. Damage includes eye lesions, which can cause blindness, and skin lesions. When syphilis is present at birth, problems can develop in the central nervous system and gastrointestinal tract (Johnson, Erbelding, & Ghanem, 2007). Most states require that pregnant women be given a blood test to detect the presence of syphilis.

Another infection that has received widespread attention recently is genital herpes. Newborns contract this virus when they are delivered through the birth canal of a mother with genital herpes (Avgil & Ornoy, 2006; Xu & others, 2007). About

An explosion at the Chernobyl nuclear power plant in the Ukraine produced radioactive contamination that spread to surrounding areas. Thousands of infants were born with health problems and deformities as a result of the nuclear contamination, including this boy whose arm did not form. *Other than radioactive contamination, what are some other types of environmental hazards to prenatal development?*

one-third of babies delivered through an infected birth canal die; another one-fourth become brain damaged. If an active case of genital herpes is detected in a pregnant woman close to her delivery date, a cesarean section can be performed (in which the infant is delivered through an incision in the mother's abdomen) to keep the virus from infecting the newborn (Baker, 2007).

AIDS is a sexually transmitted infection that is caused by the human immun-odeficiency virus (HIV), which destroys the body's immune system. A mother can infect her offspring with AIDS in three ways: (1) during gestation across the placenta, (2) during delivery through contact with maternal blood or fluids, and (3) postpartum (after birth) through breast feeding. The transmission of AIDS through breast feeding is especially a problem in many developing countries (UNICEF, 2007). Babies born to HIV-infected mothers can be (1) infected and symptomatic (show AIDS symptoms), (2) infected but asymptomatic (not show AIDS symptoms), or (3) not infected at all. An infant who is infected and asymptomatic may still develop HIV symptoms up until 15 months of age.

In the early 1990s, before preventive treatments were available, 1,000 to 2,000 infants were born with HIV infection each year in the United States. Since then, transmission of AIDS from mothers to the fetuses has been reduced dramatically (Boer & others, 2007; Kriebs, 2006). Only about one-third as many cases of newborns with AIDS appear today as in the early 1990s. This decline is due to the increase in counseling and voluntary testing of pregnant women for HIV and to the use of zidovudine (AZT) by infected women during pregnancy, and for the infant after birth (Rathbun, Lockhart, & Stephens, 2005). In many poor countries, however, treatment with AZT is limited, and HIV infection of infants remains a major problem (Kirungi & others, 2006; Rigopoulos & others, 2007).

The more widespread disease of diabetes, characterized by high levels of sugar in the blood, also affects offspring (Casson, 2006). A recent study revealed that both chronic (long-standing) and gestational (onset or first recognition during pregnancy) diabetes were significant risks for cesarean delivery and preterm birth (Rosenberg & others, 2005).

Other Parental Factors

So far, we have discussed a number of drugs, environmental hazards, maternal diseases, and incompatible blood types that can harm the embryo or fetus. Here we explore other characteristics of the mother and father that can affect prenatal and child development: nutrition, age, and emotional states and stress.

Maternal Diet and Nutrition   A developing embryo or fetus depends completely on its mother for nutrition, which comes from the mother's blood (Derbyshire, 2007a, b). The nutritional status of the embryo or fetus is determined by the mother's total caloric intake, and her intake of proteins, vitamins, and minerals. Children born to malnourished mothers are more likely than other children to be malformed.

Being overweight before and during pregnancy can also put the embryo or fetus at risk, and an increasing number of pregnant women in the United States are overweight (Catalano, 2007). Three studies found that obese women had a significant risk of fetal death (Cnattinugis & others, 1998; Kumari, 2001; Nohr & others, 2005). Other recent studies indicated that prepregnancy maternal obesity doubled the risk of stillbirth and neonatal death, and was linked with defects in the central nervous system of offspring (Anderson & others, 2005; Kristensen & others, 2005).

One aspect of maternal nutrition that is important for normal prenatal development is folic acid, a B-complex vitamin (Antony, 2007; Tamura & Picciano, 2006). As we indicated earlier in the chapter, a lack of folic acid is linked with neural tube defects in offspring, such as spina bifida (Pitkin, 2007). One recent study found that

Because the fetus depends entirely on its mother for nutrition, it is important for the pregnant woman to have good nutritional habits. In Kenya, this government clinic provides pregnant women with information about how their diet can influence the health of their fetus and offspring. *What might the information about diet be like?*

maternal use of folic acid and iron during the first month of pregnancy was associated with a lower risk of Down syndrome in offspring, although more studies are needed to confirm this connection (Czeizel & Puho, 2005). The U.S. Public Health Service recommends that pregnant women consume a minimum of 400 micrograms of folic acid per day (about twice the amount the average woman gets in one day). Orange juice and spinach are examples of foods rich in folic acid.

Eating fish is often recommended as part of a healthy diet, but pollution has made many fish a risky choice for pregnant women. Some fish contain high levels of mercury, which is released into the air both naturally and by industrial pollution (Fitzgerald & others, 2004). When mercury falls into the water, it can become toxic and accumulate in large fish, such as shark, swordfish, kin mackerel, and some species of large tuna. Mercury is easily transferred across the placenta, and the embryo's developing brain and nervous system are highly sensitive to the metal (Gliori & others, 2006). The U.S. Food and Drug Administration (2004) provided the following recommendations for women of childbearing age and young children: don't eat shark, swordfish, king mackerel or tilefish; eat up to 12 ounces (2 average meals) a week of fish and shellfish that are lower in mercury, such as shrimp, canned light tuna, salmon, pollock, and catfish.

PCB-polluted fish also pose a risk to prenatal development (Vreugdenhil & others, 2004). PCBs (polychlorinated biphenyls) are chemicals that were used in manufacturing until they were banned in the 1970s in the United States, but they are still present in landfills, sediments, and wildlife. One study kept track of the extent to which pregnant women ate PCB-polluted fish from Lake Michigan and subsequently observed their children as newborns, young children, and at 11 years of age (Jacobson & others, 1984; Jacobson & Jacobson, 2002, 2003). The women who had eaten more PCB-polluted fish were more likely to have smaller, preterm infants who were more likely to react slowly to stimuli. As preschool children, their exposure to PCBs was linked with less effective short-term memory, and at age 11 with lower verbal intelligence and reading comprehension.

Maternal Age When possible harmful effects on the fetus and infant are considered, two maternal ages are of special interest: adolescence and 35 and older (Chen & others, 2007b; Maconochie & others, 2007). One recent study revealed that the rate of stillbirth was elevated for adolescent girls and women 35 years and older (Bateman & Simpson, 2006).

The mortality rate of infants born to adolescent mothers is double that of infants born to mothers in their twenties. Although this high rate probably reflects the immaturity of the mother's reproductive system, poor nutrition, lack of prenatal care, and low socioeconomic status may also play a role (Lenders, McElrath, & Scholl, 2000). Prenatal care decreases the probability that a child born to an adolescent girl will have physical problems. However, adolescents are the least likely of women in all age groups to obtain prenatal assistance from clinics, pediatricians, and health services.

Maternal age is also linked to the risk that a child will have Down syndrome (Soergel & others, 2006). As discussed in Chapter 2, an individual with *Down syndrome* has distinctive facial characteristics, short limbs, and retardation of motor and mental abilities. A baby with Down syndrome rarely is born to a mother 16 to 34 years of age. However, when the mother reaches 40 years of age, the probability is slightly over 1 in 100 for a baby born to her to have Down syndrome, and by age 50 it is almost 1 in 10.

These adolescent mothers are participating in a program that is designed to improve their parenting skills. *What are some of the risks for infants born to adolescent mothers?*

When mothers are 35 years and older, risks also increase for low birth weight, for preterm delivery, and for fetal death. One study found that low birth weight delivery increased 11 percent and preterm delivery increased 14 percent in women 35 years and older (Tough & others, 2002). In another study, fetal death was low for women 30 to 34 years of age but increased progressively for women 35 to 39 and 40 to 44 years of age (Canterino & others, 2004).

We still have much to learn about the role of the mother's age in pregnancy and childbirth (Montan, 2007). As women remain active, exercise regularly, and are careful about their nutrition, their reproductive systems may remain healthier at older ages than was thought possible in the past. For example, in a recent study, two-thirds of the pregnancies of women 45 years and older in Australia were free of complications (Callaway, Lust, & McIntrye, 2005).

Emotional States and Stress   Tales abound about how a pregnant woman's emotional state affects the fetus. For centuries it was thought that frightening experiences—such as a severe thunderstorm or a family member's death—leave birthmarks on the child or affect the child in more serious ways. In fact, a mother's stress can be transmitted to the fetus, and we now have a better grasp of how this takes place, although the mechanisms that link fetal health and the mother's emotional states are still far from certain (King & Laplante, 2005; Talqe & others, 2007).

When a pregnant woman experiences intense fears, anxieties, and other emotions, physiological changes occur that may affect her fetus. For example, producing adrenaline in response to fear restricts blood flow to the uterine area and can deprive the fetus of adequate oxygen. Also, maternal stress may increase the level of corticotropin-releasing hormone (CRH) early in pregnancy (Kapoor & others, 2006; Sljivic & others, 2006). CRH, in turn, has been linked to premature delivery. Women under stress are about four times more likely than their low-stress counterparts to deliver babies prematurely (Dunkel-Schetter, 1998; Dunkel-Schetter & others, 2001). A mother's stress may also influence the fetus indirectly by increasing the likelihood that the mother will engage in unhealthy behaviors, such as taking drugs and engaging in poor prenatal care.

The mother's emotional state during pregnancy can influence the birth process, too. An emotionally distraught mother might have irregular contractions and a more difficult labor, which can cause irregularities in the supply of oxygen to the fetus or other problems after birth. Babies born after extended labor also may adjust more slowly to their world and be more irritable.

High maternal anxiety and stress during pregnancy might have long-term consequences for the offspring (Jones & others, 2006). One recent study revealed that infants of mothers who had a low level of CRH during pregnancy showed less fear and distress at 2 months of age than their infant counterparts whose mothers had a high level of CRH during pregnancy (Davis & others, 2005). Also, in a longitudinal study, high maternal anxiety during pregnancy was linked to higher levels of cortisol (a hormone secreted by the adrenal glands in response to stress) in offspring at 10 years of age (O'Connor & others, 2005). In another longitudinal study, preschool children whose mothers had higher concentrations of cortisol during pregnancy had higher concentrations of cortisol themselves than preschool children whose mothers had lower concentrations of cortisol during pregnancy (Gutteling, deWeerth, & Buitelaar, 2005).

Positive emotional states also appear to make a difference to the fetus. Pregnant women who are optimistic thinkers have less adverse outcomes than pregnant women who are pessimistic thinkers (Loebel & Yalli, 1999). Optimists are more likely to believe that they have control over the outcomes of their pregnancies.

Paternal Factors   So far, we have discussed how characteristics of the mother— such as drug use, disease, diet and nutrition, age, and emotional states—can influence prenatal development and the development of the child. Might there also be some paternal risk factors? Indeed, there are several. Men's exposure to lead, radiation, certain pesticides, and petrochemicals may cause abnormalities in sperm that lead to miscarriage or diseases, such as childhood cancer (Fear & others, 2007). When fathers have a diet low in vitamin C, their offspring have a higher risk of birth defects and cancer (Fraga & others, 1991). Also, it has been speculated that, when fathers take cocaine, it may attach itself to sperm and cause birth defects, but the evidence for this effect is not yet strong. In one study, long-term use of cocaine by men was related to low sperm count, low motility, and a higher number of abnormally formed sperm (Bracken & others, 1990). Cocaine-related infertility appears to be reversible if users stop taking the drug for at least one year.

The father's smoking during the mother's pregnancy also can cause problems for the offspring. In one investigation, the newborns of fathers who smoked around their wives during the pregnancy were 4 ounces lighter at birth for each pack of cigarettes smoked per day than were the newborns whose fathers did not smoke during their wives' pregnancy (Rubin & others, 1986). In another study, in China, the longer the fathers smoked, the stronger the risk that their children would develop cancer (Ji & others, 1997). In yet another study, heavy paternal smoking was associated with the risk of early pregnancy loss (Venners & others, 2004).

The father's age also makes a difference (Maconochie & others, 2007; Tang & others, 2006; Yang & others, 2007). About 5 percent of children with Down syndrome have older fathers. The offspring of older fathers also face increased risk for other birth defects, including dwarfism and Marfan syndrome, which involves head and limb deformities.

There are also risks to offspring when both the mother and father are older (Dunson, Baird, & Colombo, 2004). In one study, the risk of an adverse pregnancy outcome, such as miscarriage, rose considerably when the woman was 35 years or older and the man was 40 years of age or older (de la Rochebrochard & Thonneau, 2002).

Despite the many potential hazards during prenatal development, it is important to keep in mind that most of the time prenatal development does not go awry, and development proceeds along the positive path that we described at the beginning of the chapter.

In one study, in China, the longer the fathers smoked, the greater the risk that their children would develop cancer (Ji & others, 1997). *What are some other paternal factors that can influence the development of the fetus and the child?*

REVIEW AND REFLECT ▸ LEARNING GOAL 3

3 Describe potential hazards during prenatal development.

Review
- What is teratology? What are some general principles regarding teratogens?
- Which prescription and nonprescription drugs can influence prenatal development?
- How do different psychoactive drugs affect prenatal development?
- How do incompatible blood types influence prenatal development?
- What are some environmental hazards that can influence prenatal development?
- Which maternal diseases can affect prenatal development?
- What other parental factors affect prenatal development?

Reflect
- What can be done to convince women who are pregnant not to smoke or drink? Consider the role of health-care providers, the role of insurance companies, and specific programs targeted at women who are pregnant.

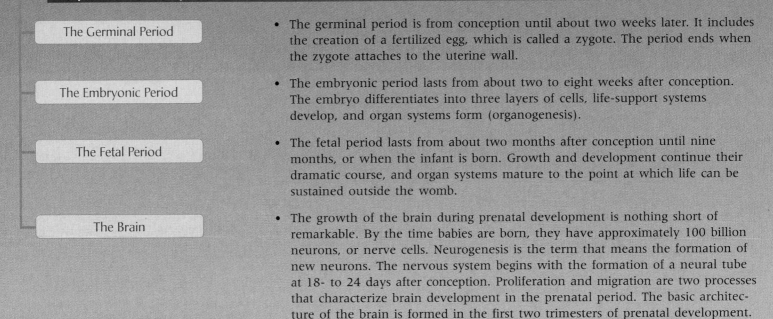

1 **WHAT IS THE COURSE OF PRENATAL DEVELOPMENT?** *Discuss the three periods of prenatal development.*

The Germinal Period

- The germinal period is from conception until about two weeks later. It includes the creation of a fertilized egg, which is called a zygote. The period ends when the zygote attaches to the uterine wall.

The Embryonic Period

- The embryonic period lasts from about two to eight weeks after conception. The embryo differentiates into three layers of cells, life-support systems develop, and organ systems form (organogenesis).

The Fetal Period

- The fetal period lasts from about two months after conception until nine months, or when the infant is born. Growth and development continue their dramatic course, and organ systems mature to the point at which life can be sustained outside the womb.

The Brain

- The growth of the brain during prenatal development is nothing short of remarkable. By the time babies are born, they have approximately 100 billion neurons, or nerve cells. Neurogenesis is the term that means the formation of new neurons. The nervous system begins with the formation of a neural tube at 18- to 24 days after conception. Proliferation and migration are two processes that characterize brain development in the prenatal period. The basic architecture of the brain is formed in the first two trimesters of prenatal development.

2 **WHAT ARE EXPECTANT PARENTS' EXPERIENCES LIKE DURING PRENATAL DEVELOPMENT?** *Characterize expectant parents' experiences during prenatal development.*

Confirming the Pregnancy and Calculating the Due Date

- A pregnancy test checks the woman's urine or blood for human chorionic gonadotropin (HCG). The length of pregnancy is computed from the first day of the woman's last menstrual period and lasts an average of 280 days, or 40 weeks.

The Three Trimesters and Preparation for Birth

- During the first trimester, the expectant mother may experience nausea and vomiting, mood swings, and feel especially tired and require more sleep. The expectant couple can benefit from taking a parent education class on pregnancy and prenatal development. Their sexual relationship may change during the first trimester, and they should discuss their feelings about sexual intercourse and do what they mutually desire. During the second trimester, the expectant mother often feels better than she did in the first trimester and better than she will feel in the third trimester. If she plans to breast feed, when colostrum begins to appear in the milk glands she should begin preparing her breasts for breast feeding. During the third trimester, the expectant mother may experience shortness of breath, swollen ankles, and other physical discomforts, and by the ninth month often looks forward to the relief from physical restrictions and to the joy of having the baby in her arms. She and her partner can learn more about labor, birth, and how to cope with the stresses of the latter part of pregnancy by taking childbirth classes.

The Expectant Mother's Nutrition, Weight Gain, and Exercise

- The best assurance of adequate caloric intake during pregnancy is a satisfactory weight gain over time. Maternal weight gain that averages 25 to 35 pounds is often linked with the best reproductive outcomes. How much and what type of exercise depends to some extent on the course of pregnancy, the expectant mother's fitness, and her customary activity level.

- Prenatal care varies extensively but usually involves medical care services with a defined schedule of visits and often includes educational, social, and nutritional services. Much needs to be done to improve prenatal care in the United States, especially for low-income families.

3 WHAT ARE SOME POTENTIAL HAZARDS TO PRENATAL DEVELOPMENT?
Describe potential hazards during prenatal development.

Some General Principles

- Teratology is the field that investigates the causes of birth defects. Any agent that can potentially cause birth defects is called a teratogen. The dose, genetic susceptibility, and time of exposure influence the severity of the damage to an unborn child and the type of defect that occurs.

Prescription and Nonprescription Drugs

- Prescription drugs that can be harmful include antibiotics, some antidepressants, and certain hormones. Nonprescription drugs that can be harmful include diet pills, aspirin, and caffeine.

Psychoactive Drugs

- Legal psychoactive drugs that are potentially harmful to prenatal development include alcohol and nicotine. Fetal alcohol syndrome is a cluster of abnormalities that appear in offspring of mothers who drink heavily during pregnancy. Even when pregnant women drink moderately (one to two drinks a day), negative effects on their offspring have been found. Cigarette smoking by pregnant women has serious adverse effects on prenatal and child development (such as low birth weight). Illegal psychoactive drugs that are potentially harmful to offspring include methamphetamine, which can produce respiratory, neurological, and other problems in the offspring; marijuana; which can result in a child's impaired information processing; cocaine, which is associated with reduced birth weight, length, and head circumference; and heroin, which produces behavior problems and may result in attention deficits later in development.

Incompatible Blood Types

- Incompatibility of the mother's and the father's blood types can also be harmful to the fetus. A woman is at risk when she has a negative Rh factor and her partner has a positive Rh factor.

Environmental Hazards

- Environmental hazards include radiation, environmental pollutants, and toxic wastes.

Maternal Diseases

- Syphilis, rubella (German measles), genital herpes, and AIDS are infectious diseases that can harm the fetus.

Other Parental Factors

- Other parental factors include maternal diet and nutrition, age, emotional states and stress, and paternal factors. A developing fetus depends entirely on its mother for nutrition. One nutrient that is especially important very early in development is folic acid. A potential hazard to prenatal development occurs when the mother consumes fish with a high mercury content. Maternal age can negatively affect the offspring's development if the mother is an adolescent or over 35. High stress in the mother is linked with less than optimal prenatal and birth outcomes. Paternal factors that can adversely affect prenatal development include exposure to lead, radiation, certain pesticides, and petrochemicals.

KEY TERMS

germinal period 85
blastocyst 85
trophoblast 85
embryonic period 85
endoderm 85

ectoderm 86
mesoderm 86
amnion 86
umbilical cord 86
placenta 86

organogenesis 86
fetal period 87
neuron 87
neurogenesis 89
teratogen 98

fetal alcohol
   syndrome (FAS) 100

MAKING A DIFFERENCE

Maximizing Positive Prenatal Outcomes

What are some good strategies during pregnancy that are likely to maximize positive outcomes for prenatal development?

- *Eat nutritiously and monitor weight gain.* The recommended daily allowances for all nutrients increase during pregnancy. The pregnant woman should eat three balanced meals a day and nutritious snacks between meals if desired. Weight gains that average 25 to 35 pounds are associated with the best reproductive outcomes.

- *Engage in safe exercise.* How much and what type of exercise is best during pregnancy depends to some degree on the course of the pregnancy, the expectant mother's fitness, and her customary activity level. Normal participation in exercise can continue throughout an uncomplicated pregnancy. It is important to remember not to overdo exercise. Exercising for shorter intervals and decreasing the intensity of exercise as pregnancy proceeds are good strategies. Pregnant women should always consult a physician before starting an exercise program.

- *Don't drink alcohol or take other potentially harmful drugs.* An important strategy for pregnancy is to totally abstain from alcohol and other drugs, such as nicotine and cocaine. In this chapter, we described the harmful effects that these drugs can have on the developing fetus. Fathers also need to be aware of potentially harmful effects they can have on prenatal development.

- *Have a support system of family and friends.* The pregnant woman benefits from a support system of family members and friends. A positive relationship with a spouse helps keep stress levels down, as does a close relationship with one or more friends.

- *Reduce stress and stay calm.* Try to maintain an even, calm emotional state during pregnancy. High stress levels can harm the fetus. Pregnant women who are feeling a lot of anxiety can reduce their anxiety through a relaxation or stress management program.

- *Stay away from environmental hazards.* We saw in this chapter that some environmental hazards, such as pollutants and toxic wastes, can harm prenatal development. Be aware of these hazards and stay away from them.

- *Get excellent prenatal care.* The quality of prenatal care varies extensively. The education the mother receives about pregnancy, labor and delivery, and care of the newborn can be valuable, especially for first-time mothers.

- *Read a good book for expectant mothers.* An excellent one is *What to Expect When You're Expecting,* which is described here.

RESOURCES FOR IMPROVING CHILDREN'S LIVES

March of Dimes

www.marchofdimes.com

A major emphasis on the part of the March of Dimes is to promote healthy pregnancy. Their Web site includes extensive information about many aspects of pregnancy and prenatal development.

National Center for Education in Maternal and Child Health (NCEMCH)

www.ncemch.org

NCEMCH answers questions about pregnancy and childbirth, high-risk infants, and maternal and child health programs. It also publishes a free guide, *Maternal and Child Health Publications.*

Pregnancy.org

www.pregnancy.org

This extensive Web site provides up-to-date information about pregnancy and prenatal development.

What to Expect When You're Expecting

by Heidi Murkoff, Arlene Eisenberg, and Sandee Hathaway (3rd ed., 2002)

New York: Workman

This highly popular book on pregnancy and prenatal development provides detailed month-by-month descriptions of what pregnancy and prenatal growth are like.

Prenatal Care Tips

Pregnant women can call this federal government toll-free number for prenatal care advice and referral to local health-care providers: 800–311–2229.

E-LEARNING TOOLS

Connect to **www.mhhe.com/santrockc10** to research the answers and complete these exercises. In addition, you'll find a number of other resources and valuable study tools for Chapter 3, "Prenatal Development," on this Web site.

Taking It to the Net

1. Mara's best friend, Aida, suffered a miscarriage after several years of trying to become pregnant. Before Mara goes to visit Aida, how can she find out more about the psychological trauma that Aida may be experiencing as a result of the miscarriage?

2. Mai, age 28, has just learned that she is pregnant. She is proud of the fact that she weighs the same as she did in high school. She is terrified of getting fat and not being able to lose the weight after the baby is born. How can Mai eat properly to keep her and her baby healthy while minimizing unnecessary and unhealthy weight gain?

3. Sven and Diana have made an application with a foreign adoption agency to adopt a child from a former Soviet Union state. The agency told them the boy they have chosen may be suffering from a mild version of fetal alcohol syndrome. How can Sven and Diana find out more about FAS before their application is approved?

Health and Well-Being, Parenting, and Education

Build your decision-making skills by trying your hand at the health and well-being, parenting, and education exercises.

Video Clips

The Online Learning Center includes the following videos for this chapter:

1. *Childbirth Education Alternatives*—1936
   A childbirth educator describes the types of childbirth classes that are available to expectant parents and the benefits of childbirth education.

2. *Teen Pregnancy and Families*—553
   Dr. Gunn describes the risk factors that are related to teen pregnancy. All involve the context (for example, poverty, ineffective schools) in which these young girls are raised.

4 Birth

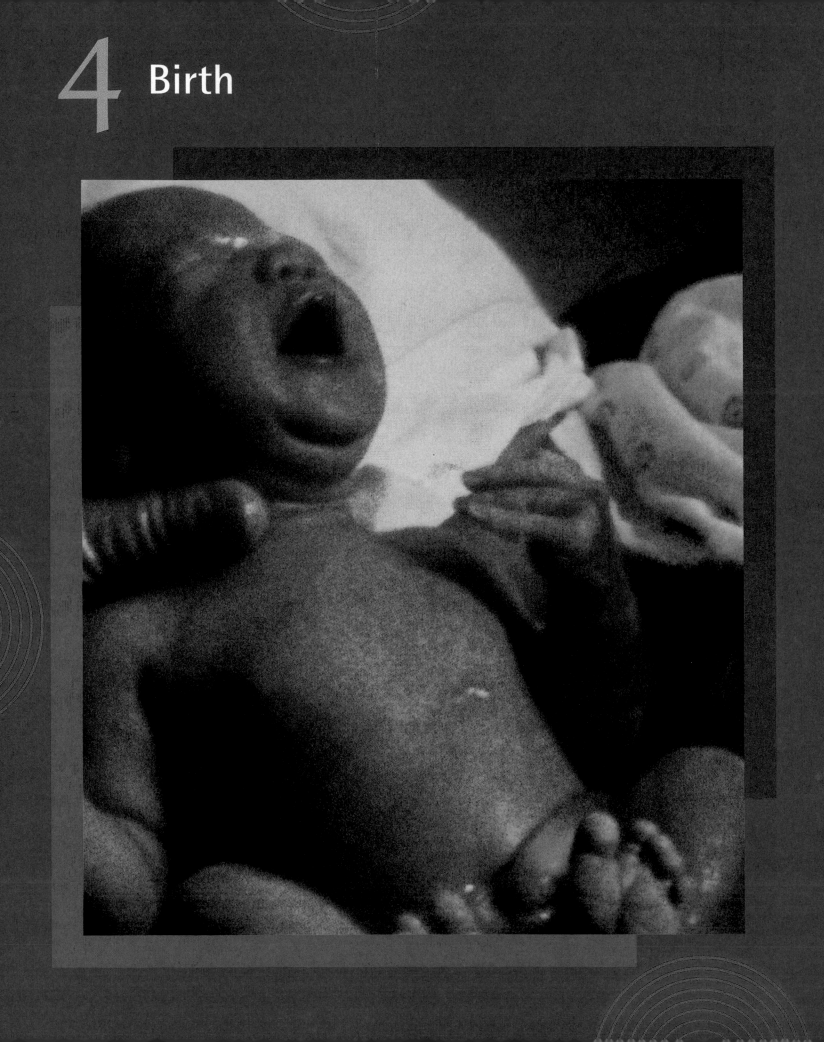

We must respect this instant of birth, this fragile moment. The baby is between two worlds, on a threshold.

—FREDERICK LEBOYER
French Obstetrician, 20th Century

Images of Children's Development
Tanner Roberts' Birth: A Fantastic Voyage

Tanner Roberts was born in a suite at St. Joseph's Medical Center in Burbank, California (Warrick, 1992, pp. E1, E11, E12). Let's examine what took place in the hours leading up to his birth. It is day 266 of his mother Cindy's pregnancy. She is in the frozen-food aisle of a convenience store and feels a sharp pain, starting in the small of her back and reaching around her middle, which causes her to gasp. For weeks, painless Braxton Hicks spasms (named for the gynecologist who discovered them) have been flexing her uterine muscles. But these practice contractions were not nearly as intense and painful as the one she just experienced. After six hours of irregular spasms, her uterus settles into a more predictable rhythm.

At 3 a.m., Cindy and her husband, Tom, are wide awake. They time Cindy's contractions with a stopwatch. The contractions are now only six minutes apart. It's time to call the hospital. A short time later, Tom and Cindy arrive at the hospital's labor-delivery suite. A nurse puts a webbed belt and fetal monitor around Cindy's middle to measure her labor. The monitor picks up the fetal heart rate. With each contraction of the uterine wall, Tanner's heartbeat jumps from its resting state of about 140 beats to 160 to 170 beats per minute. When the cervix is dilated to more than 4 centimeters, or almost half open, Cindy receives her first medication. As Demerol begins to drip into her veins, the pain of her contractions is less intense. Tanner's heart rate dips to 130 and then 120.

Contractions are now coming every three to four minutes, each one lasting about 25 seconds. The Demerol does not completely obliterate Cindy's pain. She hugs her husband as the nurse urges her to "relax those muscles. Breathe deep. Relax. You're almost there."

Each contraction briefly cuts off Tanner's source of oxygen, his mother's blood. However, in the minutes of rest between contractions, Cindy's deep breathing helps rush fresh blood to the baby's heart and brain.

At 8 a.m., Cindy's cervix is almost completely dilated and the obstetrician arrives. Using a tool made for the purpose, he reaches into the birth canal and tears the membranes of the amniotic sac, and about half a liter of clear fluid flows out. Contractions are now coming every two minutes, and each one is lasting a full minute.

By 9 a.m., the labor suite has been transformed into a delivery room. Tanner's body is compressed by his mother's contractions and pushes. As he nears his entrance into the world, the compressions help press the fluid from his lungs in preparation for his first breath. Squeezed tightly in the birth canal, the top of Tanner's head emerges. His face is puffy and scrunched. Although fiercely squinting because of the sudden light, Tanner's eyes are open. Tiny bubbles of clear mucus are on his lips. Before any more of his body emerges, the nurse cradles Tanner's head and suctions his nose and mouth. Tanner takes his first breath, a large gasp followed by whimpering, and then a loud cry. Tanner's body is wet but only slightly bloody as the doctor lifts him onto his mother's abdomen. The umbilical cord, still connecting Tanner with his mother, slows and stops pulsating. The obstetrician cuts it, severing Tanner's connection to his mother's womb. Now Tanner's blood flows not to his mother's body for nourishment, but to his own lungs, intestines, and other organs.

As the story of Tanner Roberts' birth reveals, many changes take place during the birth of a baby. In this chapter, we further explore what happens during the *birth process, measures of neonatal health and responsiveness, the development of low birth weight infants, and characteristics of the postpartum period.*

1 WHAT HAPPENS DURING THE BIRTH PROCESS?

| Stages of the Birth Process | Methods of Childbirth | Family Involvement |

| Childbirth Setting and Attendants | The Transition from Fetus to Newborn |

Nature writes the basic script for how birth occurs, but parents make important choices about conditions surrounding birth. We look first at the sequence of physical steps when a child is born.

Stages of the Birth Process

The birth process occurs in three **stages**. The first stage is the longest of the three stages. Uterine contractions are 15 to 20 minutes apart at the beginning and last up to a minute. These contractions cause the woman's cervix to stretch and open. As the first stage progresses, the contractions come closer together, appearing every two to five minutes. Their intensity increases. By the end of the first birth stage, contractions dilate the cervix to an opening of about 4 inches, so that the baby can move from the uterus to the birth canal. For a woman having her first child, the first stage lasts an average of 12 to 14 hours; for subsequent children, this stage may be shorter.

The second birth stage begins when the baby's head starts to move through the cervix and the birth canal. It terminates when the baby completely emerges from the mother's body. With each contraction, the mother bears down hard to push the baby out of her body. By the time the baby's head is out of the mother's body, the contractions come almost every minute and last for about a minute. This stage typically lasts approximately 45 minutes to an hour.

Afterbirth is the third stage, at which time the placenta, umbilical cord, and other membranes are detached and expelled. This final stage is the shortest of the three birth stages, lasting only minutes (see Figure 4.1).

Childbirth Setting and Attendants

In the United States, 99 percent of births take place in hospitals, a figure that has remained constant for several decades (Martin & others, 2005). Some women with good medical histories and low risk for problems may choose a delivery at home or in a freestanding birth center, which is usually staffed by nurse-midwives. Births at home are far more common in many other countries; for example, in Holland, 35 percent of the babies are born at home. Some critics worry that the U.S. tendency to view birth through a medical lens may lead to unnecessary medical procedures (Hausman, 2005).

afterbirth The third stage of birth, when the placenta, umbilical cord, and other membranes are detached and expelled.

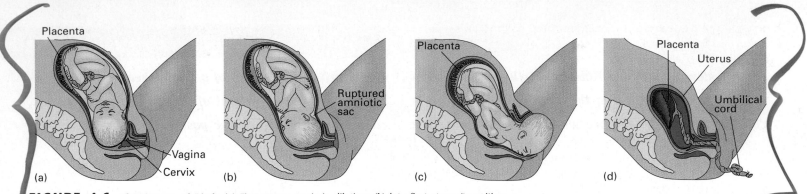

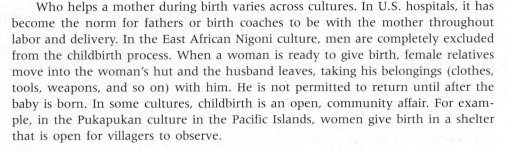

FIGURE 4.1 **The Stages of Birth** (a) First stage: cervix is dilating; (b) late first stage (transition stage): cervix is fully dilated, and the amniotic sac has ruptured, releasing amniotic fluid; (c) second stage: birth of the infant; (d) third stage: delivery of the placenta (afterbirth).

Who helps a mother during birth varies across cultures. In U.S. hospitals, it has become the norm for fathers or birth coaches to be with the mother throughout labor and delivery. In the East African Nigoni culture, men are completely excluded from the childbirth process. When a woman is ready to give birth, female relatives move into the woman's hut and the husband leaves, taking his belongings (clothes, tools, weapons, and so on) with him. He is not permitted to return until after the baby is born. In some cultures, childbirth is an open, community affair. For example, in the Pukapukan culture in the Pacific Islands, women give birth in a shelter that is open for villagers to observe.

Midwives Midwifery is the norm throughout most of the world. In Holland, more than 40 percent of babies are delivered by midwives rather than doctors (Treffers & others, 1990). But in 2003, 91 percent of U.S. births were attended by physicians, and only 8 percent of women who delivered a baby were attended by a *midwife* (Martin & others, 2005). However, the 8 percent figure in 2003 represents a substantial increase from less than 1 percent of U.S. women attended by a midwife in 1975 (Martin & others, 2005). Ninety-five percent of the midwives who delivered babies in the United States in 2003 were certified nurse-midwives. Compared to physicians, certified nurse-midwives generally spend more time with patients during prenatal visits, place more emphasis on patient counseling and education, provide more emotional support, and are more likely to be with the patient one-on-one during the entire labor and delivery process, which may explain the more positive outcomes for babies delivered by certified nurse-midwives (Davis, 2005).

Doulas In many countries, a doula attends a childbearing woman. *Doula* is a Greek word that means "a woman who helps." A **doula** is a caregiver who provides continuous physical, emotional, and educational support for the mother before, during, and after childbirth. Doulas remain with the mother throughout labor, assessing and responding to her needs. Researchers have found positive effects when a doula is present at the birth of a child (Stein, Kennell, & Fulcher, 2004). In a recent study, low-income pregnant women who were given doula support spent a shorter time in labor, and their newborn had a higher health rating at one and five minutes after birth than their low-income counterparts who did not receive doula support (Campbell & others, 2006).

In the United States, most doulas work as independent providers hired by the expectant mother. Doulas typically function as part of a "birthing team," serving as an adjunct to the midwife or the hospital's obstetric staff (Dundek, 2006). Managed care organizations are increasingly offering doula support as a part of regular obstetric care.

A woman in the African !Kung culture giving birth in a sitting position. Notice the help and support being given by another woman. *What are some cultural variations in childbirth?*

doula A caregiver who provides continuous physical, emotional, and educational support to the mother before, during, and just after childbirth.

Methods of Childbirth

U.S. hospitals often allow the mother and her obstetrician a range of options regarding their method of delivery. Key choices involve the use of medication, whether to use any of a number of nonmedicated techniques to reduce pain, and when to resort to a cesarean delivery.

Medication   Three basic kinds of drugs that are used for labor are analgesia, anesthesia, and oxytocics.

Analgesia is used to relieve pain. Analgesics include tranquilizers, barbiturates, and narcotics (such as Demerol).

Anesthesia is used in late first-stage labor and during expulsion of the baby to block sensation in an area of the body or to block consciousness. There is a trend toward not using general anesthesia, which blocks consciousness, in normal births because general anesthesia can be transmitted through the placenta to the fetus (Lieberman & others, 2005). An *epidural block* is regional anesthesia that numbs the woman's body from the waist down. Even this drug, thought to be relatively safe, has come under recent criticism because it is associated with fever, extended labor, and increased risk for cesarean delivery (Glantz, 2005).

Oxytocin is a synthetic hormone that is used to stimulate contractions; Pitocin is the most widely used oxytocin (Smith & Merrill, 2006). The benefits and risks of oxytocin as a part of childbirth continues to be debated. One recent large-scale Swedish study revealed that pregnant women who were given oxytocin during childbirth were more likely to have newborns with lower health ratings than pregnant women who were not given oxytocin during childbirth (Oscarsson & others, 2006).

Predicting how a drug will affect an individual woman and her fetus is difficult (Briggs & Wan, 2006). A particular drug might have only a minimal effect on one fetus yet have a much stronger effect on another. The drug's dosage also is a factor. Stronger doses of tranquilizers and narcotics given to decrease the mother's pain have a potentially more negative effect on the fetus than mild doses. It is important for the mother to assess her level of pain and have a voice in the decision of whether she should receive medication (Young, 2001).

A doula assisting a birth. *What types of support do doulas provide?*

Natural and Prepared Childbirth   For a brief time not long ago, the idea of avoiding all medication during childbirth gained favor in the United States. Instead, many women chose to reduce the pain of childbirth through techniques known as natural childbirth and prepared childbirth. Today, at least some medication is used in the typical childbirth, but elements of natural childbirth and prepared childbirth remain popular (Davidson, London, & Ladewig, 2008; Hogan & others, 2007).

Natural childbirth is the method that aims to reduce the mother's pain by decreasing her fear through education about childbirth and by teaching her to use breathing methods and relaxation techniques during delivery (Sandiford, 2006). This approach was developed in 1914 by English obstetrician Grantley Dick-Read. Dick-Read stressed that the doctor's relationship with the mother plays an important role in reducing her perception of pain, and that the doctor should be present, providing reassurance, during her active labor prior to delivery.

French obstetrician Ferdinand Lamaze developed a method similar to natural childbirth that is known as **prepared childbirth,** or the Lamaze method. It includes a special breathing technique to control pushing in the final stages of labor, as well as more detailed education about anatomy and physiology than Dick-Read's approach provides. The Lamaze method has become very popular in the United States. The pregnant woman's partner usually serves as a coach, who attends childbirth classes with her and helps her with her breathing and relaxation during delivery.

Many other prepared childbirth techniques have been developed (Samuels & Samuels, 1996). They usually include elements of Dick-Read's natural childbirth or

analgesia Drugs used to alleviate pain, such as tranquilizers, barbiturates, and narcotics.

anesthesia Drugs used in late first-stage labor and during expulsion of the baby to block sensation in an area of the body or to block consciousness.

oxytocin A synthetic hormone that is used to stimulate contractions.

natural childbirth Method developed in 1914 by Dick-Read, it attempts to reduce the mother's pain by decreasing her fear through education about childbirth and breathing methods and relaxation techniques during delivery.

prepared childbirth Method developed by French obstetrician Ferdinand Lamaze; this childbirth strategy is similar to natural childbirth but includes a special breathing technique to control pushing in the final stages of labor and a more detailed anatomy and physiology course.

Careers in CHILD DEVELOPMENT

Linda Pugh
Perinatal Nurse

Perinatal nurses work with childbearing women to support health and growth during the childbearing experience. Linda Pugh (Ph.D., R.N.C.) is a perinatal nurse on the faculty at the Johns Hopkins University School of Nursing. She is certified as an inpatient obstetric nurse and specializes in the care of women during labor and delivery. Pugh teaches nursing to both undergraduate and graduate students. In addition to educating professional nurses and conducting research, Pugh consults with hospitals and organizations about women's health issues.

Pugh's research interests include nursing interventions with low-income breast feeding women, discovering ways to prevent and ameliorate fatigue during childbearing, and using effective breathing exercises during labor.

Linda Pugh (*right*) with a mother and her newborn.

Lamaze's method, plus one or more other components. For instance, the Bradley method emphasizes the father's role as a labor coach (Signore, 2004). Virtually all of the prepared childbirth methods emphasize education, relaxation and breathing exercises, and support.

In sum, proponents of current prepared childbirth methods believe that when information and support are provided, women *know* how to give birth. To read about one nurse whose research focuses on fatigue during childbearing and breathing exercises during labor, see the *Careers in Child Development* profile. And to read about the increased variety of techniques now being used to reduce stress and control pain during labor, see the *Caring for Children* interlude.

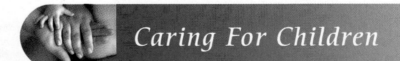

Caring For Children

FROM WATERBIRTH TO MUSIC THERAPY

The effort to reduce stress and control pain during labor has recently led to an increase in the use of some older and some newer nonmedicated techniques (Field, 2007; Simkin & Bolding, 2004; Smith & others, 2006). These include waterbirth, massage, acupuncture, hypnosis, and music therapy.

Waterbirth

Waterbirth involves giving birth in a tub of warm water. Some women go through labor in the water and get out for delivery, others remain in the water for delivery. The rationale for waterbirth is that the baby has been in an amniotic sac for many months, and that delivery in a similar environment is likely to be less stressful for the baby and the mother. Mothers get into the warm water when contractions become closer together and more intense. Getting into the water too soon can cause labor to slow or stop. Researchers have found positive results for the use of waterbirth (Enning, 2004; Simpkin & Bolding, 2004; Thoni & Moroder, 2004). In a comparison of almost 6,000 landbirths and more than 3,500 waterbirths, waterbirths resulted in a lower incidence of episiotomies (an incision made to widen the vagina for delivery), fewer perineal lacerations (the perineum is a muscle between the vagina and the rectum), fewer vaginal tears, and a lower rate of newborn complications (Geissbuehler, Stein, & Eberhard, 2004). Waterbirth has been practiced more often in European countries such as Switzerland and Sweden in recent decades than in the United States but is increasingly being included in U.S. birth plans.

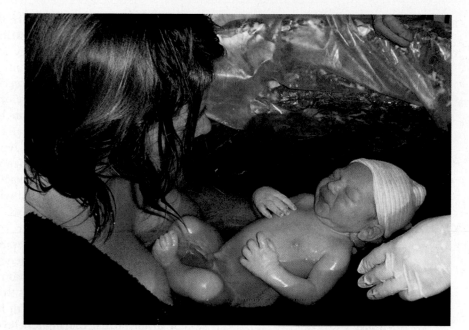

What characterizes the use of waterbirth in delivering a baby?

Massage

Massage is increasingly used as a procedure prior to and during delivery (Field, 2007). Researchers have found that massage can reduce pain and anxiety during labor (Chang, Chen, & Huang, 2006; Eogan, Daly, & O'Herlihy, 2006; Wang & others, 2005). A recent research review concluded that massage reduces the incidence of perineal trauma (damage to genitalia) following birth (Beckmann & Garrett, 2006).

Acupuncture

Acupuncture, the insertion of very fine needles into specific locations in the body, is used as a standard procedure to reduce the pain of childbirth in China, although it only recently has begun to be used in the United States for this purpose. A recent research review indicated that only a limited number of studies had been conducted on the use of acupuncture in childbirth but that it appears to be safe and may have positive effects (Smith & Crowther, 2004). One recent study found that acupuncture lowered the need for medical inductions and cesarean deliveries (Duke & Don, 2005). Another recent study revealed that acupuncture resulted in less time spent in labor and a reduction in the need for oxytocin to augment labor (Gaudernack, Forbord, & Hole, 2006). Further research is needed to determine the effectiveness of acupuncture as a childbirth procedure (Lee & Chan, 2006).

Hypnosis

Hypnosis, the induction of a psychological state of altered attention and awareness in which the individual is unusually responsive to suggestions, is also increasingly being used during childbirth (Mottershead, 2006; Spencer, 2005). Some studies have indicated positive effects of hypnosis for reducing pain during childbirth (Cyna, Andrew, & McAuliffe, 2006). However, reviews indicate that further research is needed to determine the risks and benefits of this procedure (Cyna, McAuliffe, & Andrew, 2004; Simpkin & Bolding, 2004).

Music Therapy

Music therapy during childbirth, which involves the use of music to reduce stress and manage pain, is increasing in use (Cepeda & others, 2006; Chang & Chen, 2004). Few research studies have been conducted to determine its effectiveness (Simpkin & Bolding, 2004).

Cesarean Delivery Normally, the baby's head comes through the vagina first. But if the baby is in a **breech position,** the baby's buttocks are the first part to emerge from the vagina. In 1 of every 25 deliveries, the baby's head is still in the uterus when the rest of the body is out. Breech births can cause respiratory problems. As a result, if the baby is in a breech position, what is called a cesarean section, or a cesarean delivery, is usually preformed. In a **cesarean delivery,** the baby is removed from the mother's uterus through an incision made in her abdomen.

Cesarean deliveries are safer than breech deliveries. Cesarean deliveries also are performed if the baby is lying crosswise in the uterus, if the baby's head is too large to pass through the mother's pelvis, if the baby develops complications, or if the mother is bleeding vaginally. Cesarean deliveries can be life-saving, but they do bring risks. Compared with vaginal deliveries, they involve a higher infection rate, longer hospital stays, and the greater expense and stress that accompany any surgery.

The benefits and risks of cesarean sections continue to be debated (Bailit, Love, & Dawson, 2006; London & others, 2007). Some critics believe that too many babies are delivered by cesarean section in the United States. More cesarean sections are performed in the United States than in any other country in the world. The cesarean delivery rate jumped 7.5 percent from 2002 to 2004 in the United States to 29.1 percent of all births, the highest level since these data began to be reported on birth certificates in 1989 (Hoyert & others, 2006). Higher cesarean delivery rates may be due to a better ability to identify infants in distress during birth and the increase in overweight and obese pregnant women (Coleman & others, 2005). Also, some doctors may be overly cautious and recommend a cesarean delivery to defend against a potential lawsuit.

The Transition from Fetus to Newborn

Much of our discussion of birth so far has focused on the mother. Being born also involves considerable stress for the baby. During each contraction, when the placenta and umbilical cord are compressed as the uterine muscles draw together, the supply of oxygen to the fetus is decreased. If the delivery takes too long, the baby can develop *anoxia*, a condition in which the fetus or newborn has an insufficient supply of oxygen. Anoxia can cause brain damage (Aylott, 2006).

The baby has considerable capacity to withstand the stress of birth. Large quantities of adrenaline and noradrenalin, hormones that protect the fetus in the event of oxygen deficiency, are secreted in stressful circumstances. These hormones increase the heart's pumping activity, speed up heart rate, channel blood flow to the brain, and raise the blood-sugar level. Never again in life will such large amounts of these hormones be secreted. This circumstance underscores how stressful it is to be born and also how well prepared and adapted the fetus is for birth (Van Beveren, 2007).

At the time of birth, the baby is covered with what is called *vernix caseosa*, a protective skin grease. This vernix consists of fatty secretions and dead cells, thought to help protect the baby's skin against heat loss before and during birth.

Immediately after birth, the umbilical cord is cut, and the baby is on its own. Before birth, oxygen came from the mother via the umbilical cord, but now the baby is self-sufficient and can breathe on its own. Now 25 million little air sacs in the lungs must be filled with air. These first breaths may be the hardest ones an individual takes.

What is the transition from fetus to newborn like?

breech position The baby's position in the uterus that causes the buttocks to be the first part to emerge from the vagina.

cesarean delivery The baby is removed from the mother's uterus through an incision made in her abdomen. This also is sometimes referred to as cesarean section.

Family Involvement

In the past several decades, fathers or partners increasingly have participated in childbirth. Siblings often attend the birth or visit the mother shortly afterward.

Fathers or Partners   Fathers-to-be or the mother's partner are now more likely to go to at least one meeting with the obstetrician or caregiver during the pregnancy, attend childbirth preparation classes, learn about labor and birth, and be more involved in the care of the young infant. The change is consistent with our culture's movement toward less rigid concepts of "masculine" and "feminine" and the increase of same-sex couples having children. (Draper, 2003).

For many expectant couples today, the partner or father is trained to be the expectant mother's coach during labor, helping her learn relaxation methods and special breathing techniques for labor and birth. Most health professionals now believe that, just as with pregnancy, childbirth should be an intimate, shared moment between two people who are creating a new life together. Nonetheless, some partners do not want to participate in prepared childbirth, and some women also still prefer that they not have a very active role (Johnson, 2002). In such cases, other people can provide support for childbirth—mother, sister, friend, midwife, or physician, for example.

Husbands or partners who are motivated to participate in childbirth have an important role at their wife's side. In the long stretches when there is no staff attendant present, husbands or partners can provide companionship, support, and encouragement. In difficult moments of examination or medication, they can be comforting. Initially, they may feel embarrassed to use the breathing techniques they learned in preparation classes, but they usually begin to feel more at home when they realize they are performing a necessary function for their partner during each contraction.

Some individuals question whether the father is the best coach during labor. He may be nervous and feel uncomfortable in the hospital. Never having gone through labor himself, he might not understand the expectant mother's needs as well as another woman. There is no universal answer to this issue. Some laboring women want to depend on another woman, someone who has been through labor herself. Others want their husband to intimately share the childbirth experience. Many cultures exclude men from births, just as the American culture did until the past several decades. In some cultures, the woman's mother, or occasionally a daughter, serves as her assistant.

Siblings   If a couple has a child and is expecting another, it is important for them to prepare the older child for the birth of a sibling. Sibling preparation includes providing the child with information about pregnancy, birth, and life with a newborn that is realistic and appropriate for the child's age.

Parents can prepare their older child for the approaching birth at any time during pregnancy. The expectant mother might announce the pregnancy early to explain her fatigue and vomiting. If the child is young and unable to understand the concept of waiting, parents may want to delay announcing the pregnancy until later, when the expectant mother's pregnancy becomes obvious to the child.

Parents may want to consider having the child present at the birth. Many family-centered hospitals, birth centers, and home births make this option available. Some parents wish to minimize or avoid separation from the older child, so they choose to give birth where sibling involvement is possible. These parents feel that, if there is no separation, the child will not develop separation anxiety and will not see the new baby as someone who took the mother away. Sibling involvement in the birth may enhance the attachment between the older child and the new baby. On the other hand, some children may not want to participate in the birthing process and should not be forced into it. Some preschool children may be overwhelmed by the whole process, and older children may feel embarrassed.

If the birth will be in a hospital with a typical stay of two to three days, parents need to consider the possibility that the child may feel separation anxiety by being separated from one or both parents. To ease the child's separation anxiety, the

How has the father's role in childbirth changed in the United States?

How can parents prepare a child for the birth of a sibling?

expectant mother should let the child know approximately when she will be going to the hospital, should tour the hospital with the child if possible, and, when labor begins, should tell the child where she is going. Before birth, the expectant mother can increase the partner or father's role as a caregiver, if he is not already responsible for much of the child's daily care. Parents can ask about the regulations at the hospital or birth setting and, if possible, have the child visit the mother there. As sibling visitation has become recognized as a positive emotional experience for the entire family, hospitals are increasingly allowing children to visit their mothers after the birth of the baby. Some hospitals even allow siblings in the recovery room to see both the mother and the newborn.

In addition to being separated from the mother, the child now has to cope with another emotionally taxing experience: the permanent presence of a crying newborn who requires extensive care and attention from the mother. Life is never the same for the older child after the newborn arrives. Parents who once might have given complete attention to the child now suddenly have less time available for the child—all because of the new sibling. It is not unusual for a child to ask a parent, "When are you going to take it back to the hospital?" Many children engage in regressive and attention-seeking behaviors after a new sibling arrives, such as sucking their thumb, directing anger at their parents or the baby (hitting, biting, or throwing things), wanting a bottle or the mother's breasts for themselves, or bed-wetting. These behaviors are natural and represent the child's way of coping with stress. Parents don't need to worry about these behaviors unless they persist after the child has had a reasonable amount of time to adjust to the new baby. To help the child cope with the arrival of a new baby, parents can (Simkin, Whalley, & Keppler, 2001):

- Read books to the child about living with a new baby before and after the birth.
- Plan for time alone with the older child, and do what he or she wants to do.
- Use the time when the baby is asleep and the parent is rested to give special attention to the older child.
- Give a gift to the older child in the hospital or at home.
- Tell the baby about his or her special older brother or sister when the older sibling is listening.

REVIEW AND REFLECT ▶ LEARNING GOAL 1

1 Discuss the stages, decisions involved, and transitions in birth.

Review
- What are the three stages involved in the birth process?
- What characterizes the childbirth setting and attendants?
- What are the main methods of childbirth?
- What is the fetus/newborn transition like?
- To what extent should a father and siblings be involved in the birth process?

Reflect
- Which childbirth strategies do you plan to follow if you have a child? Why?

2 WHAT ARE SOME MEASURES OF NEONATAL HEALTH AND RESPONSIVENESS?

Almost immediately after birth, after the baby and mother have become acquainted, a newborn is taken to be weighed, cleaned up, and tested for signs of developmental problems that might require urgent attention. The **Apgar Scale** is widely used to assess the health of newborns at one and five minutes after birth. The Apgar Scale evaluates infants' heart rate, respiratory effort, muscle tone, body color, and reflex irritability. An obstetrician or a nurse does the evaluation and gives the newborn a score, or reading, of 0, 1, or 2 on each of these five health signs (see Figure 4.2). A total score of 7 to 10 indicates that the newborn's condition is good. A score of 5 indicates there may be developmental difficulties. A score of 3 or below signals an emergency and indicates that the baby might not survive. The percentage of U.S. newborns with five-minute Apgar scores of 9 or 10, indicating excellent health, increased slowly from 88.6 percent in 1978 to 91.1 percent in 2003 (Martin & others, 2005). In this survey, five-minute Apgar scores of 7 or less decreased from 2.1 percent in 1978 to 1.4 percent in 1993 but has been unchanged since.

The Apgar Scale is especially good at assessing the newborn's ability to respond to the stress of delivery and the new environment (Al-Suleiman & others, 2006; Fallis & others, 2006). It also identifies high-risk infants who need resuscitation. For a more thorough assessment of the newborn, the Brazelton Neonatal Behavioral Assessment Scale or the Neonatal Intensive Care Unit Network Neurobehavioral Scale may be used.

The **Brazelton Neonatal Behavioral Assessment Scale (NBAS)** is performed within 24 to 36 hours after birth. It is also used as a sensitive index of neurological competence in the weeks or months after birth and as a measure in many studies of infant development (Hart & others, 2006; Ohgi, Gima, & Akiyama, 2006). The NBAS assesses the newborn's neurological development, reflexes, and reactions to people. The newborn is an active participant, and the score is based on the newborn's best performance. Sixteen reflexes, such as sneezing, blinking, and rooting, are assessed, along with reactions to circumstances, such as the infant's reaction to a rattle. (We have more to say about reflexes in Chapter 5, when we discuss motor development in infancy.)

The examiner rates the newborn on each of 27 items. For example, item 15 is "cuddliness." The examiner uses nine categories to assess cuddliness and scores the infant on a continuum that ranges from being very resistant to being held to being extremely cuddly and clinging. The 27 items of the NBAS are organized into four categories—physiological, motoric, state, and interaction. Based on these categories, the baby is also classified in global terms, such as "worrisome," "normal," or "superior" (Nugent & Brazelton, 2000).

Apgar Scale A widely used method to assess the health of newborns at one and five minutes after birth. The Apgar Scale evaluates infants' heart rate, respiratory effort, muscle tone, body color, and reflex irritability.

Brazelton Neonatal Behavioral Assessment Scale (NBAS) A test performed within 24 to 36 hours after birth to assess newborns' neurological development, reflexes, and reactions to people.

Score	0	1	2
Heart rate	Absent	Slow—less than 100 beats per minute	Fast—100 to 140 beats per minute
Respiratory effort	No breathing for more than one minute	Irregular and slow	Good breathing with normal crying
Muscle tone	Limp and flaccid	Weak, inactive, but some flexion of extremities	Strong, active motion
Body color	Blue and pale	Body pink, but extremities blue	Entire body pink
Reflex irritability	No response	Grimace	Coughing, sneezing, and crying

FIGURE 4.2 The Apgar Scale A newborn's score on the Apgar Scale indicates whether the baby has urgent medical problems. *What are some trends in the Apgar Scores of U.S. babies?*

A very low NBAS score can indicate brain damage, or stress to the brain that may heal in time. If an infant merely seems sluggish, parents are encouraged to give the infant attention and become more sensitive to the infant's needs. Parents are shown how the newborn can respond to people and how to stimulate such responses. These communications with parents can improve their interaction skills with both high-risk infants and healthy, responsive infants (Girling, 2006).

An "offspring" of the NBAS, the **Neonatal Intensive Care Unit Network Neurobehavioral Scale (NNNS)** provides a more comprehensive analysis of the newborn's behavior, neurological and stress responses, and regulatory capacities (Brazelton, 2004; Lester, Tronick, & Brazelton, 2004). Whereas the NBAS was developed to assess normal, healthy, term infants, T. Berry Brazelton, along with Barry Lester and Edward Tronick, developed the NNNS to assess the at-risk infant. It is especially useful for evaluating preterm infants (although it may not be appropriate for those less than 30 weeks' gestational age) and substance-exposed infants (Miller-Loncar & others, 2005). For example, the NNNS includes items to assess the infant's capacity for regulating arousal, "responsiveness to stimulation, self-soothing, and tolerance of handling" and a scale to provide information about "manifestations of drug dependence or environment-related stress" (Boukydis & others, 2004, p. 680). According to Brazelton (2004), although created to evaluate at-risk infants, the NNNS is also appropriate for assessing normal, healthy, full-term infants.

REVIEW AND REFLECT   LEARNING GOAL 2

2 Describe three measures of neonatal health and responsiveness.

Review
- How can the Apgar Scale, the Brazelton Neonatal Behavioral Assessment Scale, and the Neonatal Intensive Care Unit Network Neurobehavioral Scale be characterized?

Reflect
- What information does the Brazelton assessment provide that the Apgar does not?

3 HOW DO LOW BIRTH WEIGHT AND PRETERM INFANTS DEVELOP?

Preterm and Small for Date Infants   Consequences of Low Birth Weight   Nurturing Preterm Infants

Neonatal Intensive Care Unit Network Neurobehavioral Scale (NNNS) An "offspring" of the NBAS, the NNNS provides a more comprehensive analysis of the newborn's behavior, neurological and stress responses, and regulatory capacities.

low birth weight infants Weigh less than 5½ pounds at birth.

preterm infants Babies born three weeks or more before the pregnancy has reached its full term.

Different conditions that pose threats for newborns have been given different labels. We examine these conditions and discuss interventions for improving outcomes of preterm infants.

Preterm and Small for Date Infants

Three related conditions pose threats to many newborns: low birth weight, being preterm, and being small-for-date. **Low birth weight infants** weigh less than 5½ pounds at birth. *Very low birth weight* newborns weigh under 3 pounds and *extremely low birth weight* newborns under 2 pounds. **Preterm infants** are those born three weeks or more before the pregnancy has reached its full term—in other words,

35 or fewer weeks after conception. **Small for date infants** (also called *small for gestational age infants*) are those whose birth weight is below normal when the length of the pregnancy is considered. They weigh less than 90 percent of all babies of the same gestational age. Small for date infants may be preterm or full term. One study found that small for date infants had more than a four fold risk of death (Regev & others, 2003).

The preterm birth rate in the United States increased 18 percent from 1990 to 2004 (Hoyert & others, 2006). One of every eight U.S. births is now preterm (Ashton, 2006). The increase in preterm birth is likely due to such factors as the increasing number of births to women 35 years and older, increasing rates of multiple births, increased management of maternal and fetal conditions (for example, inducing labor preterm if medical technology indicates it will increase the likelihood of survival), increased substance abuse (tobacco, alcohol), and increased stress (Goldenberg & Culhane, 2007; Petrini, 2004). Ethnic variations characterize preterm birth. For example, in 2003, the likelihood of being born preterm was 1 in 8 for all U.S. infants but the rate was 1 in 6 for African American infants (Ashton, 2006).

There has been considerable interest generated in the role that progestin might play in reducing preterm births. In one study, weekly injections of the hormone progesterone, which is naturally produced by the ovaries, lowered the rate of preterm births by one-third (Meis & Peaceman, 2003). Recent studies provide further support for the use of progestin in the second trimester of pregnancy in reducing the risk of preterm delivery (Coomarasamy & others, 2006; Lamont & Jaqqat, 2007; Mackenzie & others, 2006). A recent survey indicated that the use of progestin to prevent preterm birth by maternal-fetal medicine surveys increased from 38 percent of these specialists to 67 percent in 2005 (Ness & others, 2006).

As we see next, in the *Diversity in Children's Development* interlude, the incidence and causes of low birth weight vary across countries.

A "kilogram kid," weighing less than 2.3 pounds at birth. *What are some possible outcomes for low birth weight infants?*

Diversity in Children's Development

INCIDENCE AND CAUSES OF LOW BIRTH WEIGHT AROUND THE WORLD

Most, but not all, preterm babies are also low birth weight babies. The incidence of low birth weight varies considerably from country to country. In some countries, such as India and Sudan, where poverty is rampant and the health and nutrition of mothers are poor, the percentage of low birth weight babies reaches as high as 31 percent (see Figure 4.3). In the United States, there has been an increase in low birth weight infants in the last two decades. The U.S. low birth weight rate of 8 percent in 2004 is considerably higher than that of many other developed countries (Hoyert & others, 2006). For example, only 4 percent of the infants born in Sweden, Finland, Norway, and Korea are low birth weight, and only 5 percent of those born in New Zealand, Australia, and France are low birth weight.

The causes of low birth weight also vary. In the developing world, low birth weight stems mainly from the mother's poor health and nutrition (Lasker & others, 2005). Diseases such as diarrhea and malaria, which are common in developing countries, can impair fetal growth if the mother becomes infected while she is pregnant. In developed countries, cigarette smoking during pregnancy is the leading cause of low birth weight (Delpisheh & others, 2006; Hankins & Longo, 2006). In both developed and developing countries, adolescents who give birth when their

(continued on next page)

small for date (small for gestational age) infants Babies whose birth weight is below normal when the length of pregnancy is considered.

FIGURE 4.3 Percentage of infants born with low birth weight in selected countries
Source: UNICEF (2005)

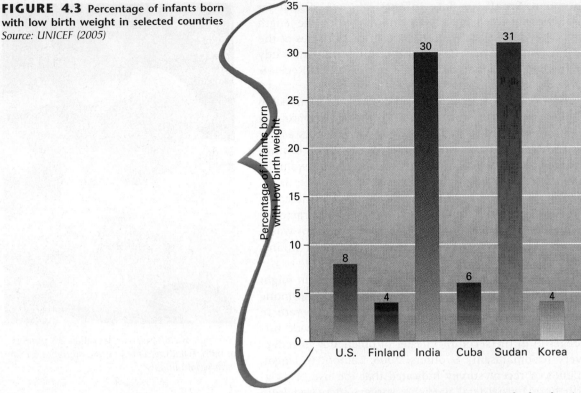

bodies have not fully matured are at risk for having low birth weight babies (Malamitsi-Puchner & Boutsikou, 2006). In the United States, the increase in the number of low birth weight infants is thought to be due to such factors as the use of drugs, poor nutrition, multiple births, and reproductive technologies (Bacak & others, 2005; Hoyert & others, 2006).

Consequences of Low Birth Weight

Although most low birth weight infants are normal and healthy, as a group they have more health and developmental problems than normal birth weight infants (Moss, 2006; Mufti, Setna, & Nazir, 2006). The number and severity of these problems increase as birth weight decreases (Kilbride, Thorstad, & Daily, 2004). Survival rates for infants who are born very early and very small have risen, but with this improved survival rate have come increases in rates of severe brain damage (Yu, 2000). The lower the birth weight, the greater the likelihood of brain injury (Watenberg & others, 2002). Approximately 7 percent of moderately low birth weight infants (3 pounds 5 ounces to 5 pounds 8 ounces) have brain injuries. This figure increases to 20 percent for the smallest newborns (1 pound 2 ounces to 3 pounds 5 ounces). Low birth weight infants are also more likely than normal birth weight infants to have lung or liver diseases.

At school age, children who were born low in birth weight are more likely than their normal birth weight counterparts to have a learning disability, attention deficit hyperactivity disorder, or breathing problems such as asthma (Hintz & others, 2005; Wocadlo & Rieger, 2006). One study revealed that 17-year-olds who were born with low birth weight were 50 percent more likely than normal birth weight individuals to have reading and mathematics deficits (Breaslau, Paneth, & Lucia, 2004). Approximately 50 percent of all low birth weight children are enrolled in special education programs.

Note that not all of these adverse consequences can be attributed solely to being born low in birth weight. Some of the less severe but more common developmental and physical delays occur because many low birth weight children come from disadvantaged environments (Malamitsi-Puchner & Boutsikou, 2006).

Nurturing Preterm Infants

Some effects of being born low in birth weight can be reversed. Intensive enrichment programs that provide medical and educational services for both the parents and children can improve short-term outcomes for low birth weight children. Federal laws mandate that services for school-age children be expanded to include family-based care for infants. At present, these services are aimed at children born with severe disabilities. The availability of services for moderately low birth weight children who do not have severe physical problems varies, but most states do not provide these services.

Currently, the two most popular Neonatal Intensive Care Unit (NICU) interventions that involve parents are breast feeding and **kangaroo care,** a way of holding a preterm infant so that there is skin-to-skin contact. Both of these interventions were uncommon until recently.

A recent survey revealed that breast feeding is now virtually universally encouraged for mothers with newborns in U.S. NICUs (Field & others, 2006). Recent surveys indicated that kangaroo care is used from 82 to 97 percent by nurses in NICUs (Engler & others, 2002; Field & others, 2006). Also in one of these surveys, massage therapy was used in 37 percent of the NICUs (Field & others, 2006).

Let's further examine kangaroo care and massage therapy. In kangaroo care, the baby, wearing only a diaper, is held upright against the parent's bare chest, much as a baby kangaroo is carried by its mother. Kangaroo care is typically practiced for two to three hours per day, skin-to-skin over an extended time in early infancy (Feldman & others, 2003; Johnson, 2007).

Why use kangaroo care with preterm infants? Preterm infants often have difficulty coordinating their breathing and heart rate, and the close physical contact with the parent provided by kangaroo care can help to stabilize the preterm infant's heartbeat, temperature, and breathing (Kennell, 2006; Ludington-Hoe & others, 2006). Further, preterm infants who experience kangaroo care have longer periods of sleep, gain more weight, decrease their crying, have longer periods of alertness, and earlier hospital discharge (Ludington-Hoe & others, 2006; Worku & Kassir, 2005). One study compared 26 low birth weight infants who received kangaroo care with 27 low birth weight infants who received standard medical/nursing care (Ohgi & others, 2002). At both 6 and 12 months of age, the kangaroo care infants were more alert and responsive, less irritable and fussy, and had a more positive mood. Another study found that preterm infants who received kangaroo care had better control of their arousal, more effectively attended to stimuli, and engaged in more sustained exploration during a toy session than a control group of preterm infants who did not receive kangaroo care (Feldman & others, 2002). Increasingly kangaroo care is being recommended for full-term infants as well (Johnson, 2005).

Many preterm infants experience less touch than full-term infants because they are isolated in temperature-controlled incubators (Chia, Selleck, & Gans, 2006). The research of Tiffany Field has led to a surge of interest in the role that massage might play in improving the developmental outcomes for preterm infants. To read about her research, see the following *Research in Children's Development interlude.*

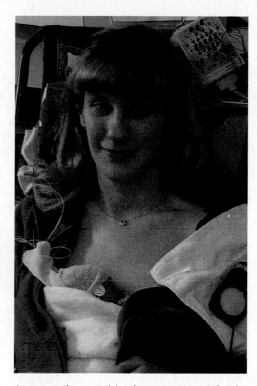

A new mother practicing kangaroo care. *What is kangaroo care?*

Research in Children's Development

TIFFANY FIELD'S RESEARCH ON MASSAGE THERAPY

Throughout history and in many cultures, caregivers have massaged infants. In Africa and Asia, infants are routinely massaged by parents or other family members for several months after birth. In the United States, interest in using touch and massage to

(continued on next page)

kangaroo care A way of holding a preterm infant so that there is skin-to-skin contact.

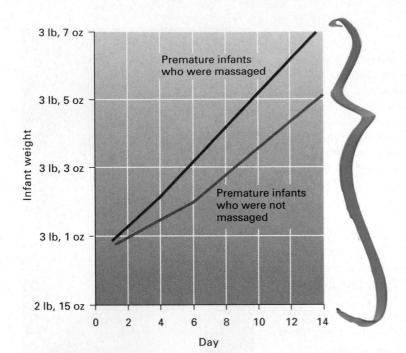

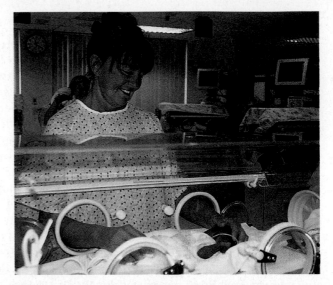

Shown here is Dr. Tiffany Field massaging a newborn infant. *What types of infants has massage therapy been shown to help?*

FIGURE 4.4 Weight Gain Comparison of Premature Infants Who Were Massaged or Not Massaged The graph shows that the mean daily weight gain of premature infants who were massaged was greater than for premature infants who were not massaged. *Besides the results of this study, what else would you want to know before concluding that massage therapy helps premature infants?*

improve the growth, health, and well-being of infants has been stimulated by the research of Tiffany Field (1998, 2001, 2003, 2007; Field, Hernandez-Reif, & Freedman, 2004; Field, Diego, & Hernandez-Reif, 2007; Field & others, 2006), director of the Touch Research Institute at the University of Miami School of Medicine.

In Field's first study in this area, massage therapy consisting of firm stroking with the palms of the hands was given three times per day for 15-minute periods to preterm infants (Field & others, 1986). The massage therapy led to 47 percent greater weight gain than standard medical treatment (see Figure 4.4). The massaged infants also were more active and alert than preterm infants who were not massaged, and they performed better on developmental tests.

In later studies, Field demonstrated the benefits of massage therapy for infants who faced a variety of problems. For example, preterm infants exposed to cocaine in utero who received massage therapy gained weight and improved their scores on developmental tests (Wheeden & others, 1993). In another investigation, newborns born to HIV-positive mothers were randomly assigned to a massage therapy group or to a control group that did not receive the therapy (Scafidi & Field, 1996). The massaged infants showed superior performance on a wide range of assessments, including daily weight gain. Another study investigated 1- to 3-month-old infants born to depressed adolescent mothers (Field & others, 1996). The infants of depressed mothers who received massage therapy had lower stress—as well as improved emotionality, sociability, and soothability—compared with the nonmassaged infants of depressed mothers.

In one study, Field and her colleagues (2004) taught mothers how to massage their full-term infants. Once a day before bedtime, the mothers massaged the babies using either light or moderate pressure. Infants who were massaged with moderate pressure "gained more weight, were greater length, performed better on the orientation scale of the Brazelton, had lower Brazelton excitability and depression scores, and exhibited less agitation during sleep" (p. 435).

In a research review of the use of massage therapy with preterm infants, Field and her colleagues (2004) concluded that the most consistent findings involve two positive results: (1) increased weight gain and (2) discharge from the hospital from three to six days earlier.

Infants are not the only ones who may benefit from massage therapy (Field, 2007). In other studies, Field and her colleagues have demonstrated the benefits of massage therapy with women in reducing labor pain (Field, Hernandez-Rief, Taylor, & others, 1997), with children who have arthritis (Field, Hernandez-Rief, Seligman, & others, 1997), with children who have asthma (Field, Henteleff, & others, 1998), with autistic children's attentiveness (Field, Lasko, & others, 1997), and with adolescents who have attention deficit hyperactivity disorder (Field, Quintino, & others, 1998).

REVIEW AND REFLECT ◆ LEARNING GOAL 3

3 Characterize the development of low birth weight and preterm infants.

Review
- What is a low birth weight infant? How can preterm and small for date infants be distinguished?
- What are the long-term outcomes for low birth weight infants?
- What is known about the roles of kangaroo care and massage therapy with preterm infants?

Reflect
- What can be done to reduce the United States' high rates of low birth weight babies?

---

4 WHAT HAPPENS DURING THE POSTPARTUM PERIOD?

Physical Adjustments	Emotional and Psychological Adjustments	Bonding

The weeks after childbirth present challenges for many new parents and their offspring. This is the **postpartum period,** the period after childbirth or delivery that lasts for about six weeks or until the mother's body has completed its adjustment and has returned to a nearly pre-pregnant state. It is a time when the woman adjusts, both physically and psychologically, to the process of childbearing.

The postpartum period involves a great deal of adjustment and adaptation. The baby has to be cared for. The mother has to recover from childbirth, to learn how to take care of the baby, and to learn to feel good about herself as a mother. The father needs to learn how to take care of his recovering wife, to learn how to take care of the baby, and to learn how to feel good about himself as a father. Many health professionals believe that the best way to meet these challenges is with a family-centered approach that uses the family's resources to support an early and smooth adjustment to the newborn by all family members. The adjustments needed are physical, emotional, and psychological. To read about one health professional who helps women to adapt in the postpartum period, see the *Careers in Child Development* profile.

Physical Adjustments

A woman's body makes numerous physical adjustments in the first days and weeks after childbirth (Border, 2006). She may have a great deal of energy or feel

postpartum period The period after childbirth when the mother adjusts, both physically and psychologically, to the process of childbearing. This period lasts for about six weeks, or until her body has completed its adjustment and has returned to a near-prepregnant state.

Careers in CHILD DEVELOPMENT

Rachel Thompson
Obstetrician/Gynecologist

Rachel Thompson is the senior member of Houston Women's Care Associates, which specializes in health care for women. She has one of Houston's most popular obstetrics/gynecology (OB/GYN) practices. Thompson's medical degree is from Baylor College of Medicine, where she also completed her internship and residency. Thompson's work focuses on many of the topics we discuss in this chapter on birth, and the postpartum period.

In addition to her clinical practice, Thompson also is a clinical instructor in the Department of Obstetrics and Gynecology at Baylor College of Medicine. Thompson says that one of the unique features of their health-care group is that the staff is comprised only of women who are full-time practitioners.

Rachel Thompson (right) talking with one of her patients at Houston Women's Care Associates.

exhausted and let down. Most new mothers feel tired and need rest. Though these changes are normal, the fatigue can undermine the new mother's sense of well-being and confidence in her ability to cope with a new baby and a new family life (Runquist, 2007).

The physical adjustments during the postpartum period are influenced by what preceded it. During pregnancy, the woman's body gradually adjusted to physical changes, but now it is forced to respond quickly. The method of delivery and circumstances surrounding the delivery affect the speed with which the mother's body readjusts (London & others, 2007).

After delivery, a mother's body undergoes sudden and dramatic changes in hormone production. When the placenta is delivered, estrogen and progesterone levels drop steeply and remain low until the ovaries start producing hormones again. The woman will probably begin menstruating again in four to eight weeks if she is not breast feeding. If she is breast feeding, she might not menstruate for several months to a year or more, though ovulation can occur during this time. The first several menstrual periods following delivery might be heavier than usual, but periods soon return to normal.

Involution is the process by which the uterus returns to its prepregnant size five or six weeks after birth. Immediately following birth, the uterus weighs 2 to 3 pounds. By the end of five or six weeks, the uterus weighs 2 to 3½ ounces. Nursing the baby helps contract the uterus at a rapid rate.

Some women and men want to resume sexual intercourse as soon as possible after the birth. Others feel constrained or afraid. A sore perineum (the area between the anus and vagina), a demanding baby, lack of help, and extreme fatigue affect a woman's ability to relax and to enjoy making love. Physicians often recommend that women refrain from having sexual intercourse for approximately six weeks following the birth of the baby.

If the woman regularly engaged in conditioning exercises during pregnancy, exercise will help her recover her former body contour and strength. With a caregiver's approval, the new mother can begin some exercises as soon as one hour after delivery. A recent study found that women who maintained or increased their exercise from prepregnancy to postpartum had better maternal well-being than women who engaged in no exercise or decreased their exercise from prepregnancy to postpartum (Blum, Beaudoin, & Caton-Lemos, 2005).

Relaxation techniques are also helpful during the postpartum period. Five minutes of slow breathing on a stressful day in the postpartum period can relax and refresh the new mother, as well as the new baby.

Emotional and Psychological Adjustments

Emotional fluctuations are common for mothers in the postpartum period. These emotional fluctuations may be due to any of a number of factors: hormonal changes, fatigue, inexperience or lack of confidence with newborn babies, or the extensive time and demands involved in caring for a newborn. For some women, emotional

involution The process by which the uterus returns to its prepregnant size.

fluctuations decrease within several weeks after the delivery, but other women experience more long-lasting emotional swings (Hall & Wittkowski, 2006).

"Baby Blues" and Postpartum Depression

As shown in Figure 4.5, about 70 percent of new mothers in the United States have what are called "baby blues." About two to three days after birth, they begin to feel depressed, anxious, and upset. These feelings may come and go for several months after the birth, often peaking about three to five days after birth. Even without treatment, these feelings usually go away after one or two weeks.

For other women, emotional fluctuations persist and can produce feelings of anxiety, depression, and difficulty in coping with stress (Morrissey, 2007; Tam & Chung, 2007). Mothers who have such feelings, even when they are getting adequate rest, may benefit from professional help in dealing with their problems. Here are some of the signs that can indicate a need for professional counseling about postpartum adaptation: excessive worrying, depression, extreme changes in appetite, crying spells, and inability to sleep.

Postpartum depression involves a major depressive episode that typically occurs about four weeks after delivery. In other words, women with postpartum depression have such strong feelings of sadness, anxiety, or despair that for at least a two-week period they have trouble coping with their daily tasks. Without treatment, postpartum depression may become worse and last for many months (Driscoll, 2006; Hanley, 2006). About 10 percent of new mothers experience postpartum depression. Between 25 to 50 percent of these depressed new mothers have episodes that last six months or longer (Beck, 2002). If untreated, approximately 25 of these women are still depressed a year later.

The hormonal changes occurring after childbirth are believed to play a role in postpartum depression (Groer & Morgan, 2007; Jolley & others, 2007). Estrogen helps some women with postpartum depression, but estrogen also has some possible problematic side effects (Grigoriadis & Kennedy, 2002). Several antidepressant drugs are effective in treating postpartum depression and appear to be safe for breast feeding women (Horowitz & Cousins, 2006). Psychotherapy, especially cognitive therapy, also is an effective treatment of postpartum depression for many women (Beck, 2006; Lasiuk & Ferguson, 2005). Also, engaging in regular exercise may help in treating postpartum depression (Daley, Macarthur, Winter, 2007).

Can a mother's postpartum depression affect the way mothers interact with their infants? A recent national survey indicated that mothers who were depressed were 1.5 times more likely to provide less healthy feeding and sleeping practices for their newborns (Paulson, Dauber, & Leiferman, 2006). In another study, a sample of 570 women and their infants were assessed three months after delivery (Righetti-Veltema & others, 2002). Ten percent of the mothers were classified as experiencing postpartum depression. Compared with nondepressed mothers, the depressed mothers had less vocal and visual communication with their infant, touched the infant less, and smiled less at the infant. The negative effects of the postpartum depression were linked to infants having eating or sleeping problems.

In addition to depression, might mothers as well as fathers have a higher incidence of psychological disorders in general in the postpartum period? A recent large-scale study followed Danish couples who had a child and those who did not during a one-year postpartum period (Munk-Olsen & others, 2006). The mothers, but not the fathers, were more likely to have a psychological disorder, such as depression or the severe disorder of schizophrenia, than couples who did not have a child born in the one-year period.

A Father's Adjustment

Although fathers may not show an increase in psychological disorders in the postpartum period, they still undergo considerable adjustment and experience considerable stress, even when they work away from home all day (Cox, 2006; Pinheiro & others, 2006). Many fathers feel that the baby comes

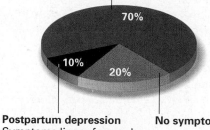

"Baby blues"
Symptoms appear 2 to 3 days after delivery and subside within 1 to 2 weeks.

70%

10% 20%

Postpartum depression
Symptoms linger for weeks or months and interfere with daily functioning.

No symptoms

FIGURE 4.5 Postpartum Blues and Postpartum Depression Among U.S. Women Some health professionals refer to the postpartum period as the "fourth trimester." Though the time span of the postpartum, period does not necessarily cover three months, the term "fourth trimester" suggests continuity and the importance of the first several months after birth for the mother.

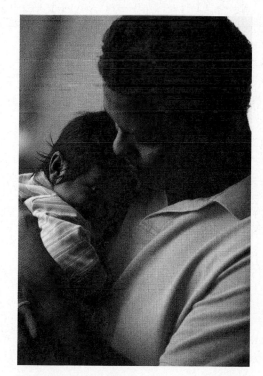

The postpartum period is a time of considerable adjustment and adaptation for both the mother and the father. Fathers can provide an important support system for mothers, especially in helping mothers care for young infants. *What kinds of tasks might the father of a newborn do to support the mother?*

postpartum depression Strong feelings of sadness, anxiety, or despair in new mothers that make it difficult for them to carry out daily tasks.

A mother bonds with her infant moments after it is born. *How critical is bonding for the development of social competence later in childhood?*

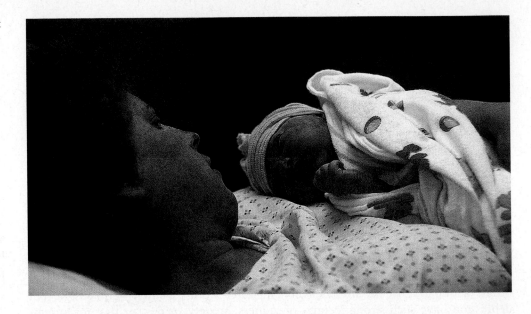

first and gets all of the mother's attention; some feel that they have been replaced by the baby. A recent national survey of more than 5,000 two-parent U.S. families in the postpartum period revealed that 14 percent of mothers and 10 percent of fathers reported depression that was at levels associated with the clinical diagnosis of depression (Paulson, Dauber, & Leiferman, 2006).

To help the father adjust, parents should set aside some special time to be together with each other. The father's postpartum reaction also likely will be improved if he has taken childbirth classes with the mother and is an active participant in caring for the baby.

For the father as well as the mother, it is important to put time and thought into being a competent parent of a young infant. Both need to become aware of the infant's needs—physical, psychological, and emotional. Both the mother and the father need to develop a sensitive, comfortable relationship with the baby.

Bonding

A special component of the parent-infant relationship is **bonding,** the formation of a connection, especially a physical bond between parents and the newborn in the period shortly after birth. Sometimes hospitals seem determined to deter bonding. Drugs given to the mother to make her delivery less painful can make the mother drowsy, interfering with her ability to respond to and stimulate the newborn. Mothers and newborns are often separated shortly after delivery, and preterm infants are isolated from their mothers even more than full-term infants.

Do these practices do any harm? Some physicians believe that during the period shortly after birth, the parents and newborn need to form an emotional attachment as a foundation for optimal development in years to come (Kennell, 2006; Kennell & McGrath, 1999). Is there evidence that close contact between mothers in the first several days after birth is critical for optimal development later in life? Although some research supports this bonding hypothesis (Klaus & Kennell, 1976), a body of research challenges the significance of the first few days of life as a critical period (Bakeman & Brown, 1980; Rode & others, 1981). Indeed, the extreme form of the bonding hypothesis—that the newborn must have close contact with the mother in the first few days of life to develop optimally—simply is not true.

Nonetheless, the weakness of the bonding hypothesis should not be used as an excuse to keep motivated mothers from interacting with their newborns. Such contact brings pleasure to many mothers. In some mother-infant pairs—including preterm

bonding A close connection, especially a physical bond between parents and their newborn in the period shortly after birth.

infants, adolescent mothers, and mothers from disadvantaged circumstances—early close contact may establish a climate for improved interaction after the mother and infant leave the hospital.

Many hospitals now offer a *rooming-in* arrangement, in which the baby remains in the mother's room most of the time during its hospital stay. However, if parents choose not to use this rooming-in arrangement, the weight of the research suggests that this decision will not harm the infant emotionally (Lamb, 1994).

REVIEW AND REFLECT   LEARNING GOAL 4

4 Explain the physical and psychological aspects of the postpartum period.

Review

- What does the postpartum period involve? What physical adjustments does the woman's body make in this period?

- What emotional and psychological adjustments characterize the postpartum period?

- Is bonding critical for optimal development?

Reflect

- If you are a female, what can you do to adjust effectively in the postpartum period? If you are a male, what can you do to help in the postpartum period?

REACH YOUR LEARNING GOALS

1 WHAT HAPPENS DURING THE BIRTH PROCESS? *Discuss the stages, decisions involved, and transitions in birth.*

Stages of the Birth Process

- The first stage of birth lasts about 12 to 14 hours for a woman having her first child. The cervix dilates to about 4 inches. The second stage begins when the baby's head starts to move through the cervix and ends with the baby's complete emergence. The third stage is afterbirth.

Childbirth Setting and Attendants

- In the United States, the vast majority of births occur in hospitals and are attended by physicians. Many hospitals now have birthing centers. Some women with good medical histories and who are at low risk for problem deliveries have babies at home. In many countries, such as Holland, much higher percentages of babies are born at home. Some births are attended by a midwife, and in many countries a doula attends.

Methods of Childbirth

- Among the methods of delivery are medicated, natural and prepared, and cesarean. The three basic kinds of drugs used in delivering a baby are analgesics, anesthesia, and oxytocics. Predicting how a particular drug will affect an individual pregnant woman and the fetus is difficult. Today the trend is toward using some medication during childbirth but keeping it to a minimum, if possible. The Lamaze method of childbirth is widely used in the United States.

The Transition from Fetus to Newborn

- In some cases, anoxia occurs. Anoxia involves an insufficient supply of oxygen in the fetus/newborn condition. Being born involves considerable stress, but the baby is well prepared and adapted to handle the stress. Large quantities of stress-related hormones (adrenaline and noradrenalin) are secreted during the fetus/newborn transition.

Family Involvement

- In the past several decades, fathers increasingly have participated in childbirth. In some cultures, the father is excluded from childbirth, as was the case in the United States until recently. Sibling preparation includes providing the child with information about the pregnancy, birth, and life with a newborn that is realistic and appropriate for the child's age.

2 WHAT ARE SOME MEASURES OF NEONATAL HEALTH AND RESPONSIVENESS? *Describe three measures of neonatal health and responsiveness.*

- For many years, the Apgar Scale has been used to assess the newborn's health. It is used one and five minutes after birth and assesses heart rate, respiratory effort, muscle tone, body color, and reflex irritability. The Brazelton Neonatal Behavioral Assessment is performed within 24 to 36 hours after birth to examine the newborn's neurological development, reflexes, and reactions to people. Recently, the Neonatal Intensive Care Unit Network Neurobehavioral Scale (NNNS) was constructed; it provides a more comprehensive analysis of the newborn's behavior, neurological and stress responses, and regulatory capacities.

3 HOW DO LOW BIRTH WEIGHT AND PRETERM INFANTS DEVELOP? *Characterize the development of low birth weight and preterm infants.*

Preterm and Small for Date Infants

- Low birth weight infants weigh less than 5½ pounds at birth. Low birth weight babies may be preterm (born three weeks or more before the pregnancy has reached full term) or small for date (also called small for gestational age, which refers to infants whose birth weight is below normal when the length of pregnancy is considered). Small for date infants may be preterm or full term.

Consequences of Low Birth Weight

- Although most low birth weight babies are normal and healthy, as a group they have more health and developmental problems than full-term babies. The number and severity of the problems increases as birth weight decreases.

Nurturing Preterm Infants

- Kangaroo care, a way of holding a preterm infant so that there is skin-to-skin contact, has positive effects on preterm infants. Massage therapy is increasingly being used with preterm infants and has positive outcomes.

4 WHAT HAPPENS DURING THE POSTPARTUM PERIOD? *Explain the physical and psychological aspects of the postpartum period.*

Physical Adjustments

- The postpartum period is the period after childbirth or delivery. It is a time when the woman adjusts, both physically and psychologically, to the process of childbearing. It lasts for about six weeks, or until the body has completed its adjustment. Physical adjustments include fatigue, involution, hormonal changes that include a dramatic drop in estrogen and progesterone, deciding when to resume sexual intercourse, and exercises to recover former body contour and strength.

Emotional and Psychological Adjustments

- The mother's emotional fluctuations are common in the postpartum period. These fluctuations may be due to hormonal changes, fatigue, inexperience or lack of confidence in caring for a newborn, or the extensive demands involved in caring for a newborn. For some, these emotional fluctuations are minimal and disappear in several weeks, but for others they can be more long-lasting. Postpartum depression involves such strong feelings of sadness, anxiety, or despair that new mothers have difficulty carrying out daily tasks. Postpartum depression affects approximately 10 percent of new mothers. The father also goes through a postpartum adjustment. He may feel that the baby now receives all his wife's attention. Some new fathers also may experience postpartum depression, especially if his partner has postpartum depression. Another adjustment for both the mother and the father is the time and thought that go into being a competent parent of a young infant.

Bonding

- Bonding refers to the occurrence of a connection, especially a physical bond, between parents and the newborn shortly after birth. Bonding has not been found to be critical in the development of a competent infant or child, although it may stimulate positive interaction between some mother-infant pairs.

KEY TERMS

afterbirth 115
doula 116
analgesia 117
anesthesia 117
oxytocin 117
natural childbirth 117
prepared childbirth 117
breech position 120

cesarean delivery 120
Apgar Scale 123
Brazelton Neonatal
    Behavioral Assessment
    Scale (NBAS) 123
Neonatal Intensive Care Unit
    Network Neurobehavioral
    Scale (NNNS) 124

low birth weight
    infants 124
preterm infants 124
small for date (small for
    gestational age)
    infants 125
kangaroo care 127
postpartum period 129

involution 130
postpartum depression 131
bonding 132

KEY PEOPLE

MAKING A DIFFERENCE

Effective Birth Strategies

Here are some birth strategies that may benefit the baby and the mother:

- *Take a childbirth class.* These classes provide information about the childbirth experience.
- *Become knowledgeable about different childbirth techniques.* We described a number of different childbirth techniques in this chapter, including Lamaze and using doulas. Obtain more detailed information about such techniques by reading a good book, such as *Pregnancy, Childbirth, and the Newborn* by Penny Simkin, Janet Whalley, and Ann Keppler (2001).
- *Use positive intervention with at-risk infants.* Massage can improve the developmental outcome of at-risk infants.

Intensive enrichment programs that include medical, educational, psychological, occupational, and physical domains can benefit low birth weight infants. Intervention with low birth weight infants should involve an individualized plan.

- *Involve the family in the birth process.* If they are motivated to participate, the husband, partner and siblings can benefit from being involved in the birth process. A mother, sister, or friend can also provide support.
- *Know about the adaptation required in the postpartum period.* The postpartum period involves considerable adaptation and adjustment by the mother. This adjustment is both physical and emotional. Exercise and relaxation techniques can benefit mothers in the postpartum period. So can an understanding, supportive husband.

RESOURCES FOR IMPROVING CHILDREN'S LIVES

Lamaze International

www.lamaze.com

Lamaze provides information about the Lamaze method and taking or teaching Lamaze classes.

The Doula Book

by Marshall Klaus, John Kennell, and Phyllis Klaus (2002)
New York: Perseus Books

Learn more about how valuable a doula can be in the childbirth process in this book.

Birth: Issues in Perinatal Care

This multidisciplinary journal on perinatal care is written for health professionals and contains articles on research and clinical practice, review articles, and commentary.

International Cesarean Network International

www.icanonline.org

This organization provides extensive information and advice about cesarean birth.

Postpartum Support International (PSI)

www.postpartum.net

PSI provides information about postpartum depression.

E-LEARNING TOOLS

Connect to **www.mhhe.com/santrockc10** to research the answers and complete these exercises. In addition, you'll find a number of other resources and valuable study tools for Chapter 4, "Birth," on this Web site.

Taking It to the Net

1. Jessica and Eric have just given birth to their first child. Eric has noticed that since the birth three months ago, Jessica has seemed a bit withdrawn and sad. He remembers from their Lamaze classes that there is a condition called postpartum depression. What can Eric do to help Jessica through this difficult time period?

2. The author of your text provides a summary of the most widely used birthing methods in the United States. What other birthing methods might a woman consider?

3. You have just given birth, and the nurse has informed you that tomorrow your baby will be assessed using the Brazelton Neonatal Behavioral Assessment Scale. What will your baby's experience be like during this assessment?

Health and Well-Being, Parenting, and Education

Build your decision-making skills by trying your hand at the health and well-being, parenting, and education exercises.

Video Clips

The Online Learning Center includes the following video for this chapter:

1. *Midwifery*—1524
   A certified midwife discusses midwives and how they differ from obstetricians.

Section Three
INFANCY

> *Babies are such a nice way to start people.*
>
> —DON HEROLD
> American Writer, 20th Century

As newborns, we were not empty-headed organisms. We had some basic reflexes, among them crying, kicking, and coughing. We slept a lot, and occasionally we smiled, although the meaning of our first smiles was not entirely clear. We ate and we grew. We crawled and then we walked, a journey of a thousand miles beginning with a single step. Sometimes we conformed; sometimes others conformed to us. Our development was a continuous creation of more complex forms. Our helpless kind demanded the meeting eyes of love. We juggled the necessity of curbing our will with becoming what we could will freely. Section 3 contains three chapters: "Physical Development in Infancy" (Chapter 5), "Cognitive Development in Infancy" (Chapter 6), and "Socioemotional Development in Infancy" (Chapter 7).

5 Physical Development in Infancy

A baby is the most complicated object made by unskilled labor.

—ANONYMOUS

| CHAPTER OUTLINE | LEARNING GOALS |

Images of Children's Development
The Stories of Latonya and Ramona: Breast and Bottle Feeding in Africa

Latonya is a newborn baby in Ghana. During her first days of life, she has been kept apart from her mother and bottle fed. Manufacturers of infant formula provide the hospital where she was born with free or subsidized milk powder. Her mother has been persuaded to bottle feed rather than breast feed her. When her mother bottle feeds Latonya, she overdilutes the milk formula with unclean water. Latonya's feeding bottles have not been sterilized. Latonya becomes very sick. She dies before her first birthday.

Ramona was born in Nigeria with a "baby-friendly" program. In this program, babies are not separated from their mothers when they are born, and the mothers are encouraged to breast feed them. The mothers are told of the perils that bottle feeding can bring because of unsafe water and unsterilized bottles. They also are informed about the advantages of breast milk, which include its nutritious and hygienic qualities, its ability to immunize babies against common illnesses, and its role in reducing the mother's risk of breast and ovarian cancer. Ramona's mother is breast feeding her. At 1 year of age, Ramona is very healthy.

For many years, maternity units in hospitals favored bottle feeding and did not give mothers adequate information about the benefits of breast feeding. In recent years, the World Health Organization and UNICEF have tried to reverse the trend toward bottle feeding of infants in many impoverished countries. They instituted the "baby-friendly" program in many countries (Grant, 1993). They also persuaded the International Association of Infant Formula Manufacturers to stop marketing their baby formulas to hospitals in countries where the governments support the baby-friendly initiatives (Grant, 1993). For the hospitals themselves, costs actually were reduced as infant formula, feeding bottles, and separate nurseries became unnecessary. For example, baby-friendly Jose Fabella Memorial Hospital in the Philippines reported saving 8 percent of its annual budget. Still, there are many places in the world where the baby-friendly initiatives have not been implemented (UNICEF, 2004).

The advantages of breast feeding in impoverished countries are substantial. However, these advantages must be balanced against the risk of passing HIV to the baby through breast milk if the mothers have the virus; the majority of mothers don't know that they are infected (Doherty & others, 2006). In some areas of Africa, more than 30 percent of mothers have the HIV virus.

(Top) An HIV-infected mother breast feeding her baby in Nairobi, Africa; *(bottom)* Rwandan mother bottle feeding her baby. *What are some concerns about breast versus bottle feeding in impoverished African countries?*

PREVIEW

It is very important for infants to get a healthy start. When they do, their first two years of life are likely to be a time of amazing development. In this chapter, we focus on the biological domain and the infant's physical development, exploring physical growth, motor development, and sensory and perceptual development.

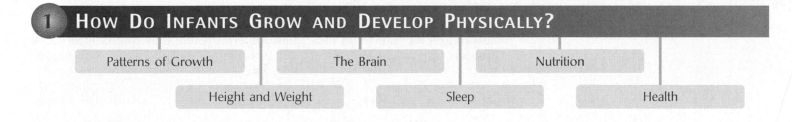

① HOW DO INFANTS GROW AND DEVELOP PHYSICALLY?

Patterns of Growth	The Brain	Nutrition

Height and Weight	Sleep	Health

Infants' physical development in the first two years of life is extensive. At birth, a newborn's head is quite large when compared to the rest of the body. They have little strength in their neck and cannot hold their head up. They have some basic reflexes. In the span of 12 months, infants become capable of sitting anywhere, standing, stooping, climbing, and usually walking. During the second year, growth decelerates, but rapid increases in such activities as running and climbing take place. Let's now examine in greater detail the sequence of physical development in infancy.

Patterns of Growth

An extraordinary proportion of the total body is occupied by the head during pre-natal development and early infancy (see Figure 5.1). The **cephalocaudal pattern** is the sequence in which the earliest growth always occurs at the top—the head—with physical growth and differentiation of features gradually working their way down from top to bottom (for example, shoulders, middle trunk, and so on). This same pattern occurs in the head area, because the top parts of the head—the eyes and brain—grow faster than the lower parts, such as the jaw.

Sensory and motor development generally proceed according to the cephalo-caudal principle. For example, infants see objects before they can control their torso, and they can use their hands long before they can crawl or walk. However, development does not follow a rigid blueprint. One study found that infants reached for toys with their feet prior to reaching with their hands (Galloway & Thelen, 2004). On average, infants first touched the toy with their feet when they were 12 weeks old and with their hands when they were 16 weeks old.

cephalocaudal pattern The sequence in which the earliest growth always occurs at the top—the head—with physical growth in size, weight, and feature differentiation gradually working from top to bottom.

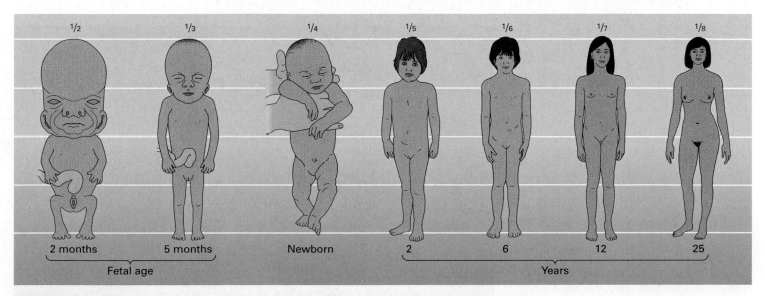

FIGURE 5.1 Changes in Proportions of the Human Body During Growth As individuals develop from infancy through adulthood, one of the most noticeable physical changes is that the head becomes smaller in relation to the rest of the body. The fractions listed refer to head size as a proportion of total body length at different ages.

Growth also follows the **proximodistal pattern,** the sequence in which growth starts at the center of the body and moves toward the extremities. For example, infants control the muscles of their trunk and arms before they control their hands and fingers, and they use their whole hands before they can control several fingers.

Height and Weight

The average North American newborn is 20 inches long and weighs 7½ pounds. Ninety-five percent of full-term newborns are 18 to 22 inches long and weigh between 5½ and 10 pounds.

In the first several days of life, most newborns lose 5 to 7 percent of their body weight before they adjust to feeding by sucking, swallowing, and digesting. Then they grow rapidly, gaining an average of 5 to 6 ounces per week during the first month. They have doubled their birth weight by the age of 4 months and have nearly tripled it by their first birthday. Infants grow about 1 inch per month during the first year, reaching approximately 1½ times their birth length by their first birthday.

Growth slows considerably in the second year of life. By 2 years of age, infants weigh approximately 26 to 32 pounds, having gained a quarter to half a pound per month during the second year; now they have reached about one-fifth of their adult weight. At 2 years of age, the average infant is 32 to 35 inches in height, which is nearly half of their adult height.

The Brain

We described the amazing growth of the brain from conception to birth in Chapter 4. By the time it is born, the infant that began as a single cell is estimated to have a brain that contains approximately 100 billion nerve cells, or neurons. Extensive brain development continues after birth, through infancy and later (Coch, Fischer, & Dawson, 2007; Nelson, 2007). Because the brain is still developing so rapidly in infancy, the infant's head should be protected from falls or other injuries, and the baby should never be shaken. *Shaken baby syndrome,* which includes brain swelling and hemorrhaging, affects hundreds of babies in the United States each year (Gerber & Coffman, 2007; Walls, 2006).

proximodistal pattern The sequence in which growth starts at the center of the body and moves toward the extremities.

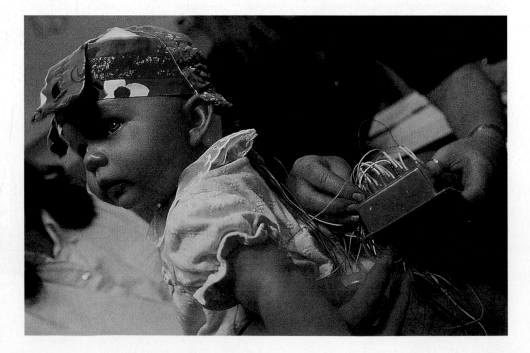

FIGURE 5.2 Measuring the Activity of an Infant's Brain By attaching up to 128 electrodes to a baby's scalp to measure the brain's activity, Charles Nelson (2003, 2005; Nelson, Thomas, & de Haan, 2006) has found that even newborns produce distinctive brain waves that reveal they can distinguish their mother's voices from another woman's, even while they are asleep. *Why is it so difficult to measure infants' brain activity?*

Studying the brain's development in infancy is not as easy as it might seem. Even the latest brain-imaging technologies (described in Chapter 1) cannot make out fine details in adult brains and cannot be used with babies (Nelson, Thomas, & de Haan, 2006). Positron-emission tomography (PET) scans pose a radiation risk to babies, and infants wriggle too much to capture accurate images using magnetic resonance imaging (MRI) (Marcus, Mulrine, & Wong, 1999). As Figure 5.2 illustrates, one way researchers have studied the infant's brain is by attaching electrodes to the scalp in order to monitor the brain's electrical activity (Nelson, 2007; Nelson, Thomas, & de Haan, 2006; Nelson, Zeanah, & Fox, 2007).

Using the electroencephalogram (EEG), which measures the brain's electrical activity, researchers have found that a spurt in EEG activity occurs at about 1½ to 2 years of age (Fischer & Bidell, 2006; Fischer & Rose, 1995). Other spurts seem to take place at about 9, 12, 15, and 18 to 20 years of age. Researchers believe that these spurts of brain activity may coincide with important changes in cognitive development. For example, the increase in EEG brain activity at 1½ to 2 years of age is likely associated with an increase in the infant's capacity for conceptualization and language, and the spurts at 15 and 20 years of age are linked to increases in reflective thinking (Immordino-Yang & Fischer, 2007).

The Brain's Development

At birth, the newborn's brain is about 25 percent of its adult weight. By the second birthday, the brain is about 75 percent of its adult weight. However, the brain's areas do not mature uniformly.

Mapping the Brain   Scientists analyze and categorize areas of the brain in numerous ways. We are most concerned with the portion farthest from the spinal cord known as the *forebrain*, which includes the cerebral cortex and several structures beneath it. The *cerebral cortex* covers the forebrain like a wrinkled cap. It has two halves, or hemispheres (see Figure 5.3). Based on ridges and valleys in the cortex, scientists distinguish four main areas, called lobes, in each hemisphere: the *frontal lobes*, the *occipital lobes*, the *temporal lobes*, and the *parietal lobes* (see Figure 5.4).

Very often, though, researchers describe areas of the cortex based not on the physical ridges and valleys but on function (see Figure 5.4). For example, the *motor cortex*, just behind the frontal lobes, processes information about voluntary movements. *The somatosensory cortex*, located at the front of the parietal lobes, processes information about body sensations. The *visual cortex* is an area in the occipital lobe

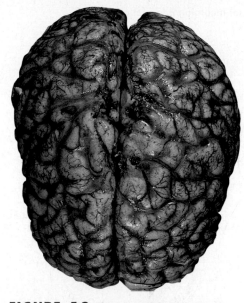

FIGURE 5.3 The Human Brain's Hemispheres The two hemispheres of the human brain are clearly seen in this photograph. It is a myth that the left hemisphere is the exclusive location of language and logical thinking or that the right hemisphere is the exclusive location of emotion and creative thinking.

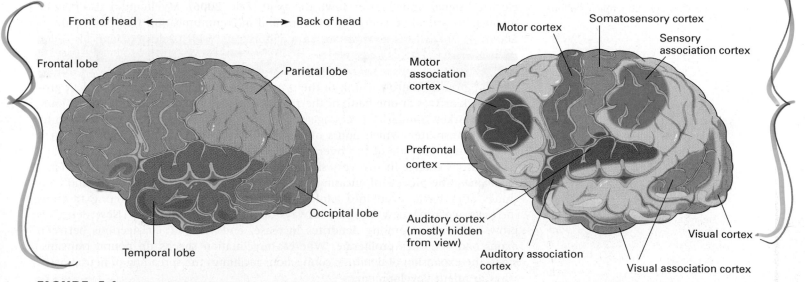

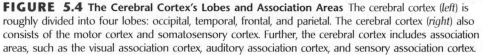

FIGURE 5.4 The Cerebral Cortex's Lobes and Association Areas The cerebral cortex (*left*) is roughly divided into four lobes: occipital, temporal, frontal, and parietal. The cerebral cortex (*right*) also consists of the motor cortex and somatosensory cortex. Further, the cerebral cortex includes association areas, such as the visual association cortex, auditory association cortex, and sensory association cortex.

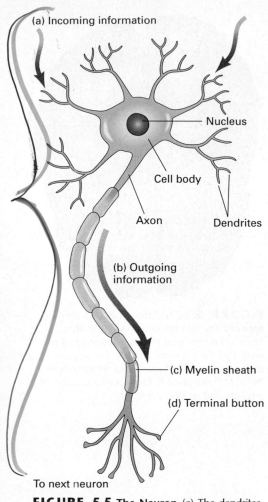

(a) Incoming information

Nucleus

Cell body

Axon   Dendrites

(b) Outgoing
information

(c) Myelin sheath

(d) Terminal button

To next neuron

FIGURE 5.5 The Neuron (a) The dendrites of the cell body receive information from other neurons, muscles, or glands through the axon. (b) Axons transmit information away from the cell body. (c) A myelin sheath covers most axons and speeds information transmission. (d) As the axon ends, it branches out into terminal buttons.

lateralization Specialization of function in one hemisphere of the cerebral cortex or the other.

that processes visual information, and the *auditory cortex* is a part of the temporal lobe that processes information about sounds. The *prefrontal cortex* is a part of the frontal lobe involved in thinking, planning, and self-regulation.

Embedded in the brain's lobes, the *association cortex* (sometimes called association areas) makes up 75 percent of the cerebral cortex. The association cortex is involved in integrating information. Figure 5.4 portrays the locations of several association areas, such as the sensory, visual, auditory, and motor association cortices.

Although these areas are found in the cerebral cortex of each hemisphere, the two hemispheres are not identical in anatomy or function (Killgore, Gruber, & Yurgelun-Todd, 2007). **Lateralization** is the specialization of function in one hemisphere of the cerebral cortex or the other. Researchers continue to be interested in the degree to which each is involved in various aspects of thinking, feeling, and behavior (Stephan, Fink, & Marshall, 2007). The most extensive research on the brain's hemispheres has focused on language (Imada & others, 2007; Salmelin, 2007). Speech and grammar are localized to the left hemisphere in most people, but some aspects of language, such as appropriate language use in different contexts and the use of metaphor and humor, involve the right hemisphere (Mitchell & Crow, 2005). Thus, language is not controlled exclusively by the brain's left hemisphere (Mills & Sheehan, 2007; Peru & others, 2006). Further, most neuroscientists agree that complex functions, such as reading, performing music, and creating art, are the outcome of communication between both sides of the brain.

At birth, the hemispheres of the cerebral cortex already have started to specialize. Newborns show greater electrical brain activity in the left hemisphere than the right hemisphere when they are listening to speech sounds (Hahn, 1987). How are the areas of the brain different in the newborn and the infant than in an adult, and why do the differences matter? Important differences have been documented at both the cellular and the structural level.

Changes in Neurons Within the brain, the type of nerve cells called neurons send electrical and chemical signals, communicating with each other. As we indicated in Chapter 4, a *neuron* is a nerve cell that handles information processing (see Figure 5.5). Extending from the neuron's cell body are two types of fibers known as axons and dendrites. Generally, the axon carries signals away from the cell body and dendrites carry signals toward it. A *myelin sheath,* which is a layer of fat cells, encases many axons (see Figure 5.5). The myelin sheath insulates axons and helps electrical signals travel faster down the axon (Zalc, 2006). Myelination also may be involved in providing energy to neurons and in communication (Haynes & others, 2006). At the end of the axon are terminal buttons, which release chemicals called *neurotransmitters* into *synapses,* which are tiny gaps between neurons' fibers. Chemical interactions in synapses connect axons and dendrites, allowing information to pass from neuron to neuron. Think of the synapse as a river that blocks a road. A grocery truck arrives at one bank of the river, crosses by ferry, and continues its journey to market. Similarly, a message in the brain is "ferried" across the synapse by a neurotransmitter, which pours out information contained in chemicals when it reaches the other side of the river.

Neurons change in two very significant ways during the first years of life. First, *myelination,* the process of encasing axons with fat cells, begins prenatally and continues after birth, even into adolescence. Second, connectivity among neurons increases, creating new neural pathways, as Figure 5.6 illustrates. New dendrites grow, connections among dendrites increase, and synaptic connections between axons and dendrites proliferate. Whereas myelination speeds up neural transmissions, the expansion of dendritic connections facilitates the spreading of neural pathways in infant development.

Researchers have discovered an intriguing aspect of synaptic connections. Nearly twice as many of these connections are made as will ever be used (Huttenlocher & Dabholkar, 1997). The connections that are used become strengthened and survive,

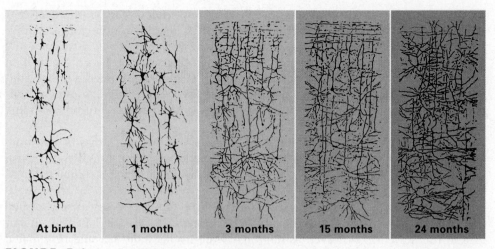

FIGURE 5.6 The Development of Dendritic Spreading Note the increase in connectedness between neurons over the course of the first two years of life.

while the unused ones are replaced by other pathways or disappear (Casey, Durston, & Fossella, 2001). In the language of neuroscience, these connections will be "pruned" (Giedd & others, 2006). For example, the more babies engage in physical activity or use language, the more those pathways will be strengthened.

Changes in Regions of the Brain   Figure 5.7 vividly illustrates the dramatic growth and later pruning of synapses in the visual, auditory, and prefrontal cortex (Huttenlocher & Dabholkar, 1997). Notice that "blooming and pruning" vary considerably by brain region (Thompson & Nelson, 2001). For example, the peak of synaptic overproduction in the visual cortex occurs at about the fourth postnatal month, followed by a

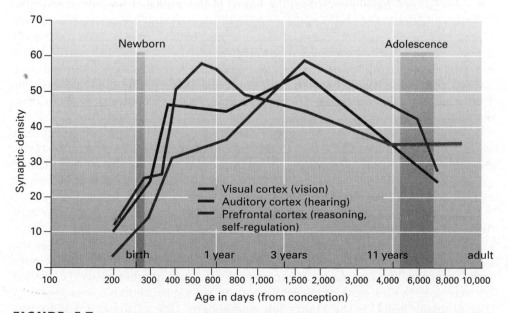

FIGURE 5.7 Synaptic Density in the Human Brain from Infancy to Adulthood The graph shows the dramatic increase and then pruning in synaptic density for three regions of the brain: visual cortex, auditory cortex, and prefrontal cortex. Synaptic density is believed to be an important indication of the extent of connectivity between neurons.

gradual retraction until the middle to end of the preschool years (Huttenlocher & Dabholkar, 1997). In areas of the brain involved in hearing and language, a similar, though somewhat later, course is detected. However, in the *prefrontal cortex,* the area of the brain where higher-level thinking and self-regulation occur, the peak of overproduction takes place at about 1 year of age; it is not until middle to late adolescence that the adult density of synapses is achieved. Both heredity and environment are thought to influence the timing and course of synaptic overproduction and subsequent retraction.

Meanwhile, the pace of myelination also varies in different areas of the brain (Dubois & others, 2007). Myelination for visual pathways occurs rapidly after birth and is completed in the first six months. Auditory myelination is not completed until 4 or 5 years of age.

In general, some areas of the brain, such as the primary motor areas, develop earlier than others, such as the primary sensory areas. The frontal lobes are immature in the newborn. However, as neurons in the frontal lobes become myelinated and interconnected during the first year of life, infants develop an ability to regulate their physiological states, such as sleep, and gain more control over their reflexes. Cognitive skills that require deliberate thinking do not emerge until later (Bell & Fox, 1992). Indeed, the prefrontal region of the frontal lobe has the most prolonged development of any brain region, with changes detectable at least into emerging adulthood (Lenroot & Giedd, 2007; Spear, 2007).

Early Experience and the Brain   What determines how these changes in the brain occur? Until the middle of the twentieth century, scientists believed that the brain's development was determined almost exclusively by genetic factors. But researcher Mark Rosenzweig (1969) was curious about whether early experiences change the brain's development. He conducted a number of experiments with rats and other animals to investigate this possibility. Animals were randomly assigned to grow up in different environments. Animals in an enriched early environment lived in cages with stimulating features, such as wheels to rotate, steps to climb, levers to press, and toys to manipulate. In contrast, other animals had the early experience of growing up in standard cages or in barren, isolated conditions.

The results were stunning. The brains of the animals growing up in the enriched environment developed better than the brains of the animals reared in standard or isolated conditions. The brains of the "enriched" animals weighed more, had thicker layers, had more neuronal connections, and had higher levels of neurochemical activity. Similar findings occurred when older animals were reared in vastly different environments, although the results were not as strong as for the younger animals. Such results give hope that enriching the lives of infants and young children who live in impoverished environments can produce positive changes in their development.

Depressed brain activity has recently been found in children who grow up in a deprived environment (Cicchetti & Toth, 2006; Nelson, Zeenah, & Fox, 2007). As shown in Figure 5.8, a child who grew up in the unresponsive and nonstimulating environment of a Romanian orphanage showed considerably depressed brain activity compared with a normal child.

The profusion of connections described earlier provides the growing brain with flexibility and resilience. Consider 16-year-old Michael Rehbein. At age 4½, he began to experience uncontrollable seizures—as many as 400 a day. Doctors said that the only solution was to remove the left hemisphere of his brain where the seizures were occurring. The first major surgery was at age 7 and another at age 10. Recovery was slow, but his right hemisphere began to reorganize and take over functions that normally occur in the brain's left hemisphere. One of these functions was speech (see Figure 5.9).

Neuroscientists believe that what wires the brain—or rewires it, in the case of Michael Rehbein—is repeated experience (Nash, 1997). Each time a baby tries to

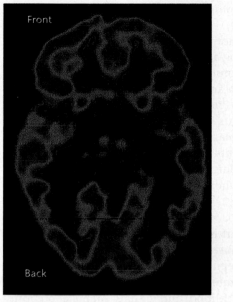

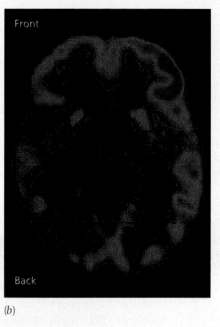

(a)   (b)

FIGURE 5.8 Early Deprivation and Brain Activity These two photographs are PET (positron emission tomography) scans—which use radioactive tracers to image and analyze blood flow and metabolic activity in the body's organs—of the brains of (a) a normal child and (b) an institutionalized Romanian orphan who experienced substantial deprivation since birth. In PET scans, the highest to lowest brain activity is reflected in the colors of red, yellow, green, blue, and black, respectively. As can be seen, red and yellow show up to a much greater degree in the PET scan of the normal child than the deprived Romanian orphan.

touch an attractive object or gazes intently at a face, tiny bursts of electricity shoot through the brain, knitting neurons together into circuits. What results are some of the behavioral milestones that we discuss in this and other chapters. For example, at about 2 months of age, the motor-control centers of the brain develop to the point at which infants can suddenly reach out and grab a nearby object. At about 4 months, the neural connections necessary for depth perception begin to form. And at about 12 months, the brain's speech centers are poised to produce one of infancy's magical moments: when the infant utters his or her first word.

In sum, neural connections are formed early in life. The infant's brain literally is waiting for experiences to determine how connections are made (Dalton & Bergenn, 2007). Before birth, it appears that genes mainly direct how the brain establishes basic wiring patterns. Neurons grow and travel to distant places awaiting further instructions. After birth, environmental experiences guide the brain's development. The inflowing stream of sights, sounds, smells, touches, language, and eye contact help shape the brain's neural connections (Nelson, 2007).

Sleep

When we were infants, sleep consumed more of our time than it does now. The typical newborn sleeps 16 to 17 hours a day, but newborns vary a lot in how much they sleep. The range is from about 10 hours to about 21 hours.

Infants also vary in their preferred times for sleeping and their patterns of sleep. Although the total amount of time spent sleeping remains somewhat consistent, an infant may change from sleeping seven or eight hours several times a day to sleeping for only a few hours three or four times a day. By about 1 month of age, many American infants have begun to sleep longer at night. By about 4 months of age, they usually have moved closer to adultlike sleep patterns,

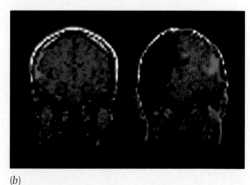

(a)

(b)

FIGURE 5.9 Plasticity in the Brain's Hemispheres (a) Michael Rehbein at 14 years of age. (b) Michael's right hemisphere (right) has reorganized to take over the language functions normally carried out by corresponding areas in the left hemisphere of an intact brain (left). However, the right hemisphere is not as efficient as the left, and more areas of the brain are recruited to process speech.

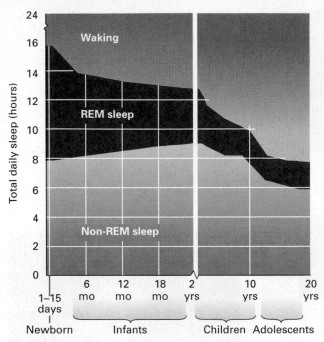

FIGURE 5.10 Developmental Changes in REM and Non-REM Sleep.

Sleep that knits up the ravelled sleave of care . . . Balm of hurt minds, nature's second course. Chief nourisher in life's feast.

—WILLIAM SHAKESPEARE
English Playwright, 17th Century

spending the most time sleeping at night and the most time awake during the day (Daws, 2000).

Cultural variations influence infant sleeping patterns. For example, in the Kipsigis culture in Kenya, infants sleep with their mothers at night and are permitted to nurse on demand (Super & Harkness, 1997). During the day, they are strapped to their mothers' backs, accompanying them on daily rounds of chores and social activities. As a result, the Kipsigis infants do not sleep through the night until much later than American infants do. During the first eight months of postnatal life, Kipsigis infants rarely sleep longer than three hours at a stretch, even at night. This sleep pattern contrasts with that of American infants, many of whom begin to sleep up to eight hours a night by 8 months of age.

REM Sleep   In *REM sleep*, the eyes flutter beneath closed lids; in *non-REM sleep*, this type of eye movement does not occur and sleep is more quiet. Figure 5.10 shows developmental changes in the average number of total hours spent in REM and non-REM sleep. By the time they reach adulthood, individuals spend about one-fifth of their night in REM sleep, and REM sleep usually appears about one hour after non-REM sleep. However, about half of an infant's sleep is REM sleep, and infants often begin their sleep cycle with REM sleep rather than non-REM sleep. A much greater amount of time is taken up by REM sleep in infancy than at any other point in the life span. By the time infants reach 3 months of age, the percentage of time they spend in REM sleep falls to about 40 percent, and REM sleep no longer begins their sleep cycle.

Why do infants spend so much time in REM sleep? Researchers are not certain. The large amount of REM sleep may provide infants with added self-stimulation, since they spend less time awake than do older children. REM sleep also might promote the brain's development in infancy (Graven, 2006).

When adults are awakened during REM sleep, they frequently report that they have been dreaming—but when they are awakened during non-REM sleep, they are much less likely to report they have been dreaming (Cartwright & others, 2006; Dement, 2005). Since infants spend more time than adults in REM sleep, can we conclude that they dream a lot? We don't know whether infants dream or not, because they don't have any way of reporting dreams.

Shared Sleeping   Sleeping arrangements for newborns vary from culture to culture (Alexander & Radisch, 2005; Berkowitz, 2004). Sharing a bed with a mother is a common practice in many cultures, such as Guatamala and China, whereas in others, such as the United States and Great Britain, newborns sleep in a crib, either in the same room as the parents or in a separate room. In some cultures, infants sleep with the mother until they are weaned, after which they sleep with siblings until middle and late childhood (Walker, 2006). Whatever the sleeping arrangements, it is recommended that the infant's bedding provide firm support and that cribs should have side rails.

In the United States, sleeping in a crib in a separate room is the most frequent sleeping arrangement for an infant. In one cross-cultural study, American mothers said they have their infants sleep in a separate room to promote the infants' self-reliance and independence (Morelli & others, 1992). By contrast, Mayan mothers in rural Guatemala had infants sleep in their bed until the birth of a new sibling, at which time the infant would sleep with another family member or in a separate bed in the mother's room. The Mayan mothers believed that the co-sleeping arrangement with their infants enhanced the closeness of their relationship with the infants and were shocked when told that American mothers have their babies sleep alone.

Shared sleeping, or co-sleeping, is a controversial issue among experts. According to some child experts, shared sleeping brings several benefits: it promotes breast feeding and a quicker response to the baby's cries, and it allows the mother to detect potentially dangerous breathing pauses in the baby (McKenna & Dade, 2005; Pelayo & others, 2006). However, shared sleeping remains a controversial issue, with some experts recommending it, others arguing against it (Mitchell, 2007; Newton & Vandeven, 2006; Pelayo & others, 2006). The American Academy of Pediatrics Task Force on Infant Positioning and SIDS (AAPTFIPS) (2000) discourages shared sleeping. The Task Force concluded that bed sharing increases the risk that the sleeping mother will roll over onto her baby or increase the risk of sudden infant death syndrome (SIDS). Recent studies have found that bed sharing is linked with a greater incidence of SIDS, especially when parents smoke (Alm, Lagercrantz, & Wennergren, 2006; Alexander & Radisch, 2005; Bajanowski & others, 2007). Also, shared sleeping is likely to place the infant at risk more if the caregivers are impaired by alcohol, smoking, or being overly tired (Baddock & others, 2007).

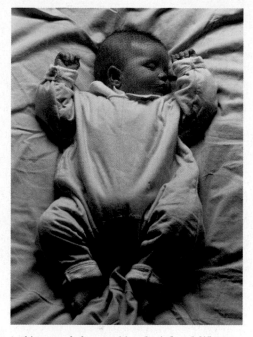

Is this a good sleep position for infants? Why or why not?

SIDS   **Sudden infant death syndrome (SIDS)** is a condition that occurs when infants stop breathing, usually during the night, and die suddenly without an apparent cause. SIDS remains the highest cause of infant death in the United States with nearly 3,000 infant deaths annually attributed to SIDS. Risk of SIDS is highest at 4 to 6 weeks of age (Matthews, Menacker, & MacDorman, 2003).

Since 1992, The American Academy of Pediatrics (AAP) has recommended that infants be placed to sleep on their backs to reduce the risk of SIDS, and the frequency of prone sleeping among U.S. infants has dropped dramatically (AAPTFIPS, 2000). Researchers have found that SIDS does indeed decrease when infants sleep on their backs rather than their stomachs or sides (Alm, Lagercrantz, & Wennergren, 2006; Mitchell, Hutchinson, & Stewart, 2007; Sharma, 2007). Among the reasons given for prone sleeping being a high-risk factor for SIDS are that it impairs the infant's arousal from sleep and restricts the infant's ability to swallow effectively (Ariagno, van Liempt, & Mirmiran, 2006).

In addition to sleeping in a prone position, researchers have found that the following are factors that are involved in SIDS:

- SIDS is less likely to occur in infants who use a pacifier when they go to sleep (Hauck, Omojokun, & Siadaty, 2006; Li & others, 2006; Mitchell, Blair, & L'Hoir, 2006).
- Low birth weight infants are 5 to 10 times more likely to die of SIDS than are their normal-weight counterparts (Horne & others, 2002).
- Infants whose siblings have died of SIDS are two to four times as likely to die of it (Lenoir, Mallet, & Calenda, 2000).
- Six percent of infants with *sleep apnea*, a temporary cessation of breathing in which the airway is completely blocked, usually for 10 seconds or longer, die of SIDS (McNamara & Sullivan, 2000).
- African American and Eskimo infants are four to six times as likely as all others to die of SIDS (Ige & Shelton, 2004).
- SIDS is more common in lower socioeconomic groups (Mitchell & others, 2000).
- SIDS is more common in infants who are passively exposed to cigarette smoke (Bajanowski & others, 2007; Markowitz, 2007).
- SIDS is more common if infants sleep in soft bedding (McGarvey & others, 2006).
- SIDS occurs more often in infants with abnormal brain stem functioning involving the neurotransmitter serotonin (Shani, Fifer, & Myers, 2007).

sudden infant death syndrome (SIDS) Occurs when an infant stops breathing, usually during the night, and suddenly dies without an apparent cause; also called crib death.

Nutrition

From birth to 1 year of age, human infants nearly triple their weight and increase their length by 50 percent. What do they need to sustain this growth?

Nutritional Needs Individual differences among infants in terms of their nutrient reserves, body composition, growth rates, and activity patterns make defining actual nutrient needs difficult (James & Ashwill, 2007; Krebs, 2007). However, because parents need guidelines, nutritionists recommend that infants consume approximately 50 calories per day for each pound they weigh—more than twice an adult's requirement per pound.

Does the same type of nutrition that makes us healthy adults also make young infants healthy? No. Diets designed for adult weight loss and prevention of heart disease may actually retard growth and development in babies. Fat is very important for babies. Nature's food—breast milk—is not low in fat or calories. No child under the age of 2 should be consuming skim milk. For growing infants, high-calorie, high-energy foods are part of a balanced diet.

Some affluent, well-educated parents almost starve their babies by feeding them the low-fat, low-calorie diet they themselves eat. In one investigation, seven babies 7 to 22 months of age were undernourished by their unwitting health-conscious parents (Lifshitz & others, 1987). The well-meaning parents substituted vegetables, skim milk, and other low-fat foods for what they called junk food. But parents who go to the opposite extreme appear to be a more widespread problem. A national study of more than 3,000 randomly selected 4- to 24-month-olds documented that many U.S. parents aren't feeding their babies enough fruits and vegetables but are feeding them too much junk food (Fox & others, 2004). Up to one-third of the babies ate no vegetables and fruit, frequently ate french fries, and almost half of the 7- to 8-month-old babies were fed desserts, sweets, or sweetened drinks. By 15 months, french fries were the most common vegetables the babies ate.

Are U.S. babies becoming increasingly overweight? A recent analysis revealed that in 1980 3.4 percent of U.S. babies less than 6 months old were overweight, a percentage that increased to 5.9 percent in 2001 (Kim & others, 2006). As shown in Figure 5.11, as younger infants become older infants, an even greater percentage are overweight. Also in this study, in addition to the 5.9 percent of infants less than 6 months old who were overweight in 2001, another 11 percent were categorized as at risk for being overweight. In this study, infants were categorized as overweight if they were above the 95th percentile for their age and gender on a weight-for-height index; they were labeled at risk for being overweight if they were between the 85th and 95th percentile.

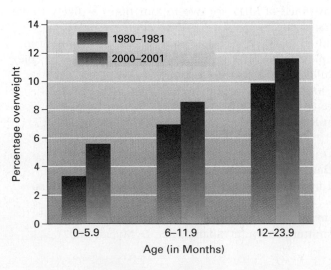

FIGURE 5.11 Percentage of Overweight U.S. Infants in 1980–1981 and 2000–2001
Note: Infants above the 95th percentile for their age and gender on a weight-for-height index were categorized as overweight.

In addition to eating too many french fries, sweetened drinks, and desserts, are there other factors that might explain this increase in overweight U.S. infants? A mother's weight gain during pregnancy, and a mother's own high weight before pregnancy, may be factors. One important factor likely is whether an infant is breast fed or bottle fed (Mayer-Davis & others, 2006). Breast fed infants have lower rates of weight gain than bottle fed infants by school age, and it is estimated that breast feeding reduces the risk of obesity by approximately 20 percent (Kolezko, 2006). Next, we explore other aspects of breast and bottle feeding.

Breast Versus Bottle Feeding   For the first 4 to 6 months of life, human milk or an alternative formula is the baby's source of nutrients and energy. For years, debate has focused on whether breast feeding is better for the infant than bottle feeding. The growing consensus is that breast feeding is better for the baby's health (Lopez Alvarez, 2007; Narramore, 2007; Schack-Nielsen & Michaelsen, 2007). Since the 1970s, breastfeeding by U.S. mothers has soared (see Figure 5.12). In 2004 more than two-thirds of U.S. mothers breast fed their newborns, and more than a third breast fed their 6-month-olds. The American Academy of Pediatrics and the American Dietetic Association strongly endorse breast feeding throughout the infant's first year (AAP Working Group on Breastfeeding, 1997; James & Dobson, 2005).

What are some of the benefits of breast feeding? They include these benefits during the first two years of life and later:

- Appropriate weight gain and lowered risk of obesity in childhood and adulthood (Li & others, 2007; Perrin, Finkle, & Benjamin, 2007)
- Fewer allergies (Host & Halken, 2005)
- Prevention or reduction of diarrhea, respiratory infections (such as pneumonia and bronchitis), bacterial and urinary tract infections, and otitis media (a middle ear infection) (Chatzimichael & others, 2007; Jackson & Nazar, 2006; Sadeharju & others, 2007)
- Denser bones in childhood and adulthood (Gibson & others, 2000)
- Reduced childhood cancer and reduced incidence of breast cancer in mothers and their female offspring (Danforth & others, 2007; Shema & others, 2007)
- Lower occurrence of type II diabetes (Das, 2007)
- Lower incidence of SIDS—in one study, for every month of exclusive breast feeding, the rate of SIDS was cut in half (Fredrickson, 1993)
- More advanced neurological and cognitive development (Eidelman & Feldman, 2004)
- Lower percentage of developmental delays in gross motor development (Sacker, Quigley, & Kelly, 2006)
- Better visual acuity (Makrides & others, 1995)

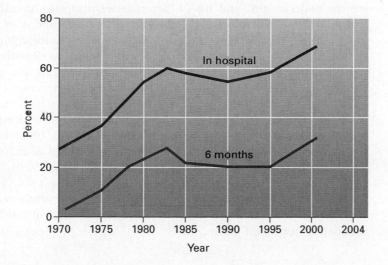

FIGURE 5.12 Trends in Breast Feeding in the United States: 1970–2001

Human milk, or an alternative formula is a baby's source of nutrients for the first 4 to 6 months. The growing consensus is that breast feeding is better for the baby's health, although controversy still swirls about the issue of breast feeding versus bottle feeding. *Why is breast feeding strongly recommended by pediatricians?*

This Honduran child has kwashiorkor. Notice the telltale sign of kwashiorkor—a greatly expanded abdomen without the appearance of such expansion in other body areas, such as arms and legs. *What are some other characteristics of kwashiorkor?*

Which women are least likely to breast feed? They include mothers who work full-time outside of the home, mothers under age 25, mothers without a high school education, African American mothers, and mothers in low-income circumstances (Heck & others, 2006; Merewood & others, 2007). In one study of low-income mothers in Georgia, interventions (such as counseling focused on the benefits of breast feeding and the free loan of a breast pump) increased the incidence of breast feeding (Ahluwalia & others, 2000). Increasingly, mothers who return to work in the infant's first year of life use a breast pump to extract breast milk that can be stored for later feeding of the infant when the mother is not present.

The AAP Work Group on Breastfeeding strongly endorses breast feeding throughout the first year of life (AAPWGB, 1997). Are there circumstances when mothers should not breast feed? Yes, a mother should not breast feed (1) when the mother is infected with AIDS or some other infectious disease that can be transmitted through her milk, (2) if she has active tuberculosis, or (3) if she is taking any drug that may not be safe for the infant (Chatzmichael & others, 2007; Giglia & Binns, 2007; Vogler, 2006).

Some women cannot breast feed their infants because of physical difficulties; others feel guilty if they terminate breast feeding early (Mozingo & others, 2000; Walshaw & Owens, 2006). Mothers may also worry that they are depriving their infants of important emotional and psychological benefits if they bottle feed rather than breast feed. Some researchers have found, however, that there are no psychological differences between breast fed and bottle fed infants (Ferguson, Harwood, & Shannon, 1987; Young, 1990).

Malnutrition in Infancy   Early weaning of infants from breast milk to inadequate sources of nutrients, such as unsuitable and unsanitary cow's milk formula, can cause protein deficiency and malnutrition in infants (Kramer, 2003). Something that looks like milk but is not, usually a form of tapioca or rice, is also often substituted for breast milk. In many of the world's developing countries, mothers used to breast feed their infants for at least two years. To become more modern, they stopped breast feeding much earlier and replaced it with bottle feeding. Comparisons of breast fed and bottle fed infants in such countries as Afghanistan, Haiti, Ghana, and Chile document that the mortality rate of bottle fed infants is as much as five times that of breast fed infants (Grant, 1997). However, as we saw in the *Images of Children's Development* opening story, a concern in developing countries is the increasing number of women who are HIV-positive and the fear that they will transmit this virus to their offspring (Doherty & others, 2006).

Two life-threatening conditions that can result from malnutrition are marasmus and kwashiorkor. **Marasmus** is caused by a severe protein-calorie deficiency and results in a wasting away of body tissues in the infant's first year. The infant becomes grossly underweight, and his or her muscles atrophy. **Kwashiorkor,** caused by severe protein deficiency, usually appears between 1 and 3 years of age. Children with kwashiorkor sometimes appear to be well fed even though they are not because the disease can cause the child's abdomen and feet to swell with water. Kwashiorkor causes a child's vital organs to collect the nutrients that are present and deprive other parts of the body of them. The child's hair also becomes thin, brittle, and colorless, and the child's behavior often becomes listless.

Even if not fatal, severe and lengthy malnutrition is detrimental to physical, cognitive, and social development (de Onis & others, 2006; Grantham-McGregor, Ani, & Fernald, 2001). In one investigation, two groups of extremely malnourished 1-year-old South African infants were studied (Bayley, 1970). The children in one group were given adequate nourishment during the next six years; no intervention took place in the lives of the other group. After the seventh year, the poorly nourished group of children performed much worse on tests of intelligence than did the adequately nourished group.

Another study linked the diets of rural Guatemalan infants with their social development at the time they entered elementary school (Barrett, Radke-Yarrow, & Klein, 1982). Children whose mothers had been given nutritious supplements during pregnancy, and who themselves had been given more nutritious, high-calorie foods in their first two years of life, were more active, more involved, more helpful with their peers, less anxious, and happier than their counterparts who had not been given nutritional supplements. The results suggest how important it is for parents to be attentive to the nutritional needs of their infants.

In further research on early supplementary feeding and children's cognitive development, Ernesto Pollitt and his colleagues (1993) conducted a longitudinal investigation over two decades in rural Guatemala. They found that early nutritional supplements in the form of protein and increased calories can have positive long-term effects on cognitive development. The researchers also found that the relation of nutrition to cognitive performance is moderated both by the time period during which the supplement is given and by the sociodemographic context. For example, the children in the lowest socioeconomic groups benefited more than did the children in higher socioeconomic groups. Although there still was a positive nutritional influence when supplementation began after 2 years of age, the effect on cognitive development was less powerful.

Adequate early nutrition is an important aspect of healthy development (Boyle & Long, 2006). In addition to sound nutrition, children need a nurturant, supportive environment (Chopra, 2003). One individual who has stood out as an advocate of caring for children is T. Berry Brazelton, who is featured in the *Careers in Child Development* profile.

Careers in CHILD DEVELOPMENT

T. Berry Brazelton
Pediatrician

T. Berry Brazelton is America's best-known pediatrician as a result of his numerous books, television appearances, and newspaper and magazine articles about parenting and children's health. He takes a family-centered approach to child development issues and communicates with parents in easy-to-understand ways.

Dr. Brazelton founded the Child Development Unit at Boston Children's Hospital and created the Brazelton Neonatal Behavioral Assessment Scale, a widely used measure of the newborn's health and well-being (which you read about in Chapter 4). He also has conducted a number of research studies on infants and children and has been President of the Society for Research in Child Development, a leading research organization.

T. Berry Brazelton, pediatrician, with a young child.

Health

Among the important aspects of infant health are immunization and accident prevention. Immunization has greatly improved children's health.

Immunization   One of the most dramatic advances in infant health has been the decline of infectious diseases over the past four decades because of widespread immunization for preventable diseases. Though many presently available immunizations can be given to individuals of any age, the recommended schedule is to begin in infancy (AAP, 2004; Bardenheier & others, 2004). The recommended age for various immunizations is shown in Figure 5.13.

Accident Prevention   Accidents are a major cause of death in infancy, especially from 6 to 12 months of age (Currie & Hotz, 2004). Infants need to be closely monitored as they gain increased locomotor and manipulative skills, along with a strong curiosity to explore the environment (Rivara, 2004). Aspiration of foreign objects, suffocation, falls, poisoning, burns, and motor vehicle accidents are among the most common accidents in infancy.

marasmus A wasting away of body tissues in the infant's first year, caused by severe protein-calorie deficiency.

kwashiorkor A condition caused by a severe deficiency in protein in which the child's abdomen and feet become swollen with water; usually appears between 1 to 3 years of age.

Age	Immunization
Birth	Hepatitis B
2 months	Diphtheria, tetanus, pertussis Polio Influenza Pneumococcal
4 months	Hepatitis B Diphtheria, tetanus, pertussis Polio Influenza Pneumococcal
6 months	Diphtheria, tetanus, pertussis Influenza Pneumococcal
1 year	Influenza Pneumococcal
15 months	Measles, mumps, rubella Influenza Varicella
18 months	Hepatitis B Diphtheria, tetanus, pertussis Polio
4 to 6 years	Diphtheria, tetanus, pertussis Polio Measles, mumps, rubella
11 to 12 years	Measles, mumps, rubella
14 to 16 years	Tetanus, diphtheria

FIGURE 5.13 Recommended Immunization Schedule of Infants and Children

Asphyxiation by foreign material in the respiratory tract is the leading cause of fatal injury in infants under 1 year of age. Toys need to be carefully inspected for potential danger. An active infant can grab a low-hanging mobile and rapidly chew off a piece. Balloons, whether partially inflated, uninflated, or popped, cause more infant choking deaths than any other kind of small object and should be kept away from infants and young children. Other choking hazards include foods such as whole grapes, nuts, hard candy, popcorn, and any uncooked hard vegetables (for example, green beans). In addition, caregivers need to mash chunky cooked foods and cut meats such as hot dogs into tiny narrow pieces to avoid choking accidents.

Burns are often not perceived to be a particular danger to infants, but several hazards exist, such as scalding water, excessive sunburn, and burns from electrical wires, sockets, and space heaters. One of the best burn safety devices is a smoke detector; parents are advised to have at least one in every level of their homes.

Automobile accidents are the leading cause of accidental deaths in children over 1 year of age. The major danger for the infant is improper restraint within the motor vehicle (Chan, Reilly, & Telfer, 2006). All infants, newborns included, should be secured in special infant car seats, rather than being held on an adult's lap or placed on the seat of the car. Infant car seats should be positioned in the backseat of the car to avoid injury from air bags.

Accidents can also harm infants in other ways. For example, sharp, jagged objects can cause skin wounds and long, pointed objects can be poked in the eye. Thus, a fork should not be given for self-feeding until the child has mastered the spoon, which usually happens by 18 months of age. Another often unrecognized danger to infants is attacks by young siblings and pets, especially dogs and cats.

We have discussed many aspects of the infant's health in this chapter. In the following *Caring for Children* interlude, we will further explore aspects of getting infants off to a healthy start in life.

Caring for Children

A HEALTHY START

The Hawaii Family Support/Healthy Start Program began in 1985 (Allen, Brown, & Finlay, 1992). It was designed by the Hawaii Family Stress Center in Honolulu, which already had been making home visits to improve family functioning and reduce child abuse for more than a decade. Participation is voluntary. Families of newborns are screened for family risk factors, including unstable housing, histories of substance abuse, depression, parents' abuse as a child, late or no prenatal care, fewer than 12 years of schooling, poverty, and unemployment. Healthy Start workers screen and interview new mothers in the hospital. They also screen families referred by physicians, nurses, and others. Because the demand for services outstrips available resources, only families with a substantial number of risk factors can participate.

Each new participating family receives a weekly visit from a family support worker. Each of the program's eight home visitors works with approximately 25 families at a time. The worker helps the family cope with any immediate crises, such as unemployment or substance abuse. The family also is linked directly with a pediatrician to ensure that the children receive regular health care. Infants are screened for developmental delays and are immunized on schedule. Pediatricians are notified when a child is enrolled in Healthy Start and when a family at risk stops participating.

The Family Support/Healthy Start Program recently hired a child development specialist to work with families of children with special needs. And, in some instances, the program's male family support worker visits a father to talk about his role in the family. The support workers encourage parents to participate in group activities held each week at the program center located in a neighborhood shopping center.

Over time, parents are encouraged to assume more responsibility for their family's health and well-being. Families can participate in Healthy Start until the child is 5 and enters public school. One study found that the Hawaiian Healthy Start program produced a lower incidence of maternal alcohol abuse and partner violence but did not reduce child abuse (Duggan & others, 2004).

The Hawaii Family Support/Healthy Start Program provides overburdened families of newborns and young children many home-visitor services. This program has been very successful in reducing abuse and neglect in families.

REVIEW AND REFLECT ▶ LEARNING GOAL 1

1 **Discuss physical growth and development in infancy**

Review
- What are cephalocaudal and proximodistal patterns?
- What changes in height and weight take place in infancy?
- What are some key features of the brain and its development in infancy?
- What changes occur in sleep during infancy?
- What are infants' nutritional needs?
- What characterizes immunization and accident prevention in infancy?

Reflect
- What three pieces of advice about the infant's physical development would you want to give a friend who has just had a baby? Why those three?

2 HOW DO INFANTS DEVELOP MOTOR SKILLS?

The Dynamic Systems View		Gross Motor Skills
	Reflexes	Fine Motor Skills

As a newborn, Ramona, whom we met in the chapter opening, could suck, fling her arms, and tightly grip a finger placed in her tiny hand. Within just two years, she would be toddling around on her own, opening doors and jars as she explored her little world. Are her accomplishments inevitable? How do infants develop their motor skills, and which skills do they develop when?

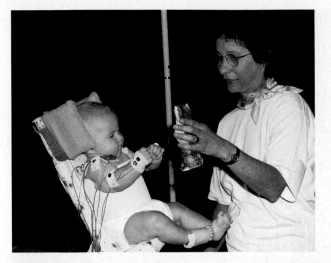

Esther Thelen is shown conducting an experiment to discover how infants learn to control their arms to reach and grasp for objects. A computer device is used to monitor the infant's arm movements and to track muscle patterns. Thelen's research is conducted from a dynamic systems perspective. *What is the nature of this perspective?*

The Dynamic Systems View

Developmentalist Arnold Gesell (1934) thought his painstaking observations had revealed how people develop their motor skills. He had discovered that infants and children develop rolling, sitting, standing, and other motor skills in a fixed order and within specific time frames. These observations, said Gesell, show that motor development comes about through the unfolding of a genetic plan, or *maturation.*

Later studies, however, demonstrated that the sequence of developmental milestones is not as fixed as Gesell indicated and not due as strongly to heredity as Gesell argued (Adolph & Berger, 2006; Adolph & Joh, 2007, 2008). In the 1990s, the study of motor development experienced a renaissance as psychologists developed new insights about *how* motor skills develop (Thelen & Smith, 1998). One increasingly influential theory is dynamic systems theory proposed by Esther Thelen.

According to **dynamic systems theory,** infants assemble motor skills for perceiving and acting. Notice that perception and action are coupled according to this theory (Smith & Breazeal, 2007; Thelen, 1995, 2001; Thelen & Smith, 2006; Thelen & Whitmeyer, 2005). In order to develop motor skills, infants must perceive something in the environment that motivates them to act and use their perceptions to fine-tune their movements. Motor skills represent solutions to the infant's goals.

How is a motor skill developed according to this theory? When infants are motivated to do something, they might create a new motor behavior. The new behavior is the result of many converging factors: the development of the nervous system, the body's physical properties and its possibilities for movement, the goal the child is motivated to reach, and the environmental support for the skill. For example, babies learn to walk only when maturation of the nervous system allows them to control certain leg muscles, when their legs have grown enough to support their weight, and when they want to move.

Mastering a motor skill requires the infant's active efforts to coordinate several components of the skill (Adolph & Berger, 2006; Adolph & Joh, 2007, 2008; Thelen & Smith, 2006). Infants explore and select possible solutions to the demands of a new task; they assemble adaptive patterns by modifying their current movement patterns. The first step occurs when the infant is motivated by a new challenge—such as the desire to cross a room—and gets into the "ball park" of the task demands by taking a couple of stumbling steps. Then, the infant "tunes" these movements to make them smoother and more effective. The tuning is achieved through repeated cycles of action and perception of the consequences of that action. According to the dynamic systems view, even universal milestones, such as crawling, reaching, and walking, are learned through this process of adaptation: infants modulate their movement patterns to fit a new task by exploring and selecting possible configurations (Adolph & Joh, 2007; Thelen & Smith, 2006).

To see how dynamic systems theory explains motor behavior, imagine that you offer a new toy to a baby named Gabriel (Thelen & others, 1993). There is no exact program that can tell Gabriel ahead of time how to move his arm and hand and fingers to grasp the toy. Gabriel must adapt to his goal—grasping the toy—and the context. From his sitting position, he must make split-second adjustments to extend his arm, holding his body steady so that his arm and torso don't plow into the toy. Muscles in his arm and shoulder contract and stretch in a host of combinations, exerting a variety of forces. He improvises a way to reach out with one arm and wrap his fingers around the toy.

Thus, according to dynamic systems theory, motor development is not a passive process in which genes dictate the unfolding of a sequence of skills over time. Rather, the infant actively puts together a skill in order to achieve a goal within the

dynamic systems theory The perspective on motor development that seeks to explain how motor behaviors are assembled for perceiving and acting.

constraints set by the infant's body and environment. Nature and nurture, the infant and the environment, are all working together as part of an ever-changing system (Adolph & Berger, 2006; Joh & Adolph, 2006; Thelen & Smith, 2006).

As we examine the course of motor development, we describe how dynamic systems theory applies to some specific skills. First, though, let's examine how the story of motor development begins with reflexes.

Reflexes

The newborn is not completely helpless. Among other things, it has some basic reflexes. For example, the newborn automatically holds its breath and contracts its throat to keep water out. **Reflexes** are built-in reactions to stimuli; they govern the newborn's movements, which are automatic and beyond the newborn's control. Reflexes are genetically carried survival mechanisms. They allow infants to respond adaptively to their environment before they have had the opportunity to learn.

The rooting and sucking reflexes are important examples. Both have survival value for newborn mammals, who must find a mother's breast to obtain nourishment. The **rooting reflex** occurs when the infant's cheek is stroked or the side of the mouth is touched. In response, the infant turns its head toward the side that was touched in an apparent effort to find something to suck. The **sucking reflex** occurs when newborns automatically suck an object placed in their mouth. This reflex enables newborns to get nourishment before they have associated a nipple with food.

Another example is the **Moro reflex,** which occurs in response to a sudden, intense noise or movement. When startled, the newborn arches its back, throws back its head, and flings out its arms and legs. Then the newborn rapidly closes its arms and legs. The Moro reflex is believed to be a way of grabbing for support while falling; it would have had survival value for our primate ancestors.

Some reflexes—coughing, sneezing, blinking, shivering, and yawning, for example—persist throughout life. They are as important for the adult as they are for the infant. Other reflexes, though, disappear several months following birth, as the infant's brain matures, and voluntary control over many behaviors develops. The rooting, sucking, and Moro reflexes, for example, all tend to disappear when the infant is 3 to 4 months old.

The movements of some reflexes eventually become incorporated into more complex, voluntary actions. One important example is the **grasping reflex,** which occurs when something touches the infant's palms. The infant responds by grasping tightly. By the end of the third month, the grasping reflex diminishes, and the infant shows a more voluntary grasp. For example, when an infant sees a mobile turning slowly above a crib, it may reach out and try to grasp it. As its motor development becomes smoother, the infant will grasp objects, carefully manipulate them, and explore their qualities. An overview of the reflexes we have discussed, along with others such as stepping and swimming, is given in Figure 5.14.

Although reflexes are automatic and inborn, differences in reflexive behavior are soon apparent. For example, the sucking capabilities of newborns vary considerably. Some newborns are efficient at forceful sucking and obtaining milk; others are not as adept and get tired before they are full. Most infants take several weeks to establish a sucking style that is coordinated with the way the mother is holding the infant, the way milk is coming out of the bottle or breast, and the infant's temperament.

Pediatrician T. Berry Brazelton (1956) observed how infants' sucking changed as they grew older. Over 85 percent of the infants engaged in considerable sucking behavior unrelated to feeding. They sucked their finger, their fists, and pacifiers. By the age of 1 year, most had stopped the sucking behavior, but as many as 40 percent of children continue to suck their thumbs after they have started school (Kessen, Haith, & Salapatek, 1970). Most developmentalists do not attach a great deal of significance to this behavior.

The Infant is by no means as helpless as it looks and is quite capable of some very complex and important actions.

—HERB PICK
*Contemporary Developmental Psychologist,
University of Minnesota*

reflexes Built-in reactions to stimuli that govern the newborn's movements, which are automatic and beyond the newborn's control.

rooting reflex A newborn's built-in reaction that occurs when the infant's cheek is stroked or the side of the mouth is touched. In response, the infant turns its head toward the side that was touched, in an apparent effort to find something to suck.

sucking reflex A newborn's built-in reaction to automatically suck an object placed in its mouth. The sucking reflex enables the infant to get nourishment before it has associated a nipple with food.

Moro reflex A neonatal startle response that occurs in reaction to a sudden, intense noise or movement. When startled, the newborn arches its back, throws its head back, and flings out its arms and legs. Then the newborn rapidly closes its arms and legs to the center of the body.

grasping reflex A neonatal reflex that occurs when something touches the infant's palms. The infants responds by grasping tightly.

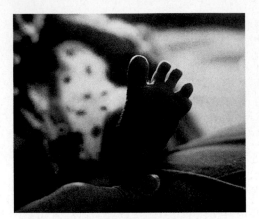

Babinski reflex

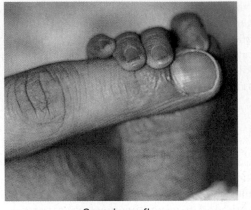

Grasping reflex

Moro reflex

Reflex	Stimulation	Infant's Response	Developmental Pattern
Blinking	Flash of light, puff of air	Closes both eyes	Permanent
Babinski	Sole of foot stroked	Fans out toes, twists foot in	Disappears after 9 months to 1 year
Grasping	Palms touched	Grasps tightly	Weakens after 3 months, disappears after 1 year
Moro (startle)	Sudden stimulation, such as hearing loud noise or being dropped	Startles, arches back, throws head back, flings out arms and legs and then rapidly closes them to center of body	Disappears after 3 to 4 months
Rooting	Cheek stroked or side of mouth touched	Turns head, opens mouth, begins sucking	Disappears after 3 to 4 months
Stepping	Infant held above surface and feet lowered to touch surface	Moves feet as if to walk	Disappears after 3 to 4 months
Sucking	Object touching mouth	Sucks automatically	Disappears after 3 to 4 months
Swimming	Infant put face down in water	Makes coordinated swimming movements	Disappears after 6 to 7 months
Tonic neck	Infant placed on back	Forms fists with both hands and usually turns head to the right (sometimes called the "fencer's pose" because the infant looks like it is assuming a fencer's position)	Disappears after 2 months

FIGURE 5.14 Infant Reflexes

Gross Motor Skills

Ask any parents about their baby, and sooner or later you are likely to hear about one or more motor milestones, such as "Cassandra just learned to crawl," "Jesse is finally sitting alone," or "Angela took her first step last week." Parents proudly announce such milestones as their children transform themselves from babies unable to lift their heads to toddlers who grab things off the grocery store shelf, chase a cat, and participate actively in the family's social life (Thelen, 1995, 2000). These milestones are examples of **gross motor skills,** which are skills that involve large-muscle activities, such as moving one's arms and walking.

The Development of Posture   How do gross motor skills develop? As a foundation, these skills require postural control (Thelen, 2001; Thelen & Smith, 2006). For example, to track moving objects, you must be able to control your head in order to stabilize your gaze; before you can walk, you must be able to balance on one leg.

gross motor skills Motor skills that involve large-muscle activities, such as walking.

Posture is more than just holding still and straight. In Thelen's (1995, 2000; Thelen & Smith, 2006) view, posture is a dynamic process that is linked with sensory information from proprioceptive cues in the skin, joints, and muscles, which tell us where we are in space; from vestibular organs in the inner ear that regulate balance and equilibrium; and from vision and hearing (Spencer & others, 2000).

Newborn infants cannot voluntarily control their posture. Within a few weeks, though, they can hold their heads erect, and soon they can lift their heads while prone. By 2 months of age, babies can sit while supported on a lap or an infant seat, but they cannot sit independently until they are 6 or 7 months of age. Standing also develops gradually during the first year of life. By about 8 months of age, infants usually learn to pull themselves up and hold on to a chair, and they often can stand alone by about 10 to 12 months of age.

Learning to Walk   Locomotion and postural control are closely linked, especially in walking upright (Adolph & Berger, 2006; Adolph & Joh, 2007, 2008). To walk upright, the baby must be able both to balance on one leg as the other is swung forward and to shift the weight from one leg to the other (Thelen & Smith, 2006).

Even young infants can make the alternating leg movements that are needed for walking. The neural pathways that control leg alternation are in place from a very early age, possibly even at birth or before. Infants engage in frequent alternating kicking movements throughout the first six months of life when they are lying on their backs. Also when 1- to 2-month-olds are given support with their feet in contact with a motorized treadmill, they show well-coordinated, alternating steps. Despite these early abilities, most infants do not learn to walk until about the time of their first birthday.

Newly crawling infant

If infants can produce forward stepping movements so early, why does it take them so long to learn to walk? The key skills in learning to walk appear to be stabilizing balance on one leg long enough to swing the other forward and shifting the weight without falling. This is a difficult biomechanical problem to solve, and it takes infants about a year to do it.

Infants also must learn what kinds of places and surfaces are safe for crawling or walking (Adolph & Berger, 2006; Adolph & Joh, 2007, 2008). Karen Adolph (1997) investigated how experienced and inexperienced crawling infants and walking infants go down steep slopes (see Figure 5.15). Newly crawling infants, who averaged about 8½ months in age, rather indiscriminately went down the steep slopes, often falling in the process (with their mothers next to the slope to catch them). After weeks of practice, the crawling babies became more adept at judging which slopes were too steep to crawl down and which ones they could navigate safely.

You might expect that babies who learned that a slope was too steep for crawling would know when they began walking whether a slope was safe. But Adolph's research indicated that newly walking infants could not judge the safety of the slopes. Only when infants became experienced walkers were they able to accurately match their skills with the steepness of the slopes. They rarely fell downhill, either refusing to go down the steep slopes or going down backward in a cautious manner. Experienced walkers perceptually assessed the situation—looking, swaying, touching, and thinking before they moved down the slope. With experience, both the crawlers and the walkers learned to avoid the risky slopes where they would fall, integrating perceptual information with the development of a new motor behavior. In this research, we again see the importance of perceptual-motor coupling in the development of motor skills.

What are some practical applications of Adolph's research? Parents should realize how accident-prone children are at this early stage of locomotion (Keen, 2005). They may seem very competent as they motor about, but they don't realize potential dangers they might encounter. It takes many weeks of walking before children learn that drop-offs, steps, and slopes are dangerous. Thus, falls and other accidents are common when infants begin to walk; caregivers should be constantly on guard.

Experienced walker

FIGURE 5.15 The Role of Experience in Crawling and Walking Infants' Judgments of Whether to Go Down a Slope Karen Adolph (1997) found that locomotor experience rather than age was the primary predictor of adaptive responding on slopes of varying steepness. Newly crawling and walking infants could not judge the safety of the various slopes. With experience, they learned to avoid slopes where they would fall. When expert crawlers began to walk, they again made mistakes and fell, even though they had judged the same slope accurately when crawling. Adolph referred to this as the *specificity of learning* because it does not transfer across crawling and walking.

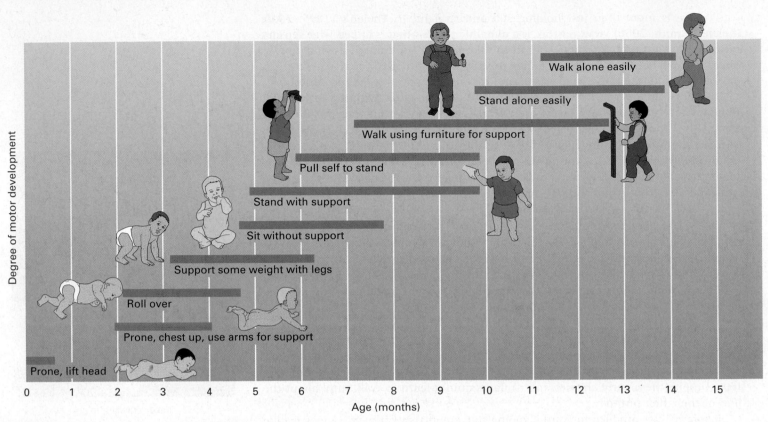

FIGURE 5.16 Milestones in Gross Motor Development

The First Year: Milestones and Variations Figure 5.16 summarizes important accomplishments in gross motor skills during the first year, culminating in the ability to walk easily. The timing of these milestones, especially the later ones, may vary by as much as two to four months, and experiences can modify the onset of these accomplishments. For example, since 1992, when pediatricians began recommending that parents keep their infants supine at night, fewer babies crawl and the age of onset of crawling is later (Davis & others, 1998). Also, some infants do not follow the standard sequence of motor accomplishments. For example, many American infants never crawl on their belly or on their hands and knees. They may discover an idiosyncratic form of locomotion before walking such as rolling, or they might never locomote until they get upright (Adolph & Joh, 2007). In the African Mali tribe, most infants do not crawl (Bril, 1999).

According to Karen Adolph and Sarah Berger (2005), "the old-fashioned view that growth and motor development reflect merely the age-related output of maturation is, at best, incomplete. Rather, infants acquire new skills with the help of their caregivers in a real-world environment of objects, surfaces, and planes" (p. 273).

Development in the Second Year The motor accomplishments of the first year bring increasing independence, allowing infants to explore their environment more extensively and to initiate interaction with others more readily. In the second year of life, toddlers become more motorically skilled and mobile. They are no longer content in a playpen and want to move all over the place. Child development experts believe that motor activity during the second year is vital to the child's competent development and that few restrictions, except for safety, should be placed on their adventures (Fraiberg, 1959).

By 13 to 18 months, toddlers can pull a toy attached to a string and use their hands and legs to climb up a number of steps. By 18 to 24 months, toddlers can

A baby is an angel whose wings decrease as his legs increase.

—FRENCH PROVERB

walk quickly or run stiffly for a short distance, balance on their feet in a squat position while playing with objects on the floor, walk backward without losing their balance, stand and kick a ball without falling, stand and throw a ball, and jump in place.

Can parents give their babies a head start on becoming physically fit and physically talented through structured exercise classes? Physical fitness classes for babies range from passive fare—with adults putting infants through the paces—to programs called "aerobic" because they demand crawling, tumbling, and ball skills. Pediatricians point out that when an adult is stretching and moving an infant's limbs, the adult can easily go beyond the infant's physical limits without knowing it. Pediatricians also recommend that exercise for infants should not be of the intense, aerobic variety. Babies cannot adequately stretch their bodies to achieve aerobic benefits.

In short, most infancy experts recommend against structured exercise classes for babies. But there are other ways of guiding infants' motor development. Caregivers in some cultures do handle babies vigorously, and this might advance motor development, as we discuss in the *Diversity in Children's Development* interlude.

Fine Motor Skills

Whereas gross motor skills involve large muscle activity, **fine motor skills** involve finely tuned movements. Grasping a toy, using a spoon, buttoning a shirt, or anything that requires finger dexterity demonstrates fine motor skills. Infants have hardly any control over fine motor skills at birth, but newborns do have many components of what will become finely coordinated arm, hand, and finger movements (Rosenblith, 1992).

The onset of reaching and grasping marks a significant achievement in infants' ability to interact with their surroundings (Oztop, Bradley, & Arbib, 2004; Rocha,

fine motor skills Motor skills that involve more finely turned movements, such as finger dexterity.

Diversity in Children's Development

CULTURAL VARIATIONS IN GUIDING INFANTS' MOTOR DEVELOPMENT

Mothers in developing countries tend to stimulate their infants' motor skills more than mothers in more modern countries (Hopkins, 1991). Jamaican mothers regularly massage their infants and stretch their arms and legs (Hopkins, 1991). Mothers in the Gusii culture of Kenya also encourage vigorous movement in their babies (Hopkins & Westra, 1988).

Do these cultural variations make a difference in the infant's motor development? When caregivers provide babies with physical guidance by physically handling them in special ways (such as stroking, massaging, or stretching) or by giving them opportunities for exercise, the infants often reach motor milestones earlier than infants whose caregivers have not provided these activities. For example, Jamaican mothers expect their infants to sit and walk alone two to three months earlier than English mothers do (Hopkins & Westra, 1990).

Nonetheless, even when infants' motor activity is restricted, many infants still reach the milestones of motor development at a normal age. For example, Algonquin infants in Quebec, Canada, spend much of their first year strapped to a cradle board. Despite their inactivity, these infants still sit up, crawl, and walk within an age range similar to that of infants in cultures who have had much greater opportunity for activity.

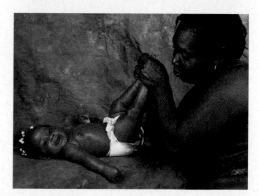

(*Top*) In the Algonquin culture in Quebec, Canada, babies are strapped to a cradle board for much of their infancy. (*Bottom*) In Jamaica, mothers massage and stretch their infants' arms and legs. *To what extent do cultural variations in the activity infants engage in influence the time at which they reach motor milestones?*

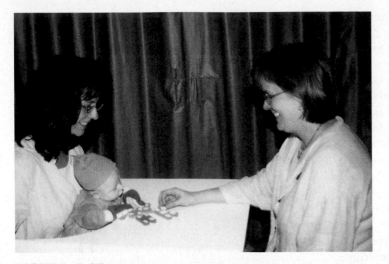

FIGURE 5.17 Infants' Use of "Sticky Mittens" to Explore Objects
Amy Needham and her colleagues (2002) found that "sticky mittens"
enhanced young infants' object exploration skills.

Silva, & Tudella, 2006). During the first two years of life, infants refine how they reach and grasp. Initially, infants reach by moving their shoulders and elbows crudely, swinging toward an object. Later, when infants reach for an object, they move their wrists, rotate their hands, and coordinate their thumb and forefinger. Infants do not have to see their own hands in order to reach for an object, (Clifton & others, 1993). Proprioceptive cues from muscles, tendons, and joints, not sight of the limb, guide reaching by 4-month-old infants.

Infants refine their ability to grasp objects by developing two types of grasps. Initially, infants grip with the whole hand, which is called the *palmer grasp*. Later, toward the end of the first year, infants grasp small objects with their thumb and forefinger, which is called the *pincer grip*. Their grasping system is very flexible. They vary their grip on an object depending on its size and shape, as well as the size of their own hands relative to the object's size. Infants grip small objects with their thumb and forefinger (and sometimes their middle finger, too), whereas they grip large objects with all of the fingers of one hand or both hands.

Perceptual-motor coupling is necessary for the infant to coordinate grasping (Keen, 2005). Which perceptual system the infant is most likely to use in coordinating grasping varies with age. Four-month-old infants rely greatly on touch to determine how they will grip an object; 8-month-olds are more likely to use vision as a guide (Newell & others, 1989). This developmental change is efficient because vision lets infants pre-shape their hands as they reach for an object.

Experience plays a role in reaching and grasping. In one study, three-month old infants participated in play sessions wearing "sticky mittens"—"mittens with palms that stuck to the edges of toys and allowed the infants to pick up the toys" (Needham, Barrett, & Peterman, 2002, p. 279) (see Figure 5.17). Infants who participated in sessions with the mittens grasped and manipulated objects earlier in their development than a control group of infants who did not receive the "mitten" experience. The experienced infants looked at the objects longer, swatted at them more during visual contact, and were more likely to mouth the objects.

Just as infants need to exercise their gross motor skills, they also need to exercise their fine motor skills (Barrett, Davis, & Needham, 2007; Keen, 2005; Needham, 2008). Especially when they can manage a pincer grip, infants delight in picking up small objects. Many develop the pincer grip and begin to crawl at about the same time, and infants at this time pick up virtually everything in sight, especially on the floor, and put the objects in their mouth. Thus, parents need to be vigilant in regularly monitoring what objects are within the infant's reach.

REVIEW AND REFLECT ◆ LEARNING GOAL 2

2 Describe infants' motor development.

Review
- What is dynamic systems theory?
- What are some reflexes that infants have?
- How do gross motor skills develop in infancy?
- How do fine motor skills develop in infancy?

Reflect
- Which view of infant motor development do you prefer—the traditional maturational view or the dynamic systems view? Why?

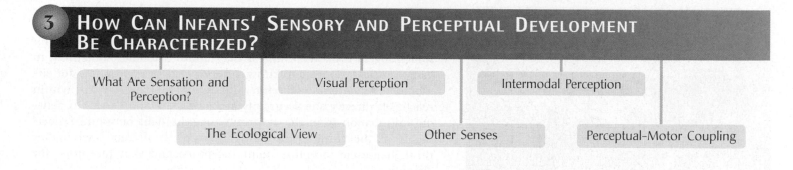

3 HOW CAN INFANTS' SENSORY AND PERCEPTUAL DEVELOPMENT BE CHARACTERIZED?

What Are Sensation and Perception?	Visual Perception	Intermodal Perception
The Ecological View	Other Senses	Perceptual-Motor Coupling

Right now, I am looking at my computer screen to make sure the words are being printed accurately as I am typing them. My perceptual and motor skills are working together. Recall that even control of posture uses information from the senses. And when people grasp an object, they use perceptual information about the object to adjust their motions.

How do these sensations and perceptions develop? Can a newborn see? If so, what can it perceive? What about the other senses—hearing, smell, taste, and touch? What are they like in the newborn, and how do they develop? Can an infant put together information from two modalities, such as sight and sound? These are among the intriguing questions that we explore in this section.

What Are Sensation and Perception?

How does a newborn know that her mother's skin is soft rather than rough? How does a 5-year-old know what color his hair is? Infants and children "know" these things as a result of information that comes through the senses. Without vision, hearing, touch, taste, smell, and other senses, we would be isolated from the world; we would live in dark silence, a tasteless, colorless, feelingless void.

Sensation occurs when information interacts with sensory *receptors*—the eyes, ears, tongue, nostrils, and skin. The sensation of hearing occurs when waves of pulsating air are collected by the outer ear and transmitted through the bones of the inner ear to the auditory nerve. The sensation of vision occurs as rays of light contact the eyes, become focused on the retina, and are transmitted by the optic nerve to the visual centers of the brain.

Perception is the interpretation of what is sensed. The air waves that contact the ears might be interpreted as noise or as musical sounds, for example. The physical energy transmitted to the retina of the eye might be interpreted as a particular color, pattern, or shape, depending on how it is perceived.

> *The experiences of the first three years of life are almost entirely lost to us, and when we attempt to enter into a small child's world, we come as foreigners who have forgotten the landscape and no longer speak the native tongue.*
>
> —SELMA FRAIBERG
> *Developmentalist and Child Advocate, 20th Century*

The Ecological View

For the past several decades, much of the research on perceptual development in infancy has been guided by the ecological view of Eleanor and James J. Gibson (E. Gibson, 1969, 1989, 2001; J. Gibson, 1966, 1979). They argue that we do not have to take bits and pieces of data from sensations and build up representations of the world in our minds. Instead, our perceptual system can select from the rich information that the environment itself provides.

According to the Gibsons' **ecological view,** we directly perceive information that exists in the world around us. The view is called *ecological* "because it connects perceptual capabilities to information available in the world of the perceiver" (Kellman & Arterberry, 2006, p. 112). Thus, perception brings us into contact with the environment in order to interact with and adapt to it. Perception is designed for action. Perception gives people such information as when to duck, when to turn their bodies through a narrow passageway, and when to put their hands up to catch something.

sensation The product of the interaction between information and the sensory receptors—the eyes, ears, tongue, nostrils, and skin.

perception The interpretation of what is sensed.

ecological view The view that perception functions to bring organisms in contact with the environment and to increase adaptation.

How would you use the Gibsons' ecological theory of perception and the concept of affordance to explain the role that perception is playing in this toddler's activity?

In the Gibsons' view, all objects have **affordances,** which are opportunities for interaction offered by objects that fit within our capabilities to perform functional activities. A pot may afford you something to cook with, and it may afford a toddler something to bang. Adults immediately know when a chair is appropriate for sitting, when a surface is safe for walking, or when an object is within reach. We directly and accurately perceive these affordances by sensing information from the environment—the light or sound reflecting from the surfaces of the world—and from our own bodies through muscle receptors, joint receptors, and skin receptors, for example.

An important developmental question is, What affordances can infants or children detect and use? In one study, for example, when babies who could walk were faced with a squishy waterbed, they stopped and explored it, then chose to crawl rather than walk across it (Gibson & others, 1987). They combined perception and action to adapt to the demands of the task.

Similarly, as we described earlier in the section on motor development, infants who were just learning to crawl or just learning to walk were less cautious when confronted with a steep slope than experienced crawlers or walkers were (Adolph, 1997; Adolph & Joh, 2007). The more experienced crawlers and walkers perceived that a slope *affords* the possibility for not only faster locomotion but also for falling. Again, infants coupled perception and action to make a decision about what do in their environment. Through perceptual development, children become more efficient at discovering and using affordances.

Studying the infant's perception has not been an easy task. The *Research in Children's Development* interlude describes some of the ingenious ways researchers study the infant's perception.

Research in Children's Development

STUDYING THE INFANT'S PERCEPTION

The creature has poor motor coordination and can move itself only with great difficulty. Although it cries when uncomfortable, it uses few other vocalizations. In fact, it sleeps most of the time, about 16 to 17 hours a day. You are curious about this creature and want to know more about what it can do. You think to yourself, "I wonder if it can see. How could I find out?"

You obviously have a communication problem with the creature. You must devise a way that will allow the creature to "tell" you that it can see. While examining the creature one day, you make an interesting discovery. When you move an object horizontally in front of the creature, its eyes follow the object's movement. The creature's head movement suggests that it has at least some vision.

In case you haven't already guessed, the creature you have been reading about is the human infant, and the role you played is that of a researcher interested in devising techniques to learn about the infant's visual perception. After years of work, scientists have developed research methods and tools sophisticated enough to examine the subtle abilities of infants and to interpret their complex actions (Bendersky & Sullivan, 2007; Field, 2007; Slater & Lewis, 2007).

affordances Opportunities for interaction offered by objects that fit within our capabilities to perform functional activities.

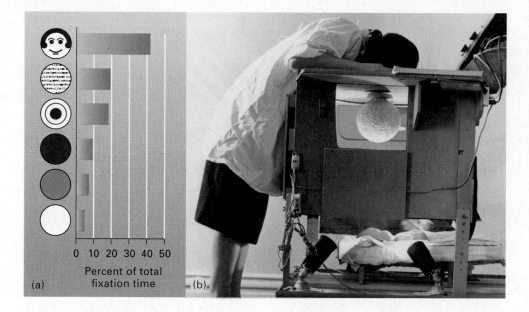

FIGURE 5.18 Fantz's Experiment on Infants' Visual Perception (*a*) Infants 2 to 3 weeks old preferred to look at some stimuli more than others. In Fantz's experiment, infants preferred to look at patterns rather than at color or brightness. For example, they looked longer at a face, a piece of printed matter, or a bull's-eye than at red, yellow, or white discs. (*b*) Fantz used a "looking chamber" to study infants' perception of stimuli.

Visual Preference Method

Robert Fantz (1963) was a pioneer in this effort. Fantz made an important discovery that advanced the ability of researchers to investigate infants' visual perception: infants look at different things for different lengths of time. Fantz placed infants in a "looking chamber," which had two visual displays on the ceiling above the infant's head. An experimenter viewed the infant's eyes by looking through a peephole. If the infant was fixating on one of the displays, the experimenter could see the display's reflection in the infant's eyes. This allowed the experimenter to determine how long the infant looked at each display. Fantz (1963) found that infants only 2 days old look longer at patterned stimuli, such as faces and concentric circles, than at red, white, or yellow discs. Infants 2 to 3 weeks old preferred to look at patterns—a face, a piece of printed matter, or a bull's-eye—rather than at red, yellow, or white discs (see Figure 5.18). Fantz' research method—studying whether infants can distinguish one stimulus from another by measuring the length of time they attend to different stimuli—is referred to as the **visual preference method**.

Habituation and Dishabituation

Another way that researchers have studied infant perception is to present a stimulus (such as a sight or a sound) a number of times. If the infant decreases its response to the stimulus after several presentations, it indicates that the infant is no longer interested in the stimulus. If the researcher now presents a new stimulus, the infant's response will recover—indicating the infant could discriminate between the old and new stimulus.

Habituation is the name given to decreased responsiveness to a stimulus after repeated presentations of the stimulus. **Dishabituation** is the recovery of an habituated response after a change in stimulation. Newborn infants can habituate to repeated sights, sounds, smells, or touches (Rovee-Collier, 2004). Among the measures researchers use in habituation studies are sucking behavior (sucking behavior stops when the young infant attends to a novel object), heart and respiration rates, and the length of time the infant looks at an object. Figure 5.19 shows the results of one study of habituation and dishabituation with newborns (Slater, Morison, & Somers, 1988).

(*continued on next page*)

visual preference method A method developed by Fantz to determine whether infants can distinguish one stimulus from another by measuring the length of time they attend to different stimuli.

habituation Decreased responsiveness to a stimulus after repeated presentation of the stimulus.

dishabituation Recovery of a habituated response after change in stimulation.

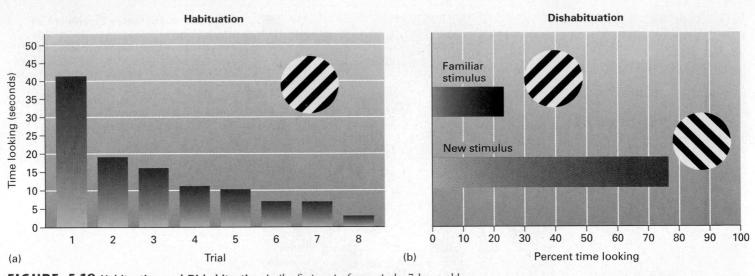

FIGURE 5.19 Habituation and Dishabituation In the first part of one study, 7-hour-old newborns were shown the stimulus in (a). As indicated, the newborns looked at it an average of 41 seconds when it was first presented to them (Slater, Morison, & Somers, 1988). Over seven more presentations of the stimulus, they looked at it less and less. In the second part of the study, infants were presented with both the familiar stimulus to which they had just become habituated to (a) and a new stimulus (shown in (b), which was rotated 90 degrees). The newborns looked at the new stimulus three times as much as the familiar stimulus.

Other Methods

To assess an infant's attention to sound, researchers often use a method called *high-amplitude sucking.* In this method, infants are given a nonnutritive nipple to suck, and the nipple is connected to "a sound generating system. Each suck causes a noise to be generated and the infant learns quickly that sucking brings about this noise. At first, babies suck frequently, so the noise occurs often. Then, gradually, they lose interest in hearing repetitions of the same noise and begin to suck less frequently. At this point, the experimenter changes the sound that is being generated. If the babies renew vigorous sucking, we infer that they have discriminated the sound change and are sucking more because they want to hear the interesting new sound" (Menn & Stoel-Gammon, 2005, p. 71).

To determine if an infant can see or hear a stimulus, researchers might look for the *orienting response,* which involves turning one's head toward a sight or sound (Keen, 2005). Another technique to determine what an infant can see is to monitor the infant's *tracking,* which consists of eye movements that follow (*track*) a moving object and can be used to evaluate an infant's early visual ability, or a startle response can be used to determine an infant's reaction to a noise (Bendersky & Sullivan, 2007).

Equipment

Technology can facilitate the use of most methods for investigating the infant's perceptual abilities. Videotape equipment allows researchers to investigate elusive behaviors. High-speed computers make it possible to perform complex data analysis in minutes. Other equipment records respiration, heart rate, body movement, visual fixation, and sucking behavior, which provide clues to what the infant is perceiving. For example, some researchers use equipment that detects if a change in infants' respiration follows a change in the pitch of a sound. If so, it suggests that the infants heard the pitch change. Thus, scientists have become ingenious at assessing the development of infants, discovering ways to "interview" them even though they cannot yet talk.

FIGURE 5.20 **Visual Acuity During the First Months of Life** The four photographs represent a computer estimation of what a picture of a face looks like to a 1-month-old, 2-month-old, 3-month-old, and 1-year-old (which approximates that of an adult).

Visual Perception

Psychologist William James (1890/1950) called the newborn's perceptual world a "blooming, buzzing confusion." More than a century later, we can safely say that he was wrong (Slater, Field, & Hernandez-Reif, 2007). Even the newborn perceives a world with some order. That world, however, is far different than the one perceived by the toddler or the adult.

Visual Acuity and Human Faces
Just how well can infants see? At birth, the nerves and muscles and lens of the eye are still developing. As a result, newborns cannot see small things that are far away. The newborn's vision is estimated to be 20/600 on the well-known Snellen chart used for eye examinations (Banks & Salapatek, 1983). In other words, an object 20 feet away is only as clear to the newborn as it would be if it were 600 feet away from an adult with normal vision (20/20). By 6 months of age, though, vision is 20/100 or better, and, by about the first birthday, the infant's vision approximates that of an adult (Banks & Salapatek, 1983).

Infants show an interest in human faces soon after birth (Slater, Field, & Hernandez-Rief, 2007). Figure 5.20 shows a computer estimation of what a picture of a face looks like to an infant at different ages from a distance of about 6 inches. Infants spend more time looking at their mother's face than a stranger's face as early as 12 hours after being born (Bushnell, 2003). By 3 months of age, infants match voices to faces, distinguish between male and female faces, and discriminate between faces of their own ethnic group and those of other ethnic groups (Kelly & others, 2007a, b; Slater & others, 2003).

Even very young infants soon change the way they gather information from the visual world, including human faces (Aslin & Lathrop, 2008). By using a special mirror arrangement, researchers projected an image of human faces in front of infants' eyes so that the infants' eye movements could be photographed (Maurer & Salapatek, 1976). As Figure 5.21 shows, the 2-month-old scans much more of the face than the 1-month-old, and the 2-month-old spends more time examining the internal details of the face. Thus, the 2-month-old gains more information about the world than the 1-month-old.

Also, as we discussed in the *Research in Child Development* interlude, young infants can perceive certain patterns. With the help of his "looking chamber, Robert Fantz (1963) revealed that even 2- to 3-week-old infants prefer to look at patterned displays rather than nonpatterned

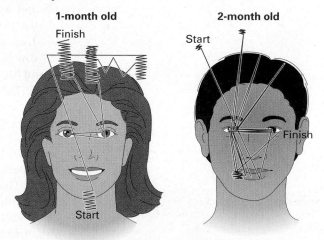

FIGURE 5.21 **How 1- and 2-Month-Old Infants Scan the Human Face**

displays. For example, they prefer to look at a normal human face rather than one with scrambled features, and prefer to look at a bull's-eye target or black-and-white stripes rather than a plain circle.

Color Vision The infant's color vision also improves (Kellman & Arterberry, 2006). By 8 weeks, and possibly by even 4 weeks, infants can discriminate some colors (Kelly, Borchert, & Teller, 1997). By 4 months of age, they have color preferences that mirror adults' color preferences in some cases, preferring saturated colors such as royal blue over pale blue, for example (Bornstein, 1975). In part, these changes in vision reflect maturation. Experience, however, is also necessary for vision to develop normally. For example, one study found that experience is necessary for normal color vision to develop (Sugita, 2004).

Perceptual Constancy Some perceptual accomplishments are especially intriguing because they indicate that the infant's perception goes beyond the information provided by the senses (Bower, 2002; Slater, Field, & Hernandez, 2007). This is the case in *perceptual constancy*, in which sensory stimulation is changing but perception of the physical world remains constant. If infants did not develop perceptual constancy, each time they saw an object at a different distance or in a different orientation, they would perceive it as a different object. Thus, the development of perceptual constancy allows infants to perceive their world as stable. Two types of perceptual constancy are size constancy and shape constancy.

Size constancy is the recognition that an object remains the same even though the retinal image of the object changes. The farther away from us an object is, the smaller its image is on our eyes. Thus, the size of an object on the retina is not sufficient to tell us its actual size. For example, you perceive a bicycle standing right in front of you as smaller than the car parked across the street, even though the bicycle casts a larger image on your eyes than the car does. When you move away from the bicycle, you do not perceive it to be shrinking even though its image on your retinas shrinks; you perceive its size as constant.

But what about babies? Do they have size constancy? Researchers have found that babies as young as 3 months of age show size constancy (Bower, 1966; Day & McKenzie, 1973). However, at 3 months of age, this ability is not full-blown. It continues to develop until 10 or 11 years of age (Kellman & Banks, 1998).

Shape constancy is the recognition that an object remains the same shape even though its orientation to us changes. Look around the room you are in right now. You likely see objects of varying shapes, such as tables and chairs. If you get up and walk around the room, you will see these objects from different sides and angles. Even though your retinal image of the objects changes as you walk and look, you will still perceive the objects as the same shape.

Do babies have shape constancy? As with size constancy, researchers have found that babies as young as 3 months of age have shape constancy (Bower, 1966; Day & McKenzie, 1973). Three-month-old infants, however, do not have shape constancy for irregularly shaped objects, such as tilted planes (Cook & Birch, 1984).

Depth Perception Decades ago, the inspiration for what would become a classic experiment came to Eleanor Gibson as she was eating a picnic lunch on the edge of the Grand Canyon. She wondered whether an infant looking over the canyon's rim would perceive the dangerous dropoff and back up. She also was worried that her own two young children would play too close to the canyon's edge and fall off. Might even infants perceive depth?

To investigate this question, Eleanor Gibson and Richard Walk (1960) constructed a miniature cliff with a dropoff covered by glass in their laboratory. They placed infants on the edge of this visual cliff and had their mothers coax them to crawl onto the glass

size constancy The recognition that an object remains the same even though the retinal image of the object changes.

shape constancy The recognition that an object's shape remains the same even though its orientation to us changes.

(see Figure 5.22). Most infants would not crawl out on the glass, choosing instead to remain on the shallow side, an indication that they could perceive depth.

The 6- to 12-month-old infants in the visual cliff experiment had extensive visual experience. Do younger infants without this experience still perceive depth? Since younger infants do not crawl, this question is difficult to answer. Two- to 4-month-old infants show differences in heart rate when they are placed directly on the deep side of the visual cliff instead of on the shallow side (Campos, Langer, & Krowitz, 1970). However, these differences might mean that young infants respond to differences in some visual characteristics of the deep and shallow cliffs, with no actual knowledge of depth. Although researchers do not know exactly how early in life infants can perceive depth, we do know, as we noted earlier, that infants develop the ability to use binocular cues to depth by about 3 to 4 months of age.

Researchers also are interested in fine-detail depth perception, which is called *stereoacuity* (Birch & others, 2005). A recent study using random-dot TV patterns showed that stereoacuity did not improve from 6 to 12 months of age but improved rapidly after 1 year of age (Takai & others, 2005).

FIGURE 5.22 Examining Infants' Depth Perception on the Visual Cliff Eleanor Gibson and Richard Walk (1960) found that most infants would not crawl out on the glass, which indicated that they had depth perception.

Nature, Nurture, and the Development of Infants' Visual Perception

There has been a longstanding interest in how strongly infants' visual perception is influenced by nature or nurture. A recent analysis concluded that much of vision develops from innate (nature) foundations and that the basic foundation of many visual abilities can be detected at birth while others unfold maturationally (Kellman & Arterberry, 2006). Environmental experiences (nurture) likely refine or calibrate many visual functions, and they may be the driving force behind some functions.

Other Senses

Other sensory systems besides vision also develop during infancy. We explore development in hearing, touch and pain, smell, and taste.

Hearing   During the last two months of pregnancy, as the fetus nestles in its mother's womb, it can hear sounds such as the mother's voice, music, and so on (Kisilevsky & others, 2004; Smith, Muir, & Kisilevsky, 2001). Two psychologists wanted to find out if a fetus that heard Dr. Seuss' classic story *The Cat in the Hat* while still in the mother's womb would prefer hearing the story after birth (DeCasper & Spence, 1986). During the last months of pregnancy, sixteen women read *The Cat in the Hat* to their fetuses. Then shortly after they were born, the mothers read either *The Cat in the Hat* or a story with a different rhyme and pace, *The King, the Mice and the Cheese* (which was not read to them during prenatal development). The infants sucked on a nipple in a different way when the mothers read the two stories, suggesting that the infants recognized the pattern and tone of *The Cat in the Hat* (see Figure 5.23). This study illustrates not only that a fetus can hear but also that it has a remarkable ability to learn even before birth.

The fetus can also recognize the mother's voice, as a recent study demonstrated (Kisilevsky & others, 2003). Sixty term fetuses (mean gestational age, 38.4 weeks) were exposed to a tape recording either of their mother or of a female stranger reading a passage. The sounds of the tape were delivered through a loudspeaker held just above the mother's abdomen. Fetal heart rate increased in response to the mother's voice but decreased in response to the stranger's voice.

Newborns will suck more rapidly on a nipple in order to listen to some sounds rather than others. Their sucking behavior indicates that they prefer a recording of

FIGURE 5.23 Hearing in the Womb
(a) Pregnant mothers read *The Cat in the Hat* to their fetuses during the last few months of pregnancy. (b) When they were born, the babies preferred listening to a recording of their mothers reading *The Cat in the Hat*, as evidenced by their sucking on a nipple that produced this recording, rather than another story, *The King, the Mice and the Cheese*.

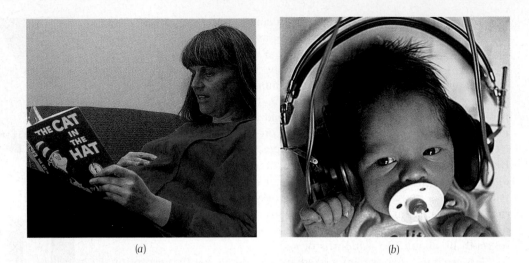

(a) (b)

their mother's voice to the voice of an unfamiliar woman, their mother's native language to a foreign language, and the classical music of Beethoven to the rock music of Aerosmith (Flohr & others, 2001; Spence & DeCasper, 1987). They are especially sensitive to the sounds of human speech.

What kind of changes in hearing take place during infancy? They involve perception of a sound's loudness, pitch, and localization:

- Immediately after birth, infants cannot hear soft sounds quite as well as adults can; a stimulus must be louder to be heard by a newborn than by an adult (Trehub & others, 1991). For example, an adult can hear a whisper from about 4 to 5 feet away, but a newborn requires that sounds be closer to a normal conversational level to be heard at that distance.
- Infants are also less sensitive to the pitch of a sound than adults are. *Pitch* is the perception of the frequency of a sound. A soprano voice sounds high pitched, a bass voice low pitched. Infants are less sensitive to low-pitched sounds and are more likely to hear high-pitched sounds (Aslin, Jusczyk, & Pisoni, 1998). By 2 years of age, infants have considerably improved their ability to distinguish sounds with different pitches.
- Even newborns can determine the general location from where a sound is coming, but by 6 months of age, they are more proficient at *localizing* sounds, detecting their origins. Their ability to localize sounds continues to improve in the second year (Litovsky & Ashmead, 1997; Morrongiello, Fenwick, & Chance, 1990; Saffran, Werker, & Warner, 2006).

Touch and Pain   Do newborns respond to touch? Can they feel pain?

Newborns do respond to touch. A touch to the cheek produces a turning of the head; a touch to the lips produces sucking movements.

Newborns can also feel pain (Gunnar & Quevado, 2007). If and when you have a son and consider whether he should be circumcised, the issue of an infant's pain perception probably will become important to you. Circumcision is usually performed on young boys about the third day after birth. Will your young son experience pain if he is circumcised when he is 3 days old? An investigation by Megan Gunnar and her colleagues (1987) found that newborn infant males cried intensely during circumcision. The circumcised infant also displays amazing resiliency. Within several minutes after the surgery, they can nurse and interact in a normal manner with their mothers. And, if allowed to, the newly circumcised newborn drifts into a deep sleep, which seems to serve as a coping mechanism.

For many years, doctors performed operations on newborns without anesthesia. This practice was accepted because of the dangers of anesthesia and because of the supposition that newborns do not feel pain. As researchers demonstrated that newborns can feel pain, the practice of operating on newborns without anesthesia is being challenged. Anesthesia now is used in some circumcisions.

The important ability to connect information about vision with information about touch develops during infancy. Coordination of vision and touch has been well documented in 6-month-olds (Rose, 1990) and in one study was demonstrated in 2- to 3-month-olds (Streri, 1987).

Smell Newborns can differentiate odors. The expressions on their faces seem to indicate that they like the way vanilla and strawberry smell but do not like the way rotten eggs and fish smell (Steiner, 1979). In one investigation, 6-day-old infants who were breast fed showed a clear preference for smelling their mother's breast pad rather than a clean breast pad (MacFarlane, 1975) (see Figure 5.24). However, when they were 2 days old, they did not show this preference, indicating that they require several days of experience to recognize this odor.

Taste Sensitivity to taste might be present even before birth. When saccharin was added to the amniotic fluid of a near-term fetus, swallowing increased (Windle, 1940). In one study, even at only 2 hours of age, babies made different facial expressions when they tasted sweet, sour, and bitter solutions (Rosenstein & Oster, 1988) (see Figure 5.25). At about 4 months of age, infants begin to prefer salty tastes, which as newborns they had found to be aversive (Harris, Thomas, & Booth, 1990).

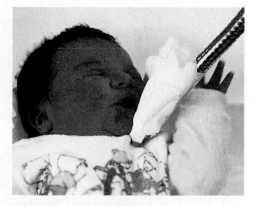

FIGURE 5.24 Newborns' Preference for the Smell of Their Mother's Breast Pad In the experiment by MacFarlane (1975), 6-day-old infants preferred to smell their mother's breast pad over a clean one that had never been used, but 2-day-old infants did not show this preference, indicating that this odor preference requires several days of experience to develop.

Intermodal Perception

Imagine yourself playing basketball or tennis. You are experiencing many visual inputs: the ball coming and going, other players moving around, and so on. However, you are experiencing many auditory inputs as well: the sound of the ball bouncing or being hit, the grunts and groans, and so on. There is good correspondence between much of the visual and auditory information: when you see the ball bounce, you hear a bouncing sound; when a player stretches to hit a ball, you hear a groan. When you look at and listen to what is going on, you do not experience just the sounds or just the sights; you put all these things together. You experience a unitary episode. This is **intermodal perception,** which involves integrating information from two or more sensory modalities, such as vision and hearing.

intermodal perception The ability to relate and integrate information from two or more sensory modalities, such as vision and hearing.

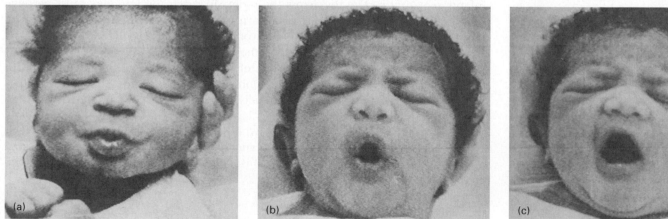

(a) (b) (c)

FIGURE 5.25 Newborns' Facial Responses to Basic Tastes Facial expressions elicited by (a) a sweet solution, (b) a sour solution, and (c) a bitter solution.

How are perception and action coupled in infants' development?

Crude exploratory forms of intermodal perception exist even in newborns (Chen, Striano, & Rakoczy, 2004). For example, newborns turn their eyes and their head toward the sound of a voice or rattle when the sound is maintained for several seconds (Clifton & others, 1981), but the newborn can localize a sound and look at an object only in a crude way (Bechtold, Bushnell, & Salapatek, 1979). These exploratory forms of intermodal perception become sharpened with experience in the first year of life (Hollich, Newman, & Jusczyk, 2005; Lewkowicz, 2003). In one study, infants as young as 3½ months old looked more at their mother when they also heard her voice and longer at their father when they also heard his voice (Spelke & Owsley, 1979); thus even young infants can coordinate visual-auditory information involving people.

Can young infants put vision and sound together as precisely as adults do? In the first six months, infants have difficulty connecting sensory input from different modes, but in the second half of the first year they show an increased ability to make this connection mentally.

Thus, babies are born into the world with some innate abilities to perceive relations among sensory modalities, but their intermodal abilities improve considerably through experience (Banks, 2005). As with all aspects of development, in perceptual development, nature and nurture interact and cooperate (Banks, 2005).

Perceptual–Motor Coupling

As we come to the end of this chapter, we return to the important theme of perceptual-motor coupling. The distinction between perceiving and doing has been a time-honored tradition in psychology. However, a number of experts on perceptual and motor development question whether this distinction makes sense (Adolph & Joh, 2007, 2008; Thelen & Whitmeyer, 2005). In particular, Esther Thelen's dynamic systems approach explores how people assemble motor behaviors for perceiving and acting; the ecological approach of Eleanor and James J. Gibson examines how perception guides action. Action can guide perception and perception can guide action. Only by moving your eyes, head, hands, and arms, and by moving from one location to another, can you fully experience your environment and learn how to adapt to it. Perception and action are coupled.

Babies continually coordinate their movements with perceptual information to learn how to maintain balance, reach for objects in space, and move across various surfaces and terrains (Adolph & Joh, 2007, 2008; Thelen & Smith, 2006; Thelen & Whitmeyer, 2005). They are motivated to move by what they perceive. Suppose infants see an attractive toy across the room. To reach the toy, they must perceive the current state of their bodies and learn how to use their limbs. Although their movements at first are awkward and uncoordinated, babies soon learn to select patterns that are appropriate for reaching their goals.

Equally important is the other part of the perception-action coupling. That is, action educates perception (Adolph & Joh, 2007, 2008; Smith & Breazeal, 2007). For example, exploring an object manually helps infants to discriminate its texture, size, and hardness. Locomoting teaches babies about how objects and people look from different perspectives and about whether surfaces will support their weight. Individuals perceive in order to move and move in order to perceive. Perceptual and motor development do not occur in isolation from one another but instead are coupled.

REVIEW AND REFLECT ◆ LEARNING GOAL 3

(3) Summarize the course of sensory and perceptual development in infancy.

Review

• What are sensation and perception?

• What is the ecological view of perception?

• How does visual perception develop in infancy?

• How do hearing, touch and pain, smell, and taste develop in infancy?

• What is intermodal perception?

• How is perceptual-motor development coupled?

Reflect

• How much sensory stimulation should caregivers provide for infants? A little? A lot? Could an infant be given too much sensory stimulation? Explain.

REACH YOUR LEARNING GOALS

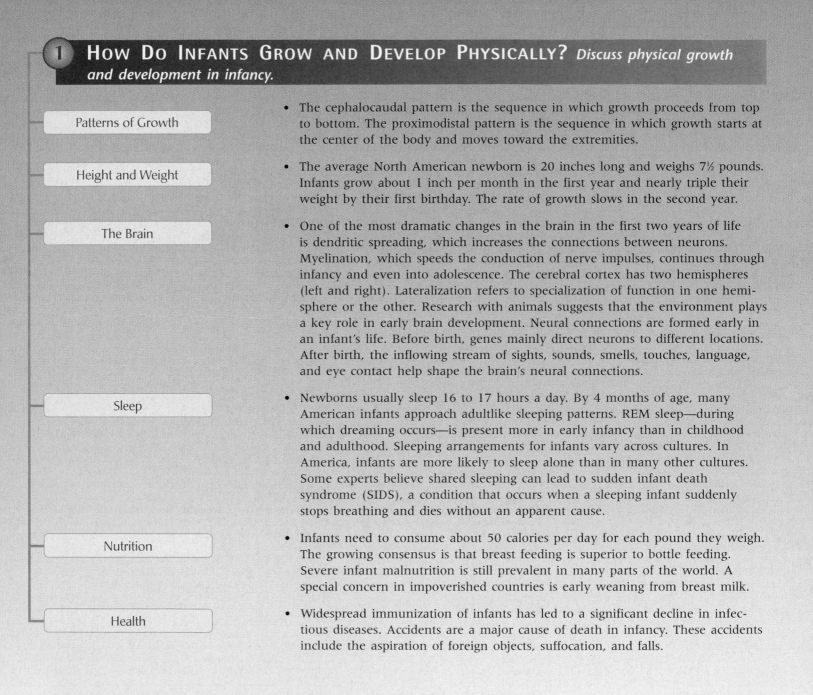

1 HOW DO INFANTS GROW AND DEVELOP PHYSICALLY? *Discuss physical growth and development in infancy.*

Patterns of Growth

- The cephalocaudal pattern is the sequence in which growth proceeds from top to bottom. The proximodistal pattern is the sequence in which growth starts at the center of the body and moves toward the extremities.

Height and Weight

- The average North American newborn is 20 inches long and weighs 7½ pounds. Infants grow about 1 inch per month in the first year and nearly triple their weight by their first birthday. The rate of growth slows in the second year.

The Brain

- One of the most dramatic changes in the brain in the first two years of life is dendritic spreading, which increases the connections between neurons. Myelination, which speeds the conduction of nerve impulses, continues through infancy and even into adolescence. The cerebral cortex has two hemispheres (left and right). Lateralization refers to specialization of function in one hemisphere or the other. Research with animals suggests that the environment plays a key role in early brain development. Neural connections are formed early in an infant's life. Before birth, genes mainly direct neurons to different locations. After birth, the inflowing stream of sights, sounds, smells, touches, language, and eye contact help shape the brain's neural connections.

Sleep

- Newborns usually sleep 16 to 17 hours a day. By 4 months of age, many American infants approach adultlike sleeping patterns. REM sleep—during which dreaming occurs—is present more in early infancy than in childhood and adulthood. Sleeping arrangements for infants vary across cultures. In America, infants are more likely to sleep alone than in many other cultures. Some experts believe shared sleeping can lead to sudden infant death syndrome (SIDS), a condition that occurs when a sleeping infant suddenly stops breathing and dies without an apparent cause.

Nutrition

- Infants need to consume about 50 calories per day for each pound they weigh. The growing consensus is that breast feeding is superior to bottle feeding. Severe infant malnutrition is still prevalent in many parts of the world. A special concern in impoverished countries is early weaning from breast milk.

Health

- Widespread immunization of infants has led to a significant decline in infectious diseases. Accidents are a major cause of death in infancy. These accidents include the aspiration of foreign objects, suffocation, and falls.

2 HOW DO INFANTS DEVELOP MOTOR SKILLS? *Describe infants' motor development.*

The Dynamic Systems View

- Thelen's dynamic systems theory seeks to explain how motor behaviors are assembled for perceiving and acting. Perception and action are coupled. According to this theory, motor skills are the result of many converging factors, such as the development of the nervous system, the body's physical properties and its movement possibilities, the goal the child is motivated to reach, and environmental support for the skill. In the dynamic systems view, motor development is far more complex than the result of a genetic blueprint.

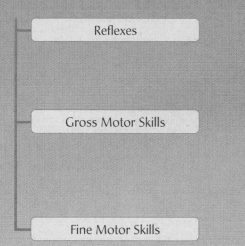

Reflexes	• Reflexes—automatic movements—govern the newborn's behavior. They include the sucking, rooting, and Moro reflexes—all of which typically disappear after three to four months, as well as such permanent reflexes as coughing and blinking. For infants, sucking is an especially important reflex because it provides a means of obtaining nutrition.
Gross Motor Skills	• Gross motor skills involve large-muscle activities. Key skills developed during infancy include control of posture and walking. Although infants usually learn to walk by their first birthday, the neural pathways that allow walking begin to form earlier. When infants reach milestones in the development of gross motor skills may vary by as much as two to four months, especially for milestones in late infancy.
Fine Motor Skills	• Fine motor skills involve finely tuned movements. The onset of reaching and grasping marks a significant accomplishment, and this becomes more refined during the first two years of life.

3 HOW CAN INFANTS' SENSORY AND PERCEPTUAL DEVELOPMENT BE CHARACTERIZED? *Summarize the course of sensory and perceptual development in infancy.*

What Are Sensation and Perception?	• Sensation occurs when information interacts with sensory receptors. Perception is the interpretation of sensation.
The Ecological View	• Created by the Gibsons, the ecological view states that we directly perceive information that exists in the world around us. Perception brings people in contact with the environment to interact with and adapt to it. Affordances provide opportunities for interaction offered by objects that fit within our capabilities to perform activities.
Visual Perception	• Researchers have developed a number of methods to assess the infant's perception, including the visual preference method (which Fantz used to determine young infants' interest in looking at patterned over nonpatterned displays), habituation and dishabituation, and tracking. The infant's visual acuity increases dramatically in the first year of life. Infants' color vision improves as they develop. Young infants systematically scan human faces. By 3 months of age, infants show size and shape constancy. In Gibson and Walk's classic study, infants as young as 6 months of age had depth perception. Much of vision develops from biological foundations, but environmental experiences can contribute to the development of visual perception.
Other Senses	• The fetus can hear several weeks prior to birth. Immediately after birth, newborns can hear, but their sensory threshold is higher than that of adults. Developmental changes in the perception of loudness, pitch, and localization of sound occur during infancy. Newborns can respond to touch and feel pain. Newborns can differentiate odors, and sensitivity to taste may be present before birth.
Intermodal Perception	• Crude, exploratory forms of intermodal perception—the ability to relate and integrate information from two or more sensory modalities —are present in newborns and become sharpened over the first year of life.
Perceptual-Motor Coupling	• Perception and action are often not isolated but rather are coupled. Individuals perceive in order to move and move in order to perceive.

KEY TERMS

cephalocaudal pattern 143
proximodistal pattern 144
lateralization 146
sudden infant death
   syndrome (SIDS) 151
marasmus 155
kwashiorkor 155

dynamic systems theory 158
reflexes 159
rooting reflex 159
sucking reflex 159
Moro reflex 159
grasping reflex 159
gross motor skills 160

fine motor skills 163
sensation 165
perception 165
ecological view 165
affordances 166
visual preference method 167

habituation 167
dishabituation 167
size constancy 170
shape constancy 170
intermodal perception 173

KEY PEOPLE

Mark Rosenzweig •••
Ernesto Pollitt •••
T. Berry Brazelton •••
Esther Thelen •••

Karen Adolph •••
Eleanor and James
   J. Gibson •••

Robert Fantz •••
William James •••
Richard Walk •••

MAKING A DIFFERENCE

Supporting the Infant's Physical Development

What are some good strategies for helping the infant develop in physically competent ways?

- *Be flexible about the infant's sleep patterns.* Don't try to put the infant on a rigid sleep schedule. By about 4 months of age, most infants have moved closer to adultlike sleep patterns.
- *Provide the infant with good nutrition.* Make sure the infant has adequate energy and nutrient intake. Provide this in a loving and supportive environment. Don't put an infant on a diet. Weaning should be gradual, not abrupt.
- *Breast feed the infant, if possible.* Breast feeding provides more ideal nutrition than bottle feeding. If because of work demands the mother cannot breast feed the infant, she should consider "pumping."
- *Toilet train the infant in a warm, relaxed, supportive manner.* Twenty months to 2 years of age is a recommended time to begin toilet training, so that it is accomplished before

the "terrible twos." Like good strategies for the infant's sleep and nutrition, toilet training should not be done in a harsh, rigid way.

- *Give the infant extensive opportunities to explore safe environments.* Infants don't need exercise classes. What they should be provided are many opportunities to actively explore safe environments. Infants should not be constricted to small, confined environments for any length of time.
- *Don't push the infant's physical development or get uptight about physical norms.* In American culture, we tend to want our child to grow faster than other children. Remember that there is wide individual variation in normal physical development. Just because an infant is not at the top of a physical chart doesn't mean parents should start pushing the infant's physical skills. Infants develop at different paces. Respect and nurture the infant's individuality.

RESOURCES FOR IMPROVING CHILDREN'S LIVES

The Amazing Infant

by Tiffany Field (2007)
Malden, MA: Blackwell

The Amazing Infant is an outstanding book on infant development, written by one of the world's leading researchers on infant development. The book accurately captures the flavor of the young infant as an active learner and one far more competent than once was believed.

Solve Your Child's Sleep Problems

by Richard Ferber (2006).
New York: Simon & Schuster

Solve Your Child's Sleep Problems helps parents recognize when their infant or child has a sleep problem and tells them what to do about it.

E-LEARNING TOOLS

Connect to **www.mhhe.com/santrockc10** to research the answers and complete these exercises. In addition, you'll find a number of other resources and valuable study tools for Chapter 5, "Physical Development in Infancy," on this Web site.

Taking It to the Net

1. Min-lee and Chung-jung are first-time parents. Min-lee insists that their 2-month-old daughter, Yu-Hsuan, can tell the difference between her mother's face and father's face, voice, and touch. Chung-jung says that is ridiculous. Who is correct?

2. Mary's mother, Robin, has just arrived from out of town and has seen her 3-month-old grandson, Troy, for the first time. Robin exclaims, "What are you feeding this roly-poly hunk? He looks overweight to me." Mary is shocked. She didn't think a baby could be overweight. Should she cut back on Troy's feedings?

3. Isabelle, who has had three children, volunteers to baby-sit for her friend Nick's 5-month-old boy so that Nick can go on a job interview. As Isabelle is undressing Alexandre, she thinks it's odd that he doesn't seem to be able to turn over in his crib. When she cradles him in her arm to bathe him, he feels "floppy" and appears to lack muscle strength. Is Alexandre evidencing any motor development delays?

Health and Well-Being, Parenting, and Education

Build your decision-making skills by trying your hand at the health and well-being, parenting, and education exercises.

Video Clips

The Online Learning Center includes the following videos for this chapter:

1. *Babinski Reflex at 2 weeks*—261
   The distinct Babinski reflex is demonstrated on this 2-week-old boy.

2. *Startle Reflex at 2 weeks*—263
   Here we see the newborn startle reflex as a 2-week-old boy reacts to a sudden bang of a tambourine.

3. *Crying at 10 Weeks*—697
   Here a 10-week-old baby boy cries and waves his arms and legs around as his mother attempts to soothe him.

4. *Auditory Tracking at 4 Months*—178
   A 4-month-old girl demonstrates auditory perception when she looks up at her mother, after hearing her mother call her name.

6 Cognitive Development in Infancy

I wish I could travel down by the road that crosses the baby's mind where reason makes kites of her laws and flies them.

—RABINDRANATH TAGORE
Bengali Poet, Essayist, 20th Century

CHAPTER OUTLINE		LEARNING GOALS

WHAT IS PIAGET'S THEORY OF INFANT DEVELOPMENT? ① Summarize and evaluate Piaget's theory of infant development.

Cognitive Processes

The Sensorimotor Stage

Evaluating Piaget's Sensorimotor Stage

HOW DO INFANTS LEARN, REMEMBER, AND CONCEPTUALIZE? ② Describe how infants learn, remember, and conceptualize.

Conditioning

Attention

Memory

Imitation

Concept Formation and Categorization

HOW ARE INDIVIDUAL DIFFERENCES IN INFANCY ASSESSED, AND DO THESE ASSESSMENTS PREDICT INTELLIGENCE? ③ Discuss infant assessment measures and the prediction of intelligence.

Measures of Infant Development

Predicting Intelligence

WHAT ARE SOME EARLY ENVIRONMENTAL INFLUENCES ON COGNITIVE DEVELOPMENT? ④ Characterize early environmental influences on cognitive development.

Nutrition

Poverty

WHAT IS THE NATURE OF LANGUAGE, AND HOW DOES IT DEVELOP IN INFANCY? ⑤ Describe the nature of language and how it develops in infancy.

Defining Language

Language's Rule Systems

How Language Develops

Biological and Environmental Influences

An Interactionist View

Images of Children's Development
The Stories of Laurent, Lucienne, and Jacqueline

Jean Piaget, the famous Swiss psychologist, was a meticulous observer of his three children: Laurent, Lucienne, and Jacqueline. His books on cognitive development are filled with these observations. Here are a few of Piaget's observations of his children in infancy (Piaget, 1952):

- At 21 days of age, "Laurent found his thumb after three attempts: prolonged sucking begins each time. But, once he has been placed on his back, he does not know how to coordinate the movement of the arms with that of the mouth and his hands draw back even when his lips are seeking them" (p. 27).
- During the third month, thumb sucking becomes less important to Laurent because of new visual and auditory interests. But, when he cries, his thumb goes to the rescue.
- Toward the end of Lucienne's fourth month, while she is lying in her crib, Piaget hangs a doll above her feet. Lucienne thrusts her feet at the doll and makes it move. "Afterward, she looks at her motionless foot for a second, then recommences. There is no visual control of her foot, for the movements are the same when Lucienne only looks at the doll or when I place the doll over her head. On the other hand, the tactile control of the foot is apparent: after the first shakes, Lucienne makes slow foot movements as though to grasp and explore" (p. 159).
- At 11 months, "Jacqueline is seated and shakes a little bell. She then pauses abruptly in order to delicately place the bell in front of her right foot; then she kicks hard. Unable to recapture it, she grasps a ball which she then places at the same spot in order to give it another kick" (p. 225).
- At 1 year, 2 months, "Jacqueline holds in her hands an object which is new to her: a round, flat box which she turns all over, shakes, (and) rubs against the bassinet. . . . She lets it go and tries to pick it up. But she only succeeds in touching it with her index finger, without grasping it. She nevertheless makes an attempt and presses on the edge. The box then tilts up and falls again" (p. 273). Jacqueline shows an interest in this result and studies the fallen box.
- At 1 year, 8 months, "Jacqueline arrives at a closed door with a blade of grass in each hand. She stretches out her right hand toward the [door] knob but sees that she cannot turn it without letting go of the grass. She puts the grass on the floor, opens the door, picks up the grass again, and enters. But when she wants to leave the room, things become complicated. She puts the grass on the floor and grasps the doorknob. But then she perceives that in pulling the door toward her she will simultaneously chase away the grass which she placed between the door and the threshold. She therefore picks it up in order to put it outside the door's zone of movement" (p. 339).

For Piaget, these observations reflect important changes in the infant's cognitive development. Piaget believed that infants go through six substages as they progress in less than two short years from Laurent's thumb sucking to Jacqueline's problem solving.

PREVIEW

Piaget's descriptions of infants are just the starting point for our exploration of cognitive development. Excitement and enthusiasm about the study of infant cognition have been fueled by an interest in what newborns and infants know, by continued fascination about innate and learned factors in the infant's cognitive development, and by controversies about whether infants construct their knowledge (Piaget's view) or know their world more directly. In this chapter, we study not only Piaget's theory of infant devel- *opment but also learning, remembering, and conceptualizing by infants; individual differences; early environmental influences on cognitive development; and language development.*

1 WHAT IS PIAGET'S THEORY OF INFANT DEVELOPMENT?

Cognitive Processes | The Sensorimotor Stage | Evaluating Piaget's Sensorimotor Stage

Poet Nora Perry asks, "Who knows the thoughts of a child?" As much as anyone, Piaget knew. Through careful observations of his own three children—Laurent, Lucienne, and Jacqueline—and observations of, and interviews with, other children, Piaget changed perceptions of the way children think about the world.

Piaget's theory is a general, unifying story of how biology and experience sculpt cognitive development. Piaget thought that, just as our physical bodies have structures that enable us to adapt to the world, we build mental structures that help us to adapt to the world. *Adaptation* involves adjusting to new environmental demands. Piaget stressed that children actively construct their own cognitive worlds; information is not just poured into their minds from the environment. He sought to discover how children at different points in their development think about the world and how systematic changes in their thinking occur.

Cognitive Processes

What processes do children use as they construct their knowledge of the world? Piaget developed several concepts to answer this question; especially important are schemes, assimilation, accommodation, organization, equilibrium, and equilibration.

Schemes   As the infant or child seeks to construct an understanding of the world, said Piaget (1954), the developing brain creates **schemes.** These are actions or mental representations that organize knowledge. In Piaget's theory, behavioral schemes (physical activities) characterize infancy, and mental schemes (cognitive activities) develop in childhood (Lamb, Bornstein, & Teti, 2002). A baby's schemes are structured by simple actions that can be performed on objects such as sucking, looking, and grasping. Older children have schemes that include strategies and plans for solving problems. For example, in the descriptions at the opening of this chapter, Laurent displayed a scheme for sucking; Jacqueline displayed a problem-solving scheme when she was able to open the door without losing her blade of grass. By the time we have reached adulthood, we have constructed an enormous number of diverse schemes, ranging from how to drive a car to balancing a budget to the concept of fairness.

Assimilation and Accommodation   To explain how children use and adapt their schemes, Piaget offered two concepts: assimilation and accommodation. **Assimilation** occurs when children use their existing schemes to deal with new information or experiences. **Accommodation** occurs when children adjust their schemes to take new information and experiences into account.

Think about a toddler who has learned the word *car* to identify the family's car. The toddler might call all moving vehicles on roads "cars," including motorcycles and trucks; the child has assimilated these objects to his or her existing scheme. But

We are born capable of learning.

—JEAN-JACQUES ROUSSEAU
Swiss-Born French Philosopher, 18th Century

schemes In Piaget's theory, actions or mental representations that organize knowledge.

assimilation Piagetian concept of the incorporation of new information into existing schemes.

accommodation Piagetian concept of adjusting schemes to fit new information and experiences.

the child soon learns that motorcycles and trucks are not cars and fine-tunes the category to exclude motorcycles and trucks, accommodating the scheme.

Assimilation and accommodation operate even in very young infants. Newborns reflexively suck everything that touches their lips; they assimilate all sorts of objects into their sucking scheme. By sucking different objects, they learn about their taste, texture, shape, and so on. After several months of experience, though, they construct their understanding of the world differently. Some objects, such as fingers and the mother's breast, can be sucked, and others, such as fuzzy blankets, should not be sucked. In other words, they accommodate their sucking scheme.

Organization   To make sense out of their world, said Piaget, children cognitively organize their experiences. **Organization** in Piaget's theory is the grouping of isolated behaviors and thoughts into a higher-order system. Continual refinement of this organization is an inherent part of development. A boy who has only a vague idea about how to use a hammer may also have a vague idea about how to use other tools. After learning how to use each one, he relates these uses, organizing his knowledge.

Equilibration and Stages of Development   Assimilation and accommodation always take the child to a higher ground, according to Piaget. In trying to understand the world, the child inevitably experiences cognitive conflict, or *disequilibrium*. That is, the child is constantly faced with counterexamples to his or her existing schemes and with inconsistencies. For example, if a child believes that pouring water from a short and wide container into a tall and narrow container changes the amount of water, then the child might be puzzled by where the "extra" water came from and whether there is actually more water to drink. The puzzle creates disequilibrium; for Piaget, an internal search for equilibrium creates motivation for change. The child assimilates and accommodates, adjusting old schemes, developing new schemes, and organizing and reorganizing the old and new schemes. Eventually, the organization is fundamentally different from the old organization; it is a new way of thinking.

In short, according to Piaget, children constantly assimilate and accommodate as they seek equilibrium. There is considerable movement between states of cognitive equilibrium and disequilibrium as assimilation and accommodation work in concert to produce cognitive change. **Equilibration** is the name Piaget gave to this mechanism by which children shift from one stage of thought to the next.

The result of these processes, according to Piaget, is that individuals go through four stages of development. A different way of understanding the world makes one stage more advanced than another. Cognition is *qualitatively* different in one stage compared with another. In other words, the way children reason at one stage is different from the way they reason at another stage. Here our focus is on Piaget's stage of infant cognitive development. In Chapters 9, 12, and 15, when we study cognitive development in early childhood, middle and late childhood, and adolescence we explore the last three Piagetian stages.

The Sensorimotor Stage

The **sensorimotor stage** lasts from birth to about 2 years of age. In this stage, infants construct an understanding of the world by coordinating sensory experiences (such as seeing and hearing) with physical, motoric actions—hence the term "sensorimotor." At the beginning of this stage, newborns have little more than reflexes with which to work. At the end of the sensorimotor stage, 2-year-olds can produce complex sensorimotor patterns and use primitive symbols. We first summarize Piaget's descriptions of how infants develop. Later we consider criticisms of his view.

Substages   Piaget divided the sensorimotor stage into six substages: (1) simple reflexes; (2) first habits and primary circular reactions; (3) secondary circular reactions;

organization Piaget's concept of grouping isolated behaviors and thoughts into a higher-order, more smoothly functioning cognitive system.

equilibration A mechanism that Piaget proposed to explain how children shift from one stage of thought to the next.

sensorimotor stage The first of Piaget's stages, which lasts from birth to about 2 years of age; infants construct an understanding of the world by coordinating sensory experiences with motoric actions.

Substage	Age	Description	Example
1 Simple reflexes	Birth to 1 month	Coordination of sensation and action through reflexive behaviors.	Rooting, sucking, and grasping reflexes; newborns suck reflexively when their lips are touched.
2 First habits and primary circular reactions	1 to 4 months	Coordination of sensation and two types of schemes: habits (reflex) and primary circular reactions (reproduction of an event that initially occurred by chance). Main focus is still on the infant's body.	Repeating a body sensation first experienced by chance (sucking thumb, for example); then infants might accommodate actions by sucking their thumb differently than they suck on a nipple.
3 Secondary circular reactions	4 to 8 months	Infants become more object-oriented, moving beyond self-preoccupation; repeat actions that bring interesting or pleasurable results.	An infant coos to make a person stay near; as the person starts to leave, the infant coos again.
4 Coordination of secondary circular reactions	8 to 12 months	Coordination of vision and touch—hand-eye coordination; coordination of schemes and intentionality.	Infant manipulates a stick in order to bring an attractive toy within reach.
5 Tertiary circular reactions, novelty, and curiosity	12 to 18 months	Infants become intrigued by the many properties of objects and by the many things they can make happen to objects; they experiment with new behavior.	A block can be made to fall, spin, hit another object, and slide across the ground.
6 Internalization of schemes	18 to 24 months	Infants develop the ability to use primitive symbols and form enduring mental representations.	An infant who has never thrown a temper tantrum before sees a playmate throw a tantrum; the infant retains a memory of the event, then throws one himself the next day.

FIGURE 6.1 Piaget's Six Substages of Sensorimotor Development

(4) coordination of secondary circular reactions; (5) tertiary circular reactions, novelty, and curiosity; and (6) internalization of schemes (see Figure 6.1).

Simple reflexes, the first sensorimotor substage, corresponds to the first month after birth. In this substage, sensation and action are coordinated primarily through reflexive behaviors, such as rooting and sucking. Soon the infant produces behaviors that resemble reflexes in the absence of the usual stimulus for the reflex. For example, a newborn will suck a nipple or bottle only when it is placed directly in the baby's mouth or touched to the lips. But soon the infant might suck when a bottle or nipple is only nearby. Even in the first month of life, the infant is initiating action and actively structuring experiences.

First habits and primary circular reactions is the second sensorimotor substage, which develops between 1 and 4 months of age. In this substage, the infant coordinates sensation and two types of schemes: habits and primary circular reactions. A *habit* is a scheme based on a reflex that has become completely separated from its eliciting stimulus. For example, infants in substage 1 suck when bottles are put to their lips or when they see a bottle. Infants in substage 2 might suck even when no bottle is present. A *circular reaction* is a repetitive action.

A **primary circular reaction** is a scheme based on the attempt to reproduce an event that initially occurred by chance. For example, suppose an infant accidentally sucks his fingers when they are placed near his mouth. Later, he searches for his fingers to suck them again, but the fingers do not cooperate because the infant cannot coordinate visual and manual actions.

Habits and circular reactions are stereotyped—that is, the infant repeats them the same way each time. During this substage, the infant's own body remains the infant's center of attention. There is no outward pull by environmental events.

Secondary circular reactions is the third sensorimotor substage, which develops between 4 and 8 months of age. In this substage, the infant becomes more object-oriented, moving beyond preoccupation with the self. The infant's schemes are not

simple reflexes Piaget's first sensorimotor substage, which corresponds to the first month after birth. In this substage, sensation and action are coordinated primarily through reflexive behaviors.

first habits and primary circular reactions Piaget's second sensorimotor substage, which develops between 1 and 4 months of age. In this substage, the infant coordinates sensation and two types of schemes: habits and primary circular reactions.

primary circular reaction A scheme based on the attempt to reproduce an event that initially occurred by chance.

secondary circular reactions Piaget's third sensorimotor substage, which develops between 4 and 8 months of age. In this substage, the infant becomes more object-oriented, moving beyond preoccupation with the self.

This 17-month-old is in Piaget's stage of tertiary circular reactions. *What might the infant do to suggest that she in this stage?*

intentional or goal directed, but they are repeated because of their consequences. By chance, an infant might shake a rattle. The infant repeats this action for the sake of its fascination. This is a *secondary circular reaction:* an action repeated because of its consequences. The infant also imitates some simple actions, such as the baby talk or burbling of adults, and some physical gestures. However, the baby imitates only actions that he or she is already able to produce.

Coordination of secondary circular reactions is Piaget's fourth sensorimotor substage, which develops between 8 and 12 months of age. To progress into this substage the infant must coordinate vision and touch, hand and eye. Actions become more outwardly directed. Significant changes during this substage involve the coordination of schemes and intentionality. Infants readily combine and recombine previously learned schemes in a coordinated way. They might look at an object and grasp it simultaneously, or they might visually inspect a toy, such as a rattle, and finger it simultaneously, exploring it tactilely. Actions are even more outwardly directed than before. Related to this coordination is the second achievement—the presence of intentionality. For example, infants might manipulate a stick in order to bring a desired toy within reach, or they might knock over one block to reach and play with another one. Similarly, when 11-month-old Jacqueline, as described in the chapter opening, placed the ball in front of her and kicked it, she was demonstrating intentionality.

Tertiary circular reactions, novelty, and curiosity is Piaget's fifth sensorimotor substage, which develops between 12 and 18 months of age. In this substage, infants become intrigued by the many properties of objects and by the many things that they can make happen to objects. A block can be made to fall, spin, hit another object, and slide across the ground. *Tertiary circular reactions* are schemes in which the infant purposely explores new possibilities with objects, continually doing new things to them and exploring the results. Piaget says that this stage marks the starting point for human curiosity and interest in novelty.

Internalization of schemes is Piaget's sixth and final sensorimotor substage, which develops between 18 and 24 months of age. In this substage, the infant develops the ability to use primitive symbols. For Piaget, a *symbol* is an internalized sensory image or word that represents an event. Primitive symbols permit the infant to think about concrete events without directly acting them out or perceiving them. Moreover, symbols allow the infant to manipulate and transform the represented events in simple ways. In a favorite Piagetian example, Piaget's young daughter saw a matchbox being opened and closed. Later, she mimicked the event by opening and closing her mouth. This was an obvious expression of her image of the event.

Object Permanence Imagine how chaotic and unpredictable your life would be if you could not distinguish between yourself and your world. This is what the life of a newborn must be like, according to Piaget. There is no differentiation between the self and world; objects have no separate, permanent existence.

By the end of the sensorimotor period, objects are both separate from the self and permanent. **Object permanence** is the understanding that objects continue to exist even when they cannot be seen, heard, or touched. Acquiring the sense of object permanence is one of the infant's most important accomplishments, according to Piaget.

How could anyone know whether an infant had a sense of object permanence or not? The principal way that object permanence is studied is by watching an infant's reaction when an interesting object disappears (see Figure 6.2). If infants search for the object, it is assumed that they believe it continues to exist.

coordination of secondary circular reactions Piaget's fourth sensorimotor substage, which develops between 8 and 12 months of age. Actions become more outwardly directed, and infants coordinate schemes and act with intentionality.

tertiary circular reactions, novelty, and curiosity Piaget's fifth sensorimotor substage, which develops between 12 and 18 months of age. In this substage, infants become intrigued by the many properties of objects and by the many things that they can make happen to objects.

internalization of schemes Piaget's sixth and final sensorimotor substage, which develops between 18 and 24 months of age. In this substage, the infant develops the ability to use primitive symbols.

object permanence The Piagetian term for understanding that objects and events continue to exist, even when they cannot directly be seen, heard, or touched.

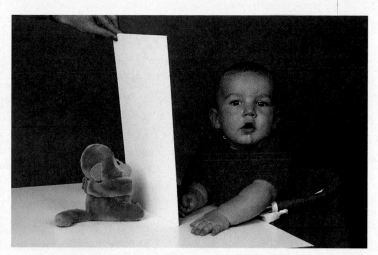

FIGURE 6.2 Object Permanence Piaget argued that object permanence is one of infancy's landmark cognitive accomplishments. For this 5-month-old boy, "out-of-sight" is literally out of mind. The infant looks at the toy monkey (*left*), but, when his view of the toy is blocked (*right*), he does not search for it. Several months later, he will search for the hidden toy monkey, reflecting the presence of object permanence.

Object permanence is just one of the basic concepts about the physical world developed by babies. To Piaget, children, even infants, are much like little scientists, examining the world to see how it works. The *Research in Children's Development* interlude that follows describes some of the ways in which adult scientists try to discover what these "baby scientists" are finding out about the world.

Research in Children's Development

OBJECT PERMANENCE AND CAUSALITY

Two accomplishments of infants that Piaget examined were the development of object permanence and the child's understanding of causality. Let's examine two research studies that address these topics.

In both studies, Renée Baillargeon and her colleagues used a research method that involves *violation of expectations*. In this method, infants see an event happen as it normally would. Then, the event is changed, often in a way that creates a physically impossible event. If infants look longer at the changed event, that indicates they are surprised by it. In other words, the infants' reaction is interpreted to indicate that the infant had certain expectations about the world that were violated.

In one study focused on object permanence, researchers showed infants a toy car that moved down an inclined track, disappeared behind a screen, and then reemerged at the other end, still on the track (Baillargeon & DeVos, 1991) (see Figure 6.3*a*). After this sequence was repeated several times, something different occurred: a toy mouse was placed *behind* the tracks but was hidden by the screen while the car rolled by (see Figure 6.3*b*). This was the "possible" event. Then, the researchers created an "impossible event": the toy mouse was placed *on* the tracks but was secretly removed after the screen was lowered so that the car seemed to go through the mouse (see Figure 6.3*c*). In this study, infants as young as 3½ months of age looked longer at the impossible event than at the possible event, indicating that they were surprised by it. Their surprise suggested that they remembered not only that the toy mouse still existed (object permanence) but its location.

Another study focused on the infant's understanding of causality (Kotovsky & Baillargeon, 1994). In this research, a cylinder rolls down a ramp and hits a toy bug at the bottom of the ramp. By 5½ and 6½ months of age, after infants have seen how far the bug will be pushed by a medium-sized cylinder, their reactions indicate that they understand that the bug will roll farther if it is hit by a large cylinder than

(continued on next page)

FIGURE 6.3 Using the Violation of Expectations Method to Study Object Permanence in Infants If infants looked longer at (c) than at (b), researchers reasoned that the impossible event in (c) violated the infants' expectations and that they remembered that the toy mouse existed.

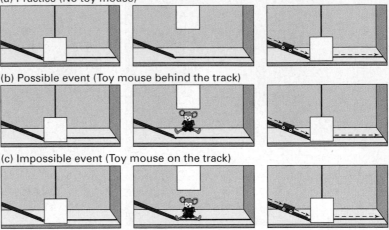

(a) Practice (No toy mouse)

(b) Possible event (Toy mouse behind the track)

(c) Impossible event (Toy mouse on the track)

if it is hit by a small cylinder. Thus, by the middle of the first year of life, these infants understood that the size of a moving object determines how far it will move a stationary object that it collides with.

The research findings discussed in this interlude and other research indicate that infants develop object permanence earlier than Piaget proposed. Indeed, as you see in the next section, a major theme of infant cognitive development today is that infants are more cognitively competent than Piaget envisioned.

Evaluating Piaget's Sensorimotor Stage

Piaget opened up a new way of looking at infants with his view that their main task is to coordinate their sensory impressions with their motor activity. However, the infant's cognitive world is not as neatly packaged as Piaget portrayed it, and some of Piaget's explanations for the cause of change are debated. In the past several decades, sophisticated experimental techniques have been devised to study infants, and there have been a large number of research studies on infant development. Much of the new research suggests that Piaget's view of sensorimotor development needs to be modified (Goswami, 2007).

The A–not–B Error   One modification concerns Piaget's claim that certain processes are crucial in transitions from one stage to the next. The data do not always support his explanations. For example, in Piaget's theory, an important feature in the progression into substage 4, *coordination of secondary circular reactions*, is an infant's inclination to search for a hidden object in a familiar location rather than to look for the object in a new location. For example, if a toy is hidden twice, initially at location A and subsequently at location B, 8- to 12-month-old infants search correctly at location A initially. But when the toy is subsequently hidden at location B, they make the mistake of continuing to search for it at location A. **A-not-B error** (also called A$\overline{B}$ error) is the term used to describe this common mistake. Older infants are less likely to make the A-not-B error because their concept of object permanence is more complete.

Researchers have found, however, that the A-not-B error does not show up consistently (Sophian, 1985). The evidence indicates that A-not-B errors are sensitive to the delay between hiding the object at B and the infant's attempt to find it (Diamond, 1985). Thus, the A-not-B error might be due to a failure in memory. Another explanation is that infants tend to repeat a previous motor behavior (Clearfield & others, 2006; Smith, 1999).

Perceptual Development and Expectations   A number of theorists, such as Eleanor Gibson (2001) and Elizabeth Spelke (1991; Spelke & Newport, 1998), stress that infants' perceptual abilities are highly developed very early in development. For

Infants know that objects are substantial and permanent at an earlier age than Piaget envisioned.

—RENÉE BAILLARGEON
Contemporary Psychologist, University of Illinois

A-not-B error Also called A$\overline{B}$ error, this occurs when infants make the mistake of selecting the familiar hiding place (A) rather than the new hiding place ($\overline{B}$) as they progress into substage 4 in Piaget's sensorimotor stage.

example, in Chapter 4 we discussed research that demonstrated the presence of intermodal perception—the ability to coordinate information from two more sensory modalities, such as vision and hearing—by 3½ months of age, much earlier than Piaget would have predicted (Spelke & Owsley, 1979).

Research also suggests that infants develop the ability to understand how the world works at a very early age. For example, by the time they are 3 months of age, infants develop expectations about future events. Marshall Haith and his colleagues (Canfield & Haith, 1991; Haith, Hazen, & Goodman, 1988) presented pictures to infants in either a regular alternating sequence (such as left, right, left, right) or an unpredictable sequence (such as right, right, left, right). When the sequence was predictable, the 3-month-old infants began to anticipate the location of the picture, looking at the side on which it was expected to appear. However, younger infants did not develop expectations about where a picture would be presented.

What kinds of expectations do infants form? Are we born expecting the world to obey basic physical laws, such as gravity, or when do we learn about how the world works? Experiments by Elizabeth Spelke (1991, 2000; Spelke & Hespos, 2001) have addressed these questions. She placed babies before a puppet stage and showed them a series of actions that are unexpected if you know how the physical world works—for example, one ball seemed to roll through a solid barrier, another seemed to leap between two platforms, and a third appeared to hang in midair (Spelke, 1979). Spelke measured and compared the babies' looking times for unexpected and expected actions. She concluded that, by 4 months of age, even though infants do not yet have the ability to talk about objects, move around objects, manipulate objects, or even see objects with high resolution, they expect objects to be solid and continuous. However, at 4 months of age, infants do not expect an object to obey gravitational constraints (Spelke & others, 1992). Similarly, research by Renée Baillargeon and her colleagues (1995, 2004; Aguiar & Baillargeon, 2002) documents that infants as young as 3 to 4 months expect objects to be *substantial* (in the sense that other objects cannot move through them) and *permanent* (in the sense that objects continue to exist when they are hidden).

In sum, researchers emphasize that infants see objects as bounded, unitary, solid, and separate from their background, possibly at birth or shortly thereafter, but definitely by 3 to 4 months of age, much earlier than Piaget envisioned. Young infants still have much to learn about objects, but the world appears both stable and orderly to them.

By 6 to 8 months, infants have learned to perceive gravity and support—that an object hanging on the end of a table should fall, that ball-bearings will travel farther when rolled down a longer rather than a shorter ramp, and that cup handles will not fall when attached to a cup (Slater, Field, & Hernandez-Reif, 2007). As infants develop, their experiences and actions on objects help them to understand physical laws (Bremner, 2007).

Many researchers conclude that Piaget wasn't specific enough about how infants learn about their world and that infants are more competent than Piaget thought (Bremner, 2007; Cohen & Cashon, 2006; Mandler, 2004, 2006; Meltzoff, 2004). As they have examined the specific ways that infants learn, the field of infant cognition has become very specialized. There are many researchers working on different questions, with no general theory emerging that can connect all of the different findings (Nelson, 1999). Their theories are local theories, focused on specific research questions, rather than grand theories like Piaget's (Kuhn, 1998). If there is a unifying theme, it is that investigators in infant development seek to understand more precisely how developmental changes in cognition take place and the big issue of nature and nurture.

A 4-month-old in Elizabeth Spelke's infant perception laboratory is tested to determine if it knows that an object in motion will not stop in midair. Spelke concluded that at 4 months babies don't expect objects like these balls to obey gravitational constraints, but that they do expect objects to be solid and continuous. Research by Spelke, Renee Baillargeon, and others suggest that infants develop an ability to understand how the world works earlier than Piaget envisioned.

1 **Summarize and evaluate Piaget's theory of infant development.**

Review
- What cognitive processes are important in Piaget's theory?
- What are some characteristics of Piaget's stage of sensorimotor development?
- What are some contributions and criticisms of Piaget's sensorimotor stage?

Reflect
- What are some implications of Piaget's theory of infant development for parenting?

2 HOW DO INFANTS LEARN, REMEMBER, AND CONCEPTUALIZE?

| Conditioning | Memory | Concept Formation and Categorization |

| Attention | Imitation |

When Piaget hung a doll above 4-month-old Lucienne's feet, as described in the chapter opening, would she remember the doll? If Piaget had rewarded her for moving the doll with her foot, would that have affected Lucienne's behavior? If he had showed her how to shake the doll's hand, could she have imitated him? If he had showed her a different doll, could she have formed the concept of a "doll"?

Questions like these might be examined by researchers taking the behavioral and social cognitive or information processing approaches introduced in Chapter 1. In contrast to Piaget's theory, these approaches do not describe infant development in terms of stages. Instead, they document gradual changes in the infant's ability to understand and process information about the world. In this section we explore what researchers using these approaches can tell us about how infants learn, remember, and conceptualize.

Conditioning

In Chapter 1, we described Pavlov's classical conditioning (in which, as a result of pairing, a new stimulus comes to elicit a response previously given to another stimulus) and Skinner's operant conditioning (in which the consequences of a behavior produce changes in the probability of the behavior's occurrence). Infants can learn through both types of conditioning. For example, if an infant's behavior is followed by a rewarding stimulus, the behavior is likely to recur.

Operant conditioning has been especially helpful to researchers in their efforts to determine what infants perceive (Wanatabe & Taga, 2006). For example, infants will suck faster on a nipple when the sucking behavior is followed by a visual display, music, or a human voice (Rovee-Collier, 1987; Rovee-Collier & Barr, 2004).

Carolyn Rovee-Collier (1987) has also demonstrated how infants can retain information from the experience of being conditioned. In a characteristic experiment, she places a 2½-month-old baby in a crib under an elaborate mobile (see Figure 6.4). She then ties one end of a ribbon to the baby's ankle and the other end to the mobile. Subsequently, she observes that the baby kicks and makes the mobile move. The movement of the mobile is the reinforcing stimulus (which increases the baby's kicking behavior) in this experiment. Weeks later, the baby is returned to the crib, but its foot is not tied to the mobile. The baby kicks, which suggests it has retained the information that if it kicks a leg, the mobile will move.

attention The focusing of mental resources.

joint attention Occurs when individuals focus on the same object or event, and an ability to track another's behavior is present, one individual directs another's attention, and reciprocal interaction is present.

Attention

Attention, the focusing of mental resources on select information, improves cognitive processing on many tasks. Even newborns can detect a contour and fix their attention on it. Older infants scan patterns more thoroughly. By 4 months, infants can selectively attend to an object. In adults, when individuals orient their attention to an object or event, the parietal lobes in the cerebral cortex are involved (Posner, 2003). It is likely that the parietal lobes are active when infants orient their attention, although research has not yet documented this. (Figure 5.4, p. 145, illustrates the location of the parietal lobes in the brain.)

Habituation and Dishabituation   Closely linked with attention are the processes of habituation and dishabituation, which we discussed in Chapter 5. If you say the same word or show the same toy to a baby several times in a row, the baby usually pays less attention to it each time. This is *habituation*—decreased responsiveness to a stimulus after repeated presentations of the stimulus. *Dishabituation* is the increase in responsiveness after a change in stimulation. Chapter 5 described some of the measures that researchers use to study whether habituation is occurring, such as sucking behavior (sucking stops when an infant attends to a novel object), heart rates, and the length of time the infant looks at an object.

Infants' attention is strongly governed by novelty and habituation (Amos & Johnson, 2006). When an object becomes familiar, attention becomes shorter, making infants more vulnerable to distraction (Oakes, Kannass, & Shaddy, 2002). One study found that 10-month-olds were more distractible than 26-month-olds (Ruff & Capozzoli, 2003).

Knowing about habituation and dishabituation can help parents interact effectively with infants. Infants respond to changes in stimulation. Wise parents sense when an infant shows an interest and realize that they may have to repeat something many times for the infant to process information. But if the stimulation is repeated often, the infant stops responding to the parent. In parent-infant interaction, it is important for parents to do novel things and to repeat them often until the infant stops responding. The parent stops or changes behaviors when the infant redirects his or her attention (Rosenblith, 1992).

Joint Attention   Another aspect of attention that is an important aspect of infant development is **joint attention,** in which individuals focus on the same object or event. Joint attention requires (1) an ability to track another's behavior, such as following someone's gaze (2) one person directing another's attention; and (3) reciprocal interaction (Butterworth, 2004). Early in infancy, joint attention usually involves a caregiver pointing or using words to direct an infant's attention. Emerging forms of joint attention occur at about 7 to 8 months, but it is not until about end of the first year that joint attention skills are frequently observed (Heimann & others, 2006; Meltzoff & Brooks, 2006). In a study conducted by Rechele Brooks and Andrew Meltzoff (2005), at 10 to 11 months of age infants first began engaging in "gaze following," looking where another person has just looked (see Figure 6.5). And by their first birthday, infants have begun to direct adults' attention to objects that capture their interest (Heimann & others, 2006).

Joint attention plays important roles in many aspects of infant development and considerably increases infants' ability to learn from other people (Striano, Reid, & Hoehl, 2006). Nowhere is this more apparent than in observations of interchanges between caregivers and infants as infants are learning language (Poulin-Dubois & Graham, 2007). When caregivers and infants frequently engage in joint attention, infants say their first word earlier and develop a larger vocabulary (Carpenter, Nagell, & Tomasello, 1998; Flom & Pick, 2003). In one study, infants' initiation of joint attention was linked to their receptive and expressive language at 3 years of age (Ulvund &

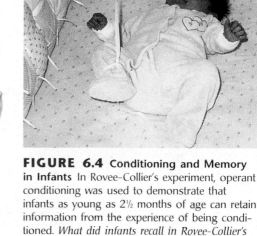

FIGURE 6.4 Conditioning and Memory in Infants In Rovee-Collier's experiment, operant conditioning was used to demonstrate that infants as young as 2½ months of age can retain information from the experience of being conditioned. *What did infants recall in Rovee-Collier's experiment?*

A mother and her infant daughter engaging in joint attention. *What about this photograph tells you that joint attention is occurring? Why is joint attention an important aspect of infant development?*

(a)   (b)

FIGURE 6.5 Gaze Following in Infancy
Researcher Rechele Brooks shifts her eyes from the infant to a toy in the foreground (*a*). The infant then follows her eye movement to the toy (*b*). Brooks and colleague Andrew Meltzoff (2005) found that infants begin to engage in this kind of behavior called "gaze following" at 10 to 11 months of age. *Why might gaze following be an important accomplishment for an infant?*

Smith, 1996). Later in the chapter in our discussion of language, we further discuss joint attention and the infant's language development.

Memory

Memory involves the retention of information over time. Attention plays an important role in memory as part of a process called *encoding*, which is the process by which information gets into memory. What can infants remember, when?

Some researchers such as Rovee-Collier have concluded that infants as young as 2 to 6 months of age can remember some experiences through 1½ to 2 years of age (Rovee-Collier, 2007; Rovee-Collier & Barr, 2004). However, critics such as Jean Mandler (2000), a leading expert on infant cognition, argue that the infants in Rovee-Collier's experiments are displaying only implicit memory. **Implicit memory** refers to memory without conscious recollection—memories of skills and routine procedures that are performed automatically. In contrast, **explicit memory** refers to the conscious memory of facts and experiences.

When people think about memory, they are usually referring to explicit memory. Most researchers find that babies do not show explicit memory until the second half of the first year (Bauer, 2005, 2006, 2007, 2008; Bauer & others, 2003; Mandler & McDonough, 1995). Then, explicit memory improves substantially during the second year of life (Bauer, 2006, 2007; Carver & Bauer, 2001). In one longitudinal study, infants were assessed several times during their second year (Bauer & others, 2000). Older infants showed more accurate memory and required fewer prompts to demonstrate their memory than younger infants.

What changes in the brain are linked to infants' memory development? From about 6 to 12 months of age, the maturation of the hippocampus and the surrounding cerebral cortex, especially the frontal lobes, make the emergence of explicit memory possible (de Haan & others, 2006; Nelson, Thomas, & de Haan, 2006) (see Figure 6.6). Explicit memory continues to improve in the second year, as these brain structures further mature and connections between them increase. Less is known about the areas of the brain involved in implicit memory in infancy.

Let's examine another aspect of memory. Do you remember your third birthday party? Probably not. Most adults can remember little if anything from the first three years of their life. This is called *infantile*, or *childhood, amnesia*. The few reported adult memories of life at age 2 or 3 are at best very sketchy (Neisser, 2004; Newcombe, 2007; Newcombe & others, 2000). Elementary school children also do not remember much of their early child years (Lie & Newcombe, 1999).

What is the cause of infantile amnesia? One reason older children and adults have difficulty recalling events from their infant and early child years is that during these early years the prefrontal lobes of the

memory A central feature of cognitive development, involving the retention of information over time.

implicit memory Memory without conscious recollection; involves skills and routine procedures that are automatically performed.

explicit memory Memory of facts and experiences.

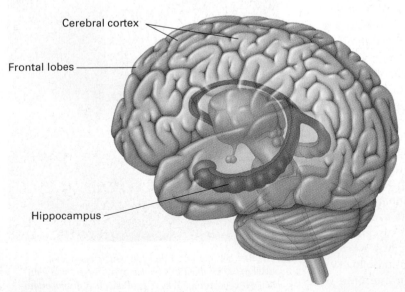

Cerebral cortex

Frontal lobes

Hippocampus

FIGURE 6.6 Key Brain Structures Involved in Memory Development in Infancy

brain are immature; this area of the brain is believed to play an important role in storing memories for events (Boyer & Diamond, 1992).

In sum, most of young infants' conscious memories appear to be rather fragile and short-lived, although their implicit memory of perceptual-motor actions can be substantial (Bauer, 2007, 2008; Mandler, 2004). By the end of the second year, long-term memory is more substantial and reliable (Bauer, 2006, 2007).

Imitation

Can infants imitate someone else's emotional expressions? If an adult smiles, will the baby follow with a smile? If an adult protrudes her lower lip, wrinkles her forehead, and frowns, will the baby show a sad face?

Infant development researcher Andrew Meltzoff (2004, 2005; Meltzoff & Moore, 1999) has conducted numerous studies of infants' imitative abilities. He sees infants' imitative abilities as biologically based, because infants can imitate a facial expression within the first few days after birth. He also emphasizes that the infant's imitative abilities do not resemble a hardwired response but rather involve flexibility and adaptability. In Meltzoff's observations of infants across first 72 hours of life, the infants gradually displayed more complete imitation of an adult's facial expression, such as protruding the tongue or opening the mouth wide (see Figure 6.7).

FIGURE 6.7 Infant Imitation Infant development researcher Andrew Meltzoff protrudes his tongue in an attempt to get the infant to imitate his behavior. *How do Meltzoff findings about imitation compare with Piagets' descriptions of infants' abilities?*

Not all experts on infant development accept Meltzoff's conclusions that newborns are capable of imitation. Some say that these babies were engaging in little more than automatic responses to a stimulus.

Meltzoff (2005) also has studied **deferred imitation,** which occurs after a time delay of hours or days. Piaget held that deferred imitation doesn't occur until about 18 months of age. Meltzoff's research suggested that it occurs much earlier. In one study, Meltzoff (1988) demonstrated that 9-month-old infants could imitate actions—such as pushing a recessed button in a box, which produced a beeping sound—that they had seen performed 24 hours earlier. Also, in a recent study, engagement in deferred imitation at 9 months of age was a strong predictor of more extensive production of communicative gestures at 14 months of age (Heimann & others, 2006). Two of the most common infant gestures are (1) extending arm to show the caregiver something the infant is holding, and (2) pointing with the arm and index finger extended at some interesting object or event.

Have researchers been able to determine which aspects of the brain are involved when infants engage in imitative behavior? It is likely that a number of brain regions are at work in infant imitation. To engage in imitation, it is necessary to attend, remember, and perform a motoric behavior. Recall from our discussion of attention that the parietal lobes likely are active when infants orient their attention, although research has not yet documented this. When infants need to remember something, recall from the previous section on infant memory that the hippocampus and frontal lobes are at work. And when infants perform a motor behavior, aspects of the cerebral cortex, such as the motor cortex and occipital lobes, are involved (Nelson, Thomas, & de Haan, 2006). (Figure 5.4, p. 154, illustrates the locations of the brain regions we have described that likely are involved in infant imitation.) Further, what are called *mirror neurons*, likely play a role in infant imitation (Nagy, 2006). A mirror neuron is a neuron that fires when an organism observes an action performed by another organism. Although not yet documented with human infants, mirror neuron pathways in the premotor cerebral cortex (a transition area between the motor cortex and the frontal lobes) and the parietal lobes have been proposed as having the potential for the perception-action coupling necessary for infants to engage in imitation (Jackon, Meltzoff, & Decety, 2006; Nagy, 2006).

Concept Formation and Categorization

Along with attention, memory, and imitation, concepts are key aspects of infants' cognitive development (Booth, 2006). To understand what concepts are, we first have to define *categories:* they group objects, events, and characteristics on the basis of common

deferred imitation Imitation that occurs after a delay of hours or days.

FIGURE 6.8 Categorization in 9- to 11-Month-Olds These are the stimuli used in the study that indicated 9- to 11-month-old infants categorize as different (birds and planes) (Mandler & McDonough, 1993).

properties. *Concepts* are ideas about what categories represent, or said another way, the sort of thing we think category members are. Concepts and categories help us to simplify and summarize information. Without concepts, you would see each object and event as unique; you would not be able to make any generalizations.

Do infants have concepts? Yes, they do, although we do not know just how early concept formation begins (Booth, 2006; Mandler, 2004; Quinn, 2007). It is not until about 7 to 9 months of age that infants form *conceptual* categories that are characterized by perceptual variability. For example, in one study of 9- to 11-year-olds, infants classified birds as animals and airplanes as vehicles even though the objects were perceptually similar—airplanes and birds with their wings spread (Mandler & McDonough, 1993) (see Figure 6.8). How could the researchers determine that the infants had these concepts? They used what is called the *object-examination test*, in which infants become familiar with objects from one category (such as birds) and then are given an object from a contrasting category (such as airplanes). How long they examine this object in comparison with a new object from the familiar category is the measure used.

Further advances in categorization occur in the second year of life (Booth, 2006). Many infants' "first concepts are broad and global in nature, such as 'animal' or 'indoor thing.' Gradually, over the first two years these broad concepts become more differentiated into concepts such as 'land animal,' then 'dog,' or to 'furniture,' then 'chair'" (Mandler, 2006, p. 1). Also in the second year, infants often categorize objects on the basis of their shape (Landau, Smith, & Jones, 1998).

In sum, the infant's advances in processing information—through attention, memory, imitation, and concept formation—is much richer, more gradual and less stage-like, and occurs earlier than was envisioned by earlier theorists, such as Piaget. As leading infant researcher Jean Mandler (2004) concluded, "The human infant shows a remarkable degree of learning power and complexity in what is being learned and in the way it is represented" (p. 304).

> ## REVIEW AND REFLECT ◆ LEARNING GOAL 2
>
> ### 2 Describe how infants learn, remember, and conceptualize.
>
> **Review**
> - How do infants learn through conditioning?
> - What is attention? What characterizes attention in infants?
> - To what extent can infants remember?
> - How is imitation involved in infant learning?
> - When do infants develop concepts, and how does concept formation change during infancy?
>
> **Reflect**
> - If a friend told you that she remembers being abused by her parents when she was 2 years old, would you believe her? Explain your answer.

3 HOW ARE INDIVIDUAL DIFFERENCES IN INFANCY ASSESSED, AND DO THESE ASSESSMENTS PREDICT INTELLIGENCE?

Measures of Infant Development

Predicting Intelligence

developmental quotient (DQ) An overall score that combines subscores in motor, language, adaptive, and personal-social domains in the Gesell assessment of infants.

So far, we have discussed how the cognitive development of infants generally progresses. We have emphasized what is typical of the largest number of infants or the average infant, but the results obtained for *most* infants do not apply to *all* infants. It is advantageous to know whether an infant is developing at a slow, normal, or advanced pace during the course of infancy. If an infant advances at an especially slow rate, then some form of enrichment may be necessary. If an infant develops at an advanced pace, parents may be advised to provide toys that stimulate cognitive growth in slightly older infants. How is an infant's cognitive development assessed?

Measures of Infant Development

Individual differences in infant cognitive development have been studied primarily through the use of developmental scales or infant intelligence tests. For example, in Chapter 4 we discussed the Brazelton Neonatal Behavioral Assessment Scale (NBAS) and the Neonatal Intensive Care Unit Network Neurobehavioral Scale (NNNS), which are used to evaluate newborns. To read about the work of one infant assessment specialist, see the *Careers in Child Development* profile.

The most important early contributor to the testing of infants was Arnold Gesell (1934). He developed a measure that helped sort out potentially normal babies from abnormal ones. This was especially useful to adoption agencies, which had large numbers of babies awaiting placement. Gesell's examination was used widely for many years and still is frequently employed by pediatricians to distinguish normal and abnormal infants. The current version of the Gesell test has four categories of behavior: motor, language, adaptive, and personal-social. The **developmental quotient (DQ)** combines subscores in these categories to provide an overall score.

The widely used **Bayley Scales of Infant Development** were developed by Nancy Bayley (1969) in order to assess infant behavior and predict later development. The current (1993) version, Bayley-II, has three components: a mental scale, a motor scale, and an infant behavior profile.

How should a 6-month-old perform on the Bayley mental scale? The 6-month-old infant should be able to vocalize pleasure and displeasure, persistently search for objects that are just out of immediate reach, and approach a mirror that is placed in front of the infant by the examiner. By 12 months of age, the infant should be able to inhibit behavior when commanded to do so, imitate words the examiner says (such as *Mama*), and respond to simple requests (such as "Take a drink").

The explosion of interest in infant development has produced many new measures, especially tasks that evaluate the ways infants process information (Rose, Feldman, & Wallace, 1992). The Fagan Test of Infant Intelligence is increasingly being used (Fagan, 1992). This test focuses on the infant's ability to process information in such ways as encoding the attributes of objects, detecting similarities and differences between objects, forming mental representations, and retrieving these representations. For example, it uses the amount of time babies look at a new object compared with the amount of time they spend looking at a familiar object to estimate their intelligence. The Fagan test elicits similar performances from infants in different cultures.

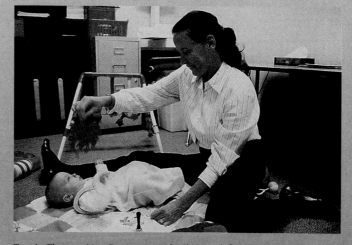
Bayley Scales of Infant Development Scales developed by Nancy Bayley that are widely used in the assessment of infant development. The current version has three components: a mental scale, a motor scale, and an infant behavior profile.

Predicting Intelligence

The infant-testing movement grew out of the tradition of IQ testing. However, IQ tests of older children pay more attention to verbal ability. Tests for infants contain far more items related to perceptual-motor development and include measures of social interaction.

Overall scores on such tests as the Gesell and the Bayley scales do not correlate highly with IQ scores obtained later in childhood. In one study conducted by Nancy Bayley, no relation was found between the Bayley scales and intelligence as measured by the Stanford-Binet at the ages of 6 and 7 (Bayley, 1943). This is not surprising because the components tested in infancy are not the same as the components tested by IQ tests.

Unlike the Gesell and Bayley scales, the Fagan test is correlated with measures of intelligence in older children. In fact, evidence is accumulating that measures of habituation and dishabituation predict intelligence in childhood and adolescence (Bornstein & Sigman, 1986; Sigman, Cohen, & Beckwith, 2000). Quicker habituation and greater amounts of looking in dishabituation reflect more efficient information processing. A review concluded that when measured between 3 and 12 months, both habituation and dishabituation are related to higher IQ scores on tests given at various times between infancy and adolescence (Kavsek, 2004).

It is important, however, not to go too far and think that connections between cognitive development in early infancy and later cognitive development are so strong that no discontinuity takes place. Some important changes in cognitive development occur after infancy, changes that we describe in later chapters.

REVIEW AND REFLECT · LEARNING GOAL 3

3 **Discuss infant assessment measures and the prediction of intelligence.**

Review
- What are some measures of individual differences in infancy?
- Do tests of infants predict intelligence later in life?

Reflect
- Parents have their 1-year-old infant assessed with a developmental scale, and the infant does very well on it. How confident should they be that the infant is going to be a genius when he or she grows up?

4 WHAT ARE SOME EARLY ENVIRONMENTAL INFLUENCES ON COGNITIVE DEVELOPMENT?

Nutrition	Poverty

So far, we have discussed a number of approaches to infants' cognitive development, but an important aspect of this development remains to be examined. What are some early environmental experiences that might influence this cognitive development? Two areas in which researchers have investigated this question are nutrition and poverty.

Nutrition

When we think about how nutrition affects development, we usually think of physical development, such as skeletal growth, body shape, and susceptibility to disease.

However, malnutrition also can restrict an infant's cognitive development (Grantham-McGregor, Ani, & Fernald, 2001).

In one study, two groups of extremely malnourished 1-year-old South African infants were examined (Bayley, 1970). The children in one group were given adequate nourishment during the next six years. No intervention took place in the lives of the other group of children. After the seventh year, the poorly nourished group of children performed worse on intelligence tests than did the adequately nourished group.

In another study, George Gutherie and his co-workers (1976) evaluated a group of severely underweight, malnourished infants in a rural area of the Philippines. They found that a combination of malnutrition, infection, and inadequate social stimulation from caregivers was associated with very low scores on the Bayley Scales of Infant Development.

In more recent research on nutrition and cognitive development which we initially discussed in Chapter 5, Ernesto Pollitt and his colleagues (1993) conducted a longitudinal study over two decades in rural Guatemala. They found that early nutritional supplements in the form of protein and increased calories can have positive long-term consequences for cognitive development. In the study, the link between nutrition and cognitive development was moderated by the time period in which the supplements were given and by the social context. For example, the children in the lowest socioeconomic groups benefited more than did the children in the higher socioeconomic groups. And, although there still was a positive nutritional influence when the supplements were given after 2 years of age, the effect was more powerful before the age of 2. In sum, good nutrition in infancy is important, not only for the child's physical development but also for the child's cognitive development.

Poverty

Researchers are increasingly interested in manipulating the early environment in children's lives when they are living in poverty, in hope that the changes will have a positive effect on their cognitive development (Powell, 2006; Ramey, Ramey, & Lanzi, 2006). Two ways this can be carried out are (1) to change parents' adaptive and responsive functioning, and (2) to provide competent educational day care.

The emphasis on children at risk for low intelligence is on prevention rather than remediation. Many low-income parents have difficulty providing an intellectually stimulating environment for their children. Programs that educate parents to be more sensitive caregivers and train them to be better teachers, as well as support services, such as high-quality Head Start programs, can make a difference in a child's intellectual development. The current trend is to conduct two-generation poverty interventions by working to improve the quality of life and skills of parents, as well as providing the child with an enriched environment (McLoyd, 1998).

The Abecedarian Intervention program at the University of North Carolina at Chapel Hill is conducted by Craig Ramey and his associates (Ramey & Campbell, 1984; Ramey & Ramey, 1998; Ramey, Ramey, & Lanzi, 2006). They randomly assigned 111 young children from low-income, poorly educated families to either an intervention group, which experienced full-time, year-round child care along with medical and social work services, or a control group, which got medical and social benefits but no child care. The child-care program included gamelike learning activities aimed at improving language, motor, social, and cognitive skills. The success of the program in improving IQ was evident by the time the children were 3 years old, at which time

What are the characteristics of effective early intervention programs for infants in poverty conditions?

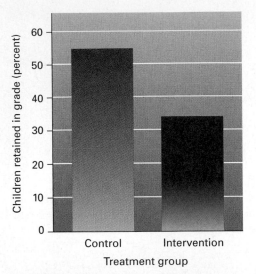

FIGURE 6.9 **Early Intervention and Retention in School** When the children in the Abecedarian program were 15 years of age, those who experienced the preschool intervention were less likely to have been retained in a grade than the children in the control group.

the children in the experimental group showed normal IQs averaging 101, a 17-point advantage over the control group. Follow-up results suggested that the effects were long-lasting. More than a decade later, at age 15, children from the intervention group still maintained an IQ advantage of 5 points over the control group children (97.7 to 92.6) (Ramey, Ramey, & Lanzi, 2001). They also did better on standardized tests of reading and math and were less likely to be held back a year in school (see Figure 6.9). Also the greatest IQ gains were by the children whose mothers had especially low IQs—below 70. At age 15, these children showed a 10-point IQ advantage over a group of children whose mothers had IQs below 70 but did not experience the child-care intervention.

Early intervention programs for infants in poverty conditions vary. Some are center-based, like the North Carolina program just described, others are home-based. Some are brief interventions; others are long-term. Some are time-intensive (such as all-day educational child care), others less intensive (such as one-hour-a-day or once-a-week sessions). In general, researchers have found that early intervention programs for infants living in poverty have the most positive developmental outcomes when (1) the program is long-lasting; (2) the program is time-intensive; (3) the program provides direct educational benefits, often in educational contexts, and does not rely on parental training alone; and (4) the program is comprehensive and multidimensional, including educational, health, and counseling services for parents, in addition to working directly with infants. We further explore intervention in the lives of children in poverty by discussing Project Head Start in Chapter 9, "Cognitive Development in Early Childhood," and by examining many factors in poverty interventions in Chapter 11, "Physical Development in Middle and Late Childhood."

REVIEW AND REFLECT ◆ LEARNING GOAL 4

4 **Characterize early environmental influences on cognitive development.**

Review
- How is nutrition linked with infants' cognitive development?
- What role does poverty play in infants' cognitive development?

Reflect
- If you were going to conduct an intervention to improve the cognitive skills of infants living in poverty, what would the intervention involve? Write down a minimum of five components in the intervention.

---

5 WHAT IS THE NATURE OF LANGUAGE, AND HOW DOES IT DEVELOP IN INFANCY?

| Defining Language | How Language Develops | An Interactionist View |

| Language's Rule Systems | Biological and Environmental Influences |

In 1799, a nude boy was observed running through the woods in France. The boy was captured when he was 11 years old. He was called the Wild Boy of Aveyron and was believed to have lived in the woods alone for six years (Lane, 1976). When found, he made no effort to communicate. He never learned to communicate effectively. Sadly, a modern-day wild child named Genie was discovered in Los Angeles in 1970. Despite intensive intervention, Genie has never acquired more than a

Rule System	Description	Examples
Phonology	The sound system of a language. A phoneme is the smallest sound unit in a language.	The word *chat* has three phonemes or sounds: /ch/ /a/ /t/. An example of phonological rule in the English language is while the phoneme /r/ can follow the phonemes /t/ or /d/ in an English consonant cluster (such as *track* or *drab*), the phoneme /l/ cannot follow these letters.
Morphology	The system of meaningful units involved in word formation.	The smallest sound units that have a meaning are called morphemes, or meaning units. The word *girl* is one morpheme, or meaning unit; it cannot be broken down any further and still have meaning. When the suffix *s* is added, the word becomes *girls* and has two morphemes because the *s* changed the meaning of the word, indicating that there is more than one girl.
Syntax	The system that involves the way words are combined to form acceptable phrases and sentences.	Word order is very important in determining meaning in the English language. For example, the sentence, "Sebastian pushed the bike" has a different meaning than "The bike pushed Sebastian."
Semantics	The system that involves the meaning of words and sentences.	Knowing the meaning of individual words—that is, vocabulary. For example, semantics includes knowing the meaning of such words as *orange*, *transportation*, and *intelligent*.
Pragmatics	The system of using appropriate conversation and knowledge of how to effectively use language in context.	An example is using polite language in appropriate situations, such as being mannerly when talking with one's teacher. Taking turns in a conversation involves pragmatics.

FIGURE 6.10 The Rule Systems of Language

speak if no one talked to them. He selected several newborns and threatened their caregivers with death if they ever talked to the infants. Frederick never found out what language the children spoke because they all died. Today, we are still curious about infants' development of language, although our experiments and observations are, to say the least, far more humane than the evil Frederick's.

Whatever language they learn, infants all over the world follow a similar path in language development. What are some key milestones in this development?

Babbling and Gestures Babies actively produce sounds from birth onward. The effect of these early communications is to attract attention (Lock, 2004; Volterra & others, 2004). Babies' sounds and gestures go through this sequence during the first year:

- *Crying*. Babies cry even at birth. Crying can signal distress, but as we discuss in Chapter 7, "Socioemotional Development in Infancy," there are different types of cries that signal different things.
- *Cooing*. Babies first coo at about 1 to 2 months. These are gurgling sounds that are made in the back of the throat and usually express pleasure during interaction with the caregiver.
- *Babbling*. In the middle of the first year, babies babble—that is, they produce strings of consonant-vowel combinations, such as "ba, ba, ba, ba."
- *Gestures*. Infants start using gestures, such as showing and pointing, at about 8 to 12 months of age. They may wave bye-bye, nod to mean "yes," show an empty cup to want more milk, and point to a dog to draw attention to it.

Deaf infants, born to deaf parents who use sign language, babble with their hands and fingers at about the same age as hearing children babble vocally (Bloom, 1998). Such similarities in timing and structure between manual and vocal babbling indicate that a unified language capacity underlies signed and spoken language (Petitto, Kovelman, & Harasymowycz, 2003).

Recognizing Language Sounds Long before they begin to learn words, infants can make fine distinctions among the sounds of the language (Jaswal & Fernald,

FIGURE 6.11 From Universal Linguist to Language-Specific Listener A baby is shown in Patricia Kuhl's research laboratory. In this research, babies listen to tape-recorded voices that repeat syllables. When the sounds of the syllables change, the babies quickly learn to look at the bear. Using this technique, Kuhl has demonstrated that babies are universal linguists until about 6 months of age, but in the next six months become language-specific listeners.

2007; Stoel-Gammon & Sosa, 2007). In Patricia Kuhl's (1993, 2000, 2007; Kuhl & others, 2006) research, phonemes from languages all over the world are piped through a speaker for infants to hear (see Figure 6.11). A box with a toy bear in it is placed where the infant can see it. A string of identical syllables is played; then the syllables are changed (for example, *ba ba ba ba*, and then *pa pa pa pa*). If the infant turns its head when the syllables change, the box lights up and the bear dances and drums, rewarding the infant for noticing the change.

Kuhl's research has demonstrated that from birth up to about 6 months of age, infants are "citizens of the world": they recognize when sounds change most of the time no matter what language the syllables come from. But over the next six months, infants get even better at perceiving the changes in sounds from their "own" language, the one their parents speak, and gradually lose the ability to recognize differences that are not important in their own language.

An example involves the English *r* and *l* sounds, which distinguish words such as *rake* and *lake* (Iverson & Kuhl, 1996; Iverson & others, 2003). In the United States, infants from English-speaking homes detect the changes from *ra* to *la* when they are 6 months old and get better at detecting the change by 12 months of age. However, in Japanese there is no such *r* or *l*. In Japan, 6-month-old infants perform as well as their American counterparts in recognizing the *r* and *l* distinction, but by 12 months of age they lose this ability.

Infants must fish out individual words from the nonstop stream of sound that makes up ordinary speech (Jusczyk, 2000; Newman & others, 2006). To do so, they must find the boundaries between words, which is very difficult for infants because adults don't pause between words when they speak. Still, infants begin to detect word boundaries by 8 months of age. For example, in one study, 8-month-old infants listened to recorded stories that contained unusual words, such as *hornbill* and *python* (Jusczyk & Hohne, 1997). Two weeks later, the researchers tested the infants with two lists of words, one made up of words in the stories, the other of new, unusual words that did not appear in the stories. The infants listened to the familiar words for a second longer, on average, than to new words.

First Words Between about 8 to 12 months of age, infants often indicate their first understanding of words. The infant's first spoken word is a milestone eagerly anticipated by every parent. This event usually occurs between 10 to 15 months of age and at an average of about 13 months. However, long before babies say their first words, they have been communicating with their parents, often by gesturing and using their own special sounds. The appearance of first words is a continuation of this communication process (Berko Gleason, 2005).

A child's first words include those that name important people (*Dada*), familiar animals (*kitty*), vehicles (*car*), toys (*ball*), food (*milk*), body parts (*eye*), clothes (*hat*), household items (*clock*), and greeting terms (*bye*). These were the first words of babies 50 years ago. They are the first words of babies today. Children often express various intentions with their single words, so that "cookie" might mean, "That's a cookie" or "I want a cookie."

On the average, infants understand about 50 words at about 13 months, but they can't say this many words until about 18 months (Menyuk, Liebergott, & Schultz, 1995). Thus, in infancy *receptive vocabulary* (words the child understands) considerably exceeds *spoken vocabulary* (words the child uses).

The infant's spoken vocabulary rapidly increases once the first word is spoken (Houston-Price, Plunkett, & Harris, 2005; Waxman & Lidz, 2006). The average 18-month-old can speak about 50 words, but by the age of 2 years can speak about 200 words. This rapid increase in vocabulary that begins at approximately 18 months is called the *vocabulary spurt* (Bloom, Lifter, & Broughton, 1985).

Like the timing of a child's first word, the timing of the vocabulary spurt varies (Bloom, 1998; Dale & Goodman, 2004). Figure 6.12 shows the range for these two language milestones in 14 children. On average, these children said their first word

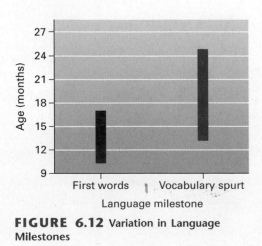

FIGURE 6.12 Variation in Language Milestones

at 13 months and had a vocabulary spurt at 19 months. However, the ages for the first word of individual children varied from 10 to 17 months and for their vocabulary spurt from 13 to 25 months.

Children sometimes overextend or underextend the meanings of the words they use (Woodward & Markman, 1998). *Overextension* is the tendency to apply a word to objects that are inappropriate for the word's meaning. For example, children at first may say *"Dada"* not only for "father" but also for other men, strangers, or boys. With time, overextensions decrease and eventually disappear. *Underextension* is the tendency to apply a word too narrowly; it occurs when children fail to use a word to name a relevant event or object. For example, a child might use the word *boy* to describe a 5-year-old neighbor but not apply the word to a male infant or to a 9-year-old male.

Two-Word Utterances

By the time children are 18 to 24 months of age, they usually utter two-word utterances. To convey meaning with just two words, the child relies heavily on gesture, tone, and context. The wealth of meaning children can communicate with a two-word utterance includes the following (Slobin, 1972):

- Identification: "See doggie."
- Location: "Book there."
- Repetition: "More milk."
- Nonexistence: "All gone thing."
- Negation: "Not wolf."
- Possession: "My candy."
- Attribution: "Big car."
- Agent-action: "Mama walk."
- Action-direct object: "Hit you."
- Action-indirect object: "Give Papa."
- Action-instrument: "Cut knife."
- Question: "Where ball?"

These examples are from children whose first language is English, German, Russian, Finnish, Turkish, or Samoan.

Notice that the two-word utterances omit many parts of speech and are remarkably succinct. In fact, in every language, a child's first combinations of words have this economical quality; they are telegraphic. **Telegraphic speech** is the use of short and precise words without grammatical markers such as articles, auxiliary verbs, and other connectives. Telegraphic speech is not limited to two words. "Mommy give ice cream" and "Mommy give Tommy ice cream" also are examples of telegraphic speech.

Biological and Environmental Influences

We have discussed a number of language milestones in infancy; Figure 6.13 summarizes the time at which infants typically reach these milestones. But what makes this amazing development possible? Everyone who uses language in some way "knows" its rules and has the ability to create an infinite number of words and sentences. Where does this knowledge come from? Is it the product of biology? Is language learned and influenced by experiences?

Biological Influences

The ability to speak and understand language requires a certain vocal apparatus as well as a nervous system with certain capabilities. The nervous system and vocal apparatus of humanity's predecessors changed over hundreds of thousands or millions of years. With advances in the nervous system and vocal structures, *Homo sapiens* went beyond the grunting and shrieking of other animals to develop speech. Although estimates vary, many experts believe that

Around the world, young children learn to speak in two-word utterances at 18 to 24 months of age. *What implications does this have for the biological basis of language?*

Age	Language milestones
Birth	Crying
1 to 2 months	Cooing begins
6 months	Babbling begins
6 to 12 months	Change from universal linguist to language-specific listener
8 to 12 months	Use gestures, such as showing and pointing Comprehension of words appears
13 months	First word spoken
18 months	Vocabulary spurt starts
18 to 24 months	Uses two-word utterances Rapid expansion of understanding of words

FIGURE 6.13 **Some Language Milestones in Infancy** Despite great variations in the language input received by infants, around the world they follow a similar path in learning to speak.

telegraphic speech The use of short and precise words without grammatical markers such as articles, auxiliary verbs, and other connectives.

get example

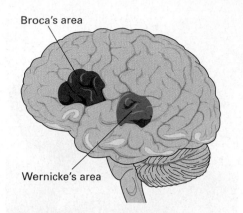

Broca's area

Wernicke's area

FIGURE 6.14 Broca's Area and Wernicke's Area Broca's area is located in the frontal lobe of the brain's left hemisphere, and it is involved in the control of speech. Wernicke's area is a portion of the left hemisphere's temporal lobe that is involved in understanding language. *How does the role of these areas of the brain relate to lateralization, which was discussed in Chapter 5?*

humans acquired language about 100,000 years ago—which, in evolutionary time, represents a very recent acquisition. It gave humans an enormous edge over other animals and increased the chances of human survival.

Some language scholars view the remarkable similarities in how children acquire language all over the world as strong evidence that language has a biological basis. There is evidence that particular regions of the brain are predisposed to be used for language (Imada & others, 2006; Opitz & Friederici, 2007; Skipper & others, 2007). Two regions involved in language were first discovered in studies of brain-damaged individuals: **Broca's area,** an area in the left frontal lobe of the brain involved in producing words, and **Wernicke's area,** a region of the brain's left hemisphere involved in language comprehension (see Figure 6.14). Damage to either of these areas produces types of **aphasia,** which is a loss or impairment of language processing. Individuals with damage to Broca's area have difficulty producing words correctly; individuals with damage to Wernicke's area have poor comprehension and often produce fluent but incomprehensible speech.

Linguist Noam Chomsky (1957) proposed that humans are biologically prewired to learn language at a certain time and in a certain way. He said that children are born into the world with a **language acquisition device (LAD),** a biological endowment that enables the child to detect certain features and rules of language, including phonology, syntax, and semantics. Children are prepared by nature with the ability to detect the sounds of language, for example, and follow rules such as how to form plurals and ask questions.

Chomsky's LAD is a theoretical construct, not a physical part of the brain. Is there evidence for the existence of a LAD? Supporters of the LAD concept cite the uniformity of language milestones across languages and cultures, evidence that children create language even in the absence of well-formed input, and biological substrates of language But as we see, critics argue that even if infants have something like a LAD, it cannot explain the whole story of language acquisition.

Environmental Influences Decades ago, behaviorists opposed Chomsky's hypothesis and argued that language represents nothing more than chains of responses acquired through reinforcement (Skinner, 1957). A baby happens to babble "Ma-ma"; Mama rewards the baby with hugs and smiles; the baby says "Mama" more and more. Bit by bit, said the behaviorists, the baby's language is built up. According to behaviorists, language is a complex learned skill, much like playing the piano or dancing.

The behaviorist view of language learning has several problems. First, it does not explain how people create novel sentences—sentences that people have never heard or spoken before. Second, children learn the syntax of their native language even if they are not reinforced for doing so. Social psychologist Roger Brown (1973) spent long hours observing parents and their young children. He found that parents did not directly or explicitly reward or correct the syntax of most children's utterances. That is, parents did not say "good," "correct," "right," "wrong," and so on. Also, parents did not offer direct corrections such as "You should say two shoes, not two shoe." However, as we see shortly, many parents do expand on their young children's grammatically incorrect utterances and recast many of those that have grammatical errors (Bonvillian, 2005).

The behavioral view is no longer considered a viable explanation of how children acquire language. But a great deal of research describes ways in which children's environmental experiences influence their language skills (Gatherhole & Huff, 2007). Many language experts argue that a child's experiences, the particular language to be learned, and the context in which learning takes place can strongly influence language acquisition (Snow & Yang, 2006; Tomasello, 2006).

Language is not learned in a social vacuum. Most children are bathed in language from a very early age (Tomasello, 2006). The Wild Boy of Aveyron, who never learned to communicate effectively, had lived in social isolation for years. The support and involvement of caregivers and teachers greatly facilitate a child's

Broca's area An area in the brain's left frontal lobe involved in speech production.

Wernicke's area An area of the brain's left hemisphere that is involved in language comprehension.

aphasia A loss or impairment of language ability caused by brain damage.

language acquisition device (LAD) Chomsky's term that describes a biological endowment that enables the child to detect the features and rules of language, including phonology, syntax, and semantics.

language learning (Berko Gleason, 2005; Pan & others, 2005; Snow & Yang, 2006). For example, one study found that when mothers immediately smiled and touched their 8-month-old infants after they babbled, the infants subsequently made more complex speech-like sounds than when mothers responded to their infants in a random manner (Goldstein, King, & West, 2003) (see Figure 6.15).

Michael Tomasello (2003, 2006) stresses that young children are intensely interested in their social world and that early in their development they can understand the intentions of other people. His *interaction view* of language emphasizes that children learn language in specific contexts. For example, when a toddler and a father are jointly focused on a book, the father might say, "See the birdie." In this case, even a toddler understands that the father intends to name something and knows to look in the direction of the pointing. Through this kind of joint attention, early in their development children are able to use their social skills to acquire language (Tomasello & Carpenter, 2007; Tomasello, Carpenter, & Liszkowski, 2007). For example, one recent study revealed that joint attention at 12 and 18 months predicted language skills at 24 months of age (Mundy & others, 2007).

In particular, researchers have found that the child's vocabulary development is linked to the family's socioeconomic status and the type of talk that parents direct to their children. To read about these links, see the *Diversity in Children's Development* interlude that follows.

FIGURE 6.15 Social Interaction and Babbling One study focused on two groups of mothers and their eighth-month-old infants (Goldstein, King, & West, 2003). One group of mothers was instructed to smile and touch their infants immediately after the babies cooed and babbled; the other group was also told to smile and touch their infants but in a random manner, unconnected to sounds the infants made. The infants whose mothers immediately responded in positive ways to their babbling subsequently made more complex, speech-like sounds, such as "da" and "gu." The research setting for this study, which underscores how important caregivers are in the early development of language, is shown above.

Diversity in Children's Development

LANGUAGE ENVIRONMENT, POVERTY, AND LANGUAGE DEVELOPMENT

What characteristics of a family make a difference to a child's language development? Socioeconomic status has been linked with how much parents talk to their children and with young children's vocabulary. Betty Hart and Todd Risley (1995) observed the language environments of children whose parents were professionals and children whose parents were on welfare. Compared with the professional parents, the parents on welfare talked much less to their young children, talked less about past events, and provided less elaboration. As indicated in Figure 6.16, the children of the professional parents had a much larger vocabulary at 36 months of age than the children of the welfare parents.

Other research has linked how much mothers speak to their infants and the infants' vocabularies. For example, in one study by Janellen Huttenlocher and her colleagues (1991), infants whose mothers spoke more often to them had markedly higher vocabularies. By the second birthday, vocabulary differences were substantial.

However, a recent study of 1- to 3-year-old children living in low-income families found that the sheer amount of maternal talk was not the best predictor of a child's vocabulary growth (Pan & others, 2005). Rather, it was maternal language

(continued on next page)

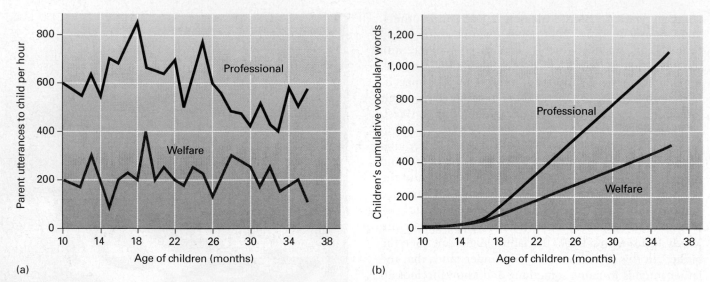

(a)

(b)

FIGURE 6.16 Language Input in Professional and Welfare Families and Young Children's Vocabulary Development (a) In this study (Hart & Risely, 1995), parents from professional families talked with their young children more than parents from welfare families. (b) All of the children learned to talk, but children from professional families developed vocabularies that were twice as large as those from welfare families. Thus, by the time children go to preschool, they already have experienced considerable differences in language input in their families and developed different levels of vocabulary that are linked to their socioeconomic context. *Does this study indicate that poverty caused deficiencies in vocabulary development?*

and literacy skills that were positively related to the children's vocabulary development. For example, when mothers used a more diverse vocabulary when talking with their children, their children's vocabulary benefited, but their children's vocabulary was not related to the total amount of their talkativeness with their children. Also, mothers who frequently used pointing gestures had children with a greater vocabulary. Pointing usually occurs in concert with speech, and it may enhance the meaning of mothers' verbal input to their children.

These research studies and others (NICHD Early Child Care Research Network, 2005) demonstrate the important effect that early speech input and poverty can have on the development of a child's language skills.

One intriguing component of the young child's linguistic environment is **child-directed speech,** language spoken in a higher pitch than normal with simple words and sentences (Newman & Hussain, 2006; Zangl & Mills, 2007). It is hard to use child-directed speech when not in the presence of a baby. As soon as you start talking to a baby, though, you shift into child-directed speech. Much of this is automatic and something most parents are not aware they are doing. Even 4-year-olds speak in simpler ways to 2-year-olds than to their 4-year-old friends. Child-directed speech has the important function of capturing the infant's attention and maintaining communication.

Adults often use strategies other than child-directed speech to enhance the child's acquisition of language, including recasting, expanding, and labeling:

- *Recasting* is rephrasing something the child has said, perhaps turning it into a question or restating the child's immature utterance in the form of a fully grammatical sentence. For example, if the child says, "The dog was barking," the adult can respond by asking, "When was the dog barking?" Effective recasting lets the child indicate an interest and then elaborates on that interest.
- *Expanding* is restating, in a linguistically sophisticated form, what a child has said. For example, a child says, "Doggie eat," and the parent replies, "Yes, the doggie is eating."

child-directed speech Language spoken in a higher pitch than normal with simple words and sentences.

- *Labeling* is identifying the names of objects. Young children are forever being asked to identify the names of objects. Roger Brown (1958) called this "the original word game" and claimed that much of a child's early vocabulary is motivated by this adult pressure to identify the words associated with objects.

Parents use these strategies naturally and in meaningful conversations. Parents do not (and should not) use any deliberate method to teach their children to talk, even for children who are slow in learning language. Children usually benefit when parents guide their children's discovery of language rather than overloading them with language; "following in order to lead" helps a child learn language. If children are not ready to take in some information, they are likely to tell you (perhaps by turning away). Thus, giving the child more information is not always better.

Remember, the encouragement of language development, not drill and practice, is the key. Language development is not a simple matter of imitation and reinforcement. To read further about ways that parents can facilitate children's language development, see the *Caring for Children* interlude.

Caring for Children

HOW PARENTS CAN FACILITATE INFANTS' AND TODDLERS' LANGUAGE DEVELOPMENT

In *Growing Up with Language*, linguist Naomi Baron (1992) provided ideas to help parents facilitate their child's language development. A summary of her ideas follows:

Infants

- *Be an active conversational partner.* Initiate conversation with the infant. If the infant is in a day-long child-care program, ensure that the baby receives adequate language stimulation from adults.
- *Talk as if the infant understands what you are saying.* Parents can generate self-fulfilling prophecies by addressing their young children as if they understand what is being said. The process may take four to five years, but children gradually rise to match the language model presented to them.
- *Use a language style with which you feel comfortable.* Don't worry about how you sound to other adults when you talk with your child. Your affect, not your content, is more important when talking with an infant. Use whatever type of baby talk with which you feel comfortable.

Toddlers

- *Continue to be an active conversational partner.* Engaging toddlers in conversation, even one-sided conversation, is the most important thing a parent can do to nourish a child linguistically.
- *Remember to listen.* Since toddlers' speech is often slow and laborious, parents are often tempted to supply words and thoughts for them. Be patient and let toddlers express themselves, no matter how painstaking the process is or how great a hurry you are in.
- *Use a language style with which you are comfortable, but consider ways of expanding your child's language abilities and horizons.* For example, using long sentences need not be problematic. Use rhymes. Ask questions that encourage answers other than "Yes" and

(continued on next page)

It is a good idea for parents to begin talking to their babies at the start. The best language teaching occurs when the talking is begun before the infant becomes capable of its first intelligible speech. *What are some other guidelines for parents to follow in helping their infants and toddlers develop their language?*

"No." Actively repeat, expand, and recast the child's utterances. Introduce new topics. And use humor in your conversation.

- *Adjust to your child's idiosyncrasies instead of working against them.* Many toddlers have difficulty pronouncing words and making themselves understood. Whenever possible, make toddlers feel that they are being understood.
- *Avoid sexual stereotypes.* Don't let the toddler's sex determine your amount or style of conversation. Many American mothers are more linguistically supportive of girls than of boys, and many fathers talk less with their children than mothers do. Cognitively enriching initiatives from both mothers and fathers benefit both boys and girls.
- *Resist making normative comparisons.* Be aware of the ages at which your child reaches specific milestones (such as the first word, first 50 words), but do not measure this development rigidly against that of other children. Such social comparisons can bring about unnecessary anxiety.

An Interactionist View

If language acquisition depended only on biology, then the Wild Boy of Aveyron and Genie (discussed earlier in the chapter) should have talked without difficulty. A child's experiences influence language acquisition. But we have seen that language does have strong biological foundations. No matter how much you converse with a dog, it won't learn to talk. In contrast, children are biologically prepared to learn language. Children all over the world acquire language milestones at about the same time and in about the same order.

Environmental influences are also very important in developmental competence in language (Gatherhole & Hoff, 2007; Tomasello, 2006). Children whose parents provide them with a rich verbal environment show many positive benefits. Parents who pay attention to what their children are trying to say, expand their children's utterances, read to them, and label things in the environment are providing valuable benefits for them (Berko Gleason, 2005).

An interactionist view emphasizes that both biology and experience contribute to language development. How much of the language is biologically determined, and how much depends on interaction with others, is a subject of debate among linguists and psychologists (Hoff & Shatz, 2007). However, all agree that both biological capacity and relevant experience are necessary.

REVIEW AND REFLECT ◆ LEARNING GOAL 5

5 **Describe the nature of language and how it develops in infancy.**

Review
- What is language?
- What are language's rule systems?
- How does language develop in infancy?
- What are some biological and environmental influences on language?
- To what extent do biological and environmental influences interact to produce language development?

Reflect
- Would it be a good idea for parents to hold large flash cards of words in front of their infant to help the infant learn language? Why or why not? What do you think Piaget would say about this activity?

REACH YOUR LEARNING GOALS

1 WHAT IS PIAGET'S THEORY OF INFANT DEVELOPMENT? *Summarize and evaluate Piaget's theory of infant development.*

Cognitive Processes

- In Piaget's theory, children construct their own cognitive worlds, building mental structures to adapt to their world. Schemes are actions or mental representations that organize knowledge. Behavioral schemes (physical activities) characterize infancy, whereas mental schemes (cognitive activities) develop in childhood. Assimilation occurs when children incorporate new information into existing schemes; accommodation refers to children's adjustment of their schemes in the face of new information. Through organization, children group isolated behaviors into a higher-order, more smoothly functioning cognitive system. Equilibration is a mechanism Piaget proposed to explain how children shift from one cognitive stage to the next. As children experience cognitive conflict in trying to understand the world, they use assimilation and accommodation to obtain equilibrium. The result is a new stage of thought. According to Piaget, there are four qualitatively different stages of thought.

The Sensorimotor Stage

- In sensorimotor thought, the first of Piaget's four stages, the infant organizes and coordinates sensations with physical movements. The stage lasts from birth to about 2 years of age Sensorimotor thought has six substages: simple reflexes; first habits and primary circular reactions; secondary circular reactions; coordination of secondary circular reactions; tertiary circular reactions, novelty, and curiosity; and internalization of schemes. One key accomplishment of this stage is object permanence, the ability to understand that objects continue to exist even though the infant is no longer observing them. Another aspect involves infants' understanding of cause and effect.

Evaluating Piaget's Sensorimotor Stage

- Piaget opened up a whole new way of looking at infant development in terms of coordinating sensory input with motoric actions. In the past decades, revisions of Piaget's view have been proposed based on research. For example, researchers have found that a stable and differentiated perceptual world is established earlier than Piaget envisioned, and infants begin to develop concepts as well.

2 HOW DO INFANTS LEARN, REMEMBER, AND CONCEPTUALIZE? *Describe how infants learn, remember, and conceptualize.*

Conditioning

- Both classical and operant conditioning occur in infants. Operant conditioning techniques have especially been useful to researchers in demonstrating infants' perception and retention of information about perceptual-motor actions.

Attention

- Attention is the focusing of mental resources, and in infancy attention is closely linked with habituation. Habituation is the repeated presentation of the same stimulus, causing reduced attention to the stimulus. If a different stimulus is presented, and the infant pays increased attention to it, dishabituation is occurring. Joint attention plays an important role in infant development, especially in the infant's acquisition of language.

Memory

- Memory is the retention of information over time. Infants as young as 2 to 6 months of age can retain information about perceptual-motor actions. However, many experts argue that what we commonly think of as memory (consciously remembering the past) does not occur until the second half of the first year of life. By the end of the second year, long-term memory is more substantial and reliable. The hippocampus and frontal lobes of the brain are involved in development of memory in infancy. The phenomenon of not being able to remember events that occurred before the age of 3—known as infantile amnesia—may be due to the immaturity of the prefrontal lobes of the brain at that age.

Imitation

- Meltzoff has shown that newborns can match their behaviors (such as protruding their tongue) to a model. His research also shows that deferred imitation occurs as early as 9 months of age. A number of brain regions are likely involved in infants' ability to engage in imitative behavior.

Concept Formation and Categorization

- Mandler argues that it is not until about 7 to 9 months of age that infants form conceptual categories, although we do not know precisely when concept formation begins. Infants' first concepts are broad. Over the first two years of life, these broad concepts gradually become more differentiated.

3   HOW ARE INDIVIDUAL DIFFERENCES IN INFANCY ASSESSED, AND DO THESE ASSESSMENTS PREDICT INTELLIGENCE? *Discuss infant assessment measures and the prediction of intelligence.*

Measures of Infant Development

- Developmental scales for infants grew out of the tradition of IQ testing of older children. These scales are less verbal than IQ tests. Gesell's scale is still widely used by pediatricians to distinguish normal and abnormal infants; it provides a developmental quotient (DQ). The Bayley scales, developed by Nancy Bayley, continue to be widely used today to assess infant development. They consist of a motor scale, a mental scale, and an infant behavior profile. Increasingly used, the Fagan Test of Infant Intelligence assesses how effectively the infant processes information.

Predicting Intelligence

- Global scores on the Gesell and Bayley scales are not good predictors of childhood intelligence. However, measures of information processing such as speed of habituation and degree of dishabituation do correlate with intelligence later in childhood. There is both continuity and discontinuity between infant cognitive development and cognitive development later in childhood.

4   WHAT ARE SOME EARLY ENVIRONMENTAL INFLUENCES ON COGNITIVE DEVELOPMENT? *Characterize early environmental influences on cognitive development.*

Nutrition

- Nutritional supplements given to malnourished infants improve their cognitive development.

Poverty

- Early intervention programs that target infants living in poverty are often more effective when they are (1) longterm, (2) time-intensive, (3) able to provide direct educational benefits, and (4) comprehensive and multidimensional.

5 WHAT IS THE NATURE OF LANGUAGE, AND HOW DOES IT DEVELOP IN INFANCY? *Describe the nature of language and how it develops in infancy.*

Defining Language	• Language is a form of communication, whether spoken, written, or signed, that is based on a system of symbols. Language consists of all the words used by a community and the rules for varying and combining them. It is characterized by infinite generativity.
Language's Rule Systems	• Phonology is the sound system of the language, including the sounds that are used and how they may be combined. Morphology refers to the units of meaning involved in word formation. Syntax is the way words are combined to form acceptable phrases and sentences. Semantics involves the meaning of words and sentences. Pragmatics is the appropriate use of language in different contexts.
How Language Develops	• Among the milestones in infant language development are crying (birth), cooing (1 to 2 months), babbling (6 months), making the transition from universal linguist to language-specific listener (7 to 11 months), using gestures (8 to 12 months), comprehension of words (8 to 12 months), first word spoken (13 months), vocabulary spurt (18 months), rapid expansion of understanding words (18 to 24 months), and two-word utterances (18 to 24 months).
Biological and Environmental Influences	• In evolution, language clearly gave humans an enormous advantage over other animals and increased their chance of survival. Broca's area and Wernicke's area are important locations for language processing in the brain's left hemisphere. Chomsky argues that children are born with the ability to detect basic features and rules of language. In other words, they are biologically prepared to learn language with a prewired language acquisition device (LAD). The behavioral view—that children acquire language as a result of reinforcement—has not been supported. Adults help children acquire language through child-directed speech, recasting, expanding, and labeling. Environmental influences are demonstrated by differences in the language development of children as a consequence of being exposed to different language environments in the home. Parents should talk extensively with an infant, especially about what the baby is attending to.
An Interactionist View	• Today, most language researchers believe that children everywhere arrive in the world with special social and linguistic capacities that make language acquisition possible. How much of the language is biologically determined, and how much depends on interaction with others, is a subject of debate among linguists and psychologists. However, all agree that both biological capacity and relevant experience are necessary.

KEY TERMS

schemes 183
assimilation 183
accommodation 183
organization 184
equilibration 184
sensorimotor stage 184

simple reflexes 185
first habits and primary
   circular reactions 185
primary circular reaction 185
secondary circular
   reactions 185

coordination of secondary
   circular reactions 186
tertiary circular reactions,
   novelty, and curiosity 186
internalization of schemes 186
object permanence 186

A-not-B error 188
attention 190
joint attention 190
memory 192
implicit memory 192
explicit memory 192

KEY PEOPLE

MAKING A DIFFERENCE

Nourishing the Infant's Cognitive Development

What are some good strategies for helping infants develop in cognitively competent ways?

- *Provide the infant with many play opportunities in a rich and varied environment.* Give the infant extensive opportunities to experience objects of different sizes, shapes, textures, and colors. Recognize that play with objects stimulates the infant's cognitive development.
- *Actively communicate with the infant.* Don't let the infant spend long bouts of waking hours in social isolation.

Infants need caregivers who actively communicate with them. This active communication with adults is necessary for the infant's competent cognitive development.

- *Don't try to overaccelerate the infant's cognitive development.* Most experts stress that infants cognitively benefit when they learn concepts naturally. The experts emphasize that restricting infants to a passive role and showing them flash cards to accelerate their cognitive development is not a good strategy.

RESOURCES FOR IMPROVING CHILDREN'S LIVES

Growing Up with Language

by Naomi Baron (1992)
Reading, MA: Addison-Wesley

Baron focuses on three representative children and their families. She explores how children put their first words together, struggle to understand meaning, and use language as a creative tool. She shows parents how they play a key role in the development of their child's language development.

How Babies Talk

by Roberta Golinkoff and Kathy Hirsh-Pasek (2000)
New York: Plume

Targeted for parents, this book by leading experts details the fascinating world of infant language. Included are activities parents can use with their infants and indicators of delayed language that can alert parents to possible language problems.

Blackwell Handbook of Language Development

edited by Erica Hoff and Marilyn Shatz (2007)
Malden, MA: Blackwell

A number of leading experts provide up-to-date discussion of many aspects of language development, including the emergence of language, the brain's role in language development, and early word learning

E-LEARNING TOOLS

Connect to **www.mhhe.com/santrockc10** to research the answers and complete these exercises. In addition, you'll find a number of other resources and valuable study tools for Chapter 6, "Cognitive Development in Infancy," on this Web site.

Taking It to the Net

1. Anthony is surveying *Time* magazine's list of top 100 people of the twentieth century. He notices that Jean Piaget made the list. Why?

2. Marco is 16 months old. He is cooing and babbling, but he has not yet uttered his first word. His father, Tony, is concerned that Marco is delayed in his language development. Should Tony be concerned? What developments in language can be expected for infants and toddlers? How might Tony identify whether Marco has a problem?

3. Poverty has serious negative consequences for children's cognitive development. Is it possible to buffer the effects of poverty through early intervention? If so, what benefits might be linked to early intervention?

Health and Well-Being, Parenting, and Education

Build your decision-making skills by trying your hand at the health and well-being, parenting, and education exercises.

Video Clips

The Online Learning Center includes the following videos for this chapter:

1. *Babbling at 7.5 months*—1264
2. *Brain Development and Cognition*—659
   Renowned brain researcher Charles Nelson describes findings from his research.
3. *Language Ability at Age 2*—2699
   While engaging in a pretend tea party with her mother, 2-year-old Abby demonstrates advancing language ability.
4. *Motherese with a 4-Year-Old*—2150
   A mother displays the unique ways that many parents speak to their infants.

7 Socioemotional Development in Infancy

We never know the love of our parents until we have become parents.

—Henry Ward Beecher
American Writer, 19th Century

LEARNING GOALS

1 Discuss emotional and personality development in infancy.

2 Describe social orientation/understanding and the development of attachment in infancy.

3 Explain how social contexts influence the infant's development.

Images of Children's Development
The Story of Darius' Fathering

Many fathers are spending more time with their infants today than in the past.

Seventeen-month-old Darius is getting excited. His father just asked him if he wants to go outside and play. Darius toddles down the hall as fast as he can to get his shoes, coat, and hat, which he knows he wears when he goes outside. He grabs his hat and says, "Play, play," which at this point in his development is what he labels going outside and exploring the yard and its flowers, bugs, and bees. On the weekend, his parents take him to the zoo, where they point out and name various animals, like lions, tigers, elephants, as Darius looks wide-eyed at the animals. When they get home, Darius' parents ask him about some of the sounds and movements the zoo animals make. Darius correctly roars at the mention of *lion* and imitates the movements of monkeys.

On weekdays, Darius' father, a writer, cares for him during the day while his mother works full-time as a landscape architect. Darius' father is doing a great job of caring for him. Darius' father keeps Darius nearby while he is writing and spends lots of time talking to him and playing with him. From their interactions, it is clear that they genuinely enjoy each other.

Last month, Darius began spending one day a week at a child-care center. His parents carefully selected the center after observing a number of centers and interviewing teachers and center directors. His parents placed him in the center one day a week because they wanted Darius to get some experience with peers and to give his father some time out from his caregiving.

Darius' father looks to the future and imagines the Little League games Darius will play in and the many other activities he can enjoy with Darius. Remembering how little time his own father spent with him, he is dedicated to making sure that Darius has an involved, nurturing experience with his father.

When Darius' mother comes home in the evening, she spends considerable time with him. Darius shows a positive attachment to both his mother and his father. By cooperating, his parents have successfully juggled their careers and work schedules to provide 17-month-old Darius with excellent child care.

PREVIEW

In Chapters 5 and 6, you read about how the infant perceives, learns, and remembers. Infants also are socioemotional beings, capable of displaying emotions and initiating social interaction with people close to them. The main topics that we explore in this chapter are emotional and personality development, social understanding and attachment, and the social contexts of the family and child care.

1 HOW DO EMOTIONS AND PERSONALITY DEVELOP IN INFANCY?

Emotional Development	Temperament	Personality Development

Anyone who has been around infants for even a brief time detects that they are emotional beings. Not only do infants express emotions, but they also vary in their temperament. Some are shy and others are outgoing. Some are active and others much less so. In this section, we explore these and other aspects of emotional and personality development in infants.

Emotional Development

Imagine your life without emotion. Emotion is the color and music of life, as well as the tie that binds people together. How do psychologists define and classify emotions, and why are they important to development? How do emotions develop during the first two years of life?

Blossoms are scattered by the wind
And the wind cares nothing, but
The blossoms of the heart
No wind can touch.

—YOUSHIDA KENKO
Buddhist Monk, 14th Century

What Are Emotions? For our purposes, we will define **emotion** as feeling, or affect, that occurs when a person is in a state or an interaction that is important to them, especially to their well-being. Emotion is characterized by behavior that reflects or expresses the pleasantness or unpleasantness of the individual's state or transactions (Barrett & others, 2007).

When we think about emotions, a few dramatic feelings such as rage or glorious joy spring to mind. Emotions can be specific and take the form of joy, fear, anger, and so on, depending on whether a transaction is a relief, a threat, a frustration, and so on. But emotions can be subtle as well, such as uneasiness in a new situation or the feeling a mother has when she holds her baby. And emotions can vary in how intense they are. For example, an infant may show intense fear or only mild fear in a particular situation.

Psychologists classify the broad range of emotions in many ways, but almost all classifications designate an emotion as either positive or negative. Positive emotions include enthusiasm, joy, and love. Negative emotions include anxiety, anger, guilt, and sadness.

Biological and Environmental Influences Emotions are influenced both by biological foundations and by a person's experience. In *The Expression of Emotions in Man and Animals*, Charles Darwin (1872/1965) argued that our facial expressions of emotion are innate, not learned; are the same in all cultures around the world; and evolved from the emotions of animals. Today, psychologists still believe that emotions, especially facial expressions of emotions, have a strong biological foundation (Goldsmith, 2002). For example, children who are blind from birth—and have never observed the smile or frown on another person's face—smile and frown in the same way that children with normal vision do. Also, facial expressions of basic emotions such as happiness, surprise, anger, and fear are the same across cultures.

Biology's importance to emotion is also apparent in the changes in a baby's emotional capacities. Certain regions of the brain that develop early in life (such as the brain stem, hippocampus, and amygdala) play a role in distress, excitement, and rage, and even infants display these emotions (Thompson, Easterbrooks, & Walker, 2003). But, as we discuss later in the chapter, infants only gradually develop the ability to regulate their emotions, and this ability seems tied to the gradual maturation of frontal regions of the cerebral cortex (discussed in Chapter 5), which can exert control over other areas of the brain (Porges, Doussard-Roosevelt, & Maiti, 1994).

These biological factors, however, are only part of the story of emotion. Emotions serve important functions in our relationships. As we discuss later in this section, emotions are the first language with which parents and infants communicate (Maccoby, 1992). Emotion-linked interchanges, as when Darius cries and his father sensitively responds, provide the foundation for the infant's developing attachment to the parent.

Social relationships, in turn, provide the setting for the development of a rich variety of emotions. When toddlers hear their parents quarreling, they often react with distress and inhibit their play (Cummings, 1987). Well-functioning families make each other laugh and may develop a light mood to defuse conflicts. Biological evolution has endowed human beings to be *emotional*, but embeddedness in relationships with others provides diversity in emotional experiences (Saarni & others, 2006).

emotion Feeling, or affect, that occurs when a person is in a state or interaction that is important to them. Emotion is characterized by behavior that reflects (expresses) the pleasantness or unpleasantness of the state a person is in or the transactions being experienced.

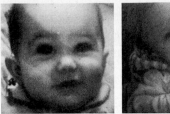

Joy   Sadness

Fear   Surprise

FIGURE 7.1 Expression of Different Emotions in Infants

Early Emotions   Leading expert on infant emotional development, Michael Lewis (2007), distinguishes between primary emotions and self-conscious emotions. **Primary emotions** are emotions that are present in humans and animals; these emotions appear in the first six months of the human infant's development. Primary emotions include surprise, interest, joy, anger, sadness, fear, and disgust (see Figure 7.1 for infants' facial expressions of some of these early emotions). In Lewis' classification, **self-conscious emotions** require self-awareness that involves consciousness and a sense of "me." Self-conscious emotions include jealousy, empathy, embarrassment, pride, shame, and guilt—most of these occurring for the first time at some point in the second half of the first year through the second year. Some experts on emotion call self-conscious emotions such as embarrassment, shame, guilt, and pride *other-conscious emotions* because they involve the emotional reactions of others when they are generated (Saarni & others, 2006). For example, approval from parents is linked to toddlers beginning to show pride when they successfully complete a task.

Researchers such as Joseph Campos (2005; Campos, Anderson, & Barbu-Roth, 2008) and Michael Lewis (2007) debate how early in the infant and toddler years the emotions that we have described first appear and their sequence. As an indication of the controversy regarding when certain emotions first are displayed by infants, consider jealousy. Some researchers argue that jealousy does not emerge until approximately 18 months of age (Lewis, 2007), whereas others emphasize that it is displayed much earlier (Draghi-Lorenz, 2007; Draghi-Lorenz, Reddy, & Costall, 2001). Consider a research study in which 6-month-old infants observed their mothers either giving attention to a lifelike baby doll (hugging or gently rocking it, for example) or to a book (Hart & Carrington, 2002). When mothers directed their attention to the doll, the infants were more likely to display negative emotions, such as anger and sadness, which may have indicated their jealousy (see Figure 7.2). On the other hand, their expressions of anger and sadness may have reflected frustration in not being able to have the novel doll to play with. Debate about the onset of an emotion such as jealousy illustrates the complexity and difficulty in indexing early emotions.

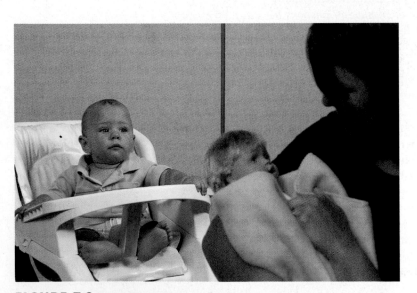

FIGURE 7.2 The Early Appearance of Jealousy An infant becomes distressed when his mother gives attention to a life-like baby doll in the laboratory of Sybil Hart at Texas Tech University.

Emotional Expression and Social Relationships
Emotional expressions are involved in infants' first relationships. The ability of infants to communicate emotions permits coordinated interactions with their caregivers and the beginning of an emotional bond between them. Not only do parents change their emotional expressions in response to infants' emotional expressions, but infants also modify their emotional expressions in response to their parents' emotional expressions. In other words, these interactions are mutually regulated. Because of this coordination, the interactions are described as *reciprocal*, or *synchronous*, when all is going well. Sensitive, responsive parents help their infants grow emotionally, whether the infants respond in distressed or happy ways (Campos, 2001; Thompson, 2006).

Cries and smiles are two emotional expressions that infants display when interacting with parents. These are babies' first forms of emotional communication.

Crying   Crying is the most important mechanism newborns have for communicating with their world. The first cry verifies that the baby's lungs have filled with air. Cries also may provide information about the health of the newborn's central nervous

primary emotions Emotions that are present in humans and other animals and emerge early in life; examples are joy, anger, sadness, fear, and disgust.

self-conscious emotions Emotions that require self-awareness, especially consciousness and a sense of "me"; example include jealousy, empathy, and embarrassment.

system. Newborns even tend to respond with cries and negative facial expressions when they hear other newborns cry (Dondi, Simion, & Caltran, 1999).

Babies have at least three types of cries:

- **Basic cry.** A rhythmic pattern that usually consists of a cry, followed by a briefer silence, then a shorter whistle that is somewhat higher in pitch than the main cry, then another brief rest before the next cry. Some infancy experts believe that hunger is one of the conditions that incite the basic cry.
- **Anger cry.** A variation of the basic cry in which more excess air is forced through the vocal cords.
- **Pain cry.** A sudden long, initial loud cry followed by breath holding; no preliminary moaning is present. The pain cry is stimulated by a high-intensity stimulus.

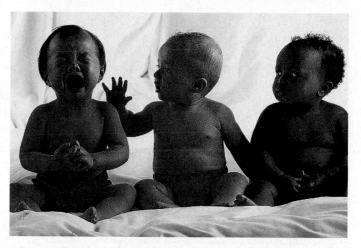

What are some different types of cries?

Most adults can determine whether an infant's cries signify anger or pain (Zeskind, Klein, & Marshall, 1992). Parents can distinguish the cries of their own baby better than those of another baby.

Smiling   The power of the infant's smiles was appropriately captured by British theorist John Bowlby (1969): "Can we doubt that the more and better an infant smiles the better he is loved and cared for? It is fortunate for their survival that babies are so designed by nature that they beguile and enslave mothers." Two types of smiling can be distinguished in infants:

- **Reflexive smile.** A smile that does not occur in response to external stimuli and appears during the first month after birth, usually during sleep.
- **Social smile.** A smile that occurs in response to an external stimulus, typically a face in the case of the young infant. Social smiling occurs as early as two months of age.

Fear   One of a baby's earliest emotions is fear, which typically first appears at about 6 months of age and peaks at about 18 months. However, abused and neglected infants can show fear as early as 3 months (Campos, 2005). The most frequent expression of an infant's fear involves **stranger anxiety,** in which an infant shows a fear and wariness of strangers.

Stranger anxiety usually emerges gradually. It first appears at about 6 months of age in the form of wary reactions. By age 9 months, the fear of strangers is often more intense, and it continues to escalate through the infant's first birthday (Emde, Gaensbauer, & Harmon, 1976).

Not all infants show distress when they encounter a stranger. Besides individual variations, whether an infant shows stranger anxiety also depends on the social context and the characteristics of the stranger.

Infants show less stranger anxiety when they are in familiar settings. For example, in one study, 10-month-olds showed little stranger anxiety when they met a stranger in their own home but much greater fear when they encountered a stranger in a research laboratory (Sroufe, Waters, & Matas, 1974). Also, infants show less stranger anxiety when they are sitting on their mothers' laps than when placed in an infant seat several feet away from their mothers (Bohlin & Hagekull, 1993). Thus, it appears that, when infants feel secure, they are less likely to show stranger anxiety.

Who the stranger is and how the stranger behaves also influence stranger anxiety in infants. Infants are less fearful of child strangers than adult strangers. They also are less fearful of friendly, outgoing, smiling strangers than of passive, unsmiling strangers (Bretherton, Stolberg, & Kreye, 1981).

basic cry A rhythmic pattern usually consisting of a cry, a briefer silence, a shorter inspiratory whistle that is higher pitched than the main cry, and then a brief rest before the next cry.

anger cry A variation of the basic cry, with more excess air forced through the vocal cords.

pain cry A sudden appearance of loud crying without preliminary moaning, followed by breath holding.

reflexive smile A smile that does not occur in response to external stimuli. It happens during the month after birth, usually during sleep.

social smile A smile in response to an external stimulus, which, early in development, typically is a face.

stranger anxiety An infant's fear and wariness of strangers; it tends to appear in the second half of the first year of life.

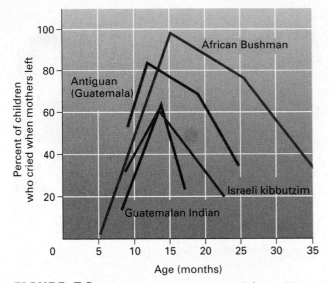

FIGURE 7.3 Separation Anxiety in Four Cultures Note that separation protest peaked at about the same time in all four cultures in this study (13 to 15 months of age) (Kagan, Kearsley, & Zelazo, 1978). However, a higher percentage (100 percent of infants in an African Bushman culture engaged in separation protest compared to only about 60 percent of infants in Guatemalan Indian and Israeli Kibbutzim cultures. *What might explain the fact that separation protest peaks at about the same time in these cultures?*

In addition to stranger anxiety, infants experience fear of being separated from their caregivers. The result is **separation protest**—crying when the caregiver leaves. Separation protest tends to peak at about 15 months among U.S. infants. In fact, one study found that separation protest peaked at about 13 to 15 months in four different cultures (Kagan, Kearsley, & Zelazo, 1978). As indicated in Figure 7.3, the percentage of infants who engaged in separation protest varied across cultures, but the infants reached a peak of protest at about the same age—just before the middle of the second year of life.

Emotional Regulation and Coping   During the first year of life, the infant gradually develops an ability to inhibit, or minimize, the intensity and duration of emotional reactions. From early in infancy, babies put their thumbs in their mouths to soothe themselves. But at first, infants mainly depend on caregivers to help them soothe their emotions, as when a caregiver rocks an infant to sleep, sings lullabies to the infant, gently strokes the infant, and so on.

The caregivers' actions influence the infant's neurobiological regulation of emotions (Saarni & others, 2006; Thompson, 2006). By soothing the infant, caregivers help infants to modulate their emotion and reduce the level of stress hormones (Gunnar & Quevado, 2007; Gunnar & Davis, 2003). Many developmentalists believe it is a good strategy for a caregiver to soothe an infant before the infant gets into an intense, agitated, uncontrolled state (McElwain & Booth-LaForce, 2006; Thompson, 1994).

Later in infancy, when they become aroused, infants sometimes redirect their attention or distract themselves in order to reduce their arousal. By 2 years of age, toddlers can use language to define their feeling states and the context that is upsetting them (Kopp & Neufeld, 2002). A toddler might say, "Feel bad. Dog scare." This type of communication may help caregivers to help the child in regulating emotion.

Contexts can influence emotional regulation (Kopp & Neufeld, 2002; Saarni & others, 2006). Infants are often affected by fatigue, hunger, time of day, which people are around them, and where they are. Infants must learn to adapt to different contexts that require emotional regulation. Further, new demands appear as the infant becomes older and parents modify their expectations. For example, a parent may take it in stride if a 6-month-old infant screams in a restaurant but may react very differently if a 1½-year-old starts screaming.

To soothe or not to soothe—should a crying baby be given attention and soothed, or does this spoil the infant? Many years ago, the behaviorist John Watson (1928) argued that parents spend too much time responding to infant crying. As a consequence, he said, parents reward crying and increase its incidence. More recently, behaviorist Jacob Gewirtz (1977) found that a caregiver's quick, soothing response to crying increased crying. In contrast, infancy experts Mary Ainsworth (1979) and John Bowlby (1989) stress that you can't respond too much to infant crying in the first year of life. They believe that a quick, comforting response to the infant's cries is an important ingredient in the development of a strong bond between the infant and caregiver. In one of Ainsworth's studies, infants whose mothers responded quickly when they cried at 3 months of age cried less later in the first year of life (Bell & Ainsworth, 1972).

Controversy still characterizes the question of whether or how parents should respond to an infant's cries (Lewis & Ramsay, 1999). However, developmentalists increasingly argue that an infant cannot be spoiled in the first year of life, which suggests that parents should soothe a crying infant. This reaction should help infants develop a sense of trust and secure attachment to the caregiver.

separation protest An infant's distressed reaction when the caregiver leaves.

Another technique for calming young infants is *swaddling*, which involves wrapping a young baby in a blanket. Swaddling is popular in many Middle Eastern countries and in the Navajo nation in the United States (Whiting, 1981). However, in the United States swaddling has generally been unpopular because it restricts freedom of movement and is thought to make babies passive (Chisolm, 1989; Saarni & others, 2006). Nonetheless, an increasing number of pediatricians recommend swaddling. Some research studies have shown positive outcomes for swaddling. In one study, newborns with brain injuries were randomly assigned to a swaddling condition (wrapping the baby in a blanket) or a massage therapy condition (Ohgi & others, 2004). Swaddling reduced the infants' crying more than the massage therapy.

Pediatricians and nurses who recommend swaddling stress that it stops the baby's uncontrolled arm and leg movements that can lead to frenzied crying (Huang & others, 2004; Karp, 2002). They also recommend tucking the baby tightly in the blanket so it does not become loose and become wrapped around the baby's face. An excellent book on how to calm a crying baby, including specific instructions on swaddling, is *The Happiest Baby on the Block* (Karp, 2002).

Temperament

Do you get upset a lot? Does it take much to get you angry, or to make you laugh? Even at birth, babies seem to have different emotional styles. One infant is cheerful and happy much of the time; another baby seems to cry constantly. These tendencies reflect **temperament,** which is an individual's behavioral style and characteristic way of responding.

Describing and Classifying Temperament How would you describe your temperament or the temperament of a friend? Researchers have described and classified the temperament of individuals in different ways. Here we examine three of those ways.

Chess and Thomas' Classification Psychiatrists Alexander Chess and Stella Thomas (Chess & Thomas, 1977; Thomas & Chess, 1991) identified three basic types, or clusters, of temperament:

- **Easy child.** This child is generally in a positive mood, quickly establishes regular routines in infancy, and adapts easily to new experiences.
- **Difficult child.** This child reacts negatively and cries frequently, engages in irregular daily routines, and is slow to accept change.
- **Slow-to-warm-up child.** This child has a low activity level, is somewhat negative, and displays a low intensity of mood.

In their longitudinal investigation, Chess and Thomas found that 40 percent of the children they studied could be classified as easy, 10 percent as difficult, and 15 percent as slow to warm up. Notice that 35 percent did not fit any of the three patterns. Researchers have found that these three basic clusters of temperament are moderately stable across the childhood years.

Kagan's Behavioral Inhibition Another way of classifying temperament focuses on the differences between a shy, subdued, timid child and a sociable, extraverted, bold child. Jerome Kagan (2000, 2002; Kagan & Fox, 2006; Kagan & Snidman, 1991) regards shyness with strangers (peers or adults) as one feature of a broad temperament category called *inhibition to the unfamiliar*. Inhibited children react to many aspects of unfamiliarity with initial avoidance, distress, or subdued affect, beginning about 7 to 9 months of age.

Kagan has found that inhibition shows considerable stability from infancy through early childhood. One study classified toddlers into extremely inhibited,

"Oh, he's cute, all right, but he's got the temperament of a car alarm."
Copyright @ The New Yorker Collection 1999 Barbara Smaller from cartoonbank.com. All Rights Reserved.

temperament An individual's behavioral style and characteristic way of emotionally responding.

easy child A child who is generally in a positive mood, who quickly establishes regular routines in infancy, and who adapts easily to new experiences.

difficult child A child who tends to react negatively and cry frequently, who engages in irregular daily routines, and who is slow to accept new experiences.

slow-to-warm-up child A child who has a low activity level, is somewhat negative, and displays a low intensity of mood.

extremely uninhibited, and intermediate groups (Pfeifer & others, 2002). Follow-up assessments occurred at 4 and 7 years of age. Continuity was demonstrated for both inhibition and lack of inhibition, although a substantial number of the inhibited children moved into the intermediate groups at 7 years of age.

Rothbart and Bates' Classification   New classifications of temperament continue to be forged. Mary Rothbart and John Bates (2006) argue that these three broad dimensions best represent what researchers have found to characterize the structure of temperament: extraversion/surgency, negative affectivity, and effortful control (self-regulation):

- *Extraversion/surgency* includes "positive anticipation, impulsivity, activity level, and sensation seeking" (Rothbart, 2004, p. 495). Kagan's uninhibited children fit into this category.
- *Negative affectivity* includes "fear, frustration, sadness, and discomfort" (Rothbart, 2004, p. 495). These children are easily distressed; they may fret and cry often. Kagan's inhibited children fit this category.
- *Effortful control (self-regulation)* includes "attentional focusing and shifting, inhibitory control, perceptual sensitivity, and low-intensity pleasure" (Rothbart, 2004, p. 495). Infants who are high on effortful control show an ability to keep their arousal from getting too high and have strategies for soothing themselves. By contrast, children low on effortful control are often unable to control their arousal; they become easily agitated and intensely emotional.

In Rothbart's (2004, p. 497) view, "Early theoretical models of temperament stressed the way we are moved by our positive and negative emotions or level of arousal, with our actions driven by these tendencies." The more recent emphasis on effortful control, however, advocates that individuals can engage in a more cognitive, flexible approach to stressful circumstances.

Biological Foundations and Experience   How does a child acquire a certain temperament? Kagan (2002, 2003) argues that children inherit a physiology that biases them to have a particular type of temperament. However, through experience they may learn to modify their temperament to some degree. For example, children may inherit a physiology that biases them to be fearful and inhibited, but they learn to reduce their fear and inhibition to some degree.

Biological Influences   Physiological characteristics have been linked with different temperaments (Rothbart & Bates, 2006). In particular, an inhibited temperament is associated with a unique physiological pattern that includes high and stable heart rate, high level of the hormone cortisol, and high activity in the right frontal lobe of the brain (Kagan, 2003; Kagan & Fox, 2006). This pattern may be tied to the excitability of the amygdala, a structure of the brain that plays an important role in fear and inhibition (Kagan, 2003; LeDoux, 1998, 2000). An inhibited temperament or negative affectivity may also be linked to low levels of the neurotransmitter serotonin, which may increase an individual's vulnerability to fear and frustration (Kramer, 1993).

What is heredity's role in the biological foundations of temperament? Twin and adoption studies suggest that heredity has a moderate influence on differences in temperament within a group of people (Plomin & others, 1994). The contemporary view is that

What are some ways that developmentalists have classified infants' temperaments? Which classification makes the most sense to you, based on your observations of infants?

temperament is a biologically based but evolving aspect of behavior; it evolves as the child's experiences are incorporated into a network of self-perceptions and behavioral preferences that characterize the child's personality (Thompson & Goodvin, 2005).

Gender, Culture, and Temperament   Gender may be an important factor shaping the context that influences the fate of temperament. Parents might react differently to an infant's temperament depending on whether the baby is a boy or a girl (Kerr, 2001). For example, in one study, mothers were more responsive to the crying of irritable girls than to the crying of irritable boys (Crockenberg, 1986).

Similarly, the reaction to an infant's temperament may depend in part of culture. For example, an active temperament might be valued in some cultures (such as the United States) but not in other cultures (such as China). Indeed, children's temperament can vary across cultures (Putnam, Sanson, & Rothbart, 2002). Behavioral inhibition is more highly valued in China than in North America, and researchers have found that Chinese children are more inhibited than Canadian infants (Chen & others, 1998). The cultural differences in temperament were linked to parent attitude and behaviors. Canadian mothers of inhibited 2-year-olds were less accepting of their infants' inhibited temperament, whereas Chinese mothers were more accepting.

In short, many aspects of a child's environment can encourage or discourage the persistence of temperament characteristics (Shiner, 2006). One useful way of thinking about these relationships applies the concept of goodness of fit, which we examine next.

Goodness of Fit and Parenting   **Goodness of fit** refers to the match between a child's temperament and the environmental demands the child must cope with (Schoppe-Sullivan & others, 2007). Suppose Jason is an active toddler who is made to sit still for long periods of time, and Jack is a slow-to-warm-up toddler who is abruptly pushed into new situations on a regular basis. Both Jason and Jack face a lack of fit between their temperament and environmental demands. Lack of fit can produce adjustment problems (Rothbart & Bates, 2006).

Some temperament characteristics pose more parenting challenges than others, at least in modern Western societies (Bates & Pettit, 2007; Rothbart & Bates, 2006; Thompson & Goodvin, 2005). When children are prone to distress, as exhibited by frequent crying and irritability, their parents may eventually respond by ignoring the child's distress or trying to force the child to "behave." In one research study, though, extra support and training for mothers of distress-prone infants improved the quality of mother-infant interaction (van den Boom, 1989). The training led the mothers to alter their demands on the child, improving the fit between the child and the environment. Also, in a longitudinal study, researchers found that a high level of fearlessness on the part of infants, when combined with harsh parenting, was linked with persistent conduct problems at age 8 (Shaw & others, 2003).

Many parents don't become believers in temperament's importance until the birth of their second child. They viewed their first child's behavior as a result of how they treated the child. But then they find that some strategies that worked with their first child are not as effective with the second child. Some problems experienced with the first child (such as those involved in feeding, sleeping, and coping with strangers) do not exist with the second child, but new problems arise. Such experiences strongly suggest that children differ from each other very early in life, and that these differences have important implications for parent-child interaction (Kwak & others, 1999; Rothbart & Putnam, 2002). To read further about some positive strategies for parenting that take into account the child's temperament, see the *Caring for Children* interlude.

An infant's temperament can vary across cultures. *What do parents need to know about a child's temperament?*

goodness of fit Refers to the match between a child's temperament and the environmental demands with which the child must cope.

Caring for Children

PARENTING AND THE CHILD'S TEMPERAMENT

What are the implications of temperamental variations for parenting? Although answers to this question necessarily are speculative, these conclusions regarding the best parenting strategies to use in relation to children's temperament were reached by temperament experts Ann Sanson and Mary Rothbart (1995):

- *Attention to, and respect for, individuality.* Good parenting involves sensitivity to the child's individual characteristics. A goal might be accomplished in one way with one child and in another way with another child, depending on the child's temperament.
- *Structuring the child's environment.* Crowded, noisy environments can pose greater problems for some children (such as a "difficult child") than others (such as an "easy child"). We might also expect that a fearful, withdrawing child would benefit from slower entry into new contexts.
- *The "difficult child" and packaged parenting programs.* Programs for parents often focus on dealing with children who have "difficult" temperaments. In some cases, "difficult child" refers to Thomas and Chess' description of a child who reacts negatively, cries frequently, engages in irregular daily routines, and is slow to accept change. In others, the concept might be used to describe a child who is irritable, displays anger frequently, does not follow directions well, or some other negative characteristic. Acknowledging that some children are harder than others to parent is often helpful, and advice on how to handle particular difficult characteristics can be useful. However, whether a particular characteristic is difficult depends on its fit with the environment. To label a child "difficult" has the danger of becoming a self-fulfilling prophecy. If a child is identified as difficult, people may treat the child in a way that actually elicits difficult behavior.

Too often, we pigeonhole children into categories without examining the context (Rothbart & Bates, 2006; Saarni, 2002). Nonetheless, caregivers need to take children's temperament into account. Research does not yet allow for many highly specific recommendations—but, in general, caregivers should (1) be sensitive to the individual characteristics of the child, (2) be flexible in responding to these characteristics, and (3) avoid applying negative labels to the child.

Personality Development

Emotions and temperament form key aspects of *personality*, the enduring personal characteristics of individuals. Let's now examine characteristics that often are thought of as central to personality development during infancy: trust and the development of self and independence.

Trust   According to Erik Erikson (1968), the first year of life is characterized by the trust versus mistrust stage of development. Following a life of regularity, warmth, and protection in the mother's womb, the infant faces a world that is less secure. Erikson proposed that infants learn trust when they are cared for in a consistent, warm manner. If the infant is not well fed and kept warm on a consistent basis, a sense of mistrust is likely to develop.

Trust versus mistrust is not resolved once and for all in the first year of life. It arises again at each successive stage of development, which can have positive or negative outcomes. For example, children who leave infancy with a sense of trust can still have their sense of mistrust activated at a later stage, perhaps if their parents are separated or divorced under conflicting circumstances.

The Developing Sense of Self   Individuals carry with them a sense of who they are and what makes them different from everyone else. They cling to this identity and begin to feel secure in the knowledge that their identity is becoming more stable. Real or imagined, the sense of self is a strong motivating force in life. When does the individual begin to sense a separate existence from others?

According to leading expert Ross Thompson (2007), studying the self in infancy is difficult mainly because infants cannot tell us how they experience themselves. Infants cannot verbally express their views of the self. They also cannot understand complex instructions from researchers.

One ingenious strategy to test infants' visual self-recognition is the use of a mirror technique, in which the infant's mother first puts a dot of rouge on the infant's nose. Then an observer watches to see how often the infant touches its nose. Next, the infant is placed in front of a mirror, and observers detect whether nose touching increases. Why does this matter? The idea is that increased nose touching indicates that the infant recognizes the self in the mirror and is trying to touch or rub off the rouge because the rouge violates the infant's view of the self. Increased touching indicates that the infant realizes that it is the self in the mirror but that something is not right since the real self does not have a dot of rouge on it.

Figure 7.4 displays the results of two investigations that used the mirror technique. The researchers found that before they were 1 year old, infants did not recognize themselves in the mirror (Amsterdam, 1968; Lewis & Brooks-Gunn, 1979). Signs of self-recognition began to appear among some infants when they were 15 to 18 months old. By the time they were 2 years old, most children recognized themselves in the mirror. In sum, infants begin to develop a self-understanding called self-recognition at approximately 18 months of age (Hart & Karmel, 1996; Lewis & others, 1989).

In one study, biweekly assessments from 15 to 23 months of age were conducted (Courage, Edison, & Howe, 2004). Self-recognition gradually emerged over this time, first appearing in the form of mirror recognition, followed by use of the personal pronoun and then by recognizing a photo of themselves. These aspects of self-recognition are often referred to as the first indications of toddlers' understanding of the mental state of me, "That they are objects in their own mental representation of the world" (Lewis, 2005, p. 363).

Late in the second year and early in the third year, toddlers show other emerging forms of self-awareness that reflect a sense of me (Thompson, 2006). For example, they refer to themselves such as by saying "me big"; they label their internal experiences such as emotions; they monitor themselves as when a toddler says, "Do it myself"; and say that things are theirs (Bates, 1990; Bretherton & others, 1986; Bullock & Lutkenhaus, 1990; Fasig, 2000).

Independence   Not only does the infant develop a sense of self in the second year of life, but independence also becomes a more central theme in the infant's life (Keller, 2007). The theories of Margaret Mahler and Erik Erikson have important implications for both self-development and independence. Mahler (1979) argues that the child goes through a separation and then an individuation process. *Separation* involves the infant's movement away from the mother. *Individuation* involves the development of self.

Erikson (1968), like Mahler, stressed that independence is an important issue in the second year of life. Erikson describes the second stage of development as the stage of autonomy versus shame and doubt. Autonomy builds as the infant's mental and motor abilities develop. At this point in development, not only can infants walk, but they can also climb, open and close, drop, push and pull, and hold and

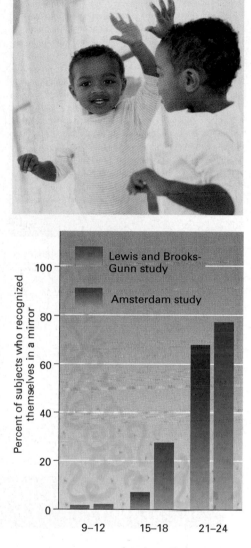

FIGURE 7.4 The Development of Self-Recognition in Infancy The graph shows the findings of two studies in which infants less than 1 year of age did not recognize themselves in the mirror. A slight increase in the percentage of infant self-recognition occurred around 15 to 18 months of age. By 2 years of age, a majority of children recognized themselves. *Why do researchers study whether infants recognize themselves in a mirror?*

Erikson stressed that autonomy versus shame and doubt is the key developmental theme of the toddler years. *What are some good strategies for parents to use with their toddlers?*

let go. Infants feel pride in these new accomplishments and want to do everything themselves, whether the activity is flushing a toilet, pulling the wrapping off a package, or deciding what to eat. It is important for parents to recognize the motivation of toddlers to do what they are capable of doing at their own pace. Then they can learn to control their muscles and their impulses themselves. But when caregivers are impatient and do for toddlers what they are capable of doing themselves, shame and doubt develop. Every parent has rushed a child from time to time. It is only when parents consistently overprotect toddlers or criticize accidents (wetting, soiling, spilling, or breaking, for example) that children develop an excessive sense of shame and doubt about their ability to control themselves and their world. As we discuss in later chapters, Erikson believed that the stage of autonomy versus shame and doubt has important implications for the individual's future development.

REVIEW AND REFLECT ⟩ LEARNING GOAL 1

1 Discuss emotional and personality development in infancy.

Review
- What is the nature of an infant's emotions, and how do they change?
- What is temperament, and how does it develop in infancy?
- What are some important aspects of personality in infancy, and how do they develop?

Reflect
- How would you describe your temperament? Does it fit one of Chess and Thomas' three styles—easy, slow to warm up, or difficult? If you have siblings, is your temperament similar or different from theirs?

2 HOW DO SOCIAL ORIENTATION/UNDERSTANDING AND ATTACHMENT DEVELOP IN INFANCY?

| Social Orientation and Understanding | Attachment and Its Development | Caregiving Styles and Attachment |

| Individual Differences in Attachment |

So far, we have discussed how emotions and emotional competence change as children develop. We have also examined the role of emotional style—in effect, we have seen how emotions set the tone of our experiences in life. But emotions also write the lyrics because they are at the core of our relationships with others.

Social Orientation/Understanding

As socioemotional beings, infants show a strong interest in the social world and are motivated to orient to it and understand it. In earlier chapters, we described many of the biological and cognitive foundations that contribute to the infant's development of social orientation and understanding. We call attention to relevant biological and cognitive factors as we explore social orientation; locomotion; intention, goal-directed behavior, and cooperation; and social referencing. Discussing biological, cognitive, and social processes together reminds us of an important aspect of development that was pointed out in Chapter 1: these processes are intricately intertwined (Diamond, 2007).

Social Orientation   From early in their development, infants are captivated by the social world. As we discussed in our coverage of infant perception in Chapter 5, young infants stare intently at faces and are attuned to the sounds of human voices, especially their caregiver's (Ramsay-Rennels & Langlois, 2007; Saffran, Werker, & Werner, 2006). Later, they become adept at interpreting the meaning of facial expressions.

Face-to-face play often begins to characterize caregiver-infant interactions when the infant is about 2 to 3 months of age. The focused social interaction of face-to-face play may include vocalizations, touch, and gestures (Leppanen & others, 2007). Such play is part of many mothers' motivation to create a positive emotional state in their infants (Laible & Thompson, 2007; Thompson, 2006).

In part because of such positive social interchanges between caregivers and infants, by 2 to 3 months of age, infants respond differently to people than objects, showing more positive emotion toward people than inanimate objects, such as puppets (Legerstee, 1997). At this age, most infants expect people to react positively when the infants initiate a behavior, such as a smile or a vocalization. This finding has been discovered using a method called the *still-face paradigm*, in which the caregiver alternates between engaging in face-to-face interaction with the infant and remaining still and unresponsive. As early as 2 to 3 months of age, infants show more withdrawal, negative emotions, and self-directed behavior when their caregivers are still and unresponsive (Adamson & Frick, 2003). The frequency of face-to-face play decreases after 7 months of age as infants become more mobile (Thompson, 2006).

Infants also learn about the social world through other contexts than face-to-face play with a caregiver (Bornstein & Tamis-LeMonda, 2007; Field, 2007). Even though infants as young as 6 months of age show an interest in each other, their interaction with peers increases considerably in the last half of the second year. Between 18 and 24 months of age, children markedly increase their imitative and reciprocal play, such as imitating nonverbal actions like jumping and running (Eckerman & Whitehead, 1999). One recent study involved presenting 1- and 2-year-olds with a simple cooperative task that consisted of pulling a lever to get an attractive toy (Brownell, & Ramani, & Zerwas, 2006) (see Figure 7.5). Any coordinated actions of the 1-year-olds appeared to be more coincidental rather than cooperative, whereas the 2-year-olds' behavior was characterized as more active cooperation to reach a goal. As increasing numbers of U.S. infants experience child care outside the home, they are spending more time in social play with other peers. Later in the chapter, we further discuss child care.

Locomotion   Recall from earlier in the chapter how important independence is for infants, especially in the second year of life. As infants develop the ability to crawl, walk, and run, they are able to explore and expand their social world. These newly developed self-produced locomotor skills allow the infant to independently initiate social interchanges on a more frequent basis (Laible & Thompson, 2007; Thompson, 2006). Remember from Chapter 5 that the development of these gross motor skills is the result of a number of factors including the development of the nervous system,

A mother and her baby engaging in face-to-face play. *At what age does face-to-face play usually begin, and when does it typically start decreasing in frequency?*

FIGURE 7.5 The Cooperation Task The cooperation on task consisted of two handles on a box, atop which was an animated musical toy, surreptitiously activated by remote control when both handles were pulled. The handles were placed far enough apart that one child could not pull both handles. The experimenter demonstrated the task, saying, "Watch! If you pull the handles, the doggie will sing" (Brownell, Ramani, & Zerwas, 2006).

the goal the infant is motivated to reach, and environmental support for the skill (Adolph & Joh, 2007, 2008; Thelen & Smith, 2006).

Intention, Goal–Directed Behavior, and Cooperation   Perceiving people as engaging in intentional and goal-directed behavior is an important social cognitive accomplishment, and this initially occurs toward the end of the first year (Laible & Thompson, 2007; Thompson, 2006). Joint attention and gaze following help the infant to understand that other people have intentions (Meltzoff, 2007; Tomasello & Carpenter, 2007). Recall from Chapter 6 that *joint attention* occurs when the caregiver and infant focus on the same object or event. We indicated that emerging aspects of joint attention occur at about 7 to 8 months, but at about 10 to 11 months of age joint attention intensifies and infants begin to follow the caregiver's gaze. By their first birthday, infants have begun to direct the caregiver's attention to objects that capture their interest (Heimann & others, 2006).

In the study on cooperating to reach a goal that was discussed earlier, 1- and 2-year-olds also were assessed with two social understanding tasks, observation of children's behavior in a joint attention task, and the parents' perceptions of the language the children use about the self and others (Brownell, Ramani, & Zerwas, 2006). Those with more advanced social understanding were more likely to cooperate. To cooperate, the children had to connect their own intentions with the peer's intentions and put this understanding to use in interacting with the peer to reach a goal.

Social Referencing   Another important social cognitive accomplishment in infancy is developing the ability to "read" the emotions of other people. **Social referencing** is the term used to describe "reading" emotional cues in others to help determine how to act in a particular situation. The development of social referencing helps infants to interpret ambiguous situations more accurately, as when they encounter a stranger and need to know whether to fear the person (de Rosnay & others, 2006; Thompson, 2006). By the end of the first year, a mother's facial expression—either smiling or fearful—influences whether an infant will explore an unfamiliar environment.

Infants become better at social referencing in the second year of life. At this age, they tend to "check" with their mother before they act; they look at her to see if she is happy, angry, or fearful. For example, in one study, 14- to 22-month-old infants were more likely to look at their mother's face as a source of information for how to act in a situation than were 6- to 9-month-old infants (Walden, 1991).

Attachment and Its Development

A small curly-haired girl named Danielle, age 11 months, begins to whimper. After a few seconds, she begins to wail. Soon her mother comes into the room, and Danielle's crying ceases. Quickly, Danielle crawls over to where her mother is seated and reaches out to be held. Danielle has just demonstrated attachment to her mother. **Attachment** is a close emotional bond between two people.

There is no shortage of theories about infant attachment. Three theorists discussed in Chapter 1—Freud, Erikson, and Bowlby—proposed influential views.

Freud argued that infants become attached to the person or object that provides oral satisfaction. For most infants, this is the mother, since she is most likely to feed the infant. Is feeding as important as Freud thought? A classic study by Harry Harlow (1958) reveals that the answer is no (see Figure 7.6).

Harlow removed infant monkeys from their mothers at birth; for six months they were reared by surrogate (substitute) "mothers." One surrogate mother was made of wire, the other of cloth. Half of the infant monkeys were fed by the wire mother, half by the cloth mother. Periodically, the amount of time the infant monkeys spent with either the wire or the cloth mother was computed. Regardless of which mother fed them, the infant monkeys spent far more time with the cloth mother. Even if the wire mother, but not the cloth mother, provided nourishment, the infant monkeys spent more time with the cloth mother. And when Harlow frightened the monkeys, those "raised" by the cloth mother ran to the mother and

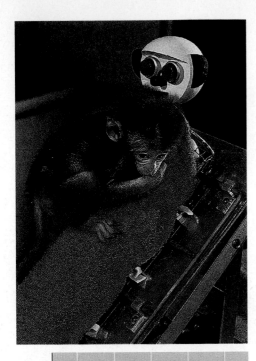

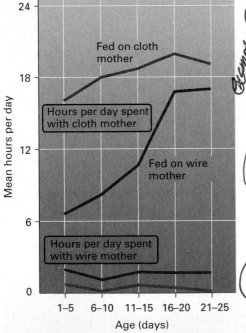

FIGURE 7.6 Contact Time with Wire and Cloth Surrogate Mothers *Regardless of whether the infant monkeys were fed by a wire or a cloth mother, they overwhelmingly preferred to spend contact time with the cloth mother. How do these results compare with what Freud's theory and Erikson's theory would predict about human infants?*

social referencing "Reading" emotional cues in others to help determine how to act in a particular situation.

attachment A close emotional bond between two people.

clung to it; those raised by the wire mother did not. Whether the mother provided comfort seemed to determine whether the monkeys associated the mother with security. This study clearly demonstrated that feeding is not the crucial element in the attachment process, and that contact comfort is important.

Physical comfort also plays a role in Erik Erikson's (1968) view of the infant's development. Recall Erikson's proposal that the first year of life represents the stage of trust versus mistrust. Physical comfort and sensitive care, according to Erikson (1968), are key to establishing a basic trust in infants. The infant's sense of trust, in turn, is the foundation for attachment and sets the stage for a lifelong expectation that the world will be a good and pleasant place to be.

The ethological perspective of British psychiatrist John Bowlby (1969, 1989) also stresses the importance of attachment in the first year of life and the responsiveness of the caregiver. Bowlby maintains both infants and its primary caregivers are biologically predisposed to form attachments. He argues that the newborn is biologically equipped to elicit attachment behavior. The baby cries, clings, coos, and smiles. Later, the infant crawls, walks, and follows the mother. The immediate result is to keep the primary caregiver nearby; the long-term effect is to increase the infant's chances of survival (Thompson, 2006).

Attachment does not emerge suddenly but rather develops in a series of phases, moving from a baby's general preference for human beings to a partnership with primary caregivers. Following are four such phases based on Bowlby's conceptualization of attachment (Schaffer, 1996):

- *Phase 1: from birth to 2 months.* Infants instinctively direct their attachment to human figures. Strangers, siblings, and parents are equally likely to elicit smiling or crying from the infant.
- *Phase 2: from 2 to 7 months.* Attachment becomes focused on one figure, usually the primary caregiver, as the baby gradually learns to distinguish familiar from unfamiliar people.
- *Phase 3: from 7 to 24 months.* Specific attachments develop. With increased locomotor skills, babies actively seek contact with regular caregivers, such as the mother or father.
- *Phase 4: from 24 months on.* Children become aware of others' feelings, goals, and plans and begin to take these into account in forming their own actions.

Bowlby argued that infants develop an *internal working model* of attachment, a simple mental model of the caregiver, their relationship, and the self as deserving of nurturant care. The infant's internal working model of attachment with the caregiver influences the infant's and later the child's subsequent responses to other people (Goldsmith, 2007; Koren-Karie, Oppenheim, & Goldsmith, 2007). The internal model of attachment also has played a pivotal role in the discovery of links between attachment and subsequent emotion understanding, conscious development, and self-concept (Thompson, 2006).

In sum, attachment emerges from the social cognitive advances that allow infants to develop expectations for the caregiver's behavior and to determine the affective quality of their relationship (Thompson, 2006). These social cognitive advances include recognizing the caregiver's face, voice, and other features, as well as developing an internal working model of expecting the caregiver to provide pleasure in social interaction and relief from distress.

Individual Differences in Attachment

Although attachment to a caregiver intensifies midway through the first year, isn't it likely that that quality of babies' attachment experiences varies? Mary Ainsworth (1979) thought so. Ainsworth created the **Strange Situation,** an observational measure of infant attachment in which the infant experiences a series of introductions, separations, and reunions with the caregiver and an adult stranger in a prescribed order. In using the Strange Situation, researchers hope that their observations will provide

What is the nature of secure and insecure attachment? How are caregiving styles related to attachment classification?

Strange Situation An observational measure of infant attachment that requires the infant to move through a series of introductions, separations, and reunions with the caregiver and an adult stranger in a prescribed order.

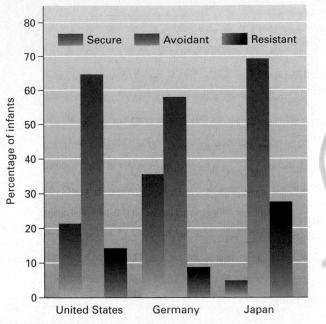

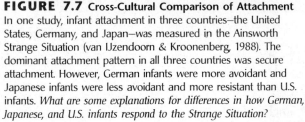

FIGURE 7.7 Cross-Cultural Comparison of Attachment
In one study, infant attachment in three countries—the United States, Germany, and Japan—was measured in the Ainsworth Strange Situation (van IJzendoorn & Kroonenberg, 1988). The dominant attachment pattern in all three countries was secure attachment. However, German infants were more avoidant and Japanese infants were less avoidant and more resistant than U.S. infants. *What are some explanations for differences in how German, Japanese, and U.S. infants respond to the Strange Situation?*

information about the infant's motivation to be near the caregiver and the degree to which the caregiver's presence provides the infant with security and confidence.

Based on how babies respond in the Strange Situation, they are described as being securely attached or insecurely attached (in one of three ways) to the caregiver:

- **Securely attached babies** use the caregiver as a secure base from which to explore the environment. When in the presence of their caregiver, securely attached infants explore the room and examine toys that have been placed in it. When the caregiver departs, securely attached infants might mildly protest, and when the caregiver returns these infants reestablish positive interaction with her, perhaps by smiling or climbing on her lap. Subsequently, they often resume playing with the toys in the room.

- **Insecure avoidant babies** show insecurity by avoiding the caregiver. In the Strange Situation, these babies engage in little interaction with the caregiver, are not distressed when she leaves the room, usually do not reestablish contact with her on her return, and may even turn their back on her. If contact is established, the infant usually leans away or looks away.

- **Insecure resistant babies** often cling to the caregiver and then resist her by fighting against the closeness, perhaps by kicking or pushing away. In the Strange Situation, these babies often cling anxiously to the caregiver and don't explore the playroom. When the caregiver leaves, they often cry loudly and push away if she tries to comfort them on her return.

- **Insecure disorganized babies** are disorganized and disoriented. In the Strange Situation, these babies might appear dazed, confused, and fearful. To be classified as disorganized, babies must show strong patterns of avoidance and resistance or display certain specified behaviors, such as extreme fearfulness around the caregiver.

Evaluating the Strange Situation Does the Strange Situation capture important differences among infants? As a measure of attachment, it may be culturally biased. For example, German and Japanese babies often show different patterns of attachment than American infants. As illustrated in Figure 7.6, German infants are more likely to show an avoidant attachment pattern, and Japanese infants are less likely to display this pattern than U.S. infants (van IJzendoorn & Kroonenberg, 1988). The avoidant pattern in German babies likely occurs because their caregivers encourage them to be independent (Grossmann & others, 1985). Also as shown in Figure 7.7, Japanese babies are more likely than American babies to be categorized as resistant. This may have more to do with the Strange Situation as a measure of attachment than with attachment insecurity itself. Japanese mothers rarely let anyone unfamiliar with their babies care for them. Thus, the Strange Situation might create considerably more stress for Japanese infants than for American infants, who are more accustomed to separation from their mothers (Miyake, Chen, & Campos, 1985). Even though there are cultural variations in attachment classification, the most frequent classification in every culture studied so far is secure attachment (Thompson, 2006; van IJzendoorn & Kroonenberg, 1988).

Some critics stress that behavior in the Strange Situation—like other laboratory assessments—might not indicate what infants do in a natural environment. But researchers have found that infants' behaviors in the Strange Situation are closely related to how they behave at home in response to separation and reunion with their mothers (Pederson & Moran, 1996). Thus, many infant researchers believe the Strange Situation continues to show merit as a measure of infant attachment.

securely attached babies Babies that use the caregiver as a secure base from which to explore the environment.

insecure avoidant babies Babies that show insecurity by avoiding the caregiver.

insecure resistant babies Babies that often cling to the caregiver, then resist her by fighting against the closeness, perhaps by kicking or pushing away.

insecure disorganized babies Babies that show insecurity by being disorganized and disoriented.

Interpreting Differences in Attachment   Do individual differences in attachment matter? Ainsworth maintains that secure attachment in the first year of life provides an important foundation for psychological development later in life. The securely attached infant moves freely away from the mother but keeps track of where she is through periodic glances. The securely attached infant responds positively to being picked up by others and, when put back down, freely moves away to play. An insecurely attached infant, by contrast, avoids the mother or is ambivalent toward her, fears strangers, and is upset by minor, everyday separations.

If early attachment to a caregiver is important, it should relate to a child's social behavior later in development. For some children, early attachments seem to foreshadow later functioning (Carlson, Sroufe, & Egeland, 2004; Egeland & Carlson, 2004; Sroufe & others, 2005a, b). In the extensive longitudinal study conducted by Alan Sroufe and his colleagues (2005a, b), early secure attachment (assessed by the Strange Situation at 12 and 18 months) was linked with positive emotional health, high self-esteem, self-confidence, and socially competent interaction with peers, teachers, camp counselors, and romantic partners through adolescence. Another study found that infants who were securely attached at 15 months of age were more cognitively and socioemotionally competent at 4 years of age than their counterparts who were insecurely attached at 15 months of age (Fish, 2004).

For some children, though, there is little continuity (Thompson & Goodvin, 2005). Not all research reveals the power of infant attachment to predict subsequent development. In one longitudinal study, attachment classification in infancy did not predict attachment classification at 18 years of age (Lewis, 1997). In this study, the best predictor of an insecure attachment classification at 18 was the occurrence of parental divorce in the intervening years. Consistently positive caregiving over a number of years is likely an important factor in connecting early attachment and the child's functioning later in development. Indeed, researchers have found that early secure attachment *and* subsequent experiences, especially maternal care and life stresses, are linked with children's later behavior and adjustment (Belsky & Pasco Fearon, 2002a, b; Thompson, 2006).

Some developmentalists point out that too much emphasis has been placed on the attachment bond in infancy. Jerome Kagan (1987, 2000), for example, emphasizes that infants are highly resilient and adaptive; he argues that they are evolutionarily equipped to stay on a positive developmental course, even in the face of wide variations in parenting. Kagan and others stress that genetic characteristics and temperament play more important roles in a child's social competence than the attachment theorists, such as Bowlby and Ainsworth, are willing to acknowledge (Bakermans-Kranenburg & others, 2007; Chaudhuri & Williams, 1999). For example, if some infants inherit a low tolerance for stress, this, rather than an insecure attachment bond, may be responsible for an inability to get along with peers.

Another criticism of attachment theory is that it ignores the diversity of socializing agents and contexts that exists in an infant's world (Cole & Tan, 2007; Kagitcibasi, 2007). A culture's value system can influence the nature of attachment (Saarni & others, 2006). In northern Germany, mothers expect infants to be independent, and their infants often show little distress upon a brief maternal separation. However, Japanese mothers are motivated to keep their infants close to them, and Japanese infants typically become upset when separated from their mother. Also, in some cultures, infants show attachments to many people. Among the Hausa (who live in Nigeria), both grandmothers and siblings provide a significant amount of care for infants (Harkness & Super, 1995). Infants in agricultural societies tend to form attachments to older siblings, who are assigned a major responsibility for younger siblings' care. Researchers recognize the importance of competent, nurturant caregivers in an infant's development (Bornstein, 2006; Parke & Buriel, 2006). At issue, though, is whether or not secure attachment, especially to a single caregiver, is critical (Lamb, 2000; Thompson, 2006).

In the Hausa culture, siblings and grandmothers provide a significant amount of care for infants. *How might these variations in care affect attachment?*

Despite such criticisms, there is ample evidence that security of attachment is important to development (Berlin & others, 2007; Laible & Thompson, 2007). Secure attachment in infancy is important because it reflects a positive parent-infant relationship and provides the foundation that supports healthy socioemotional development in the years that follow.

Caregiving Styles and Attachment

Is the style of caregiving linked with the quality of the infant's attachment? Securely attached babies have caregivers who are sensitive to their signals and are consistently available to respond to their infants' needs (Juffer & others, 2007; Main, 2000). These caregivers often let their babies have an active part in determining the onset and pacing of interaction in the first year of life. One study found that maternal sensitivity in parenting was linked with secure attachment in infants in two different cultures: the United States and Columbia (Carbonell & others, 2002).

How do the caregivers of insecurely attached babies interact with them? Caregivers of avoidant babies tend to be unavailable or rejecting (Bakermans-Kranenburg & others, 2007; Berlin & Cassidy, 2000). They often don't respond to their babies' signals and have little physical contact with them. When they do interact with their babies, they may behave in an angry and irritable way. Caregivers of resistant babies tend to be inconsistent; sometimes they respond to their babies' needs, and sometimes they don't. In general, they tend not to be very affectionate with their babies and show little synchrony when interacting with them. Caregivers of disorganized babies often neglect or physically abuse them (Cicchetti & Toth, 2006). In some cases, these caregivers are depressed.

REVIEW AND **REFLECT** ◆ **LEARNING GOAL 2**

2 **Describe social orientation/understanding and the development of attachment in infancy.**

Review
- How do social orientation/understanding develop in infancy?
- What is attachment, and how is it conceptualized?
- What are some individual variations in attachment? What are some criticisms of attachment theory?
- How are caregiving styles related to attachment?

Reflect
- How might the infant's temperament be related to a way in which attachment is classified? Look at the temperament categories we described, and reflect on how these might be more likely to show up in infants in some attachment categories than others.

---

3 **HOW DO SOCIAL CONTEXTS INFLUENCE SOCIOEMOTIONAL DEVELOPMENT IN INFANCY?**

The Family	Child Care

Now that we have explored the infant's emotional and personality development and attachment, let's examine the social contexts in which these occur. We begin by studying a number of aspects of the family and then turn to a social context in which infants increasingly spend time—child care.

The Family

The family can be thought of as a constellation of subsystems—a complex whole made up of interrelated, interacting parts—defined in terms of generation, gender, and role. Each family member participates in several subsystems. The father and child represent one subsystem; the mother and father another; the mother-father-child represent yet another; and so on.

These subsystems have reciprocal influences on each other, as Figure 7.8 highlights (Belsky, 1981). For example, Jay Belsky (1981) argues that marital relations, parenting, and infant behavior and development can have both direct and indirect effects on each other. An example of a direct effect is the influence of the parents' behavior on the child. An indirect effect is how the relationship between the spouses mediates the way a parent acts toward the child (Hsu, 2004). For example, marital conflict might reduce the efficiency of parenting, in which case marital conflict would indirectly affect the child's behavior. The simple fact that two people are becoming parents may have profound effects on their relationship.

The Transition to Parenthood   When people become parents through pregnancy, adoption, or stepparenting, they face disequilibrium and must adapt (Heincke, 2002). Parents want to develop a strong attachment with their infant, but they still want to maintain strong attachments to their spouse and friends, and possibly continue their careers. Parents ask themselves how this new being will change their lives. A baby places new restrictions on partners; no longer will they be able to rush out to a movie on a moment's notice, and money may not be readily available for vacations and other luxuries. Dual-career parents ask, "Will it harm the baby to place her in day care? Will we be able to find responsible baby-sitters?"

In a longitudinal investigation of couples from late pregnancy until 3½ years after the baby was born, couples enjoyed more positive marital relations before the baby was born than after (Cowan & Cowan, 2000; Cowan & others, 2005). Still, almost one-third showed an increase in marital satisfaction. Some couples said that the baby had both brought them closer together *and* moved them farther apart. They commented that being parents enhanced their sense of themselves and gave them a new, more stable identity as a couple. Babies opened men up to a concern with intimate relationships, and the demands of juggling work and family roles stimulated women to manage family tasks more efficiently and pay attention to their own personal growth. A study of young African American and Latino couples from 14 and 24 years of age found that fathers and mothers who had positive relationships with their own parents were more likely to show positive adjustment to parenting than their counterparts who had negative relationships with their parents (Florsheim & others, 2003).

The Bringing Home Baby project is a workshop for new parents that emphasizes strengthening the couple's relationship, understanding and becoming acquainted with the baby, resolving conflict, and developing parenting skills. Evaluations of the project revealed that parents who participated improved in their ability to work together as parents, fathers were more involved with their baby and sensitive to the baby's behavior, mothers had a lower incidence of postpartum depression symptoms, and their babies showed better overall development than participants in a control group (Gottman, Shapiro, & Parthemer, 2004; Shapiro & Gottman, 2005).

Reciprocal Socialization   For many years, socialization between parents and children was viewed as a one-way process: children were considered to be the products of their parents' socialization techniques. However, parent-child interaction is reciprocal (Kuczynski & Parkin, 2007; Parke & Buriel, 2006). **Reciprocal socialization** is socialization that is bidirectional. That is, children socialize parents just as parents socialize children. For example, the interaction of mothers and their infants is like a

Children socialize parents just as parents socialize children.

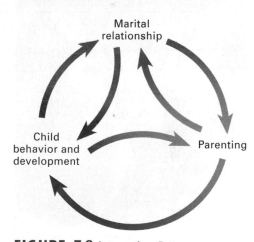

FIGURE 7.8 Interaction Between Children and Their Parents: Direct and Indirect Effects

reciprocal socialization Socialization that is bidirectional; children socialize parents, just as parents socialize children.

Caregivers often play games such as peek-a-boo and pat-a-cake. *How is scaffolding involved in these games?*

dance or a dialogue in which successive actions of the partners are closely coordinated. This coordinated dance or dialogue can assume the form of mutual synchrony in which each person's behavior depends on the partner's previous behavior (Feldman, 2006). Or it can be reciprocal in the sense that actions of the partners are matched, as when one partner imitates the other or when there is mutual smiling.

When reciprocal socialization has been studied in infancy, mutual gaze, or eye contact, plays an important role in early social interaction. In one investigation, the mother and infant engaged in a variety of behaviors while they looked at each other. By contrast, when they looked away from each other, the rate of such behaviors dropped considerably (Stern & others, 1977). In sum, the behaviors of mothers and infants involve substantial interconnection, mutual regulation, and synchronization (Moreno, Posada, & Goldyn, 2006).

An important form of reciprocal socialization is **scaffolding,** in which parents time interactions in such a way that the infant experiences turn-taking with the parents (Field, 2007). Scaffolding involves parental behavior that supports children's efforts, allowing them to be more skillful than they would be if they were to rely only on their own abilities. In using scaffolding, caregivers provide a positive, reciprocal framework in which they and their children interact. For example, in the game peek-a-boo, the mother initially covers the baby. Then she removes the cover and registers "surprise" at the infant's reappearance. As infants become more skilled at peek-a-boo, pat-a-cake, and so on, there are other caregiver games that exemplify scaffolding and turn-taking sequences. In one study, infants who had more extensive scaffolding experiences with their parents (especially in the form of turn-taking) were more likely to engage in turn-taking when they interacted with their peers (Vandell & Wilson, 1988). Engaging in turn-taking and games like peek-a-boo reflects the development of joint attention by the caregiver and infant, which we discussed in Chapter 6 (Meltzoff & Brooks, 2006; Tomasello & Carpenter, 2007).

Maternal and Paternal Caregiving   Although in many developed countries fathers are spending more time with their infants, in most countries, developed and developing, mothers continue to be more involved in caring for their infants than fathers (Parke & Buriel, 2006). Even though most fathers spend less time with their infants than mothers do, can fathers take care of infants as competently as mothers can? Male primates are notoriously low in their interest in offspring, but when forced to live with infants whose female caregivers are absent, the adult male competently rears the infants. Observations of human fathers and their infants suggest that fathers have the ability to act sensitively and responsively with their infants (Parke, 2004; Parke & Buriel, 2006). However, although fathers can be active, nurturant, involved caregivers with their infants, many do not choose to follow this pattern (Connor & White, 2006; Hofferth & Casper, 2006).

The typical father behaves differently toward an infant than the typical mother. Maternal interactions usually center on child-care activities—feeding, changing diapers, bathing. Paternal interactions are more likely to include play (Parke & Buriel, 2006). Fathers engage in more rough-and-tumble play. They bounce infants, throw them up in the air, tickle them, and so on (Lamb, 2000). Mothers do play with infants, but their play is less physical and arousing than that of fathers. Mothers tend to engage in more toy-mediated activities and are more verbal than fathers when interacting with their infants (Parke & Buriel, 2006).

Might the nature of parent-infant interaction be different in families that adopt nontraditional gender roles? This question was investigated by Michael Lamb and his colleagues (1982). They studied Swedish families in which the fathers were the primary caregivers of their firstborn, 8-month-old infants. The mothers were working full-time. In all observations, the mothers were more likely to discipline, hold, soothe, kiss, and talk to the infants than were the fathers. These mothers and fathers dealt with their infants differently, along the lines of American fathers and mothers

scaffolding Parents time interactions so that infants experience turn-taking with the parents.

following traditional gender roles. Having fathers assume the primary caregiving role did not substantially alter the way they interacted with their infants. This may be for biological reasons or because of deeply ingrained socialization patterns in cultures.

Most research that compares mothers' and fathers' parenting styles has not focused on ethnic variations and how acculturated the family is. One recent study examined how mother-infant and father engagement might be linked to infants' cognitive development as a result of acculturation in more than 1,000 Latino families and their 9-month old infants, who were all born in the United States (Cabrera & others, 2006). The majority of the Latino families were Mexican American, but the sample also included families who had come to the United States from the Dominican Republic and Central America. Mother-infant interaction was assessed by videotaping the mother and infant at home, while the mother engaged in a teaching task with the infant. Father engagement was assessed by asking fathers to rate how frequently they participated in three types of activities—literacy, caregiving, and physical play—with their infants. The parents' acculturation was assessed by examining parents' English proficiency, which was assessed by asking them to rate how well they read, write, and understand English. Infants' cognitive test scores were assessed with a shortened version of the Bayley Scales of Infant Development, which were discussed in Chapter 6. When both parents were more proficient at English, mothers had higher maternal-infant interaction scores on the teaching task, and fathers reported being more engaged with their infants. Although the Latino fathers had moderate to high levels of engagement with their infants, which is characteristic of Latino fathers, this did not translate into higher infant cognition scores. However, higher maternal interaction scores on the teaching task were linked to higher infant cognitive development scores.

How do most fathers and mothers interact differently with infants?

Child Care

Many U.S. children today experience multiple caregivers. Most do not have a parent staying home to care for them; instead, the children have some type of care provided by others—"child care." Many parents worry that child care will reduce their infants' emotional attachment to them, retard the infants' cognitive development, fail to teach them how to control anger, and allow them to be unduly influenced by their peers. How extensive is child care? Are the worries of these parents justified?

Parental Leave   Today, far more young children are in child care than at any other time in history. About 2 million children in the United States currently receive formal, licensed child care, and uncounted millions of children are cared for by unlicensed baby-sitters. In part, these numbers reflect the fact that U.S. adults cannot receive paid leave from their jobs to care for their young children. However, as described in the *Diversity in Children's Development* interlude, many countries provide extensive parental leave policies.

Diversity in Children's Development

CHILD-CARE POLICIES AROUND THE WORLD

Sheila Kammerman (1989, 2000a, b) has conducted extensive examinations of parental leave policies around the world. Policies vary in eligibility criteria, leave duration, benefit level, and the extent to which parents take advantage of these policies. Europe led the way in creating new standards of parental leave: The European Union (EU) mandated a paid 14-week maternity leave in 1992. Among advanced

(continued on next page)

How are child-care policies in many European countries, such as Sweden, different than those in the United States?

industrialized countries, the United States grants the shortest period of parental leave and is among the few countries that offers only unpaid leave (Australia and New Zealand are the others).

There are five types of parental leave from employment:

- *Maternity leave.* In some countries, the prebirth leave is compulsory as is a 6- to 10-week leave following birth.
- *Paternity leave.* This is usually much briefer than maternity leave. It may be especially important when a second child is born and the first child requires care.
- *Parental leave.* This gender-neutral leave usually follows a maternity leave and allows either women or men to share the leave policy or choose which of them will use it. In 1998, the European Union mandated a three-month parental leave.
- *Child-rearing leave.* In some countries, this is a supplement to a maternity leave or a variation on a parental leave. A child-rearing leave is usually longer than a maternity leave and is typically paid at a much lower level.
- *Family leave.* This covers reasons other than the birth of a new baby and can allow time off from employment to care for an ill child or other family members, time to accompany a child to school for the first time, or time to visit a child's school.

Sweden has one of the most extensive leave policies. Paid for by the government at 80 percent of wages, one year of parental leave is allowed (including maternity leave). Maternity leave may begin 60 days prior to the expected birth and ends six weeks after birth. Another six months of parental leave can be used until the child's eighth birthday (Kammerman, 2000a). Virtually all eligible mothers take advantage of the leave policy, and approximately 75 percent of eligible fathers take at least some part of their allowed leave. In addition, employed grandparents now have the right to take time off to care for an ill grandchild.

Variations in Child Care Because the United States does not have a policy of paid leave for child care, child care in the United States has become a major national concern (Cabrera, Hutchens, & Peters, 2006; Lamb & Ahnert, 2006). Many factors influence the effects of child care, including the age of the child, the type of child care, and the quality of the program.

The type of child care varies extensively (Lamb & Ahnert, 2006). Child care is provided in large centers with elaborate facilities and in private homes. Some child-care centers are commercial operations; others are nonprofit centers run by churches, civic groups, and employers. Some child-care providers are professionals; others are mothers who want to earn extra money.

Use of different types of child care varies by ethnicity (Johnson & others, 2003). For example, Latino families are far less likely than non-Latino White and African American families to have children in child-care centers (11 percent, 20 percent, and 21 percent, respectively, in one study (Smith, 2002). Despite indicating a preference for center-based care, African American and Latino families often rely on family-based care, especially by grandmothers. However, there has been a substantial increase in the use of center-based care by African American mothers.

The type of child care makes a difference. Researchers have found that children show more stress when they spend long hours in center-based care than in other types of care (Sagi & others, 2002). Further, children who have a fearful or easily frustrated temperament style are often the most negatively influenced by spending long hours in center-based care (Burrous, Crockenberg, & Leekes, 2005).

1. The adult caregivers

• The adults should enjoy and understand how infants and young children grow.

• There should be enough adults to work with a group and to care for the individual needs of children. The recommended ratios of adult caregivers to children of different ages are:

Age of children	Adult to children ratio
0 to 1 Year	1:3
1 to 2 Years	1:5
2 to 3 Years	1:6
3 to 4 Years	1:8
4 to 5 Years	1:10

• Caregivers should observe and record each child's progress and development.

2. The program activities and equipment

• The environment should foster the growth and development of young children working and playing together.

• A good center should provide appropriate and sufficient equipment and play materials and make them readily available.

• Infants and children should be helped to increase their language skills and to expand their understanding of the world.

3. The relation of staff to families and the community

• A good program should consider and support the needs of the entire family. Parents should be welcome to observe, discuss policies, make suggestions, and work in the activities of the center.

• The staff in a good center should be aware of and contribute to community resources. The staff should share information about community recreational and learning opportunities with families.

4. The design of the facility and the program to meet the varied demands of infants and young children, their families, and the staff

• The health of children, staff, and parents should be protected and promoted. The staff should be alert to the health of each child.

• The facility should be safe for children and adults.

• The environment should be spacious enough to accommodate a variety of activities and equipment. More specifically, there should be a minimum of 35 square feet of usable playroom floor space indoors per child and 75 square feet of play space outdoors per child.

FIGURE 7.9 What Is High-Quality Child Care? What constitutes quality child care? These recommendations were made by the National Association for the Education of Young Children. They are based on a consensus arrived at by experts in early childhood education and child development. It is especially important for parents to meet the adults who will care for their child. Caregivers are responsible for every aspect of the program's operation.

Quality also makes a difference. What constitutes a high-quality child-care program for infants? The demonstration program developed by Jerome Kagan and his colleagues (Kagan, Kearsley, & Zelazo, 1978) at Harvard University is exemplary. The child-care center included a pediatrician, a nonteaching director, and an infant-teacher ratio of 3 to 1. Teachers' aides assisted at the center. The teachers and aides were trained to smile frequently, to talk with the infants, and to provide them with a safe environment, which included many stimulating toys. No adverse effects of child care were observed in this project. To read further about what constitutes quality child care, see Figure 7.9.

Children are more likely to experience poor-quality child care if they come from families with few resources (psychological, social, and economic) (Cabrera, Hutchens, & Peters, 2006). Many researchers have examined the role of poverty in quality of child care (Giannarelli, Sonenstein, & Stagner, 2006; Phillips, 2006). One study found that extensive child care was harmful to low-income children only when the care was of low quality (Votrub-Drzal, Coley & Chase-Lansdale, 2004). Even if the child was in child care more than 45 hours a week, high-quality care was linked with fewer internalizing problems (anxiety, for example) and externalizing problems (aggressive and destructive behaviors, for example).

To read about one individual who provides quality child care to individuals from impoverished backgrounds, see the *Careers in Child Development* profile. In the *Research in Children's Development* interlude, you can read about an ongoing national study of child care and its effects.

Careers in CHILD DEVELOPMENT

Rashmi Nakhre
Child-Care Director

Rashmi, Nakhre has two master's degrees—one in psychology, the other in child development—and is director of the Hattie Daniels Day Care Center in Wilson, North Carolina. At a recent ceremony, "Celebrating a Century of Women," Rashmi received the Distinguished Women of North Carolina Award for 1999–2000.

Nakhre first worked at the child-care center soon after she arrived in the United States 25 years ago. She says that she took the job initially because she needed the money but "ended up falling in love with my job." Nakhre has turned the Wilson, North Carolina, child-care center into a model for other centers. The center almost closed several years after Nakhre began working there because of financial difficulties. Nakhre played a major role in raising funds not only to keep it open but to improve it. The center provides quality child care for the children of many Latino migrant workers.

Rashmi Nakhre, working with young children at her child-care center in Wilson, North Carolina.

Research in Children's Development

A NATIONAL LONGITUDINAL STUDY OF CHILD CARE

In 1991, the National Institute of Child Health and Human Development (NICHD) began a comprehensive, longitudinal study of child-care experiences. Data were collected on a diverse sample of almost 1,400 children and their families at 10 locations across the United States over a period of seven years. Researchers used multiple methods (trained observers, interviews, questionnaires, and testing), and they measured many facets of children's development, including physical health, cognitive development, and socioemotional development. Following are some of the results (NICHD Early Child Care Research Network, 2001, 2002, 2003, 2004, 2005, 2006).

- *Patterns of use.* Many families placed their infants in child care very soon after the child's birth, and there was considerable instability in the child-care arrangements. By 4 months of age, nearly three-fourths of the infants had entered some form of nonmaternal child care. Almost half of the infants were cared for by a relative when they first entered care; only 12 percent were enrolled in child-care centers. Socioeconomic factors were linked to the amount and type of care. For example, mothers with higher incomes and families that were more dependent on the mother's income placed their infants in child care at an earlier age. Mothers who believed that maternal employment has positive effects on children were more likely than other mothers to place their infant in nonmaternal care for more hours. Low-income families were more likely than more affluent families to use child care, but infants from low-income families who were in child care averaged as many hours as other income groups. In the preschool years, mothers who were single, those with more education, and families with higher incomes used more hours of center care than other families. Minority families and mothers with less education used more hours of care by relatives.

- *Quality of care.* Evaluations of quality of care were based on such characteristics as group size, child–adult ratio, physical environment, caregiver characteristics (such as formal education, specialized training, and child-care experience), and caregiver behavior (such as sensitivity to children). An alarming conclusion is that a majority of the child care in the first three years of life was of unacceptable low quality. Positive caregiving by nonparents in child-care settings was infrequent—only 12 percent of the children studied experienced positive nonparental child care (such as positive talk, lack of detachment and flat affect, and language stimulation)! Further, infants from low-income families experienced lower quality of child care than infants from higher-income families. When quality of caregivers' care was high, children performed better on cognitive and language tasks, were more cooperative with their mothers during play, showed more positive and skilled interaction with peers, and had fewer behavior problems. Caregiver training and good child–staff ratios were linked with higher cognitive and social competence when children were 54 months of age. Using data collected as part of the NICHD early child-care longitudinal study, a recent analysis indicated that higher-quality early child care, especially at 27 months of age, was linked to children's higher vocabulary scores in the fifth grade (Belsky & others, 2007).

What are some important findings from the National Longitudinal Study of Child Care conducted by the National Institute of Child Health and Human Development?

Higher-quality child care was also related to higher-quality mother-child interaction among the families that used nonmaternal care. Further, poor quality care was related to an increase of insecure attachment to the mother among infants who were 15 months of age, but only when the mother was low in sensitivity and responsiveness. However, child-care quality was not linked to attachment security at 36 months of age.

- *Amount of child care.* The quantity of child care predicted some child outcomes. When children spent extensive amounts of time in child care beginning in infancy, they experienced less sensitive interactions with their mother, showed more behavior problems, and had higher rates of illness (Vandell, 2004). Many of these comparisons involved children in child care for less than 30 hours a week versus those in child care for more than 45 hours a week. In general, though, when children spent 30 hours or more per week in child care, their development was less than optimal (Ramey, 2005).
- *Family and parenting influences.* The influence of families and parenting was not weakened by extensive child care. Parents played a significant role in helping children to regulate their emotions. Especially important parenting influences were being sensitive to children's needs, being involved with children, and cognitively stimulating them.

What are some strategies parents can follow in regard to child care? Child-care expert Kathleen McCartney (2003, p. 4) offered this advice:

- *Recognize that the quality of your parenting is a key factor in your child's development.*
- *Make decisions that will improve the likelihood you will be good parents.* "For some this will mean working full-time"—for personal fulfillment, income, or both. "For others, this will mean working part-time or not working outside the home."

• *Monitor your child's development.* "Parents should observe for themselves whether their children seem to be having behavior problems." They need to talk with child-care providers and their pediatrician about their child's behavior.

• *Take some time to find the best child care.* Observe different child-care facilities and be certain that you like what you see. "Quality child care costs money, and not all parents can afford the child care they want. However, state subsidies, and other programs like Head Start, are available for families in need."

REVIEW AND **REFLECT** ◆ **LEARNING GOAL 3**

3 **Explain how social contexts influence the infant's development.**

Review
• What are some important family processes in infant development?
• How does child care influence infant development?

Reflect
• Imagine that a friend of yours is getting ready to put her baby in child care. What advice would you give to her? Do you think she should stay home with the baby? Why or why not? What type of child care would you recommend?

REACH YOUR LEARNING GOALS

1 HOW DO EMOTIONS AND PERSONALITY DEVELOP IN INFANCY? *Discuss emotional and personality development in infancy.*

Emotional Development

- Emotion is feeling, or affect, that occurs when a person is in a state or an interaction that is important to them. Emotion is characterized by behavior that reflects (expresses) the pleasantness or unpleasantness of the person's state or the transaction being experienced. Psychologists believe that emotions, especially facial expressions of emotions, have a biological foundation. Biological evolution endowed humans to be emotional, but embeddedness in culture and relationships provides diversity in emotional experiences. Emotions play key roles in parent-child relationships. Infants display a number of emotions early in their development, although researchers debate the onset and sequence of these emotions. Lewis distinguishes between primary emotions and self-conscious emotions. Crying is the most important mechanism newborns have for communicating with their world. Babies have at least three types of cries—basic, anger, and pain cries. Controversy swirls about whether babies should be soothed when they cry, although increasingly experts recommend immediately responding in a caring way in the first year. Social smiling occurs as early as 2 months of age. Two fears that infants develop are stranger anxiety and separation from a caregiver (which is reflected in separation protest). As infants develop, it is important for them to engage in emotional regulation.

Temperament

- Temperament is an individual's behavioral style and characteristic way of emotional responding. Chess and Thomas classified infants as (1) easy, (2) difficult, or (3) slow to warm up. Kagan proposed that inhibition to the unfamiliar is an important temperament category. Rothbart and Bates' view of temperament emphasizes this classification: (1) extraversion/surgency, (2) negative affectivity, and (3) effortful control (self-regulation). Physiological characteristics are associated with different temperaments. Children inherit a physiology that biases them to have a particular type of temperament, but through experience they learn to modify their temperament style to some degree. Goodness of fit refers to the match between a child's temperament and the environmental demands the child must cope with. Goodness of fit can be an important aspect of a child's adjustment. Although research evidence is sketchy at this point in time, some general recommendations are that caregivers should (1) be sensitive to the individual characteristics of the child, (2) be flexible in responding to these characteristics, and (3) avoid negative labeling of the child.

Personality Development

- Erikson argued that an infant's first year is characterized by the stage of trust versus mistrust. A rudimentary form of self-recognition occurs as early as 3 months of age, but the infant develops a more complete, central form of self recognition at about 18 months of age. Independence becomes a central theme in the second year of life. Mahler argues that the infant separates herself from her mother and then develops individuation. Erikson stressed that the second year of life is characterized by the stage of autonomy versus shame and doubt.

2   HOW DO SOCIAL ORIENTATION/UNDERSTANDING AND ATTACHMENT DEVELOP IN INFANCY? *Describe social orientation/understanding and the development of attachment in infancy.*

Social Orientation/ Understanding

- Infants show a strong interest in the social world and are motivated to understand it. Infants orient to the social world early in their development. Face-to-face play with a caregiver begins to occur at 2 to 3 months of age. Newly developed self-produced locomotion skills significantly expand the infant's ability to initiate social interchanges and explore their social world more independently. Perceiving people as engaging in intentional and goal-directed behavior is an important social cognitive accomplishment, and this occurs toward the end of the first year. Social referencing increases in the second year of life.

Attachment and Its Development

- Attachment is a close emotional bond between two people. In infancy, contact comfort and trust are important in the development of attachment. Bowlby's ethological theory stresses that the caregiver and the infant are biologically predisposed to form an attachment. Attachment develops in four phases during infancy.

Individual Differences in Attachment

- Securely attached babies use the caregiver, usually the mother, as a secure base from which to explore the environment. Three types of insecure attachment are avoidant, resistant, and disorganized. Ainsworth created the Strange Situation, an observational measure of attachment. Ainsworth maintains that secure attachment in the first year of life provides an important foundation for psychological development later in life. The strength of the link between early attachment and later development has varied somewhat across studies. Some critics argue that attachment theorists have not given adequate attention to genetics and temperament. Other critics stress that they have not adequately taken into account the diversity of social agents and contexts. Cultural variations in attachment have been found, but in all cultures studied to date secure attachment is the most common classification.

Caregiving Styles and Attachment

- Caregivers of secure babies are sensitive to the babies' signals and are consistently available to meet their needs. Caregivers of avoidant babies tend to be unavailable or rejecting. Caregivers of resistant babies tend to be inconsistently available to their babies and usually are not very affectionate. Caregivers of disorganized babies often neglect or physically abuse their babies.

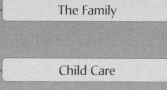

3 How Do Social Contexts Influence Socioemotional Development in Infancy? *Explain how social contexts influence the infant's development.*

The Family

Child Care

- The transition to parenthood requires considerable adaptation and adjustment on the part of parents. Children socialize parents just as parents socialize children. Mutual regulation and scaffolding are important aspects of reciprocal socialization. Belsky's model describes direct and indirect effects. The mother's primary role when interacting with the infant is caregiving; the father's is playful interaction.

- More U.S. children are in child care now than at any earlier point in history. The quality of child care is uneven, and child care remains a controversial topic. Quality child care can be achieved and seems to have few adverse effects on children. In the NICHD child-care study, infants from low-income families were more likely to receive the lowest quality of care. Also, higher quality of child care was linked with fewer child problems.

KEY TERMS

emotion 217
primary emotions 218
self-conscious emotions 218
basic cry 219
anger cry 219
pain cry 219
reflexive smile 219

social smile 219
stranger anxiety 219
separation protest 220
temperament 221
easy child 221
difficult child 221
slow-to-warm-up child 221

goodness of fit 223
social referencing 228
attachment 228
Strange Situation 229
securely attached babies 230
insecure avoidant babies 230
insecure resistant babies 230

insecure disorganized babies 230
reciprocal socialization 233
scaffolding 234

KEY PEOPLE

Michael Lewis 218
Joseph Campos 218
John Bowlby 219
John Watson 220
Jacob Gewirtz 220

Mary Ainsworth 220
Alexander Chess and Stella Thomas 221
Jerome Kagan 221

Mary Rothbart and John Bates 222
Erik Erikson 224
Ross Thompson 225

Margaret Mahler 225
Harry Harlow 228
Jay Belsky 233
Kathleen McCartney 239

MAKING A DIFFERENCE

Nurturing the Infant's Socioemotional Development

What are the best ways to help the infant develop socioemotional competencies?

- *Develop a secure attachment with the infant.* Infants need the warmth and support of one or more caregivers. The caregiver(s) should be sensitive to the infant's signals and respond nurturantly.
- *Be sure that both the mother and the father nurture the infant.* Infants develop best when both the mother and the father provide warm, nurturant support. Fathers need to seriously evaluate their responsibility in rearing a competent infant.
- *Select competent child care.* If the infant will be placed in child care, spend time evaluating different options. Be sure the infant–caregiver ratio is low. Also assess whether the adults enjoy and are knowledgeable about interacting with infants. Determine if the facility is safe and provides stimulating activities.

- *Understand and respect the infant's temperament.* Be sensitive to the characteristics of each child. It may be necessary to provide extra support for distress-prone infants, for example. Avoid negative labeling of the infant.
- *Adapt to developmental changes in the infant.* An 18-month-old toddler is very different from a 6-month-old infant. Be knowledgeable about how infants develop, and adapt to the changing infant. Let toddlers explore a wider but safe environment.
- *Be physically and mentally healthy.* Infants' socioemotional development benefits when their caregivers are physically and mentally healthy. For example, a depressed parent may not sensitively respond to the infant's signals.
- *Read a good book on infant development.* Any of T. Berry Brazelton's books are a good start. One is *Touchpoints.* Two other good books by other authors are *Infancy* by Tiffany Field and *Baby Steps* by Claire Kopp.

RESOURCES FOR IMPROVING CHILDREN'S LIVES

The Happiest Baby on the Block

by Harvey Karp (2002).
New York: Bantam

An outstanding book on ways to calm a crying baby.

Touchpoints Birth to 3

by T. Berry Brazelton and Joshua Sparrow (2006).
Cambridge, MA: Da Capo Press

Covering the period from birth through age 3, Brazelton and Sparrow focus on the concerns and questions parents have about the child's feelings, behavior, and development.

E-LEARNING TOOLS

Connect to **www.mhhe.com/santrockc10** to research the answers and complete these exercises. In addition, you'll find a number of other resources and valuable study tools for Chapter 7, "Socioemotional Development in Infancy," on this Web site.

Taking It to the Net

1. Catherine is conducting a class for new parents at a local clinic. What advice should Catherine give the parents about how parenting practices can affect a child's inborn temperament?

2. Peter and Rachel are adopting a 3-month-old infant. What are some practical things they can do to help ensure that their child develops a healthy attachment bond with them, in spite of not being with them in the first few months of life?

3. Veronica is anxious about choosing the best child-care center for her child. What are the main things she should consider as she visits the facilities on her list?

Health and Well-Being, Parenting, and Education

Build your decision-making skills by trying your hand at the health and well-being, parenting, and education exercises.

Video Chips

The Online Learning Center includes the following videos for this chapter:

1. *Sex-Typed play at Age 1—2*
   A 1-year-old girl is shown in a room surrounded by an assortment of toys. She only shows interest in the Barbie dolls, which she examines carefully from every angle.

2. *Attachment Theory—300*
   Renowned attachment researcher L. Alan Sroufe defines attachment theory and how it relates to children's social and emotional development. He states that attachment theory led to a revolution in developmental psychology. He uses examples from his own research to illustrate the significance of attachment relationships.

3. *Philosophy of Preschool Teaching—1018*
   A head teacher of a 4- year-old classroom describes her "whole child" philosophy to teaching young children.

4. *Daycare Environment at 3-Years—225*
   In this clip, we see 3-year-old Josh outside during pre-school. With the guidance of his teacher he is making a necklace out of cereal, which they discuss as he works.

Section Four
EARLY CHILDHOOD

You are troubled at seeing him spend his early years doing nothing. What! Is it nothing to be happy? Is it nothing to skip, to play, to run about all day long? Never in his life will he be so busy as now.

—JEAN-JACQUES ROUSSEAU
Swiss-Born French Philosopher, 18th Century

In early childhood, our greatest untold poem was being only 4 years old. We skipped and ran and played all the sun long, never in our lives so busy, busy being something we had not quite grasped yet. Who knew our thoughts, which we worked up into small mythologies all our own? Our thoughts and images and drawings took wings. The blossoms of our heart, no wind could touch. Our small world widened as we discovered new refuges and new people. When we said, "I," we meant something totally unique, not to be confused with any other. Section 4 consists of three chapters: "Physical Development in Early Childhood" (Chapter 8,) "Cognitive Development in Early Childhood" (Chapter 9), and "Socioemotional Development in Early Childhood" (Chapter 10).

The greatest person ever known
Is one all poets have outgrown;
The poetry, innate and untold,
Of being only four years old.

—CHRISTOPHER MORLEY
American Novelist, 20th Century

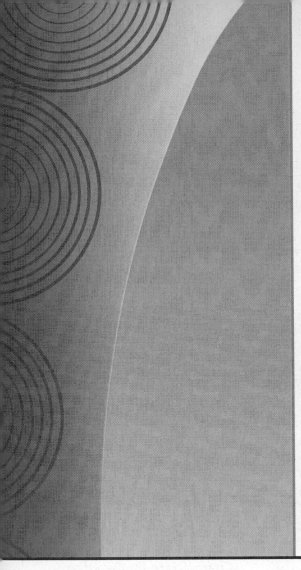

Images of Children's Development
The Story of Teresa Amabile and Her Art

Teresa Amabile remembers that, when she was in kindergarten, she rushed in every day, excited and enthusiastic about getting to the easel and painting with bright colors and big brushes. Children in Teresa's class had free access to a clay table with all kinds of art materials on it. Teresa remembers going home every day and telling her mother she wanted to draw and paint. Teresa's kindergarten experience, unfortunately, was the high point of her enthusiasm for art classes in school.

A description of Teresa's further childhood experiences with art and creativity follows (Goleman, Kaufman, & Ray, 2003, p. 60):

> The next year she entered a strict, traditional school, and things began to change. As she tells it, "Instead of having free access to art materials every day, art became just another subject, something you had for an hour and a half every Friday afternoon."
>
> Week after week, all through elementary school, it was the same art class. And a very restricted, even demoralizing one at that.

The children were not given any help in developing their skills. Also, the teacher graded the children on the art they produced, adding evaluation pressure to the situation. Teresa was aware at that time that her motivation for doing artwork was being completely destroyed. In her words, "I no longer wanted to go home at the end of the day and take out my art materials and draw or paint."

In spite of the negative instruction imposed upon her in art classes, Teresa Amabile continued her education and eventually obtained a Ph.D. in psychology. Due, in part, to her positive experiences in kindergarten, she became one of the leading researchers on creativity. Her hope is that more elementary schools will not crush children's enthusiasm for creativity, the way hers did. So many young children, like Teresa, are excited about exploring and creating, but, by the time they reach the third or fourth grade, many don't like school, let alone have any sense of pleasure in their own creativity.

PREVIEW

As twentieth-century Welsh poet Dylan Thomas artfully observed, young children do "run all the sun long." And as their physical development advances, young children's small worlds widen. We begin this chapter by examining how young children's bodies grow and change. Then we discuss the development of young children's motor skills and conclude by exploring important aspects of their health.

1 HOW DOES A YOUNG CHILD'S BODY AND BRAIN GROW AND CHANGE?

Height and Weight	The Brain	Vision

growth hormone deficiency The absence or deficiency of growth hormone produced by the pituitary gland to stimulate the body to grow.

In this section, we examine the height and weight changes for boys and girls in early childhood along with individual growth patterns. In addition, we look at how the brain and nervous system continue to develop, the expansion of young children's cognitive abilities, and how their visual acuity and depth perception continue to mature.

Height and Weight

Remember from Chapter 5, "Physical Development in Infancy," that the infant's growth in the first year is rapid. During the infant's second year, the growth rate begins to slow down, and the growth rate continues to slow in early childhood. Otherwise, we would be a species of giants. The average child grows 2½ inches in height and gains between 5 and 7 pounds a year during early childhood. As the preschool child grows older, the percentage of increase in height and weight decreases with each additional year. Figure 8.1 shows the average height and weight of children as they age from 2 to 6 years (Centers for Disease Control and Prevention, 2000). Girls are only slightly smaller and lighter than boys during these years, a difference that continues until puberty. During the preschool years, both boys and girls slim down as the trunks of their bodies lengthen. Although their heads are still somewhat large for their bodies, by the end of the preschool years most children have lost their top-heavy look. Body fat also shows a slow, steady decline during the preschool years. The chubby baby often looks much leaner by the end of early childhood. Girls have more fatty tissue than boys, and boys have more muscle tissue.

Growth patterns vary individually. Think back to your elementary school years. This was probably the first time you noticed that some children were taller than you, some shorter; some were stronger, some weaker. Much of the variation is due to heredity, but environmental experiences are involved to some extent. A review of the height and weight of children around the world concluded that the two most important contributors to height differences are ethnic origin and nutrition (Meredith, 1978). The urban, middle-socioeconomic-status, and firstborn children were taller than rural, lower-socioeconomic status, and later-born children. The children whose mothers smoked during pregnancy were half an inch shorter than the children whose mothers did not smoke during pregnancy. In the United States, African American children are taller than non-Latino White children.

Why are some children unusually short? The primary contributing influences are congenital factors (genetic or prenatal problems), growth hormone deficiency, a physical problem that develops in childhood, maternal smoking during pregnancy, or an emotional difficulty. Chronically sick children are shorter than their rarely sick counterparts. Children who have been physically abused or neglected may not secrete adequate growth hormone, which can restrict their physical growth.

Growth hormone deficiency is the absence or deficiency of growth hormone produced by the pituitary gland to stimulate the body to grow. Growth hormone deficiency may occur during infancy or later in childhood (Schwenk, 2006). As many as 10,000 to 15,000 U.S. children may have growth hormone deficiency (Stanford University Medical Center, 2007). Without treatment, most children with growth hormone deficiency will not reach a height of five feet. Treatment involves regular injections of growth hormone and usually lasts several years (Rosilio & others, 2005). Some children receive daily injections, others several times a week. Twice as many boys as girls are treated with growth hormone (Lee & Howell, 2006).

There has been a significant increase in treating short children with growth hormone therapy (Hindmarsh & Dattani, 2006). Some medical experts have expressed concern that many young children are being treated with growth hormone therapy who are merely short but don't have a growth hormone deficiency (Allen, 2006; Dunkel, 2006). In such cases, parents often perceive that there is a handicap in being short, especially in boys (Visser-van Balen, Sinnema, & Geenen, 2006).

Few studies have been conducted on the psychological and social outcomes of having a short stature in childhood. Most of those that have been carried out find little or no difference in the psychological and social functioning of short children and children who are average in height or tall (Sandberg & Colsman, 2005). For example, a research review found that although children with short stature on

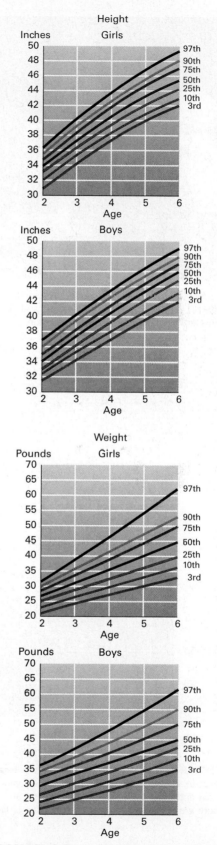

FIGURE 8.1 Height and Weight Changes from 2 Through 6 Years of Age These graphs show the percentiles of height and weight for boys and girls from 2 through 6 years of age in the United States.

The bodies of 5-year-olds and 2-year-olds are different. Notice that the 5-year-old not only is taller and weighs more but also has a longer trunk and legs than the 2-year-old. *Can you think of some other physical differences between 2- and 5-year-olds?*

average score lower than children of normal or tall stature on tests of motor skills, intelligence, and achievement, few short children score outside the normal range for these skills (Wheeler & others, 2004). One study of short children who were followed for 13 years found that they had normal psychological and social functioning (Voss, 2006), whereas another study revealed that short children are more likely to be teased (Visser-Van Balen, Sinnema, & Geenen, 2006).

The Brain

One of the most important physical developments during early childhood is the continuing development of the brain and nervous system (Durston & Casey, 2006; Nelson, Thomas, & de Haan, 2006). Although the brain continues to grow in early childhood, it does not grow as rapidly as in infancy. By the time children reach 3 years of age, the brain is three-quarters of its adult size. By age 6, the brain has reached about 95 percent of its adult volume (Lenroot & Giedd, 2006). Thus, the brain of a 5-year-old is nearly the size it will be when the child reaches adulthood, but as we see in later chapters, the development that occurs inside the brain continues through the remaining childhood and adolescent years.

The brain and the head grow more rapidly than any other part of the body. The top parts of the head, the eyes, and the brain grow faster than the lower portions, such as the jaw. Figure 8.2 reveals how the growth curve for the head and brain advances more rapidly than the growth curve for height and weight. At 5 years of age, when the brain has attained approximately 90 percent of its adult weight, the 5-year-old's total body weight is only about one-third of what it will be when the child reaches adulthood.

Neuronal Changes   In Chapters 3 and 5, we discussed the brain's development during the prenatal and infancy periods. Changes in neurons in early childhood involve connections between neurons and myelination, just as they did in infancy. Communication in the brain is characterized by the transmission of information between neurons, or nerve cells. Some of the brain's increase in size during early childhood is due to the increase in the number and size of nerve endings and receptors, which allows more effective communication to occur.

Neurons communicate with each other through *neurotransmitters* (chemical substances) that carry information across gaps (called *synapses*) between the neurons. One neurotransmitter that has been shown to increase substantially in the 3- to 6-year age period is *dopamine* (Diamond, 2001). We return to a discussion of dopamine later in this section.

Some of the brain's increase in size also is due to the increase in **myelination,** in which nerve cells are covered and insulated with a layer of fat cells (see Figure 8.3). This has the effect of increasing the speed and efficiency of information traveling through the nervous system (Jelacic, de Regt, & Weinberger, 2006). Myelination is important in the development of a number of children's abilities (Nelson, Thomas, & de Haan, 2006). For example, myelination in the areas of the brain related to hand-eye coordination is not complete until about 4 years of age. One recent fMRI study of children (mean age: 4 years) found that children with developmental delay of motor and cognitive milestones had significantly reduced levels of myelination (Pujol & others, 2004). Myelination in the areas of the brain related to focusing attention is not complete until the end of the middle or late childhood.

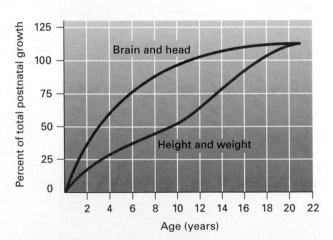

FIGURE 8.2 Growth Curves for the Head and Brain and for Height and Weight The more rapid growth of the brain and head can easily be seen. Height and weight advance more gradually over the first two decades of life.

myelination The process in which the nerve cells are covered and insulated with a layer of fat cells, which increases the speed at which information travels through the nervous system.

Structural Changes   Until recently, scientists lacked adequate technology to detect sensitive changes and view detailed maps of the developing human brain.

However, sophisticated brain-scanning techniques, such as magnetic resonance imaging (MRI), now allow us to better detect these changes (Lenroot & Giedd, 2006; Toga, Thompson, & Sowell, 2006). With high-resolution MRI, scientists have evolved spatially complex, four-dimensional growth pattern maps of the developing brain, allowing the brain to be mapped with greater sensitivity than ever before. Using these techniques, scientists have discovered that children's brains undergo dramatic anatomical changes between the ages of 3 and 15 (Thompson & others, 2000). By repeatedly obtaining brain scans of the same children for up to four years, they found that the children's brains experience rapid, distinct spurts of growth. The amount of brain material in some areas can nearly double within as little as a year, followed by a drastic loss of tissue as unneeded cells are purged and the brain continues to reorganize itself. The scientists found that the overall size of the brain did not show dramatic growth in the 3- to 15-year age range. However, what did dramatically change were local patterns within the brain.

Researchers have found that from 3 to 6 years of age, the most rapid growth takes place in the frontal lobe areas involved in planning and organizing new actions, and in maintaining attention to tasks. They have discovered that from age 6 through puberty, the most growth takes place in the temporal and parietal lobes, especially areas that play major roles in language and spatial relations.

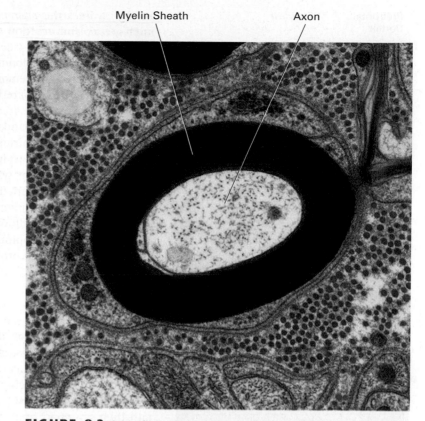

Myelin Sheath   Axon

FIGURE 8.3 **A Myelinated Nerve Fiber** The myelin sheath, shown in brown, encases the axon (white). This image was produced by an electron microscope that magnified the nerve fiber 12,000 times. *What role does myelination play in the brain's development and children's cognition?*

The Brain and Cognitive Development

The substantial increases in memory and rapid learning that characterize infants and young children are related to cell loss, synaptic growth, and myelination (Craik, 2006; Lenroot & Giedd, 2006). Somewhat amazingly, neuroscientists have found that the density of synapses peaks at 4 years of age (Lenroot & Giedd, 2006). Some leading cognitive scientists argue that the true episodic memory (memory for the when and where of life's happenings, such as remembering what one had for breakfast this morning) and self-awareness do not develop until about this time (4 years of age) (Craik, 2006). However, recall from Chapters 6 and 7 that some infant development researchers conclude that episodic memory and self-awareness emerge in infancy (Bauer, 2007, 2008).

These aspects of the brain's maturation, combined with opportunities to experience a widening world, contribute to children's emerging cognitive abilities. Consider a child who is learning to read and is asked by a teacher to read aloud to the class. Input from the child's eyes is transmitted to the child's brain, then passed through many brain systems, which translate (process) the patterns of black and white into codes for letters, words, and associations. The output occurs in the form of messages to the child's lips and tongue. The child's own gift of speech is possible because brain systems are organized in ways that permit language processing.

The brain is organized according to many neural circuits, which are neural networks composed of many neurons with certain functions. One neural circuit is thought to have an important function in the development of attention and working memory (a type of short-term memory that is like a mental workbench in performing many cognitive tasks) (Kramer & Goldman-Rakic, 2001). This neural

Prefrontal Cortex   Side view

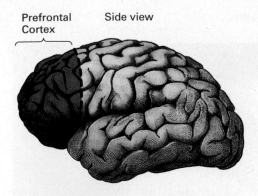

Frontal view

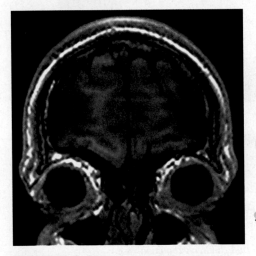

FIGURE 8.4 The Prefrontal Cortex The prefrontal cortex, the highest level in the brain, shows extensive development from 3 to 6 years of age, and as will be seen in later chapters, continues to grow through the remainder of the child and adolescent years. The prefrontal cortex plays important roles in attention, memory, and self-regulation. The top image shows a side view of the location of the prefrontal cortex. The bottom image (frontal view) is a composite of more than 100 fMRI images of the prefrontal cortex that were taken to assess individuals' speed of processing information under different conditions.

functional amblyopia An vision problem that results from not using one eye enough to avoid the discomfort of double vision produced by imbalanced eye muscles; "lazy eye."

strabismus A misalignment of the eyes in which they do not point at the same object together; crossed eyes are one type of strabismus.

circuit involves the *prefrontal cortex*, and the neurotransmitter dopamine may be a key aspect of information transmission in the prefrontal cortex and this neural circuit (Diamond, 2001) (see Figure 8.4). The maturation of the prefrontal cortex is important in the development of a number of cognitive and socioemotional skills, including attention, memory, and self-regulation (Durston & Casey, 2006).

In sum, scientists are beginning to chart connections between children's cognitive development in areas such as attention and memory, brain regions such as the prefrontal cortex, and the transmission of information at the level of the neuron such as the neurotransmitter dopamine (Nelson, Thomas, & de Haan, 2006). As advancements in technology allow scientists to "look inside" the brain to observe its activity, we will likely see an increased precision in our understanding of the brain's functioning in various aspects of cognitive development. Recently, the development of a technique called *diffusion tension imaging (DTI)*, a variation of MRI, is allowing neuroscientists to study more microstructural features of brain development in infants and children (Mukherjee & McKinstry, 2006). DTI especially provides improved imaging of the development of axons and myelination.

Vision

Visual maturity increases during the early childhood years. Only toward the end of early childhood are most children's eye muscles adequately developed to allow them to move their eyes efficiently across a series of letters. And preschool children are often farsighted, not being able to see up close as well as they can far away. By the time they enter the first grade, though, most children can focus their eyes and sustain their attention quite well (Dutton, 2003).

Depth perception continues to mature during the preschool years. However, because of young children's lack of motor coordination, they may trip and spill drinks, fall from a jungle gym, or have difficulty drawing straight lines.

What signs suggest that a child might be having vision problems and should be seen by an ophthalmologist? They include the appearance of the eyes (unusual redness of eyes or lids, crusted eyelids, styes or sores on lids, excessive tearing, unusual lid droopiness, or one eye turns in or out with fatigue) and evidence of discomfort (excessive rubbing of eyes, avoids bright light, or keeps eyes closed much of the time). In early elementary school, when children are learning to read, their eyes should be checked if they are having difficulty learning to read, if they squint at the chalkboard, or if they cover or close one eye while reading (Ip & others, 2006).

Normally, a child's eyes should be carefully examined in infancy, and children should receive regular vision screening beginning at age 3 (Adler & Millodot, 2006). Functional amblyopia and strabismus are two vision problems, which if detected and treated prior to the age of 6, can prevent the loss of vision.

Functional amblyopia, or "lazy eye," usually results from not using one eye enough to avoid the discomfort of double vision produced by imbalanced eye muscles (Anderson & Swettenham, 2006; Kim & others, 2005). Children with a lazy eye have no way of knowing that they are not seeing adequately, even though their vision is decreased because one eye is doing most of the work. Treatment may include patching the stronger eye for several months to encourage the use of the affected eye, wearing glasses, or doing eye exercises (Wyganski-Jaffe, 2005). Occasionally, surgery may be required on the muscles of the eye (Levenger & others, 2006).

Strabismus involves a misalignment of the eyes in which they do not point at the same object together. Crossed eyes are one type of strabismus (Kushner, 2006). Contact lenses may work effectively with certain kinds of strabismus. Some eye care professionals also use vision therapy to treat strabismus, in which the eyes are trained to be straight, using exercises and computerized stimulation techniques.

REVIEW AND REFLECT ▶ LEARNING GOAL 1

1 **Discuss growth and change in the young child's body and brain.**

Review
- What changes in height and weight characterize early childhood?
- How does the brain change in young children?
- What changes occur in vision in young children? What are some visual problems that can develop?

Reflect
- Think back to when you were a young child. How would you characterize your body growth? Was your growth about the same as most children your age or was it different?

2 HOW DO YOUNG CHILDREN'S MOTOR SKILLS DEVELOP?

Gross and Fine Motor Skills	Young Children's Artistic Drawings	Handedness

Running as fast as you can, falling down, getting right back up and running just as fast as you can . . . building towers with blocks . . . scribbling, scribbling, and scribbling some more . . . cutting paper with scissors. During your preschool years, you probably developed the ability to perform all of these activities.

Gross and Fine Motor Skills

Considerable progress is made in both gross and fine motor skills during early childhood. Young children develop a sense of mastery through increased proficiency in gross motor skills such as walking and running. Improvement in fine motor skills—such as being able to turn the pages of a book, one at a time—also contributes to the child's sense of mastery in the second year. First, let's explore changes in gross motor skills.

Gross Motor Skills The preschool child no longer has to make an effort simply to stay upright and to move around. As children move their legs with more confidence and carry themselves more purposefully, moving around in the environment becomes more automatic (Poest & others, 1990).

At 3 years of age, children enjoy simple movements, such as hopping, jumping, and running back and forth, just for the sheer delight of performing these activities. They take considerable pride in showing how they can run across a room and jump all of 6 inches. The run-and-jump will win no Olympic gold medals, but for the 3-year-old the activity is a source of considerable pride and accomplishment.

At 4 years of age, children are still enjoying the same kind of activities, but they have become more adventurous. They scramble over low jungle gyms as they display their athletic prowess. Although they have been able to climb stairs with one foot on each step for some time, they are just beginning to be able to come down the same way. They still often revert to putting two feet on each step.

At 5 years of age, children are even more adventuresome than when they were 4. It is not unusual for self-assured 5-year-olds to perform hair-raising stunts on practically any climbing object. Five-year-olds run hard and enjoy races with each other and their parents. A summary of development in gross motor skills during early childhood is shown in Figure 8.5.

37 to 48 Months

Throws ball underhanded (4 feet)
Pedals tricycle 10 feet
Catches large ball
Completes forward somersault (aided)
Jumps to floor from 12 inches
Hops three hops with both feet
Steps on footprint pattern
Catches bounced ball

49 to 60 Months

Bounces and catches ball
Runs 10 feet and stops
Pushes/pulls a wagon/doll buggy
Kicks 10-inch ball toward target
Carries 12-pound object
Catches ball
Bounces ball under control
Hops on one foot four hops

61 to 72 Months

Throws ball (44 feet, boys; 25 feet, girls)
Carries a 16-pound object
Kicks rolling ball
Skips alternating feet
Roller skates
Skips rope
Rolls ball to hit object
Rides bike with training wheels

FIGURE 8.5 The Development of Gross Motor Skills in Early Childhood The skills are listed in the approximate order of difficulty within each age period.

You probably have arrived at one important conclusion about preschool children: they are very, very active. Indeed, 3-year-old children have the highest activity level of any age in the entire human life span. They fidget when they watch television. They fidget when they sit at the dinner table. Even when they sleep, they move around quite a bit. Because of their activity level and the development of large muscles, especially in the arms and legs, preschool children need daily exercise.

It is important for preschool and kindergarten teachers to develop programs that encourage young children's gross motor skills (Gallahue & Ozmun, 2006; Goodway & Branta, 2003). Catherine Poest and her colleagues (1990) provided some valuable suggestions for such programs. One set of their recommendations involves developing fundamental movement skills. Careful planning is needed to ensure that a variety of motor activities appropriate to the ages and individual skills of children are provided. Beam walking is one activity that can be used. The variety of balance beam pathways helps meet the individual motor needs of young children. Challenge children to walk the beams in different directions or walk while balancing bean bags on different body parts. Decrease the width of the beams, raise the height, or set up the beams on an incline.

Competent teachers of young children also plan daily fitness activities (Frost & others, 2001). They include a daily run or gallop to music. Children love to run and get to do so too infrequently in early childhood education centers and at home. Several fast-paced fitness activities can be planned over the school year. Combine fitness with creative movement, music, and children's imaginations. Children enjoy moving like snakes, cats, bears, elephants, dinosaurs, frogs, kangaroos, seals, conductors and trains, police and police cars, pilots and airplanes, washing machines, and teeter-totters. Avoid recordings or activities that "program" children or that include group calisthenics and structured exercise routines that are not appropriate for young children.

The development of young children's gross motor skills also includes perceptual-motor activities. Teachers can ask children to copy their movements, such as putting hands on toes, hands on head, or hands on stomach. These activities help children learn body awareness and visual awareness. As the year progresses, teachers can gradually increase the difficulty of these exercises by touching body parts more difficult to name and locate (such as shoulders and elbows) (Weikart, 1987). They also can provide children with many opportunities to move to a steady beat. Children can tap and march to the tune of nursery rhymes, chants, songs, and parades. Obstacle courses are enjoyable activities for children and help them understand directions in space such as "over," "under," "around," and "through," as well as help them practice moving through space without touching any of the obstacles.

Designing and implementing a developmentally appropriate (one that's appropriate for the child's age and the child individually) movement curriculum takes time and effort. Although time consuming, such a curriculum facilitates the development of children's gross motor skills. To read further about supporting young children's motor development, see the *Caring for Children* interlude.

Caring for Children

SUPPORTING YOUNG CHILDREN'S MOTOR DEVELOPMENT

If you observe young children, you will see that they spend a great deal of time engaging in such motor activities as running, jumping, throwing, and catching. These activities can form the basis of advanced, sports-related skills. For children to progress to effective, coordinated, and controlled motor performance, interaction with, and instruction from, supportive adults can be beneficial.

How can early childhood educators support young children's motor development? When planning physical instruction for young children, it is important to keep in mind that their attention span is rather short, so instruction should be brief and to the point. Young children need to practice skills in order to learn them, so instruction should be followed with ample time for practice (Thompson, 2006).

Fitness is an important dimension of people's lives, and it is beneficial to develop a positive attitude toward it early. Preschoolers need vigorous activities for short periods of time. They can be encouraged to rest or change to a quieter activity as needed.

Movement, even within the classroom, can improve a child's stamina. Such movement activities might be as basic as practicing locomotor skills or as complex as navigating an obstacle course. A number of locomotor skills (such as walking, running, jumping, sliding, skipping, and leaping) can be practiced forward and backward. And it is important to keep practice fun, allowing children to enjoy movement for the sheer pleasure of it (Sutterby & Frost, 2006).

There can be long-term negative effects for children who fail to develop basic motor skills (Edwards & Sarwark, 2005). These children will not be as able to join in group games or participate in sports during their school years and in adulthood. However, the positive development of motor skills has other benefits besides participation in games and sports. Engaging in motor skills fulfills young children's needs and desires for movement, and exercise builds muscles, strengthens the heart, and enhances aerobic capacity.

What are some effective strategies for supporting young children's motor development?

Fine Motor Skills   At 3 years of age, children show a more mature ability to place and handle things than when they were infants. Although they have had the ability to pick up the tiniest objects between their thumb and forefinger for some time, they are still somewhat clumsy at it. Three-year-olds can build surprisingly high block towers, each block placed with intense concentration but often not in a completely straight line. When 3-year-olds play with a form board or a simple jigsaw puzzle, they are rather rough in placing the pieces. Even when they recognize the hole a piece fits into, they are not very precise in positioning the piece. They often try to force the piece in the hole or pat it vigorously.

By 4 years of age, children's fine motor coordination has improved substantially and is more precise. Sometimes 4-year-old children have trouble building high towers with blocks because in their desire to place each of the blocks perfectly, they may upset those already stacked. By age 5, children's fine motor coordination has improved. Hand, arm, and body all move together under better command of the eye. Mere towers no longer interest the 5-year-old, who now wants to build a house or a church, complete with steeple, though adults may still need to be told what each finished project is meant to be. A summary of the development of fine motor skills in early childhood is shown in Figure 8.6.

37 to 48 Months	49 to 60 Months	61 to 72 Months
Approximates a circle in drawing	Strings and laces shoelace	Folds paper into halves and quarters
Cuts paper	Cuts following a line	Traces around hand
Pastes using pointer finger	Strings 10 beads	Draws rectangle, circle, square, and triangle
Builds three-block bridge	Copies figure X	Cuts interior piece from paper
Builds eight-block tower	Opens and places clothespins (one-handed)	Uses crayons appropriately
Draws 0 and +	Builds a five-block bridge	Makes clay object with two small parts
Dresses and undresses doll	Pours from various containers	Reproduces letters
Pours from pitcher without spilling	Prints first name	Copies two short words

FIGURE 8.6 The Development of Fine Motor Skills in Early Childhood *Note:* The skills are listed in the approximate order of difficulty within each age period.

How do developmentalists measure children's motor development? The **Denver Developmental Screening Test** is a simple, inexpensive, fast method of diagnosing developmental delay in children from birth through 6 years of age. The test is individually administered and includes separate assessments of gross and fine motor skills, as well as language and personal-social ability (Brachlow, Jordan, & Tervo, 2001). Among the gross motor skills this test measures are the child's ability to sit, walk, long jump, pedal a tricycle, throw a ball overhand, catch a bounced ball, hop on one foot, and balance on one foot. Fine motor skills measured by the test include the child's ability to stack cubes, reach for objects, and draw a person.

Young Children's Artistic Drawings

In the story that opened the chapter, you read about Teresa Amabile's artistic skills and interest in kindergarten. The story revealed how these skills were restricted once she went to elementary school. Indeed, many young children show a special interest in drawing, just as Teresa did.

The unintended irregularities of children's drawings suggest spontaneity, freedom, and directness. They may use lavish colors that come close, but perhaps won't match the reality of their subjects. Form and clarity give way to bold lines flowing freely on the page. It is not the end product that matters so much, but the joy of creating, the fun of mixing colors, experimenting with different mediums, and getting messy in the process.

Young children often use the same formula for drawing different things. Though modified in small ways, one basic form can cover a range of objects. When children begin to draw animals, they portray them in the same way they portray humans: standing upright with a smiling face, legs, and arms. Pointed ears may be a clue to adults about the nature of the particular beast. As children become more sophisticated, their drawing of a cat will look more catlike to an adult. It may be resting on all four paws, tail in the air, and fur gleaming.

Not all children embrace art with equal enthusiasm, and the same child may want to draw one day but have no interest in it the next day. For most children, however, art is an important vehicle for conveying feelings and ideas that are not easily expressed in words (Thompson, 2006). Drawing and constructing also provide children with a hands-on opportunity to use their problem-solving skills to develop creative ways to represent scale, space, and motion. Parents can provide a context for artistic exploration by giving children a work space where they are not overly concerned about messiness or damage. They can make supplies available, have a bulletin board display space for the child's art, and support and encourage the child's art activity. When viewing children's art, many parents take special delight in hearing about the creative process. Questions such as "Can you tell me about this?" and "What were you thinking about when you made this?" encourage children and help parents to see the world through their children's eyes.

Developmental Changes and Stages   The development of fine motor skills in the preschool years allows children to become budding artists. There are dramatic changes in how children depict what they see. Art provides unique insights into children's perceptual worlds—what they are attending to, how space and distance are viewed, how they experience patterns and forms (Dorn, Madeja, & Sabol, 2004). Rhoda Kellogg is a creative teacher of preschool children who has observed and guided young children's artistic efforts for many decades. She has assembled an impressive array of tens of thousands of drawings produced by more than 2,000 preschool children. Adults who are unfamiliar with young children's art often view the productions of this age group as meaningless scribbles. However, Kellogg (1970) documented that young children's artistic productions are orderly, meaningful, and structured.

By their second birthday, children can scribble. Scribbles represent the earliest form of drawing. Every form of graphic art, no matter how complex, contains the

"You moved."
© The New Yorker Collection 1987 Lee Lorenz from cartoonbank.com. All Rights Reserved.

Denver Development Screening Test A test used to diagnose developmental delay in children from birth to 6 years of age; include separate assessments of gross and fine motor skills, language, and personal-social ability.

placement stage Kellogg's term for 2- to 3-year-olds' drawings that are drawn in placement patterns.

shape stage Kellogg's term for 3-year-olds' drawings consisting of diagrams in different shapes.

design stage Kellogg's term for 3- to 4-year-olds' drawings that mix two basic shapes into more complex designs.

pictorial stage Kellogg's term for 4- to 5-year-olds' drawings depicting objects that adults can recognize.

lines found in children's artwork, which Kellogg calls the 20 basic scribbles. These include vertical, horizontal, diagonal, circular, curving, waving or zigzag lines and dots. As young children progress from scribbling to picture making, they go through four distinguishable stages: placement, shape, design, and pictorial (see Figure 8.7).

Following young children's scribbles is the **placement stage,** Kellogg's term for 2- to 3-year-olds' drawings, drawn on a page in placement patterns. One example of these patterns is the spaced border pattern shown in Figure 8.7b. The **shape stage** is Kellogg's term for 3-year-olds' drawings consisting of diagrams in different shapes (see Figure 8.7c). Young children draw six basic shapes: circles, squares or rectangles, triangles, crosses, Xs, and forms. The **design stage** is Kellogg's term for 3- to 4-year-olds' drawings in which young children mix two basic shapes into a more complex design (see Figure 8.7d). This stage occurs rather quickly after the shape stage. The **pictorial stage** is Kellogg's term for 4- to 5-year-olds' drawings that consist of objects that adults can recognize (see Figure 8.7e).

Child Art in Context The title of this section, "Child Art in Context," is also the title of a book by Claire Golomb (2002), who has studied and conducted research on children's art for a number of decades. Golomb especially criticizes views of young children's art that describe it as primitive and a reflection of conceptual immaturity. She argues that children, like all novices, tend to use forms economically, and their comments indicate that their simplified version works. Rather than reflecting conceptual immaturity, Golomb views children's art as inventive problem solving.

Golomb believes that developmental changes in the way children draw are not strictly age-related but also depend on talent, motivation, familial support, and cultural values. Thus, her view contrasts with Kellogg's universal stage approach in which all children go through the same sequence in developing art skills, which we just discussed. In Golomb's view, child art flourishes in sociocultural contexts where tools are made available and where this activity is valued. In Chapter 9, "Cognitive Development in Early Childhood," we look further at young children's art, paying special attention to the role of cognitive development in their art.

Handedness

For centuries, left-handers have suffered unfair discrimination in a world designed for right-handers. Even the devil himself has been portrayed as a left-hander. For many years, teachers forced all children to write with their right hand, even if they had a left-hand tendency. Today, most U.S. teachers let children write with the hand they favor (Wenze & Wenze, 2004). However, in some cultures, such as the Republic of Malawi in southern Africa, adults still strongly encourage all children to use their right hand rather than their left hand (Zverev, 2006).

Origin and Development of Handedness What is the origin of hand preference? Genetic inheritance likely is strong. In one study, the handedness of adopted children was not related to the handedness of their adoptive parents but was related to the handedness of their biological parents (Carter-Saltzman, 1980).

Right-handedness is dominant in all cultures (it appears approximately in a ratio of 90 percent right-handers and 10 percent left-handers) and it appears before the impact of culture. For example, in one study ultrasound observations of fetal thumb sucking showed that 9 of 10 fetuses were more likely to be sucking their right hand's thumb (Hepper, Shahidullah, & White, 1990).

Thus, although adults often don't notice a child's hand preference until the toddler or early childhood years, researchers have found that hand preference occurs earlier, possibly even in the womb as we just saw (Stroganova & others, 2004). Newborns also show a preference for one side of their body over the other. In one study, 65 percent of the infants turned their head to the right when they were lying on their back in the crib (Michel, 1981). Fifteen percent preferred to face toward the left. These preferences for the right or left were linked with handedness later in development.

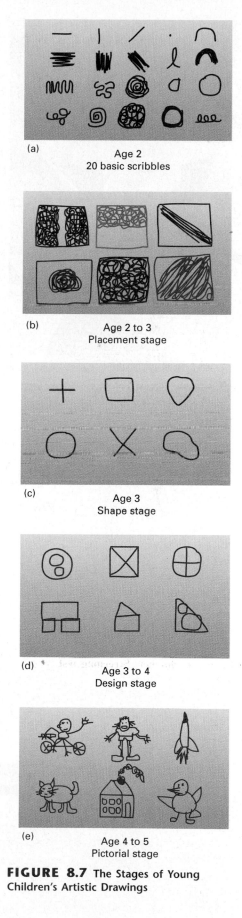

(a) Age 2
20 basic scribbles

(b) Age 2 to 3
Placement stage

(c) Age 3
Shape stage

(d) Age 3 to 4
Design stage

(e) Age 4 to 5
Pictorial stage

FIGURE 8.7 The Stages of Young Children's Artistic Drawings

Today, most teachers let children write with the hand they favor. *What are the main reasons children become left- or right-handed?*

At about 7 months of age, infants prefer grabbing with one hand or the other and this is related to later handedness (Ramsay, 1980). By 2 years of age, about 10 percent of children prefer to use their left hand. Many preschool children, though, use both hands, with a clear hand preference not completely distinguished until later in development.

Handedness, the Brain, and Language   A contemporary interest is the role of the brain in handedness (Kirveskari, Salmelin, & Hari, 2006; Magnus & Laeng, 2006; Miller & others, 2006). Approximately 95 percent of right-handed individuals process speech primarily in the brain's left hemisphere (Springer & Deutsch, 1985). However, left-handed individuals show more variation. More than half of left-handers process speech in their left hemisphere, just like right-handers. However, about one-fourth of left-handers process speech in their right hemisphere and another one-fourth process speech equally in both hemispheres (Knecht & others, 2000). Are there differences in the language development of left- and right-handers? The most consistent finding is that left-handers are more likely to have reading problems (Geschwind & Behan, 1984; Natsopoulos & others, 1998).

Handedness and Other Abilities   Although there is a tendency for left-handers to have more reading problems than right-handers, left-handers are more common among mathematicians, musicians, architects, and artists (Michelangelo, Leonardo da Vinci, and Picasso were all lefties) (Schacter & Ransil, 1996). Architects and artists who are left-handed benefit from the tendency of left-handers to have unusually good visuospatial skills and be able to imagine spatial layouts (Holtzen, 2000). Also, in one study of more than 100,000 students taking the Scholastic Aptitude Test (SAT), 20 percent of the top-scoring group was left-handed, twice the rate of left-handedness found in the general population (10 percent) (Bower, 1985).

REVIEW AND REFLECT   LEARNING GOAL 2

2 Describe changes in motor development in early childhood.

Review
- How do gross and fine motor skills change in early childhood?
- How can young children's artistic drawings be characterized?
- What is the nature of handedness?

Reflect
- Assume that you are the director of a preschool program, and the parents ask you to develop a program to teach the children how to participate in sports. Think through how you would explain to parents why most 3-year-olds are not ready for participation in sports programs. Include in your answer information about 3-year-olds' limited motor skills, as well as the importance of learning basic motor skills first and having unrealistic expectations for young children's development of sports skills.

3 WHAT ARE SOME IMPORTANT ASPECTS OF YOUNG CHILDREN'S HEALTH?

| Sleep and Sleep Problems | Nutrition | Health, Safety, and Illness |

So far, we have discussed young children's body growth and change, as well as their development of motor skills. In this section, we explore another aspect of young children's physical development—health. To learn more about young children's health, we focus on their sleep, nutrition, safety, and illness.

Sleep and Sleep Problems

Most young children sleep through the night and have one daytime nap (Davis, Parker, & Montgomery, 2004). Sometimes, though, it is difficult to get young children to go to sleep as they drag out their bedtime routine (Hoban, 2004). Helping the child slow down before bedtime often contributes to less resistance in going to bed. Reading the child a story, playing quietly with the child in the bath, or letting the child sit on the caregiver's lap while listening to music are quieting activities (Burke, Kuhn, & Peterson, 2004).

Transitional Objects   Many young children want to take a soft, cuddly object, such as a favorite blanket, teddy bear, or other stuffed animal, to bed with them. **Transitional objects** are those that children repeatedly use as bedtime companions. They usually are soft and cuddly, and most developmentalists view them as representing a transition from being a dependent person to being a more independent one. Therefore, using transitional objects at bedtime is normal behavior for young children (Steer & Lehman, 2000). In one study, children who relied on transitional objects at age 4 showed the same level of emotional adjustment at ages 11 and 16 as children who had not relied on transitional objects (Newson, Newson, & Mahalski, 1982).

Sleep Problems   Children can experience a number of sleep problems (BaHammam & others, 2006; Goll & Shapiro, 2006). One estimate indicates that more than 40 percent of children experience a sleep problem at some point in their development (Boyle & Cropley, 2004). In one study, there was a connection between children's behavioral problems and sleep problems (Smedje, Broman, & Hetta, 2001). First, children who were hyperactive during the day also were likely to toss and turn a lot during their sleep. They also were more likely to sleep walk than children who were not hyperactive. Second, children with conduct problems (for example, fighting) were more likely to resist going to bed at night. Third, children with emotional problems were more likely to have night terrors and difficulty falling asleep. In addition, children with peer problems had a shorter sleep time. Also, researchers have found children who have sleep problems also more likely to show depression and anxiety than children who do not have sleep problems (Mehl & others, 2006). And children who are overweight have more sleep problems (Eisenmann, Ekkekakis, & Holmes, 2006; Tzischinsky & Latzer, 2006).

Let's now explore these sleep problems in children: nightmares, night terrors, sleep walking, and sleep talking. **Nightmares** are frightening dreams that awaken the sleeper, more often toward the morning than just after the child has gone to bed at night. Caregivers should not worry about young children having occasional nightmares because almost every child has them. If children have nightmares persistently, it may indicate that they are feeling too much stress during their waking hours. One study found that children who experience nightmares have higher levels of anxiety than those who do not have nightmares (Mindell & Barrett, 2002).

Night terrors are characterized by a sudden arousal from sleep and an intense fear, usually accompanied by a number of physiological reactions, such as rapid heart rate and breathing, loud screams, heavy perspiration, and physical movement. In most instances, the child has little or no memory of what happened during the night terror (Mason & Pack, 2006). Night terrors are less common than nightmares and occur more often in deep sleep than do nightmares. Many children who experience night terrors return to sleep rather quickly after the night terror. Caregivers tend to be especially worried when children have night terrors, although they are usually not a serious problem (Mason & Pack, 2006).

Children usually outgrow night terrors. Although benzodiazepines (diazepam, for example) occasionally may be prescribed to be given to children at bedtime to help reduce night terrors, medication usually is not recommended (National Institutes of

transitional objects Objects that children repeatedly use as bedtime companions. These usually are soft and cuddly and probably mark the child's transition from being dependent to being more independent.

nightmares Frightening dreams that awaken the sleeper.

night terrors Characterized by sudden arousal from sleep, intense fear, and usually physiological reactions such as rapid heart rate and breathing, loud screams, heavy perspiration, and physical movement.

Health, 2007). In most cases, reassuring and comforting the child is the only treatment needed.

Somnambulism (sleep walking) occurs during the deepest stage of sleep. Approximately 15 percent of children sleep walk at least once, and from 1 to 5 percent do it regularly. Most children outgrow the problem without professional intervention (Laberge & others, 2000). Except for the danger of accidents while walking around asleep in the dark, there is nothing abnormal about sleep walking. It is safe to awaken sleep-walking children, and it is a good idea to do so because they might harm themselves. If children sleep walk regularly, parents need to make the bedroom and house as safe from harm as possible and also consult a physician to treat the child with medication (Remulla & Guilleminault, 2004).

Sleep talkers are soundly asleep as they speak, although occasionally they make fairly coherent statements for a brief period of time. Most of the time, though, you can't understand what children are saying during sleep talking. There is nothing abnormal about sleep talking, and there is no reason to try to stop it from occurring.

Nutrition

Four-year-old Bobby is on a steady diet of double cheeseburgers, french fries, and chocolate milk shakes. Between meals, he gobbles up candy bars and marshmallows. He hates green vegetables. Bobby, a preschooler, already has developed poor nutritional habits. What are a preschool child's energy needs? What is a preschooler's eating behavior like?

Energy Needs Feeding and eating habits are important aspects of development during early childhood (Knai & others, 2006). What children eat affects their skeletal growth, body shape, and susceptibility to disease (Demmelmair, von Rosen, & Koletzko, 2006). The preschool child requires up to 1,800 calories per day. Figure 8.8 shows the increasing energy needs of children as they move from infancy through the childhood years. Energy needs of individual children of the same age, sex, and size vary. However, an increasing number of children have an energy intake that exceeds what they need (Mendoza & others, 2006). A recent recommendation by the World Health Organization is that on average for children 7 years of age and younger, boys should have an 18 percent, and girls a 20 percent, reduction in energy intake (Butte, 2006).

Diet and Eating Behavior A national study found that from the late 1970s through the late 1990s, key dietary shifts took place in U.S. children: greater away-from-home consumption, large increases in total energy from salty snacks, soft drinks, and pizza; and large decreases in energy from low- and medium-fat milk and medium- and high-fat beef and pork (Nielsen, Siega-Riz, & Popkin, 2002). In this study, children's total energy intake increased from the late 1970s to late 1990s. These dietary changes occurred for children as young as 2 years of age through the adult years.

Another national assessment found that most children's diets are poor or in need of improvement (Federal Interagency Forum on Child and Family Statistics, 2002). In this assessment, only 27 percent of 2- to 5-year-old children were categorized as having good diets. Their diets worsened as they became older—only 13 percent of 6- to 9-year-old children had healthy diets.

A special difficulty that many parents encounter is getting their young children to eat vegetables (Knai & others, 2006). One study randomly assigned 156 parents with 2- to 6-year-old children to one of three conditions: (1) exposure (parents gave their child a taste of a previously disliked vegetable for 14 days), (2) information (parents were given nutritional advice and left a leaflet to read), and (3) control (no

somnambulism Sleep walking; occurs in the deepest stage of sleep.

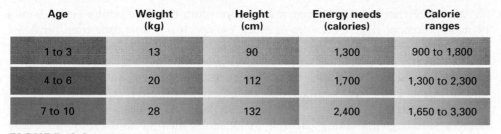

Age	Weight (kg)	Height (cm)	Energy needs (calories)	Calorie ranges
1 to 3	13	90	1,300	900 to 1,800
4 to 6	20	112	1,700	1,300 to 2,300
7 to 10	28	132	2,400	1,650 to 3,300

FIGURE 8.8 Recommended Energy Intakes for Children Ages 1 Through 10

Spinach: Divide into little piles. Rearrange again into new piles. After five or six maneuvers, sit back and say you are full.

—DELIA EPHRON
American Writer and Humorist, 20th Century

intervention) (Wardle & others, 2003). After 14 days, only children in the exposure group reported an increased liking for the previously disliked vegetable. Thus, some persistence on the part of parents in exposing children to vegetables may lead to positive results.

Another problem is that many parents do not recognize that their children are overweight. One recent study of parents with 2- to 17-year-old children found that few parents of overweight children perceived their children to be too heavy and were not worried about the children's weight (Eckstein & others, 2006).

Fat and Sugar Consumption   Although some health-conscious parents may be providing too little fat in their infants' and children's diets, other parents are raising their children on diets in which the percentage of fat is far too high (Brom, 2005; Sizer & Whitney, 2006). Our changing lifestyles, in which we often eat on the run and pick up fast-food meals, contribute to the increased fat levels in children's diets. Most fast-food meals are high in protein, especially meat and dairy products. But the average American child does not need to be concerned about getting enough protein. What must be of concern is the vast number of young children who are being weaned on fast foods that are not only high in protein but also high in fat. Eating habits become ingrained very early in life; unfortunately, it is during the preschool years that many people get their first taste of fast food (Poulton & Sexton, 1996). The American Heart Association recommends that the daily limit for calories from fat should be approximately 35 percent.

This would be a better world for children if parents had to eat the spinach.

—GROUCHO MARX
American Comedian, 20th Century

The concern is not only about excessive fat in children's diets but also about excessive sugar (Briefel & others, 2004). Consider Robert, age 3, who loves chocolate. His mother lets him have three chocolate candy bars a day. He also drinks an average of four cans of caffeinated cola a day, and he eats sugar-coated cereal each morning at breakfast. The average American child consumes almost 2 pounds of sugar per week (Riddle & Prinz, 1984). One study found that children from low-income families were more likely to have added sugar consumption than their counterparts from higher-income families (Kranz & Siega-Riz, 2002).

How does sugar consumption influence the health and behavior of young children? The association of sugar consumption with children's health problems—dental cavities and obesity, for example, has been widely documented (Hale, 2003; Lorah, 2002).

In sum, although there is individual variation in appropriate nutrition for children, their diets should be well balanced and should include fats, carbohydrates, protein, vitamins, and minerals (Boyle & Long, 2007; Wardlaw & Hempl, 2007). An occasional candy bar does not hurt, but a steady diet of hamburgers, french fries, milk shakes, and candy bars should be avoided.

"Fussy Eaters," Sweets, and Snacks   Many young children get labeled as "fussy" or "difficult eaters" when they are only trying to exercise the same rights to personal taste and appetite adults take for granted. Allow for the child's developing tastes in food. However, when young children eat too many sweets—candy bars, cola, and sweetened cereals, for example—they can spoil their appetite and then not want to eat more nutritious foods at mealtime. Thus, caregivers need to be firm in limiting the amount of sweets young children eat.

Most preschool children need to eat more often than the adults in the family because preschool children use up so much energy. It is a long time from breakfast to lunch and from lunch to dinner for the active young child. Thus, a midmorning and midafternoon snack are recommended. A good strategy is to avoid giving sweets to young children during these snack times (Skinner & others, 2004). Better choices include whole-grain bagels spread with creamy peanut butter, pureed fruit shakes, or tortillas with refried beans. Keep in mind that some foods are known choking hazards—avoid giving young children snack foods such as hard candy, nuts, any hard raw vegetable, or whole grapes.

Overweight Young Children   Being overweight has become a serious health problem in early childhood (Li & others, 2007; Torjesen, 2007). The Centers for Disease Control and Prevention (2007) has a category of obesity for adults but does not have an obesity category for children and adolescents because of the stigma the label may bring. Rather they have categories for being overweight or at risk for being overweight in childhood and adolescence. These categories are determined by body mass index (BMI), which is computed by a formula that takes into account height and weight. Only children and adolescents at or above the 95th percentile of BMI are included in the overweight category, and those at or above the 85th percentile are included in the at risk for being overweight category.

The percentages of young children who are overweight or at risk for being overweight in the United States has increased dramatically in recent decades, and the percentages are likely to grow unless changes occur in children's lifestyles (Mason & others, 2006; Podeszwa & others, 2006). In one recent study, the body mass index of more than 1,000 children was obtained from their health records at seven different times from 2 to 12 years of age (Nader & others, 2006). Eighty percent of the children who were at risk for being overweight at 3 years of age were also at risk for being overweight or were overweight at 12 years of age. Forty-percent of the children who were in the 50th BMI percentile or above at 3 years of age were at risk for being overweight or were overweight at 12 years of age.

One recent comparison of 34 countries revealed that the United States had the second highest rate of childhood obesity (Janssen & others, 2005). Childhood obesity contributes to a number of health problems (Arif & Rohrer, 2006). For example, physicians are now seeing type II (adult-onset) diabetes (a condition directly linked with obesity and a low level of fitness) in children as young as 5 years of age (Datar & Sturm, 2004).

Is being overweight associated with lower self-esteem in young children? In one study, the relation between weight status and self-esteem in 5-year-old girls was examined (Davison & Birth, 2001). The girls who were overweight had lower body self-esteem than those who were not overweight. Thus, as early as 5 years of age, being overweight is linked with lower self-esteem.

Prevention of obesity in children includes helping children and parents see food as a way to satisfy hunger and nutritional needs, not as proof of love or as a reward for good behavior (Borra & others, 2003). Snack foods should be low in fat, simple sugars, and salt, as well as high in fiber. Routine physical activity should be a daily occurrence (Robbins, Powers, & Burgess, 2008).

The Hip-Hop to Health Jr. is a family-oriented program for African American and Latino children attending Head Start programs in Chicago that is designed to reduce overweight and obesity (Fitzgibbon & others, 2002, 2005; Stolley & others 2003). The program targets African American and Latino children because they have higher rates of obesity than non-Latino White children. Weight problems are especially acute for African American and Latino young girls with 11 percent of African American and 13 percent of Latino 4- to 5-year-girls being overweight, compared with only 3 percent of non-Latino White girls (Ogden & others, 1997).

The Hip-Hop to Health Jr. program consists of a 45-minute class three times a week for 14 weeks that focuses on hands-on, fun activities that promote healthy

What are some trends in the eating habits and weight of young children?

eating, as well as a 20-minute aerobic activity each class. The parent component of the program consists of a weekly newsletter, homework assignments, and participation in an aerobics class twice a week. In a recent two-year follow-up of the Hip-Hop to Health Jr. program, children who were randomly assigned to the program had a smaller increase in body mass index compared with children who did not participate in the program (Fitzgibbon & others, 2005).

In sum, the child's life should be centered around activities, not meals (Robbins, Powers, & Burgess, 2008). To read further about a research study focused on the importance of activities in young children's lives, see the *Research in Children's Development* interlude.

Research in Childern's Development

PHYSICAL ACTIVITY IN YOUNG CHILDREN ATTENDING PRESCHOOLS

One study examined the activity level of 281 3- to 5-year-olds in nine preschools (Pate & others, 2004). The preschool children wore accelerometers, a small activity monitor, for four to five hours a day. Height and weight assessments of the children were made to calculate their BMI.

Guidelines recommend the preschool children engage in two hours of physical activity per day, divided into one hour of structured activity and one hour of unstructured free-play (National Association for Sport and Physical Education, 2002). In this study, the young children participated in an average of 7.7 minutes per hour of moderate to vigorous activity, usually in a block of time when they were outside. Over the course of eight hours of a preschool day, these children would get approximately one hour of moderate and vigorous physical activity, only about 50 percent of the amount recommended. The researchers concluded that young children are unlikely to engage in another hour per day of moderate and vigorous physical activity outside their eight hours spent in preschool and thus are not getting adequate opportunities for physical activity.

Gender and age differences characterized the preschool children's physical activity. Boys were more likely to engage in moderate or vigorous physical activity than girls. Four- and five-year-old children were more likely to be sedentary than 3-year-old children.

The young children's physical activity also varied according to the particular preschool they attended. The extent they participated in moderate and vigorous physical activity ranged from 4.4 to 10.2 minutes per hour across the nine preschools. Thus, the policies and practices of particular preschools influence the extent to which children engage in physical activity. The researchers concluded that young children need more vigorous play and organized activities.

Malnutrition in Young Children from Low-Income Families One of the most common nutritional problems in early childhood is iron deficiency anemia, which results in chronic fatigue (Bartle, 2007). This problem results from the failure to eat adequate amounts of quality meats and dark green vegetables. Young children from low-income families are most likely to develop iron deficiency anemia (Shamah & Villalpando, 2006). A recent study revealed that preschool children with iron deficiency anemia were slower to display positive affect and touch novel toys for the first time than their nonanemic counterparts (Lozoff & others, 2007).

Poor nutrition is a special concern in the lives of young children from low-income families (Greco & others, 2006). Many of these children do not get essential amounts of iron, vitamins, or protein (Walker & others, 2007). A recent study revealed that young children who had lower intakes of fresh fruit and vegetables cooked in olive oil, and higher intakes of canned fruit and vegetables, and processed salad dressing were more likely to come from lower-income, less-educated families than higher-income, more educated families (Sausenthaler & others, 2007). In part, to address this problem in the United States, the Special Supplemental Nutrition Program for Women, Infants, and Children (WIC) serves approximately 7,500,000 participants in the United States. Positive influences on young children's nutrition and health have been found for participants in WIC (Black & others, 2004; Herman, Harrison, & Jenks, 2006). For example, one study found that participating in WIC was linked with a lower risk for being overweight in young Mexican American children (Melgar-Quinonez & Kaiser, 2004). Another study revealed that WIC children who were anemic improved the most when they did not eat snacks and dried fruits (Swanson & others, 2007).

Some researchers argue that malnutrition is directly linked to cognitive deficits because of negative effects on brain development (Liu & others, 2003). However, an increasing number of researchers argue that the links between child undernutrition, physical growth, and cognitive development are more complex (Marcon, 2003). For example, nutritional influences can be viewed in the context of socioemotional factors that often coincide with undernutrition. Thus, children who vary considerably from the norm in physical growth also differ on other biological and socioemotional factors that might influence cognitive development. For example, children who are underfed often are also less supervised, less stimulated, and less educated than children who are well nourished (Wachs, 1995). As we saw earlier, poverty is an especially strong risk factor that interacts with children's nutritional status to affect physical and cognitive development (Marcon, 2003).

Malnutrition may be linked to other aspects of development in addition to cognitive deficits. One longitudinal study found that U.S. children who were malnourished at 3 years of age showed more aggressive and hyperactive behavior at age 8, had more externalizing problems at age 11, and evidenced more excessive motor behavior at age 17 (Liu & others, 2004).

Health, Safety, and Illness

The story of children's health in the past 50 years is a shift away from fighting infectious diseases toward prevention and outpatient care (Sobo, Seid, & Reyes Gelhard, 2006). In recent decades, vaccines have nearly eradicated disabling bacterial meningitis and have greatly reduced the incidence of measles, rubella, mumps, and chicken pox. In the effort to make a child's world safer, one of the main strategies is to prevent childhood injuries.

Preventing Childhood Injuries   Young children's active and exploratory nature, coupled with being unaware of danger in many instances, often puts them in situations in which they are at risk for injuries. Most of young children's cuts, bumps, and bruises are minor, but some accidental injuries can produce serious injuries or even death.

In the United States, motor vehicle accidents are the leading cause of death in young children, followed by cancer and cardiovascular disease (National Vital Statistics Reports, 2004) (see Figure 8.9). In addition to motor vehicle accidents, other accidental deaths in children involve drowning, falls, burns, and poisoning (Bessey & others, 2006).

Notice in Figure 8.9 that the seventh leading cause of death in young children in the United States involves firearms. In one cross-cultural comparison, the rate of firearm-related death among children less than 15 years of age in 26 industrialized countries was the highest in the United States (American Academy of Pediatrics, 2001). Among those industrialized countries with no firearm-related deaths in children were Japan, Singapore, and the Netherlands.

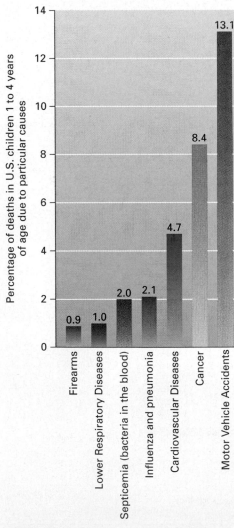

FIGURE 8.9 Main Causes of Death in Children 1 through 4 Years of Age These figures show the percentage of deaths in U.S. children 1 to 4 years of age due to particular causes in 2002 (National Vital Statistics Reports, 2004).

Many of young children's injuries can be prevented (Degutis & Greve, 2006). Among the ways this can be accomplished are regularly restraining children in automobiles, reducing access to firearms, and making homes and playgrounds safer (Jansson & others, 2006; Miller & others, 2006).

Influences on children's safety include the acquisition and practice of individual skills and safety behaviors, family and home influences, school and peer influences, and the community's actions. Notice that these influences reflect Bronfenbrenner's ecological model of development that we described in Chapter 1. Figure 8.10 shows how these ecological contexts can influence children's safety, security, and injury prevention (Sleet & Mercy, 2003). We have more to say about contextual influences on young children's health shortly.

Reducing access to firearms is a wise strategy (Schaechter & others, 2003). In 12 states that passed laws requiring that firearms be made inaccessible to children, unintentional shooting deaths of children fell almost 25 percent. In one recent study, many parents in homes with firearms reported that their children never handled the firearms, but interviews with their children contradicted the parents' perceptions (Baxley & Miller, 2006).

Deaths in young children due to automobile accidents have declined considerably in the United States since the invention of the seat belt. All U.S. states and the District of Columbia have laws that require young children to be restrained in cars, either in specially designed seats or by seat belts. In many instances, when young children are killed today in automobile accidents, they are unrestrained (Chen & others, 2005). Although many parents today use car seats or "booster seats" for their children, most don't install the seats properly. If the seat is not installed correctly, children are at risk for serious injury or death in automobile accidents (Elliott & others, 2006). Nearly all local police departments will assist parents in installing their children's car seats safely. This service is provided free of charge.

Most fatal non-vehicle-related deaths in young children occur in or around the home. Young children have drowned in bathtubs and swimming pools, been burned in fires and explosions, experienced falls from heights, and drunk or eaten poisonous substances (Schnake, Peterson, & Corden, 2005).

Playgrounds also can be a source of children's injuries (Powell, Ambardekar, & Sheehan, 2005; Sutterby & Frost, 2006). One of the major problems is that playground equipment is often not constructed over impact-absorbing surfaces, such as wood chips or sand.

Contexts of Young Children's Health
Among the contexts involved in young children's health are poverty, home and child care, environmental tobacco smoke, and exposure to lead (Gulotta & Phinney, 2000). In addition, we discuss the state of illness and health in the world's children.

Poverty and Ethnicity A special concern focuses on the health of young children living in poverty (Ramey, Ramey, & Lanzi, 2006). Low income is linked with poor health in young children (Howell, Pettit, & Kingsley, 2005). Many health problems of young children in poverty begin before birth when their mothers do not receive adequate health care, which can produce a low birth weight child and other complications that can still affect the child years later (Dubay & others, 2001). Children living in poverty may experience unsanitary conditions, live in

Individual

Development of social skills and ability to regulate emotions

Involvement in activities that promote positive attachment and prosocial skills

Acquisition of early academic skills and knowledge

Impulse control (such as not darting out into a street to retrieve a ball)

Frequent use of personal protection (such as bike helmets and safety seats)

Family/Home

High awareness and knowledge of child management and parenting skills

Caregiver participation in the child's education and social activities

Frequent parent protective behaviors (such as use of child safety seats)

Presence of home safety equipment (such as smoke alarms and cabinet locks)

School/Peers

Promotion of home/school partnerships

Availability of enrichment programs, especially for low-income families

Absence of playground hazards

Management support for safety and injury prevention

Injury prevention and safety promotion policies and programs

Community

Availability of positive activities for children and their parents

Active surveillance of environmental hazards

Effective prevention policies in place (such as pool fencing)

Commitment to emergency medical services for children and trauma care

Emphasis on safety themes

FIGURE 8.10 Characteristics That Enhance Young Children's Safety In each context of a child's life, steps can be taken to create conditions than enhance the child's safety and reduce the likelihood of injury. *How are the contexts listed in the figure related to Bronfenbrenner's theory (described in chapter 2)?*

crowded housing, and be inadequately supervised (Neumann, Gewa, & Bwibo, 2004). Children in poverty are more likely to be exposed to lead poisoning than children growing up in higher socioeconomic conditions (Morrissey-Ross, 2000). The families of many children in poverty do not have adequate medical insurance, and thus the children often receive less adequate medical care compared with children living in higher socioeconomic conditions (Olson, Tang, & Newacheck, 2005).

Ethnicity is also linked to children's health. For example, one recent study found that even when socioeconomic status was controlled, Latino, African American, and Asian American children were less likely to have a usual health-care source, health professional, doctor visit, and dental visit in the past year (Shi & Stevens, 2005). Another recent study revealed that children whose parents had limited English proficiency were three times more likely to have fair or poor health status than their English proficiency counterparts (Flores, Abreu, & Tomany-Korman, 2005).

Safety at Home and in Child Care Caregivers—whether parents at home or teachers and supervisors in child care—play an important role in the health of young children (Freedman & others, 2005; Lumeng & others, 2006;). For example, by controlling the speed of the vehicles they drive, by decreasing or eliminating their drinking—especially before driving—and by not smoking around children, caregivers enhance the likelihood that children will be healthy (Tinsley, 2003).

Young children may lack the intellectual skills—including reading ability—to discriminate between safe and unsafe household substances. And they may lack the impulse control to keep from running out into a busy street while chasing a ball. In these and many other situations, competent adult supervision and monitoring of young children is important to prevent injuries (Sleet, Schieber, & Gilchrest, 2003).

In communicating with young children, caregivers need to make the information they give to children cognitively simple (Morrongiello, Midgett, & Shields, 2001). And an important strategy is for parents to guide children in learning how to control and regulate their own health behavior (Tinsley & others, 2002).

Young children need to be encouraged to identify feelings of wellness and illness and specify them to adults. In one study, young adults with fewer illness symptoms remembered their parents as concerned with teaching self-care and the promotion of positive health behaviors (Mechanic, 1979). When they were young children, their mothers were positively oriented toward health rather than concerned with seeking medical attention and making a big deal out of minor illnesses.

Parents also influence how children cope with medical treatment (Tinsley & others, 2002). Much of this research focuses on how parents influence children's fear and coping during inpatient and outpatient pediatric medical visits (Melamed, Roth, & Fogel, 2001). Researchers have found that parents who use distraction, are less agitated, and are more reassuring have children who display lower levels of distress in these medical settings (Stephens, Barkey, & Hall, 1999).

A special concern involves the selection of the best parenting strategies with a chronically ill child. Health researcher Barbara Melamed (2002, p. 341) provided these recommendations:

- *"Balance the illness with other family needs."*
- *"Maintain clear family boundaries."* During an illness crisis, extended family members may help with chores or caring for healthy children in the family.
- *"Develop communication competence."* Think about the best ways to talk to the physicians involved, and communicate effectively about the illness to others.
- *"Attribute positive meanings to the situation."* Demonstrate how the family can be resilient in this difficult circumstance.
- *"Engage in active coping efforts."* Seek positive problem-solving solutions in dealing with stressful aspects of the child's illness.

Parents also should invest effort in finding a competent health-care provider for their children (Hickson & Clayton, 2002, p. 456). This "includes consulting sources of information and asking questions likely to provide useful information about practice characteristics that may affect the parent-doctor relationship. Parents, for example, might seek information concerning a physician's willingness to answer questions and involve parents in decision making or at least to outline options. Parents might also inquire about the physician's style of practice and philosophies about treatment, behavior management, nutrition, and other general health maintenance practices." To read about Barbara Deloin, a pediatric nurse who promotes positive parent-child experiences and positive links of families to the health-care system, see the *Careers in Child Development* profile.

Environmental Tobacco Smoke Estimates indicate that approximately 22 percent of children and adolescents in the United States are exposed to tobacco smoke in the home. An increasing number of studies reach the conclusion that children are at risk for health problems when they live in homes in which a parent smokes (Arshad, 2005; Martinez-Donate & others, 2007). If the mother smoked, her children were twice as likely to develop respiratory problems (Etzel, 1988). In one study, young children whose fathers smoked at home were more likely to have upper respiratory tract infections than those whose fathers did not smoke at home (Shiva & others, 2004). Children exposed to tobacco smoke in the home are more likely to develop wheezing symptoms and asthma than children in nonsmoking homes (Sharma & others, 2007).

Environmental tobacco smoke also affects the amount of vitamin C in children and adolescents. In one study, when parents smoked at home their 4- to 18-year-old children and adolescents had significantly lower levels of vitamin C in their blood than their counterparts in nonsmoking homes (Strauss, 2001). The more parents smoked, the less vitamin C the children and adolescents had. Children exposed to environmental smoke should be encouraged to eat foods rich in vitamin C or be given this vitamin as a supplement (Preston & others, 2003).

Exposure to Lead There is a special concern about lead poisoning in young children. Approximately 3 million children under 6 years of age are estimated to be at risk for lead poisoning, which might harm their development (Ahamed & others, 2005). As we mentioned earlier, children in poverty are at greater risk for lead poisoning than children living in higher socioeconomic conditions (Moralez, Gutierrez, & Escarce, 2005). Lead can get into children's bloodstreams through food or water that is contaminated by lead, from putting lead-contaminated fingers in their mouths, or from inhaling dust from lead-based paint (Gulson & others, 2004). The negative effects of high lead levels in children's blood include lower intelligence, lower achievement, attention deficit hyperactivity disorder, and elevated blood pressure (Canfield & others, 2003). One study found that 5-year-old children exposed to lead performed more poorly on tests of memory and problem solving (Canfield, Gendle, & Cory-Slechta, 2004). And a recent fMRI study of adults who had extensive exposure to lead from birth through early childhood showed deficits in areas of the brain,

Careers
in CHILD DEVELOPMENT

Barbara Deloin
Pediatric Nurse

Barbara Deloin is a pediatric nurse in Denver, Colorado. She practices nursing in the Pediatric Oral Feeding Clinic and is involved in research as part of an irritable infant study for the Children's Hospital in Denver. She also is on the faculty of nursing at the Colorado Health Sciences Center. Deloin previously worked in San Diego where she was coordinator of the Child Health Program for the County of San Diego.

Her research interests focus on children with special health-care needs, especially high-risk infants and children, and promoting positive parent-child experiences. She was elected president of the National Association of Pediatric Nurse Associates and Practitioners for the 2000–2001 term.

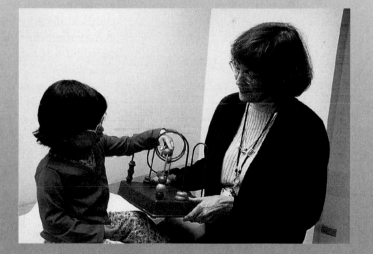

Barbara Deloin, conducting a pediatric evaluation.

such as Wernicke's area and the frontal cortex adjacent to Broca's area, that are associated with language function (Weihong & others, 2006). Because of such negative outcomes, the Centers for Disease Control and Prevention recommends that children be screened for the presence of lead contamination in their blood.

To read further about children's illness and health, see the *Diversity in Children's Development* interlude.

Diversity in Children's Development

THE STATE OF ILLNESS AND HEALTH IN THE WORLD'S CHILDREN

Each year UNICEF produces a report entitled *The State of the World's Children*. In a recent report, UNICEF (2006) emphasized the importance of information about the under-5 mortality rate of a nation. UNICEF concluded that the under-5 mortality rate is the result of a wide range of factors, including the nutritional health and health knowledge of mothers, the level of immunization, dehydration, availability of maternal and child health services, income and food availability in the family, availability of clean water and safe sanitation, and the overall safety of the child's environment.

UNICEF reports annual data on the rank of nations under-5 mortality rate. In 2004, 40 nations had a lower under-5 mortality rate than the United States with Singapore having the lowest rate of all nations (UNICEF, 2006). The relatively high under-5 mortality rate of the United States compared with other developed nations is due to such factors as poverty and inadequate health care. The devastating effects on the health of young children occur in countries where poverty rates are high (UNICEF, 2007; Wagstaff & others, 2004). The poor are the majority in nearly one of every five nations in the world (UNICEF, 2006). They often experience lives of hunger, malnutrition, illness, inadequate access to health care, unsafe water, and a lack of protection from harm (Bahl & others, 2005; Horton, 2006).

A leading cause of childhood death in impoverished countries is dehydration caused by diarrhea. In 1980, diarrhea was responsible for over 4.6 million childhood deaths. Oral rehydration therapy (ORT) was introduced in 1979 and quickly became the foundation for controlling diarrheal diseases. ORT now is given to the majority of children in impoverished countries suffering with diarrhea. Globally, the yearly number of deaths from diarrheal diseases for children under age 5 has fallen from its 1980 level to about 1.5 million in 1999 (Victora & others, 2000). Although increased immunization programs in the last several decades have led to a reduction in deaths from many diseases, measles, tetanus, and whooping cough still cause the deaths of many children around the world. In 1970, less than 10 percent of the world's children were immunized against diseases. In the beginning of the twenty-first century, approximately 75 percent of the world's children are now immunized against diseases such as tuberculosis, tetanus, and polio (Foege, 2000).

Acute respiratory infections, such as pneumonia, also have killed many children under the age of 5. Many of these children's lives could have been saved with antibiotics administered by a community health worker. Undernutrition also is a contributing factor to many deaths of children under the age of 5 in impoverished countries.

In the last decade, there has been a dramatic increase in the number of young children who have died because of HIV/AIDS transmitted to them by their parents (UNICEF, 2007). Deaths in young children due to HIV/AIDS especially occur in countries with high rates of poverty and low levels of education (Kalichman & others, 2005). For example, the uneducated are four times more likely to believe that

Many children in impoverished countries die before reaching the age of 5 from dehydration and malnutrition brought about by diarrhea. *What are some of the other main causes of death in young children around the world?*

there is no way to avoid AIDS and three times more likely to be unaware that the virus can be transmitted from mother to child (UNICEF, 2006).

Many of the deaths of young children around the world can be prevented by a reduction in poverty and improvements in nutrition, sanitation, education, and health services (Bhutta & others, 2005).

REVIEW AND REFLECT > LEARNING GOAL 3

3 Characterize the health of young children.

Review
- What is the nature of sleep and sleep problems in young children?
- What are young children's energy needs? What characterizes young children's eating behavior?
- How can the nature of children's injuries be summarized? How do contexts influence children's health?

Reflect
- If you become a parent of a young child, what precautions will you take to improve your child's health?

REACH YOUR LEARNING GOALS

1 HOW DOES A YOUNG CHILD'S BODY AND BRAIN GROW AND CHANGE?
Discuss growth and change in the young child's body and brain.

Height and Weight

- The average child grows 2½ inches in height and gains between 5 and 7 pounds a year during early childhood. Growth patterns vary individually, though. Some children are unusually short because of congenital factors, a physical problem that develops in childhood, maternal smoking during pregnancy, or an emotional difficulty.

The Brain

- By age 6, the brain has reached about 95 percent of its adult size. Some of the increase is due to increases in the number and size of nerve endings and receptors. One neurotransmitter that increases in concentration from 3 to 6 years of age is dopamine. Researchers have found that changes in local patterns in the brain occur from 3 to 15 years of age. From 3 to 6 years of age, the most rapid growth occurs in the frontal lobes. From age 6 through puberty, the most substantial growth takes place in the temporal and parietal lobes. Increasing brain maturation contributes to changes in cognitive abilities. One link involves the prefrontal cortex, dopamine, and improved attention and working memory.

Vision

- Visual maturity increases in early childhood. Some children develop vision problems such as functional amblyopia ("lazy eye") and strabismus, a misalignment of the eyes in which they do not point at the same object together.

2 HOW DO YOUNG CHILDREN'S MOTOR SKILLS DEVELOP? *Describe changes in motor development in early childhood.*

Gross and Fine Motor Skills

- Gross motor skills increase dramatically in early childhood. Children become increasingly adventuresome as their gross motor skills improve. Rough-and-tumble play often occurs, especially in boys. It is important for early childhood educators to design and implement developmentally appropriate activities for young children's gross motor skills. Three types of these activities are fundamental movement, daily fitness, and perceptual-motor. Fine motor skills also improve substantially during early childhood. The Denver Developmental Screening Test is a simple, inexpensive method of diagnosing developmental delay and includes separate assessments of gross and fine motor skills.

Young Children's Artistic Drawings

- The development of fine motor skills allows young children to become budding artists. Scribbling begins at 2 years of age, followed by four stages of drawing, culminating in the pictorial stage at 4 to 5 years of age. Golomb argues that it is important to explore the sociocultural contexts of children's art and that such factors as talent, motivation, familial support, and cultural values influence the development of children's art.

Handedness

- In today's world, the strategy is to let children use the hand they favor. Handedness likely has a strong genetic link. About 90 percent of children are right-handed and 10 percent left-handed. Left-handers are more likely to process speech in the right hemisphere of the brain than right-handers, and left-handers tend to have more reading problems. Left-handers often show up in higher than expected numbers as mathematicians, musicians, architects, and artists. Left-handers tend to have unusually good visuospatial skills.

3 WHAT ARE SOME IMPORTANT ASPECTS OF YOUNG CHILDREN'S HEALTH?
Characterize the health of young children.

Sleep and Sleep Problems

- Most young children sleep through the night and have one daytime nap. Helping the young child slow down before bedtime often leads to less resistance in going to bed. Many young children take transitional objects to bed with them; these objects represent a bridge between dependence and independence. Among the sleep problems that can develop in young children are nightmares, night terrors, and somnambulism (sleep walking), and sleep talking.

Nutrition

- Energy needs increase as children go through the early childhood years. National assessments indicate that a large majority of young children in the United States do not have a healthy diet and that over the last two decades their eating habits have worsened. Too many parents are rearing young children on diets that are high in fat and sugar. Children's diets should contain well-balanced proportions of fats, carbohydrates, protein, vitamins, and minerals. Parents should keep children's eating completely separate from discipline. A special concern is the poor nutrition of young children from impoverished families.

Health, Safety, and Illness

- Injuries are the leading cause of death in children. Motor vehicle accidents are the injuries that cause the most deaths in children. Firearm deaths are especially high in children in the United States in comparison to other countries. Among the strategies for preventing childhood injuries are restraining children in automobiles, reducing access to firearms, and making the home and playground safer. Among the contexts involved in children's health are poverty, ethnicity, home and child care, environmental tobacco smoke, and exposure to lead. The most devastating effects on the health of young children occur in countries with high poverty rates. Among the problems that low-income families face in these countries around the world are hunger, malnutrition, illness, inadequate access to health care, unsafe water, and a lack of protection from harm. In recent decades, the trend in children's illness and health is toward prevention as vaccines have been developed to reduce the number of diseases children have. Parents play an important role in young children's health. They influence their children's health by the way they behave in regard to children's illness symptoms. Parents can use a number of positive strategies in coping with the stress of having a chronically ill child. Parents need to invest effort in selecting a competent health-care provider for their children.

KEY TERMS

growth hormone
  deficiency 250
myelination 252
functional amblyopia 254

strabismus 254
Denver Developmental
  Screening Test 258
placement stage 258

shape stage 258
design stage 258
pictorial stage 258
transitional objects 261

nightmares 261
night terrors 261
somnambulism 262

KEY PEOPLE

Teresa Amabile 250

Rhoda Kellogg 258

Claire Golomb 259

MAKING A DIFFERENCE

Supporting Young Children's Physical Development

What are some good strategies for supporting young children's physical development?

- *Give young children plenty of opportunities to be active and explore their world.* Young children are extremely active and should not be constrained for long periods of time. Competent teachers plan daily fitness activities for young children. Preschool-aged children are too young for organized sports.
- *Make sure that young children's motor activities are fun and appropriate for their age.* Young children should enjoy the motor activities they participate in. Also, don't try to push young children into activities more appropriate for older children. For example, don't try to train a 4-year-old to ride a bicycle or have a 5-year-old take tennis lessons.
- *Give young children ample opportunities to engage in art.* Don't constrain young children's drawing. Let them freely create their drawings.
- *Provide young children with good nutrition.* Know how many calories preschool children need to meet their energy needs, which are greater than in infancy. Too many young children are raised on fast foods. Monitor the amount of fat and sugar in young children's diet. Nutritious midmorning and midafternoon snacks are recommended in addition to breakfast, lunch, and dinner. Make sure that young children get adequate iron, vitamins, and protein.
- *Make sure that young children have regular medical checkups that include vision testing, immunizations, and dental care.* This is especially important for children living in impoverished conditions, who are less likely to get such checkups.
- *Be a positive health role model for young children.* When you have young children with you, control the speed of the vehicle you are driving. Don't smoke in their presence. Eat healthy foods. Just by being in your presence, young children will imitate many of your behaviors.
- *Make sure that where children play is safe.* Walk through the areas where children play, and check for any potential hazards.

RESOURCES FOR IMPROVING CHILDREN'S LIVES

Child Art in Context

by Claire Golomb (2002)
Washington, DC: American Psychological Association

One of the world's leading experts on children's art reviews the latest research and presents her contextual theory of children's art. Includes many children's drawings to illustrate points related to the theory.

American Academy of Pediatrics

www.aap.org

This Web site provides extensive information about strategies for improving children's health.

How Children Learn to Be Healthy

by Barbara Tinsley (2003)
New York: Cambridge University Press

A leading expert explores the ways in which health behavior develops in children, especially focusing on the roles of parents, schools, and the media in influencing children's health.

E-LEARNING TOOLS

Connect to **www.mhhe.com/santrockc10** to research the answers and complete these exercises. In addition, you'll find a number of other resources and valuable study tools for Chapter 8, "Physical Development in Early Childhood," on this Web site.

Taking It to the Net

1. Rachel, a preschool teacher, notices that Mariah did not bring a snack to preschool today. "Mariah, did you forget your snack?" Rachel asks. "No," says Mariah. "Mommy didn't have anything to give me." Mariah's response worries Rachel, and causes her to wonder whether Mariah is receiving adequate nutrition. What are some of the consequences of nutritional deficiency in childhood? What kinds of things might alleviate this problem?

2. Greg and Keith like to take their daughter, Emily, to the local playground. Some of the equipment is old, and both

Greg and Keith are concerned about whether the equipment is safe. How common are playground injuries among preschoolers? What are some of the safety standards for playground equipment?

3. Dana's part-time job involves helping in a community center's after-school program for inner-city elementary school children. Many of the children eat too much junk food, have low energy levels, and are overweight. She wants to institute an exercise program as part of each day's activities. What are some things that Dana should keep in mind?

Health and Well-Being, Parenting, and Education

Build your decision-making skills by trying your hand at the health and well-being, parenting, and education exercises.

9 Cognitive Development in Early Childhood

The mind is an enchanting thing.

—MARIANNE MOORE
American Poet, 20th Century

CHAPTER OUTLINE

LEARNING GOALS

WHAT ARE THREE VIEWS OF THE COGNITIVE CHANGES THAT OCCUR IN EARLY CHILDHOOD? ①

Piaget's Preoperational Stage
Vygotsky's Theory
Information Processing

Describe three views of the cognitive changes that occur in early childhood.

HOW DO YOUNG CHILDREN DEVELOP LANGUAGE? ②

Understanding Phonology and Morphology
Changes in Syntax and Semantics
Advances in Pragmatics

Summarize how language develops in early childhood.

WHAT ARE SOME IMPORTANT FEATURES OF EARLY CHILDHOOD EDUCATION? ③

Variations in Early Childhood Education
Literacy and Early Childhood Education
Educating Young Children Who Are Disadvantaged
Controversies in Early Childhood Education

Evaluate different approaches to early childhood education.

A Reggio Emilia classroom in which young children explore topics that interest them.

Images of Children's Development
The Story of Reggio Emilia's Children

Reggio Emilia is an educational program for young children in the northern Italian city of Reggio Emilia. Children accepted into the program are encouraged to learn by investigating and exploring topics that interest *them* rather than follow a curriculum mandated by their teachers. A wide range of stimulating media and materials are available for children to use as they learn music, movement, drawing, painting, sculpting, collages, puppets and disguises, and photography (Strong-Wilson & Ellis, 2007). Children of single parents and children with disabilities have priority in admission; other children are admitted according to a range of needs. Parents pay on a sliding scale based on income.

In Reggio Emilia, children often explore topics in small groups, which fosters a sense of community, respect for diversity, and a collaborative approach to problem solving (Hyson, Copple, & Jones, 2006). Two co-teachers are present to serve as guides for children (Edwards, 2002). Reggio Emilia teachers consider each project an adventure. Project ideas may come from an adult's suggestion, a child's idea, or an event, such as a snowfall or something else altogether unexpected. Every project is based on what the children say and do, and teachers allow enough time for students to think and craft a project.

At the core of the Reggio Emilia approach is the image of children who are competent and have rights, especially the right to outstanding care and education. Parent participation is considered essential, and cooperation is a major theme in the schools. Many early childhood education experts believe the Reggio Emilia approach provides a supportive, stimulating context in which children are motivated to explore their world in a competent and confident manner (New, 2005, 2007).

PREVIEW

Children make a number of significant cognitive advances in early childhood. In the opening section, we explore the cognitive changes described by the major cognitive theories. Then we examine the dramatic changes in young children's language, and conclude by discussing a wide range of topics on early childhood education.

1 WHAT ARE THREE VIEWS OF THE COGNITIVE CHANGES THAT OCCUR IN EARLY CHILDHOOD?

| Piaget's Preoperational Stage | Vygotsky's Theory | Information Processing |

The cognitive world of the preschool child is creative, free, and fanciful. Preschool children's imaginations work overtime, and their mental grasp of the world improves. Our coverage of cognitive development in early childhood focuses on three theories: Piaget's, Vygotsky's, and information processing.

Piaget's Preoperational Stage

Remember from Chapter 6, "Cognitive Development in Infancy," that during Piaget's first stage of development, the sensorimotor stage, the infant progresses in the ability to organize and coordinate sensations and perceptions with physical movements and actions. The **preoperational stage,** which lasts from approximately 2 to 7 years of age, is the second Piagetian stage. In this stage, children begin to represent the world with words, images, and drawings. They form stable concepts and begin to reason. At the same time, the young child's cognitive world is dominated by egocentrism and magical beliefs.

Because Piaget called this stage "preoperational," it might sound like an unimportant waiting period. Not so. However, the label *preoperational* emphasizes that the child does not yet perform **operations,** which are reversible mental actions; they allow children to do mentally what before they could do only physically. Mentally adding and subtracting numbers are examples of operations. *Preoperational thought* is the beginning of the ability to reconstruct in thought what has been established in behavior. It can be divided into two substages: the symbolic function substage and the intuitive thought substage.

The Symbolic Function Substage

The **symbolic function substage** is the first substage of preoperational thought, occurring roughly between the ages of 2 and 4. In this substage, the young child gains the ability to mentally represent an object that is not present. This ability vastly expands the child's mental world (DeLoache, 2004). Young children use scribble designs to represent people, houses, cars, clouds, and so on; they begin to use language and engage in pretend play. However, although young children make distinct progress during this substage, their thought still has important limitations, two of which are egocentrism and animism.

Piaget's concept of **egocentrism,** which describes young children's difficulties in distinguishing between their own perspective and someone else's perspective. The following telephone conversation between 4-year-old Neta, who is at home, and her father, who is at work, typifies Neta's egocentric thought:

> **Father:** Neta, is Mommy there?
> **Neta:** (Silently nods)
> **Father:** Neta, may I speak to Mommy?
> **Neta:** (Nods again silently)

Neta's response is egocentric in that she fails to consider her father's perspective before replying. A nonegocentric thinker would have responded verbally.

Piaget and Barbel Inhelder (1969) initially studied young children's egocentrism by devising the three mountains task (see Figure 9.1). The child walks around the model of the mountains and becomes familiar with what the mountains look like from different perspectives, and she can see that there are different objects on the mountains. The child is then seated on one side of the table on which the mountains are placed. The experimenter moves a doll to different locations around the table, at each location asking the child to select from a series of photos the one photo that most accurately reflects the view that the doll is seeing. Children in the preoperational stage often pick their own view rather than the doll's view. Preschool children frequently show the ability to take another's perspective on some tasks but not others.

Animism, another limitation of preoperational thought, is the belief that inanimate objects have lifelike qualities and are capable of action (Gelman & Opfer, 2004). A young child might show animism by saying, "That tree pushed the leaf off, and it fell down," or "The sidewalk made me mad; it made me fall down." A young child who uses animism fails to distinguish the appropriate occasions for using human and nonhuman perspectives.

Possibly because young children are not very concerned about reality, their drawings are fanciful and inventive. Suns are blue, skies are yellow, and cars float on clouds in their symbolic, imaginative world. One 3½-year-old looked at a scribble he had just drawn and described it as a pelican kissing a seal (see Figure 9.2a). The symbolism is simple but strong, like abstractions found in some modern art. Twentieth-century Spanish artist Pablo Picasso commented, "I used to draw like

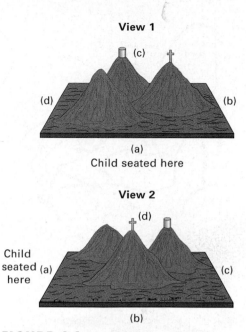

View 1

View 2

(a)
Child seated here

FIGURE 9.1 **The Three Mountains Task** View 1 shows the child's perspective from where he or she is sitting. View 2 is an example of the photograph the child would be shown, mixed in with others from different perspectives. To correctly identify this view, the child has to take the perspective of the person sitting at spot (b). Invariably, a preschool child who thinks in a preoperational way cannot perform this task. When asked what a view of the mountains looks like from position (b), the child selects a photograph taken from location (a), the child's view at the time.

preoperational stage Piaget's second stage, lasting from 2 to 7 years of age, during which time children begin to represent the world with words, images, and drawings. In this stage, they also form stable concepts, and begin to reason. At the same time, their cognitive world is dominated by egocentrism and magical beliefs.

operations In Piaget's theory, and internalized set of actions that allows children to do mentally what they formerly did physically.

symbolic function substage Piaget's first substage of preoperational thought, in which the child gains the ability to mentally represent an object that is not present (roughly between 2 and 4 years of age).

egocentrism Piaget' concept that describes children's difficulties in distinguishing between their own perspective and someone else's perspective.

animism The belief that inanimate objects have lifelike qualities and are capable of action.

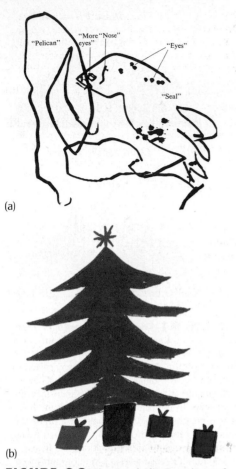

(a)

(b)

FIGURE 9.2 The Symbolic Drawings of Young Children (a) A 3½-year-old's symbolic drawing. Halfway into his drawing, the 3½-year-old artist said it was a "pelican kissing a seal." (b) This 11-year-old's drawing is neater and more realistic but also less inventive.

"I still don't have all the answers, but I'm beginning to ask the right questions."
© The New Yorker Collection, 1989, Lee Lorenz from cartoonbank.com. All Rights Reserved.

Raphael but it has taken me a lifetime to draw like young children." In the elementary school years, a child's drawings become more realistic, neat, and precise (see Figure 9.2b). Suns are yellow, skies are blue, and cars travel on roads (Winner, 1986).

The Intuitive Thought Substage The **intuitive thought substage** is the second substage of preoperational thought, occurring between approximately 4 and 7 years of age. In this substage, children begin to use primitive reasoning and want to know the answers to all sorts of questions. Consider 4-year-old Oliver, who is at the beginning of the intuitive thought substage. Although he is starting to develop his own ideas about the world he lives in, his ideas are still simple, and he is not very good at thinking things out. He has difficulty understanding events that he knows are taking place but which he cannot see. His fantasized thoughts bear little resemblance to reality. He cannot yet answer the question "What if?" in any reliable way. For example, he has only a vague idea of what would happen if a car were to hit him. He also has difficulty negotiating traffic because he cannot do the mental calculations necessary to estimate whether an approaching car will hit him when he crosses the road.

By the age of 5, children have just about exhausted the adults around them with "Why?" questions. The child's questions signal the emergence of interest in reasoning and in figuring out why things are the way they are. Following are some samples of the questions children ask during the questioning period of 4 to 6 years of age (Elkind, 1976):

"What makes you grow up?"
"Why does a woman have to be married to have a baby?"
"Who was the mother when everybody was a baby?"
"Why do leaves fall?"
"Why does the sun shine?"

Piaget called this substage *intuitive* because young children seem so sure about their knowledge and understanding yet are unaware of how they know what they know. That is, they know something but know it without the use of rational thinking.

Centration and the Limits of Preoperational Thought One limitation of preoperational thought is **centration,** a centering of attention on one characteristic to the exclusion of all others. Centration is most clearly evidenced in young children's lack of **conservation,** the awareness that altering an object's or a substance's appearance does not change its basic properties. For example, to adults, it is obvious that a certain amount of liquid stays the same, regardless of a container's shape. But this is not at all obvious to young children. Instead, they are struck by the height of the liquid in the container; they focus on that characteristic to the exclusion of others.

The situation that Piaget devised to study conservation is his most famous task. In the conservation task, children are presented with two identical beakers, each filled to the same level with liquid (see Figure 9.3). They are asked if these beakers have the same amount of liquid, and they usually say yes. Then the liquid from one beaker is poured into a third beaker, which is taller and thinner than the first two. The children are then asked if the amount of liquid in the tall, thin beaker is equal to that which remains in one of the original beakers. Children who are less than 7 or 8 years old usually say no and justify their answers in terms of the differing height or width of the beakers. Older children usually answer yes and justify their answers appropriately ("If you poured the water back, the amount would still be the same").

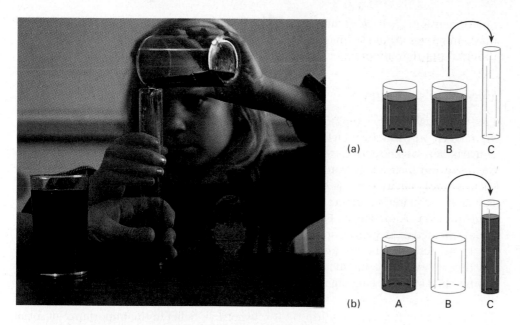

FIGURE 9.3 Piaget's Conservation Task
The beaker test is a well-known Piagetian test to determine whether a child can think operationally—that is, can mentally reverse actions and show conservation of the substance. (*a*) Two identical beakers are presented to the child. Then the experimenter pours the liquid from B into C, which is taller and thinner than A or B. (*b*) The child is asked if these beakers (A and C) have the same amount of liquid. The preoperational child says "no." When asked to point to the beaker that has more liquid, the preoperational child points to the tall, thin beaker.

In Piaget's theory, failing the conservation of liquid task is a sign that children are at the preoperational stage of cognitive development. The failure demonstrates not only centration but also an inability to mentally reverse actions. For example, in the conservation of matter example shown in Figure 9.4, preoperational children say that the longer shape has more clay because they assume that "longer is more." Preoperational children cannot mentally reverse the clay-rolling process to see that the amount of clay is the same in both the shorter ball shape and the longer stick shape.

In addition to failing to conserve volume, preoperational children also fail to conserve number, matter, length, and area. However, children often vary in their performance on different conservation tasks. Thus, a child might be able to conserve volume but not number.

Some developmentalists do not believe Piaget was entirely correct in his estimate of when children's conservation skills emerge. For example, Rochel Gelman (1969) showed that when the child's attention to relevant aspects of the conservation task is improved, the child is more likely to conserve. Gelman has also demonstrated that when adults help young children improve or focus their attention on

intuitive thought substage Piaget's second substage of preoperational thought, in which children begin to use primitive reasoning and want to know the answers to all sorts of questions (between about 4 and 7 years of age).

centration The focusing of attention on one characteristic to the exclusion of all others.

conservation The concept that an object's basic properties stay the same even though the object's appearance has been altered.

Type of conservation	Initial presentation	Manipulation	Preoperational child's answer
Number	Two identical rows of objects are shown to the child, who agrees they have the same number.	One row is lengthened and the child is asked whether one row now has more objects.	Yes, the longer row.
Matter	Two identical balls of clay are shown to the child. The child agrees that they are equal.	The experimenter changes the shape of one of the balls and asks the child whether they still contain equal amounts of clay.	No, the longer one has more.
Length	Two sticks are aligned in front of the child. The child agrees that they are the same length.	The experimenter moves one stick to the right, then asks the child if they are equal in length.	No, the one on the top is longer.

FIGURE 9.4 Some Dimensions of Conservation: Number, Matter, and Length

one dimension, such as number, their performance on another dimension, such as mass, improves. Thus, Gelman argues that conservation appears earlier than Piaget thought and that attention is especially important in explaining conservation.

Vygotsky's Theory

Like Piaget, Vygotsky (1962) was a constructivist, but Vygotsky's is a **social constructivist approach,** which emphasizes the social contexts of learning and the construction of knowledge through social interaction. In moving from Piaget to Vygotsky, our focus shifts from the individual to collaboration, social interaction, and sociocultural activity (Cole & Gajdamaschko, 2007; Daniels, Wertsch, & Cole, 2007). For Piaget, children construct knowledge by transforming, organizing, and reorganizing previous knowledge. For Vygotsky, children construct knowledge through social interaction (Hyson, Copple, & Jones, 2006; Rogoff & others, 2007). In Chapter 1, we described some basic ideas about Vygotsky's theory. Here we expand on his theory, exploring his ideas about the zone of proximal development and the young child's use of language.

The Zone of Proximal Development   Vygotsky's belief in the importance of social influences, especially instruction, on children's cognitive development is reflected in his concept of the zone of proximal development. **Zone of proximal development (ZPD)** is Vygotsky's term for the range of tasks that are too difficult for the child to master alone but that can be learned with guidance and assistance of adults or more-skilled children. Thus, the lower limit of the ZPD is the level of skill reached by the child working independently. The upper limit is the level of additional responsibility the child can accept with the assistance of an able instructor (see Figure 9.5). The ZPD captures the child's cognitive skills that are in the process of maturing and can be accomplished only with the assistance of a more-skilled person (Alvarez & del Rio, 2007; Mooney, 2006). Vygotsky (1962) called these the "buds" or "flowers" of development, to distinguish them from the "fruits" of development, which the child already can accomplish independently.

Let's consider an example that reflects the zone of proximal development (Frede, 1995, p. 125):

> A 5-year-old child is pushing a small shopping cart through the house area of his preschool. His teacher notices that he is putting fruit in the small basket and all other groceries in the larger section of the cart. She has watched him sort objects over the past few weeks and thinks that he may now be able to classify along two dimensions at the same time, with some help from her. She goes to the cash register to pretend to be the cashier and says, "We need to be careful how we divide your groceries into bags. We want to use one bag for things that go in the refrigerator, and other bags for things that will go in the cabinet." Together they devise a system with one bag for each of the following categories: food in cartons that will go into the refrigerator, loose vegetables and fruit for the refrigerator, food cartons that go in the cabinet, and food cans for the cabinet. In this example, the child's unassisted level of classification was fairly gross—fruit versus non-fruit. With the teacher's help, he was able to apply a more sophisticated form of classification.

Scaffolding   Closely linked to the idea of the ZPD is the concept of scaffolding, which was introduced in the context of parent-infant interaction in Chapter 8. **Scaffolding** means changing the level of support. Over the course of a teaching session, a more-skilled person (a teacher, parent, or advanced peer) adjusts the amount of guidance to fit the child's current performance (Daniels, 2007; de Vries, 2005). When the student is learning a new task, the skilled person may use direct instruction. As the student's competence increases, less guidance is given.

Dialogue, or discussion, is an important tool of scaffolding in the zone of proximal development. Vygotsky viewed children as having rich but unsystematic, disorganized,

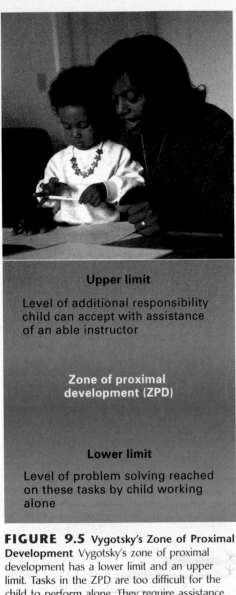

Upper limit

Level of additional responsibility child can accept with assistance of an able instructor

Zone of proximal development (ZPD)

Lower limit

Level of problem solving reached on these tasks by child working alone

FIGURE 9.5 Vygotsky's Zone of Proximal Development Vygotsky's zone of proximal development has a lower limit and an upper limit. Tasks in the ZPD are too difficult for the child to perform alone. They require assistance from an adult or a more-skilled child. As children experience the verbal instruction or demonstration, they organize the information in their existing mental structures, so they can eventually perform the skill or task alone.

social constructivist approach An approach that emphasizes the social contexts of learning and the fact that knowledge is mutually built and constructed; Vygotsky's theory is a social constructivist approach.

zone of proximal development (ZPD) Vygotsky's term for the difference between what children can achieve independently and what they can achieve with the guidance and assistance of adults or more-skilled children.

scaffolding In cognitive development, Vygotsky used this term to describe the changing support over the course of a teaching session, with the more-skilled person adjusting guidance to fit the child's current performance level.

and spontaneous ideas. In a dialogue, these ideas can be discussed in the context of the skilled helper's more systematic, logical, and rational concepts. As a result, the child's concepts become more systematic, logical, and rational. For example, a dialogue might take place between a teacher and a child when the teacher uses scaffolding to help a child understand a concept like "transportation." The teacher might ask a child to describe a method of transportation. Perhaps the child will respond "trains." In the course of a dialogue, the teacher could guide the child toward an understanding of how trains fit into the category of transportation.

Language and Thought   The use of dialogue as a tool for scaffolding is only one example of the important role of language in a child's development. According to Vygotsky, children use speech not only for social communication, but also to help them solve tasks. Vygotsky (1962) further maintained that young children use language to plan, guide, and monitor their own behavior. This use of language for self-regulation is called *private speech*. According to Vygotsky, private speech is overt from about 3 to 8 years, after which it becomes more covert. For example, when approaching a hot stove, a young child may overtly say to herself, "Nicole don't touch." For Piaget, private speech is egocentric and immature, but for Vygotsky it is an important tool of thought during the early childhood years (John-Steiner, 2007; Wertsch, 2007).

Vygotsky said that language and thought initially develop independently of each other and then merge. He emphasized that all mental functions have external, or social, origins. Children must use language to communicate with others before they can focus inward on their own thoughts. Children also must communicate externally and use language for a long period of time before they can make the transition from external to internal speech. This transition period occurs between 3 and 7 years of age and involves talking to oneself. After a while, the self-talk becomes second nature to children, and they can act without verbalizing. When this occurs, children have internalized their egocentric speech in the form of *inner speech*, which becomes their thoughts.

Vygotsky stressed that children who use a lot of private speech are more socially competent than those who don't (Santiago-Delefosse & Delefosse, 2002). He argued that private speech represents an early transition in becoming more socially communicative. For Vygotsky, when young children talk to themselves, they are using language to govern their behavior and guide themselves. For example, a child working on a puzzle might say to herself, "Which pieces first?" "I'll try green ones." "Now some blue." "No, that blue one doesn't fit there." "I'll try over here."

Researchers have found support for Vygotsky's view that private speech plays a positive role in children's development (Winsler, Carlton, & Barry, 2000; Winsler, Diaz, & Montero, 1997). Children use private speech more when tasks are difficult, when they have made errors, and when they are not sure how to proceed (Berk, 1994). Researchers have also found that children who use private speech are more attentive and improve their performance more than children who do not use private speech (Berk & Spuhl, 1995).

Teaching Strategies   Vygotsky's theory has been successfully applied to education (Daniels, 2007; Mooney, 2006). Here are some ways Vygotsky's theory can be used by educators:

1. *Assess the child's ZPD.* Like Piaget, Vygotsky did not conclude that formal, standardized tests are the best way to assess children's learning. Rather, Vygotsky argued that assessment should focus on determining the child's zone of proximal development. The

Lev Vygotsky (1896–1934), shown here with his daughter, believed that children's cognitive development is advanced through social interaction with more-skilled individuals embedded in a sociocultural backdrop. *How is Vygotsky's theory different from Piaget's?*

skilled helper presents the child with tasks of varying difficulty to determine the best level at which to begin instruction.

2. *Use the child's zone of proximal development in teaching.* Teaching should begin toward the zone's upper limit, so that the child can reach the goal with help and move to a higher level of skill and knowledge. Offer just enough assistance. You might ask, "What can I do to help you?" Or simply observe the child's intentions and attempts and provide support when needed. When the child hesitates, offer encouragement. And encourage the child to practice the skill. You may watch and appreciate the child's practice or offer support when the child forgets what to do.

3. *Use more-skilled peers as teachers.* Remember that it is not just adults that are important in helping children learn. Children also benefit from the support and guidance of more-skilled children.

4. *Monitor and encourage young children's use of private speech.* Be aware that when young children are overtly talking to themselves, it is not a sign of immaturity, but rather a positive indication of self-regulation. Thus, teachers in early childhood education programs can encourage young children to talk out loud in some situations, as when they are doing Legos. For example, a young child could say something like "Oops, that's too big—what about this one?" This type of private speech helps children focus their attention and thinking.

5. *Place instruction in a meaningful context.* Educators today are moving away from abstract presentations of material, instead providing students with opportunities to experience learning in real-world settings. For example, instead of just memorizing math formulas, students work on math problems with real-world implications.

The *Caring for Children* interlude further explores the implications of Vygotsky's theory for children's education.

Caring for Children

TOOLS OF THE MIND

Tools of the Mind is an early childhood education curriculum that emphasizes children's development of self-regulation and the cognitive foundations of literacy (Hyson, Copple, & Jones, 2006). The curriculum was created by Elena Bodrova and Deborah Leong (2001, 2007) and has been implemented in more than 200 classrooms. Most of the children in the Tools of the Mind programs are at risk because of their living circumstances, which in many instances involve poverty and other difficult conditions such as being homeless and having parents with drug problems.

Tools of the Mind is grounded in Vygotsky's (1962) theory with special attention given to cultural tools and developing self-regulation. A cultural tool is the method that teachers use to advance children's learning and thinking. (Bodrova & Leong, 2001, 2007). The zone of proximal development, scaffolding, private speech, shared activity, and play as important activity are all cultural tools that are incorporated into Tools of the Mind curriculum. In a Tools of the Mind classroom, dramatic play has a central role. Teachers guide children in creating themes that are based on the children's interests, such as treasure hunt, store, hospital, and restaurant. Teachers also incorporate field trips, visitor presentations, videos, and books in the development of children's play. They also help children develop a "play plan," which increases the maturity of their play. Play plans describe what the children expect to do in the play period, including the imaginary context, roles,

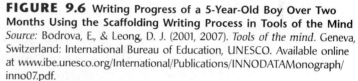

(b) Aaron's journal 2 months after using the Scaffolded Writing technique. He is now making the lines for himself and had no interaction with the story until he had completed it (a total of 4 pages of writing). The number of sentences and words per sentence continues to increase. He has become a prolific writer in a short period of time.

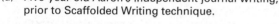

(a) Five-year-old Aaron's independent journal writing, prior to Scaffolded Writing technique.

FIGURE 9.6 Writing Progress of a 5-Year-Old Boy Over Two Months Using the Scaffolding Writing Process in Tools of the Mind
Source: Bodrova, E., & Leong, D. J. (2001, 2007). *Tools of the mind.* Geneva, Switzerland: International Bureau of Education, UNESCO. Available online at www.ibe.unesco.org/International/Publications/INNODATAMonograph/inno07.pdf.

and props to be used. The play plans increase the quality of their play and self-regulation.

Scaffolded writing is another important theme in the Tools of the Mind classroom. Teachers guide children in planning their own message by drawing a line to stand for each word the child says in their simple story. Children then repeat the message, pointing to each line as they say the word. Then, the child writes on the lines, trying to represent each word with some letters or symbols. Figure 9.6 shows how the scaffolding writing process improved a 5-year-old child's writing over the course of two months.

Research assessments of children's writing in Tools of the Mind classrooms revealed that they have more advanced writing skills than children in other early childhood programs (Bodrova & Leong, 2001, 2007). For example, they write more complex messages, use more words, spell more accurately, show better letter recognition, and have a better understanding of the concept of a sentence.

Evaluating Vygotsky's Theory How does Vygotsky's theory compare with Piaget's? We already have mentioned several comparisons, such as Vygotsky's emphasis on the importance of inner speech in development and Piaget's view that

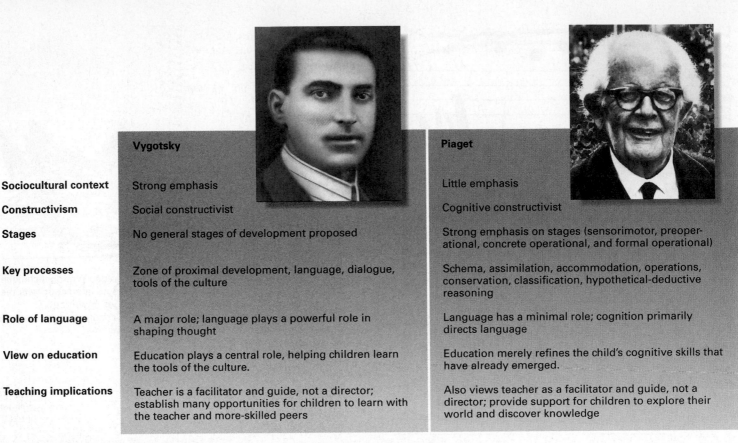

	Vygotsky	Piaget
Sociocultural context	Strong emphasis	Little emphasis
Constructivism	Social constructivist	Cognitive constructivist
Stages	No general stages of development proposed	Strong emphasis on stages (sensorimotor, preoperational, concrete operational, and formal operational)
Key processes	Zone of proximal development, language, dialogue, tools of the culture	Schema, assimilation, accommodation, operations, conservation, classification, hypothetical-deductive reasoning
Role of language	A major role; language plays a powerful role in shaping thought	Language has a minimal role; cognition primarily directs language
View on education	Education plays a central role, helping children learn the tools of the culture.	Education merely refines the child's cognitive skills that have already emerged.
Teaching implications	Teacher is a facilitator and guide, not a director; establish many opportunities for children to learn with the teacher and more-skilled peers	Also views teacher as a facilitator and guide, not a director; provide support for children to explore their world and discover knowledge

FIGURE 9.7 Comparison of Vygotsky's and Piaget's Theories

such speech is immature. Figure 9.7 compares the theories. The implication of Piaget's theory for teaching is that children need support to explore their world and discover knowledge. When Vygotsky's theory is applied to teaching, students are given many opportunities to learn with a teacher and more-skilled peers. In both Piaget's and Vygotsky's theories, teachers serve as facilitators and guides, rather than as directors and molders.

Even though their theories were proposed at about the same time, most of the world learned about Vygotsky's theory later than they learned about Piaget's theory, so Vygotsky's theory has not yet been evaluated as thoroughly. Vygotsky's view of the importance of sociocultural influences on children's development fits with the current belief that it is important to evaluate the contextual factors in learning (Cole & Gajdamaschko, 2007; Karpov, 2006).

Some critics say Vygotsky overemphasized the role of language in thinking. Also, his emphasis on collaboration and guidance has potential pitfalls. Consider these questions posed by skeptics of Vygotsky. Might facilitators be too helpful in some cases, as when a parent becomes too overbearing and controlling? Further, in some circumstances, might some children become too dependent on the help of a skilled person and benefit from doing something on their own?

Information Processing

Piaget's and Vygotsky's theories provide important ideas about how young children think, and how their thinking changes as they develop. More recently, the information-processing approach has generated research that illuminates how children process information during the preschool years. What are the limitations and advances in a young child's ability to pay attention to the environment, to remember, to develop strategies and solve problems, and to understand their own mental processes, and those of others?

short-term memory The memory component in which individuals retain information for up to 30 seconds, assuming there is no rehearsal.

Attention   Recall that in Chapter 5, "Physical Development in Infancy," we defined *attention* as the focusing of cognitive resources. The child's ability to pay attention improves significantly during the preschool years. Toddlers wander around, shift attention from one activity to another, and seem to spend little time focused on any one object or event. By comparison, the preschool child might be observed watching television for a half hour. One study videotaped young children in their homes (Anderson & others, 1985). In 99 families who were observed for 4,672 hours, visual attention to television dramatically increased during the preschool years.

In at least two ways, however, the preschool child's control of attention is still deficient:

- *Salient versus relevant dimensions.* Preschool children are likely to pay attention to stimuli that stand out, or are *salient,* even when those stimuli are not relevant to solving a problem or performing a task. For example, if a flashy, attractive clown presents the directions for solving a problem, preschool children are likely to pay more attention to the clown than to the directions. After the age of 6 or 7, children attend more efficiently to the dimensions of the task that are relevant, such as the directions for solving a problem. This change reflects a shift to cognitive control of attention, so that children act less impulsively and reflect more.
- *Planfulness.* When experimenters ask children to judge whether two complex pictures are the same, preschool children tend to use a haphazard comparison strategy, not examining all of the details before making a judgment. By comparison, elementary-school-age children are more likely to systematically compare the details across the pictures, one detail at a time (Vurpillot, 1968) (see Figure 9.8).

Preschool children's ability to control and sustain their attention is related to both their achievement-related skills and their social skills (NICHD Early Child Care Research Network, 2005; Ruff & Rothbart, 1996). For example, one recent study of more than 1,000 children found that their ability to sustain their attention at 54 months of age was linked to their school readiness (which included achievement and language skills) (NICHD Early Child Care Research Network, 2005). Also, young children who have difficulty regulating their attention are more likely than other children to experience peer rejection and to engage in aggressive behavior (Eisenberg, Spinrad, & Smith, 2004).

Young children's experiences in their home and child care can influence the development of their attention and memory. One study found that stimulating and sensitive care that occurred both early (6 to 36 months of age) and later (54 months and the first grade) in children's homes and at child care was linked to better attention and memory in the first grade (NICHD Early Child Care Research Network, 2003).

Memory   *Memory*—the retention of information over time—is a central process in children's cognitive development. In Chapter 6, we saw that most of an infant's memories are fragile and, for the most part, short-lived—except for the memory of perceptual-motor actions, which can be substantial (Mandler, 2004). Thus, we saw that to understand the infant's capacity to remember we need to distinguish *implicit memory* from *explicit memory.* Explicit memory, however, itself comes in many forms. One distinction occurs between relatively permanent or *long-term memory* and *short-term memory.*

Short-Term Memory   In **short-term memory,** individuals retain information for up to 30 seconds if there is no rehearsal of the information. Using rehearsal (repeating information after it has been presented), we can keep information in short-term memory for a much longer period. One method of assessing short-term memory is the memory-span task. You hear a short list of stimuli—usually digits—presented at a rapid pace (one per second, for example). Then you are asked to repeat the digits.

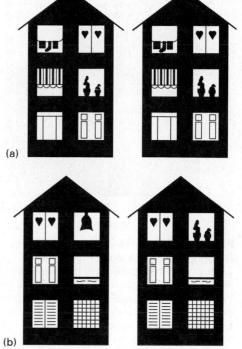

(a)

(b)

FIGURE 9.8 The Planfulness of Attention
In one study, children were given pairs of houses to examine, like the ones shown here (Vurpillot, 1968). For three pairs of houses, what was in the windows was identical (*a*). For the other three pairs, the windows had different items in them (*b*). By filming the reflection in the children's eyes, it could be determined what they were looking at, how long they looked, and the sequence of their eye movements. Children under 6 examined only a fragmentary portion of each display and made their judgments on the basis of insufficient information. By contrast, older children scanned the windows in more detailed ways and were more accurate in their judgments of which windows were identical.

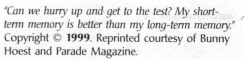

"Can we hurry up and get to the test? My short-term memory is better than my long-term memory." Copyright © **1999**. Reprinted courtesy of Bunny Hoest and Parade Magazine.

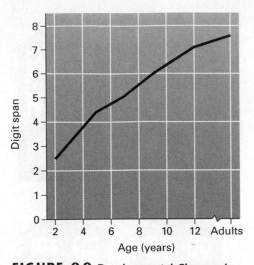

FIGURE 9.9 Developmental Changes in Memory Span In one study, from 2 years of age to 7 years of age children's memory span increased about 3 digits to 5 digits (Dempster, 1981). By 12 years of age, memory span had increased on average only another 1½ digits, to 7 digits. *What factors might contribute to the increase in memory span during childhood?*

Four-year-old Jennifer Royal was the only eyewitness to one of her playmates being shot to death. She was allowed to testify in open court and the clarity of her statements helped to convict the gunman. *What are some issues involved in whether young children should be allowed to testify in court?*

Research with the memory-span task suggests that short-term memory increases during early childhood. For example, in one investigation, memory span increased from about 2 digits in 2- to 3-year-old children to about 5 digits in 7-year-old children, yet between 7 and 13 years of age memory span increased only by 1½ digits (Dempster, 1981) (see Figure 9.9). Although 2-year-old children may only be able to remember the number sequence 5 2, by the time children reach the age of 7, they may remember the number sequence 5 2 3 7 6. Between the ages of 7 and 13, their memory can hold a sequence that is 1½ digits longer. Keep in mind, though, that memory span varies from one individual to another.

Why does memory span change with age? Rehearsal, which involves consciously repeating information, is important; older children rehearse the digits more than younger children. Speed and efficiency of processing information are important, too, especially the speed with which memory items can be identified (Schneider, 2004). For example, in one study, children were tested on their speed at repeating words presented orally (Case, Kurland, & Goldberg, 1982). Speed of repetition was a powerful predictor of memory span. Indeed, when the speed of repetition was controlled, the 6-year-olds' memory spans were equal to those of young adults.

The speed-of-processing explanation highlights a key point in the information-processing perspective: The speed with which a child processes information is an important aspect of the child's cognitive abilities (Schneider, 2004). In one study, faster processing speed on a memory-span task was linked with higher reading and mathematics achievement (Hitch, Towse, & Hutton, 2001).

How Accurate Are Young Children's Long-Term Memories?   While the toddlers' short-term memory span increases during the early childhood years, their memory also becomes more accurate. Young children can remember a great deal of information if they are given appropriate cues and prompts. Increasingly, young children are even being allowed to testify in court, especially if they are the only witnesses to abuse, a crime, and so forth. However, one study found that young children were less likely than older children to reject false suggestions about events (Ghetti & Alexander, 2004). Several factors can influence the accuracy of a young child's memory (Bruck & Ceci, 1999):

* *There are age differences in children's susceptibility to suggestion.* Preschoolers are the most suggestible age group in comparison with older children and adults (Bruck, Ceci, & Principe, 2006; Ceci, 2003). For example, preschool children are more susceptible to misleading or incorrect postevent information (Ghetti & Alexander, 2004). Despite these age differences, there is still concern about older children when they are subjected to suggestive interviews (Poole & Lindsay, 1996).

* *There are individual differences in susceptibility.* Some preschoolers are highly resistant to interviewers' suggestions, whereas others immediately succumb to the slightest suggestion (Bruck, Ceci, & Principe, 2006; Gilstrap & Ceci, 2005). One study found that children with more advanced verbal abilities and self-control were more likely to resist interviewers' suggestive questions (Clarke-Stewart, Malloy, & Allhusen, 2004). A research review found that suggestibility is linked to low self-concept, low support from parents, and mothers' insecure attachment in romantic relationships (Bruck & Melnyk, 2004).

* *Interviewing techniques can produce substantial distortions in children's reports about highly salient events.* Children are suggestible not just about peripheral details but also about the central aspects of an event (Bruck, Ceci, & Hembrooke, 1998). Their false claims have been found to persist for at least three months (Ornstein, Gordon, & Larus, 1992). Nonetheless, young children are

capable of recalling much that is relevant about an event (Fivush, 1993). When children do accurately recall an event, the interviewer often has a neutral tone, there is limited use of misleading questions, and there is an absence of any motivation for the child to make a false report (Bruck & Ceci, 1999).

To read further about false memories in children, see the following *Research in Children's Development* interlude.

Research in Children's Development

SUGGESTING FALSE EVENTS TO CHILDREN

As described in Bruck and Ceci (1999, pp. 429–430), a study by Deborah Poole and D. Stephen Lindsay revealed how parents can subtly influence their young children's memory for events. Preschool children participated in four activities (such as lifting cans with pulleys) with "Mr. Science" in a university laboratory (Poole & Lindsay, 1995). Four months later, the children's parents were mailed a storybook with a description of their child's visit to see Mr. Science. The storybook described two of the activities in which the child had participated, but it also described two in which the child had not participated. Each description ended with this fabrication of what happened when it was time to leave the laboratory: "Mr. Science wiped (child's name) hands and face with a wet-wipe. The cloth got close to (child's name) mouth and tasted real yucky."

Parents read the descriptions to their children three times. Later, the children told the experimenter that they had participated in the activities that actually had only been mentioned in the descriptions read by their parents. For example, when asked whether Mr. Science had put anything yucky in their mouth, more than half of the young children said that he had. Subsequently, when asked whether Mr. Science put something in their mouth or their parent just read this to them in a story, 71 percent of the young children said that it really happened.

This study shows how subtle suggestions can influence children's inaccurate reporting of nonevents. If such inaccurate reports are pursued in follow-up questioning by an interviewer who suspected that something sexual occurred, the result could be a sexual interpretation. This study also revealed the difficulty preschool children have in identifying the source of a suggestion (called *source-monitoring errors*). Children in this study confused their parent reading the suggestion to them with their experience of the suggestion.

In sum, whether a young child's eyewitness testimony is accurate or not may depend on a number of factors such as the type, number, and intensity of the suggestive techniques the child has experienced. It appears that the reliability of young children's reports has as much to do with the skills and motivation of the interviewer as with any natural limitations on young children's memory (Ceci, Fitneva, & Gilstrap, 2003).

According to leading experts who study children's suggestibility, research indicates that three changes need to be implemented (Bruck, Ceci, & Principe, 2006). First, interviewers should be required to electronically preserve their interviews with children. Second, a research-validated interview schedule with children needs to be developed. Third, programs need to be created to teach interviewers how to use interviewing protocols.

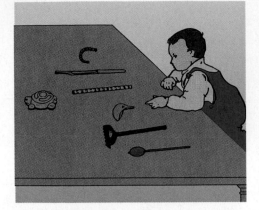

FIGURE 9.10 **The Toy-Retrieval Task in the Study of Young Children's Problem-Solving Strategies** The child needs to choose the toy rake in order to pull in the turtle. In this study (Chen & Siegler, 2000), 2-year-olds were able to learn to select the tool to obtain the toy when the experimenters showed or told them how to do so.

Strategies and Problem Solving In Chapter 1, we mentioned that information-processing theory emphasizes the importance of using good strategies. **Strategies** consist of deliberate mental activities to improve the processing of information (Pressley, 2007; Siegler, 2007). For example, rehearsing information and organizing it are two typical strategies that older children and adults use to remember more effectively. For the most part, young children do not use rehearsal and organization to remember (Miller & Seier, 1994).

Even children as young as 2 years of age can learn a strategy. For example, in a study by Zhe Chen and Robert Siegler (2000), 2-year-olds learned to select the best tool to obtain a desired toy. As Figure 9.10 illustrates, the experimenters placed young children at a table where an attractive toy was placed too far away for the child to reach it (they were not allowed to crawl on the table). On the table, between the child and the toy, were six potential tools, only one of which was likely to be useful in retrieving the tool. The experimenters either showed the child how to obtain the toy or gave the child a hint. These 2-year-olds learned the strategy.

During early childhood, the relatively stimulus-driven toddler is transformed into a child capable of flexible, goal-directed problem solving (Zelazo & Müller, 2004; Zelazo & others, 2003). For example, 3- to 4-year-olds cannot understand that a single stimulus can be described in incompatible ways from two different perspectives (Perner & others, 2002). Consider a problem in which children must sort stimuli using the rule of *color*. In the course of the color sorting, a child may describe a red rabbit as "a *red one*" to solve the problem. However, in a subsequent task, the child may need to discover a rule that describes the rabbit as just "a *rabbit*" to solve the problem. If 3- to 4-year-olds fail to understand that it is possible to provide multiple descriptions of the same stimulus, they persist in describing the stimulus as "a red rabbit." Researchers have found that at about 4 years of age, children acquire the concept of perspectives, which allows them to appreciate that a single stimulus can be described in two different ways (Frye, 1999).

Some developmental psychologists use their training in areas such as cognitive development to pursue careers in applied areas. To read about the work of Helen Schwe, an individual who followed this path, see the *Careers in Child Development* profile.

The Young Child's Theory of Mind Even young children are curious about the nature of the human mind. They have a **theory of mind,** which refers to awareness of one's own mental processes and the mental processes of others. Studies of theory of mind view the child as "a thinker who is trying to explain, predict, and understand people's thoughts, feelings, and utterances" (Harris, 2006). Children's theory of mind changes as they develop through childhood (Doherty, 2007; Flavell, 2004). The main changes occur at 2 to 3 years of age, 4 to 5 years of age, and beyond 5 years. Also, there recently has been increased interest in whether autistic children have difficulty in developing a theory of mind.

Two to Three Years of Age In this time frame, children begin to understand three mental states:

- *Perceptions.* The child realize that another person sees what is in front of her eyes and not necessarily what is in front of the child's eyes.
- *Emotions.* The child can distinguish between positive (for example, happy) and negative (sad, for example) emotions. A child might say, "Sophie feels bad."
- *Desires.* The child understands that if someone wants something, he will try to get it. A child might say, "I want my mommy."

Let's further examine young children's understanding of desires. Children refer to desires earlier and more frequently than they refer to cognitive states such as thinking and knowing (Harris, 2006). Two- to three-year-olds understand the way that desires are related to actions and to simple emotions (Harris, 2006). For example, they understand that people will search for what they want and that if they obtain it, they

strategies Deliberate mental activities to improve the processing of information.

theory of mind A concept that refers to awareness of one's own mental processes and the mental processes of others. 2–5 yrs.

Careers in CHILD DEVELOPMENT

Helen Schwe
Developmental Psychologist and Toy Designer

Helen Schwe obtained a Ph.D. from Stanford University in developmental psychology, but she now spends her days talking with computer engineers and designing "smart" toys for children. Smart toys are designed to improve children's problem-solving and symbolic thinking skills.

When she was a graduate student, Schwe worked part-time for Hasbro toys, testing its children's software on preschoolers. Her first job after graduate school was with Zowie entertainment, which was subsequently bought by LEGO. According to Helen, "Even in a toy's most primitive stage of development, . . . you see children's creativity in responding to challenges, their satisfaction when a problem is solved or simply their delight when they are having fun" (p. 50). In addition to conducting experiments and focus groups at different stages of a toy's development, Schwe also assesses the age-appropriateness of a toy. Most of her current work focuses on 3- to 5-year-old children. (Source: Schlegel, 2000, pp. 50–51)

Helen Schwe, a developmental psychologist, with some of the "smart" toys she designed.

are likely to feel happy, but if they don't they will keep searching for it and are likely to feel sad or angry (Hadwin & Perner, 1991; Wellman & Woolley, 1990).

Four to Five Years of Age Children come to understand that the mind can represent objects and events accurately or inaccurately. The realization that people can have *false beliefs*—beliefs that are not true—develops in a majority of children by the time they are 5 years old (Wellman, Cross, & Watson, 2001) (see Figure 9.11). In one study of false beliefs, young children were shown a Band-Aid box and asked what was inside (Jenkins & Astington, 1996). To the children's surprise, the box actually contained pencils. When asked what a child who had never seen the box would think was inside, 3-year-olds typically responded "pencils." However, the 4- and 5-year-olds, grinning at the anticipation of the false beliefs of other children who had not seen what was inside the box, were more likely to say "Band-Aids."

Children's understanding of thinking has some limitations in early childhood (Harris, 2006; Siegler & Alibali, 2005). They often underestimate when mental activity is likely occurring. For example, they fail to attribute mental activity to someone who is sitting quietly, reading, or talking (Flavell, Green & Flavell, 1995). Their understanding of their own thinking is also limited. One study revealed that even 5-year-olds have difficulty reporting their thoughts (Flavell, Green, & Flavell, 1995). Children were asked to think quietly about the room in their home where they kept their toothbrushes. Shortly after this, many children denied they had been thinking at all and failed to mention either a toothbrush or a bathroom. In another study, when 5-year-olds were asked to try to have no thoughts at all for about 20 seconds, they reported that they were successful at doing this (Flavell, Green, & Flavell, 2000). By contrast, most of the 8-year-olds said they engaged in mental activity during the 20 seconds and reported specific thoughts.

Beyond Age Five It is only beyond the preschool years that children have a deepening appreciation of the mind itself rather than just an understanding of mental states

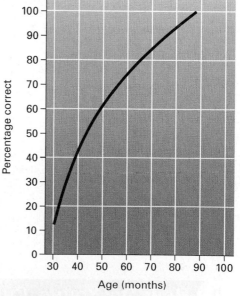

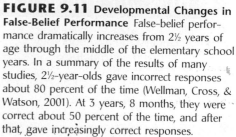

FIGURE 9.11 Developmental Changes in False-Belief Performance False-belief performance dramatically increases from 2½ years of age through the middle of the elementary school years. In a summary of the results of many studies, 2½-year-olds gave incorrect responses about 80 percent of the time (Wellman, Cross, & Watson, 2001). At 3 years, 8 months, they were correct about 50 percent of the time, and after that, gave increasingly correct responses.

The boy sitting on the sofa is autistic. *What are some characteristics of autistic children? What are some difficulties autistic children have on some theory of mind tasks?*

(Wellman, 2004). Not until middle and late childhood do children see the mind as an active constructor of knowledge or processing center (Flavell, Green, & Flavell, 1998) and move from understanding that beliefs can be false to realizing that the same event can be open to multiple interpretations (Carpendale & Chandler, 1996).

Theory of Mind and Autism   Autistic children have problems in social interaction and communication. Approximately 3 to 4 out of 1,000 children are estimated to be autistic (National Institute of Mental Health, 2004). Autism can be reliably detected as early as 3 years of age and in some cases as early as 1 year of age. Autistic children often show indifference toward others, in many instances preferring to be alone and showing more interest in objects than people. It now is accepted that autism is linked to genetic and brain abnormalities (Casanova, 2006; Iacoboni & Dapretto, 2006).

Researchers have found that autistic children have difficulty in developing a theory of mind, especially in understanding others' beliefs and emotions (Harris, 2006). Sometimes this has been referred to as "mindblindness" (Jurecic, 2006). In early research, autistic children showed deficiencies in understanding false beliefs (Baron-Cohen, Leslie, & Frith, 1985). Subsequent research has confirmed this finding (Peterson, 2005). However, it is important to consider individual variations in autistic children and particular aspects of theory of mind (Harris, 2006). Autistic children are not a homogeneous group, and some have less severe social and communication problems than others. Thus, it is not surprising that children who have less severe forms of autism don't do as poorly as those who have more severe forms of the disorder on some theory of mind tasks. For example, higher-functioning autistic children show reasonable progress in understanding others' desires (Harris, 2006). A further important consideration in thinking about autism and theory of mind is that autistic children's difficulty in understanding others' beliefs and emotions might not be due solely to theory of mind deficits but to other aspects of cognition such as problems in focusing attention or some general intellectual impairment (Renner, Grofer Klinger, & Klinger, 2006; Spencer & others, 2006).

REVIEW AND REFLECT ▶ LEARNING GOAL 1

① Describe three views of the cognitive changes that occur in early childhood.

Review
- What characterizes Piaget's stage of preoperational thought?
- What does Vygotsky's theory suggest about how preschool children construct knowledge?
- What are some important ways in which information processing changes during early childhood?

Reflect
- Should children be taught concepts such as conservation? Explain.

---

② HOW DO YOUNG CHILDREN DEVELOP LANGUAGE?

| Understanding Phonology and Morphology | Changes in Syntax and Semantics | Advances in Pragmatics |

Toddlers move rather quickly from producing two-word utterances to creating three-, four-, and five-word combinations. Between 2 and 3 years of age, they begin the transition from saying simple sentences that express a single proposition to saying complex sentences (Bloom, 1998).

Young children's understanding sometimes gets way ahead of their speech. One 3-year-old, laughing with delight as an abrupt summer breeze stirred his hair and tickled his skin, commented, "I got breezed!" Many of the oddities of young children's language sound like mistakes to adult listeners. However, from the children's point of view, they are not mistakes. They represent the way young children perceive and understand their world. As children go through their early childhood years, their grasp of the rule systems that govern language increase.

As young children learn the special features of their own language, there are extensive regularities in how they acquire that particular language (Berko Gleason, 2005). For example, children learn the prepositions *on* and *in* before other prepositions. Children learning other languages, such as Russian or Chinese, also acquire the particular features of those languages in a consistent order.

Understanding Phonology and Morphology

Recall from Chapter 6 that *phonology* is the sound system of a language, including sounds that are used and how they may be combined. During the preschool years, most children gradually become more sensitive to the sounds of spoken words and become increasingly capable of producing all the sounds of their language (National Research Council, 1999). They can even produce complex consonant clusters such as *str-* and *-mpt-*. They notice rhymes, enjoy poems, make up silly names for things by substituting one sound for another (such as *bubblegum, bubblebum, bubbleyum*), and clap along with each syllable in a phrase.

By the time children move beyond two-word utterances, they demonstrate a knowledge of morphology rules (Carlisle, 2004). Remember from Chapter 6 that *morphology* refers to the units of meaning involved in forming words. In early childhood, children begin using the plural and possessive forms of nouns (such as *dogs* and *dog's*). They put appropriate endings on verbs (such as *-s* when the subject is third-person singular and *-ed* for the past tense). They use prepositions (such as *in* and *on*), articles (such as *a* and *the*), and various forms of the verb *to be* (such as "I *was* going to the store"). Some of the best evidence for changes in children's use of morphological rules occurs in their overgeneralization of the rules, as when a preschool child say "foots" instead of "feet," or "goed" instead of "went."

In a classic experiment that was designed to study children's knowledge of morphological rules, such as how to make a plural, Jean Berko (1958) presented preschool children and first-grade children with cards such as the one shown in Figure 9.12. Children were asked to look at the card while the experimenter read aloud the words on the card. Then the children were asked to supply the missing word. This might sound easy, but Berko was interested in the children's ability to apply the appropriate morphological rule, in this case to say "wugs" with the *z* sound that indicates the plural.

Although the children's answers were not perfect, they were much better than chance. What makes Berko's study impressive is that most of the words were made up for the experiment. Thus, the children could not base their responses on remembering past instances of hearing the words. Since they could make the plurals or past tenses of words they had never heard before, this was proof that they knew the morphological rules.

Changes in Syntax and Semantics

Young children show a growing mastery of complex rules for how words should be ordered. Recall from Chapter 6 that *syntax* involves the way words are combined to form acceptable phrases and sentences. In early childhood, children show a growing mastery of complex rules for how words should be ordered (Marchman & Thal, 2005).

Consider *wh-* questions, such as "Where is Mommy going?" or "What is that boy doing?" To ask these questions properly, the child must know two important differences between *wh-* questions and affirmative statements (for instance, "Mommy is going to work" and "That boy is waiting for the school bus"). First, a

This is a wug.

Now there is another one.
There are two of them.
There are two _____.

FIGURE 9.12 Stimuli in Berko's Study of Young Children's Understanding of Morphological Rules In Jean Berko's (1958) study, young children were presented cards, such as this one with a "wug" on it. Then the children were asked to supply the missing word; in supplying the missing word, they had to say it correctly too. "Wugs" is the correct response here.

What are some advances in pragmatics that characterize children's development in early childhood?

wh- word must be added at the beginning of the sentence. Second, the auxiliary verb must be inverted—that is, exchanged with the subject of the sentence. Young children learn quite early where to put the *wh-* word, but they take much longer to learn the auxiliary-inversion rule. Thus, preschool children might ask, "Where mommy is going?" and "What that boy is doing?"

Gains in semantics also characterize early childhood. Remember that *semantics* refers to the meaning of words and sentences. Vocabulary reflects semantics, and young children's vocabulary growth is dramatic. Some experts conclude that between 18 months and 6 years of age, young children learn about one new word every waking hour (Carey, 1978; Gelman & Kalish, 2006)! By the time they enter first grade, it is estimated that children know about 14,000 words (Clark, 1993).

Advances in Pragmatics

Changes in pragmatics also characterize young children's language development (Bryant, 2005). Recall from Chapter 6 that *pragmatics* involves the appropriate use of language in different contexts. Pragmatics includes conversational skills, and a 6-year-old is simply a much better conversationalist than a 2-year-old is.

What are some of the other improvements in pragmatics during the preschool years? As children get older, they become increasingly able to talk about things that are not here (grandma's house, for example) and not now (what happened to them yesterday or might happen tomorrow, for example). A preschool child can tell you what she wants for lunch tomorrow, something that would not have been possible at the two-word stage of language development.

At about 4 years of age, children develop a remarkable sensitivity to the needs of others in conversation. One way in which they show such sensitivity is through their use of the articles *the* and *an* (or *a*). When adults tell a story or describe an event, they generally use *an* (or *a*) when they first refer to *an* animal or *an* object, and then use *the* when referring to it later. (For example, "Two boys were walking through the jungle when *a* fierce lion appeared. *The* lion lunged at one boy while the other ran for cover." Even 3-year-olds follow part of this rule; they consistently use the word *the* when referring to previously mentioned things. However, the use of the word *a* when something is initially mentioned develops more slowly. Although 5-year-old children follow this rule on some occasions, they fail to follow it on others.

Around 4 to 5 years of age, children learn to change their speech style to suit the situation. For example, even 4-year-old children speak differently to a 2-year-old than to a same-aged peer; they use shorter sentences with the 2-year-old. They also speak differently to an adult than to a same-aged peer, using more polite and formal language with the adult (Shatz & Gelman, 1973).

The advances in language that take place in early childhood lay the foundation for later development in the elementary school years, which we discuss in Chapter 12, "Cognitive Development in Middle and Late Childhood."

REVIEW AND REFLECT ▶ **LEARNING GOAL 2**

② Summarize how language develops in early childhood.

Review
- How do phonology and morphology change during early childhood?
- What characterizes young children's understanding of syntax and semantics?
- What advances in pragmatics occur in early childhood?

Reflect
- How are nature and nurture likely to be involved in the dramatic increase in a young child's spoken vocabulary?

3 WHAT ARE SOME IMPORTANT FEATURES OF EARLY CHILDHOOD EDUCATION?

> Variations in Early Childhood Education

> Educating Young Children Who Are Disadvantaged

> Literacy and Early Childhood Education

> Controversies in Early Childhood Education

To the teachers at a Reggio Emilia program (described in the chapter opening), preschool children are active learners, exploring the world with their peers, constructing their knowledge of the world in collaboration with their community, aided but not directed by the teachers. In many ways, the Reggio Emilia approach applies ideas consistent with the views of Piaget and Vygotsky discussed in this chapter. Does it matter to the children? How do other early education programs treat children, and how do the children fare? Our exploration of early childhood education focuses on variations in programs, literacy, education for children who are disadvantaged, and some controversies in early childhood education.

Variations in Early Childhood Education

There are many variations in the way young children are educated (Brewer, 2007; Driscoll & Nagel, 2008). The foundation of early childhood education has been the child-centered kindergarten.

The Child-Centered Kindergarten

In the 1840s, Friedrich Froebel's concern for quality education for young children led to the founding of the kindergarten—literally, "a garden for children." The founder of the kindergarten understood that, like growing plants, children require careful nurturing. Unfortunately, too many of today's kindergartens have forgotten the importance of careful nurturing (Krogh & Slentz, 2001).

Nurturing is still key in the **child-centered kindergarten.** It emphasizes the education of whole child and concern for his or her physical, cognitive, and socioemotional development (Follari, 2007; Hendrick & Weissman, 2006). Instruction is organized around the child's needs, interests, and learning styles. Emphasis is on the process of learning, rather than what is learned (Morrison, 2008). The child-centered kindergarten honors three principles: (1) each child follows a unique developmental pattern; (2) young children learn best through firsthand experiences with people and materials; and (3) play is extremely important in the child's total development. *Experimenting, exploring, discovering, trying out, restructuring, speaking,* and *listening* are frequent activities in excellent kindergarten programs. Such programs are closely attuned to the developmental status of 4- and 5-year-old children.

The Montessori Approach

Montessori schools are patterned after the educational philosophy of Maria Montessori (1870–1952), an Italian physician-turned-educator, who crafted a revolutionary approach to young children's education at the beginning of the twentieth century (Wentworth, 1999). Her work began in Rome with a group of children who were mentally retarded. She was successful in teaching them to read, write, and pass examinations designed for normal children. Some time later, she turned her attention to poor children from the slums of Rome and had similar success in teaching them. Her approach has since been adopted extensively in private nursery schools in the United States.

child-centered kindergarten Education that involves the whole child by considering both the child's physical, cognitive, and social development and the child's needs, interests, and learning styles.

Larry Page and Sergey Brin, founders of the highly successful Internet search engine, Google, recently said that their early years at Montessori schools were a major factor in their success (International Montessori Council, 2006). During an interview with Barbara Walters, they said they learned how to be self-directed and self-starters at Montessori (ABC News, 2005). They commented that Montessori experiences encouraged them to think for themselves and allowed them the freedom to develop their own interests.

The **Montessori approach** is a philosophy of education in which children are given considerable freedom and spontaneity in choosing activities and specially designed curriculum materials. They are allowed to move from one activity to another as they desire. The teacher acts as a facilitator rather than a director. The teacher shows the child how to perform intellectual activities, demonstrates interesting ways to explore curriculum materials, and offers help when the child requests it. "By encouraging children to make decisions from an early age, Montessori programs seek to develop self-regulated problem solvers who can make choices and manage their time effectively" (Hyson, Copple, & Jones, 2006, p. 14). The number of Montessori schools in the United States has expanded dramatically in recent years, from one school in 1959 to 355 schools in 1970 to approximately 4,000 in 2005 (Whitescarver, 2006).

Some developmentalists favor the Montessori approach, but others believe that it neglects children's social development (Chattin-McNichols, 1992). For example, while Montessori fosters independence and the development of cognitive skills, it deemphasizes verbal interaction between the teacher and child and peer interaction. Montessori's critics also argue that it restricts imaginative play and that its heavy reliance on self-corrective materials may not adequately allow for creativity and for a variety of learning styles (Goffin & Wilson, 2001).

Developmentally Appropriate and Inappropriate Education A growing number of educators and psychologists believe that preschool and young elementary school children learn best through active, hands-on teaching methods such as games and dramatic play. They know that children develop at varying rates and that schools need to allow for these individual differences (Kostelnik, Soderman, & Whiren, 2007; Miranda, 2004). They also believe that schools should focus on improving children's socioemotional development, as well as their cognitive development (Brewer, 2007; Hyson, 2007; Hyson, Copple, & Jones, 2006). Educators refer to this type of schooling as **developmentally appropriate practice,** which is based on knowledge of the typical development of children within an age span (age appropriateness), the uniqueness of the child (individual appropriateness), and sociocultural contexts (NAEYC, 1997). In contrast, developmentally inappropriate practice for young children relies on abstract paper-and-pencil activities presented to large groups (Bredekamp, 1997; McDaniels & others, 2005; Neuman & Roskos, 2005). The Reggio Emilia approach, described in the opening of the chapter, reflects developmentally appropriate practice. Figure 9.13 provides examples of developmentally appropriate and inappropriate practices for 3- through 5-year-old children.

One study compared 182 children from five developmentally appropriate kindergarten classrooms (with hands-on activities and integrated curriculum tailored to meet age group, cultural, and individual learning styles) and five developmentally inappropriate kindergarten classrooms (which had an academic, direct instruction emphasis with extensive use of workbooks/worksheets, seatwork, and rote drill/practice activities) in a Louisiana school system (Hart & others, 2003). Children from the two types of classrooms did not differ in pre-kindergarten readiness, and the classrooms were balanced in terms of sex and socioeconomic status. Teacher ratings of child behavior and scores on the California Achievement Test were obtained through the third grade. Children taught in developmentally inappropriate classrooms had slower growth in vocabulary, math application, and math computation. In another study, the academic achievement of mostly African American and Latino children who were attending Head Start was assessed in terms of whether they were in schools emphasizing developmentally appropriate or inappropriate practices (Huffman & Speer, 2000). The young children in the developmentally appropriate

Montessori approach An educational philosophy in which children are given considerable freedom and spontaneity in choosing activities and specially designed curriculum materials.

developmentally appropriate practice Education that focuses on the typical developmental patterns of children (age appropriateness), the uniqueness of each child (individual appropriateness), and sociocultural contexts. Such practice contrasts with *developmentally inappropriate practice,* which ignores the concrete, hands-on approach to learning. Direct teaching largely through abstract paper-and-pencil activities presented to large groups of young children is believed to be developmentally inappropriate.

COMPONENT	DEVELOPMENTALLY APPROPRIATE PRACTICE	DEVELOPMENTALLY INAPPROPRIATE PRACTICE
Creating a caring community of learners	To promote a positive climate for learning, teachers help children learn how to develop positive relationships with other children and adults.	Little or no effort is made to build a sense of community.
	Teachers foster group cohesiveness and create activities that meet children's individual needs.	The curriculum and environment are essentially the same for each group of children that comes through the program without considering the interests and identities of the children.
	Teachers bring each child's home culture the interests and identities of and language into the shared culture of the school.	Cultural and other individual differences are ignored.
	Teachers recognize the importance of having children work and play collaboratively.	Teachers don't help children develop feelings of caring and empathy for each other.
Teaching to enhance development and learning	Teachers plan and prepare a learning environment that fosters children's initiative, active exploration of material, and sustained engagement with other children, adults, and activities.	The environment is disorderly with little structure.
	In selecting materials, teachers consider children's developmental levels and cultural backgrounds.	The organization of the environment limits children's interaction with other children.
	Teachers maintain a safe, healthy environment and carefully supervise children.	Teachers don't adequately monitor children. Learning materials are mainly drill-and-practice, workbook-type activities rather than interesting and engaging activities.
	Teachers give children opportunities to plan and select many of their program activities from a variety of learning areas and projects.	The program provides few or no opportunities for children to make choices. Children spend too much time sitting and being quiet. Children do a lot of paper-and-pencil seatwork.
	Teachers encourage children's language and communication skills.	Teachers don't provide adequate time for children to develop concepts and skills.
	Teaching strategies involve observing and interacting with children to determine what each child is capable of doing.	Too many activities are uninteresting and unchallenging, or so difficult, that they diminish children's intrinsic motivation to learn.
	Teachers support children's play and child-chosen activities. They also provide many opportunities for children to plan, think about, reflect on, and discuss their own experiences.	Teachers spend too much time providing negative feedback and punishment.
	Activities are interesting and at the right level to challenge children and encourage their intrinsic motivation.	
	Teachers facilitate the development of social skills and self control by providing positive guidance strategies.	
Constructing appropriate curriculum	Curriculum goals assess learning in all developmental areas —physical, social, emotional, language, aesthetic, and intellectual.	Curriculum goals are narrowly focused.
	Curriculum content from various disciplines, such as math, science, or social studies, is integrated through themes, projects, play, and other learning experiences.	The curriculum is too trivial and follows a rigid plan that doesn't take into account children's interests.
	The curriculum plan designed to help children explore key ideas in disciplines appropriate for their age.	In some programs, the curriculum is not adequately planned.
	Culturally diverse and nonsexist materials are provided.	Curriculum expectations are not well matched to children's intellectual capacities and developmental characteristics.
	Teachers use a variety of approaches and daily opportunities to develop children's language and literacy skills through meaningful experiences.	Children's cultural and linguistic backgrounds are ignored.
	Children have daily opportunities for aesthetic expression through art and music, as well as daily opportunities to develop gross- and fine-motor skills.	Reading and writing instruction is too rigid.
		Instruction focuses on isolated skill development through rote memorization.
		Little effort is made to provide children with opportunities to engage in aesthetic activities.
		Little time is spent in gross or fine motor activities.

FIGURE 9.13 Examples of NAEYC Guidelines for Appropriate and Inappropriate Practices for 3- Through 5-Year-Olds *Source:* Adapted, by permission, from S. Bredekamp and C. Copple, "Developmentally Appropriate Practice for 3- through 5-year-olds," in Developmentally Appropriate Practice in Early Childhood Programs, Rev. ed., eds. S. Bredekamp and C. Copple (Washington, DC: NAEYC, 1997), 123–138.

classrooms were more advanced in letter/word identification and showed better performance in applying problems over time.

However, not all studies show significant positive benefits for developmentally appropriate education (Hyson, Copple, & Jones, 2006). Among the reasons it is difficult to generalize about research on developmentally appropriate education is that individual programs often vary, and developmentally appropriate education is an evolving concept. Recent changes in the concept have given more attention to sociocultural factors, the teacher's active involvement and implementation of systematic intentions, as well as how strong academic skills should be emphasized and how they should be taught.

Literacy and Early Childhood Education

An important emphasis in early childhood education programs is to help children develop a foundation for reading, writing, and math skills (McGhee & Richgels, 2008; Soderman & Farrell, 2008). Let's first examine reading and writing skills.

Reading and Writing   The concern about the ability of U.S. children to read and write has led to a careful examination of preschool and kindergarten children's experiences, with the hope that a positive orientation toward reading and writing can be developed early in life (Antonacci & O'Callaghan, 2006; Vacca & others, 2006). What should a literacy program for preschool children be like? Instruction should be built on what children already know about oral language, reading, and writing. Further, early precursors of literacy and academic success include language skills, phonological and syntactic knowledge, letter identification, and conceptual knowledge about print and its conventions and functions (Jalongo, 2007; Otto, 2008). A longitudinal study found that phonological awareness, letter name and sound knowledge, and naming speed in kindergarten were linked to reading success in the first and second grade (Schattschneider & others, 2004). In another longitudinal study, the number of letters children knew in kindergarten was highly correlated (.52) with their reading achievement in high school (Stevenson & Newman, 1986).

All young children should experience feelings of success and pride in their early reading and writing exercises (Graves, Juel, & Graves, 2007; Ruddell, 2006). Teachers need to help them perceive themselves as people who can enjoy exploring oral and written language. Reading should be integrated into the broad communication process, which includes speaking, listening, and writing, as well as other communication systems, such as art, math, and music (Combs, 2006; Christie, Vukellish, & Enz, 2007). Children's early writing attempts should be encouraged without concern for the proper formation of letters or correct conventional spelling. Children should be encouraged to take risks in reading and writing, and errors should be viewed as a natural part of the child's growth (Tompkins, 2006). Teachers and parents should take time to regularly read to children from a wide variety of poetry, fiction, and nonfiction (Temple & others, 2005). Teachers and parents should present models for young children to emulate by using language appropriately, listening and responding to children's talk, and engaging in their own reading and writing. And children should be encouraged to be active participants in the learning process, rather than passive recipients of knowledge. This can be accomplished by using activities that stimulate experimentation with talking, listening, writing, and reading (Barone, Hardman, & Taylor, 2006). We have much more to say about reading and writing in Chapter 12, "Cognitive Development in Middle and Late Childhood."

What should a literacy program for young children be like?

Math   Early childhood education has focused more on the development of reading skills than math skills. <u>A quality early childhood education program guides young children in developing both reading and math skills.</u> Early childhood educators need to introduce mathematical concepts, methods, and language through a range of appropriate experiences and teaching strategies (Smith, 2006; Van de Walle & Lovin, 2006). Young children especially benefit when they can explore and manipulate mathematical ideas while they are engaging in play. There is a special concern about the math skills of young children from low-socioeconomic-status (SES) families, with researchers finding that they receive less support for the development of their math skills than their higher-SES counterparts (Starkey, Klein, & Wakeley, 2004).

Although there is developmental variation in math learning by young children, they tend to follow certain sequences or learning paths as they develop. Figure 9.14 describes some skills that many children know and use early and late in the 3- to 6-year range. These are simply two points along the learning path and may have many steps in between. The learning paths described in Figure 9.14 were developed as a joint project by the National Association for the Education of Young Children and the National Council of Teachers of Mathematics (NAEYC, 2003).

Content area	Examples of typical knowledge and skills		Sample teaching strategies
	From age 3 ———————————————→ Age 6		
Number and operations	Counts a collection of 1 to 4 items and begins to understand that the last counting word tells "how many"	Counts and produces (counts out) collections up to 100 using groups of 10	Models counting of small collections and guides children's counting in everyday situations, emphasizing that we use one counting word for each object: ♡ ♡ ♡ "One. . . two. . . three. . ." Models counting by 10s while making groups of 10s (for example, 10, 20, 30. . . or 14, 24, 34. . .)
Geometry and spatial sense	Begins to match and name 2-D and 3-D shapes, first only with same size and orientation, then shapes that differ in size and orientation (such as a large triangle sitting on its point versus a small one sitting on its side)	Recognizes and names a variety of 2-D and 3-D shapes (such as quadrilaterals, trapezoids, rhombi, hexagons, spheres, cubes) in any orientation Describes basic features of shapes (such as number of sides or angles)	Introduces and labels a wide variety of shapes (such as skinny triangles, fat rectangles, prisms) that are in a variety of positions (such as a square or a triangle standing on a corner, a cylinder "standing up" or horizontal) Involves children in constructing shapes and talking about their features
Measurement	Recognizes and labels measurable attributes of objects (such as: I need a long string; Is this heavy?)	Tries out various processes and units for measurement and begins to notice different results of one method or another (such as what happens when we *don't* use a standard unit)	Uses comparing words to model and discuss measuring (such as: This book feels heavier than that block. I wonder if this block tower is taller than the desk.)
Displaying and analyzing data	Sorts objects and counts and compares the groups formed	Organizes and displays data through simple numerical representations such as bar graphs and counts the number in each group	Invites children to sort and organize collected materials by color, size, shape, etc. Asks them to compare groups to find which group has the most

FIGURE 9.14 Learning Paths and Teaching Strategies in Early Mathematics *Note:* These lists of content areas and descriptions are not exhaustive but rather presented as examples of some of the important math skills that children can learn in early childhood education and the teaching strategies that can be used.

Yolanda Garcia
Director of Children's Services/Head Start

Yolanda Garcia has been the Director of the Children's Services Department for the Santa Clara, California, County Office of Education since 1980. As director, she is responsible for managing child development programs for 2,500 3- to 5-year-old children in 127 classrooms. Her training includes two master's degrees, one in public policy and child welfare from the University of Chicago and another in education administration from San Jose State University.

Yolanda has served on many national advisory committees that have resulted in improvements in the staffing of Head Start programs. Most notably, she served on the Head Start Quality Committee that recommended the development of Early Head Start and revised performance standards for Head Start programs. Yolanda currently is a member of the American Academy of Science Committee on the Integration of Science and Early Childhood Education.

Yolanda Garcia, Director of Children's Services/Head Start, working with some Head Start children in Santa Clara, California.

Educating Young Children Who Are Disadvantaged

For many years, U.S. children from low-income families did not receive any education before they entered the first grade. Often, they began first grade already several steps behind their classmates in their readiness to learn. In the summer of 1965, the federal government began an effort to break the cycle of poverty and poor education for young children in the United States through **Project Head Start.** It is a compensatory program designed to provide children from low-income families the opportunity to acquire the skills and experiences important for success in school.

The goals and methods of Head Start programs vary greatly around the country. The U.S. Congress recently began requiring a stronger academic focus in Head Start programs. Some worry that the emphasis on academic skills will come at the expense of reduced health services and decreased emphasis on socioemotional skills (Stipek, 2004).

Head Start programs are not all created equal. One estimate is that 40 percent of the 1,400 Head Start programs are of questionable quality (Zigler & Styfco, 1994). More attention needs to be given to developing consistently high-quality Head Start programs (Bronfenbrenner, 1995). One individual who is strongly motivated to make Head Start a valuable learning experience for young children from disadvantaged backgrounds is Yolanda Garcia. To read about her work, see the *Careers in Child Development* profile.

Evaluations support the positive influence of quality early childhood programs on both the cognitive and social worlds of disadvantaged young children (Anderson & others, 2003; Chambers, Cheung, & Slavin, 2006; Ryan, Fauth, & Brooks-Gunn, 2006; Schweinhart & others, 2005; Seifert, 2006). One high-quality early childhood education program (although not a Head Start program) was the Perry Preschool program that was in operation from 1962 to 1967 in Ypsilanti, Michigan, a two-year preschool program that included weekly home visits from program personnel. In analyses of the long-term effects of the program, adults who had been in the Perry Preschool program were compared with a control group of adults from the same background who did not receive the enriched early childhood education (Schweinhart & others, 2005; Weikart, 1993). Those who had been in the Perry Preschool program had fewer teen pregnancies and higher high school graduation rates (Weikart, 1993), and at age 40 more were in the workforce, owned their own homes, had a savings account, and had fewer arrests (Schweinhart & others, 2005). In sum, ample evidence indicates that well-designed and well-implemented early childhood education programs are successful with low-income children (Barnett & Masse, 2007; Hyson, Copple, & Jones, 2006).

What is the curriculum controversy in early childhood education?

Controversies in Early Childhood Education

Four controversies in early childhood education involve (1) the curriculum, (2) whether preschool matters, (3) universal preschool education, and (4) school readiness.

Curriculum Controversy Currently, there is controversy about what the curriculum of U.S. early childhood education should be (Driscoll & Nagel, 2005; Hyson, 2007; Hyson, Copple, & Jones, 2006; Morrison, 2006; Zigler, Gilliam, & Jones, 2006). On one side are those who advocate a child-centered, constructivist approach much like that emphasized by the NAEYC along the lines of developmentally appropriate practice. On the other side are those who advocate an academic, direct instruction approach. It is important to note that NAEYC, like the direct instruction approach, emphasizes academic development—but at issue is how academic content, such as learning math and learning to read, should be infused in the curriculum and how it should be taught.

In reality, many high-quality early childhood education programs include both direct instruction and constructivist approaches. Many education experts like Lilian Katz (1999), though, worry about approaches, such as an exclusive direction instruction approach, that place too much pressure on young children to achieve and don't provide any opportunities to actively construct knowledge. Competent early childhood programs also should focus on cognitive development *and* socioemotional development, not exclusively on cognitive development (Jacobson, 2004; Kagan & Scott-Little, 2004; NAEYC, 2002).

Early childhood education should encourage adequate preparation for learning, varied learning activities, trusting relationships between adults and children, and increased parental involvement (Hildebrand, Phenice, & Hines, 2000). Too many young children go to substandard early childhood programs (Morrison, 2006). According to a report by the Carnegie Corporation (1996), four out of five early childhood programs did not meet quality standards.

Does Preschool Matter?
Is preschool a good thing for all children? According to developmental psychologist David Elkind (1988), parents who are exceptionally competent and dedicated, and who have both the time and the energy, can provide

Project Head Start Compensatory education designed to provide children from low-income families the opportunity to acquire the skills and experiences important for school success.

the basic ingredients of early childhood education in their home. If parents have the competence and resources to provide young children with a variety of learning experiences and exposure to other children and adults (possibly through neighborhood play groups), along with opportunities for extensive play, then home schooling may sufficiently educate young children. However, if parents do not have the commitment, the time, the energy, and the resources to provide young children with an environment that approximates a good early childhood program, then it *does* matter whether a child attends preschool.

Should There Be Universal Preschool Education? Especially because so many young children do not experience an environment that approximate a good early childhood program, there are increasing calls for instituting preschool education for all U.S. 4-year-old children (Zigler, Gilliam, & Jones, 2006). Attending preschool is rapidly becoming the norm for U.S. children. In 2002, 43 states funded pre-kindergarten programs, and 55 percent of U.S. 3- and 4-year-old children attended center-based programs (NAEYC, 2005). Many other 3- and 4-year-old children attend private preschool programs.

Like kindergarten, the concept of universal preschool education is that it be voluntary, not mandated, and available for any 4-year-old child. Georgia and Oklahoma are close to a universal preschool education program, and some other states, such as West Virginia, are moving in that direction. California was moving toward universal preschool education, but voters turned this down in a 2006 election. Edward Zigler and his colleagues (2006) recently argued that the United States should have universal preschool education. They emphasize that quality preschools prepare children for school readiness and academic success. Zigler and his colleagues (2006) cite research that shows quality preschool programs increase the likelihood that once children go to elementary and secondary school they will be less likely to be retained in a grade or drop out of school. They also point to analyses indicating that universal preschool would bring considerable cost savings on the order of billions of dollars because of a diminished need for remedial and justice services (Karoly & Bigelow, 2005). A number of early childhood education experts agree with Zigler and his colleagues that U.S. 4-year-olds would benefit from universal preschool education (Bennett & Masse, 2007).

Critics of universal preschool education argue that the gains attributed to preschool and kindergarten education are often overstated. They especially stress that research has not proven that nondisadvantaged children improve as a result of attending a preschool. Thus, the critics say it is more important to improve preschool education for young children who are disadvantaged rather than funding preschool education for all 4-year-old children. Some critics, especially homeschooling advocates, emphasize that young children should be educated by their parents, not by schools. Thus, controversy continues to characterize whether universal preschool education should be implemented.

School Readiness Educational reform has prompted considerable concern about children's readiness to enter kindergarten and first grade (Crompton, 2005; Halle & others, 2007). National studies suggest that 40 percent of kindergartners are not ready for first grade (Kaufmann Early Education Exchange, 2002).

The National Association for the Education of Young Children (NAEYC, 1990) stresses that government officials and educators who promote universal school readiness should commit to:

- Addressing the inequities in early life experiences, such as poverty, so that all children have access to the opportunities that promote success in school
- Recognizing and supporting individual differences in children
- Establishing reasonable and appropriate expectations for children's capabilities on school entry

Inadequate health care and economic difficulties place many children at risk for academic failure before they enter school (Naude, Pretorius, & Vijoen, 2003). Thus, it is important to provide families with access to the services and support necessary to prepare children to succeed in school. These services include basic health care, economic support, basic nutrition, adequate housing, family support services, and high-quality early childhood education programs.

Craig and Sharon Ramey (1999, 2004) reviewed scientific research on school readiness and concluded that the following six caregiver activities are necessary in the infant and early childhood years to ensure that children are ready for elementary school (Ramey & Ramey, 1999, p. 145):

1. Encourage exploration.
2. Mentor in basic skills.
3. Celebrate developmental advances.
4. Research and extend new skills.
5. Protect from inappropriate disapproval, teasing, and punishment.
6. Guide and limit behavior.

An increasing number of U.S. parents are delaying the entry of their children into the first grade with the hope that the additional year will provide their child with a competitive advantage. Borrowing the term from college athletics (in which an athlete is held out of competition for a year in hope that greater maturity and experience will produce improved performance), this strategy has been referred to as "academic redshirting." On the whole, the evidence about the short-term and long-term effects of redshirting are inconclusive (ERIC/EECE, 2002; West, Denton, & Germino-Hausken, 2000). When benefits of redshirting appear, they typically are short-lived and may in the long term be disadvantageous (Graue & DiPerna, 2000).

A related issue involves whether a child who is not doing well in kindergarten should be held back for a second year of kindergarten rather than entering the first grade. Researchers have found that this is generally not a good strategy, resulting in lower academic achievement and self-esteem (Carlton & Winsler, 1999; Hong & Radenbaugh, 2005).

In some developed countries, such as Japan, as well as in many developing countries, the goals of early childhood education are quite different from those of American programs. To read about the differences, see the *Diversity in Children's Development* interlude.

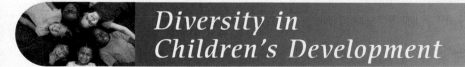

Diversity in Children's Development

EARLY CHILDHOOD EDUCATION IN JAPAN AND DEVELOPING COUNTRIES

As in America, there is diversity in Japanese early childhood education. Some Japanese kindergartens have specific aims, such as early musical training or the practice of Montessori strategies. In large cities, some kindergartens are attached to universities that have elementary and secondary schools. In most Japanese preschools, however, little emphasis is put on academic instruction.

In one study, 300 Japanese and 210 American preschool teachers, child development specialists, and parents were asked about various aspects of early childhood education (Tobin, Wu, & Davidson, 1989). Only 2 percent of the Japanese respondents

(continued on next page)

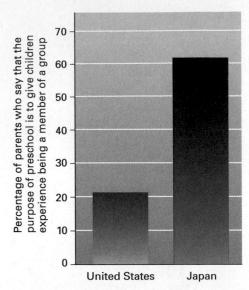

FIGURE 9.15 Comparison of Japanese and U.S. Parents' Views on the Purpose of Preschool

listed "to give children a good start academically" as one of their top three reasons for a society to have preschools. In contrast, over half the American respondents chose this as one of their top three choices. Japanese schools do not teach reading, writing, and mathematics but rather skills like persistence, concentration, and the ability to function as a member of a group. The vast majority of young Japanese children are taught to read at home by their parents.

In the comparison of Japanese and American parents, more than 60 percent of the Japanese parents said that the purpose of preschool is to give children experience being a member of the group compared with only 20 percent of the U.S. parents (Tobin, Wu, & Davidson, 1989) (see Figure 9.15). Lessons in living and working together grow naturally out of the Japanese culture. In many Japanese kindergartens, children wear the same uniforms, including caps, which are of different colors to indicate the classrooms to which they belong. They have identical sets of equipment, kept in identical drawers and shelves. This is not intended to turn the young children into robots, as some Americans have observed, but to impress on them that other people, just like themselves, have needs and desires that are equally important (Hendry, 1995).

Japan is a highly advanced industrialized country. What about developing countries—how do they compare to the United States in educating young children? The wide range of programs and emphasis on the education of the whole child—physically, cognitively, and socioemotionally—that characterizes U.S. early childhood does not exist in many developing countries (Rooparnine & Metingdogan, 2006). Economic pressures and parents' belief that education should be academically rigorous have produced teacher-centered rather child-centered early childhood education programs in most developing countries. Among the countries in which this type of early childhood education has been observed are Jamaica, China, Thailand, Kenya, and Turkey. In these countries, young children are usually given few choices and are educated in highly structured settings. Emphasis is on learning academic skills through rote memory and recitation (Lin, Johnson, & Johnson, 2003). Programs in Mexico, Singapore, Korea, and Hong Kong have been observed to be closer to those in the United States in their emphasis on curriculum flexibility and play-based methods (Cisneros-Cohernour, Moreno, & Cisneros, 2000).

What characterizes early childhood education in Japan?

A kindergarten class in Kingston, Jamaica. *What characterizes kindergarten in many developing countries like Jamaica?*

REVIEW AND **REFLECT** ◆ **LEARNING GOAL 3**

3 **Evaluate different approaches to early childhood education.**

Review
- What are some variations in early childhood education?
- What literacy and math skills should a quality early childhood education program focus on?
- What are the main efforts to educate young children who are disadvantaged?
- What are three controversies about early childhood education?

Reflect
- Might preschool be more beneficial to children from middle-income than low-income families? Why?

REACH YOUR LEARNING GOALS

1 · WHAT ARE THREE VIEWS OF THE COGNITIVE CHANGES THAT OCCUR IN EARLY CHILDHOOD? *Describe three views of the cognitive changes that occur in early childhood.*

Piaget's Preoperational Stage

- According to Piaget, in the preoperational stage children cannot yet perform operations, which are reversible mental actions, but they begin to represent the world with symbols, to form stable concepts, and to reason. During the symbolic function substage, which occurs between 2 and 4 years of age, children begin to create symbols, but their thought is limited by egocentrism and animism. During the intuitive thought substage, which stretches from 4 to 7 years of age, children begin to reason and to bombard adults with questions. Thought at this substage is called intuitive because children seem so sure about their knowledge yet are unaware of how they know what they know. Centration and a lack of conservation also characterize the preoperational stage.

Vygotsky's Theory

- Vygotsky's theory represents a social constructivist approach to development. According to Vygotsky, children construct knowledge through social interaction, and they use language not only to communicate with others but also to plan, guide, and monitor their own behavior and to help them solve problems. His theory suggests that adults should access and use the child's zone of proximal development (ZPD), which is the range of tasks that are too difficult for children to master alone but which can be learned with the guidance and assistance of adults or more-skilled children. The theory also suggests that adults and peers should teach through scaffolding, which involves changing the level of support over the course of a teaching session, with the more-skilled person adjusting guidance to fit the student's current performance level.

Information Processing

- The child's ability to attend to stimuli dramatically improves during early childhood, but the child attends to the salient rather than the relevant features of a task. Significant improvement in short-term memory occurs during early childhood. With good prompts, young children's long-term memories can be accurate, although young children can be led into developing false memories. Young children usually don't use strategies to remember, but they can learn rather simple problem-solving strategies. Theory of mind is the awareness of one's own mental processes and the mental processes of others. Children begin to understand mental states involving perceptions, desires, and emotions at 2 to 3 years of age and at 4 to 5 years of age realize that people can have false beliefs. It is only beyond the early childhood years that children have a deepening appreciation of the mind itself rather than just understanding mental states. Autistic children have difficulty in developing a theory of mind.

2 · HOW DO YOUNG CHILDREN DEVELOP LANGUAGE? *Summarize how language develops in early childhood.*

Understanding Phonology and Morphology

- Young children increase their grasp of language's rule systems. In terms of phonology, most young children become more sensitive to the sounds of spoken language. Berko's classic experiment demonstrated that young children understand morphological rules.

Changes in Syntax and Semantics

- Preschool children learn and apply rules of syntax and how words should be ordered. In terms of semantics, vocabulary development increases dramatically during early childhood.

| Advances in Pragmatics | • Young children's conversational skills improve, they increase their sensitivity to the needs of others in conversation, and they learn to change their speech style to suit the situation. |

③ WHAT ARE SOME IMPORTANT FEATURES OF EARLY CHILDHOOD EDUCATION? *Evaluate different approaches to early childhood education.*

| Variations in Early Childhood Education | • The child-centered kindergarten emphasizes the education of the whole child, with particular attention to individual variation, the process of learning, and the importance of play in development. The Montessori approach allows children to choose from a range of activities while teachers serve as facilitators. Developmentally appropriate practice (illustrated by the Reggio Emilia approach) focuses on the typical patterns of children (age appropriateness) and the uniqueness of each child (individual appropriateness). Such practice contrasts with developmentally inappropriate practice, which ignores the concrete, hands-on approach to learning. |

| Literacy and Early Childhood Education | • There has been increased interest in young children's literacy. Young children need to develop positive images of reading and writing skills through a supportive environment. Children should be active participants and be immersed in a wide range of interesting and enjoyable listening, talking, writing, and reading experiences. A quality early childhood education program also helps young children build a foundation for the development of their mathematical skills. From 3 to 6 years of age, young children develop mathematical skills in these areas: number and operations, geometry and spatial sense, measurement, and displaying and analyzing data. |

| Educating Young Children Who Are Disadvantaged | • The U.S. government has tried to break the poverty cycle with programs such as Head Start. Model programs have been shown to have positive effects on children who live in poverty. |

| Controversies in Early Childhood Education | • Controversy characterizes early childhood education curricula. On the one side are the child-centered, constructivist advocates, on the other are those who advocate a direct instruction, academic approach. Another controversy focuses on whether preschool education matters. Some parents can educate young children as effectively as a school does; however, most parents do not have the skills, time, and commitment to do so. Yet another controversy involves whether universal preschool education should be implemented. And yet another controversy focuses on school readiness, including such topics as academic redshirting and whether some children should be held back for a second year in kindergarten. |

KEY TERMS

preoperational stage 279
operations 279
symbolic function
    substage 279
egocentrism 279
animism 279

intuitive thought
    substage 281
centration 281
conservation 281
social constructivist
    approach 282

zone of proximal development
    (ZPD) 282
scaffolding 282
short-term memory 286
strategies 290
theory of mind 290

child-centered
    kindergarten 295
Montessori approach 296
developmentally appropriate
    practice 296
Project Head Start 301

KEY PEOPLE

MAKING A DIFFERENCE

Nourish the Young Child's Cognitive Development

What are some good strategies for helping young children develop their cognitive competencies?

- *Provide opportunities for the young child's development of symbolic thought.* Give the child ample opportunities to scribble and draw. Provide the child opportunities to engage in make-believe play. Don't criticize the young child's art and play. Let the child's imagination flourish.
- *Encourage exploration.* Let the child select many of the activities he or she wants to explore. Don't have the child do rigid paper-and-pencil exercises that involve rote learning. The young child should not be spending lots of time passively sitting, watching, and listening.
- *Be an active language partner with the young child.* Encourage the young child to speak in entire sentences instead of using single words. Be a good listener. Ask the child lots of questions. Don't spend time correcting the child's grammar; simply model correct grammar yourself when you talk

with the child. Don't correct the young child's writing. Spend time selecting age-appropriate books for the young child. Read books with the young child.

- *Become sensitive to the child's zone of proximal development.* Monitor the child's level of cognitive functioning. Know what tasks the child can competently perform alone and those that are too difficult, even with your help. Guide and assist the child in the proper performance of skills and use of tools in the child's zone of proximal development. Warmly support the young child's practice of these skills.
- *Evaluate the quality of the child's early childhood education program.* Make sure the early childhood program the child attends involves developmentally appropriate education. The program should be age appropriate and individual appropriate for the child. It should not be a high-intensity, academic-at-all-costs program. Don't pressure the child to achieve at this age.

RESOURCES FOR IMPROVING CHILDREN'S LIVES

National Association for the Education of Young Children (NAEYC)

202–232–8777
800–424–2460
www.naeyc.com

NAEYC is an important professional organization and advocacy group for young children and has developed guidelines for a number of dimensions of early childhood education. It publishes the excellent journal *Young Children*.

Motivated Minds: Raising Children to Love Learning

by Deborah Stipek and Kathy Seal (2001)
Hudson, OH: Owl Books

An excellent book for parents who want to guide their children's learning in a positive direction.

E-LEARNING TOOLS

Connect to **www.mhhe.com/santrockc10** to research the answers and complete these exercises. In addition, you'll find a number of other resources and valuable study tools for Chapter 9, "Cognitive Development in Early Childhood," on this Web site.

Taking It to the Net

1. Judith and Louis have a 3-year-old son, Mitchell. Many of their friends are enrolling their children in preschool. Judith and Louis do not think they can afford to enroll

Mitchell in a preschool program, although both of them think that the benefits of preschool might justify the cost. Are there significant benefits associated with preschool programs? Are there particular types of preschools that seem more beneficial for children?

2. Todd is working in a child-care center after school. He notices that there is a wide range in the children's use of language, even within age groups. Are there any guidelines that Todd can obtain that could help determine if a child is delayed in language development?

3. You are visiting a number of preschools to help your friend determine which program might be most appropriate for her 4-year-old child. You have heard that the National Association for the Education of Young Children is a great resource for both educators and parents. What kinds of tools can you find on the NAEYC Web site to assist you and your friend as you search the programs in your area?

Health and Well-Being, Parenting, and Education

Build your decision-making skills by trying your hand at the health and well-being, parenting, and education exercises.

Video Clips

The Online Learning Center includes the following videos for this chapter:

1. *Categorizing Animals and Food at Age 3—7780*
   Here we watch a 3-year-old demonstrate his ability to categorize animals and food. In the second demonstration, when presented with pictures of a zebra, turtle, bird, and kite, he makes a distinction between animals and birds.

2. *Categorizing Pictures at Age 4—7155*
   A 4-year-old is presented with pictures of a lion, bear, zebra, and wagon and asked which one is different from the others. He insists, "They're all different!" The interviewer probes him, but he is more interested in adding and subtracting pictures, which he does very well. Another set of pictures is presented to him, and again he says that all are different.

3. *Understanding Conservation (Liquid) at Age 4—2168*
   A girl proves she has an understanding of the concept of conservation when presented with Piaget's classic liquid test. This clip provides a good example of the age variation in the emergence of conservation.

4. *Memory Ability at Age 4—1606*
   Here a 4-year-old girl is presented with a sequence of numbers and asked to repeat them back. She recalls the numbers successfully and then smiles at her accomplishment.

10 Socioemotional Development in Early Childhood

Let us play, for it is yet day
And we cannot go to sleep;
Besides, in the sky the little birds fly
And the hills are all covered with sheep.

—WILLIAM BLAKE
English Poet, 19th Century

CHAPTER OUTLINE

LEARNING GOALS

WHAT CHARACTERIZES YOUNG CHILDREN'S EMOTIONAL AND PERSONALITY DEVELOPMENT?

1

Discuss emotional and personality development in early childhood.

The Self

Emotional Development

Moral Development

Gender

WHAT ROLES DO FAMILIES PLAY IN YOUNG CHILDREN'S DEVELOPMENT?

2

Explain how families can influence young children's development.

Parenting

Child Maltreatment

Sibling Relationships and Birth Order

The Changing Family in a Changing Society

HOW ARE PEER RELATIONS, PLAY, AND TELEVISION INVOLVED IN YOUNG CHILDREN'S DEVELOPMENT?

3

Describe the roles of peers, play, and television in young children's development.

Peer Relations

Play

Television

Images of Children's Development
Craig Lesley's Complicated Early Emotional and Social Life

In his memoir *Burning Fence: A Western Memoir of Fatherhood*, award-winning novelist Craig Lesley describes one memory from his early childhood:

> Lifting me high above his head, my father placed me in the crotch of the Bing cherry tree growing beside my mother's parents' house in The Dalles. A little frightened at the dizzying height, I pressed my palms into the tree's rough, peeling bark. My father stood close, reassuring. I could see his olive skin, dazzling smile, and sharp-creased army uniform.
>
> "Rudell, don't let him fall." My mother watched, her arms held out halfway, as if to catch me. . . .
>
> The cherries were ripe and robins flittered through the green leaves, pecking at the Bings. Tipping my head back I could see blue sky beyond the extended branches.
>
> "That's enough. Bring him down now." My mother's arms reached out farther.
>
> Laughing, my father grabbed me under the arms, twirled me around, and plunked me into the grass. I wobbled a little. Imprinted on my palms was the pattern of the tree bark, and I brushed off the little bark pieces on my dungarees.
>
> In a moment, my grandmother gave me a small glass of lemonade. . . .
>
> This first childhood memory of my father remains etched in my mind. . . .
>
> When I grew older, I realized that my father had never lifted me into the cherry tree. After Rudell left, I never saw him until I was fifteen. My grandfather had put me in the tree. Still, the memory of my father lifting me into the tree persists. Even today, I remain half-convinced by the details, the press of bark against my palms, the taste of lemonade, the texture of my father's serge uniform. Apparently, my mind has cross-wired the photographs of my handsome father in his army uniform with the logical reality that my grandfather set me in the crotch of the tree.
>
> Why can I remember the event so vividly? I guess because I wanted so much for my father to be there. I have no easy answers. (Lesley, 2005, pp. 8–10)

Like millions of children, Lesley experienced a family torn by divorce; he would also experience abuse by a stepfather. When his father left, Lesley was an infant, but even as a preschooler, he felt his father's absence. Once he planned to win a gift for his father so that his grandmother "could take it to him and then he'd come to see me" (Lesley, 2005, p. 16). In just a few years, the infant had become a child with a complicated emotional and social life.

PREVIEW

In early childhood, children's self-understanding, understanding of others, emotional lives and personalities develop in significant ways, and their small worlds widen. In addition to the continuing influence of family relationships, peers take on a more significant role in children's development, and play fills the days of many young children's lives.

1   WHAT CHARACTERIZES YOUNG CHILDREN'S EMOTIONAL AND PERSONALITY DEVELOPMENT?

The Self		Moral Development
	Emotional Development	Gender

Numerous changes characterize young children's socioemotional development in early childhood. Their developing minds and social experiences produce remarkable advances in the development of their self, emotional maturity, moral understanding, and gender awareness.

The Self

We learned in Chapter 7, "Socioemotional Development in Infancy," that during the second year of life children make considerable progress in self-recognition. In early childhood, their development enables young children to face the issue of initiative versus guilt and to enhance their self-understanding, as well as their understanding of others.

Initiative Versus Guilt   According to Erik Erikson (1968), the psychosocial stage that characterizes early childhood is *initiative versus guilt*. By now, children have become convinced that they are persons of their own; during early childhood, they must discover what kind of person they will become. They intensely identify with their parents, who most of the time appear to them to be powerful and beautiful, although often unreasonable, disagreeable, and sometimes even dangerous. During early childhood, children use their perceptual, motor, cognitive, and language skills to make things happen. They have a surplus of energy that permits them to forget failures quickly and to approach new areas that seem desirable—even if they seem dangerous—with undiminished zest and some increased sense of direction. On their own *initiative*, then, children at this stage exuberantly move out into a wider social world.

The great governor of initiative is *conscience*. Children now not only feel afraid of being found out, which causes shame, but they also begin to hear the inner voices of self-observation, self-guidance, and self-punishment (Bybee, 1999). Their initiative and enthusiasm may bring them not only rewards but also guilt, which lowers self-esteem.

Whether children leave this stage with a sense of initiative that outweighs their sense of guilt depends in large part on how parents respond to their children's self-initiated activities. Children who are given the freedom and opportunity to initiate motor play, such as running, bike riding, sledding, skating, tussling, and wrestling, have their sense of initiative supported. Children's initiative is also supported when parents answer their questions and do not deride or inhibit fantasy or play. In contrast, if children are made to feel that their motor activity is bad, that their questions are a nuisance, and that their play is silly and stupid, then they often develop a sense of guilt over self-initiated activities that may persist through life's later stages (Elkind, 1970).

Self-Understanding and Understanding Others   Recent research studies have revealed that young children are more pychologically aware—of themselves and others—than used to be thought (Harris, 2006; Thompson, 2006). This increased psychological awareness reflects young children's expanding psychological sophistication.

In Erikson's portrait of early childhood, the young child clearly has begun to develop **self-understanding,** which is the representation of self, the substance and

self-understanding The child's cognitive representation of self, the substance and content of the child's self-conceptions.

content of self-conceptions (Harter, 2006). Though not the whole of personal identity, self-understanding provides its rational underpinnings (Damon & Hart, 1992). Mainly through interviews, researchers have probed children's conceptions of many aspects of self-understanding (Harter, 2006).

As we saw in Chapter 7, "Socioemotional Development in Infancy," early self-understanding involves self-recognition. For example, we saw that recognizing one's body parts in a mirror takes place by approximately 18 months of age and that a sense of "me" emerges later in the second year and early in the third year. In early childhood, young children think that the self can be described by many material characteristics, such as size, shape, and color. They distinguish themselves from others through many physical and material attributes. Says 4-year-old Sandra, "I'm different from Jennifer because I have brown hair and she has blond hair." Says 4-year-old Ralph, "I am different from Hank because I am taller, and I am different from my sister because I have a bicycle." Physical activities are also a central component of the self in early childhood (Keller, Ford, & Meacham, 1978). For example, preschool children often describe themselves in terms of activities such as play. In sum, in early childhood, children often provide self-descriptions that involve body attributes, material possessions, and physical activities.

Although young children mainly describe themselves in terms of concrete, observable features and action tendencies, at about 4 to 5 years of age, as they hear others use psychological trait and emotion terms, they begin to include these in their own self-descriptions (Marsh, Ellis, & Craven, 2002; Thompson, 2006). Thus, in a self-description, a 4-year-old might say, "I'm not scared. I'm always happy."

Young children's self-descriptions are typically unrealistically positive, as reflected in the comment of the 4-year-old just described, who says he is always happy, which he is not (Harter, 2006). This occurs because they don't yet distinguish between their desired competence and their actual competence.

Children also make advances in their understanding of others in early childhood (Gelman, Heyman, Legare, 2007). As we saw in Chapter 9, "Cognitive Development in Early Childhood," young children's theory of mind includes understanding that other people have emotions and desires. And at about 4 to 5 years, children not only start describing themselves in terms of psychological traits, but they also begin to perceive others in terms of psychological traits. Thus, a 4-year-old might say, "My teacher is nice."

Something important for children to develop is understanding that people don't always give accurate reports of their beliefs (Gee & Heyman, 2007). Researchers have found that even 4-year-olds understand that people may make statements that aren't true to obtain what they want or to avoid trouble (Lee & others, 2002). For example, one recent study revealed that 4- and 5-year-olds were increasingly skeptical of another child's claim to be sick when the children were informed that the child was motivated to avoid having to go to camp (Gee & Heyman, 2007).

Individual differences characterize young children's social understanding (Thompson, 2006). Some young children are better than others at understanding what people are feeling and what they desire, for example. To some degree, these individual differences are linked to conversations caregivers have with young children about other people's feelings and desires, and children's opportunities to observe others talking about people's feelings and desires. For example, a mother might say to her 3-year-old, "You should think about Raphael's feelings next time before you hit him."

Young children are more psychologically aware of themselves and others than used to be thought. Some children are better than others at understanding people's feelings and desires—and, to some degree, these individual differences are influenced by conversations caregivers have with young children about feelings and desires.

Emotional Development

The young child's growing awareness of self is linked to the ability to feel an expanding range of emotions. Young children, like adults, experience many emotions during the course of a day. At times, they also try to make sense of other people's emotional reactions and to control their own emotions (Denham, Bassett, & Wyatt, 2007).

Self-Conscious Emotions　Recall from Chapter 8 that even young infants experience emotions such as joy and fear, but to experience *self-conscious emotions*, children must be able to refer to themselves and be aware of themselves as distinct from others (Lewis, 2002, 2007). Pride, shame, embarrassment, and guilt are examples of self-conscious emotions. Self-conscious emotions do not appear to develop until self-awareness appears in the last half of the second year of life.

During the early childhood years, emotions such as pride and guilt become more common. They are especially influenced by parents' responses to children's behavior. For example, a young child may experience shame when a parent says, "You should feel bad about biting your sister."

In one study, girls showed more shame and pride than boys (Stipek, Recchia, & McClintic, 1992). This gender difference is interesting because girls are more at risk for internalizing disorders, such as anxiety and depression, in which feelings of shame and self-criticism often are evident (Cummings, Braungart-Rieker, & Du Rocher-Schudlich, 2003).

A young child expressing the emotion of shame. *Why is shame called a "self-conscious emotion"?*

Young Children's Emotion Language and Understanding of Emotion

Among the most important changes in emotional development in early childhood are an increased ability to talk about their own and others' emotions and an increased understanding of emotion (Denham, 2006; Kuebli, 1994). Between 2 and 4 years of age, children considerably increase the number of terms they use to describe emotions (Ridgeway, Waters, & Kuczaj, 1985). They also are learning about the causes and consequences of feelings (Denham, Bassett, & Wyatt, 2007).

When they are 4 to 5 years of age, children show an increased ability to reflect on emotions. They also begin to understand that the same event can elicit different feelings in different people. Moreover, they show a growing awareness that they need to manage their emotions to meet social standards (Bruce, Olen, & Jensen, 1999). Figure 10.1 summarizes the characteristics of young children's talk about emotion and their understanding of it.

Regulation of Emotion　As we saw in Chapter 7, "Socioemotional Development in Infancy," emotion regulation is an important aspect of development (Saarni & others, 2006). Emotion regulation especially plays a key role in children's ability to manage the demands and conflicts they face in interacting with others (Denham, 2006).

Approximate age of child	Description
2 to 3 years	Increase emotion vocabulary most rapidly
	Correctly label simple emotions in self and others and talk about past, present, and future emotions
	Talk about the causes and consequences of some emotions and identify emotions associated with certain situations
	Use emotion language in pretend play
4 to 5 years	Show increased capacity to reflect verbally on emotions and to consider more complex relations between emotions and situations
	Understand that the same event may call forth different feelings in different people and that feelings sometimes persist long after the events that caused them
	Demonstrate growing awareness about controlling and managing emotions in accord with social standards

FIGURE 10.1 Some Characteristics of Young Children's Emotion Language and Understanding

An emotion-coaching parent. *What are some differences in emotion-coaching and emotion-dismissing parents?*

What role does emotion regulation play in peer relations?

✳ moral development Development that involves thoughts, feelings, and behaviors regarding rules and conventions about what people should do in their interactions with other people.

✳ Emotion–Coaching and Emotion–Dismissing Parents   Parents can play an important role in helping young children regulate their emotions (Thompson, 2006; Thompson & Lagattuta, 2005). Depending on how they talk with their children about emotion, parents can be described as taking an *emotion-coaching* or an *emotion-dismissing* approach (Katz, 1999). *Emotion-coaching parents* monitor their children's emotions, view their children's negative emotions as opportunities for teaching, assist them in labeling emotions, and coach them in how to deal effectively with emotions. In contrast, *emotion-dismissing parents* view their role as to deny, ignore, or change negative emotions. Researchers have found that when interacting with their children, emotion-coaching parents are less rejecting, use more scaffolding and praise, and are more nurturant than are emotion-dismissing parents (Gottman & DeClaire, 1997). The children of emotion-coaching parents were better at soothing themselves when they got upset, more effective in regulating their negative affect, focused their attention better, and had fewer behavior problems than the children of emotion-dismissing parents.

Emotional Regulation and Peer Relations   Emotions play a strong role in determining whether a child's peer relations are successful (Ladd, Herald, & Andrews, 2006; Saarni & others, 2006). Moody and emotionally negative children experience greater rejection by their peers, whereas emotionally positive children are more popular (Stocker & Dunn, 1990).

Emotional regulation is an important aspect of getting along with peers (Saarni & others, 2006). In one study conducted in the natural context of young children's everyday peer interactions, self-regulation of emotion enhanced children's social competence (Fabes & others, 1999). Children who made an effort to control their emotional responses were more likely to respond in socially competent ways when peers provoked them—for example, by making a hostile comment or taking something away from them. In sum, the ability to modulate one's emotions is an important skill that benefits children in their relationships with peers (Saarni & others, 2006).

Moral Development

Unlike a crying infant, a screaming 5-year-old is likely to be thought responsible for making a fuss. The parents may worry about whether the 5-year-old is a "bad" child. Although some people think children are innately good (as discussed in Chapter 1), many developmentalists believe that just as parents help their children become good readers, musicians, or athletes, parents must nurture goodness and help their children develop morally. **Moral development** involves the development of thoughts, feelings, and behaviors regarding rules and conventions about what people should do in their interactions with other people. Major developmental theories have focused on different aspects of moral development.

Moral Feelings   Feelings of anxiety and guilt are central to the account of moral development provided by Freud's psychoanalytic theory (introduced in Chapter 2). According to Freud, to reduce anxiety, avoid punishment, and maintain parental affection, children identify with parents, internalizing their standards of right and wrong, and thus form the *superego*, the moral element of personality.

Resolution of the *Oedipal conflict* plays a central role in this development. According to Freud, the young child develops an intense desire to replace the same-sex parent and enjoy the affections of the opposite-sex parent. At about 5 to 6 years of age, children recognize that their same-sex parent might punish them for their incestuous wishes. In fear of losing the parents' love and of being punished for their unacceptable sexual wishes, the child identifies with the same-sex parent, internalizing the parent's standards, and turns inward the hostility that had been aimed at the same-sex parent. This inwardly directed hostility is felt as guilt. In the psycho-analytic account of moral development, the self-punitiveness of guilt is responsible for keeping the child from committing transgressions. That is, children conform to societal standards to avoid guilt.

In short, in the psychoanalytic account of moral development, children conform to societal standards to avoid guilt. In this way, self-control replaces parental control. Freud's claims regarding the formation of the ego ideal and conscience cannot be verified. However, researchers can examine the extent to which children feel guilty when they misbehave. In one study, 106 preschool children were observed in laboratory situations in which they were led to believe that they had damaged valuable objects (Kochanska & others, 2002). In these mishaps, the behavioral indi-cators of guilt that were coded by observers included avoiding gaze (looking away or down), body tension (squirming, backing away, hanging head down, covering face with hands), and distress (looking uncomfortable, crying). Girls expressed more guilt than boys did. Children with a more fearful temperament expressed more guilt. Children of mothers who used power-oriented discipline (such as spanking, slap-ping, and yelling) displayed less guilt.

Emotions other than guilt also contribute to the child's moral develop-ment, including positive feelings. One important example is *empathy,* which is reacting to another person's feelings with an emotional response that is similar to the other's feelings (Eisenberg, 2006; Eisenberg, Fabes, & Spinrad, 2006; Johansson, 2006).

Infants have the capacity for some purely empathic responses, but empathy often requires the ability to discern another's inner psychological states, or what is called "perspective taking." For effective moral action, children need to learn how to identify a wide range of emotional states in others. They also need to learn to anticipate what kinds of action will improve another person's emotional state (Eisen-berg, Fabes, & Spinrad, 2006).

Moral Reasoning   Interest in how children think about moral issues was stimu-lated by Piaget (1932), who extensively observed and interviewed children from the ages of 4 through 12. Piaget watched children play marbles to learn how they used and thought about the game's rules. He also asked children about ethical issues—theft, lies, punishment, and justice, for example. Piaget concluded that children go through two distinct stages in how they think about morality.

- From 4 to 7 years of age, children display **heteronomous morality,** the first stage of moral development in Piaget's theory. Children think of justice and rules as unchangeable properties of the world, removed from the control of people.
- From 7 to 10 years of age, children are in a transition, showing some features of the first stage of moral reasoning and some stages of the second stage, autonomous morality.
- From about 10 years of age and older, children show **autonomous morality.** They become aware that rules and laws are created by people, and in judging an action, they consider the actor's intentions as well as the consequences.

Because young children are heteronomous moralists, they judge the rightness or goodness of behavior by considering its consequences, not the intentions of the actor. For example, to the heteronomous moralist, breaking twelve cups acciden-tally is worse than breaking one cup intentionally. As children develop into moral autonomists, intentions assume paramount importance.

The heteronomous thinker also believes that rules are unchangeable and are handed down by all-powerful authorities. When Piaget suggested to young chil-dren that they use new rules in a game of marbles, they resisted. By contrast, older children—moral autonomists—accept change and recognize that rules are merely convenient conventions, subject to change.

> *What is moral is what you feel good after and what is immoral is what you feel bad after.*
>
> —ERNEST HEMINGWAY
> *American Author, 20th Century*

Piaget extensively observed and interviewed 4- to 12-year-old children as they played games to learn how they used and thought about the games' rules.

heteronomous morality The first stage of moral development in Piaget's theory, occur-ring from 4 to 7 years of age. Justice and rules are conceived of as unchangeable properties of the world, removed from the control of people.

autonomous morality The second stage of moral development in Piaget's theory, dis-played by older children (about 10 years of age and older). The child becomes aware that rules and laws are created by people and that, in judging an action, one should consider the ac-tor's intentions as well as the consequences.

How is this child's moral thinking likely to be different about stealing a cookie depending on whether he is in Piaget's heteronomous or autonomous stage?

The heteronomous thinker also believes in **immanent justice,** the concept that if a rule is broken, punishment will be meted out immediately. The young child believes that a violation is connected automatically to its punishment. Thus, young children often look around worriedly after doing something wrong, expecting inevitable punishment. Immanent justice also implies that if something unfortunate happens to someone, the person must have transgressed earlier. Older children, who are moral autonomists, recognize that punishment occurs only if someone witnesses the wrongdoing and that, even then, punishment is not inevitable.

How do these changes in moral reasoning occur? Piaget argued that, as children develop, they become more sophisticated in thinking about social matters, especially about the possibilities and conditions of cooperation. Piaget stressed that this social understanding comes about through the mutual give-and-take of peer relations. In the peer group, where others have power and status similar to the child's, plans are negotiated and coordinated, and disagreements are reasoned about and eventually settled. Parent-child relations, in which parents have the power and children do not, are less likely to advance moral reasoning, because rules are often handed down in an authoritarian way.

Building on Piaget's ideas, Lawrence Kohlberg developed a theory of moral development that also emphasized moral reasoning and the influence of the give-and-take of peer relations. Like Piaget, Kohlberg concluded from his research that children begin as heteronomous moralists and decide whether an act is right or wrong by whether it is rewarded or punished. Later, in Chapter 13, "Socioemotional Development in Middle and Late Childhood," we examine Kohlberg's theory and his stages of moral development, the evidence his theory is based on, and its critics.

Moral Behavior   Moral behavior rather than moral reasoning or moral affect is the focus of the behavioral and social cognitive approach (Bugental & Grusec, 2006; Grusec, 2006). It holds that the processes of reinforcement, punishment, and imitation explain the development of moral behavior. When children are rewarded for behavior that is consistent with laws and social conventions, they are likely to repeat that behavior. When models who behave morally are provided, children are likely to adopt their actions. And, when children are punished for immoral behavior, those behaviors are likely to be reduced or eliminated. However, because punishment may have adverse side effects, as discussed later in this chapter, it needs to be used judiciously and cautiously.

If a 4-year-old boy has been rewarded by his mother for telling the truth when he breaks a glass at home, does that mean that he is likely to tell the truth to his preschool teacher when he knocks over a vase and breaks it? Not necessarily; the situation influences behavior. More than half a century ago, a comprehensive study of thousands of children in many situations—at home, at school, and at church, for example—found that the totally honest child was virtually nonexistent; so was the child who cheated in all situations (Hartshorne & May, 1928–1930). Behavioral and social cognitive researchers emphasize that what children do in one situation is often only weakly related to what they do in other situations. A child might cheat in class but not in a game; a child might steal a piece of candy when alone but not steal it when others are present.

Social cognitive theorists also believe that the ability to resist temptation is closely tied to the development of self-control. To achieve this self-control, children must learn to delay gratification. According to social cognitive theorists, cognitive factors are important in the child's development of self-control (Bandura, 2007a,b).

Parenting and Young Children's Moral Development   Both Piaget and Kohlberg held that parents do not provide unique or essential inputs to children's moral development. Parents, in their view, are responsible for providing role-taking opportunities and cognitive conflict, but peers play the primary role in moral development. Research

immanent justice The concept that, if a rule is broken, punishment will be meted out immediately.

reveals that both parents and peers contribute to children's moral maturity (Hastings, Utendale, & Sullivan, 2007).

In Ross Thompson's (2006; Thompson, Meyer & McGinley, 2006) view, young children are moral apprentices, striving to understand what is moral. They can be assisted in this quest by the "sensitive guidance of adult mentors in the home who provide lessons about morality in everyday experiences" (Thompson, Meyer, & McGinley, 2006). Among the most important aspects of the relationship between parents and children that contribute to children's moral development are relational quality, parental discipline, proactive strategies, and conversational dialogue.

Relational Quality   Parent-child relationships introduce children to the mutual obligations of close relationships (Thompson, 2006; Thompson, Meyer, & McGinley, 2006). Parents' obligations include engaging in positive caregiving and guiding children to become competent human beings. Children's obligations include responding appropriately to parents' initiatives and maintaining a positive relationship with parents. Thus, warmth and responsibility in the mutual obligations of parent-child relationships are important foundations for the positive moral growth in the child.

In terms of relationship quality, secure attachment may play an important role in children's moral development. A secure attachment can place the child on a positive path for internalizing parents' socializing goals and family values (Waters & others, 1990). In one study, secure attachment in infancy was linked to early conscience development (Laible & Thompson, 2002). And in a longitudinal study, secure attachment at 14 months of age served as a precursor for a link between positive parenting and the child's conscience during early childhood (Kochanska & others, 2004).

Proactive Strategies   An important parenting strategy is to proactively avert potential misbehavior by children before it takes place (Thompson, Meyer, & McGinley, 2006). With younger children, being proactive means using diversion, such as distracting their attention or moving them to alternative activities. With older children, being proactive may involve talking with them about values that the parents deem important. Transmitting these values can help older children and adolescents to resist the temptations that inevitably emerge in such contexts as peer relations and the media that can be outside the scope of direct parental monitoring.

Conversational Dialogue   Conversations related to moral development can benefit children whether they occur as part of a discipline encounter or outside the encounter in the everyday stream of parent-child interaction (Thompson, 2006; Thompson, Meyer, & McGinley, 2006). The conversations can be planned or spontaneous and can focus on topics such as past events (for example, a child's prior misbehavior or positive moral conduct), shared future events (for example, going somewhere that may involve a temptation and requires positive moral behavior), and immediate events (for example, talking with the child about a sibling's tantrums). Even when they are not intended to teach a moral lesson or explicitly encourage better moral judgment, such conversations can contribute to children's moral development.

How do caregivers contribute to young childrens' moral development?

Gender

When he was 5 years old, Craig Lesley (whose story appeared at the opening of this chapter) spent hours building forts and blazing away with a cap gun in his basement, which his grandfather had turned into a "cowboy room" (Lesley, 2005, p. 20). Would a little girl have been as delighted with the chance to play cowboy? Maybe, but even by the time they are 3 years old, most little girls prefer "feminine" toys, and most little boys prefer "masculine" toys. In other words, they display *gender-typed preferences.*

Recall that *gender* refers to the social and psychological dimensions of being male or female, and even preschool children display many of these dimensions. By the time he was 2 years old, Craig was probably aware that people can be divided into two categories. If he was like most young children, by the time he was 3 years old he had acquired a **gender identity,** which is the sense of being male or female. He had probably also begun to link dolls with girls and trucks with boys. In other words, even preschoolers begin to learn about **gender roles,** which are expectations that prescribe how females or males should think, act, and feel. During the preschool years, most children increasingly act in ways that match their culture's gender roles.

Biological Influences How do these and other gender differences come about? Biology clearly plays a role. Among the possible biological influences are chromosomes, hormones, and evolution.

Chromosomes and Hormones Biologists have learned a great deal about how sex differences develop. Recall that humans normally have 46 chromosomes arranged in pairs (see Chapter 2). The 23rd pair consists of a combination of X and Y chromosomes, usually two X chromosomes in a female and an X and a Y in a male. In the first few weeks of gestation, however, female and male embryos look alike.

Males start to differ from females when genes on the Y chromosome in the male embryo trigger the development of testes rather than ovaries; the testes secrete copious amounts of the class of hormones known as androgens, which lead to the development of male sex organs. Low levels of androgens in the female embryo allow the normal development of female sex organs.

Thus, hormones play a critical role in the development of sex differences (Berenbaum & Bailey, 2003; Lippa, 2005). The two main classes of sex hormones are estrogens and androgens, which are secreted by the *gonads* (ovaries in females, testes in males). *Estrogens,* such as estradiol, influence the development of female physical sex characteristics. *Androgens,* such as testosterone, promote the development of male physical sex characteristics.

Biology's role in creating sex differences, however, does not tell the whole story of gender differences. Consider a research study of genetic males who were born with ambiguous genitals because of a rare birth defect and who were surgically assigned to be female (Reiner & Gearhart, 2004). In this research, 16 genetically male children 5 to 16 years of age were studied; 14 of them were raised as females. Children and parents were asked detailed questions about the children's play patterns, levels of aggression, career goals, and attitudes about gender roles. The families were followed for 34 to 98 months. In the most recent assessment, 8 of the 14 individuals raised as girls had declared themselves boys, including 4 who had not been told of their surgical transformation. Nature apparently was more important than nurture in the case of these children. However, 5 of the 16 children appeared happy living as girls, implying that in some cases nurture can trump nature. Further, other research and clinical reports indicate many genetic males raised as girls appear to be well adjusted (Gooren, 2002; Slijper & others, 1998).

The Evolutionary Psychology View How might physical differences between the sexes give rise to psychological differences between males and females? Evolutionary psychology (introduced in Chapter 2) offers one answer. According to evolutionary psychology, adaptation during human evolution produced psychological differences between males and females (Buss, 2000, 2004, 2008). Because of their differing roles in reproduction, males and females faced differing pressures when the human species was evolving. In particular, because having multiple sexual liaisons improves the likelihood that males will pass on their genes, natural selection favored males who adopted short-term mating strategies. These are strategies that allow a male to win the competition with other males for sexual access to females. Therefore, say

gender identity The sense of being male or female, which most children acquire by the time they are 3 years old.

gender roles Expectations that prescribe how females or males should think, act, and feel.

evolutionary psychologists, males evolved dispositions that favor violence, competition, and risk taking.

In contrast, according to evolutionary psychologists, females' contributions to the gene pool were improved when they secured resources that ensured that their offspring would survive; this outcome was promoted by obtaining long-term mates who could provide food for a family (Geher & Miller, 2007). As a consequence, natural selection favored females who devoted effort to parenting and chose successful, ambitious mates who could provide their offspring with resources and protection.

This evolutionary unfolding, according to some evolutionary psychologists, explains key gender differences in sexual attitudes and sexual behavior. For example, in one study, men said that ideally they would like to have more than 18 sexual partners in their lifetime, whereas women stated that ideally they would like to have only 4 or 5 (Buss & Schmidt, 1993). In another study, 75 percent of the men but none of the women approached by an attractive stranger of the opposite sex consented to a request for sex (Clark & Hatfield, 1989).

Such gender differences, says David Buss (2000, 2004), are exactly the type predicted by evolutionary psychology. Buss argues that men and women differ psychologically in those domains in which they have faced different adaptive problems during evolutionary history. In all other domains, predicts Buss, the sexes will be psychologically similar.

Critics of evolutionary psychology argue that its hypotheses are backed by speculations about prehistory, not evidence, and that in any event people are not locked into behavior that was adaptive in the evolutionary past. Critics also claim that the evolutionary view pays little attention to cultural and individual variations in gender differences (Matlin, 2008; Smith, 2007).

Social Influences Many social scientists do not locate the cause of psychological gender differences in biological dispositions. Rather, they argue that these differences are due to social experiences (Denmark, Rabinowitz, & Sechzer, 2005). Explanations for how gender differences come about through experience include both social and cognitive theories.

Social Theories of Gender Three main social theories of gender have been proposed—social role theory, psychoanalytic theory, and social cognitive theory. Alice Eagly (2001; Eagly & Koenig, 2006; Wood & Eagly, 2007) proposed **social role theory,** which states that gender differences result from the contrasting roles of women and men. In most cultures around the world, women have less power and status than men have and they control fewer resources (Denmark, Rabinowitz, & Sechzer, 2005; Worell, 2006). Compared with men, women perform more domestic work, spend fewer hours in paid employment, receive lower pay, and are more thinly represented in the highest levels of organizations. In Eagly's view, as women adapted to roles with less power and less status in society, they showed more cooperative, less dominant profiles than men. Thus, the social hierarchy and division of labor are important causes of gender differences in power, assertiveness, and nurture (Betz, 2006; Eagly & Diekman, 2003).

The **psychoanalytic theory of gender** stems from Freud's view that the preschool child develops a sexual attraction to the opposite-sex parent. At 5 or 6 years of age, the child renounces this attraction because of anxious feelings. Subsequently, the child identifies with the same-sex parent, unconsciously adopting the same-sex parent's characteristics. However, developmentalists argue that gender development does not proceed as Freud proposed. Children become gender-typed much earlier than 5 or 6 years of age, and they become masculine or feminine even when the same-sex parent is not present in the family.

The social cognitive approach, discussed in Chapter 1, provides an alternative explanation of how children develop gender-typed behavior (see Figure 10.2). According to

social role theory A theory that gender difference result from the contrasting roles of men and women.

psychoanalytic theory of gender A theory deriving from Freud's view that the preschool child develops a sexual attraction to the opposite-sex parent, by approximately 5 or 6 years of age renounces this attraction because of anxious feelings, and subsequently identifies with the same sex parent, unconsciously adopting the same-sex parent's characteristics.

FIGURE 10.2 A Comparison of the Psychoanalytic and Social Cognitive Views of Gender Development Parents influence their children's development by action and example.

Theory	Processes	Outcomes
Freud's psychoanalytic theory	Sexual attraction to opposite-sex parent at 3 to 5 years of age; anxiety about sexual attraction and subsequent identification with same-sex parent at 5 to 6 years of age	Gender behavior similar to that of same-sex parent
Social cognitive theory	Rewards and punishments of gender-appropriate and -inappropriate behavior by adults and peers; observation and initiation of models' masculine and feminine behavior	Gender-typed behavior

Photo of baby with paint brush.

social cognitive theory of gender A theory that emphasizes that children's gender development occurs through the observation and imitation of gender behavior and through the rewards and punishments children experience for gender appropriate and gender-inappropriate behavior.

the **social cognitive theory of gender,** children's gender development occurs through observing and imitating what other people say and do, and through being rewarded and punished for gender-appropriate and gender-inappropriate behavior (Bussey & Bandura, 1999). From birth onward, males and females are treated differently. When infants and toddlers show gender differences, adults tend to reward them. Parents often use rewards and punishments to teach their daughters to be feminine ("Linea, you are being a good girl when you play gently with your doll") and their sons to be masculine ("Simon, a boy as big as you is not supposed to cry"). Parents, however, are only one of many sources through which children learn gender roles (Beal, 1994; Fagot, Rodgers, & Leinbach, 2000). Culture, schools, peers, the media, and other family members also provide gender-role models. For example, children also learn about gender from observing other adults in the neighborhood and on television (Fagot, Rodgers, & Leinbach, 2000). As children get older, peers become increasingly important, and we explore peer relations in later chapters. For now, let's take a closer look at the influence of parents and peers on young children's gender development.

Parental Influences   Parents, by action and by example, influence their children's gender development (Leaper & Friedman, 2007; Maccoby, 2007). Both mothers and fathers are psychologically important to their children's gender development (Grusec & Davidov, 2007). Cultures around the world, however, tend to give mothers and fathers different roles (Kagitcibasi, 2007). A recent research review provided these conclusions (Bronstein 2006):

- *Mothers' socialization strategies.* In many cultures, mothers socialize their daughters to be more obedient and responsible than their sons. They also place more restrictions on daughters' autonomy.
- *Fathers' socialization strategies.* Fathers show more attention to sons than daughters, engage in more activities with sons, and put forth more effort to promote sons' intellectual development.

Thus, according to the recent research review (Bronstein, 2006, pp. 269–270), "Despite an increased awareness in the United States and other Western cultures of the detrimental effects of gender stereotyping, many parents continue to foster behaviors and perceptions that are consonant with traditional gender role norms."

Peer Influences   Parents provide the earliest discrimination of gender roles, but before long, peers join the process of responding to and modeling masculine and feminine behavior. In fact, peers become so important to gender development that the playground has been called "gender school" (Luria & Herzog, 1985).

Peers extensively reward and punish gender behavior (Lott & Maluso, 2001). For example, when children play in ways that the culture says are sex-appropriate, their peers tend to reward them. But peers often reject children who act in a manner that is considered more characteristic of the other gender (Matlin, 2004). A little girl who brings a doll to the park may find herself surrounded by new friends; a little boy might be jeered. However, there is greater pressure for boys to conform to a traditional male role than for girls to conform to a traditional female role (Fagot, Rogers, & Leinbach, 2000).

Gender molds important aspects of peer relations. It influences the composition of children's groups, the size of groups, and interactions within a group (Maccoby, 1998, 2002):

- *Gender composition of children's groups.* Around the age of 3, children already show a preference to spend time with same-sex playmates. From 4 to 12 years of age, this preference for playing in same-sex groups increases, and during the elementary school years children spend a large majority of their free time with children of their own sex (see Figure 10.3).
- *Group size.* From about 5 years of age onward, boys are more likely to associate together in larger clusters than girls are. Boys are also more likely to participate in organized group games than girls are. In one study, same-sex groups of six children were permitted to use play materials in any way they wished (Benenson, Apostolaris, & Parnass, 1997). Girls were more likely than boys to play in dyads or triads, while boys were more likely to interact in larger groups and seek to attain a group goal.
- *Interaction in same-sex groups.* Boys are more likely than girls to engage in rough-and-tumble play, competition, conflict, ego displays, risk taking, and seeking dominance. By contrast, girls are more likely to engage in "collaborative discourse," in which they talk and act in a more reciprocal manner.

What effect do the same-sex play groups have on gender differences? In one study, researchers observed preschoolers over six months (Martin & Fabes, 2001). The more time boys spent interacting with other boys, the more their activity level, rough-and-tumble play, and sex-typed choice of toys and games increased, and the less time boys spent near adults. By contrast, the more time preschool girls spent interacting with other girls, the more their activity level and aggression decreased, and the more their girl-type play activities and time spent near adults increased.

Cognitive Influences Observation, imitation, rewards and punishment—these are the mechanisms by which gender develops according to social cognitive theory. Interactions between the child and the social environment are the main keys to gender development in this view. Some critics argue that this explanation pays too little attention to the child's own mind and understanding and that it portrays the child as passively acquiring gender roles (Martin & Ruble, 2004). Two cognitive theories—cognitive developmental theory and gender schema theory—stress that individuals actively construct their gender world:

- The **cognitive developmental theory of gender** states that children's gender typing occurs *after* children think of themselves as boys and girls. Once they consistently conceive of themselves as male or female, children prefer activities, objects, and attitudes consistent with this label.
- **Gender schema theory** states that gender typing emerges as children gradually develop gender schemas of what is gender-appropriate and gender-inappropriate in their culture. A *schema* is a cognitive structure, a network of associations that guide an individual's perceptions. A *gender schema* organizes the world in terms of female and male. Children are internally motivated to perceive the world and to act in accordance with their developing schemas.

Initially proposed by Lawrence Kohlberg (1966), the cognitive developmental theory of gender holds that gender development depends on cognition, and it applies the ideas of Piaget's cognitive developmental theory described in Chapter 9, "Cognitive Development in Early Childhood." As young children develop the conservation and categorization skills described by Piaget, said Kohlberg, they develop a concept of gender. What's more, they come to see that they will always be male or female.

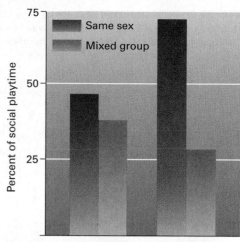

FIGURE 10.3 Developmental Changes in Percentage of Time Spent in Same-Sex and Mixed-Group Settings Observations of children show that they are more likely to play in same-sex than mixed-sex groups. This tendency increases between 4 and 6 years of age.

cognitive developmental theory of gender The theory that children's gender typing occurs after they have developed a concept of gender. Once they consistently conceive of themselves as male or female, children often organize their world on the basis of gender.

gender schema theory The theory gender typing emerges as children gradually develop gender schemas based on what is gender-appropriate & gender inappropriate in their culture.

FIGURE 10.4 The Development of Gender Behavior According to the Cognitive Developmental and Gender Schema Theories of Gender Development

Theory	Processes	Emphasis
Cognitive developmental theory	Development of gender constancy, especially around 6 to 7 years of age, when conservation skills develop; after children develop ability to consistently conceive of themselves as male or female, children often organize their world on the basis of gender, such as selecting same-sex models to imitate	Cognitive readiness facilitates gender identity
Gender schema theory	Sociocultural emphasis on gender-based standards and stereotypes; children's attention and behavior are guided by an internal motivation to conform to these gender-based standards and stereotypes, allowing children to interpret the world through a network of gender-organized thoughts	Gender schemas reinforce gender behavior

As a result, they begin to select models of their own sex to imitate. The little girl acts as if she is thinking, "I'm a girl, so I want to do girl things. Therefore, the opportunity to do girl things is rewarding."

Notice that in this view gender-typed behavior occurs only after children develop *gender constancy*, which is the understanding that sex remains the same, even though activities, clothing, and hairstyle might change (Ruble, Martin, & Berenbaum, 2006). However, researchers have found that children do not develop gender constancy until they are about 6 or 7 years old. Before this time, most little girls prefer girlish toys and clothes and games, and most little boys prefer boyish toys and games. Thus, contrary to Kohlberg's description of cognitive developmental theory, gender typing does not appear to depend on gender constancy.

Unlike cognitive developmental theory, gender schema theory does not require children to perceive gender constancy before they begin gender typing (see Figure 10.4). Instead, *gender schema theory* states that gender typing occurs when children are ready to encode and organize information along the lines of what is considered appropriate for females and males in their society (Martin & Dinella, 2001; Martin & Halverson, 1981; Ruble, Martin, & Berenbaum, 2006). Bit by bit, children pick up what is gender-appropriate and gender-inappropriate in their culture, and develop gender schemas that shape how they perceive the world and what they remember. Children are motivated to act in ways that conform with these gender schemas. Thus, gender schemas fuel gender typing (Hyde, 2007; Smith, 2007).

REVIEW AND REFLECT ◆ LEARNING GOAL 1

1 Discuss emotional and personality development in early childhood.

Review
- What changes in the self occur during early childhood?
- What changes take place in emotional development in young children?
- What are some key aspects of moral development in young children?
- How does gender develop in young children?

Reflect
- Which theory of gender development do you find most persuasive? What might an eclectic theoretical view of gender development be like? (You might want to review the discussion of an eclectic theoretical orientation in Chapter 1.)

② WHAT ROLES DO FAMILIES PLAY IN YOUNG CHILDREN'S DEVELOPMENT?

Parenting	Sibling Relationships and Birth Order

Child Maltreatment	The Changing Family in a Changing Society

Attachment to a caregiver is a key social relationship during infancy, but we saw in Chapter 7 that some experts maintain that secure attachment and the infant years have been overdramatized as determinants of life-span development. Social and emotional development is also shaped by other relationships and by temperament, contexts, and social experiences in the early childhood years and later. Consider Craig Lesley, whose story opened this chapter. As an infant he was securely attached to his mother, but his abandonment by his father also mattered. For years he missed him; he missed his love; he felt "the terrible pull of my father's blood. . . . He drew me like a lodestone" (Lesley, 2005, p. 141). In this section, we discuss social relationships of early childhood beyond attachment. We explore the different types of parenting, child maltreatment, sibling relationships, and variations in family structures.

Parenting

A few years ago, there was considerable interest in Mozart CDs that were marketed with the promise that playing them would enrich infants' and young children's brains. Some of the parents who bought them probably thought, "I don't have enough time to spend with my children so I'll just play these intellectual CDs and then they won't need me as much." Similarly, one-minute bedtime stories are being marketed for parents to read to their children (Walsh, 2000). There are one-minute bedtime bear books, puppy books, and so on. Parents who buy them know it is good for them to read with their children, but they don't want to spend a lot of time doing it. Behind the popularity of these products is an unfortunate theme which suggests that parenting can be done quickly, with little or no inconvenience (Sroufe, 2000).

What is wrong with these quick-fix approaches to parenting? Good parenting takes time and effort (Bornstein, 2006; Powell, 2005, 2006). You can't do it in a minute here and a minute there. You can't do it with CDs.

Of course, it's not just the quantity of time parents spend with children that is important for children's development—the quality of the parenting is clearly important

> *Parenting is a very important profession, but no test of fitness for it is ever imposed in the interest of children.*
>
> —GEORGE BERNARD SHAW
> *Irish Playwright, 20th Century*

Calvin and Hobbes

WHAT ASSURANCE DO I HAVE THAT YOUR PARENTING ISN'T SCREWING ME UP?

	Accepting, responsive	Rejecting, unresponsive
Demanding, controlling	Authoritative	Authoritarian
Undemanding, uncontrolling	Indulgent	Neglectful

FIGURE 10.5 Classification of Parenting Styles The four types of parenting styles (authoritative, authoritarian, indulgent, and neglectful) involve the dimensions of acceptance and responsiveness, on the one hand, and demand and control on the other. For example, authoritative parenting involves being both accepting/responsive and demanding/controlling.

authoritarian parenting A restrictive, punitive style in which parents exhort the child to follow their directions and to respect work and effort. The authoritarian parent places firm limits and controls on the child and allows little verbal exchange. Authoritarian parenting is associated with children's social incompetence.

authoritative parenting A parenting style in which parents encourage their children to be independent but still place limits and controls on their actions. Extensive verbal give-and-take is allowed, and parents are warm and nurturant toward the child. Authoritative parenting is associated with children's social competence.

neglectful parenting A style of parenting in which the parent is very uninvolved in the child's life; it is associated with children's social incompetence, especially a lack of self-control.

(Clarke-Stewart, 2006). To understand variations in parenting, let's consider the styles parents use when they interact with their children, how they discipline their children, and coparenting.

Baumrind's Parenting Styles Diana Baumrind (1971) stresses that parents should be neither punitive nor aloof. Rather, they should develop rules for their children and be affectionate with them. She has described four types of parenting styles:

- **Authoritarian parenting** is a restrictive, punitive style in which parents exhort the child to follow their directions and respect their work and effort. The authoritarian parent places firm limits and controls on the child and allows little verbal exchange. For example, an authoritarian parent might say, "You do it my way or else." Authoritarian parents also might spank the child frequently, enforce rules rigidly but not explain them, and show rage toward the child. Children of authoritarian parents are often unhappy, fearful, and anxious about comparing themselves with others, fail to initiate activity, and have weak communication skills. Sons of authoritarian parents may behave aggressively (Hart & others, 2003).

- **Authoritative parenting** encourages children to be independent but still places limits and controls on their actions. Extensive verbal give-and-take is allowed, and parents are warm and nurturant toward the child. An authoritative parent might put his arm around the child in a comforting way and say, "You know you should not have done that. Let's talk about how you can handle the situation better next time." Authoritative parents show pleasure and support in response to children's constructive behavior. They also expect mature, independent, and age-appropriate behavior by children. Children whose parents are authoritative are often cheerful, self-controlled and self-reliant, and achievement-oriented; they tend to maintain friendly relations with peers, cooperate with adults, and cope well with stress.

- **Neglectful parenting** is a style in which the parent is very uninvolved in the child's life. Children whose parents are neglectful develop the sense that other aspects of the parents' lives are more important than they are. These children tend to be socially incompetent. Many have poor self-control and don't handle independence well. They frequently have low self-esteem, are immature, and may be alienated from the family. In adolescence, they may show patterns of truancy and delinquency.

- **Indulgent parenting** is a style in which parents are highly involved with their children but place few demands or controls on them. Such parents let their children do what they want. The result is that the children never learn to control their own behavior and always expect to get their way. Some parents deliberately rear their children in this way because they believe the combination of warm involvement and few restraints will produce a creative, confident child. However, children whose parents are indulgent rarely learn respect for others and have difficulty controlling their behavior. They might be domineering, egocentric, noncompliant, and have difficulties in peer relations.

These four classifications of parenting involve combinations of acceptance and responsiveness on the one hand and demand and control on the other (Maccoby & Martin, 1983). How these dimensions combine to produce authoritarian, authoritative, neglectful, and indulgent parenting is shown in Figure 10.5.

Parenting Styles in Context Do the benefits of authoritative parenting transcend the boundaries of ethnicity, socioeconomic status, and household composition? Although some exceptions have been found, evidence linking authoritative parenting with competence on the part of the child occurs in research across a wide range of ethnic groups, social strata, cultures, and family structures (Steinberg, Blatt-Eisengart, & Cauffman, 2006; Steinberg & Silk, 2002). A recent study of more than 1,300 14- to 18-year-olds who had been adjudicated because of serious delinquent acts found that the juvenile offenders who had authoritative parents were more psychosocially mature and academically competent than those who had neglectful parents (Steinberg, Blatt-Eisengart, & Cauffman, 2006). The juvenile offenders whose parents were authoritarian or indulgent tended to score between the extremes of those whose parents were authoritative and neglectful, although those with authoritarian parents consistently functioned better than those with indulgent parents. Most of these youth came from poor, ethnic minority backgrounds.

Other research with ethnic groups suggests that some aspects of the authoritarian style may be associated with positive child outcomes (Parke & Buriel, 2006). Elements of the authoritarian style may take on different meanings and have different effects, depending on the context.

For example, Asian American parents often continue aspects of traditional Asian child-rearing practices that have sometimes been described as authoritarian. The parents exert considerable control over their children's lives. However, Ruth Chao (2001, 2005, 2007; Chao & Tseng, 2002) argues that the style of parenting used by many Asian American parents is distinct from the domineering control of the authoritarian style. Instead, Chao argues that the control reflects concern and involvement in their children's lives and is best conceptualized as a type of training. The high academic achievement of Asian American children may be a consequence of their "training" parents (Stevenson & Zusho, 2002).

An emphasis on requiring respect and obedience is also associated with the authoritarian style, but in Latino child rearing this focus may be positive rather than punitive. Rather than suppressing the child's development, it may encourage the development of a different type of self. Latino child-rearing practices encourage the development of a self and identity that is embedded in the family and requires respect and obedience (Halgunseth, Ispa, & Rudy, 2006; Harwood & others, 2002). Furthermore, many Latino families have several generations living together and helping each other (Zinn & Well, 2000). In these circumstances, emphasizing respect and obedience by children may be part of maintaining a harmonious home and may be important in the formation of the child's identity.

Even physical punishment, another characteristic of the authoritarian style, may have varying effects in different contexts. African American parents are more likely than non-Latino White parents to use physical punishment (Deater-Deckard & Dodge, 1997). However, the use of physical punishment has been linked with increased externalized child problems (such as acting out and high levels of aggression) in non-Latino White families but not in African American families. One explanation of this finding points to the need for African American parents to enforce rules in the dangerous environments in which they are more likely to live (Harrison-Hale, McLoyd, & Smedley, 2004). In this context, requiring obedience to parental authority may be an adaptive strategy to keep children from engaging in antisocial behavior that can have serious consequences for the victim or the perpetrator. As we see next, though, overall, the use of physical punishment in disciplining children raises many concerns.

Punishment For centuries, corporal (physical) punishment, such as spanking, has been considered a necessary and even desirable method of disciplining children. Use of corporal punishment is legal in every state in America. A recent national survey of U.S. parents with 3- and 4-year-old children found that 26 percent of parents reported spanking their children frequently, and 67 percent of the parents reported

According to Ruth Chao, what type of parenting style do many Asian American parents use?

indulgent parenting A style of parenting in which parents are highly involved with their children but place few demands or controls on them. Indulgent parenting is associated with children's social incompetence, especially a lack of self-control.

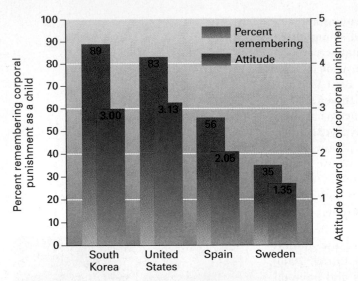

FIGURE 10.6 Corporal Punishment in Different Countries
A 5-point scale was used to assess attitudes toward corporal punish-ment with scores closer to 1 indicating an attitude against its use and scores closer to 5 suggesting an attitude favoring its use. *Why are studies of corporal punishment correlational studies, and how does that affect their usefulness?*

How do most child psychologists recommend handling a child's misbehavior?

yelling at their children frequently (Regaldo & others, 2004). A cross-cultural comparison found that individuals in the United States were among those with the most favorable attitudes toward corporal punishment and were the most likely to remem-ber it being used by their parents (Curran & others, 2001) (see Figure 10.6).

Despite the widespread use of corporal punishment, there have been surprisingly few research studies on physical punish-ment, and those that have been conducted are correlational (Baumrind, Larzelere, & Cowan, 2002; Benjet & Kazdin, 2003; Kazdin & Benjet, 2003). Clearly, it would be highly unethical to randomly assign parents to either spank or not spank their chil-dren in an experimental study. Recall that cause and effect can-not be determined in a correlational study. In one correlational study, spanking by parents was linked with children's antisocial behavior, including cheating, telling lies, being mean to others, bullying, getting into fights, and being disobedient (Strauss, Sug-arman, & Giles-Sims, 1997).

A research review concluded that corporal punishment by parents is associated with higher levels of immediate compliance and aggression by the children (Gershoff, 2002). The review also found that corporal punishment is associated with lower levels of moral internalization and mental health (Gershoff, 2002). A longitudinal study found that spanking before age 2 was related to behavioral prob-lems in middle and late childhood (Slade & Wissow, 2004). Another study revealed that children whose parents hit to slapped them in the prior two weeks showed more emotional and adjustment problems than children who had not been hit or slapped by parents in the same time frame (Aucoin, Frick, & Bodin, 2006). And a recent study discovered that a history of harsh physical discipline was linked to ado-lescent depression and externalized problems, such as juvenile delinquency (Bender & others, 2007). Some critics, though, argue that the research evidence is not yet sound enough to warrant a blanket injunction against corporal punishment, espe-cially mild corporal punishment (Baumrind, Larzelere, & Cowan, 2002; Kazdin & Benjet, 2003).

What are some reasons for avoiding spanking or similar punishments? The rea-sons include the following:

- When adults punish a child by yelling, screaming, or spanking, they are pre-senting children with out-of-control models for handling stressful situations. Children may imitate this aggressive, out-of-control behavior (Sim & Ong, 2005).
- Punishment can instill fear, rage, or avoidance. For example, spanking the child may cause the child to avoid being around the parent and to fear the parent.
- Punishment tells children what not to do rather what to do. Children should be given feedback, such as "Why don't you try this?"
- Punishment can be abusive. Parents might unintentionally become so aroused when they are punishing the child that they become abusive (Ateah, 2005; Baumrind, Larzelere, & Cowan, 2002).

Because of reasons such as these, Sweden passed a law in 1979 forbidding par-ents to physically punish (spank or slap, for example) children. Since the law was enacted, youth rates of delinquency, alcohol abuse, rape, and suicide have dropped in Sweden (Durrant, 2000). These improvements may have occurred for other rea-sons, such as changing attitudes and opportunities for youth. Nonetheless, the Swedish experience suggests that physical punishment of children may be unnec-essary. Many other countries also have passed antispanking laws.

Most child psychologists recommend handling misbehavior by reasoning with the child, especially explaining the consequences of the child's actions for others. *Time out,* in which the child is removed from a setting that offers positive reinforcement, can also be effective. For example, when the child has misbehaved, a parent might take away TV viewing for a specified time.

In Chapter 7, "Socioemotional Development in Infancy," we described the family as a system and discussed possible links between marital relationships and parenting practices (Cox & others, 2004). To read about a family systems study involving marital conflict and the use of physical punishment, see the *Research in Children's Development* interlude.

Research in Children's Development

MARITAL CONFLICT, INDIVIDUAL HOSTILITY, AND THE USE OF PHYSICAL PUNISHMENT

A longitudinal study assessed couples across the transition to parenting to investigate possible links between marital conflict, individual adult hostility, and the use of physical punishment with young children (Kanoy & others, 2003). Before the birth of the first child, the level of marital conflict was observed in a marital problem-solving discussion; answers to questionnaires regarding individual characteristics were also obtained. Thus, these characteristics of the couples were not influenced by characteristics of the child. When the children were 2 and 5 years old, the couples were interviewed about the frequency and intensity of their physical punishment of the children. At both ages, the parents' level of marital conflict was again observed in a marital problem-solving discussion.

The researchers found that both hostility and marital conflict were linked with the use of physical punishment. Individuals with high rates of hostility on the prenatal measures used more frequent and more severe physical punishment with their children. The same was evident for marital conflict—when marital conflict was high, both mothers and fathers were more likely to use physical punishment in disciplining their young children.

If parents who have a greater likelihood of using physical punishment can be identified in prenatal classes, these families could be encouraged to use other forms of discipline before they get into a pattern of physically punishing their children.

Coparenting   The relationship between marital conflict and the use of punishment highlights the importance of *coparenting*, which is the support that parents provide one another in jointly raising a child. Poor coordination between parents, undermining of the other parent, lack of cooperation and warmth, and disconnection by one parent are conditions that place children at risk for problems (McHale, 2007; McHale & Sullivan, 2007; Schoppe-Sullivan & others, 2007). For example, in one study, 4-year-old children from families characterized by low levels of mutuality and support in coparenting were more likely than their classmates to show difficulties in social adjustment on the playground (McHale, Johnson, & Sinclair, 1999). By contrast, parental cooperation and warmth are linked with children's prosocial behavior and competence in peer relations.

Parents who do not spend enough time with their children, or who have problems in child rearing, can benefit from counseling and therapy. To read about the work of marriage and family counselor Darla Botkin, see the *Careers in Child Development* profile.

Careers in CHILD DEVELOPMENT

Darla Botkin
Marriage and Family Therapist

Darla Botkin is a marriage and family therapist who teaches, conducts research, and engages in marriage and family therapy. She is on the faculty of the University of Kentucky. Darla obtained a bachelor's degree in elementary education with a concentration in special education and then went on to receive a master's degree in early childhood education. She spent the next six years working with children and their families in a variety of settings, including child care, elementary school, and Head Start. These experiences led Darla to recognize the interdependence of the developmental settings that children and their parents experience (such as home, school, and work). She returned to graduate school and obtained a Ph.D. in family studies from the University of Tennessee. She then became a faculty member in the Family Studies program at the University of Kentucky. Completing further coursework and clinical training in marriage and family therapy, she became certified as a marriage and family therapist.

Darla's current interests include working with young children in family therapy, gender and ethnic issues in family therapy, and the role of spirituality in family wellness.

Darla Botkin (*left*), conducting a family therapy session.

Child Maltreatment

Unfortunately, punishment sometimes leads to the abuse of children (Miller-Perrin & Perrin, 2007). In 2002, approximately 896,000 U.S. children were found to be victims of child abuse (U.S. Department of Health and Human Services, 2003). Eighty-four percent of these children were abused by a parent or parents. Laws in many states now require doctors and teachers to report suspected cases of child abuse, yet many cases go unreported, especially those of battered infants.

Whereas the public and many professionals use the term *child abuse* to refer to both abuse and neglect, developmentalists increasingly use the term *child maltreatment* (Cicchetti & Blender, 2004; Cicchetti & Toth, 2005, 2006). This term does not have quite the emotional impact of the term *abuse* and acknowledges that maltreatment includes diverse conditions.

Types of Child Maltreatment   The four main types of child maltreatment are physical abuse, child neglect, sexual abuse, and emotional abuse (National Clearinghouse on Child Abuse and Neglect, 2002, 2004):

- *Physical abuse* is characterized by the infliction of physical injury as a result of punching, beating, kicking, biting, burning, shaking, or otherwise harming a child. The parent or other person may not have intended to hurt the child; the injury may have resulted from excessive physical punishment (Hornor, 2005; Maguire & others, 2005).
- *Child neglect* is characterized by failure to provide for the child's basic needs (Sedlak & others, 2006; Trowell, 2006). Neglect can be physical (abandonment, for example), educational (allowing chronic truancy, for example), or emotional (marked inattention to the child's needs, for example).
- *Sexual abuse* includes fondling a child's genitals, intercourse, incest, rape, sodomy, exhibitionism, and commercial exploitation through prostitution or the production of pornographic materials (Edinburgh & others, 2006).
- *Emotional abuse (psychological abuse/verbal abuse/mental injury)* includes acts or omissions by parents or other caregivers that have caused, or could cause, serious behavioral, cognitive, or emotional problems.

Although any of these forms of child maltreatment may be found separately, they often occur in combination. Emotional abuse is almost always present when other forms are identified.

The Context of Abuse   No single factor causes child maltreatment (Cicchetti & Toth, 2005, 2006). A combination of factors, including the culture, family, and development, likely contribute to child maltreatment.

The extensive violence that takes place in American culture is reflected in the occurrence of violence in the family. A regular diet of violence appears on television screens, and parents often resort to power assertion as a disciplinary technique. In China, where physical punishment is rarely used to discipline children, the incidence of child abuse is reported to be very low.

The family itself is obviously a key part of the context of abuse. The interactions of all family members need to be considered, regardless of who performs the violent acts against the child (Kim & Cicchetti, 2004). For example, even though the father may be the one who physically abuses the child, contributions by the mother, the child, and siblings also should be evaluated.

Were parents who abuse children abused by their own parents? About one-third of parents who were abused themselves when they were young abuse their own children (Cicchetti & Toth, 2005, 2006). Thus, some, but not a majority, of parents are locked into an intergenerational transmission of abuse (Dixon, Browne, & Hamilton-Giachritsis, 2005; Leifer & others, 2004). Mothers who break out of the intergenerational transmission of abuse often have at least one warm, caring adult in their background; have a close, positive marital relationship; and have received therapy (Egeland, Jacobvitz, & Sroufe, 1988).

Children at a shelter for domestic violence in Tel Aviv, Israel.

Developmental Consequences of Abuse   Among the developmental consequences of child maltreatment are poor emotion regulation, attachment problems, problems in peer relations, difficulty in adapting to school, and other psychological problems (Cicchetti & Toth, 2005, 2006). Maltreated infants may show excessive negative affect (such as irritability and crying) or they may display blunted positive affect (rarely smiling or laughing). If young children are maltreated, they often show insecure attachment patterns in their social relationships later in development (Cicchetti & Toth, 2006). Maltreated children tend to be overly aggressive with peers or avoid interacting with peers (Bolger & Patterson, 2001). Abused and neglected children are also at risk for academic problems (Cicchetti & Toth, 2005, 2006).

Being physically abused has been linked with children's anxiety, personality problems, depression, suicide attempts, conduct disorder, and delinquency (Cicchetti & Toth, 2005, 2006; Danielson & others, 2005; Malmgren & Meisel, 2004). Later, during the adult years, maltreated children often have difficulty in establishing and maintaining healthy intimate relationships (Colman & Widom, 2004). As adults, maltreated children also show increased violence toward other adults, dating partners, and marital partners, as well as increased substance abuse, anxiety, and depression (Sachs-Ericsson & others, 2005; Shea & others, 2005). In sum, maltreated children are at risk for developing a wide range of problems and disorders (Arias, 2004; Haugaard & Hazen, 2004).

An important strategy is to prevent child maltreatment (Cicchetti & Toth, 2006; Lyons, Henly, & Schuerman, 2005). In one recent study of maltreating mothers and their 1-year-olds, two treatments were effective in reducing child maltreatment: (1) home visitation that emphasized improved parenting, coping with stress, and increasing support for the mother; and (2) parent-infant psychotherapy that focused on improving maternal-infant attachment (Cicchetti, Toth, and Rogosch, 2005).

Sibling Relationships and Birth Order

What are sibling relationships like? How extensively does birth order influence behavior?

We're wearing the blue wristband because it's time to prevent child abuse. To get with the band or learn more, visit www.preventchildabuse.org or call 1-800-688-1275 ext. 540. Prevent Child Abuse America

This print ad was created by Prevent Child Abuse America to make people aware of its national blue wristband campaign. The campaign's goal is to educate people about child abuse prevention and encourage them to support the organization.
Source: Prevent Child Abuse America

Sibling Relationships   Any of you who have grown up with siblings probably have a rich memory of aggressive, hostile interchanges. When siblings are in the presence of each other when they are 2 to 4 years of age, on average they have a conflict once every 10 minutes and then the conflicts go down somewhat from 5 to 7 years of age (Kramer, 2006). What do parents do when they encounter siblings having a verbal or physical confrontation? One study revealed that they do one of three things: (1) intervene and try to help them resolve the conflict, (2) admonish or threaten them, or (3) do nothing at all (Kramer & Perozynski, 1999). Of interest is that in families with two siblings 2 to 5 years of age, the most frequent parental reaction is do nothing at all.

Laurie Kramer (2006), who had conducted a number of research studies on siblings, says that not intervening and letting sibling conflict escalate is not a good strategy. She recently has developed a program titled More Fun with Sisters and Brothers, which teaches 4- to 8-year-old siblings social skills for developing positive interactions.

Siblings also have many pleasant, caring moments with each other (Dunn, 2005; Pomery & others, 2005; Richmond, Stocker, & Rienks, 2005). Children's sibling relationships include helping, sharing, teaching, fighting, and playing. Children can act as emotional supports, rivals, and communication partners (Noller, 2005). One recent study found that the positive aspects of children's sibling relationship were more strongly related to adjustment than was sibling conflict (Pike, Coldwell, & Dunn, 2005).

Is sibling interaction different from parent-child interaction? There is some evidence that it is. Observations indicate that children interact more positively and in more varied ways with their parents than with their siblings (Baskett & Johnson, 1982). Children also follow their parents' dictates more than those of their siblings, and they behave more negatively and punitively with their siblings than with their parents.

In some instances, siblings may be stronger socializing influences on the child than parents are (Cicirelli, 1994). Someone close in age to the child—such as a sibling—may be able to understand the child's problems and communicate more effectively than parents can. In dealing with peers, coping with difficult teachers, and discussing such taboo subjects as sex, siblings may have more influence than parents.

Is sibling interaction the same around the world? In industrialized societies, such as the United States, parents tend to delegate responsibility for younger siblings to older siblings primarily to give the parents freedom to pursue other activities. However, in nonindustrialized countries, such as Kenya, the older sibling's role as a caregiver to younger siblings has much more importance. In industrialized countries, the older sibling's caregiving role is often discretionary; in nonindustrialized countries, it is more obligatory (Cicirelli,1994).

Children's sibling relationships are characterized by both sibling rivalry and positive interchanges. *What are some characteristics of these negative and positive interactions?*

Birth Order   Whether a child has older or younger siblings has been linked to development of certain personality characteristics. For example, compared with later-born children, firstborn children are more adult-oriented, helpful, conforming, and self-controlled. Firstborns excel in academic and professional endeavors, and they have more guilt, anxiety, and difficulty in coping with stressful situations, as well as higher admission to child guidance clinics.

What accounts for such differences related to birth order? Proposed explanations usually point to variations in interactions with parents and siblings associated with being in a particular position in the family. This is especially true in the case of the firstborn child (Teti & others, 1993). The oldest child is the only one who does not have to share parental love and affection with other siblings—until another sibling comes along. An infant requires more attention than an older child; this means that the firstborn sibling receives less attention after the newborn arrives. Does this result in conflict between parents and the firstborn? In one research study, mothers became more negative, coercive, and restraining and played less with the firstborn following the birth of a second child (Dunn & Kendrick, 1982).

What is the only child like? The popular conception is that the only child is a "spoiled brat," with such undesirable characteristics as dependency, lack of self-control, and self-centered behavior. But researchers present a more positive portrayal of the only child. Only children often are achievement-oriented and display a desirable personality, especially in comparison with later-borns and children from large families (Falbo & Poston, 1993).

So far, our discussion suggests that birth order might be a strong predictor of behavior. However, an increasing number of family researchers believe that when all of the factors that influence behavior are considered, birth order itself shows limited ability to predict behavior. Think about some of the other important factors in children's lives that influence their behavior beyond birth order. They include heredity, models of competency or incompetency that parents present to children on a daily basis, peer influences, school influences, socioeconomic factors, sociohistorical factors, and cultural variations. When someone says firstborns are always like this but last-borns are always like that, the person is making overly simplistic statements that do not adequately take into account the complexity of influences on a child's development.

The one-child family is becoming much more common in China because of the strong motivation to limit the population growth in the People's Republic of China. The policy is still relatively new, and its effects on children have not been fully examined. *In general, though, what have researchers found the only child to be like?*

The Changing Family in a Changing Society

Beyond variations in the number of siblings, the families that children experience differ in many important ways. The number of children growing up in single-parent families is staggering (Martin, Emery, & Peris, 2004). As shown in Figure 10.7, the United States has the highest percentage of single-parent families compared with virtually all other countries. Children may live in families in which both parents

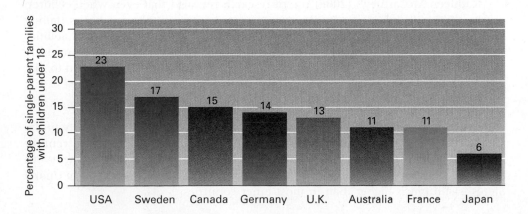

FIGURE 10.7 Single-Parent Families in Different Countries

work, or have divorced parents, or gay or lesbian parents. Differences in culture and SES (socioeconomic status) also influence their families. How do these variations in families affect children?

Working Parents More than one of every two U.S. mothers with a child under the age of 5 is in the labor force; more than two of every three with a child from 6 to 17 years of age is. Maternal employment is a part of modern life, but its effects are still debated. However, many studies have found no overall detrimental effects of maternal employment on children's development (Gottfried, Gottfried, & Bathurst, 2002; Hoffman & Youngblade, 1999).

According to Lois Hoffman (1989), because household operations have become more efficient and family size has decreased, it is not certain that American children today receive less attention when both parents work outside the home than children in the past whose mothers were not employed. Parents might spend less time than in the past keeping the house clean or pursuing hobbies. Time once split among several children might now be focused on just one or two. It also cannot be assumed that children benefit from receiving extra time and attention from stay-at-home parents. Parenting does not always have a positive effect on the child. Parents may overinvest in their children, worrying excessively and discouraging the child's independence. The needs of the growing child require parents to give increasing independence to the child, which may be easier for parents whose jobs provide an additional source of identity and self-esteem.

Although overall no detrimental effects on children's development are found when both parents work, depending on the circumstances, work can produce positive or negative effects on parenting (Crouter & McHale, 2005). Work-related stress can spill over and harm parenting, but a sense of well-being produced by work can lead to more positive parenting. Ann Crouter (2006) recently described how parents' work worlds can be brought home in negative ways. Her research reveals that when parents experience poor work conditions at their jobs, such as long hours, stressful conditions, and limited autonomy, they often become more irritable and inattentive to their children. In such negative work-spillover contexts, children show more behavioral problems and do more poorly at school.

When parents work and place their children in child care, how does that affect the children's development? Characteristics of preschoolers themselves also influence the effects of child care (Langlois & Liben, 2003). Difficult children and those with poor self-control may be especially at risk in child care (Maccoby & Lewis, 2003). Thus, it may be helpful to teach child-care providers how to foster self-regulatory skills in children (Fabes, Hannish, & Martin, 2003) and to invest more effort in building children's attachment to their child-care center or school. For example, one study revealed that when children experienced their group, class, or school as a caring community, they showed increased concern for others, better conflict resolution skills, and a decrease in problem behaviors (Solomon & others, 2000).

Kathleen McCartney's (2006) recent research revealed that even when children are in child care, regardless of the type of care or the number of hours, family characteristics are four times more likely to predict children's behavior and abilities than child-care characteristics. She concludes these results should not be surprising since the family is the primary environment that young children are exposed to, the family provides the most consistent environment over time, and measures of the family reflect genetic as well as contextual, environmental influences.

Children in Divorced Families Divorce rates changed rather dramatically in the United States and many countries around the world in the late twentieth century (Amato & Irving, 2006). The U.S. divorce rate increased dramatically in the 1960s and 1970s but has declined since the 1980s. However, the divorce rate in the United States is still much higher than in most other countries.

It is estimated that 40 percent of children born to married parents in the United States will experience their parents' divorce (Hetherington & Stanley-Hagan, 2002). Let's examine some important questions about children in divorced families:

- *Are children better adjusted in intact, never-divorced families than in divorced families?* Most researchers agree that children from divorced families show poorer adjustment than their counterparts in nondivorced families (Amato, 2006; Hetherington, 2005, 2006; Hetherington & Kelly, 2002; Huurre, Junkkari, & Aro, 2006 (see Figure 10.8). Those who have experienced multiple divorces are at greater risk. Children in divorced families are more likely than children in nondivorced families to have academic problems, to show externalized problems (such as acting out and delinquency) and internalized problems (such as anxiety and depression), to be less socially responsible, to have less competent intimate relationships, to drop out of school, to become sexually active at an early age, to take drugs, to associate with antisocial peers, to have low self-esteem, and to be less securely attached as young adults (Conger & Chao, 1996). For example, one recent study found that experiencing a divorce in childhood was associated with insecure attachment in early adulthood (Brockmeyer, Treboux, & Crowell, 2005). Another recent study revealed that when individuals experienced the divorce of their parents in childhood and adolescence, it was linked to having unstable romantic or marital relationships and low levels of education in adulthood (Amato, 2006). Nonetheless, keep in mind that a majority of children in divorced families do not have significant adjustment problems (Ahrons, 2007; Barber & Demo, 2005). One study found that 20 years after their parents had divorced when they were children, approximately 80 percent of adults concluded that their parents' decision to divorce was a wise one (Ahrons, 2004).

- *Should parents stay together for the sake of the children?* Whether parents should stay in an unhappy or conflicted marriage for the sake of their children is one of the most commonly asked questions about divorce (Hetherington, 2005, 2006). If the stresses and disruptions in family relationships associated with an unhappy, conflictual marriage that erode the well-being of children are reduced by the move to a divorced, single-parent family, divorce can be advantageous. However, if the diminished resources and increased risks associated with divorce also are accompanied by inept parenting and sustained or increased conflict, not only between the divorced couple but also among the parents, children, and siblings, the best choice for the children would be for an unhappy marriage to be retained (Hetherington & Stanley-Hagan, 2002). It is difficult to determine how these "ifs" will play out when parents either remain together in an acrimonious marriage or become divorced.

  Note that marital conflict may have negative consequences for children in the context of marriage or divorce (McDonald & Grych, 2006). A longitudinal study revealed that conflict in nondivorced families was associated with emotional problems in children (Amato, 2006)

- *How much do family processes matter in divorced families?* Family processes matter a great deal (Clarke-Stewart & Brentano, 2006; Hetherington, 2005, 2006; Kelly, 2007). When divorced parents' relationship with each other is harmonious, and when they use authoritative parenting, the adjustment of children improves (Hetherington, 2005, 2006). A number of researchers have shown that a disequilibrium, which includes diminished parenting skills, occurs in the year following the divorce—but that, by two years after the divorce, restabilization has occurred and parenting skills have improved (Hetherington, 1989).

- *What factors influence an individual child's vulnerability to suffering negative consequences as a result of living in a divorced family?* Among the factors involved in the child's risk and vulnerability are the child's adjustment prior to the

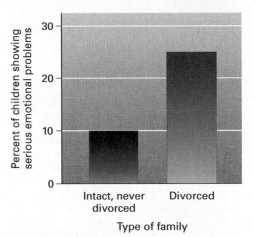

FIGURE 10.8 Divorce and Children's Emotional Problems In Hetherington's research, 25 percent of children from divorced families showed serious emotional problems compared with only 10 percent of children from intact, never-divorced families. However, keep in mind that a substantial majority (75 percent) of the children from divorced families did not show serious emotional problems.

What concerns are involved in whether parents should stay together for the sake of the children or become divorced?

As marriage has become a more optional, less permanent institution in contemporary America, children and adolescents are encountering stresses and adaptive challenges associated with their parents' marital transitions.

—E. MAVIS HETHERINGTON
Contemporary Psychologist,
University of Virginia

divorce, as well as the child's personality and temperament, gender, and custody situation (Hetherington, 2005, 2006; Hetherington & Stanley-Hagan, 2002). Children whose parents later divorce show poorer adjustment before the breakup (Amato & Booth, 1996). Children who are socially mature and responsible, who show few behavioral problems, and who have an easy temperament are better able to cope with their parents' divorce. Children with a difficult temperament often have problems in coping with their parents' divorce (Hetherington, 2000).

Earlier studies reported gender differences in response to divorce, with divorce being more negative for girls than boys in mother-custody families. However, more recent studies have shown that gender differences are less pronounced and consistent than was previously believed. Some of the inconsistency may be due to the increase in father custody, joint custody, and increased involvement of noncustodial fathers, especially in their sons' lives (Palmer, 2004). An analysis of studies found that children in joint-custody families were better adjusted than children in sole-custody families (Bauserman, 2002). Some studies have shown that boys adjust better in father-custody families, girls in mother-custody families, whereas other studies have not (Maccoby & Mnookin, 1992; Santrock & Warshak, 1979).

- *What role does socioeconomic status play in the lives of children in divorced families?* Custodial mothers experience the loss of about one-fourth to one-half of their predivorce income, in comparison with a loss of only one-tenth by custodial fathers (Emery, 1994). This income loss for divorced mothers is accompanied by increased workloads, high rates of job instability, and residential moves to less desirable neighborhoods with inferior schools (Sayer, 2006).

In sum, many factors are involved in determining how divorce influences a child's development (Hetherington, 2005, 2006). In the case of Craig Lesley, whose story opened this chapter, his parents' divorce certainly marked his life, but perhaps not quite in ways we would predict. According to Lesley, his father's "neglect motivated me to raise an alcohol-damaged Indian boy just to show the old man I could succeed as a father where he had fallen down. To be truthful, it was harder than I thought" (Lesley, 2005, p. 7). To read about some strategies for helping children cope with the divorce of their parents, see the *Caring for Children* interlude.

Caring for Children

COMMUNICATING WITH CHILDREN ABOUT DIVORCE

Ellen Galinsky and Judy David (1988) developed a number of guidelines for communicating with children about divorce:

- ***Explain the separation.*** As soon as daily activities in the home make it obvious that one parent is leaving, tell the children. If possible, both parents should be present when children are told about the separation to come. The reasons for the separation are very difficult for young children to understand. No matter what parents tell children, children can find reasons to argue against the separation. It is extremely important for parents to tell the children who will take care of them and to describe the specific arrangements for seeing the other parent.
- ***Explain that the separation is not the child's fault.*** Young children often believe their parents' separation or divorce is their own fault. Therefore, it is important to tell children that they are not the cause of the separation. Parents need to repeat this a number of times.

- *Explain that it may take time to feel better.* Tell young children that it's normal to not feel good about what is happening and that many other children feel this way when their parents become separated. It is also okay for divorced parents to share some of their emotions with children, by saying something like "I'm having a hard time since the separation, just like you, but I know it's going to get better after a while." Such statements are best kept brief and should not criticize the other parent.
- *Keep the door open for further discussion.* Tell your children to come to you anytime they want to talk about the separation. It is healthy for children to express their pent-up emotions in discussions with their parents and to learn that the parents are willing to listen to their feelings and fears.
- *Provide as much continuity as possible.* The less children's worlds are disrupted by the separation, the easier their transition to a single-parent family will be. This means maintaining the rules already in place as much as possible. Children need parents who care enough to not only give them warmth and nurturance but also set reasonable limits.
- *Provide support for your children and yourself.* After a divorce or separation, parents are as important to children as before the divorce or separation. Divorced parents need to provide children with as much support as possible. Parents function best when other people are available to give them support as adults and as parents. Divorced parents can find people who provide practical help and with whom they can talk about their problems.

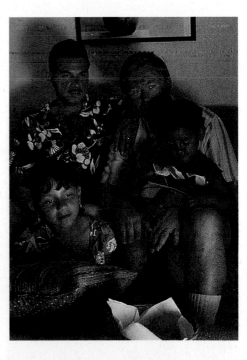

Gay Male and Lesbian Parents Increasingly, gay male and lesbian couples are creating families that include children. Approximately 20 percent of lesbians and 10 percent of gay men are parents (Patterson, 2004). There may be more than 1 million gay and lesbian parents in the United States today.

Like heterosexual couples, gay male and lesbian parents vary greatly. They may be single or they may have same-gender partners. Many lesbian mothers and gay fathers are noncustodial parents because they lost custody of their children to heterosexual spouses after a divorce.

Most children of gay and lesbian parents were born in a heterosexual relationship that ended in a divorce: in most cases, it was probably a relationship in which one or both parents only later identified themselves as gay male or lesbian. In other cases, lesbians and gay men became parents as a result of donor insemination and surrogates, or through adoption.

Parenthood among lesbians and gay men is controversial. Opponents claim that being raised by gay male or lesbian parents harms the child's development. But researchers have found few differences in children growing up with lesbian mothers or gay fathers and children growing up with heterosexual parents (Patterson, 2004; Patterson & Hastings, 2007). For example, children growing up in gay or lesbian families are just as popular with their peers, and there are no differences in the adjustment and mental health of children living in these families when they are compared with children in heterosexual families (Hyde & DeLamater, 2006; Lambert, 2005). Also, the overwhelming majority of children growing up in a gay or lesbian family have a heterosexual orientation (Tasker & Golombok, 1997).

Cultural, Ethnic, and Socioeconomic Variations Parenting can be influenced by culture, ethnicity, and socioeconomic status. In Bronfenbrenner's theory (introduced in Chapter 1), these influences are described as part of the macrosystem.

Cross-Cultural Studies Different cultures often give different answers to such basic questions as what the father's role in the family should be, what support systems are available to families, and how children should be disciplined (Harkness & Super,

2002). There are important cross-cultural variations in parenting (Kagitcibasi, 2007; Shiraev & Levy, 2007). In some countries, authoritarian parenting is widespread. For example, in the Arab world, many families today are very authoritarian, dominated by the father's rule, and children are taught strict codes of conduct and family loyalty (Booth, 2002). In one study, Chinese mothers of preschool children reported that they used more physical coercion, more encouragement of modesty, more shaming and love withdrawal, less warmth, and less democratic participation than U.S. mothers of preschool children (Wu & others, 2002).

What type of parenting is most frequent? In one study of parenting behavior in 186 cultures around the world, the most common pattern was a warm and controlling style, one that was neither permissive nor restrictive (Rohner & Rohner, 1981). The investigators commented that the majority of cultures have discovered, over many centuries, that children's healthy social development is most effectively promoted by love and at least some moderate parental control.

Cultural change is coming to families in many countries around the world (Berry, 2006; Bornstein & Cote, 2006). There are trends toward greater family mobility, migration to urban areas, separation as some family members work in cities or countries far from their homes, smaller families, fewer extended-family households, and increases in maternal employment (Brown & Larson, 2002; Larson, Brown, & Mortimer, 2003). These trends can change the resources that are available to children. For example, when several generations no longer live close by, children may lose support and guidance from grandparents, aunts, and uncles. Also, smaller families may produce more openness and communication between parents and children.

Ethnicity   Families within different ethnic groups in the United States differ in their typical size, structure, composition, reliance on kinships networks, and levels of income and education (Gonzales & others, 2007; Hernandez, Denton, & MaCartney, 2007). Large and extended families are more common among minority groups than among the White majority. For example, 19 percent of Latino families have three or more children, compared with 14 percent of African American and 10 percent of White families. African American and Latino children interact more with grandparents, aunts, uncles, cousins, and more-distant relatives than do White children.

Single-parent families are more common among African Americans and Latinos than among White Americans (Harris & Graham, 2007; McAdoo, 2006). In comparison with two-parent households, single parents often have more limited resources of time, money, and energy (Gyamfi, Brooks-Gunn, & Jackson, 2001). Ethnic minority parents also are less educated and more likely to live in low-income circumstances than their White counterparts. Still, many impoverished ethnic minority families manage to find ways to raise competent children (Hattery & Smith, 2007).

Some aspects of home life can help protect ethnic minority children from injustice. The family can filter out destructive racist messages, and parents can present alternative frames of reference to those presented by the majority. For example, TV shows may tell the 10-year-old boy that he will grow up to be either a star athlete or a bum; his parents can show him that his life holds many possibilities other than these. The extended family also can serve as an important buffer to stress (Hattery & Smith, 2007; McAdoo, 2006).

Of course, individual families vary, and how ethnic minority families deal with stress depends on many factors. Whether the parents are native-born or immigrants, how long the family has been in this country, their socioeoncomic status, and their national origin all make a difference (Berry, 2007; Fuligni & Fuligni, 2007). The characteristics of the family's social context also influence its adaptation. What are the attitudes toward the family's ethnic group within its neighborhood or city? Can the family's children attend good schools? Are there community groups that welcome people from the family's ethnic group? Do members of the family's ethnic group form community groups of their own? To read further about ethnic minority parenting, see the *Diversity in Children's Development* interlude.

What are some characteristics of families within different ethnic groups?

Diversity in Children's Development

ACCULTURATION AND ETHNIC MINORITY PARENTING

Ethnic minority children and their parents "are expected to transcend their own cultural background and to incorporate aspects of the dominant culture" into children's development. They undergo varying degrees of **acculturation,** which refers to cultural changes that occur when one culture comes in contact with another. Asian American parents, for example, may feel pressed to modify the traditional training style of parental control discussed earlier as they encounter the more permissive parenting typical of the dominant culture.

The level of family acculturation can affect parenting style by influencing expectations for children's development, parent-child interactions, and the role of the extended family (Ishii-Kuntz, 2004; Martinez & Halgunseth, 2004). For example, in one study, the level of acculturation and maternal education were the strongest predictors of maternal-infant interaction patterns in Latino families (Perez-Febles, 1992).

The family's level of acculturation also influences important decisions about child care and early childhood education (Bradley & McKelvy, 2007). For example, An African American mother might prefer to leave her children with extended family while she is at work because the kinship network is seen as a natural way to cope with maternal absence. This well-intentioned, culturally appropriate decision might, however, put the child at an educational and social disadvantage relative to other children of similar age who have the benefit of important preschool experiences that may ease the transition into early school years." Less acculturated and more acculturated family members may disagree about the appropriateness of various caregiving practices, possibly creating conflict or confusion.

How is acculturation involved in ethnic minority parenting?

The opportunities for acculturation that young children experience depend mainly on their parents and extended family. If they send the children to a child-care center, school, church, or other community setting, the children are likely to learn about the values and behaviors of the dominant culture, and they may be expected to adapt to that culture's norms. Thus, Latino children raised in a traditional family in which the family's good is considered more important than the individual's interests may attend a preschool in which children are rewarded for asserting themselves. Chinese American children whose traditional parents value behavioral inhibition (as discussed in Chapter 7) may be rewarded outside the home for being active and emotionally expressive. Over time, the differences in the level of acculturation experienced by children and by their parents and extended family may grow. (Source: Garcia Coll & Pachter, 2002, pp. 7–8)

Socioeconomic Status Low-income families have less access to resources than higher-income families (Conger & Dogan, 2007; Patterson & Hastings, 2007). The differential in access to resources includes nutrition, health care, protection from danger, and enriching educational and socialization opportunities, such as tutoring and lessons in various activities. These differences are compounded in low-income families characterized by long-term poverty (McLoyd, Aikens, & Burton, 2006).

acculturation Cultural changes that occur when one culture comes into contact with another

In America and most Western cultures, differences have been found in child rearing among different socioeconomic-status (SES) groups (Hoff, Laursen, & Tardif, 2002, p. 246):

- "Lower-SES parents (1) are more concerned that their children conform to society's expectations, (2) create a home atmosphere in which it is clear that parents have authority over children," (3) use physical punishment more in disciplining their children, and (4) are more directive and less conversational with their children.

- "Higher-SES parents (1) are more concerned with developing children's initiative" and delay of gratification, "(2) create a home atmosphere in which children are more nearly equal participants and in which rules are discussed as opposed to being laid down" in an authoritarian manner, (3) are less likely to use physical punishment, and (4) "are less directive and more conversational" with their children.

Parents in different socioeconomic groups also tend to think differently about education (Hoff, Laursen, & Tardif, 2002; Magnuson & Duncan, 2002). Middle- and upper-income parents more often think of education as something that should be mutually encouraged by parents and teachers. By contrast, low-income parents are more likely to view education as the teacher's job. Thus, increased school-family linkages especially can benefit students from low-income families.

REVIEW AND REFLECT ▶ **LEARNING GOAL 2**

2 **Explain how families can influence young children's development.**

Review
- What aspects of parenting are linked with young children's development?
- What are the types and consequences of child maltreatment?
- How are sibling relationships and birth order related to young children's development?
- How is children's development affected by having two wage-earning parents, having divorced parents, and being part of a particular cultural, ethnic, and socioeconomic group?

Reflect
- Which style or styles of parenting did your mother and father use in rearing you? What effects do you think their parenting styles have had on your development?

---

3 **HOW ARE PEER RELATIONS, PLAY, AND TELEVISION INVOLVED IN YOUNG CHILDREN'S DEVELOPMENT?**

| Peer Relations | Play | Television |

The family is an important social context for children's development. However, children's development also is strongly influenced by what goes on in other social contexts, such as in peer groups and when children are playing or watching television.

Peer Relations

As children grow older, they spend an increasing amount of time with their *peers*—children of about the same age or maturity level. Even if schools were not age graded, and children determined the composition of their groups on their own, they would sort themselves by age (Hartup, 1983).

What are the functions of a child's peer group? One of its most important functions is to provide a source of information and comparison about the world outside the family. Children receive feedback about their abilities from their peer group. Children evaluate what they do in terms of whether it is better than, as good as, or worse than what other children do. It is hard to make these judgments at home because siblings are usually older or younger.

How important are peers for development? Anna Freud (Freud & Dann, 1951) studied six children from different families who banded together after their parents were killed in World War II. The children formed a tightly knit group, dependent on one another and aloof with outsiders. Even though deprived of parental care, they neither became delinquent nor developed serious mental disorders. When peer monkeys who have been reared together are separated, they become depressed and less advanced socially (Suomi, Harlow, & Domek, 1970).

Good peer relations can be necessary for normal social development (Lynne & others, 2007). Special concerns focus on children who are withdrawn and aggressive (Bukowski, Brendgen, & Vitaro, 2007). Withdrawn children who are rejected by peers or are victimized and feel lonely are at risk for depression. Children who are aggressive with their peers are at risk for developing a number of problems, including delinquency and dropping out of school (Dodge, Coie, & Lynam, 2006; Rubin, Bukowski, & Parker, 2006).

Recall from our discussion of gender that by about the age of 3, children already prefer to spend time with same-sex rather than opposite-sex playmates, and this preference increases in early childhood. During these same years, the frequency of peer interaction, both positive and negative, picks up considerably (Hartup, 1983). Although aggressive interaction and rough-and-tumble play increase, the proportion of aggressive exchanges, compared with friendly exchanges, decreases. Many preschool children spend considerable time in peer interaction just conversing with playmates about such matters as "negotiating roles and rules in play, arguing, and agreeing" (Rubin, Bukowski, & Parker, 2006). We have much more to say about peer relations in Chapter 13, "Socioemotional Development in Middle and Late Childhood," and Chapter 16, "Socioemotional Development in Adolescence."

What are some characteristics of peer relations in early childhood?

Play

An extensive amount of peer interaction during childhood involves play, but social play is only one type of play (Seifert, 2006). *Play* is a pleasurable activity that is engaged in for its own sake, and its functions and forms vary.

Play's Functions Play is essential to the young child's health. Theorists have focused on different aspects of play and highlighted a long list of functions.

According to Freud and Erikson, play helps the child master anxieties and conflicts. Because tensions are relieved in play, the child can cope with life's problems. Play permits the child to work off excess physical energy and to release pent-up tensions. Therapists use **play therapy** both to allow the child to work off frustrations and to analyze the child's conflicts and ways of coping with them (Drews, Carey, & Schaefer, 2003). Children may feel less threatened and be more likely to express their true feelings in the context of play.

Piaget (1962) maintained that play advances children's cognitive development. At the same time, he said that children's cognitive development *constrains* the way they play. Play permits children to practice their competencies and acquired skills

play therapy Therapy that lets children work off frustrations while therapists analyze their conflicts and coping methods in a relaxed, pleasurable way. Piaget thought that cognitive structures need to be exercised, and play provides the perfect setting for this exercise. For example, children who have just learned to add or multiply begin to play with numbers in different ways as they perfect these operations, laughing as they do so.

Vygotsky (1962) also considered play to be an excellent setting for cognitive development. He was especially interested in the symbolic and make-believe aspects of play, as when a child substitutes a stick for a horse and rides the stick as if it were a horse. For young children, the imaginary situation is real. Parents should encourage such imaginary play, because it advances the child's cognitive development, especially creative thought.

Daniel Berlyne (1960) described play as exciting and pleasurable in itself because it satisfies our exploratory drive. This drive involves curiosity and a desire for information about something new or unusual. Play is a means whereby children can safely explore and seek out new information. Play encourages exploratory behavior by offering children the possibilities of novelty, complexity, uncertainty, surprise, and incongruity.

Play also increases the probability that children will converse and interact with each other (Hyson, Copple, & Jones, 2006). During this interaction, children practice the roles they will assume later in life (Sutton-Smith, 2000). In short, play releases tension, advances cognitive development, increases exploration, provides a safe haven in which children can engage in potentially dangerous behavior, and increases affiliation with peers.

Parten's Classic Study of Play   Many years ago, Mildred Parten (1932) developed an elaborate classification of children's play. Based on observations of children in free play at nursery school, Parten proposed the following types of play:

- **Unoccupied play** is not play as it is commonly understood. The child may stand in one spot or perform random movements that do not seem to have a goal. In most nursery schools, unoccupied play is less frequent than other forms of play.
- **Solitary play** happens when the child plays alone and independently of others. The child seems engrossed in the activity and does not care much about anything else that is happening. Two- and 3-year-olds engage more frequently in solitary play than older preschoolers do.
- **Onlooker play** takes place when the child watches other children play. The child may talk with other children and ask questions but does not enter into

unoccupied play Play in which the child is not engaging in play as it is commonly understood and might stand in one spot, or perform random movements that do not seem to have a goal.

solitary play Play in which the child plays alone and independently of others.

onlooker play Play in which the child watches other children play.

Mildred Parten classified play into six categories. *Study this photograph. Which of Parten's categories are reflected in the behavior of the children?*

their play behavior. The child's active interest in other children's play distinguishes onlooker play from unoccupied play.

- **Parallel play** occurs when the child plays separately from others but with toys like those the others are using or in a manner that mimics their play. The older children are, the less frequently they engage in this type of play. However, even older preschool children engage in parallel play quite often.
- **Associative play** involves social interaction with little or no organization. In this type of play, children seem to be more interested in each other than in the tasks they are performing. Borrowing or lending toys and following or leading one another in line are examples of associative play.
- **Cooperative play** consists of social interaction in a group with a sense of group identity and organized activity. Children's formal games, competition aimed at winning, and groups formed by a teacher for doing things together are examples of cooperative play. Cooperative play is the prototype for the games of middle childhood. Little cooperative play is seen in the preschool years.

Types of Play   Parten's categories represent one way of thinking about the types of play, but it omits some important types. Whereas Parten's categories emphasize the role of play in the child's social world, the contemporary perspective on play emphasizes both the cognitive and the social aspects of play. Among the most widely studied types of children's play today are sensorimotor and practice play, pretense/symbolic play, social play, constructive play, and games (Bergen, 1988).

Sensorimotor and Practice Play   **Sensorimotor play** is behavior by infants to derive pleasure from exercising their sensorimotor schemes. The development of sensorimotor play follows Piaget's description of sensorimotor thought, which we discussed in Chapter 6. Infants initially engage in exploratory and playful visual and motor transactions in the second quarter of the first year of life. For example, at 9 months of age, infants begin to select novel objects for exploration and play, especially responsive objects, such as toys that make noise or bounce. At 12 months of age, infants enjoy making things work and exploring cause and effect.

Practice play involves the repetition of behavior when new skills are being learned or when physical or mental mastery and coordination of skills are required for games or sports. Sensorimotor play, which often involves practice play, is primarily confined to infancy, whereas practice play can be engaged in throughout life. During the preschool years, children often engage in practice play. Although practice play declines in the elementary school years, practice play activities such as running, jumping, sliding, twirling, and throwing balls or other objects are frequently observed on the playgrounds at elementary schools.

Pretense/Symbolic Play   **Pretense/symbolic play** occurs when the child transforms the physical environment into a symbol. Between 9 and 30 months of age, children increase their use of objects in symbolic play. They learn to transform objects—substituting them for other objects and acting toward them as if they were these other objects. For example, a preschool child treats a table as if it were a car and says, "I'm fixing the car" as he grabs a leg of the table.

Many experts on play consider the preschool years the "golden age" of symbolic/pretense play that is dramatic or sociodramatic in nature (Fein, 1986). This type of make-believe play often appears at about 18 months of age and reaches a peak at 4 to 5 years of age, then gradually declines.

Social Play   **Social play** is play that involves interaction with peers, and it is the focus of Parten's classification. Social play increases dramatically during the preschool years.

A preschool "superhero" at play.

parallel play Play in which the child plays separately from others, but with toys like those the others are using or in a manner that mimics their play.

associative play Play that involves social interaction with little or no organization.

cooperative play Play that involves social interaction in a group with a sense of group identity and organized activity.

sensorimotor play Behavior engaged in by infants to derive pleasure from exercising their existing sensorimotor schemas.

practice play Play that involves repetition of behavior when new skills are being learned or when physical or mental mastery and coordination of skills are required for games or sports.

pretense/symbolic play Play in which the child transforms the physical environment into a symbol.

social play Play that involves social interactions with peers.

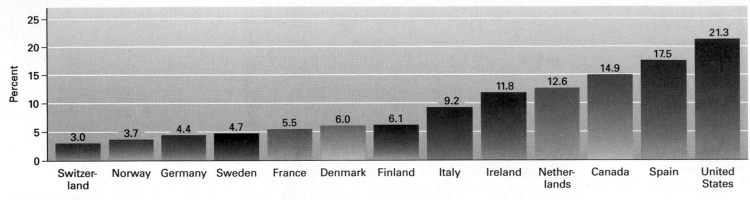

FIGURE 10.9 Percentage of 9-Year-Old Children Who Report Watching More Than Five Hours of Television per Weekday

Constructive Play **Constructive play** combines sensorimotor/practice play with symbolic representation. Constructive play occurs when children engage in the self-regulated creation of a product or a solution. Constructive play increases in the preschool years as symbolic play increases and sensorimotor play decreases. In the preschool years, some practice play is replaced by constructive play. For example, instead of moving their fingers around and around in finger paint (practice play), children are more likely to draw the outline of a house or a person in the paint (constructive play). Constructive play is also a frequent form of play in the elementary school years, both in and out of the classroom. Constructive play is one of the few playlike activities allowed in work-centered classrooms. For example, if children create a play about a social studies topic, they are engaging in constructive play.

Games **Games** are activities that are engaged in for pleasure and have rules. Often they involve competition. Preschool children may begin to participate in social games that involves simple rules of reciprocity and turn taking. However, games take on a much stronger role in the lives of elementary school children. In one study, the highest incidence of game playing occurred between 10 and 12 years of age (Eiferman, 1971). After age 12, games decline in popularity (Bergen, 1988).

In sum, play ranges from an infant's simple exercise of a new sensorimotor talent to a preschool child's riding a tricycle to an older child's participation in organized games. It is also important to note that children's play can involve a combination of the play categories we have described. For example, social play can be sensorimotor (rough-and-tumble), symbolic, or constructive.

Television

Few developments in society in the second half of the twentieth century had a greater impact on children than television (Pecora, Murray, & Wartella, 2007). Although it is only one of the many types of mass media that affect children's behavior, television is the most influential. The persuasive capabilities of television are staggering (Comstock & Scharrer, 2006).

Many children spend more time in front of the television set than they do with their parents. Just how much television do young children watch? In the 1990s, children watched an average of 26 hours of television each week, which is more than any other activity except sleep (National Center for Children Exposed to Violence, 2001). Compared with their counterparts in other developed countries, considerably more children in the United States watch television for long periods (see Figure 10.9). The 20,000 hours of television watched by the time the average American adolescent graduates from high school are greater than the number of hours spent in the classroom.

constructive play Play that combines sensorimotor and repetitive activity with symbolic representation of ideas. Constructive play occurs when children engage in self-regulated creation or construction of a product or a problem solution.

games Activities engaged in for pleasure that include rules and often competition with one or more individuals.

Television can have a negative influence on children by making them passive learners, teaching them stereotypes, providing them with violent models of aggression, and presenting them with unrealistic views of the world (Dubow, Huesmann, & Greenwood, 2007; Murray, 2007). However, television can have a positive influence on children's development by presenting motivating educational programs, increasing their world beyond their immediate environment, and providing models of prosocial behavior.

Effects of Television on Children's Aggression and Prosocial Behavior   The extent to which children are exposed to violence and aggression on television raises special concern (Murray, 2007; Pecora, Murray, & Wartella, 2007). Saturday morning cartoon shows average more than 25 violent acts per hour. What are the effects of television violence on children's aggression? Does television merely stimulate a child to go out and buy a *Star Wars* ray gun, or can it trigger an attack on a playmate? When children grow up, can television violence increase the likelihood they will violently attack someone?

In one experiment, preschool children were randomly assigned to one of two groups: one group watched television shows taken directly from violent Saturday morning cartoons on 11 days; the second group watched television cartoon shows with all of the violence removed (Steur, Applefield, & Smith, 1971). The children were then observed during play at their preschool. The preschool children who had seen the TV cartoon shows with violence kicked, choked, and pushed their playmates more than did the preschool children who watched nonviolent TV cartoon shows. Because the children were randomly assigned to the two conditions (TV cartoons with violence versus nonviolent TV cartoons), we can conclude that exposure to TV violence *caused* the increased aggression in the children in this investigation.

Other research has found links between watching television violence as a child and acting aggressively years later. For example, in one study, exposure to media violence at 6 to 10 years of age was linked with young adult aggressive behavior (Huesmann & others, 2003). In another study, long-term exposure to television violence was significantly related to the likelihood of aggression in 1,565 12- to 17-year-old boys (Belson, 1978). Boys who watched the most aggression on television were the most likely to commit a violent crime, swear, be aggressive in sports, threaten violence toward another boy, write slogans on walls, or break windows. These studies are *correlational*, so we can conclude from them that television violence is *associated with* aggressive behavior.

In addition to television violence, there is increased concern about children who play violent video games, especially those that are highly realistic (Anderson, Gentile, & Buckley, 2007). Children can become so deeply immersed in some electronic games that they experience an altered state of consciousness in which rational thought is suspended and arousing aggressive scripts are learned (Roberts, Henrikson, & Foehr, 2004). The direct rewards that players receive ("winning points") for their actions may also enhance the influence of video games.

Correlational studies indicate that children who extensively play violent electronic games are more aggressive than their counterparts who spend less time playing the games or do not play them at all (Cohen, 1995). Experiments have not yet been conducted to demonstrate increased aggression subsequent to playing violent video games, although a recent analysis of research studies concluded that playing violent video games is linked to aggression in both males and females (Anderson, Gentile, & Buckley, 2007; Carnagey, Anderson, & Bushman, 2007).

Television also can teach children that it is better to behave in positive, prosocial ways than in negative, antisocial ways (Bryant, 2007; Fisch, 2007), as Aimee Leifer (1973) demonstrated. She selected episodes from the television show *Sesame Street* that reflected positive social interchanges that taught children how to use their social skills. For example, in one interchange, two men fighting over the amount of

"Mrs. Horton, could you stop by school today?"
© Martha F. Campbell. Reprinted with permission.

How is television violence linked to children's aggression?

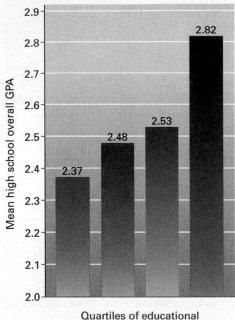

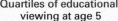

Quartiles of educational
viewing at age 5

FIGURE 10.10 Educational TV Viewing and High School Grade Point Average for Boys When boys watched more educational television (especially *Sesame Street*) as preschoolers, they had higher grade point averages in high school (Anderson & others, 2001). The graph displays the boys' early TV viewing patterns in quartiles and the means of their grade point averages. The bar on the left is for the lowest 25 percent of boys who viewed educational TV programs, the next bar the next 25 percent, and so on, with the bar on the right for the 25 percent of the boys who watched the most educational TV shows as preschoolers.

space available to them gradually began to cooperate and to share the space. Children who watched these episodes copied these behaviors, and in later social situations they applied the prosocial lessons they had learned.

Television, Cognitive Development, and Achievement In general, television has not been shown to influence children's creativity but is negatively related to their mental ability (Comstock & Scharrer, 2006). Watching television is also linked with reductions in school achievement (Comstock & Scharrer, 2006; Schmidt & Anderson, 2007). However, some types of television—such as educational programming for young children—may enhance achievement. For example, in one longitudinal study, viewing educational programs such as *Sesame Street* and *Mr. Rogers' Neighborhood* as preschoolers was associated with a host of desirable characteristics in adolescence: getting higher grades, reading more books, placing a higher value on achievement, being more creative, and acting less aggressively (Anderson & others, 2001) (see Figure 10.10). These associations were more consistent for boys than girls.

REVIEW AND REFLECT ◆ LEARNING GOAL 3

3 **Describe the roles of peers, play, and television in young children's development.**

Review
- How do peers affect young children's development?
- What are some theories and types of play?
- How does television influence young children's development?

Reflect
- What guidelines would you recommend to parents to help them to make television a more positive influence on their children's development? Consider factors such as the child's age, the child's activities other than TV, the parents' patterns of interaction with the children, and types of TV shows.

REACH YOUR LEARNING GOALS

1 WHAT CHARACTERIZES YOUNG CHILDREN'S EMOTIONAL AND PERSONALITY DEVELOPMENT? *Discuss emotional and personality development in early childhood.*

The Self

- In Erikson's theory early childhood is a period when development involves resolving the conflict of initiative versus guilt. The toddler's rudimentary self-understanding develops into the preschooler's representation of the self in terms of body parts, material possessions, and physical activities. At about 4 to 5 years of age, children also begin to use traitlike self-descriptions. Young children display more sophisticated self-understanding and understanding of others than previously thought.

Emotional Development

- Young children's range of emotions expands during early childhood as they increasingly experience self-conscious emotions such as pride, shame, and guilt. Between 2 and 4 years of age, children use an increasing number of terms to describe emotion and learn more about the causes and consequences of feelings. At 4 to 5 years of age, children show an increased ability to reflect on emotions and understand that a single event can elicit different emotions in different people. They also show a growing awareness of the need to manage emotions to meet social standards. Emotion-coaching parents have children who engage in more effective self-regulation of their emotions than do emotion-dismissing parents. Emotional regulation plays an important role in successful peer relations.

Moral Development

- Moral development involves thoughts, feelings, and behaviors regarding rules and regulations about what people should do in their interactions with others. Freud's psychoanalytic theory emphasizes the importance of feelings in the development of the superego, the moral branch of personality. In Freud's view, the superego develops through desiring to replace the same-sex parent and enjoy the opposite-sex parent's affection; children conform to societal standards to avoid guilt. Positive emotions, such as empathy, also contribute to the child's moral development. Piaget analyzed moral reasoning and concluded that children from 4 to 7 years of age display heteronomous morality, judging behavior by its consequences. According to behavioral and social cognitive theorists, moral behavior develops as a result of reinforcement, punishment and imitation, and there is considerable situational variability in moral behavior. And self-control is an important aspect of understanding children's moral behavior. Parents influence young children's moral development through the quality of parent-child relationships, being proactive in helping children avert misbehavior, and by engaging children in conversational dialogue about moral issues.

Gender

- Gender refers to the social and psychological dimensions of being male or female. Gender identity is acquired by 3 years of age for most children. A gender role is a set of expectations that prescribes how females or males should think, act, and feel. The 23rd pair of chromosomes may have two X chromosomes to produce a female, or one X and one Y chromosome to produce a male. The two main classes of sex hormones are estrogens, which are dominant in females, and androgens, which are dominant in males. Biology is not completely destiny in gender development; children's socialization experiences matter a great deal. Both psychoanalytic theory and social cognitive theory emphasize the adoption of parents' gender characteristics. Peers are especially adept at rewarding gender-appropriate behavior. Both cognitive developmental and gender schema theories emphasize the role of cognition in gender development.

2 WHAT ROLES DO FAMILIES PLAY IN YOUNG CHILDREN'S DEVELOPMENT?
Explain how families can influence young children's development.

Parenting

- Authoritarian, authoritative, neglectful, and indulgent are four main parenting styles. Authoritative parenting is the most widely used style around the world and is the style most often associated with children's social competence. However, ethnic variations in parenting styles suggest that in African American and Asian American families, some aspects of control may benefit children. Latino parents often emphasize connectedness with the family and respect and obedience in their child rearing. Physical punishment is widely used by U.S. parents, but there are a number of reasons why it is not a good choice. Coparenting has positive effects on children's development.

Child Maltreatment

- Child maltreatment may take the form of physical abuse, child neglect, sexual abuse, and emotional abuse. Child maltreatment places the child at risk for academic, emotional, and social problems. Adults who suffered child maltreatment are also vulnerable to a range of problems.

Sibling Relationships and Birth Order

- Siblings interact with each other in positive and negative ways. Birth order is related in certain ways to child characteristics, but by itself it is not a good predictor of behavior.

The Changing Family in a Changing Society

- In general, having both parents employed full-time outside the home has not been shown to have negative effects on children. However, in specific circumstances, when a mother works outside the home, such as when the infant is less than 1 year old, negative effects can occur. Divorce can have negative effects on children's adjustment, but so can an acrimonious relationship between parents who stay together for their children's sake. If divorced parents develop a harmonious relationship and practice authoritative parenting, children's adjustment improves. Researchers have found few differences between children growing up in gay or lesbian families and children growing up in heterosexual families. Cultures vary on a number of issues regarding families. African American and Latino children are more likely than White American children to live in single-parent families and larger families and to have extended family connections. Lower-SES parents create a home atmosphere that involves more authority and physical punishment with children than higher-SES parents. Higher-SES parents are more concerned about developing children's initiative and delay of gratification.

3 HOW ARE PEER RELATIONS, PLAY, AND TELEVISION INVOLVED IN YOUNG CHILDREN'S DEVELOPMENT?
Describe the roles of peers, play, and television in young children's development.

Peer Relations

- Peers are powerful socialization agents. Peers provide a source of information and comparison about the world outside the family.

Play

- Play's functions include affiliation with peers, tension release, advances in cognitive development, exploration, and provision of a safe haven. Parten developed the categories of unoccupied, solitary, onlooker, parallel, associative, and cooperative play. The contemporary perspective on play emphasizes both the cognitive and the social aspects of play. Among the most widely studied types of children's play are sensorimotor play, practice play, pretense/symbolic play, social play, constructive play, and games.

| Television |

- Television can have both negative influences (such as turning children into passive learners and presenting them with aggressive models) and positive influences (such as providing models of prosocial behavior) on children's development. TV violence is not the only cause of children's aggression, but it can induce aggression. Prosocial behavior on TV can teach children positive behavior. Television viewing has not been shown to be linked to children's creativity but is negatively related to their mental ability, although some types of educational television may enhance achievement in school.

KEY TERMS

KEY PEOPLE

MAKING A DIFFERENCE

Guiding Young Children's Socioemotional Development

How can young children's socioemotional skills be nourished? These strategies can help.

- *Look for situations to help children with their emotions.* Parents, teachers, and other adults can help children understand and handle their emotions in socially acceptable ways.
- *Present positive moral models for the child, and use emotional situations to promote moral development.* Children benefit when they are around people who engage in prosocial rather than antisocial behavior. Encourage children to show empathy and learn to deal with their emotions.
- *Be an authoritative parent.* Children's self-control and social competence benefit when both parents are authoritative.

This means being neither punitive and overcontrolling nor permissive. Authoritative parents are nurturant, engage the child in verbal give-and-take, monitor the child, and use nonpunitive control.

- *Adapt to the child's developmental changes.* Parents should use less physical manipulation and more reasoning or withholding of special privileges in disciplining a 5-year-old, as opposed to disciplining a 2-year-old.
- *Communicate effectively with children in a divorced family.* Good strategies are to explain the separation and say it is not the child's fault, explain that it may take time to feel better, keep the door open for further discussion, provide as much continuity as possible, and provide a support system for the child.

- *Provide the child with opportunities for peer interaction.* Children learn a great deal from the mutual give-and-take of peer relations. Make sure the child gets considerable time to play with peers rather than watching TV or going to an academic early childhood program all day.

- *Provide the child with many opportunities for play.* Positive play experiences can play important roles in the young child's socioemotional development.
- *Monitor the child's TV viewing.* Keep exposure to TV violence to a minimum. Develop a set of guidelines for the child's TV viewing.

RESOURCES FOR IMPROVING CHILDREN'S LIVES

The Emotional Development of Young Children

by Marylou Hyson (2004)
New York: Teachers College Press

An excellent book by a leading expert on early childhood that provides a good overview of young children' emotional development and many applications to children's emotional development in preschool and kindergarten.

The Preschool Years

by Ellen Galinsky and Judy David (1988)
New York: Times Books

The Preschool Years describes typical child development in the 3- to 5-year-old age period and provides recommendations to parents for coping with specific problems in this period of development.

For Better or For Worse: Divorce Reconsidered

by E. Mavis Hetherington and John Kelly (2002)
New York: W. W. Norton

E. Mavis Hetherington, a leading researcher, provides excellent descriptions of how divorce affects children and parents.

A World of Difference

edited by Carol Copple (2003)
Washington, DC: NAEYC

Extensive information about guiding young children's understanding of diversity and living in a diverse world.

E-LEARNING TOOLS

Connect to **www.mhhe.com/santrockc10** to research the answers and complete these exercises. In addition, you'll find a number of other resources and valuable study tools for Chapter 10, "Socioemotional Development in Young Children," on this Web site.

Taking It to the Net

1. A social worker spoke to a psychology class about how children with serious developmental delays and disabilities are more prone to being abused by their parents than are children without disabilities. What are the general risk factors for abuse for all children, and how are they compounded for children with disabilities?

2. Karen's mother is concerned about how to best help her daughter, Teresa, whose husband has abandoned her and their 5-year-old son. What are some of the challenges that Teresa may have to face, and how can her mother help her through this difficult time?

3. Jonathan and Diedre want to shield their children from the violence on television, but they are not sure how to go about it—other than by not allowing any television viewing at all. What recommendations does the APA have for parents?

4. Frieda is the middle child in a family with five siblings. She is interested in what sibling researchers have to say about the effect of birth order on sibling relationships. How does being a middle child contribute to the dynamics between Frieda and her brothers and sisters?

5. Rita's child development teacher wants each student to depict some aspect of child development from infancy to age 6 as a chronological time line represented by descriptions or illustrations. Rita has chosen the development of the self. What behaviors at 6, 12, and 18 months, and 2, 3, 4, 5, and 6 years of age represent milestones in self-awareness, self-concept, self-understanding, and self-esteem?

Health and Well-Being, Parenting, and Education

Build your decision-making skills by trying your hand at the health and well-being, parenting, and education exercises.

Video Clips

The Online Learning Center includes the following videos for this chapter:

1. *Lacking Gender Consistency at Age 4—508*
   A boy named Sal is asked to identify the gender of a male doll placed in front of him. After amusing himself by completely rotating the doll's head around, he explains that the doll is a male because of his hair. But when the interviewer puts a skirt on the doll, Sal demonstrates that he lacks an understanding of gender constancy when he explains that the doll is now a girl.

2. *Early Gender Beliefs at Age 4—25*
   When presented with a male doll, a 4-year-old boy enthusiastically identifies the doll as a boy because "It doesn't have long hair!" When the interviewer puts a skirt on the doll, Bradley believes the doll changes into a girl because "It has a dress!"

3. *Describing Friends at Age 5—99*
   Tara states that she has two special friends. She explains that these friends are special because they play together.

4. *If My Son Wore a Dress—3001*
   A good example of how parents contribute to the gender socialization of children. Here, a couple with young children describe how they would feel if their son wanted to wear a dress.

MIDDLE AND LATE CHILDHOOD

Every forward step we take we leave some phantom of ourselves behind.

—JOHN LANCASTER SPALDING
American Educator, 19th Century

In middle and late childhood, children are on a different plane, belonging to a generation and feeling all their own. It is the wisdom of the human life span that at no time are children more ready to learn than during the period of expansive imagination at the end of early childhood. Children develop a sense of wanting to make things—and not just to make them, but to make them well and even perfectly. They seek to know and to understand. They are remarkable for their intelligence and for their curiosity. Their parents continue to be important influences in their lives, but their growth also is shaped by peers and friends. They don't think much about the future or about the past, but they enjoy the present moment. Section 5 consists of three chapters. "Physical Development in Middle and Late Childhood" (Chapter 11). "Cognitive Development in Middle and Late Childhood" (Chapter 12), and "Socioemotional Development in Middle and Late Childhood" (Chapter 13).

Blessed be childhood, which brings something of heaven into the midst of our rough earthliness.

—HENRI FRÉDÉRIC AMIEL
Swiss Poet, Philosopher, 19th Century

CHAPTER OUTLINE	LEARNING GOALS

WHAT CHANGES TAKE PLACE IN BODY GROWTH, THE BRAIN, AND MOTOR DEVELOPMENT?   **1**

Skeletal and Muscular Systems

The Brain

Motor Development

1 Discuss changes in body growth, the brain, and motor development in middle and late childhood.

WHAT ARE THE CENTRAL ISSUES IN CHILDREN'S HEALTH?   **2**

Nutrition

Exercise and Sports

Overweight Children

Diseases

Accidents and Injuries

2 Characterize children's health in middle and late childhood.

WHAT ARE THE PREVALENT DISABILITIES IN CHILDREN?   **3**

Who Are Children with Disabilities?

The Range of Disabilities

Educational Issues

3 Summarize information about children with disabilities.

Images of Children's Development
The Story of Angie and Her Weight

The following comments are by Angie, an elementary-school-age girl:

> When I was eight years old, I weighed 125 pounds. My clothes were the size that large teenage girls wear. I hated my body and my classmates teased me all the time. I was so overweight and out of shape that when I took a P.E. class my face would get red and I had trouble breathing. I was jealous of the kids who played sports and weren't overweight like I was.
>
> I'm nine years old now and I've lost 30 pounds. I'm much happier and proud of myself. How did I lose the weight? My mom said she had finally decided enough was enough. She took me to a pediatrician who specializes in helping children lose weight and keep it off. The pediatrician counseled my mom about my eating and exercise habits, then had us join a group that he had created for overweight children and their parents. My mom and I go to the group once a week and we've now been participating in the program for six months. I no longer eat fast food meals and my mom is cooking more healthy meals. Now that I've lost weight, exercise is not as hard for me and I don't get teased by the kids at school. My mom's pretty happy too because she's lost 15 pounds herself since we've been in the counseling program.

Not all overweight children are as successful as Angie at reducing their weight. Indeed, being overweight in childhood has become a major national concern in the United States (Nader & others, 2006). Later in the chapter, we further explore being overweight in childhood, including its causes and outcomes.

PREVIEW

Considerable progress in children's physical development continues to take place in the middle and late childhood years. They grow taller, heavier, and stronger. They become more adept at using their physical skills. We begin the chapter by exploring the changes that characterize body growth and motor skills, then examine the central issues in children's health, and conclude by discussing children with disabilities and their education.

1 WHAT CHANGES TAKE PLACE IN BODY GROWTH, THE BRAIN, AND MOTOR DEVELOPMENT?

Skeletal and Muscular Systems	The Brain	Motor Development

The period of middle and late childhood involves slow, consistent growth. This is a period of calm before the rapid growth spurt of adolescence. Among the important aspects of body growth and proportion in this developmental period are those involving skeletal and muscular systems, the brain, and motor development.

Skeletal and Muscular Systems

During the elementary school years, children grow an average of 2 to 3 inches a year until, at the age of 11, the average girl is 4 feet, 9 inches tall, and the average boy is 4 feet, 7¾ inches tall. During the middle and late childhood years, children gain about 5 to 7 pounds a year. The weight increase is due mainly to increases in the size of the skeletal and muscular systems, as well as the size of some body organs. Muscle mass and strength gradually increase as "baby fat" decreases. The loose movements

Height (inches)

Age	Female percentiles			Male percentiles		
	25th	50th	75th	25th	50th	75th
6	43.75	45.00	46.50	44.25	45.75	47.00
7	46.00	47.50	49.00	46.25	48.00	49.25
8	48.00	49.75	51.50	48.50	50.00	51.50
9	50.25	53.00	53.75	50.50	52.00	53.50
10	52.50	54.50	56.25	52.50	54.25	55.75
11	55.00	57.00	58.75	54.50	55.75	57.25

Weight (pounds)

Age	25th	50th	75th	25th	50th	75th
6	39.25	43.00	47.25	42.00	45.50	49.50
7	43.50	48.50	53.25	46.25	50.25	55.00
8	49.00	54.75	61.50	51.00	55.75	61.50
9	55.75	62.75	71.50	56.00	62.00	69.25
10	63.25	71.75	82.75	62.00	69.25	78.50
11	71.75	81.25	94.25	69.00	77.75	89.00

Note: The percentile tells how the child compares with other children of the same age. The 50th percentile tells us that half of the children of a particular age are taller (heavier) or shorter (lighter). The 25th percentile tells us that 25 percent of the children of that age are shorter (lighter) and 75 percent are taller (heavier).

FIGURE 11.1 Changes in Height and Weight in Middle and Late Childhood

and knock-knees of early childhood give way to improved muscle tone. The increase in muscular strength is due to heredity and to exercise. Children also double their strength capabilities during these years. Because of their greater number of muscle cells, boys are usually stronger than girls. A summary of the changes in height and weight in middle and late childhood appears in Figure 11.1.

Proportional changes are among the most pronounced physical changes in middle and late childhood (Kliegman & others, 2007). Head circumference, waist circumference, and leg length decrease in relation to body height (Leifer, 2007). A less noticeable physical change is that bones continue to ossify (harden) during middle and late childhood.

The Brain

The development of brain-imaging techniques, such as MRI, has led to an increase in research on changes in the brain during middle and late childhood, and how these brain changes are linked to improvements in cognitive development (Durston & Casey, 2006; Toga, Thompson, & Sowell, 2006). One such change involves increased myelination, which characterizes many brain pathways improving the speed of processing information and communication in the higher regions of the brain, such as the cerebral cortex, and contributing to faster and more efficient processing of information on cognitive tasks (Marsh & others, 2006). Recall from our discussion in Chapter 8, "Physical Development in Early Childhood," that myelination is the process of encasing axons with fat cells.

Total brain volume stabilizes by the end of middle and late childhood, but significant changes in various structures and regions of the brain continue to occur. In particular, the brain pathways and circuitry involving the prefrontal cortex, the highest level in the brain, continue to increase (Durston & Casey, 2006). These advances in the prefrontal cortex are linked to children's improved attention, reasoning, and cognitive control (Durston & others, 2007). (See Figure 5.4, p. 145, and Figure 8.3, p. 253, for the location of the prefrontal cortex in the brain.)

Changes also occur in the thickness of the cerebral cortex (cortical thickness) in middle and late childhood (Toga, Thompson, & Sowell, 2006). One study used brain scans to assess cortical thickness in 5- to 11-year-old children (Sowell & others, 2004). Cortical thickening across a two-year time period was observed in the temporal and frontal lobe areas that function in language, which may reflect improvements in language abilities such as reading.

As children develop, activation of some brain areas increase while others decrease (Dowker, 2006; Durston & Casey, 2006). One shift in activation that occurs as children develop is from diffuse, larger areas to more focal, smaller areas (Casey & others, 2002; Durston & others, 2007; Turkeltaub & others, 2003). This shift is characterized by synaptic pruning, in which areas of the brain not being used lose synaptic connections and those being used show an increase in connections. In a recent study, researchers found less diffusion and more focal activation in the prefrontal cortex from 7 to 30 years of age (Durston & others, 2007). The activation change was accompanied by increased efficiency in cognitive performance, especially in *cognitive control*, which involves flexible and effective control in a number of areas. These areas include controlling attention, reducing interfering thoughts, inhibiting motor actions, and being flexible in switching between competing choices (Carver, Livesey, & Charles, 2001; Munkata, 2006).

Motor Development

During middle and late childhood, children's motor development becomes much smoother and more coordinated than it was in early childhood. For example, only one child in a thousand can hit a tennis ball over the net at the age of 3, yet by the age of 10 or 11 most children can learn to play the sport. Running, climbing, skipping rope, swimming, bicycle riding, and skating are just a few of the many physical skills elementary school children can master. And, when mastered, these skills are a source of great pleasure and accomplishment for children. In gross motor skills involving large muscle activity, boys usually outperform girls.

As children move through the elementary school years, they gain greater control over their bodies and can sit and attend for longer periods of time. However, elementary school children are far from being physically mature, and they need to be active. Elementary school children become more fatigued by long periods of sitting than by running, jumping, or bicycling. Physical action is essential for children to refine their developing skills, such as batting a ball, skipping rope, or balancing on a beam. An important principle of practice for elementary school children, therefore, is that they should be engaged in *active*, rather than passive, activities.

Increased myelination of the nervous system is reflected in the improvement of fine motor skills during middle and late childhood. Children's hands are used more adroitly as tools. Six-year-olds can hammer, paste, tie shoes, and fasten clothes. By 7 years of age, children's hands have become steadier. At this age, children prefer a pencil to a crayon for printing, reversal of letters is less common, and printing becomes smaller. At 8 to 10 years of age, the hands can be used independently with more ease and precision. Fine motor coordination develops to the point at which children use cursive writing rather than printing. Letter size becomes smaller and more even. At 10 to 12 years of age, children begin to show manipulative skills similar to the abilities of adults. The complex, intricate, and rapid movements needed to produce fine-quality crafts, or to play a difficult piece on a musical instrument, can be mastered. Girls usually outperform boys in fine motor skills. A summary of changes in motor skills in middle and late childhood appears in Figure 11.2.

Age	Motor Skills
6	Children can skip. Children can throw with proper weight shift and step. Girls and boys can vertically jump 7 inches. Girls can do a standing long jump of 33 inches, boys 36 inches. Children can cut and paste. Children enjoy making simple figures in clay.
7	Children can balance on one foot without looking. Children can walk 2-inch-wide balance beams. Children can hop and jump accurately into small squares. Children can participate in jumping jack exercise. Girls can throw a ball 25 feet, boys 45 feet. Girls can vertically jump 8 inches, boys 9 inches. Girls can do a standing long jump of 41 inches, boys 43 inches.
8	Children can engage in alternate rhythmic hopping in different patterns. Girls can throw a ball 34 feet, boys 59 feet. Girls can vertically jump 9 inches, boys 10 inches. Girls can perform a standing long jump of 50 inches, boys 55 inches. Children's grip strength increases. Children can use common tools, such as a hammer.
9	Girls can throw a ball 41 feet, boys 71 feet. Girls can vertically jump 10 inches, boys 11 inches. Girls can perform a standing long jump of 53 inches, boys 57 inches. Children's perceptual-motor coordination becomes smoother.
10	Children can judge and intercept pathways of small balls thrown from a distance. Girls can throw a small ball 49 feet, boys 94 feet. Girls can vertically jump 10 inches, boys 11 inches. Girls can perform a standing long jump of 57 inches, boys 51 inches.

FIGURE 11.2 Changes in Motor Skills During Middle and Late Childhood

Note that some children are able to perform these skills earlier or later than other children.

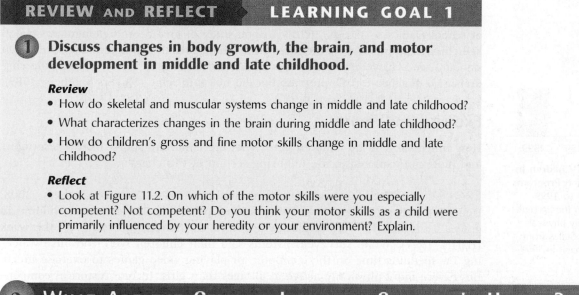

Although we have become a health-conscious nation, many children as well as adults do not practice good health habits. Too much junk food and too much couch-potato behavior describes all too many children. We begin our exploration of children's health with nutrition and exercise, then turn to a number of health problems that can emerge.

Nutrition

In the middle and late childhood years, children's average body weight doubles. Children exert considerable energy as they engage in many different motor activities. To support their growth and active lives, children need to consume more food than they did in early childhood. From 1 to 3 years of age, infants and toddlers need to consume about 1,300 calories per day. At 4 to 6 years of age, young children need to take in around 1,700 calories per day. From 7 to 10 years of age, children need to consume about 2,400 calories per day; however, depending on the child's size, the range of recommended calories for 7- to 10-year-olds is 1,650 to 3,300 per day.

Within these calorie ranges, it is important to impress on children the value of a balanced diet to promote their growth (Lissauer & Clayden, 2007). Children usually eat as their families eat, so the quality of their diet often depends largely on their family's pattern of eating. Most children acquire a taste for an increasing variety of food in middle and late childhood. However, with the increased availability of fast-food restaurants and media inducements, too many children fill up on food that has "empty calories" that do not promote effective growth (Giammattei & others, 2003). Many of these empty-calorie foods have a high content of sugar, starch, and excess fat (Wardlaw & Hampl, 2007).

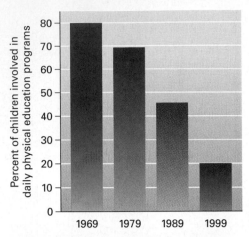

FIGURE 11.3 Percentage of Children Involved in Daily Physical Education Programs in the United States from 1969 to 1999 There has been a dramatic drop in the percentage of children participating in daily physical education programs in the United States from 80 percent in 1969 to only 20 percent in 1999.

We are underexercised as a nation. We look instead of play. We ride instead of walk. Our existence deprives us of the minimum of physical activity essential for healthy living.

—JOHN F. KENNEDY
American President, 20th Century

Both parents and teachers can help children learn to eat better. In this vein, they can help children learn about the Food Guide Pyramid and what a healthy diet entails (Gidding & others, 2006; Polnay, Hampshire, & Lakhanpaul, 2007).

Children should begin their day by eating a healthy breakfast; according to nutritionists, breakfast should make up about one-fourth of the day's calories. A nutritious breakfast helps children have more energy and be more alert in the morning hours of school (James & Ashwill, 2007). In one study of low-income elementary-school-age children, those who participated in a school breakfast program improved their standardized achievement test scores more, and had fewer absences, than the children who qualified for the program but did not participate (Meyers & others, 1989).

Exercise and Sports

How much exercise do children get? What are children's sports like? These topics and more are explored in the following section of this chapter.

Exercise Children are not getting enough exercise (Corbin & others, 2008; Dencker & others, 2006). In a 1997 national poll, only 22 percent of children in grades 4 through 12 were physically active for 30 minutes every day of the week (Harris, 1997). When surveyed, parents said their children were too busy watching TV, spending time on the computer, or playing video games to exercise much. Boys were more physically active at all ages than girls. In one historical comparison, the percentage of children involved in daily P.E. programs in schools decreased from 80 percent in 1969 to 20 percent in 1999 (Health Management Resources, 2001) (see Figure 11.3).

Television watching is linked with low activity and obesity in children (Fox, 2004; Salmon, Campbell, & Crawford, 2006). A related concern is the dramatic increase in computer use by children. Research reviews conclude that the total time that children spend in front of a television or computer screen places them at risk for reduced activity and possible weight gain (Caroli & others, 2004; Jordan, 2004). One recent study revealed that children who watched two or more hours of TV a day were less likely to participate in organized physical activities and less likely to have two more servings of a fruit a day than their counterparts who watched less than two hours of TV a day (Salmon, Campbell, & Crawford, 2006). A longitudinal study also found that a higher incidence of watching TV in childhood and adolescence was linked with being overweight, being less physically fit, and having higher cholesterol levels at 26 years of age (Hancox, Milne, & Poulton, 2004).

Some of the blame also falls on the nation's schools, many of which fail to provide daily physical education classes (Valdimarsson & others, 2006). In the 1985 School Fitness Survey, 37 percent of the children in the first through fourth grades took gym classes only once or twice a week. The investigation also revealed that parents are poor role models when it comes to physical fitness. Less than 30 percent of the parents of the children in grades 1 through 4 exercised three days a week. Roughly half said they never get any vigorous exercise. In another study, observations of children's behavior in physical education classes at four elementary schools revealed how little vigorous exercise is done in these classes (Parcel & others, 1987). Children moved through space only 50 percent of the time they were in the class, and they moved continuously an average of only 2.2 minutes. In summary, not only do children's school weeks not include adequate physical education classes, but the majority of children do not exercise vigorously, even when they are in such classes (Graham, Holt-Hale, & Parker, 2007; Kovar & others, 2007). Furthermore, most children's parents are poor role models for vigorous physical exercise (Lou, Ganley, & Flynn, 2002).

Does it make a difference if children are pushed to exercise more vigorously in elementary school? One study says yes (Tuckman & Hinkle, 1988). One hundred fifty-four elementary school children were randomly assigned either to three 30-minute running programs per week or to regular attendance in physical education classes.

Although the results sometimes varied according to sex, for the most part, the cardiovascular health, as well as the creativity, of children in the running program were enhanced. For example, the boys in this program had less body fat, and the girls had more creative involvement in their classrooms. In one study, the influence of instruction time in physical education on children's weight was explored (Datar & Sturm, 2004). One more hour of physical education in the first grade was linked to girls being less likely to be overweight.

In addition to the school, the family plays an important role in a child's exercise program (Corbin & others, 2008). A recent study revealed that 9 to 13-year-olds were more likely to engage in physical activity during their free time when the children felt safe, had a number of places to be active, and had parents who participated in physical activities with them (Heitzler & others, 2006). Indeed, a wise strategy is for parents to take up activities involving vigorous physical exercise that parents and children can enjoy together. Running, swimming, cycling, and hiking are especially recommended.

What are some good strategies for increasing children's exercise?

Sports   It is not surprising that more and more children become involved in sports every year. Both in public schools and in community agencies, children's sports programs that involve baseball, soccer, football, basketball, swimming, gymnastics, and other activities have changed the shape of many children's lives. Increasingly, newer X-treme sports have been added to the competitive arena, including skateboarding, snowboarding, off-road biking, and other high risk sports. These sports often involve complicated maneuvers, and without protective gear and proper supervision they can be dangerous for children.

Participation in sports can have both positive and negative consequences for children. Sports can provide exercise, opportunities to learn how to compete, increased self-esteem, and a setting for developing peer relations and friendships (Hoffman & others, 2005). One study revealed that participation in sports for three hours or more per week beyond regular physical education classes was related to increased physical fitness and lower fat mass in 9-year-old boys (Ara & others, 2004).

Sports also can have negative outcomes for children: the pressure to achieve and win, physical injuries, a distraction from academic work, and unrealistic expectations for success as an athlete (Cox, 2007; Williams, 2006). Few people challenge the value of sports for children when conducted as part of a school physical education or intramural program. However, some critics question the appropriateness of highly competitive, win-oriented sports teams in schools and communities, intense participation in sports at an early age, and the physical strain placed on children's bodies that can result in overuse injuries (Browne & Lam, 2006). It is important to keep in mind that learning the basic skills of a sport, as opposed to a narrow focus on winning, develops a child's self-confidence, coordination, and strength (Dweck, 2006).

What are some potential positive and negative consequences for children's participation in sports?

There is a special concern for children in high-pressure sports settings involving championship play with accompanying media publicity. Some clinicians and child developmentalists argue that such activities not only put undue stress on the participants but also teach children the wrong values—namely, a win-at-all-costs philosophy (Gould & others, 2006). The possibility of exploiting children through highly organized, win-oriented sports programs is an ever-present danger. Overly ambitious parents, coaches, and community boosters can unintentionally create a highly stressful atmosphere in children's sports. When parental, agency, or community prestige becomes the central focus of the child's participation in sports, the danger of exploitation is clearly present. Programs oriented toward such purposes often require long and arduous training sessions over many months and years, frequently leading to sports specialization at too early an age. In such circumstances, adults often transmit a distorted view of the role of the sport in the child's life, communicating to the child that the sport is the most important aspect of the child's existence. In the *Caring for Children* interlude that follows, you can read about some positive strategies for parents to follow regarding their children's sports participation.

Caring for Children

PARENTS AND CHILDREN'S SPORTS

Most sports psychologists stress it is important for parents to show an interest in their children's sports participation. Most children want their parents to watch them perform in sports. Many children whose parents do not come to watch them play in sporting events feel that their parents do not adequately support them. However, some children become extremely nervous when their parents watch them perform, or they get embarrassed when their parents cheer too loudly or make a fuss. If children request that their parents not watch them perform, parents should respect their children's wishes (Schreiber, 1990).

Parents should compliment their children for their sports performance. In the course of a game, there are dozens of circumstances when the child has done something positive, and parents should stress a child's good performance, even if the child has limited abilities. Parents can tell their children how much the children hustled in the game and how enthusiastically they played (Dweck, 2006). Even if the child strikes out in a baseball game, a parent can say, "That was a nice swing."

One of the hardest things for parents to do is to watch their children practicing or performing at a sport without helping them, to let their children make mistakes without interfering. Former Olympic swimmer Donna de Varona commented that the best way parents can help children in sports is to let them get to know themselves, and the only way they can do this is by having experiences in life. Naturally, parents want to provide their children with support and encouragement, but there is a point at which parental involvement becomes overinvolvement.

I (your author) have coached a number of young tennis players and have seen many parents who handled their roles as a nurturant, considerate parent well—but I have observed others who became too involved in their children's sport. Some parents were aware of their tendency to become too involved and backed off from pushing their children too intensely. However, some were not aware of their intrusiveness and did not back off. The worst parent had a daughter who, at the age of 9, was already nationally ranked and showed great promise. Her father went to every lesson, every practice session, every tournament. Her tennis began to consume his life. At one tournament, he stormed onto the court during one of her matches and accused his daughter's 10-year-old opponent of cheating, embarrassing his daughter and himself. I called him the next day, told him I no longer could coach his daughter because of his behavior, and recommended that he seek counseling or not go to any more of her matches.

If parents do not become too involved, they can help their children build their physical skills and help them emotionally—discussing with them how to deal with a difficult coach, how to cope with a tough loss, and how to put in perspective a poorly played game (Dweck, 2006). Parents need to carefully monitor their children as they participate in sports for signs of developing stress. If the problems appear to be beyond the intuitive skills of a volunteer coach or parent, a consultation with a counselor or clinician may be needed. Also, the parent needs to be sensitive to whether the sport in which the child is participating is the best one for the child and whether the child can handle its competitive pressures.

Some guidelines provided by the Women's Sports Foundation in its booklet *Parents' Guide to Girls' Sports* can benefit both parents and coaches of all children in sports:

The Dos

- Make sports fun; the more children enjoy sports, the more they will want to play.

- Remember that it is okay for children to make mistakes; it means they are trying.
- Allow children to ask questions about the sport and discuss the sport in a calm, supportive manner.
- Show respect for the child's sports participation.
- Be positive and convince the child that he or she is making a good effort.
- Be a positive role model for the child in sports.

The Don'ts

- Yell or scream at the child.
- Condemn the child for poor play or continue to bring up failures long after they happen.
- Point out the child's errors in front of others.
- Expect the child to learn something immediately.
- Expect the child to become a pro.
- Ridicule or make fun of the child.
- Compare the child to siblings or to more talented children.
- Make sports all work and no fun.

Now let's turn our attention to additional children's health issues. For most children, middle and late childhood is a time of excellent health. Disease and death are less prevalent in this period than in other periods of childhood and adolescence. However, some children do have health problems, such as obesity, cancer, diabetes, cardiovascular disease, asthma, and injuries due to accidents.

Overweight Children

Being overweight is an increasing health problem (Torjesen, 2007). Recall from Chapter 8, "Physical Development in Early Childhood," that being overweight is defined in terms of body mass index (BMI), which is computed by a formula that takes into account height and weight. Also, children at or above the 95th percentile of BMI are included in the overweight category, whereas children at or above the 85th percentile are described as at risk for being overweight (Centers for Disease Control and Prevention, 2007). Over the last three decades, the percentage of U.S. children who are at risk for being overweight has doubled from 15 percent in the 1970s to almost 30 percent today, and the percentage of children who are overweight has tripled during this time frame (Paxson & others, 2006). In Chapter 8, we described research that found being overweight at 3 years of age was a risk factor for being overweight at 12 years of age (Nader & others, 2006). In that study, it also was revealed that the more times that children were overweight at 7, 9, or 11 years of age, the more likely they would also be overweight at 12 years of age. Eighty percent of the children who were overweight at any time during the elementary school years remained overweight at 12 years of age. Researchers have found that being overweight as a child is a risk factor for being obese as an adult (Janssen & others, 2005). For example, a longitudinal study revealed that girls who were overweight in childhood were 11 to 30 times more likely to be obese in adulthood than girls who were not overweight in childhood (Thompson & others, 2007).

Girls are more likely than boys to be overweight (Flegal, Ogden, & Carroll, 2004). Overweight children with cardiovascular problems are more likely to come from low-socioeconomic-status families than higher-status ones (Longo-Mbenza & others, 2007). Being overweight is less common in African American than in non-Latino White children during childhood, but during adolescence this reverses.

What Factors Are Linked with Being Overweight in Childhood?   These factors are related to being overweight: heredity, blood chemistry, and environmental

FIGURE 11.4 Leptin and Obesity The *ob* mouse on the left is untreated; the one on the right has been given injections of leptin.

contexts. Overweight parents tend to have overweight children, even if they are not living in the same household (Wardlaw & Hampl, 2007). One study found that the greatest risk factor for being overweight at 9 years of age was a parent being overweight (Agras & others, 2004). Characteristics such as body type, height, body fat composition, and metabolism are inherited from parents (Walley, Blakemore, & Froguel, 2006).

Blood chemistry also is involved in being overweight. Especially important in this regard are *leptin* and *insulin.* Leptin is a protein that is released by fat cells. Leptin decreases food intake and increases energy expenditure. The importance of leptin was discovered with a strain of genetically obese mice (Campfield & others, 1995). The *ob mouse* (the label for this strain of mice) has a low metabolism, overeats, and gets extremely fat. A particular gene called *ob* produces leptin. However, because of a genetic mutation, the fat cells of *ob* mice cannot produce leptin.

Leptin has a strong influence on metabolism and eating, acting as an antiobesity hormone (Enriori & others, 2006). If *ob* mice are given daily injections of leptin, their metabolic rate increases, they become more active, and they eat less. Consequently, their weight returns to normal (see Figure 11.4). Scientists hope that at some point in the future some form of "leptin therapy" might be able to help overweight individuals lose weight (Brennan & Mantzoros, 2006; Yingzhon & others, 2006). However, this is unlikely to completely solve the current problem of being overweight in childhood or adulthood—exercise and nutrition are still very important (Fox, 2004).

A child's insulin (a hormone that controls blood glucose) level is another important factor in eating behavior and whether or not children are overweight. What children eat influences their insulin levels (Treuth & others, 2003). When children eat complex carbohydrates, such as whole-grain cereals, bread, and pasta, insulin levels go up and fall off gradually. When children consume simple sugars, such as candy bars and soft drinks, insulin levels rise sharply and then fall sharply—producing the sugar low with which many of us are all too familiar. Glucose levels in the blood are affected by these complex carbohydrates and simple sugars. Children are more likely to eat within the next several hours after eating simple sugars than after eating complex carbohydrates. And the food children eat at one meal influences what they will eat at the next meal. Thus, consuming doughnuts and candy bars, in addition to providing minimal nutritional value, sets up an ongoing sequence of what and how much children crave the next time they eat.

Environmental factors that influence whether children become overweight or not include the greater availability of food (especially food high in fat content), energy-saving devices, declining physical activity, parental monitoring of children's eating habits, the context in which a child eats, and heavy TV watching, (Metallinos-Katsaras & others, 2007; Franks & others, 2007). The American culture provides ample encouragement of overeating in children. Food is everywhere children go and easily accessed—in vending machines, fast-food restaurants, and so on. Also, the portion size that children eat in meals in the United States has grown. Fast-food restaurants capitalize on this by providing families with the opportunity to "super size" their meals at a relatively lower cost for the extra food.

Parents play an important role in children's eating habits and the likelihood they will become overweight or not (Boyle & Long, 2007; Fulkerson & others, 2007). One recent study revealed that Latino parents who monitored what their children ate had children who ate healthier foods and exercised more than their counterparts whose eating habits were not as closely monitored (Arrendono &

others, 2006). In another study, the context in which fourth to sixth-grade children ate was linked with what they ate and their tendency to be overweight (Cullen, 2001). Children who ate with their families were more likely to eat lower-fat foods (such as low-fat milk and salad dressing and lean meats), more vegetables, and drank fewer sodas than children who ate alone. Overweight children ate 50 percent of their meals in front of a TV, compared with only 35 percent of normal-weight children.

Consequences of Being Overweight in Childhood We already have mentioned an important consequence of being overweight in childhood: being overweight in childhood substantially increases the risk of being overweight in adolescence and adulthood (Nader & others, 2006; Thompson & others, 2007). Children who are overweight also are at risk for many medical and psychological problems (Daniels, 2006). Overweight children are at risk for developing pulmonary problems, such as sleep apnea (which involves upper-airway obstruction), and hip problems (Tauman & Gozal, 2006). Diabetes, hypertension (high blood pressure), and elevated blood cholesterol levels also are common in children who are overweight (Arif & Roher, 2006; Jolliffe & Jamssen, 2007). Once considered rare, hypertension in children has become increasingly common in overweight children (Daniels, 2006). Overweight children are three times more likely to develop hypertension than nonobese children (Sorof & Daniels, 2002). Social and psychological consequences of being overweight in childhood include low self-esteem, depression, and some exclusion of obese children from peer groups (Datar & Sturm, 2004). One study found that overweight children were more likely than normal-weight children to be both the victims and perpetrators of bullying (Janssen & others, 2004).

What are some concerns about children's cardiovascular health and obesity?

Treatment of Children Who Are Overweight Many experts recommend a program that involves a combination of diet, exercise, and behavior modification to help children lose weight (De Santis-Monlacl & Altshuler, 2007; Johnson & others, 2006). One study found that overweight children spent 51 percent more time in sedentary activity than children who were not overweight (Yu & others, 2002). Thus, exercise is an extremely important component of a successful weight-loss program for overweight children (Atlantis, Barnes, & Singh, 2006). Exercise increases the child's lean body mass, which increases the child's resting metabolic rate (Laforgia, Withers, & Gore, 2006). This results in more calories being burned in the resting state.

Children's activity levels not only are influenced by heredity but also by their motivation to engage in energetic activities, as well as caregivers who model an active lifestyle or provide children with opportunities to be active (Kitzman & Beech, 2006; Lindsay & others, 2006). In a typical behavior modification program, children are taught to monitor their own behavior, keeping a food diary while attempting to lose weight. The diary should record not only the type and amount of food eaten but also when, with whom, and where it was eaten. That is, do children eat in front of the TV, by themselves, or because they are angry or depressed? A diary identifies behaviors that need to be changed.

In keeping a diary, children, with the help of their parents, can calculate and keep track of the number of calories consumed. Moderate-calorie diets are more successful over the long term than are those involving extreme deprivation of calories. Educating children to modify their eating habits and learn to make wise food choices can help in weight control. For example, a year-long school-based education program was successful in reducing the consumption of carbonated drinks, which was related to a reduction in the number of overweight children (James & others, 2004).

Intervention programs with overweight children are usually conducted through schools and often focus on teaching children and parents about developing a healthy diet, exercising more, and reducing TV viewing time (Story, Kaphingst, & French, 2006). In the intervention program, Planet Health, parents and children are encouraged to work together to change their home environment, such as reducing TV time (Gortmaker & others, 1999). Other programs combine activities at school with materials sent home to parents.

A concern among researchers is that health-oriented programs are likely to be short-changed because schools are under increasing pressure to spend more time on academic topics (Paxson & others, 2006). One possible solution is to include overweight prevention in after-school programs, which conflict less with schools' academic mandates (Story, Kaphingst, & French, 2006). Another promising strategy is to provide students with healthier foods to eat at school. In 2005, several states began enacting laws that require healthier foods to be sold in vending machines at schools (Story, Kaphingst, & French, 2006). In one intervention, reducing soft drink consumption at schools was linked with a subsequent reduction in the number of 7- to 11-year-old children who were overweight (James & others, 2004). Schools also can play an important role by implementing programs that increase the amount of time children exercise (Datar & Sturm, 2004; Paxson & others, 2006).

Parents play an important role in preventing children from becoming overweight. They can encourage healthy eating habits in children by "increasing the number of family meals eaten together, making healthful foods available, and reducing the availability of sugar-sweetened beverages and sodas" (Lindsay & others, 2006, p. 173). They also can help reduce the likelihood their children will become overweight by reducing children's TV time, getting children involved in sports and other physical activities, and being healthy, physically active models themselves (Salmon, Campbell, & Crawford, 2006). As we learned in Angie's story, a combination of behavioral modification, parental involvement, and a structured program can effectively help overweight children.

What can parents do to prevent their children from being overweight or obese?

Diseases

Four childhood diseases can especially be harmful to children's development. They are (1) cancer, (2) diabetes, (3) cardiovascular disease, and (4) asthma.

Cancer Cancer is the second leading cause of death (with injuries the leading cause) in children 5 to 14 years of age in the United States. Three percent of all children's deaths in this age period are due to cancer. In the 15 to 24 age group, cancer accounts for 13 percent of all deaths. Currently, 1 in every 330 children in the United States develops cancer before the age of 19. Moreover, the incidence of cancer in children is increasing (Maule & others, 2007). Overall, approximately 25 percent of children with cancer die because of the disease during the childhood years (Hurwitz, Duncan, & Wolfe, 2004).

Childhood cancers have a different profile than adult cancers. Adult cancers attack mainly the lungs, colon, breast, prostate, and pancreas. Childhood cancers are mainly those of the white blood cells (leukemia), brain, bone, lymph system, muscles, kidneys, and nervous system. All are characterized by an uncontrolled proliferation of abnormal cells.

As indicated in Figure 11.5, the most common cancer in children is leukemia, a cancer of the tissues that make blood cells. In leukemia, the bone marrow makes an abundance of white blood cells that don't function properly. They invade the marrow and crowd out normal cells, making the child susceptible to bruising and infection (Hijiya & others, 2007). In some types of leukemia, the five-year survival rate for children is less than 25 percent (Rubnitz & others, 2006). Lymphomas arise in the lymph system. Childhood lymphomas spread to the central nervous

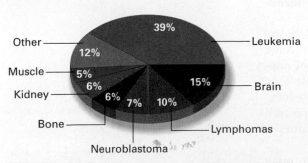

FIGURE 11.5 Types of Cancer in Children Cancers in children have a different profile than adult cancers, which attack mainly the lungs colon, breast, prostate, and pancreas.

system and bone marrow. Treatments have been developed that can cure many children with lymphoma.

When cancer strikes children, it behaves differently than it does when it attacks adults. Children frequently have a more advanced stage of cancer when they are first diagnosed. When cancer is first diagnosed in adults, it has spread to distant parts of the body in only about 20 percent of the cases; however, that figure rises to 80 percent in children. Most adult cancers result from lifestyle factors, such as smoking, diet, occupation, and exposure to other cancer-causing agents. By contrast, little is known about the causes of childhood cancers (Wakefield, 2001). Researchers are searching for possible genetic links to childhood cancers (Kennedy & D'Andrea, 2006).

Most adult cancer patients are treated in their local community by their family physician, consulting surgeon, or cancer specialist. Children with cancer are rarely treated by family physicians or pediatricians. They typically are treated by teams of physicians in children's hospitals, university medical centers, or cancer centers (Sanz, 2006).

Many children with cancer and other potentially terminal illnesses may survive for a long period of time and experience problems associated with chronic illness or physical disability (Meadows, 2006). Families initially may react with shock or denial when they find out that their child has cancer or any other type of terminal illness. Adjustment gradually follows and is usually characterized by an open admission that the illness exists. Most families move on to have realistic expectations for the child. A common pattern in parents of seriously ill children is chronic sorrow, in which acceptance of the child's illness is interspersed with periods of intense sorrow. Families with a terminally ill child benefit from the support of professionals and other families who have coped successfully with similar experiences (Friedman, Hilden, & Powaski, 2004).

Diabetes Diabetes is one of the most common chronic diseases in children and adolescents. In type I diabetes, the body produces little or no insulin (the hormone that regulates the body's blood sugar level). **Type I diabetes** is an autoimmune disease in which the body's immune system destroys insulin-producing cells. In **type II diabetes,** the most common type of diabetes, the body is able to produce insulin but it may not be enough or the body cells may be unable to use it. Risk factors for type II diabetes include being overweight and/or physically inactive, having relatives with this disease, or belonging to certain ethnic groups (Bindler & Bruya, 2006; Vivian, 2006). Native Americans, African Americans, Latinos, and Asian Americans are at greater risk for developing diabetes.

Cardiovascular Disease Recent research has documented a number of risk factors in childhood that are linked to cardiovascular disease in adulthood. The precursors of cardiovascular disease often appear at a young age, with many elementary-school-age children already possessing one or more of the risk factors, such as hypertension and obesity (Groner, Joshi, & Bauer, 2006; Kavey & others, 2006). Ethnic differences in blood pressure also are present (Li & others, 2007). A study of more than 5,000 children revealed that high blood pressure was most likely to present in Latino children (25 percent) and least characteristic of Asian American children (14 percent) (Sorof & others, 2004).

Another study examined the role of diet and exercise on cardiovascular functioning in 82 overweight 9- to 12-year-old children (Woo & others, 2004). Children were randomly assigned to either a dietary only or a dietary plus supervised exercise program for six weeks and subsequently for one year. After six weeks, both treatments were linked with a decrease in waist-hip ratio, lower cholesterol, and improved functioning of arteries. After one year, the carotid wall of the children was thinner and body fat content was lower in the children in the dietary/exercise group. To read further about research on children's cardiovascular health, see the *Research in Children's Development* interlude.

type I diabetes An autoimmune disease, in which the body's immune system destroys insulin-producing cells.

type II diabetes The most common type of diabetes, in which the body is able to produce insulin but it may not be enough or the body cells may be unable to use it.

Research in Children's Development

HEART SMART

One large-scale investigation designed to improve children's cardiovascular health is the Bogalusa Heart Study, also called Heart Smart. It involves an ongoing evaluation of 8,000 boys and girls in Bogalusa, Louisiana (Berenson, 2005; Berenson & others, 2005; Chen & others, 2005, 2007; Freedman & others, 2004, 2005, 2007; Janssen & others, 2005; Katzmarzyk & others, 2004; Li & others, 2004, 2007; Mzayek & others, 2007; Nicklas & others, 2003, 2004a, b; Rajeshwari & others, 2005; Srinivasan & others, 2006). Heart Smart intervention takes place in schools. Since 95 percent of children and adolescents aged 5 to 18 are in school, school is an efficient context in which to educate individuals about health. Special attention is given to teachers, who serve as role models. Teachers who value the role of health in life and who engage in health-enhancing behavior present children and adolescents with positive models for health. Teacher in-service education is conducted by an interdisciplinary team of specialists, including physicians, psychologists, nutritionists, physical educators, and exercise physiologists. The school's staff is introduced to heart health education, the nature of cardiovascular disease, and risk factors for heart disease. Coping behavior, exercise behavior, and eating behavior are discussed with the staff, and a Heart Smart curriculum is explained.

The Heart Smart curriculum for grade 5 includes strategies for improving cardiovascular health, eating behavior, and exercise. The physical education component of Heart Smart involves two to four class periods each week to incorporate a "Superkids-Superfit" exercise program. The physical education instructor teaches skills required by the school system plus aerobic activities aimed at cardiovascular conditioning, including jogging, racewalking, interval workouts, rope skipping, circuit training, aerobic dance, and games. Classes begin and end with five minutes of walking and stretching.

The school lunch program serves as an intervention site, where sodium, fat, and sugar levels are decreased. Children and adolescents are given reasons they should eat healthy foods, such as a tuna sandwich, and why they should not eat unhealthy foods, such as a hot dog with chili. The school lunch program includes a salad bar, where children and adolescents can serve themselves. The amount and type of snack foods sold on the school premises are monitored.

High-risk children—those with elevated blood pressure, cholesterol, and weight—are identified as part of Heart Smart (Srinivasan & others, 2006). A multidisciplinary team of physicians, nutritionists, nurses, and behavioral counselors work with the high-risk boys and girls and their parents through group-oriented activities and individual-based family counseling. High-risk boys and girls and their parents receive diet, exercise, and relaxation prescriptions in an intensive 12-session program, followed by long-term monthly evaluations.

Extensive assessment is a part of this ongoing program. Short-term and long-term changes in children's knowledge about cardiovascular disease and changes in their behavior are assessed.

Following are some results from the Bogalusa Heart Study:

- More than half of the children exceeded the recommended intake of salt, fat, cholesterol, and sugar (Nicklas & others, 1995).
- Consumption of sweetened beverages, sweets (desserts, candy), and total consumption of low-quality food were associated with being overweight in childhood (Nicklas & others, 2003).
- Adiposity (having excess body weight) beginning in childhood was related to cardiovascular problems in adulthood (Li & others, 2004).

- Higher body mass index (BMI) in childhood was linked to the likelihood of developing metabolic syndrome (a cluster of characteristics that include excessive fat around the abdomen, high blood pressure, and diabetes) in adulthood (Freedman & others, 2005).

Asthma   **Asthma** is a chronic lung disease that involves episodes of airflow obstruction. Symptoms of an asthma attack include shortness of breath, wheezing, or tightness in the chest. The incidence of asthma has risen steadily in recent decades, possibly because of increased air pollution (Pattenden & others, 2006). Asthma is the most common chronic disease in U.S. children, being present in 7 to 12 percent of them (Liu, 2002). Asthma is the primary reason for absences from school, and is responsible for a number of pediatric admissions to emergency rooms and hospitals (Sotir & others, 2006).

asthma A chronic lung disease that involves episodes of airflow obstruction.

The exact causes of asthma are not known, but it is believed that the disease results from hypersensitivity to environmental substances, which trigger an allergic reaction (Ricci & others, 2006). A recent research review concluded that the following are asthma risk factors: being male, having one or both parents with asthma, allergy sensitivity, stress early in life, infections, obesity, and exposure to environmental tobacco smoke, indoor allergens, and outdoor pollutants (Feleszko & others, 2006).

Corticosteroids, which generally are inhaled, are the most effective anti-inflammatory drugs for treating asthmatic children (Ferris & others, 2006). Often, parents have kept asthmatic children from exercising because they fear exercise will provoke an asthma attack. However, today it is believed that children with asthma should be encouraged to exercise, provided their asthma is under control, and participation should be evaluated on an individual basis (Basaran & others, 2006). Some asthmatic children lose their symptoms in adolescence and adulthood (Vonk & others, 2004).

One individual who helps children cope with their health-care experiences is child life specialist Sharon McLeod. To read about her work see the *Careers in Child Development* profile.

Accidents and Injuries

The most common cause of severe injury and death in middle and late childhood is motor vehicle accidents, either as a pedestrian or as a passenger (Leifer, 2007). Using safety-belt restraints is important in reducing the severity of motor vehicle injuries. The school-age child's motivation to ride a bicycle increases the risk of accidents. Other serious injuries involve skateboards, roller skates, and other sports equipment.

Most accidents occur in or near the child's home or school (Robertson & South, 2007). The most effective prevention strategy is to educate the child about the hazards of risk taking and improper use of equipment

Careers in CHILD DEVELOPMENT

Sharon McLeod
Child Life Specialist

Sharon McLeod is a child life specialist who is clinical director of the Child Life and Recreational Therapy Department at the Children's Hospital Medical Center in Cincinnati.

Under Sharon's direction, the goals of the Child Life Department are to promote children's optimal growth and development, reduce the stress of health-care experiences, and provide support to child patients and their families. These goals are accomplished through therapeutic play and developmentally appropriate activities, educating and psychologically preparing children for medical procedures, and serving as a resource for parents and others professionals regarding children's development and health-care issues.

Sharon says that human growth and development provides the foundation for her profession of child life specialist. She also describes her best times as a student when she conducted fieldwork, had an internship, and experienced hands-on theories and concepts she learned in her courses.

Sharon McLeod, child life specialist, working with a child at Children's Hospital Medical Center in Cincinnati.

(Snowdon & others, 2006). Appropriate safety helmets, protective eye and mouth shields, and protective padding are recommended for children who engage in active sports. Physically active school-age children are more susceptible to fractures, strains, and sprains than are their less active counterparts. Also, boys are more likely than girls to experience these injuries.

As we saw in Chapter 8, "Physical Development in Early Childhood," caregivers play a key role in preventing childhood injuries. A recent study in four developing countries (Ethiopia, Peru, Vietnam, and India) revealed that depression in caregivers was consistently linked to children's risk of injury for all types of injury assessed (burns, serious falls, broken bones, and near-fatal injury) (Howe, Hutley, & Abramsky, 2006).

REVIEW AND REFLECT ▸ LEARNING GOAL 2

2 **Characterize children's health in middle and late childhood.**

Review
- What are key aspects of children's nutrition in middle and late childhood?
- What roles do exercise and sports play in children's development?
- What is the nature of being overweight in childhood?
- What are four diseases that can especially be harmful to children?
- What is the most common cause of severe injury and death in childhood?

Reflect
- How good were your eating habits as a child? How much did you exercise in middle and late childhood? Are your eating and exercise habits today similar to or different from your eating and exercise habits as a child? Why are they similar or different?

---

3 WHAT ARE THE PREVALENT DISABILITIES IN CHILDREN?

| Who Are Children with Disabilities? | The Range of Disabilities | Educational Issues |

Our discussion of children's health has focused on nutrition and exercise. In addition, we have discussed some of the most common health problems, such as obesity, cancer, diabetes, cardiovascular disease, and asthma. In this section, we turn our attention to children with disabilities and the issues involved in their education.

Who Are Children with Disabilities?

The elementary school years are a time when children with disabilities become more sensitive about their differentness and how it is perceived by others. Approximately 10 percent of children in the United States receive special education or related services. As Figure 11.6 shows, among children with disabilities who receive special education services, more than 40 percent have a learning disability (National Center for Education Statistics, 2003). Substantial percentages of children have speech or language impairments, mental retardation, or serious emotional disturbance.

Educators now prefer to speak of "children with disabilities" rather than "handicapped children" to emphasize the person, not the disability (Hallahan & Kauffman, 2006). The term "handicapping conditions" is still used to describe impediments to the learning and functioning of individuals with a disability that have been imposed by society. For example, when children who use a wheelchair do not have adequate access to a bathroom, transportation, and so on, this is referred to as a handicapping condition.

The Range of Disabilities

In this section, we examine learning disabilities, attention deficit hyperactivity disorder, speech disorders, sensory disorders, physical disorders, emotional and behavioral disorders, and autism. In Chapter 12, we study mental retardation.

Learning Disabilities   Jalal's second-grade teacher complains that his spelling is awful. Eight-year-old Tim says reading is really hard for him, and a lot of times the words don't make much sense. Alisha has good oral language skills but has considerable difficulty in computing correct answers to arithmetic problems. Each of these students has a learning disability.

Characteristics   After examining the research on learning disabilities, leading expert Linda Siegel (2003) concluded that a definition of **learning disabilities** should include these components: (1) a minimum IQ level; (2) a significant difficulty in a school-related area (especially reading and/or mathematics); and (3) exclusion of only severe emotional disorders, second-language background, sensory disabilities, and/or specific neurological deficits. When there is a discrepency between intelligence and achievement, the possibility of a learning disability should be investigated.

A recent national survey found that 8 percent of U.S. children have a learning disability (Bloom & Dey, 2006). About three times as many boys as girls are classified as having a learning disability (Hallahan & Kauffman, 2006). Among the explanations for this gender difference are a greater biological vulnerability of boys, as well as referral bias (boys are more likely to be referred by teachers for treatment because of their disruptive, hyperactive behavior) (Liederman, Kantrowitz, & Flannery, 2005).

About 5 percent of all school-age children in the United States receive special education or related services because of a learning disability. In the federal classification of children receiving special education and related services, attention deficit hyperactivity disorder (ADHD) is included in the learning disabilities category. Because of the significant interest in ADHD today, we discuss it by itself following learning disabilities.

In the past three decades, the percentage of children classified as having a learning disability has increased substantially—from less than 30 percent of all children receiving special education and related services between 1977 and 1978 to a little more than 50 percent today. Some experts say that the dramatic increase reflects poor diagnostic practices and overidentification. They believe that teachers sometimes are too quick to label children with the slightest learning problem as having a learning disability, instead of recognizing that the problem may rest in their ineffective teaching. Other experts say the increase in children being labeled with a "learning disability" is justified (Hallahan & Kauffmann, 2006).

Dyslexia   The most common problem that characterizes children with a learning disability involves reading (Bursuck & Damer, 2007; Johnson & Morrison, 2007). Such children especially show problems with phonological skills (recall from Chapter 6 that this involves being able to understand how sounds and letters match up to make words). **Dyslexia** is a category of learning disabilities reserved for individuals who have a severe impairment in their ability to read and spell. Children with dyslexia often have difficulties in handwriting, spelling, or composition. Their writing may be extremely slow, their writing products may be virtually illegible, and they may make numerous spelling errors because of their inability to match up sounds and letters.

Disability	Number of Children	Percentage of All Children with Disabilities
Learning disabilities	2,846,000	44.4
Speech and language impairments	1,084,000	16.9
Mental retardation	592,000	9.2
Emotional disturbance	476,000	7.4

FIGURE 11.6 U.S. Children with a Disability Who Receive Special Education Services Figures are for the 2001–2002 school year and represent the four categories with the highest number and percentage of children. Both learning disability and attention deficit hyperactivity disorder are combined in the learning disabilities category (National Center for Education Statistics, 2003).

learning disability Includes three components: (1) a minimum IQ level, (2) a significant difficulty in a school-related area (especially reading and/or mathematics), and (3) exclusion of only severe emotional disorders, second-language background, sensory disabilities, and/or specific neurological deficits.

dyslexia A category of learning disabilities involving a severe impairment in the ability to read and spell.

Dyscalculia **Dyscalculia,** also known as developmental arithmetic disorder, is a learning disability that involves difficulty in math computation. It is estimated to characterize 2 to 6 percent of U.S. elementary school children (National Center for Learning Disabilities, 2007). Researchers have found that children who have math computation problems are characterized by a number of cognitive and neuropsychological deficits, including poor performance in working memory, visual perception, and visual-spatial abilities (Hallahan & others, 2006; Kucian & others, 2006). In some cases, a child will have both a reading disability and a math disability, and there are cognitive deficits that characterize both types of disabilities, such as poor working memory (Gurganus, 2007; Siegel, 2003).

Identification   Diagnosing whether a child has a learning disability is often a difficult task (Berninger, 2006). One identification procedure requires a significant discrepancy between actual achievement and expected achievement, the latter being estimated by an individually administered intelligence test. However, many educators question the adequacy of this approach (Francis & others, 2005). Another identification strategy that has been proposed is *response-to-intervention,* or *response-to-treatment,* which involves students not learning effectively in response to effective instruction (Fuchs & others, 2003). However, whether this approach can be effectively implemented is still being debated.

Initial identification of a possible learning disability is usually made by the classroom teacher. If a learning disability is suspected, the teacher calls on specialists. Individual psychological evaluations (of intelligence) and educational assessments (such as current level of achievement) are required (Mercer & Pullen, 2005). In addition, tests of visual-motor skills, language, and memory may be used. An interdisciplinary team of professionals is best suited to verify whether a student has a learning disability.

Causes and Intervention Strategies   The precise causes of learning disabilities have not yet been determined. However, some possible causes have been proposed (Bender, 2008). Learning disabilities tends to run in families with one parent having a disability such as dyslexia, although the specific genetic transmission of learning disabilities has not been discovered (Petrill & others, 2006; Shastry, 2007). Some leading researchers argue that some reading disabilities are likely due to genetics but that the majority are the result of environmental influences (Shaywitz, Lyon, & Shaywitz, 2006).

Researchers also use brain-imaging techniques, such as magnetic resonance imaging, to reveal any regions of the brain that might be involved in learning disabilities (Berninger, 2006; Shaywitz, Lyon, & Shaywitz, 2006) (see Figure 11.7). This research indicates that it is unlikely learning disabilities reside in a single, specific brain location. More likely, learning disabilities are due to problems in integrating information from multiple brain regions or subtle difficulties in brain structures and functions (National Institutes of Mental Health, 1993). Using MRI brain scans, researchers have found that two neural pathways in the brain's left hemisphere are among the brain's neural circuitry involved in reading; children with dyslexia have deficiencies in these pathways (Shaywitz, Lyon, & Shaywtiz, 2006): (1) in the back of the brain in the parietal/temporal lobe region of the cerebral cortex is a sort of phonological module where words are broken down into phonemes before they can be processed by the rest of the brain's language areas; and (2) in the back of the brain where the occipital and temporal lobes converge is a second pathway, used by skilled readers, that functions in reading whole words.

Another possibility is that some learning disabilities are caused by problems during prenatal development or delivery. A number of studies have found

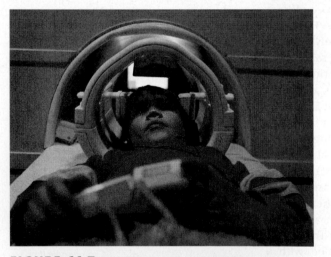

FIGURE 11.7 **Brain Scans and Learning Disabilities**
An increasing number of studies are using MRI brain scans to examine the brain pathways involved in learning disabilities. Shown here is 9-year-old Patrick Price, who has dyslexia. Patrick is going through an MRI scanner disguised by drapes to look like a child-friendly castle. Inside the scanner, children must lie virtually motionless as words and symbols flash on a screen, and they are asked to identify them by clicking different buttons.

dyscalculia Also know as developmental arithmetic disorder, this learning disability involves difficulty in math computation.

that learning disabilities are more prevalent in low birth weight infants (Litt & others, 2005).

Many interventions have focused on improving the child's reading ability, especially by improving phonological processing (Bursuck & Damer, 2007; Vukovic & Siegel, 2006). For example, in one study, instruction in phonological awareness at the kindergarten level had positive effects on reading development when the children reached the first grade (Blachman & others, 1994).

Unfortunately, not all children who have a learning disability that involves reading problems have the benefit of appropriate early intervention. Most children whose reading disability is not diagnosed until the third grade or later, and who receive standard interventions, fail to show noticeable improvements (Lyon, 1996). However, intensive instruction over a period of time by a competent teacher can remediate the deficient reading skills of many children (Bursuck & Damer, 2007).

Children with severe phonological deficits that lead to poor decoding and word recognition skills respond to intervention more slowly than do children with mild to moderate reading problems (Torgesen, 1999). Also, the success of even the best-designed reading intervention depends on the training and skills of the teacher.

Improving outcomes for children with a learning disability is a challenging task and generally has required intensive intervention for even modest improvement in outcomes (Berninger, 2006; Hallahan & others, 2006). However, no model program has proven to be effective for all children with learning disabilities (Terman & others, 1996).

Attention Deficit Hyperactivity Disorder   Matthew has attention deficit hyperactivity disorder, and the outward signs are fairly typical. He has trouble attending to the teacher's instructions and is easily distracted. He can't sit still for more than a few minutes at a time, and his handwriting is messy. His mother describes him as very fidgety.

Attention deficit hyperactivity disorder (ADHD) is a disability in which children consistently show one or more of these characteristics over a period of time: (1) inattention, (2) hyperactivity, and (3) impulsivity. Children who are inattentive have difficulty focusing on any one thing and may get bored with a task after only a few minutes. Children who are hyperactive show high levels of physical activity, almost always seeming to be in motion. Children who are impulsive have difficulty curbing their reactions and often don't think before they act. Depending on the characteristics that children with ADHD display, they can be diagnosed as (1) ADHD with predominantly inattention, (2) ADHD with predominantly hyperactivity/impulsivity, or (3) ADHD with both inattention and hyperactivity/impulsivity.

The U.S. Office of Education figures on children with a disability that were shown in Figure 11.6 include children with ADHD in the category of children with specific learning disabilities, an overall category that comprises slightly more than half of all children who receive special education services. Students with ADHD have a failure rate in school that is two to three times that of other students. About half of students with ADHD have repeated a grade by adolescence, and more than one-third eventually drop out of school.

Diagnosis and Developmental Characteristics   The number of children diagnosed and treated for ADHD has increased substantially, by some estimates doubling in the 1990s (Zentall, 2006). A recent national survey found that 7 percent of U.S. children 3 to 17 years of age had ADHD (Bloom & Dey, 2006). The disorder is diagnosed two to three times as often in boys as in girls (National Health Survey, 2005). However, there is controversy about the increased diagnosis of ADHD. Some experts attribute the increase mainly to heightened awareness of the disorder. Others are concerned that many children are being diagnosed without undergoing extensive professional evaluation based on input from multiple sources.

Many children with ADHD show impulsive behavior, such as this child who is jumping out of his seat and throwing a paper airplane at other children. *How would you handle this situation if you were a teacher and this were to happen in your classroom?*

attention deficit hyperactivity disorder (ADHD) A disability in which children consistently show one or more of the following characteristics: (1) inattention, (2) hyperactivity, and (3) impulsivity.

Signs of ADHD may be present in the preschool years. Parents and preschool or kindergarten teachers may notice that the child has an extremely high activity level and a limited attention span. They may say the child is "always on the go," "can't sit still even for a second," or "never seems to listen." Many children with ADHD are difficult to discipline, have a low frustration tolerance, and have problems in peer relations (Greene & others, 2001). Other common characteristics of children with ADHD include general immaturity and clumsiness.

Although signs of ADHD are often present in the preschool years, their classification often doesn't take place until the elementary school years (Stein & Perrin, 2003). The increased academic and social demands of formal schooling, as well as stricter standards for behavioral control, often illuminate the problems of the child with ADHD (Daley, 2006). Elementary school teachers typically report that this type of child has difficulty in working independently, completing seatwork, and organizing work. Restlessness and distractibility also are often noted. These problems are more likely to be observed in repetitive or taxing tasks, or tasks the child perceives to be boring (such as completing worksheets or doing homework).

It used to be thought that ADHD decreased in adolescence, but now it is believed that this often is not the case. Estimates suggest that ADHD decreases in only about one-third of adolescents. Increasingly, it is being recognized that these problems may continue into adulthood (Faraone, Biederman, & Mick, 2006; Seidman, 2006).

Causes and Treatment   Definitive causes of ADHD have not been found. For example, scientists have not been able to identify cause-related sites in the brain. However, a number of causes have been proposed, such as low levels of certain neurotransmitters (chemical messengers in the brain), prenatal and postnatal abnormalities, and environmental toxins, such as lead (Stein & others, 2007). Heredity also may play a role, as 30 to 50 percent of children with ADHD have a sibling or parent who has the disorder (Heiser & others, 2004). Efforts are being made to explore specific genes that might be involved in ADHD (Waldman & Gizer, 2006).

Many experts recommend a combination of academic, behavioral, and medical interventions to help students with ADHD learn and adapt more effectively (Voeller, 2004). This intervention requires cooperation and effort on the part of the parents of students with ADHD, school personnel (teachers, administrators, special educators, and school psychologists), and health-care professionals (Medd, 2003).

The most common treatment for ADHD is the use of methylphenidate, a stimulant medication (Tucha & others, 2006). About 85 to 90 percent of children with ADHD are taking this stimulant medication (the most common brand names are Ritalin and Adderall) to control their behavior (Denney, 2001). Adderall has been increasingly recommended because it has fewer side effects than Ritalin. Ritalin and Adderall speed up the nervous system and behavior of most individuals (Raphaelson, 2004). However, in many children with ADHD, the drug speeds up underactive areas of the prefrontal cortex that control attention, impulsivity, and planning. This enhanced ability to focus their attention results in what *appears* to be a "slowing down" of behavior in these children (Reeves & Schweitzer, 2004).

Methylphenidate has been found to be effective in improving the attention of many children with ADHD, but it usually does not improve their attention to the same level as that of children who do not have ADHD (Barbaresi & others, 2006; Pliszka, 2007). Researchers have found that a combination of medication (such as Ritalin) and behavior management improves the behavior of children with ADHD better than medication alone or behavior management alone (Daly & others, 2007; Greydanus, Pratt, & Patel, 2007).

However, not all children with ADHD respond positively to prescription stimulants, and some critics believe that many physicians are too quick in prescribing prescription stimulants for children with milder forms of ADHD (Doseis & others, 2003). In one study, Ritalin was less effective with children who have a high anxiety level, children who are older, and children who have less severe symptoms (Gray & Kagan,

2000). Further, in 2006, the U.S. government issued a warning about the cardiovascular risks of stimulant medications used to treat ADHD.

Some studies also have focused on the possibility that exercise might reduce ADHD (Tantillo & others, 2002). For example, researchers have found that exercise increases the levels of two neurotransmitters—dopamine and norepinephrine—that improve concentration (Ferrando-Lucas, 2006; Rebollo & Montiel, 2006). Some mental health professionals are recommending that children and youth with ADHD exercise several times a day (Ratey, 2006). They also speculate that the increase in rates of ADHD have coincided with the decrease in exercise that children are getting. Another link between ADHD and being sedentary involves watching a lot of TV. Some researchers have investigated whether heavy TV watching is linked to poor concentration in school. There have only been several studies on this link, and the findings are mixed (Cristakis & others, 2004; Stevens & Mulsow, 2006).

Speech Disorders Speech disorders include articulation disorders, voice disorders, and fluency disorders. **Articulation disorders** are problems in pronouncing sounds correctly. A child's articulation at 6 to 7 years is still not always error-free, but it should be by age 8. A child with an articulation problem may find communication with peers and the teacher difficult or embarrassing. As a result, the child may avoid asking questions, participating in discussions, or communicating with peers. Articulation problems can usually be improved or resolved with speech therapy, though it may take months or years.

Voice disorders are reflected in speech that is hoarse, harsh, too loud, too high-pitched, or too low-pitched. Children with cleft palate often have a voice disorder that makes their speech difficult to understand. If a student speaks in a way that is consistently difficult to understand, the child should be referred to a speech therapist.

Fluency disorders often involve what is commonly called "stuttering." Stuttering occurs when a child's speech has a spasmodic hesitation, prolongation, or repetition. The anxiety many children feel because they stutter can make their stuttering worse. Speech therapy is recommended.

One individual who helps children with their speech problems is Sharla Peltier. To read about her work, see the *Careers in Child Development* profile.

Sensory Disorders Sensory disorders include visual and hearing impairments. Sometimes these impairments are described as part of a larger category called "communication disorders," along with speech and language disorders.

Visual Impairments Some children may have mild vision problems that have not been corrected. If children frequently squint, hold books close to their face when they read, rub their eyes often, say that things look blurred, or mention that words move about on the page, they should be referred to appropriate professionals to have their vision checked. In many cases, they need only corrective lenses. However,

Sharla Peltier
Speech Pathologist

A speech pathologist is a health professional who works with individuals who have a communication disorder. Sharla Peltier is a speech pathologist in Manitoulin, Ontario, Canada. Peltier works with Native American children in the First Nations Schools. She conducts screening for speech/language and hearing problems and assesses infants as young as 6 months of age as well as school-age children. She works closely with community health nurses to identify hearing problems.

Diagnosing problems is only about half of what Peltier does in her work. She especially enjoys treating speech/language and hearing problems. She conducts parent training sessions to help parents understand and help with their children's language problem. As part of this training, she guides parents in improving their communication skills with their children.

Speech therapist Sharla Peltier, helping a young child improve her language and communication skills.

articulation disorders Problems in pronouncing sounds correctly.

voice disorders Disorders reflected in speech that is hoarse, harsh, too loud, too high-pitched, or too low-pitched.

fluency disorders Various disorders that involve what is commonly called "stuttering."

a small portion of children (about 1 in 1,000) have more serious visual problems and are classified as visually impaired. This includes children with low vision and blind children.

Children with **low vision** have visual acuity of between 20/70 and 20/2000 (on the Snellen scale, in which 20/20 is normal) with corrective lens. Children with low vision can read with the aid of large-print books or a magnifying glass (Douglas & others, 2004). Children who are **educationally blind** cannot use their vision in learning and must use their hearing and touch to learn. Approximately 1 in every 3,000 children is educationally blind. Almost half of these children were born blind, and another one-third lost their vision in the first year of life. Many children who are educationally blind have normal intelligence and function very well academically with appropriate supports and learning aids.

An important task when working with a visually impaired child is to determine the modality (such as touch or hearing) through which the child learns best. Preferential seating in the front of the class is also helpful.

Hearing Impairments A hearing impairment can make learning difficult for children (Connor & Zwolan, 2004). Children who are born deaf or experience a significant hearing loss in the first several years of life may not develop normal speech and language (Friend, 2008). Some children in middle and late childhood have hearing impairments that have not yet been detected (Wake & Poulakis, 2004). If children turn one ear toward the speaker, frequently ask to have something repeated, don't follow directions, or frequently complain of earaches, colds, and allergies, their hearing needs to be evaluated by a specialist, such as an audiologist (Patterson & Wright, 1990).

Many hearing-impaired children receive supplementary instruction beyond the regular classroom. Educational approaches to help children with hearing impairments learn fall into two categories: oral and manual (Hoskin & Herman, 2001):

- **Oral approaches** include using lip reading, speech reading (relies on visual cues to teach reading), and whatever hearing the child has.
- **Manual approaches** involve sign language and finger spelling. Sign language is a system of hand movements that symbolize words. Finger spelling consists of "spelling out" each word by placing the hand in different positions. A total communication approach that includes both oral and manual approaches is increasingly being used with children who are hearing impaired (Hallahan & Kauffman, 2006).

Many students with physical disabilities such as cerebral palsy cannot use a conventional keyboard and mouse. Many can use alternative keyboards effectively.

low vision Visual acuity between 20/70 and 20/2000.

educationally blind Unable to use one's vision in learning. It implies a need to use hearing and touch to learn.

oral approaches Educational approaches to help hearing-impaired children; they include lip reading, speech reading, and whatever hearing the child has.

manual approaches Educational approaches to help hearing-impaired children; they include sign language and finger spelling.

orthopedic impairments Restrictions in movement abilities due to muscle, bone, or joint problems.

Today many hearing-impaired children are educated in the regular classroom. With appropriate accommodations such as preferential seating and the assistance of hearing aids, cochlear implants, and other amplification devices, hearing-impaired children can be educated effectively (Ching & others, 2006; Litovsky, Johnstone, & Godar, 2006).

Physical Disorders Physical disorders that children may have include orthopedic impairments, such as cerebral palsy. Many children with physical disorders require special education, as well as related services. The related services may include transportation, physical therapy, school health services, and psychological services.

Orthopedic impairments involve restrictions in movement because of muscle, bone, or joint problems. Depending on the severity of the restriction, some children may have only limited restriction, whereas others cannot move at all (Morris & others, 2006). Still other children cannot control the movement of their muscles. Orthopedic impairments can be caused by prenatal or perinatal problems, or they can be due to a disease or an accident during the childhood years. With the help of adaptive devices and medical technology, many children with an orthopedic impairment function well in the classroom (Boyles & Contadino, 1997).

Cerebral palsy is a disorder that involves a lack of muscular coordination, shaking, and unclear speech. The most common cause of cerebral palsy is lack of oxygen at birth. In the most common type of cerebral palsy, which is called *spastic,* children's muscles are stiff and difficult to move. The rigid muscles often pull the limbs into contorted positions (Russman & Ashwal, 2004). In a less common type, *ataxia,* children's muscles are rigid one moment and floppy the next moment, making movements clumsy and jerky.

Computers especially help children with cerebral palsy learn. If they have the coordination to use the keyboard, they can do their written work on the computer. A pen with a light can be added to a computer and used by the child as a pointer. Children with cerebral palsy have unclear speech (Pirila & others, 2007). For these children, speech and voice synthesizers, communication boards, talking notes, and page turners can improve their communication.

Emotional and Behavioral Disorders

Most children have minor emotional difficulties at some time during their school years, but a small percentage have problems that are so serious and persistent that they are classified as having an emotional or behavioral disorder (Mash & Wolfe, 2005; Weber & Plotts, 2008). **Emotional and behavioral disorders** consist of serious, persistent problems that involve relationships, aggression, depression, fears associated with personal or school matters, as well as other inappropriate socioemotional characteristics. Approximately 8 percent of children who have a disability and require an individualized education plan fall into this classification. Boys are three times as likely as girls to have these disorders. We further discuss aggression in Chapter 13 and depression in Chapter 16.

Autism Spectrum Disorders

In Chapter 9, "Cognitive Development in Early Childhood," we indicated that autistic children have deficiencies in theory of mind, including problems in understanding others' beliefs and emotions. We also said that some autistic children have more severe disabilities than others. **Autism spectrum disorders (ASD),** also called pervasive developmental disorders, range from the severe disorder labeled *autistic disorder* to the milder disorder called *Asperger syndrome.* Children with an autism spectrum disorder are characterized as having problems in social interaction, verbal and nonverbal communication, and repetitive behaviors. They also may show atypical responses to sensory experiences (National Institute of Mental Health, 2007). Autism spectrum disorders can often be detected in children as early as 1 to 3 years of age when parents notice unusual behaviors occurring. In some cases, they report their child was different from birth, being unresponsive to people or staring at one object for a very long time. In other cases, these children seem to be developing normally for a year or two but suddenly become withdrawn or indifferent to people.

Autistic disorder is a severe autism spectrum disorder that has its onset in the first three years of life and includes deficiencies in social relationships; abnormalities in communication; and restricted, repetitive, and stereotyped patterns of behavior. Estimates indicate that approximately two to five of every 10,000 young children in the United States have an autistic disorder. Boys are about four times more likely to have an autistic disorder than girls.

Asperger syndrome is a relatively mild autism spectrum disorder in which the child has relatively good verbal language, milder nonverbal language problems, and a restricted range of interests and relationships. Children with Asperger syndrome often engage in obsessive repetitive routines and preoccupations with a particular subject.

What causes the autism spectrum disorders? The current consensus is that autism involves a brain dysfunction with abnormalities in brain structure, including the cerebellum and cerebral cortex (frontal and temporal lobes), and neurotransmitters,

cerebral palsy A disorder that involves a lack of muscular coordination, shaking, and unclear speech.

emotional and behavioral disorders These consist of serious, persistent problems that involve relationships, aggression, depression, fears associated with personal or school matters, as well as other inappropriate socioemotional characteristics.

autism spectrum disorders (ASD) Also called pervasive developmental disorders, they range from the severe disorder labeled autistic disorder to the milder disorder called Asperger syndrome. Children with these disorders are characterized by problems in social interaction, verbal and nonverbal communication, and repetitive behaviors.

autistic disorder A severe autism spectrum disorder that has its onset in the first three years of life and includes deficiencies in social relationships, abnormalities in communication, and restricted, repetitive, and stereotyped patterns of behavior.

Asperger syndrome A relatively mild autism spectrum disorder in which the child has relatively good verbal language, milder nonverbal language problems, and a restricted range of interests and relationships.

including serotonin and dopamine (Lainhart, 2006; Penn, 2006). There is some evidence that genetic factors play a role in the development of the autism spectrum disorders (Baron-Cohen, 2004). One recent study found that approximately 50 percent of boys with Asperger syndrome had a paternal history of autism spectrum disorders (Gillberg & Cederlund, 2005). There is no evidence that family socialization causes autism (Rutter & Schopler, 1987). Mental retardation is present in some children with autism, whereas others show average or above-average intelligence.

Children with autism benefit from a well-structured classroom, individualized instruction, and small-group instruction (Pueschel & others, 1995). As with children who are mentally retarded, behavior modification sometimes has been effective in helping autistic children learn (Alberto & Troutman, 2006).

Educational Issues

The legal requirement that schools serve all children with a disability is fairly recent. Beginning in the mid-1960s to mid-1970s, legislatures, the federal courts, and the U.S. Congress laid down special educational rights for children with disabilities. Prior to that time, most children with a disability were either refused enrollment or inadequately served by schools. In 1975, **Public Law 94-142,** the Education for All Handicapped Children Act, required that all students with disabilities be given a free, appropriate public education and be provided the funding to help implement this education.

In 1990, Public Law 94-142 was recast as the **Individuals with Disabilities Education Act (IDEA).** IDEA was amended in 1997 and then reauthorized in 2004 and renamed the Individuals with Disabilities Education Improvement Act. IDEA spells out broad mandates for services to all children with disabilities (Friend, 2008; Smith, 2007). These include evaluation and eligibility determination, appropriate education and an individualized education plan (IEP), and education in the least restrictive environment (LRE).

A major aspect of the 2004 reauthorization of IDEA involved aligning it with the government's No Child Left Behind (NCLB) legislation, which was designed to improve the educational achievement of all students, including those with disabilities. Both IDEA and NCLB mandate that most students with disabilities be included in general assessments of educational progress. This alignment includes requiring most students with disabilities "to take standard tests of academic achievement and to achieve at a level equal to that of students without disabilities. Whether this expectation is reasonable is an open question" (Hallahan & Kauffman, 2006, pp. 28–29). Alternate assessments for students with disabilities and funding to help states improve instruction, assessment, and accountability for educating students with disabilities are included in the 2004 reauthorization of IDEA.

Evaluation and Eligibility Determination Children who are thought to have a disability are evaluated to determine their eligibility for services under IDEA. Schools are prohibited from planning special education programs in advance and offering them on a space-available basis.

Children must be evaluated before a school can begin providing special services (Werts, Culatta, & Tompkins, 2007). Parents should be involved in the evaluation process. Reevaluation is required at least every three years (sometimes every year), when requested by parents, or when conditions suggest a reevaluation is needed. A parent who disagrees with the school's evaluation can obtain an independent evaluation, which the school is required to consider in providing special education services. If the evaluation finds that the child has a disability and requires special services, the school must provide them to the child.

The IDEA has many specific provisions that relate to the parents of a child with a disability (Friend, 2008). These include requirements that schools send notices to

Public Law 94-142 The Education for All Handicapped Children Act, created in 1975, which requires that all children with disabilities be given a free, appropriate public education and which provides the funding to help with the costs of implementing this education.

Individuals with Disabilities Education Act (IDEA) The IDEA spells out broad mandates for services to all children with disabilities (IDEA is a renaming of Public Law 94-142); these include evaluation and eligibility determination, appropriate education and the individualized education plan (IEP), and the least restrictive environment (LRE).

Increasingly, children with disabilities are being taught in the regular classroom, as is this child with mild mental retardation.

parents of proposed actions, of attendance at meetings regarding the child's placement or individualized education plan, and of the right to appeal school decisions to an impartial evaluator.

The IDEA, including its 1997 amendments, requires that technology devices and services be provided to students with disabilities if they are necessary to ensure a free, appropriate education. Two types of technology that can be used to improve the education of students with disabilities are instructional technology and assistive technology:

- **Instructional technology** includes various types of hardware and software, combined with innovative teaching methods, to accommodate students' needs in the classroom. This technology includes videotapes, computer-assisted instruction, and complex hypermedia programs in which computers are used to control the display of audio and visual images stored on videodisc. The use of telecommunication systems, especially the Internet and its World Wide Web, hold considerable promise for improving the education of students with a disability.
- **Assistive technology** consists of various services and devices to help students with disabilities function within their environment. Examples include communication aids, alternative computer keyboards, and adaptive switches. To locate such services, educators can use computer databases, such as the Device Locator System.

Appropriate Education and the Individualized Education Plan (IEP) The IDEA requires that students with disabilities have an **individualized education plan (IEP),** a written statement that spells out a program tailored specifically for the student with a disability (Lewis & Doorlag, 2006). In general, the IEP should be (1) related to the child's learning capacity, (2) specially constructed to meet the child's individual needs and not merely a copy of what is offered to other children, and (3) designed to provide educational benefits.

Amendments were made to the IDEA in 1997. Two of these involve positive behavioral support and functional behavioral assessment (U.S. Office of Education, 2000). *Positive behavioral support* focuses on culturally appropriate interventions to

instructional technology Various types of hardware and software, combined with innovative teaching methods, to accommodate students' learning needs in the classroom.

assistive technology Various services and devices to help children with disabilities function in their environment.

individualized education plan (IEP) A written statement that spells out a program tailored to a child with a disability. The plan should be (1) related to the child's learning capacity, (2) specially constructed to meet the child's individual needs and not merely a copy of what is offered to other children, and (3) designed to provide educational benefits.

attain important behavioral changes in children. *Functional behavioral assessment* involves determining the consequences (what purpose the behavior serves), antecedents (what triggers the behavior), and setting events (in which contexts the behavior occurs).

Under the IDEA, a child with a disability must be educated in the **least restrictive environment (LRE).** This means a setting that is as similar as possible to the one in which children who do not have a disability are educated. This provision of the IDEA has given a legal basis to making an effort to educate children with a disability in the regular classroom (Mastropieri & Scruggs, 2007; Smith & others, 2008). The term used to describe the education of children with a disability in the regular classroom used to be *mainstreaming.* However, that term has been replaced by the term **inclusion,** which means educating a child with special education needs full-time in the general school program.

A major aspect of the 2004 reauthorization of IDEA involved aligning it with the government's No Child Left Behind (NCLB) legislation, which mandates general assessments of educational progress that include students with disabilities (Rosenberg, Westling, & MeLeskey, 2008). This alignment includes requiring most students with disabilities "to take standard tests of academic achievement and to achieve at a level equal to that of students without disabilities. Whether this expectation is reasonable is an open question" (Hallahan & Kauffman, 2006, pp. 28–29).

Not long ago, it was considered appropriate to educate children with disabilities outside the regular classroom. However, today, schools must make every effort to provide inclusion for children with disabilities (Smith & others, 2006; Wood, 2006). These efforts can be very costly financially and very time consuming in terms of faculty effort.

The principle of least restrictive environment compels schools to examine possible modifications of the regular classroom before moving the child with a disability to a more restrictive placement (Turnbull, Turnbull, & Tompkins, 2007). Also, regular classroom teachers often need specialized training to help some children with a disability, and state educational agencies are required to provide such training (Vaughn, Bos, & Schumm, 2007).

Many legal changes regarding children with disabilities have been extremely positive. Compared with several decades ago, far more children today are receiving competent, specialized services. For many children, inclusion in the regular classroom, with modifications or supplemental services, is appropriate (Friend, 2008). However, some leading experts on special education argue that the effort to use inclusion to educate children with disabilities has become too extreme in some cases. For example, James Kauffman and his colleagues (Kauffman & Hallahan, 2005; Kauffman, McGee, and Brigham, 2004) state that inclusion too often has meant making accommodations in the regular classroom that do not always benefit children with disabilities. They advocate a more individualized approach that does not always involve full inclusion but rather options such as special education outside the regular classroom. Kauffman and his colleagues (2004, p. 620) acknowledge that children with disabilities "*do* need the services of specially trained professionals to achieve their full potential. They *do* sometimes need altered curricula or adaptations to make their learning possible." However, "we sell students with disabilities short when we pretend that they are not different from typical students. We make the same error when we pretend that they must *not* be expected to put forth extra effort if they are to learn to do some things— or learn to do something in a different way." Like general education, an important aspect of special education should be to challenge students with disabilities "to become all they can be."

One concern about special education involves disproportionate representation of students from minority backgrounds in special education programs and classes (Artiles & others, 2005). The *Diversity in Children's Development* interlude addresses this issue.

least restrictive environment (LRE) The concept that a child with a disability must be educated in a setting that is as similar as possible to the one in which children who do not have a disability are educated.

inclusion Educating a child with special education needs full-time in the general school program.

Diversity in Children's Development

DISPROPORTIONATE REPRESENTATION OF MINORITY STUDENTS IN SPECIAL EDUCATION

The U.S. Office of Education (2000) has three concerns about the overrepresentation of minority students in special education programs and classes:

- Students may be unserved or receive services that do not meet their needs.
- Students may be misclassified or inappropriately labeled.
- Placement in special education classes may be a form of discrimination.

African American students are overrepresented in special education—15 percent of the U.S. student population is African American, but 20 percent of special education students are African American. In some disabilities, the discrepancies are even greater. For example, African American students represent 32 percent of the students in programs for mild mental retardation, 29 percent in programs for moderate mental retardation, and 24 percent in programs for serious emotional disturbance.

However, it is not just a simple matter of overrepresentation of certain minority groups in special education. Latino children may be underidentified in the categories of mental retardation and emotional disturbance.

More appropriate inclusion of minority students in special education is a complex problem and requires the creation of a successful school experience for all students. Recommendations for reducing disproportionate representation in special education include (Burnette, 1998):

- Reviewing school practices to identify and address factors that might contribute to school difficulties
- Forming policy-making groups that include community members and promote partnerships with service agencies and cultural organizations
- Helping families get social, medical, mental health, and other support services
- Training more teachers from minority backgrounds and providing all teachers with more extensive course work and training in educating children with disabilities and diversity issues

---

REVIEW AND REFLECT ► LEARNING GOAL 3

③ Summarize information about children with disabilities.

Review
- Who are children with disabilities?
- What are some characteristics of the range of children's disabilities?
- What are some important issues in the education of children with disabilities?

Reflect
- Think back to your own schooling and how students with learning disabilities were or were not diagnosed. Were you aware of such individuals in your classes? Were they given special attention by teachers and/or specialists? You may know one or more individuals with a learning disability. Interview them about their school experiences. Ask them what they think could have been done better to help them with their disability.

REACH YOUR LEARNING GOALS

1 WHAT CHANGES TAKE PLACE IN BODY GROWTH, THE BRAIN, AND MOTOR DEVELOPMENT? *Discuss changes in body growth, the brain, and motor development in middle and late childhood.*

Skeletal and Muscular Systems

- The period of middle and late childhood involves slow, consistent growth. During this period, children grow an average of 2 to 3 inches a year. Muscle mass and strength gradually increase. Among the most pronounced changes are decreases in head circumference, waist circumference, and leg length in relation to body height.

The Brain

- Changes in the brain continue to occur in middle and late childhood, and these changes, such as increased myelination, are linked to improvements in cognitive functioning. In particular, pathways involving the prefrontal cortex increase—changes that are related to improved attention, reasoning, and cognitive control. During middle and late childhood, less diffusion and more focal activation occurs in the prefrontal cortex, a change that is associated with an increase in cognitive control.

Motor Development

- During the middle and late childhood years, motor development becomes much smoother and more coordinated. Children gain greater control over their bodies and can sit and attend for longer periods of time. However, their lives should be activity-oriented and very active. Gross motor skills are expanded, and children refine such skills as hitting a tennis ball, skipping rope, or balancing on a beam. Increased myelination of the nervous system is reflected in improved fine motor skills, such as handwriting development and playing a difficult piece on a musical instrument. Boys are usually better at gross motor skills, girls at fine motor skills.

2 WHAT ARE THE CENTRAL ISSUES IN CHILDREN'S HEALTH? *Characterize children's health in middle and late childhood.*

Nutrition

- In the middle and late childhood years, weight doubles, and considerable energy is expended in motor activities. To support their growth, children need to consume more calories than when they were younger. A balanced diet is important. A special concern is that too many children fill up on "empty calories" that are high in sugar, starch, and excess fat. A healthy breakfast promotes higher energy and better alertness in school.

Exercise and Sports

- Every indication suggests that children in the United States are not getting enough exercise. Television viewing, parents being poor role models for exercise, and inadequate physical education classes in schools are among the culprits. Children's participation in sports can have positive or negative consequences.

Overweight Children

- An increasing number of U.S. children are overweight, and being overweight in middle and late childhood substantially increases the risk of being overweight in adolescence and adulthood. Factors linked with being overweight in childhood include heredity, blood chemistry, and environmental contexts. Being overweight in childhood is related to a number of problems. Diet, exercise, and behavior modification are recommended in helping children to lose weight.

| Diseases | • Cancer is the second leading cause of death in children (after accidents). Childhood cancers have a different profile than adult cancers. Diabetes is also a common disease in childhood. Cardiovascular disease is uncommon in children, but the precursors to adult cardiovascular disease are often already apparent in children. Asthma is the most common chronic disease in U.S. children. |

• Cancer is the second leading cause of death in children (after accidents). Childhood cancers have a different profile than adult cancers. Diabetes is also a common disease in childhood. Cardiovascular disease is uncommon in children, but the precursors to adult cardiovascular disease are often already apparent in children. Asthma is the most common chronic disease in U.S. children.

Accidents and Injuries

• The most common cause of severe injury and death in childhood is motor vehicle accidents.

3 WHAT ARE THE PREVALENT DISABILITIES IN CHILDREN? *Summarize information about children with disabilities.*

Who Are Children with Disabilities?

• An estimated 10 percent of U.S. children receive special education or related services. More than 40 percent of these children are classified as having a learning disability. Substantial percentages also are represented by children who are mentally retarded, children with speech and language disorders, and children with serious emotional disturbance. The term "children with disabilities" is now recommended rather than "handicapped children." This is intended to focus the emphasis more on the child than the disability.

The Range of Disabilities

• Children's disabilities cover a wide range and include learning disabilities, ADHD, speech disorders, sensory disorders, physical disorders, emotional and behavioral disorders, and autism spectrum disorders. A learning disability includes three components: (1) a minimum IQ level; (2) a significant difficulty in a school-related area (especially reading or mathematics); and (3) exclusion of only severe emotional disorders, second-language background, sensory disabilities, and/or specific neurological deficits. Dyslexia is a category of learning disabilities involving a severe impairment in the ability to read and spell. Dyscalculia, also known as developmental arithmetic disorder, is a learning disability that involves difficulty in math computation. Diagnosing whether a child has a learning disability is often difficult. Various causes of learning disabilities have been proposed. Interventions with children who have a learning disability often focus on improving reading skills. Attention deficit hyperactivity disorder (ADHD) is a disability in which children consistently show problems in one or more of these areas: inattention, hyperactivity, and impulsivity. Speech disorders include articulation disorders, voice disorders, and fluency disorders. Sensory disorders include visual and hearing impairments. Physical disorders that children may have include orthopedic impairments and cerebral palsy. Emotional and behavioral disorders consist of serious, persistent problems that involve relationships, aggression, depression, fears associated with personal or school matters, as well as other inappropriate socioemotional characteristics. Autism is a severe disorder with an onset in the first three years of life, and it involves abnormalities in social relationships and communication. It also is characterized by repetitive behaviors. The current consensus is that autism involves an organic brain dysfunction. Autism spectrum disorders (ASD) is an increasingly popular term that refers to a broad range of autism disorders including the classical, severe form of autism, as well as Asperger syndrome.

Educational Issues

- Beginning in the 1960s and 1970s, the educational rights for children with disabilities were laid down. In 1975, Public Law 94-142 required all children to be given a free, appropriate public education. In 1990, Public Law 94-142 was renamed and called the Individuals with Disabilities Education Act (IDEA). Children who are thought to have a disability are evaluated to determine their eligibility for services. An individualized education plan (IEP) is a written plan that spells out a program tailored to the child with a disability. The concept of a least restrictive environment (LRE) is contained in the IDEA. The term inclusion means educating children with disabilities full-time in the general school program. The trend is toward using inclusion more.

KEY TERMS

type I diabetes 367
type II diabetes 367
asthma 369
learning disability 371
dyslexia 371
dyscalculia 372
attention deficit
    hyperactivity disorder
    (ADHD) 373

articulation disorders 375
voice disorders 375
fluency disorders 375
low vision 376
educationally blind 376
oral approaches 376
manual approaches 376
orthopedic impairments 376
cerebral palsy 377

emotional and behavioral
    disorders 377
autism spectrum disorders
    (ASD) 377
autistic disorder 377
Asperger syndrome 377
Public Law 94-142 378
Individuals with Disabilities
    Education Act (IDEA) 378

instructional technology 379
assistive technology 379
individualized education
    plan (IEP) 379
least restrictive environment
    (LRE) 380
inclusion 380

KEY PEOPLE

Linda Siegel 371   James Kauffman 380

MAKING A DIFFERENCE

Nurturing Children's Physical Development and Health

What are some good strategies for supporting children's physical development and health in the middle and late childhood years?

- *Elementary school children should participate mainly in active rather than passive activities.* This especially means reducing TV watching and increasing participation in such activities as swimming, skating, and bicycling.
- *Parents should monitor children's eating behavior.* Children need more calories now than when they were younger. However, a special concern is the increasing number of obese children. They need to have a medical checkup, to revise their diet, and to participate in a regular exercise program.

- *Elementary schools need to develop more and better physical education programs.* Only about one of every three elementary school children participates in a physical education program. Many of those who do aren't exercising much during the program.
- *Parents need to engage in physical activities that they can enjoy together with their children.* These activities include running, bicycling, hiking, and swimming.
- *Parents should try to make their children's experience in sports positive.* This means not stressing a win-at-all-costs philosophy.
- *Parents should help children avoid accidents and injuries.* Educate children about the hazards of risk taking and the improper use of equipment.

RESOURCES FOR IMPROVING CHILDREN'S LIVES

Children's HeartLink

www.childrensheartlink.org

This organization provides treatment for needy children with heart disease and support for rheumatic fever prevention programs. It also supports the education of foreign medical professionals and provides technical advice and medical equipment and supplies.

The Council for Exceptional Children (CEC)

www.cec.sped.org

The CEC maintains an information center on the education of children and adolescents with disabilities and publishes materials on a wide variety of topics.

Learning Disabilities Association of America (LDA)

www.ldaamerica/org

The LDA provides education and support for parents of children with learning disabilities, interested professionals, and others. More than 500 chapters are in operation nationwide, offering information services, pamphlets, and book recommendations.

E-LEARNING TOOLS

Connect to **www.mhhe.com/santrockc10** to research the answers and complete these exercises. In addition, you'll find a number of other resources and valuable study tools for Chapter 11, "Physical Development in Middle and Late Childhood," on this Web site.

Taking It to the Net

1. Christina's daughter, Carmella, is having a difficult time in school. Her teacher says Carmella is unable to stay focused on her schoolwork, and she often gets into trouble for speaking out of turn and for getting out of her seat. The teacher recommends to Christina that her daughter be tested for ADHD. Christina has some reservations; she recently saw a television show about the overdiagnosis of ADHD. Is ADHD overdiagnosed in children? What are some of the controversies surrounding the ADHD diagnosis? What signs and symptoms characterize ADHD?

2. Morgan, a first-grader, has not been doing well in school. His father, John, doesn't think his poor performance has to do with his intelligence, because Morgan seems to be a fast learner. He does, however, suspect that Morgan might have problems with his vision. What kinds of visual impairments are common among school-age children? What accommodations can be made to improve Morgan's school performance?

3. Monika is a first-year physical education teacher at an elementary school. When she began her job, she was dismayed when she saw how sedentary most of her students were. Are her observations common? What levels of physical fitness do we commonly see in school-age children? How can children benefit from engaging in a physical fitness program?

Health and Well-Being, Parenting, and Education

Build your decision-making skills by trying your hand at the health and well-being, parenting, and education exercises.

Video Clips

The Online Learning Center includes the following videos for this chapter:

1. *Copying Shapes at Age 7—*1125
   More advanced fine motor skills in middle childhood are demonstrated by this 7-year-old. With careful attention he copies a square, a triangle, and a circle.

2. *Obesity—*1714
   Rebecca Roach, Registered Dietician, discusses reasons for the high rate of obesity in children today.

3. *Social Worker's View on Children's Abuse and Neglect—*2000
   An elementary school social worker describes the prevalence of abuse and neglect among children and how, unfortunately, it is difficult to identify until it is too late.

12 Cognitive Development in Middle and Late Childhood

The thirst to know and understand . . .
These are the goods in life's rich hand.

—Sir William Watson
British Poet, 20th Century

CHAPTER OUTLINE	LEARNING GOALS

WHAT IS PIAGET'S THEORY OF COGNITIVE DEVELOPMENT IN MIDDLE AND LATE CHILDHOOD?

Discuss Piaget's stage of concrete operational thought, and apply Piaget's theory to education.

Concrete Operational Thought

Evaluating Piaget's Concrete Operational Stage

Applications to Education

WHAT IS THE NATURE OF CHILDREN'S INFORMATION PROCESSING?

Describe changes in information processing in middle and late childhood.

Memory

Thinking

Metacognition

HOW CAN CHILDREN'S INTELLIGENCE BE DESCRIBED?

Characterize children's intelligence.

Intelligence and Its Assessment

Types of Intelligence

Interpreting Differences in IQ Scores

Extremes of Intelligence

WHAT CHANGES IN LANGUAGE DEVELOPMENT OCCUR IN MIDDLE AND LATE CHILDHOOD? 4

Summarize language development in middle and late childhood.

Vocabulary, Grammar, and Metalinguistic Awareness

Reading

Bilingualism and Second-Language Learning

WHAT CHARACTERIZES CHILDREN'S ACHIEVEMENT? 5

Explain the development of achievement in children.

Extrinsic and Intrinsic Motivation

Mastery Motivation and Mindset

Self-Efficacy

Goal Setting, Planning, and Self-Regulation

Social Relationships and Contexts

Images of Children's Development
Marva Collins, Challenging Children to Achieve

On the first day of school, second-grade Chicago teacher Marva Collins tells her students, many of whom are repeating the second grade,

> "I know most of you can't spell your name. You don't know the alphabet, you don't know how to read, you don't know homonyms or how to syllabicate. I promise you that you will. None of you has ever failed. School may have failed you. Well, goodbye to failure, children. Welcome to success. You will read hard books in here and understand what you read. You will write every day. . . . But you must help me to help you. If you don't give anything, don't expect anything. Success is not coming to you, you must come to it." (Dweck, 2006, pp. 188–189)

Her second-grade students usually have to start off with the lowest level of reader available, but by the end of the school year, most of the students are reading at the fifth-grade level.

Collins takes inner-city children living in low-income, often poverty circumstances and challenges them to be all they can be. She won't accept failure by her students and teaches students to be responsible for their behavior every day of their lives. Collins tells students that being excellent at something is not a one-time thing but a habit, that determination and persistence are what move the world, and that thinking others will make you successful is a sure way to fail.

PREVIEW

We just saw that challenging children to succeed who had been taught to fail is an important theme of Marva Collins' teaching. Later in the chapter, we explore many aspects of achievement. First, though, we examine three main aspects of cognitive changes—Piaget's cognitive developmental theory, information processing, and intelligence—that characterize middle and late childhood. Then, following our coverage of language changes, we explore children's achievement.

1 WHAT IS PIAGET'S THEORY OF COGNITIVE DEVELOPMENT IN MIDDLE AND LATE CHILDHOOD?

| Concrete Operational Thought | Evaluating Piaget's Concrete Operational Stage | Applications to Education |

According to Piaget (1952), the preschool child's thought is preoperational. Preschool children can form stable concepts, and they have begun to reason, but their thinking is flawed by egocentrism and magical belief systems. As we discussed in Chapter 9, however, Piaget may have underestimated the cognitive skills of preschool children. Some researchers argue that under the right conditions, young children may display abilities that are characteristic of Piaget's next stage of cognitive development, the stage of concrete operational thought (Gelman, 1969). Here we cover the characteristics of concrete operational thought, an evaluation of Piaget's portrait of this stage, and applications of Piaget's ideas to education.

Concrete Operational Thought

Piaget proposed that the *concrete operational stage* lasts from approximately 7 to 11 years of age. In this stage, children can perform concrete operations, and they can reason logically as long as reasoning can be applied to specific or concrete examples. Remember that *operations* are mental actions that are reversible, and *concrete operations* are operations that are applied to real, concrete objects.

The conservation tasks described in Chapter 9 indicate whether children are capable of concrete operations. For example, recall that in one task involving conservation of matter, the child is presented with two identical balls of clay. The experimenter rolls one ball into a long, thin shape; the other remains in its original ball shape. The child is then asked if there is more clay in the ball or in the long, thin piece of clay. By the time children reach the age of 7 or 8, most answer that the amount of clay is the same. To answer this problem correctly, children have to imagine the clay rolling back into a ball. This type of imagination involves a reversible mental action applied to a real, concrete object. Concrete operations allow the child to consider several characteristics rather than focus on a single property of an object. In the clay example, the preoperational child is likely to focus on height *or* width. The concrete operational child coordinates information about both dimensions.

What other abilities are characteristic of children who have reached the concrete operational stage? One important skill is the ability to classify or divide things into different sets or subsets and to consider their interrelationships. Consider the family tree of four generations that is shown in Figure 12.1 (Furth & Wachs, 1975). This family tree suggests that the grandfather (A) has three children (B, C, and D), each of whom has two children (E through J), and that one of these children (J) has three children (K, L, and M). A child who comprehends the classification system can move up and down a level, across a level, and up and down and across within the system. The concrete operational child understands that person J can at the same time be father, brother, and grandson, for example.

Children who have reached the concrete operational stage are also capable of **seriation,** which is the ability to order stimuli along a quantitative dimension (such as length). To see if students can serialize, a teacher might haphazardly place eight sticks of different lengths on a table. The teacher then asks the students to order the sticks by length. Many young children end up with two or three small groups of "big" sticks or "little" sticks, rather than a correct ordering of all eight sticks. Another mistaken strategy they use is to evenly line up the tops of the sticks but ignore the bottoms. The concrete operational thinker simultaneously understands that each stick must be longer than the one that precedes it and shorter than the one that follows it.

Another aspect of reasoning about the relations between classes is **transitivity,** which is the ability to logically combine relations to understand certain conclusions. In this case, consider three sticks (A, B, and C) of differing lengths. A is the longest, B is intermediate in length, and C is the shortest. Does the child understand that if A is longer than B and B is longer than C, then A is longer than C? In Piaget's theory, concrete operational thinkers do; preoperational thinkers do not.

Evaluating Piaget's Concrete Operational Stage

Has Piaget's portrait of the concrete operational child stood the test of research? According to Piaget, various aspects of a stage should emerge at the same time.

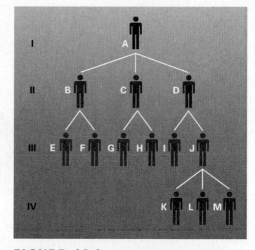

FIGURE 12.1 Classification: An Important Ability in Concrete Operational Thought A family tree of four generations (*I to IV*): The preoperational child has trouble classifying the members of the four generations; the concrete operational child can classify the members vertically, horizontally, and obliquely (up and down and across). For example, the concrete operational child understands that a family member can be a son, a brother, and a father, all at the same time.

seriation The concrete operation that involves ordering stimuli along a quantitative dimension (such as length).

transitivity The ability to logically combine relations to understand certain conclusions.

An outstanding teacher, and education in the logic of science and mathematics, are important cultural experiences that promote the development of operational thought. *Might Piaget have underestimated the roles of culture and schooling in children's cognitive development?*

In fact, however, some concrete operational abilities do not appear in synchrony. For example, children do not learn to conserve at the same time they learn to cross-classify.

Furthermore, education and culture exert stronger influences on children's development than Piaget maintained (Cole, 2005, 2006; Greenfield, Suzuki, & Rothstein-Fisch, 2006). Some preoperational children can be trained to reason at a concrete operational stage. And the age at which children acquire conservation skills is related to how much practice their culture provides in these skills. Among Wolof children in the West African nation of Senegal, for example, only 50 percent of the 10- to 13-year-olds understood the principle of conservation (Greenfield, 1966). Comparable studies among cultures in central Australia, New Guinea (an island north of Australia), the Amazon jungle region of Brazil, and rural Sardinia (an island off the coast of Italy) yielded similar results (Dasen, 1977).

Thus, although Piaget was a giant in the field of developmental psychology, his conclusions about the concrete operational stage have been challenged. In Chapter 15, after examining the final stage in his theory of cognitive development, we evaluate Piaget's contributions and the criticisms of his theory.

Neo-Piagetians argue that Piaget got some things right but that his theory needs considerable revision. They place greater emphasis on how children use attention, memory, and strategies to process information (Case, 1987, 1999; Case & Mueller, 2001; Morra & others, 2007). According to neo-Piagetians, a more accurate portrayal of children's thinking requires attention to children's strategies, the speed at which children process information, the particular task involved, and the division of problems into smaller, more precise steps (Demetriou, 2001). These are issues addressed by the information-processing approach, and we discuss some of them later in this chapter.

Another alternative to concrete operational thought comes from Vygotsky. As we discussed in Chapter 9, Vygotksy, like Piaget, held that children construct their knowledge of the world. But Vygotsky did not propose stages of cognitive development, and he emphasized the importance of social interaction, the social contexts of learning, and the young child's use of language to plan, guide, and monitor behavior (Cole & Gajda Maschko, 2007; Daniels, 2007).

Applications to Education

Piaget was not an educator, but he provided a sound conceptual framework for viewing learning and education. Following are some ideas in Piaget's theory that can be applied to teaching children (Elkind, 1976; Heuwinkel, 1996):

1. *Take a constructivist approach.* Piaget emphasized that children learn best when they are active and seek solutions for themselves. Piaget opposed teaching methods that treat children as passive receptacles. The educational implication of Piaget's view is that, in all subjects, students learn best by making discoveries, reflecting on them, and discussing them, rather than blindly imitating the teacher or doing things by rote.

2. *Facilitate, rather than direct, learning.* Effective teachers design situations that allow students to learn by doing. These situations promote students' thinking and discovery. Teachers listen, watch, and question students, to help them gain better understanding. Don't just examine what students think and the product of their learning. Rather, carefully observe them and find out how they think. Ask relevant questions to stimulate their thinking, and ask them to explain their answers.

neo-Piagetians Developmentalists who have elaborated on Piaget's theory, giving more emphasis to information-processing, strategies, and precise cognitive steps.

3. *Consider the child's knowledge and level of thinking.* Students do not come to class with empty minds. They have many ideas about the physical and natural world. They have concepts of space, time, quantity, and causality. These ideas differ from the ideas of adults. Teachers need to interpret what a student is saying and respond in a way that is not too far from the student's level. Also, Piaget suggested that it is important to examine children's mistakes in thinking, not just what they get correct, to help guide them to a higher level of understanding.

4. *Use ongoing assessment.* Individually constructed meanings cannot be measured by standardized tests. Math and language portfolios (which contain work in progress as well as finished products), individual conferences in which students discuss their thinking strategies, and students' written and verbal explanations of their reasoning can be used to evaluate progress.

5. *Promote the student's intellectual health.* When Piaget came to lecture in the United States, he was asked, "What can I do to get my child to a higher cognitive stage sooner?" He was asked this question so often here compared with other countries that he called it "the American question." For Piaget, children's learning should occur naturally. Children should not be pushed and pressured into achieving too much too early in their development, before they are ready.

6. *Turn the classroom into a setting of exploration and discovery.* What do actual classrooms look like when the teachers adopt Piaget's views? Several first- and second-grade math classrooms provide some examples (Kamii, 1985, 1989). The teachers emphasize students' own exploration and discovery. The classrooms are less structured than what we think of as a typical classroom. Workbooks and predetermined assignments are not used. Rather, the teachers observe the students' interests and natural participation in activities to determine the course of learning. For example, a math lesson might be constructed around counting the day's lunch money or dividing supplies among students. Often, games are used to stimulate mathematical thinking. For example, a version of dominoes teaches children about even-numbered combinations; a variation on tic-tac-toe replaces *X*s and *O*s with numbers. Teachers encourage peer interaction during the lessons and games because students' different viewpoints can contribute to advances in thinking.

What are some educational strategies that can be derived from Piaget's theory?

Educators have also applied Vygotsky's ideas (Alvarez & del Rio, 2007; Daniels, 2007). His theory suggests that teachers should encourage elementary school children to internalize and regulate their talk to themselves. They should provide students with opportunities to experience learning in real-world settings—for example, instead of memorizing math formulas, students should work on math problems with real-world implications. In Chapter 9, we described other ways in which teachers have applied Vygotsky's ideas.

What does a Vygotskian classroom look like? The Kamehameha Elementary Education Program (KEEP) is based on Vygotsky's theory (Tharp, 1994). Many of the learning activities take place in small groups. The key element in this program is use of the zone of proximal development (the range of tasks that are too difficult for the child to master alone but that can be learned with guidance and assistance from more-skilled peers and adults). Children might read a story and then interpret its meaning. Scaffolding is used to improve children's literary skills. The instructor asks questions, responds to students' queries, and builds on the ideas that students generate. Thousands of children from low-income families have attended KEEP public schools—in Hawaii, on an Arizona Navajo Native American reservation, and in Los Angeles. Compared with a control group of non-KEEP children, the KEEP children participated more actively in classroom discussion, were more attentive in class, and had higher reading achievement (Tharp & Gallimore, 1988).

2 WHAT IS THE NATURE OF CHILDREN'S INFORMATION PROCESSING?

Memory	Thinking	Metacognition

During middle and late childhood, most children dramatically improve their ability to sustain and control attention (Savage & others, 2006). As we discussed in Chapter 9, they pay more attention to task-relevant stimuli such as teacher instructions than to salient stimuli such as the colors in the teacher's attire. Other changes in information processing during middle and late childhood involve memory, thinking, and metacognition. In the following pages, we examine each of these areas.

Memory

In Chapter 9, we concluded that short-term memory increases considerably during early childhood but after the age of 7 does not show as much increase. **Long-term memory,** a relatively permanent and unlimited type of memory, increases with age during middle and late childhood. In part, improvements in memory reflect children's increased knowledge and their increased use of strategies to retain information (Schraw, 2006).

Knowledge and Expertise Much of the research on the role of knowledge in memory has compared experts and novices (Ericsson & others, 2006). *Experts* have acquired extensive knowledge about a particular content area; this knowledge influences what they notice and how they organize, represent, and interpret information. This in turn affects their ability to remember, reason, and solve problems. When individuals have expertise about a particular subject, their memory also tends to be good regarding material related to that subject (Gobet & Charness, 2006).

For example, one study found that 10- and 11-year-olds who were experienced chess players ("experts") were able to remember more information about chess pieces than college students who were not chess players ("novices") (Chi, 1978) (see Figure 12.2). In contrast, when the college students were presented with other stimuli, they were able to remember them better than the children were. Thus, the children's expertise in chess gave them superior memories, but only in chess.

There are developmental changes in expertise. Older children usually have more expertise about a subject than younger children do, which can contribute to their better memory for the subject.

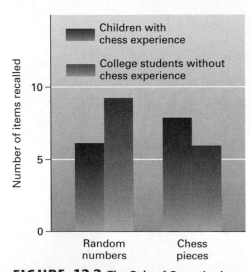

FIGURE 12.2 **The Role of Expertise in Memory** Notice that when 10- to 11- year-old children and college students were asked to remember a string of random numbers that had been presented to them, the college students fared better. However, the 10- to 11-year-olds who had experience playing chess ("experts") had better memory for the location of chess pieces on a chess board than college students with no chess experience ("novices") (Chi, 1978).

long-term memory A relatively permanent type of memory that holds huge amounts of information for a long period of time.

Strategies   If we know anything at all about long-term memory, it is that long-term memory depends on the learning activities individuals engage in when learning and remembering information (Block & Pressley, 2007; Siegler, 2006). Recall from Chapter 9 that *strategies* consist of deliberate mental activities to improve the processing of information. They do not occur automatically but require effort and work. Strategies, which are also called *control processes,* are under the learner's conscious control and can be used to improve memory (Alexander, 2006). Two important strategies are creating mental images and elaborating on information (Kellogg, 2007; Murray, 2007).

Mental imagery can help even young schoolchildren to remember pictures (Schneider & Pressley, 1997). However, for remembering verbal information, mental imagery works better for older children than for younger children (Schneider, 2004). In one study, 20 sentences were presented to first- through sixth-grade children to remember—such as "The angry bird shouted at the white dog" and "The policeman painted the circus tent on a windy day" (Pressley & others, 1987). Children were randomly assigned either to an imagery condition, in which they were told to make a picture in their head for each sentence, or to a control condition, in which they were told just to try hard. The instructions to form images helped older elementary school children (fifth-graders) but did not help the younger elementary school children (second-graders) (see Figure 12.3).

Elaboration is an important strategy that involves engaging in more extensive processing of information. When individuals engage in elaboration, their memory benefits (Terry, 2006). Thinking of examples and referencing one's self are good ways to elaborate information. Thinking about personal associations with information makes the information more meaningful and helps children to remember it. For example, if the word *win* is on a list of words a child is asked to remember, the child might think of the last time he won a bicycle race with a friend.

The use of elaboration changes developmentally (Pressley & Harris, 2006; Schneider, 2004). Adolescents are more likely to use elaboration spontaneously than are children. Elementary school children can be taught to use elaboration strategies on a learning task, but they will be less likely than adolescents to use the strategies on other learning tasks in the future. Nonetheless, verbal elaboration can be an effective strategy for processing information even for young elementary school children.

Fuzzy Trace Theory   Might something other than knowledge and strategies be responsible for the improvement in memory during the elementary school years? Charles Brainerd and Valerie Reyna (1993; Reyna, 2004; Reyna & Brainerd, 1995) argue that fuzzy traces account for much of this improvement. Their **fuzzy trace theory** states that memory is best understood by considering two types of memory representations: (1) verbatim memory trace, and (2) gist. The *verbatim memory trace* consists of the precise details of the information, whereas *gist* refers to the central idea of the information. When gist is used, fuzzy traces are built up. Although individuals of all ages extract gist, young children tend to store and retrieve verbatim traces. At some point during the early elementary school years, children begin to use gist more and, according to the theory, this contributes to the improved memory and reasoning of older children because fuzzy traces are more enduring and less likely to be forgotten than verbatim traces.

Thinking

Three important aspects of thinking are being able to think critically, creatively, and scientifically.

Critical Thinking   Currently, there is considerable interest among psychologists and educators in critical thinking (Halpern, 2007; Sternberg, Roediger, & Halpern, 2007). **Critical thinking** involves thinking reflectively and productively, as well as

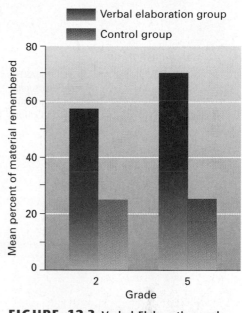

FIGURE 12.3 Verbal Elaboration and Memory Both second- and fifth-grade children remembered words better when they constructed a meaningful sentence for the word (verbal elaboration group) than when they merely heard the word and its definition (control group). The verbal elaboration worked better for the fifth-graders than the second-graders.

elaboration An important strategy that involves engaging in more extensive processing of information.

fuzzy trace theory States that memory is best understood by considering two types of memory representations: (1) verbatim memory trace and (2) gist. In this theory, older children's better memory is attributed to the fuzzy traces created by extracting the gist of information.

critical thinking Thinking reflectively and productively, as well as evaluating the evidence.

I think, therefore I am.

—RENE DESCARTES
*French Philosopher
and Mathematician,
17th Century*

S.GROSS

"For God's sake, think! Why is he being so nice to you?"
Copyright © The New Yorker Collection 1998 Sam Gross from cartoonbank.com. All Rights Reserved.

evaluating evidence. In this book, the second part of the Review and Reflect sections of each chapter challenge you to think critically about a topic or an issue related to the discussion.

Jacqueline and Martin Brooks (2001) lament that few schools really teach students to think critically and develop a deep understanding of concepts. Deep understanding occurs when students are stimulated to rethink previously held ideas. In Brooks and Brooks' view, schools spend too much time getting students to give a single correct answer in an imitative way, rather than encouraging them to expand their thinking by coming up with new ideas and rethinking earlier conclusions. They observe that too often teachers ask students to recite, define, describe, state, and list, rather than to analyze, infer, connect, synthesize, criticize, create, evaluate, think, and rethink. Many successful students complete their assignments, do well on tests and get good grades, yet they don't ever learn to think critically and deeply. They think superficially, staying on the surface of problems rather than stretching their minds and becoming deeply engaged in meaningful thinking.

Creative Thinking Cognitively competent children not only think critically, but also creatively (Kaufman, & Baer, 2006; Runco, 2006). **Creative thinking** is the ability to think in novel and unusual ways and to come up with good, unique solutions to problems. Thus, intelligence and creativity are not the same thing. This difference was recognized by J. P. Guilford (1967), who distinguished between **convergent thinking,** which produces one correct answer and characterizes the kind of thinking that is required on conventional tests of intelligence, and **divergent thinking,** which produces many different answers to the same question and characterizes creativity. For example, a typical item on a conventional intelligence test is "How many quarters will you get in return for 60 dimes?" In contrast, the following question has many possible answers: "What image comes to mind when you hear the phrase 'sitting alone in a dark room' or 'some unique uses for a paper clip'?"

It is important to recognize that children will show more creativity in some domains than others (Runco, 2006). A child who shows creative thinking skills in mathematics may not exhibit these skills in art, for example.

An important goal for parents and educators is to help children become more creative. The following *Caring for Children* interlude examines some recommendations for ways to accomplish this goal.

Caring for Children

creative thinking The ability to think in novel and unusual ways and to come up with good, unique solutions to problems.

convergent thinking Thinking that produces one correct answer and is characteristic of the kind of thinking tested by standardized intelligence tests.

divergent thinking Thinking that produces many answers to the same question and is characteristic of creativity.

brainstorming A technique in which individuals are encouraged to come up with creative ideas in a group, play off each other's ideas, and say practically whatever comes to mind.

STRATEGIES FOR INCREASING CHILDREN'S CREATIVE THINKING

Some strategies for increasing children's creative thinking include the following:

- *Have children engage in brainstorming and come up with as many ideas as possible.* **Brainstorming** is a technique in which children are encouraged to come up with creative ideas in a group, play off each other's ideas, and say practically whatever comes to mind. However, one review of research on brainstorming concluded that for many individuals, working alone can generate more ideas and better ideas than working in groups (Rickards & deCock, 2003). One reason for this is that some individuals in groups loaf, while others do most of the creative thinking. Nonetheless, there may be benefits to brainstorming, such as team building.

Whether in a group or individually, a good creativity strategy is to come up with as many new ideas as possible. The more ideas children produce, the better their chance of creating something unique. Famous twentieth-century Spanish artist Pablo Picasso produced more than 20,000 works of art; not all of them were masterpieces. Creative children are not afraid of failing or getting something wrong. They may go down twenty dead-end streets before they come up with an innovative idea. They recognize that it's okay to win some and lose some. They are willing to take risks, just as Picasso was.

What are some good strategies for guiding children in thinking more creatively?

- *Provide children with environments that stimulate creativity.* Some settings nourish creativity; others depress it (Csikszentmihalyi & Nakamura, 2006). People who encourage children's creativity often rely on children's natural curiosity. They provide exercises and activities that stimulate children to find insightful solutions to problems, rather than asking a lot of questions that require rote answers. Adults also encourage creativity by taking children to locations where creativity is valued. Science, discovery, and children's museums may offer rich opportunities to stimulate children's creativity (Gardner, 1993).

- *Don't overcontrol.* Teresa Amabile (1993) says that telling children exactly how to do things leaves them feeling that any originality is a mistake and any exploration is a waste of time. Adults are less likely to destroy children's natural curiosity if they allow children to select their own interests and support their inclinations rather than dictating activities for the children. Amabile also believes that, when adults constantly hover over children, the children feel they are being watched while they are working. When children are under constant surveillance, their creative risk taking and adventurous spirit wane. Another strategy that can harm creativity is to have grandiose expectations for a child's performance and expect the child to do something perfectly, according to Amabile.

- *Encourage internal motivation.* The excessive use of prizes, such as gold stars, money, or toys, can stifle creativity by undermining the intrinsic pleasure children derive from creative activities. Creative children's motivation is the satisfaction generated by the work itself. Competition for prizes and formal evaluations often undermine intrinsic motivation and creativity (Amabile & Hennesey, 1992).

- *Introduce children to creative people.* Think about the identity of the most creative people in your community. Teachers can invite these people to their classrooms and ask them to describe what helps them become creative or to demonstrate their creative skills. A writer, poet, musician, scientist, and many others can bring their props and productions to the class, turning it into a theater for stimulating students' creativity.

Scientific Thinking Children's problem solving is often compared to that of scientists. Both children and scientists ask fundamental questions about the nature of reality. Both also seek answers to problems that often seem utterly trivial or unanswerable to other people (such as "Why is the sky blue?"). And like scientists, children often emphasize causal mechanisms (Frye & others, 1996).

This "child as scientist" metaphor has led researchers to ask whether children generate hypotheses, perform experiments, and reach conclusions concerning the meaning of their data in ways resembling those of scientists (Clinchy, Mansfield, &

Luis Recalde holds up a seaweed specimen in one of the hands-on, high-interest learning contexts he creates for students. Recalde, a fourth- and fifth-grade science teacher in New Haven, Connecticut, uses every opportunity to make science facinating for students to learn. To help students get a better sense of what it is like to be a scientist, he brings lab coats to the classroom for students to wear. He often gives up his vacation time to help students with science projects.

Schott, 1995). In comparing children and scientists, researchers have found that preadolescents have much greater difficulty in separating their prior theories from the evidence that they have obtained. Often, when they try to learn about new phenomena, children maintain their old theories regardless of the evidence (Kuhn, Schauble, & Garcia-Mila, 1992).

Another difference between scientists and children is that children are influenced more by happenstance events than by the overall pattern of occurrences (Kuhn, 2004; Kuhn, Amsel, & O'Laughlin, 1988). Children also have difficulty designing new experiments that can distinguish conclusively among alternative causes. Instead, they tend to bias the experiments in favor of whichever hypothesis they began with, and sometimes they will see the results as supporting their original hypothesis even when the results directly contradict it (Schauble, 1990). Thus, although there are important similarities between children and scientists, there are also important differences in the degree to which they can separate theory and evidence and in their ability to design conclusive experiments (Lehrer & Schauble, 2006).

Scientists typically engage in certain kinds of thinking and behavior. For example, they regularly make careful observations; collect, organize, and analyze data; measure, graph, and understand spatial relations; pay attention to and regulate their own thinking; and know when and how to apply their knowledge to solve problems (Chapman, 2000).

These skills, which are essential to the practice of science, are not routinely taught in schools, especially elementary schools (Gullagher, 2007; Victor, Kellough, & Tai, 2008). As a result, many students are not competent at them. Many scientists and educators believe that schools need to guide students in learning how to use these skills (Bybee, Powell, & Trowbridge, 2008; Moyer, Hackett, & Everett, 2007).

Metacognition

One expert in children's thinking, Deanna Kuhn (1999), believes that to help students become better thinkers, schools should pay more attention to helping students develop skills that involve knowing about their own (and others') thinking. In other words, schools should do more to develop **metacognition,** which is cognition about cognition, or thinking about thinking (Flavell, 1999, 2004; Flavell, Miller, & Miller, 2002).

The majority of developmental studies classified as "metacognitive" have focused on *metamemory,* or knowledge about memory (DeMarie, Abshier, & Ferron, 2001). This includes general knowledge about memory, such as knowing that recognition tests are easier than recall tests. It also encompasses knowledge about one's own memory, such as a student's ability to monitor whether she has studied enough for a test that is coming up next week.

Young children do have some general knowledge about memory. By 5 or 6 years of age, children usually already know that familiar items are easier to learn than unfamiliar ones, that short lists are easier than long ones, that recognition is easier than recall, and that forgetting is more likely to occur over time (Lyon & Flavell, 1993). However, in other ways young children's metamemory is limited. They don't understand that related items are easier to remember than unrelated ones and that remembering the gist of a story is easier than remembering information verbatim (Kreutzer, Leonard, & Flavell, 1975). By the fifth grade, students understand that gist recall is easier than verbatim recall.

Young children also have only limited knowledge about their own memory. They have an inflated opinion of their memory abilities. For example, in one study a majority of young children predicted that they would be able to recall all 10 items on a list of 10 items. When tested for this, none of the young children managed this feat (Flavell, Friedrichs, & Hoyt, 1970). As they move through the elementary

Shown here is cognitive developmentalist John Flavell, who has been a pioneer in providing insights into the way children think. Among his many contributions are conducting numerous research studies that have advanced our understanding of developmental changes in metacognition.

metacognition Cognition about cognition, or thinking about thinking.

school years, children give more realistic evaluations of their memory skills (Schneider & Pressley, 1997).

In addition to metamemory, metacognition includes knowledge about strategies. In the view of Michael Pressley (2003), the key to education is helping students learn a rich repertoire of strategies that result in solutions to problems. Good thinkers routinely use strategies and effective planning to solve problems. Good thinkers also know when and where to use strategies. Understanding when and where to use strategies often results from monitoring the learning situation (Block & Pressley, 2007; Bromley, 2007).

Pressley and his colleagues (Pressley & Hilden, 2006; Pressley & others, 2001, 2003, 2004) have spent considerable time observing strategy instruction by teachers and strategy use by students in elementary and secondary school classrooms. They conclude that strategy instruction is far less complete and intense than what students need in order to learn how to use strategies effectively. They argue that education needs to be restructured so that students are provided with more opportunities to become competent strategic learners.

REVIEW AND REFLECT ▸ LEARNING GOAL 2

2 **Describe changes in information processing in middle and late childhood.**

Review
- What characterizes children's memory in middle and late childhood?
- What is involved in thinking critically, thinking creatively, and thinking scientifically?
- What is metacognition?

Reflect
- When you were in elementary school, did classroom instruction prepare you adequately for critical-thinking tasks? If you were a parent of an 8-year-old, what would you do to guide the child to think more critically and creatively?

3 HOW CAN CHILDREN'S INTELLIGENCE BE DESCRIBED?

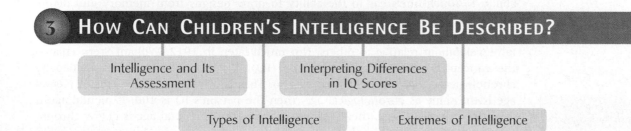

Intelligence and Its Assessment

Interpreting Differences in IQ Scores

Types of Intelligence

Extremes of Intelligence

Twentieth-century English novelist Aldous Huxley said that children are remarkable for their curiosity and intelligence. What did Huxley mean when he used the word *intelligence?* How can intelligence be assessed?

Intelligence and Its Assessment

Parents, teachers, and children themselves are likely to think and talk about children's cognitive abilities in terms different from those we have used so far. Rather than considering a child's skills as a critical thinker or scientific thinker, for example, they might ask whether a child is "smart" or intelligent.

Just what is meant by the concept of "intelligence"? Some experts describe intelligence as problem-solving skills. Others describe it as the ability to adapt to and

FIGURE 12.4 The Normal Curve and Stanford-Binet IQ Scores

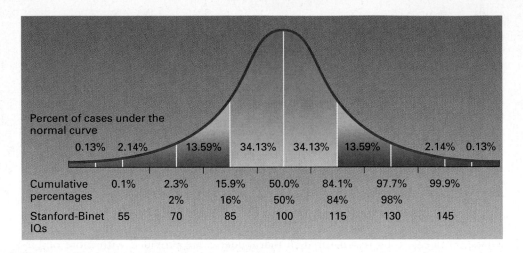

Percent of cases under the normal curve								
0.13%	2.14%		13.59%	34.13%	34.13%	13.59%	2.14%	0.13%
Cumulative percentages	0.1%	2.3%	15.9%	50.0%	84.1%	97.7%	99.9%	
		2%	16%	50%	84%	98%		
Stanford-Binet IQs	55	70	85	100	115	130	145	

learn from life's everyday experiences. Combining these ideas, we can arrive at a definition of **intelligence** as problem-solving skills and the ability to learn from and adapt to life's everyday experiences.

Interest in intelligence has often focused on individual differences and assessment. **Individual differences** are the stable, consistent ways in which people are different from each other. We can talk about individual differences in personality or any other domain, but it is in the domain of intelligence that the most attention has been directed at individual differences. For example, an intelligence test purports to inform us about whether a student can reason better than others who have taken the test. Let's go back in history and see what the first intelligence test was like.

The Binet Tests In 1904, the French Ministry of Education asked psychologist Alfred Binet to devise a method of identifying children who were unable to learn in school. School officials wanted to reduce crowding by placing students who did not benefit from regular classroom teaching in special schools. Binet and his student Theophile Simon developed an intelligence test to meet this request. The test is called the 1905 Scale. It consisted of 30 questions on topics ranging from the ability to touch one's ear to the ability to draw designs from memory and define abstract concepts.

Binet developed the concept of **mental age (MA),** an individual's level of mental development relative to others. Not much later, in 1912, William Stern created the concept of **intelligence quotient (IQ),** a person's mental age divided by chronological age (CA), multiplied by 100. That is: IQ = MA/CA $\times$ 100. If mental age is the same as chronological age, then the person's IQ is 100. If mental age is above chronological age, then IQ is more than 100. If mental age is below chronological age, then IQ is less than 100.

The Binet test has been revised many times to incorporate advances in the understanding of intelligence and intelligence tests. These revisions are called the *Stanford-Binet tests* (Stanford University is where the revisions have been done). By administering the test to large numbers of people of different ages from different backgrounds, researchers have found that scores on the Stanford-Binet approximate a normal distribution (see Figure 12.4). A **normal distribution** is symmetrical, with a majority of the scores falling in the middle of the possible range of scores and few scores appearing toward the extremes of the range.

The current Stanford-Binet is administered individually to people from the age of 2 through the adult years. It includes a variety of items, some of which require verbal responses, others nonverbal responses. For example, items that reflect a 6-year-old's performance on the test include the verbal ability to define at least six words, such as *orange* and *envelope,* as well as the nonverbal ability to trace a path

intelligence Problem-solving skills and the ability to learn from and adapt to the experiences of everyday life.

individual differences The stable, consistent ways in which people are different from each other.

mental age (MA) Binet's measure of an individual's level of mental development, compared with that of others.

intelligence quotient (IQ) A person's mental age divided by chronological age, multiplied by 100.

normal distribution A symmetrical distribution with most scores falling in the middle of the possible range of scores and few scores appearing toward the extremes of the range.

through a maze. Items that reflect an average adult's intelligence include defining words such as *disproportionate* and *regard,* explaining a proverb, and comparing idleness and laziness.

An individual's responses to the Stanford-Binet can be analyzed in terms of four content areas: verbal reasoning, quantitative reasoning, abstract/visual reasoning, and short-term memory. A general composite score is still obtained to reflect overall intelligence. The Stanford-Binet continues to be one of the most widely used tests to assess a student's intelligence (Naglieri, 2000).

The Wechsler Scales   Another set of widely used tests is called the *Wechsler scales,* developed by David Wechsler. They include the Wechsler Preschool and Primary Scale of Intelligence—Third Edition (WPPSI-III) to test children 2 years 6 months to 7 years 3 months of age; the Wechsler Intelligence Scale for Children—Fourth Edition (WISC-IV) for children and adolescents 6 to 16 years of age; and the Wechsler Adult Intelligence Scale—Third Edition (WAIS-III).

Not only do the Wechsler scales provide an overall IQ, but they also yield a number of additional composite scores (for example, the Verbal Comprehension Index, the Perceptual Reasoning Index, the Working Memory Index, and the Processing Speed Index). This allows the examiner to quickly see patterns of strengths and weaknesses in different areas of the student's intelligence. Three of the Wechsler subscales are shown in Figure 12.5.

Types of Intelligence

Is it more appropriate to think of a child's intelligence as a general ability or as a number of specific abilities? Charles Spearman (1927) said that people have both a general intelligence, which he called *g,* and specific types of intelligence, which he called *s.* As early as the 1930s, L. L. Thurstone (1938) said people have seven of these abilities, which he called primary abilities: verbal comprehension, number ability, word fluency, spatial visualization, associative memory, reasoning, and perceptual speed. More recently, Robert Sternberg and Howard Gardner have proposed influential theories that describe specific types of intelligence.

Sternberg's Triarchic Theory   Robert J. Sternberg (1986, 2004, 2006, 2007a, 2008) developed the **triarchic theory of intelligence,** which states that intelligence comes in three forms:

- *Analytical intelligence.* This refers to the ability to analyze, judge, evaluate, compare, and contrast.
- *Creative intelligence.* This consists of the ability to create, design, invent, originate, and imagine.
- *Practical intelligence.* This involves the ability to use, apply, implement, and put ideas into practice.

Sternberg (2002) says that children with different triarchic patterns "look different" in school. Students with high analytic ability tend to be favored in conventional schooling. They often do well under direct instruction, in which the teacher lectures and gives students objective tests. They often are considered to be "smart" students who get good grades, show up in high-level tracks, do well on traditional tests of intelligence and the SAT, and later get admitted to competitive colleges.

Verbal Subscales

Similarities
A child must think logically and abstractly to answer a number of questions about how things might be similar.

Example: "In what way are a lion and a tiger alike?"

Comprehension
This subscale is designed to measure an individual's judgment and common sense.

Example: "What is the advantage of keeping money in a bank?"

Nonverbal Subscales

Block Design
A child must assemble a set of multicolored blocks to match designs that the examiner shows. Visual-motor coordination, perceptual organization, and the ability to visualize spatially are assessed.

Example: "Use the four blocks on the left to make the pattern on the right."

FIGURE 12.5 Sample Subscales of the Wechsler Intelligence Scale for Children (WISC-IV) The Wechsler includes 11 subscales, 6 verbal and 5 nonverbal. Three of the subscales are shown here. Simulated items similar to those found in the *Wechsler Intelligence Scale for Children—Fourth Edition. Copyright © 2003 by Harcourt Assessment, Inc. Reproduced by permission. All rights reserved.* "Wechsler Intelligence Scale for Children" and "WISC" are trademarks of Harcourt Assessment, Inc. registered in the United States of America and/or other jurisdictions.

triarchic theory of intelligence Sternberg's theory that intelligence consists of analytical intelligence, creative intelligence, and practical intelligence.

"You're wise, but you lack tree smarts."
© The New Yorker Collection, 1988, by Donald Reilly from cartoonbank.com. All Rights Reserved. Reprinted with permission.

In contrast, children who are high in creative intelligence often are not on the top rung of their class. Many teachers have expectations about how assignments should be done, and creatively intelligent students may not conform to those expectations. Instead of giving conformist answers, they give unique answers, for which they might get reprimanded or marked down. No teacher wants to discourage creativity, but Sternberg believes that too often a teacher's desire to improve students' knowledge depresses creative thinking.

Like children high in creative intelligence, children who are practically intelligent often do not relate well to the demands of school. However, many of these children do well outside of the classroom's walls. They may have excellent social skills and good common sense. As adults, some become successful managers, entrepreneurs, or politicians, yet they have undistinguished school records.

Gardner's Eight Frames of Mind   Howard Gardner (1983, 1993, 2002; Moran & Gardner, 2006) suggests there are eight types of intelligence, or "frames of mind." These are described here, with examples of the types of vocations in which they are reflected as strengths (Campbell, Campbell, & Dickinson, 2004):

- *Verbal:* the ability to think in words and use language to express meaning (occupations: authors, journalists, speakers)
- *Mathematical:* the ability to carry out mathematical operations (occupations: scientists, engineers, accountants)
- *Spatial:* the ability to think three-dimensionally (occupations: architects, artists, sailors)
- *Bodily-kinesthetic*: the ability to manipulate objects and be physically adept (occupations: surgeons, craftspeople, dancers, athletes)
- *Musical*: a sensitivity to pitch, melody, rhythm, and tone (occupations: composers, musicians, and sensitive listeners)
- *Interpersonal*: the ability to understand and effectively interact with others (occupations: successful teachers, mental health professionals)
- *Intrapersonal*: the ability to understand oneself (occupations: theologians, psychologists)
- *Naturalist:* the ability to observe patterns in nature and understand natural and human-made systems (occupations: farmers, botanists, ecologists, landscapers)

According to Gardner, everyone has all of these intelligences but to varying degrees. As a result, we prefer to learn and process information in different ways. People learn best when they can apply their strong intelligences to the task.

Evaluating the Multiple-Intelligence Approaches   Sternberg's and Gardner's approaches have much to offer. They have stimulated teachers to think more broadly about what makes up children's competencies. And they have motivated educators to develop programs that instruct students in multiple domains. These approaches also have contributed to interest in assessing intelligence and classroom learning in innovative ways, such as by evaluating student portfolios (Kornhaber, Fierros, & Veenema, 2004; Moran & Gardner, 2006).

Still, doubts about multiple-intelligences approaches persist. If musical skill reflects a distinct type of intelligence, some critics ask, why not label the skills of outstanding chess players, prizefighters, writers, politicians, physicians, lawyers, ministers, and poets as types of intelligence? Some critics say that a research base to support the three intelligences of Sternberg or the eight intelligences of Gardner has not yet emerged. A number of psychologists think that the multiple-intelligence views have taken the concept of specific intelligences too far. For example, one expert on intelligence, Nathan Brody (2007), argues that people who excel at one type of intellectual task are likely to excel in others. Thus, individuals who do well at memorizing lists of digits are also likely to be good at solving verbal problems and spatial layout problems. The argument between those who support Spearman's

Children in the Key School form "pods," in which they pursue activities of special interest to them. Every day, each child can choose from activities that draw on Gardner's eight frames of mind. The school has pods that range from gardening to architecture to gliding to dancing. *What are some of the main ideas of Gardner's theory and its application to education?*

concept of *g* (general intelligence) and those who advocate the multiple-intelligences view is ongoing (Brody, 2007; Horn, 2007; Sternberg, 2007a).

Culture and Intelligence Differences in conceptions of intelligence occur not only among psychologists but also among cultures. What is viewed as intelligent in one culture may not be thought of as intelligent in another (Cole, 2006). For example, people in Western cultures tend to view intelligence in terms of reasoning and thinking skills, whereas people in Eastern cultures see intelligence as a way for members of a community to successfully engage in social roles (Nisbett, 2003). One study found that Taiwanese Chinese conceptions of intelligence emphasize understanding and relating to others, including when to show and when not to show one's intelligence (Yang & Sternberg, 1997).

Robert Serpell (1974, 2000) has studied concepts of intelligence in rural African communities since the 1970s. He has found that people in rural African communities, especially those in which Western schooling is not common, tend to blur the distinction between being intelligent and being socially competent. In rural Zambia, for example, the concept of intelligence involves being both clever and responsible. Elena Grigorenko and her colleagues (2001) have also studied the concept of intelligence among rural Africans. They found that people in the Luo culture of rural Kenya view intelligence as consisting of four domains: (1) academic intelligence; (2) social qualities such as respect, responsibility, and consideration; (3) practical thinking; and (4) comprehension. In another study in the same culture, children who scored highly on a test of knowledge about medicinal herbs—a measure of practical intelligence—tended to score poorly on tests of academic intelligence (Sternberg & others, 2001). These results indicated that practical and academic intelligence can develop independently and may even conflict with each other. They also suggest that the values of a culture may influence the direction in which a child develops.

Interpreting Differences in IQ Scores

The IQ scores that result from tests such as the Stanford-Binet and Wechsler scales provide information about children's mental abilities. However, interpreting what

"You can't build a hut, you don't know how to find edible roots and you know nothing about predicting the weather. In other words, you do terribly on our I.Q. test."
Copyright © 1992 by Sidney Harris. Reprinted with permission.

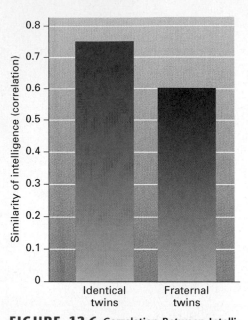

FIGURE 12.6 Correlation Between Intelligence Test Scores and Twin Status The graph represents a summary of research findings that have compared the intelligence test scores of identical and fraternal twins. An approximate .15 difference has been found, with a higher correlation (.75) for identical twins and a lower correlation (.60) for fraternal twins.

performance on an intelligence test means is debated. One issue focuses on what determines individual and group differences in these scores (Campbell, 2007; Plomin, DeFries, & Fulker, 2007).

The Influence of Genetics Arthur Jensen (1969) argued that intelligence is primarily inherited and that environment plays only a minimal role in intelligence. Jensen reviewed the research on intelligence, much of which involved comparisons of identical and fraternal twins, and which also used IQ as the indicator of intelligence. Identical twins have exactly the same genetic makeup; if intelligence is genetically determined, Jensen reasoned, identical twins' IQs should be more similar than the intelligence of fraternal twins.

The studies on intelligence in identical twins that Jensen examined showed an average correlation of .82, a very high positive association. Investigations of fraternal twins, however, produced an average correlation of .50, a moderately high positive correlation. A difference of .32 is substantial. However, a more recent research review that included many studies conducted since Jensen's original review found that the difference in the average correlation of intelligence between identical and fraternal twins was .15, substantially less than what Jensen found (Grigorenko, 2000) (see Figure 12.6).

Jensen also compared the correlation of IQ scores for identical twins reared together with those reared apart. The correlation for those reared together was .89, and for those reared apart was .78, a difference of .11. Jensen argued that if environmental factors were more important than genetic factors, the difference should have been greater.

Adoption studies have been inconclusive about the relative importance of genetics in intelligence. In most *adoption studies,* researchers determine whether the behavior of adopted children is more like that of their biological parents or their adoptive parents. In one study, the educational levels attained by biological parents were better predictors of children's IQ scores than were the IQs of the children's adoptive parents (Scarr & Weinberg, 1983). Because of the stronger genetic link between the adopted children and their biological parents, the implication is that heredity is more important than environment. Environmental effects also have been found in studies of adoption. For example, moving children into an adoptive family with a better environment than the child had in the past increased the children's IQs by an average of 12 points (Lucurto, 1990).

How strong is the effect of genetics on intelligence? The concept of heritability attempts to tease apart the effects of heredity and environment in a population. **Heritability** is the fraction of the variance in a population that is attributed to genetics. The heritability index is computed using correlational techniques. Thus, the highest degree of heritability is 1.00 and correlations of .70 and above suggest a strong genetic influence. A committee of respected researchers convened by the American Psychological Association concluded that by late adolescence, the heritability of intelligence is about .75, which reflects a strong genetic influence (Neisser & others, 1996).

An important point to keep in mind about heritability is that it refers to a specific group (population), *not* to individuals (Okagaki, 2000). Researchers use the concept of heritability to try to describe why people differ. Heritability says nothing about why a single individual, like yourself, has a certain intelligence; nor does it say anything about differences *between* groups.

Most research on heredity and environment does not include environments that differ radically. Thus, it is not surprising that many genetic studies show environment to be a fairly weak influence on intelligence (Fraser, 1995).

The heritability index has several flaws. It is only as good as the data entered into its analysis and the interpretations made from it (Sternberg, Grigorenko, & Kidd, 2005, 2006). The data are virtually all from traditional IQ tests, which some experts think are not always the best indicator of intelligence (Gardner, 2002; Sternberg, 2002). Also, the heritability index assumes that we can treat genetic and environmental influences as factors that can be separated, with each part contributing a

heritability The fraction of variance in a population that is attributed to genetics and is computed using correlational techniques.

distinct amount of influence. As we discussed in Chapter 2, genes and the environment always work together. Genes always exist in an environment, and the environment shapes their activity.

Today, most researchers agree that genetics does not determine intelligence to the extent Jensen claimed (Gottlieb, Wahlsten, & Lickliter, 2006; Ramey, Ramey, & Lanzi, 2006; Sternberg, Grigorenko, & Kidd, 2006). For most people, this means that modifications in environment can change their IQ scores considerably. Although genetic endowment may always influence a person's intellectual ability, the environmental influences and opportunities we provide children and adults do make a difference (Ramey, Ramey, & Lanzi, 2006; Sternberg, 2006).

Environmental Influences In Chapter 6, we described one study that demonstrated the influence of parents on cognitive abilities. Researchers went into homes and observed how extensively parents from welfare and middle-income professional families talked and communicated with their young children (Hart & Risley, 1995). They found that the middle-income professional parents were much more likely to communicate with their young children than the welfare parents were. How much the parents communicated with their children in the first three years of their lives was correlated with the children's Stanford-Binet IQ scores at age 3. The more parents communicated with their children, the higher the children's IQs were.

Schooling also influences intelligence (Gustafsson, 2007). The biggest effects have been found when large groups of children have been deprived of formal education for an extended period, resulting in lower intelligence. One study examined the IQ scores of children in South Africa whose schooling was delayed for four years because teachers were not available (Ramphal, 1962). Compared with children in nearby villages who had teachers, the children whose entry into school was delayed experienced a 5-point drop in IQ for every year of delay.

Another possible effect of education can be seen in rapidly increasing IQ test scores around the world (Daley & others, 2003; Flynn, 1999, 2007). IQ scores have been increasing so fast that a high percentage of people regarded as having average intelligence at the turn of the century would be considered below average in intelligence today (Howard, 2001) (see Figure 12.7). If a representative sample of people today took the Stanford-Binet test used in 1932, about one-fourth would be defined as having very superior intelligence, a label usually accorded to fewer than 3 percent of the population (Horton, 2001). Because the increase has taken place in a relatively short time, it can't be due to heredity, but rather may be due to increasing levels of education attained by a much greater percentage of the world's population or to other environmental factors such as the explosion of information to which people are exposed. The worldwide increase in intelligence test scores that has occurred over a short time frame has been called the *Flynn effect*, after the researcher who discovered it—James Flynn.

Keep in mind that environmental influences are complex (Sternberg, 2006; Sternberg, Grigorenko, & Kidd, 2006). Growing up with all the "advantages," for

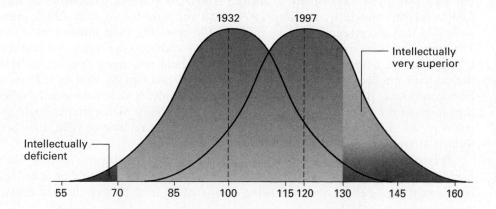

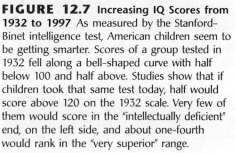

FIGURE 12.7 Increasing IQ Scores from 1932 to 1997 As measured by the Stanford-Binet intelligence test, American children seem to be getting smarter. Scores of a group tested in 1932 fell along a bell-shaped curve with half below 100 and half above. Studies show that if children took that same test today, half would score above 120 on the 1932 scale. Very few of them would score in the "intellectually deficient" end, on the left side, and about one-fourth would rank in the "very superior" range.

example, does not guarantee success. Children from wealthy families may have easy access to excellent schools, books, travel, and tutoring, but they may take such opportunities for granted and fail to develop the motivation to learn and to achieve. In the same way, "poor" or "disadvantaged" does not automatically equal "doomed."

Researchers increasingly are interested in manipulating the early environment of children who are at risk for impoverished intelligence (Campbell, 2007; Ramey, Ramey, & Lanzi, 2006). The emphasis is on prevention rather than remediation. Many low-income parents have difficulty providing an intellectually stimulating environment for their children. Programs that educate parents to be more sensitive caregivers and better teachers, as well as support services such as quality child-care programs, can make a difference in a child's intellectual development.

One review of the research on early interventions concluded that (1) high-quality center-based interventions are associated with increases in children's intelligence and school achievement; (2) the interventions are most successful with poor children and children whose parents have little education; (3) the positive benefits continue through adolescence, but are not as strong as in early childhood or the beginning of elementary school; and (4) the programs that are continued into middle and late childhood have the best long-term results (Brooks-Gunn, 2003).

Group Differences In the United States, children from African American and Latino families score below children from White families on standardized intelligence tests. On the average, African American schoolchildren score 10 to 15 points lower on standardized intelligence tests than White American schoolchildren do (Brody, 2000; Lynn, 1996). These are *average scores,* however. About 15 to 25 percent of African American schoolchildren score higher than half of White schoolchildren do, and many White schoolchildren score lower than most African American schoolchildren. The reason is that the distribution of scores for African American and White schoolchildren overlaps.

As African Americans have gained social, economic, and educational opportunities, the gap between African Americans and Whites on standardized intelligence tests has begun to narrow (Ogbu & Stern, 2001; Onwuegbuzi & Daley, 2001; Sternberg, Grigorkenko, & Kidd, 2005, 2006). This gap especially narrows in college, where African American and White students often experience more similar environments than in the elementary and high school years (Myerson & others, 1998). Also, when children from disadvantaged African American families are adopted into more-advantaged middle-socioeconomic-status families, their scores on intelligence tests more closely resemble national averages for middle-socioeconomic-status children than for lower-socioeconomic-status children (Scarr & Weinberg, 1983).

One potential influence on intelligence test performance is **stereotype threat,** the anxiety that one's behavior might confirm a negative stereotype about one's group (Steele & Aronson, 2004). For example, when African Americans take an intelligence test, they may experience anxiety about confirming the old stereotype that African Americans are "intellectually inferior." In one study, the verbal part of the GRE was given individually to African American and White students at Stanford University (Steele & Aronson, 1995). Half the students of each ethnic group were told that the researchers were interested in assessing their intellectual ability. The other half were told that the researchers were trying to develop a test and that it might not be reliable and valid (therefore, it would not mean anything in relation to their intellectual ability). The White students did equally well on the test in both conditions. However, the African American students did more poorly when they thought the test was assessing their intellectual ability; when they thought the test was just in the development stage and might not be reliable or valid, they performed as well as the White students.

Other studies have confirmed the existence of stereotype threat (Cohen & Sherman, 2005; Helms, 2005). African American students do more poorly on standardized tests if they believe they are being evaluated. If they believe the test doesn't

How might stereotype threat affect African American children's scores on tests?

stereotype threat The anxiety that one's behavior might confirm a negative stereotype about one's group.

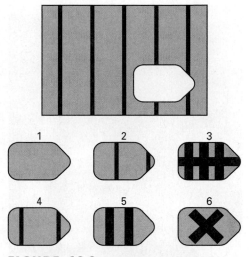

count, they perform as well as White students (Aronson, 2002; Aronson & others, 1999; Aronson, Fried, & Good, 2002). However, some critics believe the extent to which stereotype threat explains the testing gap has been exaggerated (Sackett, Hardison, & Cullen, 2004).

Biased tests may also contribute to group differences in average IQ scores. Many of the early tests of intelligence favored urban children over rural children, children from middle-SES families over children from low-income families, and White children over minority children (Miller-Jones, 1989). The standards for the early tests were almost exclusively based on White middle-SES children. And some of the items were culturally biased. For example, one item on an early test asked what you should do if you find a 3-year-old in the street. The correct answer was "Call the police." However, children from impoverished inner-city families might not choose this answer if they have had bad experiences with the police. Children living in rural areas might not have police nearby. The contemporary versions of intelligence tests attempt to reduce such cultural bias.

Even if the content of test items is appropriate, however, another problem can characterize intelligence tests. Since many items are verbal, minority groups may encounter problems in understanding the language of the items.

Creating Culture-Reduced Tests

Culture-reduced tests are tests of intelligence that are intended to limit cultural bias. Two types of culture-reduced tests have been devised. The first includes items that are familiar to children from different socioeconomic and ethnic backgrounds, or items that at least are familiar to the children taking the test. For example, a child might be asked how a bird and a dog are different, on the assumption that all children have been exposed to birds and dogs. The second type of culture-reduced test has no verbal questions. Figure 12.8 shows a sample question from the Raven's Progressive Matrices Test. Even though tests such as the Raven's Progressive Matrices are designed to be culture-fair, people with more education still score higher than those with less education do. Thus, experts such as Robert Sternberg (2007b), argue that these tests should be labeled culture-reduced rather than culture-fair because it is not possible to create a completely culture-fair test.

Why is it so hard to create culture-fair tests? Most tests tend to reflect what the dominant culture thinks is important (Greenfield, Suzuki, & Rothstein-Fisch, 2006). If tests have time limits, that will bias the test against groups not concerned with time. If languages differ, the same words might have different meanings for different language groups. Even pictures can produce bias because some cultures have less experience with drawings and photographs (Anastasi & Urbina, 1996). Within the same culture, different groups could have different attitudes, values, and motivation, and this could affect their performance on intelligence tests. Items that ask why buildings should be made of brick are biased against children who have little or no experience with brick houses. Questions about railroads, furnaces, seasons of the year, distances between cities, and so on can be biased against groups who have less experience than others with these contexts. Recall, too, that cultures define what is intelligent differently.

These attempts to produce culture-fair tests remind us that conventional intelligence tests probably are culturally biased, yet the effort to create a truly culture-fair test has not yielded a successful alternative.

Using Intelligence Tests

Psychological tests are tools. Like all tools, their effectiveness depends on the knowledge, skill, and integrity of the user. A hammer can be used to build a beautiful kitchen cabinet, or it can be used as a weapon of assault. Like a hammer, psychological tests can be used for positive purposes, or they can be badly abused. Here are some cautions about IQ that can help you avoid the pitfalls of using information about a child's intelligence in negative ways:

- *Avoid stereotyping and expectations.* A special concern is that the scores on an IQ test easily can lead to stereotypes and expectations about students (Weinstein, 2004). Sweeping generalizations are too often made on the basis of an IQ

FIGURE 12.8 Sample Item from the Raven's Progressive Matrices Test Individuals are presented with a matrix arrangement of symbols, such as the one at the top of this figure, and must then complete the matrix by selecting the appropriate missing symbol from a group of symbols, such as the ones at the bottom. Simulated item similar to those found in the *Raven's Progressive Matrices.* Copyright © 1998 by Harcourt Assessment, Inc. Reproduced with permission. All rights reserved.

culture-reduced tests Tests of intelligence that are designed to limit cultural bias.

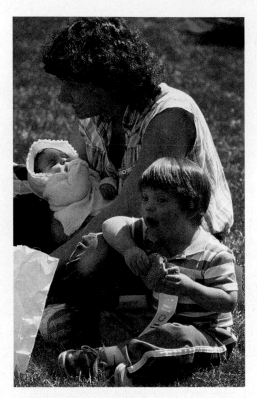

A child with Down Syndrome. *What causes a child to develop Down syndrome?*

score. An IQ test should always be considered a measure of current performance. It is not a measure of fixed potential. Maturational changes and enriched environmental experiences can advance a student's intelligence.

- *Know that IQ is not a sole indicator of competence.* Another concern about IQ tests occurs when they are used as the main or sole assessment of competence. A high IQ is not the ultimate human value. As we have seen in this chapter, it is important to consider not only students' intellectual competence in such areas as verbal skills but also their creative and practical skills.
- *Use caution in interpreting an overall IQ score.* In evaluating a child's intelligence, it is wiser to think of intelligence as consisting of a number of domains. Keep in mind the different types of intelligence described by Sternberg and Gardner. Remember that, by considering the different domains of intelligence, you can find that every child has at least one or more strengths.

Extremes of Intelligence

Intelligence tests have been used to discover indications of mental retardation or intellectual giftedness, the extremes of intelligence. At times, intelligence tests have been misused for this purpose. Keeping in mind the theme that an intelligence test should not be used as the sole indicator of mental retardation or giftedness, we explore the nature of these intellectual extremes.

Mental Retardation **Mental retardation** is a condition of limited mental ability in which an individual has a low IQ, usually below 70 on a traditional intelligence test, and has difficulty adapting to everyday life. There are several classifications of mental retardation (Hodapp & Dykens, 2006). About 89 percent of the mentally retarded fall into the mild category, with IQs of 55 to 70. About 6 percent are classified as moderately retarded, with IQs of 40 to 54; these people can attain a second-grade level of skills and may be able to support themselves as adults through some types of labor. About 3.5 percent of the mentally retarded are in the severe category, with IQs of 25 to 39; these individuals learn to talk and engage in very simple tasks but require extensive supervision. Less than 1 percent have IQs below 25; they fall into the profoundly mentally retarded classification and need constant supervision (Drew & Hardman, 2000).

Mental retardation can have an organic cause, or it can be social and cultural in origin:

- **Organic retardation** is mental retardation that is caused by a genetic disorder or by brain damage; the word *organic* refers to the tissues or organs of the body, so there is some physical damage in organic retardation. Most people who suffer from organic retardation have IQs that range between 0 and 50. However, children with Down syndrome have an average IQ of approximately 50. As discussed in Chapter 2, Down syndrome occurs when an individual has an extra copy of chromosome 21.
- **Cultural-familial retardation** is a mental deficit in which no evidence of organic brain damage can be found; individuals' IQs range from 50 to 70. Psychologists suspect that such mental deficits result from the normal variation that distributes people along the range of intelligence scores combined with growing up in a below-average intellectual environment.

Giftedness There have always been people whose abilities and accomplishments outshine others'—the whiz kid in class, the star athlete, the natural musician. People who are **gifted** have above-average intelligence (an IQ of 130 or higher) and/or superior talent for something. When it comes to programs for the gifted, most school systems with gifted programs select children who have intellectual superiority and academic aptitude. Children who are talented in the visual and

mental retardation A condition of limited mental ability in which an individual has a low IQ, usually below 70 on a traditional test of intelligence, and has difficulty adapting to everyday life.

organic retardation Mental retardation that involves some physical damage and is caused by a genetic disorder or brain damage.

cultural-familial retardation Retardation that is characterized by no evidence of organic brain damage, but the individual's IQ is between 50 and 70.

gifted Having above-average intelligence (an IQ of 130 or higher) and/or superior talent for something.

performing arts (arts, drama, dance), athletics, or other special aptitudes tend to be overlooked (Hargrove, 2005; Smith, 2005; Tassell-Baska & Stambaugh, 2006; Winner, 2000, 2006).

What are the characteristics of children who are gifted? There has been speculation that giftedness is linked with having a mental disorder. However, no relation between giftedness and mental disorder has been found. Similarly, the idea that gifted children are maladjusted is a myth, as Lewis Terman (1925) found when he conducted an extensive study of 1,500 children whose Stanford-Binet IQs averaged 150. The children in Terman's study were socially well adjusted, and many went on to become successful doctors, lawyers, professors, and scientists. Other studies support the conclusion that gifted people tend to be more mature than others, have fewer emotional problems than others, and grow up in a positive family climate (Davidson, 2000; Feldman, 2001; Smith, 2005).

Ellen Winner (1996) described three criteria that characterize gifted children, whether in art, music, or academic domains:

1. *Precocity.* Gifted children are precocious. They begin to master an area earlier than their peers. Learning in their domain is more effortless for them than for ordinary children. In most instances, these gifted children are precocious because they have an inborn high ability in a particular domain or domains.
2. *Marching to their own drummer.* Gifted children learn in a qualitatively different way than ordinary children. One way that they march to a different drummer is that they need minimal help, or scaffolding, from adults to learn. In many instances, they resist any kind of explicit instruction. They also often make discoveries on their own and solve problems in unique ways.
3. *A passion to master.* Gifted children are driven to understand the domain in which they have high ability. They display an intense, obsessive interest and an ability to focus. They are not children who need to be pushed by their parents. They motivate themselves, says Winner.

Careers in CHILD DEVELOPMENT

Sterling Jones
Supervisor of Gifted and Talented Education

Sterling Jones is program supervisor for gifted and talented children in the Detroit Public School System. Jones has been working for more than three decades with children who are gifted. He believes that students' mastery of skills mainly depends on the amount of time devoted to instruction and the length of time allowed for learning. Thus, he believes that many basic strategies for challenging children who are gifted to develop their skills can be applied to a wider range of students than once believed. He has rewritten several pamphlets for use by teachers and parents, including *How to Help Your Child Succeed* and *Gifted and Talented Education for Everyone*.

Jones has undergraduate and graduate degrees from Wayne State University and taught English for a number of years before becoming involved in the program for gifted children. He also has written materials on African Americans, such as *Voices from the Black Experience*, that are used in the Detroit schools.

Sterling Jones with some of the children in the gifted program in the Detroit Public School System.

Is giftedness a product of heredity or environment? Likely both. Individuals who are gifted recall that they had signs of high ability in a particular area at a very young age, prior to or at the beginning of formal training (Howe & others, 1995). This suggests the importance of innate ability in giftedness. However, researchers also have found that individuals with world-class status in the arts, mathematics, science, and sports all report strong family support and years of training and practice (Bloom, 1985). Deliberate practice is an important characteristic of individuals who become experts in a particular domain. For example, in one study, the best musicians engaged in twice as much deliberate practice over their lives as the least successful ones did (Ericsson, Krampe, & Tesch-Romer, 1993). To read about one individual who is making a difference in programs for children who are gifted, see the *Careers in Child Development* profile.

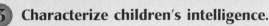

REVIEW AND REFLECT ◆ LEARNING GOAL 3

3 Characterize children's intelligence.

Review
- What is intelligence? How can the Binet tests and Wechsler scales be characterized?
- What are some different views of multiple intelligences? How can the multiple-intelligences approach be evaluated?
- What are some issues in interpreting differences in IQ scores? Explain them.
- What is the nature of children's mental retardation? How can children's giftedness be described?

Reflect
- A CD-ROM, *Children's IQ and Achievement Test*, now lets parents test their child's IQ. What might be some problems with parents giving their own children an IQ test?

4 WHAT CHANGES IN LANGUAGE DEVELOPMENT OCCUR IN MIDDLE AND LATE CHILDHOOD?

| Vocabulary, Grammar, and Metalinguistic Awareness | Reading | Bilingualism and Second-Language Learning |

Knowledge of vocabulary words appears on virtually all intelligence tests, and this as well as other aspects of language development are important aspects of children's intelligence. Children gain new skills as they enter school that make it possible to learn to read and write: these include increasingly using language to talk about things that are not physically present, learning what a word is, and learning how to recognize and talk about sounds (Berko Gleason, 2003). They have to learn the *alphabetic principle,* that the letters of the alphabet represent sounds of the language. As children develop during middle and late childhood, changes in their vocabulary and grammar also take place (Hoff, 2003).

Vocabulary, Grammar, and Metalinguistic Awareness

During middle and late childhood, changes occur in the way children's mental vocabulary is organized. When asked to say the first word that comes to mind when they hear a word, young children typically provide a word that often follows the word in a sentence. For example, when asked to respond to "dog" the young child may say "barks," or to the word "eat" say "lunch." At about 7 years of age, children begin to respond with a word that is the same part of speech as the stimulus word. For example, a child may now respond to the word "dog" with "cat" or "horse." To "eat," they now might say "drink." This is evidence that children now have begun to categorize their vocabulary by parts of speech (Berko Gleason, 2003).

The process of categorizing becomes easier as children increase their vocabulary. Children's vocabulary increases from an average of about 14,000 words at 6 years of age to an average of about 40,000 words by 11 years of age.

Children make similar advances in grammar (Chang, Dell, & Bock, 2006; Lust, 2007). During the elementary school years, children's improvement in logical reasoning and analytical skills helps them understand such constructions as the appropriate use of comparatives (*shorter, deeper*) and subjectives ("If you were president . . ."). During the elementary school years, children become increasingly able to understand and use complex grammar, such as the following sentence: *The boy who kissed his mother wore a hat.* They also learn to use language in a more connected way, producing connected discourse. They become able to relate sentences to one another to produce descriptions, definitions, and narratives that make sense. Children must be able to do these things orally before they can be expected to deal with them in written assignments.

These advances in vocabulary and grammar during the elementary school years are accompanied by the development of **metalinguistic awareness,** which is knowledge about language, such as knowing what a preposition is or the ability to discuss the sounds of a language. Metalinguistic awareness allows children "to think about their language, understand what words are, and even define them" (Berko Gleason, 2005, p. 4). It improves considerably during the elementary school years. Defining words becomes a regular part of classroom discourse, and children increase their knowledge of syntax as they study and talk about the components of sentences such as subjects and verbs (Ely, 2005).

Children also make progress in understanding how to use language in culturally appropriate ways—pragmatics. By the time they enter adolescence, most children know the rules for the use of language in everyday contexts—that is, what is appropriate to say and what is inappropriate to say.

Reading

Before learning to read, children learn to use language to talk about things that are not present; they learn what a word is; and they learn how to recognize sounds and talk about them (Berko Gleason, 2003). If they develop a large vocabulary, their path to reading is eased. Children who begin elementary school with a small vocabulary are at risk when it comes to learning to read (Berko Gleason, 2003).

Vocabulary development plays an important role in reading comprehension (Berninger, 2006; Paris & Paris, 2006). For example, a recent study revealed that a good vocabulary was linked with reading comprehension in second-grade students (Berninger & Abbott, 2005). Having a good vocabulary helps readers access word meaning effortlessly.

How should children be taught to read? Currently, debate focuses on the whole-language approach versus the basic-skills-and-phonics approach (Rasinski & Padak, 2008; Reutzel & Cooter, 2008).

The **whole-language approach** stresses that reading instruction should parallel children's natural language learning. In some whole-language classes, beginning readers are taught to recognize whole words or even entire sentences, and to use the context of what they are reading to guess at the meaning of words. Reading materials should be whole and meaningful—that is, children should be given material in its complete form, such as stories and poems, so that they learn to understand language's communicative function. Reading should be connected with listening and writing skills. Although there are variations in whole-language programs, most share the premise that reading should be integrated with other skills and subjects, such as science and social studies, and that it should focus on real-world material. Thus, a class might read newspapers, magazines, or books, and then write about and discuss them.

In contrast, the **basic-skills-and-phonics approach** emphasizes that reading instruction should teach phonics and its basic rules for translating written symbols into sounds. Early reading instruction should involve simplified materials. Only after children have learned correspondence rules that relate spoken phonemes to the alphabet letters that are used to represent them should they be given complex reading materials, such as books and poems (Rasinski & Padak, 2008).

What are the main approaches to teaching children how to read?

metalinguistic awareness Refers to knowledge about language, such as knowing what a preposition is or the ability to discuss the sounds of a language.

whole-language approach An approach to reading instruction based on the idea that instruction should parallel children's natural language learning. Reading materials should be whole and meaningful.

basic-skills-and-phonics approach The idea that reading instruction should teach both phonics and the basic rules for translating written symbols into sounds.

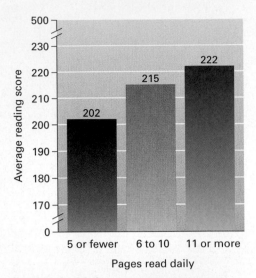

FIGURE 12.9 The Relation of Reading Achievement to Number of Pages Read Daily In the recent analysis of reading in the fourth grade in the National Assessment of Educational Progress (2000), reading more pages daily in school and as part of homework assignments was related to higher scores on a reading test in which scores ranged from 0 to 500.

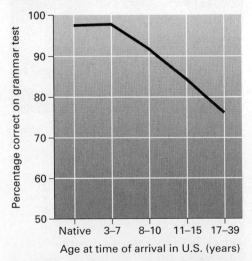

FIGURE 12.10 Grammar Proficiency and Age at Arrival in the United States In one study, ten years after arriving in the United States, individuals from China and Korea took a grammar test (Johnson & Newport, 1991). People who arrived before the age of 8 had a better grasp of grammar than those who arrived later.

Which approach is better? Research suggests that children can benefit from both approaches, but instruction in phonics needs to be emphasized (Vacca & others, 2006). An increasing number of experts in the field of reading now conclude that direct instruction in phonics is a key aspect of learning to read (Mayer, 2004; Mraz, Padak, & Rasinski, 2008).

It is important to remember that reading, like other important skills, takes time and effort (McWhorter, 2005). In a national assessment, children in the fourth grade had higher scores on a national reading test when they read 11 or more pages daily for school and homework (National Assessment of Educational Progress, 2000) (see Figure 12.9). Teachers who required students to read a great deal on a daily basis had students who were more proficient at reading than teachers who required little reading by their students.

Bilingualism and Second-Language Learning

Learning a second language is more readily accomplished by children than adolescents or adults. Adults make faster initial progress, but their eventual success in the second language is not as great as children's. For example, in one study, Chinese and Korean adults who immigrated to the United States at different ages were given a test of grammatical knowledge (Johnson & Newport, 1991). Those who began learning English when they were 3 to 7 years old scored as well as native speakers on the test, but those who arrived in the United States and started learning English in later childhood or adolescence had lower test scores (see Figure 12.10). Children's ability to pronounce words with a nativelike accent in a second language typically decreases with age, with an especially sharp drop occurring after the age of about 10 to 12 (Asher & Garcia, 1969). In sum, researchers have found that early exposure to a second language is optimal and ensures the least amount of damage to the home language and to the new language (Lesaux & Siegel, 2003; Lessow-Hurley, 2005; Petitto, Kovelman, & Harasymowycz, 2003).

Students in the United States are far behind their counterparts in many developed countries in learning a second language. For example, in Russia, schools have 10 grades, called *forms*, which roughly correspond to the 12 grades in American schools. Children begin school at age 7 in Russia and begin learning English in the third form. Because of this emphasis on teaching English, most Russian citizens under the age of 40 today are able to speak at least some English. The United States is the only technologically advanced Western nation that does not require foreign language study in high school, even for students in rigorous academic programs.

U.S. students may be missing more than the chance to acquire a skill by not learning to speak a second language. *Bilingualism*—the ability to speak two languages—has a positive effect on children's cognitive development (Gibbons & Ng, 2004). Children who are fluent in two languages perform better than their single-language counterparts on tests of control of attention, concept formation, analytical reasoning, cognitive flexibility, and cognitive complexity (Bialystok, 1999, 2001). They also are more conscious of the structure of spoken and written language and better at noticing errors of grammar and meaning, skills that benefit their reading ability (Bialystok, 1993, 1997).

In the United States, many immigrant children go from being monolingual in their home language to bilingual in that language and in English, only to end up monolingual speakers of English. This is called *subtractive bilingualism* and it can have negative effects on children, who often become ashamed of their home language.

A current controversy related to bilingualism involves bilingual education. To read about this controversy, see the *Diversity in Children's Development* interlude.

Diversity in Children's Development

BILINGUAL EDUCATION

A current controversy related to bilingualism involves the millions of U.S. children who come from homes in which English is not the primary language. What is the best way to teach these children?

For the last two decades, the preferred strategy has been *bilingual education,* which teaches academic subjects to immigrant children in their native language while slowly teaching English (Horwitz, 2008; Ovando, Combs, & Collier, 2006). Advocates of bilingual education programs argue that if children who do not know English are taught only in English, they will fall behind in academic subjects. How, they ask, can 7-year-olds learn arithmetic or history taught only in English when they do not speak the language?

Some critics of bilingual programs argue that too often it is thought that immigrant children need only one year of bilingual education. However, in general it takes immigrant children approximately three to five years to develop speaking proficiency and seven years to develop reading proficiency in English (Hakuta, Butler, & Witt, 2000). Also, immigrant children of course vary in their ability to learn English (Diaz-Rico, 2008; Echevarria, Vogt, & Short, 2008). Children who come from lower socioeconomic backgrounds have more difficulty than those from higher socioeconomic backgrounds (Hakuta, 2001). Thus, especially for immigrant children from low socioeconomic backgrounds, more years of bilingual education may be needed than they currently are receiving.

Critics who oppose bilingual education argue that as a result of these programs, the children of immigrants are not learning English, which puts them at a permanent disadvantage in U.S. society. California, Arizona, and Massachusetts have significantly reduced the number of bilingual education programs. Some states continue to endorse bilingual education, but the emphasis that test scores be reported separately for English-language learners (students whose main language is not English) in the No Child Left Behind state assessments has shifted attention to literacy in English (Snow & Kang, 2006).

What have researchers found regarding outcomes of bilingual education programs? Drawing conclusions about the effectiveness of bilingual education programs is difficult because of variations across programs in the number of years they are in effect, type of instruction, qualities of schooling other than bilingual education, teachers, children, and other factors. Further, no effectively conducted experiments that compare bilingual education with English-only education in the United States have been conducted (Snow & Kang, 2006). Some

A first- and second-grade bilingual English-Cantonese teacher instructing students in Chinese in Oakland, California. *What is the nature of bilingual education?*

experts have concluded that the quality of instruction is more important in determining outcomes than the language in which it is delivered (Lesaux & Siegel, 2003).

Research supports bilingual education in that (1) children have difficulty learning a subject when it is taught in a language they do not understand, and (2) when both languages are integrated in the classroom, children learn the second language more readily and participate more actively (Gonzales, Yawkey, & Minaya-Rowe,

(continued on next page)

2006; Hakuta, 2005). However, many of the research results report only modest rather than strong support for bilingual education, and some supporters of bilingual education now acknowledge that English-only instruction can produce positive outcomes for English-language learners (Lesaux & Siegel, 2003).

REVIEW AND REFLECT ▶ **LEARNING GOAL 4**

4 **Summarize language development in middle and late childhood.**

Review
- What are some changes in vocabulary, grammar, and metalinguistic awareness in the middle and late childhood years?
- What controversy characterizes how to teach children to read?
- What is bilingual education? What issues are involved in bilingual education?

Reflect
- What are some of the key considerations in using a balanced approach to teaching reading?

---

5 **WHAT CHARACTERIZES CHILDREN'S ACHIEVEMENT?**

| Extrinsic and Intrinsic Motivation | Self-Efficacy | Social Relationships and Contexts |

| Mastery Motivation and Mindset | Goal Setting, Planning, and Self-Regulation |

These students were given an opportunity to write and perform their own play. These kinds of self-determining opportunities can enhance students' motivation to achieve.

extrinsic motivation External incentives such as rewards and punishments.

intrinsic motivation Internal factors such as self-determination, curiosity, challenge, and effort.

We are a species motivated to do well at what we attempt, to gain mastery over the world in which we live, to explore unknown environments with enthusiasm and curiosity, and to achieve the heights of success. In this section, we explore some of the many different ways children effectively achieve their potential during middle and late childhood.

Extrinsic and Intrinsic Motivation

Extrinsic motivation involves external incentives such as rewards and punishments. The humanistic and cognitive approaches stress the importance of intrinsic motivation in achievement. **Intrinsic motivation** is based on internal factors such as self-determination, curiosity, challenge, and effort. Some individuals study hard because they want to make good grades or avoid parental disapproval (extrinsic motivation). Others study hard because they are internally motivated to achieve high standards in their work (intrinsic motivation).

One view of intrinsic motivation emphasizes self-determination (Deci & Ryan, 1994; Ryan & Deci, 2001). In this view, children want to believe that they are doing something because of their own will, not because of external success or rewards.

Researchers have found that giving children some choice and providing opportunities for personal responsibility increases their internal motivation and intrinsic interest in school tasks (Blumenfeld, Kempler, & Krajcik, 2006). For example, one study found that high school science students who were encouraged to organize

their own experiments demonstrated more care and interest in laboratory work than their counterparts who were given detailed instructions and directions (Rainey, 1965). In another study, which included mainly African American students from low-income backgrounds, teachers were encouraged to give the students more responsibility for their school program (deCharms, 1984). This consisted of opportunities to set their own goals, plan how to reach the goals, and monitor their progress toward the goals. Students were given some choice of activities to engage in and when they would do them. They also were encouraged to take personal responsibility for their behavior, including reaching the goals that they had set. Compared with a control group, students in the intrinsic motivation/self-determination group had higher achievement gains and were more likely to graduate from high school.

Phyllis Blumenfeld and her colleagues (2006) have proposed another variation on intrinsic motivation that emphasizes the importance of creating learning environments that encourage students to become cognitively engaged and take responsibility for their learning. The goal is to get students to become motivated to expend the effort to persist and master ideas rather than simply doing enough work to just get by and make passing grades. Especially important in encouraging students to become cognitively engaged and responsible for their learning is to embed subject matter content and skills learning within meaningful contexts, especially real-world situations that mesh with students' interests.

Mastery Motivation and Mindset

Becoming cognitively engaged and self-motivated to improve are reflected in children with a mastery motivation. These children also have a growth mindset that they can produce positive outcomes if they put forth the effort.

Mastery Motivation Developmental psychologists Valanne Henderson and Carol Dweck (1990) have found that children often show two distinct responses to difficult or challenging circumstances. Individuals who display **mastery motivation** are task-oriented; instead of focusing on their ability, they concentrate on learning strategies and the process of achievement rather than the outcome. Those with a **helpless orientation** seem trapped by the experience of difficulty, and they attribute their difficulty to lack of ability. They frequently say such things as "I'm not very good at this," even though they might earlier have demonstrated their ability through many successes. And, once they view their behavior as failure, they often feel anxious, and their performance worsens even further. In contrast, mastery-oriented children often instruct themselves to pay attention, to think carefully, and to remember strategies that have worked for them in previous situations. They frequently report feeling challenged and excited by difficult tasks, rather than being threatened by them (Anderman & Wolters, 2006; Dweck, Mangels, & Good, 2004).

mastery motivation An orientation in which one is task-oriented; instead of focusing on one's ability, is concerned with learning strategies.

helpless orientation An orientation in which one seems trapped by the experience of difficulty and attributes one's difficulty to a lack of ability.

One study of elementary school students found that a higher level of mastery motivation was linked to higher math and reading grades (Broussard, 2004).

Another issue in motivation involves whether to adopt a mastery or a performance orientation. Children with a **performance orientation** are focused on achievement outcomes, believing that winning is what matters most, and happiness results from winning. Does this mean that mastery-oriented individuals do not like to win and that performance-oriented individuals are not motivated to experience the self-efficacy that comes from being able to take credit for one's accomplishments? No. A matter of emphasis or degree is involved, though. For mastery-oriented individuals, winning isn't everything; for performance-oriented individuals, skill development and self-efficacy take a backseat to winning. One recent study of fifth- and seventh- grade students found that girls were more likely than boys to have mastery rather than performance goals in their approach to math achievement (Kenny-Benson & others, 2006).

Mindset   Carol Dweck's (2006) most recent analysis of motivation for achievement stresses the importance of children developing a **mindset,** which she defines as the cognitive view individuals develop for themselves. She concludes that individuals have one of two mindsets: (1) *fixed mindset,* in which they believe that their qualities are carved in stone and cannot change; or (2) *growth mindset,* in which they believe their qualities can change and improve through their effort. A fixed mindset is similar to a helpless orientation, a growth mindset in much like having mastery motivation.

In her recent book, *Mindset,* Dweck (2006) argued that individuals' mindsets influence whether they will be optimistic or pessimistic, shape their goals and how hard they will strive to reach those goals, and affect many aspects of their lives, including achievement and success in school and sports. Dweck says that mindsets begin to be shaped in childhood as children interact with parents, teachers, and coaches, who themselves have either a fixed mindset or a growth mindset. She described the growth mindset of Chicago second-grade teacher, Marva Collins, a masterful teacher we decribed at the beginning of the chapter. Collins' goal is to change apathetic, fixed-mindset children into growth-mindset children. Here's what she said to Freddie, a second-grade student who was repeating that grade, on the first day of school: " . . . we have work to do. You can't just sit in a seat and grow smart. . . . I promise, you are going to *do,* and you are going to *produce.* I am not going to let you fail" (Dweck, 2006, p. 67).

Self-Efficacy

Like having a growth mindset, **self-efficacy,** the belief that one can master a situation and produce favorable outcomes, is an important cognitive view for children to develop. Albert Bandura (1997, 2004, 2006, 2007a, b), whose social cognitive theory we described in Chapter 1, emphasizes that self-efficacy is a critical factor in whether or not students achieve. Self-efficacy has much in common with mastery motivation and intrinsic motivation. Self-efficacy is the belief that "I can"; helplessness is the belief that "I cannot" (Stipek, 2002). Students with high self-efficacy endorse such statements as "I know that I will be able to learn the material in this class" and "I expect to be able to do well at this activity."

Dale Schunk (2008; Schunk & Zimmerman, 2006) has applied the concept of self-efficacy to many aspects of students' achievement. In his view, self-efficacy influences a student's choice of activities. Students with low self-efficacy for learning may avoid many learning tasks, especially those that are challenging. By contrast, high-self-efficacy counterparts eagerly work at learning tasks. High-self-efficacy students are more likely to expend effort and persist longer at a learning task than low-self-efficacy students.

performance orientation An orientation in which one focuses on achievement outcomes; winning is what matters most, and happiness is thought to result from winning.

mindset The cognitive view, either fixed or growth, that individuals develop for themselves.

self-efficacy The belief that one can master a situation and produce favorable outcomes.

Goal Setting, Planning, and Self-Regulation

Researchers have found that self-efficacy and achievement improve when individuals set goals that are specific, proximal, and challenging (Bandura, 2001). A nonspecific, fuzzy goal is "I want to be successful." A more concrete, specific goal is "I want to do well on my spelling test this week."

Individuals can set both long-term (distal) and short-term (proximal) goals. It is okay for individuals to set some long-term goals, such as "I want to graduate from high school" or "I want to go to college," but they also need to create short-term goals, which are steps along the way. "Getting an A on the next math test" is an example of a short-term, proximal goal. So is "Doing all of my homework by 4 p.m. Sunday." David McNally (1990), author of *Even Eagles Need a Push,* advises that when individuals set goals and plan, they should be reminded to live their lives one day at a time. Have them make their commitments in bite-size chunks. A house is built one brick at a time, a cathedral one stone at a time. The artist paints one stroke at a time. The student should also work in small increments.

Another good strategy is for individuals to set challenging goals (Theobold, 2005). A challenging goal is a commitment to self-improvement. Strong interest and involvement in activities are sparked by challenges. Goals that are easy to reach generate little interest or effort. However, goals should be optimally matched to the individual's skill level. If goals are unrealistically high, the result will be repeated failures that lower the individual's self-efficacy.

It is not enough just to get individuals to set goals. It also is important to encourage them to plan how they will reach their goals. Being a good planner means managing time effectively, setting priorities, and being organized. Younger children will likely need help from parents or teachers with goal setting, planning, and organizational skills.

Individuals not only should plan their next week's activities but also monitor how well they are sticking to their plan. Once engaged in a task, they need to monitor their progress, judge how well they are doing on the task, and evaluate the outcomes to regulate what they do in the future. Researchers have found that high-achieving children often are self-regulatory learners (Eccles, 2007; Schunk, 2008). For example, high-achieving children self-monitor their learning more and systematically evaluate their progress toward a goal more than low-achieving children do (Pintrich, 2003). Encouraging children to self-monitor their learning conveys the message that children are responsible for their own behavior and that learning requires active dedicated participation by the child (Sansone & Smith, 2001).

Social Relationships and Contexts

Children's relationships with parents, peers, friends, teachers, mentors, and others can profoundly affect their achievement. So can the social contexts of ethnicity and culture.

Parents Parents' child-rearing practices are linked to children's achievement (Eccles, 2007). Here are some positive parenting practices that result in improved motivation and achievement: knowing enough about the child to provide the right amount of challenge and the right amount of support; providing a positive emotional climate, which motivates children to internalize their parents' values and goals; and modeling motivated achievement behavior, such as working hard and persisting with effort at challenging tasks.

In addition to general child-rearing practices, parents provide various activities or resources at home that may influence students' interest and motivation to pursue various activities over time (Eccles, 2007; Wigfield, Byrnes, & Eccles, 2006). For example, reading to one's preschool children and providing reading materials in the

Rhonda Nachamkin helps one of her students, Patrick Drones, with his work. Rhonda, who teaches first grade in Roswell, Georgia, has a high-energy style and approaches each unit as if it were a Hollywood production. She turns the classroom into an Egyptian tomb, New York City, and Mount Olympus. She sends parents scurrying to learn who Anubis (Egyptian god) and Prometheus (Greek Titan who stole fire) were so they can converse about these topics with their 6-year-olds. Rhonda likes to use multiple versions of fairy tales to teach reading, spelling, and analytical concepts (*Source: USA Today,* 1999).

home are positively related to students' later reading achievement and motivation (Wigfield & Asher, 1984).

Peers   Students who are more accepted by their peers and who have good social skills often do better in school and have positive academic achievement motivation (Rubin, Bukowski, & Parker, 2006; Wentzel & Looney, 2007). In contrast, rejected students, especially those who are highly aggressive, are at risk for a number of achievement problems, including getting low grades and dropping out of school (Dodge, Coie, & Lynam, 2006).

Teachers   Many children who do not do well in school consistently have negative interactions with their teachers (Stipek, 2002). They are frequently in trouble for not completing assignments, not paying attention, goofing off, or acting out. In many cases, they need structured support and discipline, but too often the classroom becomes a highly unpleasant place for them. Researchers have found that students who feel they have supportive, caring teachers are more strongly motivated to engage in academic work than students with unsupportive, uncaring teachers (McCombs, 2001; Ryan & Deci, 2000).

Nel Noddings (1992, 2001, 2006) argues that students are most likely to develop into competent human beings when they feel cared for. This requires teachers to get to know students fairly well. She stresses that this is difficult in large schools with large numbers of students in each class. She recommends that teachers remain with the same students for two to three years (voluntarily on the part of the teacher and the pupil) so that teachers would be better positioned to attend to the interests and capacities of each student.

Ethnicity   The diversity that exists among ethnic minority children is evident in their achievement. In addition to recognizing the diversity that exists within every cultural group in terms of their achievement, it also is important to distinguish between difference and deficiency (Banks, 2008; Cushner, 2006). Too often, the achievement of ethnic minority students—especially African Americans, Latinos, and Native Americans—have been interpreted as *deficits* by middle-socioeconomic-status White standards, when they simply are *culturally different and distinct* (Jones, 1994).

At the same time, many investigations overlook the socioeconomic status of ethnic minority students. In many instances, when ethnicity *and* socioeconomic status are investigated in a study, socioeconomic status predicts achievement better than ethnicity does. Students from middle- and upper-income families fare better than their counterparts from low-income backgrounds in a host of achievement situations—for example, expectations for success, achievement aspirations, and recognition of the importance of effort (Gibbs, 1989).

Sandra Graham (1986, 1990) has conducted a number of studies that reveal not only stronger socioeconomic-status than ethnic differences in achievement but also the importance of studying ethnic minority student motivation in the context of general motivational theory. Her inquiries fall within the framework of attribution theory and focus on the causes that African American students give for their achievement orientation, such as why they succeed or fail. She is struck by how consistently middle-income African American students do not fit the stereotype of being unmotivated. Like their White middle-income counterparts, they have high achievement expectations and understand that failure is usually due to a lack of effort, rather than bad luck.

A special challenge for many ethnic minority students, especially those living in poverty, is dealing with racial prejudice, conflict between the values of their group and those of the majority group,

UCLA educational psychologist Sandra Graham is shown talking with adolescent boys about motivation. She has conducted a number of studies which reveal that middle-socioeconomic-status African American students—like their White counterparts—have high achievement expectations and attribute success to internal factors such as effort rather than external factors such as luck.

and a lack of high-achieving adults in their cultural group who can serve as positive role models.

It also is important to consider the nature of the schools that primarily serve ethnic minority students (Garcia Coll, Szalacha, & Palacios, 2005). More than one-third of all African American and almost one-third of all Latino students attend schools in the 47 largest city school districts in the United States, compared with only 5 percent of all White and 22 percent of all Asian American students. Many of these ethnic minority students come from low-income families (more than half are eligible for free or reduced-cost lunches). These inner-city schools are less likely than other schools to serve more-advantaged populations or to offer high-quality academic support services, advanced courses, and courses that challenge students' active thinking skills. Even students who are motivated to learn and achieve may find it difficult to perform effectively in such contexts.

Culture In the past two decades, the poor performance of American children in math and science has become well publicized. For example, in one cross-national comparison of the math and science achievement of 9- to 13-year-old students, the United States finished 13th (out of 15) in science and 15th (out of 16) in math achievement (Educational Testing Service, 1992). In this study, Korean and Taiwanese students placed first and second, respectively. To read further research on achievement in different countries, see the *Research in Child Development* interlude.

Research in Children's Development

CHILDREN'S MATH ACHIEVEMENT IN THE UNITED STATES, CHINA, TAIWAN, AND JAPAN

Harold Stevenson's (1995, 2000; Stevenson, Hofer, & Randel, 1999; Stevenson & others, 1990) research explores reasons for the poor performance of American students. Stevenson and his colleagues have completed five cross-cultural comparisons of students in the United States, China, Taiwan, and Japan. In these studies, Asian students consistently outperform American students. And, the longer the students are in school, the wider the gap becomes between Asian and American students— the lowest difference is in the first grade, the highest in the eleventh grade (the highest grade studied).

To learn more about the reasons for these large cross-cultural differences, Stevenson and his colleagues spent thousands of hours observing in classrooms, as well as interviewing and surveying teachers, students, and parents. They found that the Asian teachers spent more of their time teaching math than did the American teachers. For example, more than one-fourth of total classroom time in the first grade was spent on math instruction in Japan, compared with only one-tenth of the time in the U.S. first-grade classrooms. Also, the Asian students were in school an average of 240 days a year, compared with 178 days in the United States.

In addition to the substantially greater time spent on math instruction in the Asian schools than the American schools, differences were found between the Asian and American parents. The American parents had much lower expectations for their children's education and achievement than did the Asian parents. Also, the American parents were more likely to believe that their children's math achievement was due to innate ability; the Asian parents were more likely to say that their children's math achievement was the consequence of effort and training (see Figure 12.11). The Asian students were more likely to do math homework

(continued on next page)

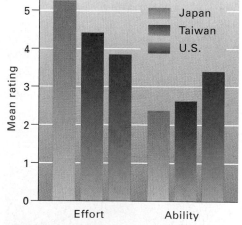

FIGURE 12.11 Mothers' Beliefs About the Factors Responsible for Children's Math Achievement in Three Countries In one study, mothers in Japan and Taiwan were more likely to believe that their children's math achievement was due to effort rather than innate ability, while U.S. mothers were more likely to believe their children's math achievement was due to innate ability (Stevenson, Lee, & Stigler, 1986). If parents believe that their children's math achievement is due to innate ability and their children are not doing well in math, the implication is that they are less likely to think their children will benefit from putting forth more effort.

Asian grade schools intersperse studying with frequent periods of activities. This approach helps children maintain their attention and likely makes learning more enjoyable. Shown here are Japanese fourth-graders making wearable masks. *What are some differences in the way children in many Asian countries are taught compared with children in the United States?*

than were the American students, and the Asian parents were far more likely to help their children with their math homework than were the American parents (Chen & Stevenson, 1989).

Critics of the cross-national comparisons argue that, in many comparisons, virtually all U.S. children are being compared with a "select" group of children from other countries, especially in the secondary school comparisons. Therefore, they conclude, it is no wonder that American students don't fare so well. That criticism holds for some international comparisons. However, even when the top 25 percent of students in different countries were compared, U.S. students did move up some, but not a lot (Mullis & others, 1998).

REVIEW AND REFLECT ▸ LEARNING GOAL 5

5 Explain the development of achievement in children.

Review
- How does extrinsic motivation differ from intrinsic motivation?
- How does mastery motivation differ from helpless and performance orientations? What is mindset, and how does it influence children's achievement?
- What is self-efficacy, and how is it involved in achievement?
- What functions do goal setting, planning, and self-monitoring play in achievement?
- How are social relationships and contexts involved in children's achievement?

Reflect
- Think about several of your own past schoolmates who showed low motivation in school. Why do you think they behaved that way? What teaching strategies might have helped them?

REACH YOUR LEARNING GOALS

1 WHAT IS PIAGET'S THEORY OF COGNITIVE DEVELOPMENT IN MIDDLE AND LATE CHILDHOOD? *Discuss Piaget's stage of concrete operational thought, and apply Piaget's theory to education.*

Concrete Operational Thought

- Concrete operational thought involves operations, conservation, classification, seriation, and transitivity. Thought is not as abstract as later in development.

Evaluating Piaget's Concrete Operational Stage

- Critics argue that some abilities emerge earlier than Piaget thought, that elements of a stage do not appear at the same time, and that education and culture have more influence on development than Piaget predicted. Neo-Piagetians place more emphasis on how children process information, strategies, speed of information processing, and the division of cognitive problems into more precise steps.

Applications to Education

- Piaget's ideas have been applied to education, which especially involves a constructivist approach that focuses on the teacher as a guide rather than a director and turns the classroom into a setting of exploration and discovery.

2 WHAT IS THE NATURE OF CHILDREN'S INFORMATION PROCESSING? *Describe changes in information processing in middle and late childhood.*

Memory

- Long-term memory increases in middle and late childhood. Knowledge and expertise influence memory. Strategies, such as imagery and elaboration, can be used by children to improve their memory. Fuzzy trace theory has been proposed to explain developmental changes in memory.

Thinking

- Critical thinking involves thinking reflectively and productively, as well as evaluating the evidence. A special concern is the lack of emphasis on critical thinking in many schools. Creative thinking is the ability to think in novel and unusual ways and to come up with good, unique solutions to problems. Guilford distinguished between convergent and divergent thinking. A number of strategies can be used to encourage children's creative thinking, including brainstorming. Children think like scientists in some ways, but in others they don't.

Metacognition

- Metacognition is thinking about thinking, or cognition about cognition. Most metacognitive studies have focused on metamemory. Pressley views the key to education as helping students learn a rich repertoire of strategies.

3 HOW CAN CHILDREN'S INTELLIGENCE BE DESCRIBED? *Characterize children's intelligence.*

Intelligence and Its Assessment

- Intelligence consists of problem-solving skills and the ability to adapt to and learn from life's everyday experiences. Interest in intelligence often focuses on individual differences and assessment. Widely used intelligence tests today include the Stanford-Binet tests and Wechsler scales. Results on these tests may be reported in terms of an overall IQ or in terms of performance on specific areas of the tests.

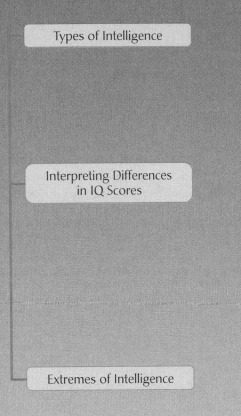

Types of Intelligence

- Spearman proposed that people have a general intelligence (*g*) and specific types of intelligence (*s*). Sternberg proposed that intelligence comes in three main forms: analytical, creative, and practical. Gardner proposes that there are eight types of intelligence: verbal, math, spatial, bodily-kinesthetic, interpersonal, intrapersonal, musical, and naturalist. The multiple-intelligence approaches have expanded our conception of intelligence, but critics argue that the research base for these approaches is not well established. Cultures, however, vary in the way they define intelligence.

Interpreting Differences in IQ Scores

- IQ scores are influenced by both genetics and characteristics of the environment. Studies of heritability indicate that genetics has a strong influence on the variance in IQ scores within a population, but environmental changes can alter the IQ scores of most people considerably. Parents, home environments, schools, and intervention programs can influence these scores. Intelligence test scores have risen considerably around the world in recent decades—called the Flynn effect—and this supports the role of environment in intelligence. Group differences in IQ scores may reflect many influences, including stereotype threat and cultural bias. Tests may be biased against certain groups because they are not familiar with a standard form of English, with the content tested, or with the testing situation. Tests are likely to reflect the values and experience of the dominant culture.

Extremes of Intelligence

- Mental retardation involves low IQ and problems in adapting to everyday life. One classification of mental retardation distinguishes organic and cultural-familial retardation. A child who is gifted has above-average intelligence and/or superior talent for something. Terman contributed to our understanding that gifted children are not more maladjusted than nongifted children. Three characteristics of gifted children are precocity, individuality, and a passion to master a domain.

4 WHAT CHANGES IN LANGUAGE DEVELOPMENT OCCUR IN MIDDLE AND LATE CHILDHOOD? *Summarize language development in middle and late childhood.*

Vocabulary, Grammar, and Metalinguistic Awareness

- Children become more analytical and logical in their approach to words and grammar. In terms of grammar, children now better understand comparatives and subjectives. They become increasingly able to use complex grammar and produce narratives that make sense. Improvements in metalinguistic awareness—knowledge about language—are evident during the elementary school years as children increasingly define words, increase their knowledge of syntax, and understand better how to use language in culturally appropriate ways.

Reading

- A current debate in reading focuses on the basic-skills-and-phonics approach versus the whole-language approach. The basic-skills-and-phonics approach advocates phonetics instruction and giving children simplified materials. The whole-language approach stresses that reading instruction should parallel children's natural language learning and giving children whole-language materials, such as books and poems. An increasing number of experts now conclude that although both approaches can benefit children, direct instruction in phonics is a key aspect of learning to read.

| Bilingualism and Second-Language Learning | • Bilingual education aims to teach academic subjects to immigrant children in their native languages while gradually adding English instruction. Researchers have found that bilingualism does not interfere with performance in either language. Success in learning a second language is greater in childhood than in adolescence. |

5 WHAT CHARACTERIZES CHILDREN'S ACHIEVEMENT? *Explain the development of achievement in children.*

| Extrinsic and Intrinsic Motivation | • Extrinsic motivation involves external incentives such as rewards and punishments. Intrinsic motivation is based on internal factors such as self-determination, curiosity, challenge, and effort. Giving children some choice and providing opportunities for personal responsibility increases intrinsic motivation. |

| Mastery Motivation and Mindset | • Individuals with a mastery motivation focus on the task rather than ability and use solution-oriented strategies. Mastery motivation is preferred over a helpless orientation (individuals seem trapped by the experience of difficulty and attribute their difficulty to lack of ability) or a performance orientation (being concerned with achievement outcomes; winning is what matters). Mindset is the cognitive view, either fixed or growth, that individuals develop for themselves. Dweck argues that a key aspect of children's development is to guide them in developing a growth mindset. |

| Self-Efficacy | • Self-efficacy is the belief that one can master a situation and produce positive outcomes. Bandura believes self-efficacy is a critical factor in whether children will achieve. |

| Goal Setting, Planning, and Self-Regulation | • Setting specific, proximal (short-term), and challenging goals benefits children's self-efficacy and achievement. Being a good planner means managing time effectively, setting priorities, and being organized. Self-monitoring is a key aspect of self-regulation and benefits children's learning. |

| Social Relationships and Contexts | • Among the social relationships and contexts that are linked to children's achievement are parenting practices, peer relationships, relationships with teachers, ethnicity, and culture. American children are more achievement-oriented than children in many countries but are less achievement-oriented than many children in Asian countries such as China, Taiwan, and Japan. |

KEY TERMS

seriation 389
transitivity 389
neo-Piagetians 390
long-term memory 392
elaboration 393
fuzzy trace theory 393
critical thinking 393
creative thinking 394
convergent thinking 394
divergent thinking 394

brainstorming 394
metacognition 396
intelligence 398
individual differences 398
mental age (MA) 398
intelligence quotient (IQ) 398
normal distribution 398
triarchic theory of intelligence 399
heritability 402

stereotype threat 404
culture-reduced tests 405
mental retardation 406
organic retardation 406
cultural-familial retardation 406
gifted 406
metalinguistic awareness 409
whole-language approach 409

basic-skills-and-phonics approach 409
extrinsic motivation 412
intrinsic motivation 412
mastery motivation 413
helpless orientation 413
performance orientation 414
mindset 414
self-efficacy 414

KEY PEOPLE

MAKING A DIFFERENCE

Supporting Children's Cognitive Development

What are the best strategies for helping elementary school children develop their cognitive skills?

- *Facilitate rather than direct children's learning.* Design situations that let children learn by doing and that actively promote their thinking and discovery. Listen, watch, and question children to help them attain a better understanding.
- *Provide opportunities for children to think critically.* Encourage children to think reflectively, rather than automatically accepting everything as correct. Ask children questions about similarities and differences in things. Ask them questions of clarification, such as "What is the main point?" and "Why?" Ask children to justify their opinion. Ask them "what if" questions.
- *Be a good cognitive role model.* Model thinking and self-reflection for the child to see and hear. When children are

around people who think critically and reflectively, they incorporate these cognitive styles into their own thinking repertoire.

- *Encourage collaboration with other children.* Children learn not only from adults but from other children as well. Cross-age teaching, in which older children who are competent thinkers interact with younger children, can be especially helpful. Collaborative problem solving teaches children how to work cooperatively with others.
- *Stimulate children's creative thinking.* Encourage children to take risks in their thinking. Don't overcontrol by telling children precisely what to do; let their originality come through. Don't set up grandiose expectations; it can hurt creativity. Encourage the child to think freely and come up with as many different ways of doing something as possible.

RESOURCES FOR IMPROVING CHILDREN'S LIVES

ERIC Database

www.eric.ed.gov

ERIC provides wide-ranging references to many educational topics, including educational practices, parent-school relations, and community programs.

National Association for Gifted Children (NAGC)

www.nagc.org

The NAGC is an association of academics, educators, and librarians. Its goal is to improve the education of gifted children. It publishes periodic reports on the education of gifted children and the journal *Gifted Children Quarterly.*

The New York Times Parent's Guide to the Best Books for Children

by Eden Lipson (2000)
New York: Crown

This revised and updated edition includes book recommendations for children of all ages. More than 1,700 titles are evaluated.

Mindset

by Carol Dweck (2006)
New York: Random House

An outstanding book that emphasizes how critical it is for parents, teachers, and other adults to guide children in developing a growth rather than a fixed mindset.

E-LEARNING TOOLS

Connect to **www.mhhe.com/santrockc10** to research the answers and complete these exercises. In addition, you'll find a number of other resources and valuable study tools for Chapter 12, "Cognitive Development in Middle and Late Childhood," on this Web site.

Taking It to the Net

1. Carla is the top student in mathematics. Mario displays exceptional talent in art class. Warren is very social and popular with his peers. What do these three students show us about different types of intelligence? How might traditional theories of intelligence miss the unique talents of these students?

2. Tae is the only Asian American student in his class. His teacher, Mr. Mantenga, does not have much experience working with Asian American students. He is under the impression that Tae is very gifted, particularly in math and in the sciences. Mr. Mantenga tries to challenge Tae with more difficult work. Is Mr. Mantenga helping Tae, or might he be basing his impressions of Tae on stereotypes? What would be helpful for Mr. Mantenga to know about Asian American children?

3. A group of parents have called a special PTA meeting to discuss the math curriculum at their children's elementary school. Apparently, students are using computers and calculators and working in groups on math "projects." The parents are alarmed that their children don't seem to be learning old-fashioned arithmetic. What happened to multiplication tables and long division?

4. Motabi is from the Congo. He is arguing with his developmental psychology classmates about the meaning of intelligence. Motabi insists that different cultures construct their own paradigms of intelligence and that intelligence in the Congo is a very different concept from intelligence in Illinois. Is there any evidence to support Motabi's argument?

Health and Well-Being, Parenting, and Education

Build your decision-making skills by trying your hand at the health and well-being, parenting, and education exercises.

Video Clips

The Online Learning Center includes the following videos for this chapter:

1. *Memory Ability at Age 7—1130*
   A boy is presented with five numbers, which are then removed from his view. He recalls all five numbers but is slightly off in the sequence. He states, "2-6-1-4-5. Same numbers, but in a different pattern."

2. *Sex Differences and School—928*
   Why are there achievement differences between boys and girls? The research is unclear, according to Dr. Eccles. She states most likely it is a two-way interaction between biological and cultural factors.

Children are busy becoming something they have not quite grasped yet, something which keeps changing.

—ALASTAIR REID
American Poet, 20th Century

CHAPTER OUTLINE

LEARNING GOALS

WHAT IS THE NATURE OF EMOTIONAL AND PERSONALITY DEVELOPMENT IN MIDDLE AND LATE CHILDHOOD? (1)

Discuss emotional and personality development in middle and late childhood.

The Self

Emotional Development

Moral Development

Gender

WHAT ARE SOME CHANGES IN PARENTING AND FAMILIES IN MIDDLE AND LATE CHILDHOOD? (2)

Describe changes in parenting and families in middle and late childhood.

Developmental Changes in Parenting

Parents as Managers

Stepfamilies

Latchkey Children

WHAT CHANGES CHARACTERIZE PEER RELATIONSHIPS IN MIDDLE AND LATE CHILDHOOD? (3)

Identify changes in peer relationships in middle and late childhood.

Developmental Changes

Peer Status

Social Cognition

Bullying

Friends

WHAT ARE SOME IMPORTANT ASPECTS OF SCHOOLS? (4)

Characterize contemporary approaches to student learning and sociocultural aspects of schooling.

Contemporary Approaches to Student Learning

Socioeconomic Status and Ethnicity

What are some of the challenges children growing up in the South Bronx face?

Images of Children's Development
Stories from the South Bronx and Pax, a Make-Believe Planet

At P.S. 30 in the South Bronx, Mr. Bedrock teaches fifth grade. One student in his class, Serafina, recently lost her mother to AIDS. When author Jonathan Kozol visited the class, he was told that two other children had taken the role of "allies in the child's struggle for emotional survival" (Kozol, 2005, p. 291).

Textbooks are in short supply for the class, and the social studies text is so out of date it claims that Ronald Reagan is the country's president. But Mr. Bedrock told Kozol that it's a "wonderful" class this year. About their teacher, 56-year-old Mr. Bedrock, one student said, "'He's getting old, . . . but we love him anyway'"(p. 292). Kozol found the students orderly, interested, and engaged. He describes one day when Mr. Bedrock is asking the students about reading charts and graphs:

> "Okay, Ashley! Get it right!"
> Before she can answer, he walks over to her desk. "If you mess it up, I'll have to punish Alejandro."
> "Hey!" says Alejandro.
> "That's not fair," says Serafina. "If someone messes up, you have to punish *her*, not someone else."
> "Unfair to Alejandro!" several children say.
> "Poor me!" says Alejandro. (p. 294)

By late childhood, most children, like these students at P.S. 30, have developed friendships, learned to interact with adults other than their parents, and developed ideas about fairness and other moral concepts.

Can children understand such concepts as discrimination, economic inequality, affirmative action, and comparable worth? Probably not, if you ask them about those terms. But Phyllis Katz (1987) found that children can understand situations that involve those concepts. Katz asked elementary-school-age children to pretend that they had taken a long ride on a spaceship to a make-believe planet called Pax. Once there, the children find problematic situations. For example, citizens of Pax who had dotted noses couldn't get jobs. Instead the jobs went to the people with striped noses. "What would you do in this situation?" Katz asked the children.

She asked them for their opinions about various situations on this faraway planet. For example, what a teacher should do when two students were tied for a prize or when they had been fighting. The elementary school children often came up with interesting solutions to problems. For example, all but two children believed that teachers should earn as much as janitors—the holdouts said teachers should make less because they stay in one room or because cleaning toilets is more disgusting and therefore deserves higher wages. All but one thought that not giving a job to a qualified applicant who had different physical characteristics (a dotted rather than a striped nose) was unfair. War was mentioned as the biggest problem on Earth, although children were not certain whether it was presently occurring. Overall, the types of rules the children believed a society should abide by were quite sensible—almost all included the need for equitable sharing of resources and work and prohibitions against aggression.

PREVIEW

The years of middle and late childhood bring many changes to children's social and emotional lives. The development of their self-conceptions, emotions, moral reasoning, and gendered behavior is significant. *Transformations in their relationships with parents and peers also occur, and schooling takes on a more academic flavor.*

1 WHAT IS THE NATURE OF EMOTIONAL AND PERSONALITY DEVELOPMENT IN MIDDLE AND LATE CHILDHOOD?

The Self		Moral Development

Emotional Development		Gender

The young students in Katz' study came up with imaginative solutions to the problems on Pax in part because of their cognitive development, as discussed in previous chapters, but their responses also reflect their socioemotional development. In this section, we explore the development of self, as well as emotional, moral, and gender development in middle and late childhood.

The Self

Among the important topics we discuss are the nature of the child's self-understanding, understanding of others, and self-esteem during the elementary school years. We also consider Erikson's view of middle and late childhood.

The Development of Self-Understanding　In middle and late childhood, especially from 8 to 11 years of age, children increasingly describe themselves with psychological characteristics and traits in contrast to the more concrete self-descriptions of younger children. Older children are more likely to describe themselves as "*popular, nice, helpful, mean, smart,* and *dumb*" (Harter, 2006, p. 526).

In addition, during the elementary school years, children become more likely to recognize social aspects of the self (Harter, 2006). They include references to social groups in their self-descriptions, such as referring to themselves as Girl Scouts, as Catholics, or as someone who has two close friends (Livesly & Bromley, 1973).

Children's self-understanding in the elementary school years also includes increasing reference to social comparison (Harter, 2006). At this point in development, children are more likely to distinguish themselves from others in comparative rather than in absolute terms. That is, elementary-school-age children are no longer as likely to think about what they do or do not do, but are more likely to think about what they can do in comparison with others.

Consider a series of studies in which Diane Ruble (1983) investigated children's use of social comparison in their self-evaluations. Children were given a difficult task and then offered feedback on their performance, as well as information about the performances of other children their age. The children were then asked for self-evaluations. Children younger than 7 made virtually no reference to the information about other children's performances. However, many children older than 7 included socially comparative information in their self-descriptions.

In sum, in middle and late childhood, self-description increasingly involves psychological and social characteristics, including social comparison.

Understanding Others　In Chapter 10, we described the advances and limitations of young children's understanding of others. In middle and late childhood, children show an increase in **perspective taking,** the ability to assume other people's perspectives and understand their thoughts and feelings. In Robert Selman's (1980) view, at about 6 to 8 years of age, children begin to understand that others may have a perspective because some people have more access to information. Then, he says, in the next several years, children become aware that each individual is aware of the other's perspective and that putting one's self in the other's place is a way of judging the other person's intentions, purposes, and actions.

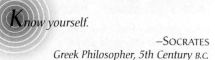

Know yourself.

—SOCRATES
Greek Philosopher, 5th Century B.C.

perspective taking The ability to assume other people's perspectives and understand their thoughts and feelings.

What are some changes in children's understanding of others in middle and late childhood?

Perspective taking is especially thought to be important in whether children develop prosocial or antisocial attitudes and behavior. In terms of prosocial behavior, taking another's perspective improves children's likelihood of understanding and sympathizing with others when they are distressed or in need (Eisenberg, Fabes, & Spinrad, 2006). In terms of antisocial behavior, some researchers have found that children who have a low level of perspective-taking skills engage in more antisocial behavior than children at higher levels (Chandler, 1973).

In middle and late childhood, children also become more skeptical of others' claims. In Chapter 10, we indicated that even 4-year-old children show some skepticism of others' claims. In middle and late childhood, children become increasingly skeptical of some sources of information about psychological traits. For example, in one study, 10- to 11-year-olds were more likely to reject other children's self-reports that they were *smart* and *honest* than were 6- to 7-year-olds (Heyman & Legare, 2005). The more psychologically-sophisticated 10- to 11-year-olds also showed a better understanding that others' self-reports may involve socially desirable tendencies than the 6- to 7-year-olds. In a recent cross-cultural comparison of 6- to 11-year-olds from the United States and China, older children showed increased skepticism of others' self-reports concerning value-laden traits, such as *honest, smart,* and *nice,* but did not show increased skepticism about less value-laden characteristics such as *outgoing, likes salty food,* and *likes the color red* (Heyman, Fu, & Lee, 2007). Older Chinese children were more likely to expect others to show modesty when talking about themselves than were their U.S. counterparts.

Later in the chapter, we further explore children's understanding of others in our discussion of the social information-processing skills and social knowledge involved in peer relations.

Self-Esteem and Self-Concept   High self-esteem and a positive self-concept are important characteristics of children's well-being (Donnellan, Trzniewski, & Robins, 2006; Harter, 2006). Investigators sometimes use the terms *self-esteem* and *self-concept* interchangeably or do not precisely define them, but there is a meaningful difference between them. **Self-esteem** refers to global evaluations of the self; it is also called *self-worth* or *self-image.* For example, a child may perceive that she is not merely a person but a *good* person. **Self-concept** refers to domain-specific evaluations of the self. Children can make self-evaluations in many domains of their lives—academic, athletic, appearance, and so on. In sum, *self-esteem* refers to global self-evaluations, *self-concept* to domain-specific evaluations.

Self-esteem reflects perceptions that do not always match reality (Baumeister & others, 2003). A child's self-esteem might reflect a belief about whether he or she is intelligent and attractive, for example, but that belief is not necessarily accurate. Thus, high self-esteem may refer to accurate, justified perceptions of one's worth as a person and one's successes and accomplishments, but it can also refer to an arrogant, grandiose, unwarranted sense of superiority over others. In the same manner, low self-esteem may reflect either an accurate perception of one's shortcomings or a distorted, even pathological insecurity and inferiority.

What are some issues involved in understanding children's self-esteem in school?

Variations in self-esteem have been linked with many aspects of children's development. However, much of the research is *correlational* rather than *experimental.* Recall from Chapter 1 that correlation does not equal causation. Thus, if a correlational study finds an association between children's low self-esteem and low academic achievement, low academic achievement could cause the low self-esteem as much as low self-esteem causes low academic achievement (Bowles, 1999).

In fact, there are only moderate correlations between school performance and self-esteem, and these correlations do not suggest that high self-esteem produces better school performance (Baumeister & others, 2003). Efforts to increase students' self-esteem have not always led to improved school performance (Davies & Brember, 1999).

self-esteem The global evaluative dimension of the self. Self-esteem is also referred to as self-worth of self-image.

self-concept Domain-specific evaluations of the self.

Children with high self-esteem have greater initiative, but this can produce positive or negative outcomes (Baumeister & others, 2003). High-self-esteem children are prone to both prosocial and antisocial actions.

In fact, a current concern is that too many of today's children grow up receiving praise for mediocre or even poor performance and as a consequence have inflated self-esteem (Graham, 2005; Stipek, 2005). They may have difficulty handling competition and criticism. This theme is vividly captured by the title of a book, *Dumbing Down Our Kids: Why American Children Feel Good About Themselves But Can't Read, Write, or Add* (Sykes, 1995).

What are some good strategies for effectively increasing children's self-esteem? See the *Caring for Children* interlude for some answers to this question.

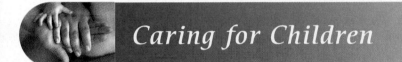

Caring for Children

INCREASING CHILDREN'S SELF-ESTEEM

Four ways children's self-esteem can be improved include identifying the causes of low self-esteem, providing emotional support and social approval, helping children achieve, and helping children cope (Bednar, Wells, & Peterson, 1995; Harter, 1999, 2006).

How can parents help children develop higher self-esteem?

- *Identify the causes of low self-esteem.* Intervention should target the causes of low self-esteem. Children have the highest self-esteem when they perform competently in domains that are important to them. Therefore, children should be encouraged to identify and value areas of competence. These areas might include academic skills, athletic skills, physical attractiveness, and social acceptance.
- *Provide emotional support and social approval.* Some children with low self-esteem come from conflicted families or conditions in which they experienced abuse or neglect—situations in which support was not available. In some cases, alternative sources of support can be arranged either informally through the encouragement of a teacher, a coach, or another significant adult, or more formally, through programs such as Big Brothers and Big Sisters.
- *Help children achieve.* Achievement also can improve children's self-esteem. For example, the straightforward teaching of real skills to children often results in increased achievement and, thus, in enhanced self-esteem. Children develop higher self-esteem because they know the important tasks that will achieve their goals, and they have performed them or similar behaviors in the past.
- *Help children cope.* Self-esteem is often increased when children face a problem and try to cope with it, rather than avoid it. If coping rather than avoidance prevails, children often face problems realistically, honestly, and nondefensively. This produces favorable self-evaluative thoughts, which lead to the self-generated approval that raises self-esteem.

Self-Regulation   One of the most important aspects of the self in middle and late childhood is the increased capacity for self-regulation. This increased capacity is characterized by deliberate efforts to manage one's behavior, emotions, and thoughts that lead to increased social competence and achievement (Laible & Thompson, 2007; Saarni & others, 2006). In Chapter 12, we described the importance of engaging in self-regulation in achievement, especially by monitoring one's progress in attaining a goal. Later in this chapter, in our discussion of emotion, we examine a number of strategies for the self-regulation of emotion, as well as coping strategies, that also reflect improvement in self-regulation during middle and late childhood.

The increased capacity in self-regulation is linked to developmental advances in the brain's prefrontal cortex, which was discussed in Chapter 11, "Physical Development in Middle and Late Childhood." Recall our discussion there of the increased focal activation in the prefrontal cortex that is linked to improved cognitive control, which includes self-regulation (Durston & others, 2007).

Industry Versus Inferiority   In Chapter 1, we described Erik Erikson's (1968) eight stages of human development. His fourth stage, industry versus inferiority, appears during middle and late childhood. The term *industry* expresses a dominant theme of this period: children become interested in how things are made and how they work. It is the Robinson Crusoe age, in that the enthusiasm and minute detail Crusoe uses to describe his activities appeal to the child's budding sense of industry. When children are encouraged in their efforts to make, build, and work—whether building a model airplane, constructing a tree house, fixing a bicycle, solving an addition problem, or cooking—their sense of industry increases. However, parents who see their children's efforts at making things as "mischief" or "making a mess" encourage children's development of a sense of inferiority.

Children's social worlds beyond their families also contribute to a sense of industry. School becomes especially important in this regard. Consider children who are slightly below average in intelligence. They are too bright to be in special classes but not bright enough to be in gifted classes. They fail frequently in their academic efforts, developing a sense of inferiority. By contrast, consider children whose sense of industry is derogated at home. A series of sensitive and committed teachers may revitalize their sense of industry (Elkind, 1970).

Emotional Development

In Chapter 10, we saw that preschoolers become more adept at talking about their own and others' emotions. They also show a growing awareness of the need to control and manage their emotions to meet social standards. In middle and late childhood children further develop their understanding and self-regulation of emotion (Saarni, 2006; Saarni & others, 2006).

Developmental Changes   Important developmental changes in emotions during the middle and late childhood years include the following (Denham, Bassett, & Wyatt, 2007; Kuebli, 1994; Thompson & Goodvin, 2005):

- *Improved emotional understanding*. For example, children in elementary school develop an increased ability to understand such complex emotions as pride and shame. These emotions become less tied to the reactions of other people; they become more self-generated and integrated with a sense of personal responsibility.
- *Increased understanding that more than one emotion can be experienced in a particular situation.*
- *Increased tendency to take into fuller account the events leading to emotional reactions.*
- *Marked improvements in the ability to suppress or conceal negative emotional reactions*. Elementary school children often intentionally hide their emotions.
- *The use of self-initiated strategies for redirecting feelings*. In the elementary school years, children become more reflective and develop better strategies to cope with emotional matters. They can more effectively manage their emotions with cognitive strategies, such as engaging in distracting thoughts.
- *A capacity for genuine empathy*.

Emotional Intelligence   One way of viewing these developments in children's ability to understand and regulate emotions is to say that they are developing social aspects of intelligence. In terms of the theories discussed in Chapter 12, they are developing what is called "practical intelligence" in Sternberg's theory and "intrapersonal" and "interpersonal" intelligence in Gardner's theory. Another approach, first proposed in 1990, identifies **emotional intelligence** as a form of social intelligence that involves the ability to monitor one's own and others' feelings and emotions, to discriminate among them, and to use this information to guide one's thinking and action (Salovey & Grewal, 2005; Salovey & Mayer, 1990).

Interest in emotional intelligence grew with the publication of Daniel Goleman's book *Emotional Intelligence* (1995). Goleman maintains that to predict an individual's competence, performance on standardized intelligence tests matters less than emotional intelligence. In Goleman's view, emotional intelligence involves four main areas:

- *Developing emotional self-awareness* (such as the ability to separate feelings from actions)
- *Managing emotions* (such as being able to control anger)
- *Reading emotions* (such as taking the perspective of others)
- *Handling relationships* (such as the ability to solve relationship problems)

Some schools have programs that are designed to help children with their emotional lives. For example, one private school near San Francisco, the Nueva School, offers a class in what is called "self science," and the list of the class's contents echoes Goleman's definition of the components of emotional intelligence. The subject of self science is feelings—the child's own and those involved in relationships. Teachers speak to issues such as hurt over being left out, envy, and disagreements.

Coping with Stress

An important aspect of children's lives is learning how to cope with stress (Taylor & Stanton, 2007). As children get older, they are able to more accurately appraise a stressful situation and determine how much control they have over it. Older children generate more coping alternatives to stressful conditions and use more cognitive coping strategies (Saarni & others, 2006). For example, older children are better than younger children at intentionally shifting their thoughts to something that is less stressful. Older children are also better at reframing, or changing one's perception of a stressful situation. For example, younger children may be very disappointed that their teacher did not say hello to them when they arrived at school. Older children may reframe this type of situation and think, "She may have been busy with other things and just forgot to say hello."

By 10 years of age, most children are able to use these cognitive strategies to cope with stress (Saarni & others, 2006). However, in families that have not been supportive and are characterized by turmoil or trauma, children may be so overwhelmed by stress that they do not use such strategies (Klingman, 2006).

The terrorist attacks on the World Trade Center in New York City and the Pentagon in Washington, D.C., on September 11, 2001, and hurricanes Katrina and Rita in September 2005, raised special concerns about how to help children cope with such stressful events. Children who have a number of coping techniques have the best chance of adapting and functioning competently in the face of traumatic events. Here are some recommendations for helping children cope with the stress of these types of events (Gurwitch & others, 2001, pp. 4–11):

- *Reassure children of their safety and security.* This may need to be done numerous times.
- *Allow children to retell events and be patient in listening to them.*
- *Encourage children to talk about any disturbing or confusing feelings.* Tell them that these are normal feelings after a stressful event.
- *Help children make sense of what happened.* Children may misunderstand what took place. For example, young children "may blame themselves, believe

What are some effective strategies to help children cope with traumatic events, such as the terrorist attacks on the United States on 9/11/2001?

emotional intelligence A form of social intelligence that involves the ability to monitor one's own and others' feelings and emotions, to discriminate among them, and to use this information to guide one's thinking and action.

things happened that did not happen, believe that terrorists are in the school, etc. Gently help children develop a realistic understanding of the event" (p. 10).

- *Protect children from reexposure to frightening situations and reminders of the trauma.* This includes limiting conversations about the event in front of the children.

Traumatic events may cause individuals to think about the moral aspects of life. Hopelessness and despair may short-circuit moral development when a child is confronted by the violence of war zones and impoverished inner cities (Nadar, 2001). Let's further explore children's moral development.

Moral Development

Remember from Chapter 10 our description of Piaget's view of moral development. Piaget proposed that younger children are characterized by *heteronomous morality*—that is, justice and rules are unchangeable. By 10 years of age, they have moved into a more advanced stage called *autonomous morality*, in which they are aware that rules are created by people and that both intentions and consequences should be considered. According to Piaget, older children consider the intentions of the individual, believe that rules are subject to change, and are aware that punishment does not always follow wrongdoing.

A second major perspective on moral development was proposed by Lawrence Kohlberg (1958, 1986). Piaget's cognitive stages of development serve as the underpinnings for Kohlberg's theory, but Kohlberg suggested that there are six stages of moral development. These stages, he argued, are universal. Development from one stage to another, said Kohlberg, is fostered by opportunities to take the perspective of others and to experience conflict between one's current stage of moral thinking and the reasoning of someone at a higher stage.

Kohlberg arrived at his view after 20 years of using a unique interview with children. In the interview, children are presented with a series of stories in which characters face moral dilemmas. The following is the most popular Kohlberg dilemma:

> In Europe a woman was near death from a special kind of cancer. There was one drug that the doctors thought might save her. It was a form of radium that a druggist in the same town had recently discovered. The drug was expensive to make, but the druggist was charging ten times what the drug cost him to make. He paid $200 for the radium and charged $2,000 for a small dose of the drug. The sick woman's husband, Heinz, went to everyone he knew to borrow the money, but he could only get together $1,000 which is half of what it cost. He told the druggist that his wife was dying and asked him to sell it cheaper or let him pay later. But the druggist said, "No, I discovered the drug, and I am going to make money from it." So Heinz got desperate and broke into the man's store to steal the drug for his wife. (Kohlberg, 1969, p. 379)

This story is one of 11 that Kohlberg devised to investigate the nature of moral thought. After reading the story, the interviewee answers a series of questions about the moral dilemma. Should Heinz have stolen the drug? Was stealing it right or wrong? Why? Is it a husband's duty to steal the drug for his wife if he can get it no other way? Would a good husband steal? Did the druggist have the right to charge that much when there was no law setting a limit on the price? Why or why not?

The Kohlberg Stages Based on the answers interviewees gave for this and other moral dilemmas, Kohlberg described three levels of moral thinking, each of which is characterized by two stages (see Figure 13.1).

Preconventional reasoning is the lowest level of moral reasoning, said Kohlberg. At this level, good and bad are interpreted in terms of external rewards and punishments.

Lawrence Kohlberg, the architect of a provocative cognitive developmental theory of moral development. *What is the nature of his theory?*

preconventional reasoning The lowest level in Kohlberg's theory of moral development. The individual's concepts of good and bad are controlled primarily by external rewards and punishment.

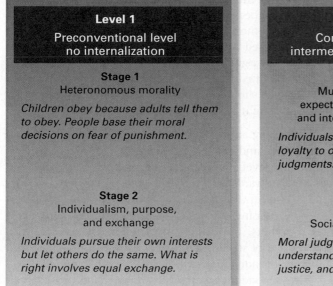

FIGURE 13.1 Kohlberg's Three Levels and Six Stages of Moral Development

- *Stage 1.* **Heteronomous morality** is the first stage in preconventional reasoning. At this stage, moral thinking is tied to punishment. For example, children think that they must obey because they fear punishment for disobedience.
- *Stage 2.* **Individualism, instrumental purpose, and exchange** is the second stage of preconventional reasoning. At this stage, individuals reason that pursuing their own interests is the right thing to do, but they let others do the same. Thus, they think that what is right involves an equal exchange. They reason that if they are nice to others, others will be nice to them in return.

Conventional reasoning is the second, or intermediate, level in Kohlberg's theory of moral development. At this level, individuals apply certain standards, but they are the standards set by others, such as parents or the government.

- *Stage 3.* **Mutual interpersonal expectations, relationships, and interpersonal conformity** is Kohlberg's third stage of moral development. At this stage, individuals value trust, caring, and loyalty to others as a basis of moral judgments. Children and adolescents often adopt their parents' moral standards at this stage, seeking to be thought of by their parents as a "good girl" or a "good boy."
- *Stage 4.* **Social systems morality** is the fourth stage in Kohlberg's theory of moral development. At this stage, moral judgments are based on understanding the social order, law, justice, and duty. For example, adolescents may reason that in order for a community to work effectively, it needs to be protected by laws that are adhered to by its members.

Postconventional reasoning is the highest level in Kohlberg's theory of moral development. At this level, the individual recognizes alternative moral courses, explores the options, and then decides on a personal moral code.

- *Stage 5.* **Social contract or utility and individual rights** is the fifth Kohlberg stage. At this stage, individuals reason that values, rights, and principles undergird or transcend the law. A person evaluates the validity of actual laws, and social systems can be examined in terms of the degree to which they preserve and protect fundamental human rights and values.

heteronomous morality Kohlberg's first state in preconventional reasoning in which moral thinking is tied to punishment.

individualism, instrumental purpose, and exchange The second Kohlberg stage of preconventional reasoning. At this stage, individuals pursue their own interests, reasoning it is the right thing to do, but also let others do the same.

conventional reasoning The second, or intermediate, level in Kohlberg's theory of moral development. At this level, individuals abide by certain standards, but they are the standards of others, such as parents or the laws of society.

mutual interpersonal expectations, relationships, and interpersonal conformity Kohlberg's third stage of moral development. At this stage, individuals value trust, caring, and loyalty to others as a basis of moral judgments.

social systems morality The fourth stage in Kohlberg's theory of moral development. Moral judgments are based on understanding the social order, law, justice, and duty.

postconventional reasoning The highest level in Kohlberg's theory of moral development. At this level, the individual recognizes alternative moral courses, explores the options, and then decides on a personal moral code.

social contract or utility and individual rights The fifth Kohlberg stage. At this stage, individuals reason that values, rights, and principles undergird or transcend the law.

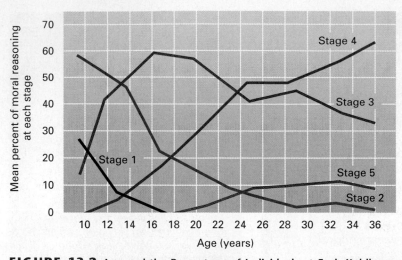

FIGURE 13.2 Age and the Percentage of Individuals at Each Kohlberg Stage In one longitudinal study of males from 10 to 36 years of age, at age 10 most moral reasoning was at stage 2 (Colby & others, 1983). At 16 to 18 years of age, stage 3 became the most frequent type of moral reasoning, and it was not until the mid-twenties that stage 4 became the most frequent. Stage 5 did not appear until 20 to 22 years of age and it never characterized more than 10 percent of the individuals. In this study, the moral stages appeared somewhat later than Kohlberg envisioned, and stage 6 was absent.

- *Stage 6.* **Universal ethical principles** is the sixth and highest stage in Kohlberg's theory of moral development. At this stage, the person has developed a moral standard based on universal human rights. When faced with a conflict between law and conscience, the person reasons that conscience should be followed, even though the decision might bring risk.

Kohlberg argued that these levels and stages occur in a sequence and are age related: before age 9, most children use level 1, preconventional reasoning based on external rewards and punishments, when they consider moral choices. By early adolescence, their moral reasoning is increasingly based on the application of standards set by others. Most adolescents reason at stage 3, with some signs of stages 2 and 4. By early adulthood, a small number of individuals reason in postconventional ways.

What evidence supports this description of development? A 20-year longitudinal investigation found that use of stages 1 and 2 decreased with age (Colby & others, 1983) (see Figure 13.2). Stage 4, which did not appear at all in the moral reasoning of 10-year-olds, was reflected in the moral thinking of 62 percent of the 36-year-olds. Stage 5 did not appear until age 20 to 22 and never characterized more than 10 percent of the individuals.

Thus, the moral stages appeared somewhat later than Kohlberg initially envisioned, and reasoning at the higher stages, especially stage 6, was rare. Although stage 6 has been removed from the Kohlberg moral judgment scoring manual, it still is considered to be theoretically important in the Kohlberg scheme of moral development.

Influences on the Kohlberg Stages   What factors influence movement through Kohlberg's stages? Although moral reasoning at each stage presupposes a certain level of cognitive development, Kohlberg argued that advances in children's cognitive development did not ensure development of moral reasoning. Instead, moral reasoning also reflects children's experiences in dealing with moral questions and moral conflict.

Several investigators have tried to advance individuals' levels of moral development by having a model present arguments that reflect moral thinking one stage above the individuals' established levels. This approach applies the concepts of equilibrium and conflict that Piaget used to explain cognitive development. By presenting arguments slightly beyond the children's level of moral reasoning, the researchers created a disequilibrium that motivated the children to restructure their moral thought. The upshot of studies using this approach is that virtually any plus-stage discussion, for any length of time, seems to promote more advanced moral reasoning (Walker, 1982).

Kohlberg maintained that peer interaction is a critical part of the social stimulation that challenges children to change their moral reasoning. Whereas adults characteristically impose rules and regulations on children, the give-and-take among peers gives children an opportunity to take the perspective of another person and to generate rules democratically. Kohlberg stressed that in principle, encounters with any peers can produce perspective-taking opportunities that may advance a child's moral reasoning.

Kohlberg's Critics   Kohlberg's theory provoked debate, research, and criticism (Lapsley, 2006; Lapsley & Narvaez, 2006; Smetana, 2006; Turiel, 2006; Walker, 2006). Key criticisms involve the link between moral thought and moral behavior, the roles of culture and the family in moral development, and the significance of concern for others.

universal ethical principles The sixth and highest stage in Kohlberg's theory of moral development. Individuals develop a moral standard based on universal human rights.

Moral Thought and Moral Behavior Kohlberg's theory has been criticized for placing too much emphasis on moral thought and not enough emphasis on moral behavior (Walker, 2004). Moral reasons can sometimes be a shelter for immoral behavior. Corrupt CEOs and politicians endorse the loftiest of moral virtues in public before their own behavior is exposed. Whatever the latest public scandal, you will probably find that the culprits displayed virtuous thoughts but engaged in immoral behavior. No one wants a nation of cheaters and thieves who can reason at the postconventional level. The cheaters and thieves may know what is right yet still do what is wrong. Heinous actions can be cloaked in a mantle of moral virtue.

The mantle of virtue is not necessarily a ruse; it is often taken on sincerely. Social cognitive theorist Albert Bandura (1999, 2002) argues that people usually do not engage in harmful conduct until they have justified the morality of their actions to themselves. Immoral conduct is made personally and socially acceptable by portraying it as serving socially worthy or moral purposes or even as doing God's will. Bandura provides the examples of Islamic extremists who mount jihad (holy war) against what they see as a tyrannical, decadent people seeking to enslave the Islamic world and antiabortion activists who bomb abortion clinics or murder doctors in order to discourage abortions.

Culture and Moral Reasoning Kohlberg emphasized that his stages of moral reasoning are universal, but some critics claim his theory is culturally biased (Miller, 2006; Shweder & others, 2006; Wainryb, 2006). Both Kohlberg and his critics may be partially correct.

This 14-year-old boy in Nepal is thought to be the sixth holiest Buddhist in the world. *How might the moral reasoning of this boy be different than Kohlberg's theory predicts?*

One review of forty-five studies in twenty-seven cultures around the world, mostly non-European, provided support for the universality of Kohlberg's first four stages (Snarey, 1987). Individuals in diverse cultures developed through these four stages in sequence as Kohlberg predicted. Stages 5 and 6, however, were not found in all cultures. Furthermore, this review found that Kohlberg's scoring system does not recognize the higher-level moral reasoning of certain cultures and thus that moral reasoning is more culture-specific that Kohlberg envisioned (Snarey, 1987).

In sum, although Kohlberg's approach does capture much of the moral reasoning voiced in various cultures around the world, his approach misses or miscontrues some important moral concepts in particular cultures (Miller, 2006, 2007; Shweder & others, 2006; Wainryb, 2006).

Families and Moral Development Kohlberg argued that family processes are essentially unimportant in children's moral development. As noted earlier, he argued that parent-child relationships usually provide children with little opportunity for give and take or perspective taking. Rather, Kohlberg said that such opportunities are more likely to be provided by children's peer relations.

Did Kohlberg underestimate the contribution of family relationships to moral development? A number of developmentalists emphasize that *inductive discipline*, which uses reasoning and focuses children's attention on the consequences of their actions for others, positively influences moral development (Hoffman, 1970). They also stress that parents' moral values influence children's developing moral thoughts (Laible & Thompson, 2007). And as we saw in Chapter 10, "Socioemotional Development in Early Childhood," parents influence young children's moral development through the quality of parent-child relationships, being proactive to avert potential misbehavior by children, in conversational dialogue (Laible & Thompson, 2007; Thompson, 2006). Nonetheless, most developmentalists agree with Kohlberg, and Piaget, that peers play an important role in the development of moral reasoning.

Gender and the Care Perspective Perhaps the most publicized criticism of Kohlberg's theory has come from Carol Gilligan (1982, 1992, 1996), who argues that Kohlberg's theory reflects a gender bias. According to Gilligan, Kohlberg's theory is based on a male norm that puts abstract principles above relationships and concern for others

Carol Gilligan is shown with some of the students she has interviewed about the importance of relationships in a female's development. *What is Gilligan's view of moral development?*

and sees the individual as standing alone and independently making moral decisions. It puts justice at the heart of morality. In contrast to Kohlberg's **justice perspective,** Gilligan argues for a **care perspective,** which is a moral perspective that views people in terms of their connectedness with others and emphasizes interpersonal communication, relationships with others, and concern for others. According to Gilligan, Kohlberg greatly underplayed the care perspective, perhaps because he was a male, because most of his research was with males rather than females, and because he used male responses as a model for his theory.

In extensive interviews with girls from 6 to 18 years of age, Gilligan and her colleagues found that girls consistently interpret moral dilemmas in terms of human relationships and base these interpretations on listening and watching other people (Gilligan, 1992, 1996; Gilligan & others, 2003). However, a meta-analysis (a statistical analysis that combines the results of many different studies) cast doubt on Gilligan's claim of substantial gender differences in moral judgment (Jaffee & Hyde, 2000). Overall, this analysis found only a small gender difference in care-based reasoning, and the difference was greater in adolescence than childhood. When differences in moral reasoning occurred, they were better explained by the nature of the dilemma than by gender. For example, both males and females tended to use care reasoning to deal with interpersonal dilemmas and justice reasoning to handle societal dilemmas.

Along with this lack of support for gender differences in moral reasoning, however, other research does find differences in how boys and girls tend to interpret situations (Eisenberg & Morris, 2004). In support of this idea, one study found that females rated prosocial dilemmas (those emphasizing altruism and helping) as more significant than did males (Wark & Krebs, 1996). Another study revealed that young adolescent girls used more care-based reasoning about dating dilemmas than did boys (Weisz & Black, 2002).

Social Conventional Reasoning   Some theorists and researchers argue that Kohlberg did not adequately distinguish between moral reasoning and social conventional reasoning (Smetana, 2006; Turiel, 2006). **Social conventional reasoning** focuses on conventional rules that have been established by social consensus in order to control behavior and maintain the social system. The rules themselves are arbitrary, such as using a fork at meals and raising your hand in class before speaking.

In contrast, moral reasoning focuses on ethical issues and rules of morality. Unlike conventional rules, moral rules are not arbitrary. They are obligatory, widely accepted, and somewhat impersonal (Turiel, 2006). Rules pertaining to lying, cheating, stealing, and physically harming another person are moral rules because violation of these rules affronts ethical standards that exist apart from social consensus and convention. Moral judgments involve concepts of justice, whereas social conventional judgments are concepts of social organization.

Prosocial Behavior   Whereas Kohlberg's and Gilligan's theories have focused primarily on the development of moral reasoning, the study of prosocial moral behavior has placed more emphasis on the behavioral aspects of moral development (Hastings, Vtendale, & Sullivar, 2007). Children engage in both immoral antisocial acts such as lying and cheating and prosocial moral behavior such as showing empathy or acting altruistically (Carlo, 2006; Hastings, Utentale, & Sullivan, 2007). Even during the preschool years, children may care for others or comfort others in distress, but prosocial behavior occurs more often in adolescence than in childhood (Eisenberg & Morris, 2004).

William Damon (1988) described how sharing develops. During their first years, when children share, it is usually not for reasons of empathy but for the fun of the social play ritual or out of imitation. Then, at about 4 years of age, a combination of empathic awareness and adult encouragement produces a sense of obligation on the part of the child to share with others. Most 4-year-olds are not selfless saints,

justice perspective The moral perspective of Lawrence Kohlberg, which puts abstract principles above relationships, and focuses on the rights of the individual; individuals independently make moral decisions.

care perspective The moral perspective of Carol Gilligan, which views people in terms of their connectedness with others and emphasizes interpersonal communication, relationships with others, and concern for others.

social conventional reasoning Thoughts about social consensus and convention, in contrast to moral reasoning, which stresses ethical issues.

however. Children believe they have an obligation to share but do not necessarily think they should be as generous to others as they are to themselves.

Children's sharing comes to reflect a more complex sense of what is just and right during middle and late childhood. By the start of the elementary school years, children begin to express objective ideas about fairness (Eisenberg, Fabes, & Spinrad, 2006). It is common to hear 6-year-old children use the word *fair* as synonymous with *equal* or *same*. By the mid to late elementary school years, children believe that equity instead sometimes means that people with special merit or special needs deserve special treatment.

Missing from the factors that guide children's sharing is one that many adults might expect to be the most influential: the motivation to obey adult authority figures. Surprisingly, a number of studies have shown that adult authority has only a small influence on children's sharing (Eisenberg, 1982). Parental advice and prodding certainly foster standards of sharing, but the give-and-take of peer requests and arguments provides the most immediate stimulation of sharing.

Moral Personality   Beyond the development of moral reasoning and specific moral feelings and prosocial behaviors, do children also develop a pattern of moral characteristics that is distinctively their own? In other words, do children develop a *moral personality,* and if so, what are its components? Researchers have focused attention on three possible components: (1) moral identity, (2) moral character, and (3) moral exemplars:

How does children's sharing change from the preschool to the elementary school years?

- *Moral identity.* Individuals have a moral identity when moral notions and moral commitments are central to their lives (Blasi, 2005). They construct the self with reference to moral categories. Violating their moral commitment would place the integrity of their self at risk (Lapsley & Narvaez, 2006).
- *Moral character.* A person with moral character has the will power, desires, and integrity to stand up to pressure, overcome distractions and disappointments, and behave morally. A person of good moral character displays moral virtues such as "honesty, truthfulness, and trustworthiness, as well as those of care, compassion, thoughtfulness, and considerateness. Other salient traits revolve around virtues of dependability, loyalty, and conscientiousness" (Walker, 2002, p. 74).
- *Moral exemplars.* Moral exemplars are people who have lived exemplary moral lives. Their moral personality, identity, character, and set of virtues reflect moral excellence and commitment.

In sum, moral development is a multifaceted, complex concept. Included in this complexity are their thoughts, feelings, behaviors, and personality.

Gender

Gilligan's claim that Kohlberg's theory of moral development reflects gender bias reminds us of the pervasive influence of gender on development. Long before elementary school, boys and girls show preferences for different toys and activities. As we discussed in Chapter 10, preschool children display a gender identity and gender-typed behavior that reflects biological, cognitive, and social influences. Here we examine gender stereotypes, gender similarities and differences, and gender-role classification.

Gender Stereotypes   According to the old ditty, boys are made of "frogs and snails" and girls are made of "sugar and spice and all that is nice." In the past, a well-adjusted boy was supposed to be independent, aggressive, and powerful. A well-adjusted girl was supposed to be dependent, nurturant, and uninterested in power. The masculine characteristics were considered to be healthy and good by society; the feminine characteristics were considered undesirable. These notions reflect **gender stereotypes,** which are broad categories that reflect general impressions and beliefs about females and males.

Recent research has found that gender stereotypes are, to a great extent, still present in today's world, in the lives of both children and adults (Hyde, 2005, 2007; Ruble, Martin, & Berenbaum, 2006). A recent study revealed that children's gender stereotyping increased from preschool through the fifth grade (Miller & others, 2007). In this study, preschoolers tended to stereotype dolls and appearance as characteristic of girls' interests and toys and behaviors (such a action heroes and hitting) as the province of boys (Miller & others, 2007). During middle and late childhood, children expanded the range and extent of their gender stereotyping in such areas as occupations, sports, and school tasks. Researchers also have found that boys' gender stereotypes are more rigid than girls' (Ruble, Martin, & Berenbaum, 2006).

Gender Similarities and Differences

What is the reality behind gender stereotypes? Let's examine some of the similarities and differences between the sexes, keeping in mind that (1) the differences are averages—not all females versus all males; (2) even when differences are reported, there is considerable overlap between the sexes; and (3) the differences may be due primarily to biological factors, sociocultural factors, or both. First, we examine physical similarities and differences, and then we turn to cognitive and socioemotional similarities and differences.

What are little boys made of?
Frogs and snails
And puppy dogs' tails.
What are little girls made of?
Sugar and spice
And all that's nice.

—J. O. HALLIWELL
English Author, 19th Century

Physical Development Women have about twice the body fat of men, most concentrated around breasts and hips. In males, fat is more likely to go to the abdomen. On the average, males grow to be 10 percent taller than females. Other physical differences are less obvious. From conception on, females have a longer life expectancy than males, and females are less likely than males to develop physical or mental disorders. Males have twice the risk of coronary disease as females.

Differences in hormones contribute to many of these physical differences between the sexes. Recall that androgens such as testosterone are male sex hormones and estrogens are female sex hormones, although both males and females produce androgens and estrogens. Male hormones promote the growth of long bones; female hormones stop such growth at puberty. Estrogen strengthens the immune system, making females more resistant to infection, for example. Female hormones also signal the liver to produce more "good" cholesterol, which makes females' blood vessels more elastic than males'. In contrast, testosterone triggers the production of low-density lipoprotein, which clogs blood vessels. Higher levels of stress hormones cause faster clotting in males but also higher blood pressure than in females.

Does gender matter when it comes to brain structure and function? Human brains are much alike, whether the brain belongs to a male or a female (Halpern, 2006). However, researchers have found some differences in the brains of males and females (Hofer & others, 2007a, b). Among the differences that have been discovered are the following:

- Female brains are smaller than male brains, but female brains have more folds; the larger folds (called convolutions) allow more surface brain tissue within the skulls of females than males (Luders & others, 2004).
- One part of the hypothalamus responsible for sexual behavior is larger in men than in women (Swaab & others, 2001).
- Portions of the corpus callosum—the band of tissues through which the brains' two hemispheres communicate—is larger in females than in males (Le Vay, 1991).
- An area of the parietal lobe that functions in visuospatial skills is larger in males than in females (Frederikse & others, 2000).
- The areas of the brain involved in emotional expression show more metabolic activity in females than in males (Gur & others, 1995).

gender stereotypes Broad categories that reflect our impressions and beliefs about females and males.

Cognitive Development   In a classic review of gender differences, Eleanor Maccoby and Carol Jacklin (1974) concluded that males have better math and visuospatial skills (the kinds of skills an architect needs to design a building's angles and dimensions), whereas females have better verbal abilities. Subsequently, Maccoby (1987) revised her conclusion about several gender dimensions. She said that the accumulation of research evidence now suggests that verbal differences between females and males have virtually disappeared but that the math and visuospatial differences still exist. For example, despite equal participation in the National Geography Bee, in most years all 10 finalists are boys (Liben, 1995).

Some experts in gender, such as Janet Shibley Hyde (2005, 2007), suggest that the cognitive differences between females and males have been exaggerated. For example, there is considerable overlap in the distributions of female and male scores on math and visuospatial tasks.

In a national study, fourth-grade boys did slightly better than girls in math and science (National Assessment of Educational Progress, 2005). Overall, though, girls were far superior students, and they were slightly better than boys in reading (see Figure 13.3). In another national study, females had better writing skills than males in grades 4, 8, and 12, with the gap widening as students progressed through school (Coley, 2001).

Socioemotional Development   Are "men from Mars" and "women from Venus"? Perhaps the gender differences that most fascinate people are those in how males and females relate to each other as people. For just about every imaginable socioemotional characteristic, researchers have examined whether there are differences between males and females. Here we examine just four: aggression, relationship communication, emotion, and prosocial behavior.

One of the most consistent gender differences is that boys are more physically aggressive than girls are (Baillargeon & others, 2007). The difference occurs in all cultures and appears very early in children's development (Ostrov & Keating, 2004). The physical aggression difference is especially pronounced when children are provoked. Both biological and environmental factors have been proposed to account for gender differences in aggression. Biological factors include heredity and hormones. Environmental factors include cultural expectations, adult and peer models, and social agents that reward aggression in boys and punish aggression in girls (Leaper & Friedman, 2007).

Although boys are consistently more physically aggressive than girls, might girls show as much or more verbal aggression, such as yelling, than boys? When verbal aggression is examined, gender differences often disappear; sometimes, though, verbal aggression is more pronounced in girls (Eagly & Steffen, 1986).

Recently, increased interest has been shown in *relational aggression*, which involves harming someone by manipulating a relationship (Crick, Ostrov, & Werner, 2006; Young, Boye, & Nelson, 2006). Relational aggression includes such behaviors as trying to make others dislike a certain individual by spreading malicious rumors about the person (Crick, 2005; Underwood, 2004). Researchers have found mixed results regarding gender and relational aggression, with some studies showing girls engaging in more relational aggression and others revealing no differences between boys and girls (Young, Boye, & Nelson, 2006).

One aspect of relationships is how people communicate. Sociolinguist Deborah Tannen (1990) distinguishes between rapport talk and report talk:

- **Rapport talk** is the language of conversation and a way of establishing connections and negotiating relationships. Females enjoy private rapport talk and conversation that is relationship oriented more than do males.
- **Report talk** is talk that gives information. Public speaking is an example of report talk. Males hold center stage through report talk with such verbal performances as story telling, joking, and lecturing with information.

"*So according to the stereotype, you can put two and two together, but I can read the handwriting on the wall.*"
Copyright © 1994 Joel Pett. Reprinted by permission.

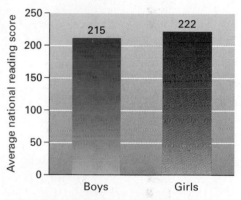

FIGURE 13.3 National Reading Scores for Boys and Girls   In the National Assessment of Educational Progress, data collected in 2005 indicated that girls did better in reading in the fourth and eighth grades (National Assessment of Educational Progress, 2005). The data for the fourth grade are shown above. An earlier assessment found that the gender difference in reading favoring girls also occurs in the twelfth grade (National Assessment of Educational Progress, 1998).

rapport talk The language of conversation and a way of establishing connections and negotiating relationships; preferred by females.

report talk Talk that provides information.

Tannen says that boys and girls grow up in different worlds of talk—parents, siblings, peers, teachers, and others talk to boys and girls differently. The play of boys and girls is also different. Boys tend to play in large groups that are hierarchically structured, and their groups usually have a leader who tells the others what to do and how to do it. Boys' games have winners and losers and often are the subject of arguments. And boys often boast of their skill and argue about who is best at what. In contrast, girls are more likely to play in small groups or pairs, and at the center of a girl's world is often a best friend. In girls' friendships and peer groups, intimacy is pervasive. Turn taking is more characteristic of girls' games than of boys' games. And much of the time, girls simply like to sit and talk with each other, concerned more about being liked by others than jockeying for status in some obvious way.

In sum, Tannen concludes that girls are more relationship-oriented than boys—and that this relationship orientation should be prized as a skill in our culture more than it currently is. Note, however, that some researchers criticize Tannen's ideas as being overly simplified and that communication between boys and girls is more complex than Tannen indicates (Dindia, 2006; Edwards & Hamilton, 2004). Further, some researchers have found similarities in boys' and girls' relationship communication strategies. In one study, in their talk men and women described and responded to problems in ways that were more similar than different (MacGeorge, 2004).

Further modification of Tannen's view is suggested by a recent *meta-analytic* review of gender differences in talkativeness (general communicative competence), affiliative speech (language used to establish or maintain connections with others, such as showing support or expanding on a person's prior remarks), and self-assertive speech (language used to influence others, such as directive statements or disagreements) (Leaper & Smith, 2004). A *meta-analysis* is a statistical analysis that combines the results of many different studies. This review confirms the criticism that Tannen overemphasizes the size of the gender difference in communication. Gender differences did occur but they were small, with girls only slightly more talkative and engaging in more affiliative speech than boys, and boys being more likely to use self-assertive speech. Perhaps the most important message from this review is that gender differences in communication often depended on the context:

- *Group size.* The gender difference in talkativeness (girls being more competent in communicating) occurred more in large groups than in dyads.
- *Speaking with peers or adults.* No average differences in talk with peers occurred, but girls talked more with adults than boys.
- *Familiarity.* The gender difference in self-assertive speech (boys using it more) was more likely to occur when talking with strangers than with familiar individuals.
- *Age.* The gender difference in affiliative speech was largest in adolescence. This may be due to adolescent girls' increased interest in socioemotional behavior traditionally prescribed for females.

Are there gender differences in emotion? Beginning in the elementary school years, boys are more likely to hide their negative emotions, such as sadness, and girls are less likely to express disappointment that might hurt others' feelings (Eisenberg, Martin, & Fabes, 1996). Beginning in early adolescence, girls say they experience more sadness, shame, and guilt, and report more intense emotions, whereas boys are more likely to deny that they experience these emotions (Ruble, Martin, & Berenbaum, 2006). Males usually show less self-regulation of emotion than females, and this low self-control can translate into behavioral problems (Else-Quest & others, 2006). In one study, children's low self-regulation was linked with greater aggression, the teasing of others, overreaction to frustration, low cooperation, and inability to delay gratification (Block & Block, 1980).

The following items are from the Bem Sex-Role Inventory. When taking the BSRI, a person is asked to indicate on a 7-point scale how well each of the 60 characteristics describes herself or himself. The scale ranges from 1 (never or almost never true) to 7 (always or almost always true).

Examples of masculine items	Examples of feminine items
Defends open beliefs	Does not use harsh language
Forceful	Affectionate
Willing to take risks	Loves children
Dominant	Understanding
Aggressive	Gentle

Scoring: The items are scored on independent dimensions of masculinity and femininity as well as androgyny and undifferentiate classifications.

FIGURE 13.4 The Bem Sex-Role Inventory Reproduced by special permission of the Publisher, Mind Garden, Inc., 1690 Woodside Road #202, Redwood City, CA 94061 USA www.mindgarden.com from the *Bem Sex-Role Inventory* by Sandra Bem. Copyright © 1978 by Consulting Psychologists Press. All rights reserved. Further reproduction is prohibited without the Publisher's written consent.

Are there gender differences in prosocial behavior? Females view themselves as more prosocial and empathic (Eisenberg & Morris, 2004). Across childhood and adolescence, females engage in more prosocial behavior (Eisenberg, Fabes, & Spinrad, 2006; Hastings, Utendale, & Sullivan, 2007). The biggest gender difference involves girls exhibiting more frequent kind and considerate behavior, with a smaller difference reflected in girls engaging in more sharing.

Gender-Role Classification Not very long ago, it was accepted that boys should grow up to be masculine and girls to be feminine. In the 1970s, however, as both females and males became dissatisfied with the burdens imposed by their stereotypic roles, alternatives to femininity and masculinity were proposed. Instead of describing masculinity and femininity as a continuum in which more of one means less of the other, it was proposed that individuals could have both masculine and feminine traits.

This thinking led to the development of the concept of **androgyny,** the presence of positive masculine and feminine characteristics in the same person (Bem, 1977; Spence & Helmreich, 1978). Figure 13.4 provides examples of some masculine and feminine characteristics. The androgynous boy might be assertive (masculine) and nurturant (feminine). The androgynous girl might be powerful (masculine) and sensitive to others' feelings (feminine). Studies have confirmed that societal changes are leading females to be more assertive (Spence & Buckner, 2000) and that sons were more androgynous than their fathers (Guastello & Guastello, 2003).

Gender experts, such as Sandra Bem, argue that androgynous individuals are more flexible, competent, and mentally healthy than their masculine or feminine counterparts. To some degree, though, which gender-role classification is best depends on the context involved. For example, in close relationships, feminine and androgynous orientations might be more desirable. One study found that girls and individuals high in femininity showed a stronger interest in caring than did boys and individuals high in masculinity (Karniol, Groz, & Schorr, 2003). However, masculine and androgynous orientations might be more desirable in traditional academic and work settings because of the achievement demands in these contexts.

Despite talk about the "sensitive male," William Pollack (1999) argues that little has been done to change traditional ways of raising boys. He says that the "boy code" tells boys that they should show little if any emotion and should act tough. Boys learn the boy code in many contexts—sandboxes, playgrounds, schoolrooms, camps, hangouts. The result, according to Pollack, is a "national crisis of boyhood." Pollack and others suggest that boys would benefit from being socialized to express their anxieties and concerns and to better regulate their aggression.

androgyny The presence of positive masculine and feminine characteristics in the same individual.

In China, females and males are usually socialized to behave, feel, and think differently. The old patriarchal traditions of male supremacy have not been completely uprooted. Chinese women still make considerably less money than Chinese men do, and, in rural China (such as here in the Lixian Village of Sichuan) male supremacy still governs many women's lives.

Gender in Context Both the concept of androgyny and gender stereotypes talk about people in terms of personality traits such as "aggressive" or "caring." However, which traits people display may vary with the situation (Galambos, 2004). Thus, the nature and extent of gender differences may depend on the context (Leaper & Friedman, 2007; Smith, 2007).

Consider helping behavior. The stereotype is that girls are better than boys at helping. But it depends on the situation. Girls are more likely than boys to volunteer their time to help children with personal problems and to engage in caregiving behavior. However, in situations in which males feel a sense of competence and that involve danger, males are more likely than females to help (Eagly & Crowley, 1986). For example, a male is more likely than a female to stop and help a person stranded by the roadside with a flat tire. Indeed, one study documented that males are more likely to help when the context is masculine in nature (MacGeorge, 2003).

"She is emotional; he is not"—that is the master emotional stereotype. However, like differences in helping behavior, emotional differences in girls and boys depend on the particular emotion involved and the context in which it is displayed (Shields, 1991). Boys are more likely to show anger toward strangers, especially male strangers, when they feel they have been challenged. Boys also are more likely to turn their anger into aggressive action. Emotional differences between girls and boys often show up in contexts that highlight social roles and relationships. For example, girls are more likely to discuss emotions in terms of relationships, and they are more likely to express fear and sadness.

The importance of considering gender in context is nowhere more apparent than when examining what is culturally prescribed behavior for females and males in different countries around the world (Denmark, Rabinowitz, & Sechzer, 2005; Matlin, 2008). Although there has been greater acceptance of androgyny and similarities in male and female behavior in the United States, in many countries gender roles have remained gender-specific. For example, in many Middle Eastern countries, the division of labor between males and females is dramatic. Males are socialized and schooled to work in the public sphere, females in the private world of home and child rearing. For example, in Iran, the dominant view is that the man's duty is to provide for his family and the woman's is to care for her family and household. China also has been a male-dominant culture. Although women have made some strides in China, the male role is still dominant. Most males in China do not accept androgynous behavior and gender equity.

REVIEW AND REFLECT ▸ LEARNING GOAL 1

1 **Discuss emotional and personality development in middle and late childhood.**

Review
- What changes take place in the self during the middle and late childhood years?
- How does emotion change during middle and late childhood?
- What is Kohlberg's theory of moral development, and how has it been criticized? How do prosocial behavior and altruism develop during the middle and late childhood years?
- What are gender stereotypes, and what are some important gender differences?

Reflect
- A 10-year-old homeless girl is caught shoplifting formula for her infant brother. Her mother is disabled and cannot care for the baby. What should her punishment be for this crime? At which Kohlberg stage should your response be placed?

② WHAT ARE SOME CHANGES IN PARENTING AND FAMILIES IN MIDDLE AND LATE CHILDHOOD?

- Developmental Changes in Parenting
- Stepfamilies
- Parents as Managers
- Latchkey Children

As children move into the middle and late childhood years, parents spend considerably less time with them. In one study, parents spent less than half as much time with their children aged 5 to 12 in caregiving, instruction, reading, talking, and playing as when the children were younger (Hill & Stafford, 1980). This drop in parent-child interaction may be even more extensive in families with little parental education. Although parents spend less time with their children in middle and late childhood than in early childhood, parents continue to be extremely important in their children's lives. In a recent analysis of the contributions of parents in middle and late childhood, the following conclusion was reached: "Parents serve as gatekeepers and provide scaffolding as children assume more responsibility for themselves and . . . regulate their own lives" (Huston & Ripke, 2006, p. 422).

Parents especially play an important role in supporting and stimulating children's academic achievement in middle and late childhood (Huston & Ripke, 2006). The value parents place on education can mean the difference in whether children do well in school. Parents not only influence children's in-school achievement, but they also make decision about children's out-of-school activities. Whether children participate in such activities as sports, music, and other activities is heavily influenced by the extent to which parents sign up children for such activities and encourage their participation (Simpkins & others, 2006).

Our further coverage of parenting and families in this section focuses on how parent-child interactions typically change in middle and late childhood, parents as managers and how elementary school children are affected by living with stepparents or by being left on their own after school.

Developmental Changes in Parenting

Parent-child interactions during early childhood often focus on matters such as modesty, bedtime regularities, control of temper, fighting with siblings and peers, eating behavior and manners, autonomy in dressing, and attention seeking. Although some of these issues—fighting and reaction to discipline, for example— are carried forward into the elementary school years, many new issues appear by the age of 7 (Maccoby, 1984). These include whether children should be made to perform chores and, if so, whether they should be paid for them; how to help children learn to entertain themselves, rather than relying on parents for everything; and how to monitor children's lives outside the family in school and peer settings.

Compared with parents of preschool children, parents of elementary school children use less physical discipline. They are more likely to use deprivation of privileges, appeals to the child's self-esteem, comments designed to increase the child's sense of guilt, and statements that the child is responsible for his or her actions.

Discipline during middle and late childhood is often easier for parents than it was during early childhood; it may also be easier than during adolescence. In middle and late childhood, children's cognitive development has matured to the point that parents can reason with children about resisting deviation and controlling their

What are some changes in the focus of parent-child relationships in middle and late childhood?

behavior. By adolescence, children's reasoning has become more sophisticated, and they may push more strongly for independence, which contributes to parenting difficulties.

During middle and late childhood, some control is transferred from parent to child. The process is gradual, and it produces *coregulation* rather than control by either the child or the parent alone. Parents continue to exercise general supervision and control, while children are allowed to engage in moment-to-moment self-regulation. The major shift to autonomy does not occur until about the age of 12 or later. School-related matters are especially important for families during middle and late childhood (Collins, Madsen, & Susman-Stillman, 2002). School-related difficulties are the number one reason that children in this age group are referred for clinical help. Children must learn to relate to adults outside the family on a regular basis—adults who interact with the child much differently than parents. During middle and late childhood, interactions with adults outside the family involve more formal control and achievement orientation.

Parents as Managers

Parents can play important roles as managers of children's opportunities, as monitors of their behavior, and as social initiators and arrangers (Parke & Buriel, 2006). Mothers are more likely than fathers to engage in managerial role in parenting.

Researchers have found that family management practices are positively related to students' grades and self-responsibility, and negatively to school-related problems (Eccles, 2007; Taylor & Lopez, 2005). Among the most important family management practices in this regard are maintaining a structured and organized family environment, such as establishing routines for homework, chores, bedtime, and so on, and effectively monitoring the child's behavior. A recent research review of family functioning in African American students' academic achievement found that when African American parents monitored their son's academic achievement by ensuring that homework was completed, restricted time spent on nonproductive distractions (such as video games and TV), and participated in a consistent, positive dialogue with teachers and school officials, their son's academic achievement benefited (Mandara, 2006).

Stepfamilies

Not only has divorce become commonplace in the United States, so has getting remarried (Goldscheider & Sassler, 2006; Hetherington, 2006). It takes time for parents to marry, have children, get divorced, and then remarry. Consequently, there are far more elementary and secondary school children than infant or preschool children living in stepfamilies.

The number of remarriages involving children has grown steadily in recent years. Also, divorces occur at a 10 percent higher rate in remarriages than in first marriages (Cherlin & Furstenberg, 1994). About half of all children whose parents divorce will have a stepparent within four years of the separation.

Remarried parents face some unique tasks. The couple must define and strengthen their marriage and at the same time renegotiate the biological parent-child relationships and establish stepparent-stepchild and stepsibling relationships (Coleman, Ganong, & Fine, 2004; Ganong, Coleman, & Hans, 2006). The complex histories and multiple relationships make adjustment difficult in a stepfamily (Hetherington & Stanley-Hagan, 2002). Only one-third of stepfamily couples stay remarried.

In some cases, the stepfamily may have been preceded by the death of a spouse. However, by far the largest number of stepfamilies are preceded by divorce rather than death (Pasley & Moorefield, 2004). Three common types of stepfamily structure are (1) stepfather, (2) stepmother, and (3) blended or complex. In stepfather families, the mother typically had custody of the children and remarried, introducing a stepfather into her children's lives. In stepmother families, the father usually had custody and remarried, introducing a stepmother into his children's lives. In a blended or complex stepfamily, both parents bring children from previous marriages to live in the newly formed stepfamily.

In Hetherington's (2006) most recent longitudinal analyses, children and adolescents who had been in a simple stepfamily (stepfather or stepmother) for a number of years were adjusting better than in the early years of the remarried family and were functioning well in comparison to children and adolescents in conflicted nondivorced families and children and adolescents in complex (blended) stepfamilies. More than 75 percent of the adolescents in long-established simple stepfamilies described their relationships with their stepparents as "close" or "very close." Hetherington (2006) concluded that in long-established simple stepfamilies adolescents seem to eventually benefit from the presence of a stepparent and the resources provided by the stepparent.

How does living in a stepfamily influence a child's development?

Children often have better relationships with their custodial parents (mothers in stepfather families, fathers in stepmother families) than with stepparents (Santrock, Sitterle, & Warshak, 1988). Also, children in simple families (stepmother, stepfather) often show better adjustment than their counterparts in complex (blended) families (Anderson & others, 1999; Hetherington & Kelly, 2002).

As in divorced families, children in stepfamilies show more adjustment problems than children in nondivorced families (Hetherington, Bridges, & Insabella, 1998; Hetherington & Kelly, 2002). The adjustment problems are similar to those found among children of divorced parents—academic problems and lower self-esteem, for example (Anderson & others, 1999). However, it is important to recognize that a majority of children in stepfamilies do not have problems. In one analysis, 25 percent of children from stepfamilies showed adjustment problems compared with 10 percent in intact, never-divorced families (Hetherington & Kelly, 2002).

Adolescence is an especially difficult time for the formation of a stepfamily (Anderson & others, 1999). This may occur because becoming part of a stepfamily exacerbates normal adolescent concerns about identity, sexuality, and autonomy.

Latchkey Children

We concluded in Chapter 10 that when both parents work outside the home it does not necessarily have negative outcomes for their children. However, the subset of children sometimes called "latchkey children" deserves further scrutiny. These children are given the key to their home, take the key to school, and then use it to let themselves into the home while their parents are still at work. Latchkey children are largely unsupervised for two to four hours a day during each school week. During the summer months, they might be unsupervised for entire days, five days a week.

How do latchkey children handle the lack of limits and structure during the latchkey hours? In one study, researchers interviewed more than 1,500 latchkey children (Long & Long, 1983). They concluded that a slight majority of these children had had negative latchkey experiences. Some latchkey children may grow up too fast, hurried by the responsibilities placed on them. Without limits and parental supervision, latchkey children find their way into trouble more easily, possibly stealing, vandalizing, or abusing a sibling. Ninety percent of the juvenile delinquents in Montgomery County, Maryland, are latchkey children. Joan Lipsitz (1983), in testifying before the Select Committee on Children, Youth, and Families, called the lack of adult supervision of children in the after-school hours a major problem. Lipsitz called it the "three-to-six o'clock problem" because it was during this time that the Center for Early Adolescence in

What are some strategies parents can adopt that benefit latchkey children?

North Carolina, when Lipsitz was director, experienced a peak of referrals for clinical help.

Although latchkey children may be vulnerable to problems, the experiences of latchkey children vary enormously, as do the experiences of all children with working parents. Parents need to give special attention to the ways in which their latchkey children's lives can be effectively monitored. Variations in latchkey experiences suggest that parental monitoring and authoritative parenting help the child cope more effectively with latchkey experiences, especially in resisting peer pressure (Galambos & Maggs, 1989; Steinberg, 1986).

For parents who work, are there good alternatives to allowing their school-children to be home by themselves after school? One study of 819 10- to 14-year-olds found that out-of-home care, whether supervised or unsupervised, was linked to delinquency, drug and alcohol use, and school problems (Coley, Morri, & Hernandez, 2004). Other research, however, found more positive outcomes for children in some after-school programs. In one study, attending a formal after-school program that included academic, recreational, and remedial activities was associated with better academic achievement and social adjustment, in comparison with other types of after-school care such as informal adult supervision or with self-care (Posner & Vandell, 1994).

Participation in five types of out-of-school care (before- and after-school programs, extracurricular activities, father care, and nonadult care—usually an older sibling) was examined in one study to determine their possible link with children's academic achievement toward the end of the first grade (NICHD Early Child Care Research Network, 2004). "Children who consistently participated in extracurricular activities during kindergarten and first grade obtained higher standardized math test scores than children who did not consistently participate in these activities. Participation in other types of out-of-school care was not related to child functioning in the first grade" (p. 280). These results, however, might reflect a difference among the parents of children in different programs. Parents who enroll their children in extracurricular activities may be more achievement-oriented and have higher achievement expectations for their children than parents who don't place their children in these activities.

One study found that low-income parents were especially dissatisfied with the quality of options available in after-school programs (Wallace Foundation, 2004). Practitioners and policymakers recommend that after-school programs have warm and supportive staff, a flexible and relaxed schedule, multiple activities, and opportunities for positive interactions with staff and peers (Pierce, Hamm, & Vandell, 1997).

REVIEW AND REFLECT ◆ LEARNING GOAL 2

2 **Describe changes in parenting and families in middle and late childhood.**

Review
- What are some important changes in parenting in middle and late childhood?
- How can parents be effective managers of children's lives?
- How does being in a stepfamily influence children's development?
- How are children likely to be affected by being left on their own after school?

Reflect
- What was your relationship with your parents like when you were in elementary school? How do you think it influenced your development?

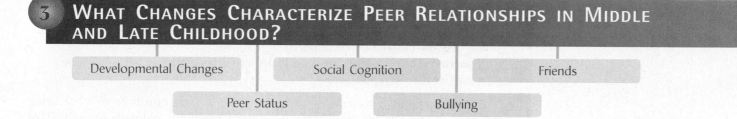

3 **WHAT CHANGES CHARACTERIZE PEER RELATIONSHIPS IN MIDDLE AND LATE CHILDHOOD?**

Developmental Changes   Social Cognition   Friends

Peer Status   Bullying

During middle and late childhood, the amount of time children spend in peer inter-action increases. Children play games with peers, function in groups, and cultivate friendships. How important are peer relationships in middle and late childhood? A longitudinal study revealed children with high levels of peer competence (popular with peers, having friends, and good social skills, for example), compared with their counterparts who were less competent in peer relationships, in middle and late childhood (Collins & van Dulmen, 2006) (1) interacted more effectively at work and had more enjoyable relationships with their co-workers in early adulthood, and (2) had more harmonious relationships with their friends, spouse or partner, and fam-ily in early adulthood. It is important to keep in mind that good peer relationships in middle and late childhood are linked to positive parenting in early childhood (Huston & Ripke, 2006).

Our further coverage in this section begins by focusing on how peer relation-ships change during middle and late childhood. We then examine variations in how children relate to their peers, such as the characteristics of popular children and of children who are bullied, before turning to the important role that friends play in children's lives.

Developmental Changes

As children enter the elementary school years, reciprocity becomes especially important in peer interchanges. Researchers estimate that the percentage of time spent in social interaction with peers increases from approximately 10 percent at 2 years of age to more than 30 percent in middle and late childhood (Rubin, Bukowski, & Parker, 2006). In one early study, a typical day in elementary school included approximately 300 episodes with peers (Barker & Wright, 1951). As chil-dren move through middle and late childhood, the size of their peer group increases, and peer interaction is less closely supervised by adults (Rubin, Bukowski, & Parker, 2006). Until about 12 years of age, children's preference for same-sex groups increases.

Peer Status

Which children are likely to be popular with their peers, and which ones are dis-liked? Developmentalists address this and similar questions by examining *sociometric status*, a term that describes the extent to which children are liked or disliked by their peer group (Ladd, Herald, & Andrews, 2006). Sociometric status is typically assessed by asking children to rate how much they like or dislike each of their class-mates. Or it may be assessed by asking children to nominate the children they like the most and those they like the least.

Developmentalists have distinguished five peer statuses (Wentzel & Asher, 1995):

- **Popular children** are frequently nominated as a best friend and are rarely disliked by their peers.
- **Average children** receive an average number of both positive and negative nominations from their peers.

What are some statuses that children have with their peers?

popular children Children who are fre-quently nominated as a best friend and are rarely disliked by their peers.

average children Children who receive an average number of both positive and negative nominations from peers.

- **Neglected children** are infrequently nominated as a best friend but are not disliked by their peers.
- **Rejected children** are infrequently nominated as someone's best friend and are actively disliked by their peers
- **Controversial children** are frequently nominated both as someone's best friend and as being disliked.

Popular children have a number of social skills that contribute to their being well liked. They give out reinforcements, listen carefully, maintain open lines of communication with peers, are happy, control their negative emotions, act like themselves, show enthusiasm and concern for others, and are self-confident without being conceited (Hartup, 1983; Rubin, Bukowski, & Parker, 1998).

Neglected children engage in low rates of interaction with their peers and are often described as shy by peers. The goal of many training programs for neglected children is to help them attract attention from their peers in positive ways and to hold that attention by asking questions, by listening in a warm and friendly way, and by saying things about themselves that relate to the peers' interests. They also are taught to enter groups more effectively.

Rejected children often have more serious adjustment problems than those who are neglected (Bukowski, Brendgen, & Vitaro, 2007; Ladd, Herald, & Andrews, 2006). One study found that children who were rejected by their peers were less likely to engage in classroom participation, more likely to express a desire to avoid school, and more likely to report being lonely than children who were accepted by their peers (Buhs & Ladd, 2001). The combination of being rejected by peers and being aggressive forecasts problems. One study evaluated 112 fifth-grade boys over a period of seven years until the end of high school (Kupersmidt & Coie, 1990). The best predictor of whether rejected children would engage in delinquent behavior or drop out of school later during adolescence was aggression toward peers in elementary school.

John Coie (2004, pp. 252–253) provided three reasons why aggressive peer-rejected boys have problems in social relationships:

- "First, the rejected, aggressive boys are more impulsive and have problems sustaining attention. As a result, they are more likely to be disruptive of ongoing activities in the classroom and in focused group play.
- Second, rejected, aggressive boys are more emotionally reactive. They are aroused to anger more easily and probably have more difficulty calming down once aroused. Because of this they are more prone to become angry at peers and attack them verbally and physically. . . .
- Third, rejected children have fewer social skills in making friends and maintaining positive relationships with peers."

Not all rejected children are aggressive (Bukowski, Brendgen, & Vitaro, 2007; Rubin, Bukowski, & Parker, 2006). Although aggression and its related characteristics of impulsiveness and disruptiveness underlie rejection about half the time, approximately 10 to 20 percent of rejected children are shy.

How can rejected children be trained to interact more effectively with their peers? Rejected children may be taught to more accurately assess whether the intentions of their peers are negative (Bierman, 2004). They may be asked to engage in role playing or to discuss hypothetical situations involving negative encounters with peers, such as when a peer cuts into a line ahead of them. In some programs, children are shown videotapes of appropriate peer interaction and asked to draw lessons from what they have seen.

One recent social skills intervention program was successful in increasing social acceptance and self-esteem and decreasing depression and anxiety in peer-rejected children (DeRosier, & Marcus, 2005). Students participated in the program once a week (50 to 60 minutes) for eight weeks. The program included instruction in

neglected children Children who are infrequently nominated as a best friend but are not disliked by their peers.

rejected children Children who are infrequently nominated as a best friend and are actively disliked by their peers.

controversial children Children who are frequently nominated both as someone's best friend and as being disliked.

how to manage emotions, how to improve prosocial skills, how to become better communicators, and how to compromise and negotiate.

Social Cognition

A boy accidentally trips and knocks another boy's soft drink out of his hand. That boy misinterprets the encounter as hostile, which leads him to retaliate aggressively against the boy who tripped. Through repeated encounters of this kind, the aggressive boy's classmates come to perceive him as habitually acting in inappropriate ways.

This encounter demonstrates the importance of *social cognition*—thoughts about social matters, such as the aggressive boy's interpretation of an encounter as hostile and his classmates' perception of his behavior as inappropriate (Gauvain & Perez, 2007). Children's social cognition about their peers becomes increasingly important for understanding peer relationships in middle and late childhood. Of special interest are the ways in which children process information about peer relations and their social knowledge (Dodge, Coie, & Lynam, 2006).

Kenneth Dodge (1983) argues that children go through five steps in processing information about their social world. They decode social cues, interpret, search for a response, select an optimal response, and enact. Dodge has found that aggressive boys are more likely to perceive another child's actions as hostile when the child's intention is ambiguous. And, when aggressive boys search for cues to determine a peer's intention, they respond more rapidly, less efficiently, and less reflectively than do nonaggressive children. These are among the social cognitive factors believed to be involved in children's conflicts.

Social knowledge also is involved in children's ability to get along with peers. They need to know what goals to pursue in poorly defined or ambiguous situations, how to initiate and maintain a social bond, and what scripts to follow to get other children to be their friends. For example, as part of the script for getting friends, it helps to know that saying nice things, regardless of what the peer does or says, will make the peer like the child more.

Bullying

Significant numbers of students are victimized by bullies (Estell, Farmer, & Cairns, 2007; Peskin & others, 2007). In one national survey of more than 15,000 sixth-through tenth-grade students, nearly one of every three students said that they had experienced occasional or frequent involvement as a victim or perpetrator in bullying (Nansel & others, 2001). In this study, bullying was defined as verbal or physical behavior intended to disturb someone less powerful. As shown in Figure 13.6, being belittled about looks or speech was the most frequent type of bullying.

Who is likely to be bullied? In the study just described, boys and younger middle school students were most likely to be affected (Nansel & others, 2001). Children who said they were bullied reported more loneliness and difficulty in making friends, whereas those who did the bullying were more likely to have low grades and to smoke and drink alcohol. Researchers have found that anxious, socially withdrawn, and aggressive children are often the victims of bullying (Hanish & Guerra, 2004). Anxious and socially withdrawn children may be victimized because they are nonthreatening and unlikely to retaliate if bullied, whereas aggressive children may be the targets of bullying because their behavior is irritating to bullies (Rubin, Bukowski, & Parker, 2006).

What are the outcomes of bullying? One study of 9- to 12-year-old children in the Netherlands found that the victims of bullies had a much higher incidence of

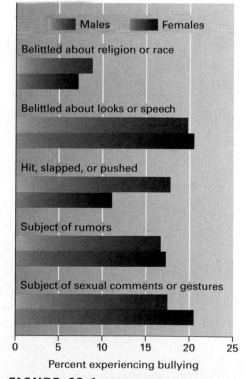

FIGURE 13.6 Bullying Behaviors Among U.S. Youth This graph shows the type of bullying most often experienced by U.S. youth. The percentages reflect the extent to which bullied students said that they had experienced a particular type of bullying. In terms of gender, note that when they were bullied, boys were more likely to be hit, slapped, or pushed than girls were.

What are some characteristics of bullying? What are some strategies to reduce bullying?

headaches, sleep problems, abdominal pain, feeling tired, and depression than children not involved in bullying behavior (Fekkes, Pijpers, & Verloove-Vanhorick, 2004). A recent study also indicated that bullies and their victims in adolescence were more likely to experience depression and engage in suicide ideation and attempt suicide than their counterparts who were not involved in bullying (Brunstein & others, 2007). Another recent study revealed that bullies, victims, or those who were both bullies and victims had more health problems (such as headaches, dizziness, sleep problems, and anxiety) than their counterparts who were not involved in bullying (Srabstein & others, 2006). To read further about bullying, see the *Research in Children's Development* interlude.

Research in Children's Development

AGGRESSIVE VICTIMS, PASSIVE VICTIMS, AND BULLIES

One study examined the extent to which aggressive victims (who provoke their peers and respond to threats or attacks with reactive aggression), passive victims (who submit to aggressors' demands), and bullies (who act aggressively toward their peers but are rarely attacked in return) showed different developmental pathways (Hanish & Guerra, 2004). The children were assessed initially in the fourth grade and then again in the sixth grade.

Peer sociometric ratings were used to identify children as aggressive victims, passive victims, bullies, uninvolved, and average. Each child received a booklet containing randomized lists (separated by gender) of the names of all children in the class. The children were asked to mark all peers' names that were applicable to certain questions. The questions included items that assessed aggression and victimization, such as "Who starts a fight over nothing?" and "Who are the children who are getting picked on?"

The results indicated that "aggressive victims became less prevalent and passive victims and bullies became more prevalent with age. Although it was common for aggressive victims and bullies to move from one group to the other across time, there was little overlap with the passive victim group" (p. 17).

To reduce bullying, teachers and schools can (Hyman & others, 2006; Limber, 2004; Milsom & Gallo, 2006):

- Get older peers to serve as monitors for bullying, and intervene when they see it taking place.
- Develop school-wide rules and sanctions against bullying, and post them throughout the school.
- Form friendship groups for children and youth who are regularly bullied by peers.
- Be aware that bullying often occurs outside the classroom, so school personnel may not actually see it taking place. Also, many victims of bullying don't report the bullying to adults. Unsupervised areas such as the playground, bus, and school corridors are common places where students are bullied. If bullying is observed in a classroom or in other locations, a decision needs to be made about whether it is serious enough to report to school authorities or parents.
- Incorporate the message of the antibullying program into places of worship, school, and other community activities where children and youth are involved.

- Encourage parents to reinforce their children's positive behaviors and model appropriate interpersonal interactions.
- Identify bullies and victims early, and use social skills training to improve their behavior. Teaching empathy, especially perspective taking, promoting self-control, and training social skills have been found to reduce the negative behavior of bullies (Macklem, 2003). Researchers have also found that when victims of bullying develop assertiveness skills, bullying is reduced (Kaiser & Raminsky, 2003; Macklem, 2003). They also have documented that improving students' social skills, including friendship skills and how to approach people, can reduce a victim's chances of being bullied (Rigby, 2002).

Friends

"My best friend is nice. She is honest and I can trust her. I can tell her my inner-most secrets and know that nobody else will find out about them. I have other friends, but she is my best friend. We consider each other's feelings and don't want to hurt each other. We help each other out when we have problems. We make up funny names for people and laugh ourselves silly. We make lists of which boys we think are the ugliest, which are the biggest jerks, and so on. Some of these things we share with other friends, some we don't." This is a description of a friendship by a 10-year-old girl. It demonstrates that children are interested in specific peers—not just any peers. They want to share concerns, interests, information, and secrets with them.

What are the functions of children's friendships?

Like adult friendships, children's friendships are typically characterized by similarity. Throughout childhood, friends are more similar than dissimilar in terms of age, sex, race, and many other factors. Friends often have similar attitudes toward school, similar educational aspirations, and closely aligned achievement orientations.

Why are children's friendships important? Children's friendships can serve six functions (Gottman & Parker, 1987):

- *Companionship*. Friendship provides children with a familiar partner and play-mate, someone who is willing to spend time with them and join in collaborative activities.
- *Stimulation*. Friendship provides children with interesting information, excitement, and amusement.
- *Physical support*. Friendship provides time, resources, and assistance.
- *Ego support*. Friendship provides the expectation of support, encouragement, and feedback, which helps children maintain an impression of themselves as competent, attractive, and worthwhile individuals.
- *Social comparison*. Friendship provides information about where the child stands vis-à-vis others and whether the child is doing okay.
- *Affection and intimacy*. Friendship provides children with a warm, close, trusting relationship with another individual. **Intimacy in friendships** is characterized by self-disclosure and the sharing of private thoughts. Research reveals that intimate friendships may not appear until early adolescence (Berndt & Perry, 1990).

Although having friends can be a developmental advantage, not all friendships are alike. People differ in the company they keep—that is, who their friends are. Developmental advantages occur when children have friends who are socially skilled and supportive. However, it is not developmentally advantageous to have coercive and conflict-ridden friendships (Rubin, Bukowski, & Parker, 2006).

The importance of friendship was underscored in a two-year longitudinal study (Wentzel, Barry, & Caldwell, 2004). Sixth-grade students who did not have a friend engaged in less prosocial behavior (cooperation, sharing, helping others), had lower grades, and were more emotionally distressed (depression, low well-being) than

intimacy in friendships Self-disclosure and the sharing of private thoughts.

their counterparts who had one or more friends. Two years later, in the eighth grade, the students who did not have a friend in the sixth grade were still more emotionally distressed.

REVIEW AND REFLECT > LEARNING GOAL 3

3 **Identify changes in peer relationships in middle and late childhood.**

Review
- What developmental changes characterize peer relations in middle and late childhood?
- How does children's peer status influence their development?
- How is social cognition involved in children's peer relations?
- What is the nature of bullying?
- What are children's friendships like?

Reflect
- If you were a school principal, what would you do to reduce bullying in your school?

---

4 WHAT ARE SOME IMPORTANT ASPECTS OF SCHOOLS?

Contemporary Approaches to Student Learning	Socioeconomic Status and Ethnicity

For most children, entering the first grade signals a change from being a "home-child" to being a "schoolchild." They take up a new role (being a student) and experience new obligations. They develop new relationships and develop new standards by which to judge themselves. School provides children with a rich source of new ideas to shape their sense of self. The children will spend many years in schools as members of small societies in which there are tasks to be accomplished, people to be socialized and socialized by, and rules that define and limit behavior, feelings, and attitudes. By the time students graduate from high school, they have spent 12,000 hours in the classroom. In short, it is justifiable to be concerned about the impact of schools on children.

Contemporary Approaches to Student Learning

Controversy swirls about the best way to teach children and how to hold schools and teachers accountable for whether children are learning.

Constructivist and Direct Instruction Approaches The **constructivist approach** is a learner-centered approach that emphasizes the importance of individuals actively constructing their knowledge and understanding with guidance from the teacher. In the constructivist view, teachers should not attempt to simply pour information into children's minds. Rather, children should be encouraged to explore their world, discover knowledge, reflect, and think critically with careful monitoring and meaningful guidance from the teacher (Eby, Herrell, & Jordan, 2006). The constructivist belief is that for too long in American education

constructivist approach A learner-centered approach that emphasizes the importance of individuals actively constructing their knowledge and understanding with guidance from the teacher.

children have been required to sit still, be passive learners, and rotely memorize irrelevant as well as relevant information (Oakes & Lipton, 2007; Silberman, 2006).

Today, constructivism may include an emphasis on collaboration— children working with each other in their efforts to know and understand (Bodrova & Leong, 2007). A teacher with a constructivist instructional philosophy would not have children memorize information rotely but would give them opportunities to meaningfully construct the knowledge and understand the material while guiding their learning (Kafai, 2006; Stiggins, 2008).

Consider an elementary school classroom that is investigating a school bus (Katz & Chard, 1989). The children write to the district's school superintendent and ask if they can have a bus parked at their school for a few days. They study the bus, discover the functions of its parts, and discuss traffic rules. Then, in the classroom, they build their own bus out of cardboard. The children are having fun, but they also are practicing writing, problem solving, and even some arithmetic. When the class has their parents' night, all that the parents want to see is the bus because their children have been talking about it at home for weeks. Many education experts believe that this is the kind of education all children deserve. That is, they believe that children should be active, constructivist learners and taught through concrete, hands-on experience.

Is this classroom more likely constructivist or direct construction?

By contrast, the **direct instruction approach** is a structured, teacher-centered approach that is characterized by teacher direction and control, high teacher expectations for students' progress, maximum time spent by students on academic tasks, and efforts by the teacher to keep negative affect to a minimum. An important goal in the direct-instruction approach is maximizing student learning time.

Advocates of the constructivist approach argue that the direct instruction approach turns children into passive learners and does not adequately challenge them to think in critical and creative ways (Oakes & Lipton, 2007). The direct instruction enthusiasts say that the constructivist approaches do not give enough attention to the content of a discipline, such as history or science. They also believe that the constructivist approaches are too relativistic and vague.

Some experts in educational psychology believe that many effective teachers use both a constructivist *and* a direct instruction approach rather than either exclusively (Bransford & others, 2006; Darling-Hammond & Bransford, 2005). Further, some circumstances may call more for a constructivist approach, others for a direction instruction approach. For example, experts increasingly recommend an explicit, intellectually engaging direct instruction approach when teaching students with a reading or a writing disability (Berninger, 2006).

Accountability
As the public and government have demanded increased accountability of how effectively schools are educating children, state-mandated tests have taken on a more powerful role (McNergney & McNergney, 2007). Most states have or are in the process of identifying objectives that every student in the state is expected to achieve. Teachers are strongly encouraged to incorporate these objectives into their classroom planning and instruction.

What are some of the most important purposes of standardized tests?

Some policymakers argue that state-mandated testing will have a number of positive effects. These include improved student performance; more time teaching the subjects' tests; high expectations for all students; identification of poorly performing schools, teachers, and administrators; and improved confidence in schools, as test scores increase.

The most visible aspect of state-mandated testing involves the No Child Left Behind (NCLB) act, the federal legislation that was signed into law in 2002. NCLB is the U.S. government's effort to hold schools and school districts accountable for the success or

direct instruction approach A structured, teacher-centered approach that is characterized by teacher direction and control, mastery of academic skills, high teacher expectations for students' progress, maximum time spent on learning tasks, and efforts to keep negative affect to a minimum.

failure of their students (Reynolds, Livingston, & Willson, 2006). The legislation shifts the responsibility to the states, with states being required to create their own standards for students' achievement in mathematics, English/language arts, and science. In 2006, states were required to give all students annual tests in grades 3 through 8.

Critics argue that the NCLB legislation will do more harm than good (Booher-Jennings, 2006; Connors, 2007). One criticism stresses that using a single score from a single test as the sole indicator of students' progress and competence represents a very narrow aspect of students' skills (Lewis, 2006, 2007). This criticism is similar to the one leveled at IQ tests, which we described in Chapter 12. To more accurately assess student progress and achievement, many psychologists and educators emphasize that a number of measures should be used, including tests, quizzes, projects, portfolios, classroom observations, and so on, rather than a single score on a single test. Also, the tests schools are using to assess achievement and progress as part of NCLB don't measure such important skills as creativity, motivation, persistence, flexible thinking, and social skills (Ercikan, 2006). Critics point out that teachers are spending far too much class time "teaching to the test" by drilling students and having them memorize isolated facts at the expense of more student-centered constructivist teaching that focuses on higher-level thinking skills, which students need for success in life. Many educational psychologists conclude that the challenge is to teach creatively within the structure imposed by NCLB (McMillan, 2007).

Despite such criticisms, the U.S. Department of Education is committed to implementing NCLB, and schools are making accommodations to meet the requirements of this law. Indeed, most educators support the importance of high expectations and high standards of excellence for students (Revelle, 2004). At issue, however, is whether the tests and procedures mandated by NCLB are the best ones for achieving these high standards (Houston, 2005).

Socioeconomic Status and Ethnicity

Children from low-income, ethnic minority backgrounds have more difficulties in school than do their middle-socioeconomic-status White counterparts. Why? Critics argue that schools have not done a good job of educating low-income, ethnic minority students to overcome the barriers to their achievement (Okagaki, 2006). Let's further explore the roles of socioeconomic status and ethnicity in schools.

Jill Nakamura, teaching in her first-grade classroom. Jill Nakamura teaches at a school located in a high-poverty area. She visits students at home early in the school year in an effort to connect with them and develop a partnership with their parents. "She holds a daily after school club for students reading below grade level . . .; those who don't want to attend must call parents to tell them. In a recent school year (2004), she "raised the percent of students reading at or above grade level from 29 percent to 76 percent" (Wong, 2004, p. 6D).

The Education of Students from Low–Income Backgrounds

Many children in poverty face problems that present barriers to their learning (McLaren, 2007; McLoyd, Aikens, & Burton, 2006). They might have parents who don't set high educational standards for them, who are incapable of reading to them, and who don't have enough money to pay for educational materials and experiences, such as books and trips to zoos and museums. They might be malnourished and live in areas where crime and violence are a way of life.

Compared with schools in higher-income areas, schools in low-income areas are more likely to have more students with low achievement test scores, low graduation rates, and small percentages of students going to college; they are more likely to have young teachers with less experience; and they are more likely to encourage rote learning (Spring, 2007, 2008). Too few schools in low-income neighborhoods provide students with environments that are conducive to learning (Tozer, Senese, & Violas, 2005). Many of the schools' buildings and classrooms are old and crumbling.

Ethnicity in Schools   More than one-third of all African American and almost one-third of all Latino students attend schools in the 47 largest city school districts in the United States, compared with only 5 percent of all White and 22 percent of all Asian American students. Many of these inner-city schools are still segregated, are grossly underfunded, and do not provide adequate opportunities for children to learn effectively. Thus, the effects of SES and the effects of ethnicity are often intertwined.

In a recent book, *The Shame of the Nation,* Jonathan Kozol (2005) described his visits to 60 U.S. schools in low-income areas of cities of 11 states. He saw many schools in which the minority population was 80 to 90 percent, concluding that school segregation is still present for many poor minority students. Kozol saw many of the inequities just summarized—unkempt classrooms, hallways, and restrooms; inadequate textbooks and supplies; and lack of resources. He also saw teachers mainly instructing students to rotely memorize material, especially as preparation for mandated tests, rather than engage in higher-level thinking. Kozol also frequently observed teachers using threatening disciplinary tactics to control the classroom.

Even outside of inner-city schools, school segregation remains a factor in U.S. education (Nieto & Bode, 2008). Almost one-third of all African American and Latino students attend schools in which 90 percent or more of the students are from minority groups (Banks, 2008).

The school experiences of students from different ethnic groups vary considerably (Bennett, 2007; Koppelman & Goodheart, 2008). African American and Latino students are much less likely than non-Latino White or Asian American students to be enrolled in academic, college preparatory programs and are much more likely to be enrolled in remedial and special education programs. Asian American students are far more likely than other ethnic minority groups to take advanced math and science courses in high school. African American students are twice as likely as Latinos, Native Americans, or Whites to be suspended from school.

Some experts say that a form of institutional racism permeates many American schools by which teachers accept a low level of performance from children of color (Ogbu & Stern, 2001; Spencer, 1999). American anthropologist John Ogbu (1989) proposed that ethnic minority students are placed in a position of subordination and exploitation in the American educational system. He argues that students of color, especially African Americans and Latinos, have inferior educational opportunities, are exposed to teachers and school administrators who have low academic expectations for them, and encounter negative stereotypes (Ogbu & Stern, 2001). In one study of middle schools in predominantly Latino areas of Miami, Latino and White teachers rated African American students as having more behavioral problems than African American teachers rated the same students as having (Zimmerman & others, 1995).

Following are some strategies for improving relationships among ethnically diverse students:

- Turn the class into a jigsaw classroom. When Elliot Aronson was a professor at the University of Texas at Austin, the school system contacted him for ideas on how to reduce the increasing racial tension in classrooms. Aronson (1986) developed the concept of "jigsaw classroom," in which students from different cultural backgrounds are placed in a cooperative group in which they have to construct different parts of a project to reach a common goal. Aronson used the term jigsaw because he saw the technique as much like a group of students cooperating to put different pieces together to complete a jigsaw puzzle. How might this work? Team sports, drama productions, and music performances are examples of contexts in which students cooperatively participate to reach a common goal.
- *Use technology to foster cooperation with students from around the world.*

Careers in CHILD DEVELOPMENT

James Comer
Child Psychiatrist

James Comer grew up in a low-income neighborhood in East Chicago, Indiana, and credits his parents with leaving no doubt about the importance of education. He obtained a bachelors degree from Indiana University. He went on to obtain a medical degree from Howard University College of Medicine, a Master of Public Health degree from the University of Michigan School of Public Health, and psychiatry training at the Yale University School of Medicine's Child Study Center. He currently is the Maurice Falk Professor of Child Psychiatry at the Yale University Child Study Center and an associate dean at the Yale University Medical School. During his years at Yale, Comer has concentrated his career on promoting a focus on child development as a way of improving schools. His efforts in support of healthy development of young people are known internationally.

Dr. Comer, perhaps, is best known for the founding of the School Development Program in 1968, which promotes the collaboration of parents, educators, and community to improve social, emotional, and academic outcomes for children. His concept of teamwork is currently improving the educational environment in more than 500 schools throughout America.

James Comer (*left*) is shown with some of the inner-city African American children who attend a school that became a better learning environment because of Comer's intervention. Comer is convinced that a strong, familylike atmosphere is a key to improving the quality of inner-city schools.

- *Encourage students to have positive personal contact with diverse other students.* Contact alone does not do the job of improving relationships with diverse others. For example, busing ethnic minority students to predominantly White schools, or vice versa, has not reduced prejudice or improved interethnic relations (Minuchin & Shapiro, 1983). What matters is what happens after children get to school. Especially beneficial in improving interethnic relations is sharing one's worries, successes, failures, coping strategies, interests, and other personal information with people of other ethnicities. When this happens, people tend to look at others as individuals rather than as members of a homogeneous group.

- *Encourage students to engage in perspective taking.* Exercises and activities that help students see others' perspectives can improve interethnic relations. This helps students "step into the shoes" of peers who are culturally different and feel what it is like to be treated in fair or unfair ways.

- *Help students think critically and be emotionally intelligent about cultural issues.* Students who learn to think critically and deeply about interethnic relations are likely to decrease their prejudice. Becoming more emotionally intelligent includes understanding the causes of one's feelings, managing anger, listening to what others are saying, and being motivated to share and cooperate.

- *Reduce bias.* Teachers can reduce bias by displaying images of children from diverse ethnic and cultural groups, selecting play materials and classroom activities that encourage cultural understanding, helping students resist stereotyping, and working with parents.

- *View the school and community as a team.* James Comer (1988, 2004) believes that a community, team approach is the best way to educate children. Three important aspects of the Comer Project for Change are (1) a governance and management team that develops a comprehensive school plan, assessment strategy, and staff development plan; (2) a mental health or school support team; and (3) a parent's program. Comer stresses that the entire school community should have a cooperative rather than an adversarial attitude. The Comer program is currently operating in more than 600 schools in 26 states. To read further about James Comer's work, see the *Careers in Child Development* profile.

- *Be a competent cultural mediator.* Teachers can play a powerful role as a cultural mediator by being sensitive to racist content in materials and classroom interactions, learning more about different ethnic groups, being sensitive to children's ethnic attitudes, viewing students of color positively, and thinking of positive ways to get parents of color more involved as partners with teachers in educating children (Jones & Fuller, 2003).

REVIEW AND REFLECT ◆ LEARNING GOAL 4

4 **Characterize contemporary approaches to student learning and sociocultural aspects of schooling.**

Review
- What are two major contemporary issues in educating children?
- How do socioeconomic status and ethnicity influence schooling?

Reflect
- Should the United States be worried about the low performance of its students in mathematics and science in comparison to Asian students? Are Americans' expectations for students too low?

1 **WHAT IS THE NATURE OF EMOTIONAL AND PERSONALITY DEVELOPMENT IN MIDDLE AND LATE CHILDHOOD?** *Discuss emotional and personality development in middle and late childhood.*

The Self

- Self-descriptions increasingly involve psychological and social characteristics, including social comparison, in middle and late childhood. Children increase their perspective taking in middle and late childhood, and their social understanding shows increasing psychological sophistication as well. Self-concept refers to domain-specific evaluations of the self. Self-esteem refers to global evaluations of the self and is also referred to as self-worth or self-image. Self-esteem is only moderately related to school performance but is more strongly linked to initiative. Four ways to increase self-esteem are to (1) identify the causes of low self-esteem, (2) provide emotional support and social approval, (3) help children achieve, and (4) help children cope. One of the most important changes in the self in middle and late childhood is children's increased capacity for self-regulation. Erikson's fourth stage of development, industry versus inferiority, characterizes the middle and late childhood years.

Emotional Development

- Developmental changes in emotion include increased understanding of complex emotions such as pride and shame, detecting that more than one emotion can be experienced in a particular situation, taking into account the circumstances that led up to an emotional reaction, improvements in the ability to suppress and conceal negative emotions, and using self-initiated strategies to redirect feelings. Emotional intelligence is a form of social intelligence that involves the ability to monitor one's own and others' feelings and emotions, to discriminate among them, and to use this information to guide one's own thinking and action. Goleman maintains that emotional intelligence involves four main areas: emotional self-awareness, managing emotions, reading emotions, and handling relationships. As children get older, they use a greater variety of coping strategies and more cognitive strategies.

Moral Development

- Kohlberg argued that moral development consists of three levels—preconventional, conventional, and postconventional—and six stages (two at each level). Kohlberg believed that these stages were age-related. Influences on movement through the stages include cognitive development, imitation and cognitive conflict, peer relations, and perspective taking. Criticisms of Kohlberg's theory have been made, especially by Gilligan, who advocates a stronger care perspective. Other criticisms focus on the inadequacy of moral reasoning to predict moral behavior, culture and family influences, and the distinction between moral reasoning and social conventional reasoning. Prosocial behavior involves positive moral behaviors such as sharing. Most sharing in the first three years is not done for empathy, but at about 4 years of age empathy contributes to sharing. By the start of the elementary school years, children express objective ideas about fairness. Recently, there has been a surge of interest in moral personality.

Gender

- Gender stereotypes are widespread around the world. A number of physical differences exist between males and females. Some experts argue that cognitive differences between males and females have been exaggerated. In terms of socioemotional differences, males are more physically aggressive than females. Tannen argues that females prefer rapport talk and males prefer report talk, but recent research indicates that Tannen's view is exaggerated. Females regulate their emotions better and engage in more prosocial behavior than males. Gender-role classification focuses on how masculine, feminine, or androgynous individuals are. Androgyny means having both positive feminine and masculine characteristics. It is important to think about gender in terms of context.

② WHAT ARE SOME CHANGES IN PARENTING AND FAMILIES IN MIDDLE AND LATE CHILDHOOD? *Describe changes in parenting and families in middle and late childhood.*

Developmental Changes in Parenting

- Parents spend less time with children during middle and late childhood than in early childhood. New parent-child issues emerge and discipline changes. Control is more coregulatory.

Parents as Managers

- Parents have important roles as managers of children's opportunities, as monitors of their behavior, and social initiators and arrangers. Mothers are more likely to function in these parental management roles than fathers.

Stepfamilies

- As in divorced families, children living in stepparent families have more adjustment problems than their counterparts in nondivorced families. However, a majority of children in stepfamilies do not have adjustment problems.

Latchkey Children

- Children who are not monitored by adults in the after-school hours may find their way into trouble more easily than other children, although contextual variations characterize latchkey children's experiences.

③ WHAT CHANGES CHARACTERIZE PEER RELATIONSHIPS IN MIDDLE AND LATE CHILDHOOD? *Identify changes in peer relationships in middle and late childhood.*

Developmental Changes

- Among the developmental changes in peer relations in middle and late childhood are increased preference for same-sex groups, an increase in time spent in peer interaction and the size of the peer group, and less supervision of the peer group by adults.

Peer Status

- Popular children are frequently nominated as a best friend and are rarely disliked by their peers. Average children receive an average number of both positive and negative nominations from their peers. Neglected children are infrequently nominated as a best friend but are not disliked by their peers. Rejected children are infrequently nominated as a best friend and are actively disliked by their peers. Controversial children are frequently nominated both as a best friend and as being disliked by peers. Rejected children are especially at risk for a number of problems.

Social Cognition

- Social information-processing skills and social knowledge are two important dimensions of social cognition in peer relations.

Bullying

- Significant numbers of children are bullied, and this can result in short-term and long-term negative effects for both the victims and bullies.

Friends

- Like adult friends, children who are friends tend to be similar to each other. Children's friendships serve six functions: companionship, stimulation, physical support, ego support, social comparison, and intimacy/affection.

Contemporary Approaches to Student Learning

- Two major contemporary issues concern how to best teach children and how to hold teachers and schools accountable for whether students are learning. The constructivist view takes a learner-centered approach, and direct instruction is a teacher-centered approach. In the United States, standardized testing of elementary school students has been mandated by both many state governments and by the No Child Left Behind federal legislation.

Socioeconomic Status and Ethnicity

- Children in poverty face many barriers to learning at school as well as at home. The effects of SES and ethnicity on schools are intertwined as many U.S. schools are segregated. Low expectations for ethnic minority children represent one of the barriers to their learning.

KEY TERMS

KEY PEOPLE

MAKING A DIFFERENCE

Guiding Children's Socioemotional Development

What are some good strategies for nourishing children's socioemotional skills?

- *Improve children's self-esteem.* This can be accomplished by identifying the causes of the child's low self-esteem, providing emotional support and social approval, and helping the child achieve.
- *Help children understand their emotions and cope with stress.* When children are experiencing considerable stress, try to remove at least one stressor from their lives. Also help the child learn effective coping strategies.

- *Nurture children's moral development.* Parents can improve their children's morality by being warm and supportive rather than punitive, using reasoning when disciplining, providing opportunities for children to learn about others' perspectives and feelings, involving children in family decision making, and modeling prosocial moral behavior.
- *Adapt to developmental changes in children.* Because parents typically spend less time with children in middle and late childhood, it is important to strengthen children's self-control. This is especially true in the case of latchkey children. As in early childhood, authoritative parenting should

continue to be the choice, rather than authoritarian or permissive parenting.

- *Improve children's peer and friendship skills.* Peer and friendship relations become increasingly important to elementary school children. Adults can talk with children about the importance of being nice, engaging in prosocial behavior, and providing support in getting peers and friends to like them. Parents also can communicate to children that being aggressive, self-centered, and inconsiderate of others harms peer and friendship relations.
- *Create schools that support children's socioemotional development.* Not only do good teachers know how to challenge and stimulate children's cognitive development, but they also know how to make children feel good about themselves. Too much of elementary school education involves negative feedback. We need more classrooms in which children are excited about learning. This learning should be designed to increase children's self-esteem, not wreck their emotional well-being. Parents need to encourage and support their children's educational accomplishments but not set unrealistic achievement expectations.

RESOURCES FOR IMPROVING CHILDREN'S LIVES

Raising Black Children

by James P. Comer and Alvin E. Poussaint (1992)
New York: Plume

Raising Black Children is an excellent book for African American parents. It includes wise suggestions that are not in most child-rearing books (almost all others are written for middle-class White parents and do not deal with special problems faced by ethnic minority parents or parents from low-income backgrounds).

National Stepfamily Resource Center

www.stepfamilies.info

This center provides a clearinghouse and support network for stepparents, remarried parents, and their children.

E-LEARNING TOOLS

Connect to **www.mhhe.com/santrockc10** to research the answers and complete these exercises. In addition, you'll find a number of other resources and valuable study tools for Chapter 13, "Socioemotional Development in Middle and Late Childhood," on this Web site.

Taking It to the Net

1. Frank is researching the latest information on bullying after his younger brother told him of his recent experiences with bullies at his junior high school. What information is available on the prevalence of bullying, the makeup of the children who bully, and why this type of behavior is increasing?
2. Jasmine is interning at a child development center during the summer. She is going to be responsible for planning a program to help kids become more aware of their own emotions as well as the feelings of others. What should she know about Daniel Goleman's theory of emotional intelligence?
3. Ellen is taking a class in gender psychology. She wants to test the theory of androgyny among her peers in her large geology lecture. She has heard that there is an online version of the test and thinks people will feel more comfortable taking it online. What conclusions can Ellen draw on the androgyny theory after taking this test?

Health and Well-Being, Parenting, and Education

Build your decision-making skills by trying your hand at the health and well-being, parenting, and education exercises.

Video Clips

The Online Learning Center includes the following videos for this chapter:

1. *Best Friends at Age 7—1120*
   John describes that he plays with his best friend and that they listen to music together.
2. *Describing Friendships at Age 8—1656*
   In this clip, a boy describes his two best friends and what they like to do together. When asked if he has any girl friends, he quickly responds, "No." But then he adds that his sisters are his friends.
3. *Self-Perception at 10 Years and 8 Years of Age—1669*
   Two Mexican-origin siblings, Laura and Jared, are asked to describe themselves. Laura responds that she works hard, tries her best, and talks too much. Jared, however, only responds that he does not talk that much.
4. *Describing Best Friends at Age 11—1722*
   An 11-year-old girl talks about her best friends and how they helped her through "sad times."

Section Six
ADOLESCENCE

In no order of things is adolescence the simple time of life.

—JEAN ERSKINE STEWART
American Writer, 20th Century

Adolescents try on one face after another, seeking to find a face of their own. Their generation of young people is the fragile cable by which the best and the worst of their parents' generation is transmitted to the present. In the end, there are only two lasting bequests parents can leave youth—one being roots, the other wings. Section 6 contains three chapters: "Physical Development in Adolescence" (Chapter 14), "Cognitive Development in Adolescence" (Chapter 15), and "Socioemotional Development in Adolescence" (Chapter 16).

14 Physical Development in Adolescence

In youth, we clothe ourselves with rainbows, and go brave as the zodiac.

—Ralph Waldo Emerson
American Poet, 19th Century

CHAPTER OUTLINE

What Is the Nature of Adolescence? ①

Positive and Negative Views of Adolescence

Developmental Transitions

What Are the Physical and Psychological Aspects of Puberty? ②

Sexual Maturation, Height, and Weight

Hormonal Changes

Timing and Variations in Puberty

Psychological Dimensions of Puberty

The Brain

What Are the Dimensions of Adolescent Sexuality? ③

Developing a Sexual Identity

The Progression of Adolescent Sexual Behaviors

Contraceptive Use

Sexually Transmitted Infections

Adolescent Pregnancy

How Can Adolescent Health and Problems Be Characterized? ④

Adolescent Health

Substance Use and Abuse

Eating Problems and Disorders

LEARNING GOALS

1 Discuss views and developmental transitions that involve adolescence.

2 Describe puberty's characteristics, developmental changes, psychological dimensions, and the development of the brain.

3 Characterize adolescent sexuality.

4 Identify adolescent problems related to health, substance use and abuse, and eating disorders.

Images of Children's Development
Stories of Adolescent Sexuality

I guess when you give a girl a sexy kiss you're supposed to open your lips and put your tongue in her mouth. That doesn't seem very sexy to me. I can't imagine how a girl would like that. What if she has braces on her teeth and your tongue gets scratched? And how are you supposed to breathe? Sometimes I wish I had an older brother I could ask stuff like this.

—Frank, age 12

I can't believe I'm so much in love! I just met him last week but I know this is the real thing. He is much more mature than the boys who have liked me before. He's a senior and has his own car. When he brought me home last night, we got so hot I thought we were going to have sex. I'm sure it will happen the next time we go out. It goes against everything I've been taught—but I can't see how it can be wrong when I'm so much in love and he makes me feel so fantastic!

—Amy, age 15

Ken and I went on a camping trip last weekend and now I'm sure that I'm gay. For a long time I've known I've been attracted to other guys, like in the locker room at school it would sometimes be embarrassing. Ken and I are great friends and lots of times we would mess around wrestling or whatever. I guessed that he felt the way I did. Now I know. Sooner or later, I'll have to come out, as they say, but I know that is going to cause a lot of tension with my parents and for me.

—Tom, age 15

I'm lucky because I have a good figure and I'm popular. I've had boyfriends since middle school and I know how to take care of myself. It's fun when you're out with a guy and you can be intimate. The only thing is, Dan and I had sex a few weeks ago and I'm wondering if I'm pregnant. He used a contraceptive, but maybe it didn't work. Or maybe I'm just late. Anyway, if I have a baby, I could deal with it. My aunt wasn't married when she got pregnant with my cousin, and it turned out okay.

—Claire, age 16

About a month ago my mom's friend's daughter tested positive for HIV. Until then my mom and stepfather never talked about sex with me, but now they're taking turns lecturing me on the theme of "don't have sex until you're married." Give me a break! Nicole and I have been together for a year and half. What do they think we do when we go out, play tiddlywinks? Besides, my real father never remarried and has girlfriends all the time. All my life I've been seeing movies and TV shows where unmarried people sleep together and the worst that happens is maybe a broken heart. I don't know that woman's daughter, but she must have been mixed up with some pretty bad characters. Me, I always use a condom.

—Sean, age 17

PREVIEW

Adolescence is an important juncture in the lives of many individuals. Puberty marks considerable biological changes, and as we just saw in the comments of adolescents, sexuality holds many mysteries and curiosities for youth. Adolescence also is a time when many health habits—good or bad—are formed and ingrained. In this chapter, we explore what adolescence is, examine its physical and psychological changes, discuss adolescent sexuality, and then describe adolescent problems and health.

1   WHAT IS THE NATURE OF ADOLESCENCE?

Positive and Negative Views of Adolescence	Developmental Transitions

As in development during childhood, genetic, biological, environmental, and social factors interact in adolescent development. During their first decade of life, adolescents experienced thousands of hours of interactions with parents, peers, and teachers, but now they face dramatic biological changes, new experiences, and new developmental tasks. Relationships with parents take a different form, moments with peers become more intimate, and dating occurs for the first time, as do sexual exploration and possibly intercourse. The adolescent's thoughts are more abstract and idealistic. Biological changes trigger a heightened interest in body image. Adolescence has both continuity and discontinuity with childhood.

Positive and Negative Views of Adolescence

There is a long history of worrying about how adolescents will turn out. In 1904, G. Stanley Hall proposed the "storm-and-stress" view that adolescence is a turbulent time charged with conflict and mood swings. However, when Daniel Offer and his colleagues (1988) studied the self-images of adolescents in the United States, Australia, Bangladesh, Hungary, Israel, Italy, Japan, Taiwan, Turkey, and West Germany, at least 73 percent of the adolescents displayed a healthy self-image. Although there were differences among them, the adolescents were happy most of the time, they enjoyed life, they perceived themselves as able to exercise self-control, they valued work and school, they expressed confidence about their sexual selves, they expressed positive feelings toward their families, and they felt they had the capability to cope with life's stresses: not exactly a storm-and-stress portrayal of adolescence.

Public attitudes about adolescence emerge from a combination of personal experience and media portrayals, neither of which produce an objective picture of how normal adolescents develop (Feldman & Elliott, 1990). Some of the readiness to assume the worst about adolescents likely involves the short memories of adults. Many adults measure their current perceptions of adolescents by their memories of their own adolescence. Adults may portray today's adolescents as more troubled, less respectful, more self-centered, more assertive, and more adventurous than they were.

However, in matters of taste and manners, the young people of every generation have seemed radical, unnerving, and different from adults—different in how they look, in how they behave, in the music they enjoy, in their hairstyles, and in the clothing they choose. It is an enormous error, though, to confuse adolescents' enthusiasm for trying on new identities and enjoying moderate amounts of outrageous behavior with hostility toward parental and societal standards. Acting out and boundary testing are time-honored ways in which adolescents move toward accepting, rather than rejecting, parental values.

Most adolescents negotiate the lengthy path to adult maturity successfully, but too large a group does not. Ethnic, cultural, gender, socioeconomic, age, and lifestyle differences influence the actual life trajectory of every adolescent (Berry, 2007; Patterson & Hastings, 2007). Different portrayals of adolescence emerge, depending on the particular group of adolescents being described (Benson & others, 2006; Wigfield & others, 2006). Today's adolescents are exposed to a complex menu of lifestyle options through the media, and many face the temptations of drug use and sexual activity at increasingly young ages. Too many adolescents are not provided with adequate opportunities and support to become competent adults (Benson & others, 2006; Conger & Dogan, 2007).

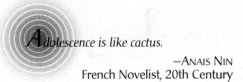

Adolescence is like cactus.

—ANAIS NIN
French Novelist, 20th Century

Growing up has never been easy. However, adolescence is not best viewed as a time of rebellion, crisis, pathology, and deviance. A far more accurate vision of adolescence describes it as a time of evaluation, of decision making, of commitment, and of carving out a place in the world. Most of the problems of today's youth are not with the youth themselves. What adolescents need is access to a range of legitimate opportunities and to long-term support from adults who deeply care about them. *What might be some examples of such support and caring?*

Developmental Transitions

Developmental transitions are often important junctures in people's lives. Such transitions include moving from the prenatal period to birth and infancy, from infancy to early childhood, and from early childhood to middle and late childhood. For adolescents, two important transitions are from childhood to adolescence and from adolescence to adulthood. Let's explore these transitions.

Childhood to Adolescence   The transition from childhood to adolescence involves a number of biological, cognitive, and socioemotional changes. Among the biological changes are the growth spurt, hormonal changes, and sexual maturation that come with puberty. In early adolescence, changes take place in the brain that allow for more advanced thinking. Also at this time, adolescents begin to stay up later and sleep later in the morning.

Among the cognitive changes that occur during the transition from childhood to adolescence are increases in abstract, idealistic, and logical thinking. As they

What are some physical, cognitive, and socioemotional changes involved in the transition from childhood to adolescence? What characterizes emerging adulthood?

ZITS By Jerry Scott and Jim Borgman

© ZITS Partnership. King Features Syndicate.

make this transition, adolescents begin to think in more egocentric ways, often sensing that they are onstage, unique, and invulnerable. In response to these changes, parents place more responsibility for decision making on the young adolescents' shoulders.

Among the socioemotional changes adolescents undergo are a quest for independence, conflict with parents, and a desire to spend more time with peers. Conversations with friends become more intimate and include more self-disclosure. As children enter adolescence, they attend schools that are larger and more impersonal than their neighborhood grade schools. Achievement becomes more serious business, and academic challenges increase. Also at this time, increased sexual maturation produces a much greater interest in romantic relationships. Young adolescents also experience greater mood swings than they did when they were children.

In sum, the transition from childhood to adolescence is complex and multidimensional, involving change in many different aspects of an individual's life (Wigfield & others, 2006). Negotiating this transition successfully requires considerable adaptation and thoughtful, sensitive support from caring adults.

Adolescence to Adulthood: Emerging Adulthood Another important transition occurs from adolescence to adulthood (Arnett, 2007; Arnett & Tanner, 2006). It has been said that adolescence begins in biology and ends in culture. That is, the transition from childhood to adolescence begins with the onset of pubertal maturation, whereas the transition from adolescence to adulthood is determined by cultural standards and experiences. Around the world, youth are increasingly expected to delay their entry into adulthood, in large part because the information society in which we now live requires that they obtain more education than their parents' generation (Hamilton & Hamilton, 2006). Thus, the transition between adolescence and adulthood can be a long one as adolescents develop more effective skills to become full members of society.

Recently, the transition from adolescence to adulthood has been referred to as **emerging adulthood** (Arnett, 2000, 2004, 2006, 2007). Like youth, the age range for emerging adulthood is approximately 18 to 25 years of age. Experimentation and exploration characterize the emerging adult. At this point in their development, many individuals are still exploring which career path they want to follow, what they want their identity to be, and which lifestyle they want to adopt (for example, single, cohabiting, or married).

emerging adulthood Occurring from approximately 18 to 25 years of age, this transitional period between adolescence and adulthood is characterized by experimentation and exploration.

Jeffrey Arnett (2006) recently concluded that five key features characterize emerging adulthood:

- *Exploring identity, especially in love and work.* Emerging adulthood is the time during which key changes in identity take place for many individuals (Kroger, 2007).
- *Experiencing instability.* Residential changes peak during early adulthood, a time during which there also is often instability in love, work, and education.
- *Being self-focused.* According to Arnett (2006, p. 10), emerging adults "are self-focused in the sense that they have little in the way of social obligations, little in the way of duties and commitments to others, which leaves with a great deal of autonomy in running their own lives."
- *Feeling in-between.* Many emerging adults don't consider themselves adolescents or full-fledged adults.
- *Experiencing the age of possibilities, a time when individuals have an opportunity to transform their lives.* Arnett (2006) describes two ways in which emerging adulthood is the age of possibilities. First, many emerging adults are optimistic about their future. Second, for emerging adults who have experienced difficult times while growing up, emerging adulthood presents an opportunity to direct their lives in a more positive direction (Masten, Obradovic, & Burt, 2006; Schulenberg & Zarrett, 2006).

REVIEW AND REFLECT ▸ **LEARNING GOAL 1**

1 **Discuss views and developmental transitions that involve adolescence.**

Review
- What are some positive and negative views of adolescence?
- What are two key developmental transitions involving adolescence?

Reflect
- You likely experienced some instances of stereotyping as an adolescent. What are some examples of the circumstances in which you feel that you were stereotyped as an adolescent?

2 WHAT ARE THE PHYSICAL AND PSYCHOLOGICAL ASPECTS OF PUBERTY?

Sexual Maturation, Height, and Weight	Timing and Variations in Puberty	The Brain

Hormonal Changes	Psychological Dimensions of Puberty

One father remarked that the problem with his teenage son was not that he grew, but that he did not know when to stop growing. As we see, there is considerable variation in the timing of the adolescent growth spurt. In addition to pubertal changes, other physical changes we explore involve sexuality and the brain.

Puberty is not the same as adolescence. For most of us, puberty ends long before adolescence does, although puberty is the most important marker of the beginning of adolescence. **Puberty** is a period of rapid physical maturation involving hormonal and bodily changes that occur primarily during early adolescence. Puberty is not a

puberty A period of rapid physical maturation involving hormonal and bodily changes that occur primarily in early adolescence.

single, sudden event (Dorn & others, 2006). We know whether a young boy or girl is going through puberty, but pinpointing puberty's beginning and end is difficult. Among the most noticeable changes are signs of sexual maturation and increases in height and weight.

Sexual Maturation, Height, and Weight

Think back to the onset of your puberty. Of the striking changes that were taking place in your body, what was the first change that occurred? Researchers have found that male pubertal characteristics develop in this order: increase in penis and testicle size, appearance of straight pubic hair, minor voice change, first ejaculation (which usually occurs through masturbation or a wet dream), appearance of kinky pubic hair, onset of maximum growth, growth of hair in armpits, more detectable voice changes, and growth of facial hair.

What is the order of appearance of physical changes in females? First, either the breasts enlarge or pubic hair appears. Later, hair appears in the armpits. As these changes occur, the female grows in height, and her hips become wider than her shoulders. **Menarche**—a girl's first menstruation—comes rather late in the pubertal cycle. Initially, her menstrual cycles may be highly irregular. For the first several years, she may not ovulate every menstrual cycle; some girls do not ovulate at all until a year or two after menstruation begins. No voice changes comparable to those in pubertal males occur in pubertal females. By the end of puberty, the female's breasts have become more fully rounded.

Marked weight gains coincide with the onset of puberty. During early adolescence, girls tend to outweigh boys, but by about age 14 boys begin to surpass girls. Similarly, at the beginning of the adolescent period, girls tend to be as tall as or taller than boys of their age, but by the end of the middle school years most boys have caught up or, in many cases, surpassed girls in height.

As indicated in Figure 14.1, the growth spurt occurs approximately two years earlier for girls than for boys. The mean age at the beginning of the growth spurt in girls is 9 years of age; for boys, it is 11 years of age. The peak rate of pubertal change occurs at 11½ years for girls and 13½ years for boys. During their growth spurt, girls increase in height about 3½ inches per year, boys about 4 inches. Boys and girls who are shorter or taller than their peers before adolescence are likely to remain so during adolescence; however, as much as 30 percent of an individual's height in late adolescence is unexplained by his or her height in the elementary school years.

Hormonal Changes

Behind the first whisker in boys and the widening of hips in girls is a flood of **hormones,** powerful chemical substances secreted by the endocrine glands and carried through the body by the bloodstream. The endocrine system's role in puberty involves the interaction of the hypothalamus, the pituitary gland, and the gonads (see Figure 14.2). The **hypothalamus** is a structure in the higher portion of the brain that monitors eating, drinking, and sex. The **pituitary gland** is an important endocrine gland that controls growth and regulates other glands. The **gonads** are the sex glands—the testes in males, the ovaries in females.

How does the hormonal system work? The pituitary sends a signal via **gonadotropins** (hormones that stimulate the testes or ovaries) to the appropriate gland to manufacture the hormone. Then the pituitary gland, through interaction with the hypothalamus, detects when the optimal level of hormones is reached and responds and maintains it with additional gonadotropin secretions (Clarkson & Herbison, 2006; Yoo & others, 2006).

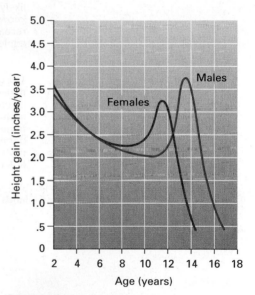

FIGURE 14.1 **Pubertal Growth Spurt** On the average, the peak of the growth spurt during puberty occurs 2 years earlier for girls (11½) than for boys (13½). *How are hormones related to the growth spurt and to the difference between the average height of adolescent boys and girls?*

menarche A girl's first menstrual period.

hormones Powerful chemical substances secreted by the endocrine glands and carried through the body by the bloodstream.

hypothalamus A structure in the higher portion of the brain that monitors eating, drinking, and sex.

pituitary gland An important endocrine gland that controls growth and regulates other glands.

gonads The sex glands—the testes in males, the ovaries in females.

gonadotropins Hormones that stimulate the testes or ovaries.

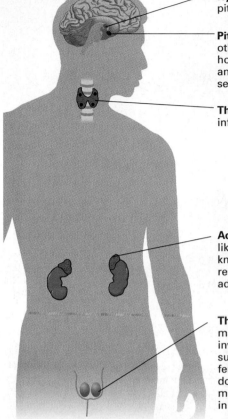

Hypothalamus: A structure in the brain that interacts with the pituitary gland to monitor the bodily regulation of hormones.

Pituitary: This master gland produces hormones that stimulate other glands. It also influences growth by producing growth hormones; it sends gonadotropins to the testes and ovaries and a thyroid-stimulating hormone to the thyroid gland. It sends a hormone to the adrenal gland as well.

Thyroid gland: It interacts with the pituitary gland to influence growth.

Adrenal gland: It interacts with the pituitary gland and likely plays a role in pubertal development, but less is known about its function than about sex glands. Recent research, however, suggests it may be involved in adolescent behavior, particularly for boys.

The gonads, or sex glands: These consist of the testes in males and the ovaries in females. The sex glands are strongly involved in the appearance of secondary sex characteristics, such as facial hair in males and breast development in females. The general class of hormones called estrogens is dominant in females, while androgens are dominant in males. More specifically, testosterone in males and estradiol in females are key hormones in pubertal development.

FIGURE 14.2 The Major Endocrine Glands Involved in Pubertal Change

Not only does the pituitary gland release gonadotropins that stimulate the testes and ovaries, but through interaction with the hypothalamus the pituitary gland also secretes hormones that either directly lead to growth and skeletal maturation or that produce growth effects through interaction with the thyroid gland, located in the neck region.

The concentrations of certain hormones increase dramatically during adolescence (Dorn & others, 2006). **Testosterone** is a hormone associated in boys with the development of genitals, an increase in height, and a change in voice. **Estradiol** is a hormone associated in girls with breast, uterine, and skeletal development. In one study, testosterone levels increased eighteenfold in boys but only twofold in girls during puberty; estradiol increased eightfold in girls but only twofold in boys (Nottelmann & others, 1987) (see Figure 14.3). Note that both testosterone and estradiol are present in the hormonal makeup of both boys and girls but that testosterone dominates in male pubertal development, estradiol in female pubertal development.

Timing and Variations in Puberty

Imagine a toddler displaying all the features of puberty—a 3-year-old girl with fully developed breasts or a boy just slightly older with a deep voice. That is what we would see by the year 2250 if the age at which puberty arrives were to keep getting younger at its present pace. In Norway today, menarche occurs at just over 13 years of age, compared with 17 years of age in the 1840s. In the United States—where children mature up to a year earlier than children in European countries—the average age of menarche declined significantly since the mid-nineteenth century (see Figure 14.4). Fortunately, however, we are unlikely to see pubescent toddlers,

testosterone A hormone associated in boys with the development of genitals, an increase in height, and a change in voice.

estradiol A hormone associated in girls with breast, uterine, and skeletal development.

since what has happened in the past century is likely the result of improved nutrition and health (Delemarre-van de Waal, 2005). The available information suggests that menarche began to occur earlier at about the time of the Industrial Revolution, a period associated with increased standards of living and advances in medical science (Petersen, 1979).

Why do the changes of puberty occur when they do, and how can variations in their timing be explained? The basic genetic program for puberty is wired into the species (Sharp & others, 2004), but nutrition, health, and other environmental factors also affect puberty's timing and makeup (Herman-Giddens, 2007; McDowell, Brody, & Hughes, 2007).

One key factor that triggers puberty for girls is body mass. Menarche occurs at a relatively consistent weight in girls. A body weight approximating 106 +/−3 pounds can trigger menarche and the end of the pubertal growth spurt. For menarche to begin and continue, fat must make up 17 percent of the girl's body weight. As a result, teenage anorexics whose weight drops dramatically, and some female athletes in sports such as gymnastics, do not menstruate (Phillips, 2003).

For most boys, the pubertal sequence may begin as early as 10 years of age or as late as 13½. It may end as early as 13 years or as late as 17 years for most boys. The normal range is wide enough that, given two boys of the same chronological age, one might complete the pubertal sequence before the other one has begun it. Menarche is considered within a normal range if it appears between the ages of 9 and 15.

Psychological Dimensions of Puberty

A host of psychological changes accompanies an adolescent's pubertal development. First, we explore whether hormonal changes are linked to psychological dimensions, then examine changes in body image, as well as early and late maturation.

Hormones and Behavior Are concentrations of hormones linked to adolescent behavior? Hormonal factors are thought to account for at least part of the increase in negative and variable emotions that characterize adolescents (Archibald, Graber, & Brooks-Gunn, 2003; Dorn & others, 2006). Researchers have found that in boys higher levels of androgens are associated with violence and acting-out problems (Van Goozen & others, 1998). There is also some indication that increased estrogen levels are linked to depression in adolescent girls (Angold, Costello, & Worthman, 1999).

However, hormonal factors alone are not responsible for adolescent behavior (DeRose & Brooks-Gunn, 2006; DeRose, Wright, & Brooks-Gunn, 2006; Graber, Brooks-Gunn, & Warren, 2006). For example, one study found that social factors accounted for two to four times as much variance as hormonal factors in young adolescent girls' depression and anger (Brooks-Gunn & Warren, 1989). Thus, hormones do not function independently with hormonal activity being influenced by many environmental factors, including parent-adolescent relationships (Booth & others, 2003). Stress, eating patterns, sexual activity, and depression can also activate or suppress various aspects of the hormone system (Archibald, Graber, & Brooks-Gunn, 2003).

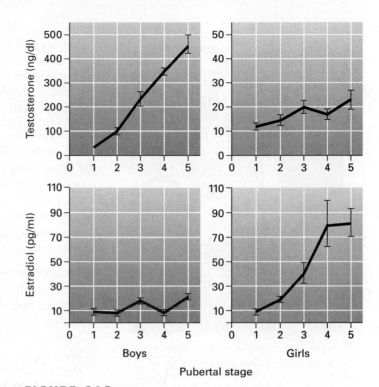

FIGURE 14.3 Hormone Levels by Sex and Pubertal Stage for Testosterone and Estradiol The five stages range from the early begining of puberty (stage 1) to the most advanced stage of puberty (stage 5). Notice the signigficant increase In testosterone in boys and the significant increase in estradiol in girls.

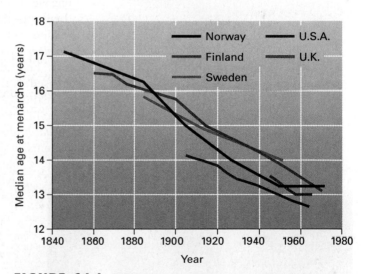

FIGURE 14.4 Median Ages at Menarche in Selected Northern European Countries and the United States from 1845 to 1969 Notice the steep decline in the age at which girls experienced menarche in four northern European countries and the United States from 1845 to 1969. Recently the age at which girls experience menarche has been leveling off.

Adolescents show a strong preoccupation with their changing bodies and develop images of what their bodies are like. *Why might adolescent males have more positive body images than adolescent females?*

Body Image One psychological aspect of puberty is certain for both boys and girls: adolescents are preoccupied with their bodies (Nishina & others, 2006; Nollen & others, 2006). In puberty, adolescents develop individual images of their bodies. Perhaps you looked in the mirror on a daily—and sometimes even hourly—basis to see if you could detect anything different in your changing body. Preoccupation with one's body image is strong throughout adolescence, but it is especially acute during puberty.

Gender Differences Gender differences characterize adolescents' perceptions of their bodies. In general, girls are less happy with their bodies and have more negative body images than boys throughout puberty (Bearman & others, 2006).

As pubertal change proceeds, girls often become more dissatisfied with their bodies, probably because their body fat increases. In contrast, boys become more satisfied as they move through puberty, probably because their muscle mass increases (Bearman & others, 2006). Here is a sampling of recent research on body image in adolescence:

- *Ethnicity*. A meta-analysis (a statistical analysis that combines the results of many studies) found that during adolescence and college, non-Latino White females had more negative body images than African American females, but during adulthood there were no differences in their body images (Grabe & Hyde, 2006). The researchers concluded that in adolescence, girls are bombarded by media images of tall, thin, non-Latino White women. By the time they are in their late twenties, many of these women may be less likely to compare themselves with media images of tall, thin women. Another revealed that the more TV non-Latino White girls watch, the more their body images subsequently worsen (Schooler & others, 2004).
- *Appearance*. Adolescent males who evaluated their appearance more positively and who said appearance was very important to them were more likely to engage in risky sexy behavior, whereas adolescent females who evaluated their appearance more positively were less likely to engage in risky behavior (Gillen, Lefkowitz, & Shearer, 2006).
- *Developmental changes*. A longitudinal study of 428 boys and girls revealed that girls' body dissatisfaction increased, whereas boys' body dissatisfaction decreased as they went through early adolescence (Bearman & others, 2006). In this study, for both boys and girls, lack of parental support and dietary restraint preceded future increases in body satisfaction.
- *Mental health problems*. A study indicated that 12- to 17-year-old girls who were patients in psychiatric hospitals and had a negative body image were more depressed, anxiety-prone, and suicidal than same-aged patients who were less concerned about their body image (Dyl & others, 2006).
- *Health*. A longitudinal study of more than 2,500 adolescents found that lower body satisfaction placed them at risk for poorer overall health (Neumark-Sztainer & others, 2006).
- *Best and worst aspects of being a boy or a girl*. The negative aspects of puberty for girls appeared in a recent study that explored 400 middle school boys' and girls' perceptions of the best and worst aspects of being a boy or a girl (Zittleman, 2006). In the views of the middle school students, at the top of the list of the worst things about being a girl was the biology of being female, which included such matters as childbirth, PMS, periods, and breast cancer. The middle school students said differential discipline (getting into trouble, being disciplined, and being blamed more than girls even when they were not at fault) is the worst thing about being a boy.

Body Art, such as tattoos and body piercing, is increasing in adolescence and emerging adulthood. *Why do youth engage in such body modification?*

Body Art An increasing number of adolescents are obtaining tattoos and getting parts of their body pierced (Armstrong, Caliendo, &

Roberts, 2006; Koch & others, 2005). Many of these youth engage in such body modification to be different, to stamp their identity as unique. In one study of adolescents, 60 percent of the students with tattoos had academic grades of As and Bs (Armstrong, 1995). In this study, the average age at which the adolescents got their first tattoo was 14 years of age. Some studies indicate that tattoos and body piercings are markers for risk taking in adolescence (Carroll & others, 2002; Deschesnes, Fines, & Demers, 2006). A recent study revealed that multiple body piercings is especially a marker for risk-taking behavior (Suris & others, 2007). However, other researchers argue that body art is increasingly used to express individuality and self-expression rather than rebellion (Armstrong & others, 2004).

Early and Late Maturation

Some of you entered puberty early, others late, and yet others on time. Adolescents who mature earlier or later than their peers perceive themselves differently (Graber, Brooks-Gunn, & Warren, 2006). In the Berkeley Longitudinal Study some years ago, early-maturing boys perceived themselves more positively and had more successful peer relations than did their late-maturing counterparts (Jones, 1965). When the late-maturing boys were in their thirties, however, they had developed a stronger sense of identity than the early-maturing boys had (Peskin, 1967). Possibly this occurred because the late-maturing boys had more time to explore life's options or because the early-maturing boys continued to focus on their advantageous physical status instead of on career development and achievement. More recent research confirms, though, that at least during adolescence, it is advantageous to be an early-maturing rather than a late-maturing boy (Simmons & Blyth, 1987).

For girls, early and late maturation have been linked with body image. In the sixth grade, early-maturing girls show greater satisfaction with their figures than do late-maturing girls, but by the tenth grade late-maturing girls are more satisfied (Simmons & Blyth, 1987) (see Figure 14.5). One possible reason for this is that in late adolescence early-maturing girls are shorter and stockier, whereas late-maturing girls are taller and thinner. Thus, late-maturing girls in late adolescence have bodies that more closely approximate the current American ideal of feminine beauty—tall and thin.

An increasing number of researchers have found that early maturation increases girls' vulnerability to a number of problems (Graber, Brooks-Gunn, & Warren, 2006; Mendle, Turkheimer, & Emery, 2007). Early-maturing girls are more likely to smoke, drink, be depressed, have an eating disorder, request earlier independence from their parents, and have older friends; and their bodies are likely to elicit responses from males that lead to earlier dating and earlier sexual experiences (Wiesner & Ittel, 2002). One study of 1,225 urban middle school girls found that those who entered puberty early experimented with alcohol and marijuana at much higher rates than their ethnic minority peers who developed later (Graber, 2003). In another study, early-maturing girls had lower educational and occupational attainment in adulthood (Stattin & Magnusson, 1990). Apparently as a result of their early physical development, early-maturing girls are exposed to social contact with older peers, which can lead to problem behaviors, (Sarigiani & Petersen, 2000).

The Brain

Along with the rest of the body, the brain is changing during adolescence, but the study of adolescent brain development is in its infancy. As advances in technology take place, significant strides will also likely be made in charting developmental changes in the adolescent brain (Nelson, Thomas, & de Haan, 2006; Steinberg, 2007). What do we know now?

Using fMRI brain scans, scientists have recently discovered that adolescents' brains undergo significant structural changes (Eshel & others, 2006; Toga, Thompson, & Sowell, 2006; Whitford & others, 2007). The **corpus callosum,** where fibers

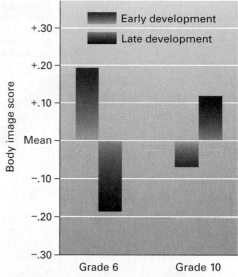

FIGURE 14.5 Early- and Late-Maturing Adolescent Girls' Perceptions of Body Image in Early and Late Adolescence

How does early and late maturation influence adolescent development? What are some of the differences in the ways girls and boys experience pubertal growth?

corpus callosum The location where fibers connect the brain's left and right hemispheres.

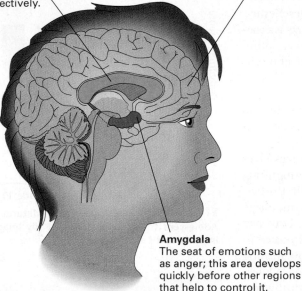

Corpus callosum
These nerve fibers connect the brain's two hemispheres; they thicken in adolescence to process information more effectively.

Prefrontal cortex
This "judgment" region reins in intense emotions but doesn't finish developing until at least age 20.

Amygdala
The seat of emotions such as anger; this area develops quickly before other regions that help to control it.

FIGURE 14.6 Changes in the Adolescent Brain

Lee Malvo, was 17-years-old, when he and John Muhammad, an adult, went on a sniper spree in 2002, terrorizing the Washington, DC, area and killing 10 people. A 2005 U.S. Supreme Court ruling stated that individuals who are 18-years-of age and under, like Malvo, cannot be given the death penalty. *Are there implications for what scientists are learning about the adolescent's brain for legal decisions, such as the death penalty?*

connect the brain's left and right hemispheres, thickens in adolescence, and this improves adolescents' ability to process information (Giedd & others, 2006). We described advances in the development of the *prefrontal cortex*—the highest level of the frontal lobes involved in reasoning, decision making, and self-control—in Chapters 8 and 11. However, the prefrontal cortex doesn't finish maturing until the emerging adult years, approximately 18 to 25 years of age, or later. However, the **amygdala**—the seat of emotions such as anger—matures earlier than the prefrontal cortex. Figure 14.6 shows the locations of the corpus callosum, prefrontal cortex, and amygdala.

Leading researcher Charles Nelson (2003; Nelson, Thomas, & de Haan, 2006) points out that although adolescents are capable of very strong emotions their prefrontal cortex hasn't adequately developed to the point at which they can control these passions. It is as if their brain doesn't have the brakes to slow down their emotions. Or consider this interpretation of the development of emotion and cognition in adolescents: "early activation of strong 'turbo-charged' feelings with a relatively un-skilled set of 'driving skills' or cognitive abilities to modulate strong emotions and motivations" (Dahl, 2004, p. 18).

Are there implications of what we now know about the adolescent's brain for the legal system? For example, can the brain research we have just discussed be used to argue that because the adolescent's brain, especially the higher-level prefrontal cortex, is still developing, adolescents should not be given a death penalty? Some scientists argue that criminal behavior in adolescence should not be excused, but that adolescents should not be given the death penalty (Fassler, 2004). Other scientists, such as Jerome Kagan (2004), stress that whether adolescents should be given the death penalty is an ethical issue, and that the brain research does not show that adolescents have a reduced blame for committing crimes. A similar stance is taken by some of the leading neuroscientists who study brain development in adolescence. Elizabeth Sowell (2004) says that scientists can't just do brain scans on adolescents and decide if they should be tried as adults. In 2005, the death penalty for adolescents (under the age of 18) was prohibited by the U.S. Supreme Court, but it still continues to be debated (Ash, 2006).

REVIEW AND REFLECT ▸ LEARNING GOAL 2

2 **Describe puberty's characteristics, developmental changes, psychological dimensions, and the development of the brain.**

Review
- What is puberty? What characterizes sexual maturation and the pubertal growth spurt?
- What are some hormonal changes in puberty?
- How has the timing of puberty changed, and what are some variations in puberty?
- What are some psychological dimensions of pubertal change?
- What developmental changes occur in the brain during adolescence?

Reflect
- Did you experience puberty early, late, or on time? How do you think the timing of your puberty influenced your development?

amygdala The seat of emotions, such as anger.

3 WHAT ARE THE DIMENSIONS OF ADOLESCENT SEXUALITY?

| Developing a Sexual Identity | Contraceptive Use | Adolescent Pregnancy |

| The Progression of Adolescent Sexual Behaviors | Sexually Transmitted Infections |

Adolescence is a time of sexual exploration and experimentation, of sexual fantasies and realities, of incorporating sexuality into one's identity. Adolescents have an almost insatiable curiosity about sexuality. They think about whether they are sexually attractive, how to do sex, and what the future holds for their sexual lives. The majority of adolescents eventually manage to develop a mature sexual identity, but most experience times of vulnerability and confusion.

Adolescence is a bridge between the asexual child and the sexual adult (Feldman, 1999). Every society gives some attention to adolescent sexuality. In some societies, adults clamp down and protect adolescent females from males by chaperoning them. Other societies promote very early marriage. Yet others allow some sexual experimentation.

In the United States, children and adolescents learn a great deal about sex from television (Collins, 2005; Ward & Friedman, 2006; Ward, Hansbrough, & Walker, 2005). The messages come from TV commercials, which use sex to sell just about everything, as well as from the content of TV shows. One study of 1,762 12- to 17-year-olds found that those who watched more sexually explicit TV shows were more likely than their counterparts who watched these shows less to initiate sexual intercourse in the next 12 months (Collins & others, 2004). Adolescents in the highest 10 percent of viewing sexually explicit TV shows were twice as likely to engage in sexual intercourse as those in the lowest 10 percent. The results held regardless of whether the exposure to explicit sex involved actual sexual behavior or just talk about sex. In a more recent study, U.S. high school students who frequently viewed talk shows and "sexy" prime-time programs were more likely to endorse sexual stereotypes than their counterparts who viewed these shows infrequently (Ward & Friedman, 2006). Also in this study, more frequent viewing and stronger identification with popular TV characters were linked with greater levels of sexual experience in adolescents. Sexual messages also come from videos, the lyrics of popular music, and Web sites (Roberts, Henriksen, & Foehr, 2004). One research review found that frequent watching of soap operas and music videos was linked with greater acceptance of casual attitudes about sex and higher expectations of engaging in sexual activity (Ward, 2003).

Sex is virtually everywhere in the American culture and is used to sell just about everything. *What evidence is cited in the text to indicate that messages from the media influence adolescents' attitudes or behavior?*

Developing a Sexual Identity

Mastering emerging sexual feelings and forming a sense of sexual identity is a multifaceted and lengthy process. It involves learning to manage sexual feelings (such as sexual arousal and attraction), developing new forms of intimacy, and learning the skills to regulate sexual behavior to avoid undesirable consequences (Crockett, Raffaelli, & Moilanen, 2003).

An adolescent's sexual identity involves activities, interests, styles of behavior, and an indication of sexual orientation (whether an individual has same-sex or other-sex attractions) (Buzwell & Rosenthal, 1996). For example, some adolescents have a high anxiety level about sex, others a low level. Some adolescents are strongly aroused sexually, others less so. Some adolescents are very active sexually, others not at all. Some adolescents are sexually inactive in response to their strong

Sexual arousal emerges as a new phenomenon in adolescence and it is important to view sexuality as a normal aspect of adolescent development.

—SHIRLEY FELDMAN
Contemporary Psychologist, Stanford University

What developmental pathways characterize attraction to same-sex individuals?

religious upbringing; others go to church regularly, yet their religious training does not inhibit their sexual activity (Thorton & Camburn, 1989).

It is commonly believed that most gay male and lesbian individuals quietly struggle with same-sex attractions in childhood, do not engage in heterosexual dating, and gradually recognize that they are gay or lesbian in mid to late adolescence (Diamond, 2003; Savin-Williams, 2006). Many gay male and lesbian youth follow this developmental pathway, but others do not. For example, many youth have no recollection of same-sex attractions and experience a more abrupt sense of their same-sex attraction in late adolescence (Savin-Williams, 2006). Researchers also have found that the majority of adolescents with same-sex attractions also experience some degree of other-sex attractions (Garofalo & others, 1999). Even though some adolescents who are attracted to same-sex individuals fall in love with these individuals, others claim that their same-sex attractions are purely physical (Savin-Williams, 2006).

In sum, gay and lesbian youth have diverse patterns of initial attraction, often have bisexual attractions, and may have physical or emotional attraction to same-sex individuals but do not always fall in love with them (Savin-Williams & Diamond, 2004).

The Progression of Adolescent Sexual Behaviors

Adolescents engage in a rather consistent progression of sexual behaviors (DeLamater & MacCorquodale, 1979). One study in which 452 individuals 18 to 25 years of age were asked about their sexual experiences found the following: kissing preceded petting, which preceded sexual intercourse and oral sex (Feldman, Turner, & Araujo, 1999). Male adolescents reported engaging in these sexual behaviors approximately one year earlier than female adolescents.

The timing of sexual initiation varies by country as well as by gender and other socioeconomic characteristics. In one study, among females, the proportion having first intercourse by age 17 ranged from 72 percent in Mali to 47 percent in the United States and 45 percent in Tanzania (Singh & others, 2000). The percentage of males who had their first intercourse by age 17 ranged from 76 percent in Jamaica to 64 percent in the United States and 63 percent in Brazil. Within the United States, male, African American, and inner-city adolescents report being the most sexually active (Feldman, Turner, & Araujo, 1999). Asian American adolescents have the most restrictive sexual timetable.

A national survey further reveals the timing of sexual activities among U.S. adolescents (Alan Guttmacher Institute, 1998):

- Eight in ten girls and seven in ten boys are virgins at age 15.
- The probability that adolescents will have sexual intercourse increases steadily with age, but one in five individuals have not yet had sexual intercourse by age 19.
- Initial sexual intercourse occurs in the mid- to late-adolescent years for a majority of teenagers, about eight years before they marry; more than one-half of 17-year-olds have had sexual intercourse.

More recent data collected in 2005 in a national U.S. survey found similar developmental trends, with 63 percent of twelfth-graders reporting that they had experienced sexual intercourse compared with 34 percent of ninth-graders (MMWR, 2006).

There has been a dramatic increase in oral sex during adolescence (Bersamin & others, 2006). In a national survey, 55 percent of U.S. 15- to 19-year-old boys and 54 percent of girls said they had engaged in oral sex (National Center for Health Statistics, 2002). What is especially worrisome about the increase in oral sex during adolescence is how casually many engage in the practice. It appears that for many adolescents oral sex is a recreational activity practiced outside of an intimate, caring relationship (Walsh & Bennett, 2004). One reason for the increase in oral sex during adolescence is the belief that oral sex is not really sex, so technically those who engage in oral sex but not sexual intercourse consider themselves technically still to be virgins. Another reason for the increase is the perception that oral sex is likely to be safer and less likely to result in sexually transmitted infections than sexual intercourse. Thus, many adolescents appear to be unaware of the health risks linked to oral sex, such as the possibility of contracting such infections, including HIV.

Adolescents who engage in sex before age 16, and experience a number of partners over time, are the least effective users of contraception and are at risk for early, unintended pregnancy and for sexually transmitted infections (Cavanaugh, 2004). Many adolescents are not emotionally prepared to handle sexual experiences, especially in early adolescence. Early sexual activity is linked with risky behaviors such as drug use, delinquency, and school-related problems (Dryfoos & Barkin, 2006). In a longitudinal study from 10 to 12 years of age to 25 years of age, early sexual intercourse and affiliation with deviant peers were linked to substance use disorders in emerging adulthood (Cornelius & others, 2007).

What are some risk factors for developing sexual problems in adolescence?

Contraceptive Use

Sexual activity is a normal activity necessary for procreation, but if appropriate safeguards are not taken it brings the risk of unintended, unwanted pregnancy and sexually transmitted infections (Carroll, 2007; Strong & others, 2008). Both of these risks can be reduced significantly by using certain forms of contraception and barriers (such as condoms).

The good news is that adolescents are increasing their use of contraceptives (Santelli & others, 2007). For example, a recent study examined trends in U.S. ninth- to twelfth-graders' contraceptive use from 1991 to 2003 (Anderson, Santelli, & Morrow, 2006). The use of condoms by males increased from 46 percent in 1991 to 63 percent in 2003. The percentage of adolescents who used either withdrawal or no method steadily declined from 33 percent in 1991 to 19 percent in 2003.

Although adolescent contraceptive use is increasing, many sexually active adolescents still do not use contraceptives, or they use them inconsistently (Davies & others, 2006). A recent study of female adolescents living in low-income circumstances revealed that those who inconsistently used contraceptives were more likely to desire to become pregnant, have less frequent communication with their partners about contraceptive use, and have a greater number of life sexual partners than their counterparts who consistently used contraceptives (Davies & others, 2006).

Psychologists are exploring ways to encourage adolescents to make less risky sexual decisions. Here an adolescent participates in an interactive video session developed by Julie Downs and her colleagues at the Department of Social and Decision Making Sciences at Carnegie Mellon University. The videos help adolescents evaluate their responses and decisions in high-risk sexual contexts.

STI	Description/cause	Incidence	Treatment
Gonorrhea	Commonly called the "drip" or "clap." Caused by the bacterium *Neisseria gonorrhoeae*. Spread by contact between infected moist membranes (genital, oral-genital, or anal-genital) of two individuals. Characterized by discharge from penis or vagina and painful urination. Can lead to infertility.	500,000 cases annually in U.S.	Penicillin, other antibiotics
Syphilis	Caused by the bacterium *Treponema pallidum*. Characterized by the appearance of a sore where syphilis entered the body. The sore can be on the external genitals, vagina, or anus. Later, a skin rash breaks out on palms of hands and bottom of feet. If not treated, can eventually lead to paralysis or even death.	100,000 cases annually in U.S.	Penicillin
Chlamydia	A common STI named for the bacterium *Chlamydia trachomatis*, an organism that spreads by sexual contact and infects the genital organs of both sexes. A special concern is that females with chlamydia may become infertile. It is recommended that adolescent and young adult females have an annual screening for this STI.	About 3 million people in U.S. annually; estimates are that 10 percent of adolescent girls have this STI.	Antibiotics
Genital herpes	Caused by a family of viruses with different strains. Involves an eruption of sores and blisters. Spread by sexual contact.	One of five U.S. adolescents and adults	No known cure but antiviral medications can shorten outbreaks
AIDS	Caused by a virus, the human immunodeficiency virus (HIV) that destroys the body's immune system. Semen and blood are the main vehicles of transmission. Common symptoms include fevers, night sweats, weight loss, chronic fatigue, and swollen lymph nodes.	More than 6,000 13- to 19-year-olds in the U.S.; epidemic incidence in sub-Saharan adolescent girls	New treatments have slowed the progression from HIV to AIDS; no cure
Genital warts	Caused by the human papillomavirus, which does not always produce symptoms. Usually appear as small, hard painless bumps in the vaginal area, or around the anus. Very contagious. Certain high-risk types of this virus cause cervical cancer and other genital cancers. In 2007, the Centers for Disease Control and Prevention recommened that all 11- and 12-year-old girls be given the vaccine, Gardasil, which helps to fight off HPV and cervical cancer.	About 5.5 million new cases annually; considered the most common STI in the U.S.	A topical drug, freezing, or surgery.

FIGURE 14.7 Sexually Transmitted Infection

Sexually Transmitted Infections

Sexually transmitted infections (STIs) are diseases that are contracted primarily through sexual contact. This contact is not limited to vaginal intercourse but includes oral-genital and anal-genital contact as well. STIs are an increasing health problem. Approximately 25 percent of sexually active adolescents are estimated to become infected with an STI each year (Alan Guttmacher Institute, 1998). Among the main STIs adolescents can get are bacterial infections (such as gonorrhea, syphilis, and chlamydia), and STIs caused by viruses—genital herpes, genital warts, and **AIDS** (acquired immune deficiency syndrome). Figure 14.7 describes these sexually transmitted infections.

No single STI has had a greater impact on sexual behavior, or created more fear, in the last two decades than AIDS. AIDS is caused by a virus, the human immunodeficiency virus (HIV), which destroys the body's immune system. Following exposure to HIV, an individual is vulnerable to germs that a normal immune system could destroy.

Through December 2005, there were 6,354 cases of AIDS in 13- to 19-year-olds in the United States (Centers for Disease Control and Prevention, 2007). Among those 20 to 24 years of age, more than 34,795 AIDS cases had been reported. Because of its long incubation period between infection with the HIV virus and AIDS diagnosis, most of the 20- to 24-year-olds were infected during adolescence.

Worldwide, the greatest concern about AIDS is in sub-Saharan Africa, where it has reached epidemic proportions (Singh & others, 2004; UNICEF, 2007). Adolescent

sexually transmitted infections (STIs)
Diseases that are contracted primarily through sexual contact. This contact is not limited to vaginal intercourse but includes oral-genital contact and anal-genital contact as well.

AIDS AIDS stands for acquired immune deficiency syndrome and is caused by a virus, the human immunodeficiency virus (HIV), which destroys the body's immune system.

girls in many African countries are especially vulnerable to infection with the HIV virus by adult men. Approximately six times as many adolescent girls as boys have AIDS in these countries. In Kenya, 25 percent of the 15- to 19-year-old girls are HIV-positive, compared with only 4 percent of this age group of boys. In Botswana, more than 30 percent of the adolescent girls who are pregnant are infected with the HIV virus. In some sub-Saharan countries, less than 20 percent of women and 40 percent of 15- to 19-year-olds reported that they used a condom the last time they had sexual intercourse (Singh & others, 2004).

There continues to be great concern about AIDS in many parts of the world, not just sub-Saharan Africa. In the United States, prevention is especially targeted at groups that show the highest incidence of AIDS. These include drug users, individuals with other STIs, young homosexual males, individuals living in low-income circumstances, Latinos, and African Americans (Centers for Disease Control and Prevention, 2004). Also, in recent years, there has been increased heterosexual transmission of the HIV virus in the United States.

Adolescent Pregnancy

In cross-cultural comparisons, the United States continues to have one of the highest adolescent pregnancy and childbearing rates in the industrialized world, despite a considerable decline in the 1990s (Centers for Disease Control and Prevention, 2002) (see Figure 14.8). The U.S. adolescent pregnancy rate is eight times as high as in the Netherlands. Although U.S. adolescents are no more sexually active than their counterparts in the Netherlands, their adolescent pregnancy rate is dramatically higher.

Why are U.S. adolescent pregnancy rates so high? We discuss possible answers to this question in the following *Diversity in Children's Development* interlude.

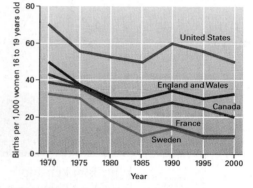

FIGURE 14.8 Cross-Cultural Comparisons of Adolescent Pregnancy Rates

Diversity in Children's Development

CROSS-CULTURAL COMPARISONS OF ADOLESCENT PREGNANCY

Three reasons as to why U.S. adolescent pregnancy rates are so high can be found in cross-cultural studies (Boonstra, 2002, pp. 9–10):

- *"Childbearing regarded as adult activity."* European countries, as well as Canada, give a strong consensus that childbearing belongs in adulthood "when young people have completed their education, have become employed and independent from their parents and are living in stable relationships. . . . In the United States, this attitude is much less strong and much more variable across groups and areas of the country."

- *"Clear messages about sexual behavior.* While adults in other countries strongly encourage teens to wait until they have established themselves before having children, they are generally more accepting than American adults of teens having sex. In France and Sweden, in particular, teen sexual expression is seen as normal and positive, but there is also widespread expectation that sexual intercourse will take place within committed relationships. (In fact, relationships among U.S. teens tend to be more sporadic and of shorter duration.) Equally strong is the expectation that young people who are having sex will take actions to protect themselves and their partners from pregnancy and sexually transmitted infections," which is much stronger in Europe than in the United States. "In keeping with this view, . . . schools in Great Britain, France, Sweden, and most of Canada" have sex education programs that

(continued on next page)

provide more comprehensive information about prevention than U.S. schools. In addition, these countries use the media more often in "government-sponsored campaigns for promoting responsible sexual behavior."

- *"Access to family-planning services.* In countries that are more accepting of teenage sexual relationships, teenagers also have easier access to reproductive health services. In Canada, France, Great Britain, and Sweden, contraceptive services are integrated into other types of primary health care and are available free or at low cost for all teenagers. Generally, teens (in these countries) know where to obtain information and services and receive confidential and nonjudgmental care. . . . In the United States, where attitudes about teenage sexual relationships are more conflicted, teens have a harder time obtaining contraceptive services. Many do not have health insurance or cannot get birth control as part of their basic health care."

Despite the negative comparisons of the United States with many other developed countries, there are encouraging trends in U.S. adolescent pregnancy rates. In 2004, births to adolescent girls fell to a record low (Child Trends, 2006). The rate of births to adolescent girls has dropped 30 percent since 1991. Reasons for these declines include increased contraceptive use and fear of sexually transmitted infections such as AIDS.

The greatest drop in the U.S. adolescent pregnancy rate in recent years has been for 15- to 17-year-old African American girls. Fear of sexually transmitted infections, especially AIDS; school/community health classes; and a greater hope for the future are the likely reasons for the recent decrease in U.S. adolescent pregnancy rates. Latino adolescents are more likely than African American and non-Latino White adolescents to become pregnant (Child Trends, 2006). Latino and African American adolescent girls who have a child are also more likely to have a second child than are non-Latino White adolescent girls.

Adolescent pregnancy creates health risks for both the baby and the mother. Infants born to adolescent mothers are more likely to have low birth weights—a prominent factor in infant mortality—as well as neurological problems and childhood illness (Dryfoos & Barkin, 2006). Adolescent mothers often drop out of school. Although many adolescent mothers resume their education later in life, they generally do not catch up economically with women who postpone childbearing until their twenties. One longitudinal study found that the children of women who had their first birth during their teens had lower achievement test scores and more behavioral problems than did children whose mothers had their first birth as adults (Hofferth & Reid, 2002).

However, often it is not pregnancy alone that leads to negative consequences for an adolescent mother and her offspring (Hillis & others, 2004; Leadbetter & Way, 2001). Adolescent mothers are more likely to come from low-income backgrounds (Hoffman, Foster, & Furstenberg, 1993; Mehra & Agrawal, 2004). Many adolescent mothers also were not good students before they became pregnant. One study found that adolescent

Careers in CHILD DEVELOPMENT

Lynn Blankenship
Family and Consumer Science Educator

Lynn Blankenship is a family and consumer science educator. She has an undergraduate degree in this area from University of Arizona. She has taught for more than 20 years, the last 14 at Tucson High Magnet School.

Blankenship was awarded the Tucson Federation of Teachers Educator of the Year Award for 1999–2000 and the Arizona Teacher of the Year in 1999.

Blankenship especially enjoys teaching life skills to adolescents. One of her favorite activities is having students care for an automated baby that imitates the needs of real babies. She says that this program has a profound impact on students because the baby must be cared for around the clock for the duration of the assignment. Blankenship also coordinates real-world work experiences and training for students in several child-care facilities in the Tucson area.

Lynn Blankenship (*center*), teaching life skills to students.

child-bearers were more likely to have a history of conduct problems, less educational attainment, and lower childhood socioeconomic status than later child-bearers (Jaffee, 2002). However, in this study, early childbearing exacerbated the difficulties associated with these risks.

Of course, some adolescent mothers do well in school and have positive outcomes (Ahn, 1994; Barnet & others, 2004; Whitman & others, 2001). Serious, extensive efforts are needed to help pregnant adolescents and young mothers enhance their educational and occupational opportunities. Adolescent mothers also need help in obtaining competent child care and in planning for the future.

All adolescents can benefit from age-appropriate family-life education (Weyman, 2003). Family and consumer science educators teach life skills, such as effective decision making, to adolescents. To read about the work of one family and consumer science educator, see the *Careers in Child Development* profile. And to learn more about ways to reduce adolescent pregnancy, see the *Caring for Children* interlude.

Caring for Children

REDUCING ADOLESCENT PREGNANCY

One strategy for reducing adolescent pregnancy, called the Teen Outreach Program (TOP), focuses on engaging adolescents in volunteer community service and stimulates discussions that help adolescents appreciate the lessons they learn through volunteerism. In one study, 695 adolescents in grades 9 to 12 were randomly assigned to either a Teen Outreach group or a control group (Allen & others, 1997). They were assessed at both program entry and at program exit nine months later. The rate of pregnancy was substantially lower for the Teen Outreach adolescents. These adolescents also had a lower rate of school failure and academic suspension.

Another group, Girls, Inc., has four programs that are intended to increase adolescent girls' motivation to avoid pregnancy until they are mature enough to make

These are not adolescent mothers, but rather adolescents who are participating in the Teen Outreach Program (TOP), which engages adolescents in volunteer community service. These adolescent girls are serving as volunteers in a child-care center for crack babies. Researchers have found that such volunteer experiences can reduce the rate of adolescent pregnancy.

(continued on next page)

responsible decisions about motherhood (Roth & others, 1998). Growing Together, a series of five two-hour workshops for mothers and adolescents, and Will Power/Won't Power, a series of six two-hour sessions that focus on assertiveness training, are for 12- to 14-year-old girls. For older adolescent girls, Taking Care of Business provides nine sessions that emphasize career planning as well as information about sexuality, reproduction, and contraception. Health Bridge coordinates health and education services—girls can participate in this program as one of their club activities. Girls who participated in these programs were less likely to get pregnant than girls who did not participate (Girls, Inc., 1991).

Currently, a major controversy in sex education is whether schools should have an abstinence-only program or a program that emphasizes contraceptive knowledge (Cabezon & others, 2005). A recent review of research found that some abstinence-only programs and some contraceptive-knowledge programs were effective in changing adolescents' sexual behavior (Bennett & Assefi, 2005). However, the positive outcomes were modest and most lasted only for a short time. Contrary to critics of contraceptive-knowledge programs, the research review found that they do not increase adolescent sexual activity. An important point to note about comparing sex education programs is that the variation in samples, interventions, and outcome measures make conclusions about which programs are most effective difficult.

REVIEW AND REFLECT LEARNING GOAL 3

3 Characterize adolescent sexuality.

Review
- How do adolescents develop a sexual identity?
- What is the progression of adolescent sexual behaviors?
- How effectively do adolescents use contraceptives?
- What are sexually transmitted infections (STIs)? What are some common STIs in adolescence?
- How high is the adolescent pregnancy rate in the United States? What are the consequences of adolescent pregnancy? How can the adolescent pregnancy rate in the United States be reduced?

Reflect
- Caroline contracted genital herpes from her boyfriend, whom she had been dating for the last three years. After breaking off the relationship and spending more time on her own, she began dating Blake. Should Caroline tell Blake about her sexually transmitted infection? If so, how and when?

4 HOW CAN ADOLESCENT HEALTH AND PROBLEMS BE CHARACTERIZED?

Adolescent Health	Substance Use and Abuse	Eating Problems and Disorders

Many health experts argue that whether adolescents are healthy depends primarily on their own behavior. To improve adolescent health, adults should aim to (1) increase adolescents' health-enhancing behaviors, such as eating nutritiously, exercising, wearing seat belts, and getting adequate sleep, and (2) reduce adolescents' health-compromising behaviors, such as drug abuse, violence, unprotected sexual intercourse, and dangerous driving.

Adolescent Health

Adolescence is a critical juncture in the adoption of behaviors relevant to health (Levine & Smolnak, 2006; Shribman, 2007). Many factors linked to poor health in adulthood begin during adolescence. Healthy behavior such as eating foods low in fat and cholesterol and engaging in regular exercise not only has immediate benefits but contributes to the delay or prevention of major causes of premature disability and mortality in adulthood—heart disease, stroke, diabetes, and cancer (Insel & Roth, 2008).

Nutrition and Exercise Concerns are growing about adolescents' nutrition and exercise (Hills, King, & Armstrong, 2007; Robbins, Power, & Burgess, 2008). In a comparison of adolescents in 28 countries, U.S. adolescents ate more junk food than adolescents in most other countries (World Health Organization, 2000). U.S. adolescents were more likely to eat fried foods and less likely to eat fruits and vegetables than adolescents in most other countries studied. U.S. adolescents are decreasing their intake of fruits and vegetables. The National Youth Risk Survey found that U.S. high school students decreased their intake of fruits and vegetables from 1999 through 2005 (MMWR, 2006) (see Figure 14.9).

In a cross-cultural study, just two-thirds of U.S. adolescents exercised at least twice a week, compared with 80 percent or more of adolescents in Ireland, Austria, Germany, and the Slovak Republic (World Health Organization, 2000). U.S. boys and girls become less active as they reach and progress through adolescence (Merrick & others, 2005). A recent study of more than 3,000 U.S. adolescents found that 34 percent were in the lowest fitness category (Carnethon, Gulati, & Greenland, 2005). Another study revealed that physical fitness in adolescence was linked to physical fitness in adulthood (Mikkelsson & others, 2006). In this study, distance running in adolescence was most predictive for adult fitness in males, whereas sit-ups were the most predictive for females.

Researchers have found that exercise in adolescence has declined in recent years and that it also declines from early through late adolescence. In 1987, 31 percent of 12- to 17-year-olds said they exercised frequently, a figure that declined to only 18 percent in 2001 (American Sports Data, 2001). In another study, physical activity declined from early to late adolescence (National Center for Health Statistics, 2000).

Ethnic differences in exercise participation rates are noteworthy, and they reflect the trend of decreasing exercise from early through late adolescence. A recent study found that Latino and African American 7- to 14-year-olds had lower aerobic fitness levels than their non-Latino White counterparts (Shaibi, Ball, & Goran, 2006). Also, as indicated in Figure 14.10, in the National Youth Risk Survey, non-Latino White boys exercised the most, African American girls the least (MMWR, 2006). Another study revealed that physical activity declined more in African American than non-Latino White girls as they went through adolescence (Kimm & Obarzanek, 2002).

Sleep Patterns Like nutrition and exercise, sleep has a huge influence on well-being. Recently there has been a surge of interest in adolescent sleep patterns (Carskadon, 2005, 2006; Carskadon, Mindell, & Drake, 2006; Chen, Wang, & Yeng, 2006; Dahl, 2006).

The National Sleep Foundation (2006) conducted a U.S. survey of 1,602 caregivers and their 11- to 17-year-olds. Forty-five percent of the adolescents got inadequate sleep on school nights (less than eight hours). Older adolescents (ninth- to twelfth-graders) got markedly less sleep on school nights than younger adolescents

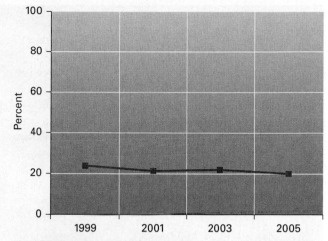

FIGURE 14.9 Percentage of U.S. High School Students Who Ate Fruits and Vegetables Five or More Times a Day, 1999 to 2005 *Note:* This shows the percentage of high school students over time who had eaten fruits and vegetables (100% fruit juice, fruit, green salad, potatoes—excluding french fries, fried potatoes, or potato chips—carrots, or other vegetables) five or more times a day during the seven days preceding the National Youth Risk Survey.

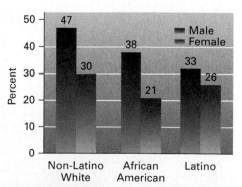

FIGURE 14.10 Exercise Rates of U.S. High School Students: Gender and Ethnicity *Note:* Data are for high school students who were physically active doing any kind of physical activity that increased their heart rate and made them breathe hard some of the time for a total of at least 60 minutes a day on 5 or more of the seven days preceding the survey.

In Mary Carskadon's sleep laboratory at Brown University, an adolescent girl's brain activity is being monitored. Carskadon (2005) says that in the morning, sleep-deprived adolescents' "brains are telling them its night time . . . and the rest of the world is saying it's time to go to school" (p. 19).

(sixth- to eighth-graders)—62 percent of the older adolescents got inadequate sleep compared with 21 percent of the younger adolescents. Adolescents who got inadequate sleep (eight hours or less) on school nights were more likely to feel more tired or sleepy, more cranky and irritable, fall asleep in school, be in a depressed mood, and drink caffeinated beverages than their counterparts who got optimal sleep (nine or more hours). In a recent study of 750 14- to 15-year-olds, getting less sleep at night was linked to higher levels of anxiety, depression, and fatigue the next day (Fuligni & Hardway, 2006).

Many adolescents stay up later at night and sleep longer in the morning than they did when they were children, and this changing timetable has physiological underpinnings (Yang & others, 2005). These findings have implications for the hours during which adolescents learn most effectively in school (Carskadon, Mindell, & Drake, 2006).

Mary Carskadon and her colleagues (2002, 2004, 2005, 2006; Carskadon, Acebo, & Jenni, 2004; Carskadon, Mindell, & Drake, 2006) have conducted a number of research studies on adolescent sleep patterns. They found that when given the opportunity adolescents will sleep an average of nine hours and 25 minutes a night. Most get considerably less than nine hours of sleep, especially during the week. This shortfall creates a sleep deficit, which adolescents often attempt to make up on the weekend. The researchers also found that older adolescents tend to be more sleepy during the day than younger adolescents. They theorized that this sleepiness was not due to academic work or social pressures. Rather, their research suggests that adolescents' biological clocks undergo a shift as they get older, delaying their period of wakefulness by about one hour. A delay in the nightly release of the sleep-inducing hormone **melatonin,** which is produced in the brain's pineal gland, seems to underlie this shift. Melatonin is secreted at about 9:30 p.m. in younger adolescents and approximately an hour later in older adolescents.

Carskadon has suggested that early school starting times may cause grogginess, inattention in class, and poor performance on tests. Based on her research, school officials in Edina, Minnesota, decided to start classes at 8:30 A.M. rather than the usual 7:25 A.M. Since then, there have been fewer referrals for discipline problems, and the number of students who report being ill or depressed has decreased. The school system reports that test scores have improved for high school students, but not for middle school students. This finding supports Carskadon's suspicion that early start times are likely to be more stressful for older than for younger adolescents.

Leading Causes of Death in Adolescence The three leading causes of death in adolescence are accidents, homicide, and suicide (National Center for Health Statistics, 2006). More than half of all deaths in adolescents ages 10 to 19 are due to accidents, and most of those, especially among older adolescents, involve motor vehicles. Risky driving habits, such as speeding, tailgating, and driving under the influence of alcohol or other drugs, may be more important causes of these accidents than is lack of driving experience. In about 50 percent of the motor vehicle fatalities involving an adolescent, the driver has a blood alcohol level of 0.10 percent, twice the level needed to be "under the influence" in some states. A high rate of intoxication is also often present in adolescents who die as pedestrians or while using recreational vehicles.

Homicide is the second leading cause of death in adolescence (National Center for Health Statistics, 2006), especially among African American male adolescents.

melatonin A sleep-inducing hormone that is produced in the brain's pineal gland.

Since the 1950s, the adolescent suicide rate has tripled. Suicide accounts for 6 percent of the deaths in the 10 to 14 age group and 12 percent of deaths in the 15 to 19 age group.

Risk Factors and Assets   Many studies have shown that factors such as poverty, ineffective parenting, and mental disorders in parents *predict* adolescent problems (Mash & Wolfe, 2007). Predictors of problems are called *risk factors*. Risk factor means that there is an elevated probability of a problem outcome in groups of people who have that factor. Children with many risk factors are said to have a "high risk" for problems in childhood and adolescence, but not every one of these children will develop problems (Spencer, 2001).

The Search Institute in Minneapolis has described 40 developmental assets that they believe adolescents need to achieve positive outcomes in their lives (Benson, 2006; Benson & others, 2006). Half of these assets are external, half internal. The 20 *external* assets include support (such as family and neighborhood), empowerment (such as adults in the community valuing youth, and youth being given useful community roles), boundaries and expectations (such as the family setting clear rules and consequences and monitoring the adolescent's whereabouts, as well as positive peer influence), and constructive use of time (such as engaging in creative activities three or more times a week and participating three or more hours a week in organized youth programs). The 20 *internal* assets include commitment to learning (such as motivation to achieve in school and doing at least one hour of homework on school days), positive values (such as helping others and demonstrating integrity), social competencies (such as knowing how to plan and make decisions and having interpersonal competencies like empathy and friendship skills), and positive identity (such as having a sense of control over life and high self-esteem). In research conducted by the Search Institute, adolescents with more assets reported engaging in fewer risk-taking behaviors, such as alcohol and tobacco use, sexual intercourse, and violence. For example, in one survey of more than 12,000 ninth- to twelfth-graders, 53 percent of the students with 0 to 10 assets reported using alcohol three or more times in the past month or getting drunk more than once in the past two weeks, compared with only 16 percent of the students with 21 to 30 assets or 4 percent of the students with 31 to 40 assets.

Among the problems that can develop in adolescence are substance use and abuse, and eating disorders. We discuss these problems here, then, in Chapter 16, explore the adolescent problems of juvenile delinquency, as well as depression and suicide.

Substance Use and Abuse

Each year since 1975, Lloyd Johnston and his colleagues at the Institute of Social Research at the University of Michigan have monitored the drug use of America's high school seniors in a wide range of public and private high schools. Since 1991, they also have surveyed drug use by eighth- and tenth-graders. In 2006, the University of Michigan study, called the Monitoring the Future Study, surveyed approximately 50,000 students in nearly 400 secondary schools.

According to this study, as Figure 14.11 illustrates, the proportions of tenth- and twelfth-grade students who used any illicit drug declined in the late 1990s and first years of the twenty-first century (Johnston & others, 2007). The United States has the highest rate of adolescent drug use of any industrialized nation. Also, the University of Michigan survey likely underestimates the percentage of adolescents who take drugs because it does not include high school dropouts, who have a higher rate of drug use than do students who are still in school.

Alcohol   How extensive is alcohol use by U.S. adolescents? Sizeable declines have occurred in recent years (Johnston & others, 2007). The percentage of U.S. eighth-graders saying that they had any alcohol to drink in the past 30 days fell from a

FIGURE 14.11 Trends in Drug Use by U.S. Eighth-, Tenth-, and Twelfth-Grade Students This graph shows the percentage of U.S. eighth-, tenth-, and twelfth-grade students who reported having taken an illicit drug in the last 12 months from 1991 to 2006 for eighth- and tenth-graders, and from 1975 to 2006 for twelfth-graders (Johnston & others, 2007).

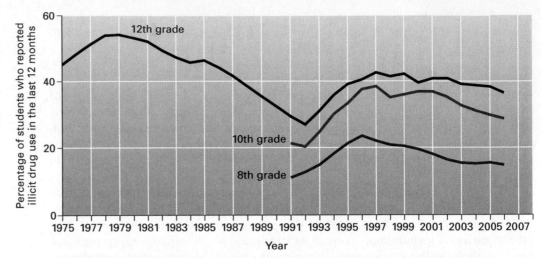

1996 high of 26 percent to 17 percent in 2006. The 30-day prevalence fell among tenth-graders from 39 percent in 2001 to 34 percent in 2006 and among high school seniors from 72 percent in 1980 to 45 percent in 2006. Binge drinking (defined in the University of Michigan surveys as having five or more drinks in a row in the last two weeks) by high school seniors declined from 41 percent in 1980 to 30 percent in 2006. Binge drinking by eighth- and tenth-graders also has dropped in recent years. A consistent gender difference occurs in binge drinking, with males engaging in this behavior more than females.

Although alcohol use by secondary school students has declined in recent years, college students show little drop in alcohol use and an increase in heavy drinking. Heavy drinking at parties among college males is common and is becoming more common (Wechsler & others, 2002).

Cigarette Smoking Cigarette smoking (in which the active drug is nicotine) is one of the most serious yet preventable health problems. One study found that smoking in the adolescent years causes permanent genetic changes in the lungs and forever increases the risk of lung cancer, even if the smoker quits (Weincke & others, 1999). The damage was much less likely among smokers in the study who started in their twenties. The early age of onset of smoking was more important in predicting genetic damage than how heavily the individuals smoked.

Smoking is likely to begin in grades 7 through 9, although sizable portions of youth are still establishing regular smoking habits during high school and college. Since 1975, cigarettes have been the substance most frequently used on a daily basis by high school seniors. Risk factors for becoming a regular smoker in adolescence include having a friend who smoked, a weak academic orientation, and low parental support (Tucker, Ellickson, & Klein, 2003).

Cigarette smoking among adolescents peaked in 1996 and 1997 and has gradually declined since then (Johnston & others, 2007). Following peak use in 1996, smoking rates for U.S. eighth-graders have fallen by 50 percent. In 2006, the percentages of adolescents who said they smoked cigarettes in the last 30 days were 22 percent (twelfth grade), 15 percent (tenth grade), and 9 percent (eighth grade).

There are a number of explanations for the decline in cigarette use by U.S. youth. These include increasing prices, less tobacco advertising reaching adolescents, more antismoking advertisements, and an increase in negative publicity about the tobacco industry (Myers & MacPherson, 2004). Since the mid-1990s, an increasing percentage of adolescents have reported that they perceive cigarette smoking as dangerous, that they disapprove of it, that they are less accepting of being around smokers, and that they prefer to date nonsmokers (Johnston & others, 2006).

Painkillers   An alarming recent trend is use of prescription painkillers by adolescents (Forrester, 2007). A 2004 survey revealed that 18 percent of U.S. adolescents had used Vicodin at some point in their lifetime, whereas 10 percent had used OxyContin (Partnership for a Drug-Free America, 2005). These drugs fall into the general class of drugs called narcotics, and they are highly addictive. In this recent national survey, 9 percent of adolescents said they had abused cough medications to intentionally get high. The University of Michigan began including OxyContin in its survey of twelfth-graders in 2002. From 2002 to 2006, adolescents' reports of using it at any time in the previous year increased (Johnston & others, 2007). Adolescents cite the medicine cabinets of their parents or of friends' parents as the main source for their prescription painkillers (Johnson & others, 2007).

A recent analysis of data from the National Survey on Drug Use and Health revealed that abuse of prescription painkillers by U.S. adolescents may become an epidemic (Sung & others, 2005). In this survey, adolescents especially at risk for abusing prescription painkillers were likely to already be using illicit drugs, came from low-socioeconomic-status families, had favorable attitudes toward illicit drugs, had detached parents, or had friends who used drugs.

The Roles of Development, Parents, and Peers   Most adolescents use drugs at some point in their development, whether limited to alcohol, caffeine, and cigarettes or extended to marijuana, cocaine, and hard drugs. Using drugs as a way of coping with stress, however, can interfere with the development of competent coping skills and responsible decision making. If they use drugs to cope with stress, many young adolescents enter adult roles of marriage and work prematurely, without adequate socioemotional growth, and risk failure in these roles. Researchers have found that drug use in childhood or early adolescence has more detrimental long-term effects on the development of responsible, competent behavior than when drug use occurs in late adolescence (Dodge & others, 2006; King & Chassin, 2007). A longitudinal study of individuals from 8 to 42 years of age found that early onset of drinking was linked to increased risk of heavy drinking in middle age (Pitkanen, Lyyra, & Pulkkinen, 2005).

One longitudinal study linked early substance abuse with several characteristics of early childhood (Kaplow & others, 2002). Risk factors at kindergarten age for substance use at 10 to 12 years of age included being male, having a parent who abused substances, having a low level of verbal reasoning by parents, and having low social problem-solving skills.

Parents, peers, and social support can play important roles in preventing adolescent drug abuse (Engels & others, 2005). Positive relationships with parents and others can reduce adolescents' drug use (Little & others, 2004). In one study, parental control and monitoring were linked with a lower incidence of problem behavior by adolescents, including substance abuse (Fletcher, Steinberg, & Williams-Wheeler, 2004). In another study, low parental involvement, peer pressure, and associating with problem-behaving friends were linked with higher use of drugs by adolescents (Simons-Morton & others, 2001). Also, a national survey revealed that parents who were more involved in setting limits, such as where adolescents went after school and what they were exposed to on TV and the Internet, were more likely to have adolescents who did not use drugs (National Center on Addiction and Substance Abuse, 2001). To read about a program created to reduce adolescent drinking and smoking, see the *Research in Children's Development* interlude.

What roles do parents play in adolescents' drug use?

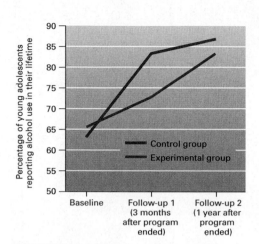

FIGURE 14.12 Young Adolescents' Reports of Alcohol Use in the Family Matters Program Note that at baseline (before the program started) the young adolescents in the Family Matters program (experimental group) and their counterparts who did not go through the program (control group) reported approximately the same lifetime use of alcohol (slightly higher use by the experimental group). However, three months after the program ended, the experimental group reported lower alcohol use, and this reduction was still present one year after the program ended, although at a reduced level.

Research in Children's Development

EVALUATION OF A FAMILY PROGRAM DESIGNED TO REDUCE DRINKING AND SMOKING IN YOUNG ADOLESCENTS

Few experimental studies have been conducted to determine if family programs can reduce drinking and smoking in young adolescents. In one experimental study, 1,326 families with 12- to 14-year-old adolescents living throughout the United States were interviewed (Bauman & others, 2002). After the baseline interviews, participants were randomly assigned either to go through the Family Matters program (experimental group) or to not experience the program (control group) (Bauman & others, 2002).

The families assigned to the Family Matters program received four mailings of booklets. Each mailing was followed by a telephone call from a health educator to "encourage participation by all family members, answer any questions, and record information" (Bauman & others, 2002, pp. 36–37). The first booklet focused on the negative consequences of adolescent substance abuse to the family. The second emphasized "supervision, support, communication skills, attachment, time spent together, educational achievement, conflict reduction, and how well adolescence is understood." The third booklet asked parents to "list things that they do that might inadvertently encourage their child's use of tobacco or alcohol, identify rules that might influence the child's use, and consider ways to monitor use. Then adult family members and the child meet to agree upon rules and sanctions related to adolescent use." Booklet four deals with what "the child can do to resist peer and media pressures for use."

Two follow-up interviews with the parents and adolescents were conducted three months and one year after the experimental group completed the program. Adolescents in the Family Matters program reported lower alcohol and cigarette use both at three months and again one year after the program had been completed. Figure 14.12 shows the results for alcohol.

Eating Problems and Disorders

Eating disorders have become increasingly common among adolescents (Kirsch & others, 2007; Stice & others, 2007). Let's now examine three eating disorders that may appear in adolescence: obesity, anorexia nervosa, and bulimia nervosa.

Obesity   The percentage of overweight adolescents has been increasing. Being overweight increased from 11 to 17 percent for U.S.12- to 19-year-olds from the early 1990s through 2004 (MMWR, 2006). As in our discussion of being overweight in Chapter 11, being overweight was determined by body mass index (BMI), which is computed by a formula that takes into account height and weight. Only adolescents at or above the 95th percentile of BMI were included in the overweight category. As discussed in Chapter 11, poor diet and inadequate exercise probably contribute to the problem. Other research indicates increases in being overweight during adolescence in European countries (Irwin, 2004; Lissau & others, 2004).

Are there ethnic variations in being overweight during adolescence in the United States? A survey by the National Center for Health Statistics (2002) found that African American girls and Latino boys have especially high risks of being overweight during adolescence. A study of 2,379 girls from 9 to 19 years of age found that the prevalence of being overweight was considerably higher for African American girls than non-Latino White girls (Kimm & Obarzanek, 2002). Another study revealed that the higher obesity rate for African American females is linked with a diet higher in calories and fat, as well as sedentary behavior (Sanchez-Johnsen & others, 2004).

There have been few cross-cultural comparisons of obesity in childhood and adolescence. However, in one study, U.S. children and adolescents (6 to 18 years of age) were four times more likely to be classified as obese than their counterparts in China and almost three times as likely to be classified as obese than their counterparts in Russia (Wang, 2000).

What types of interventions have been successful in reducing overweight in adolescents? One review indicated that clinical approaches that focus on the individual adolescent and include a combination of caloric restriction, exercise (walking or biking to school, participating in a regular exercise program), reduction of sedentary activity (watching TV, playing videogames), and behavioral therapy (such as keeping weight loss diaries and rewards for meeting goals) have been moderately effective in helping overweight adolescents lose weight (Fowler-Brown & Kahwati, 2004). In general, school-based approaches (such as instituting a school-wide program to improve eating habits) have been less effective than the clinically based individual approaches (Lytle & others, 2004). A recent research review concluded that school-based approaches for reducing adolescents' weight have modest results, with TV watching the easiest behavior to change, followed by physical activity and then nutrition (Sharma, 2006).

These adolescent girls are attending a weight-management camp. *What types of interventions have been most successful in helping overweight adolescents lose weight?*

A concern is that as schools are under increasing pressure to spend more time on academic topics that health-oriented programs are likely to be shortchanged (Paxson & others, 2006). When this is an impediment, one possibility is to include obesity prevention in after-school programs, which conflict less with schools' academic mandates (Story, Kaphingst, & French, 2006). Another promising strategy is to provide students with healthier foods to eat at school. In 2005, several states began enacting laws that require more healthy foods be sold in vending machines at schools (Story, Kaphingst, & French, 2006). In one intervention, reducing soft drink consumption at schools was linked with a subsequent reduction in the number of 7- to 11-year-old children who were overweight or obese (James & others, 2004). Schools also can play an important role by implementing programs that increase the amount of time children exercise (Datar & Sturm, 2004; Paxson & others, 2006).

Anorexia Nervosa   Although most U.S. girls have been on a diet at some point, slightly less than 1 percent ever develop anorexia nervosa (Walters & Kendler, 1994). **Anorexia nervosa** is an eating disorder that involves the relentless pursuit of thinness through starvation. It is a serious disorder that can lead to death (Agras & others, 2004). Three main characteristics of anorexia nervosa are:

- Weighing less than 85 percent of what is considered normal for a person's age and height.
- Having an intense fear of gaining weight. The fear does not decrease with weight loss.
- Having a distorted image of their body shape (Rigaud & others, 2007). Even when they are extremely thin, they see themselves as too fat. They never think they are thin enough, especially in the abdomen, buttocks, and thighs. They usually weigh themselves frequently, often take their body measurements, and gaze critically at themselves in mirrors (Seidenfeld, Sosin, & Rickert, 2004).

anorexia nervosa An eating disorder that involves the relentless pursuit of thinness through starvation.

Anorexia nervosa has become an increasing problem for adolescent girls and young adult women. *What are some possible causes of anorexia nervosa?*

Anorexia nervosa typically begins in the early to middle teenage years, often following an episode of dieting and some type of life stress (Lee & others, 2005). It is about ten times more likely to occur in females than males. When anorexia nervosa does occur in males, the symptoms and other characteristics (such as a distorted body image and family conflict) are usually similar to those reported by females who have the disorder (Araceli & others, 2005).

Most anorexics are non-Latina White adolescent or young adult females from well-educated, middle- and upper-income families and are competitive and high-achieving (Schmidt, 2003). They set high standards, become stressed about not being able to reach the standards, and are intensely concerned about how others perceive them (Striegel-Moore, Silberstein, & Rodin, 1993). Unable to meet these high expectations, they turn to something they can control: their weight. Problems in family functioning are increasingly being found to be linked to the appearance of anorexia nervosa in adolescent girls (Benninghoven & others, 2007), and a recent research review indicated that family therapy is often the most effective treatment of adolescent girls with anorexia nervosa (Bulik & others, 2007).

The fashion image in U.S. culture that emphasizes "thin is beautiful" contributes to the incidence of anorexia nervosa (Hsu, 2004; Polivy & others, 2003). This image is reflected in the saying, "You never can be too rich or too thin." The media portrays thin as beautiful in their choice of fashion models, which many adolescent girls want to emulate (Wiseman, Sunday, & Becker, 2005). And many adolescent girls who strive to be thin hang out together. A recent study of adolescent girls revealed that friends often share similar body image and eating problems (Hutchinson & Rapee, 2007). In this study, an individual girl's dieting and extreme weight-loss behavior could be predicted from her friends' dieting and extreme weight-loss behavior.

Bulimia Nervosa Whereas anorexics control their eating by restricting it, most bulimics cannot (Mitchell & Mazzeo, 2004). **Bulimia nervosa** is an eating disorder in which the individual consistently follows a binge-and-purge pattern. The bulimic goes on an eating binge and then purges by self-inducing vomiting or using a laxative. Although many people binge and purge occasionally, and some experiment with it, a person is considered to have a serious bulimic disorder only if the episodes occur at least twice a week for three months.

As with anorexics, most bulimics are preoccupied with food, have a strong fear of becoming overweight, and are depressed or anxious (Ramacciotti & others, 2005; Speranza & others, 2005). A recent study revealed that bulimics overvalued their body weight and shape, and this overvaluation was linked to higher depression and lower self-esteem (Hrabosky & others, 2007). Unlike anorexics, people who binge and purge typically fall within a normal weight range, which makes bulimia more difficult to detect.

Approximately 1 to 2 percent of U.S. women are estimated to develop bulimia nervosa (Gotesdam & Agras, 1995), and about 90 percent of bulimics are women. Bulimia nervosa typically begins in late adolescence or early adulthood. Many women who develop bulimia nervosa were somewhat overweight before the onset of the disorder, and the binge eating often began during an episode of dieting. One study of adolescent girls found that increased dieting, pressure to be thin, exaggerated emphasis on appearance, body dissatisfaction, depression symptoms, low self-esteem, and low social support predicted binge eating two years later (Stice, Presnell, & Spangler, 2002). As with anorexia nervosa, about 70 percent of individuals who develop bulimia nervosa eventually recover from the disorder (Agras & others, 2004).

bulimia nervosa An eating disorder in which the individual consistently follows a binge-and-purge eating pattern.

REVIEW AND **REFLECT**   **LEARNING GOAL 4**

4 Identify adolescent problems related to health, substance use and abuse, and eating disorders.

Review
- What are key concerns about the health of adolescents?
- What are some characteristics of adolescents' substance use and abuse?
- What are the characteristics of the major eating disorders?

Reflect
- What do you think should be done to reduce the use of drugs by adolescents?

REACH YOUR LEARNING GOALS

1 **WHAT IS THE NATURE OF ADOLESCENCE?** *Discuss views and developmental transitions that involve adolescence.*

Positive and Negative Views of Adolescence

- Many stereotypes about adolescents are too negative. The majority of adolescents today successfully negotiate the path from childhood to adulthood, although too many are not provided with adequate support and opportunities. It is important to view adolescents as a heterogeneous group. Acting out and boundary testing by adolescents moves them toward accepting, rather than rejecting, parental values.

Developmental Transitions

- Two important transitions in development are from childhood to adolescence and adolescence to adulthood. In the transition from childhood to adolescence, pubertal change is prominent, although cognitive and socioemotional changes occur as well. Emerging adulthood recently has been proposed to describe the transition from adolescence to adulthood. Five key characteristics of emerging adulthood are identity exploration (especially in love and work), instability, being self-focused, feeling in-between, and experiencing possibilities to transform one's life.

2 **WHAT ARE THE PHYSICAL AND PSYCHOLOGICAL ASPECTS OF PUBERTY?** *Describe puberty's characteristics, developmental changes, psychological dimensions, and the development of the brain.*

Sexual Maturation, Height, and Weight

- Puberty is a rapid physical maturation involving hormonal and bodily changes that take place primarily in early adolescence. A number of changes occur in sexual maturation including increased size of the penis and testicles in boys and breast growth and menarche in girls. The growth spurt involves height and weight and occurs about two years earlier for girls than boys.

Hormonal Changes

- Extensive hormonal changes characterize puberty. The pituitary gland plays an important role in these hormonal changes. Testosterone concentrations increase considerably in boys, and estradiol increases considerably in girls during puberty.

Timing and Variations in Puberty

- Puberty began occurring much earlier in the twentieth century mainly because of improved health and nutrition. The basic genetic program for puberty is wired into the nature of the species, but nutrition, health, and other environmental factors affect puberty's timing and makeup. Body mass is a key factor that triggers puberty in girls, and body fat must make up 17 percent for menarche to begin and continue. Menarche appears between ages 9 and 15. Boys can start the pubertal sequence as early as 10 years of age or as late as 17.

Psychological Dimensions of Puberty

- Researchers have found connections between hormonal changes during puberty and behavior, but environmental influences need to be taken into account. Adolescents show heightened interest in their bodies and body images. Younger adolescents are more preoccupied with these images than older adolescents. Adolescent girls often have a more negative body image than adolescent boys. Adolescents increasingly have tattoos and body piercings (body art). Some scholars conclude that body art is a sign of rebellion and is linked to risk taking, whereas others argue that increasingly body art is used to express uniqueness and self-expression rather than rebellion. Early maturation often favors boys, at least during early adolescence, but as adults, late-maturing boys have a more positive identity than early-maturing boys. Early-maturing girls are at risk for a number of developmental problems. They are more likely to smoke, drink, and have an eating disorder and are likely to have earlier sexual experiences.

The Brain

- The thickening of the corpus callosum in adolescence is linked to improved processing of information. The amygdala, which is involved in emotions such as anger, develops earlier than the prefrontal cortex, which functions in reasoning and self-regulation. This gap in development may help to explain the increase in risk-taking behavior that characterizes adolescence.

3 WHAT ARE THE DIMENSIONS OF ADOLESCENT SEXUALITY? *Characterize adolescent sexuality.*

Developing a Sexual Identity

- Adolescence is a time of sexual exploration and sexual experimentation. Mastering emerging sexual feelings and forming a sense of sexual identity are multifaceted. An adolescent's sexual identity includes sexual orientation, activities, interests, and styles of behavior. Developmental pathways for sexual minority youth are often diverse, may involve bisexual attractions, and do not always involve falling in love with a same-sex individual.

The Progression of Adolescent Sexual Behaviors

- The progression of sexual behaviors is typically kissing, petting, sexual intercourse, and oral sex. National data indicate that by age 19, four of five individuals have had sexual intercourse, although the percentage varies by gender, ethnicity, and context. Early sexual activity is a risk factor for developing sexual problems.

Contraceptive Use

- Adolescents are increasing their use of contraceptives, but large numbers still do not use them.

Sexually Transmitted Infections

- Sexually transmitted infections (STIs) are contracted primarily through sexual contact. More than one in four sexually active adolescents has an STI. Among the STIs are bacterial infections such as gonorrhea, syphilis, chlamydia, and STIs caused by viruses, such as genital herpes, genital warts, and AIDS.

Adolescent Pregnancy

- Although the U.S. adolescent pregnancy rate is still among the highest in the developed world, the rate declined considerably in the 1990s. Adolescent pregnancy often increases health risks for the mother and the offspring, although it often is not pregnancy alone that places adolescents at risk. Easy access to family-planning services and sex education programs in schools can help reduce the U.S. adolescent pregnancy rate.

4 HOW CAN ADOLESCENT HEALTH AND PROBLEMS BE CHARACTERIZED? *Identify adolescent problems related to health, substance use and abuse, and eating disorders.*

Adolescent Health

- Adolescence is a critical juncture in health because many of the factors related to poor health habits and early death in the adult years begin during adolescence. Poor nutrition, lack of exercise, and inadequate sleep are concerns. The three leading causes of death in adolescence are accidents, homicide, and suicide.

Substance Use and Abuse	• Despite recent declines in use, the United States has the highest rate of adolescent drug use of any industrialized nation. Alcohol abuse is a major adolescent problem, although its rate has been dropping in recent years, as has cigarette smoking. A recent concern is the increased use of prescription painkillers by adolescents. Drug use in childhood or early adolescence has more negative outcomes than drug use that begins in late adolescence. Parents and peers play important roles in whether adolescents take drugs.
Eating Problems and Disorders	• Eating disorders have increased in adolescence, with a substantial increase in the percentage of adolescents who are overweight. Three eating disorders that may occur in adolescence are obesity, anorexia nervosa, and bulimia nervosa.

KEY TERMS

emerging adulthood 469
puberty 470
menarche 471
hormones 471
hypothalamus 471

pituitary gland 471
gonads 471
gonadotropins 471
testosterone 472
estradiol 472

corpus callosum 475
amygdala 476
sexually transmitted
  infections (STIs) 480
AIDS 480

melatonin 486
anorexia nervosa 491
bulimia nervosa 492

KEY PEOPLE

Jeffrey Arnett 470
G. Stanley Hall 476

Daniel Offer 476
Charles Nelson 476

Mary Carskadon 486
Lloyd Johnston 487

MAKING A DIFFERENCE

Supporting Adolescent Physical Development and Health

What are some strategies for supporting and guiding adolescent physical development and health?

• *Develop positive expectations for adolescents.* Adolescents often are negatively stereotyped. These negative expectations have a way of becoming self-fulfilling prophecies and harming adult-adolescent communication. Don't view adolescence as a time of crisis and rebellion. View it as a time of evaluation, decision making, commitment, and the carving out of a place in the world.

• *Understand the many physical changes adolescents are going through.* The physical changes adolescents go through can

be very perplexing to them. They are not quite sure what they are going to change into, and this can create considerable uncertainty for them.

• *Be a good health role model for adolescents.* Adolescents benefit from being around adults who are good health models: individuals who exercise regularly, eat healthily, and don't take drugs.

• *Communicate effectively with adolescents about sexuality.* Emphasize that young adolescents should abstain from sex. If adolescents are going to be sexually active, they need to take contraceptive precautions. Adolescents need to learn about sexuality and human reproduction before they become sexually active, no later than early adolescence.

RESOURCES FOR IMPROVING CHILDREN'S LIVES

Search Institute

www.search-institute.org

The Search Institute has available a large number of resources for improving the lives of adolescents. In 1995, the Institute began distributing the excellent publications of the Center for Early Adolescence, University of North Carolina, which had just closed. The brochures and books available include resource lists and address school improvement, adolescent literacy, parent educa-

tion, program planning, and adolescent health. A free quarterly newsletter is available.

The Society for Adolescent Medicine (SAM)

www.adolescenthealth.org

SAM is a valuable source of information about competent physicians who specialize in treating adolescents. It maintains a list of recommended adolescence specialists across the United States.

E-LEARNING TOOLS

Connect to **www.mhhe.com/santrockc10** to research the answers and complete these exercises. In addition, you'll find a number of other resources and valuable study tools for Chapter 14, "Physical Development in Adolescence," on this Web site.

Taking It to the Net

1. Allison hangs out with a group of high school seniors who like to party and drink alcohol on the weekends. Even though she has heard all of the slogans and seen films about the hazards of drinking and driving, she continues to drink. "It's not as bad as doing hard drugs," she rationalizes. "Besides, practically everyone drinks in high school." However, Allison is not aware of the physiological effects drinking has on teenagers. How, specifically, might drinking affect brain development in adolescents?

2. Peter, a high school junior, has known since he was about six years old that he is gay. However, he has not told anyone at school, because he is worried that the other kids would reject and harass him. He also has not told his parents. What kinds of issues do gay youth face in high school? What is the high school environment like for most gay and lesbian youth? Are gay and lesbian youth more at risk for disorders such as depression and anxiety? What interventions might ease the coming-out process?

3. Marguerite is very concerned about her sister, Rosalina. Rosalina has lost a significant amount of weight recently, and she now refuses to eat dinner with her family. This is causing Rosalina's parents to become very upset, as food is an important part of their traditional Mexican American household. Marguerite thinks Rosalina might have an eating disorder. How might Marguerite approach Rosalina?

What are the signs and symptoms of the various eating disorders? How might Rosalina's cultural background complicate the issues around her disordered eating?

Health and Well-Being, Parenting, and Education

Build your decision-making skills by trying your hand at the health and well-being, parenting, and education exercises.

Video Clips

The Online Learning Center includes the following videos for this chapter:

1. *Girls and Body Image*—1241
   Two mature 14-year-olds talk about the social pressure for physical appearance. Brekke says that magazines greatly influence girls to look a certain way. She also describes how some girls look a certain way to be popular.

2. *15-Year-Old Girls' Relationships with Boys*—1161
   In this clip, we hear three high school students talk about how their relationships with boys have changed since middle school. They discuss how boys are more mature in high school and are often easier to talk to than girls.

3. *Talking About Teen Sex at 14*—1243
   Two mature 14-year-old girls give their opinions about teen sex. They describe that teens do not consider the long-term consequences of having sexual intercourse. They both agree that if teens are going to engage in sex, they need to be sure, think ahead, and "use precautions."

4. *Talking About Drugs at Age 14*—1245
   Two adolescent girls express their views about drug use among teens. One girl says frankly that smoking a joint is no worse than drinking a glass of wine.

The thoughts of youth are long, long thoughts.

—HENRY WADSWORTH LONGFELLOW
American Poet, 19th Century

CHAPTER OUTLINE		LEARNING GOALS

HOW DO ADOLESCENTS THINK AND PROCESS INFORMATION?　**1**

Piaget's Theory

Adolescent Egocentrism

Information Processing

1 Discuss different approaches to adolescent cognition.

WHAT CHARACTERIZES ADOLESCENTS' VALUES, MORAL EDUCATION, AND RELIGION?　**2**

Values

Moral Education

Religion

2 Describe adolescents' values, moral education, and religion.

WHAT ARE SCHOOLS FOR ADOLESCENTS LIKE?　**3**

The American Middle School

The American High School

High School Dropouts

3 Characterize schools for adolescents.

HOW DO ADOLESCENTS EXPERIENCE CAREER DEVELOPMENT AND WORK?　**4**

Career Development

Work

4 Summarize career development and work in adolescence.

Images of Children's Development
Kim-Chi and Thuy

Kim-Chi Trinh was only 9 years old in Vietnam when her father used his savings to buy passage for her on a fishing boat. It was a costly and risky sacrifice for the family, who placed Kim-Chi on the small boat, among strangers, in the hope that she eventually would reach the United States, where she would get a good education and enjoy a better life.

Kim made it to the United States and coped with a succession of three foster families. When she graduated from high school in San Diego in 1988, she had a straight-A average and a number of college scholarship offers. When asked why she excels in school, Kim-Chi says that she has to do well because she owes it to her parents, who are still in Vietnam.

Kim-Chi is one of a wave of bright, highly motivated Asians who are immigrating to America. Asian Americans are the fastest-growing ethnic minority group in the United States—two out of five immigrants are now Asian. Although Asian Americans make up only 2.4 percent of the U.S. population, they constitute 17 percent of the undergraduates at Harvard, 18 percent at MIT, 27 percent at the University of California at Berkeley, and a staggering 35 percent at the University of California at Irvine.

Not all Asian American youth do this well, however. Poorly educated Vietnamese, Cambodian, and Hmong refugee youth are especially at risk for school-related problems. Many refugee children's histories are replete with losses and trauma. Thuy, a 12-year-old Vietnamese girl, has been in the United States for two years and resides with her father in a small apartment with a cousin's family of five in the inner city of a West Coast metropolitan area (Huang, 1989). While trying to escape from Saigon, "the family became separated, and the wife and two younger children remained in Vietnam. . . . Thuy's father has had an especially difficult time adjusting to the United States. He struggles with English classes and has been unable to maintain several jobs as a waiter" (Huang, 1989, p. 307). When Thuy received a letter from her mother saying that her 5-year-old brother had died, Thuy's schoolwork began to deteriorate, and she showed marked signs of depression—lack of energy, loss of appetite, withdrawal from peer relations, and a general feeling of hopelessness. At the insistence of the school, she and her father went to the child and adolescent unit of a community mental health center. It took the therapist a long time to establish credibility with Thuy and her father, but eventually they began to trust the therapist, who was a good listener and gave them competent advice about how to handle different experiences in the new country. The therapist also contacted Thuy's teacher, who said that Thuy had been involved in several interethnic skirmishes at school. With the assistance of the mental health clinic, the school initiated interethnic student panels to address cultural differences and discuss reasons for ethnic hostility. Thuy was selected to participate in these panels. Her father became involved in the community mutual assistance association, and Thuy's academic performance began to improve.

PREVIEW

When people think of the changes that characterize adolescents, they often focus on puberty and adolescent problems. However, there are some impressive cognitive changes that occur during adolescence. We begin this chapter by focusing on these cognitive changes and then turn our attention to adolescents' values, moral education, and religion. Next, we study what schools for adolescents are like and conclude the chapter by examining career development and work in adolescence.

1 HOW DO ADOLESCENTS THINK AND PROCESS INFORMATION?

| Piaget's Theory | Adolescent Egocentrism | Information Processing |

Adolescents' developing power of thought opens up new cognitive and social horizons. Let's examine what their developing power of thought is like, beginning with Piaget's theory (1952).

Piaget's Theory

As we discussed in Chapter 12, Jean Piaget proposed that at about 7 years of age children enter the *concrete operational stage* of cognitive development. They can reason logically about concrete events and objects, and they make gains in the ability to classify objects and to reason about the relationships between classes of objects. The concrete operational stage lasts until the child is about 11 years old, according to Piaget, when the fourth and final stage of cognitive development begins, the formal operational stage.

The Formal Operational Stage What are the characteristics of the formal operational stage? Formal operational thought is more abstract than concrete operational thought. Adolescents are no longer limited to actual, concrete experiences as anchors for thought. They can conjure up make-believe situations, events that are purely hypothetical possibilities or abstract propositions, and can try to reason logically about them.

The abstract quality of thinking during the formal operational stage is evident in the adolescent's verbal problem-solving ability. Whereas the concrete operational thinker needs to see the concrete elements A, B, and C to be able to make the logical inference that, if A = B and B = C, then A = C, the formal operational thinker can solve this problem merely through verbal presentation.

Another indication of the abstract quality of adolescents' thought is their increased tendency to think about thought itself. One adolescent commented, "I began thinking about why I was thinking what I was. Then I began thinking about why I was thinking about what I was thinking about what I was." If this sounds abstract, it is, and it characterizes the adolescent's enhanced focus on thought and its abstract qualities.

Accompanying the abstract nature of formal operational thought is thought full of idealism and possibilities, especially during the beginning of the formal operational stage, when assimilation dominates. Adolescents engage in extended speculation about ideal characteristics—qualities they desire in themselves and in others. Such thoughts often lead adolescents to compare themselves with others in regard to such ideal standards. And their thoughts are often fantasy flights into future possibilities. It is not unusual for the adolescent to become impatient with these newfound ideal standards and to become perplexed over which of many ideal standards to adopt.

At the same time that adolescents think more abstractly and idealistically, they also think more logically. Children are likely to solve problems through trial-and-error; adolescents begin to think more as a scientist thinks, devising plans to solve problems and systematically testing

Might adolescents' ability to reason hypothetically and to evaluate what is ideal versus what is real lead them to engage in demonstrations, such as this protest related to better ethnic relations? What other causes might be attractive to adolescents' newfound cognitive abilities of hypothetical-deductive reasoning and idealistic thinking?

solutions. This type of problem solving requires **hypothetical-deductive reasoning,** which involves creating a hypothesis and deducing its implications, which provides ways to test the hypothesis. Thus, formal operational thinkers develop hypotheses about ways to solve problems and then systematically deduce the best path to follow to solve the problem.

One example of hypothetical-deductive reasoning involves a modification of the familiar game Twenty Questions. Individuals are shown a set of 42 color pictures, displayed in a rectangular array (six rows of seven pictures each) and are asked to determine which picture the experimenter has in mind (that is, which is "correct"). The individuals are allowed to ask only questions to which the experimenter can answer yes or no. The object of the game is to select the correct picture by asking as few questions as possible. Adolescents who are deductive hypothesis testers formulate a plan and test a series of hypotheses, which considerably narrows the field of choices. The most effective plan is a "halving" strategy (*Q:* Is the picture in the right half of the array? *A:* No. *Q:* Okay. Is it in the top half? And so on.). A correct halving strategy guarantees the answer in seven questions or less. By contrast, concrete operational thinkers may persist with questions that continue to test some of the same possibilities that previous questions could have eliminated. For example, they may ask whether the correct picture is in row 1 and are told that it is not. Later, they may ask whether the picture is *X,* which is in row 1.

Thus, formal operational thinkers test their hypotheses with judiciously chosen questions and tests. By contrast, concrete operational thinkers often fail to understand the relation between a hypothesis and a well-chosen test of it, stubbornly clinging to ideas that already have been discounted.

Evaluating Piaget's Theory   Some of Piaget's ideas on the formal operational stage have been challenged (Kuhn & Franklin, 2006). There is much more individual variation than Piaget envisioned. Only about one in three young adolescents is a formal operational thinker. Many American adults never become formal operational thinkers, and neither do many adults in other cultures.

Furthermore, education in the logic of science and mathematics promotes the development of formal operational thinking. This points recalls a criticism of Piaget's theory that we discussed in Chapter 12: culture and education exert stronger influences on cognitive development than Piaget believed (Cole, 2006; Rogoff & others, 2007).

Piaget's theory of cognitive development has been challenged on other points as well (Bauer, 2006; Cohen & Cashon, 2006). As we noted in Chapter 9, Piaget conceived of stages as unitary structures of thought, with various aspects of a stage emerging at the same time. However, most contemporary developmentalists agree that cognitive development is not as stage-like as Piaget thought (Kellman & Arterberry, 2006; Siegler, 2006). Furthermore, children can be trained to reason at a higher cognitive stage, and some cognitive abilities emerge earlier than Piaget thought (Cohen & Cashon, 2006). For example, even 2-year-olds are nonegocentric in some contexts. When they realize that another person will not see an object, they investigate whether the person is blindfolded or looking in a different direction. Some understanding of the conservation of number has been demonstrated as early as age 3, although Piaget did not think it emerged until 7. Other cognitive abilities can emerge later than Piaget thought (Kuhn & Franklin, 2006). As we noted, many adolescents still think in concrete operational ways or are just beginning to master formal operations. Even many adults are not formal operational thinkers.

Despite these challenges to Piaget's ideas, we owe him a tremendous debt. Piaget was the founder of the present field of cognitive development, and he developed a long list of masterful concepts of enduring power and fascination: assimilation, accommodation, object permanence, egocentrism, conservation, and others. Psychologists also owe him the current vision of children as active, constructive thinkers

hypothetical-deductive reasoning Piaget's formal operational concept that adolescents have the cognitive ability to develop hypotheses, or best guesses, about ways to solve problems.

(Vidal, 2000). And they have a debt to him for creating a theory that generated a huge volume of research on children's cognitive development.

Piaget was a genius when it came to observing children. His careful observations demonstrated inventive ways to discover how children act on and adapt to their world. He also showed us how children need to make their experiences fit their schemes yet simultaneously adapt their schemes to experience. Piaget revealed how cognitive change is likely to occur if the context is structured to allow gradual movement to the next higher level. Concepts do not emerge suddenly, full-blown, but instead develop through a series of partial accomplishments that lead to increasingly comprehensive understanding (Gelman & Kalish, 2006).

Adolescent Egocentrism

"Oh, my gosh! I can't believe it. Help! I can't stand it!" Tracy desperately yells. "What is wrong? What is the matter?" her mother asks. Tracy responds, "Everyone in here is looking at me." The mother queries, "Why?" Tracy says, "Look, this one hair just won't stay in place," as she rushes to the restroom of the restaurant. Five minutes later, she returns to the table in the restaurant after she has depleted an entire can of hairspray.

Tracy's reaction illustrates the egocentrism that is another characteristic of adolescent cognition. **Adolescent egocentrism** is the heightened self-consciousness of adolescents. David Elkind (1976) argues that adolescent egocentrism has two key components—the imaginary audience and personal fable. The **imaginary audience** is adolescents' belief that others are as interested in them as they themselves are, as well as attention-getting behavior—attempts to be noticed, visible, and "on stage." An adolescent might think that others are as aware of a small spot on his trousers as he is, possibly knowing that he has masturbated. Another adolescent, an eighth-grade girl, walks into her classroom and thinks that all eyes are riveted on her complexion. Adolescents sense that they are "on stage" in early adolescence, believing they are the main actors and all others are the audience.

According to Elkind, the **personal fable** is the part of adolescent egocentrism involving a sense of uniqueness and invincibility. For example, during a conversation between two 14-year-old girls, one named Margaret says, "Are you kidding, I won't get pregnant." And 13-year-old Adam describes himself, "No one understands me, particularly my parents. They have no idea of what I am feeling." Adolescents' sense of personal uniqueness makes them feel that no one can understand how they really feel. As part of their effort to retain a sense of personal uniqueness, adolescents might craft a story about the self that is filled with fantasy, immersing themselves in a world that is far removed from reality. Personal fables frequently show up in adolescent diaries.

Adolescents also often show a sense of invincibility, believing that they themselves will never suffer the terrible experiences (such as deadly car wrecks) that happen to other people. This sense of invincibility likely is involved in the reckless behavior of some adolescents, such as drag racing, drug use, suicide, and having sexual intercourse without using contraceptives or barriers against STIs.

Many adolescent girls spend long hours in front of the mirror, depleting cans of hairspray, tubes of lipstick, and jars of cosmetics. *How might this behavior be related to changes in adolescent cognitive and physical development?*

adolescent egocentrism The heightened self-consciousness of adolescents that is reflected in their belief that others are as interested in them as they are in themselves, and in their sense of personal uniqueness and invulnerability.

imaginary audience Adolescents' belief that others are as interested in them as they themselves are, as well as attention-getting behavior motivated by a desire to be noticed, visible, and "on stage."

personal fable The part of adolescent egocentrism that involves an adolescent's sense of uniqueness and invulnerability.

Information Processing

The ability to process information improves during adolescence (Byrnes, 2005; Kuhn & Franklin, 2006; Siegler, 2006). Among the areas in which this improvement occurs are memory and executive functioning.

Memory What are some aspects of memory that change during adolescence? They include short-term memory, working memory, and long-term memory.

Short-Term Memory How might short-term memory be used in problem solving? In a series of experiments, Robert Sternberg (1977) and his colleagues (Sternberg & Nigro, 1980; Sternberg & Rifkin, 1979) attempted to answer this question by giving third-grade, sixth-grade, ninth-grade, and college students analogies to solve. The main differences occurred between the younger (third- and sixth-grade) and older (ninth-grade and college) students. The older students were more likely to complete the information processing required to solve the analogy task. The children, by contrast, often stopped their processing of information before they had considered all of the necessary steps required to solve the problems. Sternberg maintains that incomplete information processing occurred because the children's short-term memory was overloaded. Solving problems, such as analogies, requires individuals to make continued comparisons between newly encoded information and previously encoded information. Sternberg argues that adolescents probably have more storage space in short-term memory, which results in fewer errors on such problems as analogies.

In addition to more storage space, are there other reasons adolescents perform better on memory span tasks and in solving analogies? Although many other factors may be involved, information-processing psychologists believe that changes in the speed and efficiency of information processing are important, especially the speed with which information can be identified.

Working Memory An increasing number of psychologists point out that the way short-term memory has been historically described is too passive and does not do justice to the amount of cognitive work that is done over the short term in memory (Kail & Hall, 2001). They prefer the concept of working memory to describe how memory works on a short-term basis (Mayer, 2003). British psychologist Alan Baddeley (1992, 2000) proposed the concept of *working memory,* which is a kind of "mental workbench" where information is manipulated and assembled to help make decisions, solve problems, and comprehend written and spoken language.

In one study, the performances of individuals from 6 to 57 years of age were examined on both verbal and visuospatial working memory tasks (Swanson, 1999). The two verbal tasks were auditory digit sequence (the ability to remember numerical information embedded in a short sentence, such as "Now suppose somebody wanted to go to the supermarket at 8651 Elm Street") and semantic association (the ability to organize words into abstract categories) (Swanson, 1999, p. 988). In the semantic association task, the participant was presented with a series of words (such as shirt, saw, pants, hammer, shoes, and nails) and then asked to remember how they go together. The two visuospatial tasks involved mapping/directions and a visual matrix. In the mapping/directions task, the participant was shown a street map indicating the route a bicycle (child/young adolescent) or car (adult) would take through a city. After briefly looking at the map, participants were asked to redraw the route on a blank map. In the visual matrix task, participants were asked to study a matrix showing a series of dots. After looking at the matrix for five seconds, they were asked to answer questions about the location of the dots. As shown in Figure 15.1, working memory increased substantially from 8 through 24 years

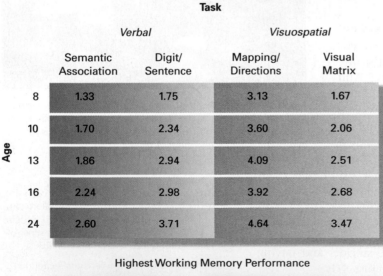

	Task			
	Verbal		*Visuospatial*	
Age	Semantic Association	Digit/ Sentence	Mapping/ Directions	Visual Matrix
8	1.33	1.75	3.13	1.67
10	1.70	2.34	3.60	2.06
13	1.86	2.94	4.09	2.51
16	2.24	2.98	3.92	2.68
24	2.60	3.71	4.64	3.47

Highest Working Memory Performance

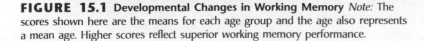

3.02 (age 45)	3.97 (age 35)	4.90 (age 35)	3.47 (age 24)

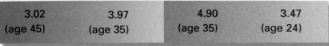

FIGURE 15.1 Developmental Changes in Working Memory *Note:* The scores shown here are the means for each age group and the age also represents a mean age. Higher scores reflect superior working memory performance.

of age no matter what the task. Thus, the adolescent years are likely to be an important developmental period for improvement in working memory (Swanson, 2005). Note that working memory continues to improve through the transition to adulthood and beyond.

Long–Term Memory Long-term memory increases substantially in the middle and late childhood years and likely continues to improve during adolescence, although this has not been well documented by researchers. If anything at all is known about long-term memory, it is that it depends on the learning activities engaged in when learning and remembering information (Pressley & Hilden, 2006; Siegler, 2006).

Executive Functioning

Attention and memory are important dimensions of information processing, but other dimensions also are important. Once adolescents attend to information and retain it, they can use the information to engage in a number of higher-order cognitive activities, such as making decisions and thinking critically. These types of higher-order, complex cognitive processes are often called *executive functioning*. Alan Baddeley (1992, 2000) recognized the importance of these higher-order cognitive processes and actually called this aspect of his cognitive model the *executive*.

It is increasingly thought that executive functioning strengthens during adolescence (Kuhn & Franklin, 2006). This executive functioning "assumes a role of monitoring and managing the deployment of cognitive resources as a function of a task demands. As a result, cognitive development and learning itself, become more effective. . . . Emergence and strengthening of this executive (functioning) is arguably the single most important and consequential intellectual development to occur in the second decade of life" (Kuhn & Franklin, 2006, p. 987). An example of how executive functioning increases in adolescence is its role in determining how attention will be allocated. We begin our examination of executive functioning by focusing on decision making.

Decision Making Adolescence is a time of increased decision making—which friends to choose, which person to date, whether to have sex, buy a car, go to college, and so on (Byrnes, 2005; Jacobs & Klaczynski, 2005; Reyna & others, 2005). How competent are adolescents at making decisions? In some reviews, older adolescents are described as more competent than younger adolescents, who in turn are more competent than children (Keating, 2004). Compared with children, young adolescents are more likely to generate different options, examine a situation from a variety of perspectives, to anticipate the consequences of decisions, and consider the credibility of sources.

One study documents that older adolescents are better at decision making than younger adolescents are (Lewis, 1981). Eighth-, tenth-, and twelfth-grade students were presented with dilemmas involving the choice of a medical procedure. The oldest students were most likely to spontaneously mention a variety of risks, to recommend consultation with an outside specialist, and to anticipate future consequences. For example, when asked a question about whether to have cosmetic surgery, a twelfth-grader said that different aspects of the situation need to be examined along with its effects on the individual's future, especially relationships with other people. By contrast, an eighth-grader presented a more limited view, commenting on the surgery's effects on getting turned down for a date, the money involved, and being teased by peers.

In sum, older adolescents often make better decisions than younger adolescents, who in turn make better decisions than children. The ability to regulate one's emotions during decision making, to remember prior decisions and their consequences, and to adapt subsequent decision making on the basis of those consequences appear to improve with age at least through the early adulthood years (Byrnes, 2005).

The error of youth is to believe that intelligence is a substitute for experience, while the error of age is to believe that experience is a substitute for intelligence.

—LYMAN BRYSON
American Author, 20th Century

What are some of the decisions adolescents have to make? What characterizes their decision making?

However, older adolescents' decision-making skills are far from perfect, as are adults' (Jacobs & Klaczynski, 2005). Indeed, some researchers have found that adolescents and adults do not differ in their decision-making skills (Quadrel, Fischoff, & Davis, 1993). Furthermore, researchers have found that adolescent decision making is linked to some personality traits. Adolescents who are impulsive and seek sensation are often not very effective decision makers, for example (Byrnes, 2005).

Being able to make competent decisions does not guarantee that one will make them in everyday life, where breadth of experience often comes into play (Jacobs & Klaczynski, 2005; Keating, 2004). For example, driver-training courses improve adolescents' cognitive and motor skills to levels equal to, or sometimes superior to, those of adults. However, driver training has not been effective in reducing adolescents' high rate of traffic accidents (Potvin, Champagne, & Laberge-Nadeau, 1988). An important research agenda is to study the ways adolescents make decisions in practical situations (Fantino & Stolarz-Fantino, 2005).

Most people make better decisions when they are calm rather than emotionally aroused. That may especially be true for adolescents. Recall from our discussion of brain development in Chapter 14 that adolescents have a tendency to be emotionally intense. Thus, the same adolescent who makes a wise decision when calm may make an unwise decision when emotionally aroused (Dahl, 2004). In the heat of the moment, then, adolescents' emotions may especially overwhelm their decision-making ability.

Adolescents need more opportunities to practice and discuss realistic decision making (Jones, Rasmussen, & Moffitt, 1997). Many real-world decisions on matters such as sex, drugs, and daredevil driving occur in an atmosphere of stress that includes time constraints and emotional involvement. One strategy for improving adolescent decision making in such circumstances is to provide more opportunities for them to engage in role-playing and group problem solving.

Another strategy is for parents to involve adolescents in appropriate decision-making activities. In one study of more than 900 young adolescents and a subsample of their parents, adolescents were more likely to participate in family decision making when they perceived themselves as in control of what happens to them and if they thought that their input would have some bearing on the outcome of the decision-making process (Liprie, 1993).

Critical Thinking Making competent decisions and reasoning logically are closely related to critical thinking, currently a buzzword in education and psychology (Sternberg, Roediger, & Halpern, 2006). **Critical thinking** is thinking reflectively and productively and evaluating evidence. In one study of fifth-, eighth-, and eleventh-graders, critical thinking increased with age, but still occurred only in 43 percent of eleventh-graders (Klaczynski & Narasimham, 1998). Many adolescents showed self-serving biases in their reasoning that included the following:

- Greater breadth of content knowledge in a variety of domains
- Increased ability to construct new combinations of knowledge
- A greater range and more spontaneous use of strategies and procedures for obtaining and applying knowledge, such as planning, considering the alternatives, and cognitive monitoring

Although adolescence is an important period in the development of critical-thinking skills, if an individual has not developed a solid basis of fundamental skills (such as literacy and math skills) during childhood, critical-thinking skills are unlikely to mature in adolescence. For the subset of adolescents who lack such fundamental skills, potential gains in adolescent thinking are not likely.

Laura Bickford is a secondary school teacher who encourages her students to think critically. To read about her work, see the *Careers in Child Development* profile.

critical thinking Thinking reflectively and productively and evaluating evidence.

Careers in CHILD DEVELOPMENT

Laura Bickford
Secondary School Teacher

Laura Bickford teaches English and journalism in grades 9 to 12 and she is Chair of the English Department at Nordhoff High School in Ojai, California.

Bickford especially believes it is important to encourage students to think. Indeed, she says that "the call to teach is the call to teach students how to think." She believes teachers need in show students the value in asking their own questions, in having discussions, and in engaging in stimulating intellectual conversations. Bickford says that she also encourages students to engage in metacognitive strategies (knowing about knowing). For example, she asks students to comment on their learning after particular pieces of projects have been completed. She requires students to keep reading logs so they can observe their own thinking as it happens.

Laura Bickford, working with students writing papers.

REVIEW AND REFLECT → LEARNING GOAL 1

1 Discuss different approaches to adolescent cognition.

Review
- What is Piaget's view on adolescent cognitive development?
- What is adolescent egocentrism?
- How does information processing change during adolescence?

Reflect
- Suppose an 8-year-old and a 16-year-old are watching a political convention on television. In view of where they are likely to be in terms of Piaget's stages of cognitive development, how would their perceptions of the proceedings likely differ?

---

2 WHAT CHARACTERIZES ADOLESCENTS' VALUES, MORAL EDUCATION, AND RELIGION?

| Values | Moral Education | Religion |

What are adolescents' values like today? How can moral education be characterized? How powerful is religion in adolescents' lives?

Values

Adolescents carry with them a set of values that influences their thoughts, feelings, and actions. **Values** are beliefs and attitudes about the way things should be. They involve what is important to us. We attach values to all sorts of things: politics,

values Beliefs and attitudes about the way things should be.

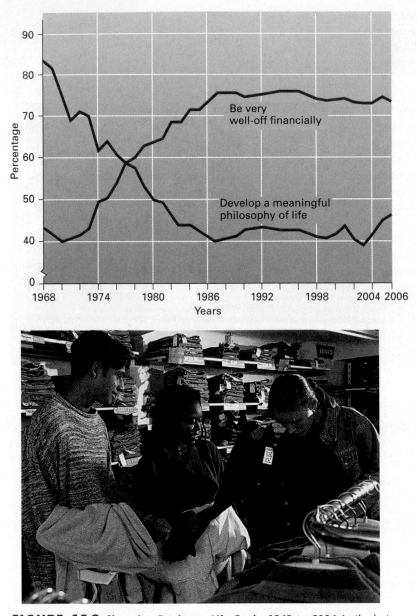

FIGURE 15.2 Changing Freshmen Life Goals, 1968 to 2006 In the last three decades, a significant change has occurred in freshmen students' life goals. A far greater percentage of today's college freshmen state that a "very important" life goal is to be well off financially, and far fewer state that developing a meaningful philosophy of life is a "very important" life goal.

religion, money, sex, education, helping others, family, friends, career, cheating, self-respect, and so on.

Changing Values Over the past two decades, adolescents have shown an increased concern for personal well-being and a decreased concern for the well-being of others, especially for the disadvantaged (Pryor & others, 2006). As shown in Figure 15.2, today's college freshmen are more strongly motivated to be well off financially and less motivated to develop a meaningful philosophy of life than were their counterparts of 20 years ago. Student commitment to becoming very well off financially as a "very important" reason for attending college was at a high level in the 2006 survey (73 percent), compared with the 1970s (50 percent in 1971).

Two aspects of values that increased during the 1960s, though, continue to characterize many of today's youth: self-fulfillment and self-expression (Conger, 1981, 1988). As part of their motivation for self-fulfillment, many adolescents show great interest in their physical health and well-being. Greater self-fulfillment and self-expression can be laudable goals, but if they become the only goals, self-destruction, loneliness, or alienation may result. Young people also need to develop a corresponding sense of commitment to others' welfare. Encouraging adolescents to have a strong commitment to others, in concert with an interest in self-fulfillment, is an important task for America during the twenty-first century.

However, there are some signs that today's college students are shifting toward a stronger interest in the welfare of our society. For example, between 1986 and 2005, there was a small increase in the percentage of college freshmen who said that they were strongly interested in participating in community action programs (26 percent in 2005 compared with 18 percent in 1986) and helping promote racial understanding (33 percent in 2005 compared with 27 percent in 1986) (Pryor & others, 2005). For successful adjustment in life, it is important to seek self-fulfillment *and* have a strong commitment to others.

Research on adolescents in seven different countries revealed that family values of compassion and social responsibility were the values that were most consistently linked with adolescent participation in community service, commitment to serving their country, and empathy for disenfranchised groups (Bowes & Flanagan, 2000). Other research on values has found that adolescents who are involved in groups that connect themselves to others in school, their communities, or faith-based institutions, report higher levels of social trust, altruism, commitments to the common good of people, and endorsements of the rights of immigrants for full inclusion in society (Flanagan, 2004; Flanagan & Faison, 2001). In this research, adolescents who were uninvolved in such groups were more likely to endorse self-interest and materialistic values.

One study of 459 students from 20 different high school classrooms participated in focus group discussions about the most important values they perceived that youth could possess. The students especially endorsed the character strengths of "leadership, practical intelligence, wisdom, love of learning, spirituality, and the capacity to love and be loved" (Steen, Kachorek, & Peterson, 2003, p. 5). Students reasoned that the strengths are mainly learned rather than innate and that they develop through ongoing real-world experiences rather than through formal instruction.

Service Learning **Service learning** is a form of education that promotes social responsibility and service to the community. In service learning, adolescents engage in activities such as tutoring, helping older adults, working in a hospital, assisting at a child-care center, or cleaning up a vacant lot to make a play area. An important goal of service learning is for adolescents to become less self-centered and more strongly motivated to help others (Benson & others, 2006; Hart, 2006; Reinders & Youniss, 2006). Service learning is often more effective when two conditions are met (Nucci, 2006): (1) giving students some degree of choice in the service activities in which they participate, and (2) providing students opportunities to reflect about their participation.

What are some of the positive effects of service learning?

Service learning takes education out into the community (Arenas & others, 2006). One eleventh-grade student worked as a reading tutor for students from low-income backgrounds with reading skills well below their grade levels. She commented that until she did the tutoring, she did not realize how many students had not experienced the same opportunities that she had when she was growing up. An especially rewarding moment was when one young girl told her, "I want to learn to read like you so I can go to college when I grow up." Thus, a key feature of service learning is that it not only benefits adolescents but also the recipients of their help.

"Adolescent volunteers tend to share certain characteristics, such as extraversion, a commitment to others, and a high degree of self-understanding" (Eisenberg & Morris, 2004, p. 174). Also, adolescent girls are more likely to volunteer to engage in service learning than adolescent boys (Eisenberg & Morris, 2004).

Researchers have found that service learning benefits adolescents in a number of ways:

- Their grades improve, they become more motivated, and they set more goals (Johnson & others, 1998; Search Institute, 1995; Serow, Ciechalski, & Daye, 1990).
- They have a deeper appreciation of the right action as reflected in more advanced moral reasoning on Kohlberg's stages and an interest in constructing the best of all possible worlds (Conrad & Hedin, 1982; Hart, Atkins, & Donnelly, 2006).
- Their self-esteem improves (Hamburg, 1997; Johnson & others, 1998).
- They have an improved sense of being able to make a difference for others (Search Institute, 1995).
- They become less alienated (Calabrese & Schumer, 1986).
- They increasingly reflect on society's political organization and moral order (Yates, 1995).
- They are more likely to volunteer in the future (Hart, Atkins, & Donnelly, 2006).

Recent figures suggest that 26 percent of U.S. public high schools require students to participate in service learning (Metz & Youniss, 2005). The benefits of service learning, both for the volunteer and the recipient, suggest that more adolescents should be required to participate in such programs (Arenas & others, 2006; Benson & others, 2006). To read further about the positive outcomes of participating in service learning, see the *Research in Children's Development* interlude.

service learning A form of education that promotes social responsibility and service to the community.

Research in Children's Development

EVALUATING A SERVICE LEARNING PROGRAM DESIGNED TO INCREASE CIVIC ENGAGEMENT

In a recent study, the possible benefits of a service learning requirement for high school students were explored (Metz & Youniss, 2005). One group of students had a service learning requirement, the other did not. Each group of students was also divided according to whether or not they were motivated to serve voluntarily. The participants in the study were 174 students (class of 2000) who were not required to engage in service learning, and 312 students (classes of 2001 and 2002) who were required to accumulate 40 hours of community service. The school was located in a middle- to upper-middle-SES suburban community outside of Boston, Massachusetts. The focus of the study was to compare the 2001 and 2002 classes, which were the first ones to have a 40-hour community service requirement, to the class of 2000, the last year in which the school did not have this requirement. For purposes of comparison, the 2001 and 2002 classes were combined into one group to be compared with the 2000 class.

The service learning requirement for the 2001 and 2002 classes was designed to give students a sense of participating in the community in positive ways. Among the most common service learning activities that students engaged in were "tutoring, coaching, assisting at shelters or nursing homes, organizing food or clothing drives, and assisting value-centered service organizations or churches" (p. 420). To obtain credit for the activities, students were required to write reflectively about the activities and describe how the activities benefited both the recipients and themselves. Students also had to obtain an adult's or supervisor's signature to document their participation.

Detailed self-reported records of students' service in grades 10 through 12 were obtained. In addition to describing the number of service hours they accumulated toward their requirement, they also were asked to indicate any voluntary services they provided in addition to the required 40 hours. Since students in the 2000 class had no required service participation, all of their service was voluntary.

The students rated themselves on four 5-point scales of civic engagement: (1) the likelihood of voting when reaching 18; (2) the likelihood they would "volunteer" or "join a civic organization" after they graduate from high school; (3) their future unconventional civic involvement (such as boycotting a product, demonstrating for a cause, or participating in a political campaign); and (4) their interest and understanding (how much they discuss politics with parents and friends, read about politics in magazines and newspapers, or watch the news on TV).

The results indicated that students who were already inclined to engage in service learning scored high on the four scales of civic engagement throughout high school and showed no increase in service after it was required. However, students who were less motivated to engage in service learning increased their civic engagement on three of the four scales (future voting, join a civic organization after graduating from high school, and interest and understanding) after they were required to participate. In sum, this research documented that a required service learning program can especially benefit the civic engagement of students who are inclined not to engage in service learning.

Moral Education

Moral education is hotly debated in educational circles (Lapsley & Narváez, 2006; Nucci, 2006). We study one of the earliest analyses of moral education, then turn to some contemporary views.

The Hidden Curriculum   More than 70 years ago, educator John Dewey (1933) recognized that, even when schools do not have specific programs in moral education, they provide moral education through a "hidden curriculum." The **hidden curriculum** is conveyed by the moral atmosphere that is a part of every school. The moral atmosphere is created by school and classroom rules, the moral orientation of teachers and school administrators, and text materials. Teachers serve as models of ethical or unethical behavior. Classroom rules and peer relations at school transmit attitudes about cheating, lying, stealing, and consideration of others. And, through its rules and regulations, the school administration infuses the school with a value system.

Character Education   **Character education** is a direct education approach that involves teaching students a basic moral literacy to prevent them from engaging in immoral behavior and doing harm to themselves or others. The argument is that such behaviors as lying, stealing, and cheating are wrong, and students should be taught this throughout their education. Every school should have an explicit moral code that is clearly communicated to students. Any violations of the code should be met with sanctions (Bennett, 1993). Instruction in specified moral concepts, such as cheating, can take the form of example and definition, class discussions and role playing, or rewarding students for proper behavior. Researchers have found that character education programs are linked to improvements in students' moral thinking and prosocial behavior, and a reduction in violence and substance abuse (Berkowitz & Bier, 2004; Berkowitz & others, 2006). The most common strategies used in effective character education program include student-centered peer discussion; interactive sessions such as class meetings and peer tutoring that promote perspective taking; and training in problem solving and decision making (Berkowitz & others, 2006).

Some character education movements are the Character Education Partnership, the Character Education Network, the Aspen Declaration on Character Education, and the publicity campaign "Character Counts." Among the books that promote character education are William Bennett's (1993) *The Book of Virtues* and William Damon's (1995) *Greater Expectations*.

Values Clarification   **Values clarification** means helping people to clarify what is important to them, what is worth working for, and what purpose their lives are to serve. In this approach, students are encouraged to define their own values and understand the values of others (Williams & others, 2003). Values clarification differs from character education in that it does not tell students what their values should be. In our chapter-opening story, we saw that Kim-Chi had clear values about doing well in school out of respect for her parents.

In values clarification exercises, there are no right or wrong answers. The clarification of values is left up to the individual student. Advocates of values clarification say it is value-free. However, critics argue that its controversial content offends community standards. They also say that because of its relativistic nature, values clarification undermines accepted values and fails to stress distinctions between right and wrong behavior.

Cognitive Moral Education   **Cognitive moral education** is a concept based on the belief that students should learn to value such aspects of life as democracy and justice as their moral reasoning develops. Kohlberg's theory, which we discussed in Chapter 13, has been the basis for a number of cognitive moral education programs. In a typical program, high school students meet in a semester-long course to discuss a number of moral issues. The instructor acts as a facilitator, rather than as a director, of the class. The hope is that students will develop more advanced notions of concepts such as cooperation, trust, responsibility, and community. Toward the end of his career, Kohlberg (1986) recognized that the moral atmosphere of the

hidden curriculum Dewey's concept that every school has a pervasive moral atmosphere, even if it doesn't have a program of moral education.

character education A direct education approach that involves teaching students a basic moral literacy to prevent them from engaging in immoral behavior and doing harm to themselves and others.

values clarification An approach to moral education that emphasizes helping people clarify what their lives are for and what's worth working for. Students are encouraged to define their own values and to understand the values of others.

cognitive moral education A concept based on the belief that students should develop such values as democracy and justice as their moral reasoning develops; Kohlberg's theory has been the basis of a number of cognitive moral education programs.

school is more important than he initially envisioned. For example, in one study, a semester-long moral education class based on Kohlberg's theory was successful in advancing moral thinking in three democratic schools, but not in three authoritarian schools (Higgins, Power, & Kohlberg, 1983).

Recall from Chapter 13 that Carol Gilligan (1982, 1996) argues that moral development should focus more on social relationships than Kohlberg does. Thus, applying Gilligan's view to moral education, emphasis should be placed on such topics as caring, sensitivity to others' feelings, and relationships. In her view, schools should better recognize the importance of relationships in the development of adolescent girls.

An Integrative Approach   Darcia Narvaez (2006) emphasizes an *integrative approach* to moral education that encompasses both the reflective moral thinking and commitment to justice advocated in Kohlberg's approach, and developing a particular moral character as advocated in the character education approach. She highlights the Child Development Project as an excellent example of an integrative moral education approach. In the Child Development Project, students are given multiple opportunities to discuss other students' experiences, which encourages empathy and perspective taking, and they participate in exercises that encourage them to reflect on their own behaviors in terms of such values as fairness and social responsibility (Solomon, Watson, & Battistich, 2002). Adults coach students in ethical decision making and guide them in becoming more caring individuals. Students experience a caring community, not only in the classroom, but also in after-school activities and through parental involvement in the program. Research evaluations of the Child Development Project indicate that it is related to an improved sense of community, an increase in prosocial behavior, better interpersonal understanding, and an increase in social problem solving (Solomon & others, 1988, 1990).

Religion

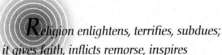

Religion enlightens, terrifies, subdues; it gives faith, inflicts remorse, inspires resolutions, and inflames devotion.

—HENRY NEWMAN
English Churchman and Writer, 19th Century

Religious issues are important to adolescents (Oser, Scarlett, & Bucher, 2006). In one survey, 95 percent of 13- to 18-year-olds said that they believe in God or a universal spirit (Gallup & Bezilla, 1992). Almost three-fourths of adolescents said that they pray, and about one-half indicated that they had attended religious services within the past week. Almost half of the youth said that it is very important for a young person to learn religious faith.

In the national study of American freshmen described earlier in the chapter in our discussion of values, in 2005, 80 percent said they attended a religious service frequently or occasionally during their senior year in high school; this percentage is down from a high of 85 percent in 1997 (Pryor & others, 2005). A similar downward trend occurred for prayer or meditation. In 2005, 63 percent of students said they pray or meditate on a weekly basis, down from a high of 67 percent in 1996. Further, in 2005, more than twice as many first-year students (17 percent) reported that they don't have a religious preference than in 1978 (8 percent). Despite the declining percentage of students who participate in religious activities, students are engaging in more discussions about religion, with 35 percent saying they frequently discussed religion in their senior year of high school compared with 30 percent in 1998 through 2003.

The Positive Role of Religion in Adolescents' Lives   Researchers have found that various aspects of religion are linked with positive outcomes for adolescents (Cotton & others, 2006; King & Benson, 2005; Oser, Scarlett, & Butcher, 2006). In one study, adolescents who viewed religion as a meaningful part of their life and a way to cope with problems were half as likely to use drugs than adolescents who did not view religion as important (Wills, Yaeger, & Sandy, 2003). In another study of 9,700 adolescents, going to church was linked with better grades for students from low-income backgrounds (Regnerus, 2001). Church attendance may benefit

Many children and adolescents show an interest in religion, and many religious institutions created by adults (such as this Muslim school in Malaysia) are designed to introduce them to religious benefits and ensure that they will carry on a religious tradition.

students because religious communities encourage socially acceptable behavior, which includes doing well in school. Church attendance also may benefit students because churches often offer positive role models for students.

Religion also plays a role in adolescents' health and whether they engage in problem behaviors (Cotton & others, 2006; King & Benson, 2006; Oman & Thoresen, 2006). Researchers have found that religious affiliation is linked to lower rates of delinquent behavior and drug use (Piko & Fitzpatrick, 2004; Steinman & Zimmerman, 2004). Also, in one recent study, adolescents with higher levels of spiritual well-being had fewer depressive symptoms and were less likely to engage in risk-taking behaviors than their counterparts with lower levels of spiritual well-being (Cotton & others, 2005). And in a recent national random sample of more than 2,000 11- to 18-year-olds, those who were higher in religiosity were less likely to smoke, drink alcohol, or use marijuana—and were more likely not be truant from school, not engage in delinquent activities, and not be depressed than their low-religiosity counterparts (Sinha, Cnaan, & Gelles, 2007).

Many religious adolescents also internalize their religion's message about caring and concern for people (Ream & Savin-Williams, 2003). For example, in one survey, religious youth were almost three times as likely to engage in community service as nonreligious youth (Youniss, McLellan, & Yates, 1999).

Religion is often an asset to the communities in which adolescents live (Ream & Savin-Williams, 2003). In some instances, religious institutions are the only organizations that initiate efforts to work with adolescents in inner cities. For inner-city youth, as well as other youth, religion offers possible answers to questions about meaning, purpose, and direction in life (Trulear, 2000).

Developmental Changes   Adolescence can be an important juncture in religious development (Benson, 2006; Oser, Scarlett, & Bucher, 2006; Scarlett, 2006). Even if children have been indoctrinated into a religion by their parents, because of advances in their cognitive development they may begin to question what their own religious beliefs truly are.

Erikson's Theory and Identity   During adolescence, especially in late adolescence and the college years, identity development becomes a central focus. In Erik Erikson's

How do religious thought and behavior change as children and adolescents develop? How are children's and adolescents' religious conceptions influenced by their cognitive development?

(1968) theory, adolescents want to know answers to questions like these: "Who am I?" "What am I all about as a person?" "What kind of life do I want to lead?" As part of their search for identity, adolescents begin to grapple in more sophisticated, logical ways with such questions as "Why am I on this planet?" "Is there really a God or higher spiritual being, or have I just been believing what my parents and the church imprinted in my mind?" "What really are my religious views?" A recent analysis of the link between identity and spirituality concluded that adolescence and emerging adulthood can serve as gateways to a spiritual identity that "transcends, but not necessarily excludes, the assigned religious identity in childhood" (Templeton & Eccles, 2006, p. 261).

Piaget's Theory and Religious Development   The cognitive developmental theory of famous Swiss psychologist Jean Piaget (1952) provides a theoretical backdrop for understanding religious development in children and adolescents. For example, in one study children were asked about their understanding of certain religious pictures and Bible stories (Goldman, 1964). The children's responses fell into three stages closely related to Piaget's theory.

In the first stage (up until 7 or 8 years of age)—*preoperational intuitive religious thought*—children's religious thoughts were unsystematic and fragmented. The children often either did not fully understand the material in the stories or did not consider all of the evidence. For example, one child's response to the question "Why was Moses afraid to look at God?" (Exodus 3:6) was "Because God had a funny face!"

In the second stage (occurring from 7 or 8 to 13 or 14 years of age)—*concrete operational religious thought*—children focused on particular details of pictures and stories. For example, in response to the question about why Moses was afraid to look at God, one child said, "Because it was a ball of fire. He thought He might burn him." Another child voiced, "It was a bright light and to look at it might blind him."

In the third stage (age 14 through the remainder of adolescence)—*formal operational religious thought*—adolescents revealed a more abstract, hypothetical religious understanding. For example, one adolescent said that Moses was afraid to look at God because "God is holy and the world is sinful." Another youth responded, "The awesomeness and almightiness of God would make Moses feel like a worm in comparison."

Other researchers have found similar developmental changes in children and adolescents. For example, in one study, at about 17 or 18 years of age, adolescents increasingly commented about freedom, meaning, and hope—abstract concepts—when making religious judgments (Oser & Gmünder, 1991).

Religious Beliefs and Parenting   Religious institutions created by adults are designed to introduce certain beliefs to children and thereby ensure that they will carry on a religious tradition. Various societies utilize Sunday schools, parochial education, tribal transmission of religious traditions, and parental teaching of children at home to further this aim.

Does this socialization work? In many cases it does (Paloutzian, 2000). In general, adults tend to adopt the religious teachings of their upbringing. For instance, individuals who are Catholics by the time they are 25 years of age, and who were raised as Catholics, likely will continue to be Catholics throughout their adult years. If a religious change or reawakening occurs, it is most likely to take place during adolescence.

However, when examining religious beliefs and adolescence, it is important to consider the quality of the parent-adolescent relationship (Ream & Savin-Williams, 2003; Regenerus, Smith, & Smith, 2004). Adolescents who have a positive relationship with their parents, or are securely attached to them, are likely to adopt their parents' religious affiliation. But when conflict or insecure attachment characterizes parent-adolescent relationships, adolescents may seek religious affiliation that is different from their parents' (Streib, 1999).

Religiousness and Sexuality in Adolescence   One area of religion's influence on adolescent development involves sexual activity. Although variability and change in church teachings make it difficult to generalize about religious doctrines, most churches discourage premarital sex. Thus, the degree of adolescent participation in religious organizations may be more important than affiliation with a particular religion as a determinant of premarital sexual attitudes and behavior. Adolescents who frequently attend religious services are likely to hear messages about abstaining from sex. Involvement of adolescents in religious organizations also enhances the probability that they will become friends with adolescents who have restrictive attitudes toward premarital sex.

A national study of 3,356 adolescent girls (mean age =16 years) focused on four aspects of religiousness: (1) attendance at religious events ("In the past 12 months, how often did you attend religious services?" and "Many churches, synagogues, and other places of worship have special activities for teenagers, such as youth groups, Bible classes, or choir. In the past 12 months, how often did you attend such youth activities?"); (2) personal conservatism ("Do you agree or disagree that the sacred scriptures of your religion are the word of God and are completely without any mistakes?" and "Do you think of yourself as a born-again Christian?"); (3) personal devotion ("How often do you pray?" and "How important is religion to you?"); and (4) religious denomination (Miller & Gur, 2002, p. 402). In this study, there was a link between engaging in personal devotion and having fewer sexual partners outside a romantic relationship. Frequent attendance at religious events was related to fear of contracting HIV or pregnancy from unprotected intercourse and planned use of birth control. Having a personal conservative orientation was linked with unprotected sex. Another study similarly found links between religion and sexuality (Fehring & others, 1998). In college students, guilt, prayer, organized religious activity, and religious well-being were associated with fewer sexual encounters.

REVIEW AND REFLECT   ▸ LEARNING GOAL 2

2 **Describe adolescents' values, moral education, and religion.**

Review
- What characterizes adolescents' values? What is service learning?
- What are some variations in moral education?
- What are adolescents' religious views and experiences?

Reflect
- What are your values? What is really important to you in life? Does the way you spend your time reflect the values that are most important to you?

---

3   WHAT ARE SCHOOLS FOR ADOLESCENTS LIKE?

| The American Middle School | The American High School | High School Dropouts |

The impressive changes in adolescents' cognition lead us to examine the nature of schools for adolescents. In Chapter 13, we discussed different ideas about the effects of schools on children's development. Here, we focus more exclusively on the nature of secondary schools.

The transition from elementary to middle or junior high school occurs at the same time as a number of other developmental changes. *What are some of these other developmental changes?*

The American Middle School

One worry of educators and psychologists is that middle schools (most often consisting of grades 6 through 8) are simply watered-down versions of high schools, mimicking their curricular and extracurricular schedules. The critics argue that unique curricular and extracurricular activities reflecting a wide range of individual differences in biological and psychological development in early adolescence should be incorporated into our junior high and middle schools. The critics also stress that many high schools foster passivity rather than autonomy, and that schools should create a variety of pathways for students to achieve an identity.

The Transition to Middle or Junior High School
The transition to middle school from elementary school interests developmentalists because, even though it is a normative experience for virtually all children, the transition can be stressful (Eccles, 2007; Wigfield & others, 2006). Why? The transition takes place at a time when many changes—in the individual, in the family, and in school—are occurring simultaneously. These changes include puberty and related concerns about body image; the emergence of at least some aspects of formal operational thought, including accompanying changes in social cognition; increased responsibility and independence in association with decreased dependency on parents; change from a small, contained classroom structure to a larger, more impersonal school structure; change from one teacher to many teachers and from a small, homogeneous set of peers to a larger, more heterogeneous set of peers; and an increased focus on achievement and performance and their assessment. This list includes a number of negative, stressful features, but there can be positive aspects to the transition. Students are more likely to feel grown up, have more subjects from which to select, have more opportunities to spend time with peers and to locate compatible friends, and enjoy increased independence from direct parental monitoring, and they may be more challenged intellectually by academic work.

When students make the transition from elementary school to middle or junior high school, they experience the **top-dog phenomenon,** the circumstance of moving from the top position (in elementary school, being the oldest, biggest, and most powerful students in the school) to the lowest position (in middle or junior high school, being the youngest, smallest, and least powerful students in the school). Researchers who have charted the transition from elementary to middle school find that the first year of middle school can be difficult for many students (Hawkins & Berndt, 1985).

Effective Middle Schools
How effective are the middle schools U.S. students attend? In 1989, the Carnegie Council on Adolescent Development issued an extremely negative evaluation of U.S. middle schools. In the report—*Turning Points: Preparing American Youth for the Twenty-First Century*—the conclusion was reached that most young adolescents attend massive, impersonal schools; learn from seemingly irrelevant curricula; trust few adults in school; and lack access to health care and counseling. The Carnegie report recommended:

- Developing smaller "communities" or "houses" to lessen the impersonal nature of large middle schools
- Lowering student-to-counselor ratios from several hundred-to-1 to 10-to-1
- Involving parents and community leaders in schools
- Developing curricula that produce students who are literate, understand the sciences, and have a sense of health, ethics, and citizenship

top-dog phenomenon The circumstance of moving from the top position (in elementary school, the oldest, biggest, and most powerful students) to the lowest position (in middle or junior high school, the youngest, smallest, and least powerful).

- Having teachers team-teach in more flexibly designed curriculum blocks that integrate several disciplines, instead of presenting students with disconnected, rigidly separated 50-minute segments
- Boosting students' health and fitness with more in-school programs and helping students who need public health care to get it

Turning Points 2000 (Jackson & Davis, 2000) continued to endorse the recommendations set forth in *Turning Points 1989*. One new recommendation in the 2000 report stated that it is important to teach a curriculum grounded in rigorous academic standards for what students should, and be able, to know. A second new recommendation was to engage in instruction to achieve higher standards and become life-long learners. These new recommendations reflect the increasing emphasis on challenging students to meet higher standards.

Extracurricular Activities   Adolescents in U.S. schools usually have a wide array of extracurricular activities they can participate in beyond their academic courses. Does participating in such school activities as sports, academic clubs, band, drama, and so on, benefit or harm adolescent development? A recent study of non-Latino White seventh- to twelfth-graders revealed that greater involvement in sports and clubs was associated with better academic adjustment (higher grades and better connectedness to school), superior psychological competencies (higher self-worth and resilience, less distress), and positive peer relations (Fredricks & Eccles, 2006). Researchers also have found that adolescents benefit from a breadth of extracurricular activities more than focusing on a single extracurricular activity (Bartko & Eccles, 2003; Morris & Kalil, 2006). More diverse involvement in extracurricular activities may help adolescents counter negative experiences in one activity (Fredricks & Eccles, 2006). Also, the more years adolescents spend in extracurricular activities, the stronger the link is with positive developmental outcomes (Fredricks & Eccles, 2006).

Of course, the quality of the extracurricular activities matters (Eccles, 2007). High-quality extracurricular activities that are likely to promote positive adolescent development include competent, supportive adult mentors, opportunities for increasing school connectedness, challenging and meaningful activities, and opportunities for improving skills (Fredricks & Eccles, 2006).

The American High School

Many high school graduates not only are poorly prepared for college, they also are poorly prepared for the demands of the modern, high-performance workplace. In a review of hiring practices at major companies, it was concluded that many companies now have sets of basic skills they want the individuals they hire to have. These include the ability to read at relatively high levels, do at least elementary algebra, use personal computers for straightforward tasks such as word processing, solve semistructured problems in which hypotheses must be formed and tested, communicate effectively (orally and in writing), and work effectively in groups with persons of various backgrounds (Hemmings, 2004).

An increasing number of educators believe that the nation's high schools need a new mission for the twenty-first century, which addresses these problems (National Commission on the High School Senior Year, 2001):

1. More support is needed to enable all students to graduate from high school with the knowledge and skills needed to succeed in postsecondary education and careers. Many parents and students, especially those in low-income and minority communities, are unaware of the knowledge and level of skills required to succeed in postsecondary education.
2. High schools need to have higher expectations for student achievement. A special concern is the senior year of high school, which has become too much of a party time rather than a time to prepare for one of life's most important

transitions. Some students who have been accepted to college routinely ignore the academic demands of their senior year. Low academic expectations harm students from all backgrounds.

3. U.S. high school students spend too much time working in low-level service jobs. Researchers have found that when tenth-graders work more than 14 hours a week their grades drop, and when eleventh-graders work 20 or more hours a week their grades drop (Greenberger & Steinberg, 1986). At the same time, shorter, higher-quality work experiences, including community service and internships, have been shown to benefit high school students.

Are American secondary schools different from those in other countries? To explore this question, see the *Diversity in Children's Development* interlude.

Diversity in Children's Development

CROSS-CULTURAL COMPARISONS OF SECONDARY SCHOOLS

Secondary schools in different countries share a number of features, but differ on others. Let's explore the similarities and differences in secondary schools in five countries: Australia, Brazil, Germany, Japan, and the United States.

Most countries mandate that children begin school at 6 to 7 years of age and stay in school until they are 14 to 17 years of age. Brazil requires students to go to school only until they are 14 years old, whereas Russia mandates that students stay in school until they are 17. Germany, Japan, Australia, and the United States require school attendance until at least 15 to 16 years of age, with some states, such as California, recently raising the mandatory age to 18.

Most secondary schools around the world are divided into two or more levels, such as middle school (or junior high school) and high school. However, Germany's schools are divided according to three educational ability tracks: (1) the main school provides a basic level of education, (2) the middle school gives students a more advanced education, and (3) the academic school prepares students for entrance to a university. German schools, like most European schools, offer a classical education, which includes courses in Latin and Greek. Japanese secondary schools have an entrance exam, but secondary schools in the other four countries do not. Only Australia and Germany have comprehensive exit exams.

The United States and Australia are among the few countries in the world in which sports are an integral part of the public school system. Only a few private schools in other countries have their own sports teams, sports facilities, and highly organized sports events.

In Brazil, students are required to take Portuguese (the native language) and four foreign languages (Latin, French, English, and Spanish). Brazil requires these languages because of the country's international character and emphasis on trade and commerce. Seventh-grade students in Australia take courses in sheep husbandry and weaving, two areas of economic and cultural interest in the country. In Japan, students take a number of Western courses in addition to their basic Japanese courses; these courses include Western literature and languages (in addition to Japanese literature and language), Western physical education (in addition to Japanese martial arts classes), and Western sculpture and handicrafts (in addition to Japanese calligraphy). The Japanese school year is also much longer than that of other countries (225 days versus 180 days in the United States, for example).

The juku, or "cramming school," is available to Japanese children and adolescents in the summertime and after school. It provides coaching to help them improve their grades and their entrance exam scores for high schools and universities. The Japanese practice of requiring an entrance exam for high school is a rarity among the nations of the world.

High School Dropouts

Dropping out of high school has been viewed as a serious educational and societal problem for many decades. By leaving high school before graduating, adolescents approach adult life with educational deficiencies that severely curtail their economic and social well-being. In this section, we study the scope of the problem, the causes of dropping out, and ways to reduce dropout rates.

High School Dropout Rates   In the last half of the twentieth century and continuing through the first several years of the twenty-first century, high school dropout rates declined overall (National Center for Education Statistics, 2007). For example, in the 1940s, more than half of 16- to 24-year-olds had dropped out of school, but in 2005 this figure had decreased to 9 percent. Figure 15.3 shows the trends in high school dropout rates from 1972 through 2005. Notice that the dropout rate of Latino adolescents remains precariously high, although it is decreasing in the twenty-first century. Statistics on Native American youth have not been adequately obtained, but estimates indicate that they likely have the highest dropout rate in the United States, with less than 50 percent completing their high school education.

Gender differences characterize U.S. dropout rates, with males more likely to drop out than females (12 versus 9 percent). The gender gap in dropout rates is especially large for Latino adolescents (32 versus 22 percent) and African American adolescents (13 versus 9 percent) (data for 2001).

The Causes of Dropping Out of School   Students drop out of school for school-related, economic, family-related, peer-related, and personal reasons. School-related problems are consistently associated with dropping out of school (Christensen & Thurlow, 2004; Sewell, 2000). In one investigation, almost 50 percent of the dropouts cited school-related reasons for leaving school, such as not liking school, being suspended, or being expelled (Rumberger, 1995). Twenty percent of the dropouts (but 40 percent of the Latino students) cited economic reasons for dropping out. Many of these students quit school and go to work to help support their families. Students from low-income families are more likely to drop out than those from middle-income families. Many school dropouts have friends who also are school dropouts. Approximately one-third of the girls who drop out of school do so for personal reasons, such as pregnancy or marriage.

Reducing the Dropout Rate   A review of school-based dropout programs found that the most effective programs provided early reading programs, tutoring,

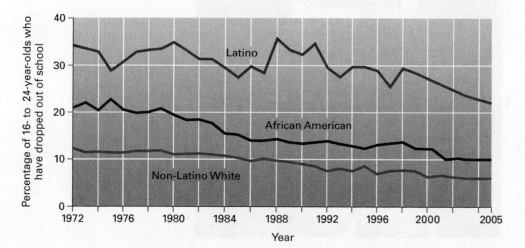

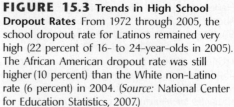

FIGURE 15.3 Trends in High School Dropout Rates From 1972 through 2005, the school dropout rate for Latinos remained very high (22 percent of 16- to 24-year-olds in 2005). The African American dropout rate was still higher (10 percent) than the White non-Latino rate (6 percent) in 2004. (*Source:* National Center for Education Statistics, 2007.)

counseling, and mentoring (Lehr & others, 2003). They also emphasized the importance of creating caring environments and relationships and offered community-service opportunities.

Clearly, then, early detection of children's school-related difficulties, and getting children engaged with school in positive ways, are important strategies for reducing the dropout rate. One program that has been very effective in reducing school dropout rates is described in the following *Caring for Children* interlude.

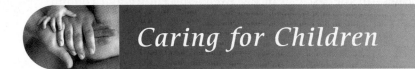

Caring for Children

THE "I HAVE A DREAM" PROGRAM

"I Have a Dream" (IHAD) is an innovative comprehensive, long-term dropout prevention program administered by the National "I Have a Dream" Foundation in New York. Since the National IHAD Foundation was created in 1986, it has grown to number over 180 projects in 64 cities and 27 states, serving more than 13,500 children ("I Have a Dream" Foundation, 2007). Local IHAD projects around the country "adopt" entire grades (usually the third or fourth) from public elementary schools, or corresponding age cohorts from public housing developments. These children— "Dreamers"—are then provided with a program of academic, social, cultural, and recreational activities throughout their elementary, middle school, and high school years. An important part of this program is that it is personal rather than institutional: IHAD sponsors and staff develop close long-term relationships with the children. When participants complete high school, IHAD provides the tuition assistance necessary for them to attend a state or local college or vocational school.

The IHAD Program was created in 1981, when philanthropist Eugene Lang made an impromptu offer of college tuition to a class of graduating sixth-graders at P.S. 121 in East Harlem. Statistically, 75 percent of the students should have dropped

These adolescents participate in the "I Have a Dream" (IHAD) Program, a comprehensive, long-term dropout prevention program that has been very successful. The IHAD program was created in 1981, when philanthropist Eugene Lang made an impromptu offer of college tuition to a class of graduating sixth-graders at P.S. 121 in East Harlem. Statistically, 75 percent of the students should have dropped out of school; instead, 90 percent graduated and 60 percent went on to college. Since the National IHAD Foundation was created in 1986, it has grown to number over 150 Projects in 57 cities and 28 states, serving some 12,000 children. *What are some other strategies for reducing high school dropout rates?*

out of school; instead, 90 percent graduated and 60 percent went on to college. Other evaluations of IHAD programs have found dramatic improvements in grades, test scores, and school attendance, as well as a reduction of behavioral problems of Dreamers. For example, in Portland, Oregon, twice as many Dreamers as control-group students had reached a math standard, and the Dreamers were less likely to be referred to the juvenile justice system (Davis, Hyatt, & Arrasmith, 1998).

REVIEW AND REFLECT ◆ LEARNING GOAL 3

3 **Characterize schools for adolescents.**

Review
- What is the transition from elementary to middle school like? What are some criticisms of, and recommendations for, improving, U.S. middle schools?
- How can the American high school be improved so that students are better prepared for the demands of the modern workplace?
- What are some of the reasons why adolescents drop out of school?

Reflect
- What was your own middle school like? How did it measure up to the Turning Points recommendations?

4 HOW DO ADOLESCENTS EXPERIENCE CAREER DEVELOPMENT AND WORK?

Career Development	Work

What characterizes career development in adolescence? Does working part-time while going to school have a positive or negative effect on adolescent development?

Career Development

What theories have been developed to direct our understanding of adolescents' career choices? What roles do exploration, decision making, and planning play in career development? How do sociocultural factors affect career development?

Theories of Career Development   Three main theories describe the manner in which adolescents make choices about career development: Ginzberg's developmental theory, Super's self-concept theory, and Holland's personality-type theory.

Ginzberg's Developmental Theory **Developmental career choice theory** is Eli Ginzberg's theory that children and adolescents go through three career choice stages: fantasy, tentative, and realistic. When asked what they want to be when they grow up, young children might answer "a doctor," "a superhero," "a teacher," "a movie star," "a sports star," or any number of other occupations. In childhood, the future seems to hold almost unlimited opportunities. Ginzberg argues that, until about the age of 11, children are in the *fantasy stage* of career choice. From the ages of 11 to 17, adolescents are in the *tentative stage* of career development, a transition from the fantasy stage of childhood to the realistic decision making of young adulthood. Ginzberg stresses that adolescents progress from evaluating their interests (11 to 12 years of age) to evaluating their capacities (13 to 14 years of age) to evaluating their values (15 to 16 years of age). Thinking shifts from less subjective to more

"Your son has made a career choice, Mildred. He's going to win the lottery and travel a lot."
Copyright © 1985. Reprinted courtesy of Bunny Hoest and Parade Magazine.

developmental career choice theory
Ginzberg's theory that children and adolescents go through three career choice stages—fantasy, tentative, and realistic.

realistic career choices at 17 to 18 years of age. Ginzberg calls the period from 17 to 18 years of age through the early twenties the *realistic stage* of career choice. During this time, the individual extensively explores available careers, then focuses on a particular career, and finally selects a specific job within the career (such as family practitioner or orthopedic surgeon, within the career of doctor).

Critics have attacked Ginzberg's theory on a number of grounds. For one, the initial data were collected from middle-socioeconomic-status youth, who probably had more career options open to them. And, as with other developmental theories (such as Piaget's), the time frames are too rigid. Moreover, Ginzberg's theory does not take into account individual differences—some adolescents make mature decisions about careers (and stick with them) at much earlier ages than specified by Ginzberg. Not all children engage in career fantasies, either. In a revision of his theory, Ginzberg (1972) conceded that lower-class individuals do not have as many options available as middle-class individuals do. Ginzberg's general point—that at some point during late adolescence or early adulthood more realistic career choices are made—probably is correct.

Super's Self-Concept Theory **Career self-concept theory** is Donald Super's theory that individuals' self-concepts play central roles in their career choices. Super argues that it is during adolescence that individuals first construct a career self-concept (Super, 1976). He emphasizes that career development consists of five phases. First, at about 14 to 18 years of age, adolescents develop ideas about work that mesh with their already existing global self-concept—this phase is called *crystallization*. Between 18 and 22 years of age, they narrow their career choices and initiate behavior that enables them to enter some type of career—the *specification* phase. Between 21 and 24 years of age, young adults complete their education or training and enter the world of work—the *implementation* phase. The decision on a specific, appropriate career is made between 25 and 35 years of age—the *stabilization* phase. Finally, after the age of 35, individuals seek to advance their careers and reach higher-status positions—the *consolidation* phase. The age ranges should be thought of as approximate rather than rigid. Super emphasizes that career exploration in adolescence is a key ingredient of the adolescent's career self-concept. He constructed the Career Development Inventory to assist counselors in promoting adolescents' career exploration.

Holland's Personality-Type Theory **Personality-type theory** is John Holland's theory that an effort should be made to match an individual's career choice with his personality (Holland, 1987). Once individuals find a career that fits with their personality, they are more likely to enjoy that career and stay in a job for a longer period of time than are individuals who work at jobs unsuitable for their personality. Holland believes six basic personality types are to be considered when matching the individual's psychological makeup with a career (see Figure 15.4):

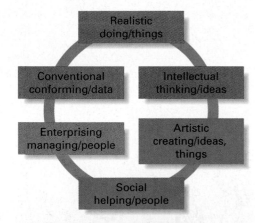

FIGURE 15.4 Holland's Model of Personality Types and Career Choices

career self-concept theory Super's theory that individuals' self-concepts play central roles in their career choices.

personality-type theory Holland's theory that an effort should be made to match an individual's career choice with his personality.

- *Realistic.* These individuals show characteristically "masculine" traits. They are physically strong, deal in practical ways with problems, and may not excel in social communication. They are best oriented toward practical careers, such as labor, farming, truck driving, and construction.
- *Intellectual.* These individuals are conceptually and theoretically oriented. They are thinkers, rather than doers. Often, they avoid interpersonal relations and are best suited to careers in math and science.
- *Social.* These individuals often show characteristically "feminine" traits, especially those associated with verbal skills and interpersonal relations. They are likely to be best equipped to enter "people" professions, such as teaching, social work, and counseling.
- *Conventional.* These youth show a distaste for unstructured activities. They are best suited for jobs as subordinates, such as bank tellers, secretaries, and file clerks.

- *Enterprising*. These individuals energize their verbal abilities toward leading others, dominating individuals, and selling people on issues or products. They are best counseled to enter careers such as sales, politics, and management.
- *Artistic*. These youth prefer to interact with their world through artistic expression, avoiding conventional and interpersonal situations in many instances, and should be oriented toward careers such as art and writing.

If all individuals were to fall conveniently into Holland's personality types, career counselors would have an easy job. But individuals are more varied and complex than Holland's theory suggests. Even Holland now admits that most individuals are not pure types. Still, the basic idea of matching individuals' abilities to particular careers is an important contribution to the career field (Brown, 1987; Lent & others, 2003). Holland's personality types are incorporated into the Strong-Campbell Vocational Interest Inventory, a widely used measure in career guidance.

Exploration, Decision Making, and Planning   Exploration, decision making, and planning play important roles in adolescents' career choices (Miller & Shevlin, 2003). In countries where equal employment opportunities have emerged—such as the United States, Canada, Great Britain, and France—the exploration of various career paths is critical in the adolescent's career development. Adolescents often approach career exploration and decision making with considerable ambiguity, uncertainty, and stress. Their career decisions often involve floundering and unplanned changes. Many adolescents not only do not know *what* information to seek about careers but also do not know *how* to seek it.

Sociocultural Influences   Not every individual born into the world can grow up to become a nuclear physicist or a doctor—there is a genetic limitation that keeps some adolescents from performing at the high intellectual levels necessary to enter such careers. Similarly, there are genetic limitations that restrict some adolescents from becoming professional football players or professional golfers. But there usually are many careers available to each of us, careers that provide a reasonable match with our abilities. Our sociocultural experiences exert strong influences on our career choices from among the wide range available. Among the important sociocultural factors that influence career development are parents and peers, schools, socioeconomic status, ethnicity, and gender.

Parents and Peers   Parents and peers are strong influences on adolescents' career choices (Vondracek & Porfelli, 2003). David Elkind (1981) argues that today's parents are pressuring their adolescents to achieve too much too soon. In some cases, though, adolescents do not get challenged enough by their parents. Consider a 25-year-old woman who vividly describes the details of her adolescence that later prevented her from seeking a competent career. From early in adolescence, both of her parents encouraged her to finish high school, but at the same time they emphasized that she needed to get a job to help them pay the family's bills. She was never told that she could not go to college, but both parents encouraged her to find someone to marry who could support her financially. This very bright girl is now divorced and feels intellectually cheated by her parents, who socialized her in the direction of marriage and away from a college education.

From an early age, children see and hear about what jobs their parents have. In some cases, parents even take their children to work with them on jobs. When we (your author and his wife) were building our house, the bricklayer brought his two sons to help with the work. They were only 14 years old, yet were already engaging in apprenticeship work with their father.

Unfortunately, some want to live vicariously through their son's or daughter's career achievements. The mother who did not get into medical school and the father who did not make it as a professional athlete may pressure their youth to achieve a career status that is beyond the youth's talents.

Parents can play an important role in the adolescent's achievement and career development. It is important for parents to neither pressure the adolescent too much nor challenge the adolescent too little.

Careers in CHILD DEVELOPMENT

Armando Ronquillo
High School Counselor/College Advisor

Armando Ronquillo is a high school counselor and college advisor at Pueblo High School, which is in a low-socioeconomic-status area in Tucson, Arizona. More than 85 percent of the students have a Latino background. Ronquillo was named top high school counselor in the state of Arizona for the year 2000. He has especially helped to increase the number of Pueblo High School students who go to college.

Ronquillo has an undergraduate degree in elementary and special education, and a master's degree in counseling. He counsels the students on the merits of staying in school and on the lifelong opportunities provided by a college education. Ronquillo guides students in obtaining the academic preparation that will enable them to go to college, including how to apply for financial aid and scholarships. He also works with parents to help them understand that "their child going to college is not only doable but also affordable."

Ronquillo works with students on setting goals and planning. He has students plan for the future in terms of 1-year (short-term), 5-year (midrange), and 10-plus-year (long-term) time periods. Ronquillo says he does this "to help students visualize how the educational plans and decisions they make today will affect them in the future." He also organizes a number of college campus visitations for students from Pueblo High School each year.

Armando Ronquillo, counseling a Latina high school student about college.

Many factors influence the parent's role in the adolescent's career development (Hargrove, Creak, & Burgess, 2002). For one, mothers who work regularly outside the home and show effort and pride in their work probably have strong influences on their adolescents' career development. A reasonable conclusion is that, when both parents work and enjoy their work, adolescents learn work values from both parents. Peers also can influence the adolescent's career development. In one study, when adolescents had friends and parents with high career standards, they were more likely to seek higher-career-status jobs, even if they came from low-income families (Simpson, 1962).

School Influences Schools, teachers, and counselors can exert a powerful influence on adolescents' career development (Heppner & Heppner, 2003). School is the primary setting where individuals first encounter the world of work. School provides an atmosphere for continuing self-development in relation to achievement and work. And school is the only institution in society that is presently capable of providing the delivery systems necessary for career education—instruction, guidance, placement, and community connections.

However, many adolescents receive little direction from school guidance counselors and do not adequately explore careers on their own. On the average, high school students spend less than three hours per year with guidance counselors, and in some schools the average is even less. School counseling has been criticized heavily, both inside and outside the educational establishment. Insiders complain about the large number of students per school counselor and the weight of noncounseling administrative duties. Outsiders complain that school counseling is ineffective, biased, and a waste of money. Short of a new profession, several options are possible (William T. Grant Foundation Commission on Work, Family, and Citizenship, 1988). First, twice the number of counselors are needed to meet all students' needs. Second, there could be a redefinition of teachers' roles, accompanied by retraining and a reduction in teaching loads, so that classroom teachers could assume a stronger role in handling the counseling needs of adolescents. The professional counselor's role in this plan would be to train and assist teachers in their counseling and to provide direct counseling in situations the teacher could not handle. Third, the whole idea of school counselors would be abandoned, and counselors would be located elsewhere—in neighborhood social service centers or labor offices, for example. (Germany forbids teachers to give career counseling, reserving this task for officials in well-developed networks of labor offices.)

Armando Ronquillo is one high school counselor who made a difference in the lives of many students. To read about his work helping youth to plot the course to college, see the *Careers in Child Development* profile.

Socioeconomic Status The channels of upward mobility open to lower-SES youth are largely educational in nature. The school hierarchy from grade school through high school, as well as through college and graduate school, is programmed to orient individuals toward some type of career. Less than 100 years ago, it was believed that only eight years of education were necessary for vocational competence, and anything beyond that qualified the individual for advanced placement in higher-status occupations. By the middle of the twentieth century, the high school diploma had already lost ground as a ticket to career success, and in today's workplace college is a prerequisite for entering a higher-status occupation.

Many of the ideas that have guided career development theory were based on experiences in middle-income and well-educated contexts. Underlying this theory is the concept that individuals have a wide range of career choices from which they can select and pursue. However, youth in low-income circumstances may have more limited career choices. Barriers such as low-quality schools, violence, and lack of access to jobs, can restrict low-income inner-city youths' access to desirable careers (Chaves & others, 2004).

Ethnicity To improve the career development of ethnic minority youth, counselors need to increase their knowledge of communication styles, values regarding the importance of the family, the impact of language fluency, and achievement expectations in various ethnic minority groups. Counselors need to be aware of and respect the cultural values of ethnic minority youth, but such values need to be discussed within the context of the realities of the educational and occupational world (Leong, 1995). For example, assertiveness training might be called for when Asian youth are following a cultural tradition of nonassertiveness.

The educational achievement and orientation of parents is also important in the career development of ethnic minority youth. In one study, African American adolescents were more likely to have U.S.-born, college-educated parents, whereas Latino adolescents were more likely to have immigrant parents with a high school education or less (Cooper, Cooper, & Chavira, 2001). In this study, resources such as help from parents, teachers and older siblings were positively linked with adolescents' higher grade point average, eligibility, and admission to more prestigious colleges.

The education and career development of Latina (the term used for Latino females) adolescents are a special concern (DeMirjyn, 2006; Lara, 2006). In one study, it was concluded that U.S. schools are doing an especially poor job of meeting the needs of America's fastest-growing minority population—Latinas (Ginorio & Huston, 2001). The study focuses on how Latinas' futures—or "possible selves"—are influenced by their families, culture, peers, teachers, and media. The report indicates that many high school counselors view success as "going away to college," yet some Latinas, because of family responsibilities, believe it is important to stay close to home. The high school graduation rate for Latinas lags behind that for girls of any other ethnic minority group, except Native Americans. Latinas also are less likely to take the SAT exam than other non-Latino White and other ethnic group females. Thus, a better effort needs to be made at encouraging Latinas' academic success and involving their families more fully in the process of college preparation (Lara, 2006).

Gender Not only Latinas, but many girls from other backgrounds have also not been adequately exposed to career possibilities. As growing numbers of females pursue careers, they are faced with questions involving career and family (Carlson & others, 2006; Kirchmeyer, 2006; Smith, 2007). Should they delay marriage and childbearing and establish their career first? Or should they combine their career, marriage, and childbearing in their twenties? Some females in the last decade have embraced the domestic patterns of an earlier historical period. They have married, borne children, and committed themselves to full-time mothering. These "stay at home moms" may work intermittently, although for the most part, they have decided to devote their efforts to raising their children, rather than working outside the home.

An increasing number of females, though, have postponed motherhood (Betz, 2006; Sax & Bryant, 2006). They develop committed, permanent ties to the workplace that resemble the pattern once reserved only for males. When they have had children, they strive to combine a career and motherhood. Although women have always had careers, today their numbers are growing at an unprecedented rate.

Work

One of the greatest changes in adolescents' lives in recent years has been the increased number of adolescents who work part-time and still attend school on a regular basis. Our discussion of adolescents and work includes information about the sociohistorical context of adolescent work, as well as the advantages and disadvantages of part-time work.

The Sociocultural Context of Work   Over the past century, the percentage of youth who worked full-time as opposed to those who were in school has decreased dramatically. In the late 1800s, fewer than 1 of every 20 high-school-age adolescents was in school. Today, more than 9 of every 10 adolescents receive high school diplomas. In the nineteenth century, many adolescents learned a trade from their father or another adult member of the community.

Even though prolonged education has kept many contemporary youth from holding full-time jobs, it has not prevented them from working on a part-time basis while going to school. Most high school seniors have had some work experience. In a national survey of 17,000 high school seniors, three of four reported some job income during the average school week (Bachman, 1982). For 41 percent of the males and 30 percent of the females, this income exceeded $50 a week. The typical part-time job for high school seniors involves 16 to 20 hours of work per week, although 10 percent work 30 hours a week or more.

In 1940, only 1 of 25 tenth-grade males attended school and simultaneously worked part-time. In the 1970s, the number increased to more than 1 of every 4. And, in the 1980s, as just indicated, 3 of 4 combined school and part-time work. Adolescents also are working longer hours now than in the past. For example, the number of 14- to 15-year-olds who work more than 14 hours per week has increased substantially in the past three decades. A similar picture emerges for 16-year-olds. In 1960, 44 percent of 16-year-old males who attended school worked more than 14 hours a week, but, by the 1980s, the figure had increased to more than 60 percent.

What kinds of jobs are adolescents working at today? About 17 percent who work do so in restaurants, such as McDonald's and Burger King, waiting on customers and cleaning up. Other adolescents work in retail stores as cashiers or salespeople (about 20 percent), in offices as clerical assistants (about 10 percent), or as unskilled laborers (about 10 percent). In one study, boys reported higher self-esteem and well-being when they perceived that their jobs were providing skills that would be useful to them in the future (Mortimer & others, 1992).

Do male and female adolescents take the same types of jobs, and are they paid equally? Some jobs are held almost exclusively by male adolescents—busboy, gardener, manual laborer, and newspaper carrier—while other jobs are held almost exclusively by female adolescents—baby-sitter and maid. Male adolescents work longer hours and are paid more per hour than female adolescents (Helson, Elliot, & Leigh, 1989).

The Advantages and Disadvantages of Part-Time Work   Does the increase in work have benefits for adolescents? In some cases, yes; in others, no. Ellen Greenberger and Laurence Steinberg (1986) examined the work experiences of students

What are some advantages and disadvantages of part-time work during adolescence?

in four California high schools. Their findings disproved some common myths. For example, generally it is assumed that adolescents get extensive on-the-job training when they are hired for work. The reality is that they got little training at all. Also, it is assumed that youth—through work experiences—learn to get along better with adults. However, adolescents reported that they rarely felt close to the adults with whom they worked. The work experiences of the adolescent did help them understand how the business world works, how to get and keep a job, and how to manage money. Working also helped adolescents learn to budget their time, take pride in their accomplishments, and to evaluate their goals. But working adolescents often have to give up sports, social affairs with peers, and sometimes sleep. And they have to balance the demands of work, school, family, and peers.

Greenberger and Steinberg asked students about their grade point averages, school attendance, and satisfaction from school, as well as the number of hours spent studying and participating in extracurricular activities since they began working. They found that the working adolescents had lower grade point averages than nonworking adolescents. More than one of four students reported that their grades dropped when they began working; only one of nine said their grades improved. But it was not just working that affected adolescents' grades—more important, it was *how long* they worked. As we indicated earlier in the chapter, tenth-graders who worked more than 14 hours a week suffered a drop in grades. Eleventh-graders worked up to 20 hours a week before their grades dropped. When adolescents spend more than 20 hours per week working, there is little time to study for tests and to complete homework assignments.

In addition to the work affecting grades, the working adolescents felt less involved in school, were absent more, and said they did not enjoy school as much as their nonworking counterparts did. The adolescents who worked also spent less time with their families—but just as much time with their peers—as their nonworking counterparts. The adolescents who worked long hours also were more frequent users of alcohol and marijuana. More recent research confirms the link between part-time work during adolescence and problem behaviors (Hansen, 1996).

Although working too many hours may be detrimental to adolescent development, work may especially benefit adolescents in low-income, urban contexts by providing them with economic benefits and adult monitoring. This may increase school engagement and decrease delinquency. In one study, low-income, urban adolescents who never worked had more school-related difficulties than those who did work (Leventhal, Graber, & Brooks-Gunn, 2001). Stable work increased the likelihood that the adolescent males in low-income, urban contexts would go to college more than the adolescent females.

Work Profiles of Adolescents Around the World   In many developing countries where it is common for adolescents to not attend school on a regular basis, boys often spend more time in income-generating labor than girls do, whereas girls spend more time in unpaid labor than boys (Larson & Verma, 1999). By early adolescence, total labor exceeds eight hours a day in many nonindustrial, unschooled populations. In literate societies, total labor "averages less than one hour per day across childhood and adolescence, with U.S. adolescents being the exception" (p. 708). For example, U.S. adolescents are far more likely to participate in paid labor than European and East Asian adolescents. As we saw earlier, many U.S. high school students work 10 or even 20 hours or more per week. One study found that U.S. high school students spent an average of 50 minutes per day working at a job, whereas North European adolescents spent an average of only 15 minutes per day working at a job (Alsaker & Flammer, 1999). In this study, employment of adolescents was virtually nonexistent in France and Russia. In another study, 80 percent of Minneapolis eleventh-graders had part-time jobs compared with only 27 percent of Japanese eleventh-graders and 26 percent of Taiwanese eleventh-graders (Fuligni & Stevenson, 1995).

Overall, the weight of the evidence suggests that spending large amounts of time in paid labor has limited developmental benefits for youth, and for some it is associated with risk behavior and costs to physical health (Larson & Verma, 1999). Some youth, though, are engaged in challenging work activities, are provided constructive supervision by adults, and experience favorable work conditions. However, in general, given the repetitive nature of most labor carried out by adolescents around the world, it is difficult to argue that working 15 to 25 hours per week in such labor provides developmental gains (Larson & Verma, 1999).

REVIEW AND REFLECT ◆ LEARNING GOAL 4

4 Summarize career development and work in adolescence.

Review
- What are three theories of career development? What characterizes career development in adolescence?
- What are adolescents' work experiences like?

Reflect
- Did you work during high school? What were some of the pluses and minuses of the experience if you did work? Are you working part-time or full-time now while you are going to college? If so, what effect does the work experience have on your academic success?

REACH YOUR LEARNING GOALS

1 HOW DO ADOLESCENTS THINK AND PROCESS INFORMATION? *Discuss different approaches to adolescent cognition.*

Piaget's Theory

- During the formal operational stage, Piaget's fourth stage of cognitive development, thought is more abstract, idealistic, and logical than during the concrete operational stage. Adolescents become capable of hypothetical-deductive reasoning. However, many adolescents are not formal operational thinkers but are consolidating their concrete operational thought. Piaget made a number of important contributions to understanding children's development, but his theory has undergone considerable criticism.

Adolescent Egocentrism

- Elkind proposed that adolescents, especially young adolescents, develop an egocentrism that includes both an imaginary audience (the belief that others are as preoccupied with the adolescent as the adolescent is) and a personal fable (a sense of uniqueness and invulnerability).

Information Processing

- Three aspects of memory that improve during adolescence are short-term memory, working memory, and long-term memory. Higher-order cognitive processes such as making decisions and thinking critically are often called executive functioning. It is increasingly thought that executive functioning strengthens during adolescence. Adolescence is a time of increased decision making. Older adolescents make better decisions than younger adolescents, who in turn are better at this than children are. Being able to make competent decisions, however, does not mean they actually will be made in everyday life, where breadth of experience comes into play. Adolescence is an important transitional period in critical thinking because of such cognitive changes as increased speed, automaticity, and capacity of information processing; more breadth of content knowledge; increased ability to construct new combinations of knowledge; and increased use of spontaneous strategies.

2 WHAT CHARACTERIZES ADOLESCENTS' VALUES, MORAL EDUCATION, AND RELIGION? *Describe adolescents' values, moral education, and religion.*

Values

- Values are the beliefs and attitudes about the way things should be. Over the last two decades, first-year college students have shown an increased concern for personal well-being and a decreased interest in the welfare of others. Service learning is a form of education that promotes social responsibility and service to the community. Service learning is increasingly required by schools and has positive effects on adolescent development.

Moral Education

- The hidden curriculum is a term used by Dewey to describe his belief that even when schools do not have specific moral education programs, every school does provide a moral education. Character education is a direct education approach that advocates teaching adolescents moral literacy. Values clarification emphasizes helping students to clarify what purpose their lives are to serve and what is worth working for. Cognitive moral education (often based on Kohlberg's theory) states that students should develop such values as democracy and justice as their moral reasoning develops. Recently, an integrative moral education approach has been advocated.

Religion

- Many children and adolescents show an interest in religion, and religious institutions are designed to introduce them to religious beliefs. Adolescence may be a special juncture in religious development for many individuals. Various aspects of religion are linked with positive outcomes in adolescent development. Erikson's ideas on identity can be applied to understanding the increased interest in religion during adolescence. Piaget's theory provides a theoretical foundation for understanding developmental changes in religion. When adolescents have a positive relationship with parents, and/or are securely attached to them, they often adopt their parents' religious beliefs. Links have been found between adolescent sexuality and religiousness.

③ WHAT ARE SCHOOLS FOR ADOLESCENTS LIKE? *Characterize schools for adolescents.*

The American Middle School

- The transition to middle or junior high school coincides with many physical, cognitive, and socioemotional changes. The transition involves moving from the top-dog position to the lowest position, and this transition is often difficult for many children. Criticisms of U.S. middle schools indicate they are too massive and impersonal, and that curricula are often irrelevant. Recommendations for improving U.S. middle schools include developing small communities of students within the schools, having lower student-counselor ratios, and raising academic standards. Participation in extracurricular activities is associated with positive academic and psychological outcomes.

The American High School

- An increasing number of educators believe that U.S. high schools need a new mission for the twenty-first century; one that involves more support for graduating with the knowledge and skills to succeed in college and a career, higher expectations for achievement, and less time spent working in low-level service jobs.

High School Dropouts

- Many school dropouts have educational deficiencies that limit their economic and social well-being for much of their adult lives. Progress has been made in lowering the dropout rate for African American youth, but the dropout rate for Native American and Latino youth remains very high. Native American youth likely have the highest dropout rate. Males are more likely to drop out than females. Dropping out of school is associated with demographic, family-related, peer-related, school-related, economic, and personal factors.

4 HOW DO ADOLESCENTS EXPERIENCE CAREER DEVELOPMENT AND WORK?

Summarize career development and work in adolescence.

Career Development

- Three theories of career development are Ginzberg's developmental career choice theory, Super's career self-concept theory, and Holland's personality-type theory. Ginzberg's theory argues that children and adolescents go through three career choice stages: fantasy, tentative, and realistic. Super's theory is that the individual's self-concept plays a central role in career choice and involves these phases: crystallization, specification, implementation, stabilization, and consolidation. Holland stresses that an individual's career choice should fit with her personality type: realistic, intellectual, social, conventional, enterprising, or artistic. Explorations of career options is a critical aspect of adolescents' career development. Too many youth flounder and make unplanned career choices. Sociocultural influences include parents and peers, schools, socioecononomic status, ethnicity, and gender. The channels of opportunity for adolescents from low-income families are primarily educational.

Work

- Adolescents are not as likely to hold full-time jobs today as they were in the nineteenth century. There has been a tremendous increase in the percentage of adolescents who work part-time and go to school, which has both advantages (such as managing money) and disadvantages (such as relation to low grades when working too many hours). Profiles of adolescent work vary around the world. In many developing countries, boys engage in considerably more paid labor than girls, who participate in more unpaid labor at home. U.S. adolescents engage in more work than their counterparts in many other developed countries. There appears to be little developmental advantage for most adolescents when they work 15 to 25 hours per week.

KEY TERMS

hypothetical-deductive
   reasoning 502
adolescent egocentrism 503
imaginary audience 503
personal fable 503

critical thinking 506
values 507
service learning 509
hidden curriculum 511

character education 511
values clarification 511
cognitive moral education 511
top-dog phenomenon 516

developmental career choice
   theory 521
career self-concept theory 522
personality-type theory 522

MAKING A DIFFERENCE

Supporting Adolescents' Cognitive Development

What are some good strategies for nourishing adolescents' cognitive development?

- *Provide support for adolescents' information processing.* Provide opportunities and guide adolescents in making good decisions, especially in real-world settings; stimulate adolescents to think critically; and encourage them to engage in self-regulatory learning.
- *Give adolescents opportunities to discuss moral dilemmas.* Provide adolescents with group opportunities to discuss the importance of cooperation, trust, and caring.
- *Create better schools for adolescents.* Schools for adolescents need to emphasize socioemotional development as well as cognitive development.
- Take individual variation in adolescents seriously.

- Develop curricula that involve high expectations for success and the support to attain that success.
- Develop smaller communities.
- Involve parents and community leaders more.
- Break down the barriers between school and work to reduce the high school dropout rate.
- *Provide adolescents with information about careers.* Adolescents do not get adequate information about careers. Career decision making needs to be given a higher priority in schools.
- *Don't let adolescents work too many hours while going to school.* Parents need to monitor how many hours adolescents work during the school year. A rule of thumb is that working more than 20 hours a week in the eleventh and twelfth grades lowers grades.

RESOURCES FOR IMPROVING CHILDREN'S LIVES

Turning Points 2000

by Gayle Davis and Anthony Jackson (2000)

This follow-up to earlier Turning Points recommendations includes a number of strategies for meeting the educational needs of adolescents, especially young adolescents.

E-LEARNING TOOLS

Connect to **www.mhhe.com/santrockc10** to research the answers and complete these exercises. In addition, you'll find a number of other resources and valuable study tools for Chapter 15, "Cognitive Development in Adolescence," on this Web site.

Taking It to the Net

1. Roger has two daughters: Ellen, who is a senior in high school; and Lisa, who is in the eighth grade. Roger remembers that Ellen had a very difficult time when she transitioned from middle school to high school, and he wants to make the process easier for Lisa. What kinds of things would help Lisa ease the transition? What makes this process so stressful for young teenagers?

2. LaTricia is an excellent student. She is on the debate team, and she makes extremely convincing arguments for the issues she is debating. However, when it comes to picking an outfit to wear in the morning, LaTricia has much more difficulty. She often stands in front of the closet, seemingly overwhelmed with the choices. Why might LaTricia be so skilled at challenging academic tasks, yet still have trouble with daily choices?

3. Steven is a high school junior. He was always a C student throughout elementary school and middle school. Now he is in danger of failing two of his classes. Steven is tired of school and wants to drop out. What might help Steven improve his grades and stay in school? What academic, social, and emotional factors might be contributing to Steven's school failure?

Health and Well-Being, Parenting, and Education

Build your decision-making skills by trying your hand at the health and well-being, parenting, and education exercises.

Video Clips

The Online Learning Center includes the following videos for this chapter:

1. *Thoughts on School*—1991
   Three adolescent friends describe experiences with school and what they like and dislike about school.

2. *Non-College-Bound Adolescents*—923
   A discussion of the unique problems faced by non-college-bound adolescents.

16 Socioemotional Development in Adolescence

In case you're worried about what's going to become of the younger generation, it's going to grow up and start worrying about the younger generation.

—ROGER ALLEN
Contemporary American Writer

CHAPTER OUTLINE

LEARNING GOALS

WHAT CHARACTERIZES EMOTIONAL AND PERSONALITY DEVELOPMENT IN ADOLESCENCE?   ①

Self-Esteem

Identity

Emotional Development

1 Discuss changes in the self and emotional development during adolescence.

WHAT IS THE NATURE OF PARENT-ADOLESCENT RELATIONSHIPS?   ②

Autonomy and Attachment

Parent-Adolescent Conflict

2 Describe changes that take place in adolescents' relationships with their parents.

WHAT ASPECTS OF PEER RELATIONSHIPS ARE IMPORTANT IN ADOLESCENCE?   ③

Friendships

Peer Groups

Dating and Romantic Relationships

3 Characterize the changes that occur in peer relations during adolescence.

WHY IS CULTURE AN IMPORTANT CONTEXT FOR ADOLESCENT DEVELOPMENT?   ④

Cross-Cultural Comparisons

Ethnicity

4 Explain how culture influences adolescent development.

WHAT ARE SOME SOCIOEMOTIONAL PROBLEMS IN ADOLESCENCE?   ⑤

Juvenile Delinquency

Depression and Suicide

The Interrelation of Problems and Successful Prevention/Intervention Programs

5 Identify adolescent problems in socioemotional development and strategies for helping adolescents with problems.

Jewel Cash

Images of Children's Development
Jewel Cash, Teen Dynamo

The mayor of the city says that she is "everywhere." She recently persuaded the city's school committee to consider ending the practice of locking tardy students out of their classrooms. She also swayed a neighborhood group to support her proposal for a winter jobs program. According to one city councilman, "People are just impressed with the power of her arguments and the sophistication of the argument" (Silva, 2005, pp. B1, B4). She is Jewel E. Cash, and she is just 16 years old.

A junior at Boston Latin Academy, Jewel was raised in one of Boston's housing projects by her mother, a single parent. Today she is a member of the Boston Student Advisory Council, mentors children, volunteers at a women's shelter, manages and dances in two troupes, and is a member of a neighborhood watch group—among other activities. Jewel is far from typical, but her activities illustrate that cognitive and socioemotional development allows even adolescents to be capable, effective individuals.

PREVIEW

Significant changes characterize socioemotional development in adolescence. These changes include increased efforts to understand one's self, searching for identity, and emotional fluctuations. Changes also occur in the social contexts of adolescents' lives, with transformations occurring in relationships with families and peers in cultural contexts. Adolescents are also at risk for developing socioemotional problems, such as delinquency and depression.

1 WHAT CHARACTERIZES EMOTIONAL AND PERSONALITY DEVELOPMENT IN ADOLESCENCE?

| Self-Esteem | Identity | Emotional Development |

Jewel Cash told an interviewer from the *Boston Globe,* "I see a problem and I say, 'How can I make a difference?'... I can't take on the world, even though I can try. . . . I'm moving forward but I want to make sure I'm bringing people with me" (Silva, 2005, pp. B1, B4). Jewel's confidence, sense of self, and emotional maturity sound at least as impressive as her activities. This section examines how adolescents develop characteristics like these. How much did you understand yourself during adolescence, and how did you acquire the stamp of your identity? This section examines self-esteem, identity, and emotional development during adolescence.

Self-Esteem

Recall from Chapter 13 that *self-esteem* is the overall way we evaluate ourselves, and that self-esteem is also referred to as self-image or self-worth. One recent study found that adolescents who had low self-esteem had lower levels of mental health, physical health, and economic prospects as adults than adolescents with high self-esteem (Trzesniewski & others, 2006). Another recent study revealed that self-esteem increased during emerging adulthood (18 to 25 years of age) (Galambos, Barker, & Krahn, 2006).

Controversy characterizes the extent to which self-esteem changes during adolescence and whether there are gender differences in adolescents' self-esteem (Donnellan & others, 2006; Harter, 2006). In one study, both boys and girls had particularly high self-esteem in childhood, but their self-esteem dropped considerably during adolescence (Robins & others, 2002). The self-esteem of girls declined more than the self-esteem of boys during adolescence in this study. Another study also found that the self-esteem of girls declined during early adolescence, but it found that the self-esteem of boys increased in early adolescence (Baldwin & Hoffman, 2002). In this study, high adolescent self-esteem was related to positive family relationships.

Some critics argue that developmental changes and gender differences in self-esteem during adolescence have been exaggerated (Harter, 2002). For example, in one analysis of research studies on self-esteem in adolescence, it was concluded that girls have only slightly more negative self-esteem than do boys (Kling & others, 1999). Despite the differing results and interpretations, the self-esteem of girls is likely to decline at least somewhat during early adolescence.

Why would the self-esteem of girls decline during early adolescence? One explanation points to girls' negative body images during pubertal change. Another explanation involves the greater interest young adolescent girls take in social relationships and society's failure to reward that interest. To read further about self-esteem in adolescence, see the *Research in Children's Development* interlude.

Research in Children's Development

ADOLESCENTS' SELF-IMAGES

One study examined the self-image of 675 adolescents (289 males and 386 females) from 13 to 19 years of age in Naples, Italy (Bacchini & Magliulo, 2003). Self-image was assessed using the Offer Self-Image Questionnaire (Offer, Ostrov, & Howard, 1989), which consists of 130 items grouped into 11 scales that define five different aspects of self-image:

- The *psychological self* (made up of scales that assess impulse control, emotional tone, and body image)
- The *social self* (consists of scales that evaluate social relationships, morals, and vocational and educational aspirations)
- The *coping self* (composed of scales to measure mastery of the world, psychological problems, and adjustment)
- The *familial self* (made up of only one scale that evaluates how adolescents feel about their parents)
- The *sexual self* (composed of only one scale that examines adolescents' feelings and attitudes about sexual matters)

The adolescents had positive self-images, with their scores being above a neutral score (3.5) on all 11 scales. For example, the adolescents' average body self-image score was 4.2. The aspect of their lives in which adolescents had the most positive self-image involved their educational and vocational aspirations (average score of 4.8). The lowest self-image score was for impulse control (average score of 3.9). These results support the view that adolescents have a more positive perception of themselves than is commonly believed.

Gender differences were found on a number of the self-image scales, with boys consistently having more positive self-images than did girls. Keep in mind, though, that as we indicated earlier, even though girls reported lower self-images than boys, their self-images still were mainly in the positive range.

What are some important dimensions of identity?

"Who are you?" said the Caterpillar. Alice replied, rather shyly, "I—I hardly know, Sir, just at present—at least I know who I was when I got up this morning, but I must have changed several times since then."

—LEWIS CARROLL
English Writer, 19th Century

identity versus identity confusion Erikson's fifth developmental stage, which occurs at about the time of adolescence. At this time, adolescents are faced with deciding who they are, what they are all about, and where they are going in life.

Identity

Who am I? What am I all about? What am I going to do with my life? What is different about me? How can I make it on my own? These questions reflect the search for an identity. By far the most comprehensive and provocative theory of identity development is Erik Erikson's. In this section, we examine his views on identity. We also discuss contemporary research on how identity develops and how social contexts influence that development.

What Is Identity?   Identity is a self-portrait composed of many pieces, including these:

- The career and work path the person wants to follow (vocational/career identity)
- Whether the person is conservative, liberal, or middle-of-the-road (political identity)
- The person's spiritual beliefs (religious identity)
- Whether the person is single, married, divorced, and so on (relationship identity)
- The extent to which the person is motivated to achieve and is intellectual (achievement, intellectual identity)
- Whether the person is heterosexual, homosexual, or bisexual (sexual identity)
- Which part of the world or country a person is from and how intensely the person identifies with his or her cultural heritage (cultural/ethnic identity)
- The kind of things a person likes to do, which can include sports, music, hobbies, and so on (interest)
- The individual's personality characteristics, such as being introverted or extraverted, anxious or calm, friendly or hostile, and so on (personality)
- The individual's body image (physical identity)

At the bare minimum, identity involves commitment to a vocational direction, an ideological stance, and a sexual orientation. We put these pieces together to form a sense of ourselves continuing through time within a social world.

Synthesizing the identity components can be a long and drawn-out process, with many negations and affirmations of various roles and faces. Identity development gets done in bits and pieces. Decisions are not made once and for all, but have to be made again and again. Identity development does not happen neatly, and it does not happen cataclysmically (Kroger, 2003, 2007).

Erikson's View   Questions about identity surface as common, virtually universal, concerns during adolescence. Some decisions made during adolescence might seem trivial: whom to date, whether or not to break up, which major to study, whether to study or play, whether or not to be politically active, and so on. Over the years of adolescence, however, such decisions begin to form the core of what the individual is all about as a human being—what is called his or her identity.

It was Erik Erikson (1950, 1968) who first understood how central questions about identity are to understanding adolescent development. That identity is now believed to be a key aspect of adolescent development is a result of Erikson's masterful thinking and analysis. His ideas reveal rich insights into adolescents' thoughts and feelings, and reading one or more of his books is worthwhile. A good starting point is *Identity: Youth and Crisis* (1968). Other works that portray identity development are *Young Man Luther* (1962) and *Gandhi's Truth* (1969).

Erikson's theory was introduced in Chapter 1. Recall that his fifth developmental stage, which individuals experience during adolescence, is **identity versus identity confusion.** During this time, said Erikson, adolescents are faced with deciding who they are, what they are all about, and where they are going in life.

These questions about identity occur throughout life, but they become especially important for adolescents. Erikson points out that adolescents face an overwhelming

Position on Occupation and Ideology	Identity Status			
	Identity diffusion	Identity foreclosure	Identity moratorium	Identity achievement
Crisis	Absent	Absent	Present	Present
Commitment	Absent	Present	Absent	Present

FIGURE 16.1 Marcia's Four Statuses of Identity According to Marcia, an individual's status in developing an identity can be described as identity diffusion, identity foreclosure, identity moratorium, or identity achievement. The status depends on the presence or absence of (1) a crisis or exploration of alternatives and (2) a commitment to an identity. *What is the identity status of most young adolescents?*

number of choices. As they gradually come to realize that they will be responsible for themselves and their own lives, adolescents search for what those lives are going to be.

The search for an identity during adolescence is aided by a **psychosocial moratorium,** which is Erikson's term for the gap between childhood security and adult autonomy. During this period, society leaves adolescents relatively free of responsibilities and free to try out different identities. Adolescents in effect search their culture's identity files, experimenting with different roles and personalities. They may want to pursue one career one month (lawyer, for example) and another career the next month (doctor, actor, teacher, social worker, or astronaut, for example). They may dress neatly one day, sloppily the next. This experimentation is a deliberate effort on the part of adolescents to find out where they fit in the world. Most adolescents eventually discard undesirable roles.

Youth who successfully cope with conflicting identities emerge with a new sense of self that is both refreshing and acceptable. Adolescents who do not successfully resolve this identity crisis suffer what Erikson calls identity confusion. The confusion takes one of two courses: individuals withdraw, isolating themselves from peers and family, or they immerse themselves in the world of peers and lose their identity in the crowd.

Developmental Changes   Although questions about identity may be especially important during adolescence, identity formation neither begins nor ends during these years. It begins with the appearance of attachment, the development of the sense of self, and the emergence of independence in infancy; the process reaches its final phase with a life review and integration in old age. What is important about identity development in adolescence, especially late adolescence, is that for the first time, physical development, cognitive development, and socioemotional development advance to the point at which the individual can sort through and synthesize childhood identities and identifications to construct a viable path toward adult maturity.

How do individual adolescents go about the process of forming an identity? Eriksonian researcher James Marcia (1980, 1994) argues that Erikson's theory of identity development contains four *statuses* of identity, or ways of resolving the identity crisis: identity diffusion, identity foreclosure, identity moratorium, and identity achievement. What determines an individual's identity status? Marcia classifies individuals based on the existence or extent of their crisis or commitment (see Figure 16.1). **Crisis** is defined as a period of identity development during which the individual is exploring alternatives. Most researchers use the term *exploration* rather than crisis. **Commitment** is personal investment in identity.

The four statuses of identity are:

- **Identity diffusion,** the status of individuals who have not yet experienced a crisis or made any commitments. Not only are they undecided about occupational and ideological choices, they are also likely to show little interest in such matters.
- **Identity foreclosure** is the status of individuals who have made a commitment but not experienced a crisis. This occurs most often when parents hand

psychosocial moratorium Erikson's term for the gap between childhood security and adult autonomy.

crisis Marcia's term for a period of identity development during which the individual is exploring alternatives.

commitment Marcia's term for the part of identity development in which individuals show a personal investment in identity.

identity diffusion Marcia's term for individuals who have not yet experienced a crisis (explored alternatives) or made any commitments.

identity foreclosure Marcia's term for individuals who have made a commitment but have not experienced a crisis.

down commitments to their adolescents, usually in an authoritarian way, before adolescents have had a chance to explore different approaches, ideologies, and vocations on their own.

- **Identity moratorium** is the status of individuals who are in the midst of a crisis but whose commitments are either absent or are only vaguely defined.
- **Identity achievement** is the status of individuals who have undergone a crisis and made a commitment.

Let's explore some examples of Marcia's identity statuses. Thirteen-year-old Sarah has neither begun to explore her identity in any meaningful way nor made an identity commitment; she is identity diffused. Eighteen-year-old Tim's parents want him to be a medical doctor, so he is planning on majoring in premedicine in college and has not explored other options; he is identity foreclosed. Nineteen-year-old Sasha is not quite sure what life paths she wants to follow, but she recently went to the counseling center at her college to find out about different careers; she is in identity moratorium status. Twenty-one-year-old Marcelo extensively explored several career options in college, eventually getting his degree in science education, and is looking forward to his first year of teaching high school students; he is identity achieved. These examples focused on the career dimension of identity, but remember that identity has a number of dimensions.

In Marcia's terms, young adolescents are primarily in the identity statuses of diffusion, foreclosure, or moratorium. In order to move to the status of identity achievement, young adolescents need three things (Marcia, 1987, 1996): (1) they must be confident that they have parental support, (2) they must have an established sense of industry, and (3) they must be able to adopt a self-reflective stance toward the future.

> *Once formed, an identity furnishes individuals with a historical sense of who they have been, a meaningful sense of who they are now, and a sense of who they might become in the future.*
>
> —JAMES MARCIA
> *Contemporary Psychologist,*
> *Simon Fraser University*

Beyond Erikson Some researchers believe the most important identity changes take place during *emerging adulthood,* the period from about 18 to 25 years of age (Arnett, 2007; Cote, 2006; Kroger, 2007). For example, Alan Waterman (1985, 1989, 1992) has found that from the years preceding high school through the last few years of college, the number of individuals who are identity achieved increases, whereas the number of who are identity diffused decreases. Many young adolescents are identity diffused. College upperclassmen are more likely than high school students or college freshmen to be identity achieved.

The timing of changes in identity status may depend on the particular area of life involved. For example, for religious beliefs and political ideology, many college students have identity-foreclosure and identity-moratorium status. Many college students are still wrestling with ideological commitments (Arehart & Smith, 1990; Harter, 1990).

Recall from Chapter 14 that one of emerging adulthood's themes is not having many social commitments, which gives individuals considerable independence in developing a life path (Arnett, 2006, 2007). James Cote (2006) argues that because of this freedom, developing a positive identity in emerging adulthood requires considerable self-discipline and planning. Without this self-discipline and planning, emerging adults are likely to drift and not follow any particular direction. Cote also stresses that emerging adults who obtain a higher education are more likely to be on a positive identity path. Those who don't obtain a higher education, he says, tend to experience frequent job changes, not because they are searching for an identity but rather because they are just trying to eek out a living in a society that rewards higher education.

Resolution of the identity issue during adolescence or emerging adulthood does not mean that identity will be stable through the remainder of life (Kroger, 2007; Pals, 2006). Many individuals who develop positive identities follow what are called "MAMA" cycles; that is, their identity status changes from *m*oratorium to *a*chievement to *m*oratorium to *a*chievement (Archer, 1989). These cycles may

identity moratorium Marcia's term for individuals who are in the midst of a crisis, but their commitments are either absent or vaguely defined.

identity achievement Marcia's term for individuals who have undergone a crisis and have made a commitment.

be repeated throughout life (Francis, Fraser, & Marcia, 1989). Marcia (2002) argues that the first identity is just that—it is not, and should not be expected to be, the final product.

In short, questions about identity come up throughout life. An individual who develops a healthy identity is flexible and adaptive, open to changes in society, in relationships, and in careers (Adams, Gulotta, & Montemayor, 1992). This openness assures numerous reorganizations of identity throughout the individual's life.

Family Influences   Parents are important figures in the adolescent's development of identity. For example, one study found that poor communication between mothers and adolescents, as well as persistent conflicts with friends, was linked to less positive identity development (Reis & Youniss, 2004). Do parenting styles influence identity development? Parents who encourage adolescents to participate in family decision making—*democratic* parents—foster identity achievement. In contrast, parents who control the adolescent's behavior without giving the adolescent an opportunity to express opinions—*autocratic* parents—encourage identity foreclosure. *Permissive* parents, who provide little guidance to adolescents and allow them to make their own decisions, promote identity diffusion (Enright & others, 1980).

The search for balance between the need for autonomy and the need for connectedness becomes especially important to identity during adolescence. Developmentalist Catherine Cooper and her colleagues (Carlson, Cooper, & Hsu, 1990; Cooper & Grotevant, 1989; Grotevant & Cooper, 1985, 1998) found that the presence of a family atmosphere that promotes both individuality and connectedness is important in the adolescent's identity development:

- **Individuality** consists of two dimensions: self-assertion (the ability to have and communicate a point of view) and separateness (the use of communication patterns to express how one is different from others).
- **Connectedness** also consists of two dimensions: mutuality, which involves sensitivity to and respect for others' views, and permeability, which involves openness to others' views.

In general, Cooper's research indicates that identity formation is enhanced by family relationships that are both individuated, which encourages adolescents to develop their own point of view, and connected, which provides a secure base from which adolescents can explore their widening social worlds. When connectedness is strong and individuation weak, adolescents often have an identity-foreclosure status. When connectedness is weak, adolescents often reveal identity confusion (Archer & Waterman, 1994).

Ethnic Identity   Throughout the world, ethnic minority groups have struggled to maintain their ethnic identities while blending in with the dominant culture (Erikson, 1968). **Ethnic identity** is an enduring aspect of the self that includes a sense of membership in an ethnic group, along with the attitudes and feelings related to that membership (Phinney, 1996). Erikson thought that this struggle for a separate ethnic identity within the larger culture has been the driving force in the founding of churches, empires, and revolutions throughout history.

Many aspects of sociocultural contexts may influence ethnic identity (Berry, 2007; Phinney & Ong, 2007). Ethnic identity tends to be stronger among members of minority groups than among members of mainstream groups. For example, in one study, the exploration of ethnic identity was higher among ethnic minority college students than among White non-Latino college students (Phinney & Alipuria, 1990). Time is another aspect of the context that influences ethnic identity. The indicators of identity often differ for each succeeding generation of immigrants (Berry, 2007; Phinney & Ong, 2007). First-generation immigrants are likely to be secure in their identities and unlikely to change much; they may or may not develop a new identity. The degree to which they begin to feel "American" appears to be related

Michelle Chin, age 16: "Parents do not understand that teenagers need to find out who they are, which means a lot of experimenting, a lot of mood swings, a lot of emotions and awkwardness. Like any teenager, I am facing an identity crisis. I am still trying to figure out whether I am a Chinese American or an American with Asian eyes."

individuality Individuality consists of two dimensions: self-assertion (the ability to have and communicate a point of view) and separateness (the use of communication patterns to express how one is different from others).

connectedness Connectedness consists of two dimensions: mutuality (sensitivity to and respect for others' views) and permeability (openness to others' views).

ethnic identity An enduring, basic aspect of the self that includes a sense of membership in an ethnic group and the attitudes and feelings related to that membership.

Researcher Margaret Beale Spencer, shown here talking with adolescents, believes that adolescence is often a critical juncture in the identity development of ethnic minority individuals. Most ethnic minority individuals consciously confront their ethnicity for the first time in adolescence.

to whether or not they learn English, develop social networks beyond their ethnic group, and become culturally competent in their new country. Second-generation immigrants are more likely to think of themselves as "American," possibly because citizenship is granted at birth. For second-generation immigrants, ethnic identity is likely to be linked to retention of their ethnic language and social networks. In the third and later generations, the issues become more complex. Broad social factors may affect the extent to which members of this generation retain their ethnic identities. For example, media images may either discourage or encourage members of an ethnic group from identifying with their group or retaining parts of its culture. Discrimination may force people to see themselves as cut off from the majority group and encourage them to seek the support of their own ethnic culture.

The immediate contexts in which ethnic minority youth live also influence their identity development (Spencer, 2006). In the United States, many ethnic minority youth live in pockets of poverty, are exposed to drugs, gangs, and crime, and interact with youth and adults who have dropped out of school or are unemployed. Support for developing a positive identity is scarce. In such settings, programs for youth can make an important contribution to identity development.

Researchers are increasingly finding that a positive ethnic identity is linked to positive outcomes for ethnic minority adolescents (Umana-Taylor, 2006; Umana-Taylor, Bhanot, & Shin, 2006). Consider these three studies:

- Ethnic identity was related to higher school engagement and lower aggression (Van Buren & Graham, 2003)
- A stronger ethnic identity was associated with higher self-esteem in African American, Latino, and Asian American youth (Bracey, Bamaca, & Umana-Taylor, 2004).
- The strength of ninth-grade students' ethnic identification was a better predictor of their academic success than the specific ethnic labels they used to describe themselves (Fuligni, Witkow, & Garcia, 2005). In this study, the ethnic groups most likely to incorporate more of their family's national origin and cultural background into their ethnic identification were Mexican and Chinese immigrants.

Emotional Development

Adolescence has long been described as a time of emotional turmoil (Hall, 1904). In its extreme form, this view is too stereotypical because adolescents are not constantly in a state of "storm and stress." Nonetheless, early adolescence is a time when emotional highs and lows increase (Rosenblum & Lewis, 2003; Scaramella & Conger, 2004). Young adolescents can be on top of the world one moment and down in the dumps the next. In many instances, the intensity of their emotions seems out of proportion to the events that elicit them (Steinberg & Levine, 1997). Young adolescents might sulk a lot, not knowing how to adequately express their feelings. With little or no provocation, they might blow up at their parents or siblings, which could involve using the defense mechanism of displacing their feelings onto another person.

Reed Larson and Maryse Richards (1994) found that adolescents reported more extreme emotions and more fleeting emotions than their parents did. For example, adolescents were five times more likely to report being "very happy" and three times more likely to report being "very sad" than their parents (see Figure 16.2). These findings lend support to the perception of adolescents as moody and changeable (Rosenblum & Lewis, 2003).

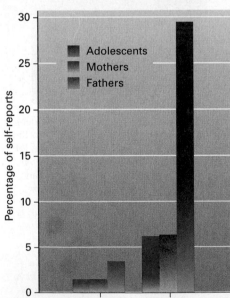

FIGURE 16.2 Self-Reported Extremes of Emotion by Adolescents, Mothers, and Fathers Using the Experience Sampling Method In the study by Reed Larson and Maryse Richards (1994), adolescents and their mothers and fathers were beeped at random times by researchers using the experience sampling method. The researchers found that adolescents were more likely to report more emotional extremes than their parents.

Researchers have also found that from the fifth through the ninth grades, both boys and girls experience a 50 percent decrease in being "very happy" (Larson & Lampman-Petraitis, 1989). In this same study, adolescents were more likely than preadolescents to report mildly negative mood states.

It is important for adults to recognize that moodiness is a *normal* aspect of early adolescence, and most adolescents make it through these moody times to become competent adults. Nonetheless, for some adolescents, such emotions can reflect serious problems. For example, rates of depressed moods become more elevated for girls during adolescence (Nolen-Hoeksema, 2007). We will have more to say about depression later in the chapter.

What causes the emotional swings of early adolescence? As we saw in Chapter 14, significant hormonal changes characterize puberty. Emotional fluctuations in early adolescence may be related to the variability of hormones during this time period. Moods become less extreme as adolescents move into adulthood, and this decrease in emotional fluctuation may be due to adaptation to hormone levels over time (Rosenbaum & Lewis, 2003).

Researchers have discovered that pubertal change is associated with an increase in negative emotions (Archibald, Graber, & Brooks-Gunn, 2003; Brooks-Gunn, Graber, & Paikoff, 1994; Dorn, Williamson, & Ryan, 2002). However, most researchers conclude that hormonal influences are small, and that when they occur they usually are associated with other factors, such as stress, eating patterns, sexual activity, and social relationships (Rosenbaum & Lewis, 2003; Susman, Dorn, & Schiefelbein, 2003; Susman & Rogol, 2004).

Indeed, environmental experiences may contribute more to the emotions of adolescence than hormonal changes. Recall from Chapter 14 that in one study, social factors accounted for two to four times as much variance as hormonal factors in young adolescent girls' depression and anger (Brooks-Gunn & Warren, 1989). In sum, both hormonal changes and environmental experiences are involved in the changing emotional landscape of adolescence.

Being able to control one's emotions is an important aspect of adolescent development. For example, one study revealed the importance of emotion regulation and mood in academic success (Gumora & Arsanio, 2002). Even when their level of cognitive ability was controlled, young adolescents who said they experienced more negative emotion regarding academic routines had lower grade point averages.

REVIEW AND REFLECT ▸ LEARNING GOAL 1

1 **Discuss changes in the self and emotional development during adolescence.**

Review
- What are some changes in self-esteem that take place in adolescence?
- How does identity develop in adolescence?
- What factors affect emotional development in adolescence?

Reflect
- Where are you in your identity development? Get out a sheet of paper and list each of the pieces of identity (vocational, political, religious, relationship achievement/intellectual, sexual, gender, cultural/ethnic, interest, personality, and physical) in a column on the left side of the paper. Then write the four identity statuses (diffused, foreclosed, moratorium, and achieved) across the top of the page. Next to each dimension of identity, place a check mark in the appropriate space that reflects your identity status for the particular aspect of identity. If you checked diffused or foreclosed for any of the dimensions, think about what you need to do to move on to a moratorium status in those areas.

② WHAT IS THE NATURE OF PARENT–ADOLESCENT RELATIONSHIPS?

Autonomy and Attachment   Parent–Adolescent Conflict

In Chapter 13, we discussed how, during middle and late childhood, parents spend less time with their children than in early childhood. We saw that discipline during these years involves an increased use of reasoning and deprivation of privileges, and that there is a gradual transfer of control from parents to children, producing coregulation. Adolescence typically alters the relationship between parents and their children. Among the most important aspects of family relationships in adolescence are those that involve autonomy, attachment, and parent-adolescent conflict.

Autonomy and Attachment

When I was a boy of 14, my father was so ignorant I could hardly stand to have the man around. But when I got to be 21, I was astonished at how much he had learnt in 7 years.

—MARK TWAIN
American Writer and Humorist, 20th Century

Jewel, whom we met in the chapter opening, has an unusual relationship with her mother. When Jewel was a child, her mother would take her to community events around the city. Now the two still often attend events together, and Jewel jokes that her mother is her press secretary (Silva, 2005).

If Jewel and her mother instead matched stereotypes, Jewel would probably be doing all that she could to escape her mother's company. Jewel's actual behavior illustrates the dangers of overgeneralization, but it is, after all, the typical adolescent that we're most interested in. With most adolescents, parents are likely to find themselves engaged in a delicate balancing act, weighing competing needs for autonomy and control, for independence and connection.

The Push for Autonomy The typical adolescent's push for autonomy and responsibility puzzles and angers many parents. Parents see their teenager slipping from their grasp. They may have an urge to take stronger control as the adolescent seeks autonomy and responsibility. Heated emotional exchanges may ensue, with either side calling names, making threats, and doing whatever seems necessary to gain control. Parents may seem frustrated because they *expect* their teenager to heed their advice, to want to spend time with the family, and to grow up to do what is right. Most parents anticipate that their teenager will have some difficulty adjusting to the changes that adolescence brings, but few parents imagine and predict just how strong an adolescent's desires will be to spend time with peers or how much adolescents will want to show that it is they—not their parents—who are responsible for their successes and failures.

The ability to attain autonomy and gain control over one's behavior in adolescence is acquired through appropriate adult reactions to the adolescent's desire for control (Collins & Steinberg, 2006). At the onset of adolescence, the average individual does not have the knowledge to make appropriate or mature decisions in all areas of life. As the adolescent pushes for autonomy, the wise adult relinquishes control in those areas in which the adolescent can make reasonable decisions but continues to guide the adolescent to make reasonable decisions in areas in which the adolescent's knowledge is more limited. Gradually, adolescents acquire the ability to make mature decisions on their own.

Gender differences characterize autonomy-granting in adolescence. In general, boys are given more independence than girls. In one study, this was especially true in U.S. families with a traditional gender-role orientation (Bumpus, Crouter, & McHale, 2001).

What are strategies parents can use to guide adolescents in effectively handling their increased motivation for autonomy?

The Role of Attachment Recall from Chapter 7 that one of the most widely discussed aspects of socioemotional development in infancy is secure attachment to caregivers. In the past decade, researchers have explored whether secure attachment also might be an important concept in adolescents' relationships with their parents (Furman, 2007; Zimmerman, 2007). For example, Joseph Allen and his colleagues (Allen, 2007; Allen, Kuperminc, & Moore, 2005; Allen & others, 1998, 2002) found that securely attached adolescents were less likely than those who were insecurely attached to engage in problem behaviors, such as juvenile delinquency and drug abuse.

Other research has examined possible links between secure attachment to parents and good relations with peers. Researchers have found that securely attached adolescents had better peer relations than their insecurely attached counterparts (Kobak, 1999; Laible, Carlo, & Raffaeli, 2000). However, the correlations between adolescent-parent attachments and adolescent outcomes are moderate, indicating that the success or failure of parent-adolescent attachments does not necessarily guarantee success or failure in peer relationships (Buhrmester, 2003).

Clearly, secure attachment with parents can be an asset for the adolescent, fostering the trust to engage in close relationships with others and laying the foundation for skills in close relationships. But a significant minority of adolescents from strong, supportive families nonetheless struggle in peer relations for a variety of reasons, such as being physically unattractive, maturing late, and experiencing cultural and SES discrepancies. On the other hand, some adolescents from troubled families find a positive, fresh start with peer relations that can compensate for their problematic family backgrounds.

Balancing Freedom and Control We have seen that parents play very important roles in adolescent development (Collins & Steinberg, 2006; Harold, Colarossi, & Mercier, 2007). Although adolescents are moving toward independence, they still need to stay connected with families (Bradshaw & Garbarino, 2004). The following studies document the important roles that parents play in adolescents' development:

- In the National Longitudinal Study on Adolescent Health (Council of Economic Advisors, 2000) of more than 12,000 adolescents, those who did not eat dinner with a parent five or more days a week had dramatically higher rates of smoking, drinking, marijuana use, getting into fights, and initiation of sexual activity.
- In another study, parents who played an active role in monitoring and guiding their adolescents' development were more likely to have adolescents with positive peer relations and lower drug use than parents who had a less active role (Mounts, 2002).

A recent longitudinal study provides further evidence of links between adolescents' relationship with their parents and their behavior (Goldstein & others, 2005). Young adolescents' perceptions of autonomy and warmth in relationships with parents in the seventh grade were linked with the adolescents' participation in risky peer contexts (such as going along with a peer to engage in deviant behavior) in the eighth grade, which in turn was related to the adolescents' engagement in deviant behavior (such as delinquency or drug use) in the eleventh grade. In terms of autonomy, young adolescents who perceived that they had a high degree of freedom over their daily activities (such as how late they could stay out and whether they could date) participated in extensive unsupervised interactions with peers, which in turn was related to deviant behaviors in the eleventh grade. Also, young adolescents who perceived their parents as too intrusive tended to frequently interact with peers who engaged in deviant behavior, which in turn was linked with deviant behavior in the eleventh grade. Thus, it is important for parents to maintain a delicate balance between not permitting too much freedom with peers and being too intrusive in their young adolescents' lives. Another important result in this study was that young adolescents who indicated they had less positive relationships with their parents tended to have an extreme peer orientation, which in turn was linked to engaging in deviant behavior in the eleventh grade.

Parent-Adolescent Conflict

While attachment to parents remains strong for many adolescents, the connectedness is not always smooth. Early adolescence is a time when conflict with parents escalates beyond childhood levels. This increase may be due to a number of factors: the biological changes of puberty, cognitive changes involving increased idealism and logical reasoning, social changes focused on independence and identity, maturational changes in parents, and expectations that are violated by parents and adolescents. Researchers have found that early-maturing adolescents experience more conflict with their parents than those who mature on time or late (Collins & Steinberg, 2006). Many adolescents compare their parents to an ideal standard and then criticize their flaws.

Many parents see their adolescent changing from a compliant child to someone who is noncompliant, oppositional, and resistant to parental standards. When this happens, parents tend to clamp down and put more pressure on the adolescent to conform to parental standards. Parents often expect their adolescents to become mature adults overnight, instead of understanding that the journey takes 10 to 15 years. Parents who recognize that this transition takes time handle their youth more competently and calmly than those who demand immediate conformity to adult standards. The opposite tactic—letting adolescents do as they please without supervision—is also unwise.

Although parent-adolescent conflict increases in early adolescence, it does not reach the tumultuous proportions G. Stanley Hall envisioned at the beginning of the twentieth century (Collins & Steinberg, 2006; Smetana, Campione-Barr, & Metzger, 2006). Rather, much of the conflict involves the everyday events of family life, such as keeping a bedroom clean, dressing neatly, getting home by a certain time, and not talking forever on the phone. The conflicts usually do not involve major dilemmas, such as drugs and delinquency.

It is not unusual to hear parents of young adolescents ask, "Is it ever going to get better?" Things usually do get better as adolescents move from early to late adolescence. Conflict with parents often escalates during early adolescence, remains somewhat stable during the high school years, and then lessens as the adolescent reaches 17 to 20 years of age. Parent-adolescent relationships may become more positive if adolescents go away to college than if they attend college while living at home (Sullivan & Sullivan, 1980).

It is not enough for parents to understand children. They must accord children the privilege of understanding them.
—MILTON SAPIRSTEIN
American Psychiatrist, 20th Century

The everyday conflicts that characterize parent-adolescent relationships may actually serve a positive developmental function. These minor disputes and negotiations facilitate the adolescent's transition from being dependent on parents to becoming an autonomous individual. For example, in one study, adolescents who expressed disagreement with their parents explored identity development more actively than did adolescents who did not express disagreement with their parents (Cooper & others, 1982). Recognizing that conflict and negotiation can serve a positive developmental function can tone down parental hostility. Understanding parent-adolescent conflict, though, is not simple (Conger & Ge, 1999).

In sum, the old model of parent-adolescent relationships suggested that as adolescents mature they detach themselves from parents and move into a world of autonomy apart from parents. The old model also suggested that parent-adolescent conflict is intense and stressful throughout adolescence. The new model emphasizes that parents serve as important attachment figures and support systems as adolescents explore a wider, more complex social world. The new model also emphasizes that, in most families, parent-adolescent conflict is moderate rather than severe and

Old Model		New Model
Autonomy, detachment from parents; parent and peer worlds are isolated		Attachment and autonomy; parents are important support systems and attachment figures; adolescent-parent and adolescent-peer worlds have some important connections
Intense, stressful conflict throughout adolescence; parent-adolescent relationships are filled with storm and stress on virtually a daily basis		Moderate parent-adolescent conflict is common and can serve a positive developmental function; conflict greater in early adolescence

FIGURE 16.3 Old and New Models of Parent-Adolescent Relationships

that the everyday negotiations and minor disputes are normal and can serve the positive developmental function of helping the adolescent make the transition from childhood dependency to adult independence (see Figure 16.3).

Still, a high degree of conflict characterizes some parent-adolescent relationships. One estimate of the proportion of parents and adolescents who engage in prolonged, intense, repeated, unhealthy conflict is about one in five families (Montemayor, 1982). While this figure represents a minority of adolescents, it indicates that 4 to 5 million American families encounter serious, highly stressful parent-adolescent conflict. And this prolonged, intense conflict is associated with a number of adolescent problems—movement out of the home, juvenile delinquency, school dropout, pregnancy and early marriage, membership in religious cults, and drug abuse (Brook & others, 1990). To read about some strategies for parenting adolescents, see the *Caring for Children* interlude.

Caring for Children

STRATEGIES FOR PARENTING ADOLESCENTS

Following are some effective strategies parents can use to increase the likelihood that adolescents will develop in positive ways:

1. *Show them warmth and respect, and avoid the tendency to be too controlling or too permissive.*
2. *Demonstrate sustained interest in their lives.* Parents need to spend time with their adolescents and monitor their lives.
3. *Understand and adapt to their cognitive and socioemotional development.*
4. *Communicate expectations for high standards of conduct and achievement.*
5. *Display constructive ways of dealing with problems and conflict.* Moderate conflict is a normal part of the adolescent's desire for independence and search for an identity.
6. *Model behaviors expected from children.* When parents state rules about such matters as drinking, driving, finances, and societal duties, and then don't adhere to the rules themselves, adolescents wonder why the rules should apply to them.
7. *Understand that adolescents don't become adults overnight.* Adolescence is a long journey.

3 WHAT ASPECTS OF PEER RELATIONSHIPS ARE IMPORTANT IN ADOLESCENCE?

Friendships   Peer Groups   Dating and Romantic Relationships

Peers play powerful roles in the lives of adolescents. When you think back to your adolescent years, many of your most enjoyable moments probably were spent with peers—on the telephone, in school activities, in the neighborhood, at dances, or just hanging out. But peer relations can have positive or negative effects on adolescents. For example, having friends who are into school, sports, or religion is likely to have a positive influence on the adolescent. However, hanging out with the wrong peers can lead to varied problems. Consider the results of these three recent studies:

- Hanging out with antisocial peers in adolescence was a stronger predictor of substance abuse than relationships with parents (Nation & Heflinger, 2006).
- Higher levels of antisocial peer involvement in early adolescence (13 to 16 years of age) were linked with higher rates of delinquent behavior in late adolescence (17 to 18 years of age (Laird & others, 2005).
- Deviant peer affiliation was related to adolescents' depressive symptoms (Connell & Dishion, 2006).

Peer relations undergo important changes in adolescence, including changes in friendships and in peer groups and the beginning of romantic relationships. Being overlooked or, worse yet, being rejected can have damaging effects on children's development that sometimes are carried forward to adolescence (Bukowski, Brendgen, & Vitaro, 2007; Rubin, Bukowski, & Parker, 2006).

Friendships

For most children, being popular with their peers is a strong motivator. The focus of their peer relations is on being liked by classmates and being included in games or lunchroom conversations. Beginning in early adolescence, however, teenagers typically prefer to have a smaller number of friendships that are more intense and intimate than those of young children.

Harry Stack Sullivan (1953) was the most influential theorist to discuss the importance of adolescent friendships. In contrast to other psychoanalytic theorists who focused almost exclusively on parent-child relationships, Sullivan argued that friends are also important in shaping the development of children and adolescents.

What changes take place in friendship during the adolescent years?

Everyone, said Sullivan, has basic social needs, such as the need for tenderness (secure attachment), playful companionship, social acceptance, intimacy, and sexual relations. Whether or not these needs are fulfilled largely determines our emotional well-being. For example, if the need for playful companionship goes unmet, then we become bored and depressed; if the need for social acceptance is not met, we suffer a lowered sense of self-worth.

During adolescence, said Sullivan, friends become increasingly important in meeting social needs. In particular, Sullivan argued that the need for intimacy intensifies during early adolescence, motivating teenagers to seek out close friends. If adolescents fail to forge such close friendships, they experience loneliness and a reduced sense of self-worth.

Many of Sullivan's ideas have withstood the test of time (Buhrmester, 2005). For example, adolescents report disclosing intimate and personal information to their friends more often than do younger children (Buhrmester, 1998) (see Figure 16.4). Adolescents also say they depend more on friends than on parents to satisfy their needs for companionship, reassurance of worth, and intimacy. The ups and downs of experiences with friends shape adolescents' well-being (Berndt, 2002).

Although most adolescents develop friendships with individuals who are close to their own age, some adolescents become best friends with younger or older individuals. Do older friends encourage adolescents to engage in delinquent behavior or early sexual behavior? Adolescents who interact with older youth do engage in these behaviors more frequently, but it is not known whether the older youth guide younger adolescents toward deviant behavior or whether the younger adolescents were already prone to deviant behavior before they developed the friendship with the older youth (Billy, Rodgers, & Udry, 1984).

Peer Groups

Unlike children, whose groups are usually informal collections of friends or neighborhood acquaintances, adolescents are often members of formal and heterogeneous groups, including adolescents beyond their friends and neighborhood acquaintances. For example, try to recall the student council, honor society, or football team at your junior high school. These organizations probably included many people you had not met before and may have included adolescents from various ethnic groups.

Do these and other peer groups matter? Yes, they do. Researchers have found that the standards of peer groups, and the influence of crowds and cliques, become increasingly important during adolescence.

Peer Pressure Young adolescents conform more to peer standards than children do. Around the eighth and ninth grades, conformity to peers—especially to their antisocial standards—peaks (Leventhal, 1994). At this point, adolescents are most likely to go along with a peer to steal hubcaps off a car, draw graffiti on a wall, or steal cosmetics from a store counter. U.S. adolescents are more likely to put pressure on their peers to resist parental influence than Japanese adolescents are (Rothbaum & others, 2000).

Cliques and Crowds Cliques and crowds assume more important roles in the lives of adolescents than children (Brown, 2004; Verkooijen, de Vries, & Nielsen, 2007). **Cliques** are small groups that range from two to about twelve individuals and average about five to six individuals. The clique members are usually of the same sex and about the same age.

Cliques can form because adolescents engage in similar activities, such as being in a club or on a sports team. Some cliques also form because of friendship. Several adolescents may form a clique because they have spent time with each other and enjoy each other's company. Not necessarily friends, they often develop a friendship if they stay in the clique.

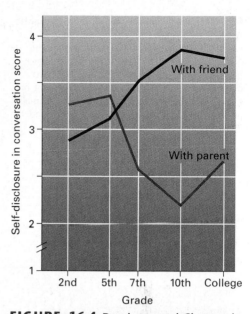

FIGURE 16.4 Developmental Changes in Self-Disclosing Conversations Self-disclosing conversations with friends increased dramatically in adolescence while declining in an equally dramatic fashion with parents. However, self-disclosing conversations with parents began to pick up somewhat during the college years. The measure of self-disclosure involved a 5-point rating scale completed by the children and youth, with a higher score representing greater self-disclosure. The data shown represent the means for each age group.

Most adolescents conform to the mainstream standards of their peers. However, the rebellious or anticonformist adolescent reacts counter to the mainstream peer group's expectations. These adolescents deliberately move away from the actions or beliefs this group advocates.

clique A small group that ranges from two to about twelve individuals, averaging about five to six individuals, and can form because adolescents engage in similar activities.

FIGURE 16.5 **Age of Onset of Romantic Activity** In this study, announcing that "I like" someone occurred earliest, followed by going out with the same person three or more times, having an exclusive relationship for over two months, and finally planning an engagement or marriage (which characterized only a very small percentage of participants by the twelfth grade) (Buhrmester, 2001).

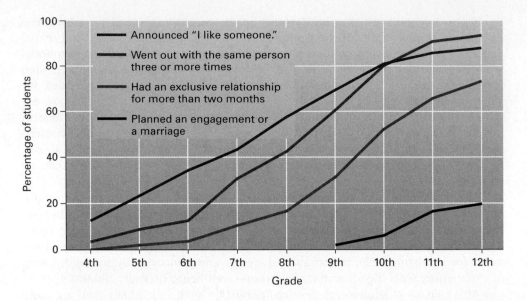

What do adolescents do in cliques? They share ideas and hang out together. Often they develop an in-group identity in which they believe that their clique is better than other cliques.

Crowds are larger than cliques and less personal. Adolescents are usually members of a crowd based on reputation, and they may or may not spend much time together. Many crowds are defined by the activities adolescents engage in (such as "jocks" who are good at sports or "druggies" who take drugs) (Brown, 2004). Reputation-based crowds often appear for the first time in early adolescence and usually become less prominent in late adolescence (Collins & Steinberg, 2006).

In one study, crowd membership was associated with adolescent self-esteem (Brown & Lohr, 1987). The crowds included jocks (athletically oriented), populars (well-known students who led social activities), normals (middle-of-the-road students who made up the masses), druggies or toughs (known for illicit drug use or other delinquent activities), and nobodies (low in social skills or intellectual abilities). The self-esteem of the jocks and the populars was highest, whereas that of the nobodies was lowest. One group of adolescents not in a crowd had self-esteem equivalent to that of the jocks and the populars; this group was the independents, who indicated that crowd membership was not important to them. Keep in mind that these data are correlational; self-esteem could increase an adolescent's probability of becoming a crowd member, just as crowd membership could increase the adolescent's self-esteem.

Dating and Romantic Relationships

Adolescents spend considerable time either dating or thinking about romantic relationships. Dating can be a form of recreation, a source of status, a setting for learning about close relationships, as well as a way of finding a mate.

Developmental Changes in Romantic Relationships Can you remember confiding to a friend in middle school or junior high that you "liked" someone? Or what is was like when you first had an exclusive relationship with someone, "going out" with that person and only that person? One study found that 40 percent of the sixth-graders studied had announced that "I like" someone (Buhrmester, 2001) (see Figure 16.5). But it wasn't until the tenth grade that half of the adolescents had had a romantic relationship that lasted two months or longer. By the twelfth grade, a quarter of the adolescents still had not had a romantic relationship that lasted two months or longer. Another study found that 35 percent of 15- to 16-year-olds, and almost

crowd A larger group structure than a clique, a crowd is usually formed based on reputation, and members may or may not spend much time together.

60 percent of 17- and 18-year-olds, had had dating relationships that endured for 11 months or longer (Carver, Joyner, & Udry, 2003).

In their early exploration of romantic relationships, today's adolescents often find comfort in numbers and begin hanging out together in mixed-sex groups. Sometimes they just hang out at someone's house or get organized enough to get someone to drive them to a mall or a movie (Peterson, 1997). Or they may try *cyberdating*—"dating" over the Internet—as another alternative to traditional dating (Thomas, 1998). Cyberdating is popular especially among middle school students. Of course, cyberdating is hazardous since one does not know who is really at the other end of the computer link. By the time they reach high school and are able to drive, most adolescents are more interested in real-life dating.

The functions of dating and romantic relationships also tend to change over the course of adolescence. Young adolescents are likely to see romantic relationships, not as a way of fulfilling attachment or sexual needs, but as a context for exploring how attractive they are, how they should romantically interact with someone, and how all of this looks to the peer group (Brown, 1999). In one study of heterosexual adolescents, young adolescents frequently mentioned companionship, intimacy, and support as positive aspects of romantic relationships, but not love and security (Feiring, 1996). Also, the young adolescents described physical attraction more in terms of cute, pretty, or handsome than in sexual terms (such as being a good kisser). (Possibly the failure to discuss sexual interests was due to the adolescents' discomfort in talking about such personal feelings with an unfamiliar adult.) Attachment and sexual needs become central to these relationships only after adolescents learn how to interact with romantic partners (Bouchey & Furman, 2003; Furman & Shaeffer, 2003).

What are dating relationships like in adolescence?

Romantic Relationships in Gay and Lesbian Youth Recently, researchers have begun to study romantic relationships in gay, lesbian, and bisexual youth (Savin-Williams, 2006). Many sexual minority youth date other-sex peers, which can help them to clarify their sexual orientation or disguise it from others (Savin-Williams & Diamond, 2004). Most gay and lesbian youth have had some same-sex sexual experience, often with peers who are "experimenting" and then go on to a primarily heterosexual orientation. However, relatively few have same-sex romantic relationships because of limited opportunities and social disapproval of same-sex relationships (Diamond, 2003). In one study, gay and lesbian youth rated the breakup of a current romance as their second most stressful problem, second only to disclosure of their sexual orientation to their parents (D'Augelli, 1991).

Gender Differences How adolescents behave on a date depends on their **dating scripts,** which are cognitive models that guide dating interactions. In one study of heterosexual adolescents, first dates were highly scripted along gender lines that gave males more power than females (Rose & Frieze, 1993). The male's script involved initiating the date (asking for and planning it), controlling the public domain (driving and opening doors), and initiating sexual interaction (making physical contact, making out, and kissing). The female's script focused on the private domain (concern about appearance, enjoying the date), participating in the structure of the date established by the male (being picked up, having doors opened), and responding to sexual overtures. Gender differences also occur in the motivations that adolescents bring to dating. In one study of heterosexual adolescents, 15-year-old girls were more likely to describe romance in terms of interpersonal qualities, the boys in terms of physical attraction (Feiring, 1996).

Sociocultural Contexts and Dating The sociocultural context exerts a powerful influence on adolescents' dating patterns. This influence may be seen in differences in dating patterns among ethnic groups within the United States. For example, one study found that Asian American adolescents were less likely to be involved

dating scripts The cognitive models that individuals use to guide dating interactions.

What are some ethnic variations in dating during adolescence?

How is emotion involved in adolescent romantic relationships?

in a romantic relationship in the past 18 months than African American or Latino adolescents (Carver, Joyner, & Udry, 2003).

Values, religious beliefs, and traditions often dictate the age at which dating begins, how much freedom in dating is allowed, whether dates must be chaperoned by adults or parents, and the roles of males and females in dating. For example, Latino and Asian American cultures have more conservative standards regarding adolescent dating than does the Anglo-American culture. Dating may become a source of conflict within a family if the parents have immigrated from cultures in which dating begins at a late age, little freedom in dating is allowed, dates are chaperoned, and adolescent girl dating is especially restricted. When immigrant adolescents choose to adopt the ways of the dominant U.S. culture (such as unchaperoned dating), they often clash with parents and extended-family members who have more traditional values.

In one study, Latina young adults in the midwestern United States reflected on their experiences in dating during adolescence (Raffaeli & Ontai, 2003). They said that their parents placed strict boundaries on their romantic involvement. As a result, the young women said that their adolescent dating experiences were filled with tension and conflict. Over half of the Latinas engaged in "sneak dating" without their parents' knowledge.

Dating and Adjustment Researchers have linked dating and romantic relationships with various measures of how well adjusted adolescents are (Barber, 2006; Fisher, 2006). Not surprisingly, one study of tenth-grade adolescents found that those who dated were more likely than those who did not date to be accepted by their peers and to be perceived as more physically attractive (Furman, Ho, & Low, 2005). Another recent study of 14- to 19-year-olds found that adolescents who were not involved in a romantic relationship had more social anxiety than their counterparts who were dating or romantically involved (La Greca & Harrison, 2005). But tenth-grade adolescents who dated also had more externalized problems such as delinquency and engaged in substance use (as well as genital sexual behavior) more than their counterparts who did not date (Furman, Ho, & Low, 2005).

Dating and romantic relationships at an unusually early age have been linked with several problems (Smetana, Campione-Barr, & Metzger, 2006). Early dating and "going with" someone is associated with adolescent pregnancy and problems at home and school (Florsheim, 2003). In one study, girls' early romantic involvement was linked with lower grades, less active participation in class discussion, and school-related problems (Buhrmester, 2001).

REVIEW AND **REFLECT** ◆ **LEARNING GOAL 3**

3 **Characterize the changes that occur in peer relations during adolescence.**

Review
- What changes take place in friendship during adolescence?
- What are adolescents' peer groups like?
- What is the nature of adolescent dating and romantic relationships?

Reflect
- What were your peer relationships like during adolescence? What peer groups were you involved in? How did they influence your development? What were your dating and romantic relationships like in adolescence? If you could change anything about the way you experienced peer relations in adolescence, what would it be?

4 WHY IS CULTURE AN IMPORTANT CONTEXT FOR ADOLESCENT DEVELOPMENT?

Cross-Cultural
Comparisons

Ethnicity

We live in an increasingly diverse world, one in which there is increasing contact between adolescents from different cultures and ethnic groups. In this section, we explore how adolescents vary cross-culturally and how ethnicity affects U.S. adolescents and their development.

Cross-Cultural Comparisons

What are the world's youth like? What traditions remain for adolescents around the globe? What circumstances are changing adolescents' lives?

Some experts argue that adolescence too often is thought of in a "Eurocentric" way (Nsamenang, 2002). Others note that advances in transportation and telecommunication are spawning a global youth culture in which adolescents everywhere wear the same type of clothing and have similar hairstyles, listen to the same music, and use similar slang expressions (Schegel, 2000). But cultural differences among adolescents have by no means disappeared (Larson & Wilson, 2004; Shiraev & Levy, 2007).

Traditions and Changes in Adolescence Around the Globe   Consider some of the variations of adolescence around the world (Brown & Larson, 2002):

- Two-thirds of Asian Indian adolescents accept their parents' choice of a marital partner for them (Verma & Saraswathi, 2002).
- In the Philippines, many female adolescents sacrifice their own futures by migrating to the city to earn money that they can send home to their families.
- In the Middle East, many adolescents are not allowed to interact with the other sex, even in school (Booth, 2002).
- Street youth in Kenya and other parts of the world learn to survive under highly stressful circumstances (Nsamenang, 2002). In some cases abandoned by their parents, they may engage in delinquency or prostitution to provide for their economic needs.
- Individuals in the United States are marrying later than in past generations, whereas youth in Russia are marrying earlier to legitimize sexual activity (Stetsenko, 2002).

Thus, depending on the culture being observed, adolescence may involve many different experiences (Larson & Wilson, 2004).

Some cultures have retained their traditions regarding adolescence, but rapid global change is altering the experience of adolescence in many places, presenting new opportunities and challenges to young people's health and well-being. Around the world, adolescents' experiences may differ (Brown & Larson, 2002; Larson & Wilson, 2004).

Health   Adolescent health and well-being have improved in some respects but not in others. Overall, fewer adolescents around the world die from infectious diseases and malnutrition now than in the past (Call & others, 2002; World Health Organization, 2002). However, a number of adolescent health-compromising behaviors (especially illicit drug use and unprotected sex) are increasing in frequency (Blum & Nelson-Mmari, 2004). Extensive increases in the rates of HIV in adolescents have occurred in many sub-Saharan countries (World Health Organization, 2002).

Gender   Around the world, the experiences of male and female adolescents continue to be quite different (Brown & Larson, 2002; Larson & Wilson, 2004). Except in a few areas, such as Japan, the Philippines, and Western countries, males have far greater access to educational opportunities than females. In many countries, adolescent females have less freedom to pursue a variety of careers and engage in various leisure acts than males. Gender differences in sexual expression are widespread, especially in India, Southeast Asia, Latin America, and Arab countries where there are far more restrictions on the sexual activity of adolescent females than on males. These gender differences do appear to be narrowing over time, however. In some countries, educational and career opportunities for women are expanding, and in some parts of the world control over adolescent girls' romantic and sexual relationships is weakening.

Family In some countries, adolescents grow up in closely knit families with extensive extended-kin networks "that provide a web of connections and reinforce a traditional way of life" (Brown & Larson, 2002, p. 6). For example, in Arab countries, "adolescents are taught strict codes of conduct and loyalty" (p. 6). However, in Western countries such as the United States, parenting is less authoritarian than in the past, and much larger numbers of adolescents are growing up in divorced families and stepfamilies.

In many countries around the world, current trends "include greater family mobility, migration to urban areas, family members working in distant cities or countries, smaller families, fewer extended-family households, and increases in mothers' employment" (Brown & Larson, 2002, p. 7). Unfortunately, many of these changes may reduce the ability of families to provide time and resources for adolescents.

The typical relationship between parents and adolescents varies among cultures. For example, in some cultures there is less parent-adolescent conflict than in others. American psychologist Reed Larson (1999) spent six months in India studying middle-socioeconomic-status adolescents and their families. He observed that in India there seems to be little parent-adolescent conflict, and that many families likely would be described as "authoritarian" in Baumrind's categorization (discussed in Chapter 10). Researchers also have found considerably less conflict between parents and adolescents in Japan than in the United States (Rothbaum & others, 2000).

The extent to which adolescents push for autonomy also varies. Larson observed that in India many adolescents do not go through a process of breaking away from their parents, and that parents choose their youths' marital partners. In one study, U.S. adolescents sought autonomy earlier than Japanese adolescents (Rothbaum & others, 2000). In the transition to adulthood, Japanese youth are less likely to live outside the home than Americans (Hendry, 1999).

School In general, the number of adolescents in school in developing countries is increasing. However, schools in many parts of the world—especially Africa, South Asia, and Latin America—still do not provide education to all adolescents. Indeed, there has been a decline in the percentage of Latin American adolescents who have access to secondary and higher education (Welti, 2002). Furthermore, many schools do not provide students with the skills they need to be successful in adult work.

Peers Some cultures give peers a stronger role in adolescence than others (Brown, 2004; Brown & Larson, 2002). In most Western nations, peers figure prominently in adolescents' lives, in some cases taking on roles that are otherwise assumed by parents. Among street youth in South America, the peer network serves as a surrogate family that supports survival in dangerous and stressful settings. In other regions of the world, such as in Arab countries, peers have a very restrictive role, especially for girls (Booth, 2002).

In sum, adolescents' lives are characterized by a combination of change and tradition. Researchers have found both similarities and differences in the experiences of adolescents in different countries (Larson & Wilson, 2004). To read about how adolescents around the world spend their time, see the *Diversity in Children's Development* interlude.

Street youth in Rio de Janeiro. *What are some cultural variations in adolescent peer relations?*

Diversity in Children's Development

HOW ADOLESCENTS AROUND THE WORLD SPEND THEIR TIME

Reed Larson and Suman Verma (Larson, 2001; Larson & Verma, 1999) have examined how adolescents spend their time in work, play, and developmental activities such as school. Figure 16.6 summarizes the average daily time use by adolescents in different regions of the world (Larson & Verma, 1999). U.S. adolescents spend about 60 percent as much time on schoolwork as East Asian adolescents do, which is mainly due to U.S. adolescents doing less homework.

What U.S. adolescents have in greater quantities than adolescents in other industrialized countries is discretionary time (Larson & Wilson, 2004). About 40 to 50 percent of U.S. adolescents' waking hours (not counting summer vacations) is spent in discretionary activities compared with 25 to 35 percent in East Asia and 35 to 45 percent in Europe. Whether this additional discretionary time is a liability or an asset for U.S. adolescents, of course, depends on how they use it.

According to Larson (2001), for optimal development, U.S. adolescents may have too much unstructured time because when adolescents are allowed to choose what they do with their time, they typically engage in unchallenging activities such as hanging out and watching TV. Although relaxation and social interaction are important aspects of adolescence, it seems unlikely that spending large numbers of hours per week in unchallenging activities fosters development. Structured voluntary activities may provide more promise for adolescent development than unstructured time, especially if adults give responsibility to adolescents, challenge them, and provide competent guidance in these activities (Larson, 2001).

How do East Asian and U.S. adolescents spend their time differently?

Activity	Nonindustrial, unschooled populations	Postindustrial, schooled populations		
		United States	**Europe**	**East Asia**
Household labor	5 to 9 hours	20 to 40 minutes	20 to 40 minutes	10 to 20 minutes
Paid labor	0.5 to 8 hours	40 to 60 minutes	10 to 20 minutes	0 to 10 minutes
Schoolwork	—	3.0 to 4.5 hours	4.0 to 5.5 hours	5.5 to 7.5 hours
Total work time	6 to 9 hours	4 to 6 hours	4.5 to 6.5 hours	6 to 8 hours
TV viewing	*Insufficient data*	1.5 to 2.5 hours	1.5 to 2.5 hours	1.5 to 2.5 hours
Talking	*Insufficient data*	2 to 3 hours	*Insufficient data*	45 to 60 minutes
Sports	*Insufficient data*	30 to 60 minutes	20 to 80 minutes	0 to 20 minutes
Structured voluntary activities	*Insufficient data*	10 to 20 minutes	1.0 to 20 minutes	0 to 10 minutes
Total free time	4 to 7 hours	6.5 to 8.0 hours	5.5 to 7.5 hours	4.0 to 5.5 hours

Note. The estimates in the table are averaged across a 7-day week, including weekdays and weekends. Time spent in maintenance activities like eating, personal care, and sleeping is not included. The data for nonindustrial, unschooled populations come primarily from rural peasant populations in developing countries.

FIGURE 16.6 Average Daily Time Use of Adolescents in Different Regions of the World

Rites of Passage Another variation in the experiences of adolescents in different cultures is whether the adolescents go through a rite of passage. Some societies have elaborate ceremonies that signal the adolescent's move to maturity and achievement of adult status (Kottak, 2004). A **rite of passage** is a ceremony or

rite of passage A ceremony or ritual that marks an individual's transition from one status to another. Most rites of passage focus on the transition to adult status.

These Congolese Kota boys painted their faces as part of a rite of passage to adulthood. *What rites of passage do American adolescents have?*

ritual that marks an individual's transition from one status to another. Most rites of passage focus on the transition to adult status. In many primitive cultures, rites of passage are the avenue through which adolescents gain access to sacred adult practices, to knowledge, and to sexuality. These rites often involve dramatic practices intended to facilitate the adolescent's separation from the immediate family, especially the mother. The transformation is usually characterized by some form of ritual death and rebirth, or by means of contact with the spiritual world. Bonds are forged between the adolescent and the adult instructors through shared rituals, hazards, and secrets to allow the adolescent to enter the adult world. This kind of ritual provides a forceful and discontinuous entry into the adult world at a time when the adolescent is perceived to be ready for the change.

Africa has been the location of many rites of passage for adolescents, especially sub-Saharan Africa. Under the influence of Western culture, many of the rites are disappearing today, although some vestiges remain. In locations where formal education is not readily available, rites of passage are still prevalent.

Do we have such rites of passage for American adolescents? We certainly do not have universal formal ceremonies that mark the passage from adolescence to adulthood. Certain religious and social groups do have initiation ceremonies that indicate that an advance in maturity has been reached—the Jewish bar or bat mitzvah, the Catholic confirmation, and social debuts, for example.

School graduation ceremonies come the closest to being culture-wide rites of passage in the United States. The high school graduation ceremony has become nearly universal for middle-class adolescents and increasing numbers of adolescents from low-income backgrounds. Nonetheless, high school graduation does not result in universal changes; many high school graduates continue to live with their parents, continue to be economically dependent on them, and continue to be undecided about career and lifestyle matters.

Another rite of passage for increasing numbers of American adolescents is sexual intercourse (Halonen & Santrock, 1999). By 19 years of age, four out of five American adolescents have had sexual intercourse.

Ethnicity

It is important for adolescents to learn to take the perspective of individuals from ethnic and cultural groups that are different from theirs and think, "If I were in their shoes, what kind of experiences might I have had?" "How would I feel if I were a member of their ethnic or cultural group?" "How would I think and behave if I had grown up in their world?" Such perspective taking often increases an adolescent's empathy and understanding of individuals from ethnic and cultural groups different from their own (Banks, 2006).

Earlier in this chapter, we explored the identity development of ethnic minority adolescents. Here we further examine immigration and the relationship between ethnicity and socioeconomic status.

Immigration   Relatively high rates of immigration are contributing to the growth of ethnic minorities in the United States (Berry, 2007; Phinney & Ong, 2007). Immigrants often experience stressors uncommon to, or less prominent among, longtime residents such as language barriers, dislocations and separations from support networks, changes in SES status, and the dual struggle to preserve identity and to acculturate (Chun & Akutsu, 2003).

Stanley Sue (1990) argues that the adjustment of immigrants to their new country may be complicated by the fact that both native-born Americans and immigrants may be torn between two values related to ethnic issues—assimilation and pluralism:

- **Assimilation** is the absorption of ethnic minority groups into the dominant group, which often means the loss of some or virtually all of the behavior

assimilation The absorption of ethnic minority groups into the dominant group, which often involves the loss of some or virtually all of the behavior and values of the ethnic group.

and values of the ethnic group. Individuals who endorse assimilation usually advocate that ethnic minority groups become more American.

- **Pluralism** is the coexistence of distinct ethnic and cultural groups in the same society, each of which maintains its cultural differences.

Many of the families that have immigrated in recent decades to the United States, such as Mexican Americans and Asian Americans, come from collectivist cultures in which family obligation and duty to one's family is strong (Fuligni & Fuligni, 2007). For adolescents, this family obligation may take the form of assisting parents in their occupations and contributing to the family's welfare (Parke & Buriel, 2006). This often means helping out in jobs in construction, gardening, cleaning, or restaurants. In some cases, the large number of hours immigrant youth work in such jobs can be detrimental to their academic achievement.

Jason Leonard, age 15: "I want America to know that most of us black teens are not troubled people from broken homes and headed to jail. . . . In my relationships with my parents, we show respect for each other and we have values in our house. We have traditions we celebrate together, including Christmas and Kwanzaa."

Ethnicity and Socioeconomic Status

Much of the research on ethnic minority adolescents has failed to tease apart the influences of ethnicity and socioeconomic status. Ethnicity and socioeconomic status can interact in ways that exaggerate the influence of ethnicity because ethnic minority individuals are overrepresented in the lower socioeconomic levels of American society (Doucet & Hamon, 2007; Wilson, 2007). Consequently, researchers too often have given ethnic explanations for aspects of adolescent development that were largely due instead to socioeconomic status. For example, decades of research on group differences in self-esteem failed to consider the socioeconomic status of African American and White children and adolescents. When African American adolescents from low-income backgrounds are compared with White adolescents from middle-income backgrounds, the differences often are large but not informative because of the confounding of ethnicity and socioeconomic status (Scott-Jones, 1995).

Although some ethnic minority youth have middle-income backgrounds, economic advantage does not entirely enable them to escape the burdens of ethnic minority status (Banks, 2008; Harris & Graham, 2007). Middle-income ethnic minority youth still encounter much of the prejudice, discrimination, and bias associated with being a member of an ethnic minority group. Often characterized as a "model minority" because of their strong achievement orientation and family cohesiveness, Japanese Americans still experience stress associated with ethnic minority status (Sue, 1990).

Not all ethnic minority families are poor. However, poverty contributes to the stressful life experiences of many ethnic minority adolescents (Hattery & Smith, 2007). Thus, many ethnic minority adolescents experience a double disadvantage: (1) prejudice, discrimination, and bias because of their ethnic minority status; and (2) the stressful effects of poverty.

Recent studies provide insight into the discrimination experienced by ethnic minority adolescents. In one study, discrimination of seventh- to tenth-grade African American students was related to their lower level of psychological functioning, including perceived stress, symptoms of depression, and lower perceived well-being; more positive attitudes toward African Americans were associated with more positive psychological functioning in adolescents (Sellers & others, 2006). Figure 16.7 shows the percentage of African American adolescents who reported experiencing different types of racial hassles in the past year. Also, in a study of Latino youth, discrimination was negatively linked, and social and parental support were positively related to their academic success (DeGarmo & Martinez, 2006).

Type of Racial Hassle	Percent of Adolescents Who Reported the Racial Hassle in the Past Year
Being accused of something or treated suspiciously	71.0
Being treated as if you were "stupid", being "talked down to"	70.7
Others reacting to you as if they were afraid or intimidated	70.1
Being observed or followed while in public places	69.1
Being treated rudely or disrespectfully	56.4
Being ignored, overlooked, not given service	56.4
Others expecting your work to be inferior	54.1
Being insulted, called a name or harassed	52.2

FIGURE 16.7 African-American Adolescents' Reports of Racial Hassles in the Past Year

pluralism The coexistence of distinct ethnic and cultural groups in the same society, each of which maintains its cultural differences.

REVIEW AND REFLECT **LEARNING GOAL 4**

4 **Explain how culture influences adolescent development.**

Review
- What are some comparisons of adolescents in different cultures? How do adolescents around the world spend their time? What are rites of passage?
- How does ethnicity influence adolescent development?

Reflect
- What is your ethnicity? Have you ever been stereotyped because of your ethnicity? How different is your identity from the mainstream culture?

5 WHAT ARE SOME SOCIOEMOTIONAL PROBLEMS IN ADOLESCENCE?

| Juvenile Delinquency | Depression and Suicide | The Interrelation of Problems and Successful Prevention/ Intervention Programs |

In Chapter 13, we described these adolescent problems: substance abuse, sexually transmitted infections, and eating disorders. Here, we examine the problems of juvenile delinquency, depression and suicide, and the interrelation of problems and successful programs for prevention/intervention.

Juvenile Delinquency

The label **juvenile delinquent** is applied to an adolescent who breaks the law or engages in behavior that is considered illegal. Like other categories of disorders, juvenile delinquency is a broad concept; legal infractions range from littering to murder. Because the adolescent technically becomes a juvenile delinquent only after being judged guilty of a crime by a court of law, official records do not accurately reflect the number of illegal acts juvenile delinquents commit. Estimates of the number of juvenile delinquents in the United States are sketchy, but FBI statistics indicate that at least 2 percent of all youth are involved in juvenile court cases.

U.S. government statistics reveal that 8 of 10 cases of juvenile delinquency involve males (Snyder & Sickmund, 1999). In the last two decades, however, there has been a greater increase in female delinquency than in male delinquency (Snyder & Sickmund, 1999). For both male and female delinquents, rates for property offenses are higher than for other rates of offenses (such as offenses against persons, drug offenses, and public order offenses). Arrests of adolescent males for delinquency still are much higher than for adolescent females.

Delinquency rates among minority groups and lower-socioeconomic-status youth are especially high in proportion to the overall population of these groups. However, such groups have less influence over the judicial decision-making process in the United States and, therefore, may be judged delinquent more readily than their White, middle-socioeconomic-status counterparts.

In the Pittsburgh Youth Study, a longitudinal study focused on more than 1,500 inner-city boys, three developmental pathways to delinquency were (Loeber & Farrington, 2001; Loeber & others, 1998; Stoutheimer-Loeber & others, 2002):

- *Authority conflict.* Youth on this pathway showed stubbornness prior to age 12, then moved on to defiance and avoidance of authority.

juvenile delinquent An adolescent who breaks the law or engages in behavior that is considered illegal.

- *Covert.* This pathway included minor covert acts, such as lying, followed by property damage and moderately serious delinquency, then serious delinquency.
- *Overt.* This pathway included minor aggression followed by fighting and violence.

One issue in juvenile justice is whether an adolescent who commits a crime should be tried as an adult (Redding, 2005). In one study, trying adolescent offenders as adults increased rather than reduced their crime rate (Myers, 1999). The study evaluated more than 500 violent youth in Pennsylvania, which has adopted a "get tough" policy. Although these 500 offenders had been given harsher punishment than a comparison group retained in juvenile court, they were more likely to be rearrested—and rearrested more quickly—for new offenses once they were returned to the community. This suggests that the price of short-term public safety attained by prosecuting juveniles as adults might increase the number of criminal offenses over the long run.

A distinction is made between early-onset—before age 11—and late-onset—after 11—antisocial behavior. Early-onset antisocial behavior is associated with more negative developmental outcomes than late-onset antisocial behavior (Schulenberg & Zarrett, 2006). Early-onset antisocial behavior is more likely to persist into emerging adulthood and is associated with more mental health and relationship problems (Roisman, Aguilar, & Egeland, 2004; Stoutheimer-Loeber & others, 2004).

Causes of Delinquency   What causes delinquency? Many causes have been proposed, including heredity, identity problems, community influences, and family experiences. Erik Erikson (1968), for example, maintains that adolescents whose development has restricted them from acceptable social roles, or made them feel that they cannot measure up to the demands placed on them, may choose a negative identity. Adolescents with a negative identity may find support for their delinquent image among peers, reinforcing the negative identity. For Erikson, delinquency is an attempt to establish an identity, although a negative one.

Although delinquency is less exclusively a phenomenon of lower socioeconomic status than it was in the past, some characteristics of lower-class culture might promote delinquency. The norms of many lower-SES peer groups and gangs are antisocial, or counterproductive, to the goals and norms of society at large. Getting into and staying out of trouble are prominent features of life for some adolescents in low-income neighborhoods (Flannery & others, 2003). Adolescents from low-income backgrounds may sense that they can gain attention and status by performing antisocial actions. Being "tough" and "masculine" are high-status traits for lower-SES boys, and these traits are often measured by the adolescent's success in performing and getting away with delinquent acts. Furthermore, adolescents in communities with high crime rates observe many models who engage in criminal activities. These communities may be characterized by poverty, unemployment, and feelings of alienation toward the middle class. Quality schooling, educational funding, and organized neighborhood activities may be lacking in these communities (Sabol, Coulton, & Korbin, 2004).

Certain characteristics of family support systems are also associated with delinquency (Cavell & others, 2007; Feinberg & others, 2007). Parents of delinquents are less skilled in discouraging antisocial behavior and in encouraging skilled behavior than are parents of nondelinquents. Parental monitoring of adolescents is especially important in determining whether an adolescent becomes

What are some factors that are linked to whether adolescents engage in delinquent acts?

A current concern is gang violence. *What are some reasons that adolescents join a gang?*

a delinquent (Coley, Morris, & Hernandez, 2004; Patterson, DeBaryshe, & Ramsey, 1989). Family discord and inconsistent and inappropriate discipline also are associated with delinquency (Bor, McGee, & Fagan, 2004). An increasing number of studies have also found that siblings can have a strong influence on delinquency (Bank, Burraston, & Snyder, 2004; Conger & Reuter, 1996). In one study, high levels of hostile sibling relationships and older sibling delinquency were linked with younger sibling delinquency in both brother and sister pairs (Slomkowski & others, 2001). Having delinquent peers greatly increases the risk of becoming delinquent (Dodge, Coie, & Lynam, 2006; Laird & others, 2005; Lauber, Marshall, & Meyers, 2005).

Youth Violence Youth violence is a special concern in the United States today (Barton, 2005). Estimates indicate that there are more than 750,000 gang members in more than 24,000 gangs in the United States, with the average age of gang members being 17 to 18 years (Egley, 2002). Gangs often engage in violent and criminal activities and use these activities as an indication of gang identity and loyalty (Lauber, Marshall, & Meyers, 2005).

Among the risk factors that increase the likelihood an adolescent will become a gang member are disorganized neighborhoods characterized by economic hardship, having other family members in a gang, drug use, lack of family support, and peer pressure (Lauber, Marshall, & Meyers, 2005). Also, a recent study found that peer rejection, doing poorly in school, and engaging in antisocial behavior were linked with whether middle school students were members of a gang (Dishion, Nelson, & Yasui, 2005).

School violence is an issue of national concern in the United States (Molina, Dulmus, & Sowers, 2005). A national survey found that in 2005, 13.6 percent of U.S. high school students reported that they had been in a physical fight on school property, and 6.5 percent said they carry a weapon on school property (Eaton & others, 2006). The good news is that there has been a decline in violence-related behaviors in schools. In the national survey just mentioned, from 1991 to 2005, physical fighting declined from 16 percent to 13.5 percent, and weapon carrying in schools declined from 12 percent of students to 6.5 percent. However, being injured in a fist fight remained stable, and not going to school because of safety concerns increased from 4.4 percent of students in 1993 to 6 percent of students in 2005. And violence figures for some subgroups of adolescents increased. Being threatened or injured with a weapon on school property increased for ninth-grade students and for African American students.

Since the late 1990s, a series of school shootings gained national attention. In April 1999, in Littleton, Colorado, two Columbine High School students, Eric Harris and Dylan Klebold, shot and killed 12 students and a teacher, wounded 23 others, and then killed themselves. In May 1998, slightly built Kip Kinkel strode into a cafeteria at Thurston High School in Springfield, Oregon, and opened fire on his fellow students, murdering two and injuring many others. Later that day, police went to his home and found his parents lying dead on the floor, also victims of Kip's violence. In 2001, 15-year-old Charles "Andy" Williams fired shots at Santana High School in Southern California, killing two classmates and injuring 13 others. According to students at the school, Andy was a victim of bullying and had joked the previous weekend of his violent plans, but no one took him seriously after he later said he was just kidding.

Is there any way psychologists can predict whether a youth will turn violent? It's a complex task, but researchers have pieced together some clues (Cowley, 1998). Violent youth are overwhelmingly male, and many are driven by feelings of powerlessness. Violence seems to infuse these youth with a sense of power. In one study based on data collected in the National Longitudinal Study of Adolescent Health, secure attachment to parents, living in an intact family, and attending church services with parents were linked with lower incidences of violent behavior in seventh- through twelfth-graders (Franke, 2000).

Small-town shooting sprees attract attention, but youth violence is far greater in poverty-infested areas of inner cities. Urban poverty fosters powerlessness and rage, and many inner-city neighborhoods provide almost daily opportunities to observe violence. Many urban youth who live in poverty also lack adequate parent involvement and supervision (Tolan, 2001).

James Garbarino (1999, 2001) says there is a lot of ignoring that goes on in these kinds of situations. Parents often do not want to acknowledge what might be a very upsetting reality. Harris and Klebold were members of the "Trenchcoat Mafia" clique of Columbine outcasts. The two even had made a video for a school media class the previous fall that depicted them walking down the halls at the school, shooting other students. Allegations were made that a year earlier the sheriff's department had been given information that Harris had bragged openly on the Internet that he and Klebold had built four bombs. Kip Kinkel had an obsession with guns and explosives, a history of abusing animals, and a nasty temper when crossed. When police examined his room, they found two pipe bombs, three larger bombs, and bomb-making recipes Kip had downloaded from the Internet. Clearly, some signs were present in these students' lives to suggest that they had some serious problems, but it is still very difficult to predict whether youth like these will act on their anger and sense of powerlessness to commit murder.

Garbarino (1999, 2001) has interviewed a number of youth killers. He concludes that nobody really knows precisely why a tiny minority of youth kill, but that it might be a lack of a spiritual center. In the youth killers he interviewed, Garbarino often found a spiritual or emotional emptiness in which the youth sought meaning in the dark side of life.

Some interventions can reduce or prevent youth violence (Barton, 2004; Carnegie Council on Adolescent Development, 1995). Prevention efforts should include developmentally appropriate schools, supportive families, and youth and community organizations. At a more specific level, one promising strategy for preventing youth violence is the teaching of conflict management as part of health education in elementary and middle schools. To build resources for such programs, the Carnegie Foundation is supporting a national network of violence prevention practitioners based at the U.S. Department of Education, linked with a national research center on youth violence at the University of Colorado.

These are some of the Oregon Social Learning Center's recommendations for reducing youth violence (Walker, 1998, p. 1C):

- *Recommit to raising children safely and effectively.* This includes engaging in "parenting practices that produce healthy, well-adjusted children. Such practices involve consistent, fair discipline that is never harsh or severely punitive, careful monitoring and supervision, positive family management techniques, involvement in the child's daily life, daily debriefings about the child's experiences, and teaching problem-solving strategies."
- *Make prevention a reality.* Too often lip service is given to prevention strategies without investing in them at the necessary levels to make them effective.
- *"Give greater support to our schools, which are struggling to educate an increasingly diverse and at-risk student population."*
- *"Forge effective partnerships among families, schools, social service systems, public safety, churches, and other agencies to create the socializing experiences that will give all of our youth a chance to develop along positive lines."*

One individual whose goal is to reduce violence in adolescence and help at-risk adolescents cope more effectively with their lives is Rodney Hammond. To read about his work, see the *Careers in Child Development* profile.

Charles "Andy" Williams, escorted by police after being arrested for killing two classmates and injuring 13 others at Santana High School. *What factors might contribute to youth murders?*

Careers in CHILD DEVELOPMENT

Rodney Hammond
Health Psychologist

Rodney Hammond described his college experiences, "When I started as an undergraduate at the University of Illinois, Champaign-Urbana, I hadn't decided on my major. But to help finance my education, I took a part-time job in a child development research program sponsored by the psychology department. There, I observed inner-city children in settings designed to enhance their learning. I saw first-hand the contribution psychology can make, and I knew I wanted to be a psychologist" (American Psychological Association, 2003, p. 26).

Rodney Hammond went on to obtain a doctorate in school and community college with a focus on children's development. For a number of years, he trained clinical psychologists at Wright State University in Ohio and directed a program to reduce violence in ethnic minority youth. There, he and his associates taught at-risk youth how to use social skills to effectively manage conflict and to recognize situations that could lead to violence. Today, Hammond is Director of Violence Prevention at the Centers for Disease Control and Prevention in Atlanta. Hammond says that if you are interested in people and problem solving, psychology is a wonderful way to put these together. (Source: American Psychological Association, 2003, pp. 26–27)

Rodney Hammond, counseling an adolescent girl about the risks of adolescence and how to effectively cope with them.

Depression and Suicide

What is the nature of depression in adolescence? What causes an adolescent to commit suicide?

Depression Depression is more likely to occur in adolescence than in childhood and more likely to occur in adulthood than adolescence. Further, adolescent girls consistently have higher rates of depression than adolescent boys (Graber, 2004; Logsdon, 2004; Nolen-Hoeksema, 2007). Among the reasons for this gender difference are that

Depression is more likely to occur in adolescence than in childhood, and female adolescents are more likely than male adolescents to be depressed.

- Females tend to ruminate in their depressed mood and amplify it.
- Females' self-images, especially their body images, are more negative than males'.
- Females face more discrimination than males do.
- Puberty occurs earlier for girls than for boys, and as a result girls experience a piling up of changes and life experiences in the middle school years, which can increase depression.

Certain family factors place adolescents at risk for developing depression (Graber, 2004). These include having a depressed parent, emotionally unavailable parents, parents who have high marital conflict, and parents with financial problems. For example, a recent study revealed that parent-adolescent conflict and low parental support were linked to adolescent depression (Sheeber & others, 2007).

Poor peer relationships also are associated with adolescent depression (Kistner, 2006). Not having a close relationship with a best friend, having less contact with friends, and experiencing peer rejection all increase depressive tendencies in adolescents. Problems in adolescent romantic relationships can also trigger depression, especially for girls (Davila & Steinberg, 2006).

The experience of difficult changes or challenges also is associated with depressive symptoms in adolescence (Compas & Grant, 1993), and parental divorce increases depressive symptoms in adolescents. Also, when adolescents go through puberty at the same time as they move from elementary school to middle or junior high school, they report being depressed more than do adolescents who go through puberty after the school transition.

Onset of depression in early adolescence is linked with more negative outcomes than onset of depression in late adolescence (Schulenberg & Zarrett, 2006). For example, the early onset is associated with further recurrences of depression and with an increased risk of being diagnosed with an anxiety disorder, substance abuse, eating disorder, suicide attempt, and unemployment at a future point in development (Graber, 2004).

Suicide   Suicide behavior is rare in childhood but escalates in adolescence and then increases further in emerging adulthood (Park & others, 2006). Suicide is the third leading cause of death in 10- to 19-year-olds today in the United States (National Center for Health Statistics, 2006). After increasing to high levels in the 1990s, suicide rates in adolescents have declined in recent years. In 2004, 4,214 U.S. individuals from 15 to 24 years of age committed suicide (Minino, Heron, & Smith, 2006). Emerging adults have triple the rate of suicide as adolescents (Park & others, 2006).

Although a suicide threat should always be taken seriously, far more adolescents contemplate or attempt it unsuccessfully than actually commit it (Mazza, 2005). In a national study, in 2005, 17 percent of U.S. high school students said that they had seriously considered or attempted suicide in the last 12 months (Eaton & others, 2006). As shown in Figure 16.8, this percentage has declined since 1991. In the national survey, in 2005, 2.3 percent reported a suicide attempt that resulted in an injury, poisoning, or drug overdose that had been treated by a doctor. Females were more likely to attempt suicide than males, but males were more likely to succeed in committing suicide. In emerging adulthood, males are six times as likely to commit suicide as females (National Center for Injury Prevention and Control, 2006). Males use more lethal means, such as guns, in their suicide attempts, whereas adolescent females are more likely to cut their wrists or take an overdose of sleeping pills—methods less likely to result in death.

One issue focuses on whether lesbian and gay male adolescents are especially vulnerable to suicide. In one study of 12,000 adolescents, approximately 15 percent of lesbian and gay male youth said that they had attempted suicide compared with 7 percent of heterosexual youth (Russell & Joyner, 2001). However, Richard Savin-Williams (2001) found that lesbian and gay male adolescents were only slightly more likely than heterosexual adolescents to attempt suicide. He argues that most studies have exaggerated the suicide rates for lesbian and gay male adolescents because they survey only the most disturbed youth who are attending support groups or hanging out at shelters for lesbian and gay male youth.

Distal, or earlier, experiences often are involved in suicide attempts as well. The adolescent may have a long-standing history of family instability and unhappiness. Just as a lack of affection and emotional support, high control, and pressure for achievement by parents during childhood are related to adolescent depression, such combinations of family experiences also are likely to show up as distal factors in adolescents' suicide attempts. One recent review of research found a link that adolescents who had been physically or sexually abused

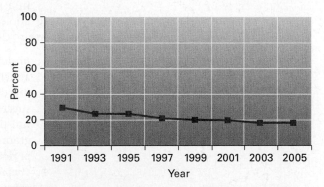

FIGURE 16.8 Percentage of U.S. Ninth- to Twelfth-Grade Students Who Seriously Considered Attempting Suicide in the Previous 12 Months from 1991 to 2005

were more likely to have suicidal thoughts than adolescents who had not experienced such abuse (Evans & others, 2005). Adolescents who attempt suicide may also lack supportive friendships. One study found that social isolation was linked with suicide attempts in adolescent girls (Bearman & Moody, 2004).

Just as genetic factors are associated with depression, they also are associated with suicide. The closer a person's genetic relationship to someone who has committed suicide, the more likely that person is to also commit suicide.

What is the psychological profile of the suicidal adolescent? Suicidal adolescents often have depressive symptoms (Hallfors & others, 2004; Kaslow & others, 2004; Werth, 2004). Although not all depressed adolescents are suicidal, depression is the most frequently cited factor associated with adolescent suicide. A sense of hopelessness, low self-esteem, and high self-blame are also associated with adolescent suicide (Harter & Whitesell, 2001; O'Donnell & others, 2004). A recent study also revealed that overweight middle school students were more likely to think about, plan, and attempt suicide than their counterparts who were not overweight (Whetstone, Morrissey, & Cummings, 2007).

The Interrelation of Problems and Successful Prevention/Intervention Programs

We have described some of the major adolescent problems in this chapter and in Chapter 14: substance abuse; juvenile delinquency; school-related problems, such as dropping out of school; adolescent pregnancy and sexually transmitted infections; depression; and suicide.

The most at-risk adolescents have more than one problem. Researchers are increasingly finding that problem behaviors in adolescence are interrelated (Mason, Hitchings, & Spoth, 2007; Thompson, Ho, & Kingree, 2007). For example, heavy substance abuse is related to early sexual activity, lower grades, dropping out of school, and delinquency. Early initiation of sexual activity is associated with the use of cigarettes and alcohol, the use of marijuana and other illicit drugs, lower grades, dropping out of school, and delinquency. Delinquency is related to early sexual activity, early pregnancy, substance abuse, and dropping out of school. In 1990, it was estimated that as many as 10 percent of all adolescents in the United States have serious multiple-problem behaviors (for example, adolescents who have dropped out of school, are behind in their grade level, are users of heavy drugs, regularly use cigarettes and marijuana, and are sexually active but do not use contraception) (Dryfoos, 1990). In 1990, it was estimated that another 15 percent of adolescents participate in many of these behaviors but with slightly lower frequency and less deleterious consequences. These high-risk youth often engage in two- or three-problem behaviors (Dryfoos, 1990; Dryfoos & Barkin, 2006). Recently, it was estimated that in 2005 the 15 percent figure had increased to 20 percent of all U.S. adolescents (Dryfoos & Barkin, 2006).

In a review of the programs that have been successful in preventing or reducing adolescent problems, adolescence researcher Joy Dryfoos (1990; Dryfoos & Barkin, 2006) described the common components of successful programs:

1. *Intensive individualized attention.* In successful programs, high-risk children are attached to a responsible adult, who gives the child attention and deals with the child's specific needs. This theme occurs in a number of programs. In a successful substance-abuse program, a student assistance counselor is available full-time for individual counseling and referral for treatment. Successful programs often require highly trained personnel, and they extend over a long period (Dryfoos & Barkin, 2006).

2. *Community-wide multiagency collaborative approaches.* The basic philosophy of community-wide programs is that a number of different programs and services have to be in place. In one successful substance-abuse program, a community-wide health promotion campaign has been implemented that uses

local media and community education, in concert with a substance-abuse curriculum in the schools.

3. *Early identification and intervention.* Reaching children and their families before children develop problems, or at the beginning of their problems, is a successful strategy (Aber & others, 2006; Pianta, 2005).

Here are two prevention programs/research studies that merit attention:

- *High Scope.* One preschool program serves as an excellent model for the prevention of delinquency, pregnancy, substance abuse, and dropping out of school. Operated by the High Scope Foundation in Ypsilanti, Michigan, the Perry Preschool has had a long-term positive impact on its students. This enrichment program, directed by David Weikart, services disadvantaged African American children. They attend a high-quality two-year preschool program and receive weekly home visits from program personnel. Based on official police records, by age 19 individuals who had attended the Perry Preschool program were less likely to have been arrested and reported fewer adult offenses than a control group. The Perry Preschool students also were less likely to drop out of school, and teachers rated their social behavior as more competent than a control group who did not receive the enriched early experience.

- *Fast Track.* Another program that seeks to prevent adolescent problems is called Fast Track (Dodge, 2001; Dodge & the Conduct Problems Prevention Research Group, 2007; Lochman & the Conduct Problems Prevention Research Group, 2007; Milan, Pinderhuges, & the Conduct Problems Prevention Research Group, 2006). High-risk children who show conduct problems at home and at kindergarten were identified. Then, during the elementary school years, the at-risk children and their families are given support and training in parenting, problem-solving and coping skills, peer relations, classroom atmosphere and curriculum, academic achievement, and home-school relations. Ten project interventionists work with the children, their families, and schools to increase the protective factors and decrease the risk factors in these areas. Thus far, the results show that the intervention effectively improved parenting practices and children's problem-solving and coping skills, peer relations, reading achievement, and problem behavior at home and school during the elementary school years compared with a control group of high-risk children who did not experience the intervention. However, more recent analysis of the Fast Track participants indicated that long-term outcomes were positive only for the highest-risk group of children (Dodge & others, 2007). The intervention reduced their likelihood of developing conduct disorder by half (41 percent to 21 percent).

REVIEW AND REFLECT   LEARNING GOAL 5

5 **Identify adolescent problems in socioemotional development and strategies for helping adolescents with problems.**

Review

- What is juvenile delinquency? What causes it? What is the nature of youth violence?
- What is the nature of depression and suicide in adolescence?
- How are adolescent problems interrelated? What are some components of successful prevention/intervention programs for adolescents?

Reflect

- Are the consequences of risk taking in adolescence today more serious than in the past? If so, why?

REACH YOUR LEARNING GOALS

① WHAT CHARACTERIZES EMOTIONAL AND PERSONALITY DEVELOPMENT IN ADOLESCENCE? *Discuss changes in the self and emotional development during adolescence.*

Self-Esteem

- Some researchers have found that self-esteem declines in early adolescence for both boys and girls, but the drop for girls is greater. Other researchers caution that these declines are often exaggerated and actually are small.

Identity

- Identity development is complex and is done in bits and pieces. Erikson argues that identity versus identity confusion is the fifth developmental stage, which individuals experience during adolescence. A psychosocial moratorium during adolescence allows the personality and role experimentation that are important aspects of identity development. Identity development begins during infancy and continues through old age. James Marcia proposed four identity statuses—identity diffusion, foreclosure, moratorium, and achievement—that are based on crisis (exploration) and commitment. Some experts argue the main changes in identity occur in emerging adulthood rather than adolescence. Individuals often follow *moratorium-achievement-moratorium-achievement* (MAMA) cycles in their lives. Parents are important figures in adolescents' identity development. Democratic parenting facilitates identity achievement; autocratic and permissive parenting do not. Identity development is also facilitated by family relations that promote both individuality and connectedness. Throughout the world, ethnic minority groups have struggled to maintain their identities while blending into the majority culture.

Emotional Development

- Adolescents report more extreme and fleeting emotions than their parents, and as individuals go through early adolescence they are less likely to report being very happy. However, it is important to view moodiness as a normal aspect of early adolescence. Although pubertal change is associated with an increase in negative emotions, hormonal influences are often small, and environmental experiences may contribute more to the emotions of adolescence than hormonal changes.

② WHAT IS THE NATURE OF PARENT-ADOLESCENT RELATIONSHIPS? *Describe changes that take place in adolescents' relationships with their parents.*

Autonomy and Attachment

- Many parents have a difficult time handling the adolescent's push for autonomy, even though the push is one of the hallmarks of adolescence. Adolescents do not simply move into a world isolated from parents; attachment to parents increases the probability that an adolescent will be socially competent.

Parent-Adolescent Conflict

- Parent-adolescent conflict increases in adolescence. The conflict is usually moderate rather than severe, and the increased conflict may serve the positive developmental function of promoting autonomy and identity. A subset of adolescents experiences is high parent-adolescent conflict, which is linked with negative outcomes.

3 | WHAT ASPECTS OF PEER RELATIONSHIPS ARE IMPORTANT IN ADOLESCENCE? *Characterize the changes that occur in peer relations during adolescence.*

Friendships

- Harry Stack Sullivan was the most influential theorist to discuss the importance of adolescent friendships. He argued that there is a dramatic increase in the psychological importance and intimacy of close friends in early adolescence. Adolescents share intimate, personal information with friends more frequently than do children. Adolescent friendships typically are more intense than childhood friendships.

Peer Groups

- Children groups are less formal and less heterogeneous than adolescent groups. The pressure to conform to peers is strong during adolescence, especially during the eighth and ninth grades. Cliques and crowds assume more importance in the lives of adolescents than in the lives of children. Membership in certain crowds—especially jocks and populars—is associated with increased self-esteem. Independents also show high self-esteem.

Dating and Romantic Relationships

- Dating can have many functions. Younger adolescents often begin to hang out together in mixed-sex groups. Many gay and lesbian youth date other-sex peers, which can help them to clarify their sexual orientation or disguise it from others. Male and female adolescents engage in different dating scripts. Culture can exert a powerful influence on adolescent dating. Dating shows mixed connections with adjustment during adolescence. Early dating is linked with developmental problems.

4 | WHY IS CULTURE AN IMPORTANT CONTEXT FOR ADOLESCENT DEVELOPMENT? *Explain how culture influences adolescent development.*

Cross-Cultural Comparisons

- There are both similarities and differences in adolescents across different countries. With technological advances, a youth culture with similar characteristics may be emerging. However, there still are many variations in adolescents across cultures. In some countries, traditions are being continued in the socialization of adolescents, whereas in others, substantial changes in the experiences of adolescents are taking place. Adolescents often fill their time with different activities, depending on the culture in which they live. Rites of passage are ceremonies that mark an individual's transition from one status to another, especially into adulthood. In primitive cultures, rites of passage are often well defined. In contemporary America, rites of passage to adulthood are ill-defined.

Ethnicity

- Many of the families that have immigrated in recent decades to the United States come from collectivist cultures in which there is a strong sense of family obligation. Much of the research on ethnic minority adolescents has not teased apart the influences of ethnicity and socioeconomic status. Because of this failure, too often researchers have given ethnic explanations for characteristics that were largely due to socioeconomic factors. While not all ethnic minority families are poor, poverty contributes to the stress of many ethnic minority adolescents.

5   WHAT ARE SOME SOCIOEMOTIONAL PROBLEMS IN ADOLESCENCE?

Identify adolescent problems in socioemotional development and strategies for helping adolescents with problems.

Juvenile Delinquency

- A juvenile delinquent is an adolescent who breaks the law or engages in conduct that is considered illegal. Heredity, identity problems, community influences, and family experiences have been proposed as causes of juvenile delinquency. An increasing concern is the high rate of violence among youth, especially in gangs and at school. Violent youth are overwhelmingly male and often driven by feelings of powerlessness. Although school-related violence has declined, violence such as being injured or threatened at school has increased for some subgroups.

Depression and Suicide

- Adolescents have a higher rate of depression than children. Female adolescents are more likely to have mood and depressive disorders than male adolescents are. Adolescent suicide is the third leading cause of death in U.S. adolescents. Both proximal (recent) and distal (earlier) factors are likely involved in suicide's causes.

The Interrelation of Problems and Successful Prevention/ Intervention Programs

- Researchers are increasingly finding that problem behaviors in adolescence are interrelated. Dryfoos found a number of common components in successful programs designed to prevent or reduce adolescent problems: they provide individual attention to high-risk adolescents, they develop community-wide intervention, and they include early identification and intervention.

KEY TERMS

identity versus identity
   confusion 538
psychosocial
   moratorium 539
crisis 539

commitment 539
identity diffusion 539
identity foreclosure 539
identity moratorium 540
identity achievement 540

individuality 541
connectedness 541
ethnic identity 541
clique 549
crowd 550

dating scripts 551
rite of passage 555
assimilation 556
pluralism 557
juvenile delinquent 558

KEY PEOPLE

Erik Erikson 538
James Marcia 539
Alan Waterman 540

Reed Larson and Maryse
   Richards 542
G. Stanley Hall 546

Harry Stack Sullivan 548
Stanley Sue 556

Richard Savin-Williams 563
Joy Dryfoos 564

MAKING A DIFFERENCE

Supporting Adolescents' Socioemotional Development

What are some good strategies for helping adolescents improve their socioemotional competencies?

- *Let adolescents explore their identity.* Adolescence is a time of identity exploration. Adults should encourage adolescents

to try out different options as they seek to find what type of life they want to pursue.

- *Understand the importance of autonomy and attachment.* A common stereotype is that parents are less important in adolescent development than in child development. However, parents continue to play a crucial role in the adolescent's development. They need their parents as a resource and support system, especially in stressful times. Value the adolescent's motivation for independence. However, continue to monitor the adolescent's whereabouts, although less intrusively and directly than in childhood.

- *Keep parent-adolescent conflict from being turbulent, and use good communication skills with the adolescent.* Adolescents' socioemotional development benefits when conflict with parents is either low or moderate. Keep communication channels open with the adolescent. Be an active listener and show respect for the adolescent's advancing developmental status. As with childhood, authoritative parenting is the best choice in most situations. Communicate expectations for high standards of achievement and conduct.

- *Recognize the importance of peers, youth organizations, and mentors.* Respected peers need to be used more frequently in programs that promote health and education. Adolescents need greater access to youth organizations staffed by caring peers and adults. Mentors can play a strong role in supporting adolescents' socioemotional development.

- *Help adolescents better understand the nature of differences, diversity, and value conflicts.* Adolescents need to be encouraged to take the perspective of adolescents from diverse ethnic backgrounds.

- *Give adolescents individualized attention.* One of the reasons that adolescents develop problems is that they have not been given adequate attention.

- *Provide better community-wide collaboration for helping youth.* In successful programs, a number of different services and programs cooperate to help adolescents.

- *Prevent adolescent problems through early identification and intervention.* The seeds of many adolescent problems are already in place in childhood.

RESOURCES FOR IMPROVING CHILDREN'S LIVES

Adolescence: Growing Up in America Today

by Joy Dryfoos and Carol Barkin (2006)
New York: Oxford University Press.

Dryfoos' recent update of 1990 book on at-risk adolescents contains extensive information about programs and strategies for improving adolescents' lives.

You and Your Adolescent

by Laurence Steinberg and Ann Levine (2nd ed., 1997)
New York: HarperCollins

You and Your Adolescent provides a broad, developmental overview of adolescence, with parental advice mixed in along the way.

E-LEARNING TOOLS

Connect to **www.mhhe.com/santrockc10** to research the answers and complete these exercises. In addition, you'll find a number of other resources and valuable study tools for Chapter 16, "Socioemotional Development in Adolescence," on this Web site.

Taking It to the Net

1. Marissa is 12 years old, and she has already begun puberty. She is much taller than her classmates, and she has well-developed breasts and other secondary sex characteristics. Marissa is embarrassed about the sudden physical changes in her body, and she feels very insecure. Moreover, Marissa, who has always done very well in school, is learning very quickly that the "brains" in school are not very popular. What factors may be contributing to Marissa's struggles? What can family members and teachers do to support adolescent girls during the early stages of development?

2. Shawn just learned that a classmate of his, Glenn, was hospitalized for depression and suicidality. Shawn was very surprised when he heard this; he saw Glenn as very popular and never would have guessed that he was depressed. How common is it for adolescents to be depressed? How commonly does adolescent suicide occur? How can friends, family members, and teachers determine whether someone is depressed and/or suicidal? What can they do to support the depressed/suicidal adolescent?

3. Shelley's mother is Euro-American, and her father is Japanese. Many people who do not know her have a hard time identifying her ethnic background, and she is constantly asked, "What are you?" There are a couple of other students of color at her school, although few of them openly identify as biracial or multiracial. Shelley is now in the process of figuring out who she is. What are some of the challenges biracial or multiracial adolescents face? How might the process of identity development progress?

Health and Well-Being, Parenting, and Education

Build your decision-making skills by trying your hand at the health and well-being, parenting, and education exercises.

Video Clips

The Online Learning Center includes the following videos for this chapter:

1. *Relationships with Parents at Age 16*—1982
   In this clip, three adolescent friends describe their relationships with their parents. They describe "normal" fights, and they discuss differences between their relationships with their mothers versus fathers.

2. *Ethnic and Racial Identity in Adolescence*—2259
   Two African American girls discuss candidly their feelings about being Black. One describes being Black as being a mixture of many cultures. The other says it's hard to be African American because there is no distinct culture for Blacks.

3. *Talking About Ethnic Identity in Adolescence*—1994
   Students view the diversity among them, as well as among their peers, very positively. They admit that they are different from one another, because of their ethnic backgrounds, but they each benefit from one another because of these differences.

A

accommodation Piagetian concept of adjusting schemes to fit new information and experiences. 183

acculturation Cultural changes that occur when one culture comes into contact with another. 339

active (niche-picking) genotype-environment correlations Correlations that exist when children seek out environment they find compatible and stimulating. 75

adolescence The developmental period of transition from childhood to early adulthood, entered at approximately 10 to 12 years of age and ending at 18 to 22 years of age. 17

adolescent egocentrism The heightened self-consciousness of adolescents that is reflected in their belief that others are as interested in them as they are in themselves, and in their sense of personal uniqueness and invulnerability. 503

adoption study A study in which investigators seek to discover whether, in behavior and psychological characteristics, adopted children are more like their adoptive parents, who provided a home environment, or more like their biological parents, who contributed their heredity. Another form of the adoption study is to compare adopted and biological siblings. 74

affordances Opportunities for interaction offered by objects that fit within our capabilities to perform functional activities. 166

afterbirth The third stage of birth, when the placenta, umbilical cord, and other membranes are detached and expelled. 115

AIDS AIDS stands for acquired immune deficiency syndrome and is caused by a virus, the human immunodeficiency virus (HIV), which destroys the body's immune system. 480

amnion The life-support system that is a thin bag or envelope that contains a clear fluid in which the developing embryo floats. 86

amygdala The seat of emotions, such as anger. 476

analgesia Drugs used to alleviate pain, such as tranquilizers, barbiturates, and narcotics. 117

androgyny The presence of positive masculine and feminine characteristics in the same individual. 441

anesthesia Drugs used in late first-stage labor and during expulsion of the baby to block sensa-

tion in an area of the body or to block consciousness. 117

anger cry A variation of the basic cry, with more excess air forced through the vocal cords. 219

animism The belief that inanimate objects have lifelike qualities and are capable of action. 279

anorexia nervosa An eating disorder that involves the relentless pursuit of thinness through starvation. 491

A-not-B error Also called AB error, this occurs when infants make the mistake of selecting the familiar hiding place (A) rather than the new hiding place ($\overline{B}$) as they progress into substage 4 in Piaget's sensorimotor stage. 188

Apgar Scale A widely used method to assess the health of newborns at one and five minutes after birth. The Apgar Scale evaluates infants' heart rate, respiratory effort, muscle tone, body color, and reflex irritability. 123

aphasia A loss or impairment of language ability caused by brain damage. 204

articulation disorders Problems in pronouncing sounds correctly. 375

Asperger syndrome A relatively mild autism spectrum disorder in which the child has relatively good verbal language, milder nonverbal language problems, and a restricted range of interests and relationships. 377

assimilation Piagetian concept of the incorporation of new information into existing schemes. 183

assimilation The absorption of ethnic minority groups into the dominant group, which often involves the loss of some or virtually all of the behavior and values of the ethnic group. 556

assistive technology Various services and devices to help children with disabilities function in their environment. 379

associative play Play that involves social interaction with little or no organization. 343

asthma A chronic lung disease that involves episodes of airflow obstruction. 369

attachment A close emotional bond between two people. 228

attention The focusing of mental resources. 191

attention deficit hyperactivity disorder (ADHD) A disability in which children consistently show one or more of the following characteristics: (1) inattention, (2) hyperactivity, and (3) impulsivity. 373

authoritarian parenting A restrictive punitive style in which parents exhort the child to follow

their directions and to respect work and effort. The authoritarian parent places firm limits and controls on the child and allows little verbal exchange. Authoritarian parenting is associated with children's social incompetence. 326

authoritative parenting A parenting style in which parents encourage their children to be independent but still place limits and controls on their actions. Extensive verbal give-and-take is allowed, and parents are warm and nurturant toward the child. Authoritative parenting is associated with children's social competence. 326

autism spectrum disorders (ASD) Also called pervasive developmental disorders, they range from the severe disorder labeled autistic disorder to the milder disorder called Asperger syndrome. Children with these disorders are characterized by problems in social interaction, verbal and nonverbal communication, and repetitive behaviors. 377

autistic disorder A severe autism spectrum disorder that has its onset in the first three years of life and includes deficiencies in social relationships, abnormalities in communication, and restricted, repetitive, and stereotyped patterns of behavior. 377

autonomous morality The second stage of moral development in Piaget's theory, displayed by older children (about 10 years of age and older). The child becomes aware that rules and laws are created by people and that, in judging an action, one should consider the actor's intentions as well as the consequences. 317

average children Children who receive an average number of both positive and negative nominations from peers. 447

B

basic cry A rhythmic pattern usually consisting of a cry, a briefer silence, a shorter inspiratory whistle that is higher pitched than the main cry, and then a brief rest before the next cry. 219

basic-skills-and-phonics approach The idea that reading instruction should teach both phonics and the basic rules for translating written symbols into sounds. 409

Bayley Scales of Infant Development Scales developed by Nancy Bayley that are widely used in the assessment of infant development. The current version has three components: a mental scale, a motor scale, and an infant behavior profile. 195

behavior genetics The field that seeks to discover the influence of heredity and environment on individuals differences in human traits and development. 74

biological processes Changes in an individual's body. 16

blastocyst The inner layer of cells that develops during the germinal period. These cells later develop into the embryo. 85

bonding A close connection, especially a physical bond between parents and their newborn in the period shortly after birth. 132

brainstorming A technique in which individuals are encouraged to come up with creative ideas in a group, play off each other's ideas, and say practically whatever comes to mind. 394

Brazelton Neonatal Behavioral Assessment Scale (NBAS) A test performed within 24 to 36 hours after birth to assess newborns' neurological development, reflexes, and reactions to people. 123

breech position The baby's position in the uterus that causes the buttocks to be the first part to emerge from the vagina. 120

Broca's area An area in the brain's left frontal lobe involved in speech production. 204

Bronfenbrenner's ecological theory An environmental systems theory that focuses on five environmental systems: microsystem, mesosystem, exosystem, macrosystem, and chronosystem. 30

bulimia nervosa An eating disorder in which the individual consistently follows a binge-and-purge eating pattern. 192

C

care perspective The moral perspective of Carol Gilligan, which views people in terms of their connectedness with others and emphasizes interpersonal communication, relationships with others, and concern for others. 436

career self-concept theory Super's theory that individuals' self-concepts play central roles in their career choices. 522

case study An in-depth look at a single individual. 34

centration The focusing of attention on one characteristic to the exclusion of all others. 281

cephalocaudal pattern The sequence in which the earliest growth always occurs at the top—the head—with physical growth in size, weight, and feature differentiation gradually working from top to bottom. 143

cerebral palsy A disorder that involves a lack of muscular coordination, shaking, and unclear speech. 377

cesarean delivery The baby is removed from the mother's uterus through an incision made in her abdomen. This also is sometimes referred to as cesarean section. 120

character education A direct education approach that involves teaching students a basic moral literacy to prevent them from engaging in immoral behavior and doing harm to themselves and others. 511

child-centered kindergarten Education that involves the whole child by considering both the child's physical, cognitive, and social development and the child's needs, interests, and learning styles. 295

child-directed speech Language spoken in a higher pitch than normal with simple words and sentences. 206

chromosomes Threadlike structures made up of deoxyribonucleic acid, or DNA. 61

clique A small group that ranges from two to about twelve individuals, averaging about five to six individuals, and can form because adolescents engage in similar activities. 549

cognitive developmental theory of gender The theory that children's gender typing occurs after they have developed a concept of gender. Once they consistently conceive of themselves as male of female, children often organize their world on the basis of gender. 323

cognitive moral education A concept based on the belief that students should develop such values as democracy and justice as their moral reasoning develops; Kohlberg's theory has been the basis of a number of cognitive moral education programs. 511

cognitive processes Changes in an individual's thought, intelligence, and language. 17

commitment Marcia's term for the part of identity development in which individuals show a personal investment in identity. 539

connectedness Connectedness consists of two dimensions: mutuality (sensitivity to and respect for others' views) and permeability (openness to others' views). 541

conservation The concept that an object's basic properties stay the same even though the object's appearance has been altered. 281

constructive play Play that combines sensorimotor and repetitive activity with symbolic representation of ideas. Constructive play occurs when children engage in self-regulated creation or construction of a product or a problem solution. 344

constructivist approach A learner-centered approach that emphasizes the importance of individuals actively constructing their knowledge and understanding with guidance from the teacher. 452

context The settings, influenced by historical, economic, social, and cultural factors, in which development occurs. 9

continuity-discontinuity issue The issue regarding whether development involves gradual, cumulative change (continuity) or distinct stages (discontinuity). 19

controversial children Children who are frequently nominated both as someone's best friend and as being disliked. 448

conventional reasoning The second, or intermediate, level in Kohlberg's theory of moral development. At this level, individuals abide by certain standards, but they are the standards of others, such as parents or the laws of society. 433

convergent thinking Thinking that produces one correct answer and is characteristic of the kind of thinking tested by standardized intelligence tests. 394

cooperative play Play that involves social interaction in a group with a sense of group identity and organized activity. 343

coordination of secondary circular reactions Piaget's fourth sensorimotor substage, which develops between 8 and 12 months of age. Actions become more outwardly directed, and infants coordinate schemes and act with intentionality. 186

corpus callosum The location where fibers connect the brain's left and right hemispheres. 475

correlation coefficient A number based on statistical analysis that is used to describe the degree of association between two variables. 35

correlational research A research design whose goal is to describe the strength of the relationship between two or more events or characteristics. 35

creative thinking The ability to think in novel and unusual ways and to come up with good, unique solutions to problems. 394

crisis Marcia's term for a period of identity development during which the individual is exploring alternatives. 539

critical thinking Thinking reflectively and productively, and evaluating evidence. 393

critical thinking Thinking reflectively and productively and evaluating the evidence. 506

cross-cultural studies Comparisons of one culture with one or more other cultures. These provide information about the degree to which children's development is similar, or universal, across cultures, and to the degree to which it is culture-specific. 9

cross-sectional approach A research strategy in which individuals of different ages are compared at one time. 37

crowd A larger group structure than a clique, a crowd is usually formed based on reputation, and members may or may not spend much time together. 550

cultural-familial retardation Retardation that is characterized by no evidence of organic brain damage, but the individual's IQ is between 50 and 70. 406

culture The behavior patterns, beliefs, and all other products of a group that are passed on from generation to generation. 9

culture-reduced tests Tests of intelligence that are designed to limit cultural bias. 405

D

dating scripts The cognitive models that individuals use to guide dating interactions. 551

deferred imitation Imitation that occurs after a delay of hours or days. 193

Denver Development Screening Test A test used to diagnose developmental delay in children from birth to 6 years of age; includes separate assessments of gross and fine motor skills, language, and personal-social ability. 258

descriptive research A research design that has the purpose of observing and recording behavior. 35

design stage Kellogg's term for 3- to 4-year-olds' drawings that mix two basic shapes into more complex designs. 258

development The pattern of movement or change that begins at conception and continues through the human life span. 195

developmental career choice theory Ginzberg's theory that children and adolescents go through three career choice stages—fantasy, tentative, and realistic. 521

developmental quotient (DQ) An overall score that combines subscores in motor, language, adaptive, and personal-social domains in the Gesell assessment of infants. 194

developmentally appropriate practice Education that focuses on the typical developmental patterns of children (age appropriateness), the uniqueness of each child (individual appropriateness), and sociocultural contexts. Such practice contrasts with *developmentally inappropriate practice*, which ignores the concrete, hands-on approach to learning. Direct teaching largely through abstract paper-and-pencil activities presented to large groups of young children is believed to be developmentally inappropriate. 296

difficult child A child who tends to react negatively and cry frequently, who engages in irregular daily routines, and who is slow to accept new experiences. 221

direct instruction approach A structured, teacher-centered approach that is characterized by teacher direction and control, mastery of academic skills, high teacher expectations for students' progress, maximum time spent on learning tasks, and efforts to keep negative effect to a minimum. 453

dishabituation Recovery of a habituated response after a change in stimulation. 167

divergent thinking Thinking that produces many answers to the same question and is characteristic of creativity. 394

DNA A complex molecule with a double helix shape; that contains genetic information. 61

doula A caregiver who provides continuous physical, emotional, and educational support to the mother before, during, and just after childbirth. 116

Down syndrome A chromosomally transmitted form of mental retardation, caused by the presence of an extra copy of chromosome 21. 64

dynamic systems theory The perspective on motor development that seeks to explain how motor behaviors are assembled for perceiving and acting. 158

dyscalculia Also known as developmental arithmetic disorder, this learning disability involves difficulty in math computation. 372

dyslexia A category of learning disabilities involving a severe impairment in the ability to read and spell. 371

E

early childhood The developmental period that extends from the end of infancy to about 5 to 6 years of age, sometimes called the preschool years. 17

early-later experience issue The issue of the degree to which early experiences (especially infancy) or later experiences are the key determinants of the child's development. 19

easy child A child who is generally in a positive mood, who quickly establishes regular routines in infancy, and who adapts easily to new experiences. 221

eclectic theoretical orientation An orientation that does not follow any one theoretical approach, but rather selects from each theory whatever is considered the best in it. 32

ecological view The view that perception functions to bring organisms in contact with the environment and to increase adaptation. 165

ectoderm The outermost layer of cells, which becomes the nervous system and brain, sensory receptors (ears, nose, and eyes, for example), and skin parts (hair and nails, for example). 86

educationally blind Unable to use one's vision in learning. It implies a need to use hearing and touch to learn. 375

egocentrism Piaget's concept that describes children's difficulties in distinguishing between their own perspective and someone else's perspective. 279

elaboration An important strategy that involves engaging in more extensive processing of information. 393

embryonic period The period of prenatal development that occurs two to eight weeks after conception. During the embryonic period, the rate of cell differentiation intensifies, support systems for the cells form, and organs appear. 85

emerging adulthood Occurring from approximately 18 to 25 years of age, this transitional period between adolescence and adulthood is characterized by experimentation and exploration. 469

emotion Feeling, or affect, that occurs when a person is in a state or interaction that is important to them. Emotion is characterized by behavior that reflects (expresses) the pleasantness or unpleasantness of the state a person is in or the transactions being experienced. 217

emotional and behavioral disorders These consist of serious, persistent problems that involve relationships, aggression, depression, fears associated with personal or school matters, as well as other inappropriate socioemotional characteristics. 377

emotional intelligence A form of social intelligence that involves the ability to monitor one's own and others' feelings and emotions, to discriminate among them, and to use this information to guide one's thinking and action. 431

endoderm The inner layer of cells, which develops into digestive and respiratory systems. 85

epigenetic view Emphasizes that development is the result of an ongoing, bidirectional interchange between heredity and environment. 76

equilibration A mechanism that Piaget proposed to explain how children shift from one stage of thought to the next. 184

Erikson's theory Includes eight stages of human development. Each stage consists of a unique developmental task that confronts individuals with a crisis that must be resolved. 23

estradiol A hormone associated in girls with breast, uterine, and skeletal development. 472

ethnic gloss Using an ethnic label such as African American or Latino in a superficial way that portrays an ethnic group as being more homogeneous than it really is. 40

ethnic identity An enduring, basic aspect of the self that includes a sense of membership in an ethnic group and the attitudes and feelings related to that membership. 541

ethnicity A characteristic based on cultural heritage, nationality, race, religion, and language. 9

ethology Stresses that behavior is strongly influenced by biology, is tied to evolution, and is characterized by critical or sensitive periods. 29

evocative genotype-environment correlations Correlations that exist when the child's characteristics elicit certain types of physical and social environments. 75

evolutionary psychology Emphasizes the importance of adaptation, reproduction, and "survival of the fittest" in shaping behavior. 58

experiment A carefully regulated procedure in which one or more of the factors believed to influence the behavior being studied are manipulated, while all other factors are held constant. 36

explicit memory Memory of facts and experiences. 192

extrinsic motivation External incentives such as rewards and punishments 412

F

fertilization A stage in reproduction whereby an egg and a sperm fuse to create a single cell, called a zygote. 61

fetal alcohol syndrome (FAS) A cluster of abnormalities that appears in the offspring of mothers who drink alcohol heavily during pregnancy. 100

fetal period The prenatal period of development that begins two months after conception and lasts for seven months, on the average. 87

fine motor skills Motor skills that involve more finely tuned movements, such as finger dexterity. 163

first habits and primary circular reactions Piaget's second sensorimotor substage, which develops between 1 and 4 months of age. In this substage, the infant coordinates sensation and two types of schemes: habits and primary circular reactions. 185

fluency disorders Various disorders that involve what is commonly called "stuttering." 375

fragile X syndrome A genetic disorder involving an abnormality in the X chromosome, which becomes constricted and often breaks. 65

functional amblyopia A vision problem that results from not using one eye enough to avoid the discomfort of double vision produced by imbalanced eye muscles; "lazy eye." 254

fuzzy trace theory States that memory is best understood by considering two types of memory representations: (1) verbatim memory trace and (2) gist. In this theory, older children's better memory is attributed to the fuzzy traces created by extracting the gist of information. 393

G

games Activities engaged in for pleasure that include rules and often competition with one or more individuals. 344

gender The psychological and sociocultural dimension of being female or male. 9

gender identity The sense of being male or female, which most children acquire by the time they are 3 years old. 320

gender roles Expectations that prescribe how females or males should think, act, and feel. 320

gender schema theory The theory that gender typing emerges as children gradually develop gender schemas based on what is gender-appropriate and gender-inappropriate in their culture. 323

gender stereotypes Broad categories that reflect our impressions and beliefs about females and males. 438

genes Units of hereditary information composed of DNA. Genes direct cells to reproduce themselves and manufacture the proteins that maintain life. 61

genetic epistemology The study of how children's knowledge changes over the course of their development. 15

genotype A person's genetic heritage; the actual genetic material. 62

germinal period The period of prenatal development that takes place in the first two weeks after conception. It includes the creation of the zygote, continued cell division, and the attachment of the zygote to the uterine wall. 85

gifted Having above-average intelligence (an IQ of 130 or higher) and/or superior talent for something. 406

gonadotropins Hormones that stimulate the testes or ovaries. 471

gonads The sex glands—the testes in males, the ovaries in females. 471

goodness of fit Refers to the match between a child's temperament and the environmental demands with which the child must cope. 223

grasping reflex A neonatal reflex that occurs when something touches the infant's palms. The infant responds by grasping tightly. 159

gross motor skills Motor skills that involve large-muscle activities, such as walking. 160

growth hormone deficiency The absence or deficiency of growth hormone produced by the pituitary gland to stimulate the body to grow. 250

H

habituation Decreased responsiveness to a stimulus after repeated presentation of the stimulus. 167

helpless orientation An orientation in which one seems trapped by the experience of difficulty and attributes one's difficulty to a lack of ability. 413

heritability The fraction of variance in a population that is attributed to genetics and is computed using correlational techniques. 402

heteronomous morality Kohlberg's first stage in preconventional reasoning in which moral thinking is tied to punishment. 317

heteronomous morality The first stage of moral development in Piaget's theory, occurring from 4 to 7 years of age. Justice and rules are conceived of as unchangeable properties of the world, removed from the control of people. 433

hidden curriculum Dewey's concept that every school has a pervasive moral atmosphere, even if it doesn't have a program of moral education. 511

hormones Powerful chemical substances secreted by the endocrine glands and carried through the body by the bloodstream. 471

hypothalamus A structure in the higher portion of the brain that monitors eating, drinking, and sex. 471

hypothesis A specific assumption or prediction that can be tested to determine its accuracy. 19

hypothetical–deductive reasoning Piaget's formal operational concept that adolescents have the cognitive ability to develop hypotheses, or best guesses, about ways to solve problems. 502

I

identity achievement Marcia's term for individuals who have undergone a crisis and have made a commitment. 540

identity diffusion Marcia's term for individuals who have not yet experienced a crisis (explored meaningful alternatives) or made any commitments. 539

identity foreclosure Marcia's term for individuals who have made a commitment but have not experienced a crisis. 539

identity moratorium Marcia's term for individuals who are in the midst of a crisis, but their commitments are either absent or vaguely defined. 540

identity versus identity confusion Erikson's fifth developmental stage, which occurs at about the time of adolescence. At this time, adolescents are faced with deciding who they are, what they are all about, and where they are going in life. 538

imaginary audience Adolescents' belief that others are as interested in them as they themselves are, as well as attention-getting behavior motivated by a desire to be noticed, visible, and "on stage." 503

immanent justice The concept that, if a rule is broken, punishment will be meted out immediately. 318

implicit memory Memory without conscious recollection; involves skills and routine procedures that are automatically performed. 192

inclusion Educating a child with special education needs full-time in the general school program. 380

individual differences The stable, consistent ways in which people are different from each other. 398

individualism, instrumental purpose, and exchange The second Kohlberg stage of preconventional reasoning. At this stage, individuals pursue their own interests, reasoning it is the right thing to do, but also let others do the same. 433

individuality Individuality consists of two dimensions: self-assertion (the ability to have and communicate a point of view) and separateness (the use of communication patterns to express how one is different from others). 541

individualized education plan (IEP) A written statement that spells out a program tailored to a child with a disability. The plan should be (1) related to the child's learning capacity, (2) specially constructed to meet the child's individual needs and not merely a copy of what is offered to other children, and (3) designed to provide educational benefits. 379

Individuals with Disabilities Education Act (IDEA) The IDEA spells out broad mandates for services to all children with disabilities (IDEA is a renaming of Public Law 94-142); these include evaluation and eligibility determination, appropriate education and the individualized education plan (IEP), and the least restrictive environment (LRE). 378

indulgent parenting A style of parenting in which parents are highly involved with their children but place few demands or controls on them. Indulgent parenting is associated with children's social incompetence, especially a lack of self-control. 327

infancy The developmental period that extends from birth to 18 to 24 months of age. 17

infinite generativity The ability to produce an endless number of meaningful sentences using a finite set of words and rules. 199

information-processing theory Emphasizes that individuals manipulate information, monitor it, and strategies about it. Central to this theory are the processes of memory and thinking. 27

innate goodness view The idea, presented by Swiss-born French philosopher Jean-Jacques Rousseau, that children are inherently good. 14

insecure avoidant babies Babies that show insecurity by avoiding the caregiver. 230

insecure disorganized babies Babies that show insecurity by being disorganized and disoriented. 230

insecure resistant babies Babies that often cling to the caregiver, then resist her by fighting against the closeness, perhaps by kicking or pushing away. 230

instructional technology Various types of hardware and software, combined with innovative teaching methods, to accommodate students' learning needs in the classroom. 379

intelligence Problem-solving skills and the ability to learn from and adapt to the experiences of everyday life. 398

intelligence quotient (IQ) A person's mental age divided by chronological age, multiplied by 100. 398

intermodal perception The ability to relate and integrate information from two or more sensory modalities, such as vision and hearing. 173

internalization of schemes Piaget's sixth and final sensorimotor substage, which develops between 18 and 24 months of age. In this substage, the infant develops the ability to use primitive symbols. 186

intimacy in friendships Self-disclosure and the sharing of private thoughts. 451

intrinsic motivation Internal factors such as self-determination, curiosity, challenge, and effort. 412

intuitive thought substage Piaget's second substage of preoperational thought, in which children begin to use primitive reasoning and want to know the answers to all sorts of questions (between about 4 and 7 years of age). 281

involution The process by which the uterus returns to its prepregnant size. 130

J

joint attention Occurs when individuals focus on the same object or event, and an ability to track another's behavior is present, one individual directs another's attention, and reciprocal interaction is present. 191

justice perspective The moral perspective of Lawrence Kohlberg, which puts abstract principles above relationships, and focuses on the rights of the individual; individuals independently make moral decisions. 436

juvenile delinquent An adolescent who breaks the law or engages in behavior that is considered illegal. 558

K

kangaroo care A way of holding a preterm infant so that there is skin-to-skin contact. 127

Klinefelter syndrome A genetic disorder in which males have an extra X chromosome, making them XXY instead of XY. 65

kwashiorkor A condition caused by a severe deficiency in protein in which the child's abdomen and feet become swollen with water; usually appears between 1 to 3 years of age. 155

L

laboratory A controlled setting in which many of the complex factors of the "real world" are removed. 33

language A form of communication, whether spoken, written, or signed, that is based on a system of symbols. 199

language acquisition device (LAD) Chomsky's term that describes a biological endowment that enables the child to detect the features and rules of language, including phonology, syntax, and semantics. 204

lateralization Specialization of function in one hemisphere of the cerebral cortex or the other. 146

learning disability Includes three components: (1) a minimum IQ level, (2) a significant difficulty in a school-related area (especially reading and/or mathematics), and (3) exclusion of only severe emotional disorders, second-language background, sensory disabilities, and/or specific neurological deficits. 371

least restrictive environment (LRE) The concept that a child with a disability must be educated in a setting that is as similar as possible to the one in which children who do not have a disability are educated. 380

longitudinal approach A research strategy in which the same individuals are studied over a period of time, usually several years or more. 37

long-term memory A relatively permanent type of memory that holds huge amounts of information for a long period of time. 392

low birth weight infants Weigh less than 5 1/2 pounds at birth. 124

low vision Visual acuity between 20/70 and 20/2000. 376

M

manual approaches Educational approaches to help hearing-impaired children; they include sing language and finger spelling. 376

marasmus A wasting away of body tissues in the infant's first year, caused by severe protein-calorie deficiency. 155

mastery motivation An orientation in which one is task-oriented; instead of focusing on one's ability, is concerned with learning strategies 413

meiosis A specialized form of cell division that occurs to form eggs and sperm (or gametes). 61

melatonin A sleep-inducing hormone that is produced in the brain's pineal gland 486

memory A central feature of cognitive development, involving the retention of information over time. 192

menarche A girl's first menstrual period. 471

mental age (MA) Binet's measure of an individual's level of mental development, compared with that of others. 398

mental retardation A condition of limited mental ability in which an individual has a low IQ, usually below 70 on a traditional test of intelligence, and has difficulty adapting to everyday life. 406

mesoderm The middle layer of cells, which becomes the circulatory system, bones, muscles, excretory system, and reproductive system. 86

metacogntion Cognition about cognition, or thinking about thinking. 396

metalinguistic awareness Refers to knowledge about language, such as knowing what a preposition is or the ability to discuss the sounds of a language. 409

middle and late childhood The developmental period that extends from about 6 to 11 years of age, sometimes called the elementary school years. 17

mindset The cognitive view, either fixed or growth, that individuals develop for themselves. 414

mitosis Cellular reproduction in which the cell's nucleus duplicates itself with two new cells being formed, each containing the same DNA as the parent cell, arranged in the same 23 pairs of chromosomes. 61

Montessori approach An educational philosophy in which children are given considerable freedom and spontaneity in choosing activities and specially designed curriculum materials. 296

moral development Development that involves thoughts, feelings, and behaviors regarding rules and conventions about what people should do in their interactions with other people. 316

Moro reflex A neonatal startle response that occurs in reaction to a sudden, intense noise or movement. When startled, the newborn arches its back, throws its head back, and flings out its arms and legs. Then the newborn rapidly closes its arms and legs to the center of the body. 159

morphology Units of meaning involved in word formation. 199

mutual interpersonal expectations, relationships, and interpersonal conformity Kohlberg's third stage of moral development. At this stage, individuals value trust, caring, and loyalty to others as a basis of moral judgments. 433

myelination The process in which the nerve cells are covered and insulated with a layer of fat cells, which increases the speed at which information travels through the nervous system. 252

N

natural childbirth Method developed in 1914 by Dick-Read, it attempts to reduce the mother's pain by decreasing her fear through education about childbirth and breathing methods and relaxation techniques during delivery. 118

naturalistic observation Observing behavior in real-world settings. 33

nature-nurture issue The issue regarding whether development is primarily influenced by nature or nurture. 18

neglected children Children who are infrequently nominated as best friend but are not disliked by their peers. 448

neglectful parenting A style of parenting in which the parent is very uninvolved in the child's life; it is associated with children's social incompetence, especially a lack of self-control. 326

Neonatal Intensive Care Unit Network Neurobehavioral Scale (NNNS) An "offspring" of the NBAS, the NNNS provides a more comprehensive analysis of the newborn's behavior, neurological and stress responses, and regulatory capacities. 124

neo-Piagetians Developmentalists who have elaborated on Piaget's theory, giving more emphasis to information-processing, strategies, and precise cognitive steps. 390

neurogenesis The formation of new neurons. 89

neurons The term for nerve cells, which handle information processing at the cellular level. 87

nightmares Frightening dreams that awaken the sleeper. 261

night terrors Characterized by sudden arousal from sleep, intense fear, and usually physiological reactions such as rapid heart rate and breathing, loud screams, heavy perspiration, and physical movement. 261

nonshared environment experiences The child's own unique experiences, both within the family and outside the family, that are not shared by another sibling. Thus, experiences occurring within the family can be part of the "nonshared environment." 76

normal distribution A symmetrical distribution with most scores falling in the middle of the possible range of scores and few scores appearing toward the extremes of the range. 398

O

object permanence The Piagetian term for understanding that objects and events continue to exist, even when they cannot directly be seen, heard, or touched. 186

onlooker play Play in which the child watches other children play. 342

operations In Piaget's theory, an internalized set of actions that allows children to do mentally what they formerly did physically. 279

oral approaches Educational approaches to help hearing-impaired children; they include lip reading, speech reading, and whatever hearing the child has. 376

organic retardation Mental retardation that involves some physical damage and is caused by a genetic disorder or brain damage. 406

organization Piaget's concept of grouping isolated behaviors and thoughts into a higher-order, more smoothly functioning cognitive system. 184

organogenesis Process of organ formation that takes place during the first two months of prenatal development. 86

original sin view Advocated during the Middle Ages, the belief that children were born into the world as evil beings and were basically bad. 13

orthopedic impairments Restrictions in movement abilities due to muscle, bone, or joint problems. 376

oxytocin A synthetic hormone that is used to stimulate contractions. 117

P

pain cry A sudden appearance of loud crying without preliminary moaning, followed by breath holding. 219

parallel play Play in which the child plays separately from others, but with toys like those the others are using or in a manner that mimics their play. 343

passive genotype-environment correlations Correlations that exist when the biological parents, who are genetically related to the child, provide a rearing environment for the child. 74

perception The interpretation of what is sensed. 165

performance orientation An orientation in which one focuses on achievement outcomes; winning is what matters most, and happiness is thought to result from winning. 414

personal fable The part of adolescent egocentrism that involves an adolescent's sense of uniqueness and invulnerability. 503

personality-type theory Holland's theory that an effort should be made to match an individual's career choice with his personality. 522

perspective taking The ability to assume other people's perspectives and understand their thoughts and feelings. 427

phenotype The way an individual's genotype is expressed in observed and measurable characteristics. 62

phenylketonuria (PKU) A genetic disorder in which an individual cannot properly metabolize phenylalanine an amino acid. PKU is now easily detected—but if left untreated, results in mental retardation and hyperactivity. 65

phonology The sound system of the language, including the sounds that are used and how they may be combined. 199

Piaget's theory States that children actively construct their understanding of the world and go through four stages of cognitive development. 25

pictorial stage Kellogg's term for 4- to 5-year-olds' drawings depicting objects that adults can recognize. 258

pituitary gland An important endocrine gland that controls growth and regulates other glands. 471

placement stage Kellogg's term for 2- to 3-year-olds' drawings that are drawn in placement patterns. 258

placenta Consists of a disk-shaped group of tissues in which small blood vessels from the mother and the offspring intertwine but don't join. 86

play therapy Therapy that lets children work off frustrations while therapists analyze their conflicts and coping methods. 341

pluralism The coexistence of distinct ethnic and cultural groups in the same society, each of which maintains its cultural differences. 557

popular children Children who are frequently nominated as a best friend and are rarely disliked by their peers. 447

postconventional reasoning The highest level in Kohlberg's theory of moral development. At this level, the individual recognizes alternative moral courses, explores the options, and then decides on a personal moral code. 433

postpartum depression Strong feelings of sadness, anxiety, or despair in new mothers that make it difficult for them to carry out daily tasks. 131

postpartum period The period after childbirth when the mother adjusts, both physically and psychologically, to the process of childbearing. This period lasts for about six weeks, or until her body has completed its adjustment and has returned to a near-prepregnant state. 129

practice play Play that involves repetition of behavior when new skills are being learned or when physical or mental mastery and coordination of skills are required for games or sports. 343

pragmatics The appropriate use of language in different contexts. 200

preconventional reasoning The lowest level in Kohlberg's theory of moral development. The individual's concepts of good and bad are controlled primarily by external rewards and punishment. 432

prenatal period The time from conception to birth. 17

preoperational stage Piaget's second stage, lasting from 2 to 7 years of age, during which time children begin to represent the world with words, images, and drawings. In this stage, they also form stable concepts, and begin to reason. At the same time, their cognitive world is dominated by egocentrism and magical beliefs. 279

prepared childbirth Method developed by French obstetrician Ferdinand Lamaze; this childbirth strategy is similar to natural childbirth but includes a special breathing technique to control pushing in the final stages of labor and a more detailed anatomy and physiology course. 118

pretense/symbolic play Play in which the child transforms the physical environment into a symbol. 343

preterm infants Babies born three weeks or more before the pregnancy has reached its full term. 124

primary circular reaction A scheme based on the attempt to reproduce an event that initially occurred by chance. 185

primary emotions Emotions that are present in humans and other animals and emerge early in life; examples are joy, anger, sadness, fear, and disgust. 218

Project Head Start Compensatory education designed to provide children from low-income families the opportunity to acquire the skills and experiences important for school success. 301

proximodistal pattern The sequence in which growth starts at the center of the body and moves toward the extremities. 144

psychoanalytic theories Describe development as primarily unconscious and heavily colored by emotion. Behavior is merely a surface characteristic, and the symbolic workings of the mind have to be analyzed to understand behavior. Early experiences with parents are emphasized. 22

psychoanalytic theory of gender A theory deriving from Freud's view that the preschool child develops a sexual attraction to the opposite-sex parent, by approximately 5 or 6 years of age renounces this attraction because of anxious feelings, and subsequently identifies with the same-sex parent, unconsciously adopting the same-sex parent's characteristics. 321

psychosocial moratorium Erikson's term for the gap between childhood security and adult autonomy. 539

puberty A period of rapid physical maturation involving hormonal and bodily changes that occur primarily in early adolescence. 470

Public Law 94-142 The Education for All Handicapped Children Act, created in 1975, which requires that all children with disabilities be given a free, appropriate public education and which provides the funding to help with the costs of implementing this education. 378

R

rapport talk The language of conversation and a way of establishing connections and negotiating relationships; preferred by females. 439

reciprocal socialization Socialization that is bidirectional; children socialize parents, just as parents socialize children. 233

reflexes Built-in reactions to stimuli that govern the newborn's movements, which are automatic and beyond the newborn's control. 159

reflexive smile A smile that does not occur in response to external stimuli. It happens during the month after birth, usually during sleep. 219

rejected children Children who are infrequently nominated as a best friend and are actively disliked by their peers. 448

report talk Talk that provides information. 439

rite of passage A ceremony or ritual that marks an individual's transition from one status to another. Most rites of passage focus on the transition to adult status. 555

rooting reflex A newborn's built-in reaction that occurs when the infant's cheek is stroked or the side of the mouth is touched. In response, the infant turns its head toward the side that was touched, in an apparent effort to find something to suck. 159

S

scaffolding In cognitive development, Vygotsky used this term to describe the changing support over the course of a teaching session, with the more-skilled person adjusting guidance to fit the child's current performance level. 234

scaffolding Parents time interactions so that infants experience turn-taking with the parents. 282

schemes In Piaget's theory, actions or mental representations that organize knowledge. 183

scientific method An approach that can be used to obtain accurate information. It includes these steps: (1) conceptualize the problem, (2) collect data, (3) draw conclusions, and (4) revise research conclusions and theory. 19

secondary circular reactions Piaget's third sensorimotor substage, which develops between 4 and 8 months of age. In this substage, the infant becomes more object-oriented, moving beyond preoccupation with the self. 185

securely attached babies Babies that use the caregiver as a secure base from which to explore the environment. 230

self–concept Domain-specific evaluations of the self. 428

self–conscious emotions Emotions that require self-awareness, especially consciousness and a sense of "me"; examples include jealousy, empathy, and embarrassment. 218

self–efficacy The belief that one can master a situation and produce favorable outcomes. 414

self–esteem The global evaluative dimension of the self. Self-esteem is also referred to as self-worth or self-image. 428

self–understanding The child's cognitive representation of self, the substance and content of the child's self-conceptions. 313

semantics The meaning of words and sentences. 200

sensation The product of the interaction between information and the sensory receptors— the eyes, ears, tongue, nostrils, and skin. 165

sensorimotor play Behavior engaged in by infants to derive pleasure from exercising their existing sensorimotor schemas. 343

sensorimotor stage The first of Piaget's stages, which lasts from birth to about 2 years of age; infants construct an understanding of the world by coordinating sensory experiences with motoric actions. 184

separation protest An infant's distressed reaction when the caregiver leaves. 220

seriation The concrete operation that involves ordering stimuli along a quantitative dimension (such as length). 389

service learning A form of education that promotes social responsibility and service to the community. 509

sexually transmitted infections (STIs) Diseases that are contracted primarily through sexual contact. This contact is not limited to vaginal intercourse but includes oral-genital contact and anal-genital contact as well. 480

shape constancy The recognition that an object's shape remains the same even though its orientation to us changes. 170

shape stage Kellogg's term for 3-year-olds' drawings consisting of diagrams in different shapes. 258

shared environment experiences Siblings' common experiences, such as their parents' personalities and intellectual orientation, the family's socioeconomic status, and the neighborhood in which they live. 76

short–term memory The memory component in which individuals retain information for up to 30 seconds, assuming there is no rehearsal. 286

sickle–cell anemia A genetic disorder that affects the red blood cells and occurs most often in people of African descent. 74

simple reflexes Piaget's first sensorimotor substage, which corresponds to the first month after birth. In this substage, sensation and action are coordinated primarily through reflexive behaviors. 185

size constancy The recognition that an object remains the same even though the retinal image of the object changes. 170

slow–to–warm–up child A child who has a low activity level, is somewhat negative, and displays a low intensity of mood. 221

small for date (small for gestational age) infants Babies whose birth weight is below normal when the length of pregnancy is considered. 125

social cognitive theory The view of psychologists who emphasize behavior, environment, and cognition as the key factors in development. 28

social cognitive theory of gender A theory that emphasizes that children's gender development occurs through the observation and imitation of gender behavior and through the rewards and punishments children experience for gender-appropriate and gender-inappropriate behavior. 322

social constructivist approach An approach that emphasizes the social contexts of learning and the fact that knowledge is mutually built and constructed; Vygotsky's theory is a social constructivist approach. 282

social contract or utility and individual rights The fifth Kohlberg stage. At this stage, individuals reason that values, rights, and principles undergird or transcend the law. 433

social conventional reasoning Thoughts about social consensus and convention, in contrast to moral reasoning, which stresses ethical issues. 436

social play Play that involves social interactions with peers. 343

social policy The government's course of action to promote the welfare of its citizens. 11

social referencing "Reading" emotional cues in others to help determine how to act in a particular situation. 228

social role theory A theory that gender differences result from the contrasting roles of men and women. 321

social smile A smile in response to an external stimulus, which, early in development, typically is a face. 219

social systems morality The fourth stage in Kohlberg's theory of moral development. Moral judgments are based on understanding the social order, law, justice, and duty. 433

socioeconomic status (SES) The grouping of people with similar occupational, educational, and economic characteristics. 9

socioemotional processes Changes in an individual's relationships with other people, changes in emotions, and changes in personality. 17

solitary play Play in which the child plays alone and independently of others. 342

somnambulism Sleep walking; occurs in the deepest stage of sleep. 262

standardized test A test with uniform procedures for administration and scoring. Many standardized tests allow a person's performance to be compared with the performance of other individuals. 34

stereotype threat The anxiety that one's behavior might confirm a negative stereotype about one's group. 404

strabismus A misalignment of the eyes in which they do not point at the same object together; crossed eyes are one type of strabismus. 254

Strange Situation An observational measure of infant attachment that requires the infant to move through a series of introductions, separations, and reunions with the caregiver and an adult stranger in a prescribed order. 229

stranger anxiety An infant's fear and wariness of strangers; it tends to appear in the second half of the first year of life. 219

strategies Deliberate mental activities to improve the processing of information. 290

sucking reflex A newborn's built-in reaction to automatically suck an object placed in its mouth. The sucking reflex enables the infant to get nourishment before it has associated a nipple with food. 159

sudden infant death syndrome (SIDS) A condition that occurs when an infant stops breathing, usually during the night, and suddenly dies without an apparent cause. 151

symbolic function substage Piaget's first substage of preoperational thought, in which the child gains the ability to mentally represent an object that is not present (roughly between 2 and 4 years of age). 279

syntax The ways words are combined to form acceptable phrases and sentences. 199

T

tabula rasa view The idea, proposed by John Locke, that children are not innately bad but are like a "blank tablet." 13

telegraphic speech The use of short and precise words without grammatical markers such as articles, auxiliary verbs, and other connectives. 203

temperament An individual's behavioral style and characteristic way of emotionally responding. 221

teratogen From the Greek word *tera*, meaning "monster," any agent that can potentially cause a birth defect or negatively alter cognitive or behavioral outcomes. The field of study that investigates the causes of birth defects is called teratology. 98

tertiary circular reactions, novelty, and curiosity Piaget's fifth sensorimotor substage, which develops between 12 and 18 months of age. In this substage, infants become intrigued by the many properties of objects and by the many things that they can make happen to objects. 186

testosterone A hormone associated in boys with the development of genitals, an increase in height, and a change in voice. 472

theory An interrelated, coherent set of ideas that helps to explain and make predictions. 19

theory of mind A concept that refers to awareness of one's own mental processes and the mental processes of others. 290

top-dog phenomenon The circumstance of moving from the top position (in elementary school, the oldest, biggest, and most powerful students) to the lowest position (in middle or junior high school, the youngest, smallest, and least powerful). 516

transitional objects Objects that children repeatedly use as bedtime companions. These usually are soft and cuddly and probably mark the child's transition from being dependent to being more independent. 261

transitivity The ability to logically combine relations to understand certain conclusion. 389

triarchic theory of intelligence Sternberg's theory that intelligence consists of analytical intelligence, creative intelligence, and practical intelligence. 399

trophoblast The outer layer of cells that develops in the germinal period. These cells provide nutrition and support for the embryo. 85

Turner syndrome A chromosomal disorder in females in which either an X chromosome is missing, making the person XO instead of XX, or the second X chromosome is partially deleted. 65

twin study A study in which the behavioral similarity of identical twins is compared with the behavioral similarity of fraternal twins. 74

type I diabetes An autoimmune disease, in which the body's immune system destroys insulin-producing cells. 367

type II diabetes The most common type of diabetes, in which the body is able to produce insulin but it may not be enough or the body cells may be unable to use it. 367

umbilical cord Contains two arteries and one vein, and connects the baby to the placenta. 86

universal ethical principles The sixth and highest stage in Kohlberg's theory of moral development. Individuals develop a moral standard based on universal human rights. 434

unoccupied play Play in which the child is not engaging in play as it is commonly understood and might stand in one spot, or perform random movements that do not seem to have a goal. 342

values Beliefs and attitudes about the way things should be. 507

values clarification An approach to moral education that emphasizes helping people clarify what their lives are for and what's worth working for. Students are encouraged to define their own values and to understand the values of others. 511

visual preference method A method used to determine whether infants can distinguish one stimulus from another by measuring the length of time they attend to different stimuli. 167

voice disorders Disorders reflected in speech that is hoarse, harsh, too loud, too high-pitched, or too low-pitched. 375

Vygotsky's theory A sociocultural cognitive theory that emphasizes how culture and social interaction guide cognitive development. 26

W

Wernicke's area An area of the brain's left hemisphere that is involved in language comprehension. 204

whole-language approach An approach to reading instruction based on the idea that instruction should parallel children's natural language learning. Reading materials should be whole and meaningful. 409

X

XYY syndrome A chromosomal disorder in which males have an extra Y chromosome. 65

Z

zone of proximal development (ZPD) Vygotsky's term for the difference between what children can achieve independently and what they can achieve with the guidance and assistance of adults or more-skilled children. 282

zygote A single cell formed through fertilization. 61

REFERENCES

A

Abel, E. L. (2006). Fetal alcohol syndrome: A cautionary note. *Current Pharmacy Design, 12,* 1521–1529.

Aber, J. L., Bishop-Josef, S. J., Jones, S. M., McLern, T., & Phillips, D. A. (2006). *Child development and social policy.* Washington, DC: American Psychological Association.

Adams, G. R., Gulotta, T. P., & Montemayor, R. (Eds.). (1992). *Adolescent identity formation.* Newbury Park, CA: Sage.

Adams, G., & Snyder, K. (2006). Child care subsidies and low-income parents. In N. Cabrera, R. Hutchens, H. E. Peters, & L. Peters (Eds.), *From Welfare to childcare.* Mahwah, NJ: Erlbaum.

Adamson, L., & Frick, J. (2003). The still face: A history of a shared experimental paradigm. *Infancy, 4,* 451–473.

Adgent, M. A. (2006). Environmental tobacco smoke and sudden infant death syndrome: A review. *Birth Defects Research, 77,* 69–85.

Adler, D., & Millodot, M. (2006). The possible effect of undercorrection on myopic progression in children. *Clinical and Experimental Optometry, 89,* 315–321.

Adolph, K. E. (1997). Learning in the development of infant locomotion. *Monographs of the Society for Research in Child Development, 62* (3, Serial No. 251).

Adolph, K. E., & Berger, S. E. (2005). Physical and motor development. In M. H. Bornstein & M. E. Lamb (Eds.), *Developmental psychology* (5th ed.). Mahwah, NJ: Erlbaum.

Adolph, K. E., & Berger, S. E. (2006). Motor development. In W. Damon & R. Lerner (Eds), *Handbook of child psychology* (6th ed.). New York: Wiley.

Adolph, K. E. & Joh, A. S. (2007). Motor development: How infants get into the act. In A. Slater & M. Lewis (Eds.), *Introduction to infant development* (2nd ed.), New York: Oxford University Press.

Adolph, K. E., & Joh, A. S. (2008, in press). Multiple learning mechanisms in the development of action. In A. Needham & A. Woodward (Eds.), *Learning and the infant mind.* New York: Oxford University Press.

Agras, W. S., Hammer, L. D., McNicholas, F., & Kraemer, H. C. (2004). Risk factors for childhood overweight: A prospective study from birth to 9.5 years. *Journal of Pediatrics, 145,* 20–25.

Aguiar, A., & Baillargeon, R. (2002). Developments in young infants' reasoning about occluded objects. *Cognitive Psychology, 45,* 263–336.

Ahmed, M., Verma, S., Kumar, A., & Siddiqui, M. K. (2005). Environmental exposure to lead and its correlation with biochemical indices in children. *Science of the Total Environment, 346,* 48–55.

Ahluwalia, I. B., Tessaro, I., Grumer-Strawn, L. M., MacGowan, C., & Benton-Davis, S. (2000). Georgia's breastfeeding promotion program for low-income women. *Pediatrics, 105,* E-85–E-87.

Ahn, N. (1994). Teenage childbearing and high school completion: Accounting for individual heterogeneity. *Family Planning Perspectives, 26,* 17–21.

Ahrons, C. (2004). *We're still family.* New York: HarperCollins.

Ahrons, C. R. (2007). Family ties after divorce: Long-term implications for children. *Family Process, 46,* 53–65.

Ainsworth, M. D. S. (1979). Infant-mother attachment. *American Psychologist, 34,* 932–937.

Alan Guttmacher Institute. (1998). *Teen sex and pregnancy.* New York: Author.

Alberto, P. A., & Troutman, A. C. (2006). *Applied analysis for teachers* (7th ed.). Upper Saddle River, NJ: Prentice Hall.

Aldridge, J., & Goldman, R. (2007). *Current issues and trends in education* (2nd ed.). Boston: Allyn & Bacon.

Alexander, P. A. (2006). Psychology in learning and instruction. Upper Saddle River, NJ: Prentice Hall.

Alexander, R. T., & Radisch, D. (2005). Sudden infant death syndrome risk factors with regards to sleep position, sleep surface, and co-sleeping. *Journal of Forensic Science, 50,* 147–151.

Allen, D. B. (2006). Growth hormone therapy for short stature: Is the benefit worth the burden? *Pediatrics, 118,* 343–348.

Allen, J. P. (2007, March). *A transformational perspective on the attachment system in adolescence.* Paper presented at the meeting of the Society for Research in Child Development, Boston.

Allen, J. P., Kuperminc, G. P., Moore, C. (2005, April). *Stability and predictors of change in attachment security across adolescence.* Paper presented at the Meeting of the Society for Research on Child Development, Atlanta.

Allen, J. P., Marsh, P. A., McFarland, F. C., McElhaney, K. B., Land, D. J., Jodl, K. M., et al. (2002). Attachment and autonomy as predictors of the development of social skills and deviance during mid-adolescence. *Journal of Consulting and Clinical Psychology, 70,* 56–66.

Allen, J. P., Moore, C., Kuperminc, G., & Bell, K. (1998). Attachment and adolescent psychosocial functioning. *Child Development, 69,* 1406–1419.

Allen, J. P., Philliber, S., Herring, S., & Kuperminc, G. P. (1997). Preventing teen pregnancy and academic failure: Experimental evaluation of a developmentally-based approach. *Child Development, 68,* 729–742.

Allen, M., Brown, P., & Finlay, B. (1992). *Helping children by strengthening families.* Washington, DC: Children's Defense Fund.

Alm, B. Lagercrantz, H., & Wennergren, G. (2006). Stop SIDS—sleeping solitary supine, sucking smoother, stopping smoking substitutes. *Acta Pediatrica, 95,* 260–262.

Almeida, A. M., Murakami, Y., Baker, A., Maeda, Y., Roberts, I. A., Kinoshita, A., Layton, D. M., & Karadimitris, A. (2007). Targeted therapy for inherited GPI deficiency. *New England Journal of Medicine, 356,* 1641–1647.

Alsaker, F. D., & Flammer, A. (1999). *The adolescent experience: European and American adolescents in the 1990s.* Mahwah, NJ: Erlbaum.

Al-Suleiman, S. A., Al-Janna, F. E., Rhaman, J., & Rhaman, M. S. (2006). Obstetric complications and perinatal outcomes in triplet pregnancies. *Journal of Obstetrics and Gynecology, 26,* 200–204.

Altarac, M., & Saroha, E. (2007). Lifetime prevalence of learning disability among U.S. children. *Pediatrics, 119* (Suppl. 1), S77–S83.

Alvarez, A., & del Rio, P. (2007). Inside and outside the zone of proximal development: An eco-functional reading of Vygotsky. In H. Daniels, J. Wertsch, & M. Cole (Eds.), *The Cambridge companion to Vygotsky.* New York: Cambridge University Press.

Alvik, A., Haldorsen, T., Groholt, B., & Lindemann, R. (2006). Alcohol consumption before and during pregnancy comparing concurrent and retrospective reports. *Alcohol: Clinical and Experimental Research, 30,* 510–515.

Amabile, T. M. (1993). Commentary. In D. Goleman, P. Kaufman, & M. Ray. *The Creative Spirit.* New York: Plume.

Amabile, T. M., & Hennessy, B. A. (1992). The motivation for creativity in children. In A. K. Boggiano & T. S. Pittman (Eds.), *Achievement and motivation.* New York: Cambridge.

Amato, P. R. (2006). Marital discord, divorce, and children's well-being: Results from a 20-year longitudinal study of two generations. In A. Clarke-Stewart & J. Dunn (Eds.), *Families count.* New York: Cambridge University Press.

Amato, P. R., & Booth, A. (1996). A prospective study of divorce and parent-child relationships. *Journal of Marriage and the Family, 58,* 356–365.

Amato, P., & Irving, S. (2006). Historical trends in divorce and dissolution. In M. A. Fine & J. H. Harvey (Eds.), *Handbook of divorce and relationship dissolution.* Mahwah, NJ: Erlbaum.

American Academy of Pediatrics. (2001). Falls from heights: Windows, roofs, and balconies. *Pediatrics, 107,* 1188–1191.

American Academy of Pediatrics. (2004). Recommended childhood and adolescent immunization schedule—United States, January–June 2004. *Pediatrics. 113,* 142–143.

American Academy of Pediatrics (AAP) Work Group on Breastfeeding. (1997). Breastfeeding and the use of human milk. *Pediatrics, 100,* 1035–1039.

American Academy of Pediatrics Task Force on Infant Positioning and SIDS. (2000). Changing concepts of sudden infant death syndrome. *Pediatrics, 105,* 650–656.

American Psychological Association. (2003). *Psychology: Scientific problem solvers.* Washington. DC: Author.

American Public Health Association. (2006). *Understanding the health culture of recent immigrants to the United States.* Retrieved July 28, 2006, from www.apha.org/ppp/red/Intro.htm

American Sports Data. (2001). *Superstudy of sports participation.* Hartsdale, NY: Author.

Amos, D., & Johnson, S. P. (2006). Learning by selection: Visual search and object perception in young infants. *Developmental Psychology, 42,* 1236–1245.

Amsterdam, B. K. (1968). *Mirror behavior in children under two years of age.* Unpublished doctoral dissertation. University of North Carolina, Chapel Hill.

Anastasi, A., & Urbina, S. (1996). *Psychological testing* (7th ed.). Upper Saddle River, NJ: Prentice Hall.

Anderman, E. M., & Wolters, C. A. (2006). Goals, values, and affect: Influences on student motivation. In P. A. Alexander & P. H. Winne (Eds.), *Handbook of educational psychology* (2nd ed.). Mahwah, NJ: Erlbaum.

Anderson, C. A., & Bushman, B. J. (2001). Effects of violent video games on aggressive behavior, aggressive cognition, aggressive affect, physiological arousal, and prosocial behavior: A meta-analytic review of the scientific literature. *Psychological Science, 12,* 353–359.

Anderson, C. A., Gentile, D. A., & Buckley, K. E. (2007). *Violent video game effects on children and adolescents.* New York: Oxford University Press.

Anderson, D. R., Huston, A. C., Schmitt, K., Linebarger, D. L., & Wright, J. C. (2001). Early childhood viewing and adolescent behavior: The recontact study. *Monographs of the Society for Research in Child Development, 66,* (1, Serial No. 264).

Anderson, D. R., Lorch, E. P., Field, D. E., Collins, P., & Nathan, J. (1985, April). *Television viewing at home: Age trends in visual attention and time with TV.* Paper presented at the biennial meeting of the Society for Research in Child Development, Toronto.

Anderson, E., Greene, S. M., Hetherington, E. M., & Clingempeel, W. G. (1999), The dynamics of parental remarriage. In E. M. Hetherington (Ed.), *Coping with divorce, single parenting, and remarriage.* Mahwah, NJ: Erlbaum.

Anderson, J. E., Santelli, J. S., & Morrow, B. (2006). Trends in adolescent contraceptive use, unprotected and poorly protected sex, 1991–2003. *Journal of Adolescent Health, 38,* 734–739.

Anderson, J. L., Waller, D. K., Canfield, M. A., Shaw, G. M., Watkins, M. L., & Werler, M. M. (2005). Maternal obesity, gestational diabetes, and central nervous system birth defects. *Epidemiology, 16,* 87–92.

Anderson, L. M., Shinn, C., Fullilove, M. T., Serimshaw, S. C., Fielding, J. E., Normand, J., & Carande-Kulis, V. G. (2003). The effectiveness of early childhood development programs: A systematic review. *American Journal of Preventive Medicine, 24* (Supp. 3), 32–46.

Anderson, S. J., & Swettenham, J. B. (2006). Neuroimaging in human amblyopia. *Neuroimaging in Human Amblyopia, 14,* 21–35.

Angold, A., Costello, E. J., & Worthman, C. M. (1999). Puberty and depression: The roles of age, pubertal status and pubertal timing. *Psychological Medicine, 28,* 51–61.

Antonacci, P. A. P., & O'Callaghan, C. M. (2006). *A handbook for literacy instructional and assessment strategies, K-8.* Boston: Allyn & Bacon.

Antony, A. C. (2007). In utero physiology: Role of folic acid in nutrient delivery and fetal development. *American Journal of Clinical Nutrition, 85* (Suppl.), 598S–603S.

Ara, I., Vicente-Rodriguez, G., Jimenez-Ramirez, J., Dorado, C., Serrano-Sanchez, J. A., & Calbet, J. A. (2004). Regular participation in sports is associated with enhanced physical fitness and lower body mass in prepubertal boys. *International Journal of Obesity and Related Metabolic Disorders, 28,* 1585–1593.

Araceli, G., Castro, J., Cesena, J., & Toro, J. (2005). Anorexia nervosa in male adolescents: Body image, eating attitudes, and psychological traits. *Journal of Adolescent Health, 36,* 221–226.

Archer, S. L. (1989). The status of identity: Reflections on the need for intervention. *Journal of Adolescence, 12,* 345–359.

Archer, S. L., & Waterman, A. S. (1994). Adolescent identity development: Contextual perspectives. In C. B. Fisher & R. M. Lerner (Eds.), *Applied developmental psychology.* New York: McGraw-Hill.

Archibald, A. B., Graber, J. A., & Brooks-Gunn, J. (2003). Pubertal processes and physical growth in adolescence. In G. R. Adams & M. Berzonsky (Eds.), *Handbook on adolescence.* Malden, MA: Blackwell.

Archibald, A. B., Graber, J.A., & Brooks-Gunn, J. (2003). Pubertal processes and physical growth in adolescence. In G. R. Adams & M. Berzonsky (Eds.). *Handbook on adolescence.* Malden, MA: Blackwell

Arehart, D. M., & Smith, P. H. (1990). Identity in adolescence: Influences on dysfunction and psychosocial task issues. *Journal of Youth and Adolescence, 19,* 63–72.

Arenas, A., Bosworth, K., Kwadayi, H. P., & Compare, A. (2006). Civic service through schools: An international perspective. *Journal of Comparative Education, 36,* 23–40.

Arendt, R., Angelopoulos, J., Salvator, A., & Singer, L. (1999). Motor development of cocaine-exposed children at age two years. *Pediatrics, 103,* 86–92.

Aries, P. (1962). *Centuries of childhood* (R. Baldrick, Trans.). New York: Knopf.

Ariagno, R. L., Van Liempt, S., & Mirmiran, M. (2006). Fewer spontaneous arousals during prone sleep in preterm infants at 1 and 3 months corrected age. *Journal of Perinatology, 26,* 306–312.

Arias, I. (2004). The legacy of child maltreatment: Long-term health consequences for women. *Journal of Women's Health, 13,* 468–473.

Arif, A. A., & Rohrer, J. F. (2006). The relationship between obesity, hyperglycemia symptoms, and health-related quality of life among Hispanic and non-Hispanic white children and adolescents. *BMC Family Practice, 7,* 3.

Armstrong, M. L. (1995) Adolescent tattoos: educating and pontificating. *Pediatric Nursing, 21* (6), 561–564.

Armstrong, M. L., Caliendo, C., & Roberts, A. E. (2006). Genital piercings: What is known and what people with genital piercings tell us. *Urologic Nursing, 26,* 173–180.

Armstrong, M. L., Roberts, A. E., Owen, D. C., & Koch, J. R. (2004). Contemporary college students and body piercing. *Journal of Adolescent Health, 35,* 58–61.

Arnett, J. J. (2000). Emerging adulthood *American Psychologist, 55,* 469–480.

Arnett, J. J. (2004). *Emerging adulthood.* New York: Oxford University Press.

Arnett, J. J. (2006). Emerging adulthood: Understanding the new way of coming of age. In J. J. Arnett & J. L. Tanner (Eds.), *Emerging adults in America.* Washington, DC: American Psychological Association.

Arnett, J. J. (2007). Socialization in emerging adulthood: From the family to the wider world, from socialization to self-socialization. In J. E. Grusec & P. D. Hastings (Eds.), *Handbook of socialization.* New York, Guilford.

Arnett, J. J., & Tanner, J. L. (Eds.) (2006). *Advances in emerging adulthood.* Washington, DC: American Psychological Association.

Aron, A., Aron, E., & Coups, E. (2008). *Statistics for the behavioral and social sciences.* Upper Saddle River, NJ: Prentice Hall.

Aronson, E. (1986, August). *Teaching students things they think they already know about: The case of prejudice and desegregation.* Paper presented at the meeting of the American Psychological Association, Washington, DC.

Aronson, J. (2002). Stereotype threat: Contending and coping with unnerving Expectations. *Improving academic achievement.* San Diego: Academic Press.

Aronson, J. M., Lustina, M. J., Good, C., Keough, K., Steele, C. M., & Brown, J. (1999). When white men can't do math: Necessary and sufficient factors in stereotype threat. *Journal of Experimental Social Psychology, 35,* 29–46.

Aronson, J. M., Fried, C. B., & Good. C. (2002). Reducing the effects of stereotype threat on African American college students by shaping theories of intelligence. *Journal of Experimental Social Psychology. 38,* 113–125.

Arredondo, E. M., Elder, J. P., Ayala, G. X., Campbell, N., Baquero, B., & Duerksen, S. (2006). Is parenting style related to children's healthy eating and physical activity in Latino families? *Health Education Research, 21,* 862–871.

Arshad, S. H. (2005). Primary prevention of asthma and allergy. *Journal of Allergy and Clinical Immunology, 116,* 3–14.

Artiles, A. J., Rueda, R., Salazar, J. J., & Higareda, I. (2005). Within-group diversity in minority disproportionate representation: English language learners in urban school districts. *Exceptional Children, 71,* 283–300.

Ash, P. (2006). Adolescents in adult court: Does the punishment fit the criminal? *The Journal of the American Academy of Psychiatry and the Law, 34,* 145–149.

Asher, J., & Garcia, R. (1969). The optimal age to learn a foreign language. *Modern Language Journal, 53,* 334–341.

Ashkenazi, A., & Silberstein, S. D. (2006). Hormone-related headache: Pathophysiology and treatment. *CNS Drugs, 20,* 125–141.

Ashton, D. (2006). Prematurity—infant mortality: The scourge remains. *Ethnicity & Disease, 16* (Suppl. 2), S3–S58.

Aslin, R. N., Jusczyk, P. W., & Pisoni, D. B. (1998). Speech and auditory processing during infancy: Constraints on and precursors to lanquaqe. In W. Damon (Ed.), *Handbook of child psychology* (5th ed. Vol.2) New York:Wiley.

Aslin, R. N., & Lathrop, A. L. (2008, in press). Visual perception. In M. Haith & J. Benson (Eds.), *Handbook of infant and early childhood development.* London: Elsevier.

Assanand, S., dias, M., Richardson, E., & Waxler-Morrison, N. (1990). The South Asians. In N. Waxler-Morrison, J. M. Anderson, & E. Richardson (Eds.), *Cross-cultural caring.* Vancouver, BC: UBC Press.

Ateah, C. A. (2005). Maternal use of physical punishment in response to child misbehavior: Implications for child abuse prevention. *Child Abuse and Neglect, 29,* 169–185.

Atlantis, E., Barnes, E. H., & Singh, M. A. (2006). Efficacy of exercise for treating overweight in children and adolescents: A systematic review. *International Journal of Obesity, 30,* 1027–1040.

Aucoin, K. J., Frick, P. J., & Bodin, S. D. (2006). Corporal punishment and child adjustment. *Journal of Applied Developmental Psychology, 27,* 527–541.

Avgil, M., & Ornoy, A. (2006). Herpes simplex virus and Epstein-Barr virus infections in pregnancy: Consequences of neonatal or intrauterine infection. *Reproductive Toxicology, 21,* 436–445.

Aylott, M. (2006). The neonatal energy triangle. Part 1: Metabolic adaptation. *Pediatric Nursing 18,* 38–42.

B

Bacak, S. J., Baptiste-Roberts, K., Amon, E., Ireland, B., & Leet, T. (2005). Risk factors for neonatal mortality among extremely-low-birth-weight infants. *American Journal of Obstetrics and Gynecology, 192,* 862–867.

Bacchini, D., & Magliulo, F. (2003). Self-image and perceived self-efficacy during adolescence. *Journal of Youth and Adolescence, 32,* 337–350.

Bachman, J. G. (1982, June 28). *The American high school student: A profile based on national survey data.* Paper presented at a conference entitled "The American High School Today and Tomorrow," Berkeley, CA.

Baddeley, A. (1992). Working memory. *Science, 255,* 556–560.

Baddeley, A. (2000). Short-term and working memory. In E. Tulving & F. I. M. Craik (Eds.), *The Oxford handbook of memory.* New York: Oxford University Press.

Baddock, S. A., Galland, B. C., Taylor, B. J., & Bolton, D. P. (2007). Sleep arrangements and behavior of bed-sharing families in the home setting. *Pediatrics, 119,* e200–e2007.

BaHammam, A., AlFaris, E., Shaikh, S., & Bin Saeed, A. (2006). Prevalence of sleep problems and habits of Saudi primary school children. *Annals of Saudi Medicine, 26,* 7–13.

Bahl, R., Frost, C., Kirkwood, B. R., Edmond, K., Martines, J., Bhandari, N., & Arthur, P. (2005). Infant feeding patterns and risk of death and hospitalization in the first half of infancy: Multicentre cohort study. *Bulletin of the World Health Organization, 83,* 418–426.

Bailey, B. N., Delaney-Black, V., Covington, C. Y., Ager, J., Janisse, J., Hannigan, J. H., & Sokol, R. J. (2004). Prenatal exposure to binge drinking and cognitive and behavioral outcomes at age 7 years. *American Journal of Obstetrics and Gynecology, 191,* 1037–1043.

Bailit, J. L., Love, T. E., & Dawson, N. V. (2006). Quality of obstetric care and risk-adjusted primary cesarean delivery rates. *American Journal of Obstetrics and Gynecology, 194,* 402–407.

Baillargeon, R. (1995). The object concept revisited: New directions in the investigation of infants' physical knowledge, In C. E. Granrud (Ed.), *Visual perception and cognition in infancy.* Hillsdale, NJ: Erlbaum.

Baillargeon, R. (2004). The acquisition of physical knowledge in infancy: A summary in eight lessons. In U. Goswami (Ed.), *Blackwell handbook of childhood cognitive development.* Malden, MA: Blackwell.

Baillargeon, R. H., Zoccolillo, M., Keenna, K., Cote, S., Perusse, D., Wu, H-X., Boivin, M., & Tremblay, R. E. (2007). Gender differences in physical aggression: A prospective population-based survey of children before and after two years of age. *Developmental Psychology, 43,* 13–26.

Baillarqeon, R., & Devos, J. (1991). Object permanence in young children: Further evidence. *Child Development, 62,* 1227–1246.

Bajanowski, T., Brinkmann, B., Mitchell, E. A., Vennemann, M. M., Leukel, H. W., Larsch, K. P., Beike, J., & the GeSID Group. (2007, in press). Nicotine and cotinine in infants dying from sudden infant death syndrome. *International Journal of Legal Medicine.*

Bakeman, R., & Brown, J. V. (1980). Early interaction: Consequences for social and mental development at three years. *Child Development, 51,* 437–447.

Baker, D. A. (2007). Consequences of herpes simplex virus in pregnancy and their prevention. *Current Opinions in Infectious Diseases, 20,* 73–76.

Bakermans-Kranenburg, M. J., Breddels-Van Bardewijk, F., Juffer, M. K., Velderman, M. H., & van IJzenddorn, M. H. (2007). Insecure mothers with temperamentally reactive infants. In F. Juffer, M. J. Bakermans-Kranenburg, & M. H. van IJzendoorn (Eds.), *Promoting positive parenting.* Mahwah, NJ: Erlbaum.

Baldwin, S., & Hoffman, J. P. (2002). The dynamics of self-esteem: A growth curve analysis. *Journal of Youth and Adolescence, 31,* 101–113.

Ballem, K. D., & Plunkett, K. (2005). Phonological specificity in children at 1; 2. *Journal of Child Language, 32,* 159–173.

Baltes, P. B., Lindenberger, U., & Staudinger, U. (2006). Life span theory in developmental psychology. In W. Damon & R. Lerner (Eds.), *Handbook of child psychology* (6th ed.). New York: Wiley.

Bandura, A. (1997). *Self-efficacy.* New York: W. H. Freeman.

Bandura, A. (1998, August). *Swimming against the mainstream: Accentuating the positive aspects of humanity.* Paper presented at the meeting of the American Psychological Association, San Francisco.

Bandura, A. (1999). Moral disengagement in the perpetuation of inhumanities. *Personality and Social Psychology Review, 3,* 193–209.

Bandura, A. (2001). Social cognitive theory. *Annual Review of Psychology* (Vol. 52). Palo Alto, CA: Annual Reviews.

Bandura, A. (2002). Selective moral disengagement in the exercise of moral agency. *Journal of Moral Education, 31,* 101–119.

Bandura, A. (2004, May). *Toward a psychology of human agency.* Paper presented at the meeting of the American Psychological Society, Chicago.

Bandura, A. (2005). Evolution of social cognitive theory. In K. G. Smith & M. A. Hitt (Eds.), *Great minds in management* (pp. 9–35). Oxford: Oxford University Press.

Bandura, A. (2006). Toward a psychology of human agency. *Perspectives on Psychological Science, 1,* 164–180.

Bandura, A. (2007a). Self-efficacy in health functioning. In S. Ayers & others (Eds.), *Cambridge handbook of psychology, health, and medicine.* New York: Cambridge University Press.

Bandura, A. (2007b). Social cognitive theory. In W. Donsbach (Ed.), *International encyclopedia of communication.* Thousand Oaks, CA: Sage.

Bank, L., Burraston, B., & Snyder, J. (2004). Sibling conflict and ineffective parenting as predictors of adolescent boys' antisocial behavior and peer difficulties: Additive and interactive effects. *Journal of Research on Adolescence, 14,* 99–125.

Banks, J. A. (2006). *Cultural diversity and education* (5th ed.). Boston: Allyn & Bacon.

Banks, J. A. (2008). *Introduction to multicultural education* (4th ed.). Boston: Allyn & Bacon.

Banks, M. S. (2005). The benefits and costs of combining information between and within the senses. In J. J. Reiser, J. J. Lockman, & C. A. Nelson (Eds.), *The role of action in learning and development.* Mahwah, NJ: Erlbaum.

Banks, M. S., & Salapatek, P. (1983). Infant visual perception. In P. H. Mussen (Ed.), *Handbook of child psychology* (4th ed., Vol. 2). New York: Wiley.

Barbaresi, W. J., Katusic, S. K., Colligan, R. C., Weaver, A. L., Leibson, C. L., & Jacobsen, S. J. (2006). Long-term stimulant medication treatment of attention-deficit/hyperactivity disorder: Results from a population-based study. *Journal of Developmental and Behavioral Pediatrics, 27,* 1–10.

Barber, B. L. (2006). To have loved and lost . . . Adolescent romantic relationships and rejection. In A. C. Crouter & A. Booth (Eds.), *Romance and sex in adolescence and emerging adulthood.* Mahwah, NJ: Erlbaum.

Barber, B., & Demo, D. H. (2005). The kids are alright (at least, most of them): Links between divorce and dissolution and child well-being. In M. Fine & J. Harvey (Eds.), *Handbook of divorce and relationship dissolution.* Mahwah, NJ: Erlbaum.

Bardenheir, B. H., Yusuf, H. R., Rosenthal, J., Santoli, J. M., Shefer, A. M., Rickert, D. L., & Chu, S. Y. (2004). Factors associated with underimmunization at 3 months of age in our medically underserved areas. *Public Health Reports, 119,* 479–485.

Barker, R., & Wright, H. F. (1951). *One boy's day.* New York: Harper & Row.

Barnet, B., Arroyo, C., Devoe, M., & Duggan, A. K. (2004). Reduced school dropout rates among adolescent mothers receiving school-based prenatal care. *Archives of Pediatric and Adolescent Medicine, 158,* 262–268.

Baron-Cohen, S. (2004). Autism research in to causes and intervention. *Pediatric Rehabilitation, 7,* 73–78.

Baron-Cohen, S., Leslie, A. M., & Frith, U. (1985). Does the autistic child have a "theory of mind"? *Cognition, 21,* 37–46.

Barone, D., Hardman, D., & Taylor, J. (2006). *Reading first in the classroom.* Boston: Allyn & Bacon.

Barrett, D. E., Radke-Yarrow, M., & Klein, R. E. (1982). Chronic malnutrition and child behavior: Effects of calorie supplementation on social and emotional functioning at school age. *Developmental Psychology, 18,* 541–556.

Barrett, L. F., Mesquita, B., Ochsner, K. N., & Gross, J. J. (2007). The experience of emotion. *Annual Review of Psychology* (Vol. 58). Palo Alto, CA: Annual Reviews.

Barrett, T. M., Davis, E. F., & Needham, A. (2007). Learning about tools in infancy. *Developmental Psychology, 43,* 352–368.

Barron, J., Petrilli, F., Strath, L., & McCaffrey, R. (2007). Successful interventions for smoking cessation in pregnancy. *MCN American Journal of Maternal and Child Nursing, 32,* 42–47.

Bartko, T. W., & Eccles, J. S. (2003). Adolescent participation in structured and unstructured activities: A person-oriented analysis. *Journal of Youth and Adolescence, 32,* 233–241.

Bartle, C. (2007). Developing a service for children with iron deficiency anemia. *Nursing Standard, 21,* 44–49.

Barton, W. H. (2004). Bridging juvenile justice and positive youth development. In S. F. & M. A. Hamilton (Eds.), *The youth development handbook.* Thousand Oaks, CA: Sage.

Barton, W. H. (2005). Juvenile justice policies and programs. In J. M. Jenson & M. W. Fraser (Eds.). *Social policy for children and families.* Thousand Oaks, CA: Sage.

Basaran, S., Guler-Uysal, F., Ergen, N., Seydaoglu, G., Bingol-Karakoe, G., & Ufuk Altintas, D. (2006). Effects of physical exercise on quality of life, exercise capacity, and pulmonary function in children with asthma. *Journal of Rehabilitation Medicine and Science, 38,* 130–135.

Baskett, L. M., & Johnson, S. M. (1982). The young child's interaction with parents versus siblings. *Child Development, 53,* 643–650.

Bateman, B. T., & Simpson, L. L. (2006). Higher rate of stillbirth at the extremes of reproductive age: A large nationwide sample of deliveries in the United States. *American Journal of Obstetrics and Gynecology, 194,* 840–845.

Bates, A. S., Fitzgerald, J. F., Dittus, R. S., & Wollinsky, F. D. (1994). Risk factors for underimmunization in poor urban infants. *Journal of the American Medical Association, 272,* 105–1109.

Bates, E. (1990). Language about me and you: Pronomial reference and the emerging concept of self. In D. Cicchetti & M. Beeghly (Eds.), *The self in transition: Infancy to childhood* (pp. 165–182). Chicago: University of Chicago Press.

Bates, J. E., & Pettit, G. S. (2007). Temperament, parenting, and socialization. In J. E. Grusec & P. D. Hastings (Eds.), *Handbook of socialization.* New York: Guilford.

Bauer, P. J. (2005). Developments in declarative memory. *Psychological Science, 16,* 41–47.

Bauer, P. J. (2006). Event memory. In W. Damon & R. Lerner (Eds.), *Handbook of child psychology* (6th ed.). New York: Wiley.

Bauer, P. J. (2007). *Remembering the times of our lives.* Mahwah, NJ: Erlbaum.

Bauer, P. J. (2008, in press). Learning and memory: Like a horse and carriage. In A. Needham & A. Woodward (Eds.), *Learning and the infant mind.* New York: Oxford University Press.

Bauer, P. J., Wenner, J. A., Dropik, P. L., & Wewerka, S. S. (2000). Parameters of remembering and forgetting in the transition from infancy to early childhood. *Monographs of the Society for Research in Child Development, 65* (4, Serial No. 263).

Bauer, P. J., Wiebe, S. A., Carver, L. J., Waters, J. M., & Nelson, C. A. (2003). Developments in long-term explicit memory late in the first year of life: Behavioral and electrophysiological indices. *Psychological Science, 14,* 629–635.

Bauman, K. E., Ennett, S. T., Foshee, V. A., Pemberton, M., King, T. S., & Koch, G. G. (2002). Influence of a family program on adolescent smoking and drinking prevalence. *Prevention Science, 3,* 35–42.

Baumeister, R. F., Campbell, J. D., Krueger, J. I., & Vohs, K. D. (2003). Does high self esteem cause better performance, interpersonal success, happiness, or healthier lifestyles? *Psychological Science in the Public Interest, 4* (No. 1), 1–44.

Baumrind, D. (1971). Current patterns of parental authority. *Developmental Psychology Monographs, 4* (1, Pt. 2).

Baumrind, D., Larzelere, R. E., & Cowan, P. A. (2002). Ordinary physical punishment: Is it harmful? Comment on Gershoff. *Psychological Bulletin, 128,* 590–595.

Bauserman, R. (2002). Child adjustment in joint-custody versus sole-custody arrangements: A meta-analytic review. *Journal of Family Psychology, 16,* 91–102.

Baxley, F., & Miller, M. (2006). Parental misperceptions about children and firearms. *Archives of Pediatric and Adolescent Medicine, 160,* 542–547.

Bayley, N. (1943). Mental growth during the first three years. In R. G. Barker, J. S. Kounin, & H. F. Wright (Eds.), *Child behavior and development.* New York: McGraw-Hill.

Bayley, N. (1969). *Manual for the Bayley Scales of Infant Development.* New York: Psychological Corporation.

Bayley, N. (1970). Development of mental abilities. In P. H. Mussen (Ed.), *Manual of child psychology* (3rd ed., Vol. 1). New York: Wiley.

Beal, C. R. (1994). *Boys and girls: The development of gender roles.* Boston: McGraw-Hill.

Bearman, P. S., & Moody, J. (2004). Suicide and friendships among American adolescents. *American Journal of Public Health, 94,* 89–95.

Bearman, S. K., Presnall, K., Martinez, E., & Stice, E. (2006). The skinny on body dissatisfaction: A longitudinal study of adolescent girls and boys. *Journal of Youth and Adolescence, 35,* 217–229.

Bech, B. H., Obel, C., Henriksen, T. B., & Olsen, J. (2007). Effect of reducing caffeine intake on birth weight and length of gestation: Randomized controlled trial. *British Medical Journal, 334,* 409.

Bechtold, A. G., Busnell, E. W., & Salapatek, P. (1979, April.) *Infants' visual localization of visual and auditory targets.* Paper presented at the meeting of the Society for Research in Child Development, San Francisco.

Beck, C. T. (2002). Theoretical perspectives of postpartum depression and their treatment implications. *American Journal of Maternal/Child Nursing, 27,* 282–287.

Beck, C. T. (2006). Postpartum depression: It isn't just the blues. *American Journal of Nursing, 106,* 40–50.

Beckmann, M. M., & Garrett, A. J. (2006). Antenatal perineal massage for reducing perineal trauma. *Cochrane Database of Systematic Reviews, 1,* CD005123.

Bednar, R. L., Wells, M. G., & Peterson, S. R. (1995). *Self-esteem* (2nd ed.). Washington, DC: American Psychological Association.

Beeghly, M., Martin, B., Rose-Jacobs, R., Cahral, H., Heeren, T., Augustyn, M., Bellinger, D., & Frank, D. A. (2006). Prenatal cocaine exposure and children's language functioning at 6 and 9.5 years: Moderating effects of child age, birthweight, and gender. *Journal of Pediatric Psychology, 31,* 98–115.

Bell, K. N., & Oakley, G. P. (2006). Tracking the prevention of folic acid–preventable spina bifida and anencephaly. *Birth Defects Research A: Clinical and Molecular Teratology, 76,* 654–657.

Bell, M. A., & Fox, N. A. (1992). The relations between frontal brain electrical activity and cognitive development during infancy. *Child Development, 63,* 1142–1163.

Bell, S. M., & Ainsworth, M. D. S. (1972). Infant crying and maternal responsiveness. *Child Development, 43,* 1171–1190.

Bellinger, D. C. (2005). Teratogen update: Lead and pregnancy. *Birth Defects Research, 73,* 409–420.

Bellinger, D., Leviton, A., Waternaux, C., Needleman, H., & Rabinowitz, M. (1987). Longitudinal analysis of prenatal and postnatal lead exposure and early cognitive development. *New England Journal of Medicine, 316,* 1037–1043.

Belsky, J. (1981). Early human experience: A family perspective. *Developmental Psychology, 17,* 3–23.

Belsky, J., & Pasco Fearon, R. (2002a). Early attachment security, subsequent maternal sensitivity, and later child development: Does continuity in development depend upon continuity of caregiving? *Attachment and Human Development, 4,* 361–387.

Belsky, J., & Pasco Fearon, R. (2002b). Infant-mother attachment security, contextual risk, and early development: A moderational analysis. *Development and Psychopathology, 14,* 293–310.

Belsky, J., Vandell, D. L., Burchinal, M., Clarke-Stewart, A., McCartney, K., Owen, M. T., & the NICHD Early Child Care Research Network (2007). Are there long-term effects of early child care. *Child Development, 78,* 681–701.

Belson, W. (1978). *Television violence and the adolescent boy.* London: Saxon House.

Bender, H. L., Allen, J. P., McElhaney, K. B., Antonishak, J., Moore, C. M., Kello, H. O., & Davis, S. M. (2007). Use of harsh physical discipline and developmental outcomes in adolescence. *Development and Psychopathology, 19,* 227–242.

Bender, W. N. (2008). *Learning disabilities* (6th ed.). Boston: Allyn & Bacon.

Bendersky, M. & Sullivan, M. (2007). Basic methods in infant research. In A. Slater & M. Lewis (Eds.), *Introduction to infant development* (2nd ed.). New York: Oxford University Press.

Benenson, J. F., Apostolaris, N. H., & Parnass, J. (1997). Age and sex differences in dyadic and group interaction. *Developmental Psychology, 33,* 538–543.

Benjet, C., & Kazdin, A. E. (2003). Spanking children: The controversies, findings, and new directions. *Clinical Psychology Review, 23,* 197–224.

Bennett, C. I. (2007). *Comprehensive multicultural education* (6th ed.). Boston: Allyn & Bacon.

Bennett, S. E., & Assefi, N. P. (2005). School-based teenage pregnancy prevention programs: A systematic review of randomized controlled trials. *Journal of Adolescent Health, 36,* 72–81.

Bennett, W. (1993). *The book of virtues.* New York: Simon & Schuster.

Benninghoven, D., Tetsch, N., Kunzendorf, S., & Jantschek, G. (2007). Body image in patients with eating disorders and their mothers, and the role of family functioning. *Comprehensive Psychiatry, 48,* 118–123.

Benson, P. L. (2006). *All kids are our kids.* San Francisco: Jossey-Bass.

Benson, P. L. (2006). The science of child and adolescent spiritual development: Definitional, theoretical, and field-building challenges. In E. C. Roehlkepartain, P. E. King, & L. M. Wagener (Eds.), *The handbook of spiritual development in childhood and adolescence.* Thousand Oaks, CA: Sage.

Benson, P. L., Scales, P. C., Hamilton, S. F., & Sesma, A. (2006). Positive youth development: Theory, research, and applications. In W. Damon & R. Lerner (Eds.), *Handbook of child psychology* (6th ed.). New York: Wiley.

Berenbaum, S. A., & Bailey, J. M. (2003). Effects on gender identity of prenatal androgens and genital appearance: Evidence from girls with congenital adrenal hyperplasia. *Journal of Endocrinology and Metabolism, 88,* 1102–1106.

Berensen, G. S. (2005). Obesity—A critical issue in preventive cardiology: The Bogalusa Heart Study. *Preventive Cardiology, 8,* 234–241.

Berensen, G. S., Srinivasan, S. R., & the Bogalusa Heart Study Group. (2005).

Cardiovascular risk factors in youth with implications for aging: The Bogalusa Heart Study. *Neurobiology of Aging, 26,* 303–307.

Bergen, D. (1988). Stages of play development. In D. Bergen (Ed.), *Play as a medium for learning and development.* Portsmouth, NH: Heinemann.

Berk, L. E. (1994). Why children talk to themselves. *Scientific American, 271* (5), 78–83.

Berk, L. E., & Spuhl, S. T. (1995). Maternal interaction, private speech, and task performance in preschool children. *Early Childhood Research Quarterly, 10,* 145–169.

Berko Gleason, J. (2003). Unpublished review of J. W. Santrock's *Life-span development* (9th ed.). (New York: McGraw-Hill).

Berko Gleason, J. (2005). The development of language: In J. Berko Gleason, *The development of language* (6th ed.). Boston: Allyn & Bacon.

Berko, J. (1958). The child's learning of English morphology. *Word, 14,* 150–177.

Berkowitz, C. D. (2004). Cosleeping: Benefits, risks, and cautions. *Advances in Pediatrics, 51,* 329–349.

Berkowitz, M. W., & Bier, M. C. (2004). Research-based character education. *Annals of the American Academy of Political and Social Science, 591,* 72–85.

Berkowitz, M. W., Sherblom, S., Bier, M., & Battistich, V. (2006). Educating for positive youth development. In M. Killen & J. Smetana (Eds.), *Handbook of moral development.* Mahwah, NJ: Erlbaum.

Berlin, L. J., Ziv, Y., Amaya-Jackson, L., & Greenberg, M. T. (2007). *Enhancing early attachments.* New York: Guilford.

Berlin, L., & Cassidy, J. (2000). Understanding parenting: Contributions of attachment theory and research. In J. D. Osofsky & H. E. Fitzgerald (Eds.), *WAIMH handbook of infant mental health* (Vol. 3). New York: Wiley.

Berlyne, D. E (1960). *Conflict, arousal, and curiosity.* New York: McGraw-Hill.

Bern, S. L. (1977). On the utility of alternative procedures for assessing psychological androgyny. *Journal of Consulting and Clinical Psychology, 45,* 196–205.

Berndt, T. J. (2002). Friendship quality and social development, *Current Directions in Psychological Science, 11,* 7–10.

Berndt, T. J., & Perry, T. B. (1990). Distinctive features and effects of early adolescent friendships. In R. Montemayor (Ed.), *Advances in adolescent research.* Greenwich, CT: JAI Press.

Berninger, V. W. (2006). Learning disabilities. In W. Damon & R. Lerner (Eds.), *Handbook of child psychology* (6th ed.). New York: Wiley.

Berninger, V. W., & Abbott, R. (2005, April). *Paths leading to reading comprehension in at-risk and normally developing second grade readers.* Paper

presented at the meeting of the Society for Research in Child Development, Atlanta.

Berry, J. W. (2006). Acculturation. In M. H. Bornstein & L. R. Cote (Eds.), *Acculturation and parent-child relationships.* Mahwah, NJ: Erlbaum.

Berry, J. W. (2007). Acculturation. In J. E. Grusec & P. D. Hastings (Eds.), *Handbook of socialization.* New York: Guilford.

Bersamin, M. M., Walker, S., Fisher, D. A., & Grube, J. W. (2006). Correlates of oral sex and vaginal intercourse in early and middle adolescence. *Journal of Research on Adolescence, 16,* 59–68.

Bertenthal, B. (2005). Theories, methods, and models: Discussion of the chapters by Newcombe, Thelen, & Whitmeyer. In J. J. Reiser, J. J. Lockman, & C. A. Nelson (Eds.), *The role of action in learning and development.* Mahwah, NJ: Erlbaum.

Bessey, P. Q., Arons, R. R., Dimaggio, C. J., & Yurt, R. W. (2006). The vulnerabilities of age: Burns in children and older adults. *Surgery, 140,* 705–715.

Best, J. M. (2007, in press). Rubella. *Seminars in Fetal and Neonatal Medicine.*

Bethesda, MD: National Institute on Drug Abuse.

Betz, N. E. (2006). Women's career development. In J. Worell & C. D. Goodheart (Eds.), *Handbook of girls' and women's psychological health.* New York: Oxford University Press.

Bhutta, Z. A., Darmstadt, G. L., Hasan, B. S., & Haws, R. A. (2005). Community-based interventions for improving perinatal and neonatal health outcomes in developing countries: A review of the evidence. *Pediatrics, 113,* 519–616.

Bialystok, E. (1993). Metalinguistic awareness: The development of children's representations in language. In C. Pratt & A. Garton (Eds.), *Systems of representation in children.* London: Wiley.

Bialystok, E. (1997). Effects of bilingualism and biliteracy on children's emerging concepts of print. *Developmental Psychology, 33,* 429–440.

Bialystok, E. (1999). Cognitive complexity and attentional control in the bilingual mind. *Child Development, 70,* 537–804.

Bialystok, E. (2001). *Bilingualism in development: Language, literacy, and cognition.* New York: Cambridge University Press.

Bierman, K. L. (2004). *Peer rejection.* New York: Guilford.

Billman, J. (2003). *Observation and participation in early childhood settings: A practicum guide* (2nd ed.). Boston: Allyn & Bacon.

Billson, F. A., Fitzgerald, B. A., & Provis, J. M. (1985). Visual deprivation in infancy and childhood: Clinical aspects. *Australian and New Zealand Journal of Ophthalmology, 13,* 279–286.

Billy, J. O. G., Rodgers, J. L., & Udry, J. R. (1984). Adolescent sexual behavior and friendship choice. *Social Forces, 62,* 653–678.

Bindler, R. M., & Bruya, M. A. (2006). Evidence for identifying children at risk for being overweight, cardiovascular disease, and type 2 diabetes in primary care. *Journal of Pediatric Health Care, 20,* 82–87.

Birch, E. E., Fawcett, S. L., Morale, S. E., Weakley, D. R., & Wheaton, D. H. (2005). Risk factors for accommodative estrapia among hypermetropic children. *Investigations in Ophthalmology and Vision Science, 46,* 526–529.

Birren, J. E. (Ed.). (2007). Encyclopedia of Gerontology (2nd ed.). Oxford, UK: Elsevier.

Bishop, D. V., Laws, G., Adams, C., & Norbury, C. F. (2006). High heritability of speech and language impairments in 6-year-old twins demonstrated using parent and teacher report. *Behavior Genetics, 36,* 173–184.

Bjorklund, D. F. (2006). Mother knows best: Epigenetic inheritance, maternal effects, and the evolution of human intelligence. *Developmental Review, 26,* 213–242.

Bjorklund, D. F. (2007). *Why youth is not wasted on the young.* Malden, MA: Blackwell.

Bjorklund, D. F., & Pellegrini, A. D. (2002). *The origins of human nature.* New York: Oxford University Press.

Blachman, B. A., Ball, E., Black, R., & Tangel, D. (1994). Kindergarten teachers develop phenome awareness in low-income inner-city classrooms: Does it make a difference? In B. A. Blachman (Ed.), *Reading and writing.* Mahwah, NJ: Erlbaum.

Black, M. M., & others. (2004). Special Supplemental Nutrition Program for Women, Infants, and Children participation and infants' growth and health: A multisite surveillance study. *Pediatrics, 114,* 169–176.

Blasi, A. (2005). Moral character: A psychological approach. In D. K. Lapsley & F. C. Power (Eds.) *Character psychology and character education.* Notre Dame, IN: University of Notre Dame Press.

Block, C. C., & Pressley, M. (2007). Best practices in teaching comprehension. In L. B. Gambrell, L. M. Morrow, & M. Pressley (Eds), *Best practices in literacy instruction.* New York: Guilford.

Block, J. H., & Block, J. (1980). The role of ego-control and ego-resiliency in the organization of behavior. In W. A. Collins (Ed.), *Minnesota symposium on child psychology* (Vol. 13). Minneapolis: University of Minnesota Press.

Bloom, B. (1985). *Developing talent in young people.* New York: Ballentine.

Bloom, B., & Dev, A. N. (2006). Summary health statistics for U.S. children: National Health Interview Survey, 2004. *Vital Health Statistics, 227,* 1–85.

Bloom, L. (1998). Language acquisition in developmental context. In W. Damon (Ed.), *Handbook of child psychology* (5th ed., Vol. 5). New York: Wiley.

Bloom, L., Lifter, K., & Broughton, J. (1985). The convergence of early cognition and language in the second year of life: Problems in conceptualization and measurement. In M. Barrett (Ed.), *Single word speech.* London: Wiley.

Blum, J. W., Beaudoin, C. M., & Caton-Lemos, L. (2005). Physical activity patterns and maternal well-being in postpartum women. *Maternal and Child Health Journal, 8,* 163–169.

Blum, R., & Nelson-Mmari, K. (2004). Adolescent health from an international perspective. In R. Lerner & L. Steinberg (Eds.), *Handbook of adolescent psychology.* New York: Wiley.

Blumenfeld, P. C., Kempler, T. M., & Krajcik, J. S. (2006). Motivation and cognitive engagement in learning environments. In R. K. Sawyer (Ed.). *Cambridge handbook of learning sciences.* New York: Cambridge University Press.

Bodrova, E., & Leong, D. J. (2001). *Tools of the mind.* Geneva: International Bureau of Education, UNESCO. Retrieved August 10, 2005 from www.ibe.unesco.org/International/Publications/ INNODATA, Monograph/inno07.pdf

Bodrova, E., & Leong, D. J. (2007). *Tools of the mind* (2nd ed.). Geneva: International Bureau of Education, UNESCO.

Boer, K., Nellen, J. F., Patel, D., Timmermans, S., Tempelman, C., Wibaut, M., Sluman, M. A., van der Ende, M. E., & Godfried, M. H. (2007). The AmRo study: Pregnancy outcomes in HIV-1-infected women under effective highly active antiretroviral therapy and a policy of vaginal delivery. *British Journal of Obstetrics and Gynecology, 114,* 148–155.

Bohlin, G., & Hagekull, B. (1993). Stranger wariness and sociability in the early years. *Infant Behavior and Development, 16,* 53–67.

Bojesen, A., & Gravholt, C. H. (2007). Klinefelter syndrome in clinical practice. *Nature Clinical Practice: Urology, 4,* 192–204.

Bolger, K. E., & Patterson, C. J. (2001). Developmental pathways from child maltreatment to peer rejection. *Child Development, 72,* 339–351.

Bonvillian, J. (2005). Unpublished review of J. W. Santrock's *Topical life-span development* (3rd ed.). New York: McGraw-Hill.

Boonstra, H. (2002, February). Teen pregnancy: Trends and lessons learned. *The Guttmacher Report on Public Policy,* pp. 7–10.

Booth, A. (2006). Object function and categorization in infancy: Two mechanisms of facilitation. *Infancy, 10,* 145–169.

Booth, A., Johnson, D. R., Granger, D. A., Crouter, A. C., & McHale, S. (2003). Testosterone and child and adolescent adjustment: The moderating role of parent-child relationships. *Developmental Psychology, 39,* 85–98.

Booth, M. (2002). Arab adolescents facing the future: Enduring ideals and pressures to change. In B. B. Brown, R. W. Larson, & T. S. Saraswathi (Eds.), *The world's youth.* New York: Cambridge University Press.

Bor, W., McGee, T. R., & Fagan, A. A. (2004). Early risk factors for adolescent antisocial behavior: An Australian longitudinal study. *Australian and New Zealand Journal of Psychiatry, 38,* 365–372.

Borders, N. (2006). After the afterbirth: A critical review of postpartum health relative to method of delivery. *Journal of Midwifery and Women's Health, 51,* 242–248.

Borkowski, J. G., Farris, J. R., Whitman, T. L., Carothers, S. S., Weed, K., & Keogh, D. A. (Eds.). (2007). *Risk and resilience.* Mahwah, NJ: Erlbaum.

Bornstein, M. H. (2006). Parenting science and practice. In W. Damon & R. Lerner (Eds.), *Handbook of child psychology* (6th ed.). New York: Wiley.

Bornstein, M. H., Arterberry, M. E., & Mash, C. (2005). Perceptual development. In M. H. Bornstein & M. E. Lamb (Eds.), *Developmental psychology* (5th ed.). Mahwah, NJ: Erlbaum.

Bornstein, M. H., & Cote, L. R. (Eds.). (2006). *Acculturation and parent-child relationships.* Mahwah, NJ: Erlbaum.

Bornstein, M. H., & Sigman, M. D. (1986). Continuity in mental development from infancy. *Child Development, 57,* 251–274.

Bornstein, M. H., & Tamis-LeMonda, C. S. (2007). Infants at play: Development, functions, and partners. In A. Slater & M. Lewis (Eds.), *Introduction to infant development.* Malden, MA: Blackwell.

Borra, S. T., Kelly, L., Shirreffs, M. B., Neville, K., & Geiger, C. J. (2003). Developing health messages. *Journal of the American Dietary Association, 103,* 721–728.

Bouchard, T. J. (1995, August). *Heritability of intelligence.* Paper presented at the meeting of the American Psychological Association, New York.

Bouchard, T. J., Lykken, D. T., McGue, M., Segal, N. L., & Tellegen, A. (1990). Source of human psychological differences. The Minnesota Study of Twins Reared Apart. *Science, 250,* 223–228.

Bouchey, H. A., & Furman, W. (2003). Dating and romantic relationships in adolescence. In G. Adams & M. Berzonsky (Eds.), *Blackwell handbook of adolescence.* Malden, MA: Blackwell.

Boukydis, C. F. Z., Bigsby, R., & Lester, B. M. (2004). Clinical use of the Neonatal Intensive Care Unit Network Neurobehavioral Scales. *Pediatrics, 113* (Suppl.), S679–S689.

Bower, B. (1985). The left hand of math and verbal talent. *Science News, 127,*263.

Bower, T. G. R. (1966). Slant perception and shape constancy in infants. *Science,* 151, 832–834.

Bower, T. G. R. (2002). Space and objects. In A. Slater & M. Lewis (Eds.), *Introduction to infant development.* New York: Oxford University Press.

Bowes, J., & Flanagan, C. A. (2000, July). *The relationship of empathy, sympathy, and altruism in adolescence: International comparisons.* Paper presented at the meeting of the International Society for the Study of Behavioral Development, Beijing, China.

Bowlby, J. (1969). *Attachment and loss* (Vol. 1). London: Hogarth Press.

Bowlby, J. (1989). *Secure and insecure attachment.* New York: Basic Books.

Bowles, T. (1999). Focusing on time orientation to explain adolescent self concept and academic achievement: Part II. Testing a model. *Journal of Applied Health Behaviour, I,* 1–8.

Boyer, K., & Diamond, A. (1992). Development of memory for temporal order in infants and young children. In A. Diamond (Ed.), *Development and neural bases of higher cognitive function.* New York: New York Academy of Sciences.

Boyle, J., & Cropley, M. (2004). Children's sleep: Problems and solutions. *Journal of Family Health Care, 14,* 61–63.

Boyle, M. A., & Long, S. (2007). *Personal nutrition* (6th ed.). Belmont, CA: Wadsworth.

Boyles, N. S., & Contadino, D. (1997). *The learning differences sourcebook.* Los Angeles: Lowell House.

Bracey, J. R., Bamaca, M. Y., & Umana-Taylor, A. J. (2004). Examining ethnic identity among biracial and monoracial adolescents. *Journal of Youth and Adolescence, 33,* 123–132.

Brachlow, A., Jordan, A. E., & Tervo, R. (2001). Developmental screenings in rural settings: A comparison of the child developmental review and the Denver II Developmental Screening Test. *Journal of Rural Health, 17,* 156–159.

Bracken, M. B., Eskenazi, B., Sachse, K., McSharry, J., Hellenbrand, K., & Leo-Summers, L. (1990). Association of cocaine use with sperm concentration, motility, and morphology. *Fertility and Sterility, 53,* 315–322.

Bradley, R. H., & McKelvey, L. (2007). Managing the differences within: Immigration and early childhood education in the United States. In J. E. Lansford, K. Deater-Deckhard, & M. H. Bornstein (Eds.), *Immigrant families in contemporary society.* New York: Guilford.

Bradshaw, C. P., & Garbarino, J. (2004). Using and building family strengths to promote youth development. In S. F. Hamilton & M. A. Hamilton (Eds.), *The youth development handbook.* Thousand Oaks, CA: Sage.

Brainerd, C. J., & Reyna, V. E. (1993). Domains of fuzzy-trace theory. In M. L. Howe &

R. Pasnak (Eds.), *Emerging themes in cognitive development*. New York: Springer.

Bransford, J., & others. (2006). Learning theories in education. In P. A. Alexander & P. H. Winne (Eds.), *Handbook of educational psychology* (2nd ed.). Mahwah, NJ: Erlbaum.

Brazelton, T. B. (1956). Sucking in infancy. *Pediatrics, 17*, 400–404.

Brazelton, T. B., (2004). Preface: The Neonatal Intensive Care Unit Network Neurobehavioral Scale. *Pediatrics, 113* (Suppl.) S632–S633.

Bredekamp, S. (1997). NAEYC issues revised position statement on developmentally appropriate practice in early childhood programs. *Young Children, 52*, 34–40.

Bremner, G. (2007). Perception and knowledge of the world. In A. Slater & M. Lewis (Eds.), *Introduction to infant development* (2nd ed.). Malden, MA: Blackwell.

Brennan, A. M., & Mantzoros, C. S. (2006). Drug insight: The role of leptin in human pathophysiology—emerging clinical applications. *Nature Clinical Practice: Endocrinology and Metabolism, 2*, 318–327.

Breslau, N., Paneth, N. S., & Lucia, V. C. (2004). The lingering academic deficits of low birth weight children. *Pediatrics, 114*, 1035–1040.

Bretherton, I., Fritz, J., Zahn-Waxler, C., & Ridgeway, D. (1986). Learning to talk about emotions: A functionalist perspective. *Child Development, 57*, 529–548.

Bretherton, I., Stolberg, U., & Kreye, M. (1981). Engaging strangers in proximal interaction: Infants' social initiative. *Developmental Psychology, 17*, 746–755.

Brewer, J. A. (2007). *Introduction to early childhood education* (6th ed.). Boston: Allyn & Bacon.

Briefel, R. R., Redy, K., Karwe, V., Jankowski, L., & Hendricks, K. (2004). Toddler's transition to table foods: Impact on nutrient intakes and food patterns. *Journal of the American Dietic Association, 104*, 38–44.

Briggs, G. G., & Wan, S. R. (2006). Drug therapy during labor and delivery, Part 1. *American Journal of Health-System Pharmacy, 63*, 1038–1047.

Briken, P., Habermann, N., Berner, W., & Hill, A. (2006). XYY chromosome abnormality in sexual homicide perpetrators. *American Journal of Medical Genetics B: Neuropsychiatry and Genetics, 141*, 198–200.

Bril, B. (1999). Dires sur l'enfant selon les cultures. Etat des lieux et perspectives. In B. Brill, P. R. Dasen, C. Sabatier, & B. Krewer (Eds.), *Propossur l'enfant et l'adolescent. Quels enfants pour quelles cultures?* Paris: L'Harmattan.

Brockmeyer, S., Treboux, D., & Crowell, J. A. (2005, April). *Parental divorce and adult children's attachment status and marital relationships*. Paper presented at the meeting of the Society for Research in Child Development, Atlanta.

Brody, N. (2000). Intellignece. In A. Kazdin (Ed.), *Encyclopedia of psychology*. Washington DC, & New York:American Psychological Association and Oxford University Press.

Brody, N. (2007). Does education influence intelligence? In P. C. Kyllonen, R. D. Roberts, & L. Stankov (Eds.), *Extending intelligence*. Mahwah, NJ: Erlbaum.

Brodzinsky, D. M., Lang, R., & Smith, D. W. (1995). Parenting adopted children. In M. H. Bornstein (Ed.), *Handbook of parenting* (Vol. 3). Hillsdale, NJ: Erlbaum.

Brodzinsky, D. M., & Pinderhughes, E. (2002). Parenting and child development in adoptive families. In M. H. Bornstein (Ed.), *Handbook of parenting* (Vol. 1). Mahwah, NJ: Erlbaum.

Brodzinsky, D. M., Schechter, D. E., Braff, A. M., & Singer, L. M. (1984). Psychological and academic adjustment in adopted children. *Journal of Consulting and Clinical Psychology, 52*, 582–590.

Brom, B. (2005). *Nutrition Now* (4th ed.). Belmont, CA: Wadsworth.

Bromage, D. I. (2006). Prenatal diagnosis and selective abortion: A result of the cultural turn? *Medical Humanities, 32*, 38–42.

Bromley, K. (2007). Best practices in teaching writing. In L. B. Gambrell, L. M. Morrow, & M. Pressley (Eds.), Best practices in literacy instruction. New York: Guilford.

Bronfenbrenner, U. (1986). Ecology of the family as a context for human development: Research perspectives. *Developmental Psychology, 22*, 723–742.

Bronfenbrenner, U. (1995, March). *The role research has played in Head Start*. Paper presented at the meeting of the Society for Research in Child Development, Indianapolis.

Bronfenbrenner, U. (2000). Ecological theory. In A. Kazdin (Ed.), *Encyclopedia of psychology*. Washington, DC, & New York: American Psychological Association and Oxford University Press.

Bronfenbrenner, U. (2004). Making human beings human. Thousand Oaks. CA. Sage.

Bronfenbrenner, U., & Morris, P. (1998). The ecology of developmental processes. In W. Damon (Ed.), *Handbook of child psychology* (5th ed., Vol. 1). New York: Wiley.

Bronfenbrenner, U., & Morris, P. A. (2006). The ecology of developmental processes. In W. Damon & R. Lerner (Eds.), *Handbook of child psychology* (6th ed.). New York: Wiley.

Bronstein, P. (2006). The family environment: Where gender role socialization begins. In J. Worell & C. D. Goodheart (Eds.), *Handbook of girls' and women's psychological health*. New York: Oxford University Press.

Brook, J. S., Brook, D. W., Gordon, A. S., Whiteman, M., & Cohen, P. (1990). The psychological etiology of adolescent drug use: A family interactional approach. *Genetic Psychology Monographs, 116* No. 2.

Brooker, R. J., Widmaier, E. P., Graham, L, & Stiling, P. (2008). *Biology*. New York: McGraw-Hill.

Brooks, J. G., & Brooks, M. G. (2001). *The case for constructivist classrooms.* (2nd ed.). Upper Saddle River, NJ: Erlbaum.

Brooks, R., & Meltzoff, A. N. (2005). The development of gaze following and its relation to language. *Developmental Science, 8*, 535–543.

Brooks-Gunn, J. (2003). Do you believe in magic?: What we can Expect from early childhood programs. *Social Policy Report, Society for Research in Child Development, XVII* (No. 1). 1–13.

Brooks-Gunn, J., Graber, J. A., & Paikoff, R. L. (1994). Studying links between hormones and negative affect: Models and measures. *Journal of Research on Adolescence, 4*, 469–486.

Brooks-Gunn, J., & Warren, M. P. (1989). The psychological significance of secondary sexual characteristics in 9- to 11-year-old girls. *Child Development, 59*, 161-169.

Brosco, J. P., Mattingly, M., & Sanders, L. M. (2006). Impact of specific medical interventions on reducing the prevalence of mental retardation. *Archives of Pediatric and Adolescent Medicine, 160*, 302–309.

Broussard, S. C. (2004). The relationship between classroom motivation and academic achievement in elementary-school-aged children. *Family and Consumer SciencesResearch Journal, 33*, 106–120.

Brown, B. B. (1999). "You're going with whom?!": Peer group influences on adolescent romantic relationship. In W. Furman, B. B. Brown, & C. Feiring (Eds.), *The development of romantic relationships in adolescence*. Cambridge: Cambridge University Press.

Brown, B. B. (2004). Adolescent's relationship with peers. In R. Lerner & L. Steinberg (Eds.), *Handbook of adolescent Psychology*. New York: Wiley.

Brown, B. B. (Ed.), (2007). *Key indicators of child and youth well-being*. Mahwah, NJ: Erlbaum.

Brown, B. B., & Larson, R. W. (2002). The kaleidoscope of adolescence: Experiences of the world's youth at the beginning of the 21st century. In B. B. Brown, R. W. Larson, & T. S. Saraswathi (Eds.), *The world's youth*. New York: Cambridge University Press.

Brown, B. B., & Lohr, M. J. (1987). Peer-group affiliation and adolescent self-esteem: An integration of ego-identity and symbolic-interaction theories. *Journal of Personality and Social Psychology, 52*, 47–55.

Brown, D. (1987). The status of Holland's theory of vocational choice. *Career Development Quarterly, 36*, 13–24.

Brown, M., Keynes, R., & Lumsden, A. (2001). *The developing brain.* New York: Oxford University Press.

Brown, R. (1958). *Words and things.* Glencoe IL: Free Press.

Brown, R. (1973). *A first language: The early stages.* Cambridge, MA: Harvard University Press.

Browne, G. J., & Lam, L. T. (2006). Concussive head injury in children and adolescents related to sports and other leisure physical activities. *British Journal of Sports Medicine, 40,* 163–168.

Brownell, C. A., Ramani, G. B., & Zerwas, S. (2006). Becoming a social partner with peers: Cooperation and social understanding in one- and two-year-olds. *Child Development, 77,* 803–821.

Bruce, J. M., Olen, K., & Jensen, S. J. (1999, April). *The role of emotion and regulation in social competence.* Paper presented at the meeting of the Society for Research in Child Development, Albuquerque.

Bruck, M., & Ceci, S. J. (1999). The suggestibility of children's memory. *Annual Review of Psychology, 50,* 419–439.

Bruck, M., Ceci, S. J., & Hembrooke, H. (1998). Reliability and credibility of young children's reports: From research to policy and practice. *American Psychologist, 53*(2), 136–151.

Bruck, M., Ceci, S. J., & Principe, G. F. (2006). The child and the law. In W. Damon & R. Lerner (Eds.), *Handbook of child psychology* (6th ed.). New York: Wiley.

Bruck, M., & Melnyk, L. (2004). Individual differences in children's suggestibility: A review and a synthesis. *Applied Cognitive Psychology, 18,* 947–996.

Brunstein Klomek, A., Marrocco, F., Kleinman, M., Schofeld, I. S., & Gould, M. S. (2007). Bullying, depression, and suicidality in adolescents. *Journal of the American Academy of Child and Adolescent Psychiatry, 46,* 40–49.

Bryant, J. A. (Ed.). (2007). *The children's television community.* Mahwah, NJ: Erlbaum.

Bryant, J. B. (2005). Language in social contexts: Communicative competence in the preschool years. In J. Berko Gleason (Ed.), *The development of language* (6th ed.). Boston: Allyn & Bacon.

Bryant, J. B. (2005). Language in social contexts: The development of communicative competence. In J. Berko Gleason, *The development of language* (6th ed.). Boston: Allyn & Bacon.

Bugental, D. B., & Grusec, J. E. (2006). Socialization processes. In W. Damon & R. Lerner (Eds.). *Handbook of child psychology* (6th ed.). New York: Wiley.

Buhrmester, D. (1998). Need fulfillment, interpersonal competence, and the developmental contexts of early adolescent friendship. In W. M. Bukowski & A. F. Newcomb (Eds.). *The company they keep: Friendship in childhood and adolescence.* New York: Cambridge University Press.

Buhrmester, D. (2001, April). *Romantic development: Does age at which romantic involvement start matter?* Paper presented at the meeting of the Society for Research in Child Development, Minneapolis.

Buhrmester, D. (2003). Unpublished review of J. W. Santrock's *Adolescence* (10th ed.). New York: McGraw-Hill.

Buhrmester, D. (2005, April). *The antecedents of adolescents' competence in close relationships: A six-year-study.* Paper presented at the meeting of the Society for Research in Child Development. Atlanta.

Buhs, E. S., & Ladd, G. W. (2001). Peer rejection as an antecedent of young children's school adjustment: An examination of mediating processes. *Developmental Psychology, 37,* 550–560.

Bukowski, W. M., Brendgen, M., & Vitaro, F. (2007). Peers and socialization: Effects on externalizing and internalizing problems. In J. E. Grusec & P. D. Hastings (Eds.), *Handbook of socialization.* New York: Guilford.

Bulik, C. M., Berkman, N. D., Brownley, K. A., Sedway, J. A., & Lohr, K. N. (2007, in press). Anorexia nervosa treatment: A systematic review of randomized controlled trials. *International Journal of Eating Disorders.*

Buller, D. J. (2005). Evolutionary psychology: The emperor's new paradigm. *Trends in Cognitive Science, 9,* 277–283.

Bullock, M., & Lutkenhaus, P. (1990). Who am I? Self-understanding in toddlers. *Merrill-Palmer Quarterly, 36,* 217–238.

Bumpas, M. F., Crouter, A. C., & McHale, M. (2001). Parental autonomy granting during adolescence: Exploring gender differences in context. *Developmental Psychology, 37,* 163–173.

Burden, M. J., Jacobson, S. W., Sokol, R. J., & Jacobson, J. L. (2005). Effects of prenatal alcohol exposure on attention and working memory at 7.5 years of age. *Alcoholism: Clinical and Experimental Research, 29,* 443–452.

Burke, R. V., Kuhn, B. R., & Peterson, J. L. (2004). Brief report: A "storybook" ending to children's bedtime problems–the use of a rewarding social story to reduce bedtime resistance and frequent nighttime waking. *Journal of Pediatric Psychology, 29,* 389–396.

Burnette, J. (1998). Reducing the disproportionate representation of minority students in special education. *ERIC/OSEP Digest, No. E566.*

Burrous, E., Crockenberg, S., & Leerkes, E. (2005, April). Developmental history of care and control, anger and depression: Correlates of maternal sensitivity in toddlerhood. Poster presented at the Biennial Meetings of the Society for Research in Child Development, Atlanta.

Bursuck, W. D., & Damer, M. (2007). *Reading instruction for students who are at risk or have disabilities.* Boston: Allyn & Bacon.

Bushnell, I. W. R. (2003). Newborn face recognition. In O. Pascalis & A. Slater (Eds.), *The development of face processing in infancy and early childhood.* New York: NOVA Science.

Buss, D. M. (1995). Psychological sex differences: Origins through sexual selection. *American Psychologist, 50,* 164–168.

Buss, D. M. (2000). Evolutionary psychology. In A. Kazdin (Ed.), *Encyclopedia of psychology.* Washington, DC, & New York: American Psychological Association and Oxford University Press.

Buss, D. M., (2004). *Evolutionary Psychology* (2nd ed.). Boston: Allyn & Bacon.

Buss, D. M. (2008). *Evolutionary psychology* (3rd ed.). Boston: Allyn & Bacon.

Buss, D. M., & Schmitt, D. P. (1993). Sexual strategies theory: An evolutionary perspective on human mating. *Psychological Review, 100,* 204–232.

Bussey, K., & Bandura A. (1999). Social cognitive theory of gender development and differentiation. *Psychological Review, 106,* 676–713.

Butte, N. F. (2006). Energy requirements of infants and children. *Nestle Nutrition Workshop Series: Pediatric Program, 58,* 19–32.

Butte, N. F., & King, J. C. (2005). Energy requirements during pregnancy and lactation. *Public Health Nutrition, 8,* 1010–1027.

Butterworth, G. (2004). Joint visual attention in infancy. In G. Bremner & A. Slater (Eds.), *Theories of infant development.* Malden, MA: Blackwell.

Buzwell, S., & Rosenthal, D. (1996). Constructing a sexual self: Adolescents' sexual self-perceptions and sexual risk-taking. *Journal of Research on Adolescence, 6,* 489–513.

Bybee, J. (Ed.). (1999). *Guilt and children.* San Diego: Academic Press.

Bybee, R. W., Powell, J. C., & Trowbridge, L. W. (2008). *Teaching secondary science* (9th ed.). Upper Saddle River, NJ: Prentice Hall.

Byrnes, J. P. (2005). The development of regulated decision making. In J. E. Jacobs & P. A. Klaczynski (Eds.), *The development of judgment and decision making in children and adolescents.* Mahwah, NJ: Erlbaum.

C

Cabezon, C., Vigil, P., Rojas, I., Leiva, M. E., Riquelme, R., Aranda, W., & Garcia, C. (2005). Adolescent pregnancy prevention: An abstinence-centered randomized controlled intervention in a Chilean public high school. *Journal of Adolescent Health, 36,* 64–69.

Cabrera, N. J., Shannon, J. D., West, J., & Brooks-Gunn, J. (2006). Parental interactions with Latino infants: Variation by country of origin and English proficiency. *Child Development, 77,* 1190–1207.

Cabrera, N., Hutchens, R., & Peters, H. E. (Eds.), (2006). *From welfare to childcare.* Mahwah, NJ: Erlbaum.

Cairns, R. B., & Cairns, B. D. (2006). The making of developmental psychology. In W. Damon & R. Lerner (Eds.), *Handbook of child psychology* (6th ed.). New York: Wiley.

Calabrese, R. L., & Schumer, H. (1986). The effects of service activities on adolescent alienation. *Adolescence, 21,* 675–687.

Call, K. A. Riedel, A., Hein, K., McLoyd, V., Kpke, M., & Petersen, P. (2002). Adolescent health and well-being in the 21st century: A global perspective. *Journal of Research on Adolescence, 12,* 69–98.

Callaway, L. K., Lust, K., & McIntyre, H. D. (2005). Pregnancy outcomes in women of very advanced maternal age. *Obstetric and Gynecology Survey, 60,* 562–563.

Campbell, D. A., Lake, M. F., Falk, M., & Backstrand, J. R. (2006). A randomized controlled trial of continuous support by a lay doula. *Journal of Obstetrics and Gynecology: Neonatal Nursing, 35,* 456–464.

Campbell, F. A. (2007). The malleability of the cognitive development of children of low-income African-American families: Intellectual test performance over twenty-one years. In P. C. Kyllonen, R. D. Roberts, & L. Stankov (Eds.), *Extending intelligence.* Mahwah, NJ: Erlbaum.

Campbell, L., Campbell, B., & Dickinson D. (2004). *Teaching and learning through multiple intelligences* (3rd ed.). Boston: Allyn & Bacon.

Campbell, M. K., & Mottols, M. F. (2001). Recreational exercise and occupational safety during pregnancy and birth weight: A case control study. *American Journal of Obstetrics and Gynecology, 184,* 403–408.

Campfield, L. A., Smith, F. J., Gulsez, Y., Devos, R., & Burn, P. (1995). Mouse OB protein: Evidence for a peripheral signal linking adiposity and central neural networks. *Science, 269,* 546–549.

Campos, J. J., (2001, April). *Emotion in emotional development: Problems and prospects.* Paper presented at the meeting of the Society for Research in Child Development Minneapolis.

Campos, J. J., (2005). Unpublished review of J.W. Santrock's *Life-span development (11th ed.).* (New York: McGraw-Hill)

Campos, J. J., Langer, A., & Krowitz, A. (1970). Cardiac responses on the visual cliff in prelocomotor human infants. *Science, 170,* 196–197.

Canfield, R. L., Gendle, M. H., Cory-Slechta, D. A. (2004). Impaired neuropsychological functioning in lead-exposed children. *Developmental Neuropsychology, 26,* 513–540.

Canfield, R. L., & Haith, M. M. (1991). Young infants' visual expectations for symmetric and asymmetric stimulus sequences. *Developmental Psychology, 27,* 198–208.

Canfield, R. L., Henderson, C. R., CorySlechta, D. A., Cox, Jusko, T. A., & Lamphear, B. P. (2003). Intellectual impairment in children with blood lead concentrations below 10 microg per deciliter. *New England Journal of Medicine, 348,* 1517–1526.

Canterino, J. C., Ananth, C. V., Smulian, J., Harrigan, J. T., & Vintzileos, A. M. (2004). Maternal age and risk of fetal death in singleton gestations: United States, 1995–2000. *Obstetrics and Gynecology Survey, 59,* 649–650.

Carbonell, O. A., Altze, G., Bustamante, M. R., & Quiceno, J. (2002). Maternal caregiving and infant security in two cultures. *Developmental Psychology, 38,* 67–78.

Carel, J. C. (2005). Growth hormone in Turner syndrome: Twenty years after, what can we tell our patients? *Journal of Clinical Endocrinology and Metabolism, 90,* 3793–3794.

Carey, S. (1978). The child as word learner. In M. Halle, J. Bresnan, & G. A. Miller (Eds.), *Linguistic theory and psychological reality* (pp. 264–293). Cambridge, MA: MIT Press.

Carlisle, J. F. (2004). Morphological processes that influence learning to read. In C. A. Stone, E. R. Silliman, B. J. Ehren, & K. Apel (Eds.), *Handbook of language and literacy.* New York: Guilford.

Carlo, G. (2006). Care-based and altruistically-based morality. In M. Killen & J. Smetana (Eds.), *Handbook of moral development.* Mahwah, NJ: Erlbaum.

Carlson, C., Cooper, C., & Hsu, J. (1990, March). *Predicting school achievement in early adolescence: The role of family process.* Paper presented at the meeting of the Society for Research in Adolescence, Atlanta.

Carlson, D. S., Kaacmar, K. M., Wayne, J. H., & Grzywacz, J. G. (2006). Measuring the positive side the work-family interface: Development and validation of a work-family enrichment scale. *Journal of Vocational Behavior, 68,* 131–164.

Carlson, E. A., Sroufe, L. A., & Egeland, B. (2004). The construction of experience: A longitudinal study of representation and behavior. *Child Development, 75,* 66–83.

Carlton, M. P., & Winsler, A. (1999). School readiness: The need for a paradigm shift. *School Psychology Review, 28,* 338–352.

Carnagey, N. L., Anderson, C. A., & Bushman, B. J. (2007, in press). The effect of video game violence on physiological desensitization to real-life violence. *Journal of Experimental Social Psychology.*

Carnegie Corporation. (1989). *Turning points: Preparing youth for the 21st century.* New York: Author.

Carnegie Corporation. (1996). *Report on education for children 3–10 years of age.* New York: The Carnegie Foundation.

Carnegie Council on Adolescent Development (1995). *Great transitions.* New York: The Carnegie Corporation.

Carnethon, M. R., Gulati, M., & Greenland, P. (2005). Prevalence of cardiovascular disease correlates of low cardio-respiratory fitness in adolescents and adults. *Journal of the American Medical Association, 294,* 2981–2988.

Caroli, M., Argentieri, L., Cardone, M., & Masi, A. (2004). Role of television in childhood obesity prevention. *International Journal of Obesity and Related Metabolic Disorders, 28* (Suppl. 3), S104–S108.

Carpendale, J. I., & Chandler, M. J. (1996). On the distinction between false belief understanding and subscribing to an interpretive theory of mind. *Child Development, 67,* 1686–1706.

Carpenter, J., Nagell, K., & Tomasello, M. (1998). Social cognition, joint attention, and communicative competence from 9 to 15 months of age. *Monographs of the Society for Research in Child Development, 70* (1, Serial No. 279).

Carroll, J. L. (2007). *Sexuality now* (2nd ed.). Belmont, CA: Wadsworth.

Carroll, S. T., Riffenburgh, R. H., Roberts, T. A., & Myhre, E. D. (2002) Tattoos and body piercings as indicators of adolescent risk-taking behaviors. *Pediatrics, 109* (6), 1021–1027.

Carskadon, M. A. (Ed.). (2002). *Adolescent sleep patterns.* New York: Cambridge University Press.

Carskadon, M. A. (2004). Sleep difficulties in young people. *Archives of Pediatric and Adolescent Medicine, 158,* 597–598.

Carskadon, M. A. (2005). Sleep and circadian rhythms in children and adolescents: Relevance for athletic performance of young people. *Clinical Sports Medicine, 24,* 319–328.

Carskadon, M. A. (2006, March). *Too little, too late: Sleep bioregulatory processes across adolescence.* Paper presented at the meeting of the Society for Research on Adolescence, San Francisco.

Carskadon, M. A., Acebo, C., & Jenni, O. G. (2004). Regulation of adolescent sleep: Implications for behavior. *Annals of the New York Academy of Science's 102,* 276–291.

Carskadon, M. A., Mindell, J., & Drake, C. (2006, September). *Contemporary sleep patterns in the USA: Results of the 2006 National Sleep Foundation Poll* Paper presented at the European Sleep Research Society, Innsbruck, Austria.

Carter-Saltzman, L. (1980). Biological and sociocultural effects on handedness: Comparison between biological and adoptive families. *Science, 209,* 1263–1265.

Cartwright, R., Agargun, M. Y., Kirkby, J., & Friedman, J. K. (2006). Relation of dreams to waking concerns. *Psychiatry Research, 141,* 261–270.

Carver, A. C., Livesey, D. J., & Charles, M. (2001). Age related changes in inhibitory control as measured by stop signal task performance. *The International Journal of Neuroscience, 107,* 43–61.

Carver, K., Joyner, K., & Udry, J. R. (2003). National estimates of romantic relationships. In P. Florsheim (Ed.), *Adolescent romantic relations and sexual behavior.* Mahwah, NJ: Erlbaum.

Carver, L. I, & Bauer, P. J. (2001). The dawning of a past: The emergence of long-term explicit memory in infancy. *Journal of Experimental Psychology: General, 130,* (4), 726–745.

Casavnova, M. F. (2006). Neuropathological and genetic findings in autism: The significance of a putative minicolumnopathy. *Neuroscientist, 12,* 435–441.

Case, R. (1987). Neo-Piagetian theory: Retrospect and prospect. *International Journal of Psychology, 22,* 773–791.

Case, R. (1999). Conceptual development in the child and the field: A personal view of the Piagetian legacy. In E. K. Skolnick, K. Nelson, S. A. Gelman, & P. H. Miller (Eds.), *Conceptual development.* Mahwah, NJ: Erlbaum.

Case, R., Kurland, D. M., & Goldberg, J. (1982). Operational efficiency and the growth of short-term memory span. *Journal of Experimental Child Psychology, 33,* 386–404.

Case, R., & Mueller, M. P. (2001). Differentiation, integration, and covariance mapping as fundamental processes in cognitive and neurological growth. In J. L. McClelland & R. S. Siegler (Eds.), *Mechanisms of cognitive development.* Mahwah, NJ: Erlbaum.

Casey, B. J., Durston, S., & Fossella, J. A. (2001). Evidence for a mechanistic model of cognitive control. *Clinical Neuroscience Research, 1,* 267–282.

Casey, B. J., Thomas, K. M., Davidson, M. C., Kunz, K., & Franzen, P. L. (2002). Dissociating striatal and hippocampal function developmentally with a stimulus-response compatibility task. *Journal of Neuroscience, 22*(19), 8647–8652.

Casson, I. F. (2006) Pregnancy in women with diabetes—after the CEMACH report, what now? *Diabetic Medicine, 23,* 481–484.

Catalano, P. M. (2007). Management of obesity in pregnancy. *Obstetrics and Gynecology, 109,* 419–433.

Caughey, A. B., Hopkins, L. M., & Norton, M. E. (2006). Chorionic villus sampling compared with amniocentesis and the difference in the rate of pregnancy loss. *Obstetrics and Gynecology, 108,* 612–616.

Cavanaugh, S. E. (2004). The sexual debut of girls in adolescence: The intersection of race, pubertal timing, and friendship group characteristics. *Journal of Research on Adolescence, 14,* 285–312.

Cavell, T. A., Hymel, S., Malcolm, K. T., & Seay, A. (2007). Socialization and interventions for antisocial youth. In J. E. Grusec & P. D. Hastings (Eds.), *Handbook of socialization.* New York: Guilford.

Ceci, S. J. (2003). Cast in six ponds and you'll reel in something: Looking back on 25 years of research. *American Psychologist, 58,* 855–864.

Ceci, S. J., Fitneva, S. A., & Gilstrap, L. L. (2003). Memory development and eye witness testimony. In A. Slater, & G. Bremner (Eds.), *An introduction to developmental psychology,* Malden, MA: Blackwell.

Centers for Disease Control and Prevention. (2000), *CDC growth charts: United States.* Atlanta: Author.

Centers for Disease Control and Prevention. (2002). *Adolescent pregnancy.* Atlanta: Author.

Centers for Disease Control and Prevention. (2004, October 8). Smoking during pregnancy—United States, 1990–2002. *MMWR Morbidity and Mortality Report, 53,* 911–915.

Centers for Disease Control and Prevention. (2007). *Diseases and conditions.* Atlanta: Author.

Cepeda, M. S., Carr, D. B., Lau, J., & Alvarez, H. (2006). Music for pain relief. *Cochrane Database of Systematic Reviews, 2,* CD004843.

Chambers, B., Cheung, A. C. K., & Slavin, R. F. (2006). Effective preschool programs for children at risk of school failure: A best-evidence synthesis. In B. Spodek & O. N. Saracho (Eds.), *Handbook of research on the education of young children.* Mahwah, NJ: Erlbaum.

Chan, L., Reilly, K. M., & Telfer, J. (2006). Odds of critical injuries in unrestrained pediatric victims of motor vehicle collision. *Pediatric Emergency Care, 22,* 622–629.

Chan, W. S. (1963). *A source book in Chinese philosophy.* Princeton, NJ: Princeton University Press.

Chandler, M. (1973). Egocentrism and antisocial behavior: The assessment and training of social perspective-taking skills. *Developmental Psychology, 9,* 326–332.

Chang, F., Dell, G. S., & Bock, K. (2006). Becoming syntactic. *Psychological Review, 113,* 234–272.

Chang, L., Smith, L. M., LoPresti, C., Yonekura, M. L., Kuo, J., Walot, I., & Ernst, T. (2004). Smaller subcortical volumes and cognitive deficits in children with prenatal methamphetamine exposure. *Psychiatry Research, 132,* 95–106.

Chang, M. Y., Chen, C. H., & Huang, K. F. (2006). A comparison of massage effects on labor pain using the McGill Pain Questionnaire. *Journal of Nursing Research, 14,* 190–197.

Chang, S. C., & Chen, C. H. (2004). The application of music therapy in maternal nursing. *Hu Li Za Zhi, 51,* 61–66.

Chang, S. C., O'Brien, K. O., Nathanson, M. S., Mancini, J., & Witter, F. R. (2003). Characteristics and risk factors for adverse birth outcomes in pregnant black adolescents. *Journal of Obstetrics and Gynecology Canada, 25,* 751–759.

Chao, R. (2001). Extending research on the consequences of parenting style for Chinese Americans and European Americans. *Child Development, 72,* 1832–1843.

Chao, R. K. (2005, April). *The importance of Guan in describing control of immigrant Chinese.* Paper presented at the meeting of the Society for Research in Child Development, Atlanta.

Chao, R. K. (2007, March). *Research with Asian Americans: Looking back and moving forward.* Paper presented at the meeting of the Society for Research in Child Development, Boston.

Chao, R. K., & Tseng, V. (2002). Parenting of Asians. In M. H. Bornstein (Ed.), *Handbook of parenting* (2nd ed. Vol. 4). Mahwah, NJ: Erlbaum.

Chapman, O. L. (2000). Learning science involves language, experience, and modeling. *Journal of Applied Developmental Psychology, 21,* 97–108.

Chattin-McNichols, J. (1992). *The Montessori controversy.* Albany, NY: Delmar.

Chatzimichael, A., Tsalkidis, A., Cassimos, D., Gardikis, S., Tripsianis, G., Deftereos, S. Ktenidou-Kartali, S., & Tsanaksas, I. (2007). The role of breastfeeding and passive smoking on the development of severe bronchiolitis in infants. *Minerva Pediatrica, 59,* 199–206.

Chauhuri, J. H., & Williams, P. H. (1999, April). *The contribution of infant temperament and parent emotional availability to toddler attachment.* Paper presented at the meeting of the Society for Research in Child Development, Albuquerque.

Chaves, A. P., Diemer, M. A., Blustein, D. L., Gallagher, L. A., DeVoy, J. E., Casares, M. T., & Perry, J. C. (2004). Conceptions of work: The view from urban youth. *Journal of Counseling Psychology, 51,* 257–286.

Chen W., Srinivasan, S. R., Li, S., Xu, J., & Berensen, G. S. (2007 in press). Clustering of long-term trends in metabolic syndrome variables from childhood to adulthood in Blacks and Whites: The Bogalusa Heart Study. *American Journal of Epidemiology.*

Chen, C., & Stevenson, H. W. (1989). Homework: A cross-cultural comparison. *Child Development, 60,* 551–561.

Chen, I. G., Durbin, D. R., Elliott, M. R., Kallan, M. J., & Winston, F. K. (2005). Trip characteristics of vehicle crashes involving child passengers. *Injury Prevention, 11,* 219–224.

Chen, M. Y., Wang, E. K., & Jeng, Y. J. (2006). Adequate sleep among adolescents is positively associated with health status and health-related behaviors. *BMC Public Health, 6,* 59.

Chen, W., Srinivasan, S. R., Li, S., Xu, J., & Berensen, G. S. (2005). Metabolic syndrome variables at low levels in childhood are beneficially associated with adulthood cardiovascular risk: The Bogalusa Heart Study. *Diabetes Care, 28,* 126–131.

Chen, X., Hastings, P. D., Rubin, K. H., Chen, H., Cen, G., & Stewart, S. L. (1998). Childrearing attitudes and behavioral inhibition in Chinese and Canadian toddlers: A cross-cultural study. *Developmental Psychology, 34,* 677–686.

Chen, X., Striano, T., & Rakoczy, H. (2004). Auditory-oral matching behaviors in newborns. *Developmental Science, 7,* 42–47.

Chen, X. K., Wen, S. W., Fleming, N., Demissie, K., Rhoads, G. G., & Walker, M. C. (2007b, in press). Teenage pregnancy and adverse birth outcomes: A large population based retrospective cohort study. *International Journal of Epidemiology.*

Chen, X. K., Wen, S. W., Yang, Q., & Walker, M. C. (2007a). Adequacy of prenatal care and neonatal mortality in infants born to mothers with and without antenatal high-risk conditions. *Australian and New Zealand Journal of Obstetrics and Gynecology, 47,* 122–127.

Chen, Z., & Siegler, R. S. (2000). Across the great divide: Bridging the gap between understanding of toddlers' and older children's thinking. *Monograph of the Society for Research in Child Development, 65* (No. 2).

Cherlin, A. J., & Furstenberg, F. F. (1994). Stepfamilies in the United States: A reconsideration. *Annual Review of Sociology* (Vol. 20).

Chess, S., & Thomas, A. (1977). Temperamental individuality from childhood to adolescence. *Journal of Child Psychiatry, 16,* 218–226.

Cheung, A. P. (2006). Assisted reproductive technology: Both sides now. *Journal of Reproductive Medicine, 51,* 283–292.

Chi, M. T. (1978). Knowledge structures and memory development, In R. S. Siegler (Ed.), *Children's thinking: What develops?* Hillsdale, NJ: Erlbaum.

Chia, P., Sellick, K., & Gan, S. (2006). The attitudes and practices of neonatal nurses in the use of kangaroo care. *Australian Journal of Advanced Nursing, 23,* 20–27.

Child Trends (2006, April). *Fast facts at a glance.* Washington, DC: Author.

Children's Defense Fund. (2001). *Children's welfare and mental health.* Retrieved January 6, 2007, from www.childrensdefense.org

Ching, T. Y., van Wanrooy, E., Hill, M., & Incerti, P. (2006). Performance in children with hearing aids or cochlear implants: Bilateral stimulation and binaural hearing. *International Journal of Audiology, 45* (Suppl.), S108–S112.

Chisholm, J. S. (1989). Biology, culture and the development of temperament: A Navajo example. In J. K. Nugent, B. Lester, & T. B. Brazelton (Eds.), *The cultural context of infancy: Vol. 1. Biology, culture, and infant development* (pp. 341–364). Norwood, NJ: Ablex.

Chomsky, N. (1957). *Synatactic structures.* The Hague: Mouton.

Chopra, M. (2003). Risk factors for undernutrition of young children in a rural area of South Africa. *Public Health Nursing, 6,* 645–652.

Christakis, D. A., Zimmerman, F. J., DiGuiuseppe, D. L., & McCarty, C. A. (2004). Early television exposure and subsequent attentional problems in children. *Pediatrics, 113,* 708–713.

Christensen, S. L., & Thurlow, M. L. (2004). School dropouts: Prevention, considerations, interventions, and challenges. *Current Directions in Psychological Science, 13,* 36–39.

Christie, J. F., Vukellich, C., & Enz, B. J. (2007). *Teaching language and literacy.* Boston: Allyn & Bacon.

Chun, K. M., & Akutsu, P. D. (2003). Acculturation among ethnic minority families. In K. M. Chun, P. B. Organista, & G. Marin (Eds.). *Acculturation.* Washington, DC: American Psychological Association.

Cicchetti, D., & Blender, J. A. (2004, December 14). A multiple-levels-of-analysis approach to the study of developmental processes in maltreated children. *Proceedings of the National Academy of Science USA, 101,* 17325–17326.

Cicchetti, D., & Toth, S. L. (2005). Child maltreatment. *Annual Review of Clinical Psychology,* (Vol. 1). Palo Alto, CA: Annual Reviews.

Cicchetti, D., & Toth, S. L. (2006). Developmental psychopathology and preventive intervention. In W. Damon & R. Lerner (Eds.), *Handbook of child psychology* (6th ed.). New York: Wiley.

Cicchetti, D., Toth, S. L., & Rogusch, F. A. (2005). *A prevention program for child maltreatment.* Unpublished manuscript, University of Rochester, Rochester, NY.

Cicirelli, V. G. (1994). Sibling relationships in cross-cultural perspective. *Journal of Marriage and Family, 56,* 7–20.

Cipriano, L. E., Rupar, C. A., & Zaric, G. S. (2007). The cost effectiveness of expanding newborn screening for up to 21 inherited metabolic disorders using tandem mass spectrometry: Results from a decision-analytic model. *Value Health, 10,* 83–97.

Cisneros-Cohernour, E. J., Moreno, R. P., & Cisneros, A. A. (2000). Curriculum reform in Mexico: Kindergarten teachers' challenges and dilemmas. Proceedings of the Lilian Katz Symposium. In D. Rothenberg (Ed.), *Issues in early childhood education: Curriculum reform, teacher education, and dissemination of information.* Urbana-Champaign: University of Illinois.

Clark, E. (1993). *The Lexicon in acquisition.* New York: Cambridge University Press.

Clark, R. D., & Hatfield, E. (1989). Gender differences in receptivity to sexual offers. *Journal of Psychology and Human Sexuality, 2,* 39–55.

Clarke-Stewart, K. A., (2006). What have we learned: Proof that families matter, policies for families and children, prospects for future research. In A. Clarke-Stewart & J. Dunn (Eds.), *Families Count.* New York: Cambridge University Press.

Clarke-Stewart, K. A., & Brentano, C. (2006). *Divorce: Causes and Consequences.* New Haven, CT: Yale University Press.

Clarke-Stewart, K. A., Malley, L. C., & Allhusen, V. D. (2004). Verbal ability, self-control, and close relationships with parents protect children against misleading statements. *Applied Cognitive Psychology, 18,* 1037–1058.

Clarkson, J., & Herbison, A. E. (2006). Development of GABA and glutamate signaling at the GnRH neuron in relation to puberty. *Molecular and Cellular Endocrinology 254–255,* 32–38.

Clearfield, M. W., Diedrich, F. J., Smith, L. B., & Thelen, E. (2006). Young infants reach correctly in A-not-B tasks: On the development of stability and perseveration. *Infant Behavior and Development, 29,* 435–444.

Clifton, R. K., Morrongiello, B. A., Kulig, J. W., & Dowd, J. M. (1981). Developmental changes in auditory localization in infancy. In R. N. Aslin, J. R. Alberts, & M. R. Petersen (Eds.), *Development of perception* (Vol. 1). Orlando, FL: Academic Press.

Clifton, R. K., Mulr, D. W., Ashmead, D. H., & Clarkson, M. G. (1993). Is visually guided reaching in early infancy a myth? *Child Development, 64,* 1099–1110.

Clinchy, B. M., Mansfield, A. F., & Schott, J. L. (1995, March). *Development of narrative and scientific modes of thought in middle childhood.* Paper presented at the meeting of the Society for Research in Child Development, Indianapolis.

Cnattinugius, S., Bergstrom, R., Lipworth, L., & Kramer, M. S. (1998). Prepregnancy weight and the risk of adverse pregnancy out comes. *New England Journal of Medicine, 338,* 147–152.

Coch, D., Fischer, K. W., & Dawson, G. (Eds.) (2007). *Human behavior, learning, and the developing brain: Typical development.* New York: Guilford.

Cogswell, M. E., Perry, G. S., Schieve, L. A., & Dietz, W. H. (2001). Obesity in women of childbearing age: Risks, prevention, and treatment. *Primary Care Update in Obstetrics and Gynecology, 8,* 89–105.

Cohen, G. L., & Sherman, D. K. (2005). Stereotype threat and the social and scientific contexts of the race achievement gap. *American Psychologist, 60,* 270–271.

Cohen, L. B. (1995). Violent video games: Aggression, arousal, and desensitization in young adolescent boys. Doctoral dissertation, University of Southern California. *Dissertation Abstracts International, 57* (2-B), 1463. University Microfilms No. 9616947.

Cohen, L. B., & Cashon, C. H. (2006). Infant cognition. In W. Damon & R. Lerner (Eds.), *Handbook of child psychology* (6th ed.). New York: Wiley.

Coie, J. (2004). The impact of negative social experiences on the development of antisocial behavior. In J. B. Kupersmidt & K. A. Dodge (Eds.), *Children's peer relations: From development to intervention*. Washington, DC: American Psychological Association.

Colby, A., Kohlberg, L., Gibbs, J., & Lieberman, M. (1983). A longitudinal study of moral judgment. *Monographs of the Society for Research in Child Development* (Serial No. 201).

Cole, M. (2005). Culture and cognitive development in phylogenetic, historical, and ontogenetic perspective. In W. Damon & R. Lerner (Eds.), *Handbook of child psychology* (6th ed.). New York: Wiley.

Cole, M. (2005). Culture and development. In M. H. Bornstein & M. E. Lamb (Eds), *Developmental science* (5th ed.). Mahwah, NJ: Erlbaum.

Cole, M. (2006). Culture and cognitive development in phylogentic. historical, and ontogenetic perspective. In w. Damon R. Levner Leds.). *Handbook of child psychology* (6th ed.). New York: Wiley.

Cole, M., & Gajdamaschko, N. (2007). Vygotsky and culture. In H. Daniels, J. Wertsch, & M. Cole (Eds.), *The Cambridge companion to Vygotsky*. New York: Cambridge University Press.

Cole, P. M., & Tan, P. Z. (2007). Emotion socialization from a cultural perspective. In J. E. Grisec & P. D. Hastings (Eds.), *Handbook of socialization*. New York: Guilford.

Coleman, M., Ganong, L., & Fine, M. (2004). Communication in stepfamilies. In A. L. Vangelisti (Ed.), *Handbook of family communication*. Mahwah, NJ: Erlbaum.

Coleman, V. H., Erickson, K., Schulkin, J., Zinberg, S., & Sachs, B. P. (2005). Vaginal birth after cesarean delivery: Practice patterns of obstetricians-gynecologists. *Journal of Reproductive Medicine, 50,* 261–266.

Coley, R. (2001). *Differences in the gender gap: Comparisons across racial/ethnic groups in education and work.* Princeton: Educational Testing Service.

Coley, R. L., Li-Grining, C. P., & Chase-Landsdale, P. L. (2006). Low-income families' child care experiences. In N. Cabrera, R. Hutchens, H. E. Peters, & L. Peters (Eds.), *From welfare to childcare.* Mahwah, NJ: Erlbaum.

Coley, R. L., Morris, J. E., & Hernandez, D. (2004). Out-of-school care and problem behavior trajectories among low-income adolescents: Individual, family, and neighborhood characteristics and added risks. *Child Development, 75,* 948–965.

Collins, R. L. (2005). Sex on television and its impact on American youth: Background and results from the RAND television and adolescent sexuality study. *Child and Adolescent Psychiatry Clinics of North America, 14,* 371–385.

Collins, R. L., Elliott, M. N., Berry, S. H., Kanocouse, D. E., Kunkel, D., Hunter, S. B., & Miu, A. (2004). Watching sex on television predicts adolescent initiation of sexual behavior. *Pediatrics, 114,* e280–e289.

Collins, W. A., Madsen, S. D., & Susman-Stillman, A. (2002). Parenting during middle childhood. In M. Bornstein (Ed.), *Handbook of parenting* (2nd ed.). Mahwah, NJ: Erlbaum.

Collins, W. A., & Steinberg, L. (2006). Adolescent development in interpersonal context. In W. Damon & R. Lerner (Eds.), *Handbook of child psychology* (6th ed.). New York: Wiley.

Collins, W. A., & van Dulmen, M. (2006). The significance of middle childhood peer competence for work and relationships in early childhood. In A. C. Huston & M. N. Ripke (Eds.), *Developmental context in middle childhood.* New York: Cambridge University Press.

Colman, R. A., & Widom, C. S. (2004). Childhood abuse and neglect and adult intimate relationships: A prospective study. *Child Abuse and Neglect, 28,* 1133–1151.

Combs, M. (2006). *Readers and writers in the primary grades* (3rd ed.). Upper Saddle River, NJ: Prentice Hall.

Comer, J. (2004). *Leave no child behind.* New Haven, CT: Yale University Press.

Comer, J. P. (1988). Educating poor minority children. *Scientific American, 259,* 42–48.

Commoner, B. (2002). Unraveling the DNA myth: The spurious foundation of genetic engineering. *Harper's Magazine, 304,* 39–47.

Compas, B. E., & Grant, K. E. (1993, March). *Stress and adolescent depressive symptoms: Underlying mechanisms and processes.* Paper presented at the biennial meeting of the Society for Research in Child Development, New Orleans.

Comstock, G., Scharrer, E. (2006). Media and popular culture. In W. Damon & R. Lerner (Eds.), *Handbook of child psychology* (6th ed.). New York: Wiley.

Conger, J. J. (1981). Freedom and commitment: Families, youth, and social change. *American Psychologist, 36,* 1475–1484.

Conger, J. J. (1988). Hostages to the future: Youth, values, and the public interest. *American Psychologist, 43,* 291–300.

Conger, R. D., & Chao, W. (1996). Adolescent depressed mood. In R. L. Simons (Ed.), *Understanding differences between divorced and intact families: Stress, interaction, and child outcome.* Thousand Oaks, CA: Sage.

Conger, R. D., & Dogan, S. J. (2007). Social class and socialization in families. In J. E. Grusec & P. D. Hastings (Eds.), *Handbook of socialization.* New York: Guilford.

Conger, R. D., & Ge, X. (1999). Conflict and cohesion in parent-adolescent relations: Changes in emotional expression. In M. J. Cox & J. Brooks-Gunn (Eds.), *Conflict and cohesion in families.* Mahwah, NJ: Erlbaum.

Conger, R., & Reuter, M. (1996). Siblings, parents, and peers: A longitudinal study of social influences in adolescent risk for alcohol use and abuse. In G. H. Brody (Ed.), *Sibling relationships: Their causes and consequences.* Norwood, NJ: Ablex.

Connell, A. M., & Dishion, T. J. (2006). The contribution of peers to monthly variation in adolescent depressed mood: A short-term longitudinal study with time-varying predictors. *Developmental Psychopathology, 18,* 139–154.

Conner, M. E., & White, J. L. (Eds.). (2006). *Black fathers.* Mahwah, NJ: Erlbaum.

Connor, C. M., & Zwolan, T. A. (2004). Examining multiple sources of influence on the reading comprehension skills of children who use cochlear implants. *Journal of Speech, Language, and Hearing Research. 47,* 509–526.

Connors, J. (2007). Causalities of reform. *Phi Delta Kappan, 88,* 518–522.

Conrad, D., & Hedin, D. (1982). The impact of experiential education on adolescent development. In D. Conrad & D. Hedin (Eds.), *Child and Youth Services* (special issue): *Youth participation and experiential education, 4,* 57–76.

Conway, K. S., & Kutinova, A. (2006). Maternal health: Does prenatal care make a difference? *Health Economics, 15,* 461–488.

Cook, M., & Birch, R. (1984). Infant perception of the shapes of tilted plane forms. *Infant Behavior and Development, 7,* 389–402.

Coomarasamy, A., Thangaratinam, S., Gee, H., & Khan, K. S. (2006). Progesterone for the prevention of preterm birth: A critical evaluation of evidence. *European Journal of Obstetrics and Gynecology: Reproductive Biology, 129,* 111–118.

Cooper, C. R., Cooper, R. G., & Chavira, G. (2001). *Bridging multiple worlds: How African American and Latino youth in academic outreach programs navigate math pathways to college.* Unpublished manuscript, University of California at Santa Cruz.

Cooper, C. R., & Grotevant, H. D. (1989, April). *Individuality and connectedness in the family and adolescent's self and relational competence.* Paper presented at the meeting of the Society for Research in Child Development, Kansas City.

Cooper, C. R., Grotevant, H. D., Moore, M. S., & Condon, S. M. (1982, August). *Family support and conflict: Both foster adolescent identity and role taking.* Paper presented at the meeting of the American Psychological Association, Washington, DC.

Corbett, T. (2007). Social indicators as policy tool: Welfare reform as a case study. In B. Brown (Ed.), *Key indicators of child and youth well-being.* Mahwah, NJ: Erlbaum.

Corbin, C. B., Welk, G. J., Corbin, W. R., & Welk, K. A. (2008). *Concepts of fitness and wellness* (7th ed.). New York: McGraw-Hill.

Cornelius, J. R., Clark, D. B., Reynolds, M., Kirisci, L., & Tarter, R. (2007). Early age of first sexual intercourse and affiliation with deviant peers predict development of SUD: A prospective longitudinal study. *Addictive Behavior, 32,* 850–854.

Corsini, R. J. (1999). *The dictionary of psychology.* Philadelphia: Brunner/Mazel.

Cote, J. E. (2006). Emerging adulthood as an institutionalized moratorium: Risks and benefits to identity formation. In J. J. Arnett & J. L. Tanner (Eds.), *Emerging adults in America.* Washington, DC: American Psychological Association.

Cotton, S., Larkin, E., Hoopes, A., Comer, B. A., & Rosenthal, S. L. (2005). The impact of adolescent spirituality on depressive symptoms and health risk behaviors. *Journal of Adolescent Health, 36,* 529.

Cotton, S., Zebracki, M. A., Rosenthal, S. L., Tsevat, J., & Drotar, D. (2006). Religion/spirituality and adolescent health outcomes: A review. *Journal of Adolescent Health, 38,* 472–480.

Council of Economic Advisors. (2000). *Teens and their parents in the 21st century: An examination of trends in teen behavior and the role of parent involvement.* Washington, DC: Author.

Couperus, J. W., & Nelson, C. A. (2006). Early brain development and plasticity. In K. McCartney & D. Phillips (Eds.), *Blackwell handbook of early childhood development.* Malden, MA: Blackwell.

Courage, M. L., Edison, S. C., & Howe, M. L. (2004). Variability in the early development of visual selfrecognition. *Infant Behavior and Development, 27,* 509–532.

Cowan, C. P., & Cowan, P. A. (2000). *When partners become parents.* Mahwah, NJ: Erlbaum.

Cowan. P., Cowan. C., Ablow. J., Johnson, V. K., & Measelle, J. (2005) *The family context of parenting in children's adaptation to elementary school.* Mahwah, NJ; Erlbaum.

Cowley, G. (1998, April 6). Why children turn violent. *Newsweek,* pp. 24–25.

Cox, J. (2006). Postnatal depression in fathers. *Lancet, 366,* 982.

Cox, M. J., Burchinal, M., Taylor, L. C., Frosch, B., Goldman, B., & Kanoy, K. (2004). The transition to parenting: Continuity and change in early parenting behavior and attitudes. In R. D. Conger, F. O. Lorenz, & K. A. S. Wickrama (Eds.), *Continuity and change in family relations.* Mahwah, NJ: Erlbaum.

Cox, R. H. (2007). *Sport psychology* (6th ed.). New York: McGraw-Hill.

Craik, F. I. M. (2006). Brain-behavior relations across the lifespan: A commentary. *Neuroscience and Biobehavioral Reviews, 30,* 885–892.

Crick, N. R. (2005, April). *Gender and psychopathology.* Paper presented at the meeting of the Society for Research in Child Development, Atlanta.

Crick, N. R., Ostrov, J. M., & Werner, N. E. (2006). A longitudinal study of relational aggression, physical aggression, and children's social-psychological adjustment. *Journal of Abnormal Child Psychology, 34,* 127–138.

Crockenberg, S. B. (1986). Are temperamental differences in babies associated with predictable differences in caregiving? In J. V. Lerner & R. M. Lerner (Eds.), *Temperament and social interaction during infancy and childhood.* San Francisco: Jossey-Bass.

Crockett, L. J., Raffaelli, M., & Moilanen, K. (2003). Adolescent sexuality: Behavior and meaning. In G. Adams & M. Berzonsky (Eds.), *Blackwell handbook of adolescence.* Malden, MA: Blackwell.

Crompton, D. (2005). Building bridges with early childhood education. *Young Children, 60.* (No. 2), 6.

Crossman, A. M., Scullin, M. H., & Melnyk, L. (2004). Individual and developmental differences in suggestibility. *Applied Cognitive Psychology, 18,* 941–945.

Crouter, A. C. (2006). Mothers and fathers at work. In A. Clarke-Stewart & J. Dunn (Eds.), *Families count.* New York: Cambridge University Press.

Crouter, A. C., & McHale, S. (2005). The long arm of the job revisited: Parenting in dual-earner families. In T. Luster & L. Okagaki (Eds.), *Parenting.* Mahwah, NJ: Erlbaum.

Crowley, K., Callahan, M. A., Tenenbaum, H. R., & Allen, E. (2001). Parents explain more to boys than to girls during shared scientific thinking. *Psychological Science, 12,* 258–261.

Csaba, A., Bush, M. C., & Saphier, C. (2006). How painful are amniocentesis and chorionic villus sampling? *Prenatal Diagnosis, 26,* 35–38.

Csikszentmihalyi, M., & Nakamura, J. (2006). Creativity though the life span from an evolutionary systems perspective. In C. Hoare (Ed.), *Handbook of adult development and learning.* New York: Oxford University Press.

Cullen, K. (2001). *Context and eating behavior in children.* Unpublished research, Children's Nutrition Research Center, Baylor School of Medicine, Houston.

Cummings, E. M. (1987). Coping with background anger in early childhood. *Child Development, 58,* 976–984.

Cummings, E. M., Braungart-Rieker, J. M., & Du Rocher-Schudlich, T. (2003). Emotion and personality development. In I. B. Weiner (Ed.), *Handbook of psychology* (Vol. 6). New York: Wiley.

Cummings, M. (2006). *Human heredity* (7th ed.). Pacific Grove, CA: Brooks Cole.

Curran, K., DuCette, J., Eisenstein, J., & Hyman, I. A. (2001, August). *Statistical analysis of the cross-cultural data: The third year.* Paper presented at the meeting of the American Psychological Association, San Francisco.

Currie, J., & Hotz, V. J. (2004). Accidents will happen? Unintentional childhood injuries and the effects of child care regulations. *Journal of Health Economics 23,* 25–29.

Cushner, K. H. (2006). *Human diversity in action* (3rd ed.). New York: McGraw-Hill.

Cyna, A. M., Andrew, M. I., & McAuliffe, G. L. (2006). Antenatal self-hypnosis for labor and childbirth: A pilot study. *Anesthesia and Intensive Care, 34,* 464–469.

Cyna, A. M., McAuliffe, G. L., & Andrew, M. I. (2004). Hypnosis for pain relief in labor and childbirth: A systematic review. *British Journal of Anesthesia, 93,* 505–511.

Czeizel, A. E., & Puho, E. (2005). Maternal use of nutritional supplements during the first month of pregnancy and decreased risk of Down's syndrome: Case-control study. *Nutrition, 21,* 698–704.

D

Dahl, R. E. (2004). Adolescent brain development: A period of vulnerabilities and opportunities. *Annals of the New York Academy of Sciences, 1021,* 1–22.

Dahl, R. E. (2006). Sleeplessness and aggression in youth. *Journal of Adolescent Health, 38,* 641–642.

Dale, P., & Goodman, J. (2004). Commonality and differences in vocabulary growth. In M. Tomasello & D. I. Slobin (Eds.), *Beyond nature-nurture.* Mahwah, NJ: Erlbaum.

Daley, A. J., Macarthur, C., & Winter, H. (2007). The role of exercise in treating postpartum depression: A review of the literature. *Journal of Midwifery and Women's Health, 52,* 56–62.

Daley, D. (2006). Attention deficit hyperactivity disorder: A review of the essential facts. *Child: Care, Health, and Development, 32,* 193–204.

Daley, T. C., Whaley, S. E., Sigman, M. D., Espinosa, M. P., & Neumann, C. (2003). IQ on the rise: The Flynn effect in rural Kenyan children. *Psychological Science, 14,* 215–219.

Dalton, T. C., & Bergenn, V. W. (2007). *Early experience, the brain, and consciousness.* Mahwah, NJ: Erlbaum.

Daly, B. P., Creed, T., Xanthopoulos, M., & Brown, R. T. (2007). Psychosocial treatments for children with attention deficit hyperactivity disorder. *Neuropsychology Review, 17,* 73–89.

Damon, W. (1988). *The moral child.* New York: Free Press.

Damon, W. (1995). *Greater expectations.* New York: Free Press.

Damon, W., & Hart, D. (1992). Self-understanding and its role in social and moral development. In M. H. Bornstein & M. E. Lamb (Eds.), *Developmental psychology: An advanced textbook* (3rd ed.). Hillsdale, NJ: Erlbaum.

Damon, W., Lerner, R. (Eds.), *Handbook of child psychology* (6th ed.). New York: Wiley.

Danforth, K. N., Tworoger, S. S., Hecht, J. L., Rosner, B. A., Colditz, G. A., & Hankinson, S. E. (2007). Breastfeeding and risk of ovarian cancer in two prospective cohorts. *Cancer Causes Control, 18,* 517–523.

Daniels, H. (2007). Pedagogy. In H. Daniels, J. Wertsch, & M. Cole (Eds.), *The Cambridge companion to Vygotsky.* New York: Cambridge University Press.

Daniels, H., Wertsch, J., & Cole, M. (Eds.). (2007). *The Cambridge companion to Vygotsky.* New York: Cambridge University Press.

Daniels, P., Noe, G. F., & Mayberry, R. (2006). Barriers to prenatal care among Black women of low socioeconomic status. *American Journal of Health Behavior, 30,* 188–198.

Daniels, S. R. (2006). The consequences of childhood overweight and obesity. *Future of Children, 16,* (No. 1), 47–67.

Danielson, C. K., De Arellano, M. A., Kilpatrick, D. G., Saunders, B. E., & Resnick, H. S. (2005). Child maltreatment in depressed adolescents: Differences in symptomatology based on history of abuse. *Child Maltreatment, 10,* 37–48.

Darling-Hammond, L., & Bransford, J. (Eds.). (2005). *Preparing teachers for a changing world.* San Francisco: Jossey-Bass.

Darwin, C. (1859). *On the origin of species.* London: John Murray.

Darwin, C. (1965). *The expression of the emotions in man and animals.* Chicago: University of Chicago Press. (Original work published 1872.)

Das, U. N. (2007). Breastfeeding prevents type 2 diabetes mellitus: But, how and why? *American Journal of Clinical Nutrition, 85,* 1436–1437.

Dasen, P. R. (1977). Are cognitive processes universal? A contribution to cross-cultural Piagetian psychology. In N. Warran (Ed.), *Studies in cross-cultural psychology* (Vol. 1). London: Academic Press.

Datar, A., & Sturm, R. (2004). Physical education in elementary school and body mass index: Evidence from the early childhood longitudinal study. *American Journal of Public Health, 94,* 1501–1506.

Dattillio, F. M. (Ed.). (2001). Case studies in couple and family therapy. New York: Guilford.

D'Augelli, A. R. (1991). Gay men in college: Identity processes and adaptations. *Journal of College Student Development, 32,* 140–146.

Davidson, J. (2000). Giftedness. In A. Kazdin (Ed.), *Encyclopedia of psychology.* Washington, DC, & New York: American Psychological Association and Oxford University Press.

Davidson, M. R., London, M. L., & Ladewig, P. A. (2008). *Olds' maternal-newborn nursing and women's health across the lifespan* (8th ed.). Upper Saddle River, NJ: Prentice Hall.

Davies, J., & Brember, I. (1999). Reading and mathematics attainments and self-esteem in years 2 and 6–An eight-year cross-sectional study. *Educational Studies, 25,* 145–157.

Davies, S. L., DeClemente, R. J. Wingood, G. M., Person, S. D., Dix, E. S., Harrington, K., Crosby, R. A., & Oh, K. (2006). Predictors of inconsistent contraceptive use among adolescent girls: Findings from a prospective study. *Journal of Adolescent Health, 39,* 43–49.

Davila, J., & Steinberg, S. J. (2006). Depression and romantic dysfunction during adolescence. In T. E. Joiner, J. S. Brown, & J. Kistner (Eds.), *The Interpersonal, cognitive, and social nature of depression.* Mahwah, NJ: Erlbaum.

Davis, A. E., Hyatt, G., & Arrasmith, D. (1998, February). "I Have a Dream" program. Class One Evaluation Report, Portland, OR: Northwest Regional Education Laboratory.

Davis, B. E., Moon, R. Y., Sachs, M. C., & Ottolini, M. C. (1998). Effects of sleep position on infant motor development. *Pediatrics, 102,* 1135–1140.

Davis, D. K. (2005). Leading the midwifery renaissance. *RCM Midwives, 8,* 264–268.

Davis, E. P., Glynn, L. M., Dunkel-Schetter, C., Hobel, C., Chiez-Demet, A., & Sandman, C. A. (2005). Corticotropin-releasing hormone during pregnancy is associated with infant temperament. *Developmental Neuroscience, 27,* 299–305.

Davis, K. F., Parker, K. P., & Montgomery, G. L. (2004). Sleep in infants and young children: Part one: Normal sleep. *Journal of Pediatric Health Care, 18,* 65–71.

Davison, K. K., & Birth, L. L. (2001). Weight status, parent reaction, and self-concept in five-year-old girls. *Pediatrics, 107,* 46–53.

Daws, D. (2000). *Through the night.* San Francisco: Free Association Books.

Day, N. L., Goldschmidt, L., & Thomas, C. A. (2006). Prenatal marijuana exposure contributes to the prediction of marijuana use at age 14. *Addiction, 101,* 1313–1322.

Day, N. L., Leech, S. L., Richardson, G. A., Cornelius, M. D., Robles, N., & Larkby, C. (2002). Prenatal alcohol exposure predicts continued deficits in offspring size at 14 years of age. *Alcohol: Clinical and Experimental Research, 26,* 1584–1591.

Day, R. H., & McKenzie, B. E. (1973). Perceptual shape constancy in early infancy. *Perception, 2,* 315–320.

de Haan, M., Mishkin, M., Baldewig, T., & Vargha-Khadem, F. (2006). Human memory development and its dysfunction after early hippcampal injury. *Trends in Neuroscience, 29,* 374–381.

de la Rocheborchard, E., & Thonneau, F. (2002). Paternal age and maternal age are risk factors for miscarriage: Results of a multicentre European study. *Human Reproduction, 17,* 1649–1656.

de Moraes Barros, M. C., Guinsburg, R., de Araujo Peres, C., Mitsuhiro, S., Chalem, E., & Laranjeira, R. R. (2006). Exposure to marijuana during pregnancy alters neurobehavior in the early neonatal period. *Journal of Pediatrics, 149,* 781–787.

de Onis, M., de Onis, M., Onyango, A. W., Borghi, E., Garza, C., & Yang, H. (2006). Comparison of the World Health Organization (WHO) child growth standards and the National Center for Health Statistics/WHO international growth reference: Implications for child health programs. *Public Health Nutrition, 9,* 942–947.

de Rosnay, M., Cooper, P. J., Tsigaras, N., & Murray, L. (2006). Transmission of social anxiety from mother to infant: An experimental study using a social referencing paradigm. *Behavior Research and Therapy, 44,* 1165–1175.

De Santis-Moniaci, D., & Altshuler, L. (2007). Comprehensive behavioral treatment of overweight and the pediatric practice. *Pediatric Annals, 36,* 102–108.

de Vries, P. (2005). Lessons from home: Scaffolding vocal improvisation and song acquisition in a 2-year-old. *Early Childhood Education Journal, 32,* 307–312.

Deater-Deckard, K., & Dodge K. (1997). Externalizing behavior problems and discipline revisited: non-linear effects and variation by culture, context and gender. *Psychological Inquiry, 8,* 161–175.

DeCasper, A. J., & Spence, M. J. (1986). Prenatal maternal speech influences newborn's perception of speech sounds. *Infant Behavior and Development, 9,* 133–150.

deCharms, R. (1984). Motivation enhancement in educational settings. In R. Ames & C. Ames (Eds.), *Research on motivation in education* (Vol. 1). Orlando: Academic Press.

Deci, E., & Ryan, R. (1994). Promoting self-determined education. *Scandinavian Journal of Educational Research, 38,* 3–14.

DeGarmo, D. S., & Martinez, C. R. (2006). A culturally informed model of academic well-being for Latino youth: The importance of discriminatory experiences and social support. *Family Relations, 55,* 267–278.

Degutis, L. C., & Greve, M. (2006). Injury prevention. *Emergency Medical Clinics of North America, 24,* 871–888.

DeLamater, J., & MacCorquodale, P. (1979). *Premarital sexuality.* Madison: University of Wisconsin Press.

Delemarre-van de Waal, H. A. (2005). Secular trend of timing puberty. *Endocrine Development, 8,* 1–14.

DeLoache, J. S. (2004). Early development of the understanding and use of symbolic art: facts. In U. Goswami (Ed.), *Blackwell handbook of childhood cognitive development.* Malden, MA: Blackwell.

Delpisheh, A., Attia, E., Drammond, S., & Brabin, B. J. (2006). Adolescent smoking in pregnancy and birth outcomes. *European Journal of Public Health, 16,* 168–172.

DeMarie, D., Abshier, D. W., & Ferron, J. (2001, April). *Longitudinal study of predictors of memory improvement over the elementary school years: Capacity, strategies, and metamemory revisited.* Paper presented at the meeting of the Society for Research in Child Development, Minneapolis.

Dement, W. C. (2005). History of sleep medicine. *Neurologic Clinics, 23,* 964–965.

Demetriou, A. (2001, April). *Towards a comprehensive theory of intellectual development: Integrating psychometric and post—Piagetian theories.* Paper presented at the meeting of the Society for Research in Child Development, Minneapolis.

DeMirjyn, M. (2006, April). *Surviving the system: Narratives of Chicana/Latina undergraduates.* Paper presented at the meeting of the American Educational Research Association, San Francisco.

Demmelmair, H., von Rosen, J., & Koletzko, B. (2006). Long-term consequences of early nutrition. *Early Human Development, 82,* 567–574.

Dempster, F. N. (1981). Memory span: Sources of individual and developmental differences. *Psychological Bulletin, 80,* 63–100.

Dencker, M., Thorsson, O., Karlsson, M. K., Linden, C., Svensson, J., Wollmer, P., & Anderson, L. B. (2006). Daily physical activity and its relation to aerobic fitness in children aged 8–11 years. *European Journal of Applied Physiology, 96,* 587–592.

Denham, S. A. (2006). The emotional basis of learning and development in early childhood education. In B. Spodak & O. N. Saracho (Eds.), *Handbook of research on the education of young children* (2nd ed.). Mahwah, NJ: Erlbaum.

Denham, S. A., Bassett, H. H., & Wyatt, T. (2007). The socialization of emotional competence. In J. E. Grusec & P. D. Hastings (Eds.), *Handbook of socialization.* New York: Guilford.

Denmark, F. L., Rabinowitz, V. C., & Sechzer, J. A. (2005). *Engendering psychology: Women and gender revisited* (2nd ed.). Boston: Allyn & Bacon.

Denmark, F. L., Russo, N. F., Frieze, I. H., & Eschuzur, J. (1988). Guidelines for avoiding sexism in psychological research: A report of the ad hoc committee on nonsexist research. *American Psychologist, 43,* 582–585.

Denny, C. B. (2001). Stimulant effects in attention deficit hyperactivity disorder. *Journal of Clinical Child Psychology, 30,* 98–109.

Derbyshire, E. (2007a). Nutrition in pregnant teenagers: How nurses can help. *British Journal of Nursing, 16,* 144–145.

Derbyshire, E. (2007b). The importance of adequate fluid and fiber intake during pregnancy. *Nursing Standard, 21,* 40–43.

DeRose, L. M., & Brooks-Gunn, J. (2006). Transition into adolescence: The role of pubertal processes. In L. Balter & C. S., Tamis-LeMonda (Eds.), *Child psychology: A handbook of contemporary issues.* New York: Psychology Press.

DeRose, L. M., Wright, A. J., & Brooks-Gunn, J. (2006). Does puberty account for the differential in depression? In C. L. M. Keyes & S. H. Goodman (Eds.), *Women and depression: A handbook for the social, behavioral, and biomedical sciences.* New York: Cambridge University Press.

DeRosier, M. E., & Marcus, S. R. (2005). Building friendships and combating bullying: Effectiveness of S. S. Grin at one-year follow-up. *Journal of Clinical Child and Adolescent Psychology, 34,* 140–150.

DeSantis, L. (1998). Building healthy communities with immigrants and refugees. *Journal of Transcultural Nursing, 9,* 20–31.

Deschesnes, M., Fines, P., & Demers, S. (2006). Are tattooing and body piercing indicators of risk-taking behaviors among high school students? *Journal of Adolescence, 29,* 379–393.

Dewey, J. (1933). *How we think.* Lexington, MA: D.C. Heath.

Diamond, A. D. (1985). Development of the ability to use recall to guide action, as indicated by infants' performance on AB. *Child Development, 56,* 868–883.

Diamond, A. D. (2001). A model system for studying the role of dopamine in the prefrontal cortex during early development in humans: Early and continuously treated phenylketonuria. In C. Nelson & M. Luciana (Eds.), *Handbook of developmental cognitive neuroscience.* Cambridge, MA: MIT Press.

Diamond, A. D. (2007). Interrelated and interdependent. *Developmental Science, 10,* 152–158.

Diamond, L. M. (2003). Love matters: Romantic relationships among sexual-minority adolescents. In P. Florsheim (Ed.), *Adolescent romantic relationships and sexual behavior.* Mahwah, NJ: Erlbaum.

Diaz-Rico, L. T. (2008). *A course for teaching English learners.* Boston: Allyn & Bacon.

Echevarria, J., Vogt, M., & Short, D. J. (2008). *Making content comprehensible for English learners* (3rd ed.). Boston: Allyn & Bacon.

Dietrich, R. S., & Cohen, I. (2006). Fetal MR imaging. *Magnetic Resonance Imaging Clinics of North America, 14,* 503–522.

Dindia, K. (2006). Men are from North Dakota, women are from South Dakota. In K. Dindia & D. J. Canary (Eds.), *Sex differences and similarities in communication.* Mahwah, NJ: Erlbaum.

Dishion, T. J., Nelson, S. E., & Yasui, M. (2005) Predicting early adolescent gang involvement from middle school adaptation. *Journal of Clinical Child and Adolescent Psychology, 34,* 62–73.

Dixon, L., Browne, K., & Hamilton-Giachritsis, C. (2005). Risk factors of parents abused as children: A mediational analysis of the intergenerational continuity of child maltreatment (Part I). *Journal of Child Psychology and Psychiatry and Allied Disciplines, 46,* 47–57.

Dodge, K. A. (1983). Behavioral antecedents of peer social status. *Child Development, 54,* 1386–1399.

Dodge, K. A. (2001). The science of youth violence prevention: Progressing from developmental psychopathology to efficacy to effectiveness in public policy. *American Journal of Preventive Medicine, 20,* 63–70.

Dodge, K. A., & the Conduct Problems Prevention Research Group. (2007, March). *The impact of Fast Track on adolescent conduct disorder.* Paper presented at the meeting of the Society for Research in Child Development, Boston.

Dodge, K. A., Coie, J. D., & Lynam, D. R. (2006). Aggression and antisocial behavior in youth. In W. Damon & R. Lerner (Eds.), *Handbook of child psychology* (6th ed.). New York. Wiley.

Dodge, K. A., Malone, P. S., Lansford, J. E., Miller-Johnson, S., Pettit, G. S., & Bates, J. E. (2006). Toward a dynamic developmental model of the role of parents and peers in early onset substance abuse. In A. Clarke-Stewart & J. Dunn (Eds.), *Families count.* New York: Cambridge University Press.

Doherty, M. (2007). *Theory of mind.* Philadelphia: Psychology Press.

Doherty, T., Chopra, M., Nkonki, L., Jackson, D., & Greiner, T. (2006). Effects of the HIV epidemic on infant feeding in South Africa: "When they see me coming with the tins they laugh at me." *Bulletin of the World Health Organization, 84,* 90–96.

Dondi, M., Simion, F., & Caltran, G. (1999). Can newborns discriminate between their own cry and the cry of another newborn infant? *Developmental Psychology, 35* (2), 418–426.

Donnellan, M. B., Trzesniewski, K. H., & Robins, R. W. (2006). Personality and self-esteem development in adolescence. In D. K.

Mroczek & T. D. Little (Eds.), *Handbook of personality development.* Muhwah, NJ: Erlbaum.

Dorn, C. M., Madeja, S. S., & Sahol, F. R. (2004). *Assessing expressive learning* Mahwah, NJ: Erlbaum.

Dorn, L. D., Dahl, R. E., Woodward, H. R., & Biro, F. (2006). Defining the boundaries of early adolescence: A user's guide to assessing pubertal status and pubertal timing in research with adolescents. *Applied Developmental Science, 10,* 30–56.

Dorn, L. D., Williamson, D. E., & Ryan, N. D. (2002, April). *Maturational hormone differences in adolescents with depression and risk for depression.* Paper presented at the meeting of the Society for Research on Adolescence, New Orleans.

Doseis, S., Zito, J. M., Safer, D. J., Soeken, K. L., Mitchell, J. W., Ellwood, L. C. (2003). Parental perceptions and satisfaction with stimulant medication for attention deficit hyperactivity disorder. *Journal of Developmental and Behavioral Pediatrics, 24,* 155–162.

Doucet, F., & Hamon, R. R. (2007). A nation of diversity: Demographics of the United States of America and their implications for diverse families. In B. S. Trask & R. R. Hamon (Eds.), *Cultural diversity and families.* Thousand Oaks, CA: Sage.

Douglas, G., Grimley, M., McLinden, M., & Watson, L. (2004). Reading errors made by children with low vision. *Ophthalmic and Physiological Optics, 24,* 319–322.

Dowan, M. K. (2006). *Microbiology.* New York: McGraw-Hill.

Dowker, A. (2006). What can functional brain imaging studies tell us about typical and atypical cognitive development in children. *Journal of Physiology, Paris, 99,* 333–341.

Dragi-Lorenz, R. (2007, July). *Self-conscious emotions in young infants and the direct perception of self and others in interaction.* Paper presented at the meeting of the International Society for Research on Emotions, Sunshine Coast, Australia.

Draghi-Lorenz, R., Reddy, V., & Costall, A. (2001). Rethinking the development of "nonbasic" emotions: A critical review of existing theories. *Developmental Review, 21,* 263–304.

Draper, J. (2003). Men's passage to fatherhood: An analysis of the contemporary relevance of transition theory. *Nursing Inquiry, 10,* 66–77.

Drew, C., & Hardman, M. L. (2000). *Mental retardation* (7th ed.). Columbus, OH: Merrill.

Drewes, A. A., Carey, L. J., & Schaefer, C. E. (2003). *School-based play therapy.* New York: Wiley.

Driscoll, A., & Nagel, N. G. (2005). *Early childhood education, birth-8 (3rd ed.).* Boston: Allyn & Bacon.

Driscoll, A., & Nagel, N. G. (2008). *Early childhood education* (4th ed.). Boston: Allyn & Bacon.

Driscoll, J. W. (2006). Postpartum depression: The state of the science. *Journal of Perinatal and Neonatal Nursing, 20,* 40–42.

Dryfoos, J. G. (1990). *Adolescents at risk: Prevalence or prevention,* New York: Oxford University Press.

Dryfoos, J. G., Barkin, C. (2006). *Adolescence: Growing up in America today.* New York: Oxford University Press.

Dubay, L. Joyee, T., Kaestner, R., & Kenney, G. M. (2001). Changes in prenatal care timing and low birth weight by race and socioeconomic status: Implications for the Medicaid expansions for pregnant women. *Health Services Research, 36,* 373–398.

Dubois, J., Dehaene-Lambertz, G., Perrin, M., Mangin, J. F., Cointepas, Y., Ducheesnay, E., Le Bihan, D., & Hertz-Pannier, L. (2007, in press). Asynchrony of the early maturation of white matter bundles in healthy infants: Quantitative landmarks revealed noninvasively by diffusion tensor imaging. *Human Brain Mapping.*

Dubow, E. F., Huesmann, L. R., & Greenwood, D. (2007). Media and youth socialization. In J. E. Grusec & P. D. Hastings (Eds.), *Handbook of socialization.* New York: Guilford.

Duffy, T. M., & Kirkley, J. R. (Eds.). (2004). *Learner-centered theory and practice in distance education.* Mahwah, NJ: Erlbaum.

Duggan, A., Fuddy, L., Burrell, L., Higman, S. M., McFarlane, E., Windham, A., & Sia, C. (2004). Randomized trial of statewide home visiting program to prevent child abuse: Impact in reducing parental risk factors. *Child Abuse and Neglect, 28,* 623–643.

Duke, K., & Don, M. (2005). Acupuncture use for prebirth treatment. *Complementary Therapy in Clinical Practice, 11,* 121–126.

Dundek, L. H. (2006). Establishment of a Somali doula program at a large metropolitan hospital. *Journal of Perinatal and Neonatal Nursing, 20,* 128–137.

Dunkel, L. (2006). Management of children with idiopathic short stature. *European Journal of Endocrinology, 155* (Suppl. 1), S35–S38.

Dunkel-Schetter, C. (1998). Maternal stress and preterm delivery. *Prenatal and Neonatal Medicine, 3,* 39–42.

Dunkel-Schetter, C., Gurung, R. A. R., Lobel, M., & Wadhwa, P. D. (2001). Stress processes in pregnancy and birth. In A. Baum, T. A. Revenson, & J. E. Singer (Eds.), *Handbook of health psychology.* Mahwah, NJ: Erlbaum.

Dunn, J. (2005). Commentary: Siblings in their families. *Journal of Family Psychology, 19,* 654–657.

Dunn, J., & Kendrick, C. (1982). *Siblings.* Cambridge, MA: Harvard University Press.

Dunson, D. B., Baird, D. D., & Columbo, B. (2004). Increased fertility with age in men and women. *Obstetrics and Gynecology, 103,* 51–56.

Durrant, J. E. (2000). Trends in youth crime and well-being since the abolition of corporal punishment in Sweden. *Youth and Society, 3,* 437–455.

Durston, S., & Casey, B. J. (2006). What have we learned about cognitive development from neuroimaging? *Neuropsychologia, 44,* 2149–2157.

Durston, S., Davidson, M. C., Tottenham, N. T., Galvan, A., Spicer, J., Fossella, J. A., & Casey, B. J. (2007, in press). A shift from diffuse to focal cortical activity with development. *Developmental Science.*

Dutton, G. N. (2003). Cognitive vision, its disorders and differential diagnosis in adults and children: Knowing where and what things are, *Eye, 17,* 289–304.

Dweck, C. S. (2006). *Mindset.* New York: Random House.

Dweck, C. S., Mangels, J. A., & Good, C. (2004). Motivational effects on attention, cognition, and performance. In D. Yun Dai & R. J. Sternberg (Eds.), *Motivation, emotion, and cognition.* Mahwah, NJ: Erlbaum.

Dyl, J., Kittler, J., Phillips, K. A., & Hunt, J. I. (2006). Body dysmorphic disorder and other clinically significant body image concerns in adolescent psychiatric inpatients: Prevalence and clinical characteristics. *Child Psychiatry and Human Development, 36,* 369–382.

E

Eagly, A. H. (2002). Social role theory of sex differences and similarities. In J. Worrell (Ed.), *Encyclopedia of women and gender.* San Diego: Academic Press.

Eagly, A. H., & Crowley, M. (1986). Gender and helping: A meta-analytic review of the social psychological literature. *Psychological Bulletin, 108,* 233–256.

Eagly, A. H. & Diekman, A. B. (2003). The malleability of sex differences in response to social roles. In L. G. Aspinwall & V. M. Staudinger (Eds.), *A psychology of human strengths.* Washington, DC: American Psychological Association.

Eagly, A. H., & Koenig, A. M. (2006). Social role theory of sex differences and similarities: Implications for prosocial behavior. In K. Dindia & D. J. Canary (Eds.), *Sex differences and similarities in communication.* Mahwah, NJ: Erlbaum.

Eagly, A. H., & Steffen, V. J. (1986). Gender and aggressive behavior: A meta-analytic review of the social psychological literature. *Psychological Bulletin, 100,* 309–330.

Eaton, D. K., & others (2006, June 9). Youth risk behavior surveillance—United States, 2005. *MMWR, 55,* 1–108.

Eby, J. W., Herrell, A., & Jordan, M. L. (2006). *Teaching K-12 schools: A reflective action* *approach* (4th ed.). Upper Saddle River, NJ: Prentice Hall.

Eby, R. (2005). Language and literacy in the school years. In J. Berko Gleason, *The development of language* (6th ed.). Boston: Allyn & Bacon.

Eccles, J. S. (2007). Families, schools, and developing achievement-related motivations and engagement. In J. E. Grusec & P. D. Hastings (Eds.), *Handbook of socialization*. New York: Guilford.

Eccles J. S., & Gootman, J. A. (Eds.). (2002). *Community programs to promote youth development.* Washington, DC: National Academy Press.

Eccles, J. S., Brown, B., & Templeton, J. (2007). A developmental framework for selecting indicators of well-being during the adolescent and young adult years. In B. Brown (Ed.), *Key indicators of child and youth well-being.* Mahwah, NJ: Erlbaum.

Eckerman, C. & Whitehead, H. (1999). How toddler peers generate coordinated action: A cross-cultural exploration. *Early Education & Development, 10,* 241–266.

Eckstein, K. C., Mikhail, L. M., Ariza, A. J., Thompson, J. S., Millard, S. C., Binns, H. J., & the Pediatric Practice Research Group. (2006). Parents' perceptions of their child's weight and health. *Pediatrics, 117,* 681–690.

Edelman, M. W. (1992). *The measure of our success.* Boston: Beacon Press.

Edelman, M. W. (2000). Commentary in *The state of America's children.* Washington, DC: Children's Defense Fund.

Edelman, M. W. (2004, October 28). *Interfaith service for justice for children and the poor.* Presentation, Children's Defense Fund, Washington, DC.

Edinburgh, L., Saewye, E., Thao, T., & Levitt, C. (2006). Sexual exploitation of very young Hmong girls. *Journal of Adolescent Health, 39,* 111–118.

Educational Testing Service. (1992, February). *Cross-national comparisons of 9–13 year olds' science and math achievement.* Princeton, NJ: Author.

Edwards, C. P. (2002). Three approaches from Europe: Waldorf, Montessori, and Reggio Emilia. *Early Childhood Practice and Research, 4,* 364–40.

Edwards, R., & Hamilton, M. A. (2004). You need to understand my gender role: An empirical test of Tannen's model of gender and communication. *Sex Roles, 50,* 491–504.

Edwards, S. L., & Sarwark, J. F. (2005). Infant and child motor development. *Clinical and Orthopedic Related Research, 434,* 33–39.

Egeland, B. (2007). Understanding developmental processes of resilience and psychology: Implications for policy and practice. In A. Masten (Ed.), *Multilevel dynamics in developmental psychology.* Mahwah, NJ: Erlbaum.

Egeland, B., & Carlson, B. (2004). Attachment and psychopathology. In L. Atkinson & S. Goldberg (Eds.), *Attachment issues in*

psychopathology and intervention. Mahwah, NJ: Erlbaum.

Egeland, B., Jacobvitz, D., & Sroufe, L. A. (1988). Breaking the cycle of abuse. *New Directions for Child Development, 11,* 77–92.

Egley, A. (2002), *National youth gang survey trends from 1996 to 2000.* Washington, DC: U.S. Department of Justice, Office of Justice Programs, Office of Juvenile Justice and Delinquency Prevention.

Eidelman, A. I., & Feldman, R. (2004). Positive effect of human milk on neurobehavioral and cognitive development of premature infants. *Advances in Experimental Medicine and Biology, 554,* 359–364.

Eiferman, R. R. (1971). Social play in childhood. In R. Herron & B. Sutton-Smith (Eds.), *Child's play.* New York: Wiley.

Eisenberg, N. (Ed.). (1982). *The development of prosocial behavior.* New York: Wiley.

Eisenberg, N. (2006). Empathy-related responding in children. In M. Killen & J. G. Smetana (Eds.), *Handbook of moral development.* Mahwah, NJ: Erlbaum.

Eisenberg, N., Fabes, R. A., & Spinrad, T. L. (2006). Prosocial development. In W. Damon & R. Lerner (Eds.), *Handbook of child psychology* (6th ed.). New York: Wiley.

Eisenberg, N., Martin, C. L., & Fabes, R. A. (1996). Gender development and gender effects. In D. C. Berliner & R. C. Calfee (Eds.), *Handbook of educational psychology.* New York: Macmillan.

Eisenberg, N., & Morris, A. S. (2004). Moral cognitions and social responding in adolescence. In R. Lerner & L. Steinberg (Eds.), *Handbook of adolescent psychology.* New York: Wiley.

Eisenberg, N., Spinrad, T. L., & Smith, C. L. (2004). Emotion-related regulation: Its conceptualization, relations to social functioning, and socialization. In P. Philippot & R. S. Feldman (Eds.), *The regulation of emotion.* Mahwah, NJ: Erlbaum.

Eisenmann, J. C., Ekkekakis, P., & Holmes, M. (2006). Sleep duration and overweight among Australian children and adolescents. *Acta Pediatrica, 95,* 956–963.

Elkind, D. (1970, April 5). Erik Erikson's eight ages of man. *New York Times Magazine.*

Elkind, D. (1976). *Child development and education: A Piagetian perspective.* New York: Oxford University Press.

Elkind, D. (1981). *The hurried child.* Reading, MA: Addison-Wesley.

Elkind, D. (1988, January). Educating the very young: A call for clear thinking. *NEA Today,* pp. 22–27.

Elliott, M. R., Kallan, M. J., Durbin, D. R., & Winston, F. K. (2006). Effectiveness of child safety seats versus seat belts in reducing risk for

death in children in passenger vehicle crashes. *Archives of Pediatric and Adolescent Medicine, 160,* 617–621.

Elliott, V. S. (2004). Methamphetamine use increasing. Retrieved March 15, 2004, from www.amaassn.org/amednews/2004/07/26/hlsc0726.htm

Else-Ouest, N. M., Hyde, J. S., Goldsmith, H. H., & Van Hulle, C. (2006). Gender differences in temperament: A meta-analysis. *Psychological Bulletin, 132,* 33–72.

El-Toukhy, T., Khalaf, Y., & Braude, P. (2006). IVF results: Optimize not maximize. *American Journal of Obstetrics and Gynecology, 194,* 322–331.

Emde, R. N., Gaensbauer, T. G., & Harmon, R. J. (1976). Emotional expression in infancy: A biobehavioral study. *Psychological Issues: Monograph Series, 10* (37).

Emery, R. E. (1994). *Renegotiating family relationships.* New York: Guilford Press.

Engels, R. C., Vermulst, A. A., Dubas, J. S., Bot, S. M., & Gerris, J. (2005). Long-term effects of family functioning and child characteristics on problem drinking in young adulthood. *European Addiction Research, 11,* 32–37.

Enger, E. (2007). *Concepts in biology* (12th ed.). New York: McGraw-Hill.

Engler, A. J., Ludington-Hoe, S. M., Cusson, R. M., Adams, R., Bahsen, M., Brumbaugh, E., Coates, P., Grief, J., McHargue, L., Ryan, D. L., Settle, M., & Williams, D. (2002). Kangaroo care: National survey of practice, Knowledge, barriers, and perceptions. *American Journal of Maternal/Child Nursing, 27,* 146–153.

Enning, C. (2004). Waterbirth: Contemporary application for historic concepts. *Midwifery Today, 70,* 45.

Enright, R. D., Lapsley, D. K., Dricas, A. S., & Fehr, L. A. (1980). Parental influence on the development of adolescent autonomy and identity. *Journal of Youth and Adolescence, 9,* 529–546.

Enriori, P. J., Evans, A. E., Sinnayah, P., & Cowley, M. A. (2006). Leptin resistance and obesity. *Obesity, 14,* (Suppl. 5), S254–S258.

Ensembl Human. (2007). *Explore the Homo sapiens genome.* Retrieved April 28, 2007, from www.ensemble.org/Homo_sapiens/index.html

Eogan, M., Daly, L., & O'Herlihy, C. (2006). The effect of regular antenatal perineal massage on postnatal pain and anal sphincter injury: A prospective observational study. *Journal of Maternal-Fetal and Neonatal Medicine, 19,* 225–229.

Ercikan, K. (2006). Developments in assessment of student learning. In P. A. Alexander & P. H. Winne (Eds.), *Handbook of educational psychology* (2nd ed.). Mahwah, NJ: Erlbaum.

ERIC/EECE. (2002). Academic redshirting. *ERIC Clearinghouse on Elementary and Early Childhood Education,* pp. 1–15.

Ericsson, K. A., Charness, N., Feltovich, P. J., & Hoffman, R. R. (Eds.). (2006). *The Cambridge handbook of expertise and expert performance.* New York: Cambridge University Press.

Ericsson, K. A., Krampe, R., & Tesch-Romer, C. (1993). The role of deliberate practice in the acquisition of expert performance. *Psychological Review, 100,* 363–406.

Erikson, E. H. (1950). *Childhood and society.* New York: W. W. Norton.

Erikson, E. H. (1960). *Identity: Youth and crisis.* New York: W.W. Norton.

Erikson, E. H. (1962). *Young man Luther.* New York: W. W. Norton.

Erikson, E. H. (1968). *Identity: Youth and crisis.* New York. W. W. Norton.

Erikson, E. H. (1969). *Gandhi's truth.* New York: W. W. Norton.

Eshel, N., Nelson, E. E., Blair, R. J., Pine, D. S., & Ernst, M. (2006, in press). Neural substrates of choice selection in adults and adolescents: Development of the ventrolateral prefrontal and anterior cingulated cortices. *Neuropsychologia.*

Estell, D. B., Farmer, T. W., & Cairns, B. D. (2007). Bullies and victims in rural African American youth: Behavioral characteristics and social network placement. *Aggressive Behavior, 33,* 145–159.

Etzel, R. (1988, October). *Children of smokers.* Paper presented at the American Academy of Pediatrics meeting, New Orleans.

Evans, E., Hawton, K., Rodham, K., & Deeks, J. (2005). The prevalence of suicide phenomena in adolescents: A systematic review of population based studies. *Suicide and Life-Threatening Behavior, 35,* 239–250.

Evans, G. W., English, G. W. (2002). The environment of poverty. *Child Development, 73,* 1238–1248.

F

Fabes, R. A., Eisenberg, N., Jones, S., Smith, M., Gutherie, I., Poulin, R., Shepard, S., & Friedman, J. (1999). Regulation, emotionality, and preschoolers' socially competent peer interactions. *Child Development, 70,* 432–442.

Fabes, R. A., Hanish, L. D., & Martin, C. L. (2003). Children at play: The role of peers in understanding the effects of child care. *Child Development, 74,* 1039–1043.

Fagan, J. F. (1992). Intelligence. A theoretical viewpoint. *Current Directions in Psychological Science, 1,* 82–86.

Fagot, B. I. (1995). Parenting boys and girls. In M. H. Bornstein (Ed.), *Handbook of parenting* (Vol. 1). Hillsdale, NJ: Erlbaum.

Fagot, B. I., Rodgers, C. S., & Leinbach, M. D. (2000). Theories of gender socialization. In T. Eckes & H. M. Trautner (Eds.), *The developmental social psychology of gender.* Mahwah, NJ: Erlbaum.

Falbo, T., & Poston, D. L. (1993). The academic, personality, and physical outcomes of only children in China. *Child Development, 64,* 18–35.

Fallis, W. M., Hamelin, K., Synomds, J., & Wang, X. (2006). Maternal and newborn outcomes related to maternal warming during cesarean delivery. *Journal of Obstetric, Gynecologic, and Neonatal Nursing, 35,* 324–331.

Fantino, E., & Stolarz-Fantino, S. (2005). Decision-making: Context matters. *Behavioural Processes, 69,* 165–171.

Fantz, R. L. (1963). Pattern vision in newborn infants. *Science, 140,* 296–297.

Faraone, S. V., Biederman, J., & Mick, E. (2006). The age-dependent decline of attention deficit hyperactivity disorder: A meta-analysis of follow-up studies. *Psychological Medicine, 36,* 159–165.

Fasig, L. (2000). Toddlers' understanding of ownership: Implications for self-concept development. *Social Development, 9,* 370–382.

Fassler, D. (2004, May 8). Commentary in "Teen brains on trial", *Science News Online,* p. 1.

Fear, N. T., Hey, K., Vincent, T., & Murphy, M. (2007). Paternal occupation and neural tube defects: A case-control study based on the Oxford Record Linkage Study register. *Pediatric and Perinatal Epidemiology, 21,* 163–168.

Federal Interagency Forum on Child and Family Statistics. (2002). *American children Key national indicators of well-being.* Washington, DC: U. S. Government Printing Office.

Fehring, R. J., Cheever, K. H., German, K., & Philpot, C. (1998). Religiosity and sexual activity among older adolescents. *Journal of Religion and Health, 37,* 229–239.

Fein, G. G. (1986). Pretend play. In D. Görlitz & J. F. Wohlwill (Eds.), *Curiosity, imagination, and play.* Hillsdale, NJ: Erlbaum.

Feinberg, M. E., Button, T. M., Neiderhiser, J. M., Reiss, D., & Hetherington, E. M. (2007). Parenting and antisocial behavior and depression: Evidence of genotype x parenting environment interaction. *Archives of General Psychiatry, 64,* 457–465.

Feinberg, M. E., & Hetherington, E. M. (2001). Differential parenting as a within-family variable. *Journal of Family Psychology, 15,* 22–37.

Feiring, C. (1996). Concepts of romance in 15-year-old adolescents. *Journal of Research on Adolescence, 6,* 181–200.

Fekkes, M., Pijpers, F. I., & Verloove-Vanhorick, S. P. (2004). Bullying behavior and associations with psychosomatic complaints and depression in victims. *Journal of Pediatrics, 144,* 17–22.

Feldman, H. D. (2001, April). *Contemporary developmental theories and the concept of talent.* Paper presented at the meeting of the Society for Research in Child Development, Minneapolis.

Feldman, R. (2006). From biological rhythms to social rhythms: Physiological precursors of mother-infant synchrony. *Developmental Psychology, 42,* 175–188.

Feldman, R., Weller, A., Sirota, L., & Eidelman, A. I. (2002). Skin-to-skin contact (kangaroo care) promotes self-regulation in premature infants: Sleep-wake cyclicity, arousal modulation, and sustained exploration. *Developmental Psychology, 38,* 194–207.

Feldman, R., Weller, A., Sirota, L., & Eidelman, A. I. (2003). Testing a family intervention hypothesis: The contribution of mother-infant skin-to-skin (kangaroo care) to family interaction, proximity, and touch. *Journal of Family Psychology, 17,* 94–107.

Feldman, S. S. (1999). Unpublished review of J. W. Santrock's *Adolescence,* 8th ed. (New York: McGraw-Hill).

Feldman, S. S., & Elliott, G. R. (1990). Progress and promise of research on normal adolescent development. In S. S. Feldman & G. Elliott (Eds.), *At the threshold: The developing adolescent.* Cambridge, MA: Harvard University Press.

Feldman, S. S., Turner, R., &Aruajo, K. (1999). Interpersonal context as an influence on sexual timetables of youths: Gender and ethnic effects. *Journal of Research on Adolescence, 9,* 25–52.

Feleszko, W., & others. (2006). Parental tobacco smoking is associated with IL-13 secretion in children with allergic asthma. *Journal of Allergy and Clinical Immunology, 117,* 97–102.

Ferguson, D. M., Harwood, L. J., & Shannon, F. T. (1987). Breastfeeding and subsequent social adjustment in 6- to 8-year-old children. *Journal of Child Psychology and Psychiatry, 28,* 378–386.

Fernandes, O., Sabharwal, M., Smiley, T., Pastuszak, A., Koren, G., & Einarson, T. (1998). Moderate to heavy caffeine consumption during pregnancy and relationship to spontaneous abortion and abnormal fetal growth: A meta-analysis. *Reproductive Toxicology, 12,* 435–444.

Ferrando-Lucas, M. T. (2006). Attention deficit hyperactivity disorder: Its etiological factors and endophenotypes. *Revista de Neurologia (Spanish), 42,* (Suppl.) S9–S11.

Ferris, T. G., Kuhlthau, K., Ausiello, J., Perrin, J., & Kahn, R. (2006). Are minority children the last to benefit from a new technology? Technology diffusion and inhaled corticosteroids for asthma. *Medical Care, 44,* 81–86.

Field, T. M. (1998). Massage therapy effects. *American Psychologist, 53,* 1270–1281.

Field, T. M. (2001). Massage therapy facilitates weight gain in preterm infants. *Current Directions in Psychological Science, 10,* 51–55.

Field, T. M. (2002). Infants' need for touch. *Human Development, 45,* 100–103.

Field, T. M. (2003). Stimulation of preterm infants. *Pediatrics Review, 24,* 4–11.

Field, T. M. (2007). *The amazing infant.* Malden, MA: Blackwell.

Field, T. M., Diego, M., & Hernandez-Reif, M. (2007). Massage therapy research. *Developmental Review, 27,* 75–89.

Field, T. M., Grizzle, N., Scafidi, F., & Schanberg, S. (1996). Massage and relaxation therapies' effects on depressed adolescent mothers. *Adolescence, 31,* 903–911.

Field, T. M., Henteleff, T., Hernandez-Reif, M., Martines, E., Mavunda, K., Kuhn, C., & Schanberg, S. (1998). Children with asthma have improved pulmonary functions after massage therapy. *Journal of Pediatrics, 132,* 854–858.

Field, T. M., Hernandez-Reif, M., Feijo, L., & Freedman, J. (2006). Prenatal, perinatal, and neonatal stimulation. *Infant Behavior and Development, 29,* 24–31.

Field, T. M., Hernandez-Reif, M., Freedman, J. (2004, Fall). Stimulation programs for preterm infants. *SRCD Social Policy Reports, XVIII* (No. 1), 1–20.

Field, T. M., Hernandez-Reif, M., Seligman, S., Krasnegor, J., & Sunshine, W. (1997). Juvenile rheumatoid arthritis: Benefits from massage therapy. *Journal of Pediatric Psychology, 22,* 607–617.

Field, T. M., Hernandez-Reif, M., Taylor, S., Quinitino, O., & Burman, I. (1997). Labor pain is reduced by massage therapy. *Journal of Psychosomatic Obstetrics and Gynecology, 18,* 286–291.

Field, T. M., Lasko, D., Mundy, P., Henteleff, T., Kabat, S., Talpins, S., & Dowling, M. (1997). Brief report: Autistic children's attentiveness and responsivity improve after touch therapy. *Journal of Autism and Developmental Disorders, 27,* 333–338.

Field, T. M., Quintino, O., Henandez-Reif, M., & Koslosky, G. (1998). Adolescents with attention deficit hyperactivity disorder benefit from massage therapy. *Adolescence, 33,* 103–108.

Field, T. M., Schanberg, S. M., Scafidi, F., Bauer, C. R., Vega-Lahr, N., Garcia, R., Nystrom, J., & Kuhn, C. M. (1986). Tactile/kinesthetic stimulation effects on preterm neonates. *Pediatrics, 77,* 654–658.

Finn, M. V. (2006). Evolution and ontogeny of stress response to social challenges in the human child. *Developmental Review, 26,* 138–174.

Fisch, S. M. (2007). Peeking behind the scenes: Varied approaches to the production of educational television. In J. A. Bryant (Ed.), *The children's television community.* Mahwah, NJ: Erlbaum.

Fischer, K. W., & Bidell, T. R. (2006). Dynamic development of action and thought. In W. Damon & R. Lerner (Eds.), *Handbook of child psychology* (6th ed.). New York: Wiley.

Fischer, K. W., & Rose, S. P. (1995, Fall). Concurrent cycles in the dynamic development of brain and behavior. *SRCD Newsletter,* pp. 3–4, 15–16.

Fish, M. (2004). Attachment in infancy and preschool in low socioeconomic status rural Appalachian children: Stability and change and relations to preschool and kindergarten competence. *Developmental Psychopathology, 16,* 293–312.

Fisher, H. E. (2006). Broken hearts: The nature and risks of romantic rejection. In A. C. Crouter & A. Booth (Eds.), *Romance and sex in adolescence and emerging adulthood.* Mahwah, NJ: Erlbaum.

Fitzgerald, E. F., Hwang, S. A., Lannguth, K., Cayo, M., Yang, B. Z., Bush, S., Worswick, P., & Lauzon, T. (2004). Fish consumption and other environmental exposures and their associations with serum PCB concentrations among Mohawk women at Akwesasne. *Environmental Research, 94,* 160–170.

Fitzgibbon, M. L., Stolley, M. R., Dyer, A. R., VanHorn, L., & Kaufer Chistroffel, K. (2002). A community-based obesity prevention program for minority children: Rationale and study design for Hip to Health Jr. *Preventive Medicine, 34,* 289–297.

Fitzgibbon, M. L., Stolley, M. R., Schiffer, L., Van Horn, L., Kaufer Christoffel, L., & Dyer, A. (2005). Two-year follow-up results for Hip-Hop to Health Jr: A randomized controlled trial for overweight prevention in preschool minority children. *Journal of Pediatrics, 146,* 618–625.

Fivush, R. (1993). Developmental perspectives on autobiographical recall. In G. S. Goodman, & B. Bottoms (Eds.), *Child victims and child witnesses: Understanding and improving testimony.* New York: Guilford.

Flanagan, C. (2004). Volunteerism, leadership, political Socialization, and Civic Engagement. In R. Lerner L. Steinberg (Eds.), Handbook of adolescent psychology (2nd ed.). New York: Wiley.

Flanagan, C., & Fiason, N. (2001). Youth civic development: Implications of research for social policy and programs. *SRCD Social Policy Report. XV* (No. 1), 1–14.

Flannery, D. J., Hussey, D., Biebelhausen, L., & Wester, K. (2003). Crime, delinquency, and youth gangs. In G. Adams & M. Berzonsky (Eds.), *Blackwell handbook of adolescence.* Malden, MA: Blackwell.

Flavell, J. H. (1999). Cognitive development: Children's knowledge about the mind. *Annual Review of Psychology* (Vol. 50). Palo Alto, CA: Annual Reviews.

Flavell, J. H. (2004). Theory-of-mind development: Retrospect and prospect. *Merrill-Palmer Quarterly, 50,* 274–290.

Flavell, J. H., Friedrichs, A., & Hoyt, J. (1970). Developmental changes in memorization processes. *Cognitive Psychology, 1,* 324–340.

Flavell, J. H., Green, F. L., & Flavell, E. R. (1995). Young children's knowledge about thinking. *Monographs of the Society for Research in Child Development, 60* (1, Serial No. 243).

Flavell, J. H., Green, F. L., & Flavell, E. R. (1998). The mind has a mind of its own: Developing knowledge about mental uncontrollability. *Cognitive Development, 13,* 127–138.

Flavell, J. H., Friedrichs, A., & Hoyt, J. (1970). Developmental changes in memorization processes. *Cognitive Psychology, 1,* 324–340.

Flavell, J. H., Green, F. L. & Flavell, E. R. (2000). Development of children's awareness of their own thoughts. Journal of Cognition and Development, 1, 97–112.

Flavell, J. H., Miller, P. H., & Miller, S. (2002). *Cognitive development* (4th ed.). Upper Saddle River, NJ: Prentice Hall.

Flegal, K. M., Ogden, C. L., & Carroll, M. D. (2004). Prevalence and trends in Mexican-American adults and children. *Nutrition Review, 62,* S144–S148.

Fletcher, A. C., Steinberg, L., & Williams-Wheeler, M. (2004). Parental influences on adolescent problem behavior: Revisiting Stattin and Kerr. *Child Development, 75,* 781–796.

Flint, M. S., Baum, A., Chambers, W. H., & Jenkins, F. J. (2007, in press). Induction of DNA damage, alteration of DNA repair, and transcriptional activation by stress hormones. *Psychoneuroendocrinology.*

Flohr, J. W., Atkins, D. H., Bower, T. G. R., & Aldridge, M. A. (2001, April). *Infant music preferences.* Paper presented at the meeting of the Society for Research in Child Development, Minneapolis.

Flom, R., & Pick, A. D. (2003). Verbal encouragement and joint attention in 18-month-old infants. *Infant Behavior and Development, 26,* 121–134.

Flores, G., Abreu, M., & Tomany-Korman, S. C. (2005). Limited English proficiency, primary language at home, and disparities in children's health care: How language barriers are measured matters. *Public Health Reports, 120,* 418–420.

Florsheim, P. (Ed.). (2003). *Adolescent romantic relations and sexual behavior.* Mahwah, NJ: Erlbaum.

Florsheim, P., Sumida, E., McCann, C., Winstanley, M., Fukui, R., Seefedlt, T., & Moore, D. (2003). The transition to parenthood among young African American and Latino couples: Relational predictors of risk for parental dysfunction. *Journal of Family Psychology, 17,* 65–79.

Flynn, J. R. (1999). Searching for justice: The discovery of IQ gains over time. *American Psychologist, 54,* 5–20.

Flynn, J. R. (2007). The history of the American mind in the 20th century: A scenario to explain gains over time and a case for the irrelevance of *g.* In P. C. Kyllonen, R. D. Roberts, & L. Stankov (Eds.), *Extending intelligence.* Mahwah, NJ: Erlbaum.

Foege, W. (2000). The power of immunization. *The progress of nations.* New York: UNICEF.

Follari, L. (2007). *Foundations and best practices in early childhood education.* Upper Saddle River, NJ: Prentice Hall.

Fontenot, H. B. (2007). Transition and adaptation to adoptive motherhood. *Journal of Obstetrics, Gynecologic, and Neonatal Nursing, 36,* 175–182.

Forrester, M. B. (2007). Oxycodone abuse in Texas, 1998–2004. *Journal of Toxicology and Environmental Health A, 70,* 534–538.

Forrester, M. B., & Merz, R. D. (2007). Genetic counseling utilization by families with offspring affected by birth defects, Hawaii, 1986–2003. *American Journal of Medical Genetics A, 143,* 1045–1052.

Fowler-Brown, A., & Kahwati, L. C. (2004). Prevention and treatment of overweight in children and adolescents. *American Family Physician, 69,* 2591–2598.

Fox, K. R. (2004). Childhood obesity and the role of physical activity. *Journal of Research in Social Health, 124,* 34–39.

Fox, M. K., Pac, S., Devaney, B., & Jankowski, L. (2004). Feeding infants and toddlers study: What foods are infants and toddlers eating? *American Dietetic Association Journal, 104* (Suppl.), S22–S30.

Fraga, C. G., Motchnik, P. A., Shigenaga, M. K., Helbock, H. J., Jacob, R. A., & Ames, B. N. (1991). Ascorbic acid protects against endogenous oxidative DNA damage in human sperm. *Proceedings of the National Academy of Sciences of the United States, 88,* 11003–11006.

Fraiberg, S. (1959). *The Magic years.* New York: Scribner's.

Francis, D. J., Fletcher, J. M., Stuebing, K. K., Lyon, G. R., Shaywitz, B. A., & Shaywitz, S. E. (2005). Psychometric approaches to the identification of LD: IQ and achievement scores are not sufficient. *Journal of Learning Disabilities, 38,* 98–108.

Francis, J., Fraser, G., & Marcia, J. E. (1989). *Cognitive and experimental factors in moratorium-achievement (MAMA) cycles.* Unpublished manuscript, Department of Psychology, Simon Fraser University, Burnaby, British Columbia.

Franke, T. M. (2000, winter). The role of attachment as a protective factor in adolescent violent behavior. *Adolescent & Family Health, 1,* 29–39.

Franks, A., Kelder, S. H., Dino, G. A., Horn, K. A., Gortmaker, S. L., Wiecha, J. L., & Simoes, E. J. (2007). School-based programs: Lessons learned from CATCH, Planet Health, and Not-On-Tobacco. *Preventing Chronic Disease, 4,* A33.

Fraser, S. (Ed.). (1995). *The bell curve wars: Race, intelligence, and the future of America.* New York: Basic Books.

Fratelli, N., Papageorghiou, A. T., Prefumo, F., Bakalis, S., Homfray, T., & Thilaganathan,

B. (2007, in press). Outcome of prenatally diagnosed agenesis of the corpus callosum. *Prenatal Diagnosis.*

Frede, E. C. (1995). The role of program quality in producing early childhood program benefits. *The Future of Children* (Vol. 5, No. 3), 115–132.

Frederikse, M., Lu, A., Aylward, E., Barta, P., Sharma, T., & Pearlson, G. (2000). Sex differences in inferior lobule volume in schizophrenia. *American Journal of Psychiatry, 157,* 422–427.

Fredricks, J. A., & Eccles, J. S. (2006). Extracurricular involvement and adolescent adjustment: Impact of duration, number of activities, and breadth of participation. *Applied Developmental Science, 10,* 132–146.

Fredrickson, D. D. (1993). Breastfeeding research priorities, opportunities, and study criteria: What we learned from the smoking trial. *Journal of Human Lactation, 3,* 147–150.

Freedman, D. S., Khan, L. K., Serdula, M. K., Dietz, W. H., Srinivasan, S. R., & Berensen, G. S. (2004). Inter-relationships among childhood BMI, childhood height and adult obesity: The Bogalusa Heart Study. *International Journal of Obesity and Related Metabolic Disorders, 28,* 10–16.

Freedman, D. S., Khan, L. K., Serdula, M. K., Dietz, W. H., Srinivasan, S. R., & Berensen, G. S. (2005). The relation of childhood BMI to adult adiposity: The Bogalusa Heart Study. *Pediatrics, 115,* 22–27.

Freedman, D. S., Mei, Z., Srinivasan, S. R., Berensen, G. S., & Dietz, W. H. (2007). Cardiovascular risk factors and excess adiposity among overweight children and adolescents: The Bogalusa Heart Study. *Journal of Pediatrics, 150,* 12–17.

Freedman, L. P., Waldman, R. J., de Pinho, H., Wirth, M. E., Chowdhury, A. M., & Rosenfield, A. (2005). Transforming health systems to improve the lives of women and children. *Lancet, 365,* 997–1000.

Freeman, S., & Herron, J. C. (2007). *Evolutionary analysis* (4th ed.). Upper Saddle River, NJ: Prentice Hall.

Freud, A., & Dann, S. (1951). Instinctual anxiety during puberty. In A. Freud (Ed.), *The ego and its mechanisms of defense.* New York: International Universities Press.

Freud, S. (1917). *A general introduction to psychoanalysis.* New York: Washington Square Press.

Friedman, D. L., Hilden, J. M., & Pulaski, K. (2004). Issues and challenges in palliative care for children with cancer. *Current Oncology Reports, 6,* 431–437.

Friend, M. (2008). Special education (2nd ed.). Boston: Allyn & Bacon.

Frost, J. L., Thorton, C., Brown, J., Sutterby, J. A., & Therrell, J. (2001). *The developmental benefits and use patterns of overhead equipment on playgrounds.* Research commissioned by Game Time, a Playcore company, Fort Payne, AL.

Frye, D. (1999). Development of intention: The relation of executive function of theory of mind. In P. D. Zelazo, J. W. Astington, & D. R. Olson (Eds.), *Developing theories of intention: Social understanding and self-control.* Mahwah, NJ: Erlbaum.

Frye, D., Zelazo, P. D., Brooks, P. J., & Samuels, M. C. (1996). Inference and action in early causal reasoning. *Developmental Psychology, 32,* 120–131.

Fuchs, D., Mock, D., Morgan, P. L., & Young, C. L. (2003). Responsiveness-to-intervention: Definitions, evidence, and implications for the learning disabilities construct. *Learning Disabilities Research & Practice, 18,* 157–171.

Fuligni, A. J., & Fuligni, A. S. (2007). Immigrant families and the educational achievement of their children. In J. E. Lansford, K. Deater-Deckhard, & M. H. Bornstein (Eds.), *Immigrant families in contemporary society.* New York: Guilford.

Fuligni, A. J., & Hardway, C. (2006). Daily variation in adolescents' sleep, activities, and psychological well-being. *Journal of Research on Adolescence, 16,* 353–378.

Fuligni, A. J., & Stevenson, H. W. (1995). Time use and mathematics achievement among American, Chinese, and Japanese high school students. *Child Development, 66,* 830–842.

Fuligni, A. J., Witkow, M., & Garcia, C. (2005, April). *Ethnic identity and the academic adjustment of adolescents from Mexican, Chinese, and European backgrounds.* Paper presented at the meeting of the Society for Research in Child Development, Atlanta.

Fulkerson, J. A., Strauss, J., Neurmark-Sztainer, D., Story, M., & Boutelle, K. (2007). Correlates of psychosocial well-being among overweight adolescents: The role of the family. *Journal of Consulting and Clinical Psychology, 75,* 181–186.

Furman, Ho, M. & Low, S. (2005, April). *Adolescent dating experiences and adjustment.* Paper presented at the meeting of the Society for Research in Child Development, Atlanta.

Furman, W. C. (2007, March). *The conceptualization of attachment in adolescents' relationships.* Paper presented at the meeting of the Society for Research in Child Development, Boston.

Furman, W., & Shaffer, L. (2003). The role of romantic relationships in adolescent development. In P. Florsheim (Ed.), *Adolescent romantic relations and sexual behavior.* Mahwah, NJ: Erlbaum.

Furth, H. G., & Wachs, H. (1975). *Thinking goes to school.* New York: Oxford University Press.

G

Galambos, N. L. (2004). Gender and gender role development in adolescence. In R. Lerner & L. Steinberg (Eds.), *Handbook of adolescence.* New York: Wiley.

Galambos, N. L., Barker, E. T., & Krahn, H. J. (2006). Depression, self-esteem, and anger in emerging adulthood: Seven-year trajectories. *Developmental Psychology, 42*, 350–365.

Galambos, N. L., & Maggs, J. L. (1989, April). *The afterschool ecology of young adolescents and self-reported behavior.* Paper presented at the biennial meeting of the Society for Research in Child Development, Kansas City.

Galinsky, E., & David, J. (1988). *The preschool years: Family strategies that work—from experts and parents.* New York: Times Books.

Gallagher, J. J. (2007). *Teaching science for understanding.* Upper Saddle River, NJ: Prentice Hall.

Gallahue, D. L., & Ozmun, J. C. (2006). Motor development in young children. In B. Spodek & O. N. Saracho (Eds.), *Handbook of research on the education of young children* (2nd ed.). Mahwah, NJ: Erlbaum.

Galloway, J. C., & Thelen, E. (2004). Feet first: Object exploration in young infants. *Infant Behavior & Development, 27*, 107–112.

Gallup, G. W., & Bezilla, R. (1992). *The religious life of young Americans,* Princeton, NJ: Gallup Institute.

Ganong, L., Coleman, M., & Hans, J. (2006). Divorce as prelude to stepfamily living and the consequences of re-divorce. In M. A. Fine & J. H. Harvey (Eds.), *Handbook of divorce and relationship dissolution.* Mahwah, NJ: Erlbaum.

Garbarino, J. (1999). *Lost boys: Why our sons turn violent and how we can save them.* New York: Free Press.

Garbarino, J. (2001). Violent children. *Archives of Pediatrics and Adolescent Medicine, 155*, 1–2.

Garcia Coll, C. T., Szalacha, L. A., & Palacios, N. (2005). Children of Dominican, Portuguese, and Cambodian immigrant families: Academic attitudes and pathways during middle childhood. In C. R. Cooper, C. T. Garcia Coll, W. T. Bartko, H. M. Davis & C. Chatman (Eds.), *Developmental pathways through middle childhood.* Mahwah, NJ: Erlbaum.

Garcia Coll, C., & Pachter, L. M. (2002). Ethnic and minority parenting. In M. H. Bornstein (Ed.), *Handbook of parenting* (2nd ed., Vol. 4). Mahwah, NJ: Erlbaum.

Gardner, H. (1983). *Frames of mind.* New York: Basic Books.

Gardner, H. (1993). *Multiple intelligences.* New York: Basic Books.

Gardner, H. (2002). The pursuit of excellence through education. In M. Ferrari (Ed.), *Learning from extraordinary minds.* Mahwah, NJ: Erlbaum.

Garmezy, N. (1993). Children in poverty: Resilience despite risk. Psychiatry, 56, 127–136.

Garofalo, R., Wolf, R. C., Wissow, L. S., Woods, E. R., & Goodman, E. (1999). Sexual orientation and risk of suicide attempts among a representative sample of youth. *Archives of Pediatrics and Adolescent Medicine, 153*, 487–493.

Gathercole, V. C. M., & Hoff, E. (2007). Input and the acquisition of language: Three questions. In E. Hoff & M. Shatz (Eds.), *Blackwell handbook of language development.* Malden, MA: Blackwell.

Gaudernack, L. C., Forbord, S., & Hole, E. (2006). Acupuncture administered after spontaneous rupture of membranes at term significantly reduces the length of birth and use of oxytocin. *Acta Obstetricia et Gynecologica Scandinavica, 85*, 1348–1353.

Gauvain, M., & Perez, S. M. (2007). The socialization of cognition. In J. E. Grusec & P. D. Hastings (Eds.), *Handbook of socialization.* Mahwah, NJ: Erlbaum.

Geary, D. C. (2006). Evolutionary developmental psychology: Current status and future directions. *Developmental Review, 26*, 113–119.

Gee, C. L., & Heyman, G. D. (2007, in press). Children's evaluation of other people's self-descriptions. *Social Development.*

Geher, G., & Miller, G. (Eds.) (2007). *Mating intelligence.* Mahwah, NJ: Erlbaum.

Geissbuehler, V., Stein, S., & Eberhard, J. (2004). Waterbirths compared to landbirths: An observational study of nine years. *Journal of Perinatal Medicine, 32*, 308–314.

Gelhorn, H., Stallings, M., Young, S., Corley, R., Rhee, S. H., Christian, H., & Hewitt, J. (2006). Common and specific genetic influences on aggressive and nonaggressive conduct disorder domains. *Journal of the American Academy of Child and Adolescent Psychiatry, 45*, 570–577.

Gelman, R. (1969). Conservation acquisition: A problem of learning to attend to relevant attributes. *Journal of Experimental Child Psychology, 7*, 67–87.

Gelman, S. A., Heyman, G. D., & Legare, C. H. (2007, in press). Developmental changes in the coherence of essentialist beliefs about psychological characteristics. *Child Development.*

Gelman, S. A., & Kalish, C. W. (2006). Conceptual development. In W. Damon & R. Lerner (Eds.), *Handbook of child psychology* (6th ed.) New York: Wiley.

Gelman, S. A., & Opfer, J. E. (2004). Development of the animate-inanimate distinction. In U. Goswami (Ed.), *Blackwell handbook of childhood cognitive development.* Malden, MA: Blackwell.

Gennetian, L. A., Crosby, D. A., & Huston, A. C. (2006). Welfare and child care policy effects on very young children's child care experiences. In N. Cabrera, R. Hutchens, H. E. Peters, & L. Peters (Eds.), *From welfare to childcare.* Mahwah, NJ: Erlbaum.

Gennetian, L. A., & Miller, C. (2002). Children and welfare reform: A view from an experimental welfare reform program in Minnesota. *Child Development, 73*, 601–620.

Gerber, P., & Coffman, K. (2007, in press). Nonaccidental head trauma in infants. *Child's Nervous System.*

Gershoff, E. T. (2002). Corporal punishment by parents and associated child behaviors and experiences: A meta-analysis and theoretical review. *Psychological Bulletin, 128*, 539–579.

Geschwind, N., & Behan, P. O. (1984). Laterality, hormones, and immunity. In N. Geschwind & A. M. Galaburda (Eds.), *Cerebral dominance: The biological foundations.* Cambridge, MA: Harvard University Press.

Gesell, A. (1934). *An atlas of infant behavior.* New Haven, CT: Yale University Press.

Gesell, A. L. (1938). *Infancy and human growth.* New York: Macmillan.

Gewirtz, J. (1977). Maternal responding and the conditioning of infant crying: Directions of influence within the attachment-acquisition process. In B. C. Etzel, J. M. LeBlanc, & D. M. Baer (Eds.), *New developments in behavioral research.* Hillsdale, NJ: Erlbaum.

Ghetti, S., & Alexander, K. W. (2004). "If it happened, I would remember It": Strategic use of event memorability in the rejection of false autobiographical events. *Child Development, 75*, 542–561.

Ghi, T., Pilu, G., Falco, P., Segata, M., Carletti, A., Cocchi, G., Santini, D., Bonasoni, P., Tani, G., & Rizzo, N. (2006). Prenatal diagnosis of open and closed spina bifida. *Ultrasound in Obstetrics and Gynecology, 28*, 899–903.

Giammattei, J., Blix, G., Marshak, H. H., Wollitzer, A. O., & Pettitt, D. J. (2003). Television watching and soft drink consumption: Associations with obesity in 11- to 13-year-old schoolchildren. *Archives of Pediatric and Adolescent Medicine, 157*, 882–886.

Giannarelli, F., Sonenstein, E., & Stagner, M. (2006). Child care arrangements and help for low-income families with young children: Evidence from the National Survey of America's Families. In N. Cabrera, R. Hutchens, & H. E. Peters (Eds.), *From welfare to childcare.* Mahwah, NJ: Erlbaum.

Gibbons, J., & Ng, S. H. (2004). Acting bilingual and thinking bilingual. *Journal of Language & Social Psychology, 23*, 4–6.

Gibbs, J. C. (2003). Moral development & reality. Thousand Oaks, CA: Sage.

Gibson, E. J. (1969). *Principles of perceptual learning and development.* New York: Appleton-Century-Crofts.

Gibson, E. J. (1989). *Exploratory behavior in the development of perceiving, acting, and the acquiring of knowledge. Annual Review of Psychology, 39.* Palo Alto, CA: Annual Reviews.

Gibson, E. J. (2001). *Perceiving the affordances.* Mahwah, NJ: Erlbaum.

Gibbs, J. T. (1989). Black American adolescents. In J. T. Gibbs & L. N. Huang (Eds.), *Children of color*. San Francisco: Jossey-Bass.

Gibson, E. J., Riccio, G., Schmuckler, M. A., Stoffregen, T. A., Rosenberg, D., & Taormina, J. (1987). Detection of the traversability of surfaces by crawling and walking infants. *Journal of Experimental Psychology: Human Perception and Performance, 13,* 533–544.

Gibson, E. J., & Walk, R. D. (1960). The "visual cliff." *Scientific American, 202,* 64–71.

Gibson, J. H., Harries, M., Mitchell, A., Godfrey, R., Lunt, M., & Reeve, J. (2000). Determinants of bone density and prevalence of osteopenia among female runners in their second to seventh decades of age. *Bone, 26,* 591–598.

Gibson, J. J. (1966). The senses considered as perceptual. systems. Boston: Houghton Mifflin.

Gibson, J. J. (1979). *The ecological approach to visual perception.* Boston: Houghton Mifflin.

Gidding, S. S., & others (2006). Dietary recommendations for children and adolescents: A guide for practitioners. *Pediatrics, 117,* 544–549.

Giedd, J. N. & others. (2006). Puberty-related Influences on brain development. *Molecular and Cellular Endocrinology, 254–255,* 155–162.

Giequel, C., & Le Boue, Y. (2006). Hormonal regulation of fetal growth. *Hormone Research, 65* (Suppl. 3), 28–33.

Giglia, R. C., & Binns, C. W. (2007). Alcohol and breastfeeding: What do Australian mothers know? *Asia Pacific Journal of Clinical Nutrition, 16* (Suppl. 1), S473–S477.

Gillberg, C., & Cederlund, M. (2005). Asperger syndrome: Familial and prenatal factors. *Journal of Autism and Developmental Disorders, 35,* 159–166.

Gillen, M. M., Lefkowitz, E. S., & Sherer, C. L. (2006). Does body image play a role in risky sexual behaviour and attitudes? *Journal of Youth and Adolescence, 35,* 230–242.

Gilligan, C. (1982). *In a different voice.* Cambridge, MA: Harvard University Press.

Gilligan, C. (1992, May). *Joining the resistance: Girls' development in adolescence.* Paper presented at the symposium on development and vulnerability in close relationships, Montreal, Quebec.

Gilligan, C. (1996). The centrality of relationships in psychological development: A puzzle, some evidence, and a theory. In G. G. Noam & K. W. Fischer (Eds.), *Development and vulnerability in close relationships.* Hillsdale, NJ: Erlbaum.

Gilligan, C., Spencer, R., Weinberg, M. K., & Bertsch, T. (2003). On the listening guide: A voice-centered relational model. In P. M. Carnic & J. E. Rhodes (Eds.), *Qualitative research in psychology.* Washington, DC: American Psychological Association.

Gilstrap, L. L., & Ceci, S. J. (2005). Reconceptualizing children's suggestibility: Bidirectional and temporal properties. *Child Development, 76,* 40–53.

Ginorio, A. B., & Huston, M. (2001). *Si! Se Puede! Yes, we can: Latinas in school.* Washington, DC: AAUW.

Ginzberg, E. (1972). Toward a theory of occupational choice: A restatement. *Vocational Guidance Quarterly, 20,* 169–176.

Girling, A. (2006). The benefits of using the Neonatal Behavioral Assessment Scale in health visiting practice. *Community Practice, 79,* 118–120.

Girls, Inc. (1991). *Truth, trusting, and technology: New research on preventing adolescent pregnancy.* Indianapolis: Author.

Glantz, J. C. (2005). Elective induction vs. spontaneous labor associations and outcomes. *Journal of Reproductive Medicine, 50,* 235–240.

Gliori, G., Imm., P., Anderson, H. A. & Knobeloch, L. (2006). Fish consumption and advisory awareness among expectant women. *Wisconsin Medicine Journal, 105,* 41–44.

Gobet, E., & Charness, N. (2006). Expertise in chess. In K. A. Ericsson, N. Charness, P. J. Feltovich, & R. R. Hoffman (Eds.), *The Cambridge handbook of expertise and expert performance.* New York: Cambridge University Press.

Godding, V., Bonnier, C., Flasse, L., Michael, M., Longueville, E., Lebecque, P., Robert, A., & Galanti, L. (2004). Does in utero exposure to heavy maternal smoking induce nicotine withdrawal symptoms in neonates? *Pediatric Research, 55,* 645–651.

Goffin, S. G., & Wilson, C. S. (2001). *Curriculum models and early childhood education.* Upper Saddle River, NJ: Prentice Hall.

Goldberg, A. E., & Sayer, A. (2006). Lesbian couples' relationship quality across the transition to parenthood. *Journal of Marriage and the Family, 68,* 87–100.

Goldenberg, R. L., & Culhane, J. F. (2007). Low birth weight in the United States. *American Journal of Clinical Nutrition, 85* (Suppl.), S584–S590.

Goldman, R. (1964). *Religious thinking from childhood to adolescence.* London: Routledge & Kegan Paul.

Goldscheider, F., & Sassler, S. (2006). Creating stepfamilies: Integrating children into the study of union formation. *Journal of Marriage and the Family, 68,* 275–291.

Goldsmith, D. F. (2007). Challenging children's negative internal working models. In D. Oppenheim & D. F. Goldsmith (Eds.), *Attachment theory in clinical work with children.* New York: Guilford.

Goldsmith, H. H. (2002). Genetics of emotional development. In R. J. Davidson, K. R. Scherer, & H. H. Goldsmith (Eds.), *Handbook of affective sciences,* New York: Oxford University Press.

Goldstein, M. H., King, A. P., & West, M. J. (2003). Social interaction shapes babbling: Testing parallels between birdsong and speech. *Proceedings of the National Academy of Sciences, 100* (13), 8030–8035.

Goldstein, S. E., Davis-Kean, P. E., & Eccles, J. S. (2005). Parents, peers, and problem behavior: A longitudinal investigation of the impact of relationship perceptions and characteristics on the development of adolescent problem behavior. *Developmental Psychology, 41,* 401–413.

Goleman, D. (1995). *Emotional intelligence.* New York: Basic Books.

Goleman, D., Kaufman, P, & Ray, M. (1993). *The creative spirit* New York: Plume.

Goll, J. C., & Shapiro, C. M. (2006). Sleep disorders presenting as common pediatric problems. *Canadian Medical Association Journal, 174,* 617–619.

Golomb, C. (2002). Child art in context. Washington, Dc: American Psychological Association.

Golombok, S., MacCallum, F., & Goodman, E. (2001). The "test-tube" generation: Parent-child relationships and the psychological well-being of in vitro fertilization children at adolescence. *Child Development, 72,* 599–608.

Gonzales, N. A., Dumka, L. E., Muaricio, A. M., & German, M. (2007). Building bridges: Strategies to promote academic and psychological resilience for adolescents of Mexican origin. In J. E. Lansford, K. Deater Deckhard, & M. H. Bornstein (Eds.), *Immigrant families in contemporary society.* New York: Guilford.

Gonzales, V., Yawkey, T. D., & Minaya-Rowe, L. (2006). *English-as-a-second language (ESL) teaching and learning.* Boston: Allyn & Bacon.

Goodway, J. D., & Branta, C. F. (2003). Influence of a motor skill intervention on fundamental motor skill development of disadvantaged preschool children. *Research Quarterly for Exercise and Sport, 74,* 36–46.

Gooren, L. J. (2002). Psychological consequences. *Seminars in Reproductive Medicine, 20,* 285–296.

Gortmaker, S. L., Peterson, K., Wiecha, J., Sobol, A. M., Dixit, S., Fox, M. K., & Laird, N. (1999). Reducing obesity via a school-based interdisciplinary intervention among youth. *Archives of Pediatric and Adolescent Medicine, 153,* 409–418.

Goswami, U. (2006). The foundations of psychological understanding. *Developmental Science, 9,* 545–550.

Goswami, U. (2007). *Cognitive development.* Philadelphia: Psychology Press.

Gotesdam, K. G., & Agras, W. S. (1995). General population-based epidemiological survey of eating disorders in Norway. *International Journal of Eating Disorders, 18,* 119–126.

Gottfried, A. E., Gottfried, A. W., & Bathurst, K. (2002). Maternal and dual-earner employment status and parenting. In M. H. Bornstein (Ed.), *Handbook of parenting* (2nd ed., Vol. 2.) Mahwah, NJ: Erlbaum.

Gottlieb, G. (2005). Unpublished review of Santrocks Topical life-span development (3rd ed.). New York: McGraw-Hill.

Gottlieb, G. (2007). Probabalistic epigenesis. *Developmental Science, 10,* 1–11.

Gottman, J. M., & DeClaire, J. (1997). *The heart of parenting: Raising an emotionally intelligent child.* New York: Simon & Schuster.

Gottlieb, G., Wahlsten, D., & Lickliter, R. (2006). The significance of biology for human development: A developmental psychobiological systems view. In W. Damon & R. Lerner (Eds.), *Handbook of child psychology* (6th ed.). New York: Wiley.

Gottman, J. M., & Parker, J. G. (Eds.). (1987). *Conversations of friends.* New York: Cambridge University Press.

Gottman, J. M., Shapiro, A. F., Parthemer, J. (2004). Bringing baby home: A preventative intervention program for expectant couples. *International Journal of Childbirth Education, 19,* 28–30.

Gotz, I., & Gotz, M, (2006). How and why parents change their attitudes to prenatal diagnosis. *Clinical Child Psychology and Psychiatry, 11,* 293–300.

Gould, D., Lauer, L., Rolo, C., Jannes, C., & Pennisi, N. (2006). Understanding the role parents play in tennis success: A national survey of junior tennis coaches. *British Journal of Sports Medicine, 40,* 632–636.

Gould, S. J. (1981). *The mismeasure of man.* New York: W. W. Norton.

Grabe, S., & Hyde, J. S. (2006). Ethnicity and body dissatisfaction among women in the United States: A meta-analysis. *Psychological Bulletin, 132,* 622–640.

Graber, J. A. (2003). *Early puberty and drug use.* Unpublished data, Department of Psychology, University of Florida, Gainesville, FL.

Graber, J. (2004). Internalizing problems during adolescence. In R. Lerner & L. Steinberg (Eds.), *Handbook of adolescent psychology.* New York: Wiley.

Graber, J. A., Brooks-Gunn, J., & Warren, M. P. (2006). Pubertal effects on adjustment in girls: Moving from demonstrating effects to identifying pathways. *Journal of Youth and Adolescence, 35,* 391–401.

Graham, G. M., Holt-Hale, S., & Parker, M. A. (2007). *Children moving* (7th ed.). New York: McGraw-Hill.

Graham, J. M., & Shaw, G. M. (2005). Gene-environment interactions in rare diseases that include common birth defects. *Birth Defects*

Research, Part A, Clinical and Molecular Teratology, 73, 865–867.

Graham, S. (1986, August). *Can attribution theory tell us something about motivation in blacks?* Paper presented at the meeting of the American Psychological Association, Washington, DC.

Graham, S. (1990). Motivation in Afro-Americans. In G. L. Berry & J. K. Asamen (Eds.), *Black students: Psychosocial issues and academic achievement,* Newbury Park, CA: Sage.

Graham, S. (1992). Most of the subjects were white and middle class. *American Psychologist, 47,* 629–637.

Graham, S. (2005, February 16). Commentary in USA TODAY, p. 2D.

Graham, S. (Ed.). (2006). Our children too: A history of the first 25 years of the Society for Research in Child Development. *Monographs of the Society for Research in Child Development* (Vol. 71, No. 1), 1–227.

Grant, J. P. (1993). *The state of the world's children.* New York: UNICEF and Oxford University Press.

Grant, J. P. (1997). *The state of the world's children.* New York: UNICEF and Oxford University Press.

Grantham-McGregor, C, Ani, C, & Fernaid, L., (2001). The role of nutrition in intellectual development. In R. J. Sternberg & E. L. Girogorenko (Eds.), *Environmental effect on cognitive abilities,* Mahwah, NJ: Erlbaum.

Graue, M. E., & DiPerna, J. (2000). Redshirting and early retention: Who gets the "gift of time" and what are its outcomes? *American Educational Research Journal, 37,* 509–534.

Graven, S. (2006). Sleep and brain development. *Clinical Perinatology, 33,* 693–706.

Graves, M., Juel, C., & Graves, B. (2007). *Teaching reading in the 21st century* (4th ed.). Boston: Allyn & Bacon.

Gray, J. R., & Kagan J. (2000). The challenge of determining which children with attention deficit hyperactivity disorder will respond positively to methylphenidate. *Journal of Applied Developmental Psychology, 21,* 471–489.

Gray, K. A., Day, N. L., Leech, S., & Richardson, G. A. (2005). Prenatal marijuana exposure: Effect on child depressive symptoms at ten years of age. *Neurotoxicology and Teratology, 27,* 439–448.

Graziano, A. M., & Raulin, M. L. (2007). *Research method* (6th ed.). Boston: Allyn & Bacon.

Greco, L., Balungi, J., Amono, K., Iriso, R., & Corrado, B. (2006). Effect of low-cost food on the recovery and death rate of malnourished children. *Journal of Pediatric Gastroenterology and Nutrition, 43,* 512–517.

Greenberger, E., & Steinberg, L. (1986). *When teenagers work: The psychological social costs of adolescent employment.* New York: Basic Books.

Greene, R. W., Biederman, J., Faraone, S. V., Monuteaux, M. C., Mick, E., DuPre, E. P.,

Fine, C. S., & Goring, J. C. (2001). Social impairment in girls with ADHD. *Journal of the American Academy of Child and Adolescent Psychiatry, 40,* 704–710.

Greenfield, P. M. (1966). On culture and conservation. In J. S. Bruner, R. P. Oliver, & P. M. Greenfield (Eds.), *Studies in cognitive growth.* New York: Wiley.

Greenfield, P. M., Suzuki, L. K., Rothstein-Fisch, C. (2006). Cultural Pathways through human development. In W. Damon R. Lerner (Eds.), *Handbook of child psychology* (6th ed.). New York: Wiley.

Greenough, W. T. (1999, April). *Experience, brain development, and links to mental retardation.* Paper presented at the meeting of the Society for Research in Child Development, Albuquerque.

Greenough, W. T. (2001, April). *Nature and nurture in the brain development process.* Paper presented at the meeting of the Society for Research in Child Development, Minneapolis.

Greenough, W. T., Klintsova, A. Y., Irvan, S. A., Galvez., R., Bates, K. E., & Weller, I. J. (2001). Synaptic regulation of protein synthesis and the fragile X protein. *Proceedings of the National Academy of Science, USA, 98,* 7101–7106.

Gregory, M., Boddington, P., Dimond, R., Atkinson, P., Clarke, A., & Collins, P. (2007). Communicating about haemophilia within the family: The importance of context and of experience. *Haemophilia, 13,* 189–198.

Gregory, R. J. (2007). *Psychological testing* (5th ed.). Boston: Allyn & Bacon.

Greydanus, D. E., Pratt, H. D., & Patel, D. R. (2007). Attention deficit hyperactivity disorder across the lifespan: The child, adolescent, and adult. *Disease-A-Month, 53,* 70–131.

Grigorenko, E. (2000). Heritability and intelligence. In R. J. Sternberg (Ed.), *Handbook of intelligence.* New York: Cambridge University Press.

Grigorenko, E. L., Geissler. P., Prince, R., Okatcha. F., Nokes, C., Kenney, D. A., Bundy. D. A., & Sternberg, R. J. (2001). The organization of Luo conceptions of intelligence. A study of implicit theories in a Kenyan village. *International Journal of Behavioral Development, 25,* 367–378.

Grigoriadis, S., & Kennedy, S. H. (2002). Role of estrogen in the treatment of depression. *American Journal of Therapy, 9,* 503–509.

Groer, M. W., & Morgan, K. (2007). Immune, health, and endocrine characteristics of depressed postpartum mothers. *Psychoneuroimmunology, 32,* 133–138.

Groner, J. A., Joshi, M., & Bauer, J. A. (2006). Pediatric precursors of adult cardiovascular disease: Noninvasive assessment of early vascular changes in children and adolescents. *Pediatrics, 118,* 1683–1691.

Gronlund, N. W. (2006). *Assessment of student achievement* (8th ed.). Boston: Allyn & Bacon.

Gropman, A. L., & Adams, D. R. (2007). A typical patterns of inheritance. *Seminars in Pediatric Neurology, 14*, 34–45.

Grossmann, K., Grossmann, K. E., Spangler, G., Suess, G., & Unzner, L. (1985). Maternal sensitivity and newborns' orientation responses as related to quality of attachment in northern Germany. In I. Bretherton & E. Waters (Eds.), Growing points of attachment theory and research. *Monographs of the Society for Research in Child Development, 50* (1–2, Serial No. 209).

Grotevant, H. D., & Cooper, C. R. (1985). Patterns of interaction in family relationships and the development of identity exploration in adolescence. *Child Development, 56*, 415–428.

Grotevant, H. D., & Cooper, C. R. (1998). Individuality and connectedness in adolescent development: Review and prospects for research on identity, relationships, and context. In E. Skoe & A. von der Lippe (Eds.), *Personality development in adolescence: A cross-national and life-span perspective.* London: Routledge.

Grotevant, H. D., van Dulmen, M. H. M., Dunbar, N., Nelson-Christinedaughter, J., Christensen, M., Fan, X., & Miller, B. C. (2006). Antisocial behavior of adoptees and nonadoptees: Prediction from early history and adolescent relationships. *Journal of Research on Adolescence, 16*, 105–131.

Grusec, J. E. (2006). Development of moral behavior and conscience. In M. Killen & J. G. Smetana (Eds.), *Handbook of moral development.* Mahwah, NJ: Erlbaum.

Grusec, J. E., & Davidov, M. (2007). Social-ization in the family: The roles of parents. In J. E. Grusec & P. D. Hastings (Eds.), *Handbook of socialization.* New York: Guilford.

Grusec, J. E., & Hastings, P. D. (Eds.). (2007). *Handbook of Socialization.* New York: Guilford.

Guastello, D. D., & Guastello, S. J. (2003). Androgyny, gender role behavior, and emotional intelligence among college students and their parents. *Sex Roles, 49*, 663–673.

Guilford, J. P. (1967). *The structure of intellect.* New York: McGraw-Hill.

Gulotta, C. S., & Phinney, J. W. (2000). Inter-vention models for mothers and children at risk for injuries, *Clinical, Child, and Family Psychology Review, 3*, 25–36.

Gulson, B. L., Mizon, K. J., Davis, J. D., Palmer, J. M., & Vimpani, G. (2004). Identifi-cation of sources of lead in children in a primary zinc-lead smelter environment. *Environmental Health Perspectives, 112*, 52–60.

Gumora, G., & Arsenio, W. (2002). Emotional-ity, emotion regulation, and school performance in middle school children. *Journal of School Psychology, 40*, 395–413.

Gunnar, M. R., & Davis, E. P. (2003). Stress and emotion in early childhood. In I. B. Weiner (Ed.), *Handbook of psychology* (Vol. 6). New York: Wiley.

Gunnar, M. R., & Quevedo, K. (2007). The neurobiology of stress and development. *Annual Review of Psychology, Vol. 58.* Palo Alto, CA: Annual Reviews.

Gunnar, M. R., Malone, S., & Fisch, R. O. (1987). The psychobiology of stress and coping in the human neonate: Studies of the adrenocortical activity in response to stress in the first week of life. In T. Field, P. McCabe, & N. Scheiderman (Eds.). *Stress and coping.* Hillsdale, NJ: Erlbaum.

Gunnar, M., & Quevado, K. (2007). The neu-robiology of stress and development. *Annual Re-view of Psychology* (Vol. 58) Palo Alto, CA: Annual Reviews.

Gur, R. C., Mozley, L. H., Mozley, P. D., Resnick, S. M., Karp, J. S., Alavi, A., Arnold, S. E., & Gur, R. E. (1995). Sex differ-ences in regional cerebral glucose metabolism during a resting state. *Science, 267*, 528–531.

Gurgan, T., & Demirol, A. (2007). Unresolved issues regarding assisted reproduction technol-ogy. *Reproductive Biomedicine Online, 14* (Suppl. 1), S40–S43.

Gurganus, S. P. (2007). *Math instruction for stu-dents with learning problems.* Boston: Allyn & Bacon.

Gurwitch, R. H., Silovksy, J. F., Schultz, S., Kees, M., & Burlingame, S. (2001). *Reactions and guidelines for children following trauma/disaster.* Norman, OK: Department of Pediatrics, University of Oklahoma Health Sciences Center.

Gustafsson, J-E. (2007). Schooling and intelli-gence: Effects of track of study on level and pro-file of cognitive abilities. In P. C. Kyllonen, R. D. Roberts, & L. Stankov (Eds.), *Extending intelligence.* Mahwah, NJ: Erlbaum.

Gutherie, G. M., Masangkay, Z., & Gutherie, H. A. (1976). Behavior, malnutrition, and mental development, *Journal of Cross-Cultural Psychology, 7*, 169–180.

Gutteling, B. M., de Weerth, C., & Buitelaar, J. K. (2005). Maternal prenatal stress and 4–6 year old children's salivary cortisol concentra-tions pre- and postvaccination. *Stress, 7*, 257–260.

Gyamfi, P., Brooks-Gunn, J., & Jackson, A. P. (2001). Associations between employment and financial and parental stress in low-income single Black mothers. In M. C. Lennon (Ed.), *Welfare, work, and well-being.* New York: Haworth Press.

H

Hadwin, J., & Perner, J. (1991). Pleased and surprised: Children's cognitive theory of emo-tion. *British Journal of Developmental Psychology, 9*, 215–234.

Hahn, C. S., & DiPietro, J. A. (2001). In vitro fertilization and the family: Quality of parenting, family functioning, and child psychosocial adjustment. *Developmental Psychology, 37*, 37–48.

Hahn, W. K. (1987). Cerebral lateralization of function: From infancy through childhood. *Psychological Bulletin, 101*, 376–392.

Haith, M. M., Hazen, C., & Goodman, G. S. (1988). Expectation and anticipation of dynamic visual events by 3.5 month old babies. *Child Development, 59*, 467–479.

Hakuta, K. (2001, April). *Key policy Milestones and directions in The education of English language learners.* Paper prepared for the Rockefeller Foundation Symposium, Leveraging change: An Emerging framework for educational equity, Washington, DC.

Hakuta, K. (2005, April). *Bilingualism at the intersection of research and public policy.* Paper presented at the meeting of the Society for Research in Child Development, Atlanta.

Hakuta, K., Butler, Y. G., & Witt, D. (2000). *How long does it take English learners to attain profi-ciency?* Berkeley, CA: The University of California Linguistic Minority Research Institute Policy Report 2000–1.

Hale, K. J. (2003). Oral health risk assessment timing and establishment of the dental home. *Pediatrics, 111*, 1113–1116.

Halgunseth, L. C., Ispa, J. M., & Rudy, D. (2006). Parental control in Latino families: An integrated review of the literature. *Child Development, 77*, 1282–1297.

Hall, G. S. (1904). *Adolescence* (Vols. 1 & 2). Englewood Cliffs, NJ: Prentice Hall.

Hall, P. L., & Wittkowski, A. (2006). An exploration of negative thoughts as a normal phenomenon after childbirth. *Journal of Midwifery and Women's Health, 51*, 321–330.

Hallahan, D. P., & Kauffman, J. M. (2006). Exceptional learners (10th ed.). Boston: Allyn & Bacon.

Hallahan, D. P., Lloyd, J. W., Kauffman, J. M., Weiss, M. P., & Martinez, E. A. (2006). *Learning disabilities* (3rd ed.). Boston: Allyn & Bacon.

Halle, T., Reidy, M., Moorehouse, M., Zaslow, M., Walsh, C., Margie, N. G., & Dent, A. (2007). Progress in the development of school readiness. In B. Brown (Ed.), *Key indicators of child and youth well-being.* Mahwah, NJ: Erlbaum.

Hallfors, D. D. Waller, M. W., Ford, C. A., Halpern, C. T., Brodish, P. H., & Iritani, B. (2004). Adolescent depression and suicide risk: Association with sex and drug behavior. *American Journal of Preventive Medicine, 27*, 224–231.

Halonen, J., & Santrock, J. W. (1999). *Psycho-logy: Contexts and application.* Boston: McGraw-Hill.

Halpern, D. F. (2006). Assessing gender gaps in learning. In P. A. Alexander & P. H. Winne (Eds.), *Handbook of educational Psychology* (2nd ed.). Mahwah, NJ: Erlbaum.

Halpern, D. F. (2007). The nature and nurture of critical thinking. In R. J. Sternberg, H. Roediger, & D. Halpern (Eds.), *Critical thinking in psychology.* New York: Cambridge University Press.

Hamburg, D. A. (1997). Meeting the essential requirements for healthy adolescent development in a transforming world. In R. Takanishi & D. Hamburg (Eds.), *Preparing adolescents for the 21st century.* New York: Cambridge University Press.

Hamilton, S. F., & Hamilton, M. A. (2006). School, work, and emerging adulthood. In J. J. Arnett & J. L. Tanner (Eds.), *Emerging adults in America.* Washington, DC: American Psychological Association.

Hancox, R. J., Milne, B. J., & Poulton, R. (2004). Association between child and adolescent television viewing and adult health: A longitudinal birth cohort study. *Lancet, 364,* 257–262.

Hankins, G. D., & Longo, M. (2006). The role of stillbirth prevention and late preterm (near-term) births. *Seminars in Perinatology, 30,* 20–23.

Hanley, J. (2006). The assessment and treatment of postnatal depression. *Nursing Times, 102,* 24–26.

Hannish, L. D., & Guerra, N. G. (2004). Aggressive victims, passive victims, and bullies: Developmental continuity or developmental change? *Merrill-Palmer Quarterly, 50,* 17–38.

Hansen, D. (1996, April). *Adolescent employment and psychosocial outcomes: A comparison of two employment contexts.* Paper presented at the meeting of the Society for Research on Adolescence, Boston.

Hargrove, B. K., Creagh, M. G., & Burgess, B. L. (2003). Family interaction patterns as predictors of vocational identity and career decision-making self-efficacy. *Journal of Vocational Behavior, 61,* 185–201.

Hargrove, K. (2005). What makes a "good" teacher "great"? *Gifted Child Today, 28,* 30–31.

Harkness, S., & Super, C. M. (1995). Culture and parenting. In M. H. Bornstein (Ed.), *Handbook of parenting* (Vol. 3). Hillsdale, NJ: Erlbaum.

Harkness, S., & Super, C. M. (2002). Culture and parenting. In M. H. Bornstein (Ed.), *Handbook of parenting* (2nd ed., Vol. 2). Mahwah, NJ: Erlbaum.

Harlow, H. F. (1958). The nature of love. *American Psychologist, 13,* 673–685.

Harold, R. D., Colarossi, L. G., & Mercier, L. R. (2007). *Smooth sailing or stormy waters: Family transitions through adolescence and their implications for practice and policy.* Mahwah, NJ: Erlbaum.

Harris, G., Thomas, A., & Booth, D. A. (1990). Development of salt taste in infancy. *Developmental Psychology, 26,* 534–538.

Harris, J. B. (1998). *The nurture assumption: Why children turn out the way they do: Parents matter less than you think and peers matter more.* New York: Free Press.

Harris, L. (1997). *A national poll of children and exercise.* Washington, DC: Lou Harris & Associates.

Harris, P. L. (2006). Social cognition. In W. Damon & R. Lerner (Eds.), *Handbook of child psychology* (6th ed.). New York: Wiley.

Harris, Y. R., & Graham, J. A. (2007). *The African American child.* New York: Springer.

Harrison-Hale, A. O., McLoyd, V. C., & Smedley, B. (2004). Racial and ethnic status: Risk and protective processes among African-American families. In K. L. Maton, C. J. Schellenbach, B. J. Leadbetter, & A. L. Solarz (Eds.), *Investing in children, families, and communities.* Washington, DC: American Psychological Association.

Hart, B., & Risley, T. R. (1995). *Meaningful differences.* Baltimore, MD: Paul Brookes.

Hart, C. H., Yang, C., Charlesworth, R., & Burts, D. C. (2003, April). *Early childhood teachers' curriculum beliefs, classroom practices, and children's outcomes: What are the connections?* Paper presented at the biennial meeting of the Society for Research in Child Development, Tampa, FL.

Hart, D. (2006). Service commitment and care exemplars. In M. Killen & J. G. Smetana (Eds.), *Handbook of moral development.* Mahwah, NJ: Erlbaum.

Hart, D., Atkins, R., & Donnelly, T. M. (2006). Community service and moral development. In M. Killen & J. Smetana (Eds.), *Handbook of moral development.* Mahwah, NJ: Erlbaum.

Hart, D., Burock, D., London, B., & Atkins, R. (2003). Prosocial development, antisocial development, and moral development. In A. M. Slater & G. Bremner (Eds.), *An introduction to developmental psychology.* Malden, MA: Blackwell.

Hart, D., & Karmel, M. P. (1996). Self-awareness and self-knowledge in humans, great apes, and monkeys. In A. Russon, K. Bard, & S. Parker (Eds.), *Reaching into thought.* New York: Cambridge University Press.

Hart, S., & Carrington, H. (2002). Jealousy in 6-month-old infants. *Infancy, 3,* 395–402.

Hart, S. L., Boylan, L. M., Carroll, S. R., Musick, Y. A., Kuratko, C., Border, B. G., & Lampe, R. M. (2006). Brief report: Newborn behavior differs with docosahexaenoic acid levels in breast milk. *Journal of Pediatric Psychology, 31,* 221–226.

Harter, S. (1990). Processes underlying adolescent self-concept formation. In R. Montemayor, G. R. Adams, & R. P. Gulotta (Eds.), *From childhood to adolescence: A transitional period?* Newbury Park, CA: Sage.

Harter, S. (1999). *The construction of the self.* New York: Guilford.

Harter, S. (2002). Unpublished review of Santrock's, *Child development* (10th Ed.). New York: McGraw-Hill.

Harter, S. (2006). The self. In W. Damon & R. Lerner (Eds.), *Handbook of child psychology* (6th ed.). New York: Wiley.

Harter, S., & Whitesell, N. (2001, April). *What we have learned from Columbine: The impact of self-esteem on suicidal and violent ideation among adolescents.* Paper presented at the meeting of the Society for Research in Child Development, Minneapolis.

Hartshorne, H., & May, M. S. (1928–1930). *Moral studies in the nature of character: Studies in the nature of character.* New York: Macmillan.

Hartup, W. W. (1983). The peer system. In P. H. Mussen (Ed.), *Handbook of child psychology* (4th ed., Vol. 4). New York: Wiley.

Hartup, W. W. (1999, April). *Peer relations and the growth of the individual child.* Paper presented at the meeting of the Society for Research in Child Development, Albuquerque.

Hartwell, L. (2008). *Genetics* (3rd ed.). New York: McGraw-Hill.

Harwood, R., Leyendecker, B., Carlson, V., Asencio, M., & Miller, A. (2002). Parenting among Latino families in the U.S. In M. H. Bornstein (Ed.), *Handbook of parenting* (2nd ed.). Mahwah, NJ: Erlbaum.

Hastings, P. D., Utendale, W. T., & Sullivan, C. (2007). The socialization of prosocial behavior. In J. E. Grusec & P. D. Hastings (Eds.), *Handbook of socialization.* New York: Guilford.

Hattery, A. J., & Smith, E. (2007). *African American families.* Thousand Oaks: Sage.

Hauck, F. R., Omojokun, O. O., & Siadaty, M. S. (2005). Do pacifiers reduce the risk of sudden infant death syndrome? A meta-analysis. *Pediatrics, 116,* e717–e723.

Haugaard, J. J., & Hazan, C. (2004). Adoption as a natural experiment. *Developmental Psychopathology, 15,* 909–926.

Haugaard, J. J., & Hazan, C. (2004). Recognizing and treating uncommon behavioral and emotional disorders in children and adolescents who have been severely maltreated: Reactive attachment disorder. *Child Maltreatment, 9,* 154–160.

Hausman, B. L. (2005). Risky business: Framing childbirth in hospital settings. *Journal of Medical Ethics, 26,* 23–38.

Hawkins, J. A., & Berndt, T. J. (1985, April). *Adjustment following the transition to junior high school.* Paper presented at the biennial meeting of the Society for Research in Child Development, Toronto.

Haynes, R. L., Folkerth, R. D., Szweda, L. I., Volpe, J. J., & Kinney, H. C. (2006). Lipid peroxidation during cerebral myelination. *Journal of Neuropathology and Experimental Neurology, 65,* 894–904.

Health Management Resources. (2001). *Child health and fitness.* Boston: Author.

Heck, K. E., Braveman, P., Cubbin, C., Chavez, G. F., & Kiely, J. L. (2006). Socioeconomic status and breastfeeding initiation among California mothers. *Public Health Reports, 121*, 51–59.

Heimann, M., Strid, K., Smith, L., Tjus, T., Ulvund, S. E., & Melzoff, A. N. (2006). Exploring the relation between memory, gestural communication, and the emergence of language in infancy: A longitudinal study. *Infant and Child Development, 15*, 233–249.

Heinicke, C. M. (2002). The transition to parenting. In M. H. Bornstein (Ed.), *Handbook of parenting* (2nd ed.). Mahwah, NJ: Erlbaum.

Heiser, P., Friedel, S., Dempfile, A., Kongrad, K., Smidt, J., Grabarkiewicz, J., Herpertz-Dahlann, B., Remschmidt, H., & Hebebrand, J. (2004). Molecular genetic aspects of attention deficit/hyperactivity disorder. *Neuroscience and Biobehavioral Reviews, 28*, 625–641.

Heitzler, C. D., Martin, S. L., Duke, J., & Huhman, M. (2006). Correlates of physical activity in a national sample of children aged 9–13 years. *Preventive Medicine, 42*, 254–260.

Hellstrom-Lindahl D., & Nordberg, A. (2002). Smoking during pregnancy: A way to transfer the addiction to the next generation? Respiration, 69, 289–293.

Helms, J. E. (2005). Stereotype threat might explain the black-white test-score difference. *American Psychologist, 60*, 269–270.

Helson, R., Elliot, T., & Leigh, J. (1989). Adolescent antecedents of women's work patterns. In D. Stern & D. Eichorn (Eds.), *Adolescence and work*. Hillsdale, NJ: Erlbaum.

Hemmings, A. (2004). *Coming of age in U.S. high schools*. Mahwah, NJ: Erlbaum.

Henderson, V. L., & Dweck, C. S. (1990). Motivation and achievement. In S. S. Feldman & G. R. Elliott (Eds.), *At the threshold: The developing adolescent*. Cambridge, MA: Harvard University Press.

Hendrick J., & Weissman, P. (2006). *The whole child* (8th ed.). Upper Saddle River, NJ: Prentice Hall.

Hendry, J. (1995). *Understanding Japanese society*. London: Routledge.

Hendry, J. (1999). *Social anthropology*. New York: Macmillan.

Henriksen, T. B., Hjollund, N. H., Jensen, T. K., Bonde, J. P., Andersson, A. M., Kolstad, H., Ernst, E., Giwereman, A., Skakkebaek, N. E., & Olsen, J. (2004). Alcohol consumption at the time of conception and spontaneous abortion. *American Journal of Epidemiology, 160*, 661–667.

Hepper, P. (2007). The foundations of development. In A. Slater & M. Lewis (Eds.), *Introduction to infant development* (2nd ed.). New York: Oxford University Press.

Hepper, P. G., Shahidullah, S., & White, R. (1990). Origins of fetal handedness. *Nature, 347*, 431.

Heppner, M. J., & Heppner, P. P. (2003). Identifying process variables in career counseling: A research agenda. *Journal of Vocational Behavior, 62*, 429–452.

Herbst, M. A., Mercer, B. M., Beasley, D., Meyer, N., & Carr, T. (2003). Relationship of prenatal care and perinatal morbidity in low-birth-weight infants. *American Journal of Obstetrics and Gynecology, 189*, 930–933.

Herman, D. R., Harrison, G. G., & Jenks, E. (2006). Choices made by low-income women provided with an economic supplement for fresh fruit and vegetable purchase. *Journal of the American Dietetic Association, 106*, 740–744.

Herman-Giddens, M. E. (2007). The decline in the age of menarche in the United States: Should we be concerned? *Journal of Adolescent Health, 40*, 201–203.

Hernandez, D. J., Denton, N. A., & Macartney, S. E. (2007). Family circumstances of children in immigrant families. In J. E. Lansford, K. Deater-Deckhard, & M. H. Bornstein (Eds.), *Immigrant families in contemporary society*. New York: Guilford.

Heshmat, S., & Lo, K. C. (2006). Evaluation and treatment of ejaculatory duct obstruction in infertile men. *Canadian Journal of Urology, 13* Suppl. 1, 18–21.

Hetherington, E. M. (1989). Coping with family transitions: Winners, losers, and survivors. *Child Development, 60*, 1–14.

Hetherington, E. M. (1993). An overview of the Virginia Longitudinal Study of Divorce and Remarriage with a focus on early adolescence. *Journal of Family Psychology, 7*, 39–56.

Hetherington, E. M. (2000). Divorce. In A. Kazdin (Ed.), *Encyclopedia of psychology*. Washington, DC, & New York: American Psychological Association and Oxford University Press.

Hetherington, E. M. (2005). Divorce and the Adjustment of children. *Pediatrics in Review, 26*, 163–169.

Hetherington, E. M. (2006). The influence of conflict, marital problem solving, and parenting on children's adjustment in nondivorced, divorced, and remarried families. In A. Clarke-Stewart & J. Dunn (Eds.), *Families count*. New York: Oxford University Press.

Hetherington, E. M. (2006). The influence of conflict, marital problem solving, and parenting on children's adjustment in nondivorced, divorced, and remarried families. In A. Clarke-Stewart & J. Dunn (Eds.), *Families count*. New York: Oxford University Press.

Hetherington, E. M., Bridges, M., & Insabella, G. M. (1998). What matters? What does not? Five perspectives on the association between marital transitions and children's adjustment. *American Psychologist, 53*, 167–184.

Hetherington, E. M., Reiss, D., & Plomin, R. (Eds.). (1994). *Separate social worlds of siblings: The impact of nonshared environment on development*. Hillsdale, NJ: Erlbaum.

Hetherington, E. M., & Kelly, J. (2002). *For better or for worse: Divorce reconsidered*. New York: W. W. Norton.

Hetherington, E. M., & Stanley-Hagan, M. (2002). Parenting in divorced and remarried families. In M. H. Bornstein (Ed.), *Handbook of parenting* (2nd ed., Vol. 3). Mahwah, NJ: Erlbaum.

Heuwinkel, M. K. (1996). New ways of learning 5 new ways of teaching. *Childhood Education, 72*, 27–31.

Heyman, G. D., Fu, G., & Lee, K. (2007, in press). Evaluating claims people make about themselves: The development of skepticism. *Child Development*.

Heyman, G. D., & Legare, C. H. (2005). Children's evaluation of sources of information about traits. *Developmental Psychology, 41*, 636–647.

Hickson, G. B., & Clayton, E. W. (2002). Parents and children's doctors. In M. H. Bornstein (Ed.), *Handbook of parenting* (Vol. 5). Mahwah, NJ: Erlbaum.

Higgins, A., Power, C., & Kohlberg, L. (1983, April). *Moral atmosphere and moral judgment*. Paper presented at the biennial meeting of the Society for Research in Child Development, Detroit.

Hijiya, N., & others. (2007). Cumulative incidence of secondary neoplasms as a first event after childhood acute lymphoblastic leukemia. *Journal of the American Medical Association, 297*, 1207–1215.

Hildebrand, V., Phenice, A., & Hines, R. P. (2000). *Knowing and serving diverse families*. Columbus, OH: Merrill.

Hill, C. R., & Stafford, F. P. (1980). Parental care of children: Time diary estimate of quantity, predictability, and variety. *Journal of Human Resources, 15*, 219–239.

Hill, M. A. (2007). Early human development. *Clinical Obstetrics and Gynecology, 50*, 2–9.

Hillis, S. D., Anda, R. F., Dube, S. R., Felitti, V. J., Marchbanks, P. A., & Marks, J. S. (2004). The association between adverse childhood experiences and adolescent pregnancy, long-term psychological consequences, and fetal death. *Pediatrics, 113*, 320–327.

Hills, A. P., King, N. A., & Armstrong, T. P. (2007). The contribution of physical activity and sedentary behaviors of the growth and development of children and adolescents: Implications for overweight and obesity. *Sports Medicine, 37*, 533–545.

Hindmarsh, P. C., & Dattani, M. T. (2006). Use of growth hormone in children. *Nature Clinical Practice: Endocrinology and Metabolism, 2,* 260–268.

Hintz, S. R., Kendrick, D. E., Vohr, B. R., Poole, W. K., Higgins, R. D., and the National Institute of Child Health and Human Development Neonatal Research Network. (2005). Changes in neurodevelopment outcomes at 18 and 22 months' corrected age among infants of less than 25 weeks' gestational age born in 1993–1999. *Pediatrics, 115,* 1645–1651.

Hitch, G. J., Towse, J. N., & Hutton, U. (2001). What limits children's working memory span? Theoretical accounts and applications for scholastic development. *Journal of Experimental Psychology: General, 130,* 184–198.

Hoban, T. F. (2004). Sleep and its disorders in children. *Seminars in Neurology, 24,* 327–340.

Hodapp, R. M., & Dykens, E. M. (2006). Mental retardation. In W. Damon & R. Lerner (Eds.), *Handbook of child psychology.* Mahwah, NJ: Erlbaum.

Hofer, A., Siedentopf, C. M., Ischebeck, A., Rettenbacher, M. A., Verius, M., Felber, S., & Fleischhacker, W. (2007a). Sex differences in brain activation patterns during processing of positively and negatively balanced emotional stimuli. *Psychological Medicine, 37,* 109–119.

Hofer, A., Seidentopf, C. M., Ischebeck, A., Rettenbacher, M. A., Verius, M., Felber, S., & Fleischhacker, W. (2007b). Gender differences in regional cerebral activity during the perception of emotion: A functional MRI study. *Neuroimage, 132,* 854–862.

Hofer, S. M., Sliwinski, M. J. (2006). Design and analysis of longitudinal studies on aging. In J. E. Birren K. W. Schaie (Eds.), *Handbook of the psychology of aging* (6th ed.). San Diego: Academic Press.

Hoff, E. (2003). Language development in childhood. In I. B. Weiner (Ed.), *Handbook of psychology* (Vol. VI), New York: Wiley.

Hoff, E., Laursen, B., & Tardif, T. (2002). Socioeconomic status and parenting. In M. H. Bornstein (Ed.), *Handbook of parenting* (2nd ed.). Mahwah, NJ: Erlbaum.

Hoff, E., & Shatz, M. (Eds.). (2007). *Blackwell handbook of language development.* Malden, MA: Blackwell.

Hoffereth, S. L., & Casper, L. M. (Eds.). (2006). *Handbook of measurement issues in family research.* Mahwah, NJ: Erlbaum.

Hofferth, S. L., & Reid, L. (2002). Early childbearing and children's achievement behavior over time. *Perspectives on sexual and reproductive health, 34,* 41–49.

Hoffman S., Foster, E., & Furstenberg, F. (1993). Reevaluating the costs of teenage childbearing. *Demography, 30,* 1–13.

Hoffman, J. R., Kang, J., Faigenbaum, A. D., & Ratamess, N. A. (2005). Recreational sports participation is associated with enhanced physical fitness in children. *Research in Sports Medicine, 13,* 149–161.

Hoffman, L. W. (1989). Effects of maternal employment in the two parent family. *American Psychologist, 44,* 283–292.

Hoffman, L. W., & Youngblade, L. M. (1999). *Mothers at work: Effects on children's well-being.* New York: Cambridge.

Hoffman, M. L. (1970). Moral development. In P. H. Mussen (Ed.), *Manual of child psychology* (3rd ed., Vol. 2). New York: Wiley.

Hogan, M. A., Glazebrook, R., Brancato, V., & Rogers, J. (2007). *Maternal-newborn nursing: Review and rationales* (2nd ed.). Upper Saddle River, NJ: Prentice Hall.

Holland, J. L. (1987). Current status of Holland's theory of careers: Another perspective. *Career Development Quarterly, 36,* 24–30.

Hollich, G., Newman, R. S., & Jusczyk, P. W. (2005). Infants' use of synchronized visual information to separate streams of speech. *Child Development, 76,* 598–613.

Holloway, J. W., & Koppelmann, G. H. (2007). Identifying novel genes contributing to asthma pathogenesis. *Current Opinion in Allergy and Clinical Immunology, 7,* 69–74.

Holtzen, D. W. (2000). Handedness and professional tennis. *International Journal of Neuroscience, 105,* 101–119.

Hong, G., & Raudenbush, S. W. (2005). Effects of kindergarten retention policy on children's cognitive growth in reading and mathematics. *Educational Evaluation and Policy Analysis, 27,* 205–224.

Hopkins, B. (1991). Facilitating early motor development: An intracultural study of West Indian mothers and their infants living in

Hopkins, B., & Westra, T. (1988). Maternal handling and motor development: An intracultural study. *Genetic Psychology Monographs, 14,* 377–420.

Hopkins, B., & Westra, T. (1990). Motor development, maternal expectations, and the role of handling. *Infant Behavior and Development, 13,* 117–122.

Horn, J. (2007). Spearman, *g,* expertise, and the nature of human cognitive capacity. In P. C. Kyllonen, R. D. Roberts, & L. Stankov (Eds.), *Extending intelligence.* Mahwah, NJ: Erlbaum.

Horne, R. S., Franco, P., Adamson, T. M., Groswasser, J., & Kahn, A. (2002). Effects of body position on sleep and arousal characteristics in infants. *Early Human Development, 69,* 25–33.

Hornor, G. (2005). Physical abuse: Recognition and reporting. *Journal of Pediatric Health Care, 19,* 4–11.

Horowitz, J. A., & Cousins, A. (2006). Postpartum depression treatment rates for at-risk women. *Nursing Research, 55* (Suppl. 2), S23–S27.

Horton, D. M. (2001). The disappearing bell curve. *Journal of Secondary Gifted Education, 12,* 185–188.

Horton, R. (2006). The coming decade for global action on child health. *Lancet, 367,* 3–5.

Horwitz, E. K. (2008). *Becoming a language teacher.* Boston: Allyn & Bacon.

Hoskin, J., & Herman, R. (2001). The communication, speech, and gesture of a group of hearing impaired children. *International Journal of Language and Communication Disorders, 36* (Suppl.), 206–209.

Host, A., & Halken, S. (2005). Primary prevention of food allergy in infants who are at risk. *Current Opinions in Allergy and Clinical Immunology, 5,* 255–259.

Houston, P. D. (2005, February). NCLB: Dreams and nightmares. *Phi Delta Kappan,* 469–470.

Houston-Price, C., Plunkett, K., & Harris, P. (2005). Word-learning wizardry at 1; 6. *Journal of Child Language, 32,* 175–189.

Howard, R. W. (2001). Searching the real world for signs of rising population intelligence. *Personality & Individual Differences, 30,* 1039–1058.

Howe, L. D., Huttly, S. R., & Abramsky, T. (2006). Risk factors for injuries in young children in four developing countries: The Young Lives Study. *Tropic Medicine and International Health, 11,* 1557–1566.

Howe, M. J. A., Davidson, J. W., Moore, D. G., & Sloboda, J. A. (1995). Are there early childhood signs of musical ability? *Psychology of Music, 23,* 162–176.

Howell, E. M., Pettit, K. L., & Kingsley, G. T. (2005). Trends in maternal and infant health in poor urban neighborhoods: Good news from the 1990s, but challenges remain. *Public Health Reports, 120,* 409–417.

Hoyert, D. L., Mathews, T. J., Menacker, F., Strobino, D. M., & Guyer, B. (2006). Annual summary of vital statistics: 2004. *Pediatrics, 117,* 168–183.

Hrabosky, J. I., Masheb, R. M., White, M. A., & Grilo, C. M. (2007). Overvaluation of shape and weight in binge eating disorder. *Journal of Consulting and Clinical Psychology, 75,* 175–180.

Hsu, H-C. (2004). Antecedents and consequences of separation anxiety in first-time mothers: Infant, mother, and social-contextual characteristics. *Infant Behavior and Development, 27,* 113–133.

Hsu, L. K. (2004). Eating disorders: Practical interventions. *Journal of the American Medical Women's Association, 59,* 113–124.

Huang, C. M., Tung, W. S., Kuo, L. L., & Ying-Ju, C. (2004). Comparison of pain responses of premature infants to the heelstick between containment and swaddling. *Journal of Nursing Research, 12,* 31–40.

Huang, L. N. (1989). Southeast Asian refugee children and adolescents. In J. T. Gibbs & L. N. Huang (Eds.), *Children of color.* San Francisco: Jossey-Bass.

Huesmann, L. R., Moise-Titus, J. Podolski, C., & Eron, L. D. (2003). Longitudinal relations between exposure to TV violence and their aggressive and violent behavior in young adulthood: 1977–1992. *Developmental Psychology, 39,* 201–221.

Huffman, L. R., & Speer, P. W. (2000). Academic performance among at-risk children: The role of developmentally appropriate practices. *Early Childhood Research Quarterly, 15,* 167–184.

Huisman, T. A., & Kellenberger, C. J. (2007, in press). MR imaging characteristics of the normal fetal gastrointestinal tract and abdomen. *European Journal of Radiology.*

Huizink, A. C., & Mulder, E. J. (2006). Maternal smoking, drinking, or cannabis use during pregnancy and neurobehavioral and cognitive functioning in human offspring. *Neuroscience and Biobehavioral Research, 30,* 24–41.

Hurt, H., Brodsky, N. L., Roth, H., Malmud, F., & Giannetta, J. M. (2005). School performance of children with gestational cocaine exposure. *Neurotoxicology and Teratology, 27,* 203–211.

Hurwitz, C. A., Duncan, J., & Wolfe, J. (2004). Caring for a child with cancer at the close of life: "There are people who make it, and I'm hoping I'm one of them." *Journal of the American Medical Association, 292,* 2141–2149.

Hurwitz, L. M., & others. (2006). Radiation dose to the fetus from body MDCT during early gestation. *American Journal of Roentgenology, 186,* 871–876.

Huston, A. C. (1983). Sex-typing. In P. H. Mussen (Ed.). *Handbook of child psychology* (4th ed., Vol. 4). New York: Wiley.

Huston, A. C., & Ripke, N. N. (2006). Experiences in middle and late childhood and children's development. In A. C. Huston & M. N. Ripke (Eds.), *Developmental contexts in middle childhood.* New York: Cambridge University Press.

Hutchinson, D. M., & Rapee, R. M. (2007, in press). Do friends share similar body image and eating problems? The role of social networks and peer influences in early adolescence. *Behavior Research and Therapy.*

Huttenlocher, J., Haight, W., Bruk, A., Seltzer, M., & Lyons, T. (1991). Early vocabulary growth: Relation to language input and gender. *Developmental Psychology, 27,* 236–248.

Huttenlocher, P. R., & Dabholkar, A. S. (1997). Regional differences in synaptogenesis in human cerebral cortex. *Journal of Comparative Neurology, 37* (2), 167–178.

Huurre, T., Junkkari, H., & Aro, H. (2006). Long-term psychosocial effects of parental divorce: A follow-up study from adolescence to adulthood. *European Archives of Psychiatry and Clinical Neuroscience, 256,* 256–263.

Hvas, A. M., Nexos, E., & Nielsen, J. B. (2006). Vitamin B(12) and vitamin B(6) supplementation is needed among adults with phenylketonuria (PKU). *Journal of Inherited Metabolic Disorders, 29,* 47–53.

Hyde, J. S. (2005). The gender similarities hypothesis. *American Psychologist, 60,* 581–592.

Hyde, J. S. (2007). *Half the human experience* (7th ed.). Boston: Houghton Mifflin.

Hyde, J. S., & DeLamater, J. (2006). *Human sexuality (9th ed.).* New York: McGraw-Hill.

Hyman, I., Kay, B., Tabori, A., Weber, M., Mahon, M., & Cohen, I. (2006). Bullying: Theory, research, and interventions. In C. M. Evertson & C. S. Weinstein (Eds.), *Handbook of classroom management: Research, practice, and contemporary issues.* Mahwah, NJ: Erlbaum.

Hyson, M. (2007). Curriculum. In R. New & M. Cochran (Eds.), *Early childhood education: An international encyclopedia of early childhood education.* New York: Greenwood.

Hyson, M. C., Copple, C., & Jones, J. (2006). Early childhood development and education. In W. Damon & R. Lerner (Eds.), *Handbook of child psychology* (6th ed.). New York: Wiley.

I

"I Have a Dream" Foundation. (2003). *About vs. Retrieved January 5, 2007, from www.ihad.org.*

Iacoboni, M., & Dapretto, M. (2006). The mirror neuron system and the consequences of its dysfunction. *Nature Reviews: Neuroscience, 7,* 942–951.

Ige, F., & Shelton, D. (2004). Reducing the risk of sudden infant death syndrome (SIDS) in African-American communities. *Journal of Pediatric Nursing, 19,* 290–292.

Imada, T., Zhang, Y., Cheour, M., Taulu, S., Ahonen, A., & Kuhl, P. K. (2007). Infant speech perception activates Broca's area: A developmental magnetoencephalography study. *Neuroreport, 17,* 957–962.

Immordino-Yang, M. H., & Fisher, K. W. (2007). Dynamic development of hemispheric biases in three cases: Cognitive/hemispheric cycles, music, and hemispherectomy. In D. Coch, G. Dawson, & K. W. Fischer (Eds.), *Human behavior, learning, and the developing brain.* New York: Guilford.

Insel, P. M., & Roth, W. T. (2008). *Core concepts in health Update* (10th ed.). New York: McGraw-Hill.

International Montessori Council. (2006). Much of their success on prime-time television. Retrieved March 24, 2006, from www.Montessori.org/enews/barbara_walters.html

Ip, J. M., Robaei, D., Rochtchina, E., & Mitchell, P. (2006). Prevalence of eye disorders in young children with eyestrain complaints. *American Journal of Ophthalmology, 142,* 495–497.

Irwin, C. E. (2004). Eating and physical activity during adolescence: Does it make a difference in adult health status? *Journal of Adolescent Health, 34,* 459–460.

Ishii-Kuntz, M. (2004). Asian American families. In M. Coleman & L. Ganong (Eds.), *Handbook of contemporary families.* Thousand Oaks, CA: Sage.

Itti, E., Gaw Gonzalo, I. T., Pawlikowska-Haddal, A., Boone, K. B., Mlikotic, A., Itti, L., Mishkin, F. S., & Swerdloff, R. S. (2006). The structural brain correlates of cognitive deficits in adults with Klinefelter's syndrome. *Journal of Clinical Endocrinology and Metabolism, 91,* 1423–1427.

Iverson, P. & Kuhl, P. K. (1996). Influences of phonetic identification and category goodness on American listeners' perception of /r/ and /l/. *Journal of the Acoustical Society of America, 99,* 1130–1140.

Iverson, P., Kuhl, P. K., Akahane-Yamada, R., Diesch, E., Tohkura, Y., Ketterman, A., & Siebert, C. (2003). A perceptual interference account of acquisition difficulties in non-native phonemes. *Cognition 87,* B47–57.

J

Jackson, A., & Davis, G. (2000). *Turning points 2000.* New York: Teachers College Press.

Jackson, K. M., & Nazar, A. M. (2006). Breastfeeding, the immune response, and longterm health. *Journal of the American Osteopathic Association, 106,* 203–207.

Jackson, P. L., Meltzoff, A. N., & Decety, J. (2006). Neural circuits involved in imitation and perspective-taking. *NeuroImage, 31,* 429–439.

Jackson, S. L. (2006). *Research methods and statistics: A critical thinking approach* (2nd ed.). Belmont, CA: Wadsworth.

Jackson, S. L. (2008). *Research methods.* Belmont, CA: Wadsworth.

Jacobs, J. E., & Klaczynski, P. A. (Eds.). (2005). *The development of judgment and decision making in children and adolescents.* Mahwah, NJ: Erlbaum.

Jacobson, J. L., & Jacobson, S. W. (2002). Association of prenatal exposure to an environmental contaminant with intellectual function in childhood. *Journal of Toxicology—Clinical Toxicology, 40,* 467–475.

Jacobson, J. L., & Jacobson, S. W. (2003). Prenatal exposure to polychlorinated biphenyls and attention at school age. *Journal of Pediatrics, 143,* 780–788.

Jacobson, J. L., Jacobson, S. W., Fein, G. G., Schwartz, P. M., & Dowler, J. (1984). Prenatal exposure to an environmental toxin: A test of the multiple-effects model. *Developmental Psychology, 20*, 523–532.

Jacobson, L. (2004). Pre-K standards said to slight social, emotional skills. *Education Week, 23* (No. 42), 13–14.

Jaffee, S. R. (2002). Pathways to adversity in young adulthood among early childbearers. *Journal of Family Psychology, 16*, 38–49.

Jaffee, S., & Hyde, J. S. (2000). Gender differences in moral orientation: A meta-analysis. *Psychological Bulletin, 126*, 703–726.

Jalongo, M. R. (2007). *Early childhood language arts* (4th ed.). Boston: Allyn & Bacon.

James, D. C. & Dobson, B. (2005). Position of the American Dietetic Association: Promoting and supporting breastfeeding. *Journal of the American Dietetic Association, 105*, 810–818.

James, J., Thomas, P., Cavan, D., & Kerr, D. (2004). Preventing childhood obesity by reducing consumption of carbonated drinks: Cluster randomized trial. *British Medical Journal, 328*, 1237.

James, S. R., & Ashwill, J. (2007). *Nursing care of children* (3rd ed.). London: Elsevier.

James, W. (1890/1950). *The principles of psychology*. New York: Dover.

Jansen, I. (2006). Decision making in child-birth: The influence of traditional structures in a Ghanaian village. *International Nursing Review, 53*, 41–46.

Janssen, I., Craig, W. M., Boyce, W. F., & Picikett, W. (2004). Associations between overweight and obesity with bullying behaviors in school-aged children. *Pediatrics, 113*, 1187–1194.

Janssen, I., Katzmarzyk, P. T., Boyce, W. F., Vereecken, C., Mulvihill, C., Roberts, C., Currie, C., & Pickett, W. (2005). Comparison of overweight and obesity prevalence in schoolaged youth from 34 countries and their relationships with physical activity and dietary patterns. *Obesity Reviews, 6*, 123–132.

Janssen, I., Katzmarzyk, P. T., Srinivasan, S. R., Chen, W., Malina, R. M., Boucharad, C., & Berenson, G. S. (2005). Utility of childhood BMI in the prediction of adulthood disease: Comparison of national and international references. *Obesity Research, 13*, 1106–1115.

Jansson, B., De Leon, A. P., Ahmed, N., & Jansson, V. (2006). Why does Sweden have the lowest childhood injury mortality in the world? The roles of architecture and public pre-school services. *Journal of Public Health Policy, 27*, 146–165.

Jaswal, V. K., & Fernald, A. (2007). Learning to communicate. In A. Slater & M. Lewis (Eds.), *Introduction to infant development* (2nd ed.). New York: Oxford University Press.

Jelacic, S., de Regt, D., & Weinberger, E. (2006). Interactive digital MR atlas of the pediatric brain. *Radiographics, 26*, 497–501.

Jenkins, J. M., & Astington, J. W. (1996). Cognitive factors and family structure associated with theory of mind development in young children. *Developmental Psychology, 32*, 70–78.

Jensen, A. R. (1969). How much can we boost IQ and scholastic achievement? *Harvard Educational Review, 39*, 1–123.

Ji, B. T., Shu, X. O., Linet, M. S., Zheng, W., Wacholde, S., Gao, Y. T., Ying, D. M., & Jin, E. (1997). Paternal cigarette smoking and the risk of childhood cancer among offspring of nonsmoking mothers. *Journal of the National Cancer Institute, 89*, 238–244.

Joh, A. S. & Adolph, K. E. (2006). Learning from falling. *Child Development, 77*, 89–102.

Johansson, E. (2006). Children's morality: Perspectives and research. In B. Spodak & N. Saracho (Eds.), *Handbook of research on the education of young children* (2nd ed.). Mahwah, NJ: Erlbaum.

Johnson, A. N. (2005). Kangaroo holding beyond the NICU. *Pediatric Nursing, 31*, 53–56.

Johnson, A. N. (2007). Factors influencing implementation of kangaroo holding in a special care nursery. *MCN American Journal of Maternal Child Nursing, 32*, 25–29.

Johnson, D. B., Gerstein, D. E., Evans, A. E., & Wooward-Lopez, G. (2006). Preventing obesity: A life cycle perspective. *Journal of the American Dietetic Association, 106*, 97–102.

Johnson, D. J., Jaeger, E., Randolph, S. M., Cauce, A., Ward, J., & National Institute of Child Health and Human Development Early Child Care Research Network (2003). Studying the effects of early child care experiences on the development of children of color in the United States. *Child Development, 74*, 1227–1244.

Johnson, G. B. (2008). *The living world* (5th ed.). New York: McGraw-Hill.

Johnson, H. L., Erbelding, E. J., & Ghanem, K. G. (2007). Sexually transmitted infections during pregnancy. *Current Infectious Disease Reports, 9*, 125–133.

Johnson, J. S., & Newport, E. L. (1991). Critical period effects on universal properties of language: The status of subjacency in the acquisition of a second language. *Cognition, 39*, 215–258.

Johnson, M. K., Beebe, T., Mortimer, J. T., & Snyder, M. (1998). Volunteerism in adolescence: A process perspective. *Journal of Research on Adolescence, 8*, 309–332.

Johnson, M. P. (2002). The implications of unfulfilled expectations and perceived pressure to attend the birth on men's stress levels following birth attendance: A longitudinal study.

Journal of Psychosomatic Obstetrics and Gynecology, 23, 173–182.

Johnson, R. S., & Morrison, M. (2007). Toward a resolution of inconsistencies in the phonological deficit theory of reading disorders: Phonological reading difficulties are more severe in high-IQ poor readers. *Journal of Learning Disabilities, 40*, 66–79.

John-Steiner, V. (2007). Vygotsky on thinking and speaking. In H. Daniels, J. Wertsch, & M. Cole (Eds.), *The Cambridge companion to Vygotsky*. New York: Cambridge University Press.

Johnston, L. D., O'Malley, P. M., Bachman, J. G., & Schulenbeg, J. E. (2007). *Monitoring the future national results on adolescent drug use: Overview of key findings, 2006*. Bethesda, MD: National Institute of Drug Abuse.

Jolley, S. N., Ellmore, S., Barnad, K. E., & Carr, D. B. (2007). Dysregulation of the hypothalamic-pituitary-adrenal axis in postpartum depression. *Biological Research for Nursing, 8*, 210–222.

Jolliffe, C. J., & Jansen, I. (2007). Vascular risks and management of obesity in children and adolescents. *Vascular Health and Risk Management, 2*, 171–187.

Jones, A., Godfrey, K. M., Wood, P., Osmond, C., Goulden, P., & Phillips, D, I, (2006). Fetal growth and the adrenocortical response to psychological stress. *Journal of Clinical Endocrinology and Metabolism, 91*, 1868–1871.

Jones, B. F., Rasmussen, C. M., & Moffit, M. C. (1997). *Real-life problem solving*. Washington, DC: American Psychological Association.

Jones, H. W. (2007). Iatrogenic multiple births: A 2003 checkup. *Fertility and Sterility, 87*, 453–455.

Jones, J. M. (1994). The African American: A duality dilemma? In W. J. Lonner & R. Malpass (Eds.). *Psychology and culture*. Needham Heights, MA: Allyn & Bacon.

Jones, M. C. (1965). Psychological correlates of somatic development. *Child Development, 36*, 899–911.

Jones, T. G., & Fuller, M. L. (2003). *Teaching Hispanic children*. Boston: Allyn & Bacon.

Jordan, A. (2004). The role of the media in children's development: An ecological perspective. *Journal of Developmental and Behavioral Pediatrics, 25*, 196–206.

Joseph, J. (2006). *The missing gene*. New York: Algora.

Juffer, F., Bakermans-Kranenburg M. J., & van IJzendoorn, M. H. (2007). *Promoting positive parenting*. Mahwah, NJ: Erlbaum.

Jurecic, A. (2006). Mindblindness: Autism, writing, and the problem of empathy. *Literature and Medicine, 25*, 1–23.

Jusczyk, P. W. (2000). *The discovery of spoken language*. Cambridge, MA: MIT Press.

Jusczyk, P. W., & Hohne, E. A. (1997). Infants' memory for spoken words. *Science, 277*, 1984–1986.

K

Kaecht, S., Drager, B., Deppe, M., Bobe, L., Lohmann, H., Floel, A., Ringelstein, E. B., & Henningsen, H. (2000). Handedness and hemispheric language dominance in healthy humans. *Brain, 135*, 2512–2518.

Kafai, Y. B. (2006). Constructivism. In R. K. Sawyer (Ed.), *The Cambridge handbook of the learning sciences.* New York: Cambridge University Press.

Kagan, J. (1987). Perspectives on infancy. In J. D. Osofsky (Ed.), *Handbook on infant development* (2nd ed.). New York: Wiley.

Kagan, J. (1992). Yesterday's promises, tomorrow's promises. *Developmental Psychology, 28*, 990–997.

Kagan, J. (2000). Temperament. In A. Kazdin (Ed.), *Encyclopedia of psychology.* Washington, DC, & New York: American Psychological Association and Oxford University Press.

Kagan, J. (2002). Behavioral inhibition as a temperamental category. In R. J. Davidson K. R. Scherer, & H. H. Goldsmith (Eds.), *Handbook of affective sciences.* New York: Oxford University Press.

Kagan, J. (2003). Biology, context, and development. *Annual Review of Psychology* (Vol. 54). Palo Alto, CA: Annual Reviews.

Kagan, J. (2004, May 8). Commentary in "Teen brains on trial", *Science News Online*, p. 2.

Kagan, J. J., Kearsley, R. B., & Zelazo, P. R. (1978). *Infancy: Its place in human development.* Cambridge, MA: Harvard University Press.

Kagan, J., & Fox, N. (2006). Biology, culture, and temperamental biases. In W. Damon & R. Lerner (Eds.), *Handbook of child psychology* (6th ed.). New York: Wiley.

Kagan, J., & Snidman, N. (1991). Infant predictors of inhibited and uninhibited behavioral profiles. *Psychological Science, 2*, 40–44.

Kagan, S. L., & Scott-Little, C. (2004). Early learning standards. *Phi Delta Kappan, 82*, 388–395.

Kagitcibasi, C. (2007). *Family, self, and human development across cultures.* Mahwah, NJ: Erlbaum.

Kail, R., & Hall, L. K. (2001). Distinguishing short-term memory from working memory. *Memory and Cognition, 29*, 1–9.

Kaiser, B., & Rasminsky, J. S. (2003). *Challenging behavior in young children: Understanding, preventing, and responding effectively.* Boston: Pearson.

Kalant, H. (2004). Adverse effects of cannabis on health: An update of the literature since 1996. *Progress in Neuropsychopharmacology and Biological Psychiatry, 28*, 849–863.

Kalichman, S. C., Simbayi, L. C., Jooste, S., Cherry, C., & Cain, D. (2005). Poverty-related stressors and HIV AIDS transmission risks in two South African communities. *Journal of Urban Health, 82*, 237–249.

Kamerman, S. B. (1989). Child care, women, work, and the family: An international overview of child-care services and related policies. In J. S. Lande, S. Scarr, & N. Gunzenhauser (Eds.), *Caring for children: Challenge to America.* Hillsdale, NJ: Erlbaum.

Kamerman, S. B. (2000a). Parental leave policies. *Social Policy Report of the Society for Research in Child Development, XIV* (No. 2), 1–15.

Kamerman, S. B. (2000b). From maternity to paternity child leave policies. *Journal of the Medical Women's Association, 55*, 98–99.

Kamii, C. (1985). *Young children reinvent arithmetic: Implications of Piaget's theory.* New York: Teachers College Press.

Kamii, C. (1989). *Young children continue to reinvent arithmetic.* New York: Teachers College Press.

Kanaka-Gantenbein, C. (2006). Hormone replacement therapy in Turner syndrome. *Pediatric Endocrinology Review, 3* Suppl. 1, 214–218.

Kanoy, K., Ulku-Steiner, B., Cox, M., & Burchinal, M. (2003). Marital relationship and individual psychological characteristics that predict physical punishment of children. *Journal of Family Psychology, 17*, 20–28.

Kaplow, J. B., Curran, P. J., Dodge, K. A., & the Conduct Problems Prevention Research Group. (2002). Child, parent, and peer predictors of early-onset substance use: A multisite longitudinal study. *Journal of Abnormal Child Psychology, 30*, 199–216.

Kapoor, A., Dunn, E., Kostaki, A., Andrews, M. H., & Matthews, S. G. (2006). Fetal programming of hypothalamo-pituitary-adrenal function: Prenatal stress and glucocorticoids. *Journal of Physiology, 572*, 31–44.

Karniol, R., Grosz, E., & Schorr, I. (2003). Caring, gender-role orientation, and volunteering. *Sex Roles, 49*, 11–19.

Karoly, L. A. & Bigelow. J. H. (2005). *The economics of investing in universal preschool education in California.* Santa Monica, CA: RAND Corporation.

Karp, H. (2002). *The happiest baby on the block.* New York: Bantam.

Karpin, I., & Bennett, B. (2006). Genetic technologies and the regulation of reproductive decision-making in Australia. *Journal of Law and Medicine, 14*, 127–134.

Karpov, Y. V. (2006). *The neo-Vygotskian approach to child development.* New York: Cambridge University Press.

Kaslow, N. J., & others. (2004). Person factors associated with suicidal behavior among African women and men. *Cultural Diversity and Ethnic Minority Psychology, 10*, 5–22.

Katz, L. (1999). Curriculum disputes in early childhood education. *ERIC Clearinghouse on Elementary and Early Childhood Education*, Document EDO-PS-99-13.

Katz, L. F. (1999, April). *Toward a family-based hyper vigilance model of childhood aggression: The role of the mother's and the father's meta-emotion philosophy.* Paper presented at the meeting of the Society for Research in Child Development, Albuquerque.

Katz, L., & Chard, S. (1989). *Engaging the minds of young children: The project approach.* Norwood, NJ: Ablex.

Katz, P. A. (1987, August). *Children and social issues.* Paper presented at the meeting of the American Psychological Association, New York.

Katzmarzyk, P. T., Srinivasan, S. R., Chen, W., Malina, R. M., Bouchard, C., & Berensen, G. S. (2004). Body mass index, waist circumference, and clustering of cardiovascular disease risk factors in a biracial sample of children and adolescents. *Pediatrics, 114*, e198–e205.

Kauffman Early Education Exchange (2002). *Set for success: Building a strong foundation for school readiness based on the social-emotional development of young children. 1* (No. 1). Kansas City: The Ewing Marion Kauffman Foundation.

Kauffman, J. M., & Hallahan, D. P. (2005). *Special education.* Boston: Allyn & Bacon.

Kauffman, J. M., McGee, K., & Brigham, M. (2004). Enabling or disabling? Observations on changes in special education. *Phi Delta Kappan, 85*, 613–620.

Kaufman, J. C., & Baer, J. (Eds.). (2006). *Creativity and reason in cognitive development.* New York: Cambridge University Press.

Kaufman, W., & Groters, S. (2006). Developmental neuropathology in DNT studies—a sensitive tool for the detection and characterizations of developmental neurotoxicants. *Reproductive Toxicology, 22*, 196–223.

Kavey, R. E., Allada, V., Daniels, S. R., Hayman, L. L., McCrindle, B. W., Newburger, J. W., Parekh, R. S., & Steinberger, J. (2006, in press). Cardiovascular risk reduction in high-risk pediatric patients. *Circulation.*

Kavsek, M. (2004). Predicting IQ from infant visual habituation and dishabituation: A meta-analysis. *Journal of Applied Developmental Psychology, 25*, 369–393.

Kazdin, A. E., & Benjet, C. (2003). Spanking children: Evidence and issues. *Current Directions in Psychological Science, 12*, 99–103.

Keating, D. P. (2004). Cognitive and brain development. In R. Lerner & L. Steinberg (Eds.), *Handbook of adolescence* (2nd ed.). New York: Wiley.

Keen, R. (2005a). Unpublished review of J. W. Santrock's *Topical life-span development* (3rd ed.), New York: McGraw-Hill.

Keller, A., Ford, L., & Meacham, J. (1978). Dimensions of self-concept in preschool children. *Developmental Psychology, 14*, 483–489.

Keller, H. (2007). *Cultures of infancy.* Mahwah, NJ: Erlbaum.

Kellman, P. J., & Arterberry, M. E. (2006). Infant visual perception. In W. Damon & R. Lerner (Eds.), *Handbook of child psychology* (6th ed.). New York: Wiley.

Kellman, P. J., & Banks, M. S. (1998). Infant visual perception. In W. Damon(Eds.), *Handbook of child psychology* (5th ed., Vol. 2). New York:

Kellogg, R. (1970). *Understanding children's art: Readings in developmental psychology today.* Del Mar, CA: CRM.

Kellogg, R. T. (2007). *Fundamentals of cognitive psychology.* Thousand Oaks, CA: Sage.

Kelly, D. J., & others. (2007a, in press). Cross-race preferences for same-race faces extend beyond the African versus Caucasian contrast. *Infancy.*

Kelly, D. J., & others. (2007b, in press). Three-month-olds, but not newborns, prefer own-race faces. *Developmental Science.*

Kelly, J. B. (2007). Children's living arrangements following separation and divorce: Insights from empirical and clinical research. *Family Process, 46*, 35–52.

Kennedy, R. D., & D'Andrea, A. D. (2006). DNA repair pathways in clinical practice: Lessons from pediatric cancer susceptibility syndromes. *Journal of Clinical Oncology, 24*, 3799–3808.

Kennell, J. H. (2006). Randomized controlled trial of skin-to-skin contact from birth versus conventional incubator for physiological stabilization in 1200 g to 2199 g newborns. *Acta Paediatica (Sweden), 95*, 15–16.

Kennell, J. H., & McGrath, S. K. (1999). Commentary: Practical and humanistic lessons from the third world for perinatal caregivers everywhere. *Birth, 26*, 9–10.

Kenney-Benson, G. A., Pomerantz, E. M., Ryan, A. M., & Patrick, H. (2006). Sex differences in math performance: The role of children's approach to schoolwork. *Developmental Psychology, 42*, 11–26.

Kerr, M. (2001). Culture as a context for temperament. In T. D. Wachs & G. A. Kohnstamm (Eds.), *Temperament in context.* Mahwah, NJ: Erlbaum.

Kessen, W., Haith, M. M., & Salapatck, P. (1970). Human infancy. In P. H. Mussen (Ed.), *Manual of child psychology* (3rd ed., Vol. 1). New York: Wiley.

Kilbride, H. W., Thorstad, K., & Daily, D. K. (2004). Preschool outcome of less than 801-gram preterm infants compared with full-term siblings. *Pediatrics, 113*, 742–747.

Killgore, W. D., Gruber, S. A., & Yurelun-Todd, D. A. (2007, in press). Depressed mood and lateralized prefrontal activity during a Stroop task in adolescent children. *Neuroscience Letters.*

Kim, A. H., Chen, J., Ottar-Pfeifer, W., Holgado, S., Stager, D. R., Parks, M. M.Beauchamp, G. R., Scott, W., Marsh, M. J., & Tong, P. Y. (2005). Screening for amblyopia in preverbal children with photoscreening photographs: IV. *Binocular Vision and Strabismus Quarterly, 20*, 71–80.

Kim, J., & Cicchetti, D. (2004). A longitudinal study of child maltreatment, mother-child relationship quality and maladjustment: The role of self-esteem and social competence. *Journal of Abnormal Child Psychology, 32*, 341–354.

Kim, J., Peterson, K. E., Scanlon, K. E., Fitzmaurice, G. M., Must, A., Oken, E., Rifas-Shiman, S. L., Rich-Edwards, J. W., & Gillman, M. W. (2006). Trends in overweight from 1980 through 2001 among preschool-aged children enrolled in a health maintenance organization. *Obesity, 14*, 1107–1112.

Kimm, S. Y., & Obarzanek, E. (2002). Childhood obesity: A new pandemic of the new millennium. *Pediatrics, 110*, 1003–1007.

King, K. M., & Chassin, L. (2007). A prospective study of the effects of age of initiation of alcohol and drug use on young adult substance dependence. *Journal of Studies on Alcohol and Drugs, 68*, 256–265.

King, P. E., & Benson, P. L. (2006). Spiritual development and adolescent wellbeing and thriving. In E. C. Roehkepartain, P. E. King, L. Wagner, & P. L. Benson (Eds.), *Handbook of spiritual development in childhood and adolescence.* Thousand Oaks, CA: Sage.

King, S., & Laplante, D. P. (2005). The effects of prenatal maternal stress on children's cognitive development: Project Ice Storm. *Stress 8*, 35–45.

Kirchmeyer, C. (2006). The different effects of family on objective career success across gender: A test of alternative explanations. *Journal of Vocational Behavior, 68*, 323–346.

Kirsch, G., McVey, G., Tweed, S., & Katzman, D. K. (2007). Psychosocial profiles of young adolescent females seeking treatment for an eating disorder. *Journal of Adolescent Health, 40*, 351–356.

Kirungi, W. L., Musinguzi, J., Madraa, E., Muluma, N., Cllejja, T., Ghys, P., & Bessinger, R. (2006). Trends in antenatal HIV prevalence in urban Uganda associated with uptake of preventive sexual behavior. *Sexually Transmitted Infections, 82*, (Suppl. 1), i36–i41.

Kirveskari, E., Slmelin, R., & Hari, R. (2006). Neuromagnetic responses to vowels vs. tones reveal hemispheric specialization. *Clinical Neurophysiology, 117*, 643–648.

Kisilevsky, B. S., Hains, S. M., Lee, K., Xic, X., Huang, H., Ye, H. H., Zhang, K., & Wang, Z. (2003). Effects of experience on fetal voice recognition. *Psychological Science, 14*, 220–224.

Kisilevsky, S., Hains, S. M., Jacquet, A. Y., Granier-Deferre, C., & Lecanuet, J. P. (2004). Maturation of fetal responses to music. *Developmental Science, 7*, 550–559.

Kistner, J. (2006). Children's peer acceptance, perceived acceptance, and risk of depression. In T. E. Joiner, J. S. Brown, & J. Kistner (Eds.), *The interpersonal, cognitive, and social nature of depression.* Mahwah, NJ: Erlbaum.

Kitzmann, K. M., & Beech, B. M. (2006). Family-based interventions for pediatric obesity: Methodological and conceptual challenges from family psychology. *Journal of Family Psychology, 20*, 175–189.

Klaczynski, P. A., & Narasimham, G. (1998). Development of scientific reasoning biases: Cognitive versus ego-protective explanations. *Developmental Psychology, 34*, 175–187

Klaus, M., & Kennell, H. H. (1976). *Maternal-infant bonding.* St. Louis: Mosh.

Klesges, L. M., Johnson, K. C., Ward, K. D., & Barnard, M. (2001). Smoking cessation in pregnant women. *Obstetrics and Gynecological Clinics of North America, 28*, 269–282.

Kliegman, R. M., Behrman, R. E., Jenson, H. B., & Stanton, B. F. (2007). *Nelson textbook of pediatrics* (18th ed.). London: Elsevier.

Kling, K. C., Hyde, J. S., Showers, C. J., & Buswell, B. N. (1999). Gender differences in self-esteem: A meta-analysis. *Psychological Bulletin, 125*, 470–500.

Klingman, A. (2006). Children and war trauma. In W. Damon & R. Lerner (Eds.), *Handbook of child psychology* (6th ed.). New York: Wiley.

Knai, C., Pomerleau, J., Lock, K., & McKee, M. (2006). Getting children to eat more fruits and vegetables: A systematic review. *Preventive Medicine, 42*, 85–95.

Knobloch, J., Shaughnessy, J. D., & Ruther, U. (2007, in press). Thalidomide increases limb deformities by perturbing the Bmp/Dkk1? Wnt signaling pathway. *FASEB Journal.*

Kobak, R. (1999). The emotional dynamics of disruptions in attachment relationships: Implications for theory, research, and clinical intervention. In J. Cassidy & P. Shaver (Eds.). *Handbook of attachment.* New York: Guilford.

Kobayashi, K., Tajima, M., Toishi, S., Fujimori, K. Suzuki, Y., & Udagama, H. (2005). Fetal growth restriction associated with measles virus infection during pregnancy. *Journal of Perinatal Medicine, 33*, 67–68.

Koch, J. R., Roberts, A. E., Armstrong, M. R., & Owen, D. C. (2005). College students, tattoos, and sexual activity. *Psychological Reports, 97*, 887–890.

Kochanska, G., Gross, J. N., Lin, M., & Nichols, K. E. (2002). Guilt in young children:

Development, determinants, and relations with a broader set of standards. *Child Development, 73,* 461–482.

Kochanska, G., Aksan, N., Knaack, A., & Rhines, H. M. (2004). Maternal parenting and children's conscience: Early security as a moderator. *Child Development, 75,* 1229–1242.

Kochi, C., Longui, C. A., Lemos-Marini, S. H., Guerra-Junior, G., Melo, M. B., Calliari, L. E., & Monte, O. (2007). The influence of parental origin of X chromosome genes on the stature of patients with 45 X Turner syndrome. *Genetics and Molecular Research, 18,* 1–7.

Kohlberg, L. (1958). *The development on modes of moral thinking and choice in the years 10 to 16.* Unpublished doctoral dissertation, University of Chicago.

Kohlberg, L. (1966). A cognitive-developmental analysis of children's sex-role concepts and attitudes. In E. E. Maccoby (Ed.), *The development of sex differences.* Palo Alto, CA: Stanford University Press.

Kohlberg, L. (1969). Stage and sequence: The cognitive-developmental approach to socialization. In D. A. Goslin (Ed.), *Handbook of socialization theory and research.* Chicago: Rand McNally.

Kohlberg, L. (1986). A current statement on some theoretical issues. In S. Modgil & C. Modgil (Eds.), *Lawrence Kohlberg.* Philadelphia: Falmer.

Koletzko, B. (2006). Long-term consequences of early feeding and later obesity risk. *Nestle Nutrition Workshop Series: Pediatric Program, 58,* 1–18.

Kopp, C. B., & Neufeld, S. J. (2002). Emotional development in infancy. In R. Davidson & K. Scherer (Eds.), *Handbook of affective sciences.* New York: Oxford University Press.

Koppelman, K., & Goodheart, L. (2008). *Understanding human differences* (2nd ed.). Boston: Allyn & Bacon.

Koren-Karie, N., Oppenheim, D., & Goldsmith, D. (2007). Keeping the inner world of the child in mind. In D. Oppenheim & D. Goldsmith (Eds.), *Attachment theory in clinical work with children.* New York: Guilford.

Kornhaber, M., Fierros, E., & Veenema, S. (2004). Multiple intelligences. Boston: Allyn & Bacon.

Kostelnik, M. J., Soderman, A. K., & Whiren, A. P. (2007). *Developmentally appropriate curriculum* (4th ed.). Upper Saddle River, NJ: Prentice Hall.

Kotovsky, L., & Baillargeon, R. (1994). Calibration based reasoning about collision events in 11 -month-old infants. *Cognition, 51,* 107–129.

Kottak, C. P. (2004). *Cultural anthropology* (10th ed). New York: McGraw-Hill.

Kottak, C. P., & Kozaitis, K. A. (2008). *On being different: Diversity and multiculturalism in the United States* (3rd ed.). New York: McGraw-Hill.

Koukoura, O., Sifakis, S., Stratoudakis, G., Manta, N., Kaminopetros, P., & Koumantakis, E. (2006). A case report of recurrent anencephaly and literature review. *Clinical and Experimental Obstetrics and Gynecology, 33,* 185–189.

Kovar, S. K., Combs, C. A., Campbell, K., Napper-Owen, G., & Worrell, V. J. (2007). *Elementary classroom teachers as movement educators* (2nd ed.). New York: McGraw-Hill.

Kozol, J. (2005). *The shame of the nation.* New York: Crown.

Kramer, L. (2006, July 10). Commentary in "How your siblings make you who you are", by J. Kluger. *Time,* pp. 46–55.

Kramer, L., Perozynski, L. (1999). Parental beliefs about managing sibling conflict. *Developmental Psychology, 35,* 489–499.

Kramer, L. S., & Goldman-Rakic, P. S. (2001). Prefrontal microcircuits. *Journal of Neuroscience, 21,* 3788–3796.

Kramer, M. (2003). Commentary: Breastfeeding and child health, growth, and survival. *International Journal of Epidemiology, 32,* 96–98.

Kramer, M. S., & McDonald, S. W. (2006). Aerobic exercise for women during pregnancy. *Cochrane Database of Systematic Reviews, 3,* CD000180.

Kramer, P. (1993). *Listening to Prozac.* New York: Penguin Books.

Kranz, S., & Siega-Riz, A. M. (2002). Sociodemographic determinants of added sugar intake in preschoolers 2 to 5 years old. *Journal of Pediatrics, 140,* 667–672.

Krebs, N. F. (2007). Food choices to meet nutritional needs of breast-fed infants and toddlers on mixed diets. *Journal of Nutrition, 137,* 511S–517S.

Kreutzer, M., Leonard, C., & Flavell, J. H. (1975). An interview study of children's knowledge about memory. *Monographs of the Society for Research in Child Development. 40* (1, Serial No. 159).

Kriebs, J. M. (2006). Changing the paradigm: HIV in pregnancy. *Journal of Perinatal and Neonatal Nursing, 20,* 71–73.

Kristensen, J., Vesteraard, M., Wisborg, K., Kesmodel, U., & Secher, N. J. (2005). Prepregnancy weight and the risk of stillbirth and neonatal death. *British Journal of Obstetrics and Gynecology, 112,* 403–408.

Kroger, J. (2003). Identity development in adolescence. In G. Adams & M. Berzonsky (Eds.), Blackwell handbook of adolescence. Malden, MA: Blackwell.

Kroger, J. (2007). *Identity development: Adolescence through adulthood.* (2nd ed.). Thousand Oaks, CA: Sage.

Krogh, K. L., & Slentz, S. I. (2001). *Teaching young children.* Mahwah, NJ: Erlbaum.

Kucian, K., Loenneker, T., Dietrich, T., Dosch, M., Martin, E., & von Aster, M. (2006). Impaired neural networks for approximate calculation in dyscalculic children: A functional MRI study. *Behavioral and Brain Function, 2,* 31.

Kuczynski, L., & Parkin, C. N. (2007). Agency and bidirectionality in socialization: Interactions, transactions, and relational dialectics. In J. E. Grusec & P. D. Hastings (Eds.), *Handbook of socialization.* New York: Guilford.

Kuebli, J. (1994, March). Young children's understanding of everyday emotions. *Young Children,* pp. 36–48.

Kuhl, P. K. (1993). Infant speech perception: A window on psycholinguistic development. *International Journal of Psycholinguistics, 9,* 33–56.

Kuhl, P. K. (2000). A new view of language acquisition. *Proceedings of the National Academy of Science, 97.* (22) 11850–11857.

Kuhl, P. K. (2007). Is speech learning "gated" by the social brain? *Developmental Science, 10,* 110–120.

Kuhl, P. K., Stevens, E., Hayashi, A., Deguchi, T., Kiritani, S., & Iverson, P. (2006). Infants show a facilitation for native language phonetic perception between 6 and 12 months. *Developmental Science, 9,* F13–F21.

Kuhn, D. (1998). Afterword to Volume 2: Cognition, perception, and language. In W. Damon (Ed.), *Handbook of child psychology* (5th ed., Vol. 2). New York: Wiley.

Kuhn, D. (1999). Metacognitive development. In L. Balter & S. Tamis-Lemonda (Eds.), *Child psychology: A handbook of contemporary issues.* Philadelphia: Psychology Press.

Kuhn, D. (2004). What is scientific thinking, and how does it develop? In U. Goswami (Ed.), *Blackwell handbook of childhood cognitive development.* Malden, MA: Blackwell.

Kuhn, D., & Franklin, S. (2006). The second decade: What develops (and how)? In W. Damon & R. Lerner (Eds.), *Handbook of child psychology* (6th ed.). New York: Wiley.

Kuhn, D., Amsel, E., & O'Laughlin, M. (1988). *The development of scientific thinking skills.* Orlando, FL: Academic Press.

Kuhn, D., Schauble, L., & Garcia-Mila, M. (1992). Cross-domain development of scientific reasoning. *Cognition and Instruction, 9,* 285–327.

Kumar, R., Gautam, G., Gupta, N. P., Aron, M., Dada, R., Kucheria, K., Gupta, S. K., & Mitra, A. (2006). Role of testicular fine-needle aspiration cytology in infertile men with clinical obstructive azoospermia. *National Medical Journal of India, 19,* 18–20.

Kumari, A. S. (2001). Pregnancy outcome in women with morbid obesity. *International Journal of Gynecology and Obstetrics, 73,* 101–107.

Kupersmidt, J. B., & Coie, J. D. (1990). Preadolescent perr status, aggression, and school adjustment as predictors of externalizing problems in adolescence. *Child Development, 61,* 1350–1363.

Kupperman, M., Learman, L. A., Gates, E., Gregorich, S. E., Nease, R. F., Lewis, J., & Washington, A. E. (2006). Beyond race or ethnicity and socioeconomic status: Predictors of prenatal testing for Down syndrome. *Obstetrics and Gynecology, 107,* 1087–1097.

Kushner, B. J. (2006). Perspective on strabismus, 2006. *Archives of Ophthalmology, 124,* 1321–1326.

Kwak, H. K., Kim, M., Cho, B. H., & Ham, Y. M. (1999, April). *The relationship between children's temperament, maternal control strategies, and children's compliance.* Paper presented at the meeting of the Society for Research in Child Development, Albuquerque.

L

La Greca, A. M., & Harrison, H. M. (2005). Adolescent peer relations, friendships, and romantic relationships: Do they predict social anxiety and depression? *Journal of Clinical Child and Adolescent Psychology, 34,* 49–61.

Laberge, L., Tremblay, R. E., Vitarao, F., & Montplaiser, J. (2000). Development of parasomnias from childhood to early adolescence. *Pediatrics, 106,* 67–74.

Ladd, G. W., Herald, S. L., & Andrews, R. K. (2006). Young children's peer relations and social competence. In B. Spodak & O. N. Saracho (Eds.), *Handbook of research on the education of young children* (2nd ed.). Mahwah, NJ: Erlbaum.

Laforgia, J., Withers, R. T., & Gore, C. J. (2006). Effects of exercise intensity and duration on the excess post-exercise oxygen consumption. *Journal of Sports Science, 24,* 1247–1264.

Laible, D. J., & Thompson, R. A. (2007). Early socialization: A relationship perspective. In J. E. Grusec & P. D. Hastings (Eds.), *Handbook of socialization.* New York: Guilford.

Laible, D. J., Carlo, G., & Raffaell, M. (2000). The differential relations of parent and peer attachment to adolescent adjustment. *Journal of Youth and Adolescence, 29,* 45–53.

Laible, D. J., & Thompson, R. A. (2002). Early parent-child conflict: Lessons in emotion, morality, and relationships. *Child Development, 73,* 1187–1203.

Laifer-Narin, S., Budorick, N. E., Simpson, L. L., & Platt, L. D. (2007). Fetal magnetic resonance imaging: A review. *Current Opinion in Obstetrics and Gynecology, 19,* 151–156.

Lainhart, J. E. (2006). Advances in autism neuroimaging research for the clinician and geneticist. *American Journal of Medical Genetics, C: Seminars in Medical Genetics, 142,* 33–39.

Laird, R. D., Pettit, G. S., Dodge K. A., & Bates, J. E. (2005). Peer relationship antecedents of delinquent behavior in late adolescence: Is there evidence of demographic group differences in developmental processes? *Development and Psychopathology, 17,* 127–144.

Lamb, M. E. (1994). Infant care practices and the application of knowledge. In C. B. Fisher & R. M. Lerner (Eds.), *Applied developmental psychology.* New York: McGraw-Hill.

Lamb, M. E. (2000). The history of research on father involvement: An overview. *Marriage and Family Review, 29,* 23–42.

Lamb, M. E., & Ahnert, M. E. (2006). Nonparental child care. In W. Damon & R. Lerner (Eds.), *Handbook of child psychology* (6th ed.). New York: Wiley.

Lamb, M. E., Bornstein, M. H., & Teti, D. M. (2002). *Development in infancy* (4th ed.). Mahwah, NJ: Erlbaum.

Lamb, M. E., Frodi, A. M., Hwant, C. P., Frodi, M., & Steinberg, J. (1982). Mother and father-infant interaction involving play and holding in traditional and nontraditional. Swedish families. *Developmental Psychology, 18,* 215–221.

Lamb, M. E., & Sternberg, K. J. (1992). Sociocultural perspectives in nonparental childcare. In M. E. Lamb, K. J. Sternberg, C. Hwang, & A. G. Broberg (Eds.), *Child care in context.* Hillsdale, NJ: Erlbaum.

Lambert, S. (2005). Gay and lesbian families: What we know and where to go from here. *Family Journal, 13,* 43–51.

Lamont, R. F., & Jaggat, A. N. (2007). Emerging drug therapies for preventing spontaneous labor and preterm birth. *Expert Opinion on Investigational Drugs, 16,* 337–345.

Landau, B., Smith, L., & Jones, S. (1998). Object perception and object naming in early development. *Trends in Cognitive Science, 2,* 19–24.

Lane, H. (1976). *The wild boy of Aveyron.* Cambridge, MA: Harvard University Press.

Langlois, J. H., & Liben, L. S. (2003). Child care research. An editorial perspective. *Child Development, 74,* 969–1226.

Lapsley, D. K. (2006). Moral stage theory. In M. Killen & J. G. Smetana (Eds.), *Handbook of moral development.* Mahwah, NJ: Erlbaum.

Lapsley, D. K., & Narvaez, D. (2006). Character education. In W. Damon & R. Lerner (Eds.), *Handbook of child psychology* (6th ed.). New York: Wiley.

Lara, L. E. (2006, April). *Young Latinas and their relation to the new technologies.* Paper presented at the meeting of the American Educational Research Association, San Francisco.

Larson, R. & Richards, M. H. (1994). *Divergent realities.* New York: Basic Books.

Larson, R. W. (1999, September). Unpublished review of J. W. Santrock's *Adolescence* (8th ed.). New York: McGraw-Hill.

Larson, R. W. (2001). How U. S. children and adolescents spend their time: What it does (and doesn't) tell us about their development. *Current Directions in Psychological Science, 10,* 160–164.

Larson, R. W., Brown, B., & Mortimer, J. (2003). *Adolescents' preparation for the future: Perils and promises.* Malden, MA: Blackwell.

Larson, R., & Lampman-Petraitis, C. (1989). Daily emotional states as reported by children and adolescents. Child Development, 60, 1250–1260.

Larson, R. W., & Varma, S. (1999). How children and adolescents spend time across the world: Work, play, and developmental opportunities. *Psychological Bulletin, 125,* 701–736.

Larson, R. W., & Wilson, S. (2004). Adolescence across place and time: Globalization and the changing pathways to adulthood. In R. Lerner, & L. Steinberg (Eds.), *Handbook of Adolescent Psychology.* New York, Wiley.

Lasiuk, G. C., & Ferguson, L. M. (2005). From practice to midrange theory and back again: Beck's theory of postpartum depression. *Advanced Nursing Science, 28,* 127–136.

Lasker, J. N., Coyle, B., Li, K., & Ortynsky, M. (2005). Assessment of risk factors for low birth weight deliveries. *Health Care for Women International, 26,* 262–280.

Latimer, J. (2007). Becoming informed: Genetic counseling, ambiguity, and choice. *Health Care Analysis, 15,* 13–23.

Lauber, M. O., Marshall, M. L., & Meyers, J. (2005). Gangs. In S. W. Lee (Ed.), *Encyclopedia of school psychology.* Thousand Oaks, CA: Sage.

Leadbeater, B. J. R., & Way, N. (2001). *Growing up fast.* Mahwah, NJ: Erlbaum:

Leaper, C., & Friedman, C. K. (2007). The socialization of gender. In J. E. Grusec & P. D. Hastings (Eds.), *Handbook of socialization.* New York: Guilford.

Leaper, C., & Smith, T. E. (2004). A meta-analytic review of gender variations in children's language use: Talkativeness, affiliative speech, and assertive speech. *Developmental Psychology, 40,* 993–1027.

LeDoux, J. E. (1998). *The emotional brain: The mysterious underpinnings of emotional life.* New York: Simon & Schuster.

LeDoux, J. E. (2000). Emotion circuits in the brain. *Annual Review of Neuroscience, 23,* 155–184.

Lee, A., & Chan, S. (2006). Acupuncture and anesthesia. *Best Practices in Research and Clinical Anesthesia, 20,* 303–314.

Lee, H. Y., Lee, E. L., Pathy, P., & Chan, Y. H. (2005). Anorexia nervosa in Singapore: An eight-year retrospective study. *Singapore Medical Journal, 46,* 275–281.

Lee, J. M., & Howell, J. D. (2006). Tall girls: The social shaping of a medical therapy. *Archives of Pediatric and Adolescent Medicine, 160,* 1035–1059.

Lee, K., Cameron, C. A., Doucette, J., Talwar, V. (2002). Phantoms and fabrications: Young children's detection of implausible lies. *Child Development, 73,* 1688–1702.

Lee, Y. M., & Simpson, L. L. (2007). Major fetal structural malformations: The role of new imaging modalities. *American Journal of Medical Genetics, C, 145,* 33–44.

Legerstee, M. (1997). Contingency effects of people and objects on subsequent cognitive functioning in 3-month-old infants. *Social Development, 6,* 307–321.

Lehr, C. A., Hanson, A., Sinclair, M. F., & Christensen, S. L. (2003). Moving beyond dropout prevention towards school completion. *School Psychology Review, 32,* 342–364.

Leifer, A. D. (1973). *Television and the development of social behavior.* Paper presented at the meeting of the International Society for the Study of Behavioral Development, Ann Arbor, MI.

Leifer, G. (2007). *Introduction to maternity and pediatric nursing* (5th ed.). London: Elsevier.

Leifer, M., Kilbane, T., Jacobsen, T., & Grossman, G. (2004). A three-generational study of transmission of risk for sexual abuse. *Journal of Clinical Child and Adolescent Psychology, 33,* 662–665.

Lenders, C. M., McElrath, T. F., & Scholl, T. O. (2000). Nutrition in pregnancy. *Current Opinions in Pediatrics, 12,* 291–296.

Lenoir, C. P., Mallet, E., & Calenda, E. (2000). Siblings of sudden infant death syndrome and near miss in about 30 families: Is there a genetic link? *Medical Hypotheses, 54,* 408–411.

Lenroot, R. K., & Giedd, J. N. (2006). Brain development in children and adolescents: Insights from anatomical magnetic resonance imaging. *Neuroscience and Biobehavioral Reviews, 30,* 718–729.

Lenroodt, R. L., & Giedd, J. N. (2007). The structural development of the human brain as measured longitudinally with magnetic resonance imaging. In D. Coch, G. Dawson, & K. W. Fischer (Eds.), *Human behavior, learning, and the developing brain.* New York: Guilford.

Lent, R. W., Brown, S. D., Nota, L., & Sorest, S. (2003). Testing social cognitive interest and choice hypotheses across Holland types in Italian high school students. *Journal of Vocational Behavior, 62,* 101–118.

Leong, F. T. I. (1995). Introduction and overview. In F. T. I. Leong (Ed.), *Career development and vocational behavior in racial and ethnic minorities.* Hillsdale, NJ: Erlbaum.

Leppanen, J. M., Moulson, M., Vogel-Farley, V. K., & Nelson, C. A. (2007). An ERP study of emotional face processing in the adult and infant brain. *Child Development, 78,* 232–245.

Lesaux, N. K., & Siegel, L. S. (2003). The development of reading in children who speak English as a second language. *Developmental Psychology, 39,* 1005–1019.

Lesley, C. (2005). *Burning fence: A western memoir of fatherhood.* New York: St. Martin's Press.

Lessow-Hurley, J. (2005). *The foundations of dual language instruction* (4th ed.). Boston: Allyn & Bacon.

Lester, B. M., Tronick, E. Z., & Brazelton, T. B. (2004). The Neonatal Intensive Care Unit Network Neurobehavioral Scale procedures. *Pediatrics, 113* (Suppl.) S641–S667.

Lester, B. M., Tronick, E. Z., LaGasse, L., Seifer, R., Bauer, C. R., Shankaran, S., Bada, H. S., Wright, L. L., Smeriglio, V. L., Lu, J., Finnegan, L. P., & Maza, P. L. (2002). The maternal lifestyle study: Effects of substance exposure during pregnancy on neurodevelopmental outcome in 1-month-old infants. *Pediatrics, 110,* 1182–1192.

LeVay, S. (1991). A difference in the hypothalamic structure between heterosexual and homosexual men. *Science, 253,* 1034–1037.

Levenger, S., Nemet, P., Hirsh, A., Kremer, I., & Nemet, A. (2006). Refractive eye surgery in treating functional amblyopia in children. *Binocular Vision and Strabismus Quarterly, 21,* 231–234.

Leventhal, A. (1994, February). *Peer conformity during adolescence: An integration of developmental, situational, and individual characteristics.* Paper presented at the meeting of the Society for Research on Adolescence, San Diego.

Leventhal, T., Graber, J. A., & Brooks-Gunn, J. (2001). *Adolescent transitions into young adulthood.* Unpublished manuscript, Center for Children and Families, Columbia University.

Levine, M. P., & Smolak L. (2006). *Prevention of eating problems and disorders.* Mahwah, NJ: Erlbaum.

Lewis, A. C. (2006). Clean up the test mess. *Phi Delta Kappan, 87,* 643–644.

Lewis, A. C. (2007). Looking beyond NCLB. *Phi Delta Kappan, 88,* 483–484.

Lewis, C. G. (1981). How adolescents approach decisions: Changes over grades seven to twelve and policy implications. *Child Development, 52,* 538–554.

Lewis, M. (1997). *Altering fate: Why the past does not predict the future.* New York: Guilford Press.

Lewis, M. (2002). Early emotional development. In A. Slater & M. Lewis (Eds.), *Introduction to infant development.* New York: Oxford University Press.

Lewis, M. (2005). Selfhood. In B. Hopkins (Ed.), *The Cambridge Encyclopedia of child development.* Cambridge, UK: Cambridge University Press.

Lewis, M. (2007). Early emotional development. In A. Slater & M. Lewis (Eds.), Introduction to infant development. (2nd ed.). New York: Oxford University Press.

Lewis, M., & Brooks-Gunn, J. (1979). *Social cognition and the acquisition of the self.* New York: Plenum.

Lewis, M., & Ramsay, D. S. (1999). Effect of maternal soothing and infant stress response. *Child Development, 70,* 11–20.

Lewis, M., Sullivan, M. W., Sanger, C., & Weiss, M. (1989). Self-development and self-conscious emotions. *Child Development, 60,* 146–156.

Lewis, R. (2007). *Human genetics* (7th ed.). New York: McGraw-Hill.

Lewis, R. B., & Doorlag, D. (2006). *Teaching special students in general education classrooms* (7th ed.). Upper Saddle River, NJ: Prentice Hall.

Lewkowicz, D. J. (2003). Learning and discrimination of audiovisual events in human infants: The hierarchical relation between intersensory temporal synchrony and rhythmic pattern cues. *Developmental psychology, 39,* 795–804.

Li, C., Goran, M. I., Kaur, H., Nollen, N., & Ahluwalia, J. S. (2007). Developmental trajectories of overweight during childhood: Role of early life factors. *Obesity, 15,* 760–761.

Li, D. K., Willinger, M., Petitti, D. B., Odulil, R. K., Liu, L., & Hoffman, H. J. (2006). Use of a dummy (pacifier) during sleep and risk of sudden infant death syndrome (SIDS): Population based case-control study. *British Medical Journal, 332,* 18–22.

Li, S., Chen, W., Srinivasan, S. R., Tang, R., Bond, M. G., & Berenson, G. S. (2007, in press). Race (black-white) and gender divergences in the relationship of cardiovascular risk factors to carotid artery intima-media thickness in adulthood: The Bogalusa Heart Study. *Atherosclerosis.*

Li, X., Li, S., Ulusovy, E., Chen, W., Srinivasan, S. R., & Berensen, G. S. (2004). Childhood adiposity as a predictor of cardiac mass in adulthood: The Bogalusa Heart Study. *Circulation, 110,* 3488–3492.

Liben, L. S. (1995). Psychology meets geography: Exploring the gender gap on the national geography bee. *Psychological Science Agenda, 8,* 8–9.

Lidral, A. C., & Murray, J. C. (2005). Genetic approaches to identify disease genes for birth defects with cleft lip/palate as a model. *Birth Defects Research, 70,* 893–901.

Lie, E., & Newcombe, N. (1999). Elementary school children's explicit and implicit memory for faces of preschool classmates. *Developmental Psychology, 35,* 102–112.

Lieberman, E., Davidson, K., Lee-Parritz, A., & Shearer, E. (2005). Changes in fetal position during labor and their association with epidural analgesia. *Obstetrics and Gynecology, 105,* 974–982.

Liederman, J., Kantrowitz, L., & Flannery, K. (2005). Male vulnerability to reading disability is not likely to be a myth: A call for new data. *Journal of Learning Disabilities, 38,* 109–129.

Lifshitz, F., Pugliese, M. T., Moses, N., & Weyman-Daum, M. (1987). Parental health beliefs as a cause of nonorganic failure to thrive. *Pediatrics, 80,* 175–182.

Limber, S. P. (2004). Implementation of the Olweus Bullying Prevention Program in American schools: Lessons learned from the field. In D. L. Espelage, & S. M. Swearer (Eds.), *Bullying in American schools.* Mahwah, NJ: Erlbaum.

Lin, M., Johnson, J. E., & Johnson, K. M. (2003). Dramatic play in Montessori kindergartens in Taiwan and Mainland China. Unpublished manuscript, Department of Curriculum and Instruction, Pennsylvania State University, University Park, PA.

Lindsay, A. C., Sussner, K. M., Kim, J., & Gortmaker, S. (2006). The role of parents in preventing childhood obesity. *Future of Children, 16,* (No. 1), 169–186.

Lippa, R. A. (2005). *Gender, nature, and nurture* (2nd ed.). Mahwah, NJ: Erlbaum.

Liprie, M. L. (1993). Adolescents' contributions to family decision making. In B. H. Settles, R. S. Hanks, & M. B. Sussman (Eds.), *American families and the future: Analyses of possible destinies.* New York: Haworth Press.

Lipsitz, J. (1983, October). *Making it the hard way: Adolescents in the 1980s.* Testimony presented at the Crisis Intervention Task Force, House Select Committee on Children, Youth, and Families, Washington, DC.

Lissau, I., Overpeck, M. D., Ruan, W. J., Due, P., Holstein, B. E., & Hediger, M. L. (2004). Body mass index and overweight in adolescents in 13 European countries, Israel, and the United States. *Archives of Pediatrics & Adolescent Medicine, 158,* 27–33.

Lissauer, T., & Clayden, G. (2007). *Illustrated textbook of pediatrics* (3rd ed.). London: Elsevier.

Litovsky, R. Y., & Ashmead, D. H. (1997). Development of binaural and spatial hearing in infants and children. In R. H. Gilkey & T. R. Anderson (Eds.), *Binaural and spatial hearing in real and virtual environments,* Mahwah, NJ: Erlbaum.

Litovsky, R. Y., Johnstone, P. M., & Godar, S. P. (2006). Benefits of bilateral cochlear implants and/or hearing aids in children. *International Journal of Audiology, 45* (Suppl.), S78–S91.

Litt, J., Taylor, H. G., Klein, N., & Hack, M. (2005). Learning disabilities in children with very low birthweight: Prevalence, neuropsychological correlates, and educational interventions. *Journal of Learning Disabilities, 38,* 130–141.

Little, H. A., Rowe, C. L., Dakof, G. A., Ungaro, R. A., & Henderson, C. E. (2004). Early intervention for adolescent substance abuse: Pretreatment to posttreatment outcomes of a randomized clinical trial comparing multidimensional family therapy and peer group treatment. *Journal of Psychoactive Drugs, 36,* 49–63.

Liu, A. H. (2002). Early intervention for asthma prevention in children. *Allergy and Asthma Processes, 23,* 289–293.

Liu, J., Raine, A., Venables, P. H., Dalais, C., & Mednick, S. A. (2003). Malnutrition at age 3 years and lower cognitive ability at age 11 years: Independence from psychosocial adversity. *Archives of Pediatric and Adolescent Medicine, 157,* 593–600.

Liu, J., Raine, A., Venables, P. H., & Mednick, S. A. (2004). Malnutrition at 3 years and externalizing behavior problems at age 8, 11, and 17 years. *American Journal of Psychiatry, 161,* 2005–2013.

Lively, W., & Bromley, D. (1973). *Person perception in childhood and adolescence.* New York: Wiley.

Lochman, J., & the Conduct Problems Prevention Research Group. (2007, March). *Fast Track intervention outcomes in the middle school years.* Paper presented at the meeting of the Society for Research in Child Development, Boston.

Lock, A. (2004). Preverbal communication. In U. Goswami (Ed.), *Blackwell handbook of childhood cognitive development.* Malden, MA: Blackwell.

Loebel, M., & Yali, A. M. (1999, August). *Effects of positive expectancies on adjustments to pregnancy.* Paper presented at the meeting of the American Psychological Association, Boston.

Loeber, R., & Farrington, D. P. (Eds.). (2001). *Child delinquents: Development, intervention and service needs.* Thousand Oaks, CA: Sage.

Loeber, R., Farrington, D. P., Stouthamer-Loeber, M., Moffitt, T., & Caspi, A. (1998). The development of male offending: Key findings from the first decade of the Pittsburgh Youth Study. *Studies in Crime and Crime Prevention, 7,* 141–172.

Loehlin, J. C., Horn, J. M., & Ernst, J. L. (2007). Genetic and environmental influences on adult life outcomes: Evidence from the Texas adoption project. *Behavior Genetics, 37,* 463–476.

Logsdon, M. C. (2004). Depression in adolescent girls: Screening and treatment strategies for primary care providers. *Journal of the American Women's Medical Association, 59,* 101–106.

London, M. L., Ladewig, P. A., Ball, J. W., & Bindler, R. A. (2007). *Maternal and child nursing care* (2nd ed.). Upper Saddle River, NJ: Prentice Hall.

Long, T. & Long, L. (1983). *Latchkey children.* New York: Penguin.

Longo-Mbenza, B., Lukoki, L. E. & M'buyambia-Kabangu, J. R. (2007, in press). Nutritional status, socioeconomic status, heart rate, and blood pressure in African school children and adolescents. *International Journal of Cardiology.*

Lopez Alvarez, M. J. (2007). Proteins in human milk. *Breastfeeding Review, 15,* 5–16.

Lorah, C. (2002). New age, new meals, old problem. *Dentistry Today, 21,* 50–53.

Lorenz, K. Z. (1965). *Evolution and the modification of behavior.* Chicago: University of Chicago Press.

Lott, B., & Maluso, D. (2001). Gender development: Social learning. In J. Worell (Ed.), *Encyclopedia of women and gender.* San Diego: Academic Press.

Lou, J. E., Ganley, T. J., & Flynn, A. J. (2002). Exercise and children's health. *Current Sports Medicine Reports, 1,* 349–353.

Loughlin, K. R. (2007). Urologic radiology during pregnancy. *Urology Clinics of North America, 34,* 23–26.

Lozoff, B., Corapci, F., Burden, M. J., Kaciroti, N., Angulo-Baaroso, R., Sazawal, S., & Black, M. (2007). Preschool-aged children with iron deficiency anemia show altered affect and behavior. *Journal of Nutrition, 137,* 683–689.

Lucurto, C. (1990). The malleability of IQ as judged from adoption studies. *Intelligence, 14,* 275–292.

Luders, E., Narr, K. L., Thompson, P. M., Rex, D. E., Jancke, L., Steinmetz, H., & Toga, A. W. (2004). Gender differences in cortical complexity. *Nature Neuroscience, 1,* 799–800.

Ludington-Hoe, S. M., Lewis, T., Morgan, K., Cong, X., Anderson, L., & Reese, S. (2006). Breast and infant temperatures with twins during kangaroo care. *Journal of Obstetric, Gynecologic, and Neonatal Nursing, 35,* 223–231.

Lumeng, J. C., Appugliese, D., Cabral, H. J., Bradley, R. H., & Zuckerman, B. (2006). Neighborhood safety and overweight status in children. *Archives of Pediatric and Adolescent Medicine, 160,* 25–31.

Luria, A., & Herzog, E. (1985, April). *Gender segregation across and within settings.* Paper presented at the biennial meeting of the Society for Research in Child Development, Toronto.

Lust, B. C. (2007). *Child language.* New York: Cambridge University Press.

Lynn, R. (1996). Racial and ethnic differences in intelligence in the U. S. on the Differential Ability Scale. *Personality and Individual Differences, 26,* 271–273.

Lynne, S. D., Graber, J. A., Nichols, T. R., Brooks-Gunn, J., & Botvin, G. J. (2007). Links between pubertal timing, peer influences, and externalizing behaviors among urban students followed through middle school. *Journal of Adolescent Health, 181,* e7–e13.

Lyon, G. R. (1996). Learning disabilities. *The Future of Children, 6* (1), 54–76.

Lyon, T. D., & Flavell, J. H. (1993). Young children's understanding of forgetting over time. *Child Development, 64,* 789–800.

Lyons, S. J., Henly, J. R., & Schuerman, J. R. (2005). Informal support in maltreating families: Its effects on parenting practices. *Children and Youth Services Review, 27,* 21–38.

Lytle, L. A., Murray, D. M., Perry, C. L., Story, M., Birnbaum, A. S., Kubik, M. Y., & Varnell, S. (2004). School-based approaches to affect adolescents' diets: Results from the TEENS study. *Health Education and Behavior, 31,* 270–287.

M

Maccoby, E. E. (1984). Middle childhood in the context of the family. In *Development during middle childhood.* Washington, DC: National Academy Press.

Maccoby, E. E. (1987, November). Interview with Elizabeth Hall: All in the family. *Psychology Today,* pp. 54–60.

Maccoby, E. E. (1992). The role of parents in the socialization of children: An historical overview. *Developmental Psychology, 28,* 1006–1018.

Maccoby, E. E. (1998). The two sexes: Growing up apart, coming together. Cambridge, MA: Harvard University Press.

Maccoby, E. E. (2002). Gender and group processes. *Current Directions in Psychological Science, 11,* 54–58.

Maccoby, E. E. (2007). Historical overview of socialization research and theory. In J. E. Grusec & P. D. Hastings (Eds.), *Handbook of socialization.* New York: Guilford.

Maccoby, E. E., & Jacklin, C. N. (1974). *The psychology of sex differences.* Palo Alto, CA: Stanford University Press.

Maccoby, E. E., & Lewis, C. C. (2003). Less daycare or better daycare? *Child Development, 74,* 1069–1073.

Maccoby, E. E., & Martin, J. A. (1983). Socialization in the context of the family: Parent-child interaction. In P. H. Mussen (Ed.), *Handbook of child psychology* (4th ed., Vol. 4). New York: Wiley.

Maccoby, E. E., & Mnookin, R. H. (1992). *Dividing the child: Social and legal dilemmas of custody.* Cambridge, MA: Harvard University Press.

MacFarlane, J. A. (1975). Olfaction in the development of social preferences in the human neonate. In *Parent-infant interaction.* Ciba Foundation Symposium No. 33. Amsterdam: Elsevier.

MacGeorge, E. L. (2003). Gender differences in attributions and emotions in helping contexts. *Sex Roles, 48,* 175–182.

MacGeorge, E. L. (2004). The myth of gender cultures: Similarities outweigh differences in men's and women's provisions of and responses to supportive communication. *Sex Roles, 50,* 143–175.

Mackenzie, R., Walker, M., Armson, A., & Hannah, M. E. (2006). Progesterone for the prevention of preterm birth among women at increased risk: A systematic review and meta-analysis of randomized control trials. *American Journal of Obstetrics and Gynecology, 194,* 1234–1242.

Macklem, G. L. (2003). *Bullying and teasing: Social power in children's groups.* New York: Kluwer Academic/Plenum.

Maconochie N., Doyle, P., Prior, S., & Simmons, R. (2007). Risk factors for first trimester miscarriage—results from a UK-population-based case control study. *British Journal of Obstetrics and Gynecology, 114,* 170–176.

Madan, A., Palaniappan, L., Urizar, G., Wang, Y., Fortmann, S. P., & Gouuld, J. B. (2006). Socioicultural factors that affect pregnancy outcomes in two dissimilar immigrant groups in the United States. *Journal of Pediatrics, 148,* 341–346.

Mader, S. S. (2007). *Biology* (9th ed.). New York: McGraw-Hill.

Magnus, R., & Laeng, B. (2006). Drawing on the other side of the brain. *Laterality, 11,* 71–89.

Magnuson, K. A., & Duncan, G. J. (2002). Poverty and parenting. In M. H. Bornstein (Ed.), *Handbook of parenting.* Mahwah, NJ: Erlbaum.

Maguire, S., Mann, M. K., Sibert, J., & Kemp, A. (2005). Are there patterns of bruising in childhood which are diagnostic or suggestive of abuse? A systematic review. *Archives of Diseases in Childhood, 90,* 182–186.

Mahler, M. (1979). *Separation-individuation* (Vol. 2). London: Jason Aronson.

Main, M. (2000). Attachment theory. In A. Kazdin (Ed.), *Encyclopedia of psychology.* Washington, DC, & New York: American Psychological Association and Oxford University Press.

Makrides, M., Neumann, M., Simmer, K., Pater, J., & Gibson, R. (1995). Are long-chain polyunsaturated fatty acids essential nutrients in infancy? *Lancet, 345,* 1463–1468.

Malamitsi-Puchner, A., & Boutsikou, T. (2006). Adolescent pregnancy and perinatal outcome. *Pediatric Endocrinology Reviews, 3* (Suppl 1), 170–171.

Malmgren, K. W., & Meisel, S. M. (2004). Examining the link between child maltreatment and delinquency for youth with emotional and behavioral disorders. *Child Welfare, 83,* 175–188.

Mandara, J. (2006). The impact of family functioning on African American males' academic achievement: A review and clarification of the empirical literature. *Teachers College Record, 108,* 206–233.

Mandler, J. M. (2000). Perceptual and conceptual processes in infancy. *Journal of Cognition and Development, 1,* 3–36.

Mandler, J. M. (2004). *The foundations of the mind: Origins of conceptual thought.* New York: Oxford University Press.

Mandler, J. M. (2006). *Jean Mandler.* Retrieved January 15, 2006, from http://cogsci.ucsd.edu/~jean/

Mandler, J. M., & McDonough, L. (1993). Concept formation in infancy. *Cognitive Development, 8,* 291–318.

Mandler, J. M., & McDonough, L. (1995). Longterm recall in infancy. *Journal of Experimental Child Psychology, 59,* 457–474.

Mannessier, L., Alie-Daram, S., Roubinet, F., & Brossard, Y. (2000). Prevention of fetal hemolytic disease: It is time to take action. *Transfusions in Clinical Biology, 7,* 527–532.

Marchman, V., & Thal, D. (2005). Words and grammar. In M. Tomasello & D. I. Slobin (Eds.), *Beyond nature-nature.* Mahwah, NJ: Erlbaum.

Marcia, J. E. (1980). Ego identity development. In J. Adelson (Ed.), *Handbook of adolescent psychology.* New York: Wiley.

Marcia, J. E. (1987). The identity status approach to the study of ego identity development. In T. Honess & K. Yardley (Eds.), *Self and identity: Perspectives across the lifespan.* London: Routledge & Kegan Paul.

Marcia, J. E. (1994). The empirical study of egoidentity. In H. A. Bosma, T. L. G. Graafsma, H. D. Grotevars, & D. J. De Levita (Eds.), *Identity and development.* Newbury Park, CA: Sage.

Marcia, J. E. (1996). Unpublished review of J. W. Santrock's *Adolescence,* (7th ed.). Dubuque, IA: Brown & Benchmark.

Marcia, J. E. (2002). Identity and psychosocial development in adulthood. *Identity, 2,* 7–28.

Marcon, R. A. (2003). The physical side of development. *Young Children, 58,* 80–87.

Marcus, D. L., Mulrine, A., & Wong, K. (1999, September 13). How kids learn. *U.S. News & World Report,* pp. 44–50.

Markowitz, S. (2007, in press). The effectiveness of cigarette regulations in reducing cases of sudden infant death syndrome. *Journal of Health Economics.*

Marsh, H., Ellis, L., & Craven, R. (2002). How do preschool children feel about themselves? Unraveling measurement and multidimensional self-concept structure. *Developmental Psychology, 38,* 376–393.

Marsh, R., Zhu, H., Schultz, R. T., Quackenbush, G., Royal, J., Skudlarksi, P., & Peterson, B. S. (2006). A developmental fMRI study of self-regulatory control. *Human Brain Mapping, 27,* 848–863.

Martin, C. L., & Dinella, L. (2001). Gender development: Gender schema theory. In J. Worell (Ed.), *Encyclopedia of women and gender.* San Diego: Academic Press.

Martin, C. L., & Fabes, R. A. (2001). The stability and consequences of young children's same-sex peer interactions. *Developmental Psychology, 37,* 431–446.

Martin, C. L., & Halverson, C. F. (1981). A schematic processing model of sex typing and stereotyping in children. *Child Development, 52,* 1119–1134.

Martin, C. L., & Ruble, D. (2004). Children's search for gender cues. *Current Directions in Psychological Science, 13,* 67–70.

Martin, D. W. (2008). *Doing psychology experiments* (7th ed.). Belmont, CA: Wadsworth.

Martin, J. A., Hamilton, B. E., Sutton, P. D., Ventura, S. J., Menacker, F., & Munson, M. L. (2005, September). Births: Final data for 2003. *National Vital Statistics Reports, 54* (No. 2), 1–116.

Martin, J. A., Kochanek, K. D., Strobino, D. M., Guyer, B., & MacDorman, M. F. (2005). Annual summary of vital statistics—2003. *Pediatrics, 115,* 619–634.

Martin, M. T., Emery, R., & Peris, T. S. (2004). Children and parents in single-parent families. In M. Coleman & L. Ganong (Eds.), *Handbook of contemporary families.* Thousand Oaks, CA: Sage.

Martinez, E., & Halgunseth, L. (2004). Hispanics/Latinos. In M. Coleman & L. Ganong (Eds.), *Handbook of contemporary families.* Thousand Oaks, CA: Sage.

Martinez-Donate, M. P., Hovell, M. F., Hofsteer, C. R., Gonzalez-Perez, G. J., Adams, M. A., & Kotay, A. (2007). Correlates of home smoking bans among Mexican-Americans. *American Journal of Health Promotion, 21,* 229–236.

Mash, E. J. & Wolfe, D. (2007). *Abnormal child psychology* (3rd ed., media edition). Belmont, CA: Wadsworth.

Mason, T. B., & Pack, A. I. (2006). Sleep terrors in childhood. *Journal of Pediatrics, 147,* 388–392.

Mason, W. A., Hitchings, J. E., & Spoth, R. L. (2007). Emergence of delinquency and depressed mood throughout adolescence as predictors of late adolescent problem substance use. *Psychology of Addictive Behaviors, 21,* 13–24.

Massey, Z., Rising, S. S., & Ickovics, J. (2006). Centering Pregnancy group prenatal care: Promoting relationship-centered care. *Journal of Obstetric, Gynecologic, and Neonatal Nursing, 35,* 286–294.

Masten, A. S. (2001). Ordinary magic: Resilience processes in development. *American Psychologist, 56,* 227–238.

Masten, A. S. (2004). Regulatory processes, risk, and resilience in adolescent development. *Annals of the New York Academy of Science, 102,* 310–319.

Masten, A. S. (2006). Developmental psychopathology: Pathways to the future. *International Journal of Behavioral Development, 31,* 46–53.

Masten, A. S., Burt, K., & Coatsworth, J. D. (2006). Competence and psychopathology in development. In D. Cicchetti & D. Cohen (Eds.), *Developmental psychopathology, Vol. 3, Risk, disorder and psychopathology (2nd ed.)* New York: Wiley.

Masten, A. S., Obradovic, J., & Burt, K. B. (2006). Resilience in emerging adulthood. In J. J. Arnett & J. L. Tanner (Eds.), *Emerging adults in America.* Washington, DC: American Psychological Association.

Mastropieri, M. A., & Scruggs, T. E. (2007). *Inclusive classroom* (3rd ed.). Upper Saddle River, NJ: Prentice Hall.

Mathews, T. J., Menacker, F., & MacDorman, M. F. (2003). Infant mortality statistics from the 2001 period linked birth/infant death data set. *National Vital Statistics Reports, 52,* 1–28.

Matijasevich, A., Barros, F. C., Sntos, I. S., & Yemini, A. (2006). Maternal caffeine consumption and fetal death: A case-control study in Uruguay. *Pediatric and Perinatal Epidemiology, 20,* 100–109.

Matlin, M. W. (2004). *The psychology of women* (5th ed.), Belmont, CA: Wadsworth.

Matlin, M. W. (2008). *The psychology of women* (6th ed.). Belmont, CA: Wadsworth.

Matthews, J. D., & Cramer, E. P. (2006). Envisioning the adoption process to strengthen gay- and lesbian-headed families: Recommendations for adoption professionals. *Child Welfare, 85,* 317–340.

Maule, M. M., Merietti, F., Pastore, G., Magnani, C., & Richiardi, L. (2007). Effects of maternal age and cohort of birth on incidence time trends of childhood acute lymphoblastic leukemia. *Cancer Epidemiology, Biomarkers, and Prevention, 16,* 347–351.

Maurer, D., & Salapatek, P. (1976). Developmental changes in the scanning of faces by young infants. *Child Development, 47,* 523–527.

Mayer, R. E. (2003). Memory and information processes. In I. B. Weiner (Ed.), *Handbook of psychology* (Vol. VII). New York: Wiley.

Mayer, R. E. (2004). Teaching of subject matter. *Annual Review of Psychology,* Vol. 55. Palo Alto, CA: Annual Reviews.

Mayer-Davis, E. J., Rifas-Shiman, S. L., Zhou, L., Hu, F. B., Colditz, G. A., & Gillman, M. W. (2006). Breast-feeding and risk for childhood obesity: Does maternal diabetes or obesity status matter? *Diabetes Care, 29,* 2231–2237.

Mayes, L. (2003). Unpublished review of J. W. Santrock's *Tropical life-span development* (2nd ed.) New York: McGraw-Hill.

Mazza, J. J. (2005). Suicide. In S. W. Lee (Ed.), *Encyclopedia of school psychology.* Thousand Oaks, CA: Sage.

Mbonye, A. K., Neema, S., & Magnussen, P. (2006). Treatment-seeking practices for malaria in pregnancy among rural women in Mukono district, Uganda. *Journal of Biosocial Science, 38,* 221–237.

McAdoo, H. P. (2006). *Black Families* (4th ed.). Thousand Oaks, CA: Sage.

McBurney, D. H. & White, T. L. (2007). *Research methods* (7th ed.). Belmont, CA: Wadsworth.

McCartney, K. (2003, July 16). Interview with Kathleen McCartney in A. Bucuvalas, "Child care and behavior." *HGSE News,* pp. 1–4. Cambridge, MA: Harvard Graduate School of Education.

McCartney, K. (2006). The family-child-care mesosystem. In A. Clarke-Stewart & J. Dunn (Eds.), *Families count.* New York: Cambridge University Press.

McCombs, B. L. (2001, April). *What do we know about learners and learning? The learner-centered framework.* Paper presented at the meeting of the American Educational Research Association, Seattle.

McDaniel, S. G., Issac, M., Brooks, H., & Hatch, A. (2005). Confronting K-3 challenges in an era of accountability. *Young Children, 60* (No. 2), 20–26.

McDonald, R., & Grych, J. H. (2006). Young children's appraisals of interparental conflict: Measurement and links with adjustment problems. *Journal of Family Psychology, 20,* 88–99.

McDowell, M. A., Brody, D. J., & Hughes, J. P. (2007). Has age of menarche changed? Results from the National Health and Nutrition Examination Survey. *Journal of Adolescent Health, 40,* 227–231.

McElwain, N. L., & Booth-LaForce, C. (2006). Maternal sensitivity to infant distress and nondistress as predictors of infant-mother attachment security. *Journal of Family Psychology, 2,* 247–255.

McGarvey, C., McDonnell, M., Hamilton, K., O'Regan, M., & Matthews, T. (2006). An 8 year study of risk factors for SIDS: Bed-sharing versus non-bed-sharing. *Archives of Disease in Childhood, 91,* 318–323.

McGee, L. M., & Richgels, D. J. (2008). *Literacy's beginnings* (5th ed.). Boston: Allyn & Bacon.

McHale, J. (2007). *Charting the bumpy road of coparenthood.* Washington, DC: Zero to Three Press.

McHale, J., Johnson, D., & Sinclair, R. (1999). Family dynamics, preschoolers' family representations, and preschool peer relationships. *Early Education and Development, 10,* 373–401.

McHale, J. & Sullivan, M. (2007, in press). Family systems. In M. Hersen & A. Gross (Eds.), Handbook of clinical psychology, Volume II: Children and adolescents. New York: Wiley.

McLaren, P. (2007). *Life in schools* (5th ed.). Boston: Allyn & Bacon.

McLoyd, V. C. (1998). Children in poverty: Development, public policy, and practice, In W. Damon (Ed.), *Handbook of child psychology* (5th ed., Vol. 4). New York: Wiley.

McLoyd, V. C., Aikens, N. L., & Burton, L. M. (2006). Childhood poverty, policy, and practice. In W. Damon & R. Lerner (Eds.), *Handbook of child psychology* (6th ed.). New York: Wiley.

McMillan, J. H. (2007). *Classroom assessment* (4th ed.). Boston: Allyn & Bacon.

McNally, D. (1990). *Evers eagles need a push.* New York: Dell.

McNamara, F, & Sullivan, C. E. (2000). Obstructive sleep apnea in infants. *Journal of Pediatrics, 136,* 318–323.

McNergney, R. F., & McNergney, J. M. (2007). *Education* (5th ed.). Boston: Allyn & Bacon.

McWhorter, K. (2005). *Efficient and flexible reading* (7th ed.). Boston: Allyn & Bacon.

Meadows, A. T. (2006). Pediatric cancer survivorship: Research and clinical care. *Journal of Clinical Oncology, 24,* 5160–5165.

Mechanic, D. (1979). Correlates of physician utilization: Why do major multivariate studies of physician utilization find trivial psychosocial and organizational effects? *Journal of Health and Social Behavior, 20,* 389–396.

Medd, S. E. (2003). Children with ADHD need our advocacy. *Journal of Pediatric Health Care, 17,* 102–104.

Mehl, R. C., O'Brien, L. M., Jones, J. H., Dreisbach, J. K., Mervis, C. B., & Gozal, D. (2006). Correlates of sleep and pediatric bipolar disorder. *Sleep, 29,* 193–197.

Mehra, S., & Agrawal, D. (2004). Adolescent health determinants for pregnancy and child health outcomes among the urban poor. *Indian Pediatrics, 41,* 137–145.

Meis, P. J., & Peaceman, A. M. (2003). Prevention of recurrent preterm delivery by 17-alpha-hydroxyprogesterone caproate. *New England Journal of Medicine, 348,* 2379–2385.

Melamed, B. G. (2002). Parenting the ill child. In M. H. Bornstein (Ed.), *Handbook of parenting* (Vol. 5). Mahwah, NJ: Erlbaum.

Melamed, B. G., Roth, B., & Fogel, J. (2001). Childhood health issues across the life span. In A. Baum. T. A. Revenson. & J. E. Singer (Eds.). *Handbook of health psychology.* Mahwah. NJ: Erlbaum.

Melgar-Quinonez, H. R., & Kaiser, L. L. (2004). Relationship of child-feeding practices to overweight in low-income Mexican-American preschool-aged children. *Journal of the American Dietetic Association, 104,* 1110–1119.

Meltzoff, A. N. (1988). Infant imitation and memory: Nine-month-old infants in immediate and deferred tests. *Child Development, 59,* 217–225.

Meltzoff, A. N. (2004). Imitation as a mechanism of social cognition: Origins of empathy, theory of mind, and the representation of action. In U. Goswami (Ed.), *Blackwell handbook of childhood cognitive development.* Malden, MA: Blackwell.

Metzoff, A. N. (2005). Imitation. In B. Hopkins (Ed.), *Cambridge encyclopedia of child development.* Cambridge: Cambridge University Press.

Meltzoff, A. N. (2007). "Like me": A foundation for social cognition. *Developmental Science, 10,* 126–134.

Meltzoff, A. N., & Brooks, R. (2006). Eyes wide shut: The importance of eyes in infant gaze following and understanding of other minds. In R. Flom, K. Lee, & D. Muir (Eds.), *Gaze following: Its development and significance.* Mahwah, NJ: Erlbaum.

Meltozoff, A. N., & Moore, M. K. (1999). A new foundation for cognitive development in infancy: The birth of the representational infant. In E. K. Skolnick, K. Nelson, S. A. Gelman, & P. H. Miller (Eds.), *Conceptual development.* Mahwah, NJ: Erlbaum.

Mendle, J., Turkheimer, E., & Emery, R. E. (2007). Detrimental psychological outcomes associated with early pubertal timing in adolescent girls. *Developmental Review, 27,* 151–171.

Mendoza, J. A., Drewnowski, A., Cheadle, A., & Christakis, D. A. (2006). Dietary energy density is associated with selected predictors of obesity in U. S. children. *Journal of Nutrition, 136,* 1318–1322.

Menias, C. O., Elsayes, K. M., Peterson, C. M., Huete, A., Gratz, B. I., & Bhalla, S. (2007). CT of pregnancy-related complications. *Emergency Radiology, 13,* 299–306.

Menn, L., & Stoel-Gammon, C. (2005), Phonoloqical development: Learning Sounds and sound patterns. In J. Berko Gleason (Ed.), *The development of language* (6th ed.). Boston: Allyn & Bacon.

Menyuk, P., Liebergott, J., & Schultz, M. (1995). *Early language development in full-term and premature infants.* Hillsdale, NJ: Erlbaum.

Mercer, C. D., & Pullen, P. C. (2005). *Students with learning disabilities* (6th ed.). Upper Saddle River, NJ: Prentice Hall.

Meredith, N. V. (1978), Research between 1960 and 1970 on the standing height of young children in different parts of the world. In H. W. Reece & L. P. Lipsitt (Eds.), *Advances in child development and behavior* (Vol. 12). New York: Academic Press.

Merewood, A., Patel, B., Newton, K. N., MacAuley, L. P., Chamberlin, L. B., Francisco, P., & Mehta, S. D. (2007). Breastfeeding duration rates and factors affecting continued breastfeeding among infants born at an inner-city U.S. baby-friendly hospital. *Journal of Human Lactation, 23,* 157–164.

Merrick, J., Morad, M., Halperin, I., & Kandel, I. (2005). Physical fitness and adolescence. *International Journal of Adolescent Medicine, 17,* 89–91.

Metallinois-Katsaras, E. S., Freedson, P. S., Fulton, J. E., & Sherry, B. (2007). The association between an objective measure of physical activity and weight status in preschoolers. *Obesity, 15,* 686–694.

Metz, E. C., & Youniss, J. (2005). Longitudinal gains in civic development through school-based required service. *Political Psychology, 26,* 413–437.

Meyers, A. F., Sampson, A. E., Weitzman, M., Rogers, B. L., & Kayne, H. (1989). School breakfast program and school performance. *American Journal of Diseases of Children, 143,* 1234–1239.

Michal, G. I. (1981). Right-handedness: A consequence of infant supine head-orientation preference? *Science, 212,* 685–687.

Mikkelsson, L., Kaprio, J., Kautiainen, H., Kujala, U., Mikkelsson, M., & Nupponen, H. (2006). School fitness tests as predictors of adult health-related fitness. *American Journal of Human Biology, 18,* 342–349.

Milan, S., Pinderhughes, E. E., & the Conduct Problems Prevention Research Group. (2006). Family instability and child maladjustment trajectories during elementary school. *Journal of Abnormal Child Psychology, 34,* 43–56.

Millar, R., & Shevlin, M. (2003). Predicting career information-seeking behavior of school pupils using the theory of planned behavior. *Journal of Vocational Behavior, 62,* 26–42.

Miller, B., Baig, M., Hayes, J., & Elton, S. (2006). Injury outcomes in children following automobile, motorcycle, and all-terrain vehicle accidents: An institutional review. *Journal of Neurosurgery, 105* (Suppl. 3), S182–S186.

Miller, B. C., Fan, X., Christensen, M., Grotevant, H. D., & von Dulmen, M. (2000). Comparisons of adopted and nonadopted adolescents in a large, nationally representative sample. *Child Development, 71,* 1458–1473.

Miller, C. F., Lurye, L., Zosuls, K., & Rubles, D. N. (2007). *Developmental changes in the accessibility of gender stereotypes.* Unpublished manuscript, Department of Family Resources and Human Development, Arizona State University.

Miller, J. G. (2006). Insights into moral development from cultural psychology. In M. Killen & J. G. Smetana (Eds.), *Handbook of moral development.* Mahwah, NJ: Erlbaum.

Miller, J. G. (2007). Cultural psychology of moral development. In S. Kitayama & D. Cohen (Eds.), *Handbook of cultural psychology.* New York: Guilford.

Miller, J. W., Javadev, S., Dodrill, C. B., & Ojemann, G. A. (2006). Gender differences in handedness and speech lateralization related to early neurological results. *Neurology, 65,* 1974–1975.

Miller, L., & Gur, M. (2002). Religiousness and sexual responsibility in adolescent girls. *Journal of Adolescent Health, 31,* 401–406.

Miller, P. H., & Seier, W. I. (1994). Strategy utilization deficiencies in children: When, where, and why. In H. W. Reese (Ed.), *Advances in child development and behavior* (Vol. 24). New York: Academic Press.

Miller-Jones, D. (1989). Culture and testing. *American Psychologist, 44,* 360–366.

Miller-Loncar, C., Lester, B. M., Selfer, R., Lagasse, L. L., Bauer, C. R., Shankaran, S., Bada, H. S., Wright, L. L., Smeriglio, V. L., Bigsby, R., & Liu, J. (2005). Predictors of motor development in children prenatally exposed to cocaine. *Neurotoxicology and Teratology, 27,* 213–220.

Miller-Perrin, C. L., & Perrin, R. D. (2007). *Child maltreatment* (2nd ed.). Thousand Oaks, CA: Sage.

Mills, D. L., & Sheehan, N. (2007). Experience and developmental changes in the organization of language-relevant brain activity. In D. Coch, G. Dawson, & K. W. Fischer (Eds.), *Human behavior, learning, and the developing brain.* New York: Guilford.

Milsom, A., & Gallo, L. L. (2006). Bullying in middle schools: Prevention and intervention. *Middle School Journal, 37,* 12–19.

Mindell, J. A., & Barrett, K. M. (2002). Nightmares and anxiety in elementary-aged children: Is there a relationship? *Child Care: Health and Development, 28,* 317–322.

Minino, A. M., Heron, M. P., & Smith, B. L. (2006). Deaths: Preliminary data 2004. *National Vital Statistics Report, 54,* 1–49.

Minuchin, P. O., & Shapiro, E. K. (1983). The school as a context for social development. In P. H. Mussen (Ed.), *Handbook of child psychology* (4th ed., Vol. 4). New York: Wiley.

Miranda, M. L. (2004). The implications of developmentally appropriate practices for the kindergarten general music classroom. *Journal of Research in Music Education, 52,* 43–53.

Mitchell, E. A. (2007). Recommendations for sudden infant death syndrome prevention: A discussion document. *Archives of Disease in Childhood, 92,* 155–159.

Mitchell, E. A., Blair, P. S., & L'Hoir, M. P. (2006). Should pacifiers be recommended to prevent sudden infant death syndrome? *Pediatrics, 117,* 1811–1812.

Mitchell, E. A., Hutchinson, L., & Stewart, A. W. (2007, in press). The continuing decline in SIDS mortality. *Archives of Disease in Childhood.*

Mitchell, E. A., Stewart, A. W., Crampton, P., & Salmond, C. (2000). Deprivation and sudden infant death syndrome. *Social Science and Medicine, 51,* 147–150.

Mitchell, K. S., & Mazzeo, S. E. (2004). Binge eating and psychological distress in ethnically diverse undergraduate men and women. *Eating Behavior, 5,* 157–169.

Mitchell, R. L., & Crow, T. J. (2005). Right hemisphere language functions and schizophrenia: The forgotten hemisphere. *Brain, 128,* 963–978.

Miyake, K, Chen, S., & Campos, J. (1985). Infants' temperament, mothers' mode of interaction and attachment in Japan: An interim report. In I. Bretherton & F. Waters (Eds.), Growing points of attachment theory and research. *Monographs of the Society for Research in Child Development, 50* (1–2, Serial No. 109), 276–297.

MMWR (2006, June 9). Youth risk behavior surveillance—United States, 2005 (Vol. 255). Atlanta: Centers for Disease Control and Prevention.

Molina, I. A., Dulmus, C. N., Sowers, K. M. (2005). Secondary prevention for youth violence: A review of selected school-based programs. *Brief Treatment & Crisis Intervention, 5,* 1–3.

Molse, K. J. (2005). Fetal RhD typing with free DNA I maternal plasma. *American Journal of Obstetrics and Gynecology, 192,* 663–665.

Montan, S. (2007). Increased risk in the elderly parturient. *Current Opinion in Obstetrics and Gynecology, 19,* 110–112.

Montemayor, R. (1982). The relationship between parent-adolescent conflict and the amount of time adolescents spend with parents, peers, and alone. *Child Development, 53,* 1512–1519.

Mooney, C. G. (2006). *Theories of childhood.* Upper Saddle River, NJ: Prentice Hall.

Moore, D. (2001). *The dependent gene.* New York: W. H. Freeman.

Moos, M. K. (2006). Prenatal care: Limitations and opportunities. *Journal of Obstetric, Gynecologic, and Neonatal Nursing, 35,* 278–285.

Moralez, L. S., Gutierrez, P., & Escarce, J. J. (2005). Demographic and socioeconomic factors associated with blood levels among Mexican-American children and adolescents in the United States. *Public Health Reports, 120,* 448–454.

Moran, S., & Gardner, H. (2006). Extraordinary achievements. In W. Damon & R. Lerner (Eds.). Handbook of Child psychology (6th ed.). New York: Wiley.

Morelli, G. A., Rogoff, B., Oppenheim, D., & Goldsmith, D. (1992). Cultural variation in infants' sleeping arrangements: Questions of independence. *Developmental Psychology, 28,* 604–613.

Moreno, A., Posada, G. E., & Goldyn, D. T. (2006). Presence and quality of touch influence coregulation in mother-infant dyads. *Infancy, 9,* 1–20.

Morongiello, B. A., Midgett, C., & Shields, R. (2001). Don't run with scissors: Young children's knowledge of home safety rules. *Journal of Pediatric Psychology, 26,* 105–115.

Morra, S., Gobbo, C., Marini, Z., & Sheese, R. (2007). *Cognitive development: Neo-Piagetian perspectives.* Mahwah, NJ: Erlbaum.

Morris, C., Kurinczuk, J. J., Fitzpatrick, R., & Rosenbaum, P. L. (2006). Do the abilities of children with cerebral palsy explain their activities and participation? *Developmental Medicine and Child Neurology, 48,* 954–961.

Morris, P., & Kalil, A. (2006). Out of school time use during middle childhood in a low-income sample: Do combinations of activities affect achievement and behavior? In A. Huston & M. Ripke (Eds.), *Middle childhood: Contexts of development.* New York: Cambridge University Press.

Morrison, G. S. (2006). *Fundamentals of early childhood education* (4th ed.). Upper Saddle River, NJ: Prentice Hall.

Morrison, G. S. (2008). *Fundamentals of early childhood education* (5th ed.). Upper Saddle River, NJ: Prentice Hall.

Morrissey, M. V. (2007). Suffer no more in silence: Challenging the myths of women's mental health in childbearing. *International Journal of Psychiatric Nursing Research, 12,* 1429–1438.

Morrissey-Ross, M. (2000). Lead poisoning and its elimination, *Public Health Nursing, 17,* 229–230.

Morrongiello, B. A., Fenwick, K. D., & Chance, G. (1990). Sound localization acuity in very young infants: An observer-based testing procedure. *Developmental Psychology, 26,* 75–84.

Mortimer, J. T., Finch, M., Shanahan, M., & Ryu, S. (1992). Work experience, mental health, and behavioral adjustment in adolescence. *Journal of Research on Adolescence, 2,* 24–57.

Moss, T. J. (2006). Respiratory consequences of preterm birth. *Clinical and Experimental Pharmacology and Physiology, 33,* 280–284.

Mottershead, N. (2006). Hypnosis: Removing labor from birth. *Practicing Midwife, 9,* 26–27, 29.

Mounts, N. S. (2002). Parental management of adolescent peer relationships in context: The role of parenting style. *Journal of Family Psychology, 16,* 58–69.

Moyer, R. H., Hackett, J. K., & Everett, S. A. (2007). *Teaching science as investigations.* Upper Saddle River, NJ: Prentice Hall.

Mozingo, J. N., Davis, M. W., Droppleman, P. G., & Merideth, A. (2000). "It wasn't working." Women's experiences with short-term breast feeding. *American Maternal Journal of Nursing, 25,* 120–126.

Mraz, M., Padak, N. D., & Rasinski, T. V. (2008). *Evidence-based instruction in reading.* Boston: Allyn & Bacon.

Mufti, P., Setna, F., & Nazir, K. (2006). Early neonatal mortality: Effects of interventions on survival of low birth babies weighing 1000–2000g. *The Journal of the Pakistan Medical Association, 56,* 174–176.

Muhler, M. R., Hartmann, C., Werner, W., Meyer, O., Bollmann, R., & Klingebiel, R. (2007). Fetal MRI demonstrates glioependymal cyst in a case of sonographic unilateral ventriculomegaly. *Pediatric Radiology, 37,* 391–395.

Mukherjee, P., & McKinstry, R. C. (2006). Diffusion tensor imaging and tractography of human brain development. *Neuroimaging Clinics of North America, 16,* 19–43.

Mullis, L. V. S., Martin, M. O., Beaton, A. E., Gonzales, E. J., Kelly, D. L., & Smith, T. A. (1998). *Mathematics and science achievement in the final year of secondary school.* Chestnut Hill, MA: Boston College, TIMSS International Study Center.

Munakata, Y. (2006). Information processing approaches to development. In W. Damon & R. Lerner (Eds.), *Handbook of child psychology* (6th ed.). New York: Wiley.

Mundy, P., Block, J., Delgado, C., Pomares, Y., Van Hocke, A. V., & Parlade, M. V. (2007). Individual difference and the development of joint attention in infancy. *Child Development, 78,* 938–954.

Munk-Olsen, T., Laursen, T. M., Pedersen, C. B., Mors, O., & Mortensen, B. (2006). New parents and mental disorders. *Journal of the American Medical Association, 296,* 2582–2589.

Munshi, A., & Duvvuri, S. (2007). Genomic imprinting—the story of the other half and the conflicts of silencing. *Journal of Genetic and Genomics, 34,* 93–103.

Murray, E. A. (2007). Visual memory. *Annual Review of Neuroscience* (Vol. 29). Palo Alto, CA: Annual Reviews.

Murray, J. P. (2007). TV violence: Research and controversy. In N. Pecora, J. P. Murray, & E. A. Wartella (Eds.), *Children and television.* Mahwah, NJ: Erlbaum.

Myers, A., & Hansen, C. (2006). *Experimental psychology* (6th ed.). Belmont, CA: Wadsworth.

Myers, D. L. (1999). *Excluding violent youths from juvenile court: The effectiveness of legislative waiver.* Doctoral dissertation, University of Maryland, College Park, MD.

Myers, M. G., & MacPherson, L. (2004). Smoking cessation efforts among substance abusing adolescents. *Drug and Alcohol Dependency, 73,* 209–213.

Myerson, J., Rank, M. R., Raines, F. Q., & Schnitzler, M. A. (1998). Race and general cognitive ability: The myth of diminishing returns in education. *Psychological Science, 9,* 139–142.

Mzayek, F., Hassig, S., Sherwin, R., Hughes, J., Chen, W., Srinivasan, S., & Berensen, G. (2007, in press). The association of birth weight with developmental trends in blood pressure from childhood through mid-adulthood: The Bogalusa Heart Study. *American Journal of Epidemiology.*

N

Nadar, K. (2001). Treatment methods for childhood trauma. In J. P. Wilson, M. J. Friedman, & J. Lindy (Eds.), *Treating psychological trauma and PTSD.* New York: Guilford Press.

Nader, P., O'Brien, M., Houts, R., Bradley, R., Belsky, J., Corsnoe, R., Friedman, S., Mei, Z., & Susman, E. J. (2006). Identifying risk for obesity in early childhood. *Pediatrics, 118,* e594–e601.

NAEYC. (1990). NAEYC position statement on school readiness. *Young Children, 46,* 21–28.

NAEYC. (1997). *Principles of child development and learning that inform developmentally appropriate practice* (Position statement). Washington, DC: Author.

NAEYC. (2002). *Early learning standards: Creating the conditions for success.* Washington, DC: Author.

NAEYC. (2003). Learning paths and teaching strategies in early mathematics. *Young children, 58* (No. 1), 41–44.

NAEYC. (2005). *Critical facts about young children and early childhood in the United States.* Washington, DC: Author.

Nagel, H. T., Kneght, A. C, Kloosterman, M. D., Wildschut, H. I., Leschot, N. J., & Vandenbussche, F. P. (2007). Prenatal diagnosis in the Netherlands, 1991–2000: Number of invasive procedures, indications, abnormal results, and terminations of pregnancies. *Prenatal Diagnosis, 27,* 251–257.

Naglieri, J. (2000). Stanford-Binet Intelligence Scale. In A. Kazdin (Ed.), *Encyclopedia of psychology.* Washington, DC, & New York: American Psychological Association and Oxford University Press.

Nagy, E. (2006). From imitation to conversation: The first dialogues with human neonates. *Infant and Child Development, 15,* 223–232.

Naigles, L. R., & Swensen, L. D. (2007). Syntactic support for word learning. In E. Hoff & M. Shatz (Eds.), *Blackwell handbook of language development.* Malden, MA: Blackwell.

Nansel, T. R., Overpeck, M., Pilla, R., Ruan, W., Simons-Morton, B., & Scheidt, P. (2001). Bullying behaviors among U.S. youth. *Journal of the American Medical Association, 285,* 2094–2100.

Nardi, P. M. (2006). *Doing survey research* (2nd ed.). Boston: Allyn & Bacon.

Narramore, N. (2007). Supporting breastfeeding mothers on children's wards: An overview. *Pediatric Nursing, 19,* 18–21.

Narvaez, D. (2006). Integrative ethical education. In M. Killen & J. Smetana (Eds.), *Handbook of moral development.* Mahwah, NJ: Erlbaum.

Nash, J. M. (1997, February 3). Fertile minds. *Time,* pp. 50–54.

Nation, M., & Heflinger, C. A. (2006). Risk factors for serious alcohol and drug use: The role of psychosocial variables in predicting the frequency of substance abuse among adolescents. *American Journal of Alcohol Abuse, 32,* 415–433.

National Assessment of Educational Progress (1998). *National report: 1998.* Washington, DC: National Center for Education Statistics.

National Assessment of Educational-Progress. (2000). *The nation's report card.* Washington, DC: National Center for Education Statistics.

National Assessment of Educational Progress. (2005). *The nation's report card.* Washington, DC: National Center for Education Statistics.

National Association for Sport and Physical Education, *Active start: A statement of physical activity guidelines for children birth to five years.* Reston, VA: National Association for Sport and Physical Education Publication.

National Center for Addiction and Substance Abuse. (2001). *2000 teen survey.* New York: National Center for Addiction and Substance Abuse, Columbia University.

National Center for Children Exposed to Violence. (2001). *Statistics.* New Haven, CT: Author.

National Center for Education Statistics. (2003). *Digest of education statistics, table 52.* Washington, DC: Author.

National Center for Education Statistics. (2007). *The condition of education 2007.* NCES 2007-064. Indicator 23. Washington, DC: U.S. Department of Education.

National Center for Health Statistics. (2000). *Health United States, 2000, with adolescent health chartbook.* Bethesda, MD: U.S. Department of Health and Human Services.

National Center for Health Statistics (2002). *Sexual behavior and selected health measures: Men and women 15–44 years of age, United States, 2002,* PHS 2003–1250. Atlanta: Centers for Disease Control and Prevention.

National Center for Health Statistics. (2002) Prevalence of overweight among children and adolescents: United States 1999–2000 (Table 71). *Health United States, 2002.* Atlanta, GA: Centers for Disease Control and Prevention.

National Center for Health Statistics. (2006). *Death rates.* Atlanta: Centers for Disease Control and Prevention.

National Center for Health Statistics. (2006). *Health United States.* Atlanta: Centers for Disease Control and Prevention.

National Center for Injury Prevention and Control. Fatal injury reports (online database). Retrieved March 16, 2006, from www.cdc.gov/ncipc/wisqars/

National Center for Learning Disabilities. (2007). *Learning disabilities.* Retrieved January 5, 2007, from www.ncid.org.

National Clearinghouse on Child Abuse and Neglect. (2002). *What is child maltreatment?* Washington, DC: Administration for Children and Families.

National Clearinghouse on Child Abuse and Neglect. (2004). *What is child abuse and neglect?* Washington, DC: U.S. Department of Health and Human Services.

National Commission on the High School Senior Year (2001). *Youth at the crossroads: Facing high school and beyond.* Washington, DC: The Education Trust.

National Health Survey. (2005). *ADHD.* Atlanta: Center for Disease Control and Prevention.

National Institute of Mental Health. (2004). *Autism spectrum disorders.* Bethesda, MD: Author.

National Institute of Mental Health. (2007). *Autism spectrum disorders (pervasive developmental disorders).* Retrieved January 6, 2007, from www.nimh.nih.gov/Publicat/autism.cfm.

National Institutes of Health. (2007). Night terror. Retrieved January 19, 2007, from *www.nih.nih.gov/medlineplus/ency/article/000809.htm.*

National Institutes of Mental Health. (1993). *Learning disabilities* (NIH publication No. 93–3611). Bethesda, MD: Author.

National Research Council. (1999). *How people learn.* Washington, DC: National Academy Press.

National Sleep Foundation (2006). *2006 Sleep in America poll.* Washington, DC: Author.

National Vital Statistics Reports. (2004, March 7). Deaths: Leading causes for 2002. Atlanta: Centers for Disease Control and Preventions.

Natsopoulos, D., Klosseoglou, G., Xeroxmeritou, A., & Alevriadou, A. (1998). Do the hands talk on the mind's behalf? Differences in language between left- and right-handed children. *Brain and language, 64,* 182–214

Naude, H., Pretorius, E., & Vijoen, J. (2003). The impact of impoverished language development on preschoolers' readiness-to-learn during the foundation phase. *Early Child Development and Care, 173,* 271–291.

Nava-Ocampo, A. A. & Koren, G. (2007). Human teratogens and evidence-based teratogen risk counseling: The Mother risk approach. *Clinical Obstetrics and Gynecology, 50,* 123–131.

Needham, A. (2008, in press). Learning in infants' object perception, object-directed action, and tool use. In A. Needham & A. Woodward (Eds.), *Learning and the infant mind.* New York: Oxford University Press.

Needham, A., Barrett, T., & Peterman, K. (2002). A pick-me-up for infants' exploratory skills: Early simulated experiences reaching for objects using " sticky mittens" enhances young infants' object exploration skills. *Infant Behavior and Development, 25,* 279–295.

Neisser, U. (2004). Memory development: New questions and old. *Developmental Review, 24,* 154–158.

Neisser, U., Boodoo, G., Bouchard, T. J., Boykin, A. W., Brody, N., Ceci, S. J., Halpern, D. F., Loehlin, J. C., Perloff, R. J., Sternberg, R., & Urbina, S. (1996). Intelligence: Knowns and unknowns. *American Psychologist, 51,* 77–101.

Nelson, C. A. (2003). Neural development and lifelong plasticity. In R. M. Lerner, F. Jacobs, & D. Wertlieb (Eds.), *Handbook of applied developmental science* (Vol. 1). *Thousand* Oaks, CA: Sage.

Nelson, C. A. (2007). A developmental cognitive neuroscience approach to the study of a typical development: A model system involving infants of diabetic mothers. In D. Coch, G. Dawson, & K. W. Fischer (Eds.), *Human behavior, learning, and the developing brain.* New York: Guilford.

Nelson, C. A., Thomas, K. M., & de Haan, M. (2006). Neural bases of cognitive development. In W. Damon, R. Lerner, (Eds.), *Handbook of child psychology* (6th ed.). New York: Wiley.

Nelson, C. A., Zeanah, C., & Fox, N. A. (2007, in press). The effects of early deprivation on brain-behavioral development: The Bucharest Early Intervention Project. In D. Romer & E. Walker (Eds.), *Adolescent psychopathology and the developing brain: Integrating brain and prevention science.* New York: Oxford University Press.

Nelson, K. (1999). Levels and modes of representation: Issues for the theory of conceptual change and development. In E. K. Skolnick, K. Nelson, S. A. Gelman, & P. H. Miller (Eds.), *Conceptual development.* Mahwah, NJ: Erlbaum.

Ness, A., Dias, T., Damus, K., Burd, I., & Berghella, V. (2006). Impact of recent randomized trials on the use of progesterone to prevent preterm birth: A 2005 follow-up survey.

American Journal of Obstetrics and Gynecology, 195, 1174–1179.

Nester, E. W., Anderson, D. G., Roberts, C. E., & Nester, M. T. (2007). *Microbiology* (5th ed.). New York: McGraw-Hill.

Neuman, S. B., & Roskos, K. (2005). Whatever happened to developmentally appropriate practice in early literacy? *Young Children, 60* (No. 4), 22–27.

Neumann, C. G., Gewa, C., & Bwibo, N. B. (2004). Child nutrition in developing countries. *Pediatric Annals, 33,* 658–674.

Neumark-Sztainer, D., Paxton, S. J., Hannan, P. J., Haines, J., & Story, M. (2006). Does body satisfaction matter? Five-year longitudinal associations between body satisfaction and health behaviors in adolescent females and males. *Journal of Adolescent Health, 39,* 244–251.

New, R. (2005). The Reggio Emilia approach: Provocations and partnerships with U.S. early childhood educators. In J. I. Roopnarine & J. E. Johnson (Eds.), *Approaches to early childhood education* (4th ed.). Columbus, OH: Merrill/Prentice Hall.

New, R. (2007, in press). Reggio Emilia as cultural activity. *Theory into Practice.* Strong-Wilson, T., & Ellis, J. (2007, in press). Children and place: Reggio Emilia's environment as a third teacher. *Theory into practice.*

Newcomb, M. D., & Bentler, P. M. (1989). Substance use and abuse among children and teenagers. *American Psychologist, 44,* 242–248.

Newcombe, N. (2007). The development of implicit and explicit memory. In N. Cowan & M. Courage (Eds.), *The development of memory in childhood.* Philadelphia: Psychology Press.

Newcombe, N. S., Drummey, A. B., Fox, N. A., Lile, E., & Ottinger-Alberts, W. (2000). Remembering early childhood: How much, how, and why (or why not). *Current Directions in Psychological Science, 9,* 55–58.

Newell, K., Scully, D. M., McDonald, P. V., & Baillargeon, R. (1989). Task constraints and infant grip configurations. *Developmental Psychobiology, 22,* 817–832.

Newman, B. M., & Newman, P. R. (2007). *Theories of human development.* Mahwah, NJ: Erlbaum.

Newman, R. S., & Hussain, I. (2006). Changes in preferences for infant-directed speech in low and moderate noise by 4.5- to 13-month-olds. *Infancy, 10,* 61–76.

Newman, R. S., Ratner, N. B., Jusczyk, A. E., Jusczyk, P. W., & Dow, K. A. (2006). Infants' early ability to segment the conversational speech signal predicts late language development: A retrospective analysis. *Developmental Psychology, 42,* 643–655.

Newson, J., Newson, E., & Mahalski, P. A. (1982). Persistant infant comfort habits and their sequelae at 11 and 16 years. *Journal of Child Psychology and Psychiatry, 23,* 421–436.

Newton, A. W., & Vandeven, A. M. (2006). Unexplained infant death: A review of sudden infant death syndrome, sudden unexplained infant death, and child maltreatment facilities in shaken baby syndrome. *Current Opinions in Pediatrics, 18,* 196–200.

NICHD Early Child Care Research Network. (2001). Nonmaternal care and family factors in early development: An overview of the NICHD study of Early Child Care. *Journal of Applied Developmental Psychology, 22,* 457–492.

NICHD Early Child Care Research Network. (2002). Structure Process Outcome: Direct and indirect effects of child care quality on young children's development. *Psychological Science, 13,* 199–206.

NICHD Early Child Care Research Network. (2003). Do children's attention processes mediate the link between family predictors and school readiness. *Developmental Psychology, 39,* 581–593.

NICHD Early Child Care Research Network. (2003). Does amount of time spent in child care predict socioemotional adjustment during the transition to kindergarten? *Child Development, 74,* 976–1005.

NICHD Early Child Care Research Network. (2004). Are child developmental outcomes related to before-land after-school care arrangement? *Child Development, 75,* 280–295.

NICHD Early Child Care Research Network, (2004). Type of child care and children's development at 54 months. *Early Childhood Research Quarterly, 19,* 203–230.

NICHD Early Child Care Research Network. (2005). Duration and developmental timing of poverty and children's cognitive and social development from birth through third grade. *Child Development, 76,* 795–810.

NICHD Early Child Care Research Network. (2005). Predicting Individual differences in attention, memory, and planning in first graders from experiences at home, child care, and school. *Developmental Psychology, 41,* 99–114.

NICHD Early Child Care Research Network, (2006). Infant-mother attachment classification: Risk and protection in relation to changing maternal caregiving quality. *Developmental Psychology, 42,* 38–58.

Nicklas, T. A., Demory-Luce, D., Yang, S. J., Baranowski, T., Zakeri, I., & Berensen, G. (2004b). Children's food consumption patterns have changed over two decades (1973–1994): The Bogalusa Heart Study. *Journal of the American Dietetic Association, 104,* 1127–1140.

Nicklas, T. A., Morales, M., Linares, A., Yang, S. J., Baranowski, T., De Moor, C., & Berensen, G. (2004a). Children's meal patterns have changed over a 21-year-period: The Bogalusa Heart Study. *Journal of the American Dietetic Association, 104,* 753–761.

Nicklas, T. A., Webber, L. S., Jonson, C. S., Srinivasan, S. R., & Berensen, G. S. (1995). Foundations for health promotion with youth: A review of observation from the Bogalusa Heart Study. *Journal of Health Education, 26,* S18–S26.

Nicklas, T. A., Yang, S. J., Baranowski, T., Zakeri, I., & Berensen, G. (2003). Eating patterns and obesity in children. The Bogalusa Heart Study. *American Journal of Preventive Medicine, 25,* 9–16.

Nielsen, S. J., Siega-Riz, A. M., & Popkin, B. M. (2002). Trends in energy intake in U. S. between 1977 and 1996: Similar shifts seen across age groups. *Obesity Research, 10,* 370–378.

Nieto, S., & Bode, P. (2008). *Affirming diversity* (5th ed.) Boston: Allyn & Bacon.

Nisbett, R. (2003). *The geography of thought.* New York: Free Press.

Nishina, A., Ammon, N., Bellmore, A., & Graham, S. (2006). Body dissatisfaction and physical development among ethnic minority adolescents. *Journal of Youth and Adolescence, 35,* 179–191.

Noakes, P. S., Thomas, R., Lane, C., Mori, T. A., Barden, A. E., Devadason, S. G., & Prescott, S. L. (2007, in press). Maternal smoking is associated with increased infant oxidative stress at 3 months of age. *Thorax.*

Noddings, N. (1992). *The challenge to care in the schools.* New York: Teachers College Press.

Noddings, N. (2001). The care tradition: Beyond "add women and stir." *Theory into Practice, 40,* 29–34.

Noddings, N. (2006). *Critical lessons: What our schools should teach.* New York: Cambridge University Press.

Nohr, E. A., Bech, B. H., Davies, M. J., Fryenberg, M., Henriksen, T. B., & Olsen, J. (2005). Prepregnancy obesity and fetal death: A study with the Danish National Birth Cohort. *Obstetrics and Gynecology, 106,* 250–259.

Nolen-Hoeksema, S. (2007). *Abnormal psychology* (4th ed.). New York: McGraw-Hill.

Nollen, N., Kaur, H., Pulvers, K., Choi, W., Fitzgibbon, M., Li, C., Nazir, N., & Ahluwalia, J. S. (2006). Correlates of ideal body size among Black and White adolescents. *Journal of Youth and Adolescence, 35,* 276–284.

Noller, P. (2005). Sibling relationships in adolescence: Learning and growing together. *Personal Relationships, 12,* 1–22.

Norgard, B., Puho, E., Czeilel, A. E., Skriver, M. V., & Sorensen, H. T. (2005). Aspirin use during early pregnancy and the risk of congenital abnormalities. *American Journal of Obstetrics and Gynecology, 192,* 922–923.

Nottelmann, E. D., Susman, E. J., Blue, J. H., Inoff-Germain, G., Dorn, L. D., Loriaux, D. L., Cutler, G. B., & Chrousos, G. P. (1987). Gonadal and adrenal hormone correlates of adjustment in early adolescence. In R. M. Lerner & T. T. Foch (Eds.), *Biological-psychological interactions in early adolescence.* Hillsdale, NJ: Erlbaum.

Nsamenang, A. B. (2002). Adolescence in sub-Saharan Africa: An image constructed from Africa's triple heritage. In B. B. Brown, R. W. Larson, & T. S. Saraswathi (Eds.), *The world's youth.* New York: Cambridge University Press.

Nucci, L. (2006). Education in the moral domain. In M. Killen & J. G. Smetana (Eds.), *Handbook of moral development.* Mahwah, NJ: Erlbaum.

Nugent, K., & Brazelton, T. B. (2000). Preventive infant mental health: Uses of the Brazelton scale. In J. D. Osofsky & H. E. Fitzgerald (Eds.), *WAIMH Handbook of infant mental health* (Vol. 2). New York: Wiley.

O

Oakes, J., & Lipton, M. (2007). *Teaching to change the world* (3rd ed.). New York: McGraw-Hill.

Oakes, L. M., Kannass, K. N., & Shaddy, D. J. (2002). Developmental changes in endogenous control of attention: The role of target familiarity on infants' distraction latency. *Child Development, 73,* 1644–1655.

Oakley, G. P. (2007). When will we eliminate folic acid–preventable spina bifida? *Epidemiology, 18,* 367–368.

O'Connor, T. G., Ben-Shlomo, Y., Heron, J., Golding, J., Adams, D., & Glover, V. (2005). Prenatal anxiety predicts individual differences in cortisol in pre-adolescent children. *Biological Psychiatry, 58,* 211–217.

O'Donnell, L., O'Donnell, C., Wardlaw, D. M., & Stueve, A. (2004). Risk and resiliency factors influencing suicidality among urban African American and Latino youth. *American Journal of Community Psychology, 33,* 37–49.

Oepkes, D., & others (2006). Doppler ultrasonography versus amniocentesis to predict fetal anemia. *New England Journal of Medicine, 355,* 156–164.

Offer, D., Ostrov. E., & Howard, K. I. (1989). *The offer self-image questionnaire for adolescents: A manual.* Chicago: Michael Reese-Hospital.

Offer, D., Ostrov E., Howard, K. I., & Atkinson, R. (1988). *The teenage world: Adolescents' self-image in ten countries.* New York: Plenum.

Ogbu, J. U. (1989, April). *Academic socialization of Black children: An inoculation against future failure?* Paper presented at the meeting of the Society for Research in Child Development, Kansas City.

Ogbu, J., & Stern, P. (2001). Caste status and intellectual ability. In R. J. Sternberg & E. L. Grigorenko (Eds.), *Environmental effects on cognitive abilities.* Mahwah, NJ: Erlbaum.

Ogden, C. L., Troiano, R. P., Briefel, Kuczmarksi, R. J., Flegal, K. M., & Johnson, C. L. (1997). Prevalence of overweight in preschool children in the United States, 1971 through 1994. *Pediatrics, 99,* E1.

Ohgi, S., Akiyama, T., Arisawa, K., & Shigemori, K. (2004). Randomized controlled trial of swaddling versus massage in the management of excessive crying in infants with cerebral injuries. *Archives of Disease in Childhood, 89,* 212–216.

Ohgi, S., Fukuda, M., Moriuchl, H., Kusumoto, T., Akiyama, T., Nugetn, J. K., Brazelton, T. B., Arisawa, K., Takahashi, T., & Saitoh, H. (2002). Comparison of kangaroo care and standard care: Behavioral organization, development, and temperament in healthy, low birth weight infants through 1 year. *Journal of Perinatology, 22,* 374–379.

Ohgi, S., Gima, H., & Akiyama, T. (2006). Neonatal behavioral profile and crying in premature infants at term age. *Acta Paediatrica, 95,* 1375–1380.

Okagaki, L. (2000). Determinants of intelligence: Socialization of intelligence. In A. Kazdin (Ed.), *Encyclopedia of psychology.* Washington, DC, & New York: American Psychological Association and Oxford University Press.

Okagaki, L. (2006). Ethnicity, learning. In P. A. Alexander & P. H. Winne (Eds.), *Handbook of educational psychology* (2nd ed.). Mahwah, NJ: Erlbaum.

Olds, S. B., London, M. L., Ladewig, P. A. (1988). *Maternal newborn nursing* (3rd ed.). Boston: Addison Wesley.

Olson, L. M., Tang, S. F., & Newacheck, P. W. (2005). Children in the United States with discontinuous health insurance coverage. *New England Journal of Medicine, 353,* 418–419.

Oman, D., & Thoresen, C. E. (2006). Religion, spirituality, and children's physical health. In E. C. Roehlkepartain, P. E. King, & L. M. Wagener (Eds.), *The handbook of spiritual development in childhood and adolescence.* Thousand Oaks, CA: Sage.

Onwuegbuze, A. J., & Daley, C. E. (2001). Racial differences in IQ revisited: A synthesis of nearly a century of research. *Journal of Black Psychology, 27,* 209–220.

Opitz, B., & Friederici, A. D. (2007, in press). Neural basis of processing sequential and hierarchical structures. *Human Brain Mapping.*

Ornstein, P., Gordon, B. N., & Larus, D. (1992). Children's memory for a personally experienced event: Implications for testimony. *Applied Cognition and Psychology, 6,* 49–60.

Oscarsson, M. E., Amer-Wahlin, I., Rydhstroem, H., & Kallen, K. (2006).

Outcome in obstetric care related to oxytocin use: A population-based study. *Acta Obstetricia et Gynecologica Scandinavica, 85,* 1094–1098.

Oser, F., & Gmunder, P. (1991). *Religious judgement: A developmental perspective.* Birmingham, AL: Religious Education Press.

Oser, F., Scarlett, W. G., & Bucher, A. (2006). Religious and spiritual development through the lifespan. In W. Damon & R. Lerner (Eds.), *Handbook of child psychology* (6th ed.). New York: Wiley.

Ostrov, J. M., Keating, C. F. (2004). Gender differences in preschool aggression during free play and structured interactions: An observational study. *Social Development, 13,* 255–277.

Otto, B. W. (2008). *Literacy development in early childhood.* Upper Saddle River, NJ: Prentice Hall.

Ovando, C. J., Combs, M. C., & Collier, V. P. (2006). *Bilingual and ESL classrooms* (4th ed.). New York: McGraw-Hill.

Oztop, E., Bradley, N. S., & Arbib, M. A. (2004). Infant grasp learning: A computational model. *Experimental Brain Research, 158,* 480–503.

P

Paisley, T. S., Joy, E. A., & Price, R. J. (2003). Exercise during pregnancy. *Current Sports Medicine Reports, 2,* 325–330.

Palmer, S. E. (2004). Custody and access issues with children whose parents are separated or divorced. *Canadian Journal of Community Mental Health, 4* (Suppl.) 25–38.

Palo Alto, CA: Annual Reviews.

Palomaki, G. E., Steinort, K., Knight, G. J., & Haddow, J. E. (2006). Comparing three screening strategies for combining first- and second-trimester Down syndrome markers. *Obstetrics and Gynecology, 107,* 1170.

Paloutzian, R. F. (2000). *Invitation to the psychology of religion* (3rd ed.). Needham Heights, MA: Allyn & Bacon.

Pals, J. L. (2006). Constructing the "springboard effect": Causal connections, self-making, and growth within the life story. In D. P. McAdams, R. Josselson, & A. Lieblich (Eds.), *Identity and story.* Washington, DC: American Psychological Association.

Pan, B. A. (2005). Semantic development. In J. Berko Gleason, *The development of language* (6th ed.). Boston: Allyn & Bacon.

Pan, B. A., Rowe, M. L., Singer, J. D., & Snow, C. E. (2005). Maternal correlates of growth in toddler vocabulary production in low-income families. *Child Development, 76,* 763–782.

Pan, L., Ober, C., & Abney, M. (2007). Heritability estimation of sex-specific effects on human quantitative traits. *Genetic Epidemiology, 31,* 338–347.

Pang, V. O. (2005). *Multicultural education* (3rd ed.). New York: McGraw-Hill.

Parazzini, F., Chatenoud, L., Surace, M., Tozzi, L., Salerio, B., Bettoni, G., & Benzi, G. (2003). Moderate alcohol drinking and risk of preterm birth. *European Journal of Clinical Nutrition, 57,* 1345–1349.

Parcel, G. S., Simons-Morton, G. G., O'Hara, N. M., Baranowski, T., Kolbe, L. J., & Bee, D. E. (1987). School promotion of healthful diet and exercise behavior: An integration of organizational change and social learning theory interventions. *Journal of School Health, 57,* 150–156.

Paris, S. G., & Paris, A. H. (2006). Assessment of early reading. In W. Damon & R. Lerner (Eds.), *Handbook of child psychology* (6th ed.). New York: Wiley.

Park, M. J., Paul Mulye, T., Adams, S. H., Brindis, C. D., & Irwin, C. E. (2006). The health status of young adults in the United States. *Journal of Adolescent Health, 39,* 305–317.

Parke, R. D. (2004). Development in the family. *Annual Review of Psychology* (Vol. 55). Palo Alto, CA: Annual Reviews.

Parke, R. D., & Buriel, R. (2006). Socialization in the family: Ethnic and ecological perspectives. In W. Damon & R. Lerner (Eds.), *Handbook of child psychology* (6th ed.). New York: Wiley.

Parten, M. (1932). Social play among preschool children. *Journal of Abnormal Social Psychology, 27,* 243–269.

Partnership for a Drug-Free America. (2005). *Partnership Attitude Tracking Study.* New York: Author.

Pasley, K., & Moorefield, B. S. (2004). Stepfamilies. In M. Coleman & L. Ganong (Eds.), *Handbook of contemporary families.* Thousand Oaks, CA: Sage.

Pate, R. R., Pfeiffer, K. A., Trost, S. G., Ziegler, P., & Dowda, M. (2004). Physical activity among children attending preschools. *Pediatrics, 114,* 1258–1263.

Pattenden, S., Hoek, G., Braun-Fahrländer, C., Forastiere, F., Kosheleva, A., Neuberger, M., & Fletcher, T. (2006). NO2 and children's respiratory symptoms in the PATY study. *Occupational and Environmental Medicine, 63,* 828–835.

Patterson, C. J. (2004). What differences does a civil union make? Changing public policies and the experiences of same-sex couples: Comment on Solomon, Rothblum, and Balsam (2004). *Journal of Family Psychology, 18,* 287–289.

Patterson, C. J. (2006). Children of lesbian and gay parents. *Current Directions in Psychological Science, 15,* 241–244.

Patterson, C. J., & Hastings, P. D. (2007). Socialization in the context of family diversity.

In J. E. Grusec & P. D. Hastings (Eds), *Handbook of socialization*. New York: Guilford.

Patterson, G. R., De Baryshe, B. D., & Ramsey, E. (1989). A developmental perspective on antisocial behavior. *American Psychologist, 44,* 329–355.

Patterson, K., & Wright, A. E. (1990, Winter). The speech, language, or hearing-impaired child: At-risk academically. *Childhood Education,* pp. 91–95.

Paulson, J. F., Dauber, S., & Leiferman, J. A. (2006). Individual and combined effects of postpartum depression in mothers and fathers on parenting behavior. *Pediatrics, 118,* 659–668.

Pavlov, I. P. (1927). In G. V. Anrep (Trans.), *Conditioned reflexes.* London: Oxford University Press.

Paxson, C., Donahue, E., Orleans, C. T., & Grisso, J. A. (2006). Introducing the issue. *Future of Children, 16,* (No. 1), 3–17.

Pecora, N., Murray, J. P., & Wartella, E. A. (Eds.). (2007). *Children and television.* Mahwah, NJ: Erlbaum.

Pederson, D. R., & Moran, G. (1996). Expressions of the attachment relationship outside of the Strange Situation. *Child Development, 67,* 915–927.

Pelayo, R., Owens, J., Mindell, J., & Sheldon, S. (2006). Bed sharing with unimpaired parents is not an important risk for sudden infant death syndrome: Letter to the editor, *Pediatrics, 117,* 993–994.

Penagarikano, O., Mulle, J. G., & Warren, S. T. (2007, in press). The pathophysiology of fragile X syndrome. *Annual Review of Genomics and Human Genetics.*

Penn, H. E. (2006). Neurobiological correlates of autism: A review of recent research. *Child Neuropsychopathology, 12,* 57–79.

Perez-Febles, A. M. (1992). *Acculturation and interactional styles of Latina mothers and their infants.* Unpublished honors thesis, Brown University, Providence, RI.

Perner, J., Stummer, S., Sprung, M., & Doherty, M. (2002). Theory of mind finds its Piagetian perspective: Why alternative naming comes with understanding belief. *Cognitive Development, 17,* 1451–1472.

Perrin, E. M., Finkle, J. P., & Benjamin, J. T. (2007). Obesity prevention and the primary care pediatrician's office. *Current Opinion in Pediatrics, 19,* 354–361.

Peru, A., Moro, V., Tellini, P., & Tassinari, G. (2006). Suggestive evidence for an involvement of the right hemisphere in the recovery of childhood aphasia: A 3-year follow-up case. *Neurocase, 12,* 179–190.

Peskin, H. (1967). Pubertal onset and ego functioning. *Journal of Abnormal Psychology, 72,* 1–15.

Peskin, M. F., Tortolero, S. R., Markham, C. M., Addy, R. C., & Baumier, E. R. (2007). Bullying and victimization an internalizing symptoms among low-income Black and Hispanic students. *Journal of Adolescent Health, 40,* 372–375.

Peterson, C. C. (2005). Mind and body: Concepts of human cognition, physiology, and false belief in children with autism or typical development. *Journal of Autism and Developmental Disorders, 35,* 487–497.

Peterson, K. S. (1997, September 3). In high school, dating is a world into itself. *USA Today,* pp. 1–2D.

Petesen, A. C. (1979, January). Can puberty come any faster? *Psychology Today,* pp. 45–56.

Petrill, S. A., Deater-Deckhard, K., Thompson, L. A., Dethorne, L. S., & Schatschneider, C. (2006). Reading skills in early readers: Genetic and shared environmental influences. *Journal of Learning Disabilities, 39,* 48–55.

Petrini, J. (2004). *Preterm birth: A public health priority.* White Plains, NY: National March of Dimes.

Pettito, L. A., Kovelman, I., & Harasymowycz, U. (2003, April). *Bilingual language development: Does learning the new damage the old.* Paper presented at the meeting of the Society for Research in Child Development, Tampa.

Pfeifer, M., Goldsmith, H. H., Davidson, R. J., & Rickman, M. (2002). Continuity and change in inhibited and uninhibited children. *Child Development, 73,* 1474–1485.

Phillips, D. (2006). Child care as risk or protection in the context of welfare reform. In N. Cabrera, R. Hutchens, & H. E. Peters (Eds.), *From welfare to childcare.* Mahwah, NJ: Erlbaum.

Phillips, S. (2003). Adolescent health. In I. B. Weiner (Ed.), *Handbook of psychology* (Vol. IX). New York: Wiley.

Phinney, J. S. (1996). When we talk about American ethnic groups, what do we mean? *American Psychologist, 51,* 918–927.

Phinney, J. S. (2006). Ethnic identity exploration in emerging adulthood. In J. J. Arnett & J. L. Tanner (Eds.), *Emerging adults in America.* Washington, DC: American Psychological Association.

Phinney, J. S., & Alipuria, L. L. (1990). Ethnic identity in college students from four ethnic groups. *Journal of Adolescence, 13,* 171–183.

Phinney, J. S., & Ong, A. D. (2007). Ethnic identity in immigrant families. In J. E. Lansford, K. Deater-Deckard, & M. H. Bornstein (Eds.), *Immigrant families in contemporary society.* New York: Guilford.

Piaget, J. (1932). *The moral judgment of the child.* New York: Harcourt Brace Jovanovich.

Piaget, J. (1952). *The origins of intelligence in children.* (M. Cook, Trans.). New York: International Universities Press.

Piaget, J. (1954). *The construction of reality in the child.* New York: Basic Books.

Piaget, J. (1962). *Play, dreams, and imitation.* New York. W. W. Norton.

Piaget, J., & Inhelder, B. (1969). *The child's conception of space* (F. J. Langdon & J. L. Lunger, Trans.). New York: W. W. Norton.

Pierce, G. F., Lillicrap, D., Pipe, S. W., & Vandenriessche, T. (2007). Gene therapy, bioengineered clotting factors, and novel technologies for hemophilia treatment. *Journal of Thrombosis and Haemostasis, 5,* 901–906.

Pierce, K. M., Hamm, J. V., & Vandell, D. L. (1997, April). *Experiences in after-school programs and children's adjustment at school and at home.* Paper presented at the meeting of the Society for Research in Child Development, Washington, DC.

Pike, A., Coldwell, J., & Dunn, J. (2005). Sibling relationships in early/middle childhood: Links with individual adjustment. *Journal of Family Psychology, 19,* 523–532.

Piko, B., & Fitzpatrick, K. M. (2004). Substance use, religiosity and other protective factors among Hungarian adolescents. *Addictive Behaviors, 29,* 1095–1107.

Pinette, M. G., Wax, J., Blackstone, J., Crtin, A., & McCrann, D. (2004). Timing of early amniocentesis as a function of membrane fusion. *Journal of Clinical Ultrasound, 32,* 8–11.

Pinheiro, R. T., Magalhaes, P. V., Horta, B. L., Pnheiro, K. A., da Silva, R. A., & Pinto, R. H. (2006). Is paternal postpartum depression associated with maternal postpartum depression? Population-based study in Brazil. *Acta Psychiatrica Scandinavia, 113,* 230–232.

Pintrich, P. R. (2003). Motivation and classroom learning. In I. B. Weiner (Ed.), *Handbook of psychology* (Vol. VII). New York: Wiley.

Pipe, M-E., Lamb, M. E., Orbach, Y., & Cederborg, A-C. (Eds.), (2007). *Child sexual abuse.* Mahwah, NJ: Erlbaum.

Pirila, S., van der Meere, J., Pentikainen, T., Russu–Niemi, P., Korpela, R., Kilpinen, J., & Nieminen, P. (2007). Language and motor speech skills in children with cerebral palsy. *Journal of Communication Disorders, 40,* 116–128.

Pitkanen, T., Lyyra, A. L., & Pulkkinen, L. (2005). Age of onset of drinking and the use of alcohol in adulthood: A follow-up study from age 8–42 for females and males. *Addiction, 100,* 652–661.

Pitkin, R. M. (2007). Folate and neural tube defects. *American Journal of Clinical Nutrition, 85,* (Suppl.) S285–S288.

Planta, R. C. (2005). Prevention. In H. W. Lee (Ed.), *Encyclopedia of school psychology.* Thousand Oaks, CA: Sage.

Pliszka, S. R. (2007). Pharmacologic treatment of attention deficit hyperactivity disorder: Efficacy, safety, and mechanisms of action. *Neuropsychology Review, 17,* 61–72.

Plomin, R. (2004). Genetics and developmental psychology. *Merrill-Palmer Quarterly, 50,* 341–352.

Plomin, R., & Schalkwyck, L. C. (2007). Microarrays. *Developmental Science, 10,* 19–23

Plomin, R., DeFries, J. C., Craig, I. W., & McGuffin, P. (Eds.). (2003). *Behavioral genetics in the postgenomic era.* Washington, DC: APA Books.

Plomin, R., DeFries, J. C., & Fulker, D. W. (2007). *Nature and nurture during infancy and childhood.* Mahwah, NJ: Erlbaum.

Plomin, R., Reiss, D., Hetherington, E. M., & Howe, G. W. (1994). Nature and nurture: Contributions to measures of the family environment. *Developmental Psychology, 30,* 32–43.

Podeszwa, D. A., Stanko, K. J., Mooney, J. F., Cramer, K. E., & Mendelow, M. J. (2006) An analysis of the functional health of obese children and adolescents utilizing the PODC instrument. *Journal of Pediatric Orthopedics, 26,* 140–143.

Poest, C. A., Williams, J. R., Witt, D. D., & Atwood, M. E. (1990). Challenge me to move: Large muscle development in young children. *Young Children, 45,* 4–10.

Polivy, J., Herman, C. P., Mills, J., & Brock, H. (2003). Eating disorders in adolescence. In G. Adams & M. Berzonsky (Eds.), *Blackwell handbook of adolescence.* Malden, MA: Blackwell.

Pollack, W. (1999). *Real boys.* New York: Owl Books.

Pollard, I. (2007). Neuropharmacology of drugs and alcohol in mother and fetus. *Seminars in Fetal and Neonatal Medicine, 12,* 106–113.

Pollitt, E. P., Gorman, K. S., Engle, P. L., Martorell, R, & Rivera, J. (1993). Early supplementary feeding and cognition. *Monographs of the Society for Research in Child Development, 58* (7, Serial No. 235).

Pollitt, E. P., Gorman, K. S., Engle, P. L., Martorell, R, & Rivera, J. (1993). Early supplementary feeding and cognition. *Monographs of the Society for Research in Child Development, 58* (7, Serial No. 235).

Polnay, L., Hampshire, A., & Lakhanpaul, M. (2007). *Manual of pediatrics.* London: Elsevier.

Pomery, E. A., Gibbons, F. X., Gerrard, M., Cleveland, M. J., Brody, G. H., & Wills, T. A. (2005). Families and risk: Protective analyses of familial and social influences on adolescent substance abuse. *Journal of Family Psychology, 19,* 560–570.

Poole, D. A., & Lindsay, D. S. (1995). Interviewing preschoolers: Effects of nonsuggestive techniques, parental coaching and leading questions on reports of nonexperienced events. *Journal of Experimental Child Psychology, 60,* 129–154.

Poole, D. A., & Lindsay, D. S. (1996). *Effects of parents' suggestions, interviewing techniques, and age on young children's event reports.* Paper presented at the NATO Advanced Study Institute, Porte de Bourgenay, France.

Porath, A. J., & Fried, P. A. (2005). Effects of prenatal cigarette and marijuana exposure on drug use among offspring. *Neurotoxicology and Teratology, 27,* 267–277.

Porges, S. W., Doussard-Roosevelt, J. A., & Maiti, A. K. (1994). Vagal tone and the physiological regulation of emotion. In N. A. Fox (Ed.), *Emotion regulation: Behavioral and biological considerations. Monographs of the Society for Research in Child Development, 59* (Serial No. 240), 167–196.

Posner, J. K., & Vandell, D. L. (1994). Low-income children's after-school care: Are there benefits of after-school programs? *Child Development, 65,* 440-456.

Posner, M. I. (2003). Imaging a science of mind. *Trends in Cognitive Science, 7,* 450–453.

Potvin, L., Champagne, F., & Laberge-Nadeau, C. (1988). Mandatory driver training and road safety: The Quebec experience. *American Journal of Public Health, 78,* 1206–1212.

Poudevigne, M. S., & O'Connor, P. J. (2006). A review of physical activity patterns in pregnant women and their relationship to psychological health. *Sports Medicine, 36,* 19–38.

Poulin-Dobois, D., & Graham, S. A. (2007). Cognitive processes in early word learning. In E. Hoff & M. Shatz (Eds.), *Blackwell handbook of language development.* Malden, MA: Blackwell.

Poulton, S., & Sexton, D. (1996). Feeding young children Developmentally appropriate considerations for supplementing family care. *Childhood Education, 73,* 66–71.

Powell, D. R. (2005). Searching for what works in parenting interventions. In T. Luster & L. Okagaki (Eds.), *Parenting* (2nd ed.). Mahwah, NJ: Erlbaum.

Powell, D. R. (2006). Families and early childhood interventions. In W. Damon & R. Lerner (Eds.), *Handbook of child psychology* (6th ed.). New York: Wiley.

Powell, E. C., Ambardekar, E. J., & Sheehan, K. M. (2005). Poor neighborhood: Safe Playgrounds. *Journal of Urban Health, 83,* 403–410.

Pressley, M. (2003). Psychology of literacy and literacy instruction. In I. B. Weiner (Ed.), *Handbook of Psychology.* New York: Wiley.

Pressley, M. (2007). Achieving best practices. In L. B. Gambrell, L. M. Morrow, & M. Pressley (Eds.), *Best practices in literacy instruction.* New York: Guilford.

Pressley, M., Allington, R., Wharton-McDonald, R., Block, C. C., & Morrow, L. M. (2001). *Learning to read: Lessons from exemplary first grades.* New York: Guilford.

Pressley, M., Cariligia-Bull, T., Deane, S., & Schneider, W. (1987). Short-term memory, verbal competence, and age as predictors of imagery instructional effectiveness. *Journal of Experimental Child Psychology, 43,* 194–211.

Pressley, M., Dolezal, S. E, Raphael, L. M., Welsh, L. M., Bogner, K., & Roehrig, A. D. (2003). *Motivating primary-grades teachers.* New York: Guilford.

Pressley, M., & Harris, K. R. (2006). Cognitive strategies instruction. In P. A. Alexander & P. H. Winne (Eds.), *Handbook of educational psychology* (2nd ed.). Mahwah, NJ: Erlbaum.

Pressley, M., & Hilden, K. (2006). Cognitive strategies. In W. Damon & R. Lerner (Eds.), *Handbook of child psychology* (6th ed.). New York: Wiley.

Pressley, M., Raphael, L. Gallagher, D., & DiBella, J. (2004). Providence–St. Mel school: How a school that works for African-American students works. *Journal of Educational Psychology, 96,* 216–235.

Preston, A. M., Rodrigquez, C., Rivera, C. E., & Sahai, H. (2003). Influence of environmental tobacco smoke on vitamin C status in children. *American Journal of Clinical Nutrition, 77,* 167–172.

Pryor, J. H., Hurtado, S., Saenz, V. B., Korn, J. S., Santos, J. L., & Korn, W. S. (2006). *The American freshman: National norms for fall 2006.* Los Angeles: Higher Education Research Institute, UCLA.

Pryor, J. H., Hurtado, S., Saenz, V. B., Lindholm, J. A., Korn, W. S., & Mahoney, K. M. (2005). The American freshman: National norms for fall 2005. Los Angeles: Higher Education Research Institute, UCLA.

Pueschel, S. M., Scola, P. S., Weidenman, L. E., & Bernier, J. C. (1995). *The special child.* Baltimore: Paul Brookes.

Pujol. J., Lopez-Sala, A., Sebastian-Galles, N., Deus, J., Cardoner, N., Soriano-Mas, C., Moreno, A., & Sans, A. (2004). Delayed myelination in children with developmental delay detected by volumetric MRI. *Neuroimage, 22,* 897–903.

Putnam, S. P., Sanson, A. V., & Rothbart, M. K. (2002). Child temperament and parenting. In M. H. Bornstein (Ed.), *Handbook of parenting* (2nd ed.). Mahwah, NJ: Erlbaum.

Q

Quadrel, M. J., Fischoff, B., & Davis, W. (1993). Adolescent (in) vulnerability. *American Psychologist, 48,* 102–116.

Quadrelli, R., Quadrelli, A., Mechoso, B., Laufer, M., Jaumandreu, C., & Vaglio, A. (2007). Parental decisions to abort or continue a pregnancy following prenatal diagnosis of chromosomal abnormalities in a setting where termination pregnancy is not legally available. *Prenatal Diagnosis, 27,* 228–232.

Quinn, P. C. (2007). Categorization. In A. Slater & M. Lewis (Eds.), *Introduction to infant development* (2nd ed.). New York: Oxford University Press.

R

Raffaelli, M., & Ontai, L. L. (2004). Gender socialization in Latino/a families: Results from two retrospective studies. *Sex Roles, 50,* 287–299.

Rainey, R. (1965). The effects of directed vs. nondirected laboratory work on high school chemistry achievement. *Journal of Research in Science Teaching, 3,* 286–292.

Rajeshwari, R., Yang, S. J., Niclas, T. A., & Berensen, G. S. (2005). Secular trends in children's sweetened-beverage consumption (1973 to 1994): The Bogalusa Heart Study. *Journal of the American Dietetic Association, 105,* 208–214.

Ramacciotti, C. E., Coli, E., Paoli, R., Gabriellini, G., Schulte, F., Castrogiovanni, S., Dell'Osso, L., & Garfinkel, P. E. (2005). The relationship between binge eating disorder and non-purging bulimia nervosa. *Eating and Weight Disorders, 10,* 8–12.

Ramey, C. T., & Campbell, F. A. (1984). Preventive education for high-risk children: Cognitive consequences of the Carolina Abecedarian Project. *American Journal of Mental Deficiency, 88,* 515–523.

Ramey, C. T., & Ramey, S. L. (1998). Early prevention and early experience. *American Psychologist, 53,* 109–120.

Ramey, C. T., & Ramey, S. L. (2004). Early learning and school readiness: Can early intervention make a difference? *Merrill-Palmer Quarterly, 50,* 471–491.

Ramey, C. T., Ramey, S. L., & Lanzi, R. G. (2001). Intelligence and experience. In R. J. Sternberg & E. L. Grigorenko (Eds.), *Environmental effects on cognitive abilities.* Mahwah, NJ: Erlbaum.

Ramey, C. T., Ramey, S. L., & Lanzi, R. G. (2006). Children's health and education. In W. Damon & R. Lerner (Eds.), *Handbook of child psychology* (6th ed.). New York: Wiley.

Ramey, S. L. (2005). Human developmental science serving children and families: Contributions of the NICHD study of early child care. In NICHD Early Child Care Research Network (Eds.), *Child care and development.* New York: Guilford.

Ramey, S. L., & Ramey, C. T. (1999). *Going to school: How to help your child succeed.* New York: Goddard Press.

Ramphal, C. (1962). *A study of three current problems in education.* Unpublished doctoral dissertation, University of Natal, India.

Ramsay, D. S. (1980). Onset of unimanual handedness in infants. *Infant Behavior and Development, 3,* 377–385.

Ramsey-Rennels, J. L., & Langlois, J. H. (2007). How infants perceive and process faces. In A. Slater & M. Lewis (eds.), *Introduction to infant development* (2nd ed.). Malden, MA: Blackwell.

Raphaelson, M. (2004). Stimulants and attention-deficit hyperactivity disorder. *Journal of the American Medical Association, 292,* 2214.

Rasinski, T. V., & Padak, N. (2008). *From phonics to fluency* (2nd ed.). Boston: Allyn & Bacon.

Ratey, J. (2006, March 27). Commentary in L. Szabo, "ADHD treatment is getting a workout." *USA Today,* p. 6D.

Rathbun, R. C., Lockhart, S. M., & Stephens, J. R. (2006). Current HIV treatment guidelines—a review. *Current Pharmacology Design, 12,* 1045–1063.

Raven, P. H., Johnson, G. B., Mason, K. A., Losos, J., & Singer, S. (2008). *Biology* (8th ed.). New York: McGraw-Hill.

Ravid, D., Levie, R., & Ben-Zvi, G. A. (2004). Morphological disorders. In L. Verhoeven & H. Van Balkom (Eds.), *The classification of language disorders.* Mahwah, NJ: Erlbaum.

Ream, G. L. & Savin-Williams, R. (2003). Religious development in adolescence. In G. Adams & M. Berzonsky (Eds.), *Blackwell handbook of adolescence.* Malden, MA: Blackwell.

Rebollo, M. A., & Montiel, S. (2006). Attention and the executive functions. *Revista de Neurologia (Spanish), 42,* (Suppl.) S3–S7.

Redding, R. E. (2005). Adult punishment for juvenile defenders: Does it reduce crime? In N. E. Dowd, D. G. Singer, & R. F. Wilson (Eds.), *Handbook of children, culture, and violence.* Thousand Oaks, CA: Sage.

Reddy, U. M., Wapner, R. J., Rebar, R. W., & Tasca, R. J. (2007). Infertility, assisted reproductive technology, and adverse pregnancy outcomes: Executive summary of a National Institute of Child Health and Human Development workshop. *Obstetrics and Gynecology, 109,* 967–977.

Reed, S. K. (2007). *Cognitive psychology* (7th ed.). Belmont, CA: Wadsworth.

Reeves, G., & Schweitzer, J. (2004). Pharmacological management of attention deficit hyperactivity disorder. *Expert Opinions in Pharmacotherapy, 5,* 1313–1320.

Regalado, M., Sareen, H., Inkelas, M., Wissow, L. S., & Halfon, N. (2004). Parents' discipline of young children: Results from the National Survey of Early Childhood Health. *Pediatrics, 113,* 1952–1958.

Regev, R. H., Lusky, A., Dolfin, T., Litmanovitz, I., Arnon, S., Reichman, B., & the Israel Neonatal Network. (2003). Excess mortality and morbidity among small-for-gestational-age premature infants: A population based study. *Journal of Pediatrics, 143,* 186–191.

Regnerus, M. D. (2001). *Making the Grade: The Influence of Religion upon the Academic Performance of Youth in Disadvantaged Communities.* Report 01-04, Center for Research on Religion and Urban Civil Society, University of Pennsylvania.

Regnerus, M. D., Smith, C., & Smith, B. (2004). Social context in the development of religiosity. *Applied Developmental Science, 8,* 27–38.

Reid, P. T., & Zalk, S. R. (2001). Academic environments: Gender and ethnicity in U.S. higher education. In J. Worrell (Ed.), *Encyclopedia of women and gender.* San Diego: Academic Press.

Reinders, H., & Youniss, J. (2006). School-based required community service and civic development in adolescence. *Applied Developmental Science, 10,* 2–12.

Reiner, W. G., & Gearhart, J. P. (2004). Discordant sexual identity in some genetic males with cloacal exstrophy assigned to female sex at birth. *New England Journal of Medicine, 350,* 333–341.

Reis, O., & Youniss, O. (2004). Patterns of identity change and development in relationships with mothers and friends. *Journal of Adolescent Research, 19,* 31–44.

Remner, G. (2007). Perception and knowledge of the world. In A. Slater & M. Lewis (Eds.), *Introduction to infant development* (2nd ed.). Malden, MA: Blackwell.

Remulla, A., & Guilleminault, C. (2004). Somnambulism (sleepwalking). *Expert Opinions in Pharmacotherapy, 5,* 2069–2074.

Renner, P., Grofer Klinger, L., & Klinger, M. R. (2006). Exogenous and endogenous attention orienting in autism spectrum disorders. *Child Neuropsychology, 12,* 361–382.

Reutzel, D. R., & Cooter, R. B. (2008). *Teaching children to read* (5th ed.). Upper Saddle River, NJ: Prentice Hall.

Revelle, S. P. (2004). High standards + high-stakes = high achievement in Massachusetts. *Phi Delta Kappan, 85,* 591–597.

Reyna, V. F. (2004). How people make decisions that involve risk: A dual-process approach. *Current Directions in Psychological Science, 13,* 60–66.

Reyna, V. F., & Brainerd, C. J. (1995). Fuzzy-trace theory: An interim analysis. *Learning and Individual Differences, 7,* 1–75.

Reyna, V. G., Adam, M. B., Walsk, M. E., LeCroy, C. W., Muller, K., & Brainerd, C. J. (2005). The development of judgment and decision making from childhood to adolescence. In J. E. Jacobs & P. A. Klaczynski (Eds.), *The development of judgment and decision making in children and adolescents.* Mahwah, NJ: Erlbaum.

Reynolds, C. R., Livingston, R., & Willson, V. (2006). *Measurement and assessment in education.* Boston: Allyn & Bacon.

Ricci, G., Patrizi, A., Baldi, E., Menna, G., Tabanelli, M., & Masi, M. (2006). Long-term follow-up of atopic dermatitis: Retrospective analysis of related risk factors and association with concomitant allergic diseases. *Journal of the American Academy of Dermatology, 55*, 765–771.

Richardson, G. A., Ryan, C., Willford, J., Day, N. L., & Goldschmidt, L. (2002). Prenatal alcohol and marijuana exposure: Effects on neuropsychological outcomes at 10 years. *Neurotoxicology and Teratology, 24*, 309–320.

Richmond, M. K., Stocker, C. M., & Rienks, S. L. (2005). Longitudinal associations between sibling relations quality, parental differential treatment, and children's adjustment. *Journal of Family Psychology, 19*, 550–559.

Rickards, T., & deCock, C. (2003). Understanding organizational creativity: Toward a paradigmatic approach. In M. A. Runco (Ed.), *Creativity research handbook.* Cresskill, NJ: Hampton Press.

Riddle, D. B., & Prinz, R. (1984, August). *Sugar consumption in young children.* Paper presented at the meeting of the American Psychological Association, Toronto.

Ridgeway, D., Waters, E., & Kuczaj, S. A. (1985). Acquisition of emotion-descriptive' language: Receptive and productive vocabulary norms for ages 18 months to 6 years. *Developmental Psychology, 21*, 901–908.

Rifas-Shiman, S. L., Rich-Edwards, J. W., Willett, W. C., Kleinman, K. P., Oken, E., & Gillman, M. W. (2006). Changes in dietary intake from the first to the second trimester of pregnancy. *Pediatric and Perinatal Epidemiology, 20*, 35–42.

Rigaud, D., Verges, B., Colas-Linhart, N., Petiet, A., Moukkaddem, M., Van Wymelbeke, V., & Brondel, L. (2007, in press). Hormonal and psychological factors linked to the increased thermic effect of food in malnourished fasting anorexia nervosa. *Journal of Clinical Endocrinology and Metabolism.*

Rigby, K. (2002). *New perspectives on bullying.* London: Jessica Kingsley Publishers.

Righetti-Veltema, M., Conne-Perreard, E., Bousquest, A., & Manzano, J. (2002). Postpartum depression and mother-infant relationship at 3 months old. *Journal of Affective Disorders, 70*, 291–306.

Rigopoulos, D., Gregoriou, S., Paparizos, V., & Katsambas, A. (2007). AIDS in pregnancy. Part II: Treatment in the era of highly active antiretroviral therapy and management of obstetric, anesthetic, and pediatric issues. *Skinmed, 6*, 79–84.

Riley, E. H., Fuentes-Afflick, E., Jackson, R. A., Escobar, G. J., Brawarsky, P., Schrieber, M., & Haas, J. S. (2005). Correlates of prescription drug use during pregnancy. *Journal of Women's Health, 14*, 401–409.

Rivara, F. P. (2004). Modification of the home environment for the reduction of injuries. *Archives of Pediatric and Adolescent Medicine, 158*, 513.

Rizzo, M. S. (1999, May 8). Genetic counseling combines science with a human touch. *Kansas City Star*, p. 3.

Robbins, G., Powers, D., & Burgess, S. (2008). *A fit way of life.* New York: McGraw-Hill.

Roberts, D. F., Henriksen, L., & Foehr, U. G. (2004). Adolescents and the media. In R. Lerner & L. Steinberg (Ed.), *Handbook of adolescent psychology* (2nd ed.). New York: Wiley.

Robertson, D. M., & South, M. (2007). *Practical pediatrics* (6th ed.). London: Elsevier.

Robins, R. W., Trzesniewski, K. H., Tracey, J. L., Potter, J., & Gosling, S. D. (2002). Age differences in self-esteem from age 9 to 90. *Psychology and Aging, 17*, 423–434.

Rocha, N. A. C. F., Silva, F. P. S., & Tudella, E. (2006). The impact of object size and rigidity on infant reaching. *Infant Behavior and Development, 29*, 251–261.

Rode, S. S., Chang, P., Fisch, R. O., & Sroufe, L. A. (1981). Attachment patterns of infants separated at birth. *Developmental Psychology, 17*, 188–191.

Rogoff, B., Moore, L., Najafi, B., Dexter, A., Correa-Chavez, M., & Solis, J. (2007). Children's development of cultural repertoires through participation in everyday routines and practices. In J. E. Grusec & P. D. Hastings (Eds.), *Handbook of socialization.* New York: Guilford.

Rohner, R. P., & Rohner, E. C. (1981). Parental acceptance-rejection and parental control: Cross-cultural codes. *Ethnology, 20*, 245–260.

Roisman, G. I., Aguilar, B., & Egeland, B. (2004). Antisocial behavior in the transition to adulthood: The independent and interactive roles of development history and emerging developmental tasks. *Development and Psychopathology, 16*, 857–872.

Roopnarine, J. L., & Metindogan, A. (2006). Early childhood education research in cross-national perspective. In B. Spodek & O. N. Saracho (Eds.), *Handbook of research on the education of young children.* Mahwah, NJ: Erlbaum.

Rose, S. A. (1990). Cross-modal transfer in human infants: What is being transferred? *Annals of the New York Academy of Sciences, 608*, 38–47.

Rose, S. A., Feldman, J. F., & Wallace, I. F. (1992). Infant information processing in relation to six-year cognitive outcomes. *Child Development, 63*, 1126–1141.

Rose, S., & Frieze, I. R. (1993). Young singles' contemporary dating scripts. *Sex Roles, 28*, 499–509.

Rosenberg, M. S., Westling, D. L., & McLeskey, J. (2008). *Special education for today's teachers.* Upper Saddle River, NJ: Prentice Hall.

Rosenberg, T. J., Garbers, S., Lipkind, H., & Chiasson, M. A. (2005). Maternal obesity and diabetes as risk factors for adverse pregnancy outcomes: Differences among 4 racial/ethnic groups. *American Journal of Public Health, 95*, 1545–1551.

Rosenblith, J. F. (1992). *In the beginning* (2nd ed.). Newbury Park, CA: Sage.

Rosenblum, G. D., & Lewis, M. (2003). Emotional development in adolescence. In G. Adams & M. Berzonsky (Eds.), *Blackwell handbook of adolescence.* Malden, MA: Blackwell.

Rosenstein, D., & Oster, H. (1988). Differential facial responses to four basic tastes in newborns. *Child Development, 59*, 1555–1568.

Rosenzweig, M. R. (1969). Effects of heredity and environment on brain chemistry, brain anatomy, and learning ability in the rat. In M. Monosevitz, G. Lindzey, & D. D. Thiessen (Eds.), *Behavioral genetics.* New York: Appleton-Century-Crofts.

Rosilio, M., Carel, J. C., Ecosse, E., & Chaussainon, J. L. (2005). Adult height of prepubertal short children born small for gestational age treated with GH. *European Journal of Endocrinology, 152*, 835–843.

Rosnow, R. L., & Rosenthal, R. (2008). *Beginning behavioral research* (6th ed.). Upper Saddle River, NJ: Prentice Hall.

Ross, C., & Kirby, G. (2006). Welfare-to-work transitions for parents of infants. In N. Cabrera, R. Hutchens, H. E. Peters, & L. Peters (Eds.), *From welfare to childcare.* Mahwah, NJ: Erlbaum.

Roth, J. L., Brooks-Gunn, J., Murray, L., & Foster, W. (1998). Promoting healthy adolescents: Synthesis of youth development program evaluations. *Journal of Research on Adolescence, 8*, 423–459.

Rothbart, M. K., (2004). Temperament and the pursuit of an integrated developmental psychology. *Merrill-Palmer Quarterly, 50*, 492–505.

Rothbart, M. K., & Bates, J. E. (2006). Temperament. In W. Damon & R. Lerner (Eds.), *Handbook of child psychology* (6th ed.). New York: Wiley.

Rothbart, M. K., & Putnam, S. P. (2002). Temperament and socialization. In L. Pulkkinen & A. Caspi (Eds.), *Paths to successful development.* New York: Cambridge University Press.

Rothbaum, F., Poll, M., Azuma, H., Miyake, K., & Weisz, J. (2000). The development of close relationships in Japan and the United States: Paths of symbiotic harmony and generative tension. *Child Development, 71*, 1121–1142.

Rothbaum, F., & Trommsdorff, G. (2007). Do roots and wings complement or oppose one another?: The socialization of relatedness and autonomy in cultural context. In J. E. Grusec & P. D. Hastings (Eds.), *Handbook of socialization.* New York: Guilford.

Rovee-Collier, C. & Barr, R. (2004). Infant learning and memory. In G. Bremner & A. Fogel (Eds.), *Blackwell handbook of infant development*. Malden, MA: Blackwell.

Rovee-Collier, C. (1987). Learning and memory in children. In J. D. Osofsky (Ed.), *Handbook of infant development* (2nd ed.). New York: Wiley.

Rovee-Collier, C. (2007). The development of infant memory. In N. Cowan & M. Courage (Eds.), *The development of memory in childhood*. Philadelphia: Psychology Press.

Roza, S. J., Verburg, B. O., Jaddoe, V. W., Hofman, A., Mackenbach, J. P., Steegers, E. A., Witteman, J. C., Verhulst, F. C., Tiemeir, H. (2007). Effects of maternal smoking in pregnancy on prenatal brain development: The Generation R study. *European Journal of Neuroscience, 25,* 611–627.

Rubin, K. H., Bukowski, W., & Parker, J. G. (2006). Peer interactions, relationships, and groups. In W. Damon & R. Lerner (Eds.), *Handbook of child psychology* (6th ed.). New York: Wiley.

Ruble, D. (1983). The development of social comparison processes and their role in achievement-related self-socialization. In E. Higgins, D. Ruble, & W. Hartup (Eds.), *Social cognitive development: A social-cultural perspective.* New York: Cambridge University Press.

Ruble, D. N., Martin, C. L., & Berenbaum, S. A. (2006). Gender development. In W. Damon & R. Lerner (Eds.), *Handbook of child psychology* (6th ed.). New York: Wiley.

Rubnitz, J. E., Razzouk, B. I., Lensing, S., Pounds, S., Pui, C. H., & Ribeiro, R. C. (2006). Prognostic factors and outcome of recurrence in childhood acute myeloid leukemia. *Cancer, 109,* 157–163.

Ruddell, R. B. (2006). *Teaching children to read and write* (4th ed.). Boston: Allyn & Bacon.

Ruff, H. A., & Capozzoli, M. C. (2003). Development of attention and distractibility in the first 4 years of life. *Developmental Psychology, 39,* 877–890.

Ruff, H. A., & Rothbart, M. K. (1996). *Attention in early development.* New York: Oxford University Press.

Rumberger, R. W. (1995). Dropping out of middle school: A multilevel analysis of students and schools. *American Education Research Journal, 3,* 583–625.

Runco, M. A. (Ed.). (2006). *Creativity research handbook.* Creskill, NJ: Hampton Press.

Runquist, J. (2007). Persevering through postpartum fatigue. *Journal of Obstetric, Gynecologic, and Neonatal Nursing, 36,* 28–37.

Russell, S. T., Joyner, K. (2001). Adolescent sexual orientation and suicide risk: Evidence from a national study. *American Journal of Public Health, 91,* 1276–1281.

Russman, B. S., & Ashwal, S. (2004). Evaluation of the child with cerebral palsy. *Seminars in Pediatric Neurology, 11,* 47–57.

Rutter, M. (2007). Gene-environment interdependence. *Developmental Science, 10,* 12–18.

Rutter, M., & Schopler, E. (1987). Autism and pervasive developmental disorders: Concepts and diagnostic issues. *Journal of Autism and Pervasive Developmental Disorders, 17,* 159–186.

Ryan, R. & Deci, E. (2000). Self-determination theory and the facilitation of intrinsic motivation, social development, and well-being. *American Psychologist, 55,* 68–78.

Ryan, R. M., & Deci, E. L. (2001). When rewards compete with nature. In C. Sansone & J. M. Harackiewicz (Eds.), *Intrinsic and extrinsic motivation.* San Diego: Academic Press.

Ryan, R. M., Fauth, R. C., & Brooks-Gunn, J. (2006). Childhood poverty: Implications for school readiness and early childhood education. In B. Spodek & O. N. Saracho (Eds.), *Handbook of research on the education of young children.* Mahwah, NJ: Erlbaum.

Ryan, S. D., Pearlmutter, S., & Groza, V. (2004). Coming out of the closet: Opening agencies to gay and lesbian adoptive parents. *Social Work, 49,* 85–95.

S

Saarni, C. (2002). Unpublished review of J. W. Santrock's *Life-span development* (10th ed.). New York: McGraw-Hill.

Saarni, C. (2006). Emotion regulation and personality development in childhood. In D. K. Mroczek & T. D. Little (Eds.), *Handbook of personality development.* Mahwah, NJ: Erlbaum.

Saarni, C., Campos, J., Camras, L. A., & Witherington, D. (2006). Emotional development. In W. Damon & R. Lerner (Eds.), *Handbook of child psychology* (6th ed.). New York: Wiley.

Sabol, W. J., Coulton, C. J., & Korbin, J. E. (2004). Building community capacity for violence prevention. *Journal of Interpersonal Violence, 19,* 322–340.

Sachs-Ericsson, N., Blazer, D., Plant, A. E., & Arnow, B. (2005). Childhood sexual and physical abuse and the 1-year prevalence of medical problems in the National Comorbidity Study. *Health Psychology, 24,* 32–40.

Sacker, A., Quigley, M. A., & Kelly, Y. J. (2006). Breastfeeding and developmental delay: Findings from the millennium cohort study. *Pediatrics, 118,* e682–e689.

Sackett, P. R., Hardison, C. M., & Cullen, M. J. (2004). On interpreting stereotype threat as accounting for African-American White differences in cognitive tests. *American Psychologist, 59,* 7–13.

Sadeharju, K., & others (2007). Maternal antibodies in breast milk protect the child from enterovirus infections. *Pediatrics, 119,* 941–946.

Saffran, J. R., Werker, J. F., & Werner, L. A. (2006). The infant's auditory world: Hearing, speech, and the beginnings of language. In W. Damon & R. Lerner (Eds.), *Handbook of child psychology* (6th ed.). New York: Wiley.

Sagi, A., Koren-Karie, N., Gini, M., Ziv, Y., & Joels, T. (2002). Shedding further light on the effects of various types and quality of early child care on infant-mother attachment relationship: The Haifa study of early child care. *Child Development. 73,* 1166–1186.

Salmelin, R. (2007). Clinical neurophysiology of language: The MEG approach. *Clinical Neurophysiology, 118,* 237–254.

Salmon, J., Campbell, K. J., & Crawford, D. A. (2006). Television viewing habits associated with obesity risk factors: A survey of Melbourne schoolchildren. *Medical Journal of Australia, 184,* 64–67.

Salovey, P., & Grewal, D. (2005). The science of emotional intelligence. *Current Directions in Psychological Science, 14,* 281–285.

Salovy, P., & Mayer, J. D. (1990). Emotional intelligence. *Imagination, Cognition, and Personality, 9,* 185–211.

Samuels, M., & Samuels, N. (1996). *New well pregnancy book.* New York: Fireside.

Sanchez-Johnsen, L. A., Fitzgibbon, M. L., Martinovich, Z., Stolley, M. R., Dyer, A. R., & Van Horn, L. (2004). Ethnic differences in correlates of obesity between Latin-American and black Women. *Obesity Research, 12,* 652–660.

Sandberg, D. E., & Colsman, M. (2005). Growth hormone treatment of short stature: Status of the quality of life rationale. *Hormone Research, 63,* 275–283.

Sandefur, G. D., & Meier, A. (2007). The family environment: Structure, material resources, and child care. In B. Brown (Ed.), *Key indicators of child and youth well-being.* Mahwah, NJ: Earlbaum.

Sandiford, R. (2006). Keeping it natural. *Nursing Times, 102,* 22–23.

Sanson, A., & Rothbart, M. K. (1995). Child temperament and parenting. In M. H. Bornstein (Ed.), *Handbook of parenting* (Vol. 4). Hillsdale, NJ: Erlbaum.

Sansone, C., & Smith, J. L. (2001). Interest and self-regulation. In C. Sansone & J. M. Harakiewicz (Eds.), *Intrinsic and extrinsic motivation.* San Diego: Academic Press.

Santelli, J. S., Lindberg, L. D., Finer, L. B., & Singh, S. (2007). Explaining recent declines in adolescent pregnancy in the United States: The contribution of abstinence and improved contraceptive use. *American Journal of Public Health, 97,* 150–156.

Santelli, J., Ott, M. A., Lyon, M., Rogers, J., Summers, D., & Schleifer, R. (2006). Abstinence and abstinence-only education: A review of U.S. policies and programs. *Journal of Adolescent Health, 38,* 72–81.

Santiago-Delefosse, M. J., & Delefosse, J. M. O. (2002). Three positions on child thought and language. *Theory and Psychology, 12,* 723–747.

Santrock, J. W., Sitterle, K. A., & Warshak, R. A. (1988). Parent-child relationships in stepfather families. In P. Bronstein & C. P. Cowan (Eds.), *Fatherhood today: Men's changing roles in the family.* New York: Wiley.

Santrock, J. W., & Warshak, R. A. (1979). Father custody and social development in boys and girls. *Journal of Social Issues, 35,* 112–125.

Sanz, M. A. (2006). Treatment of acute promyelocytic leukemia. *Hematology,* 147–155.

Sarigiani, P. A., & Petersen, A. C. (2000). Adolescence: Puberty and biological maturation. In A. Kazdin (Ed.), *Encyclopedia of psychology.* Washington, DC, & New York: American Psychological Association and Oxford University Press.

Saudino, K. J. (2005). Behavioral genetics and child temperament. *Journal of Developmental and Behavioral Pediatrics, 26,* 214–223.

Sausenthaler, S., Kompauer, I., Mielck, A., Borte, M., Herbarth, O., Schaaf, B., von Berg, A., & Heinrich, J. (2007). Impact of parental education and income equality on children's food intake. *Public Health Nutrition, 10,* 24–33.

Savage, R., Cornish, K., Manly, T., & Hollis, C. (2006). Cognitive processes in children's reading and attention: The role of working memory, divided attention, and response inhibition. *British Journal of Psychology, 97,* 365–385.

Savin-Williams, R. C. (2001). *Mom, dad, I'm gay.* Washington, DC: American Psychological Association.

Savin-Williams, R. C. (2006). *The new gay teenager.* Cambridge, MA: Harvard University Press.

Savin-Williams, R. C., & Diamond, L. (2004). Sex. In R. Lerner & L. Steinberg (Eds.), *Handbook of adolescent psychology.* New York: Wiley.

Sax, L. J., & Bryant, A. N. (2006). The impact of college on sex-atypical career choices of men and women. *Journal of Vocational Behavior, 68,* 52–63.

Sayal, K., Heron, J., Golding, J., & Emond, A. (2007). Prenatal alcohol exposure and gender differences in childhood mental health problems: A longitudinal population-based study. *Pediatrics, 119,* e426–e434.

Sayer, L. C. (2006). Economic aspects of divorce and relationship dissolution. In M. A. Fine & J. H. Harvey (Eds.), *Handbook of divorce and relationship dissolution.* Mahwah, NJ: Erlbaum.

Scafidi, F., & Field, T. M. (1996). Massage therapy improves behavior in neonates born to HIV-positive mothers. *Journal of Pediatric Psychology, 21,* 889–897.

Scaramella, L. V., & Conger, R. D. (2004). Continuity versus discontinuity in parent and adolescent negative effect. In R. D. Conger, F. O. Lorenz, & K. A. S., Wickrama (Eds.), *Continuity and change in family relations.* Mahwah, NJ: Erlbaum.

Scarlett, W. G. (2006). Toward a developmental analysis of religious and spiritual development. In E. C. Roehkepartain, P. E. King, L. Wagner, & P. L. Benson (Eds.), *Handbook of spiritual development in childhood and adolescence.* Thousand Oaks, CA: Sage.

Scarr, S. (1993). Biological and cultural diversity: The legacy of Darwin for development. *Child Development, 64,* 1333–1353.

Scarr, S., & Weinberg, R. A. (1983). The Minnesota adoption studies: Genetic differences and malleability. *Child Development, 54,* 182–259.

Schachter, S. C., & Ransil, B. I. (1996). Handedness distributions in nine professional groups. *Perceptual and Motor Skills, 82,* 51–63.

Schack-Nielson, L., & Michaelsen, K. F. (2007). Advances in our understanding of the biology of human milk and its effect on offspring. *Journal of Nutrition, 137,* 503S–510S.

Schaechter, J., Duran, I., De Marchena, J., Lemard, G., & Villar, M. E. (2003). Are "accidental" gun deaths as rare as they seem? *Pediatrics, 111,* 741–744.

Schaffer, H. R. (1996). *Social development.* Cambridge, MA: Blackwell.

Schaie, K. W. (2007). Generational differences: The age-cohort period model. In J. E. Birren, (Ed.). *Encyclopedia of Gerontoloogy* (2nd ed.). Oxford, UK: Elsevier.

Schattschneider, C., Fletcher, J. M., Francis, D. J., Carlson, C. D., & Foorman, B. R. (2004). Kindergarten prediction of reading skills: A longitudinal comparative analysis. *Journal of Educational Psychology, 96,* 265–282.

Schauble, L. (1990). Belief revision in children: The role of prior knowledge and strategies for generating evidence. *Journal of Experimental Child Psychology, 49,* 31–57.

Schegel, A. (2000). The global spread of adolescent culture. In L. J. Crockett & R. K. Silbereisen (Eds.), *Negotiating adolescence in times of social change.* New York: Cambridge University Press.

Scheinfeld, N., & Bangalore, S. (2006). Facial edema induced by isotretinoin use: A case and a review of the side effects of isotretinoin. *Journal of Drugs and Dermatology, 5,* 467–468.

Schindler, S. & others (2007). The effects of large neutral amino acid supplements in PKU: An MRS and neuropsychological study. *Molecular Genetics and Metabolism, 91,* 48–54.

Schlegel, M. (2000). All work and play. *Monitor on Psychology 31* (No. 11), 50–51.

Schmidt, M. D., Pekow, P., Freedson, P. S., Markenson, G., & Chasan-Taber, L. (2006). Physical activity patterns during pregnancy in a diverse population of women. *Journal of Women's Health, 15,* 909–918.

Schmidt, M. E., & Anderson, D. R. (2007). The impact of television on cognitive development and achievement. In N. Pecora, J. P. Murray, & E. A. Wartella (Eds.), *Children and television.* Mahwah, NJ: Erlbaum.

Schmidt, U. (2003). Aetiology of eating disorders in the 21st century: New answers to old questions. *European Child and Adolescent Psychiatry, 12* (Suppl 1) S1130–S1137.

Schmitt, D. P., & Pilcher, J. J. (2004). Evaluating evidence of psychological adaptation: How do we know one when we see one? *Psychological Science, 15,* 643–649.

Schnake, E. M., Peterson, N. M., & Corden, T. E. (2005). Promoting water safety: The physician's role. *Wisconsin Journal of Medicine, 104,* 45–49.

Schneider, W. (2004). Memory development in childhood. In P. Smith & C. Hart (Eds.), *Blackwell handbook of childhood cognitive development.* Malden, MA: Blackwell.

Schneider, W., & Pressley, M. (1997). *Memory development from 2 to 20* (2nd ed.). Mahwah, NJ: Erlbaum.

Schooler, D., Ward, L. M., Merriwether, A., & Caruthers, A. (2004). Who's that girl: Television's role in the body image development of young White and Black women. *Psychology of Women Quarterly, 28,* 38–47.

Schoppe-Sullivan, S. J., Mangelsdorf, S. C., Brown, G. L., & Sokolowski, M. S. (2007). Goodness-of-fit in family context: Infant temperament, marital quality, and early coparenting behavior. *Infant Behavior and Development, 30,* 82–96.

Schrag, S. G., & Dixon, R. L. (1985). Occupational exposure associated with male reproductive dysfunction. *Annual Review of Pharmacology and Toxicology, 25,* 467–592.

Schraw, G. (2006). Knowledge structures and processes. In P. A. Alexander & P. H. Winne (Eds.), *Handbook of educational psychology* (2nd ed.). Mahwah, NJ: Erlbaum.

Schreiber, L. R. (1990). *The parent's guide to kids' sports.* Boston: Little, Brown.

Schulenberg, J. E., & Zarett, N. R. (2006). Mental health during emerging adulthood: Continuity and discontinuity in courses, causes, and functions. In J. J. Arnett & J. L. Tanner (Eds.), *Emerging adults in America.* Washington, DC: American Psychological Association.

Schunk, D. H. (2008). *Learning theories* (5th ed.). Upper Saddle River, NJ: Prentice Hall.

Schunk, D. H., & Zimmerman, B. J. (2006). Competence and control beliefs. In P. A. Alexander & P. H. Wynne (Eds.), *Handbook of educational psychology* (2nd ed.). Mahwah, NJ: Erlbaum.

Schweinhart, L. J., Montie, J., Xiang, Z., Barnett, W. S., Belfield, C. R., & Nores, M. (2005). *Lifetime effects: The High/Scope Perry Preschool Study through age 40.* Ypsilanti, MI: High/Scope Press.

Schwenk, W. F. (2006). Growth hormone therapy—established uses in short children. *Acta Pediatrica Supplement, 95,* S6–S8.

Scott-Jones, D. (1995, March). *Incorporating ethnicity and socioeconomic status in research with children.* Paper presented at the meeting of the Society for Research in Child Development, Indianapolis.

Scourfield, J., Van den Bree, M., Martin, N., & McGuffin, P. (2004). Conduct problems in children and adolescents: A twin study. *Archives of General Psychiatry, 61,* 489–496.

Search Institute. (1995). *Barriers to participation in youth programs.* Unpublished manuscript, the Search Institute, Minneapolis.

Sedlak, A. J., Schultz, D., Wells, S. J., Lyons, P., Doueck, H. J., & Gragg, F. (2006). Child protection and justice systems processing of serious abuse and neglect cases. *Child Abuse and Neglect, 30,* 657–677.

Seidenfeld; M. E., Sosin, E., & Rickert, V. I. (2004). Nutrition and eating disorders in adolescents. *Mt. Sinai Journal of Medicine, 71,* 155–161.

Seidman, L. J. (2006). Neuropsychological functioning in people with ADHD across the lifespan. *Clinical Psychology Review, 26,* 466–485.

Seifert, K. L. (2006). Cognitive development and the education of young children. In B. Spodak & N. Saracho (Eds.), *Handbook of research on the education of young children* (2nd ed.). Mahwah, NJ: Erlbaum.

Sellers, R. M., Copeland-Linder, N., Martin, P. P., & Lewis, R. L. (2006). Racial identity matters: The relationship between racial discrimination and psychological functioning in African American adolescents. *Journal of Research on Adolescence, 16,* 187–216.

Selman, R. L. (1980). *The growth of interpersonal understanding.* New York: Academic Press.

Serow, R. C., Ciechalski, J., & Daye, C. (1990). Students as volunteers. *Urban Education, 25,* 157–168.

Serpell, R. (2000). Culture and intelligence. In A. Kazdin (Ed.), *Encyclopedia of psychology.* Washington, DC, & New York: American Psychological Association and Oxford University Press.

Sewell, T. E. (2000). School dropout. In A. Kazdin (Ed.), *Encyclopedia of psychology.* Washington, DC, & New York: American Psychological Association and Oxford University Press.

Shaibi, G. Q., Ball, G. D., & Goran, M. I. (2006). Aerobic fitness among Caucasian, African American, and Latino youth. *Ethnicity and Disease, 16,* 120–125.

Shamah, T., & Villalpando, S. (2006). The role of enriched foods in infant and child nutrition. *British Journal of Nutrition, 96* (Suppl. 1), S73–S77.

Shani, R., Fifer, W. P., & Myers, M. M. (2007). Identifying infants at risk for sudden infant death syndrome. *Current Opinion in Pediatrics, 19,* 145–149.

Shankaran, S., Lester, B. M., Das, A., Bauer, C. R., Bada, H. S., Lagasse, L., & Higgins, R. (2007). Impact of maternal substance use during pregnancy on childhood outcome. *Seminars in Fetal and Neonatal Medicine, 12,* 143–150.

Shapiro, A. F., and Gottman, J. M. (2005). Effects on marriage of a psycho-education intervention with couples undergoing the transition to parenthood, evaluation at 1-year post-intervention. *Journal of Family Communication, 5,* 1–24.

Sharma, A. R., McGue, M. K., & Benson, P. L. (1996). The emotional and behavioral adjustment of adopted adolescents: Part I: Age at adoption. *Children and Youth Services Review, 18,* 101–114 Juffer, F., & van Ijzendoorn, M. H. (2005). Behavior problems and mental health referrals of international adoptees: A meta-analysis. *Journal of the American Medical Association, 293,* 2501–2513.

Sharma, B. R. (2007). Sudden infant death syndrome: A subject of microlegal research. *American Journal of Forensic Medicine and Pathology, 28,* 69–72.

Sharma, H. P., Hansel, N. N., Matsui, E., Diette, G. B., Eggleston, P., & Breysse, P. (2007). Indoor environmental influences on children's asthma. *Pediatric Clinics of North America, 54,* 103–120.

Sharma, M. (2006). School-based interventions for childhood and adolescent obesity. *Obesity Review, 7,* 261–269.

Sharp, L., Cardy, A. H., Cotton, S. C., & Little, J. (2004). CYP 17 gene polymorphisms: Prevalence and associations with hormone levels and related factors, a Huge review. *American Journal of Epidemiology, 160,* 729–740.

Shastry, B. S. (2007). Assessment of the contribution of the LOC387715 gene polymorphism in a family with exudative age-related macular generation and heterozygous CFH variant (Y402H). *Journal of Human Genetics, 52,* 384–387.

Shatz, M., & Gelman, R. (1973). The development of communication skills: Modifications in the speech of young children as a function of the listener. *Monographs of the Society for Research in Child Development, 38* (Serial No. 152).

Shaw, D., Gilliom, M., Ingoldsby, E. M., & Nagin, D. S. (2003). Trajectories leading to school-age conduct problems. *Developmental Psychology, 39,* 189–200.

Shaywitz, B. A., Lyon, G. R., & Shaywitz, S. E. (2006). The role of functional magnetic resonance imaging in understanding reading and dyslexia. *Developmental Neuropsychology, 30,* 613–632.

Shea, A., Walsh, C., MacMillan, H., & Steiner, M. (2005). Child maltreatment and HPA axis dysregulation: Relationship to major depressive disorder and post traumatic stress disorder in females. *Psychoneuroendocrinology, 30,* 162–178.

Sheeber, L. B., Davis, B., Leve, C., Hops, H., & Tildesley, E. (2007). Adolescents' relationships with their mothers and fathers: Associations with depressive disorder and subdiagnostic symptomatology. *Journal of Abnormal Psychology, 116,* 144–154.

Shema, L., Ore, L., Ben-Shachar, M., Haj, M., & Linn, S. (2007, in press). The association between breastfeeding and breast cancer occurrence among Israeli Jewish women: A case control study. *Journal of Cancer Research and Clinical Oncology.*

Shi, L., & Stevens, G. D. (2005). Disparities in access to care and satisfaction among U. S. children: The roles of race/ethnicity and poverty status. *Public Health Report, 120,* 431–441.

Shields, S. A. (1991). Gender in the psychology of emotion. In K. T. Strongman (Ed.), *International Review of Studies of Emotion* (Vol. 1). New York: Wiley.

Shiner, R. L. (2006). Temperament and personality in childhood. In D. K. Mrocezek & T. D. Little (Eds.), *Handbook of personality development.* Mahwah, NJ: Erlbaum.

Shiraev, E., & Levy, D. (2007). *Cross-cultural psychology: Critical thinking and critical applications* (3rd ed.). Boston: Allyn & Bacon.

Shiva, F., Nasiri, M., Sadeghi, B., & Padyab, M. (2004). Effects of passive smoking on common respiratory symptoms in young children. *Acta Pediatrics, 92,* 1394–1397.

Shribman, S. (2007). Adolescence: An opportunity not to be missed. *Lancet, 369,* 1788–1799.

Shweder, R., Goodnow, J., Hatano, G., LeVine, R. A., Markus, H., & Miller, P. (2006). The cultural psychology of development. In W. Damon & R. Lerner (Eds.), *Handbook of child psychology* (6th ed.). New York: Wiley.

Siega-Ritz, A. M., Siega-Ritz, A. M., & Laraira, B. (2006). The implications of maternal overweight and obesity on the course of pregnancy and birth outcomes. *Maternal and Child Health Journal, 10* (Suppl. 7), S153–S156.

Siegel, L. S. (2003). Learning disabilities. In I. B. Weiner (Ed.), *Handbook of psychology,* (Vol. VI). New York: Wiley.

Siegler, R. S. (2006). Microgenetic analysis of learning. In W. Damon & R. Lerner (Eds.). *Handbook of child psychology* (6th ed.). New York: Wiley.

Siegler, R. S. (2007). Cognitive variability. *Developmental Science 10*, 104–109.

Siegler, R. S., & Alibali, M. W. (2005). *Children's thinking* (4th ed.). Upper Saddle River, NJ: Prentice Hall.

Sigman, M., Cohen, S. E., & Beckwith, L. (2000). Why does infant attention predict adolescent intelligence? In D. Muir & A. Slater (Eds.), *Infant development: Essential readings.* Malden, MA: Blackwell.

Signore, R. J. (2004). Bradley method offers option for natural childbirth. *American Family Physician, 70*, 650.

Silberman, M. (2006). *Teaching actively.* Boston: Allyn & Bacon.

Silva, C. (2005, October 31). When teen dynamo talks, city listens. *Boston Globe.* pp. B1, B4.

Sim, T. N., & Ong, L. P. (2005). Parent punishment and child aggression in a Singapore Chinese preschool sample. *Journal of Marriage and the Family, 67*, 85–99.

Simkin, P., Whalley, J., & Keppler, A. (2001). *Pregnancy, childbirth, and the newborn* (rev. and updated ed.). Minnetonka, MN: Meadowood Publishers.

Simmons, R. G., & Blyth, D. A. (1987). *Moving into adolescence.* Hawthorne, NY: Aldine.

Simons-Morton, B., Haynie, D. L., Crump, A. D., Eitel, P., & Saylor, K. E. (2001). Peer and parent influences on smoking and drinking among early adolescents. *Health Education and Behavior, 28*, 95–107.

Simpkin, P., & Bolding, A. (2004). Update on nonpharmacological approaches to relieve labor pain and prevent suffering. *Journal of Midwifery and Women's Health, 49*, 489–504.

Simpkins, S. D., Fredricks, J. A., Davis-Kean, P. E., & Eccles, J. S. (2006). Healthy mind, healthy habits: The influence of activity involvement in middle childhood. In A. C. Huston & M. N. Ripke (Eds.), *Developmental contexts in middle childhood.* New York: Cambridge University Press.

Simpson, R. L. (1962). Parental influence, anticipatory socialization, and social mobility. *American Sociological Review, 27*, 517–522.

Singh, S., Darroch, J. E., Vlasoff, M., & Nadeau, J. (2004). *Adding it up: The benefits of investing in sexual and reproductive health care.* New York: The Alan Guttmacher Institute.

Singh, S., Wulf, D., Samara, R., & Cuca, Y. P. (2000). Gender differences in the timing of first intercourse. Data from 14 countries. *International Family Planning Perspectives, 26*, 21–28, 43.

Sinha, J. W., Cnaan, R. A., & Gelles, R. J. (2007). Adolescent risk behaviors and religion: Findings from a national study. *Journal of Adolescence, 30*, 231–249.

Sizer, F., & Whitney, E. (2006). *Nutrition* (10th ed.), Belmont, CA: Wadsworth.

Skinner, B. F. (1938). *The behavior of organisms: An experimental analysis.* New York: Appelton-Century-Crofts.

Skinner, B. F. (1957). *Verbal behavior.* New York: Appleton-Century-Crofts.

Skinner, J. D., Ziegler, P., Pac, S., & Devaney, B. (2004). Meal and snack patterns of infants and toddlers. *Journal of the American Dietic Association.* 104. 65–70.

Skipper, J. I., Goldin-Meadow, S., Nusbaum, H. C., & Small, S. L. (2007). Speech-associated gestures, Broca's area, and the human mirror system. *Brain and Language, 101*, 260–277.

Slade, E. P., & Wissow, L. S. (2004). Spanking in early childhood and later behavior problems: A prospective study. *Pediatrics, 113*, 1321–1330.

Slater, A., Field, T., & Hernandez-Reif, M. (2007). The development of the senses. In A. Slater & M. Lewis (Eds.), *Introduction to infant development* (2nd ed.). New York: Oxford University Press.

Slater, A., Morison, V., & Somers, M. (1988). Orientation discrimination and cortical function in the human newborn. *Perception.* 17, 597–602.

Slater, A., Quinn, P., Lewkowicz, D. J., Hayes, R. & Brookes, H. (2003). Learning of arbitrary adult voice-face pairings at three months of age. In O. Pascalis & A. Slater (Eds.), *The development of face processing in infancy and early childhood.* New York: NOVA Science.

Slater, A., & Lewis, M. (Eds.) (2007). *Introduction to infant development* (2nd ed.). New York: Oxford University Press.

Sleet, D. A., & Mercy, J. A. (2003). Promotion of safety, security, and well-being. In M. H. Bornstein, L. Davidson, C. L. M., Keyes, & K. A. Moore (Eds.), *Well-being* Mahwah, NJ: Erlbaum.

Sleet, D. A., Schieber, R. A., & Gilchrist, J. (2003). Health promotion policy and politics: Lessons from childhood injury prevention. *Health Promotion and Practice, 4*, 103–108.

Slijper, F. M., Drop, S. L., Molennar, J. C., & de Muinck Keizer-Schrama, S. M. (1998). Long-term psychological evaluation of intersex children. *Archives of Sexual Behavior, 27*, 125–144.

Sljivic, S., & others. (2006). Possible interactions of genetic and immuno-neuroendocrine regulatory mechanisms in pathogenesis of congenital anomalies. *Medical Hypotheses, 67*, 57–64.

Slobin, D. (1972, July). Children and language: They learn the same way around the world. *Psychology Today*, 71–76.

Slomkowski, C., Rende, R., Conger, K. J., Simons, R. L., & Conger, R. D. (2001). Sisters, brothers, and delinquency: Social influence during early and middle adolescence. *Child Development, 72*, 271–283.

Slombowksi, C., Rende, R., Novak, S., Lloyd-Richardson, E., & Niaura, R. (2005).

Sibling effects on smoking in adolescence: Evidence for social influence from a genetically informative design. *Addiction, 100*, 430–438.

Slykerman, R. F., Thompson, J. M., Clark, P. M., Becroft, D. M., Robinson, E., Pryor, J. E., Wild, C. J., & Mitchell, E. A. (2007). Determinants of developmental delay in infants aged 12 months. *Pediatric and Perinatal Epidemiology, 21*, 121–128.

Smedje, H., Broman, J. E., & Hetta, J. (2001). Associations between disturbed sleep and behavioral difficulties in 635 children aged six to eight years: A study based on parent's perceptions. *European Journal of Child and Adolescent Psychiatry, 10*, 1–9.

Smetana, J. G. (2006). Social domain theory. In M. Killen & J. G. Smetana (Eds.), *Handbook of moral development.* Mahwah, NJ: Erlbaum.

Smetana, J., Campione-Barr, N., & Metzger, A. (2006). Adolescent development in interpersonal and societal contexts. *Annual Review of Psychology.* (Vol. 57). Palo Alto, CA: Annual Reviews.

Smith, A. C., Choufani, S., Ferreira, J. C., & Weksberg, R. (2007). Growth regulation, imprinted genes, and chromosome 11p15.5. *Pediatric Research, 61*, 43R–47R.

Smith, B. (2007). *The psychology of Sex and Gender.* Boston: Allyn & Bacon.

Smith, C. A., & Crowther, C. A. (2004). Acupuncture for the induction of labor. *Cochrane Database of Systematic Review, 1*, CD0029262.

Smith, C. A., Collins, C. T., Cyna, A. M., & Crowther, C. A. (2006). Complementary and alternative therapies for pain management in labor. *Cochrane Database of Systematic Reviews, 4*, CD003521.

Smith, D. (2005). *Working with gifted and talented pupils in the secondary school.* Thousand Oaks, CA: Sage.

Smith, D. D. (2007). *Introduction to special education* (6th ed.). Boston: Allyn & Bacon.

Smith, J. G., & Merrill, D. C. (2006). Oxytocin for induction of labor. *Clinical Obstetrics and Gynecology, 49*, 594–608.

Smith, K. (2002). *Who's minding the kids? Child care arrangements: Spring 1977.* Current Population Reports, P70–86. Washington, DC: U.S. Census Bureau.

Smith, L., Muir, D. W., & Kisilevsky, B. (2001, April). *Preterm infants' responses to auditory stimulation of varying intensity.* Paper presented at the meeting of the Society for Research in Child Development, Minneapolis.

Smith, L. A., Oyeku, S. O., Homer, C., & Zuckerman, B. (2006). Sickle cell disease: A question of equity and quality. *Pediatrics, 117*, 1763–1770.

Smith, L. B. (1999). Do infants possess innate knowledge structures? The con side. *Developmental Science, 2*, 133–144.

Smith, L. B., & Breazeal, C. (2007). The dynamic lift of developmental processes. *Developmental Science, 10,* 61–68.

Smith, L. M., Chang, L., Yonekura, M. L., Gilbride, K., Kuo, J., Poland, R. E., Walot, L., & Ernst, T. (2001). Brain proton magnetic resonance spectroscopy and imaging in children exposed to cocaine in utero. *Pediatrics, 107,* 227.

Smith, R. A., & Davis, S. (2007). *The psychologist as detective* (4th ed.). Upper Saddle River, NJ: Prentice Hall.

Smith, S. S. (2006). *Early childhood mathematics* (3rd ed.). Upper Saddle River, NJ: Prentice Hall.

Smith, T. E. C., Polloay, E. A., Patton, J. R., & Dowdy, C. A. (2006). *Teaching students with special needs in inclusive settings* (4th ed., Update). Boston: Allyn & Bacon.

Smith, T. E. C., Polloway, E. A., Patton, J. R., & Dowdy, C. A. (2008). *Teaching students with special needs in inclusive settings* (5th ed.). Boston: Allyn & Bacon.

Snarey, J. (1987, June). A question of morality. *Psychology Today,* pp. 6–8.

Snow, C. E., & Kang, J. Y. (2006). Becoming bilingual, biliterate, and bicultural. In W. Damon & R. Lerner (Eds.), *Handbook of child psychology* (6th ed.). New York: Wiley.

Snowdon, A. W., Polgar, J., Patrick, L., & Stamler, L. (2006). Parent's knowledge about and use of child safety systems. *Canadian Journal of Nursing Research, 38,* 98–114.

Snyder, H. N., & Sickmund, M. (1999, October). *Juvenile offenders and victims: 1999 national report.* Washington, DC: National Center for Juvenile Justice.

Sobo, E. J., Seid, M., & Reves Gelhard, L. (2006). Parent-identified barriers to pediatric health care: A process-oriented approach. *Health Services Research, 41,* 148–172.

Soderman, A. K., & Farrell, P. (2008). *Creating literacy-rich preschools and kindergartens.* Boston: Allyn & Bacon.

Soergel, P., Pruggmayer, M., Schwerdtfeger, R., Mulhaus, K., & Scharf, A. (2006). Screening for trisomy 21 with maternal age, fetal nuchal translucency, and maternal serum biochemistry at 11–14 weeks: A regional experience from Germany. *Fetal Diagnosis and Therapy, 21,* 264–268.

Solomon, D., Battistich, V., Watson, M., Schaps, E., & Lewis, C. (2000). A six-district study of educational change: Direct and mediated effects of the Child Development Project. *Social Psychology of Education, 4,* 3–51.

Solomon, D., Watson, M, Schapes, E., Battistich, V., & Solomon, J. (1990). Cooperative learning as part of a comprehensive program designed to promote prosocial development. In S. Sharan (Ed.), *Cooperative learning: Theory and research* New York: Praeger.

Solomon, D., Watson, M. S., & Battistich, V. A. (2002). Teaching and school effects on moral/ prosocial development. In V. Richardson (Ed.), *Handbook for research on teaching.* Washington, DC: American Educational Research Association.

Solomon, D., Watson, M. S., Delucchi, K., Schaps, E., & Battistich, V. (1988). Enhancing children's prosocial behavior in the classroom. *American Educational Research Journal, 25,* 527–554.

Sonek, J. (2007). First trimester ultrasonography in screening and detection of fetal abnormalities. *American Journal of Genetics C, 145,* 45–61.

Sophian, C. (1985). Perseveration and infants' search: A comparison of two- and three-location tasks. *Developmental Psychology, 21,* 187–194.

Sorof, J. M., & Daniels, S. (2002). Obesity hypertension: A problem of epidemic proportions. *Hypertension, 404,* 441–447.

Sorof, J. M., Lai, D., Turner, J., Poffenberger, T., & Portman, R. J. (2004). Overweight, ethnicity, and the prevalence of hypertension in school-aged children. *Pediatrics, 113,* 475–482.

Sotir, M., Yeats, K., Miller, W., & Shy, C. (2006). Comparison of asthma-related functional consequences and health care utilization among children with and without upper respiratory infection-triggered wheezing. *Journal of Asthma, 43,* 629–632.

Sowell, E. (2004, July). Commentary in M. Beckman, "Crime, culpability, and the adolescent brain." *Science Magazine, 305,* 599.

Sowell, E. R., Thompson, P. M., Leonard, C. M., Welcome, S. E., Kan, E., & Toga, A. W. (2004). Longitudinal mapping of cortical thickness and brain growth in children. *Journal of Neuroscience, 24,* 8223–8231.

Spafford, C. S., & Grosser, G. S. (2005). *Dyslexia and reading difficulties* (2nd ed.). Boston: Allyn & Bacon.

Spear, L. P. (2007). Brain development and adolescent behavior. In D. Coch, G. Dawson, & K. W. Fischer (Eds.), *Human behavior, learning, and the developing brain.* New York: Guilford.

Spearman, C. E. (1927). *The abilities of man.* New York: Macmillan.

Spelke, E. S. (1979). Perceiving bimodally specified events in infancy. *Developmental Psychology, 5,* 626–636.

Spelke, E. S. (1991). Physical knowledge in infancy: Reflections on Piaget's theory. In S. Carey & R. Gelman (Eds.), *The epigenesis of mind: Essays on biology and cognition.* Hillsdale, NJ: Erlbaum.

Spelke, E. S. (2000). Core knowledge. *American Psychologist, 55,* 1233–1243.

Spelke, E. S., Breinlinger, K., Macomber, J., & Jacobson, K. (1992). Origins of knowledge. *Psychological Review, 99,* 605–632.

Spelke, E. S., & Hespos. S. J. (2001). Continuity, competence, and the object concept. In E. Dupoux (Ed.), *Language, brain, and behavior.* Cambridge, MA: Bradford/MIT Press.

Spelke, E. S. & Newport, E. L. (1998). Nativism, empiricism, and the development of knowledge. In W. Damon (Ed.), *Handbook of child psychology* (5th ed., Vol. 2). New York: Wiley.

Spelke, E. S., & Owsley, C. J. (1979). Intermodal exploration and knowledge in infancy. *Infant Behavior and Development, 2,* 13–28.

Spence, J. T., & Buckner, C. E. (2000). Instrumental and expressive traits, trait stereotypes, and sexist attitudes: What do they signify? *Psychology of Women Quarterly, 24,* 44–62.

Spence, J. T., & Helmreich, R. (1978). *Masculinity and feminity: Their psychological dimensions.* Austin: University of Texas Press.

Spence, M. J., & DeCasper, A. J. (1987). Prenatal experience with low-frequency maternal voice sounds influences neonatal perception of maternal voice samples. *Infant Behavior and Development, 10,* 133–142.

Spencer, J. P., Vereijken, B., Diedrich, F. J., & Thelen, E. (2000). Posture and the emergence of manual skills. *Developmental Science, 3,* 216–233.

Spencer, M. B. (1999). Social and cultural influences on school adjustment: The application of the identity-focused cultural ecological perspective. *Educational Psychologist, 34,* 43–57.

Spencer, M. B. (2001). Resiliency and fragility factors associated with the contextual experiences of low-resource urban African-American male youth and families. In A. Booth & A. C. Crouter (Eds.), *Does it take a village?* Mahwah, NJ: Erlbaum.

Spencer, M. B. (2006). Phenomendogy and ecological systems theory: Development of diverse groups. In W. Damon & R. Lerner (Eds.), *Handbook of child psychology* (6th ed.). New York: Wiley.

Spencer, M. D., Moorhead, T. W., Lymer, G. K., Job, D. E., Muir, W. J., Hoare, P., Owens, D. G., Lawrie, S. M., & Johnstone, E. C. (2006). Structural correlates of intellectual impairment and autistic features in adolescents. *Neuroimage, 33,* 1136–1144.

Spencer, S. (2005). Giving birth on the beach: Hypnosis and psychology. *Practicing Midwife, 8,* 27–29.

Speranza, M., Corcos, M., Loas, G., Stephan, P., Guilbaud, O., Perez-Diaz, F., Venisse, J. L., Bizouard, P., Halfon, O., Flament, M., & Jeammet, P. (2005). Depressive personality dimensions and alexithymia in eating disorders. *Psychiatry Research, 135,* 153–163.

Spohr, H. L., Willms, J., & Steinhausen, H. C. (2007). Fetal alcohol spectrum disorders in young adulthood. *Journal of Pediatrics, 150,* 175–179.

Spring, J. (2007). *Deculturalization and the struggle for equality* (5th ed.). New York: McGraw-Hill.

Spring, J. (2008). *American education* (13th ed.). New York: McGraw-Hill.

Springer, S. P., & Deutsch, G. (1985). *Left brain, right brain.* San Francisco: Freeman.

Sprinthall, R. C. (2007). *Basic statistical analysis* (8th ed.). Boston: Allyn & Bacon.

Spry, M., Scott, T., Pierce, H., & D'Orazio, J. A. (2007). DNA repair pathways and hereditary cancer susceptibility syndromes. *Frontiers in Bioscience, 12,* 4191–4207.

Srabstein, J. C., McCarter, R. J., Shao, C., & Huang, Z. J. (2006). Morbidities associated with bullying behaviors in adolescents: School based study of American adolescents. *International Journal of Adolescent Medicine and Health, 18,* 587–596.

Srinivasan, S. R., Frontini, M. G., Xu, J., & Berenson, G. S. (2006). Utility of non-high density cholesterol levels in predicting adult dyslipidemia and other cardiovascular risks. *Pediatrics, 118,* 201–206.

Sroufe, L. A. (2000, Spring). The inside scoop on child development: Interview. *Cutting through the hype.* Minneapolis: College of Education and Human Development, University of Minnesota.

Sroufe, L. A. (2007). Commentary: The place of development in developmental psychology. In A. Masten (Ed.), *Multilevel dynamics in developmental psychology.* Mahwah, NJ: Erlbaum.

Sroufe, L. A., Egeland, B., Carlson, E., & Collins, W. A. (2005). The place of early attachment in developmental context. In K. E. Grossman, K. Krossman, & E. Waters (Eds.), *The power of longitudinal attachment research: From infancy and childhood to adulthood.* New York: Guilford.

Sroufe, L. A., Egeland, B., Carlson, E., & Collins, W. A. (2006). The place of early attachment in developmental context. In K. E. Grossman, K. Krossman, & E. Waters (Eds.), *The power of longitudinal attachment research: From infancy and childhood to adulthood.* New York: Guilford.

Sroufe, L. A., Waters, E., & Matas, L. (1974). Contextual determinants of infant affectional response. In M. Lewis & L. Rosenblum (Eds.), *Origins of fear.* New York: Wiley.

Stanford University Medical Center. (2007). *Growth hormone deficiency.* Palo Alto, CA: Author.

Starkey, P., Klein, A., & Wakeley, A. (2004). Enhancing young children's mathematical knowledge through a pre-kindergarten mathematics intervention. *Early Childhood Research Quarterly, 19,* 99–120.

Stattin, H., & Magnusson, D. (1990). *Pubertal maturation in female development: Paths through life* (Vol. 2). Hillsdale, NJ: Erlbaum.

Steele, C. M., & Aronson, J. (1995). Stereotype threat and the intellectual test performance of African-Americans. *Journal of Personality and Social Psychology, 69,* 797–811.

Steele, C. M., & Aronson, J. A. (2004). Stereotype threat does not live by Steele and Aronson (1995) alone. *American Psychologist, 59,* 47–48.

Steen, T. A., Kachorek, L. V., & Peterson, C. (2003). Character strengths among youth. *Journal of Youth and Adolescence. 32,* 5–16.

Steer, A. J., & Lehman, E. B. (2000). Attachment to transitional objects. *American Journal of Orthopsychiatry, 70,* 340–350.

Stein, D. J., Fan, J., Fossella, J., & Russell, V. A. (2007). Inattention and hyperactivity-impulsivity: Psychobiological and evolutionary underpinnings. *CNS Spectrum, 12,* 190–196.

Stein, M. T., Kennell, J. H., & Fulcher, A. (2004). Benefits of a doula present at the birth of a child. *Journal of Developmental and Behavioral Pediatrics, 25* (Suppl. 5), S89–S92.

Stein, M. T., & Perrin, J. M. (2003). Diagnosis and treatment of ADHD in school-age children in primary care settings: A synopsis of the AAP practice guidelines. *Pediatric Review, 24,* 92–98.

Steinberg, L. D. (2007). Risk taking in adolescence. *Current Directions in Psychological Science, 16,* 55–59.

Steinberg, L. D. (1986). Latchkey children and susceptibility to peer pressure: An ecological analysis. *Developmental Psychology, 22,* 433–439.

Steinberg, L. D., Blatt-Eisengart, I., & Cauffman, E. (2006). Patterns of competence and adjustment among adolescents from authoritative, authoritarian, indulgent, and neglectful homes: A replication in a sample of serious juvenile offenders. *Journal of Research on Adolescence, 16,* 47–58.

Steinberg, L. D., & Levine, A. (1997). *You and your adolescent* (2nd ed.). New York: Harper Perennial.

Steinberg, L. D., & Silk, J. S. (2002). Parenting adolescents. In M. Bornstein (Ed.), *Handbook of parenting* (2nd ed., Vol. 1). Mahwah, NJ: Erlbaum.

Steiner, J. E. (1979). Human facial expressions in response to taste and smell stimulation. In H. Reese & L. Lipsitt (Eds.), *Advances in child development* (Vol. 13). New York: Academic Press.

Steinman, K. J. & Zimmerman, M. A. (2004). Religious activity and risk behavior among African-American adolescents: Concurrent and developmental effects. *American Journal of Community Psychology, 33* (3), 151–161.

Stephan, K. E., Fink, G. R., & Marshall, J. C. (2007). Mechanisms of hemispheric specialization: Insights from analyses of connectivity. *Neuropsychologia, 45,* 209–228.

Stephens, B. K., Barkey, M. E., & Hall, H. R. (1999). Techniques to comfort children during stressful procedures. *Advances in Mind-Body Medicine. 15,* 49–60.

Stern, D. N., Beebe, B., Jaffe, J., & Bennett, S. L. (1977). The infant's stimulus world during social interaction: A study of caregiver behaviors with particular reference to repetition and timing. In H. R. Schaffer (Ed.), *Studies in mother-infant interaction.* London: Academic Press.

Sternberg, R. J. (1977). *Intelligence, information processing, and analogical reasoning: The componential analysis of human abilities.* Hillsdale, NJ: Erlbaum.

Sternberg, R. J. (1986). *Intelligence applied.* San Diego: Harcourt Brace Jovanovich.

Sternberg, R. J. (2002). Intelligence: The triarchic theory of intelligence. In J. W. Gutherie (Ed.), *Encyclopedia of education* (2nd ed.). New York: Macmillan.

Sternberg, R. J. (2004). Individual differences in cognitive development. In U. Goswami (Ed.), *Blackwell handbook of childhood cognitive development.* Malden, MA: Blackwell.

Sternberg, R. J. (2006). *Cognitive psychology* (4th ed.). Belmont, CA: Wadsworth.

Sternberg, R. J. (2007). g, g's, or jeez: Which is the best model for developing abilities, competence, and expertise? In P. C. Kyllonen, R. D. Roberts, & L. Stankov (Eds.), *Extending intelligence.* Mahwah, NJ: Erlbaum.

Sternberg, R. J. (2007b). Unpublished review of J. W. Santrock's *Child development* (12th ed.). New York: McGraw-Hill.

Sternberg, R. J. (2008, in press). The triarchic theory of successful intelligence. In N. Salkind (Ed.), *Encyclopedia of educational psychology.* Thousand Oaks, CA: Sage.

Sternberg, R. J., & Rifkin, B. (1979). The development of analogical reasoning processes. *Journal of Experimental Child Psychology, 27,* 195–232.

Sternberg, R. J., Grigorenko, E. L., & Kidd, K. K. (2005). Intelligence, race, and genetics. *American Psychologist, 60,* 46–59.

Sternberg, R. J., & Nigro, C. (1980). Developmental patterns in the solution of verbal analogies. *Child development, 51,* 27-38

Sternberg, R. J., Grigorenko, E. L., & Kidd, K. K. (2006). Racing toward the finish line. *American Psychologist, 61,* 178–179.

Sternberg, R. J., Nokes, K., Geissler, P. W., Prince, R., Okatcha, F., Bundy, D. A., & Grigorenko, E. L. (2001). The relationship between academic and practical intelligence: A case study in Kenya. *Intelligence, 29,* 401–418.

Sternberg, R. J., Roediger, H., & Halpern, D. (eds.) (2006). *Critical thinking in psychology.* Mahwah, NJ: Erlbaum.

Stetsenko, A. (2002). Adolescents in Russia: Surviving the turmoil and creating a brighter future. In B. B. Brown, R. W. Larson, & T. S. Saraswathi (Eds.), *The World's youth.* New York: Cambridge University Press.

Steur, F. B., Applefield, J. M., & Smith, R. (1971). Televised aggression and interpersonal aggression of preschool children. *Journal of Experimental Child Psychology, 11,* 442–447.

Stevens, T., & Mulsow, M. (2006). There is no meaningful relationship between television exposure and symptoms of attention-deficit/hyperactivity disorder. *Pediatrics, 117,* 665–672.

Stevenson, H. W. (1995). Mathematics achievement of American students: First in the world by the year 2000? In C. A. Nelson (Ed.), *Basic and applied perspectives on learning, cognition, and development.* Minneapolis: University of Minnesota Press.

Stevenson, H. W. (2000). Middle childhood: Education and schooling. In A. Kazdin (Ed.), *Encyclopedia of psychology.* Washington, DC, & New York: American Psychological Association and Oxford University Press.

Stevenson, H. W., Hofer, B. K., & Randel, B. (1999). *Middle childhood: Education and schooling.* Unpublished manuscript, Dept. of Psychology, University of Michigan, Ann Arbor.

Stevenson, H. W., Lee, S., & Stigler, J. W. (1986). Mathematics achievement of Chinese, Japanese, and American children. *Science. 231.* 693–699.

Stevenson, H. W., Lee, S., Chen, C., Stigler, J. W., Hsu, C., & Kitamura, S. (1990). Contexts of achievement. *Monograph of the Society for Research in Child Development, 55* (Serial No. 221).

Stevenson, H. W., & Newman, R. S. (1986). Long-term prediction of achievement and attitudes in mathematics and reading. *Child Development, 57,* 646–659.

Stevenson, H. W., & Zusho, A. (2002). Adolescence in China and Japan: Adapting to a changing environment. In B. B. Brown, R. W. Larson, & T. S. Saraswathi (Eds.), *The world's youth.* New York: Cambridge University Press.

Stice, E., Presnell, K., Gau, J., & Shaw, H. (2007). Testing mediators of intervention effects in randomized controlled trials: An evaluation of two eating disorder programs. *Journal of Consulting and Clinical Psychology, 75,* 20–32.

Stice, E., Presnell, K., & Spangler, D. (2002). Risk factors for binge eating onset in adolescent girls: A 2-year prospective investigation. *Health Psychology, 21,* 131–138.

Stiggins, R. (2008). *Introduction to student-involved assessment for learning* (5th ed.). Upper Saddle River, NJ: Prentice Hall.

Stipek, D. J. (2002). *Motivation to learn* (4th ed.). Boston: Allyn & Bacon.

Stipek, D. J. (2004). Head Start: Can't we have our cake and eat it too? *Education Week, 23* (No. 34), 52–53.

Stipek, D. J. (2005, February 16). Commentary in *USA TODAY,* p. 1D.

Stipek, D., Recchia, S., & McClintic, S. (1992). Self-evaluation in young children. *Monographs of the Society for Research in Child Development, 57* (1, Serial No. 226).

Stocker, C., & Dunn, J. (1990). Sibling relationships in adolescence: Links with friendships and peer relationships. *British Journal of Developmental Psychology, 8,* 227–244.

Stoel-Gammon, C., & Sosa, A. V. (2007). Phonological development. In E. Hoff & M. Shatz (Eds.), *Blackwell handbook of language development.* Malden, MA: Blackwell.

Stolley, M. R., Fitzgibbon, M. L., Dyer, A., Van Horn, L., Kaufer Christoffel, K., & Schiffer, L. (2003). Hip-Hop to Health Jr., an obesity prevention program for minority preschool children: Baseline characteristics of the participants. *Preventive Medicine, 36,* 320–329.

Story, M., Kaphingst, K. M., & French, S. (2006). The role of schools in obesity prevention. *Future of Children, 16,* (No. 1), 109–142.

Stouthamer-Loeber, M., Loeber, R., & Wei, E. Farrington, D. P., & Wikstrom, P. H. (2002). Risk and promotive effects in the explanation of serious delinquency in boys. *Journal of Consulting and Clinical Psychology, 20,* 111–123.

Stouthamer-Loeber, M., Wei, E., Loeber, R., & Masten, A. (2004). Desistance from persistent serious delinquency in the transition to adulthood. *Development and Psychopathology, 16,* 897–918.

Strauss, M. A., Sugarman, D. B., & Giles-Sims, J. (1997). Spanking by parents and subsequent anti-social behavior in children. *Archives of Pediatrics and Adolescent Medicine, 151,* 761–767.

Strauss, R. S. (2001). Environmental tobacco smoke and serum vitamin C levels in children. *Pediatrics, 107,* 540–542.

Streib, H. (1999). Off-road religion? A narrative approach to fundamentalist and occult orientation of adolescents. *Journal of Adolescence, 22,* 255–267.

Streissguth, A. P., Martin, D. C., Sandman, B. M., Kirchner, G. L., & Darby, B. L. (1984). Intrauterine alcohol and nicotine exposure: Attention and reaction time in four-year-old children. *Developmental Psychology, 20,* 533–543.

Streri, A. (1987) Tactile discrimination of shape and intermodal transfer in two-to three-month-old infants. *British Journal of Developmental Psychology, 5,* 213–220.

Striano, T., Reid, V. M., & Hoehl, S. (2006). Neural mechanisms of joint attention in infancy. *European Journal of Neuroscience, 23,* 2819–2823.

Striegel-Moore, R. H., Silberstein, L. R., & Rodin, J. (1993). The social self in bulimia nervosa: Public self-consciousness, social anxiety, and perceived fraudulence. *Journal of Abnormal Psychology, 102,* 297–303. (p. 406)

Stringer, M., Ratcliffe, S. J., Evans, E. C., & Brown, L. P. (2005). The cost of prenatal care attendance and pregnancy outcomes in low-income working women. *Journal of Obstetrical, Gynecologic, and Neonatal Nursing, 34,* 551–560.

Stroganova, T. A., Pushina, N. P., Orekhova, E. V., Posikera, I. N., & Tsetlin, M. M. (2004). Functional brain asymmetry and individual differences in hand preference in early ontogeny, *Human Physiology, 30,* 20–30.

Strong, B., Yarber, W., Sayad, B., & DeVault, C. (2008). *Human sexuality* (6th ed.). New York: McGraw-Hill.

Sue, S. (1990, August). *Ethnicity and culture in psychological research and practice.* Paper presented at the meeting of the American Psychological Association, Boston.

Sugita, Y. (2004). Experience in early infancy is indispensable for color perception. *Current Biology, 14,* 1267–1271.

Sullivan, H. S. (1953). *The interpersonal theory of psychiatry.* New York: W. W. Norton.

Sullivan, K., & Sullivan, A. (1980). Adolescent-parent separation. *Developmental Psychology, 16,* 93–99.

Sung, H. E., Richter, L., Vaughan, R., Johnson, P. B., & Thom, B. (2005). Nonmedical use of prescription opioids among teenagers in the United States: Trends and correlates. *Journal of Adolescent Health, 37,* 44–51.

Suomi, S. J., Harlow, H. F., & Domek, C. J. (1970). Effect of repetitive infant-infant separations of young monkeys. *Journal of Abnormal Psychology, 76,* 161–172.

Super, C., & Harkness, S. (1997). The cultural structuring of child development. In J. W. Berry, Y. H. Poortinga, & J. Pandey (Eds.), *Handbook of cross-cultural psychology: Theory and method.* Vol. 2. Boston: Allyn & Bacon.

Super, D. E. (1976). *Career education and the meanings of work.* Washington, DC: U.S. Office of Education.

Suris, J. C., Jeannin, A., Chossis, I., & Michaud, P. A. (2007). Piercing among adolescents: Body art as a risk marker: A population-based study. *Journal of Family Practice, 56,* 126–130.

Susman, E. J., Dorn, L. D., & Schiefelbein, V. L. (2003). Puberty, sexuality, and health. In R. M. Lerner, M. A. Easterbrooks, & J. Mistry (Eds.), *Comprehensive handbook of psychology: Developmental psychology* (Vol. 6). New York: Wiley.

Susman, E. J., & Rogol, A. (2004). Puberty and psychological development. In R. Lerner & L. Steinberg, (Eds.), *Handbook of adolescence.* New York: Wiley.

Sutterby, J. A., & Frost, J. (2006). Creating play environments for early childhood: Indoors and out. In B. Spodek & O. N. Saracho (Eds.), *Handbook of research on the education of young children* (2nd ed.). Mahwah, NJ: Erlbaum.

Sutton-Smith, B. (2000). Play. In A. Kazdin (Ed.), *Encyclopedia of psychology.* Washington, DC, & New York: American Psychology Association and Oxford University Press.

Swaab, D. F., Chung, W. C., Kruijver, F. P., Hofman, M. A., & Ishunina, T. A. (2001). Structural and functional sex differences in the human hypothalamus. *Hormones and Behavior, 40,* 93–98.

Swanson, B. J., Roman-Shriver, C. R., Shriver, B. J., & Goodell, L. S. (2007, in press). A comparison between improvers and non-improvers among children with anemia enrolled in the WIC program. *Maternal and Child Health Journal.*

Swanson, H. L. (1999). What develops in working memory? A life-span perspective. *Developmental Psychology, 35,* 986–1000.

Swanson, H. L. (2005). Memory. In S. W. Lee (Ed.), *Encyclopedia of school psychology.* Thousand Oaks, CA: Sage.

Sykes, C. J. (1995). *Dumbing down our kids: Why American children feel good about themselves but can't read write, or add.* New York: St. Martin's Press.

T

Tager-Flusberg, H. (2005). Morphology and syntax in the preschool years. In J. Berko Gleason, *The development of language* (6th ed.). Boston: Allyn & Bacon.

Takai, Y., Sato, M., Tan, R., & Hirai, T. (2005). Development of stereo acuity: Longitudinal design using a computer-based random-dot stereo test. *Japanese Journal of Ophthalmology, 49,* 1–5.

Talaro, K. P. (2008). *Foundations of microbiology* (6th ed.). New York: McGraw-Hill.

Talge, N. M., Neal, C., Glover, V., & the Early Stress, Translational Research and Prevention Science Network: Fetal and Neonatal Experience on Child and Adolescent Mental Health. (2007). Antenatal maternal stress and long-term effects on neurodevelopment: How and why? *Journal of Child Psychology and Psychiatry, 48,* 245–261.

Tam, W. H., & Chung, T. (2007). Psychosomatic disorders in pregnancy. *Current Opinion in Obstetrics and Gynecology, 19,* 126–132.

Tamura, T., & Picciano, M. F. (2006). Folate and human reproduction. *American Journal of Human Reproduction, 83,* 993–1016.

Tang, C. H., Wu, M. P., Liu, J. T., Liu, H. C., & Hsu, C. C. (2006). Delayed parenthood and the risk of cesarean delivery—is paternal age an independent risk factor? *Birth, 33,* 18–26.

Tannen, D. (1990). *You just don't understand!* New York: Ballantine.

Tantillo, M., Kesick, C. M., Hynd, G. W., & Dishman, R. K. (2002). The effects of exercise on children with attention-deficit hyperactivity disorder. *Medical Science and Sports Exercise, 34,* 203–212.

Tappia, P. S., & Gabriel, C. A. (2006). Role of nutrition in the development of the fetal cardiovascular system. *Expert Review of Cardiovascular Therapy, 4,* 211–215.

Tasker, F. L., & Golombok, S. (1997). *Growing up in a lesbian family: Effects on child development.* New York: Guilford.

Tassell-Baska, J., & Stambaugh, T. (2006). *Comprehensive curriculum for gifted learners* (3rd ed.). Boston: Allyn & Bacon.

Tauman, R., & Gozal, D. (2006). Obesity and obstructive sleep apnea in children. *Pediatric Respiratory Reviews, 7,* 247–259.

Taylor, F. M. A., Ko, R., & Pan, M. (1999). Prenatal and reproductive health care. In E. J. Kramer, S. L. Ivey, & Y. W. Ying (Eds.), *Immigrant women's health.* San Francisco: Jossey-Bass.

Taylor, R. D., & Lopez, E. I. (2005). Family management practice, school achievement, and problem behavior in African American adolescents: Mediating processes. *Applied Developmental Psychology, 26,* 39–49.

Taylor, S. E., & Stanton, A. L. (2007). Coping resources, Coping processes, and mental health. *Annual Review of Clinical Psychology,* (Vol. 3). Palo Alto, CA: Annual Reviews.

Temple, C. A., MaKinster, J. G., Buchmann, L. G., Logue, J., Mrvova, G., & Gearan, M. (2005). *Intervening for literacy.* Boston: Allyn & Bacon.

Templeton, J. L., & Eccles, J. S. (2006). The relation between spiritual development and identity processes. In E. Roehlkepartain, P. E. King, L. Wagener, & P. L. Benson (Eds.), *The handbook of spirituality in childhood and adolescence.* Thousand Oaks, CA: Sage.

Tenenbaum, H. R., Callahan, M., Alba-Speyer, C., & Sandoval, L. (2002). Parent child science conversations in Mexican descent families: Educational background, activity, and past experience as moderators. *Hispanic Journal of Behavioral Sciences, 24,* 225–248.

Terman, D. L., Larner, M. B., Stevenson, C. S., & Behrman, R. E. (1996). Special education for students with disabilities: Analysis and recommendations. *The Future of Children, 6* (1), 4–24.

Terman, L. (1925). *Genetic studies of genius. Vol. 1: Mental and physical traits of a thousand gifted children.* Stanford, CA: Stanford University Press.

Terry, W. S. (2006). Learning and memory (3rd ed.). Boston: Allyn & Bacon.

Teti, D. (2001). Retrospect and prospect in the psychological study of sibling relationships. In J. P. McHale & W. S. Grolnick (Eds.), *Retrospect and prospect in the psychological study of families.* Mahwah, NJ: Erlbaum.

Teti, D. M., Sakin, J., Kucera, E., Caballeros, M., & Corns, K. M. (1993, March). *Transitions to siblinghood and security of firstborn attachment:*

Psychosocial and psychiatric correlates of changes over time. Paper presented at the biennial meeting of the Society for Research in Child Development, New Orleans.

Thapar, A., Fowler, T., Rice, F., Scourfield, J., Van Den Bree, M., Thomas, S., Harold, G., & Hay, D. (2003). Maternal smoking during pregnancy and attention deficit hyperactivity disorder symptoms in offspring. *American Journal of Psychiatry, 160,* 1985–1989.

Tharp, R. G. (1994). Intergroup differences among Native Americans in socialization and child cognition: An orthogenetic analysis. In P. M. Greenfield & R. Cocking (Eds.), *Crosscultural roots of minority child development.* Mahwah, NJ: Erlbaum.

Tharp, R. G., & Gallimore, R. (1988). *Rousing minds to life: Teaching, learning, and schooling in social context.* New York: Cambridge University Press.

Thelen, E. (1995). Motor development: A new synthesis. *American Psychologist, 50,* 79–95.

Thelen, E. (2000). Perception and motor development. In A. Kazdin (Ed.), *Encyclopedia of psychology.* Washington, DC, & New York: American Psychological Association and Oxford University Press.

Thelen, E. (2001). Dynamic mechanisms of change in early perceptual-motor development. In J. L. McClelland & R. S. Siegler (Eds.), *Mechanisms of cognitive development.* Mahwah, NJ: Erlbaum.

Thelen, E., Corbetta, D., Kamm, K., Spencer, J. P., Schneider, K., & Zernicke, R. F. (1993). The transition to reaching: Mapping intention and intrinsic dynamics. *Child Development, 64,* 1058–1098.

Thelen, E., & Smith, L. B. (1998). Dynamic systems theory. In W. Damon (Ed.), *Handbook of child psychology* (5th ed., Vol. 1.), New York: Wiley.

Thelen, E., & Smith, L. B. (2006). Dynamic development of action and thought. In W. Damon & R. Lerner (Eds.), *Handbook of child psychology* (6th ed.). New York: Wiley.

Thelen, E., & Whitmeyer, V. (2005). Using dynamic systems theory to conceptualize the interface of perception, action, and cognition. In J. J. Reiser, J. J. Lockman, & C. A. Nelson (Eds.), *The role of action in learning and development.* Mahwah, NJ: Erlbaum.

Theobold, M. A. (2005). *Increasing student motivation.* Thousand Oaks, CA: Sage.

Thomas, A., & Chess, S. (1991). Temperament in adolescence and its functional significance. In R. M. Lerner, A. C. Petersen, & J. Brooks-Gunn (Eds.), *Encyclopedia of adolescence* (Vol. 2). New York: Garland.

Thomas, K. (1998, November 4). Teen cyberdating is a new wrinkle for parents, too. *USA Today,* p. 9D.

Thompson, C. M. (2006). Repositioning the visual arts in early childhood education: A decade of reconsideration. In B. Spodek & O. N.

Saracho (Eds.), *Handbook of research on the education of young children* (2nd ed.). Mahwah, NJ: Erlbaum.

Thompson, D. R., Obarzanek, E., Franko, D. L., Barton, B. A., Morrison, J., Biro, F. M., Daniels, S. R., & Striegel-Moore, R. H. (2007). Childhood overweight and cardiovascular disease risk factors: The National Heart, Lung, and Blood Institute Growth and Health Study. *Journal of Pediatrics, 150,* 18–25.

Thompson, M. P., Ho, C. H., & Kingree, J. B. (2007). Prospective associations between delinquency and suicidal behaviors in a nationally representative sample. *Journal of Adolescent Health, 40,* 232–237.

Thompson, P. M., Giedd, J. N., Woods, R. P., MacDonald, D., Evans, A. C., & Toga, A. W. (2000). Growth patterns in the developing brain detected by using continuum mechanical tensor maps. *Nature, 404,* 190–193.

Thompson, R. A. (1994). Emotion regulation: A theme in search of a definition. *Monographs of the Society for Research in Child Development, 59* (Serial No. 240), 2–3.

Thompson, R. A. (2006). The development of the person. In W. Damon & R. Lerner (Eds.), *Handbook of child psychology* (6th ed.). New York: Wiley.

Thomson, R. A. (2007). Unpublished review of J. W. Santrock's, *Children* (10th ed.). New York: McGraw-Hill.

Thompson, R. A., Easterbrooks, M. A., & Walker, L. (2003). Social and emotional development in infancy. In I. B. Weiner (Ed.), *Handbook of psychology* (Vol. 6). New York: Wiley.

Thompson, R. A., & Goodvin, R. (2005). The individual child: Temperament, emotion, self, and personality. In M. H. Bornstein & M. E. Lamb (Eds.), *Developmental psychology* (5th ed.). Mahwah, NJ: Erlbaum.

Thompson, R. A., & Lagattuta, K. H. (2005). Feeling and understanding: Early emotional development. In K. McCartney & D. Phillips (Eds.), *The Blackwell handbook of early childhood development.* Malden, MA: Blackwell.

Thompson, R. A., Meyer, S., & McGinley, M. (2006). Understanding values in relationships: The development of conscience. In M. Killen & J. Smetana (Eds.), *Handbook of moral development.* Mahwah, NJ: Erlbaum.

Thompson, R. A., & Nelson, C. A. (2001). Developmental science and the media. *American Psychologist, 56,* 5–15.

Thoni, A., & Moroder, L. (2004). Waterbirth: A safe and natural delivery method. Experience after 1355 waterbirths in Italy. *Midwifery Today, 70,* 44–48.

Thorton, A., & Camburn, D. (1989). Religious participation and sexual behavior and attitudes. *Journal of Marriage and the Family, 49,* 117–128.

Thornton, P. L., Kieffer, E. C., Salbarian-Pena, Y., Odoms-Young, A., Willis, S. K., Kim, H., & Salinas, M. A. (2006). Weight, diet, and physical activity-related health beliefs and practices among pregnant and postpartum Latino women: The role of social support. *Maternal and Child Health Journal, 10,* 95–104.

Thurstone, L. L. (1938). *Primary mental abilities.* Chicago: University of Chicago Press.

Tinsley, B. J. (2003). *How children learn to be healthy.* New York: Cambridge University Press.

Tinsley, B. J., Markey, C. N., Ericken, A. J., Kwasman, A., & Ortiz, R. V. (2002). Health promotion for parents. In M. H. Bornstein (Ed.), *Handbook of parenting* (Vol. 5). Mahwah, NJ: Erlbaum.

Tobin, J. J., Wu, D. Y. H., & Davidson, D. H. (1989). *Preschool in three cultures.* New Haven, CT: Yale University Press.

Toga, A. W., Thompson, P. M., & Sowell, E. R (2006). Mapping brain maturation. *Trends in Neuroscience, 29,* 148–159.

Tolan, P. H. (2001). Emerging themes and challenges in understanding youth violence. *Journal of Clinical Child Psychology, 30,* 233–239.

Tomasello, M. (2003). *Constructing a language: A usage based theory of language acquisition.* Cambridge, MA: Harvard University Press.

Tomasello, M. (2006). Acquiring linquistic constructions. In W. Damon & R. Lerner (Eds.), Handbook of child psychology (6th ed). New York: Wiley.

Tomasello, M., & Carpenter, M. (2007). Shared intentionality. *Developmental Science, 10,* 121–125.

Tomasello, M., Carpenter, M., & Liszkowski, U. (2007). A new look at infant pointing. *Child Development, 78,* 705–722.

Tompkins, G. E. (2006). *Literacy for the 21st century* (4th ed.). Upper Saddle River, NJ: Prentice Hall.

Torgesen, J. K. (1999). Reading disabilities. In R. Gallimore, L. P. Bernheimer, D. L. MacMillan, D. L. Speece, & S. Vaughan (Eds.), *Developmental perspectives on children with learning disabilities.* Mahwah, NJ: Erlbaum.

Torjesen, I. (2007). Tackling the obesity burden. *Nursing Times, 103,* 23–24.

Tough, S. C., Newburn-Cook, C., Johnston, D. W., Svenson, L. W., Rose, S., & Belik, J. (2002). Delayed childbearing and its impact on population rate changes in lower birth weight, multiple birth, and preterm delivery. *Pediatrics, 109,* 399–403.

Tozer, S. E., Senese, G., & Violas, P. C. (2005). *School and society* (5th ed.). New York: McGraw-Hill.

Treffers, P. E., Eskes, M., Kleiverda, G., & van Alten, D. (1990). Home births and minimal medical interventions. *Journal of the American Medical Association, 246,* 2207–2208.

Trehub, S. E., Schneider, B. A., Thorpe, L. A., & Judge, P. (1991). Observational measures of auditory sensitivity in early infancy. *Developmental Psychology, 27,* 40–49.

Treuth, M. S., Sunehag, A. L., Trautwein, L. M., Bier, D. M., Haywood, M. W., & Butte, N. F. (2003). Metabolic adaptation to high-fat and high-carbohydrate diets in children and adolescents. *American Journal of Clinical Nutrition, 77,* 479–489.

Trimble, J. E. (1988, August). *The enculturation of contemporary psychology.* Paper presented at the meeting of the American Psychological Association, New Orleans.

Trowell, J. (2006). Child abuse and neglect: Attachment, development, and intervention. *Journal of Child Psychology and Psychiatry, 47,* 533–534.

Trulear, H. D. (2000). *Faith-based institutions and high-risk youth: First report to the field.* Philadelphia, PA: Public/Private Ventures.

Trzesniewski, K. H., Donnellan, M. B., Caspi, A., Moffitt, T. E., Robins, R. W., & Poultin, R. (2006). Adolescent low self-esteem is a risk factor for adult poor health, criminal behavior, and limited economic prospects. *Developmental Psychology, 42,* 381–390.

Tucker, J. S., Ellickson, P. L., & Klein, M. S. (2003). Predictors of the transition to regular smoking during adolescence and young adulthood. *Journal of Adolescent Health, 32,* 314–324.

Tuckman, B. W., & Hinkle, J. S. (1988). An experimental study of the physical and psychological effects of aerobic exercise on school children. In B. G. Melamed, K. A. Matthews, D. K. Routh, B. Stabler, & N. Schneiderman (Eds.), *Child health psychology.* Hillsdale, NJ: Erlbaum.

Turiel, E. (2006). The development of morality. In W. Damon & R. Lerner (Eds.), *Handbook of child psychology* (6th ed.). New York: Wiley.

Turkeltaub, P. E., Gareau, L., Flowers, D. L., Zeffiro, T. A., & Eden, G. F. (2003). Development of neural mechanisms for reading. *Nature Neuroscience, 6,* 767–773.

Turnbull, A., Turnbull, H. R., & Tompkins, J. R. (2007). *Exceptional lives* (5th ed.). Upper Saddle River, NJ: Prentice Hall.

Tzischinsky, O., & Latzer, Y. (2006). Sleep-wake cycles in obese children with and without binge-eating episodes. *Journal of Pediatric Child Health, 42,* 68–693.

U

U.S. Department of Energy. (2001). *The human genome project.* Washington, DC: Author.

U.S. Department of Health and Human Services. (2003). *Child abuse and neglect statistics.* Washington, DC: Author.

U.S. Food and Drug Administration. (2004, March 19). An important message for pregnant woman and women of childbearing age who may become pregnant about the risk of mercury in fish. Washington, DC: Author.

U.S. Office of Education. (2000). *To assure a free and appropriate public education of all children with disabilities.* Washington, DC: Author.

Uba, L. (1992). Cultural barriers to health care for Southeast Asian refugees. *Public Health Reports, 107,* 544–549.

Ulvund, S. E., & Smith, L. (1996). The predictive validity of nonverbal communicative skills in infants with perinatal hazards. *Infant Behavior and Development, 19,* 441–449.

Umana-Taylor, A. J. (2006, March). *Ethnic identity, acculturation, and enculturation: Considerations in methodology and theory.* Paper presented at the meeting of the Society for Research on Adolescence, San Francisco.

Umana-Taylor, A. J., Bhanot, R., & Shin, N. (2006). Ethnic identity formation in adolescence: The critical role of families. *Journal of Family Issues, 27,* 390–414.

Underwood, M. K. (2004). Gender and peer relations: Are the two cultures really all that different? In J. B. Kupersmidt & K. A. Dodge (Eds.), *Children's peer relations: From development to intervention.* Mahwah, NJ: Erlbaum.

UNICEF. (2004). *State of the world's children: 2004.* Geneva: Author.

UNICEF. (2006). *The state of the world's children 2006.* Geneva: Author.

UNICEF. (2007). *The state of the world's children 2007.* Geneva: Author.

Urbano, M. T., & Tait, D. M. (2004). Can the irradiated uterus sustain a pregnancy? *Clinical Oncology, 16,* 24–28.

USA Today. (1999). *All-USA TODAY Teacher Team.* Retrieved January 15, 2004, from www.usatoday.com/news/education/1999

V

Vacca, J. A. L., Vacca, R. T., Gove, M. K., Burkey, L. C., Lenhart, L. A., & McKeon, C. A. (2006). *Reading and learning to read* (6th ed.). Boston: Allyn & Bacon.

Vahratian, A., Siega-Riz, A. M., Savitz, D. A., & Throp, J. M. (2004). Multivitamin use and risk of preterm birth. *American Journal Epidemiology, 160,* 886–892.

Valdimarsson, O., Linden, C., Johnell, O., Gardsell, P., & Karlsson, M. K. (2006). Daily physical education in the school curriculum in prepubertal girls during 1 year is followed by an increase in bone mineral accrual and bone width—data from the prospective controlled Malmo pediatric osteoporosis prevention study. *Calcified Tissue International, 78,* 65–71.

Van Beveren, T. T. (2007, January). *Personal conversation.* Richardson, TX: Department of Psychology, University of Texas at Dallas.

Van Buren, E., & Graham, S. (2003). *Redefining ethnic identity: Its relationship to positive and negative school adjustment outcomes for minority youth.* Paper presented at the meeting of the Society for Research in Child Development, Tampa.

Van de Walle, J. A., & Lovin, L. A. (2006). *Teaching student-centered mathematics: Grades K-3.* Boston: Allyn & Bacon.

van den Boom, D. C. (1989). Neonatal irritability and the development of attachment. In G. A. Kohnstamm, J. E. Bates, & M. K. Rothbart (Eds.), *Temperament in childhood.* New York: Wiley.

Van Goozen, S. H. M. Matthys, W., Cohen-Kettenis, P. T., Thisjssen, J. H. H., & van Engeland, H. (1998). Adrenal androgens and aggression in conduct disorder prepubertal boys and normal control. *Biological Psychiatry, 43,* 156–158.

van Ijzendoorn, M. H., Juffer, F., & Poelhuis, C. W. (2005). Adoption and cognitive development: A meta-analytic comparison of adopted and nonadopted children's IQ and school performance. *Psychological Bulletin, 131,* 301–316.

van IJzendoorn, M. H., & Kroonenberg, P. M. (1988). Cross-cultural patterns of the Strange Situation. *Child Development, 59,* 147–156.

Vandell, D. L. (2004). Early child care: The known and unknown. *Merrill-Palmer Quarterly, 50,* 387–414.

Vandell, D. L., & Wilson, K. S. (1988). Infants' interactions with mother, sibling, and peer: Contrasts and relations between interaction systems. *Child Development, 48,* 176–186.

Vargas, L., & Koss-Chiono, J. (1999). *Working with Latino youth.* San Francisco. Jossey-Bass.

Vaughn, S. S., Bos, C. S., & Schumm, J. S. (2007). *Teaching students who are exceptional, diverse, and at risk in the general education classroom* (4th ed.). Boston: Allyn & Bacon.

Venners, S. A., Wang, X., Chen, C., Wang, L., Chen, D., Guang, W., Huang, A., Ryan, L., O'Conner, J., Lasley, B., Overstreet, J., Wilcox, A., & Xu, X. (2005). Paternal smoking and pregnancy loss: A prospective study using a biomarker of pregnancy. *American Journal of Epidemiology, 159,* 993–1001.

Verkooijen, K. T., de Vries, N. K., & Nielsen, G. A. (2007). Youth crowds and substance use: The impact of perceived group norm and multiple group identification. *Psychology of Addictive Behaviors, 21,* 55–61.

Verma, S., & Saraswathi, T. S. (2002). Adolescence in India: Street urchins or silicon valley millionaires? In B. B. Brown, R. W. Larson, & T. S. Saraswathi (Eds.), *The world's youth.* New York: Cambridge University Press.

Victor, E., Kellough, R. D., & Tai, R. H. (2008). *Science education* (11th ed.). Upper Saddle River, NJ: Prentice Hall.

Victora, G. C., Bryce, J., Fontaine, O., & Monasch, R. (2000). Reducing deaths from diarrhea through oral rehydration therapy. *Bulletin of the World Health Organization, 78,* 1246–1255.

Vidal, F. (2000). Piaget's theory. In A. Kazdin (Ed.), *Encyclopedia of psychology.* Washington, DC, & New York: American Psychological Association and Oxford University Press.

Villamor, E., & Cnattingius, S. (2006). Interpregnancy weight change and risk of adverse pregnancy outcomes: A population-based study. *Lancet, 368,* 1136–1138.

Visootsak, J., & Sherman, S. (2007). Neuropsychiatric and behavioral aspects of trisomy 21. *Current Psychiatry Reports, 9,* 135–140.

Visser-van Balen, H., Sinnema, G., & Geenen, R. (2006). Growing up with idiopathic short stature: Psychosocial development and hormone treatment. A critical review. *Archives of Disease in Childhood, 91,* 433–439.

Vivian, E. M. (2006). Type 2 diabetes in children and adolescents—the next epidemic? *Current Medical Research and Opinion, 22,* 297–306.

Voeller, K. K. (2004). Attention-deficit hyperactivity disorder. *Journal of Child Neurology, 19,* 798–814.

Vogler, G. P. (2006). Behavior genetics and aging. In J. E. Birren & K. W. Schaie (Eds.), *Handbook of the psychology of aging* (6th ed.). San Diego: Academic Press.

Volterra, M. C., Caselli, O., Capirci, E., & Pizzuto, E. (2004). Gesture and the emergence and development of language. In M. Tomasello & D. I. Slobin (Eds.), *Beyond nature-nurture.* Mahwah, NJ: Erlbaum.

Vondracek, F. W., & Porfeli, E. J. (2003). The world of work and careers. In G. Adams & M. Berzonsky (Eds.), *Blackwell handbook of adolescence.* Malden, MA: Blackwell.

Vonk, J. M., Postma, D. S., Boezen, H. M., Grol, M. H., Schouten, J. P., Koeter, G. H., & Gerritsen, J. (2004). Childhood factors associated with asthma remission after year follow up. *Thorax, 59,* 925–929.

Voss, L. D. (2006). Is short stature a problem? The psychological view. *European Journal of Endocrinology, 155* (Suppl. 1), S39–S45.

Votruba-Drzal, E., Coley, R. L., & Chase-Lansdale, P. L. (2004). Child care and low-income children's development: Direct and moderated effects. *Child Development, 75,* 296–312.

Voydanoff, P. (2007). *Work, family, and community.* Mahwah, NJ: Erlbaum.

Vreugdenhil, H. J., Mulder, P. G., Emmen, H. H., & Weisglas-Kuperus, N. (2004). Effects of perinatal exposure to PCBs on neuropsychological functions in the Rotterdam cohort at 9 years of age. *Neuropsychology, 18,* 185–193.

Vukovic, R. K., & Siegel, L. S. (2006). The double-deficit hypothesis: A comprehensive analysis of the evidence. *Journal of Learning Disabilities, 39,* 25–47.

Vurpillot, E. (1968). The development of scanning strategies and their relation to visual differentiation. *Journal of Experimental Child Psychology, 6,* 632–650.

Vygotsky, L. S. (1962). *Thought and language.* Cambridge, MA: MIT Press.

W

Wachs, T. D. (1995). Relation of mild-to-moderate malnutrition to human development: Correlational studies. *Journal of Nutrition Supplement, 125,* 2245s–2254s.

Wagstaff, A., Bustreo, F., Bryce, J., Claeson, M., and the WHO-World Bank Child Health and Poverty Working Group. (2004). Child health: Reaching the poor. *American Journal of Public Health, 94,* 726–736.

Wainright, J. L., & Patterson, C. J. (2005, April). *Adjustment among adolescents living with same-sex couples: Data from the National Longitudinal Study of Adolescent Health.* Paper presented at the meeting of the Society for Research in Child Development, Atlanta.

Wainryb, C. (2006). Moral development in culture: Diversity, tolerance, and justice. In M. Killen & J. G. Smetana (Eds.), *Handbook of moral development.* Mahwah, NJ: Erlbaum.

Wake, M., & Poulakis, Z. (2004). Slight and mild hearing loss in primary school children. *Journal of Pediatrics and Child Health, 40,* 11–13.

Wakefield, J. (2001). Toxic inheritance: Father's job may mean cancer for kids. *Environmental Health Perspectives, 109,* 193–196.

Walden, T. (1991). Infant social referencing. In J. Garber & K. Dodge (Eds.), *The development of emotional regulation and deregulation.* New York: Cambridge University Press.

Waldman, I. D., & Gizer, I. R. (2006). The genetics of attention deficit hyperactivity disorder. *Clinical Psychology Review, 26,* 396–432.

Walker, H. (1998, May 31). Youth violence: Society's problem. *Eugene Register Guard,* p. 1C.

Walker, L. J., (1982). The sequentiality of Kohlberg's stages of moral development. *Child Development, 53,* 1130–1136.

Walker, L. J. (2002). In W. Damon (Ed.), *Bringing in a new era of character education.* Stanford, CA: Hoover Press.

Walker, L. J. (2004). Progress and prospects in the psychology of moral development. *Merrill-Palmer Quarterly, 50,* 546–557.

Walker, L. J. (2006). Gender and morality. In M. Killen & J. G. Smetana (Eds.), *Handbook of moral development.* Mahwah, NJ: Erlbaum.

Walker, S. (2006). Unpublished review of J. W. Santrock's *Topical life- span development,* (3rd ed.). New York: McGraw-Hill.

Walker, S. O., Petrill, S. A., & Plomin, R. (2005). A genetically sensitive investigation of the effects of the school environment and socioeconomic status on academic achievement in seven-year-olds. *Educational Psychology, 25,* 55–63.

Walker, S. P., Wachs, T. D., Gardner, J. M., Lozoff, B., Wasserman, G. A., Pollitt, E., Carter, J. A., & The International Child Development Steering Group. (2007). Child development risk factors for adverse outcomes in developing countries. *Lancet, 369,* 145–157.

Wallace Foundation. (2004). *Out-of-school learning: All work and no play.* New York City: Author.

Walley, A. J., Blakemore, A. I., & Froguel, P. (2006). Genetics of obesity and the prediction of risk for health. *Human Molecular Genetics, 15,* (Suppl. 2), R124–R130.

Walls, C. (2006). Shaken baby syndrome education: A role for nurse practitioners with families of small children. *Journal of Pediatric Health Care, 20,* 304–310.

Walsh, D., & Bennett, N. (2004). *WHY do they act that way?: A survival guide to the adolescent brain for you and your teen.* New York: Free Press.

Walsh, L. A. (2000, Spring). The inside scoop on child development: Interview, *Cutting through the hype.* Minneapolis: College of Education and Human Development, University of Minnesota.

Walsh, L. V. (2006). Beliefs and rituals in traditional birth, attendant practice in Guatemala. *Journal of Transcultural Nursing, 17,* 148–154.

Walshaw, C. A., & Owens, J. M. (2006). Low breastfeeding rates and milk insufficiency. *British Journal of General Practice, 56,* 379.

Walters, E., & Kendler, K. S. (1994). Anorexia nervosa and anorexia-like symptoms in a population based twin sample. *American Journal of Psychiatry, 152,* 62–71. **Agras, W. S., & others.** (2004). Report of the National Institutes of Health workshop on overcoming barriers to treatment research in anorexia nervosa. *International Journal of Eating Disorders, 35,* 509–521.

Wang, J. Q. (2000, November). *A comparison of two international standards to assess child and adolescent obesity in three populations.* Paper presented at the meeting of American Public Health Association, Boston.

Wang, S. M., DeZinno, P., Fermo, L., William, K., Caldwell-Andrews, A. A., Bravemen, F., & Kain, Z. N. (2005). Complementary and alternative medicine for low-back pain in pregnancy: A cross-sectional survey. *Journal of Alternative and Complementary Medicine, 11,* 459–464.

Ward, L. M. (2003). Understanding the role of entertainment media in the sexual socialization of American youth: A review of empirical research. *Developmental Review, 23,* 347–388.

Ward, L. M., & Friedman, K. (2006). Using TV as a guide: Associations between television viewing and adolescents' sexual attitudes and behavior. *Journal of Research on Adolescence, 16,* 133–156.

Ward, L. M., Hansbrough, E., & Walker, E. (2005). Contributions of music video exposure to Black adolescents' gender and sexual schemas. *Journal of Adolescent Research, 20,* 141–166.

Wardlaw, G. M., Hempl, J. (2007). *Perspectives in nutrition.* (7th ed.). New York: McGraw-Hill.

Wardle, J., Cooke, E. J., Gibson, E. L., Sapochnik, M., Sheiham, A., & Lawson, M. (2003). Increasing children's acceptance of vegetables; A randomized trial of parent-led exposure. *Appetite, 40,* 155–162.

Wark, G. R., & Krebs, D. L. (1996). Gender and dilemma differences in real-life moral judgment. *Developmental Psychology, 32,* 220–230.

Warrick, P. (1992, March 1). The fantastic voyage of Tanner Roberts. *Los Angeles Times.* pp. E1, E11, E12.

Warshak, R. A. (2004, January). Personal communication, Department of Psychology, University of Texas at Dallas, Richardson.

Wasserman, M., Bender, D., & Lee, S. Y. (2007). Use of preventive maternal and child health services by Latina women: A review of published intervention studies. *Medical Care Research and Review, 64,* 4–45.

Watamabe, H., & Taga, G. (2006). General to specific development of movement patterns and memory for contingency between actions and events in young infants. *Infant Behavior and Development, 29,* 402–422.

Watemberg, N., Silver, S., Harel, S., & Lerman-Sagie, T. (2002). Significance of microencephaly among children with developmental abilities. *Journal of Child Neurology. 17,* 117–122.

Waterman, A. S. (1985). Identity in the context of adolescent psychology. In A. S. Waterman (Ed.), *Identity in adolescence: Processes and contents.* San Francisco: Jossey-Bass.

Waterman, A. S. (1989). Curricula interventions for identity change: Substantive and ethical considerations. *Journal of Adolescence, 12,* 389–400.

Waterman, A. S. (1992). Identity as an aspect of optimal psychological functioning. In G. R. Adams,

T. P. Gullotta, & R. Montemayor (Eds.), *Adolescent identity formation.* Newbury Park, CA: Sage.

Waters, E., Kondo-Ikemura, K., Posada, G., & Richters, J. E. (1990). Learning to love: Mechanisms and milestones. In M. Gunnar & L. A. Sroufe (Eds.), *Minnesota symposia on child psychology, 23.* Mahwah, NJ: Erlbaum.

Watson, D. L. & Tharp, R. G. (2007). *Self-directed behavior* (9th ed.). Belmont, CA: Wadsworth.

Watson, J. B. (1928). *Psychological care of infant and child.* New York: W. W. Norton.

Watson, J. B., & Rayner, R. (1920). Conditioned emotional reactions. *Journal of Experimental Psychology, 3,* 1–14.

Waxman, S. R., & Lidz, J. L. (2006). Early word learning. In W. Damon & R. Lerner (Eds.). *Handbook of child psychology* (6th ed.). New York: Wiley.

Weaver, R. F. (2008). *Molecular biology* (4th ed.). New York: McGraw-Hill.

Weber. J., & Plotts, C. (2008). Emotional and behavioral disorders (5th ed.). Boston: Allyn & Bacon.

Wechsler, H., Lee, J. E., Kuo, M., Seibring, M., Nelson, T. F., & Lee, H. (2002). Trends in college binge drinking during a period of increased prevention efforts: Findings from 4 Harvard School of Public Health college alcohol study surveys: 1993–2001. *Journal of American College Health, 50,* 203–217.

Wegman, M. E. (1987). Annual summary of vital statistics—1986. *Pediatrics, 80,* 817–827.

Weihong, Y., Holland, S. K., Cecil, K. M., Dietrich, K. N., Wessel, S. D., Altaye, M., Hornung, R. W., Ris, M. D., Egelhoff, J. C., & Lanphear, B. P. (2006). The impact of early childhood lead exposure on brain organization: A functional magnetic resonance imaging study of language function. *Pediatrics, 188,* 971–977.

Weikart, P. S. (1987). *Round the circle: Key experiences in movement for children ages 3 to 5.* Ypsilanti, MI: High/Scope Press.

Weikert, D. P. (1993), [Long-term positive effects in the Perry Preschool Head Start Program.] Unpublished data, High Scope Foundation, Ypsilanti, MI.

Weineke, J. K., Thurston, S. W., Kelsey, K. T., Varkonyi, A., Wain, J. C., Mark, E. J., & Christiani, D. C. (1999). Early age at smoking initiation and tobacco carcinogen DNA damage in the lung. *Journal of the National Cancer Institute, 91,* 614–619.

Weinstein, R. S. (2004). *Reaching higher: The power of expectations in schooling.* Cambridge, MA: Harvard University Press.

Weisz, A. N., & Black, B. M. (2002). Gender and moral reasoning: African American youth respond to dating dilemmas. *Journal of Human Behavior in the Social Environment, 5,* 35–52.

Wellman, H. M. (2004). Understanding the psychological world: Developing a theory of mind. In U. Goswami (Ed.), *Blackwell handbook of childhood cognitive development.* Malden, MA: Blackwell.

Wellman, H. M., Cross, D., & Watson, J. (2001). Meta-analysis of theory-of-mind development: The truth about false belief. *Child Development, 72,* 655–684.

Wellman, H. M. & Woolley, J. D. (1990). From simple desires to ordinary beliefs: The early development of everyday psychology. *Cognition, 35,* 245–275.

Welti, C. (2002). Adolescents in Latin America: Facing the future with skepticism. In B. B. Brown, R. W. Larson, & T. S. Saraswathi (Eds.), *The world's youth.* New York: Cambridge.

Wentworth, R. A. L. (1999). *Montessori for the millennium.* Mahwah, NJ: Erlbaum.

Wentzel, K. R., & Asher, S. R. (1995). The academic lives of neglected, rejected, popular, and controversial children. *Child Development, 66,* 754–763.

Wentzel, K. R, Barry, C. M., & Caldwell, K. A. (2004). Friendships in middle school: Influences on motivation and school adjustment. *Journal of Educational Psychology, 96,* 195–203.

Wentzel, K. R., & Looney, L. (2007). Socialization in school settings. In J. E. Grusec & P. D. Hastings (Eds.), *Handbook of socialization.* New York: Guilford.

Wenze, G. T., & Wenze, N. (2004). Helping left-handed children adapt to school expectations. *Childhood Education, 81,* 25–31.

Werth, J. L. (2004). The relationships among clinical depression, suicide, and other actions that may hasten death. *Behavioral Science and the Law, 22,* 627.

Werts, M. G., Culatta, R. A., & Tompkins, J. R. (2007). *Fundamentals of special education* (3rd ed.). Upper Saddle River, NJ: Prentice Hall.

Wertsch, J. V. (2007). Mediation. In H. Daniels, J. Wertsch, & M. Cole (Eds.), *The Cambridge companion to Vygotsky.* New York: Cambridge University Press.

West, J., Denton, K., & Germino-Hausken, E. (2000). *America's kindergartners.* Washington, DC: National Center for Education Statistics.

Weyman, A. (2003). Promoting sexual health to young people. *Journal of Research on Social Health, 123,* 6–7.

Wheeden, A., Scafidi, F. A., Field, T., Ironson, G., Valdeon, C. & Bandstra, E. (1993). Massage effects on cocaine-exposed preterm neonates. *Journal of Developmental and Behavioral Pediatrics, 14,* 318–322.

Wheeler, P. G., Bresnahan, K., Shephard, B. A., Lau, J., & Balk, E. M. (2004). Short stature and functional impairments: A systematic review. *Archives of Pediatric and Adolescent Medicine, 158,* 236–243.

Whetstone, L. M., Morrissey, S. L., & Cummings, D. M. (2007). Children at risk: The association between perceived weight status and suicidal thoughts and attempts in middle school youth. *Journal of School Health, 77,* 59–66.

Whitescarver, K. (2006, April). *Montessori rising: Montessori education in the United States, 1955–present.* Paper presented at the meeting of the American Education Research Association, San Francisco.

Whitfield, K. E., King, G., Moller, S., Edwards, C. L., Nelson, T., & Vandenbergh, D. (2007). Concordance rates for smoking among African-American twins. *Journal of the American Medical Association, 99,* 213–217.

Whitford, T. J., Rennie, C. J., Grieve, S. M., Clark, C. R., Gordon, E., & Williams, L. M. (2007). Brain maturation in adolescence. *Human Brain Mapping, 28,* 228–237.

Whiting, B. B., & Edwards, C. P. (1988). *Children of different worlds.* Cambridge, MA: Harvard University Press.

Whiting, J. (1981). Environmental constraint on infant care practices. In R. L. R. M. Monroe, & B. B. Whiting (Ed.), *Handbook of cross-cultural human development.* New York: Garland STPM Press.

Whitman, T. L., Borkowski, J. G., Keogh, D. A., & Weed, K. (2001). *Interwoven lives.* Mahwah, NJ: Erlbaum.

Wiesner, M., & Ittel, A. (2002). Relations of pubertal timing and depressing symptoms to substance use in early adolescence. *Journal of Early Adolescence, 22,* 5–23.

Wigfield, A., & Asher, S. R. (1984). Social and motivational influences on reading. In P. D. Pearson, R. Barr, M. L. Kamil, & P. Mosenthal (Eds.), *Handbook of reading research.* New York: Longman.

Wigfield, A., Byrnes, J. P., & Eccles, J. S. (2006). Developing during early adolescence. In P. A. Alexander & P. H. Winne (Eds.), *Handbook of educational psychology* (2nd ed.). Mahwah, NJ: Erlbaum.

Wigfield, A., Eccles, J. S., Schiefele, U., Roeser, R., & Davis-Kean, P. (2006). Development of achievement motivation. In W. Damon & R. Lerner (Eds.), *Handbook of child psychology* (6th ed.). New York: Wiley.

William T. Grant Foundation Commission on Work, Family, and Citizenship. (1988, February). *The forgotten half: Noncollege-bound youth in America.* New York: William T Grant Foundation.

Williams, D. D., Yancher, S. C., Jensen, L. C., & Lewis, C. (2003). Character education in a public high school: A multi-year inquiry into unified studies. *Journal of Moral Education, 32,* 3–33.

Williams, J. H. (2006). *Applied sport psychology* (5th ed.). New York: McGraw-Hill.

Williams, J. H., & Ross, L. (2007, in press). Consequences of prenatal toxin exposure for mental health in children and adolescents: A systematic review. *European Child and Adolescent Psychiatry.*

Wills, T. A., Yaeger, A. M., & Sandy, J. M. (2003). Buffering effect of religiosity for adolescent substance use. *Psychology of Addictive Behaviors, 17,* 24–31.

Wilson, M. N. (2007). Poor fathers involvement in the lives of their children. In D. R. Crane & T. B. Heaton (Eds.), *Handbook of families and poverty.* Thousand Oaks, CA: Sage.

Windle, W. F. (1940). *Physiology of the human fetus.* Philadelphia: W. B. Saunders.

Winner, E. (1986, August.). Where pelicans kiss seals. *Psychology Today,* pp. 24–35.

Winner, E. (1996). *Gifted children: Myths and realities.* New York: Basic Books.

Winner, E. (2000). The origins and ends of giftedness. *American Psychologist, 55,* 159–169.

Winner, E. (2006). Development in The arts. In W. Damon & R. Lerner (Eds.), *Handbook of child psychology* (6th ed.) New York: Wiley.

Winsler, A., Carlton, M. P., & Barry, M. J. (2000). Age-related changes in preschool children's systematic use of private speech in a natural setting. *Journal of Child Language, 27,* 665–687.

Winsler, A., Diaz, R. M., & Montero, I. (1997). The role of private speech in the transition from collaborative to independent task performance in young children. *Early Childhood Research Quarterly, 12,* 59–79.

Wiseman, C. V., Sunday, S. R., & Becker, A. E. (2005). Impact of the media on adolescent boy image. *Child and Adolescent Psychiatric Clinics of North America, 14,* 453–471.

Wltkin, H. A., Mednick, S. A., Schulsinger, R., Bakkestrom, E., Christiansen, K. O., Goodenbough, D. R., Hirchhorn, K., Lunsteen, C., Owen, D. R., Philip, J., Ruben, D. B., & Stocking, M. (1976). Criminality in XYY and XXY men. *Science, 193,* 547–555.

Wocadlo, C., & Rieger, I. (2006). Educational and therapeutic resource dependency at early school age in children who were born very preterm. *Early Human Development, 82,* 29–37.

Wong, A. H., Gottesman, I. I., & Petronis, A. (2005). Phenotypic differences in genetically identical organisms: The epigenetic perspective. *Human Molecular Genetics, 15 (No. 1),* 11–18.

Wong, T. B. (2004, October 14). *USA Today's* 2004 all-USA team. *USA Today,* p. 6 D.

Woo, K. S., Chook, P., Yu, C. W., Suung, R. Y., Qiao, M., Leung, S. S., Law, C. W., Metreweli, C., & Celermajer, D. S. (2004). Effects of diet and exercise on obesity-related vascular dysfunction in children. *Circulation, 109,* 1981–1986.

Wood, J. W. (2006). *Teaching students in inclusive settings* (5th ed.). Upper Saddle River, NJ: Prentice Hall.

Wood, W., & Eagly, A. H. (2007). Social structural origins of sex differences in human mating. In S. W. Gangestad & J. A. Simpson (Eds.), *The evolution of mind.* New York: Guilford.

Woodward, A. L., & Markman, E. M. (1998). Early word learning. In D. Kuhn & R. S. Siegler (Eds.). *Handbook of child psychology* (5th ed., Vol. 2). New York: Wiley.

Worell, J. (2006). Pathways to healthy development: Sources of strength and empowerment. In J. Worell & C. D. Goodheart (Eds.), *Handbook of girls' and women's psychological health.* New York: Oxford University Press.

Worell, J., & Goodheart, C. D. (Eds.). (2006). *Handbook of girls' and women's psychological health: Gender and well-being across the life span.* New York: Oxford University Press.

Worku, B., & Kassie, A. (2005). Kangaroo mother care: A randomized controlled trial on effectiveness of early kangaroo care for low birthweight infants in Addis Ababa, Ethiopia. *Journal of Tropical Pediatrics, 51,* 93–97.

World Health Organization (2000, February 2). *Adolescent health behavior in 28 countries.* Geneva: Author.

World Health Organization. (2002). *The world health report 2002.* Geneva, Author.

Wu, P., Robinson, C. C., Yang, C., Hart, C. H., Olsen, S. F., & Porter, C. L. (2002). Similarities and differences in mothers' parenting of preschoolers in China and the United States. *International Journal of Behavioural Development, 26,* 481–491.

Wyganski-Jaffe, T. (2005). The effect on pediatric ophthalmologists of the randomized trial of patching regiments for treatment of moderate amblyopia. *Journal of the American Optometric Association, 9,* 208–211.

X

Xu, F., Markowitz, L. E., Gottlieb, S. L., & Berman, S. M. (2007). Seroprevalence of herpes simplex virus types 1 and 2 in pregnant women in the United States. *American Journal of Obstetrics and Gynecology, 196,* e1–e6.

Xu, Y., Cook, T. J., & Knipp, G. T. (2006). Methods for investigating placental fatty acid Transport. *Methods of Molecular Medicine, 122,* 265–284.

Y

Yang, C. K., Kim, J. K., Patel, S. R., & Lee, J. H. (2005). Age-related changes in sleep/wake patterns among Korean teenagers. *Pediatrics, 115* (Suppl 1), S250–S256.

Yang, Q., Wen, S. W., Leader, A., Chen, X. K., Lipson, J. & Walker, M. (2007). Paternal age and birth defects: How strong is the association. *Human Reproduction, 22,* 696–701.

Yang, S., & Sternberg, R. J. (1997). Taiwanese Chinese people's conceptions of intelligence. *Intelligence, 25,* 21–36.

Yang, S. N., Liu, C. A., Chung, M. Y., Huang, H. C., Yeh, G. C., Wong, C. S., Lin, W. W., Yang, C. H., & Tao, P. L. (2006). Alterations of postsynaptic density proteins in the hippocampus of rat offspring from the morphine-addicted mother: Beneficial effects of dextromethorphan. *Hippocampus, 16,* 521–530.

Yang, Y., May, Y., Ni, L., Zhao, S., Li, L., Zhang, J., Fan, M., Liang, C., Cao, J., & Xu, L. (2003). Lead exposure through gestation-only caused long-term memory deficits in young adult offspring. *Experimental Neurology, 184,* 489–495.

Yates, M. (1995, March). *Community service and political-moral discussions among Black urban adolescents.* Paper presented at the meeting of the Society for Research in Child Development, Indianapolis.

Yingzhon, Y., Dorma, Y., Rili, G., & Kubo, K. (2006). Regulation of body weight by leptin, with special reference to hypoxia-induced regulation. *Internal Medicine, 45,* 941–946.

Yoo, H. J., Choi, K. M., Ryu, O. H., Suh, S. I., Kim, N. H., Baik, S. H., & Choi, D. S. (2006). Delayed puberty due to pituitary stalk dysgenesis and ectopic neurophyophysis. *Korean Journal of Internal Medicine, 21,* 68–72.

Young, D. (2001). The nature and management of pain: What is the evidence? *Birth, 28,* 149–151.

Young, E. L., Boye, A. E., & Nelson, D. A. (2006). Relational aggression: Understanding, identifying, and responding in schools. *Psychology in the Schools, 43,* 297–312.

Young, K. T. (1990). American conceptions of infant development from 1955 to 1984: What the experts are telling parents. *Child Development, 61,* 17–28.

Youniss, J., McLellan, J. A., & Yates, M. (1999). Religion, community service, and identity in American youth. *Journal of Adolescence, 22,* 243–253.

Yu, C. W., Sung, R. Y., So, R., Lam, K., Nelson, E. A., Li, A. M., Yuan, Y., & Lam, P. K. (2002). Energy expenditure and physical activity of obese children: Cross-sectional study. *Hong Kong Medical Journal, 8,* 313–317.

Yu, V. Y. (2000). Developmental outcome of extremely preterm infants. *American Journal of Perinatology, 17,* 57–61.

Z

Zalc, B. (2006). The acquisition of myelin: A success story. *Novartis Foundation Symposium, 276,* 15–21.

Zangl, R., & Mills, D. L. (2007). Increased brain activity to infant-directed speech in 6- and 13-month-old infants. *Infancy, 11,* 31–62.

Zelazo, P. D., & Muller, U. (2004). Executive function in typical and atypical development. In U. Goswami (Ed.), *Blackwell handbook of cognitive development.* Malden, MA: Blackwell.

Zelazo, P. D., Muller, U., Frye, D., & Marcovitch, S. (2003). The development of executive function in early childhood. *Monographs of the Society for Research in Child Development, 68* (3, Serial No. 274).

Zentall, S. S. (2006). *ADHD and education.* Upper Saddle River, NJ: Prentice Hall.

Zeskind, P. S., Klein, L., & Marshall, T. R. (1992). Adults' perceptions of experimental modifications of durations and expiratory sounds in infant crying. *Developmental Psychology, 28,* 1153–1162.

Zhang, L., Jie, C., Obie, C., Abidi, F., Schwartz, C. E., Stevenson, R. E., Valle, D., & Wang, T. (2007). X chromosome cDNA microarray screening identifies a functional PLP2 promoter polymorphism enriched in patients with X-linked mental retardation. *Genome Research, 17,* 641–648.

Zigler, E. F., & Styfco, S. J. (1994). Head Start: Criticisms in a constructive context. *American Psychologist, 49,* 127–132.

Zigler, E., Gilliam, W. S., & Jones, S. M. (2006). *A vision for universal preschool education.* New York: Cambridge University Press.

Zimmerman, P. (2007, March). *Attachment in adolescence.* Paper presented at the meeting of the Society for Research in Child Development, Boston.

Zimmerman, R. S., Khoury, E., Vega, W. A., Gil, A. G., & Warheit, G. J. (1995). Teacher and student perceptions of behavior problems among a sample of African American, Hispanic, and non-Hispanic White students. *American Journal of Community Psychology, 23,* 181–197.

Zinn, M. B., & Wells, B. (2000). Diversity within Latino families: New lessons for family social science. In D. M., Demo, K. R. Allen, & M. A. Fine (Eds.), *Handbook of family diversity.* New York: Oxford University Press.

Zitanova, I., Korytar, P., Sobotova, H., Horakova, L., Sustrova, M., Pueschel, S., & Durackova, Z. (2006). Markers of oxidative stress in children with Down syndrome. *Clinical Chemistry and Laboratory Medicine, 44,* 306–310.

Zittleman, K. (2006, April). *Being a girl and being a boy: The voices of middle schoolers.* Paper presented at the meeting of the American Educational Research Association, San Francisco.

Zverev, Y. P. (2006). Cultural and environmental pressure against left-hand preference in urban and semi-urban Malawi. *Brain and Cognition, 60,* 295–303.

CREDITS

Title page: Corbis RF
Prologue: © Bachmann/Photo Network/Grant Heilman

Section Openers

1: © Ariel Skelley/CORBIS; **2:** © Petit Format/Nestle/Photo Researchers; **3:** Courtesy of Northern Telecom; **4:** (c) Ariel Skelley/Corbis; **5:** © Ariel Skelley/CORBIS; **6:** © Ariel Skelley/Corbis

Chapter 1

Opener: © Franciso Cruz/Superstock; **p. 6 (top):** © Seana O'Sullivan/ CORBIS/Sygma; **p. 6 (bottom):** © AP/Wide World Photos; **p. 8:** Courtesy of Luis Vargas; **p. 9:** © National Association for the Education of Young Children/photo © Robert Maust/Photo Agora; **p. 10 (top):** © Nancy Agostini; **p. 10 (bottom):** © AFP/CORBIS; **p. 11:** © Dain Gair Photographic/Index Stock; **p. 12:** © Nathan Benn/CORBIS; **1.3:** Photo © Erich Lessing/ Art Resource, NY/Painting by A.I>G. Velasquez, *Infanta Margarita Teresa in white garb*, Kunsthi-storisches Museum, Vienna, Austria; **1.4:** © Archives of the History of American Psychology/Louise Bates Ames Gift; **1.6 (Prenatal):** © Dr. Landrum B. Shettles; (Infancy): Courtesy of John Santrock; (Early childhood): © Joe Sohm/The Image Works; (middle childhood): © CORBIS website; (Adolescence): © James Shaffer; **p. 20:** © PhotoDisc website; **p. 22:** © Bettmann/CORBIS; **p. 24:** © Sarah Putnam/Index Stock; **p. 25:** © Yves DeBraine/Stock Photo; **p. 26:** © Courtesy of A.R. Lauria/Dr. Michael Cole/Laboratory of Human Cognition; **p. 28 (top):** © AP/Wide World Photos **(bottom):** © Bettmann/CORBIS; **p. 29:** © Nina Leen/Time/ Life Magazine/Getty News Service; **p. 31:** Courtesy of Urie Bronfenbrenner; **1.13 (Freud):** © Bettmann/ CORBIS; (Pavlov): © CORBIS; (Piaget): © Yves deBraine/Stock Photo; (Vygotsky): © A.R. Lauria/Dr. Michael Cole, Laboratory of Human Cognition, University of California, San Diego; (Skinner): © Harvard University News Office; (Erikson): © UPI/Bettmann/CORBIS; (Bandura): © Bettmann/CORBIS; (Bronfenbrenner): Courtesy of Urie Bronfenbrenner; **p. 33:** © Ray Stott/The Image Works; **p. 34:** © Bettmann/CORBIS; **p. 35:** © Sovereign/Photo-take; **p. 38:** © McGraw-Hill Higher Educaton, John Thoeming, photographer; **p. 40:** Courtesy of Pamela Trotman Reid; **p. 41 (left):** © Kevin Fleming/CORBIS; **p. 41 (right):** © Ed Honowitz/Stone/Getty Images; **p. 49:** Courtesy of Valerie Pang; **p. 52:** Courtesy of Katherine Duchen Smith, Certified Pediatric Nurse Practitioner, Ft. Collins, Colorado

Chapter 2

Opener: © Design Pics/CORBIS RF; **p. 56 (top):** © Enrico Ferorelli; **p. 56 (bottom):** © Frans Lemmens/zefa/CORBIS; **p. 59:** © David Wilkie;

p. 61: © Rick Rickman; **2.3 (left & right):** © Custom Medical Stock Photo; **p. 64:** © Joel Gordon 1989; **p. 66:** © Andrew Eccles/JBGPHOTO.COM; **p. 67:** Courtesy of Holly Ishmael; **p. 68:** © Jacques Pavlosky/sygma/CORBIS; **p. 69:** © Reuters/Corbis; **p. 71:** © AP/Wide World Photos; **p. 73:** © Sondra Dawes/The Image Works; **p. 74:** © Myrleen Ferguson Cate/Photo Edit; **p. 76:** © Duomo/Corbis

Chapter 3

Opener: © Lennart Nilsson; **p. 84:** © John Santrock; **3.3a:** © Lennart Nilsson; **3.3b&c:** © Petit Format/Nestle/Photo Researchers; 3.4: © Lennart Nilsson/Albert Bonniers Forlag AB; **p. 89 (bottom):** 2006 Spina Bifida camp photo; **p. 92 (top):** © David Young-Wolff/Photo Edit; **p. 92 (bottom):** © Vol. 15/PhotoDisc; **p. 95 (top):** Courtesy of Elizabeth Noble; **p. 95 (bottom):** © Sharon Schindler Rising, Centering Pregnancy Program; **p. 97:** © Vivianne Moos/CORBIS; **p. 100:** Courtesy of Ann Streissguth; **p. 101:** © Will & Deni McIntyre/Photo Researchers; **p. 102:** © John Chiasson; **p. 103:** © R.I.A./Gamma/Eyedea; **p. 104:** © Betty Press/Woodfin Camp & Associates; **p. 106:** © Karen Kasmauski/CORBIS; **p. 107:** © David Butow/CORBIS

Chapter 4

Opener: © SIU/Peter Arnold, Inc.; **p. 116:** M.Shostak/Anthro-Photo; **p. 117:** © Brand X/CORBIS Royalty Free; **p. 118:** Courtesy of Linda Pugh; **p. 119:** © Dr. Holly Beckwith; **p. 120:** © Tom Galliher/CORBIS; **p. 121:** © Rubber Ball Productions/Getty RF; **p. 122:** © Brand X/CORBIS RF; **4.2:** © Stephen Marks, Inc./The Image Bank/Getty Images; **p. 125:** © Charles Grupton/Stock Boston; **p. 127:** Courtesy of Dr. Susan M. Ludington; **p. 128:** © Dr. Tiffany Field; **p. 130:** Courtesy of Rachel Thompson; **p. 131:** © Ariel Skelley/ CORBIS; **p. 132:** © James G. White

Chapter 5

Opener: © George Disario/The Stock Market/CORBIS; **p. 142 (top):** © Wendy Stone/CORBIS; **p. 142 (bottom):** © Dave Bartruff/CORBIS; **5.2:** © 1990 Kenneth Jarecke/Contact Press Images; **5.3:** © A. Glauberman/Photo Researchers; **5.8a&b:** Courtesy of Dr. Harry T. Chugani, Children's Hospital of Michigan; **5.9a:** © David Grubin Productions Inc. Reprinted by permission; **5.9b:** Courtesy of Dana Boatman, Ph.D., Department of Neurology, John Hopkins University. Reprinted with permission from *The Secret Life of the Brain*, © 2001 by the National Academy of Sciences, the National Academies Press, Washington, D.C.; **p. 151:** © Tom Rosenthal/SuperStock; **p. 154 (top):** © Vol. DV251 Digital Vision/Getty Images; **p. 154 (bottom):** © Bob Dammrich/The Image Works; **p. 155:** Courtesy

of Dr. T. Berry Brazelton; **p. 157:** Courtesy of The Hawaii Family Support/Healthy Start Program; **p. 158:** Courtesy of Esther Thelen; **5.14a:** © Elizabeth Crews/The Image Works; **5.14b:** © James G. White; **5.14c:** © Petit Format/Photo Researchers, Inc.; **5.15a&b:** © Karen Adolph, New York University; **p. 163 (top):** Michael Greenlar/The Image Works; **p. 163 (bottom):** © Frank Bailey Studio; **5.17:** Courtesy Amy Needham; **p. 165:** © Mika/zefa/CORBIS; **5.18:** Adapted from "The Origin of Form and Perception" by R. L. Fantz © 1961 by *Scientific American*. Photo © by David Linton; **5.20 (all)** Courtesy of Dr. Charles Nelson; **5.22:** © Enrico Ferorelli; **5.23a:** © Michael Siluk; **5.23b:** © Dr. Melanie J. Spence, University of Texas at Dallas; **5.24:** © Jean Guichard/Sygma/CORBIS; **5.25 (all):** D. Rosenstein and R. Oster, "Differential Facial Response to Four Basic Tastes in Newborns" in *Child Development*, Volume 59, **pp. 1561–1563.** Reprinted with permission of the Society for Research in Child Development; **p. 173 (bottom):** © Philip Kaake/Corbis

Chapter 6

Opener: © Spencer Grant/Photo Edit; **p. 186:** © PunchStock; **6.2a&b:** © Doug Goodman/Photo Researchers; **p. 189:** © Joe McNally; **6.4:** Courtesy of Carolyn Rovee-Collier; **6.5a&b:** Photos from: Meltzoff, A. N., & Brooks, R. (2007). Intersubjectivity before language: Three windows on preverbal sharing. In S. Bråten (Ed.), On being moved: From mirror neurons to empathy **(pp. 149–174).** Philadelphia, PA: John Benjamins.; **p. 192:** © Tom Stewart/CORBIS; **6.7:** © Andrew Meltzoff; **6.8:** From Jean Mandler, University of California, San Diego. Reprinted by permission of Oxford University Press; **p. 195:** © John Santrock; **p. 197:** © Peter Byron/Photo Researchers; **6.11a&b:** © 2003 University of Washington, Institute for Learning and Brain Sciences (I-LABS); **p. 203:** © Anthony Bannister/Animals Animals/Earth Scenes; **6.15:** © Michael Goldstein, Cornell University; **p. 207:** © John Carter/PhotoResearchers

Chapter 7

Opener: © Jamie Marcial/SuperStock; **p. 216:** © Rick Gomez/CORBIS; **7.1 (all):** © Michael Lewis, Institute for the Study of Child Development, Robert Wood Johnson Medical School; **7.2:** © Sybil L. Hart, Texas Tech University; **p. 219:** © Andy Cox/Stone/Getty Images; **p. 222:** © Michael Tcherevkoff/The Image Bank/Getty Images; **p. 223:** © Judith Oddie/Photo Edit; **7.4:** © Digital Vision/Getty RF; **p. 226:** © Vol. 63 PhotoDisc/Getty Images; **p. 227:** © Britt Erlanson/ Image Bank/Getty; **7.5:** Courtesy Celia A. Brownell, University of Pittsburgh; **7.6:** © Martin Rogers/Stock Boston; **p. 229:** © David

Young-Wolff/Photo Edit; **p. 231:** © Penny Tweedie/Stone/Getty Images; **7.8:** © BrandX-Pictures/Getty Images; **p. 234 (top):** © National Geographic/Getty RF; **p. 234 (bottom):** © Stephanie Rausser/Taxi/Getty Images; **p. 235:** © John Henley/CORBIS; **p. 236:** © Schwartzwald Lawrence/CORBIS; **p. 238:** Courtesy of Rashmi Nakhre, the Hattie Daniels Day Care Center; **p. 239:** © Lawrence Migdale/Stone/Getty Images

Chapter 8

Opener: © Tom & Dee Ann McCarthy/CORBIS; **p. 252:** © Bob Daemmrich/The Image Works; **8.3:** © Photo Researchers; **8.4:** © Sam Gilbert, Institute of Cognitive Neuroscience, UK; **p. 256:** © Nestor Bachmann/dpa/Corbis; **p. 260:** © Eyewire Vol. EP078/Getty Images; **p. 264:** © L. Perez/zefa/CORBIS; **p. 269:** Courtesy of Barbara Deloian; **p. 270:** © AP/Wide World Photos

Chapter 9

Opener: © Ariel Skelley/The Stock Market/CORBIS; **p. 278:** From 'Open Window' © 1994 Municipality of Reggio Emilia Infant-toddler Centers and Preschools Published by Reggio Children; **9.3:** © Paul Fusco/Magnum Photos; **p. 282:** © Bob Daemmrich/The Image Works; **p. 283:** © James Wertsch/Washington University at St. Louis; **9.7 (left):** © A. R. Lauria/Dr. Michael Cole, Laboratory of Human Cognition, University of California, San Diego; **9.7 (right):** © Bettmann/CORBIS; **p. 288:** © 2007 JamesKamp.com; **p. 291:** © Nita Winter; **p. 292:** © AP/Wide World Photos; **p. 294:** © Ellen Senisi/The Image Works; **p. 296:** © AP/Wide World Photos; **p. 298:** © Ariel Skelley/Corbis; **p. 300:** Courtesy of Yolanda Garcia; **p. 301:** © Ronnie Kaufman/The Stock Market/CORBIS; **p. 304 (left):** © Karen Kasmauski/Corbis; **p. 304 (right):** © SOS Children's Villages (www.sos-usa.org)

Chapter 10

Opener: © Ariel Skelley/Corbis; **p. 314:** © CORBIS/Royalty-Free; **p. 315:** © Michael Lewis, Institute for the Study of Child Development, Robert Wood Johnson Medical School; **p. 316 (top):** © LWA-Dann Tardif/zefa/CORBIS; **p. 316 (bottom):** © Catherine Ledner/Stone/Getty Images; **p. 317:** © Yves De Braine/Black Star/Stock Photo; **p. 318:** © Randy Faris/CORBIS; **p. 319:** © Corbis RF; **10.5:** © Ariel Skelley/Corbis; **p. 322:** © Digital Stock; **p. 327:** © Jose Luis Pelaez/CORBIS; **p. 328:** © PunchStock; **p. 330:** D. Botkin (2000). Family play therapy: A creative approach to including young children in family therapy. *Journal of Systematic Therapies,* 19, 30-41.; **p. 331:** © David M. Wells/CORBIS; **p. 332 (top):** © Prevent Child Abuse America. Also reprinted by permission of Grant and Tamia Hill; **p. 332 (bottom left):** © Thomas Hoeffgen/Taxi/ Getty Images; **p. 332 (bottom right):** © Corbis RF; **p. 333:** © Ariel Skelley/CORBIS; **p. 335:** © PunchStock; **p. 337:** © S. Gazin/The Image Works; **p. 338:** © Karen Kasmauski/Woodfin Camp & Associates; **p. 341:** © Ariel Skelley/CORBIS; **p. 339:** © Spencer Grant/Photo Edit; **p. 342:** © Richard Hutchings/Photo Edit; **p. 343:** © Bryan F. Peterson; **p. 345:** © Franco Vogt/ CORBIS

Chapter 11

Opener: © Michael Pole/The Stock Market/CORBIS; **p. 361 (top):** © Aerial Skelley/CORBIS; **p. 361 (bottom):** © Gabe Palmer/CORBIS; **11.4: p. 365:** © Felicia Martinez/Photo Edit; **p. 366:** © CORBIS/Royalty-Free; **p. 369:** Courtesy of Sharon McLeod; **11.7:** © AP/Wide World Photos; **p. 373** © David Young-Wolff/Photo Edit; **p. 375:** Courtesy of Charla Peltier; **p. 376:** Used by permission of Don Johnston Inc.; **p. 379:** © Richard Hutchings/Photo Researchers

Chapter 12

Opener: © Gabe Palmer/CORBIS; **p. 390:** © M & E Bernheim/Woodfin Camp & Associates; **p. 391:** © Gabe Palmer/Corbis; **p. 395:** © Francisco Cruz/SuperStock; **p. 396 (top):** © Stan Godlewski Photography; **p. 396 (bottom):** © John Flavell; **p. 401:** © Joe McNally; **p. 404:** © Will & Deni McIntyre/CORBIS; **p. 406:** © Jill Cannefax; **p. 407:** Courtesy of Sterling Jones; **p. 409:** © Richard Howard; **p. 411:** © Elizabeth Crews; **p. 412:** © Elizabeth Crews/ The Image Works; **p. 416 (top):** © Michael A. Schwarz Photography, Inc.; **p. 416 (bottom):** Courtesy of Sandra Graham; **p. 418:** © Eiji Miyazawa/Stock Photo

Chapter 13

Opener: © Rolf Bruderer/CORBIS; **p. 426:** © Joseph Sohm/Visions of America/Corbis; **p. 428 (top):** © Paul Edmondson/Corbis; **p. 428 (bottom):** © Photophile/Tom Tracy; **p. 429:** © Jose Luis Pelaez, Inc./Corbis; **p. 431:** © AFP/CORBIS; **p. 435:** © Raghu-Rai/Magnum Photos; **p. 436:** © Keith Carter; **p. 437:** © Norbert Schaefer/CORBIS; **p. 442:** © Catherine Gehm; **p. 443:** © Ariel Skelley/CORBIS; **p. 445:** © Michael Newman/Photo Edit; **p. 446:** © Getty Royalty Free; **p. 448:** © Corbis Royalty Free; **p. 450:** © Catherine Ledner/Stone/Getty Images; **p. 451:** © Jiang Jin/SuperStock Royalty Free; **p. 453:** © Elizabeth Crews; **p. 454:** © Bob Daemmrich/ The Image Works; **p. 455:** © 2004, USA Today. Reprinted with permission; **p. 456:** © John S. Abbott

Chapter 14

Opener: © Mug Shots/The Stock Market/CORBIS; **p. 468 (top):** © M. Regine/The Image Bank/Getty Images; **p. 468 (bottom left):** © Marleen Ferguson/Photo Edit; **p. 468 (bottom right):** © Chuck Savage/The Stock Market/Corbis; **p. 474 (top):** © Jon Feingerssh/The Stock Market/CORBIS; **p. 474 (bottom):** © Corbis Royalty Free; **p. 475:** © David Young-Wolff/Photo Edit; **p. 476:** © Davis Turner-Pool/Getty Images; **p. 477:** © Joel Gordon 1995; **p. 478:** © Marilyn Humphries; **p. 479 (top):** © Lawrence Migdale/Stock Boston; **p. 479 (bottom):** © Michael Ray; **p. 482:** Courtesy Lynn Blankinship; **p. 483:** © 1998 Frank Fournier; **p. 486:** © Jim LoScalzo; **p. 489:** © Chuck Savage/CORBIS; **p. 491:** © Karen Kasmausk/Corbis; **p. 492:** © Tony Freeman/Photo Edit

Chapter 15

Opener: © Vol. RFCD697/CORBIS; **p. 501:** © David Young-Wolff/Photo Edit; **p. 503:** © Stewart Cohen/Stone/Getty Images; **p. 506:** © Big Cheese Photo/SuperStock RF; **p. 507:** Courtesy of Laura Bickford; **15.2:** © Penny Tweedie/Stone/Getty Images; **p. 509:** © David Young-Wolff/Photo Edit; **p. 513 (top):** © Stone/Getty Images; **p. 513 (bottom):** © Bob Daemmrich/The Image Works; **p. 516:** © Super-Stock Royalty Free; **p. 518:** © Fujifots/The Image Works; **p. 520:** Courtesy of I Have a Dream-Houston, Houston, TX; **p. 523:** © Bill Stanton; **p. 524:** Courtesy of Dr. Armando Ronquillo; **p. 526:** © Dennis MacDonald/Photo Edit

Chapter 16

Opener: © George Disario/The Stock Market/CORBIS; **p. 536:** © Matthew J. Lee, The Boston Globe; **p. 538:** © Dominic Rouse/The Image Bank/Getty Images; **p. 541:** © USA Today Library, photo by Robert Deutsch; **p. 542:** ourtesy of Margaret Beale Spencer; **p. 544:** © Myrleen Ferguson Cate/Photo Edit; **16.3:** © Spencer Grant/Photo Edit; **p. 548:** © Tony Freeman/Photo Edit; **p. 549:** © Michael Siluk/ The Image Works; **p. 551:** © Tessa Codrington/ Stone/Getty Images; **p. 552 (top):** © Tom & Dee Ann McCarthy/CORBIS; **p. 552 (bottom):** © David De Lossy/The Image Bank/Getty Images; **p. 554:** © AFP/CORBIS; **p. 555:** © Getty Royalty Free; **p. 556:** © Daniel Laine; **p. 557:** © USA Today Library, photo by H. Darr Beiser; **p. 559:** © Chuck Savage/Corbis; **p. 560:** © Mark Richards/Photo Edit; **p. 561:** © Charlie Neuman/SDUT/Zuma; **p. 562 (top):** Courtesy of Rodney Hammond, National Center for Injury Prevention and Control, CDCP; **p. 562 (bottom):** © Jim Smith/Photo Researchers

Text and Line Art Credits

Prologue: P. 1 From the book *100 Ways to Build Self-Esteem and Teach Values* (formerly *Full Esteem Ahead*). Copyright © 1994, 2003, by Diane Loomans. Reprinted with permission of H.J. Kramer/New World Library, Novato, CA. www.newworldlibrary.com. Toll-free 800/972-6657 ext. 52.

Chapter 1

Figure 1.12 "Bronfenbrenner's Ecological Theory of Development," from C.B. Kopp & J.B. Krakow, 1982, *Child Development in the Social Context*, p. 648. Addison-Wesley Longman, Inc. Reprinted by permission of Pearson Education, Inc., Upper Saddle River, NJ. **Figure 1.15** From Crowley, et al., 2001, "Parents Explain More to Boys Than Girls During Shared Scientific Thinking," *Psychological Science*, 12, 258–261. Reprinted by permission of Blackwell Publishers.

Chapter 2

P. 58 Excerpt from D. Bjorklund & A. Pellegrini, *The Origins of Human Nature*, American Psychological Association, 2002, pp. 336–340. Copyright © 2002 by the American Psychological Association. Reprinted by permission. **Figure 2.1** From Bonner, John, T.; *The Evolution of Culture in Animals*. Copyright © 1980 Princeton University Press. Reprinted by permission of Princeton University Press. **P. 71** Excerpt from D. Brodzinsky & E. Pinderhughes, 2002, "Parenting and Child Development in Adoptive Families," in M. Bornstein (ed.) *Handbook of Parenting*, Vol. I, pp. 280–282. Mahwah, NJ: Lawrence Erlbaum.

Education of Young Children. www.naeyc.org. Note: The current position statement can be found online at: http://www.naeyc.org/about. positions/pdf/PSDAP98.PDF **Figure 9.14** Reprinted with permission from the National Association for the Education of Young Children. www.naeyc.org. **Figure 9.1** From Santrock, *Life-Span Development*, 9th ed., Figure 8.18. Copyright © 2004 The McGraw-Hill Companies. Reproduced with permission of The McGraw-Hill Companies.

Chapter 10

P. 312 From *Burning Fence: A Western Memoir of Fatherhood*, by Craig Lesley, pp. 8–10. Copyright © 2005 by Craig Lesley and reprinted by permission of St. Martin's Press, LLC. **Figure 10.7** From the U.S. Census Bureau. **Figure 10.9** From D.F. Robitaille and R.A. Gardner, *The IEA Study of Mathematics II: Contexts and Outcomes of School Mathematics*. Reprinted by permission.

Chapter 11

Figure 11.1 From *Nelson Textbook of Pediatrics*, R.E. Behman & V.C. Vaughan, eds. W.B. Saunders, 1987. Copyright © 1987 Elsevier. Used with permission. **Figure 11.2** From B.J. Cratty, *Perceptual and Motor Development in Infants and Children*. Prentice-Hall, 1979. Reprinted by permission of Pearson Education, Inc., Upper Saddle River, NJ. **Figure 11.3** Data presented by Health Management Resources, 2001. *Child Health and Times*. Boston: Health Management Resources. **Figure 11.6** "U.S. Children with a Disability Who Receive Special Education Services," from Santrock, *Life-Span Development*, 11th ed., Fig. 10.3. Copyright © 2008 The McGraw-Hill Companies. Reproduced with permission of The McGraw-Hill Companies.

Chapter 12

Figure 12.1 From John Santrock, *Life Span Development*, 10th ed., Figure 10.4. Copyright © 2006 The McGraw-Hill Companies. Reproduced with permission of The McGraw-Hill Companies. **Figure 12.2** From "The Role of Expertise in Memory," from M.T.H. Chi, "Knowledge Structures and Memory Development," in R.S. Siegler (Ed.) *Children's Thinking: What Develops?* Mahwah, NJ: Lawrence Erlbaum. Reprinted by permission obtained via The Copyright Clearance Center. **Figure 12.3** Based on M. Pressley, et al., "Short-Term Memory, Verbal Competence, and Age as Predictors of Imagery Instructional Effectiveness," *Journal of Experimental Child Psychology*, 43, 194–211. **Figure 12.4** From Santrock, *Psychology*, 7th ed., Figure 10.1. Copyright © 1997 The McGraw-Hill Companies. Reproduced with permission of The McGraw-Hill Companies. **Figure 12.7** From "The Increase in IQ Scores from 1932 to 1997," by Dr. Ulric Neisser. Reprinted by permission. **Figure 12.10** Reprinted from Johnson & Newport, 1991, "Critical Period Effects on Universal Language: The Status of Subjacency in Acquisition of a Second Language,"

Cognition, 39(3), 215–258. Copyright © 1991 Elsevier.

Chapter 13

Figure 13.2 From Colby et al., 1983, "A Longitudinal Study of Moral Judgment," *Monographs of the Society for Research in Child Development*, Serial No. 201. Reprinted with permission from the Society for Research in Child Development. **Figure 13.3** "National Reading Scores," from Santrock, *Life-Span Development*, 11th ed. Copyright © 2008 The McGraw-Hill Companies. Reproduced with permission of The McGraw-Hill Companies. **Figure 13.4** Reproduced by special permission of the Publisher, Mind Garden, Inc., 855 Oak Grove, Suite 215, Menlo Park, CA 94025 USA. www.mindgarden.com from the *Bem Sex Role Inventory*, by Sandra Bem. Copyright © 1978 by Consulting Psychologists Press, Inc. All rights reserved. Further reproduction is prohibited without the Publisher's written consent. **Figure 13.5** "Percentage of Same Sex Couples with Children," from Santrock, *Life-Span Development*, 11th ed., Fig. 15.9. Copyright © 2008 The McGraw-Hill Companies. Reproduced with permission of The McGraw-Hill Companies. **Figure 13.6** From Nansel, et al., 2001, "Bullying Behaviors Among U.S. Youth," *Journal of the American Medical Association*, Vol. 285, pp. 2094–2100.

Chapter 14

Figure 14.1 From J.M. Tanner, et al., "Standards from Birth to Maturity for Height, Weight, Height Velocity: British Children," *Archives of Diseases in Childhood*, 41. Copyright © 1966. Used by permission of BMJ Publishing Group. **Figure 14.3** From Santrock, *Adolescence*, 8th ed., Figure 3.4. Copyright © 2001 The McGraw-Hill Companies. Reproduced with permission of The McGraw-Hill Companies. **Figure 14.6** "The Prefrontal Cortex," from *U.S. News & World Report*, Special Issue, "Mysteries of the Teen Years," May 1, 2005. Copyright © 2005 U.S. News & World Report, L.P. Reprinted with permission. **Figure 14.8** From Darroch, et al., 2000, *Teenage Sexual and Reproductive Behavior in Developed Countries: Can Progress Be Made?* Occasional Report, Alan Guttmacher Institute, New York, No. 13, p. 4. Reprinted by permission of the Alan Guttmacher Institute. **P. 481** From H. Boonstra, February 2002, "Teen Pregnancy: Trends and Lessons Learned," *The Guttmacher Report on Public Policy*, pp. 9–10. Reprinted by permission of the Alan Guttmacher Institute. **Figure 14.9** "Percentage of U.S. High School Students Who Ate Fruits and Vegetables ≥ Five Times a Day, 1999 to 2005," after data presented by the MMWR, 9 June 2006. *Youth Risk Behavior Surveillance-United States*, 2005, Vol. 255. Atlanta: Center for Disease Control & Prevention. **Figure 14.10** "Exercise Rates of U.S. High School Students by Gender and Ethnicity," after data presented by the MMWR, 9 June 2006. *Youth Risk Behavior Surveillance-United States*, 2005, Vol. 255. Atlanta: Center for Disease Control & Prevention.

Figure 14.11 "Trends in Drug Use by U.S. Eighth-, Tenth-, and Twelfth-Grade Students," from L.D. Johnston, P.M. O'Malley, & J.G. Bachman, 2001, *The Monitoring of the Future: National Results on Adolescent Drug Use*. Washington, DC: National Institute on Drug Abuse. **Figure 14.12** "Young Adolescents' Reports of Alcohol Use in the Family Matters Program," from K.E. Bauman, S.T. Ennett, et al., 2002, "Influence of a Family Program on Adolescent Smoking and Drinking Prevalence," *Prevention Science*, 3. pp. 35–42. With kind permission of Springer Science and Business Media.

Chapter 15

Figure 15.1 From H. Lee Swanson, "What Develops in Working Memory? A Life-Span Perspective," *Developmental Psychology*, 34(4), 986–1000. Copyright © 1998 by the American Psychological Association. Reprinted by permission. **Figure 15.2** Graph from L. J. Sax, A. W. Astin, J. A. Lindholm, W. S. Korn, V. B. Saenz, and K. M. Mahoney (2003). The American Freshman: National Norms for Fall 2003 Los Angeles: Higher Education Research Institute, UCLA. Data from L. J. Sax, S. Hurtado, J. A. Lindholm, A. W. Astin, W. S. Korn, and K. M. Mahoney (2004) The American Freshman: Norms for Fall 2004 Los Angeles: Higher Education Research Institute, UCLA. Used with permission. **Figure 15.4** Reproduced by special permission of the publisher, Psychological Assessment Resources, Inc., 16204 North Florida Avenue, Lutz, FL 33549, from *Making Vocational Choices*, Third Edition. Copyright © 1973, 1985, 1992, 1997 by Psychological Assessment Resources, Inc. All rights reserved.

Chapter 16

Figure 16.2 From *Divergent Realities* by Reed Larson. Cambridge, MA: Perseus Books. Reprinted by permission of Basic Books, a member of Perseus Books Group. **Figure 16.5** "Age of Onset of Romantic Activity," from "Romantic Development: Does Age at Which Romantic Involvement Starts Matter?" by Duane Buhrmester, April 2001, paper presented at the meeting of the Society for Research in Child Development, Minneapolis, MN. **Figure 16.6** From R.W. Larson, 2001, "How U.S. Children and Adolescents Spend Time: What it Does (and Doesn't) Tell Us About Their Development," *Current Directions in Psychological Science*, 10/e, Table 1, p. 160–164. Reprinted by permission of Blackwell Publishers. **Figure 16.7** After Sellers, et al., 2006, "Racial Identity Matters," *Journal of Research on Adolescence*, 16(2), 187–216, Table 1. Reprinted by permission of Blackwell Publishers. **Figure 16.8** "Percentage of U.S. 9th- to 12th-Grade Students Who Seriously Considered Attempting Suicide in the Previous 12 Months from 1991 to 2005," *National Risk Behavior Survey 1991–2005: Trends in the Prevalance of Suicide Ideating and Attempts*. Centers for Disease Control & Prevention.

NAME INDEX